THE NEW
CAMBRIDGE MODERN HISTORY

ADVISORY COMMITTEE

G.N.CLARK J.R.M.BUTLER J.P.T.BURY

THE LATE E.A.BENIANS

VOLUME IV

THE DECLINE OF SPAIN AND
THE THIRTY YEARS WAR
1609–48/59

THE NEW CAMBRIDGE MODERN HISTORY

VOLUME IV
THE DECLINE OF SPAIN AND
THE THIRTY YEARS WAR
1609–48/59

EDITED BY
J. P. COOPER

CAMBRIDGE
AT THE UNIVERSITY PRESS
1971

Published by the Syndics of the Cambridge University Press
Bentley House, 200 Euston Road, London NW1 2DB
American Branch: 32 East 57th Street, New York, N.Y.10022

© Cambridge University Press 1970

Library of Congress Catalogue Card Number: 57–14935

ISBN: 0 521 07618 8

First published 1970
Reprinted 1971

Printed in Great Britain
at the University Printing House, Cambridge
(Brooke Crutchley, University Printer)

CONTENTS

INTRODUCTORY

CHAPTER I

GENERAL INTRODUCTION

By J. P. COOPER, *Fellow and Lecturer in Modern History, Trinity College, Oxford*

CONTENTS

CHAPTER II

THE EUROPEAN ECONOMY 1609–50

By F. C. SPOONER, *Professor of Economic History, University of Durham*

CHAPTER III

THE EXPONENTS AND CRITICS OF ABSOLUTISM

By R. MOUSNIER, *Professor of Modern History at the Sorbonne*

CONTENTS

CHAPTER IV

THE SCIENTIFIC MOVEMENT AND ITS INFLUENCE 1610–50

By A. C. CROMBIE, *University Lecturer in the History of Science,*
University of Oxford, and Fellow of Trinity College
and M. A. HOSKIN, *University Lecturer in the History of Science,*
University of Cambridge, and Fellow of Churchill College

CHAPTER V

CHANGES IN RELIGIOUS THOUGHT

By G. L. MOSSE, *Professor of History, University of Wisconsin*

CONTENTS

CONTENTS

CONTENTS

THE CENTRAL CONFLICTS

CHAPTER IX

SPAIN AND EUROPE 1598–1621

By H. R. TREVOR-ROPER, *Regius Professor of Modern History,
University of Oxford, and Fellow of Oriel College*

CHAPTER X

THE STATE OF GERMANY (to 1618)

By G. D. RAMSAY, *Fellow and Tutor in Modern History,
St Edmund Hall, Oxford*

CONTENTS

CHAPTER XI

THE THIRTY YEARS WAR

By E. A. BELLER, *Professor of History, Princeton University*

CONTENTS

CHAPTER XII

THE LOW COUNTRIES

By E. H. KOSSMANN, *Professor of Modern History, Rijksuniversiteit, Groningen*

CONTENTS

CHAPTER XIII

SWEDEN AND THE BALTIC 1611–54

By M. ROBERTS, *Professor of Modern History, the Queen's University, Belfast*

CONTENTS

THE UNMAKING AND REMAKING OF STATES

CONTENTS

CHAPTER XVI

FRENCH INSTITUTIONS AND SOCIETY 1610–61

By R. Mousnier

CONTENTS

CHAPTER XVII

THE HABSBURG LANDS 1618–57

By V-L. TAPIE, *Professor of Modern History at the Sorbonne,
Membre de l'Institut*

CONTENTS

CHAPTER XVIII

THE FALL OF THE STUART MONARCHY

By J. P. COOPER

CONTENTS

CHAPTER XIX

THE ENDING OF POLISH EXPANSION AND THE SURVIVAL OF RUSSIA

I. POLAND–LITHUANIA 1609–48

By H. JABLONOWSKI, *Professor of East European History,*
Rheinische Friedrich-Wilhelms-Universität, Bonn

2. RUSSIA 1613–45

By J. L. H. KEEP, *Reader in Russian Studies, School of Slavonic and*
East European Studies, University of London

CONTENTS

THE FRONTIERS OF EUROPE

CHAPTER XX

THE OTTOMAN EMPIRE 1617–48

By V. J. PARRY, *Reader in the History of Near and Middle East,*
School of Oriental and African Studies, University of London

CHAPTER XXI

EUROPE AND ASIA

By J. B. HARRISON, *Reader in the History of India,*
School of Oriental and African Studies, University of London

CONTENTS

CHAPTER XXII

THE EUROPEAN NATIONS AND THE ATLANTIC

By E. E. RICH, *Vere Harmsworth Professor of Imperial and Naval History in the University of Cambridge, and Master of St Catharine's College*

CONTENTS

CHAPTER XXIII

LATIN AMERICA 1610–60

By W. BORAH, *Professor of History, University of California, Berkeley*

CHAPTER I

GENERAL INTRODUCTION

U NDENIABLY the first half of the seventeenth century in Europe (or for that matter in China and to a lesser extent India) was an eventful period, full of conflicts. In China a dynasty collapsed amidst peasant revolts and for the last time nomadic invaders conquered the settled lands. In Europe there were more widespread and prolonged wars than ever before, the assassination of one king and the execution of another, while revolts of whole kingdoms and provinces against their rulers took place from Ireland to the Ukraine, from Muscovy to Naples and from Portugal to Anatolia. But has this period in Europe any distinctive character or significance for those who feel a need to find such things in history? Recent fashions would cause many historians to answer No for a variety of reasons. The most general one would be that to make Europe the centre of a general history is at once anachronistic and parochial, a quaint attempt to prolong nostalgic memories of the domination of the world by western European culture and power, which ended in 1942, if not before. As Europe's place in the world has changed, so has our perspective of history. Still obsessed by the view which tacitly dominated so many earlier European historians that power is the essential subject of history and that only success and never failure deserve study, some historians were so disorientated by Europe's loss of power and so beguiled by the rhetoric of the new leaders of Afro-Asian states and by counting the heads of the big battalions that they became prophets, unmaking the past in order to gratify an imaginary present and an improbable future. This first intoxication has scarcely survived the demise of those first leaders. But one curious result has been the proliferation of posts and courses for teaching African history to a much greater extent that those dealing with Asian civilizations which really do have long recorded histories. All states feel a need to supply or invent a history for themselves and this need is now partly met for African ones, as a kind of penitential exercise by their former rulers. This may be politically or morally edifying, the development of techniques for using oral tradition even advances genuine knowledge, but as far as the seventeenth century is concerned, it cannot substantially alter the perspectives of European or world history.

More persuasively and presumably democratically it can be argued that it is arrogant and inappropriate to concentrate on 100,000,000 Europeans to the exclusion of two or three times as many Asians. As yet, despite their trans-Atlantic conquests and command of oceanic routes, Europeans were not decisively superior in political organization, in military or other technology to Asiatic societies and empires, by whom they were generally treated as dubious parasites. The answer must be that while knowledge of the economies and societies of Europe is still very imperfect, it is far worse for those of Asia, but also that it was to be European powers which conquered and transformed Asia. This is something which will always be a major episode of world history, whatever changes in political power and academic fashions the future may hold. Transformations in the organization of war, especially war by sea, began to make European powers decisively stronger in the seventeenth century. The development of science was to have even greater long-term effects in providing Europeans with greater power, but the seventeenth century was more decisive in changing educated Europeans' ways of viewing the world than in giving them immediate command of new means to change it.

Even if these reasons for concentrating on Europe are acceptable, the first half of the seventeenth century may not make an intelligible or profitable period of study. Men of the time, Galileo, Bacon, Descartes, Gassendi, saw themselves as apostles or discoverers of new systems of knowledge which broke with past traditions. Historians of science may dispute some of 'the new philosophy's' claims, but not that there was continuity of development before and after the middle of the century. However, searchers for landmarks might note that in 1609 Kepler's *New Astronomy* broke with the tradition of treating the planets' motions as circular and presented the universe as a machine, while in 1659 Huygens constructed his perfected pendulum clock: 'the first apparatus that embodies in its construction the laws of the new dynamics . . . not of empirical trial and error' (Koyré). The façade of Maderna's Santa Susanna in Rome (finished in 1603) is generally considered the first fully typical baroque composition. Again there was no neat break in mid-century; while the years from around 1640 to 1670 might be considered the apogee of high baroque in Italy, its influence outside Italy continued to be strong, though not without new rivals. But in economic history the early or middle decades of the century have often been seen as the decisive turning point of a secular trend from expansion to depression. More recently many historians have seen the seventeenth century and more especially the years before 1660 as a period of economic and political crisis, without agreeing as to its causes or even its most important symptoms. This again requires a longer perspective within which to put the fate of a mere two generations. The limitations of the period are both arbitrary and a matter of convenience, but within them are important problems which can be identified, even if we cannot adequately explain them.

To consider such a period mainly through the history of individual states is also open to serious objection. This again is partly a matter of convenience, since in fact individual historians generally study particular societies in depth. The unevenness of information as between different countries and its total quantity for all Europe make effective synthesis unlikely. There are also other reasons. The view that the central process in European history was the building of nation-states is now unfashionable among historians, though its political influence has never been stronger outside Europe and remains powerful in Europe itself. Everywhere in former colonial territories men are attempting to create states with national identities. Such an approach could distort the past when dominated by a teleological drive to demonstrate that the European states of the early twentieth century were both inevitable and morally right. It can also mean that state and nation building, like the ultimate withering away of the state after the dictatorship of the proletariat, can be used to justify almost anything for the sake of national survival, future glory or present welfare. Nevertheless this approach to the seventeenth century does emphasize features of real importance. For it was then that the multi-national monarchy of the Spanish Habsburgs collapsed as an effective power, while the future belonged to states, France, England, the United Netherlands and Sweden, which had achieved a degree of identity and unity. Yet all these countries ruled or wished to rule over territories with separate histories, languages or cultures. The seventeenth century also saw the building up of another multi-lingual empire from a number of territories with diverse historical traditions by the Austrian Habsburgs and the growth of political fragmentation in Germany, despite ties of common language and culture.

Because international relations were dominated by dynastic considerations, because the rights of provinces, groups, or even individuals, to renounce the suzerainty of particular monarchs were not yet entirely fictional, because of the lack of both the concept and reality of modern linear frontiers between states and because of the international character of much of the culture of courts and ruling groups, the criteria of modern nationalism (meaningless as these often are) were scarcely applicable. It is easy for those of other nations to mock the anachronistic results of projecting backwards the artificial constructs of Irish, Magyar, Rumanian, German or English nationalism, but they are reminders of how much our conceptions of the past are influenced by later, even recent, events.

This may be made more precise by a negative example. If the Ukraine had emerged as an independent national state in the nineteenth or twentieth centuries, our interpretation of the significance of events in eastern Europe in the seventeenth might be considerably modified, as both English and Irish views on their history have been modified by the existence of the Irish Republic. Perhaps ideally such events should not influence historians, but in real life they do. The variety of interpretations which have been put on the career of Bohdan Khmelnytsky and the treaty of Pereiaslavl of 1654 (the very use of the word treaty has been the subject of prolonged controversies) by Polish, Russian and Ukrainian historians in the last fifty years is an extreme illustration of this, and is not solely due either to difficulties in interpreting the evidence or the deliberate distortions of facts to serve current political purposes.[1]

This also suggests that consideration of a relatively short period can be useful in so far as it reminds us of the unforeseeable and unexpected character of what now seem clear or inevitable general trends. In one very general sense European history can be seen as a brutal history of the assertion of power inside and outside Europe. Those nationalisms which appear valid and real rather than quaint or romantic expressions of antiquarianism are those which acquired sufficient power to assert themselves. If the accumulation of power has seemed the primary object of European states in modern times, it has also been argued that no ruler or state before Napoleon claimed to justify aggression and conquest on grounds of national and cultural superiority or destiny. Undoubtedly such claims became much more clear cut in the nineteenth century, culminating in those of Hitler, Mussolini and Stalin. But if the Habsburgs themselves belonged to a supra-national dynastic tradition of imperialism, the Spaniards who bore the main burden of imperial defence in the early seventeenth century did not see things in the same way. The Castilians' sense of their destiny to conquer and rule was resented by the other Iberian peoples. The popular demand to enforce rules of *limpieza* (the exclusion of those with Jewish and Moorish blood from honour and office) was both a perversion of Christianity and a variant of the almost universal belief that noble blood was superior to that of commoners, but above all it shows a fierce sense of identity and exclusiveness. There was a popular saying 'Let us acknowledge God's grace in making us men, not beasts, Christians, not Moors, Spaniards not men of another nation' and another among Castilian *hidalgos* 'I swear to God I am as noble as the king and more so as he is half Flemish'. Quevedo saw the struggle with the Dutch as one for domination of the world.

Again some nations claimed to be specially chosen by God; this conception was propagated for England by Foxe's *Book of Martyrs* and culminated in Milton's apologetics and historical projects. The Scots had an older tradition which the Covenanters invoked.[2] The Swedes saw themselves as heirs of the Goths, descendants of Japheth, the oldest nation in the world, world conquerors and teachers of the ancient Greeks. These myths were systematized by Johannes Magnus with further inspiration from the prophecies by Paracelsus and Tycho Brahe of the Lion of the North as the precursor of the second coming and universal peace.[3] Now

---

[1] Cf. C. B. O'Brien, *Muscovy and the Ukraine . . . 1654–1667* (Berkeley, 1963); S. Kot, *Georges Niemirycz* (The Hague, 1960); D. Doroshenko, *History of the Ukraine* (Edmonton, 1939); S. Quillitzsch, 'Der ukrainische Befreiungskampf im 17 Jahrhundert', *Deutsch-Slawischen Beziehungen*, Vol. I (1956), pp. 1–38.

[2] See below, Chapter XVIII, p. 567.

[3] M. Roberts, *Gustavus Adolphus*, Vol. I (1953), pp. 509–16, 523–6.

all these exaltations of chosen nations have millenarian and universalist implications, just as Campanella chose first the Spanish and then the French monarchy as the instrument to inaugurate his general Utopia. But they also fed national pride and self-consciousness in a way that the Ottomans' total identification with a mission of conquest for Islam failed to do: they were so lacking in any pride in pure Turkish descent that the word Turk was generally used in a derogatory sense of nomads and peasants.[1]

If national failings were most often invoked by propaganda aiming to serve dynastic and religious ends, the notion of Europe and agreed boundaries for it had emerged by the early seventeenth century. This not so much replaced as modified the old idea of Christendom. Europe and Christendom became largely interchangeable terms; whereas once Christendom had meant all Christians everywhere, Christians were now essentially Europeans: 'Jesus Christ is their way, their truth, their life; who hath long since given a Bill of Divorce to ingratefull Asia where he was borne, and Africa the place of his flight . . . and is become almost wholly and onely European', as Samuel Purchas put it in 1625. He went on to claim a supremacy in Asian trade which was very far from being established, and a power in technology which was at best only beginning.[2] If increasing knowledge of other lands led Europeans to define themselves in terms of the differences between themselves and others, the comparisons were not always favourable to Europe. In the sixteenth century Busbecq and others had made comparisons which favoured the Ottomans. But in the seventeenth century suggestions that Europeans were warlike barbarians, unworthy of their Christian heritage, when compared with the natural innocence of Amerindians, or the civilized wisdom of the Chinese, became more frequent. The first view was pioneered by Montaigne's reflections on the Brazilians and the standard answer was provided by Botero who argued there was no civilization without cities. The first full accounts of the Chinese appeared in the late sixteenth century and stressed their prosperity and unwarlike character. The Jesuit Ricci began a long tradition which by the later seventeenth century had represented Chinese culture and government as the product of enlightened despotism, but already in the first decade of the century an Italian merchant, Francesco Carletti, anticipated Voltaire in his praise of China.[3] By 1641 the *libertin* and atheist, La Mothe Le Vayer, in his *Les Vertus des païens* hailed the Chinese as practising natural religion in its purest form, while benefiting from the rule of the disciples of Confucius, another, but unmartyred, Socrates.

If Purchas inflated naïve pride into a premature anticipation of things to come, Europe as a political entity was a conception increasingly in-

[1] B. Lewis, *The Emergence of Modern Turkey* (1961), Chapter I.
[2] D. Hay, *Europe, the Emergence of an Idea* (Edinburgh, 1957), Chapters 6 and 7, p. 110.
[3] F. Chabod, *Storia dell'idea d'Europa* (Bari, 1962), pp. 64–89.

voked in diplomatic propaganda. Richelieu claimed to be saving not only German liberties from Habsburg hegemony but also Europe. Jurists were still dominated by Roman or Old Testament precedents in their discourses on the *jus gentium*, despite the inappropriateness of the circumstances of a chosen people or of an empire with universalist claims to their contemporary situation of sovereign states without superiors. As full of classical and biblical learning as any of his predecessors, Grotius turned from *ius gentium* to *jus inter gentes*.

He seems to have been the first to adopt fully the basic axiom common to his successors: that the State is sovereign, subject to no exterior controls and amenable mainly to considerations of its own self-interest. He aimed to show that on those terms it is in the interest of the State to accept the rule of law, since to preserve its existence there must be some community of nations.[1]

States had equal rights, even if they had not equal powers to assert them, but over-assertion of power would in the long run be detrimental to the interests of the powerful. This may have contributed to developing some sense of a European community of nations. Grotius had been counsel for the Dutch East India Company and had used the sovereignty of Asiatic states as an argument to reject Portuguese claims based on papal authority, but the recognition of a community of nations which included European and Asiatic ones on genuinely equal terms was to be deferred both by Europeans' assertion of their power[2] and by China's refusal to recognize other states except as tributaries of her emperor.

If there came to be general agreement that the frontier of Europe itself was on the Don, this was also a period in which what proved to be lasting boundaries and divisions were achieved. White Russia and Smolensk, Kiev and the Left Bank Ukraine went to Muscovy, Portugal became independent of the Spanish Habsburgs and the religious geography of Germany was substantially settled by the Thirty Years War until the twentieth century. Outside Europe the frontiers between Persia and the Ottoman Empire which Murad IV established are still substantially those between Turkey, Iraq and Persia. Spain ceased to have a monopoly of settlement in the Caribbean and was no longer able to control or limit the settlement of North America by others. In the east Asian archipelago, Spain's hold on the Philippines was finally consolidated, although by 1650 the Dutch had established themselves as the predominant European power. By the mid-seventeenth century Russian traders and trappers had reached the Pacific through Siberia and were in contact with the Chinese on the River Amur.

There was some sense of a European culture, though as yet Russia was regarded as largely alien to it. Religious and political controversies like

[1] G. Mattingly, *Renaissance Diplomacy* (1955), p. 294; Vol. III in this series, Chapter VI; and below, Chapter III, pp. 111–12.
[2] See below, Chapter XXII, p. 671.

those between Bellarmine and James I had a European audience, as did more narrowly academic ones, such as Casaubon's refutation of Baronius, demonstrating that the Hermetic writings were post-Christian. All these were in Latin, like most academic writings. French, Spanish and Italian vernacular cultures were all international in the sense that their influence was felt throughout Europe. Italian influence on painting and architecture was stronger over a wider area of Europe than in the sixteenth century. But it is as well to remember that those whom we now recognize as the greatest writers, thinkers or artists were not necessarily widely influential in Europe in their own times. While Rubens, Bernini and to a lesser extent van Dyck had great European reputations, Vermeer and Velasquez did not. While Tasso, Cervantes, Quevedo, even Marino, were read all over Europe by 1650, neither Shakespeare nor Corneille had an international readership. Descartes is still read and Bacon much mentioned, if less studied, today, but in this period Justus Lipsius was probably more widely read than either.

The literary and linguistic influences of French and Spanish, unlike those of Italian, were ultimately more closely connected with exercise of political power. The influence of Castilian language and culture was at its height not only in the lands directly ruled from Madrid, but also in Bohemia, Austria and Germany.[1] Direct influence of Spanish literature went further still; over twenty Jacobean plays derive from Spanish sources, some by way of French translations, but many directly. Fletcher and Massinger both probably knew Spanish. Not only Cervantes' fiction, but many picaresque novels were translated into English, French, Italian and German. Aleman's *Guzmán de Alfarache* (1599, 1604), 'the first full-length realistic novel in European literature', was a best-seller outside Spain and directly shaped the form of the German masterpiece, Grimmelshausen's *Simplicissimus* (1669). The direct influence of Spanish on French and English literature was perhaps strongest in the first half of the seventeenth century, but the number and popularity of translations continued to grow thereafter.

The tasks of the more general historian have become so complex that he has little hope of accomplishing anything except the provision of easy targets for criticism by his more specialized colleagues. Historians of art often feel that such historians make extravagant and crude assertions about the geographical and chronological range of baroque art, its content, style and social significance. Some historians of literature complain of the useless proliferation of themes and categories borrowed from historians of art and science. Other historians tend to feel that those who specialize in cultural history use out-of-date analyses and crude concepts

[1] H. Tiemann, *Das Spanische Schrifttum in Deutschland von der Renaissance bis zur Romantik* (Hamburg, 1936).

when they refer to the social, political and economic background. Likewise many economic historians believe that understanding of the fundamental structure of history and society is only accessible to those trained in statistical and analytical techniques, though they may disagree about how to apply them in demography or price history. Thus the mere historian, the man who tries to study events in some general way, was never more at a discount. But general synthesis was almost equally difficult when diplomatic, political, and constitutional history were thought to be the fundamentals. All anyone can hope to do is to interest others in trying to produce better answers or better questions, as well as more knowledge, while resisting temptations to use particular concepts, such as 'conjoncture', 'the great chain of being', 'Baroque sensibility', or modern myths such as 'dissociation of sensibility', or the 'organic society', as keys to too many, or in the last two cases to any, doors.

If the general economic and social conditions in which states were trying to build up their power are now a major concern of historians, it is only comparatively recently that they have thought in terms of phases of general economic growth and depression. Political and cultural history since the Middle Ages or earlier was usually seen as a progression, subjected to temporary interruptions. States rose and declined, but this was usually seen as a transference of power to new leaders, while the general power of Europe in relation to other areas of the world clearly grew between say 1400 and 1800, or 1700. Since economic factors were mainly considered in relation to policies pursued by governments in order to build up states and because economic historians were mainly concerned with the evolution of economic institutions and organization, and of techniques of production, such developments either implied or assumed over-all long-term growth. Some areas were backward, such as Russia, some areas admittedly declined, as did Spain, but this was compensated by growth and advance elsewhere. As the study of economic history developed, historians such as Pirenne rejected concepts of steady evolution in favour of ones of a more cyclical character. Historians have become increasingly interested in stressing disjunctions, price revolutions, or crises. Similar interests have been pursued in political and cultural history. In recent years the seventeenth century has been seen as above all a century of revolution and crisis. Marxist interpretations still stress the older evolutionary pattern in so far as they see the crisis as contributing to 'the transition from feudalism to capitalism' and to the ultimate strengthening of 'progressive forces', notably those favouring industrial capitalism. But there tends to be general agreement that the disturbances of the seventeenth century were to some appreciable extent reactions to economic crises and depression, when growth of population and resources were often checked with brutal suddenness, even though important intellectual and cultural developments, especially in science and religion, took place.

Thus there is currently a general notion of an economic decline, or depression, beginning in the first half of the seventeenth century, signalled by exceptionally violent price fluctuations and intensified by prolonged warfare, so that the century began 'and lived under the sign of depression, contraction, deflation'. Baroque art has been seen as in part a manifestation, conditioned by this social and economic background; a highly emotional escape from the miseries of the world which still reflects its conflicts and suffering. It has also been claimed that late medieval preoccupation with death, the charnel house and the transitoriness of things reappears as a leading motif of baroque.[1] However this may be, we should at least note that stylistic analysis has always stressed the tensions, complications and disjunctions of Mannerist art and architecture and contrasted them with the harmonious and integrated syntheses achieved by baroque and its exuberance, or even self-confidence.

The most important general economic symptoms are held to be the behaviour of prices; in comparison with the sixteenth century fluctuations were more violent and the general trend ceased to rise, turning to stagnation or decline. There has been considerable disagreement about when the turning point, or reversal of trend, took place: 1619, 1630, 1640, 1650 have all been suggested, while some have preferred to see it as a cumulative process, affecting different parts of Europe at different times and only completed for all Europe after the mid-seventeenth century. There has been even more disagreement about the nature and causes of the period's political and social crises,[2] except that once again they are held to be somehow related to economic difficulties and depression.

Many economic historians have come to believe that they can assess the general trend of an economy by the study of prices. At one time the history of prices seemed so fundamental and all-powerful a source of knowledge that some historians were prepared to infer demographic trends from them. Wiser counsels may now have prevailed, but there is still a belief, mostly strongly held in France, that the study of prices can reveal a basic structure whose long-term changes were largely independent of wars and political events. Sometimes issues have been further confused by speaking of price history as though it were quantitative. No doubt it aspires to be, and a price series can be thought of as measuring something. The difficulty may be to decide what it is measuring and what validity it has as evidence. The accepted view is that a continuous rise in price is evidence of economic growth. However, this depends upon a number of assumptions, not all of them verifiable, about the relationship of price movements to growth in pre-industrial societies with large subsistence sectors. If we

[1] J. Rousset, *La Littérature de l'Age Baroque en France* (1954), Chapter IV. For a sweeping rejection see H. Peyre, 'Commonsense remarks on French Baroque', *Studies in Seventeenth-Century Literature*, ed. J. J. Demarest (Ithaca, 1962), pp. 1–19.
[2] E.g. T. H. Aston (ed.), *Crisis in Europe 1560–1660* (1965).

say that in sixteenth-century Europe population and towns grew, along with the volume of trade and shipping and the output of the textile industries, more land was cultivated and so on; all these propositions seem probable, but we cannot quantify them and produce continuous series of statistics. Thus such innumerate propositions seem inferior in value to price series, though these are often discontinuous, fail to cover most products other than grain and only cover some areas. Price series, especially when presented as index numbers, silver equivalents, or moving averages, remain the basis for acts of faith, rather than quantitative evidence about the development of the economy. Lack of other evidence may force us to use them as a guide to the direction of economic change, but we must recognize that radical criticism of such procedures is possible. To take price series alone as revealing the fundamental pattern of economic change and then fit other pieces of evidence into that pattern, or explain them away, if they fail to fit into it, is a dangerous procedure which has sometimes been a perhaps unconscious consequence of the first raptures of the quest for *une histoire totale*.

It may be worth briefly categorizing some of the main economic interpretations offered in recent years. This cannot do justice to the ingenuity and learning of their authors, but may indicate their general characteristics, even at the cost of over-simplification. (1) The explanations offered by Chaunu[1] and Goubert[2] may be taken together since they both regard detailed analyses of trends and cycles in prices as a fundamental guide. Chaunu concentrates on international trade and Goubert on the economic history of one region with particular attention to demographic factors; both infer trends of production from indirect evidence, though to differing extents, and both agree that the European economy had moved into depression by about 1650. (2) Abel[3] and Slicher van Bath[4] regard price trends as important, but are concerned with relating them to agricultural production rather than with cyclical analysis and international trade. They see the period from the mid-seventeenth century as the beginning of a period of prolonged depression, contrasting with the expansion of the sixteenth century, and characterized by depressed cereal prices, high real wages, growth of pastoral farming and rural industry. (3) Romano[5] has attempted a general explanation embracing prices, credit, monetary factors, international trade, industrial and agricultural production, which aims to show that a decisive break happened between 1619 and 1622,

[1] P. Chaunu, *Séville et l'Atlantique*, Vol. VIII, 2, pt. ii; 'Le renversement de la tendance majeure des prix et des activités au XVIIe siècle', *Studi in Onore di A. Fanfani*, vol. IV (1962); 'Réflexions sur le tournant des années 1630–50', *Cahiers d'Histoire*, vol. XII (1967).

[2] P. Goubert, *Beauvais et le Beauvaisis de 1600 à 1730* (1960), pp. 493–512, 599–624.

[3] W. Abel, *Agrarkrisen und Agrarkonjunktur in Mitteleuropa vom 13 bis zum 19 Jahrhundert* (1935); *Geschichte des deutschen Landwirtschaft* (1962).

[4] B. Slicher van Bath, *The Agrarian History of Western Europe* (1963).

[5] R. Romano, 'Tra XVI e XVII secolo una Crisi Economica 1619–22', *Rivista Storica Italiana*, Vol. LXXIV (1962), pp. 480–531.

turning the whole economy towards depression. (4) Baehrel[1] and Le Roy Ladurie,[2] like Goubert, are concerned with particular regions, but have produced more direct evidence of production and the movement of rents and incomes and their relationship to prices. Both believe that their findings have some validity beyond their particular regions and do not agree with (1) and (3) that there was a decisive break before 1650.

Fifthly and finally there are various Marxist explanations. Some, while still seeing the whole century as assisting structural changes from feudalism to capitalism, allow that there were social and economic crises especially in the first half of the century and that the whole period was one of relative economic stagnation compared with the sixteenth century.[3] But some Polish historians, though agreeing that Poland and other countries declined economically, deny that this was true of the European economy in general.[4] Topolski denies that there was 'a general economic crisis in the sense of stagnation or recession caused by a slackening of economic activity'. There was a diversity of developments in the various European countries, so that the regression of the Polish economy was partly due to its exploitation by more advanced countries such as the Netherlands, England and Sweden. As Malowist puts it 'the border regions became in some ways a kind of economic colony of the west', which needed their grain, timber products and raw materials and found them a valuable market for manufactured and colonial goods. This exploitation was to the advantage of western mercantile and industrial interests and of the Polish magnates at the expense of Polish towns, artisans, merchants and peasants. Topolski explicitly denies that regression in Poland was due to war whose ravages after 1626 and still more after 1648 only accelerated a process which had already begun and would presumably have produced similar results eventually without the wars. On the effects of war Topolski has the tacit or explicit support of almost all the historians mentioned. Only Le Roy Ladurie allows considerable importance to the fiscal pressures produced by war. Goubert considers that war had only local and temporary effects on grain prices, always very much less than those of bad harvests, so that it seems implied that war had only relatively peripheral social and economic significance.

Chaunu's explanation has already had considerable influence. Because of this and its great range in space, time and information, it is desirable to give a fuller, though still highly schematic, account of it. He argues that there was a chronic shortage of money in sixteenth- and seventeenth-

[1] R. Baehrel, *Une Croissance; La Basse-Provence Rurale* (1961).

[2] E. Le Roy Ladurie, *Les Paysans de Languedoc* (1966).

[3] A. Klima and J. Macurek, 'La question de la transition du feudalisme au capitalisme', XI *Congres Int. des Sciences Historiques* (1960), *Rapports*, Vol. IV, pp. 85–140; E. Hobsbawm, 'The General Crisis of the Seventeenth Century', in *Crisis in Europe*, ed. Aston.

[4] J. Topolski, 'La régression économique en Pologne XVIe–XVIIIe siècles', *Acta Poloniae Historica* Vol. VII (1962); M. Malowist, 'The development of the Baltic countries in the sixteenth and seventeenth centuries', *Econ. Hist. Rev.* (1959).

century Europe which is a main reason for the progressive devaluation of moneys of account (see Map 1, below p. 87). Thus the silver arriving in Seville eased the shortage of trading capital sufficiently to encourage investment in trade and shipping. High prices encouraged economic activity, but continuing inflation meant that a given quantity of silver bought less, while expanding trade needed more working capital. For the growth of trade to continue, the growth of the American mines' output had to be faster than the rise in prices and the increase in the volume of trade, since contemporary instruments of credit required bullion backing. These conditions were met in the generation before 1600, but thereafter silver shipments did not increase, they were roughly fifteen per cent lower for the next two decades and fell increasingly steeply after 1625. The volume of shipping used in Seville's trans-Atlantic trade reached its peak 1608–10, then, after a period of hesitations around a rather lower level, turned decisively downwards after 1622 (see Fig. 3, below p. 90). Chaunu considers that it is impossible to measure production directly so that indices of the volume of activity on the great sea-routes are the best evidence available. Seville's Atlantic trade was the motor of Europe's economic expansion as it faltered and then lost power, so the trend of the whole economy turned from expansion to stagnation or decline. The crisis of the early 1620s was ultimately due to the failure to finance a growing volume of trade. This in turn was due to failure to find new mines and new populations to exploit. 'When the expansion of the Spanish Atlantic economy ceased, Europe was plunged into a prolonged crisis from which it did not emerge until the second great colonial expansion, that of the Dutch, English and French colonial empires provided a new stimulus to economic advance.'

Thus Chaunu is a theorist of the economic frontier, claiming that 'occupation of space appears to play the same role in the economies of the fifteenth to eighteenth centuries which advances in technology play in economies of the last hundred years'. The chronology of decline in Europe, or of the change from growth to slower growth, differed by regions. In Mediterranean Europe, Spain and Spanish America, it began around 1600, but was later in the Netherlands, the Baltic, Brazil and the Indian Ocean. Considering prices Chaunu finds, between the period of expansion and that of contraction, an episode of varying length in different countries when prices rise more slowly or move along a plateau. The decisive change follows after two or three cyclical crises; it comes earlier in the west than in the east and in the south than in the north, earlier on the coasts as against the interior of the continent.

Although Chaunu's original assertion that international prices at Amsterdam showed the direct and immediate effect of the decline of Seville's trade has been accepted by some historians, it ought not to have survived an actual inspection of the fragmentary price series cited from

Posthumus' *History of Prices in Holland*. The reversal of trend in Dutch domestic prices came after 1650, or even 1660, thirty or forty years after the decisive crisis at Seville. The causal connections between the two remain obscure. Chaunu has rightly described the decline of Seville's trade as the collapse of a monopoly, but he pays little attention to the problem of whether the volume of Atlantic trade may not have increased after 1620, or 1630, as it was redistributed to the benefit of the Dutch and English. Estimates of Brazil's sugar production suggest that it doubled between 1600 and 1650 and that most of the increase took place after 1630. Again Chaunu only pays attention to trade through the Sound in order to accept Romano's view that its volume declined after the 1620s in step with Seville's. As we shall see this view is mistaken and it is arguable that the trade through the Sound was more important for Europe than Seville's trade had ever been; it certainly employed an enormously greater volume of shipping.

But before pursuing these questions, we should note that the interpretation of the seventeenth century as essentially a period of crisis and depression and that of long-term trends in grain prices as indices of economic growth have both been challenged. Falling grain prices are not incompatible with growth, and the trends of the sixteenth and seventeenth centuries could be explained by the bunching of good and bad harvests.[1] More generally Schöffer has suggested a different perspective for the seventeenth century.[2] Until the eighteenth century a large proportion of the population, more especially urban populations, were liable to suffer severely as a result of comparatively slight dislocations. A bad harvest, an epidemic, shortage of current coin, military looting and requisitioning could have quite disproportionate effects. The purchasing power of the population was so low that the prosperity of much trade and industry, domestic and foreign, depended on the behaviour of a small élite. When such precarious demands failed the whole economy might be shaken. Fluctuation and instability were thus built into the structures of economic and social life. Schöffer agrees that the seemingly limitless prospects of expansion outside Europe of the sixteenth century were checked in the seventeenth, and allows an agrarian recession after 1650. But he argues that it is difficult to infer continuous economic crisis or severe depression from the evidence of prices alone. He suggests that it is quite possible to see the seventeenth century as one of growing economic stability and rising real wages with declining silver imports contributing to that stability. As population growth slackened there may have been not only more money in circulation than in the sixteenth century, but also more per head of population. Clearly there were tremendous shifts of economic and political

[1] M. Morineau, 'D'Amsterdam à Seville, de quelle realité l'histoire des prix est-elle le miroir?' *Annales* (1968).

[2] I. Schöffer, 'Did Holland's Golden Age coincide with a period of Crisis?' *Acta Historiae Neerlandica*, Vol. I (1966).

power from southern to north-western Europe, but such shifts could also make for greater stability, ' . . . a period of solidifying and organizing. Inside Europe prices, currency circulation became more settled and stable. The state grew more than the economy.'

This is a reminder that the older conception of state-building as the main subject of European history has not been entirely replaced by studying economic and social structures and trends. The fragility of demographic structures and those of international trade both suggest that states had a limited amount of economic potential to exploit, quite apart from limited means of influencing their economies in peacetime. Thus bad harvests might have more serious or widespread direct effects than war. Yet the indirect effects of war—prolonged fiscal pressures, the prevalence of inducements to finance tax-farming and war rather than trade, the persistent spread of disease and diversion of man-power—must have had longer-term economic effects at least as important as those of bad harvests and conceivably more important than those of the failure to find new silver mines. A vigorously expanding economy could doubtless afford more expensive and extensive wars than a declining one, but the example of Spain suggests that the will to fight wars could multiply economic difficulties. Again, countries whose wealth was based to a greater extent on sea-power and maritime trade could profit by open or undeclared wars. But it is difficult to see that Spain, allegedly the economically dominant country around 1600, was in a really strong position in terms of wealth or growth of economic power between 1580 and 1620.

If we consider the impact of war on Europe in the sixteenth century, Italy, Germany, the Netherlands, France, Spain, England and Scotland were all seriously affected directly or indirectly between 1540 and 1559. By 1559 the most serious results had been in the finances of all the states concerned, but the most serious economic effects had probably been on Italy. The Italian economy seems to have recovered and probably grew after 1560, but from the 1560s wars, rebellions and civil wars increasingly affected the Netherlands, France, Spain, Portugal, England and Ireland, while Italy was less directly affected. From the 1590s the northern and southern Netherlands and France recovered; trade and industry then expanded to new levels. In France this ended in the 1630s and in the Netherlands later. The economy which did not recover, but declined, was that of Spain, or more particularly Castile, which had put most resources into war. Although the economies of the Netherlands and England recovered from the crisis of the early 1620s, that of northern Italy did not: there the Mantuan war at least assisted the demographic disaster of 1630.[1] It may seem superficial to suggest that the multiple effects of war were enough to check economic expansion between the 1620s and 1660, but it is

[1] See below, Chapter II, p. 76.

worth noticing that the countries more protected from the full effects of land war and more dependent on maritime trade, the northern Netherlands, England and Portugal, did best. The exception here is Venice, but she was involved in a crippling war for Crete, when her trade and sea-power had already been declining for a generation.

For the moment economic hypotheses and analysis must be postponed in order to consider some general social factors. One of the great virtues of Abel, Slicher van Bath, Romano and Baehrel is that they emphasize the primary importance of agriculture. Most historians would agree that both population and agricultural production increased in Europe during the sixteenth century and that probably the cultivated area increased,though whether either substantially surpassed the peaks of the fourteenth century is unclear.

This process of internal colonization slackened and in some areas probably ceased altogether in the seventeenth century. Abel and Slicher see this check as happening after 1650, but Romano sees it as a product of the crisis of the early 1620s, a view which is unpersuasive for Europe in general. More plausibly he points to what was an almost universal European phenomenon, the increasing pressures on rural populations by owners of land and seigneurial rights. We may add that such pressures were often increased and new burdens added as a result of the fiscal necessities of states fighting wars.

Now the traditional élite of owners of land and seigneurial rights had been the nobility, so it is worth attempting some crude approximations of their characteristics and behaviour as a social group. As a corollary to the view that the building of nation-states was the essence of European history, most historians in the first decades of this century saw the emergence of 'new monarchies' allying themselves with the urban middle classes, especially with lawyers and merchants, to attack the traditional privileges of the nobles, discipline their unruliness and transform them by introducing new men with a new tradition of serving the state. What were the mercantilist policies which such monarchies pursued, but basically those of medieval city-states adapted to the needs of larger units, national states? Such concepts produced now-hackneyed phrases about an apparently eternally rising middle class displacing an effete and immemorial nobility and were later reinforced by the supposed effects of the price revolution in promoting capitalism and eroding noble incomes. Yet it is arguable that the monarchies of the sixteenth and seventeenth centuries were more successful in eroding the privileges and political power of their towns than those of their nobilities. The independence and direct political power of towns declined everywhere in Europe, except in the United Provinces and Switzerland.

The way in which men of the time regarded nobility reveals a number of tensions and contradictions in their ways of thinking and acting. Their conceptions also demand an effort of imagination from us. One great modern assumption, or platitude, is that environment is all-important, so that its dominance is often assumed by historians, sociologists and journalists without troubling about evidence. The comparable conceptions of the past were often based on assumptions about heredity and blood. Such conceptions now seem the more distasteful, because of their associations with virulent racialism. Although there have been great advances in knowledge of genetically determined factors in the history of individuals, the possibility that such factors might have important social consequences lacks the respectability and acceptability of environmental assumptions. If we are uncomfortable with the notion of a nobility of blood, so in fact were many people in the sixteenth and seventeenth centuries. It conflicted obviously enough with Christian precepts and there was a very strong medieval tradition, reinforced by much humanist rhetoric, that the only true nobility was that conferred by virtue. Such views had a certain practical convenience in so far as they justified the ennoblement of new men and helped to explain what was already apparent long before the sixteenth century: that many or most nobles were not the direct heirs of Visigothic, Frankish, Norman, Sarmatian, or Trojan nobles. The question as to what made a man noble also involved political theory; there were sayings in many countries to the effect that a king could make a lord or a knight, but not a gentleman. Before considering views about the origin of nobility, we should notice that, though the word noble was usually reserved for the peerage in England, and though in Spain there was a distinction between nobles and *hidalgos*, in France, Poland and other countries it included those without titles who in England were called the gentry. Nobility will here be used in this comprehensive sense and it should also be remembered that the father's status and privileges as a noble were inherited by all his sons, not only by the eldest as in the English peerage.

Most jurists (and the continental treatises on nobility were almost all by jurists or clergy) held that the effective origin of nobility was in grants by public authority. This is put in its most extreme form by a commentator on Louis XIV's commissions to verify noble titles: 'It is an error to believe that Nature has anything to do with differences of status, they are solely the work of the Prince and civil laws . . .' On the other hand from 1578 the king of Poland could not make a commoner noble without the assent of the Diet. Although Bartolus and his successors accepted the general principle of origin in public authority, they also acknowledged the theory of blood and what were still ideals and prejudices of social life in the seventeenth century, when they said that the nobility of the newly ennobled was less perfect than that of older nobles until four generations had passed and that the most perfect nobility was that by immemorial prescription (a lineage without known origins among commoners). Medieval tradition also defended the theory of blood as well as that of virtue. The origin of gentility was in the blessing of Noah; from Japheth, the blessed (incidentally the traditional ancestor of Europeans), descended nobles and from Ham, the accursed, the base and unfree. However there were those, like Raleigh, who held that nobles were the descendants of those chosen by original popular compact and those, like Bodin, who saw their origin in violence and oppression, while others saw them as descendants of conquerors, such as the Franks. Moreno de Vargas (*Discursos de la Nobleza de España*, 1636) like many of his predecessors quoted St Jerome—*Nobilitates mundi nihil aliud esse quam inveteratae divitiae*. In their more realistic and historical moments Spanish, French and Italian writers acknowledged that nobility was often the result of wealth, rather than virtue or valour. Moreno remarked (fo. 51 v) that those living in small places, where the other inhabitants were poor, could use their power to escape taxes and thus become accepted as nobles.

Before considering the legal privileges of nobles in more detail, it is worth having some notion of their numbers. At the one extreme was Biscaya where all the native-born were *hidalgos*, at the other the Grison cantons where no noble privileges were recognized. The countries with the highest proportion of nobles were probably Castile and Poland, each with about 10% of the total population; Hungary may have approached this proportion, it was certainly over 5%. In England taking a very wide definition including lawyers, clergy, military and naval officers, Gregory King's estimates suggest about 4% for c. 1688. A narrower definition might perhaps give 2–3% c. 1660. In France c. 1700 it was perhaps 1%, but must have been higher in 1650, though probably under 2%. In Piedmont c. 1700 it was some 1·5% and was almost certainly lower in the early seventeenth century. It was probably under 1% in Lombardy, a little over 1% in Verona and Naples, perhaps 4% in Imola; well under 1% in Bohemia in 1618 and probably in Catalonia, it was 0·33 per cent in Sweden around 1610. Thus a very numerous nobility was 5–10% of the population. Countries with small nobilities had 1% or less, such as Sweden, Bohemia, much of Italy and possibly much of Germany. France and England occupy a middling position with somewhat under and over 2% respectively.[1] These percentages are very rough approximations, but at least they indicate how numerically small this important element was.

Another broad distinction is that between the mainly town-dwelling nobilities of Castile and Italy and the mainly rural nobilities of England,

[1] The Breton nobility is reckoned the most numerous of any French province and numbered some 40,000 or more in 1668, about 2% of the estimated population. J. Meyer, *La Noblesse Bretonne au XVIIIe Siècle* (1966), Vol. I, pp. 55–6.

France, Germany and Poland. In Castile and Italy nobles dominated most towns and through them the countryside, in Poland and Brandenburg the nobles dominated the countryside and had reduced most of the towns to economic and political insignificance. In France, England and western Germany the towns retained a greater independent identity, economically, socially and politically, though there was considerable interaction between them and rural gentry. In all cases such relationships were influenced by the character of royal authority and administration. The numbers of nobles often varied considerably in different regions of the same kingdom. In Castile they were more numerous in the north-west than in Andalusia; in Poland they were 27 to 31% of the population in Masovia, in Little Poland 6·3% and in Great Poland 7·6%. In Wales the gentry were notoriously more numerous than anywhere in England and Brittany had the same reputation in France. The more numerous the nobles in a given region, the greater the number of poor ones, and the fewer they were, the higher the proportion of rich ones.

This brings us to the other distinctive feature of nobilities as social groups, their inclusion of many of the wealthiest and some of the poor in their societies. The very poor nobles were a much smaller proportion of those who were poor, than the rich nobles were of those who were wealthy —the exception to the latter would be the United Provinces. While gradations of wealth and status have seldom coincided exactly in any society, the discrepancies in the seventeenth century could be very much greater than in capitalist or communist societies today. There were many officials, lawyers, merchants, even artisans and peasants who were wealthier than appreciable numbers of nobles, except in countries like Bohemia and Sicily where the number of nobles was small and where younger sons could usually be provided for in the church. In all these societies there was great emphasis on rights of precedence and many quarrels turned on the order of seating in church, of receiving the sacraments, in leaving church, in public processions and at banquets and so on. There were hierarchies inside and outside the nobility. Within the nobility titles, whether recently conferred or not, gave precedence, but among those with the same title ancientness of lineage gave precedence and was generally more esteemed than recently acquired titles.

All nobilities had to a greater or lesser extent a sense of common identity and privileges which belonged to all their members, irrespective of titles and wealth. Both were perhaps most strongly developed in Poland, where there were no legal distinctions between higher and lower nobility and there was insistence that legally all were equal (though even there the wealthy came to be called *nobiles* and the poor *generosi*). The other extreme is England where specific legal privileges were confined to peers of parliament and descended only to the eldest male heir; the rest, however ancient their lineage or great their fortunes, were counted as gentry.

However they did still enjoy a measure of informally privileged treatment in so far as the full rigour of the law was usually reserved for the poor and humble. It was a common saying among French country gentlemen that they were as noble as the king. The comparison seemed blasphemous to Loyseau and other jurists, but it stressed a corporate pride and a desire for equality within the nobility.

The most important privilege possessed by most nobilities, except the English, was fiscal. The exemption of French nobles from the *taille* and the distinction between nobles and *pecheros* in Castile, the immunities from taxation, or preferential rates of tax, belonging to nobles' fiefs and demesnes in most countries, commemorated times when nobles were supposed to have given personal military service. The fiscal privileges of nobles were seriously eroded in France and Castile in our period, but the general tendency for indirect taxes to grow was very marked all over Europe. This was partly influenced by nobles' privileges, though also by a general disinclination of the wealthy to see their incomes taxed and by considerations of fiscal convenience. An important and long-lasting attitude was transmitted beyond Europe by this conception of privilege. Although the Council of the Indies had not favoured the creation of a colonial nobility or sale of titles, the fact that the only *pecheros*, those burdened with tributes and services, in Spanish America were Indians, Negroes and mulattoes, meant that all white colonists were noble, according to the definition of nobility in Castile.[1] It was altogether fitting that Quevedo's *El Buscón*, Pablo, whose consuming, but constantly thwarted desire, was to be accepted as an *hidalgo* and obliterate his tainted parentage, should end by sailing to the Indies.

In Poland nobles were subject to laws providing accusatory procedures and milder penalties, instead of the inquisitorial procedures and severer penalties of the law governing peasants and townspeople. Most nobilities had special customs relating to the inheritance of property, especially that in the form of fiefs: these varied between different regions, as did customs of peasant or bourgeois inheritance. However there were special legal devices creating unbarrable entails of land, such as the Spanish *mayorazgo*, though by the seventeenth century this was not exclusively used by nobles. In Sicily and the Roman lands such limitations by *fidei commissa* had developed considerably by the sixteenth century, though in most of Italy, France and the Habsburg lands the main growth was after 1600, while in England the strict settlement developed after 1640.[2] Such devices were of most importance for comparatively large landowners. But there were also older privileges belonging to all nobles.

[1] R. Konetzke, 'La formación de la nobleza en Indias', *Estudios Americanos*, Vol. III (1951), pp. 329–57.
[2] S. J. Woolf, *Studi sulla Nobilita Piemontese nell'epocà del'Assolutismo* (Turin, 1963), pp. 150–3 and below, p. 583.

In Spain and France and most other countries nobles were exempt from billeting and could not be pressed as common soldiers, though they might owe personal service to the prince. In most countries the habitual wearing of swords was restricted to nobles and everywhere they claimed exemption from certain forms of punishment, particularly flogging and usually hanging. In England there were no legal rules as elsewhere, but there seems to have been strong conventional feeling that gentlemen ought to be exempt from flogging. In Spain nobles were exempt from torture, except when heresy and treason were involved; they could not be arrested for debt, nor could execution be had on their houses, clothes, arms, or horses. Spanish law, like that of most countries, granted these privileges to foreign nobles who were residents.

In some ways the most remarkable privilege recognized almost everywhere, except in Germany and England, was that the bastard of a noble was born noble, though he did not inherit his father's rank. After 1600 in France his nobility required confirmation by letters patent which was apparently never refused. This custom shows the strength of the notion of blood transmitted in the male line. In France, the Netherlands, Italy, Germany and Poland some religious houses and cathedral chapters required entrants to prove noble descent for at least three or four generations. In theory in Spain places in the military orders could only be held by nobles and in Castile in most towns half the places in the corporation were reserved for nobles.

Two other general conventions with important, if contradictory, social implications are the notion of derogation and its opposite, that certain attainments or occupations automatically conferred nobility. All societies accepted the general idea that there were some occupations whose nature was so base and servile that they were incompatible with nobility, though, unlike other countries, England did not have formal rules about this. This idea goes back to Aristotle and the Greek notion of base and mechanical occupations. The definitions varied, one of the crucial differences being whether to trade as a merchant was incompatible with nobility, as it was in France, Naples, Ferrara, Germany, the southern Netherlands, but not in Spain, Venice, Genoa, Milan, Tuscany, Poland and England. Clearly social conventions exerted pressure whatever rules the law laid down; Spanish nobles were not famous as merchants, though in Seville many were attracted into trade in the sixteenth century. The rules of derogation again emphasize the notion of blood: children born before derogation inherited nobility, a noble recovered his status when he ceased to practise a degrading occupation. The ideal noble 'lived nobly' on the proceeds of his land, not by gainful occupations. This ideal was acknowledged by writers in Italy such as Alessandro Sardo (*Discorsi*, 1587).[1] Nearly every-

---

[1] M. Berengo, *Nobili e mercanti nella Lucca del Cinquecento* (Turin, 1965), pp. 252–62, gives a general sketch.

where it was agreed that retail trade and most handicrafts (with the famous exception of glassmaking in France) were degrading.

This feeling about derogation was thought by contemporaries to be strongest in France and more attempt was probably made to enforce the rules there than in most countries, though the feeling was also very strong in Germany and Naples. There are general complaints by Spanish writers about the numbers of poor nobles in degrading occupations, though they seem to have been more concerned about unworthy offices rather than trades. But outside the Basque provinces the *relaciones* of 1575–80 show that in New Castile the great majority of hidalgos did not 'plough or traffic', though there were a few who worked on the land, and even fewer as craftsmen, such as carpenters or cobblers.[1] Similar feelings existed in England, but remained a social prejudice without legal sanctions: opinion would have found the notion of a gentleman as a shopkeeper or craftsman comically unacceptable, but not as a merchant or *entrepreneur*, though they might be less esteemed in theory than landowners.

Agriculture presented difficulties in this context. There was a strong classical tradition which extolled it as honourable, though in many countries poor peasants were among the most exploited and least esteemed members of society. In France and Spain it was allowed that a poor noble might cultivate his own land, but not those of others. In Italy and Germany this degree of tolerance seems to have been lacking, but in some regions of Poland poor nobles were often working tenants or even shepherds. Domestic service was another occupation where distinctions were uneasy. By tradition waiting on a king or a great lord was honourable, but generally speaking by the seventeenth century such service was coming to be more ceremonious than real, if it were still to be honourable.[2] In Poland foreigners were struck by the numbers of poor nobles performing actual domestic services to magnates, while wearing their hats and insisting on other marks of respect for their status.[3] German law incorporated the conception of degrading occupations more strongly than elsewhere: *Unehrlichkeit* and *Anrüchigkeit* due to opprobrious trades, including those of shepherds, millers, tailors, jailers, hangmen and scavengers, excluded men from all judicial procedures and meant that they, their children, or even grandchildren, were excluded from other crafts.

If some writers, like Gutierrez de los Rios,[4] arrived at the somewhat unexpected conclusion that agriculture was a liberal art, not everyone in Spain accepted their seemingly more obvious contention that painting

---

[1] N. Salomon, *La Campagne de Nouvelle Castile à la Fin du XVIe Siècle* (1964), pp. 290–1.

[2] E.g. C. Loyseau, *Traité des Ordres* . . . (1610), p. 50, para 34.

[3] A. Guagninus, *Sauromatia Europea* (1578) in *Respublica* . . . *Regni Poloniae* (Elzevir, 1628), pp. 263–4.

[4] *Noticia General Para la Estimación des las Artes y de la Manera en que Se conocen las liberales de las que son Mecánicas y Serviles.* . . . (Madrid, 1600), book IV, c. 3.

and sculpture belonged to the same category. In 1563 the statutes of the Order of Santiago classified painters as 'vile and mechanical'. Architects, helped by their connections with the science of fortification, gained greater acceptance as an honourable profession beyond Italy in the seventeenth century; this was so even in Germany, despite hostility to their mechanical associations with masons, which Count Rochus von Linar had experienced.[1] But much older and deeper tensions arose from questions about the privileges that university degrees and legal offices should confer. These seemed to go against the traditional conception that the noble's true vocation was that of arms. However, Bartolus and his successors had insisted that doctors of laws acquired nobility; the title-page of Moreno's book has the slogan *Las Letras y las armas dan Nobleza Conservala el Valor y la Riqueza*. Indeed Moreno says that all doctors, masters and licentiates of the universities of Salamanca, Valladolid, Alcalá de Henares and Bologna enjoyed the full privileges of nobility, while those of other universities had such privileges, except the fiscal immunities.[2] There was some dispute as to the nobility of doctors in France, but it was generally recognized in some form—in Provence it was transmitted to their children, in Dauphiné and Normandy it was only personal.[3] Most cathedral chapters in Germany accepted doctorates as the equivalent to proofs of nobility. The English accepted university graduates as gentry. In many countries nobles enjoyed preferential treatment at universities and were often excused part of the requirements for degrees. Although a good many nobles in addition to those intending to enter the church did attend universities and colleges, there was hostility between *letrados* and robe, the nobilities of privilege and office in Spain and France, on the one hand, and the nobles of lineage. This is equally apparent in Moreno's diatribes and in Loyseau's 'the insolence of minor country gentlemen is so great . . . that it is impossible to live in peace with them . . . they are birds of prey whose only occupation . . . is to live off others and to persecute each other'. He includes graduates and officers of justice and finance in the Third Estate, remarking that officers formerly came from the nobility as in Rome, but that French nobles 'despise letters and embrace idleness'.[4] This has yet to be confirmed by systematic research, though some French nobles spoke as though knowledge of Latin was almost a derogation. The French seem to have gone further than most countries in providing special academies for nobles which concentrated on fencing, riding, dancing, writing and elementary mathematics applied to surveying and fortification, without any Latin. Paradoxically this owed something to a humanist tradition, supported by Vives and

[1] E. Hempel, *Baroque Art and Architecture in Central Europe* (1965), pp. 10, 28, 31.
[2] Fo. 16. Fray Juan Benito Guardiola's *Tratado de Nobleza . . .* (Madrid, 1595) does not seem to allow this to graduates of other universities.
[3] G.-A. de la Roque, *Traité de la Noblesse . . .* (Rouen, 1678), Chapter 42.
[4] Loyseau, *Traité . . .* pp. 57, 95-9.

others, which stressed the educational value of the mechanical arts. Most nobles in Poland, Austria, Hungary and many parts of Germany must have known Latin, since it was an officially spoken, as well as written language, for many lay purposes. In general the more really poor nobles there were, the more numerous ill-educated ones were likely to be.

Even in France the situation was more complex than Loyseau's remarks might imply. Some high robe families had genuine noble origins, they all usually owned land and seigneurial rights so that they had common interests with the rural nobles. In Bavaria the lesser nobility became more intermingled with the urban patriciates; many families became office-holders in the court and administration of the dukes and electors and some rose by this means into the ranks of the higher nobility.[1] Nevertheless there was a general tendency from the sixteenth century onwards for the older nobility to try to close their ranks and enforce distinctions between themselves and the newly ennobled. In France this took the form of sweeping demands for abolition of sale of office and reservation of certain offices, or a proportion of them, for nobles. These were unsuccessful, but from 1600 onwards the crown did make increasing efforts to check usurpation of noble status, though these were often unpopular with the lesser nobles. In Spain there was a hardening of attitudes against the newly privileged so that by the mid-seventeenth century those without noble parents and grandparents were excluded from the military orders and from the municipalities of Madrid and some other cities where there was a monopoly of government by nobles.[2] In Westphalia the urban patriciate of the larger towns had been very little behind the lesser nobility in social esteem and had intermarried with them in the fifteenth century. By the later sixteenth century there was a marked cleavage between them, with the nobles attempting to exclude the patricians from the *Landtag* and the chapter of Munster.[3]

While most of the pressure in these directions came from the poorer nobles, it was the rich nobles, the magnates (not all of them from old families), who were most successful in maintaining or increasing their power and wealth in most countries during the seventeenth century. Rules about derogation hurt poor nobles by restricting their choice of occupation, without inconveniencing rich ones, just as special laws of entail were only of use to those with adequate lands to settle. The most important and universal inheritance of poor nobles were the conceptions of blood, lineage and honour. In practice their best means of enforcing some sort of solidarity and equality among all nobles, whatever their rank or wealth, was through notions of honour, enforced by the duel. A noble

[1] F. W. Euler, in *Deutscher Adel 1430–1555*, ed. H. Rössler (Darmstadt, 1965), pp. 91–2.
[2] Dominguez Ortiz, *La sociedad española en el siglo XVII*, Vol. I (Madrid, 1963), pp. 195, 258.
[3] G. Theuerkauf in *Deutscher Adel*, pp. 160–71.

could only refuse a challenge and still preserve his reputation, if the challenger was not noble. The rise of the duel accompanied the decline of the tournament. In the thirteenth century the tournament had been realistic, bloody and relatively cheap. A poor knight could compete and make his name. Fifteenth- and sixteenth-century tournaments were so expensive as to become largely the preserve of princes, their favourites and magnates. The duel was cheap and deadly and put the poor noble on a genuine equality with the rich. A man could make a reputation (however dubious in the eyes of moralists and clerical or lay authority) with his sword. Buckingham may have been the last practitioner of the tournament in England and it seems to have died out all over Europe in this period. *Manège*, the management of great horses, was the fashionable conspicuous expenditure of the rich, usually requiring indoor riding schools; its relevance to warfare is dubious, but it has left its mark on equestrian portraits.

The duel on the point of honour seems to have developed in France from the early sixteenth century and produced a distinctive code which had absolute force in controlling the behaviour and reputation of nobles. It is generally thought to have originated in Italy and clearly owed much to the rules about duels and challenges between soldiers which receive so much attention in treatises on martial law. By the later sixteenth century duelling was a distinctive feature of the behaviour of nobles all over Europe. Francis I and Henri II had tried to control duels by reviving judicial combat, Henri IV by prohibiting them, unless they had explicit permission, while his successors tried to prohibit them absolutely, as did James I in England and the Spanish Kings. A chorus of jurists and divines supported such prohibitions, which were particularly ineffective in this period, though duels became less frequent in Spain and France in the later seventeenth century.

Yet Bodin had said 'the Prince can dispose of a subject's life and goods, but has no power over his honour'. Here we have a code of conduct which was in direct defiance of the rules laid down by church and state and of course with the tradition which identified true nobility with virtue. If there is an impression that more duels were fought in France than elsewhere, the conception of honour was certainly of the greatest importance in Spanish life and literature. It is convenient to concentrate on Spain, because the conception has been much analysed there, but this does not imply that it was unimportant elsewhere. '"Honour" and "dishonour" depend upon the consciousness of the individual; "fame" and "infamy" upon that of society.' Honour is equated with life and dishonour with death, for infamy is a social death. Hence the essential proposition of the code of honour is that honour is more valuable than life, or that life without honour is impossible. Hence the obligation to accept any challenge from an appropriate challenger, to punish verbal insults, give the lie. To refuse is to accept infamy or social death. Yet, as Caro Baroja points out, there were Castilian proverbs which took a different line: 'most honour, most pain', 'honour alone is a poor inheritance', 'between honour and wealth, the last is first'.[1] (We may add there were similar English and French proverbs.) A further complication in the Spanish situation was *limpieza*, the idea of being dishonoured by the possession of Moorish or Jewish blood, or by an ancestor condemned by the Inquisition. Although it is true that the imposition of the rules about *limpieza* was popular, since many *pecheros* were 'pure', while many noble families were 'tainted', it can also be seen as a move by poor nobles against the rich ones whose blood was more likely to be 'tainted'.

The duty to kill to defend honour or avenge dishonour was a major theme in Spanish plays, including those of the highly religious Calderón. This and the fact that the plays as printed and performed were licensed and approved by the church has led some to argue that the code expressed in the plays was accepted in ordinary life and approved by casuists in dealing with actual conduct. But it can be shown that the essential proposition that honour is more important than life was rejected by many casuists, though they agreed that honour and reputation were more valuable than property. The dramatists themselves may have used the imperatives of this code as a convention of proven popularity with their audiences rather than as a serious account of real life.[2] Most authorities condemned duelling, but some Spanish and Italian casuists thought it could be justifiable and at least one Spanish casuist accepted the right of nobles to kill commoners who persisted in repeating insults to their honour.[3] Loyseau savagely regarded the propensity of French nobles towards duelling as an 'attribute of divine providence so that as in nature the most dangerous animals exterminate each other so does our nobility which is not only the most valiant, but also the most violent and insolent in the world'.

Nobles had to be prepared to use force against each other in order to live honourably and to some extent their living and status might depend on the use of force against others. If their status and privileges were generally acknowledged by the rest of society, poor nobles were more likely to have to assert their claims to recognition and precedence personally, while rich ones could leave it to their clients or servants. To a greater or lesser extent most societies connived at the revenging of supposed insults to nobles by commoners, whether to the point of murder as sometimes happened in Spain or Prague, or the beatings or mutilations by noblemen's servants with which French writers might be threatened

[1] J. Caro Baroja, 'A historical account of several conflicts', in *Honour and Shame*, ed. J. Peristiany (1965), pp. 81–137.
[2] C. A. Jones, 'Honour in Spanish Golden Age Drama', *Bull. Hispanic Studies*, Vol. 35 (1958), pp. 199–210.
[3] Dominguez Ortiz, *La sociedad española* . . . , p. 286.

and which occasionally happened. But the naked use of force in order to secure power and livelihood were still part of the way of life of many nobles in south-western France, whether in leading peasants against tax-collectors, or maintaining possession of disputed lands and levying illegal dues.[1] Alliances between bandits and nobles in order to exploit peasants and travellers had been traditional in sixteenth-century Catalonia, in the papal states, Naples and Sicily. Such habits died out in Catalonia after about 1618 and among the Roman nobility in the late sixteenth century, but they continued in Naples and Sicily. There it was not just a matter of poor nobles sharing profits with bandits, but of the use of outlaws and bandits to intimidate communes and their elected officials; if need be, murdering those who resisted the illegal demands of a local magnate.

Fynes Moryson, whose personal observations were made in the 1590s, provides some comparative impressions of the incidence of violence in the social life of nobles. He considered that among the Germans few were killed or seriously hurt in combat, owing to their peaceable nature and lack of taking offence. This he contrasted not only with France, but also with England, where men 'being most impatient of reproaches and the law giving ridiculous satisfactions for injuries by word and all wrongs, excepting maimes, it hath been accounted a disgracefull course to seeke remedy that way and most injuries have commonly been revenged by the Sword in single combat . . .'. Because the law again gave no satisfaction for words, quarrels and brawls were frequent in Holland. He found few single combats in Italy, the original home of duelling, as premeditated murder for revenge was more usual. In Prague ' . . . manslaughters committed by Gentlemen against strangers and those of meaner condition are much more frequent [than in Germany] because Gentlemen can only be judged in Parliament [the Estates] which are not often called and are then tried by Gentlemen who are partiall in the cause and commonly acquit or delude Justice by delaies . . .'. The greatest contrast was in Switzerland, where the law was severe against brawls and provided satisfactions so that even among soldiers there were few murders; 'all bystanders are bound to keep the peace and a man who kills another can only escape capital punishment if he can prove self-defence'. Nevertheless the wearing of swords was more widespread than in most countries.

Another comparison which rightly interested Moryson was that between enjoyment of hunting rights in different countries. He considered that there was more hunting of deer and more hawking in England and Scotland and that the English gentry had many more parks for keeping deer than elsewhere in Europe. He rightly pointed out that in most parts of Germany 'all Hunting is forbidden to any but absolute Princes in their

[1] Y.-M. Bercé, 'La Noblesse rurale . . . sous Louis XIII', *Annales du Midi* (1964), pp. 44–59.

own territories', except hunting of 'hurtful beasts', such as foxes and wolves, 'only in some parts the Hunting of Hares is permitted to Gentlemen, as in Saxony . . .'. In Denmark nobles could only hunt 'in their own grounds of inheritance', elsewhere only the king could hunt. The higher nobility in Bohemia had full hunting rights over their lands. There, in Saxony and other parts of Germany, the unauthorized killing of deer and wild boar, even though they were spoiling crops, was punishable by death, while he claimed that in Austria the lords' leave was needed to kill sparrows. In Flanders nobles had the right to hunt hares, pheasants and partridges, whereas in Holland and Friesland partridges and seafowl were taken by the vulgar. Moryson thought Italy unsuited to hunting and saw very little going on there and in Poland. Although there was a great deal in France, they hunted in the open fields and had few parks, while only great men could afford to keep hawks. Moryson only saw hawking once in Poland and once in Bohemia 'never ells . . . I did in any place see any exercise either of Hunting or Hawking which so frequently offers itself to passengers neere the high wayes of England' which . . . 'hath more fallow Deer than all Europe. No Kingdom in the World hath so many Dovehouses.' Again the great exception is Switzerland where 'Hunting . . . is free for all men, they having few gentlemen . . . In like manner all sorts of men have freedom to fish in all rivers, brooks or lakes, being in the Territories of their particular Cantons or Commonwealths. And like freedom have they to hawke and take all kinds of birds by nets and like Arts . . .'[1]. In fact the rights of non-nobles to hunt in France had been finally abolished in the sixteenth century, except in the case of wolves and foxes. In England property qualifications for keeping dogs, ferrets or nets and for using guns or bows for hunting were imposed in 1606 and penalties on poaching were increased.

Moryson makes other observations which, though doubtless subjective, are of general interest. He found the 'French use great liberty of conversation and small reverence to superiors', despising English gentlemen for wearing great lords' liveries 'even for a festival day' and giving them so much deference. French visitors in their turn were struck by the ceremoniousness of the English court, compared with that of Henri IV. Moryson remarked that in English inns gentlemen expected to eat in their chambers or sit at table only with gentry, whereas in Germany commoners sat at the same table, but lower down, receiving poorer service for the same price. He thought the Germans used their wives as servants, but did not 'exact respect from their children' who 'shake hands with them instead of raising their hats and asking blessing on their knees as in England'. He also marvelled that

[1] Moryson, *An Itinerary* (1617), pp. 85, 148, 151, 169, 200, 221–2, 261, 287; *Shakespeare's Europe*, ed. C. Hughes (1903), pp. 159, 354–5, 367, 387, 397, 468; Corpus Christi Coll., Oxford, MS 94, fos. 215, 538–9, 544, 646.

the Gentlemen howsoever sometimes learned yet proudly despise Graduates of the University, no less or more than Merchants which I found not onely by common practice, but also by my private experience. For conversing with a Gentleman, he perceiving I spake Latin better than he thought became a Gentleman, asked me how long I did study in the University . . . [and] did after esteem me as a Pedant . . .

Moryson wondered that, despite 'Gentlemen first rising by learning, warfare and traffic, they only judge warfare worthy to raise and continue Gentlemen . . .'. We might guess that these were the prejudices of lesser and poorer nobles. For it is certain that many Austrian and German nobles were well educated and that they had a distinctive culture based on knowledge not only of Latin, but also of modern Romance languages. It has been said that the basic works of that culture were Cicero's *De Officiis*, Petrarch's *Canzoniere* and Ariosto's *Orlando Furioso* and that the dominant tone of European culture derived from the patronage and tastes of nobles and courts, to which non-noble readers and writers largely conformed, or aspired.[1]

While there is much truth in this, yet proverbial wisdom and long-standing ethical and religious traditions contradicted or were sceptical of noble values. However, though literature, art and proverbial lore may mostly reflect noble or peasant ways of life, the lack of much explicit literary concern with the ways of life of bourgeois and artisans does not show that these did not have distinctive values and cultures of their own. The evangelists of both Protestantism and the Counter-Reformation disapproved of popular magical superstitions and of both popular and noble tastes for bloody and adulterous chivalric romances. The first great picaresque novel *Guzmán de Alfarache* was a deliberate moralizing alternative to these romances, 'a "truthful" literature in response to the explicit demands of the Counter-Reformation'.[2] Yet if the moral intention wore thin in Alemán's successors the success of the new genre did not in fact transform popular taste: 'novels of chivalry . . . were reprinted in the form of chap-books, until very near our own times and . . . especially in the south of Spain . . . were the favourite reading of drovers and farm hands . . .'. In France chap-books based on the Charlemagne romances were also a staple of popular reading throughout the seventeenth and eighteenth centuries. Such works presented a mythical medieval society and were almost exclusively concerned with the deeds of kings and nobles and a perpetual crusade against the infidel. French popular literature presented a world of myth and miracles, of saints, giants and magic which was alien not only to the general trend of intellectual development among the learned, but also to the humanistic elements in the ideal and actual education of nobles. Spanish popular literature seems to have been

[1] O. Brunner, *Adeliges Landleben und Europäischer Geist* (Salzberg, 1949); *Neue Wege der Sozialgeschichte* (Göttingen, 1956), 'Osterreichische Adelsbibliotheken'.
[2] A. A. Parker, *Literature and the Delinquent* (Edinburgh, 1967), p. 22.

peculiar in that influence of oral tradition was much stronger on 'official literature' than in France or England, particularly on verse plays. More Spanish chap-books were probably in verse and they certainly included more poems from well-known writers and more adaptations of their plays and stories.[1]

Thus, small as the numbers of nobles were in proportion to the rest of the population, attitudes deriving from their culture not only influenced the literature and art of the educated but also that accessible to the un-educated. If Corneille's plays have heroes who embodied stoic and chivalric virtues of ideal nobles, supported by pride and the quest for glory, they also share with the chap-books' romances the justification of noble rebellions against injustice and tyranny. But however widespread its influence this culture, sympathetic to the ideals of the nobility, did not enjoy an undisputed monopoly; the Christian, medieval and humanistic traditions all had elements which were hostile to its assumptions and which still survived in the writings of divines, jurists and moralists. Moreover the economic interests and political aspirations of great and poor nobles might differ considerably. The conventions and legal rules about derogatory occupations, personal service, or living nobly, also differed appreciably between different countries. The ideals of the nobility, tacitly and explicitly expressed in their own behaviour and culture, might conflict with many of the realities of everyday life, but they also strongly influenced the cultural ideals of much of the rest of the population, espe-cially through plays and chap-books. Such conflicts and contrasts grew stronger as a result of royal policies and fiscal necessities. There was pressure to reduce noble fiscal privileges and excesses of duelling, but more important and more general were the sales of titles and privileges of nobility and of royal rights of jurisdiction and taxation over local communities. There was an almost universal tendency for great nobles, who included some men or families recently risen to greatness, to con-solidate or maintain their power as a group and for lesser ones to become more dependent upon serving kings or magnates for their survival, less able to pursue effectively and independently their own political and social aims.

The European nobilities were economically heterogeneous groups of diverse origins. Although all accepted ideologies which proclaimed that they ought either to be closed groups, or at worst groups which co-opted new members according to strict rules, reality was different. In most countries many, perhaps most noble families had been recruited by prescription, often in defiance of legal rules, and such recruitment con-tinued. This produced paradoxical situations; perhaps the most extreme

[1] Baroja, 'A historical account . . .', in *Honour and Shame*, pp. 113, 116; R. Mandrou, *De la culture populaire au 17e et 18e siècles* (1964); E. M. Wilson, *Some Aspects of Spanish Literary History* (Oxford, 1966).

was that in Poland, where the king could not create new nobles without the consent of the Diet, yet the Diet made no serious attempt to control or prevent recruitment by prescription so that by 1630 thousands of cases of usurpation of nobility were alleged.[1] It was in absolutist France that the strictest efforts were made to control the acquisition of nobility by prescription. These were particularly vigorous from the late 1650s and the lesser nobility of some regions attempted organized protest and resistance. The state was always the most serious potential or actual competitor of the nobles, whether in trying to assert its own monopoly of violence and power, or in competing with them in exploiting rural populations and in some cases urban ones. The divisions of the spoils and power and their stability naturally varied in different countries. The forces affecting policies and political arrangements also varied, but everywhere, except in Holland and Zeeland in the northern Netherlands, the Swiss cantons and the duchy of Württemberg, the nobility remained an important social and political group. In most of Europe, whether under limited or absolute monarchies they still formed the most important group in terms of prestige. But everywhere there were other self-consciously organized social groupings, even in the aristocratic republics of Venice and Poland.

By risking insecure generalizations and sweeping comparisons, we may be able to see some of the distinctive common features of European societies. In sixteenth- and seventeenth-century China there were also considerable discrepancies between the legal rules and cultural conventions concerning the status of occupations and reality; for instance mercantile wealth and military success were in theory little esteemed, but in fact gave access to power and prestige. The privileged élite, the *shen-shih*, with their wives and children, were perhaps two to three per cent of the population in the seventeenth century and were recruited by examination, purchase and success in military affairs. Their privileges were conferred because they were actual or potential officials, but for the great majority they were not hereditary, though the sons of the privileged and wealthy had a much better chance of acquiring privileged status than those of commoners. Their variety of origins, great discrepancies in wealth and power and the fact that many were landowners make the *shen-shih* roughly comparable as a privileged group with the European nobility in the inclusive sense used here. Although social mobility measured in terms of access of commoners to official positions was less in seventeenth-century China than under the early Ming, it may well have been greater than in Europe in the sense that there may have been more opportunities, though still very limited ones, to rise from the peasantry. In fact there is no information yet available either about rates at which commoners entered Europe's

[1] J. Bardach, in *Gouvernés et Gouvernants, Recueils de la Soc. J. Bodin*, Vol. xxv (1965), p. 281.

privileged groups, or about downward mobility, remotely comparable to that for China.[1] But it is clear that there was considerable upward and downward mobility among European nobilities, especially in the larger ones such as Poland's. If downward mobility was facilitated by lack of primogeniture in China (though clan custom did not always favour equal partition), extinction in the male line was facilitated by lack of polygamy in Europe. The most important differences seem to be in the relationships of social groups to the state, the extent to which they could acquire power and prestige independently of the state and the extent to which the state apparatus could control the life of communities.

If access to the centre of power may have been more open in China, the government exercised a more monolithic monopoly of power and propagated a more uniform officially approved culture. There may be distortion through concentrating on the intentions and working of governments of China, where 'history was written by officials for officials' so that the sources concentrate on the workings of bureaucracy rather than of society. Nevertheless there were many centres of power in Europe, simply because there were many states, while within each state there were groups corporately conscious of rights, either specifically conceded by or customarily entrenched against it. Conflicting explanations were available; for some theorists of natural law, like Suarez, and for all defenders of absolutism the authority of communities derived from the state, for Althusius and his followers the state was a federation or even confederation of communities. In China, towns were primarily the seats of administration by officials of a central government which exercised more control than the most absolute European monarchy. European towns usually enjoyed a more indirect relationship with central authorities which recognized their corporate privileges and identities. If their independence had generally declined since the Middle Ages and if their militias were now unable to defend them in serious warfare, they were still important for preventing popular disturbances and the excesses which the passage of friendly troops inflicted on the countryside. Even in absolute monarchies towns were often still left with discretion as to the means by which they raised some of the taxes imposed. In the *Ständestaat* as it survived in the Habsburg lands, most of Germany, Poland and the southern Netherlands, administration was shared between officials some of whom were only responsible to the ruler and others to the estates. The tutelage of more centralized administrations over local communities was growing generally, particularly in France, but it never entirely effaced their traditions and in many ways local oligarchies grew stronger. The status of village com-

---

[1] W. Eberhard, *Social Mobility in Traditional China* (Leiden, 1962); R. M. Marsh, *The Mandarins; The Circulation of Elites in China 1600–1900* (Glencoe, 1961); Ping-ti Ho, *The Ladder of Success in Imperial China* (1962); J. M. Menzel (ed.), *The Chinese Civil Service* (Boston, 1963).

munities varied, but they often did enjoy some corporate identity, recognized by rulers and seigneurs, though usually much less effective independence than towns, except in some mountainous regions. Some were controlled and exploited by towns, especially in Spain, Italy and Switzerland, though almost everywhere many more were controlled by seigneurs. For fiscal reasons higher authorities found it convenient to deal with village assemblies, or elected representatives, who could bind the community by their acts. Village syndics and assemblies survived as legal entities over much of Europe. (They existed in some English villages, but not as a general pattern fostered by central authority as in France, though they did become generalized in the township meetings of New England.) Their recognition was due mainly to their serving the convenience of others, but such institutions also served their members' purposes in regulating use of commons, waste, fallows, disposal of garbage and so on and, if need be, by collective litigation and agreements.

Chinese local government was highly centralized and left little discretion or initiative to officials: in theory the same was true of local finances, though in fact the fees and perquisites of officials were not effectively controlled. The non-official privileged élite were the spokesmen of local interests, but they had no legally defined role. Indeed they were forbidden to form associations, meddle in administration, petition on behalf of commoners or to publish essays or choose personal names without official approval. Despite sale of privileges, there were no checks on the government's power to degrade men from privileged status and such penalties were much more frequent in Chinese than in European law. Urban gilds, clans, village headmen and meetings performed important functions with direct or tacit official approval in regulating social life, especially in arbitrating to settle all kinds of disputes and applying local customs, helped by general reluctance to resort to official courts. Villages and towns did not form collective legal entities, created by individuals acting together and recognized by the administration, though they might have informal arrangements for settling their affairs, as long as the government did not choose to intervene. There were no procedures for challenging official decisions within the rules of law acknowledged by the government, as there were in European absolutist states, where litigation about conflicts of jurisdiction, execution of decrees and the assessment of taxes was frequent. In China the check on official action came from within the administration through the censorate, not through litigation; there '. . . the legal system was a system of control (though there were gaps in this) and the distribution of rights was only secondary and incidental'. European courts often performed administrative and police functions in this period, but in China judicial functions were part of the repressive duties of administrators; even for the privileged groups 'legal involvement was something to be feared and avoided' and there was extreme reluctance wholly to acquit a defendant.[1]

From the sixteenth century Christianity became less plausible in its universalist aspirations, more ambiguous and contradictory in its public prescriptions, not only because Christians were becoming identified with Europeans, but also because of the splits caused by the Reformation. Protestants and Catholics shared a common and continuing theological and intellectual inheritance, incorporating the old methods of Aristotelian scholasticism, together with newer ones of humanistic rhetoric and of critical or even comparative study of Roman law. Within the Catholicism of the Counter-Reformation there were conflicting views of man's place in the world; the Christian stoicism of Lipsius exalted human reason and ancient wisdom which Bérulle condemned as delusions and pride of those naturally wretched, ignorant and sinful. The religious orders themselves were divided by choices between hierarchical and missionary conceptions of the church. The growth of scepticism, the 'new Pyrrhonism', in the later sixteenth century did not involve any immediate breach with religion, since it mainly provided another weapon in the apologetics of relevation. Nevertheless in so far as it was used publicly to attack rational theology and support fideism, or privately by *libertins* to put all revealed religions on an equal footing, it did face even the most orthodox with intellectual choices. Thus long before the 'new philosophy' had provided a new cosmology, still less had much impact on education or the universities, European scholars were forced to consider alternative ways of interpreting their religion and legal and political institutions and had to choose between alternative methods of organizing and interpreting knowledge. If this was true within the major religious confessions or within the officially approved universities of one country, within European culture taken as a whole the available choices and possible conflicts were naturally much greater.

The monolithic character of Chinese culture can doubtless be exaggerated and the Taoist tradition had enduring importance as an unofficial alternative. Nevertheless the official culture and ideology appear to have been much more successful in presenting universal and unambiguous precepts and interpretations, public discussion and criticism of which was more severely restricted and politically dangerous, though a private life of religious contemplation or intellectual dissent might be possible. The seventeenth century saw in the 'School of Han Learning' the development of 'a discipline of historical and textual criticism' which led to the rejection of large parts of the official canonical writings 'as being interpolated,

[1] E. Balazs, *Chinese Civilization and Bureaucracy* (1964); Ch'ü T'ung-Tsu, *Local Government in China under the Ch'ing* (Harvard, 1962); Kung-Chuan Hsiao, *Rural China; Imperial Control in the Nineteenth Century* (1960); S. van der Sprenkel, *Legal Institutions in Manchu China* (1962), p. 128; D. Bodde and C. Morris, *Law in Imperial China* (Harvard, 1967), p. 197.

altered, not genuine, or intentionally falsified'. There was also a great deal of colloquial literature which was regarded officially and with justification as subversive. The common denominator of these movements of criticism and reform and of their immediate failure has been seen as anti-absolutism.[1] The ideal of official Confucianism seemed to see the state as indistinguishable from society.

This continued domination by a rigidly defined official ideology can be seen partly as a response to the needs of controlling and colonizing a vast area whose populations were originally ethnically and culturally distinct, and whose speech and environments were still very different.

The desire to unite Europe in some similar fashion had not entirely vanished by the seventeenth century. If after 1600 the greatest successes eventually went to small states, the United Provinces, Sweden and ultimately England, so that to us this seems a distinctive feature of the century, it was not only Utopian advocates of universal monarchy, such as Campanella, or those with millenarian expectations, such as Comenius, who foresaw a very different future for Europe. At a less visionary level, from the Battle of the White Mountain down to at least the Peace of Prague (1635) the possibility of a refashioning of the empire under the emperor's effective domination and of a Habsburg hegemony over continental Europe seemed far greater than at any time since Charles V's victories at Pavia or Mühlberg. There were still those like Guillén de la Camera who believed that after Nördlingen the Spanish Empire would endure for ever, or like Fray Benito de Peñalosa who rejoiced at the depopulation of Spain, caused by her divine mission to defend and propagate the faith. Fear and hatred of the Jews and Jewish blood seemed to increase Spaniards' determination to see themselves as a chosen race, characteristics they shared with militant Calvinists. A courtly sonnet hailed Philip IV as the hero who would free Asia, destroy heresy, inaugurate the universal rule of perfect law, *un Solo Pastor y un solo Imperio*.[2]

Our knowledge of what was to be tends to discount the reality of such fears and hopes, encourages us to believe that all real prospects of Habsburg hegemony had died with Philip II. Similarly the undoubted progress of Catholic restoration by 1600 can be too easily accepted as making the religious settlements of 1648 and later inevitable. Yet from a more immediate point of view the later sixteenth century was equally remarkable for the fact that the rulers of Poland, Austria, Bohemia, Hungary and France had been forced to abandon the enforcement of Catholic uniformity and to allow *de facto* or formal rights to dissidents. If the Counter-

[1] E. Balazs, *Political Theory and Administrative Reality in Traditional China* (1965), pp. 5–29.
[2] O. H. Green, *Spain and the Western Tradition*, Vol. IV (1966), pp. 5–9, 14–16.

Reformation had already made considerable progress in Germany and Poland by 1600, it was the Habsburg victories after 1618 which made the Bohemian lands, Austria and ultimately Hungary safe for Catholicism and provided conditions which assisted the growth of Catholic intolerance in Poland. The Rome of Urban VIII and Bernini was the cultural and spiritual capital of those lands reconquered for Catholicism. Yet when Santa Maria della Vittoria was built to commemorate the White Mountain still greater conquests seemed possible, but by the time the culminating splendour of the new Rome, Bernini's Piazza of St Peter's, was begun in 1656, such hopes had already gone. Nevertheless in 1635 when the Hall of the Realms at the new Buen Retiro Palace at Madrid was first displayed, its iconography celebrated more than the mere survival of the Spanish monarchy under the leadership of Olivares, and catalogued what were to have been definitive victories over heresy from Bahia to Switzerland. The fears of then obscure provincials, such as Pym and Cromwell, were not necessarily delusions of Protestant fervour, exploited by the propaganda of Richelieu or the defeated Camerarius. Both Bernini's Rome and the Hall of the Realms were built to celebrate triumphs which were not to be, but which were not necessarily impossible.

This was a Europe where there were nations with God-given destinies, though not nation-states. Everywhere men were told that all political authority was sacred, that all rulers were responsible to God. If there was dispute about the nature and amount of authority which God had given them over their subjects, there was agreement that royal authority was a kind of personal property. As legitimate kings, unlike tyrants, were bound to respect the property rights of their subjects, so their subjects must respect the rights of kings. With the exception of Poland and the empire, the elective and explicitly contractual elements in European monarchies had weakened during the sixteenth century and this trend culminated in the conversion of conquered Bohemia to what now seemed the normal and proper form of hereditary succession. Attempts by kings to settle details of government by their last wills, as magnates might settle the management of their estates, were often frustrated by assemblies, courts or councils. This also happened in France where absolutist theories interpreted fundamental law more and more narrowly until by the early seventeenth century only the law regulating monarchial succession was outside the scope of the king's sovereign power. But if the king's inheritance of his crown was analogous to the subject's right to inherit property, then the pursuit of dynastic interests and inheritances were as legitimate as the subject's enjoyment of his property rights. Externally the conception of inalienable property rights possessed by kings or dynasties was both a practical and legalistic stumbling block to universalist aspirations. Internally kings' and subjects' property rights did conflict. Perhaps the most serious conflicts arose in war, whether fought for dynastic interests or merely defensively. Then all kings and states invoked emergency powers, to over-ride normal customary or legal procedures which implied some regulation of or consent to taxes, forced loans, or requisitions and so encroached upon their subjects' property rights, which all agreed it was a main purpose of society and government to protect.

Even after 1618 most kings spent more time in hunting than in leading armies or directing wars, though state portraits might show the unmilitary Philip IV and Charles I in equestrian postures of command. James I, though devoted to hunting, was untypical in his wish to be remembered as a peacemaker. The iconography of Rubens' *Triumph of Peace*, planned in the early 1620s for the Banqueting House at Whitehall, commemorates hopes and achievements more unfounded than, and as ephemeral as those in the Hall of the Realms, but expected the union of Christendom by very different means.[1] Rubens' ceiling symbolizes more than James' failures in foreign policy, for his inability to pay for it reminds us of the failure of most European states to reform their finances and administrations effectively during the two decades of comparative peace and prosperity before 1620. Those decades were not particularly peaceful around the Baltic and were neither peaceful nor prosperous in the Muscovy of the Time of Troubles. They were also a time of disaster for the Ottomans; revolts in the Balkans and throughout Anatolia were followed by defeats by the Persians. The major immediate cause of Ottoman difficulties was the earlier Persian war which they had ended victoriously in 1590.[2] Similarly war or civil war had strained the governments and resources of Spain, France, the Netherlands, England and the Habsburg lands. By 1609 all these states were faced with the need to revivify their ordinary means of peacetime administration and above all to restore their finances.

Most governments wished to restore or increase their authority in ecclesiastical affairs. This might mean trying to increase the effectiveness of national churches by trying to settle disputes and grievances concerning them, as in France or England. All states, with the exception of Transylvania, aspired to religious uniformity, not diversity, as their ideal and many were increasingly repressive towards dissenters. In the sixteenth century secular encroachments on church property happened everywhere. Even in Spain, where there were no direct Protestant threats, the crown sold and exploited church lands and rights. By contrast the seventeenth century saw the church generally recovering or even increasing its property. In most countries serious threats of secularization and alienation, or resistance to paying tithes, diminished and had virtually ceased by 1660. The main secular demands on the churches' wealth were taxes and contributions to pay for wars. Governments certainly tried to

[1] Per Palme, *Triumph of Peace* (1957), pp. 260–2.
[2] See Vol. III in this series, pp. 371–6 and below, Chapter xx, p. 626.

increase these, but in so far as they had become more explicitly committed to defend ecclesiastical property and authority in its traditional forms this limited the expedients available for dealing with debts and fiscal problems.

By 1610 it might have seemed that France had solved and England was about to solve their immediate financial problems and that Spain would make some concerted attempt to deal with hers. By 1621 it was apparent that they had not; in all three countries ordinary revenue did not cover actual expenditure, governments' debts were large and their credit poor. The countries which seemed to be stronger financially were the United Provinces, Denmark and Sweden. Sweden's achievement was the more remarkable since it took place during almost continuous and not always successful war, but in the long run, though Sweden's administration and power were effectively transformed, her pursuit of security and Baltic interests proved beyond her financial resources. The country where there was most discussion about the plight of the economy and the government's finances and least done to remedy them was Spain. The only problem which Philip III chose to tackle was the unreal, if highly emotive one, of the Moriscos. Their expulsion (1609–14) was approved by the church, the Inquisition and the mass of Castilians against the opposition of the nobility and wealthier townsmen of the kingdoms of Valencia and Aragon. This can be seen as a last stage in making Spain and its culture closed and inward-looking, concerned above all to defend its purity and honour, a process whose sixteenth-century landmarks had included the rejection of Erasmian influences and the prohibition of studies abroad. More immediately it may have been an attempt to conciliate Castilians at the expense of Aragonese interests for the failure of the peace to lighten their fiscal burdens. What is certain is that it ruined much of Valencia's economy immediately, while ultimately stimulating even greater French immigration into Aragon and exacerbating the general difficulties already caused by rural depopulation and lack of man-power.

In 1615 Philip III's total expenditure was more than in 1608 and not more than ten per cent below the highest years of the 1590s, when the crown's receipts from American silver had been twice as great and the yield of Castile's taxes much higher. Yet reforms comparable to Sully's were possible in Philip III's dominions, as the count of Lemos showed in Naples (1610–16). In 1612 there was a deficit of 1,600,000 ducats, over half the average receipts. This was cut by reducing interest on debts, by more efficient accounting and collection, by increasing rents of tax-farms and by raising new customs duties and an extraordinary *donativo*. Ordinary expenditure was reduced, revenues were reallocated, most of them going to a new department the *Cassa Militare*, which, as assigned annuities and rents fell in, should have an increasing surplus which would pay off the 10,000,000 debt, whose interest was 800,000 ducats a year. By

1616 the deficit equalled the amount of interest, but Lemos' successor, the aggressive Osuna,[1] rapidly undid his achievements. By 1621 the deficit was nearly 4,000,000, the debt perhaps 20,000,000 ducats and the economy had been severely shaken by devaluations in 1617, 1618 and 1620.[2]

In England and France anticipations and assignments had eroded ordinary revenues and ensured permanent deficits so that nominally short-term debts were often left unpaid to the detriment of royal credit. The Notables in 1627 were told that the French deficit had long averaged some 5,000,000 to 6,000,000 *livres* a year, despite considerable increases in indirect taxation, sales of offices and other expedients. This was due to the expenses of civil war and of pensions and rewards to magnates. Louis XIII, unlike Philip III, Philip IV, James I and Charles I, proved capable of controlling and reducing the expenses of his court and household, though reforming statesmen, like Sully, Cranfield, Olivares, Richelieu, or Strafford still expected substantial rewards for themselves and their creatures. Not that more austerity and less magnificence by courts and governments would necessarily have changed the course of international relations and of economic and commercial developments. But in so far as there was a general failure by states to maintain or increase their financial strength down to 1620, when international and economic circumstances were relatively favourable, of which the most extreme example is the conduct of Philip III and Lerma, this restricted their freedom of action in conducting war and foreign policy and so influenced the character of the war. While the great debasements and manipulations of coinage in Poland and Germany after 1616 may have economic causes, they were also the result of the greed and financial difficulties of rulers and towns. The governments involved in war after 1618 had less realizable, or unmortgaged, fiscal resources than a hundred or even fifty years before. They were more dependent on tax-farmers and financiers.

The financial failures of peacetime conditioned the conduct of war most obviously in attempts to make it pay for itself. These were not new, but the contribution systems of Wallenstein, the imperialists and the Swedes were more systematic and longer lasting in their effects. War at sea had always relied on such hopes, but again the activities of the Dutch West India Company and the Dunkirkers were greater and lasted longer. Statesmen, like Richelieu and Olivares, were well aware that to decide on war was to precipitate financial, political and administrative crises, whose outcome was unpredictable, though they hoped to control them. Rulers invoked extraordinary powers to deal with the emergency and once armies were raised, they could, if necessary, be maintained by applying the contribution-system or something like it to their own subjects, over-

[1] See below, Chapter IX, pp. 275–6.
[2] G. Galasso, *Mezzogiorno medievale e moderno* (Turin, 1965), ' . . . le finanze napoletane nella prima meta del Seicento'

riding local authorities and the traditional apparatus of fiscal administration. But once raised, armies and their commanders were not fully controllable by their governments at home and still less abroad, arrears of pay and promises of rewards to commanders often meant the failure or prolongation of peace negotiations, of which the most famous example is the Swedish quest for *satisfactio* after 1636. If rulers claimed emergency powers and often possessed greater means of asserting them, these threatened both to transform and destroy their governments. Fiscal pressures could produce popular revolts which might directly or indirectly involve the ruling groups of whole provinces. At the same time that emergency administrative and judicial commissions claimed greater power for the state, rulers were often selling off or mortgaging their traditional authority and powers. Sales of offices, jurisdictions, lands, rights, privileges, titles and honours could change the character of ruling groups and their political, economic and social relationships with governments and the rest of the population. The actions of governments seemed to become identified with the interests of tax-farmers, financiers and armies and alien to those of most of their subjects. The war became not so much one of attrition, but a gamble as to which tottering conglomeration of alienated local interests and exhausted taxpayers could avoid collapsing for longer than its enemies. The counterpart to this in diplomacy was the general use of that method of 'continual negotiation' which Richelieu made famous. At any given moment one or more of the belligerents had more than usually urgent reasons for making peace. But entering the war in the first place had involved such dangers and losses that the longer it lasted, the more it seemed that there was little more to be lost by gambling on a change of fortune and the difficulties of opponents. As the stakes spent on war grew higher, the more necessary it seemed for the temporarily stronger party in the negotiations to secure some real gains, hence the difficulty of reaching any settlement. Initially both Spain and France made some attempt to solve their financial problems by traditional methods of consultation, before turning to more desperate expedients.

In willingly accepting the renewal of war in 1621 Olivares was the heir of the imperial past; to find means to fight the war, he had no choice but also to try to be the heir of the *arbitristas*. The most important part of the latter inheritance was the attempt to restore the economy and the crown's credit by founding a national banking system. Plans for banks managed by municipalities and the crown had been discussed under Philip II; in 1599 the Cortes approved such a scheme and granted taxes on condition that it was implemented. Despite complaints, nothing was done, but after 1617 discussions revived; in 1621 a junta was appointed and at last in 1623 a decree was published. Banks and pawnshops were to be set up in 119 towns and financed by a forced loan of a twentieth from lay and clerical estates over 2,000 ducats, converted into perpetual annuities at 3%. All ecclesiastical and charitable foundations were to deposit their funds and the banks would have a monopoly of loans, selling redeemable annuities at 5% and lending at 7%. The Cortes opposed the forced loan and finally only granted taxes on condition that the king financed the banks and withdrew their monopoly of lending (1626). An attempt to set up a Crown banking company in 1627, managed by Italian financiers and chartered to conduct lotteries, deal in foreign exchange and have a monopoly of *censos*, was defeated in the same way in 1628 and 1629.[1]

These schemes attempted to tackle fundamental problems, even if all that they promised would have been unlikely to happen. Although they would have strengthened the crown's bargaining power with the hated foreign financiers, they offended clergy, nobles, *letrados* and the richer townsmen. Apart from paying the forced loan, men of property would suffer from the monopoly of lending and control of interest rates. One of Spain's longstanding problems was the strong preference such men showed for *censos* [redeemable rent charges] against other forms of investment; men even sold land to buy them and the clergy used them extensively. Thus the banks' monopoly would have reduced the income of all holders of *censos*, because it would eventually become impossible to get a higher return than 5% on any loan. This was expected to stimulate more productive investments. But the banks were not necessarily attractive to debtors who would have had to pay the normal 7%, while greater nobles had often obtained royal privileges which forced their creditors to accept rates well below this.[2] Thus the Cortes rejected the *arbitristas*, expressed an explicit preference for increasing indirect taxes[3] and by implication chose the way of debasements and arbitrary expedients. It was also a warning that if the ruling groups of Castile would not accept Olivares' plans, the prospects of the other Iberian kingdoms accepting them were poor. In the long run no one trusted the monarchy to keep its promises and the non-Castilians were unlikely to exchange their relative immunity from the fiscal burdens of empire for promises of the de-Castilianization of its rewards in the Union of Arms.[4]

The plans for reforming the French monarchy put to the Assembly of Notables of 1626 were as comprehensive as anything considered by the councils of Castile, and some of them also had long histories. A favourite expedient for improving French finances and credit was the redemption of the alienated rights and lands of the royal demesne. This had been urged by the States General in 1614 and earlier and had actually been begun by Sully. Richelieu wished to raise a forced loan at low interest from the towns and clergy to provide a fund to complete its redemption during the

[1] E. J. Hamilton, 'Spanish Banking Schemes before 1700', *Journal of Pol. Economy*, Vol. LVII (1949).
[2] B. Bennassar, *Valladolid au siècle d'or* (Paris, 1967), pp. 258–72, 557–67.
[3] *Actas de las Cortes de Castilla*, Vol. XXXIX, pp. 5–20.
[4] See below, Chapter XV, p. 463.

next six years. The Notables doubted whether any loan would be used for this purpose. Despite Richelieu's promises, they neither accepted his plan nor offered any real remedies for the financial difficulties. However, they did approve the plans for reviving commercial and maritime power, which themselves were in part a reply to Olivares' attempts to achieve the same results. For the time being Richelieu thought it possible to conduct a war or expensive foreign policies, while simultaneously pursuing administrative reforms and mercantilist plans at home. By 1629 he thought a choice had to be made, and so seems to show better judgment than Olivares, but for Olivares there was no alternative to attempting structural reforms while fighting a war. The attitude of the Cortes of Castile made such an attempt both essential to finance the war and unlikely to succeed. Neither they nor other statesmen could overcome the difficulty that creditors would never trust absolute rulers who claimed uncontrolled emergency powers to keep long-term financial promises.

Before examining how the cost of war was met and its effects, it is worth considering to what extent conditions outside Europe helped to make it possible for so many European states to engage in prolonged warfare and what turning points in the struggle were decisive for changing the distribution of power in Europe. As the Ottomans continued to be distracted by internal dissensions down to 1627 and after that were still concentrating their resources on a renewed war with Persia (1623–39), there was no serious threat to distract the Habsburgs in Hungary. Central and eastern Europe and the Ottomans had turned their backs on each other, apart from border skirmishes, as Spain and the Ottomans had done in the last two decades of the sixteenth century. This also assisted the Poles in expanding into White Russia and above all into the Ukraine, without producing an immediate need for strengthening the military and administrative power of the crown. However, the failure of the Polish kings to defend their Baltic provinces and interests against the Swedes gives a misleading impression of Polish power. Poland was still the greatest military power in eastern Europe, when the nobles chose to unite their forces behind the crown. The Diet refused to support Sigismund III's and Ladislas IV's Baltic plans and by treating Ladislas' plans against the Turks in the same way helped to precipitate the Cossack revolt of 1648. But to defend their Ukrainian colonization they raised 100,000 men for the Chocim campaign of 1621 against the Turks and Tartars, and 120,000 against Bohdan Khmelnytsky in 1651. Thus Ottoman weakness after the death of Murad IV indirectly contributed to the eclipse of Poland by encouraging Ladislas' plans. In western Europe power shifted as a result of the renewal of direct conflict between France and Spain.

Olivares, looking back after the catastrophe of 1640, thought that Spain's defeats had their origins in the Mantuan war (1628–31). Until then the Habsburgs had been victorious, but viewed from Madrid the situation was unsatisfactory. Spanish money and sometimes Spanish troops had made possible the reconquest of Bohemia and the victories of the Catholic League and Wallenstein in Germany, yet it had proved impossible to get any promise of a general league against the Dutch from either the emperor or the princes, who resented Spain's occupation of the Lower Palatinate. Olivares had also hoped to ruin the Dutch by closing the Baltic to them; by 1628 these plans had been frustrated by the caution of the Hansa towns and Wallenstein's refusal to act under Spain's direction.[1] Wallenstein had second thoughts as a result of his failure at Stralsund, but Madrid had decided (September 1628) to concentrate its resources securing the Mantuan territories.[2] Castile's finances were being put in better order by the forced debt conversion of 1627 which gave financiers *juros* [annuities] and freed the revenues pledged to them and by the new banking company's devaluation of the inflated copper coinage. The Mantuan territory of Montferrat and Casale's control of a pass to Italy threatened the security of the Milanese and the land-route to the Netherlands, hence Olivares' decision to deny the inheritance to the French duke of Nevers to whom the last duke had willed it when he died at the end of 1627. While there were grounds for disputing the legality of the duke's will, Spain had not appealed to them but to the immediate force of arms. In so doing Spain had flouted dynastic property rights, challenged France and further disturbed her relations with the emperor, since Montferrat was an imperial fief.

At the same time important decisions had to be taken about the Netherlands. The Stadholder Frederick Henry was willing to negotiate a renewal of the truce of 1609 which the infanta and Spinola urged should be accepted. But Olivares argued that this would be disastrous to Spain, as it had been before. The Dutch would capture her trade in both the Indies; the cost of fighting the war prevented them from devoting all their resources to increasing their sea-power. The only solution was to win the war by buying the intervention of the emperor and the German princes. Philip IV followed neither course; he allowed negotiations with the Dutch, but set his terms impossibly high, while failing to send the funds necessary for buying support in the empire. The result of Spain and Savoy's occupation of Montferrat and the siege of Casale was not direct French intervention, but the sending of an ambassador to Madrid. Both sides wished to avoid an immediate clash, but for different reasons. Time was not on Spain's side. In October La Rochelle surrendered, leaving Richelieu free to concentrate on intervention in Italy; at about the same time came news of Piet Heyn's capture of the treasure-fleet in September. Faced with a sudden lack of immediate resources, Olivares wished to accept the

---

[1] See below, Chapter VII, p. 228.
[2] R. Rodenas Vilar, *La Politica Europea de España durante la Guerra de Treinta Años (1624–30)* (Madrid, 1967), p. 146.

Dutch terms for a truce and concentrate on defeating France. A majority of the Council of State supported him, but again Philip refused their advice and decided to try to meet the crisis by bluff.[1]

The result was disaster in 1629. The French defeated Savoy, relieved Casale and established themselves in Italy, while Frederick Henry, encouraged by French subsidies, besieged Bois-le-Duc and eventually took it in September. Now it was Spain which had to appeal to the emperor for assistance. The sending of an imperial army to Italy not only weakened Ferdinand's position in Germany and so made still more remote any hope of a German alliance to defeat the Dutch, but it also gave the emperor the possibility of settling the Mantuan question unilaterally with the French, without consulting Madrid. This the French envoys at Ratisbon succeeded in doing in 1630 by playing on the emperor's hopes that they would not incite opposition to the election of his son as king of the Romans. The French over-reached themselves in denouncing the agreement made at Ratisbon, but the final settlement at the Treaty of Cherasco (1631) by giving France direct control of access to Italy by the acquisition of Pinerolo and Casale was more dangerous to Spain than the peaceful succession of Nevers to the Mantuan inheritance would have been. This result cost Spain by Olivares' reckoning over 10,000,000 ducats. It had also severely strained French government and finances and forced Louis XIII to choose between pursuing far-reaching reforms and costly anti-Habsburg foreign policy, but Richelieu could still buy time free from direct involvement in war.[2] Spain resumed the quest for a truce with the United Provinces, only to find that they were now mainly interested in the negotiations as a means of encouraging rebellion in the south. Spain had lost opportunities for limiting her commitments and had ensured that they would increase. By 1632 financing the war by means involving a large measure of consultation with traditional assemblies and of respect for *fueros* had reached its limits. Henceforward greater resort to force and extraordinary measures were essential and the change is to some extent symbolized by the setting up of the *Junta de Ejecución* in 1634 which replaced the traditional Council of State as the centre of decision-making. By 1636 these methods had apparently overcome disaster in Germany and near-disaster in the Netherlands, were raising large forces intended to expel the Dutch from northern Brazil, and had forced Richelieu to declare open war on Spain and face defeat and invasion in northern France. Although Richelieu and Olivares were engaged almost continuously in secret peace negotiations from 1636, these reversals of the disasters from 1628 to 1633 must have strengthened Olivares' conviction that his will power, energy and gambler's nerve could prevail over the deficiencies produced by exhaustion and dissension in Spain's dominions for long enough to impose her terms abroad.

[1] *Ibid.* pp. 166–70, 180–1. [2] See below, Chapter XVI, pp. 488–9.

Thus the declaration of war between France and Spain in 1635 did prove a real turning point in international relations. Eventually Spain had to accept the long-mooted peace with the United Provinces and yet was unable to keep the emperor in the war against France. Even before 1648 this phase of the war had decisively affected the governments and economies of the belligerents. As Spain was the country ultimately worst affected it is worth attempting a rough analysis of its fiscal régime, and its peculiarities.[1] By comparison with France one obvious contrast is that the weight of indirect taxation was very much heavier in Castile. However it should be remembered that since the sixteenth century there had been a general tendency for states to increase the relative contribution of indirect taxes and that if Spain was the most extreme example of this, the other country where they were probably as important was the United Provinces. Thanks to its long regalist tradition the Spanish crown certainly got greater contributions from its clergy than the French, though it is impossible to assess the relative proportions of clerical wealth taken by the two crowns. Another and greater contrast with France is the profit made from manipulating the coinage; there was no debasement in France, though the money of account was devalued and changes in mint ratios and the nominal values of coins were made. France's monetary system was not as stable as that of the United Provinces or England, but it was less violently disturbed than those of Castile or Germany or Poland, while the manipulations of Castile's coinage continued for much longer than in any other country, with the possible exception of the Ottoman Empire. In both Spain and France customs duties on overseas trade were a far less important part of revenue than in the United Provinces or England, or Denmark. In both Spain and France contracts with and advances from financiers were important. Both states ruined their credit; in the short run the French financiers seemed to have had the better bargain and by the 1650s seemed to be in full control of financial administration, while Spain's were more frequently the victims of the crown's necessities and of their unpopularity. Both countries' wars were financed by repudiations of assignments of revenue, sales of annuities, offices and privileges, forced loans, requisitions and billeting of troops. While Spain's finances had been even more desperate for even longer than those of France, it may be that her financial administration was better informed about the true current state of her affairs than the French one. Spain's troubles were certainly not due to her government's ignorance of what was happening.

The importance of the manipulation of Castile's coinage is shown by the fact that it provided 48,000,000 ducats for the crown 1621–58, against 34,000,000 from American silver. After 1640 America provided only 11,000,000 ducats and coinage 30,000,000. In the first twenty years of his

[1] Based on A. Dominguez Ortiz, *Politica y Hacienda de Felipe IV* (Madrid, 1960).

44

reign Philip IV's receipts averaged about 18,000,000 ducats a year,[1] but some 6,000,000 were assigned to the payment of *juros* [annuities] which already amounted to 5,600,000 in 1621. Of the remaining receipts, perhaps 10% came from direct taxes, mostly clerical subsidies, supplemented by occasional *donativos*. The largest item, some 90,000,000 (averaging 4,500,000 a year) were the *servicios* voted by the Cortes which mostly consisted of indirect taxes on foodstuffs [the *millones*]. There was also from 1631 a royal tax on salt, while the old *alcabalas* [sales tax], now assigned or alienated, amounted to nearly 3,000,000, so that by the 1630s taxes on consumption were about 10,000,000 ducats a year or more on a population probably somewhat under 6,000,000. The next largest item in the unassigned receipts, some 37,000,000, came from the *Cruzada* [sale of bulls of indulgence], ordinary clerical subsidies and the revenues of the military orders, followed by the coinage yielding nearly 18,000,000. Then came 16,000,000 from *Media anata* of *juros*. In 1634 half the interest due to foreigners owning *juros* was withheld, in 1635 and 1636 the whole, while natives received a third and a half respectively; in 1637–40 half from both, in 1641 the whole and from 1645 always a half and from 1648 more than a half. Except in the most desperate crises widows, poor nobles, hospitals, nunneries and endowments for festivals of the Blessed Sacrament were exempt, those whose interest was withheld had to accept it in the form of *juros* of the same face value. The crown got a secure and regular revenue of some 2,500,000 ducats, ruined its credit and reduced the market price of *juros* to half their face value which had usually equalled their market price in the sixteenth century.[2] The crown had to force purchase of *juros* in 1637, 1640, 1646 and 1649, assigning a quota to corporations, office-holders and individuals in each region.

The *donativo* had seemed to offer hope of escape from such expedients. They were in theory benevolences from those best able to pay, but even the successful ones of 1590 and 1624 were used by nobles as opportunities for obtaining royal privileges to extend or convert *censos* on their lands at lower rates of interest. That of 1629 was in large part a sale of privileges and pardons to towns and individuals. The towns were allowed to sell common lands, or break up pastures and above all to raise additional excises or dues especially on their rural *pecheros*. In 1632 the attempt to make the *donativo* more an appeal to individual patriotism led to resistance and failure; it raised only 1,000,000 ducats against some 4,000,000 each from those of 1624 and 1629. In 1635 the crown tried to avoid bargains with the towns, but individuals still obtained pardons and privileges, in particular the nobles were exempted from personal military

---

[1] These are receipts accounted for in Dominguez Ortiz, *Politica y Hacienda*, appendix I, but average receipts for the whole reign were probably about 20,000,000 ducats a year, *ibid.* p. 182.

[2] A. Castillo Pintado, 'Los Juros de Castilla . . . ' *Hispania*, Vol. XXIII (1963), p. 63.

service. This again raised about 4,000,000, but was in fact the last *donativo* to raise a large sum. In 1637 preparations for a 25% tax on *censos* were made, but came to nothing in face of particularly strong opposition from the clergy and the Basque provinces. In 1640 a plan for a graded capitation tax also failed. The only regular direct tax paid by the titled nobility was the *lanzas* instituted in 1631, by which they and the bishops agreed individually to pay for contingents of troops. Its yield was supposed to be 400,000 ducats, but by 1660 was only 150,000. Presumably the yield was better maintained under Olivares and in fact the magnates were forced to contribute very heavily to the war in his last years. From 1635 to 1640 some 3,600,000 ducats was raised for the army. By 1643 the duke of Medinaceli had contributed half a million ducats. Such exactions were the main cause of the magnates' growing hostility to the court and to Olivares whose fall inaugurated a régime of comparative immunity for the greater nobles.

Traditionally the Cortes of Castile, like the French States General, had always opposed sale of offices and the crown had repeatedly broken promises to end the practice. But by the 1630s the Cortes hoped to reduce the burdensomeness of the *servicios* by agreeing to the creation and sale of new municipal offices and the sale of fiscal and legal offices. It is impossible to estimate the yield from sale of offices; it must have been considerable, though probably not as important as in France in the 1630s. There sales of new offices, of increased wages of old ones, *droit annuel* and so on averaged over a third of the cash receipts of the central treasury. But the yield of the highest year, some 36,000,000 livres, was only just over half the assessment of the *taille* and its military supplements in 1639 at 69,000,000. By 1640 creation of new offices and additional wages had satiated demand and was lowering their price;[1] sale of new offices as a major expedient was exhausted. The crown continued to force its officers to buy increases in wages which it was then unable to pay, just as Philip IV had to force his officers and subjects to buy *juros*. But the great contrast was in the role of indirect taxes whose gross yield was about 38% of the *taille* and its supplements as assessed in 1639, though the proportion rose in the 1640s. The total taxation of the clergy averaged under 2,000,000 a year 1615–66, but nearly half of this consisted of tenths which had already been alienated to pay *rentes*. The *dons gratuits* voted by the clergy averaged under half a million *livres* 1626–36 and from 1636 to 1645 900,000, while in 1645–56 they declined to rather less than the first figure.[2] Spain certainly got more from its clergy, especially in the 1630s, though it is impossible to say precisely how much. The fact that French clergy's taxation averaged over 3,500,000 *livres* a year from 1666 to 1715 and that the *dons gratuits* alone averaged nearly 5,000,000 1690–1715 suggests that they had escaped lightly in the earlier period.

[1] See below, Chapter XVI, pp. 495–6.
[2] P. Blet, *Le Clergé de France et la Monarchie* (Rome, 1959), Vol. II, pp. 391–4.

By comparison with 1626, the assessment of the *taille* had doubled by
1636 and, including the military supplements, more than trebled by 1639.
Its incidence is best illustrated by local examples, though there were considerable regional variations. In the *généralité* of Caen the *taille* was
1,075,000 *livres* in 1631, just under 2,300,000 in 1635, 3,200,000 in 1638
and about the same in 1643, with additional military charges of 700,000,
an almost fourfold increase 1631–8. But by 1639 40% of the assessment
was in arrears, as against 19·6% in 1629. As with the office-holders,
the willingness and capacity of the *taillables* to pay increasing levies was
being exhausted. In Montpellier (in a *pays d'état*) the *taille* was about
30,000 *livres* in 1600, had doubled by 1627 and was 100,000 in 1640. The
assessment of the small town of Espalion in Rouergue increased from
1,266 *livres* in 1618 to over 6,800 in 1643. In the *généralité* of Bordeaux the
taille increased from a little over 1,000,000 between 1610 and 1632 to
2,000,000 in 1635, 3,000,000 in 1644 and almost 4,000,000 in 1648—
including military charges it was about 5,000,000. But this did not account
for all the charges; financial officials were entitled to fees, parishes had to
pay dues for garrisons, militia, billeting, so that their total expenses could
be twice the amount of the *taille*. Many towns, including important ones
such as Bordeaux, were exempt from the *taille*, but they were still liable to
provide subsistence for troops, raise forced loans and contributions for the
crown, which were levied by additional *octrois* or other indirect taxes.
Others were not directly assessed and could evade part of their quota by
overcharging neighbouring villages. All towns ran into debt and their
inability to meet further demands led to increasing intervention in their
affairs by *intendants* or governors, tax-farmers and royal officials. In 1647
the government doubled municipal *octrois*, but disposed of half or more
of them itself. By 1660 Amiens had a debt of 315,975 *livres*, four or five
times its average annual receipts in the 1650s. Admittedly Amiens was in a
frontier province, but everywhere the accumulation of municipal and
communal debts was one of the most important consequences of the war
and was responsible for the extension of the monarchy's administrative
tutelage. For as arrears and debts piled up, the legal expenses of village
communities grew as they had to pay the expenses of imprisoned collectors
of the *taille*, or of seizures and other legal processes.

Growing municipal and communal indebtedness were everywhere the
result of states' increasing fiscal demands and difficulties, though the social
and administrative consequences were not necessarily the same as in
France. The most spectacular example is perhaps that of Naples, which
of all the Spanish dominions was most open to fiscal pressure from
Madrid and contributed most to its war effort, especially after 1636.[1] By
then the debt had risen from about 30,000,000 ducats in 1626 (when the
deficit was already 6,800,000) to 40,000,000, but had doubled by 1648

[1] R. Villari, *La Rivolta Antispagnola a Napoli. Le Origini 1585–1647* (Bari, 1967).

to 80,000,000. Communal debts, mainly the result of the crown's exactions, were 54,000,000 in 1637. The kingdom was sending abroad some 3,500,000 a year towards the war. Part of this was raised by new taxes on export of oil and silk and on consumption of oil, flour, salt and grain at Naples, which were immediately alienated to financiers. But much was raised by in effect devaluing the obligations for which old direct and indirect taxes had already been alienated and by selling titles, offices, rights and jurisdiction over communes and lands of the royal demesne.

The chief beneficiary after 1636 was Bartolomeo Aquino, who with his partners eventually established a near-monopoly of revenues and advances. He had been a merchant and during his supremacy as a financier many who continued as merchants went bankrupt. His first victims were foreigners who held assignments of revenues from solvent communes and were forced to exchange them for assignments on insolvent ones. The raising of new direct and indirect taxes in a period of depression meant that the yield of older taxes fell. Already by 1637 old investors had lost 50% of their capital, but the crown's credit was only beginning its decline; by 1646–7 Aquino was paying only 10–15% of their nominal value for the new obligations on its revenues. In the meantime he and others had also bought up old assignments and pensions at give-away prices. Fiscal officials, holders of assigned taxes, and the creditors of communes all had the right to send *commissari* to collect their money as best they could. Increasingly this was done by means of sequestrations which had to be carried out by force, just as the tax farmers and *intendants* in France had to raise special troops to enforce payment of taxes.

But in some of his contracts Aquino was acting as agent on a 10% commission for nobles buying assignments of customs and direct taxes. He was also a means to sales of titles and offices and above all of portions of royal demesne declared inalienable in 1620. Aquino's monopoly was destroyed by the revolution of 1648, but he had assisted the last phase of social changes, which proved more enduring. The most obvious symbol of these changes was the increase in the number of titled nobility: 133 in 1601, 161 in 1613, 271 in 1631, 341 in 1640, 434 in 1675, while the number of untitled barons remained roughly constant at a little under 500. The period of greatest growth was 1620 to 1650 and the greatest increase was in the highest titles of prince and duke. Aquino himself became prince of Caramanico and a number of Genoese and Tuscans acquired lands and titles in Naples. Even in 1600 few of the holders of titles had held them for as long as a century.

The most conspicuous new recruits in the later period were financiers, merchants and lesser nobles who had made their fortunes as office-holders and councillors. But many old-established baronial families also prospered and were promoted; in 1600 many of the magnates were heavily in debt and a good deal of land was sold on this account, but after about

1620 they seem generally to have been more successful in exploiting their estates. Communes made optimistic leases of seigneurial rights at rents which fell into arrears, as prices stagnated, or fell, and fiscal pressures increased. Once in debt to a baron, they might be forced to surrender administrative independence and valuable tolls or lands. Such bargains could also be enforced by hiring bandits to threaten and murder. Both new and old nobles were the chief gainers from the crown's increasing financial difficulties, while merchants, townspeople, peasants and lesser office-holders were the losers.

Politically the nobles prevented the crown from lightening the weight of taxation by successfully opposing the introduction of a tax on rent charges and of stamp duties, which would have injured their interests. They added to the viceroy's difficulties by denouncing the financiers in Parliament, by encouraging smuggling and resistance to *commissari* and royal officials in communes under their protection, while at the same time buying up direct taxes and rights over royal demesne. In the provinces, despite their protests and appeals to the crown, more and more communities were at the mercy of barons and cut off from effective help by royal courts and officials. To get supply from Parliament in 1639 the viceroy withdrew the edict of 1637 which subjected baronial jurisdiction over offences involving firearms to royal control and so threatened to control their strong-arm men. Increasing baronial exploitation of provincial townspeople and peasants meant heavier taxes on the merchants, artisans and labourers of Naples. The attempts to bring to justice a few extremist nobles who were involved in plots with France, and the summoning of representatives from all the communes in 1647 to discuss the financial disorders which predictably led to a flood of complaints against the barons might suggest that the crown wished to revive Osuña's policy of seeking popular allies against the nobility. But if the crown had ever been free to do so, this was no longer possible, its power was irrevocably mortgaged to the nobility.

In 1647 towns and peasants rose against domination and exploitation by the baronage. These had been intensified by the crown's fiscal necessities,[1] which were the immediate occasion of the rising in Naples itself provoked by a new tax on fruit. There Masaniello led the people not only against the urban nobles, the financiers and tax collectors, but also against the bandits belonging to the barons' retinues, and sought support from the country. Neither in Naples nor the provinces did the rebels begin by attacking Spanish rule. Indeed they appealed to a more or less mythical paternalistic king for justice and redress. The leaders of communes wanted to become the immediate subjects of the crown as a guarantee of

[1] R. Villari, *Mezzogiorno e contadini nell'età moderna* (Bari, 1961), pp. 118–42; G. Pepe, *Il Mezzogiorno d'Italia sotto gli Spagnoli. La Tradizione Storiografico* (Florence, 1952), pp. 137–41, 213–20.

local particularism. This appeal to legitimate authority against injustice and usurpation gave the movement real power in the provinces by uniting peasants and urban oligarchies, so that the barons were helpless and could only flee or make concessions. Their only hope was in rallying to the viceroy and awaiting the arrival of Spanish troops. This helped to ensure that Naples would throw off Spanish allegiance and proclaim a republic. Mazarin was unwilling to assist a republic, while few nobles were willing to seek French intervention which would complete the victory of their enemies. Mazarin's reluctance, and his determination to thwart the ambitions of the duke of Guise, ensured the eventual submission of Naples.

Yet the very importance of the peasants in the revolt had made its success doubtful. Apart from disliking destruction of property and violence, the better-off townspeople were economically and socially the rivals of the barons in exploiting peasants and artisans. Already by 1600 the ruling groups in the communes of Calabria had been shifting the basis of taxation required to meet both *donativi* and communal debts from hearth taxes to indirect and capitation taxes from which those 'living nobly' in occupations not involving manual labour were exempt.[1] The clergy claimed similar exemption, though some of them often sympathized with popular grievances and sometimes joined the revolts. They could not afford a renewal of peasant refusals to pay tithe which had been frequent in the grain-producing areas in the late sixteenth century. The clergy and urban leaders also wished to save their investments in public and communal debts and offices. They needed a reformed régime, the restoration of 'popular liberties' and an equal share with the nobility in government which Genoino had been advocating since 1620,[2] not a transformation of society. When Naples submitted in 1648, the barons were free to reconquer their fiefs and repudiate any concessions made in 1647. Some reforms of financial administration did take place in the next twenty years, but the gains made by the baronage were not seriously affected.

A comparison with Sicily underlines the importance of fiscal exploitation and its results in Naples. It is generally agreed that Sicily suffered much less from Spanish exactions than Naples. Although the parliament of Sicily never fought any major battles, Madrid recognized it as a forum for hearing grievances and granting favours which still had some potential for real resistance. The parliament of Naples did not meet again after 1642, but the continued existence of that of Sicily safeguarded the island's privileges. The viceroys, like the parliament, were anxious it should be spared and regularly pleaded the country's poverty and exhaustion. Much the same pleas came from Naples, but they were less heeded

[1] F. Caracciolo, 'Fisco e contribuenti in Calabria . . . ' *Nuovo Rivista Storica*, Vol. XLVII (1963), pp. 504–38.
[2] M. Schipa, *Masaniello* (Bari, 1925).

in Madrid, which was used to asking for what its subjects believed to be impossible. Moreover, in the case of Catalonia over-estimation of its resources through sheer ignorance was part of Olivares' miscalculations. Perhaps the Sicilian barons' tradition of loyalty to Spain made Madrid less exigent than towards the Neapolitans whose propensities towards other allegiances had been greater.

For Sicilian men of property rent charges were of great importance: everyone invested in the state's financial difficulties by buying assignments of revenues and privileges. The crown sold its demesne and offices, while creating titles at much the same rate as in Naples. The towns were ruled by nobles who at Messina were exceptional in still having active mercantile interests. They all sought privileges for themselves and their towns and were likely to invest in offices. They also invested in rent charges and mortgages on baronial estates, as did the church. The barons always claimed to be chronically in debt, but were able to raise money to buy titles, privileges and rights to taxes. The most important privilege was that granted in 1610 of buying *merum et mixtum imperium* [full criminal and civil jurisdiction] over their fiefs. The crown also protected them from their creditors and upset investors by forcing reductions of interest and withholding interest payments on its obligations. The parliament was prepared to grant special *donativi* to guarantee the interest payments. The crown recognized the importance of investments in rent charges when in 1642 it refused the barons' request for a forced reduction of the interest on their debts.[1]

The universal complaints of ruin as a result of war and its costs were probably more exaggerated in Sicily than in Naples. For certainly the export trade of Sicily had grown in value. The export of corn though subject to harvest fluctuations remained at the average level reached in the later sixteenth century.[2] Messina's exports of silk rose by over a third between the 1590s and 1620s and maintained this average level, though with greater fluctuations in the 1650s and 1660s. Production may have been growing between 1620 and 1650 and then reached a plateau. The average value of the silk exported was at least a third greater than that of corn.[3] While prosperity of exports does not demonstrate general prosperity, there was also considerable internal colonization. In the sixteenth century twelve new communes were founded; in the seventeenth seventy-six with a population of 63,000, of which fifty-eight were founded before 1653. There was a general tendency for peasants to migrate from the more

[1] V. Titone, *La Sicilia della Dominazione Spagnola all'Unita* (Bologna, 1955), pp. 23–4, 289–320; G. Tricoli, 'Una battaglia parlamentare . . . del secolo XVII', *Melanges A. Marongiu* (Brussels, 1968), pp. 213–45.

[2] F. Braudel, *La Méditerrané et le Monde méditerranéen . . .* (2nd ed. 1966), Vol. I, pp. 541, 545–8.

[3] M. Aymard, 'Commerce et production de la soie sicilienne au XVI et XVII siècles', *Mélanges d'Archéologie et d'Histoire*, Vol. LXXVII (1965), pp. 609–40.

heavily taxed communes of the royal demesne to the baronial ones, and the new communes were especially attractive to new settlers because of initially very light dues and rents.[1] To some limited extent baronial debts must have helped to finance this colonization. In the long run it may have increased exhaustion and erosion of the soil and feudal abuses, but in our period it provided at least some peasants with more attractive choices than existed in Castile or Naples.

Possibly these circumstances may help to explain why the popular risings of 1647, occasioned by bad harvests in 1646, were less bloody and prolonged than those in Naples, though their first targets were the same—high indirect taxes and noble privileges. In Palermo the mass uprising was soon controlled by the *maestranze* [gilds], whose leader d'Alesio produced a programme very similar to Genoino's: an equal share in government for the people (by which was meant the better-off townspeople) with the nobility and a more equal distribution of taxes. Concessions and procrastination by the viceroy to d'Alesio undermined the support of the *maestranze*. Although there were revolts in many other towns, Messina maintained its traditional hostility to Palermo and the other towns made no attempt to organize any kind of general authority, or to assist each other, as was done to some extent in Naples. The capitulations granted to d'Alesio were disregarded; the attempt to reform the fiscal system by abolishing indirect taxes on food was abandoned, as after a short time was the appointment of popular consuls to the senates of Palermo and Catania. One lasting result of the revolt, apart from reminding everyone from the gilds upwards of the delicate balance of interrelated interests over which the viceroy presided, was a reduction in the exemptions to the indirect taxes which were to be supervised by a new financial deputation of nobles and clergy elected from the holders of obligations. This was meant to ensure the regular payment of interest, though at a lower rate.

In Milan, whither most of the money raised in Naples went, Spanish fiscal exactions were probably less than in Naples, but greater than in Sicily. But the direct effects of war were greater, above all in the continual passage and quartering of troops. Once again the government was selling its regalian rights, offices and titles, though there was no great increase in the number of fiscal offices until after 1650. The urban patriciates were relatively more important than in the south.[1] (Of 270 titled nobility and 433 feudatories in 1700, 157 and 207 had been granted since 1646 and 158 and 205 respectively came from Milan's patriciate.) They had ceased to be directly involved in industry or trade, but ensured their monopoly of high

[1] C. A. Garufi, 'Patti Agrari e Comuni Feudale di Nuova Fondazione in Sicilia', Pt II *Archivio Storico Siciliano*, Third Series, Vol. II (1947).

[2] Chiefly based on B. Caizzi, 'Le Classi Sociali', *Storia di Milano*, Vol. XI, Pt V (Fondazione Treccani degli Alfieri, 1958) and *Il Comasco sotto il Dominio Spagnolo* (Como, 1955).

municipal, administrative and judicial offices by requiring long and expensive academic studies and proofs of nobility. From 1593 the college of Jurisconsults in Milan decided to exclude anyone who was active in mercantile trading. Such families invested in public debt, private lending and foreign exchange transactions, as well as in land and feudal rights. Investments in rent charges, mortgages and public debt meant as elsewhere that men could 'live nobly' and they or their descendants would be accepted as noble. The buying of jurisdictional and regalian rights over communities from the crown in the form of fiefs held on a variety of conditions was comparatively easy and required money, not proofs of nobility. The purchasers included besides patricians, financiers, merchants and traders but, given the decline of trade and industry, financiers predominated among the new men. Infeudation of lands and communities took place on a large scale, despite the efforts of communes to buy immunity. Some feudatories had very large possessions and others very small ones. The nobles owned almost half the total land and the church perhaps a quarter, though the proportions were higher in the plain.

As returns from land were low, the older noble families who were not patricians with offices needed more than their legal privileges of partial exemption from taxes. They sought favours and additional sources of income. Magnates piled up arrears of taxes and sought remissions, while lesser nobles tended to suffer and go under. Thus there was a growth of great estates as well as in recruitment to the nobility. Both land and money became concentrated into fewer hands. There had been some growth of small peasant proprietorship in the plains in the sixteenth century, but this was checked and there were sales and temporary abandonment of holdings; south of Como the worst period for sales of peasant property was 1620–50. In the mountainous regions great estates were less dominant and conditions were better for small owners. In Milan and the other cities wealth and power had gone from merchants, traders and *entrepreneurs* to office-holders and nobles, including new men who were financiers.

Declining industry and international trade and a preference for investing cash in rent charges and land were not peculiar to Spanish Italy. Similar phenomena can be found in Genoa, Florence and Venice. Sharply falling production of woollen and silk textiles in the old urban centres from the early seventeenth century was compensated partly by growing production in villages and other towns, but little of this was exported. By the later seventeenth century Italy, like Spain or Poland, had become mainly an exporter of primary products, such as silk, olive oil, wine, rice or sulphur, in its trade with north-western Europe. Its earnings from shipping and banking had declined, but its industrial self-sufficiency, especially in textiles, was much greater than that of Spain or Poland. It has been argued that the crucial period when the Venetian nobility increasingly turned away from commercial activities to investment in land was between about 1570 and 1630.[1] Milanese capitalists from about the 1590s showed a radical change in business interests towards concentrating investment in financial affairs, accepting risks for the sake of quick returns. Both in Venice and Milan urban trade and industry were increasingly heavily burdened with taxes and high labour costs. Monetary disorder and debasement, which was also the product of financial difficulties, encouraged concentration on foreign exchange transactions. The most fully documented examples of this are the Lucini family partnerships, whose profits were used to acquire 1,100,000 *lire* of real property and 800,000 in charges on public, communal and private revenues. After 1615 they largely withdrew from the foreign exchanges; this may be taken as a symptom of the general malaise about the economic and political future, anticipating the crisis of money and credit in 1619, which inaugurated prolonged war and economic depression.[2]

Thus it can be argued that already the patterns of economic behaviour in northern Italy were changing decisively before the war could have had any effect. Yet these changes and the growing sense of insecurity were certainly influenced by the financial difficulties of Spain and other states before 1618. Its coincidence with the outbreak of general war made the monetary crisis of 1619–23 in Milan so serious. Its effects and the direct impact of the Mantuan war were reinforced by the plague of 1630. Returns from land also fell catastrophically. The accounts of a great estate show a net return of about 3% before 1623, perhaps nearer 4% before 1610. After 1623 it was scarcely 1% and in some years showed a loss. By the 1640s expenditure on repairs and improvements had fallen by nearly a half, fiscal charges amounted to nearly half the gross receipts and there was an average annual deficit of expenses over receipts of 2,330 *lire* compared with an average surplus of 14,700 *lire* 1600–23.[3] To survive, nobles had to depend on favours, borrowing, income from offices and obligations. The price of land fell very considerably, so that for those with cash profitable purchases could be made, or usurious contracts. But the great rush to buy land by moneyed men had been in the first three decades of the century. Those who could consolidate their estates and wait saw their incomes revive again after 1659 and still more after 1670, while economic life in the towns still stagnated.

The Milanese differed from the south in the apparent absence of wide-

---

[1] C. M. Cipolla, 'The Economic Decline of Italy'; S. J. Woolf, 'Venice and the Terraferma' in *Crisis and Change in the Venetian Economy*, ed. B. Pullan (1968), pp. 127–45, 175–203.

[2] A. de Maddalena, 'L'immobilizzazione della ricchezza nella Milano spagnola . . .', *Annale dell'Istituto di Storia Ec. e Soc. dell'Università di Napoli*, Vol. VI (1965), pp. 39–72; 'Affaires et gens d'affaires Lombardes sur les foires de Bisenzone', *Annales* (1967), pp. 939–90.

[3] A. de Maddalena, 'I bilanci dal 1600 al 1647 di una azienda fondiaria lombarda', *Rivista Int. di Scienze Economiche e Commerciale*, Vol. II (1955), pp. 510–25, 671–98.

spread popular revolts. To attribute this simply to the continuous presence of considerable garrisons and the fact that it was a more active theatre of war, when it was the presence of troops and the nearness of war which produced revolt in Catalonia, may seem superficial, but at least emphasizes the different traditions of government in the two dominions. Spanish power was weak in 1647–8, so the examples of Naples and Sicily suggest that in most of Europe rebellions which failed to gain noble support and probably some external assistance were doomed. England comes nearest to being the exception, but there the Scots gave crucial aid and even the Commonwealth had some leaders and support from important families of landed gentry. The revolt of the Ukraine is perhaps the nearest thing to a successful peasant rising, but most of its leaders had ambitions very different from the mass of their followers and it ultimately depended on foreign aid. In Portugal the widespread peasant rising against taxes of 1637 failed, where a popular revolt with noble support in 1640 was successful and received French aid. Catalonia had both French aid and a popular uprising which both compelled and rallied noble support.

Equally noble conspiracies did not guarantee success of themselves, even when there were considerable popular and noble grievances to exploit, as those of Medina-Sidonia and Ayamonte in Andalusia in 1641, van der Bergh in the southern Netherlands or the marquess of Acaya in Naples. Pseudo-Marxist explanations that the Bohemian revolt mainly failed because the nobles refused to seek peasant support seem unrealistic, but do point to an obvious but important limitation. The Old English in Ireland were uneasy in joining a rebellion against Protestant landlords, even though their titles were based on confiscation. Plots by magnates in France in the twenty years after 1629 failed to achieve much popular support, during a period of widespread popular revolts. Condé and the princely Frondeurs did get some popular support most notably in Bordeaux and to some extent in Paris. Popular revolts were usually antifiscal in origin, but war often increased dependence or identification of interests in relationships between crowns and great nobles. They could afford to buy for cash, or as rewards for loyalty and service, the crown's regalian rights, and became defenders of a prerogative they held in pawn. As communes or peasants fell into debt, or government obligations fell in value, there were bargains to be snatched by those who had cash, or power to borrow it. But, as we have seen, fiscal pressures meant that peasants were less able to pay rents and seigneurial dues; quartering of troops was particularly ruinous to both peasants and landlords.

Thus a noble's credit both in the literal sense of being able to go on owing large sums to the state or individuals and in the sense of prestige was more necessary than ever to maintain his status, and essential if he wanted to increase his power and wealth. If in peacetime no king's revenues were enough to satisfy all his magnates and their followers, the pressures of war finance made royal favours more valuable and the magnates' support more necessary. Too much pressure could impair even the loyalty of Castilian grandees, as Olivares demonstrated. The nobles of Portugal and Catalonia were nearer to the court than those of Italy, yet seemed as cut off from its opportunities. Catalonia had little in the way of royal demesne and regalian rights which could be auctioned off as in Italy. By the 1640s most European nobilities had undergone an inflation of titles, new men had bought their way in and more land and wealth had been concentrated in great estates. Some broad resemblances can be seen in Castile, Naples, Sicily, Bohemia, Austria, France and Sweden, in so far as magnates were actively or passively allied with governments, financiers, jurist councillors and military *entrepreneurs* in exploiting war. The main victims at home or abroad were rural populations, but to varying degrees towns, office-holders and lesser nobles were under increasing pressure.

War and war finance tended to destroy the plausibility of royal governments as dispensers of protection and justice to their subjects. A general slogan of popular revolts was 'Long Live the king without the taxes'. The sheer lack of protection was at its worst in Germany, where peasants' attempts to defend and revenge themselves against troops led to savage reprisals. Towns and communes might pay large sums to remain the direct vassals of the crown, yet great nobles in Castile and Italy could often protect their estates and vassals from the worst excesses of royal troops and tax-farmers; flight from villages under royal jurisdiction to those under private ones was not peculiar to Sicily. In France there was a constant struggle by rural nobles, royal officers and town oligarchs to reduce the burden of the *taille* on their own tenants and peasants at the expense of others. Thus the *intendants* seemed to play an ambiguous part, they were simultaneously the instruments of the tax-farmers imposing collection, *contrainte solidaire*, distraints by armed force and also of attempts to ensure more equitable assessments. Both processes involved over-riding the interests of local officers and nobles.

Peasants and the poor could be incited to rebel in the name of provincial liberties against new taxes, or new royal officials by both urban oligarchies (including royal officers) and nobles. This was the complement to services of protection against distraints and billeting which seigneurs might provide at other times and which might also unite *taillables* and privileged even against the *intendants*' attempts at equitable assessment. Peasant revolts in France were usually directed against tax-farmers and fiscal officials. Unlike the rebels of 1647 in Naples, they seldom attacked nobles or seigneurial dues. In the more peaceful conditions of 1614, villages in Champagne had complained about hunting rights, abuses of seigneurial justice, arbitrary raising of dues, and the abuses produced by clientage in assessing the *taille*.[1] Perhaps pressure of war finance made such grievances less dominant, but the areas which later saw peasant risings do not include Champagne, which was a heavily garrisoned frontier province. In the later sixteenth century provinces as far apart as Languedoc and Picardy had seen effective resistance to paying tithes which apparently ceased under Louis XIII. Tithes were not the first target of most peasant disturbances, though they are put first in what seems the least negative and most spontaneous programme, that of 'the peasant commune' of Poitou in 1636.[2]

The peasants took most of the risks and were the chief victims of repression, frequently conducted by provincial governors, or clients of magnates, assisted by officers of the high robe from Paris. The *intendants* were not usually regarded by provincial governors as rivals to their authority; magnates, like Condé and Longueville, co-operated with and protected them from the resentments of provincial nobles and officers. Again what Parisian merchants, the Parlements, officers and the lesser nobility had in common was resentment of taxation and financial mismanagement. All had selfish reasons for their violent attacks on the way the royal finances had inflicted misery on the masses, but that does not make the misery less real. They were unable to maintain any unity or pursue common objectives together. Yet they had one dominating common hatred, the financiers and tax-farmers, and all wanted a *Chambre de Justice* to punish and mulct them. The lesser nobles' demands show their jealousy of the magnates, as well as of the high robe. The nobles of Champagne sought reductions of court expenses and pensions and that all governors of provinces and towns should be resident, holding office for three years only: followed by a year without office in which complaints could be heard.[3] The noble assemblies of 1651–2 were particularly concerned about ensuring protection from exactions and quartering of troops and suggested raising companies of nobles to protect their provinces. Mazarin's triumph meant the restoration of the financiers and most of the magnates, even Condé was restored to his governorships in 1659. The *Chambre de Justice* had to wait for the personal rule of Louis XIV.

The triumph of the financiers after the Fronde contrasts with their fate in Spain in the 1650s even though Fouquet was later to be made a scapegoat for their unpopularity. Although some French financiers were foreigners, the greatest being Barthélemy d'Herwarth, in Spain native Castilians were of very minor importance. Down to the suspension of payments in 1627 Genoese bankers dominated the crown's affairs. There-

[1] Y. Durand (ed.), *Cahiers du Doléances des Paroisses du Bâilliage de Troyes* (1966), pp. 58–9, 65–7.
[2] R. Mousnier (ed.), *Lettres . . . au Chancelier Séguier*, Vol. II (1964), pp. 1105–6; cf. p. 1164.
[3] R. Mousnier, J. Labaut, Y. Durand (eds.), *Deux Cahiers de la Noblesse (1649–51)* (1963), pp. 142, 152–3, 82–3.

after some of them continued with more restricted operations, but they were largely replaced by Portuguese financiers. This development owed something to Olivares' desire to keep Spain's trade out of foreign hands, but more to the zeal of the Portuguese inquisition under Philip II's rule. Many of Castile's Jews had gone to Portugal and remained there. By 1600 the traditions of Jewish culture and religion were virtually dead in Spain, while in Portugal common usage made Jew and businessman synonymous. By 1620 the Inquisition's success in detecting alleged Judaizers and encouraging search for purity of blood had led them to complain that a third of the population was Jewish. The pressure was such that the descendants of families which had been driven out of Castile began to return to it as a refuge and resume their medieval role in royal finance.

Philip III sold pardons and privileges to the *conversos* and in 1628–9 they bought freedom to trade, marry and settle in Spain, the basis for their preponderance in the crown's *asientos*. In 1640 there were 2,000 Portuguese merchants in Seville and some 4,000 at Madrid. Olivares protected them from the Inquisition and even considered relaxing the laws about purity; their favour and prosperity was a major reason for his unpopularity. Even in the 1630s the Inquisition had tried and ruined at least two prominent financiers; with the revolt of Portugal and Olivares' fall, the Portuguese became more unpopular than ever and the Inquisition had greater freedom. By the 1650s wholesale arrests and condemnations of Portuguese were taking place. Many of the wealthy fled abroad, but a few could still buy real immunity. The Cortizos family kept their fortunes, bought titles, places in the Order of Calatrava and even offices in the Inquisition. Some lesser men continued as farmers of revenues, despite persecutions and confiscations. The crown gained from the confiscations, but finally ruined its credit and any hope of keeping the bulk of overseas trade out of foreign hands. However, the continual arrests and public humiliations at *autos* of monopolists, financiers and tax-farmers by identifying and punishing the authors of fiscal grievances may have given both commoners and nobles satisfactions which elsewhere could only be attempted by rebellions. In this idiosyncratic and distasteful way Castilian government and society remained united in a hypocritical parody of its former strength, while in the mid-seventeenth, as in the fifteenth century, French absolutism was the product of disunion and deadlock between rival groups, of public weakness, rather than of its own strength.

A special case of entry to the greater landed nobility by financiers is that of military *entrepreneurs* which was particularly important in Bohemia,[1] and to a lesser extent in Austria and Germany. Such *entrepreneurs* advanced credit to princes (sometimes borrowing from bankers and merchants as Hans de Witte did for Wallenstein) to raise and equip troops. As war continued they accumulated larger credits in the form of

[1] See below, Chapter XVII.

arrears. There were some 1,500 military *entrepreneurs* in the empire during the Thirty Years War, most of them were originally noble and some had also been wealthy. The physical risks might be greater than in ordinary lending, but if a colonel or commander lived, he could hope to acquire titles and land. The Bavarian Count von Sporck (1601–79) was the son of a peasant, but left 3,000,000 *thalers*. By the late 1630s there was a high proportion of commoners owning regiments in the imperial army. Over the whole period they were outnumbered by those born noble, who were often originally poor, but might acquire titles and landed estates.[1]

In Bohemia and Austria the war caused a concentration of land into greater estates at the expense of the lesser nobility. In Bohemia this process was more the result of forfeitures and the endowment of great military *entrepreneurs*, than in Austria where the old knightly class declined and a newly created nobility of civil and military office-holders increased. In Brandenburg the elector recovered control of his demesnes which had been mortgaged to the Estates and extended them, while the lesser nobility survived to a much greater extent to become a nobility of service as army officers. In Sweden the war created a much more numerous nobility, often of foreign origin, endowed with revenues alienated by the crown; but also much concerned with office-holding. The lesser nobles resented the patronage secured by the council families and their allies among the new men, who had found fortunes and titles in the German war. These poorer nobles were willing to support absolutism for the sake of secure wages as military or civil officers. In Denmark, where the crown had about half the land, there had been concentration of estates in the hands of the high nobility whose indebtedness also grew. After 1643 war and the disruption of foreign trade weakened them further and the price of land fell. There absolutism after 1660 removed the legal restrictions on commoners buying noble land, created many new nobles and changed the old nobility into something much more like a nobility of service.

In England there were honours and titles to sell but little or nothing to go with them in the way of privileges or jurisdiction. The kings nominated judges and sometimes sold their places, but they did not sell jurisdiction. What profits were to be made from sale of office in the central government went mostly to other office-holders. Sales of crown land were an important part of extraordinary finance down to the 1650s, but the crown lands were an insignificant part of the country's land, compared with Denmark. There were no permanent direct or indirect taxes to be alienated. Its unpaid justices of the peace constituted a kind of nobility of service which was not necessarily less responsive to royal commands than corporations or holders of venal offices. As a result of the civil war new men and families temporarily dominated local government. But the traditional order which was restored, though more oligarchic, was not a closed

[1] F. Redlich, *The German Military Enterpriser* (Wiesbaden, 1964), Vol. I.

oligarchy based either on claims to absolutist tutelage over local communities or on the alienation of royal authority to holders of hereditary fiefs.

One of the major themes of the period is certainly the transformation and consolidation of noble power. But we lack detailed analyses of the origins of even the greater nobility in most countries and means of comparing rates of change with other periods, let alone estimates of their relative wealth and power. However, it is clear that almost everywhere there was a great increase in the number of higher titles and that both old and new families could profit from the financial difficulties of princes. In many countries there was a growth of great estates partly at the expense of the lesser nobles. The lesser nobles' best chance of survival seems to have been by becoming a service nobility, as in Brandenburg and Sweden; to some extent this must also have happened in France with maintenance of a large standing army after 1659. In Italy and Spain there seems to have been a sharing of state and economic power with the greater nobles, who in a sense take over, or at least become the main beneficiaries of absolutist monarchies, whereas in Poland though magnates were still the main beneficiaries, the constitutional forms were a negation of absolutism.

Castile perhaps provides the other example of a state where a very numerous nobility accepted magnate predominance with even less open social disturbance. While the dominance of *letrados* in sixteenth-century administration may sometimes be exaggerated, the growing importance of councillors of 'cape and sword' after 1600 is undeniable. Perhaps this led to an identification of interests between robe and sword such as took place in eighteenth-century France. Another possibly important mechanism was the way *limpieza* and the Inquisition operated. The purity laws had certainly been used to embarrass the higher nobility and the town oligarchies in the sixteenth century. Under Philip III the nobles complained at length of the consequences of esteeming 'a common person who is *limpio* more than a hidalgo who is not . . .'. In 1624 crown decreed restrictions of proofs and above all of disproofs of *limpieza* and ordered the destruction of all writings purporting to show impure descent of families (almost always important noble ones). The concentration of the Inquisition's attention on the Portuguese provided a convenient and popular diversion. By the 1650s it was said that nobles of mixed blood felt safe enough to speak disdainfully of the Inquisition. A French observer expressed astonishment at the urban character of the nobles and their lack of hunting rights and the fact that artisans and tradesmen dressed like nobles and wore swords. He exaggerated, but his comments point to a victory for noble aspirations which unified Castilian society, when other victories eluded it.

These trends among nobilities may be seen as one of the results of the many attempts to reform states in this period. The demands of rebels for the restoration of ancient privileges and levels of taxation had as little success as the plans of lawyers for restoring constitutions, or of statesmen and pamphleteers for reforming taxation, balancing budgets and increasing national wealth. The conscious plans were swamped by the needs of war which themselves produced expedients, with important and lasting effects, such as the *intendants* in France, the introduction of the excise and land tax in England. Even in Spanish Italy a certain amount of redress of some of the worst fiscal abuses happened after 1660. Yet it can be argued that the most successful of all the attempts to carry out general plans for reforming states in a period full of such plans was the reform of the Ottoman state.

By the mid-seventeenth century the Ottomans had produced a number of treatises, as concerned with the diagnostics of decline and its remedies as those of the much more prolific Spanish *arbitristas*.[1] The Ottoman reformers tended to be pessimistic and had all had direct experience of government, unlike some of the *arbitristas*. Like the French they wanted to abolish sale of office as the root of all evil, like the Scots and English Puritans they wanted to restore the direct rigour of the Sacred Law. They saw (less reluctantly than the leaders of the New Model Army) that this could only be done by a man of the sword. What can easily be overlooked is that in the short run they were much more successful than their western counterparts. Murad IV and the Köprülü Vezirs really did produce effective reforms, as the revival of efficiently kept tax registers and records shows. They were far more ruthless in dealing with tax-farmers and usurpations of revenues, lands and rights than western governments. Their immediate success was perhaps partly due to the fact that what they were trying to restore was not a mythical past of Anglo-Saxon, or Frankish liberties, of primitively pure Christianity, or a Christian *imperium*, but a government which really had existed and flourished a couple of generations ago and whose records and achievements were carefully studied.

This was also their undoing. They found themselves restoring a system of government and above all a military machine which was inappropriate to its tasks. In temporarily restoring something like the old order, they also restored its contradictions which had already produced the near collapse of the early seventeenth century. The Ottoman government was remarkably successful in mobilizing resources; this remained true even after the great defeats of the late seventeenth century. It was its increasing inability to make effective use of those resources above all in war which mattered. As always it could borrow the latest weapons, or experts in engineering and artillery from western Europe. What it could not borrow effectively were the tactics, drill and organization of European field armies which could provide a defensive pattern which was virtually unbeatable

[1] B. Lewis, 'Ottoman observers of Ottoman decline', *Islamic Studies* (Karachi), Vol. 1 (1962), pp. 71–87.

by Ottoman formations, as Montecuccoli first demonstrated at St Gotthard (1664).

Some Ottoman reformers saw the crucial importance of European sea-power, but plans for promoting overseas trade and native industry do not seem to have occupied them seriously. Traditional Ottoman policies might almost be called the opposite of mercantilism in that it favoured foreign merchants and taxed exports highly. However, in European states fiscal necessity usually over-rode all other considerations in executing policies, and realization of the desirability of promoting native industry, trade and shipping was no guarantee that such results would happen, as the examples of Spain and Poland show. Once the supreme example of a state effectively organized for large-scale war, the Ottoman Empire was in danger of becoming unable to deal with the new techniques and organization of war which were emerging.

Clearly war had important effects on European societies, though even here it can be argued that it merely accelerated trends already apparent before 1618. This has been argued even more strongly concerning the economic effects of war, where Germany provides a particularly important problem. As we have seen, the worsening of the condition of peasants and the growth of large noble estates were certainly not peculiar to Germany, but equally Germany was not the only country affected by the pressures of war, though they were certainly more direct and terrible there. The Thirty Years War can also be seen as not having seriously affected the obedience of German prices to the general behaviour and trends of European ones. Slicher van Bath has argued that 'When the average price level remains for a very long time below that of an equally long period immediately preceding it, we can speak of a fundamental change.' Measured in silver equivalents the price of rye behaves in this way in Germany, falling by 40% or more, comparing 1650–99 with 1600–49, and so indicating a prolonged agrarian depression in Europe especially in arable farming.[1] Yet making the same comparison the international price of rye at Amsterdam and Danzig fell by 7% and 1% respectively. Domestic prices of grain in the Netherlands fell very little or even rose slightly and the same is true of England. French prices in silver did not fall nearly so far as German ones and nominal prices of wheat at Beauvais, Toulouse and Paris rose by about 30%. The only prices which seem to follow the German pattern are Italian ones; wheat at Bassano, Pavia and Siena fell by over 25%, as did rye at Milan. Germany and northern Italy probably lost more population than other areas, 1620–40. A European model built on German prices may be deceptive.

However, this process has been taken a stage further by arguing that German prices and economic trends 'are part of a general European

[1] *The Agrarian History of Western Europe*, pp. 206–10.

crisis' and are 'completely in harmony with the long-term movement of prices in Western Europe . . . When the depression of the decade 1640–50 began in Germany, it was one that hit the whole European economy and was not exclusively due to the Thirty Years War.'[1] By looking at prices exclusively in silver the two decades after 1600 can be seen as a period of falling grain prices, heralding depression or crisis. Clearly the wholesale debasements preceding the war do indicate economic difficulties. Yet quite apart from these, German grain prices 1600–50 show more violent fluctuations than in the sixteenth century. This is not true of the southern Netherlands and does not seem to be true of some French series. The short- and long-term behaviour of German prices during and after the war seems to have peculiar characteristics which may be due to the exceptionally strong impact of war.

TABLE I. *Shipping through the Sound (index numbers)*

	Total no. of passages	Total of Dutch and Frieslanders	Tonnage of Dutch and Frieslanders
1590–9	100	100	100
1614–23	90	97	132
1624–31	53	51	75
1635–44	65	56	107
1646–53	62	62	136

Source; P. Jeannin, 'Les comptes du Sund . . .', *Revue Historique*, Vol. ccxxxi (1964), p. 75.

If the volume of maritime trade is any indication of production or prosperity, Jeannin's work on the Sound tolls is of the greatest importance. The volume of shipping was commanded by the amount of grain exported and over 80% consisted of Dutch ships. There was a slump in the 1570s and 1580s, then, as Table 1 shows, a boom in the 1590s (followed by a decline) then new growth until 1623. The slump 1624–31 was caused first by bad harvests 1622–4 and then by the Swedish blockade of the Vistula. Expansion was resumed in 1635 and the peak of the whole series was reached in 1649–50. The lasting fall in volume came after 1653, not after 1623. This was mainly because western Europe became more self-sufficient in grain. However the value of exports from the Baltic may have risen, since industrial materials, such as iron hemp and flax, increased. Earlier exports of flax, hemp and potash had increased considerably after 1618, remaining at a high level after 1624. Swedish exports of bar iron were growing rapidly from the 1620s. From 1630 to 1650 the amount exported from the Baltic and the volume of Dutch shipping were

[1] H. Kamen, 'Economic and social consequences of the Thirty Years War', *Past and Present*, no. 39 (1968), pp. 44–61.

all rising, while prices at Amsterdam were stable. There was clearly expansion as well as recovery from the slump of the 1620s.

These exports of industrial materials point to industrial growth in western Europe. The cloth industries of Reims and Amiens recovered from the disasters of the late sixteenth century and then expanded until about 1635, after which production fell. The textile industries of the southern Netherlands recovered and the linen industry expanded down to 1640. The woollen industries of Gand and Bruges probably reached higher outputs than in the sixteenth century. In the north the growth of Leiden's cloth output slackened 1620–33, but then went on to reach its peak 1654–65. Despite the decline of the old draperies in England after 1618, the new draperies expanded until 1640 and a silk industry was established. Some of this growth was no doubt at the expense of Italy, just as some of the growth of shipping and trade was at her expense and that of the Iberian Powers. The longer and cruder index of shipping through the Sound in Table 2 suggests that there was no sudden fall after 1660 and that the level remained appreciably greater than that of a hundred years earlier.

TABLE 2. *Dutch ships westwards through the Sound (annual averages)*

	(1) No. of ships	(2) Snapper* total in 1,000s lasts	(3) Jeannin† average Dutch ships in lasts	(4) (1) × (3) in 1,000s lasts
1562–8	1,343	98·7	40	53·7
1574–80	1,014	60·9	40	40·6
1581–90	1,321	79·4	47	63·6
1591–1600	1,601	102·6	{70 {60	{112·0 { 96·1
1601–10	1,337	96·7	72	95·3
1611–20	1,684	139·8	84	141·5
1621–30	1,048	111·0	95	99·8
1631–40‡	1,004	124·0	110	110·4
1641–50	1,156	161·8	140*	—
1651–7	887	124·2	140*	—
1661–70	681	95·3	140*	—

* F. Snapper, *Oorlogsinvloeden op de Overzeese Handel van Holland 1551–1719* (Amsterdam, 1959), pp. 312–14.

† Jeannin, *Le Navire et l'économie maritime du Nord de l'Europe; 3e Colloque Internat. d'histoire maritime* (Paris, 1960), pp. 58–61; ships at Königsberg.

‡ Eight years only.

The agrarian sector was doubtless more fundamental. Here again there are indications of early depression east of the Elbe (see Fig. 5, below, p. 93) and the amount of land reclaimed in the Netherlands fell sharply after 1664 (see Fig. 4, below, p. 92). It has also been argued that grain yields fell generally in the seventeenth century, but there is no convincing evidence of this except for Poland. There are indications that yields in England may have risen, but elsewhere it seems likely that yields remained stationary. However, one new crop with higher yields, maize, was spreading in northern Spain, Italy and southern France. Its use in Italy has been regarded as an impoverishment of popular diet, but in the long run it must have made subsistence easier.

Information about the movement of rent remains extremely patchy. As we have seen in Lombardy the return from land fell after 1623. In England rents rose considerably and probably faster than prices 1600–40. They soon recovered from the Civil War, but probably failed to go on rising in the 1660s. In the southern Netherlands a few leases show rents rising much faster than prices from 1600 to the 1640s, then falling. French experience was various. In Beauvaisis and Haut Poitou rents rose till 1650. In Picardy rents returned 1600–30 to levels reached before 1570, were reduced again by war and then recovered temporarily to higher levels in the 1660s. Rents of small parcels of land near Paris fell steeply in the 1590s; they then rose steadily 1600–70, but only passed their former levels in the 1630s. In Languedoc and Provence rents also rose until about 1670. In Languedoc they had risen no faster than grain prices in the sixteenth century, but after 1600 they rose considerably faster; by 1650 measured in grain they had risen 50–100%, in money 100–150%.

Probably the main reason for increasing rents was competition for holdings as population had increased. The farmer's margin of profit was under twofold attack. Le Roy Ladurie considers that direct taxation had not risen faster than prices down to 1610. From about 1625 this changed; by 1650 taxes calculated in grain at constant prices had more than doubled. The *taille* took 6·2% of gross revenue in the 1580s and 13% in 1650. It had become a heavier burden than tithe and apparently replaced it as the main target of peasant unrest. It should be remembered that indirect taxes had also risen considerably and that the *taille* in Languedoc was less burdensome than in many other regions. In Languedoc seigneurial dues were of minor importance, but in other regions, such as Burgundy, they were the means whereby landowners increased their share of revenue from land at the peasants' expense. In such circumstances individual peasants as well as village communities became indebted and sales of peasant strips and communal lands and rights often followed.

Many purchasers were officers, not only from the high robe as at Dijon, but also lesser ones who had largely replaced merchants as the municipal oligarchs at Amiens. Some in Burgundy and elsewhere belonged to old noble families or were village oligarchs [*coqs de village*]. But many bought rent charges because they wanted a secure income. Historians generally deplore such manifestations of *rentier* ambitions with their avoidance of entrepreneurial risks, as a victory for attitudes hostile to rational economic behaviour. Yet given the risk of trade and of direct exploitation of land, especially in the 1640s and 1650s, was the preference for security so irrational? The borrowers by means of rent charges were probably mainly nobles and peasants, but at Amiens it was the peasants who were most likely to end by losing their land. Although rent charges were clearly an important form of investment in most of Europe, we are still very ignorant of their real economic significance in different countries and how interest rates really worked. Interest rates were falling everywhere in this period, though again the chronology and significance of this remains obscure. But it would seem that large and long-term borrowers were in a much better position than in the sixteenth century, while peasants were usually the last to feel the benefit of falling interest rates. They were the victims of war and peace throughout most of Europe west and east of the Elbe. Upon their acceptance of their fate and upon the interplay of other political and social groups which sometimes gave some of them hopes of protection or even prosperity, the history of this as of other periods is founded.

If peasants, apart from the *coqs de village*, were victims of society, even poor ones might help to victimize local scapegoats as witches. Witchcraft can be seen as a mechanism which by attributing misfortunes, especially sickness, to ill will by others makes life endurable for those who lack knowledge and means to control the hazards of living at the margins of subsistence. From the fifteenth century churchmen distinguished between natural and demoniac ('black') magic. This distinction might ensure immunity for intellectuals reviving hermetic traditions but not for village sorcerers, normally engaged in fortune telling, curative spells, or divining for lost objects, though always liable to be suspected of interfering with fertility in men, animals and plants. Witch hunts, led by evangelists of Protestant or Catholic reform or by learned magistrates, meant wholesale torture of suspects nominated by local resentments. This produced confessions of the Satanic compacts and Sabbats prescribed by learned handbooks, followed by executions of widening circles of alleged participants. In this period there were probably more victims than ever, particularly in Germany; yet James I, Spanish inquisitors, the German Jesuit Spee and French *parlementaires* all became convinced that the standard procedures and confessions were false. The same arguments had had no effect in the sixteenth century, but now they gradually influenced judicial proceedings. The machinery of witch-hunting had perhaps over-reached itself by successfully establishing its beliefs at a really popular level. By 1650 *libertins* blamed such beliefs on popular superstition, while in France and the Basque lands popular demands for extirpation of witches were increasingly thwarted by higher judicial authorities. If some economic historians think of this period as 'the end of the long sixteenth century', it was also the beginning of a long seventeenth century in which the cultural traditions and social and political structures of Europe's *ancien régime* matured.

CHAPTER II

THE EUROPEAN ECONOMY 1609–50

THE structures and activity of the international economy probably changed more substantially in the sixteenth century than in the century which followed. In the earlier period the opportunitities offered by a series of remarkable explorations and maritime discoveries progressively altered the volume of commerce and industry, and indeed the general perspectives of the world as then known. Vasco da Gama, during his notable voyage in 1497–8, managed to turn the southern cape of Africa and open a new way to the old riches of the Indies, to the pepper and spices, the silks, cottons and pearls, the perfumes, drugs and other merchandise which through the centuries had largely coloured the conspicuous consumption of Europe. In another direction the frail expedition of Christopher Columbus, touching land in the West Indies in October 1492, led the way for fleets of successors to a fresh continent across the Atlantic. This held forth immense stocks of precious metals and tropical produce, which Europe did not have but was eager to exploit. However, the arrival of these resources—sometimes new, often in abundance—did not find its full explanation in the wavering fortunes of discovery, conquest and plunder. As the new territories grew in stature, they disgorged materials which found their place as commodities in a highly developed market system. Europe received them, not free but at the cost of increased output from her economy. These international outlets came in the wake of territorial conquest and implied expanding export sectors beyond the natural growth of European trade. They helped to widen the outlook on a world of apparently unknown possibilities, encouraging a penchant for intrepid adventure, to which the only limit seemed to be the capacity for enterprise and endeavour. All this contributed collectively a massive human achievement.

But in the seventeenth century the panorama had clearly changed. Although the scale of economic enterprise in real terms was considerably greater than a century before, the rate of growth was less significant. Although Europe had grown more populous, more skilful and more wealthy, its activity had also become relatively less flexible, albeit more lethargic. It is possible that as economic development progressed, marginal returns from new resources fell. Indeed, the volume of transactions seemed to have risen beyond the capacities of those resolute, tight-mouthed and calculating merchant magnates, the Fuggers and Welsers of Augsburg, the Spinolas and Grimaldis of Genoa, the Stroganovs in Russia, to name a few, who in spite of all their outstanding achievements were relayed by great corporative undertakings, companies under joint management, which took the lead. The East India Company in England and the famous Vereenigde Oostindische Compagnie of the United Provinces, for example, asserted monopoly rights and acted under the shadow and protection of their respective states. In time these commercial organizations became more diversified, with objectives often indistinguishable from the policies of government. They embodied mercantile theories and advice emanating from such men as Laffemas and Montchrétien, Thomas Mun and Gerald Malynes, Johann Risingh, Duarte Gomes Solis and other advisers in Europe. State protection, whether effective or presumptive, had the disadvantage that commercial and industrial activity came to bear a mounting burden of impositions inseparable from political aggrandizement. Royal regulations, navigation acts and attitudes, which have been conveniently lumped together under the title of *Mercantilism*, were the price to pay for changing structures of power and initiative in the different economies. As in many other spheres of life Europe faced a surfeit of government. Only more successful times, turned to advantage by the convinced champions of free trade, could prune the exigencies of Leviathan, embodiment of state power.

Such concepts nevertheless take us beyond the period of this chapter which within the limits of 1609 and 1650 admittedly has a certain unity by the norms of traditional history. It opens on the one hand with the Twelve Years Truce (9 April 1609) signed by the deputies of Philip III of Spain and of the Estates of the insurgent United Provinces; and closes on the other hand with the Peace of Westphalia (24 October 1648), which combined both the Treaty of Osnabrück and the separate Treaty of Münster. The Peace of 1648 was destined to settle many of the outstanding power problems so ferociously disputed in the Thirty Years War, but left Spain and France to fight on until the settlement in the Treaty of the Pyrenees (1659). Can the international economy claim an equally valid compartment in the history of Europe?

It would be simple enough indeed to find economic analogies to the limits of this period. Did not, after all, the Spanish monarchy again declare itself bankrupt in 1607, unpapering another crack in this dominant economy on the high tide of its affairs, at the beginning of a century filled with rebuffs and bitterness? Was not 1609 also the founding year for the great Wisselbank of Amsterdam, that unmistakable sign of the financial ascendancy of the astute and nimble Dutch Republic? And again, at the close of the period, we find the whole or almost the whole of Europe in 1648–52 shaken by a cycle of violent price fluctuations, a severe crisis of subsistence typical of the seventeenth century, and perhaps of all economies before the Industrial Revolution.

Yet such events, whether haphazard, isolated or linked together, do not make the setting of this chapter. It is necessary to establish the unity of the first half of the seventeenth century as a phase in the economic development of Europe justifiable in itself. Between 1609 and 1650 or perhaps more precisely between 1590 and 1650, a culminating point and watershed was reached in that long phase of prosperity—the long sixteenth century as Fernand Braudel has aptly called it—which had sustained the economic evolution of Europe since the mid-fifteenth century. The final surge, already filled with hesitations and uncertainties, covered the first half of the seventeenth century. It was a double phenomenon.

In the first place, the turning point of this long development was spread over a fairly wide period of time, commensurately long we should say with the phase which preceded it. It would indeed be difficult, when dealing with such long secular movements, to fix a precise year, an exact crisis valid for the entire international economy. The movement was similar to the turn of a high tide, when some time must pass at slack water before the observer can say for certain that the ebb has set in. This chapter covers a similar reversal in the economic history of Europe. It probably lasted half a century.

The second aspect: the economic down-turn was not of the same nature for all the countries of the continent of Europe. The evolution of this polyvalent economy followed a complex pattern, and long-term growth and recession did not necessarily affect all the regions of Europe in the same way. For some, as in the case of Spain and many Mediterranean countries, the turn of the sixteenth century proved to be a major crisis affecting their position at the head of European affairs and foreshadowed decline. This was an absolute upset, unseating a dominant economy and its dependants. For other economies, as the later developments in Holland and England were to show, the series of setbacks in the early seventeenth century were only stages in a march to economic pre-eminence, a series of difficult crises, which the whole of Europe shared in varying degrees. Being less directly absorbed in the concentration of power characterized by the rise of Spain, they resisted longer than the others. Such a difference in economic temperament serves to emphasize the inherent disparity of Europe, which the prosperity of the sixteenth century had confronted, accentuated but failed entirely to resolve.

This dramatic period covered in large measure by the years 1609 to 1650 constitutes a part of what has been aptly described as the crisis of the seventeenth century. This was a huge movement, much wider than the material civilization of Europe itself, which was obliged to hesitate, pause and re-form. Such a crisis was not confined to one year alone, to one place, to one catastrophe. It took form slowly in the context of the whole of Europe in half a century of slumps, bankruptcies and shocks of war, and in effect prepared for a new phase in the long continuity of economic history. The problem in its full complexity still remains relatively new. The empirical data for the discussion often leave much to be desired and the tentative conclusions presented here must wait for future studies to clear up the many obscure aspects of changes in this period. In this chapter, the varying crisis in different sectors—population; money, prices and wages; trade and production—must claim our attention in turn, through at least some thirty years of European war, with its inevitable wastages and destruction.

I

The problems of population growth in the early seventeenth century, perhaps typically of pre-industrial economies, remained fundamental to economic activity. The level of human population indeed implied at once the available supply of labour—the working force and intelligence to husband the land and ply the crafts—and at the same time constituted the potential aggregate consumption of the different communities. Since population growth was in the nature of a cumulative process, sustained quantitative changes or even retardation in the rate of increase may be understood to have had wide repercussions which are difficult to estimate not only in absolute terms but also in the risks and uncertainties encountered by economic enterprise.

Through the long growth of the sixteenth century, the inhabitants experienced increases in numbers, relatively of considerable significance. In 1600, according to Joseph Kulischer, Europe—that is the larger Europe west of the Urals—could claim some 95,000,000. By 1650, another estimate by Carr-Saunders sets this population at some 100,000,000. These figures, however, are extremely uncertain and others can be suggested in their place. The still valid data and methods of Julius Beloch propose, for a smaller-sized Europe however, an overall figure in the region of 80,000,000 about which the population fluctuated.

The Europe from the Atlantic to the Urals of some 100,000,000 held a position in the world roughly the same as today, about one-fifth of the earth's population. According to the same estimates, Asia added some 330,000,000; Africa stood at about the same level as Europe, although this is no doubt hasty and over-generous; America, 13,000,000; and Oceania, 1,000,000. Total: 545,000,000. In my opinion a lower figure, perhaps even as low as some 450–460,000,000, would be more acceptable. The margin of error in these estimates remains significantly high. The whole question indeed is largely undecided and open to conjecture.

The distribution of the different regional populations also probably altered during the period under survey. It would be difficult to follow such changes in a period as brief as the first half of the seventeenth century, but estimates by A. P. Usher and Julius Beloch exist for the whole century. Some countries, important at the beginning, had declined in numbers by the end of the century. Germany passed from about 20,000,000 to 15,500,000 and the Low Countries from 3,000,000 to 2,700,000.

France, however, with the territories solidly acquired by Mazarin and Louis XIV in 1648 and 1659, probably rose from about 16,000,000 to 20,000,000. These three groups together registered a slight decrease from 39,000,000 in 1600 to 38,200,000 in 1700. Spain and Italy also may have declined from 8,000,000 and 13,000,000 to 7,300,000 and 11,300,000 respectively in 1700. But can we accept all these assessments as correct?

By the middle of the seventeenth century it is possible that the total population of Europe had suffered a notable recession. In some areas this was apparently severe. The inhabitants of Italy may have declined by twenty per cent; of Germany in general by a third, of Bohemia by half, of Moravia by a third. A recent estimate for northern France suggests that a fall in population levels set in after 1640. On the outer fringe of Europe, there were signs of depopulation in Anatolia. All this tends to corroborate the hypothesis of an over-all decline by the middle of the century. But the data are still based on regional estimates and it is often difficult to assess fully the aggregate effects of inter-regional migrations. By the end of the century, however, this temporary depression had probably been overcome and declines in some areas were compensated by advances in others. Germany in particular had managed in all probability by about 1700 to repair its great losses and return to the population level of 1600.

There is a further indicator of internal population changes in the density of inhabitants. About 1600, the three most densely populated countries were: Italy (with 114 to the square mile); the Netherlands (with 104); and France (with 88). By 1700 the Austrian Netherlands showed a remarkable human concentration (137 per square mile compared with 98 for the United Provinces): Italy had 102; France, 95. Again such estimates are tentative, but the conclusions tend to coincide with the general knowledge of the period. At least to some extent, losses in the south of Europe were adjusted by gains in the north—in the Low Countries, the British Isles and Scandinavia, which went ahead by comparison with the Mediterranean countries and the Iberian Peninsula.

The general readjustment in Europe's population was also apparent in the relative positions of the great cities. In the first half of the seventeenth century some of the notable centres of the 'Mediterranean' economy tended to lag or even decline—such as Messina, Palermo, Seville and Antwerp, the financial hub of Spanish affairs in the north. Others such as Amsterdam, Madrid and Vienna advanced—the two latter, both continental capitals and administrative centres for vast empires, may be considered as important signs of structural change. During the seventeenth century two other great capitals of Europe—Paris and London—managed to pass the mark of 400,000 inhabitants. Paris, wealthy, brilliant but dangerous as the Fronde revealed, was soon to drive the *grand monarque* to the magnificence of Versailles; London, thriving and looking to the prosperity ahead, was destined to surpass in size all the other cities of Europe.

London, indeed, was an example of exceptional urban success. When John Stow first published his *Survey* (1598), it had a well-established position as port, capital and economic focus of the country. It absorbed citizens in search of work or amusement. It offered asylum from persecution in other parts of Europe, as the Flemings crowding into Billingsgate indicated. By 1603, with perhaps as many as 170,000 inhabitants, it was already disproportionately large for England, standing out, as James I disdainfully remarked, 'like a head of a rickety child'. And there were protests. In 1596 the council had complained to the Middlesex magistrates of 'the multitudes of base tenements and houses of unlawful and disorderly resort in the suburbs'. But the city continued to grow majestically through the seventeenth century, sprawling beyond the medieval walls and moats, often still in place, out into the liberties and still again into the outparishes. At the end of the century, Gregory King proposed a likely population of 550,000 inhabitants. The deaths recorded in the bills of mortality also give some idea of this expansion.

TABLE 3

Period	City (97 parishes)	Liberties	Outparishes
1604–23	48,000	74,000	31,000
1624–43	58,000	98,000	55,000
1644–63	59,000	109,000	70,000
1664–83	61,000	120,000	189,000
1684–1703	56,000	134,000	145,000

While the recorded deaths in the City remained almost stationary, they doubled in the liberties and quintupled in the outparishes. By the 1660s the outparishes returned the greatest number, although this superiority over the combined totals from the City and the liberties became permanent only after the 1680s. London in the seventeenth century, indeed, bore the mark of success, surviving the Great Plague (1665) and the Fire (1666). On all sides, as F. J. Fisher has observed, the capital displayed itself as a notable centre of conspicuous consumption.

If in all probability the total population of Europe stagnated or even receded in the middle of the seventeenth century, there were some very good reasons. The inhabitants faced the severe setbacks which most societies have experienced when pushed to the limits of their resources. The perennial scourges of mankind—famine, pestilence and war—struck the communities of Europe perhaps more insistently, more disastrously during this period.

The famines of the type suffered by the *Ancien Régime* were more often due to a series of bad harvests which exhausted the meagre reserves in hand. Their severity in the early seventeenth century has been linked to the deterioration in climatic conditions, to that long spell of cold and unfavourable weather experienced in Europe after 1600. The evidence of larch trees at Berchtesgaden suggests that growth was twice as great before 1600 as after. In Switzerland and Iceland, glaciers probably reached their first maximum limits in the middle of the seventeenth century. The existence of this long-term climatic fluctuation, however, in the present state of our empirical knowledge, must remain an open question.

Certainly, there were cases of exceptional harvest failures and famines. In Russia, in 1601, a catastrophic dearth lasted three years, which caused, so it was reported, some 120,000 deaths in Moscow alone, and brought the starving peasants crowding into the city for alms. When this finally was refused, they left to die by the roadside in great numbers. Western Europe, notwithstanding its relative commercial sophistication, suffered two severe bouts of dearth: in 1628-30 and in 1648-52.

The first cycle probably reached its peak in the spring of 1629. In Udine, between May 1627 and May 1629, the price of wheat quadrupled, and the cheaper grains, such as rye and maize, the staple diet of the poor and the greatest sufferers, rose even more steeply. In England in 1630, the price of wheat rose above sixty shillings the quarter. But these grim years in Europe have little to compare with the disasters which tightened conditions in other parts of the world at this time. In India, in the Gujerat, a Dutch observer records a terrible series of years

an excessive drought, so that the crops withered and the cattle starved in the fields, then in 1631 such continuous and unusual heavy rains that the rivers overflowed and covered the land, destroying whole stretches of country, towns and many villages, and ruining the standing crops, which were most promising. The result was a great famine and horrible mortality both of men and cattle . . .

Grain prices rose twenty times; cannibalism was rife

but a still more horrible sight was seen: the village named Susuntra, where human flesh was sold openly in the market . . . in the years which followed, these calamities began to cease and food began to grow at the former price, but still the present days and abundance of provisions are not to be compared with former times. May God Almighty preserve all Christian countries from such plagues . . .

The second cycle of high food prices was exceptionally acute in 1649-50. Cloudbursts in 1649 and consequent harvest failures prepared the way for winter and early spring months of extreme difficulty. The phenomenon was present over large areas of Europe, in Italy and England, in France and Poland. Between 1645-6 and 1649-50, the price of wheat more or less doubled in England and France, and trebled in Italy. In Lwow in Poland the price of oats between 1643 and 1651 rose eight times (see Fig. 1).

The direct effects of famines on the total size of Europe's population, however, are difficult to measure with certainty. Crop failures, or even a series of crop failures, wrought their disastrous effects not so much

73

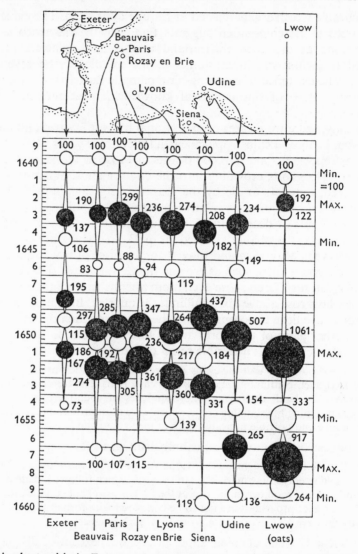

Fig. 1. A wheat crisis in Europe, 1639–60 [reference: F. Braudel and F. C. Spooner, *Cambridge Economic History of Europe*, Vol. IV, ed. E. E. Rich and C. H. Wilson (1967)]. The movement of prices is shown as an index, based on the period from the fourth quarter 1639 to the first quarter 1640 (= 100).

directly through famine deaths as indirectly through the diseases associated with pernicious undernourishment. Any question of food shortages turned inevitably on the not less important question of the adequacy of food consumption.

The standards of nutrition probably deteriorated in the seventeenth century. This has been suggested in the case of Poland. In Italy after the difficult years of the 1620s and 1630s there were signs of inferior diets. In Udine the cheaper maize, destined to become the staple food of the poor, appeared in the official market lists from September 1622. There also from 1668, mixtures of grains and pulses were officially quoted— wheat and rye; wheat, rye and lentils; maize, sorghum and buckwheat; and others—substitutes and signs of distress, which disappeared only after the middle of the eighteenth century. In Sweden, the food budgets for the manor of Gripsholm show a decline in the daily intake of calories:

TABLE 4

Year	Daily consumption of calories
1555	4,166
1638	2,480
1653	2,883
1661	2,920

It would be very convenient to accept this example of Gripsholm as evidence of growing malnutrition and exposure to disease in the general crisis of the seventeenth century. But can these food estimates in Scandinavia prove the case?

It is within the realm of possibility that other biological factors also played a part in the changing structure of Europe's population, including overcrowding, insecurity and general stress. Certainly, severe epidemics struck Europe in the seventeenth century. The housing problems of the cities faced town authorities with the dangers of filth and poor hygiene. London was no exception. Piped water was a rarity, and households even after the opening of the new river in 1613 were largely supplied by water carriers from the public conduits. The crowded suburbs, with buildings quickly thrown up to meet the pressure for housing, became breeding grounds for disease and particularly for rat-borne plague. The plagues of 1603, 1625, 1636 and later the great plague of 1665, according to Charles Creighton, appeared first and made their greatest ravages in the suburbs. The plague of 1636, to cite another notable instance, was severe in Newcastle (Northumberland), growing rapidly to meet the expanding coal trade.

Scarcely a year passed without a serious outbreak of some sort or other. There were bouts of fever, cholera, the 'sweating sickness', as well as the plague which made its last serious appearances as an epidemic sickness in the seventeenth century. The form of war typhus associated with Europe reached a peak in the Thirty Years War with the inevitable sieges, pitched battles and pillaging of marauding armies. England came to know its gravity in 1643 in the Civil War. And heavy plague years were often bad years for deaths from other diseases: in London typhus fever in

4-2

1625 and 1636, and smallpox in 1641, claimed many victims. Dysentery— the 'griping of the guts' as the mortality bills described it after 1658— appeared more frequently in the records of the seventeenth century.

Although plague did not strike alone, it was the great killer. In Italy in the wake of the dearths of 1628–9 the plague of 1630 made terrible inroads on the population. In that year alone, according to Julius Beloch, a million and a half died in the peninsula, of whom two-thirds perished in the plain of Lombardy. Bologna, the city and district taken together, lost 29,698; Venice, Chioggia and Malamocco 46,490 (about 35% of the inhabitants); Padua about 17,000 (44%); Verona, city and suburbs together, 31,000 (59%); Parma about 20,000 (50%); Cremona about 25,000 (60%). The plague of 1656 was less severe but nevertheless was notable in Liguria and the kingdom of Naples. The cities of Genoa and Naples probably lost as many as half of their inhabitants. These figures, clearly, can be accepted only after allowing for some measure of exaggeration and margins of error in counting.

Such losses sometimes halved the urban populations and left scars which were difficult to efface. Milan, which had had a population of 180,216 in the time of Borromeo, after 1630 claimed about 100,000. After the great plague in 1630, Bologna had fallen from 65,000 to 46,747 in 1631. Venice with a population of 142,804 in 1624, held 98,244 in 1633. There the pestilence made its greatest inroads on the poor, as can be seen from the changing percentages between the main social groups:

TABLE 5

Year	Nobles (nobiles)	Burgesses (cittadini)	Inhabitants (popolani)
	%	%	%
1624	3·9	7·4	88·7
1633	4·0	10·6	85·4

Genoa with 68,000 inhabitants in 1608 was reduced to 38,360 in 1660.

The Netherlands also suffered heavy losses. Haarlem lost 5,723 in the plague of 1655. Leiden, with 44,745 inhabitants in 1622, lost 9,897 in 1624–5, 14,582 in 1635, and 10,529 in 1655. Amsterdam sustained nine noteworthy attacks between 1617 and 1664, of which four were particularly grave: 11,795 deaths in 1624 (or 1 in 9); 17,193 in 1636 (1 in 7); 16,727 in 1655 (1 in 8); and 24,148 in 1664 (1 in 6). This great financial centre paid heavily indeed for the prosperous expansion of its affairs.

And in London, the same terrible record. In 1603 some 30,000 are said to have died from the plague. The same disease claimed 35,417 in the period from May to November 1625. In the year of the Great Plague of 1665, the deaths recorded were as follows:

TABLE 6

Year	Plague	Fever	Smallpox	Total deaths
1665	68,596	5,257	655	97,306

These were clearly greater than in 1630, 1636, and 1647, when the losses could represent perhaps as many as a quarter of the inhabitants.

The third great setback to the population of Europe was the destruction of war. For thirty years this misfortune coursed across the battle-grounds of Germany, and although most countries on the continent felt its effects, the empire was the greatest sufferer. Here and there according to the estimates of Günther Franz the losses were immense, but not all the regions were affected in the same way. Some areas—the north-west fringe, Austria and the cantons of Switzerland—came through the trials almost unscathed. Others were less gravely tested: Moravia, Saxony and Silesia had losses of 15 to 20%. The rest of Germany, however, bore the brunt of the conflict. Some regions lost 40%; Bohemia, Brandenburg, Magdeburg, Thuringia, Bavaria and Franconia were reduced by half. Some estimates for Mecklenburg, Pomerania, Coburg and Hesse, the Palatinate and Würtemberg put the losses at 60 to 70%, while in pockets between Augsburg, Nüremburg and Stuttgart the losses in some rural districts could have risen as high as four-fifths, towns being reduced to the level of villages. With the direct losses of war came disease and starvation, heaping disaster on disaster. Much still remains to be known about these dark and sorry years in German history.

TABLE 7

Origin	Destination	In percentages 1590–4	1655–9
Low Countries	Amsterdam	50·4	53·6
	Leiden	15·5	41·2
	Middelburg	18·0	43·9
Belgium	Amsterdam	34·3	5·0
	Leiden	53·3	15·2
	Middelburg	72·1	30·5
France	Amsterdam	1·8	3·7
	Leiden	26·8	18·2
	Middelburg	5·8	13·6
Germany	Amsterdam	11·2	28·8
	Leiden	3·0	21·6
	Middelburg	1·9	3·3
Others	Amsterdam	1·8	6·9
	Leiden	1·3	3·2
	Middelburg	2·2	8·7

Yet the absolute level of such losses still remains open to conjecture. It is difficult to dissociate deaths from the redistribution of population through emigration. There were open cities, places of refuge, such as Amsterdam, London, Constantinople and many others, ready to absorb migrants. Something of the scale of such movements can be seen from the origins of newcomers to Amsterdam, Leiden and Middelburg, between 1590–4 and 1655–9 (see Table 7).

After some sixty years the majority of the newcomers to these cities arrived from the drift to the cities in the Netherlands, or from Germany rather than, as at the end of the sixteenth century, from the Low Countries under Spanish control. Both these areas in turn had been trouble-spots and so the exodus from theatres of war thus contributed to the general redistribution of population.

II

The link between population problems and the waning prosperity of the sixteenth century is by no means easy to measure from the tentative estimates of population: redistribution and migrations, as we have seen, cloud the issues. The sectors of money and prices, however, fix more precisely both the turning points and the changing relationships between the different regions of the international economy in the early seventeenth century.

Monetary problems received a good deal of publicity in the writings of contemporary bullionists and mercantilists. Bullion served ultimately to adjust trading balances and underwrite a credit system, which was rarely able to venture very far from final settlements in coin. The prosperity of the long sixteenth century had been marked by an astonishing increase in the precious metals at the disposal of Europe, from Africa, from Europe itself, and finally from the extraordinary mines of Mexico and Peru. By far the greater part had been counted through the House of Trade—the *Casa de la Contratación*—in Seville. Spain became the pressure point for the monetary circulations of Europe.

This state of affairs underwent radical changes in the early seventeenth century, even though at first sight little seemed to have altered. The fleets of galleons arrived irregularly under heavy convoy from the New World. Only once did they fail to make port and this was a day indeed for jubilation among the enemies of Spain. In 1628 Admiral Pieter Pieterzoon Heyn (1578–1629), commanding the squadrons of the Dutch West India Company, waylaid and captured the larger part of the treasure-fleet, taking it in triumph to Amsterdam to provide the company shareholders with a 50% dividend. But this was a rare event. Spain did not easily relinquish her position as the centre for bullion in Europe. All the documents bear witness to this reality. After 1685, when Cadiz assumed the place of Seville, the centre of high pressure had hardly shifted.

The real crisis came when that pressure began to fade. The shipments of bullion reached their peak point in the decade of the 1590s and declined through the seventeenth century (see Fig. 2). By the 1640s the cargoes of gold were 8% of those in the 1590s and silver had fallen to 39%.

TABLE 8. *Average annual imports of gold and silver in Seville from the New World, in kilograms*

Period	Gold	Silver
1591–1600	1,945	270,763
1641–50	155	105,643

Various explanations have been proposed for this failure to maintain the position of the sixteenth century: difficulties of labour, mining and extraction; of obtaining cheap mercury for the amalgamation process. In addition, it must be observed that in the eighteenth century (see Fig. 6) when the New World again experienced expanding production of precious metals, it was Mexico not Peru which led the way. To all appearances, Peru was the greatest loser in the early seventeenth century. The drain of silver to the East directly across the Pacific has also been suggested as a possible factor. The recent study of Pierre Chaunu, however, rejects this hypothesis and shows that the movement of Spanish trade between Acapulco and Manila followed the general trend of trade in the Atlantic: it was in decline from the decade 1606–15. The problem was probably more general. The production of gold and silver like other industrial sectors fell victim to the relentless law of diminishing marginal returns and declining profits. From the monetary point of view an important turning point was taken. The sixteenth century had passed its prime.

Yet, while the additions to the stocks of gold and silver money declined, the requirements for circulating medium continued to grow with advancing prosperity, expanding transactions and rising price-levels in some cases prolonged through the Thirty Years War. Silver was particularly required for settling debtor trading balances. Bullion flowed from Spain, where it was relatively abundant, to the less well-endowed areas of Europe's economy: to Poland, eastern Europe and Russia, whose commercial systems grew more and more accustomed to a money economy; to the Levant, India, the East Indies and China, where silver coins especially the famous Spanish piece of eight reals gave merchants the advantage of a buyer's market. From Venice alone in 1610–14, the silver Spanish reals officially exported to the Levant amounted to six per cent of the silver being imported at Seville. Although this was an important trading centre, it was not the only outlet. We must also take into account

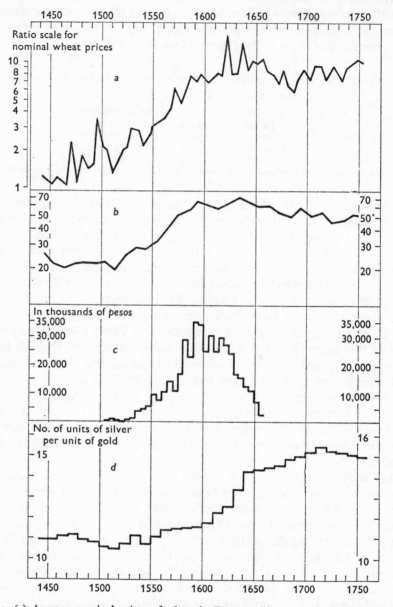

Fig. 2. (*a*) Average nominal prices of wheat in Europe; (*b*) average prices of wheat in grams of silver per hectolitre; (*c*) the value of imports of gold and silver at Seville [reference: E. J. Hamilton, *American Treasure and the Price Revolution in Spain 1501–1650* (Cambridge, Mass., 1934)]; (*d*) the bimetallic ratios in Europe (ten-yearly averages).

the trade from ports such as Genoa, the financial dependency of Spain, from Leghorn, Naples, Marseilles, Barcelona . . . And in the north, the great East India Companies of Holland and England, the expeditions from France and Denmark commandeered silver for export with official permission. These were some indications of the demands on the declining supplies, and of the potential monetary difficulties, which characterized the early seventeenth century.

In effect, a whole mercantile system was placed in jeopardy. Spain had attracted the attention of the great financial *entrepreneurs*, who found through Spain the required opening into both the bullion markets of Europe and the trade with the New World. The Fuggers and Welsers of Germany, the Spinolas of Genoa had not hesitated to throw themselves into the Spanish venture, forming liaisons which often, officially at least, lasted until the failures of the first half of the seventeenth century. This commercial activity enlivened the whole economic system, with its relays of fairs and bourses to adjust balances and settle international accounts. If this system had enjoyed smooth continuity, any change would at once have been more easily evident. In reality, however, the monetary and financial systems tended to respond to the irregular cadence of the treasure fleets arriving in Seville. Before these galleons made port, the money markets were tight, as merchants in their letters all over Europe testified. After the unloading of the treasure fleet, the markets one after another reported easier monetary conditions. For the early seventeenth century, the periods of tight money appeared longer and more persistently, precipitating shortages and even failures. These uncertainties acted as a restraining force on the interaction and expansion of the international economy at large.

Such shortages naturally did not pass unheeded. The first serious effects, paradoxically enough, were felt in Spain, unsettled by the expenses of grandiose politics, increasingly unstable, as though the system was rotting at the core. There, too, the government intervened in the conscious effort to expand the monetary circulation and cull profits and revenue for itself. It ordered the minting of large quantities of copper *maravedis*. These were small coins which had their most severe repercussions on the daily life of the country. The estimates by Earl J. Hamilton of the quantities of this coin put into circulation are:

TABLE 9

Period	Value of copper coins issued, in *ducados* (each worth 375 *maravedis*)
1599–1606	22 millions
1617–19	5 millions
1621–6	14 millions

The nominal value of these masses of copper coin was further increased by restamping at higher currency rates in 1603, 1636, 1641 and 1651. In addition, the situation was aggravated by vast quantities of counterfeit copper money smuggled into the country. In this coinage the monarchy found only a stop-gap relief measure in a fevered effort to fill the coffers. Later the repercussions became all too evident and prepared the royal bankruptcies of 1607 and 1627.

The economic consequences were indeed disastrous. Inevitably, the copper currency clogged the circulation, and true to the so-called Gresham's Law, drove out the more valuable silver and gold coins. At first, during the Twelve Years Truce, the effects were not painfully apparent. The premium on silver was about 1% in 1603, and rose slowly to 3% in 1619. But with the outbreak of the Thirty Years War and the renewed conflict with the United Provinces (1621), this premium rose unchecked, with peaks during the silver difficulties of 1626-8 and 1641-2. It reached 50% by the mid-seventeenth century. Such unstable monetary conditions constituted in reality a progressive devaluation, and were not mastered in Spain until the 1680s. The pernicious effects impressed observers abroad, as well as statesmen in Spain. They were pointed out as a lesson to all.

Other governments used this expedient but with greater caution. France, although it had already used copper currency since 1578, introduced moderate quantities after 1609. In Sweden, copper currency assumed a more important role. There the mining and production of copper was under the close control of the Swedish monarchy and had at first prospered from the demand of the mints in Spain. Gustavus Adolphus, himself hard pressed to finance his military campaigns in Europe, turned to this expedient in 1624. Copper coinage assumed a particular importance after 1626 when the foreign demand for Swedish copper fell after the stop on minting in Spain. The Swedish *daler*, veritable plates of copper, became so cumbersome that later in the eighteenth century they were carried on special sleds. This sort of difficulty later assured the success of the credit facilities offered by the Bank of Sweden, founded in 1656, which issued the first bank-notes of Europe. Copper currency flowed abroad. Further east in Moscow, copper provoked a further incident, when the coinage, begun in 1656, culminated in a runaway inflation after 1661 and the famous 'copper riots' in 1663.

In Germany, the governments also tampered with the currency during the *Kipper- und Wipperzeit*, a spell of monetary debasements and coin-clipping which shook the country at the outbreak of the Thirty Years War. These debasements were examples of hyperinflation even when measured by the official valuations. In Munich and Augsburg between 1617 and 1622 the silver equivalent of the *Rechnungsgulden* fell 88%; in Frankfurt between 1612 and 1622 the devaluation was 72%; in Leipzig between

1619 and 1622, 82%; in Vienna between 1619 and 1622, 74%; in Strasbourg between 1619 and 1622, 66%. These brusque movements formed relatively short interludes, but the different economies were shaken and trade disrupted at a particularly delicate moment in the history of the empire. Only in the last decade of the seventeenth century was Europe able to overcome these difficulties, all too often provoked by government interference.

A second aspect of the monetary crisis, which cannot be dissociated from the general insufficiency of monetary resources, was the rapid appreciation of gold. This resulted partly from the preponderance of silver over gold brought from the New World, which was particularly apparent in the first half of the seventeenth century. More silver was imported in 1601-60 than in 1503-1600, but far less gold. In 1503-1600 the ratio of silver to gold by weight was about 48 to 1; in 1601-60, this ratio had risen to about 340 to 1.

TABLE 10. *Total gold and silver imported in Seville from the New World, in kilograms*

Period	Gold	Silver	Ratio by weight
1503-1600	153,564	7,439,142	1 : 48.44
1601-60	27,769	9,447,673	1 : 340.22

The value of gold in terms of silver consequently tended to increase. This was further augmented as gold was preferred for hoarding, since it tended to retain its value more easily than silver. About 1550, the average value of gold to silver in Europe was at an average ratio of about 1 to 11; by 1600 this had almost reached 1 to 12. By 1650 it had advanced to 1 to $14\frac{1}{2}$, and by 1700 to about 1 to 15 or $15\frac{1}{2}$ (see Fig. 2). It remained roughly at this level until after the 'Great Crisis' of 1873. The period of greatest change in the ratio of gold to silver was in the first half of the seventeenth century.

This rapid transformation in the structures of gold values was most apparent in the highly advanced economies and particularly in the upper levels of the monetary system of Europe concerned with international trade and finance. The economic growth of the sixteenth century had been accompanied by a growing volume of bills of exchange passing through the great fairs and exchanges—the fairs of Medina del Campo, of Lyons and of Piacenza; through the exchanges of Venice, Paris, London or Amsterdam . . . These exchanges were often adjusted to a fictitious gold currency which thus assumed the role of an international accounting system, even though the actual payments may have been made in silver.

For Spain there was the gold *escudo* or *pistole*; for France the *écu d'or au soleil*; for the fairs of Piacenza the *scudi d'oro*; and many others. The relative appreciation of gold threatened to disrupt the established relationship between contracts and payments in real coin.

The first was part of a complex change in the international economy itself. As the balance of economic affairs tended to shift away from the older centres of southern Europe to the smaller but more progressive economies of the north, the customary markets, fairs and commercial centres became less involved in trading bulk merchandise, but nevertheless retained a primacy in exchange and financial dealings. It is not surprising, therefore, in the face of the changes in gold values, that here and there a double monetary system evolved, which on the one hand left the domestic system of accounts flexible to devaluations and freely convertible into gold and silver, but on the other hand stabilized the system of international payments by retaining customary values. The difference between the two levels of monetary circulation in effect showed that the international network of exchanges tended to diverge from the uncertainties of some of the domestic currency systems which were susceptible to devaluation and government manipulation. This was evident in the case of Spain and France. About 1600, in Spain the gold *escudo* (valued at 400 *maravedis*) and in France the gold *écu au soleil* (at 60 *sols*) were both real gold coins and standards of value for bills of exchange. The gold devaluation in Spain of 23 November 1609 and in France of September 1602 raised the *escudo* to 440 *maravedis* and the *écu* to 65 *sols* in specie; but left the values of the *escudo* and the *écu* in bills of exchange at their old values, that is 400 *maravedis* and 60 *sols* respectively. Did this retention of the old system of exchange rates show that the international accounting had reached such an advanced level of homogeneity that merchants were little inclined to disrupt their habitual methods in dealings with countries of such major importance?

A second aspect of these changes was the establishment of the public banks. Some were already in existence such as the Banco dello Spirito Santo in Naples, or the venerable Banco di San Giorgio in Genoa. The latter, at the heart of the powerful mercantile republic in league with Spain, showed renewed vitality and reflected the changing needs: in 1606 it opened a new *cartulario* in *scudi di cambi* and later in 1625 another in *moneta di Reali*. Other banks were created to suit the needs of government finance. Venice had its Banco della Piazza di Rialto (founded in 1587 and dissolved in 1637) and its Banco Giro (founded in 1619). In Amsterdam the famous Wisselbank was established by the ordinance of 31 January 1609. This was followed by similar banks in Middelburg in 1616, in Delft in 1621 and in Rotterdam in 1635. The Girobank was set up in Hamburg in 1619. Nüremberg had its bank from 1621. There were unsuccessful attempts to set up public banks in Spain in 1603 (by the Pragmatic of

Valladolid) and in France in 1607. Ostensibly they had the limited purpose of easing government finance, as well as of avoiding the dangers of defective currency and the risks entailed in shifting bullion and specie. But gradually they formed a means of facilitating international payments. In the Banco della Piazza of Venice (by the decree of the Senate of 1593), and in the Wisselbank (by the foundation charter of 1609), bills of exchange were ordered to be settled in the bank ledgers. In Venice this system was underwritten by the huge state reserves of gold and silver kept in the *Deposito Grande* (in 1609 these amounted to 9,173,170 ducats worth 204,290 kilograms of silver). In Amsterdam the average deposits (officially at 100%) in the vaults of the bank between 1650 and 1654 amounted to 8,520,211 florins, which (allowing for the premium on bank money), was equivalent to some 89,770 kilograms of silver. The massive position of Venice is thus demonstrated. These public banks formed relay points in the financial circuits and added stability to a network of exchanges distinct from the domestic monetary systems prone to devaluation. In the Banco Giro of Venice at least by 1621 there was a premium of 20% on converting bank money into current money. In Amsterdam, the premium was lower, reaching the level of about 4% in the 1670s.

In the face of changing monetary conditions it is probable that the volume of credit also expanded in the first two decades of the seventeenth century. Merchants and financiers made increased use of endorsing bills of exchange and of the *patto di ricorsa* (which offered a brief period of credit during the time the bill circulated before being returned). In the Banco dello Spirito Santo in Naples, the balance of credits rose from 46,210 ducats in 1600 to 841,285 ducats on 10 June 1622. But such commercial confidence was relatively short-lived. The uncertainties imposed by the renewal of war and the pressures of government finance served only to emphasize the inflexibilities of the credit potential of Europe, where the monetary system remained largely tied to the restrictions of gold and silver.

In the last resort, the gap between bullion supplies and the expansion of the different monetary systems inevitably resulted in devaluations. These in turn classified the relative positions of the various regional economies, where some more than others succeeded in maintaining their standing. The more important national moneys of account, when reduced to their equivalents in silver, show the following changes between 1580-9 and 1650-4 (see Map I).

From these percentages, it can readily be seen that the economies of north-western Europe offered strong resistance. On the other hand, Poland, underdeveloped and largely dependent on agricultural products to sustain her position in the international markets, suffered most of all. At the outbreak of the Thirty Years War she shared in the wave of debasements of Germany, but did not recover to the same extent as her German and Austrian neighbours. In a decade between 1617 and 1627 the *grosz* lost more than half its equivalent in silver. Again in the devaluations of 1663, it lost another half, although on this occasion Danzig avoided the collapse, refusing no doubt to pay its share of the war and leaving the continental cities, such as Krakow, Warsaw, Poznan, Lublin, Lwow and others to carry the burden. In this respect there was also an economic partition of Poland.

TABLE II

Country	Name of money of account	Index of silver values in 1650–4 (1580–9 = 100)
England	Pound sterling	96·77
Holland	*Guilder*	84·23
Augsburg	*Rechnungsgulden*	83·68
Spanish Netherlands	Florin	80·39
Austria	*Rechengulden*	79·43
Frankfurt	*Rechnungsgulden*	79·21
Venice	*Lira*	76·51
France	*Livre tournois*	68·47
Spain	*Maravedi*	66·41
Genoa	*Lira*	55·41
Poland	*Grosz*	38·91

Finally, the writings of the mercantilists in the early seventeenth century underlined the effect of these monetary difficulties on contemporaries. The economy of the sixteenth century had grown accustomed to relatively large additions of bullion to smooth the working of international trade, to encourage the relays of merchants and substantiate their forecasts. The sagging conditions which obtained in the early seventeenth century often provoked confused explanations. 'We live', said Montchrétien in 1615, 'not so much from trade in raw materials as from gold and silver.' The importance of money supplies held the attention of Malynes in the *Lex Mercatoria*, 'for if Money be wanting, trade doth decrease although commodities be abundant and good cheap'. And again in his *Treatise of the Canker of England's Commonwealth* (1601): 'the more ready money, either in specie or by exchange that our merchants should make their return by, the more employment would they make upon our home commodities advancing the price thereof which price would augment the quantity by setting more people on work'. The bullionists did not shrink from linking the quantity of specie with prices and full employment. Swelling reserves of bullion, rising prices and a mounting level of employment were the outward signs of inner economic well-being: their derangement had causal links with depression. Their theories, even if discredited, form a pungent comment on the contemporary monetary difficulties and general economic conditions.

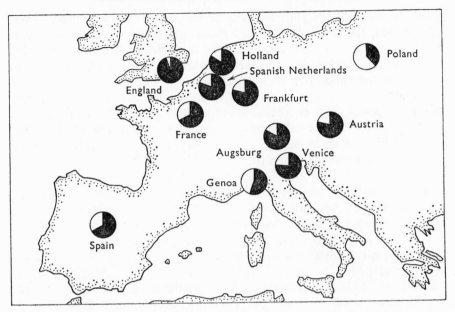

Map 1. Index of silver devaluation in Europe, 1650-4. The segment in white shows the proportion of devaluation; the full circle represents the base-period 1580-9 (= 100).

The study of the movements and structures of prices has, like that of money, added greatly to our knowledge of the international economy, for both the phases of development and the regional differences which were fundamental to the early seventeenth century.

The first problem is one of general chronology. The transition from the prolonged inflation of the sixteenth century to the stable and then falling prices more characteristic of the seventeenth century is not a simple question. It presupposes that the prices of goods circulating in regional or international markets can be expressed in common monetary terms, usually in silver. In reality, the economic activity over large areas of Europe was mainly destined to satisfy home or local needs. It is therefore difficult to find a commodity widely served by international trade. Grain prices have firstly the advantage of being most abundantly recorded but secondly the disadvantage of relating to a bulky commodity, difficult to transport and store—two factors which loomed large in the final price.

The silver prices of wheat show relatively clearly the down-turns in the different regions of Europe. The most highly advanced regions of Europe, which had been flooded with silver currency during the sixteenth century, were the first to experience a change in price trends. In Spain, the dominant economy, the inflation of silver prices apparently ended about 1600, and it is probable that the defeat of the Invincible Armada and the ensuing material difficulties coincided with a profound change in the economic

87

development of Spain. Italy also shared this experience. In Udine, Siena and Naples, the last decade of the sixteenth century was probably the high-tide mark to a long-term rise in prices. In south-east France, in Grenoble and Dauphiné, the level for the 1590s was higher than any decade in the preceding or succeeding quarter-century, although the evidence is confused by the wars of the League. In general, it is probable that grain prices in silver for the towns in the western basin of the Mediterranean reached their culminating point at the turn of the century, and consequently for them the first half of the seventeenth century meant recession in the levels of silver prices (see Fig. 2).[1]

Further north the conditions were somewhat different. In Germany and Austria, the prolonged rise in price levels continued through the sixteenth century until the eve or the outbreak of the Thirty Years War and the monetary debasements of the *Kipperjahre*. The evidence, however, is very confused through the disturbances of war, but it is probable that from this peak point and at least by the 1630s a serious recession in price levels developed in the towns of Germany and Austria. In Speyer, Leipzig and Frankfurt this falling trend continued in the prices of all or almost all commodities until 1656–60; in Würzburg, Augsburg and Munich it lasted until 1671. There were brief crises *en route* due to Imperial or Swedish occupations, as in the case of Augsburg in 1626 and 1633–5, in Würzburg in 1631 and 1634, in Munich in 1632 and 1648–9. After 1656–60 and 1671, prices began to rise again in Germany and Central Europe, thus ending the serious recession which had marked the Thirty Years War and its immediate consequences. Some economic historians, and notably Maurice Elsas, have not hesitated to attribute this phenomenon to the loss of population and the heavy destruction of war. In general, we may assume that the price recession during the Thirty Years War and progressive rise after 1656 and 1671 were different from the long-term experience of Europe and indicate that the price systems of Germany and Austria tended to detach themselves and form a particular case.

Again in the north, Holland and England, enjoying relatively stable monetary conditions in the first half of the seventeenth century, offered a longer resistance to the downward pressures on prices. The inflation in almost all sectors continued until the 1640s. Only in the final stages of the Thirty Years War did the level of prices begin to fall, following a downward trend which continued until the first quarter of the eighteenth century. The down-turn in these small progressive economies of the north in effect set the closing limit to the long inflation of silver prices in the sixteenth century, inaugurated with the crumbling of the dominant economy of Spain. Spread over almost half a century, it emphasizes the fundamental disparity of the international economy.

[1] For a more extensive demonstration of this, see *Cambridge Economic History of Europe*, Vol. IV, pp. 470–5.

The relative size and importance of this economy is certainly shown by the differences in price levels from region to region. The price range between those areas with high silver prices, such as Spain and Italy, and those with low silver prices as in Poland, had hardly advanced closer than a ratio of 1 to 6, or at most 1 to 5 in the first half of the seventeenth century. This gap was the natural mainspring of the grain trade, even when high transport costs were involved. Risks were considerable and the rates of marine insurance were high. In Amsterdam the rates during the Thirty Years War for Constantinople were as high as 18% in 1626; for Danzig 5% in 1630, although these fell to 5% and 2% respectively in November 1648 after the signing of peace. The dangers and losses of war, high freight costs and a low level of capital investment all combined to maintain considerable differentials between regional prices.

The third discrepancy which the growth of the sixteenth century had emphasized was the gap between the sectors of agriculture and industry. The long inflation, furthered by the pressure of a hungry population, culminated in the astonishing rise in the prices of farm products, particularly of grain. The agricultural sector probably enjoyed, as wheat prices show, a privileged position until the end of the Thirty Years War, attracting investment and bringing marginal lands into cultivation. This was accompanied no doubt by an increase, in the Ricardian sense, in the rents of the better lands. Hans-Helmut Wächter has shown the fall in marginal profits in the case of east Prussia after 1620 and during the Thirty Years War. There the position was reversed in favour of a general contraction of the area under cultivation (see Fig. 5). In general the downturn in the price of grain implied also a reversed relationship between very sensitive agricultural and industrial sectors.

However, the inflation of the long sixteenth century meant also relative stability and closer integration of the international economy in commercial prosperity. Economic growth naturally experienced its ups and downs but these tended to be submerged in the progressive upward movement. When this pressure began to wane, the equilibrium in the international economy was impaired. The downturns in the economy, at least as far as the available evidence from grain prices suggests, were followed by phases of violent cyclic fluctuations. In the case of Spain after 1600 H. T. Davis, using the data of Earl Hamilton, has shown that the amplitude of fluctuations tended to increase. In Udine a phase of clearly defined major cycles of greater range than before appeared after 1627 (1627-36, 1636-40, 1640-6, 1646-50, 1650-3, 1653-9); and in Beauvais in France, after 1640 (1639-45, 1645-50, 1650-7, 1657-8). The cyclic nature of price movements especially during periods of crop failures was probably a European phenomenon. In the two decades 1640-60, culminating in the crisis of subsistence in 1649-50, the chronology of price cycles was valid with slight variations in Exeter, Paris, Lyons, Beauvais,

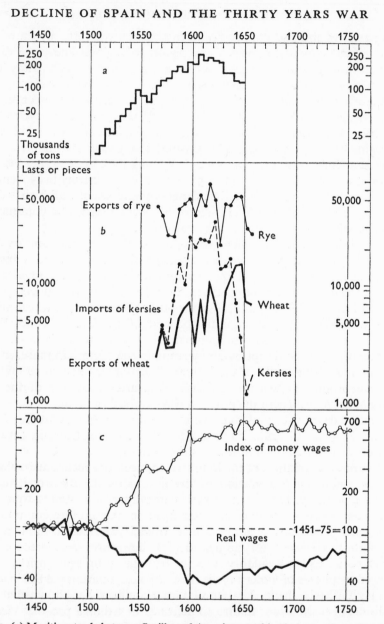

Fig. 3. (*a*) Maritime trade between Seville and America, combined tonnage inward and outward bound [reference: H. and P. Chaunu, *Séville et l'Atlantique 1504 à 1650* (8 vols. and *annexe graphique,* Paris, 1955–60)]; (*b*) Baltic trade (five-yearly averages)—wheat, rye, kersies [reference: N. Bang, *Tabeller over Skibsfart og Varetransport gennem Øresund 1497–1660* (2 parts in 3 vols. Copenhagen, 1906–22)]; (*c*) builders' wage-rates in England (five-yearly averages) [reference: S. Hopkins and E. H. Phelps Brown, 'Seven centuries of prices of consumables, compared with builders' wage-rates', *Economica* (1956)].

Udine, Siena and Lwow. The violence of these cycles was a sign of profound economic disturbances. In the space of a decade, grain prices rose as much as five times in the case of Udine and ten times in the exceptional case of the price of oats in Lwow.

A final aspect of the structure of prices: the question of wages and the price of labour. The growth of the sixteenth century, according to some economic historians, implied also a fall in the living standards of labour. The cost of living and especially of food rose and the money wages of labour tended to lag behind. Hence the real equivalents of those money wages tended to fall. This has been established in the majority of cases. In Valencia the real wages of building craftsmen fell until about 1600. The available evidence for Germany and Austria tends to confirm this conclusion, although in these cases real wages tended to rise during the Thirty Years War until 1660-70. In England real wages of building craftsmen fell throughout the sixteenth century but reached a turning point about 1610-14 (see Fig. 3). From this reversal, the rising trend implied that builders were receiving better remuneration.

Although this evidence for wage history gives little indication of the level of employment or of the labour force available, the important feature remains: wage trends changed at the beginning of the seventeenth century. For the period covered by this chapter, the international economy in general faced both the easing of price inflation and the rising levels of real wages and, by implication, rising production costs with their inevitable problems and difficulties.

III

Yet the first call on human endeavour was to produce food. Agriculture largely dominated the structures of production. The farms, harnessed to natural productive forces, were the foremost industries of Europe, and the crafts with their capital requirements and uncertain outlets were at a disadvantage against this entrenched position. Agriculture continued to thrive in the early seventeenth century. In the Netherlands, B. H. Slicher van Bath has shown that the draining of the polders progressed during the early seventeenth century, in step with the rising grain prices in the market of Amsterdam (see Fig. 4). This land reclamation increased in the years 1590-1614; further progress was made in the next quarter of a century 1615-39. Then decline set in, and the average for 1640-64 was well below that for the previous half-century. In east Prussia, as we have already mentioned, the expansion in agriculture changed fundamentally after 1620 when the war disturbances had their full effect (see Fig. 5).

The grain cargoes passing through the Sound from the Baltic confirm this impression of thriving agriculture. The tolls show that the exports of rye rose from 473,714 lasts in 1600-9 to 578,415 lasts in 1640-9; and wheat from 51,496 lasts to 160,551 lasts in the same period. Thus rye was

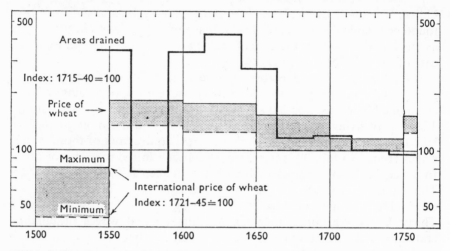

Fig. 4. Index of areas drained and wheat prices in the Netherlands (1721–45 = 100) [reference: B. H. Slicher van Bath, *De agrarische Geschiedenis van West-Europa (500–1850)* (Utrecht, 1960)].

nine times more important than wheat in the first decade, and only four and a half times in the 1640s (see Fig. 3). Yet what justification can the Sound tolls offer for such affirmations? The quantitative evidence is not to be taken at its face value and deservedly has been subjected to considerable criticism from scholars, in particular Aksel Christensen, Astrid Friis, Alfred Huhnhäuser, Pierre Jeannin and Walther Vogel. The extent of smuggling remains a large and perhaps unknown factor. This would modify the absolute totals of tonnage and merchandise reported passing in and out of the Baltic. It could also adjust the relative quantities of goods: for example, before the reform of 1618, rye carried less duty than wheat and as a result, in passing the customs, wheat was often declared as rye. Such considerations qualify the conclusions drawn from the apparently increasing shipments of wheat.

In view of this, the expansion of the grain trade is difficult to explain. Ostensibly, it revealed a growing taste for luxury, wheat being destined for white bread and the tables of the well-to-do. Could it have been merely a further sign of the increasing wealth of the economies of the north? Or was it another indication of the difficult conditions in the grainlands of the Baltic countries, obliged to export their cereals?

This grain trade in effect emphasized the outstanding real advantages maintained by the economies of northern and eastern Europe. Such a bulky trade required transport, warehouses and barges. It needed merchants prepared to carry the risks of commodity markets during good and bad years. Amsterdam was able to provide these advantages. And the producing areas of Poland, concentrated in the great estates, offered

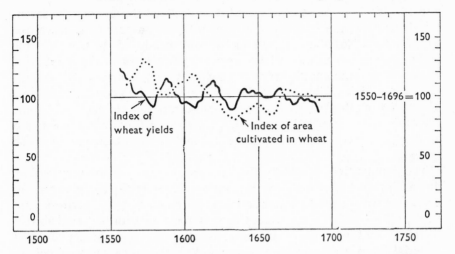

Fig. 5. Index of trends of grain production in eastern Prussia (1550–1696 = 100) [reference: H.-H. Wächter, *Ostpreussische Domänenvorwerke im 16. und 17. Jahrhundert* (Würzburg, 1958)].

natural resources of fertile lands and abundant labour, both tied and servile, symbols of her agrarian economy.

However, the grain markets did not all continue to enjoy prosperity, as can be inferred from the changing secular trends in grain prices. The 'agricultural crisis', which marked the later seventeenth century and reached a serious situation in the 1730s and 1740s, later received vociferous attention in the writings and theories of the Physiocrats. It had one notable effect in the shift away from grain to livestock raising.

Conditions were different in the manufacturing sectors of the international economy. The crafts distributed here and there in cities and in the surrounding countryside were all too often held together by the commercial capital of merchants who provided the raw materials and carried away the finished goods. As Adam Smith astutely observed, small advantages in production could create a considerable competitive position in foreign markets. The manufacturing sectors were far more fragile in the face of the market demand in Europe. The textile and metallurgical sectors in particular experienced dramatic changes in the early seventeenth century.

Textiles were especially susceptible. Some centres in the Mediterranean producing cloth for export began to lose ground from the end of the century. In Spain the prosperity of cloth workers in some areas lasted until the 1590s. In Italy, the early seventeenth century, and not least the difficulties of the 1620s and the consequences of the plague of 1630, reserved hard times for the cloth industries. In Venice, the output of the great Arte della Lana had reached peak years in 1601 and 1602 (28,601 and 28,729 pieces respectively), and then declined throughout the seventeenth century, the falling production following a parabolic curve (see Fig. 6). By 1650, about 10,000 pieces were produced. In Como in the early seventeenth century there were 60 workshops producing 8,000–10,000 pieces annually; by 1650 there were 4 manufactories with an output of 400 pieces. Florence in the 1590s produced 13,000–14,000 pieces of woollen cloth a year, but by the mid-century it claimed only some 5,000 pieces. Italian cloth production fell away before declining demand and aggressive competition in the Levant mainly from Dutch and English traders.

The competition offered by England did not conceal the very serious difficulties she herself suffered. Her export economy depended largely on wool and wool products, amounting to as much as 75%, perhaps even 90% of the total value exported. Changes in markets for her cloth abroad therefore had profound repercussions on the economic activity and material life of the country as a whole. A further potential weakness in England's position was the imbalance in the destination of the exports; at the beginning of the seventeenth century about three-quarters of the cloth export went to Germany and the United Provinces, less than one-eighth to the Baltic, almost one-sixteenth to each of France and the Levant, and the rest to Italy, Barbary and Russia. And a third weakness: England did not control the complete processing of her cloth. The greater part exported was undressed—for example, 72% from London in 1606—for finishing abroad in the more advanced cloth centres, mainly in the Netherlands for the markets in eastern and central Europe, but also in Paris and Venice, where the cloths were dyed and given the 'Italian' finish appreciated in the Levant. The combination of these potential weaknesses covered in prosperous years was particularly susceptible to shocks. In 1614, a good year, 127,215 shortcloths were exported; but the position of the industry worsened at the end of the second decade of the seventeenth century.

At this point Alderman Cockayne proposed to set up a consortium—the famous *Project*—for finishing the cloth in England, with the monopoly of the export trade thus taken out of the hands of the Merchant Adventurers. By October 1617 this scheme had clearly failed and the former conditions were re-established. This restoration was the prelude to a depression beginning with the commercial slump of 1619–20, which coincided with the difficult years at the outbreak of the Thirty Years War, the monetary debasements in Germany and Austria, and the devaluations in Poland of 1619–23—all important markets for English cloth. Exports dropped. Shortcloths fell from 102,332 pieces in 1618 to 75,631 pieces in 1622. This crisis eventually marked a distinct break in the position of the older English draperies, henceforth to decline. The industries sought newer lines and the production improved in the lighter cloths—bays,

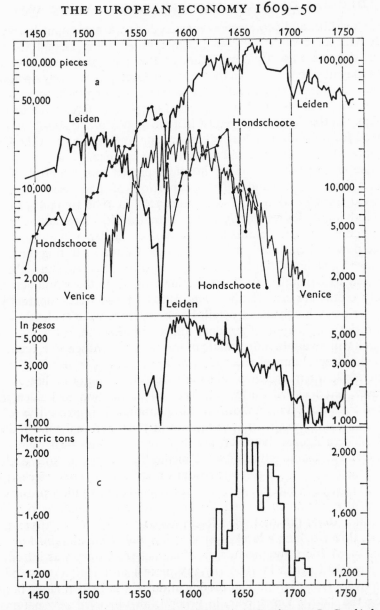

Fig. 6. (a) The production of cloth in Leiden [reference: N. Posthumus, *De Geschiedenis van de Leidsche Lakenindustrie* (3 vols. The Hague, 1908–39)], Hondschoote [reference: E. Coornaert, *La draperie-sayetterie d'Hondschoote* (*XIVe–XVIIe siècles*) (Paris, 1930)], and Venice [reference: D. Sella, 'Les mouvements longs de l'industrie lainière', *Annales; Economies, Sociétés, Civilisations* (1957)]; (b) of silver in Potosi, Peru [reference: M. Moreyra y Paz-Soldán, *En torno a dos valiosos documentos sobre Potosí*]; and (c) of copper in Sweden (five-yearly average) [reference: F. R. Tegengren, *Sveriges ädlare malmer och bergwerk* (Stockholm, 1924)].

Spanish cloths, and *perpetuanos*—destined for warmer countries. English cloth had some outlets in the Levant: in 1634 the Levant Company exported some 17,000 pieces, although the average for the 1620s and 1630s may have been more in the region of 6,000 pieces yearly, in addition to the quantities sent indirectly, for example, via Leghorn. In 1628 3,346 'Spanish' cloths were sent to northern Europe; this figure rose to 13,517 in 1640. On the other hand, whilst in 1606 75·9% of the shortcloths were shipped from London by English merchants to Germany and the United Provinces, this percentage had fallen to 51·9 by 1640.

These crisis years of 1620–3 in effect passed more control of cloth exports in English hands. The proportion of undressed shortcloths exported from London fell from about 72% in 1606 to 34·8% in 1640. The cloth industries were obliged to reform, the older lines falling away to make room for lighter cloths and alternative outlets.

The powerful cloth industries of the Low Countries during these years also faced a series of difficulties and transformations. At first sight these appeared to be similar to those in England, since the manufactures of quality cloths for export and long-distance trade were apparently the most seriously involved. In detail, however, there were evidently important variations in type of product and of markets served which future research will no doubt differentiate more clearly. Hondschoote, recovering from the deep slump of the 1580s, enjoyed increasing production until about 1638, when 27,466 pieces were exported. Many of her weavers, however, left to swell the population and production of Leiden in the United Provinces. There, cloth working continued to grow. The total of cloth of all sorts reached 144,723 pieces in 1664, before a general decline set in. These figures, however, conceal a radical transformation of the industry. The manufacture of some of the older types of cloth declined: says after 1617 (53,568 pieces); fustians after 1624 (33,986 pieces); bays after 1633 (23,785 pieces); velvets after 1637–8 (13,454 pieces). But other lines prospered: *lakens* forged ahead, enjoying a spectacular rise in the 1630s and 1640s (1630: 1,780 pieces; 1640: 10,805 pieces; 1651: 22,069 pieces), thus reaching a level of production which it maintained until the 1720s. In addition, the production of camlets and warp was introduced, which reached peaks in 1669 (67,335 pieces) and 1664 (19,350 pieces) respectively (see Fig. 6). The modification of the Leiden cloth industry during the Thirty Years War, in general, also evolved new patterns of supplying long-distance markets.

The mining and metallurgical sectors also prospered during the Thirty Years War. This was the great opportunity for Sweden with her rich mines of iron and copper under close royal patronage and control. The famous copper company—the Kopparkompaniet founded in 1619—benefited at first from the demand for copper money in Spain. The stop on this, in 1626, pushed Gustavus Adolphus to find other outlets, partly in copper coinage for Sweden. The production of copper, however, doubled during the war, reaching a peak in 1650 with 2,941 metric tons (see Fig. 6). This was the highest point in the seventeenth century; peace meant recession. At the beginning of the eighteenth century, however, her copper surpassed that of central Europe, and in spite of the Dutch promotion of production in Japan for use in the Far East, held a foremost place in world markets.

Iron was another contribution from Sweden. During the sixteenth century its production had grown under direct crown encouragement especially from Gustavus I (1523–60), who brought in German technicians. Malleable bar iron became increasingly important from 1540, and after 1600, although twice as expensive, exceeded the older osmund iron in export value. This trend became typical of the seventeenth century: between 1600 and 1720 Swedish iron production increased five times. The exports rose during the Thirty Years War, and most spectacularly after 1627. The average annual exports of bar iron from the Baltic, if we turn once more to the uncertain evidence of the Sound tolls, increased seven-fold in a quarter-century:

TABLE 12

Period	Average annual exports from the Baltic in metric tons
1620–4	1,179
1645–9	7,747
1650–4	5,362

Estimates from other sources propose the following annual figures for exports from Sweden:

TABLE 13

Year	Estimated annual exports from Sweden in metric tons
c. 1620	6,650 (bar iron and osmund)
c. 1640	10,600 (bar iron)
c. 1650	17,300 (bar iron)

The conclusion of the peace faced Sweden with recession but by then her position in the metal markets had been firmly established. Eli Heckscher estimated that Sweden supplied about a third of the requirements of Europe in 1720. England was an important customer, and on the eve of the Civil War her forges worked between 14,000 and 32,000 metric tons of iron bar. About 1720, some 40% of her requirements of iron probably came from Sweden.

Finally, another growth sector: the coal industry of England. Between the 1550s and the 1680s, according to John U. Nef, the production of

coal increased 14 times, a relative development far greater than in the
following centuries:

TABLE 14

Period	Total coal produced in metric tons
1551–60	206,681
1681–90	2,934,874
1781–90	10,132,302

The shipments of coal from Newcastle, in consequence, followed this
trend, particularly noticeable in the first half of the seventeenth century:

TABLE 15

Year	Quantity of coal shipped in metric tons
Michaelmas 1591–Michaelmas 1592	110,356
Michaelmas 1608–Michaelmas 1609	235,490
Christmas 1633–Christmas 1634	445,472
June 1658–June 1659	520,671

And the consumption increased in London. There the imports passed
from 34,208 in 1591–2 to 260,037 metric tons in 1667–8. Thus by the
middle of the seventeenth century one of the pillars of England's future
economy was firmly established.

IV

How then to conclude a résumé all too brief for the problems involved?
The central feature has been the pause in the long economic development
of Europe. Although it is probable that over large areas of the continent
per capita incomes could change only within relatively confined limits, it
may be assumed that there was a check and even reduction in particular
aggregate national incomes during this period. The economic crisis was
noticeable above all in the growth of the commercial system which had
sustained Europe, and indeed the world, during the sixteenth century.

Spain held a central and dominant position in that commercial prosperity, and the turn of the sixteenth century was indeed her crisis. The
defeat of the Invincible Armada, the declining cargoes of bullion from
America after 1600, the long recession in the transatlantic trade of Seville
after the peak years of 1607–9 (see Fig. 3), the royal bankruptcies of 1596,
1607, 1627 and 1645—all these foreshadowed her experience of growing
debility and frustration in the seventeenth century. The financial tensions
of the far-stretched politics of Spain, reprieved with the Truce of 1609,
mounted again with the renewal of the war against the Dutch in 1621 (see
Map 2). The royal bankruptcy of 1627 dragged down above all the

Genoese merchants and financiers, who had long been her persistent though not disinterested supporters. Their discomfiture proved the moment for the Portuguese, profiting by their difficulties and forecasting the revolt of 1640, in their case successful, leading to independence, but for the rebel Catalans to defeat and repression. Later the bankruptcy of 1647 finally published the incapacity of Spain, and prepared the way for the peace settlements of Westphalia in the following year, and eventually of the Pyrenees (1659).

Yet the long and progressive abdication of Spain was reprieved during the Twelve Years Truce, when the international economy gained a brief respite. Then, in 1618, the outbreak of war in Germany and the great commercial crisis of 1619–20, which although neither the deciding moments for Europe, nor the sole turning points to end the sixteenth century, were nevertheless huge catastrophes. This moment of truth unmasked the unsubstantiated bravado of Spain, and inevitably also the confusion and weakness of the trading communities of southern Europe, already in difficulties.

The failure of Spain to dominate in the struggle against Holland, renewed with the end of the Truce in 1621, resolved itself into a general European conflict. This confirmed the ascendancy of the thriving economies of the north, above all of the Netherlands. In the seventeenth century the Dutch achieved their 'golden age', almost against the prevailing trends in the international economy. This in itself was a considerable achievement.

Yet fortune smiled on the Dutch traders and investors, and with good reason. In an age of difficult transport Holland was naturally endowed with a commanding geographical position, with thrifty merchants recruited from the four corners of Europe, with an integrated transport system of canals and waterways, of warehouses, barges and a mercantile marine equipped with the successful and economical 'fluit', manned by a dozen hands, the cargo ship *par excellence*. Towards the end of the century, the yearly trading fleets were astonishingly large: 800 fluits to the Baltic and 400 to St Ubes in Portugal for salt; 200 to 250 whalers, 300 to 350 herring boats . . . Little wonder that Holland was able to expand and capture the profits which went with scale of enterprise.

The great trading companies outlined this range of commerce: the Russia Grain Company (1608); the Northern Company (1614) for whaling and based on Spitzbergen; the New Netherlands Company (1614) for North America between the 40th and 45th parallels; and the West India Company (1621). By the Treaty of The Hague of 1669, the Dutch controlled the timber trade of Norway. And not least there was the trade to the East Indies. Almost symbolically, Cornelius Houtman, a Dutch merchant resident in Lisbon, sailed in 1595 with a fleet for the Indies and returned in 1597 richly furnished. The United East India Company (1602) in league with the sultan of Bantam, found footing from 1619 in Batavia in Java. From this vantage point, with factories along the coast from Persia and India to China and Japan, established in the key port of Malacca captured from the Portuguese in 1641, they scooped up profits to raise the concentration of capital in Holland. By 1650, the governor general in Batavia reported that the cumulative profits to date exceeded 75,000,000 florins with a capital of more than 12,500,000 resting in the Indies. It had been accomplished in half a century.

The Dutch, however, did not have an open field. The competition was severe from the Portuguese (from whom they seized Elmina in 1637), and not least from England. The conflict was joined in all fields of lucrative profit. Their Northern Company of 1614 had the aim of rebutting English attacks. In the Far East, the aggressive situation was such that a treaty of partnership was made in 1619 between the English and Dutch Companies. This *entente* ended in the massacre of Amboyna (1623), when the Dutch violently asserted their ascendancy, beheaded the small colony, and effectively cleared out the competition of their English rivals. Their predominancy on the seven seas found a block in the English Navigation Act (1651), and finally in war, the Anglo-Dutch War of 1652-3, first of these open hostilities to mark the seventeenth century.

Although the economic development of Europe apparently underwent a sharp relapse in commercial prosperity, there were compensations. The initiative in the north of Europe showed that fundamentally the international economy was endowed with strength and continuity. The transformations, which were evident in the case of the textile industries, were symptoms of the versatility of a mercantile system responsive to new conditions. This element of continuity was most apparent in the character and direction of capital investment.

In the face of difficult times ahead, the commercial fortunes sought alternative outlets and sources of profit. De la Vega in his *Confusion de Confusiones* (1688) acutely describes the speculation among the merchants of Amsterdam. Although in February 1610 the Estates had forbidden the selling of shares *in blanco*, the proclivity to speculate was amply testified in the boom and crash of the Tulip Mania in 1636-7. Indeed, the diversion of funds into other fields prolonged and consolidated the capital gains established in the commercial prosperity of the sixteenth century.

These funds no doubt turned more substantially to land and real estate. This was traditionally common to the commercial centres of Europe: merchants were accustomed to lay out wealth in land. But after the commercial difficulties of the 1620s it probably became more important. Aldo de Maddalena in the case of Lombardy has shown the growing investment in land from the 1620s. In Lyons, it is not surprising to find a young notary such as Le Grangier in the early 1620s leaving aside his father's business in the fairs to deal extensively in property and marriage contracts. According to W. Hoskins, the surge in rebuilding rural England was at its height in the years 1590 to 1640. But these agrarian and land problems are complex and scholars have not yet agreed on the explanations to offer. Certainly they were set in sharp relief in the mid-seventeenth century.

The outbreak and spread of the war in Germany after 1618 offered a second reprieve from economic stagnation. The Thirty Years War grew more serious with the deepening animosity between Spain and France, in open conflict after 1635. The building and commissioning of fleets, the manufacture of arms and munitions, the fortifications, the raising of armies, were all fresh opportunities. The Dutch financiers, notably from Amsterdam, were not slow to respond. A company of Amsterdam merchants in 1619 financed a gun foundry in Thuringia. Louis de Geer (1587–1652) invested heavily in the mines and production of Sweden. In 1627 the Swedish crown granted him the monopoly of founding iron canon, which he held until 1648. These Swedish iron cannon led the market, being preferred to those offered from England at the same price. Elias Trip, his partner, also deeply involved in the metal trade, had cannon foundries, gun shops and powder factories in Amsterdam, supplying armies and attracting buyers from all over Europe, among them the French agents of Richelieu. The boom in Swedish iron and copper helped to prolong the prosperity of the sixteenth century, but these easy market conditions did not survive the peace.

Thirdly, a major outlet for investment in the seventeenth century was found in the state. As the opportunities for trading in the private sector grew more intractable, merchants became more willing to take up government loans which offered hopes of monopolies and protection. Alvaro Castillo has shown how the *asientos* (or loans to the Spanish monarchy) increased after 1610, as the trans-Atlantic trade of Seville declined. Yet, this sector apparently did not survive after 1640–2, and collapsed in the final exhaustion of Spain (see Map 2). The syndicates for raising royal revenues in England, and the tax-farmers in France were further signs of investment in the state, hungry for funds and ready to grant privileges in return for the means to buttress power or sustain grandiose policies.

The capital assets threatened by difficult conditions again found relief in the great companies, armed to seize the initiative and win outstanding profits. The English East India Company in the first half-century offered, for example, an average return on capital of 82%. Indeed the great companies, such as in England and Holland, became so large that in time their interests combined with those of government. The Dutch West India Company (1621) was a direct instrument of war, plundering the trade routes to bring a stream of Spanish and Portuguese prize cargoes to Holland, making landings and annexing territories in the West Indies and in Brazil. In Holland itself, the Thirty Years War was a saga of intrigue

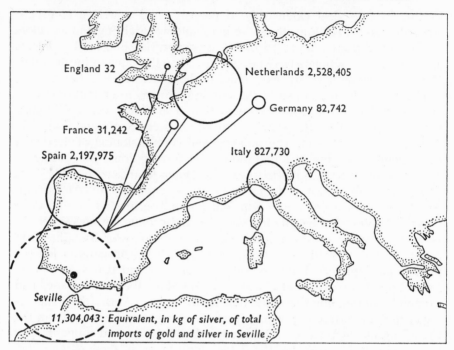

Map 2. Payments of Spanish *asientos*, 1580–1626 (converted into
kilograms of silver) [reference: A. Castillo].

between on the one hand the war party buttressed by the great companies,
on occasion bribed by France, and on the other hand the peace party aiming
for truce with Spain. Inevitably, in such an uneasy alliance with mercantile
interests, the state, ready with monopolies for trade and manufactures, was
obliged to enter more deeply into economic affairs. The policies of the great
statesmen—Richelieu in France, Olivares in Spain, Oxenstierna in Sweden,
Strafford and Cromwell in England—all bore witness to the way in which
economic difficulties flowed to swell the power of state. This is perhaps the
most eloquent lesson of the early seventeenth century, unnerved before an
unpromising future, but at the same time gifted with a propensity to
create or rather to consolidate the gains achieved.

Lastly, in a much larger context, capital flows faced new technological
horizons through changes in the level of knowledge. Between Galileo
Galilei (1564–1642) and Sir Isaac Newton (1642–1727) complex advances
in the understanding of the natural world brought wider perspectives,
although clearly these transformations—the *scientific revolution*—pass the
period of this chapter. In the field of mathematics and engineering, for
example, considerable contributions were made in the second quarter of
the seventeenth century by Galileo, Torricelli, Pascal and Descartes.

Among the later mercantilists, Sir William Petty set out with computations and *Political Arithmetic* to measure the scale of aggregate economic activity. Nor did concepts suggesting a closed society pass unchallenged, as the debate in France in the 1680s of the Ancients against the Moderns revealed. These are only brief references to a prodigious movement but it is evident that over a wide range of techniques and knowledge the seventeenth century did not constitute a retrograde movement.

Yet all this looked to the future. At the time, there seemed to be little more than a repetition of difficulties and a deepening of human misery, accompanied relentlessly by the increasing power of governments and behind them of aristocracies and ruling minorities. The state swallowed up loyalties and obligations, organized conflicts, and became the funnel for expenditures. In the outward manoeuvres and realities of war it set the targets, its own targets, refusing to allow commercial and industrial financiers to press ahead unhampered by national restrictions. It submitted *entrepreneurs* to its own wilful behests and almost at once left them stranded. In the final analysis this aspect of the destiny of Europe is inseparable from the movement of the international economy which this chapter has all too briefly outlined.

CHAPTER III

THE EXPONENTS AND CRITICS OF ABSOLUTISM

ETWEEN 1610 and 1659 absolutism triumphed almost everywhere in Europe. Although in England monarchical absolutism failed, parliamentary absolutism was victorious. States were threatened by great wars and by the disruptions of wars of religion. Men's minds were challenged by theories of popular sovereignty, of contract and tyrannicide, and by new mechanistic views of the universe. There were economic crises, some caused by the falling volume of silver arriving from America, others by bad harvests, famines and epidemics, which were perhaps more frequent than in the sixteenth century. The remedy for these troubles seemed to be a political power less shackled by laws, customs and privileges, and better able to impose a common purpose upon the members of the body politic. At the centre of all the theoretical conflicts were the two principles of sovereignty and of *raison d'état*, developed by Jean Bodin and Machiavelli respectively. Sovereignty was defined by Bodin as 'the supreme power in the State not bound by the laws . . . not recognising any superior'; its attributes are to legislate, to raise armies, make war and peace, pass final judgements on cases, raise taxes, coin money, etc. *Raison d'état* covered whatever actions the prince might have to take in order to secure the safety and growth of the state. Bodin and Machiavelli were criticized, but almost all their critics borrowed their fundamental ideas while attempting to Christianize or adapt them. Our study of political concepts cannot be restricted to the ideas of theorists. We must try to consider what statesmen, administrators and members of different social groups thought of absolutism, what ideas and slogans moved men to act—and their relationship to their whole environment. Such a history of political ideas has scarcely begun to be attempted.

The conflict of political ideas in Europe did not contradict the unity of European civilization. Europe began as Christendom and it was from Christianity that all the theoreticians began. A small number of essential ideas circulated, originating from two principal centres, Spain and the Netherlands. For the Catholics these centres were the universities of Salamanca and Louvain and for the Protestants those of the United Provinces, especially Leiden. The political teaching of Justus Lipsius, professor at the University of Leiden until 1592, then, after his conversion, at Louvain, was spread by Bernegger. He was professor of history and political science at the University of Strasbourg from 1613 to 1640 and attracted students from Germany, Hungary, Denmark and Switzerland.

Buckler continued the work of Bernegger at Strasbourg and a pupil of Buckler, Bosius, taught the doctrines of Lipsius at Jena from 1656 to 1676. Bernegger's son-in-law, Heim Freins, became chancellor of the University of Uppsala in 1642 and spread the theories of Lipsius in Sweden. Gustavus Adolphus learnt them from another pupil of Bernegger, Skytte, his historiographer. There were many French students at the University of Leiden; Guez de Balzac studied there in 1615, writing a *Discours Politique* against absolutism, though in 1631 he became a defender of absolute monarchy. The University of Salamanca, where the disciples of Vittoria had revived the teaching of Thomism, trained the great Spanish Jesuit Suarez and many others, who went to the Roman colleges, to the universities of Louvain, Alcala, and Coimbra, spreading the political teachings of neo-Thomism among Jesuits and other ecclesiastics and thence to lay circles.

Books were important in spreading political ideas. The multiplication of editions and translations of political works testified to the profound interest in them. Bodin's *Republique* appeared in 1576 and had nine Latin editions between 1586 and 1650, seventeen French editions between 1576 and 1753, while there were Italian, English and German translations. The *Politica* of Althusius had eight editions between 1603 and 1654. Justus Lipsius' *Politica* had an edition a year until 1618, thirty-one Latin editions in the seventeenth century, besides Dutch, French, English, German and Polish translations. Even lesser works had success: Balzac's *Prince* had four editions between 1631 and 1662, Philippe de Bethune's *Conseiller d'état* had five between 1632 and 1665. Battles of the books aroused public attention; such as those of James I with Cardinal Bellarmine and Cardinal du Perron. James sent his apologia against Bellarmine to all the princes, who received it coolly. However, James was much read by Italian jurists, who considered him the ideal prince. Bellarmine in 1619 dedicated his *De Officio Principis* to Ladislas, son of Sigismund III of Poland. The monk Paolo Sarpi fought from 1605 to 1607 on behalf of the Republic of Venice against the Roman Curia and against Bellarmine; their polemics found echoes in many pulpits.

Theorists and polemicists corresponded with each other and with princes. Paolo Sarpi corresponded with the French jurists Jacques Leschassier, with Jacques Gillot and with de L'Isle-Groslot, and obtained a profound knowledge of Gallican doctrines for his struggle against the pope. Campanella corresponded with Père Joseph after 1628 and advised Richelieu upon Italian affairs in order to further his plans for national independence, a prerequisite for absolutism. Political refugees were important. Grotius, exiled from Holland, wrote the *De Jure Belli Ac Pacis*, in France in 1623 and 1624, before publishing it at Frankfurt in 1625 and becoming Swedish ambassador in France from 1635 to 1645. Hobbes published the *De Cive* in Paris in 1642 and wrote the *Leviathan* there.

The essential condition of absolutism was sovereignty which recognized no superior. But the European sovereigns, whether kings or republics, had to face the pretensions of the pope. On several occasions there were controversies which grouped together English, French, and Italian theorists against the pope and led to attempts at union between them and the German Protestants. From 1605 to 1607 there was the papal interdict against Venice whose legislation had limited the acquisition of real property by the church. In 1606 the pope forbade English Catholics to take the oath demanded by James I after the Gunpowder Plot. Under Henri IV the Parlement of Paris refused to accept the decrees of the Council of Trent which had confirmed the church's rights to fiscal immunity and to jurisdiction over the laity in marriages, wills, contracts and offences concerning the faith. Finally there was the murder of Henri IV (1610) by a maniac, inspired by the doctrines of the Monarchomachs and by the Jesuit Mariana's views on tyrannicide. These conflicts produced an important European literature. The Spanish Jesuits supported papal claims. Mariana's *De Rege et Regis Institutione*, which first appeared in 1598 was reprinted in 1610 on this occasion. It revived the old theory expressed by Boniface VII in the Bull *Unam Sanctam*. By divine right the pope has two swords, the temporal and the spiritual; he entrusts the temporal to the princes, but they remain responsible to him for its use and are his vicars. The pope institutes them, supervises them and, if necessary, judges and deposes them. When he releases subjects from their oath of allegiance, it becomes lawful for anyone to kill the tyrant. Except for the defence of tyrannicide, this was the favorite theory of the Roman Curia. More important was the work of the theologian Suarez who dominated Catholic thought in the seventeenth century. His *De Legibus* (1612) and his *Defensio Fidei* (1613), directed against the apology of James I, were approved by the pope and by Philip III of Spain. For Suarez, church and state were two societies, each natural and perfect in its own fashion, but differing in their origin and structure. All things spiritual and their jurisdiction belonged to the church, while all temporal matters belonged to the state. It was inconceivable that one head, the king, should control both spiritual and temporal jurisdictions, as James I claimed. The king ought not to usurp the functions of the church, while the pope had no direct authority over states, though he had an indirect power. The spiritual was superior to the temporal because it had God for its end and the pope's authority came directly from God, while that of the princes came indirectly through the people. The pope was spiritually superior to temporal princes; he had the right and duty to advise princes for the spiritual advantage to the church. He could constrain them by ecclesiastical censures, in cases of immorality, of flagrant tyranny, or of scandals to the faith. If a prince became a heretic he could be deposed and his subjects released from their allegiance. Thus the pope could legitimately forbid Catholics to take the oath demanded by James I. This theory of *potestas indirecta* was, apart from some nuances, held by Cardinal Bellarmine in *De Potestate Summi Pontificis* (1610); *De Officio Principis Christiani* (1619), and expounded by Cardinal du Perron to the French Estates General (1615).

These theories were opposed by James I, who summarized part of the Protestant political tradition. For Luther, the authority of the state, like all authority, came from God and the people ought to submit to it, even if it were tyrannical, though the prince ought to respect the two tables of the law. Calvin held that magistrates were the vicars of God and were owed absolute obedience by the people even in cases of tyranny. James I's principal works were *The Trew Law of Free Monarchies* (1598), the *Basilikon Doron* (1599), *An Apologie for the Oath of Allegience* (1607) and *A Defence of the Right of Kings against Cardinal Perron* (1615). James claimed that he was personally chosen by God to govern his people, was invested directly by God with his sovereignty and was accountable to God alone. The pope had no concern in this and this was why James demanded from his Catholic subjects an oath that the pope had no right to depose the king, nor to dispose of his dominions, nor to authorize any foreign prince to invade them, nor to discharge any of his subjects from their allegiance, nor to authorize anyone to bear arms against the king, or threaten his person and that they would defend the king and his heirs if the pope excommunicated them. Paul V forbade the taking of this oath because it wounded the Catholic faith and jeopardized the safety and salvation of souls. Bellarmine declared that it denied the primacy of the Apostolic See and transferred authority over the English church from the successor of St Peter to the successor of Henry VIII.

But the opinions of the Curia, of Suarez and of Bellarmine were only theologically probable. A Catholic who did not profess them did not cease to be a Catholic, as the affair of the Interdict against Venice showed. The Venetians considered that their laws were of long standing and similar to those of other states, while the pope was only seeking a pretext to extend his jurisdiction and to attack in Venice the right of all princes. Venice declared herself resolved to continue Catholic, while defending herself. The magistrates ensured that the churches remained open, despite the interdict, and were supported by the great majority. The republic consulted jurists in Padua, Milan, France, and Spain, and took the monk Paolo Sarpi as their adviser. He, together with several theologians, published the *Trattato dell'Interdetto*. God had ordained two forms of government, one spiritual, the other temporal. Each of these is supreme in its own sphere and independent of the other, having no right to interfere with the other. Thus the pope has no power to annul the laws of princes on temporal matters, or to dethrone them, or to release their subjects from allegiance. Ecclesiastics have no sanction by divine law to be exempt from secular authority. If the prince has conceded any exemption, he still has full power over their persons and goods in case of public necessity. The pope is only infallible in things necessary for the faith, his censures against princes ought to be examined by theologians. If they certify that the censures are invalid, the prince can forbid their execution. The pope's pretensions extended beyond primacy towards a totalitarian power, while the Jesuits made it a *supra divinitas*. The Venetian theologians were strongly influenced by James I, whom Paolo Sarpi described as 'a most wise king', but they perhaps owed even more to the French Gallicans. Sarpi admired the Gallicans as defenders of the universal church who, in fighting for princely power, fought also for the glory of Christ and the liberty of Italy.

Gallicanism was more vigorous than ever thanks to the opposition of the Parlement of Paris to the reception of the decrees of the Council of Trent and to horror at doctrines of tyrannicide. According to the Gallicans, Christ had distinguished between what was God's and what was Caesar's. The temporal power which belonged to Caesar was as divine as the spiritual power. Like the spiritual power, it came immediately from God and was of equal authority within its independent sphere. The pope's power was purely spiritual; he might excommunicate and lay interdicts, but he could not depose princes nor release their subjects from their allegiance. The king of France was not subordinate to the pope in temporal matters because of his spiritual primacy. Nor was he the vassal of the pope in virtue of the donation of Constantine to which the French people had never consented. After the assassination of Henri IV the Parlement of Paris condemned Mariana's and suppressed Bellarmine's books on papal power, they asked Richer, syndic of the faculty of theology of Paris (the Sorbonne), to provide a statement of Gallican views. In December 1611 they required Jesuits resident in France to subscribe to four principal doctrines from the faculty: the superiority of councils over the pope, the absolute independence of temporal power belonging to sovereign princes by immediate divine right, the confessor's obligation to reveal to the magistrates plots against the sovereign, the submission of ecclesiastics to secular power. In 1614 the *Defensio Fidei* of Suarez was condemned to be burnt by the hangman, but the king's council suspended the execution of the decree. In the Estates General of 1614 the third Estate asked the king to make Gallican doctrine on the power of kings a fundamental law of the kingdom. As Du Perron had shown that these doctrines were only theologically probable, the king's council was unwilling to make them an article of faith and so cause a schism. It forbade further discussion of them, while affirming that they were the views of the kingdom. In 1626 the Parlement and the Sorbonne condemned the Jesuit Santarelli's book (1624) on the pope's absolute power to depose kings. Richelieu ordered the publication of a treatise on the liberties of the Gallican church by Pierre and Jacques Dupuy in 1638, and in 1641 the *De Concordia Sacerdotii et Imperii* by the *conseiller d'état* Pierre de Marca, which was condemned and placed on the Index in 1642.

Thus the Curia and its theoreticians did not abate their claims. However the kings found good arguments for rejecting the pope's supremacy in temporal affairs and often in spiritual affairs in varying degrees. There were no effective obstacles to absolutist doctrines here.

The authority of the emperor might have provided another limitation on princely sovereignty, but only in the German part of the empire was this still a practical problem. The Italian states and princes, although they were nominally within the empire, claimed to be and effectively were sovereign states. But the emperor did not renounce any of his claims. They were defended by Reinking, a professor at the Lutheran University of Giessen, in the *Tractatus de Regimine Saeculari et Ecclesiastico* (1619). This insisted upon the continuity of the Roman and the Holy Roman Empires. The *Lex Regia*, restated in the *Institutes of Justinian* and remaining the law of the Holy Roman Empire, stated *quod principi placuit legis habet vigorem*, since the people had transferred to the prince its *imperium* and *potestas*. Thus the emperor was the *summus magistratus christiani orbis* and a truly absolute monarch. As a disciple of Bodin, Reinking declared the emperor was *legibus solutus*, but bound to respect the commandments of God, natural law and the laws which he had sworn to observe. The emperor ought to have an unlimited supremacy and be able to abrogate or modify laws decreed by other princes. The book became the bible of the imperialists and Ferdinand II in 1630 said that he completely accepted it. The theologian Witzendorff restated its conclusions in his *Discursus de Status et Administrationis Imperii Romanii* in 1641.

But most people denied imperial absolutism, while the princes claimed to be absolute in their own estates. Jurists and politicians invoked the fundamental laws of the empire, the Golden Bull of 1356, the ordinances of the Diets, imperial capitulations, which were supposed to assure to each prince *Landeshoheit*, territorial superiority, equivalent to sovereignty. Bodin has already *Republique*, II, VI, described it as 'an aristocratic state where sovereignty resides in the seven electors and some three hundred princes'. Althusius elaborated a theory based upon an idealization of the political realities of the empire in his *Politica*, first published in 1603, greatly enlarged in 1610, and frequently reprinted until 1654. According to him the empire was a true state, formed by the drawing together of provinces. It was an organic union for the spiritual and bodily health of its members. Only this state could fulfil the vital needs of its citizens and so its sovereign magistrate, the emperor, had to have supreme spiritual and temporal powers. But he was only the steward of this supreme power which belonged to the community. He was elected in the name of the community by the College of Electors who 'represented absolutely' the will of the empire. He subscribed to the fundamental laws of the community and to any explanations added by the electors; he pledged himself to administer the state according to the laws prescribed by God which were the laws of reason and the state itself. Purely an executive agent, he was watched over by the Electoral College who kept him within the proper bounds and could resist him if he became a tyrant. The confederated provinces retained their autonomy.

Protestantism inspired many to go further. Theologians following Calvin, and still more Beza, had declared resistance to the emperor in the defence of religion lawful and thus denied the Roman Catholic affiliation of the Holy Roman Empire. In 1609 the Protestant princes told Rudolf II 'his majesty well knows that a great difference exists and ought to exist between the German Empire, its state, members and subjects and the former Roman Empire'. The *Lex Regia* did not apply to the empire, as the jurist Conring undertook to show. The law of Lothar was a fable, for Roman law had only been introduced into Germany in the thirteenth century. German law was customary law and the true *Lex Regia* was the emperor's capitulation at his election, while his coronation oath was an oath of allegiance to the empire. Thus the empire was above the emperor and if he broke his oath the state ought to protect the empire if necessary by force. This was the view of the rector of the University of Jena, Hortleder, in 1608 and he imparted it to his pupil, Duke John Ernest of Saxe-Weimar and to his brother and successor, William, who both fought against the emperor.

Moreover, the court of Saxe-Weimar also encouraged at the University of Jena, the school of Arumæus, the great adversary of Reinking, a Calvinist and professor at Jena from 1602 to 1637. In his *Discursus Academici ad Auream Bullam* (1617) and in his *Commentarius de Comitiis Romano-Germanici imperii* (1630), Arumæus distinguished within the Empire a double sovereignty (*majestas*), the *majestas realis*, which was the highest and belonged to the *stände* and the *majestas personalis*, which belonged to the emperor and was subordinate to the *majestas realis*. The empire was a limited monarchy with aristocratic government. Limnæus belonged to the school of Arumæus and in *Juris Publici Imperii Romano-germanici Libri IX* (1629–32), maintained that the electoral capitulation was the juridical basis of imperial power, that the laws of the empire were not the work of the emperor alone, but of all the states of the empire, while the emperor was the steward of the empire which was an aristocracy. Limnaus was a counsellor of William, Duke of Saxe-Weimar, and in 1631 became a counsellor of the margrave of Ansbach and tutor to his son.

But even more influential was the *Dissertatio de Ratione Status in Imperio Romano Germanico* (1640), written by the Swedish German

P. Chemnitz under the pseudonym of Hippolitus a Lapide. It showed that in the empire it was no longer a question *de religione* but *de regione* and called upon the states to fight for their liberties against the power of Austria. Sovereignty belonged to the empire and the estates grouped in the Diet, not to the emperor. The Diet had the *summa et absoluta seu legibus soluta potestas*, not the emperor. The empire was above the laws and the emperor and could modify the fundamental laws, change the emperor. If the emperor threatened sovereignty and liberty of the empire, it was a duty to fight the emperor as an enemy of the empire. The emperor had no right to make war or peace, to raise taxes or troops, without the consent of the electors. He did not possess supreme jurisdiction and was only the agent and executant to the empire's decisions. Each member of the empire had the right to raise troops and make alliances, even with foreigners, without the emperor's consent. The emperor's power ought to be no greater than that of a doge of Venice, while the House of Austria ought to be completely removed from the empire. Although the emperor had the book burnt its main points were incorporated, thanks to France, in the Treaties of Westphalia.

The French insisted that the Diet should take part in the negotiations and its sovereignty was guaranteed in those treaties. Article eight of the Treaty of Osnabruck confirmed the electors, princes and states of the empire in their ancient rights, privileges and liberties, both in temporal and spiritual matters, including the right to make alliances among themselves and with foreign powers. It thus recognized the sovereignty of the members of the empire and provided for their free assembly to conduct all imperial affairs, to make laws, to make war or peace or alliances and to raise taxes and soldiers. The Treaty of Münster contained the same provisions and the Diet which met for the execution of these treaties became permanent, presiding over the division of the empire into a multitude of petty sovereign states. The emperor's pretensions to absolutism had been finally defeated.

The existence of an international community of states which observed certain rules in their relationships might imply some limitation upon the absolute prince's sovereign power. Suarez maintained that mankind was everywhere bound together by the natural precepts of love and mutual pity. It consisted of an association of states bound together by the need which they had for each other. Relationships between states ought to be regulated by obligations accepted by common agreement, the law of nations. While Suarez suggested principles for public international law, Grotius developed and applied them in the *De Jure Belli ac Pacis* (1625). He recognized the existence of a human society whose members had common interests, notably in enjoying free and peaceful relationships. This society consists of sovereign states: the law of nations is 'that which has gained the force of law by the will of all nations, or of several of them in relationship to each other', demonstrated by 'the constant usage and witness of those having knowledge thereof'. Thus the law of nations arose from the free consent of states, legally equal, to laws inspired by God's will and by natural law, the product of reason. Some of these rules were open to dispute; Grotius, as a good Dutchman, defended the freedom of the seas and was opposed by the Englishman Selden, who argued that the sea could be appropriated and occupied and that British dominion over it extended to the opposite coast (*Mare Clausum*, 1635). But whatever rules were allowed, such as the right to make war in self-defence, or to preserve the necessities of life, or rights to free passage of persons and goods, or to free intercourse with distant nations, etc., such rules arose from a consensus and did not limit sovereignty or princely absolutism.

Absolutism seemed the answer to a deeply felt want in most European states. Theologians of the post-Tridentine Thomist revival had to try to assimilate absolutism and the principles of Bodin and Machiavelli. Suarez founded his work upon Thomist philosophical realism and on the decrees of the Council of Trent, in accordance with which he interpreted the political circumstances of his own time. From realism he took the fundamental idea of unchanging natural essences persisting beneath changing appearances. Society, the family, the city and the state correspond to unchanging necessities of human nature. 'Man is a social animal whose true nature inclines to a communal life.' The family alone is insufficient to satisfy all man's needs, hence families are joined together in cities and cities in principalities and monarchies, since the state is the necessary condition for man's full development. Suarez, like Aristotle, saw the state as a moral organism, *corpus politicum mysticum*, uniting wills, not by a contract, but by a consensus among men who freely decide to found a society. Although men are free to decide to found this society, they cannot change either its ends or its structure, for society has an unalterable nature, willed by God. And since man, according to the Council of Trent, is free to choose between good and evil, but needs guidance in order to strive for greater virtue and glory, society is characterized by a subordination of each to superior authority. Public power derives from natural law and is sovereign and so has power to make laws. Men are born free and sovereignty in the first instance is in the whole body of men forming a society. But after their voluntary agreement to adhere to the political structure ordained by God as the author of nature, public authority is embodied in a supreme magistrate who may be a popular assembly, a college of aristocrats, or a monarch. Monarchy is the best form, since it most nearly resembles the order of the universe. But men's choice, their agreement on the first principles, fixes irrevocably the form of government. The people have no further rights over the state, since it is only a state when it possesses full sovereign power. Public authority is of divine origin: the king as a sovereign rules as the viceregent of God so that obedience is due to him according to natural law, as the quasi-proprietor of public power, he is absolute. But he becomes a tyrant if he uses his power against the common good which is the end of the state.

This powerful theological construct was propagated by the Jesuits, but was excluded from the Protestant states where philosophical nominalism and belief in predestination triumphed. Even in Catholic states it was accepted, to a greater or lesser extent, according to circumstances, as the pages which follow will show.

But Muscovy is an exception to the rest of Europe, though the Muscovites regarded themselves as Europeans because they were Christians. They even claimed to be the only truly orthodox Christians. Moscow was the third and last Rome; the czar, the only Christian emperor. He recognized no superior and was an autocrat. The patriarchs of Moscow taught that the Holy Ghost was in him to govern man and the Czar Alexis said 'God has blest us, the Czar, and has given us to govern and judge faithfully our people in the East, West, South and North'. This notion of the sovereign as the direct agent of God is a principle common to absolutism throughout Europe. But Russian absolutism had another basis; Muscovy was the private property of the Kalita family. The state was the hereditary property of a dynasty, but after the death of Feydor Ivanovitch in 1598 the Kalita family became extinct. The problem of the time of troubles from 1598 to 1613 was to discover a czar by birth. When the Zemsky Sobor of 1613 declared Mikhail Romanof, czar, it was because he was the nephew of the last Kalita and was said to be 'elected by God before his birth'. But the fact remained that the state had survived without a czar during the time of troubles. Thus the state began to be distinguished from the person of the sovereign. There was also some temporary weakening of the old ideas of autocracy, but they ended by reasserting themselves.

The word absolutism was also to be found in Polish documents. The Kings Sigismund III and Ladislas IV, were accused of claiming absolute power when they asked the Diet to provide permanent taxes for the crown and a standing army in order to preserve the state. Although the Polish Diet had greatly reduced the king's powers, Poland was not a *Ständestaat*, for although the Diet comprised three estates—the King, the Senate and Chamber of Deputies—only nobles were represented. Poland was a republic of nobles, with an elective king of very limited powers. The constitution was based on the unbridled individualism of the nobles, guaranteed by the 'fundamental laws'. The rights of the individual noble were respected to such an extent that all nobles were regarded as equal, thus excluding the use of distinguishing titles; all decisions had to be unanimous, while each deputy in the Diet had a limited and specific mandate.

In Poland absolutism only existed in the power that each noble had over the inhabitants of his domain. Over-mighty subjects were kings and the state was a mirage.

The rule of unanimity paralysed the Diets and even endangered the country's defence. In March 1606 Sigismund III convoked a Diet in order to reform the constitution by establishing majority rule, a permanent tax and a standing army. The bishops and some of the laymen supported majority rule, which would have removed sovereignty from the individual nobles and restored it to the Diet. But the opposition accused the king of aspiring to *absolutum dominium*. Some of the nobles, led by Zebrodowsky, claimed that the king had broken the fundamental law, and rebelled. They were defeated, but the Diet of 1609 guaranteed the inviolability of the constitution. Subsequent attempts at reform were equally unsuccessful. State sovereignty was not only shattered by the principle of unanimity, but individual sovereignty was still further reinforced and guaranteed by the progressive establishment of the *liberum* veto which was permanently established by the Diet of 1652. At the end of the statutory six weeks the Diet had not reached agreement and the king demanded a prolongation; the deputy Ladislas Sicinski announced his veto and left. As it seemed impossible to constrain individual members, the Diet was declared dissolved. Henceforward such interrupted Diets became more frequent. Attempts to abolish the *liberum* veto and to adopt majority rule failed. Neither the king nor the Diet possessed full sovereignty; Poland's unreformed and irreformable constitution brought its defeats, loss of territories and ultimate extinction.

In the Holy Roman Empire the *Ständestaat* prevailed. Such a state was based upon the sacred rights of corporations, communities and individuals, guaranteed by fundamental laws. There was also a dualism between the prince and 'the estates', the nobility, the clergy and towns, whose deputies met in Diets. These had to be consulted about everything concerning the country's welfare. They had to give their consent to war, peace, and alliances, and to levying taxes which were often collected under the supervision of their own officials. Their committees and officials might also supervise the whole administration of the state. Althusius was the theorist of this kind of state; man is a social animal who needs society in order to live a truly human life. In every society authority is needed to allocate common resources, organize work, and arrange co-operation. The family, the village, the province and the state, has each an organic form, the grouping together of whose successive units produces a larger organism. The province was the natural unit of the *Ständestaat*. There each order, the church, the nobles, the craftsmen and peasants had its own deputies to consider its own affairs and to join with the other orders in considering more general matters. The head of the province, whether count, duke or prince, had the attributes of sovereignty, but on important matters convoked the Estates and gave their decisions the force of law by agreeing to execute them.

The Diets generally controlled the princes because they controlled finance, but there were often conflicts. In East Friesland, for example, both the count and the Estates claimed to be sovereign so that there were two financial administrations, two armies and two sets of diplomats. The Estates, led by the town of Emden, negotiated with the Dutch, and the count with the English. Elsewhere there were even more extreme ideas; about 1610 Von Tschernembl told the Estates of Upper Austria that the people, i.e. the nobility, were really sovereign: 'the people choose their prince and can also reject him . . . the territory decides for itself whether its ruler shall be hereditary . . .'.

This type of state persisted most strongly in the early seventeenth century in small countries. In the larger ones, such as Bohemia, Bavaria, or France, transformation into absolute monarchy had begun. The principal political cause of this was the Thirty Years War which showed that the *Ständestaat* was incapable of the rapid and energetic actions necessary for defence and so facilitated the growth of military despotism. In Brandenburg after 1631 the Swedish army provided the example of raising taxes by requisitioning without the consent of the Estates which was later followed by the Elector George William. The development of absolutism in Brandenburg-Prussia had special characteristics, owing to economic and social circumstances: the decline of the towns and the growth of demesne farming dependent upon serf labour. This resulted in the preponderance of the landed nobility, Junkers, who eventually recognized the prince's absolutism, while obtaining their own monopoly of social privileges. Such developments owed much to theories which justified the claims of princes while undermining those of their opponents. Suarez and Bellarmine greatly helped Maximilian of Bavaria and the Emperors Ferdinand II and Ferdinand III. Lutheranism always extolled the omnipotence of princes; while Calvinism did so when the prince was a Calvinist. The electors of Brandenburg found Calvinist councillors their best helpers in promoting absolutism. This can be seen in the religiosity of the *Confessio Sigismundi* (1614)—which was perhaps not written by the Elector John Sigismund but by his spiritual adviser—and also in the Great Elector's political testament, where the king owes homage to God who protects him and will bless his enterprises, if he does not suffer his household to be polluted with mistresses, operas, comedies, masques, etc.; such pietistic attitudes went very well with ideas of sovereignty and *raison d'état*.

For these political theorists, jurists and statesmen, whether Protestant or Catholic, were strongly influenced by Bodin's conception of sovereignty and by Machiavelli's of *raison d'état*. According to Hippolitus a Lapide, *raison d'état* was 'a certain political consideration towards which all councils and all actions in the state are directed . . . so that by it was attained more speedily and successfully the supreme end, the safety and growth of the state'. Sovereignty and *raison d'état* were the active principles which enabled the modern state to break the resistance of provincial estates, of privileged orders, corporations and individuals. Through them princes were able to develop new ideas of law in the course of their quest for absolutism. The *salus publica* allowed the over-riding of old ideas of sacrosanct rights and constant changes of laws and customs so that the law was a perpetually fluctuating response to the maxim *salus publica, suprema lex*. The literature of *raison d'état* flourished in the Holy Roman Empire and was profoundly influenced by the Italians, Botero and Ammirato, who were much admired at Ferdinand II's court. *Raison d'état* was expounded in the books of Christopher Besold, professor of law at Tübingen (*Politicorum libri duo*, 1618), in those of Reinking, Conring, Hippolitus a Lapide and in the *Manuale Politicum de Ratione Status, seu Idole Principum* by the imperial councillor Von Efferen (1630). Conring produced a dissertation on *ratio status* under the name of Heinrich Vossging and dedicated it to the Great Elector in 1651. By then *raison d'état* was a common subject of conversation and jurists had made it into a special category of law. Clapmarius' *De arcanis rerum publicarum libri sex* (1605, reprinted 1644), identified *arcana dominationis* and reason of state, understanding it as *jus dominationis* which gave the sovereign the right to over-ride common law, *jus commune seu ordinarium*, in the name of *bonum publicum*. J. A. Struve (*Syntagma Juris Civilis*, 1658) wrote: 'Law is a disposition, a rule prescribed according to some principle by a superior, according to which men's actions are guided in such a way that they may be just.' Thus the prince's will and the state's power become the foundation of positive law. Such conceptions encouraged princes to act and influenced their actions. This can be seen when Ferdinand II altered the constitution and privileges of the towns and estates of Bohemia in the ordinance of 10 May 1627, or still more clearly in the execution of Wallenstein (1634) where the necessity of the state over-rode positive law and customary forms of trial.

Italy, apart from Venice and Savoy, was a province of Spain, dominated by the thought of Suarez and Bellarmine. Bodin and Machiavelli were also influential there and the humanist notion of the hero persisted, while Tacitus, the historian of the empire, became more popular than Livy, the historian of the republic. Political writers were associated with the courts of Italian princes, themselves seeking absolute power, though often clients of Spain. Ideas such as those of Botero were current: the mainspring of any state is the obedience of its subjects, this depends upon the prince's virtue; he is a hero of superhuman intelligence who leads a perfect life and deserves absolute power. Thus *quicquid principi placuit legis habet vigorem*, the prince is *legibus solutus, superiorem non recognoscens*.

Gamberti developed the same theme in his *Idea di un Principe et Eroe Christiano* (1659). The Italians also claimed that the prince was the vicar of God. G. Gucci in *Il Principe Christiano Politico* (1630) held that his omnipotence came immediately from God, while the majority held it came indirectly through the consent of man, as did Canonieri in *L'Introductione alla Politica* (1640), but by this transfer the subjects renounced all their power. The *Lex Regia* was considered the foundation of princely absolutism. The prince himself possessed all sovereign power and, although Bodin was officially proscribed, he influenced Zuccolo (*Il Secolo dell'Oro*, 1629), and R. Della Torre (*Astrolobio di Stato*, 1647), etc. Every sovereign prince had the same power within his state as that possessed by the Roman emperors. They all agreed that the prince ought to respect natural law, the law of nations and, in ordinary circumstances, any just and reasonable laws. Italians inclined to limit the prince's absolute power to a greater extent than Bodin.

Naturally the adaptations of Machiavelli to the Council of Trent by distinctions between bad *raison d'état* and good *raison d'état*, serving Christian ends, made by the Jesuit Botero (*Ragion di Stato*, 1589) and Ammirato (*Discorsi supra Cornelio Tacito*, 1598) were influential. According to Zuccolo (*La Ragion di Stato*, 1621): 'Not only councillors in the courts and doctors in the schools, but barbers and the most humble craftsmen in the shops . . . discussed and disputed about *raison d'état* and persuaded themselves that they knew what things are done by *raison d'état* and what not.' Many others admitted that *raison d'état* justified departures from equity when the state's existence was at stake. Although Paolo Sarpi, as a convinced anti-Jesuit, was opposed to Botero, he believed that the state's integrity and sovereignty should be preserved at any price. In his letter to the Doge Antonio Priuli of 26 November 1628, he describes a conversation with the Prince of Condé in which he maintained that Christ's Kingdom was not of this world, and that religion was concerned with heavenly things, while government was of this world and that therefore religion and government could neither meet nor conflict. This amounted to making the safety or preservation of the state the only moral imperative of government. Even an anti-Machiavellian like Campanella was obliged to acknowledge that the Jews had been defeated when they refused to fight on the Sabbath so that the Maccabees had held that 'in times of necessity, men must always fight', thus showing there was a *raison d'état*. That kingdom which he nominated to realize his City of the Sun (1602) (first Spain, *Monarchia Hispanica*, 1620, then France, *Monarchie delle Nationi*, 1635) was to be allowed *raison d'état*.

In Spain Suarez' and Bellarmine's ideas triumphed with the crown's approval. They were adapted to the particular circumstances of Spain by some fifty political writers, including Jesuits, lawyers, judges, councillors, soldiers and ambassadors. They wrote mostly in Spanish, but a still wider audience could be reached by translating political maxims into visual emblems. Thus the clock became the symbol of the king keeping the various wheels in unison, while a river divided into many branches illustrated the maxim that division of forces weakens. Besides books of emblems such as F. D. Saavedra's *Political Idea of a Christian Prince Expressed in a Hundred and One Symbols* (Paris, 1660), there were processions with tableaux and epigrams of political import at all the chief festivals in Spain and the Spanish possessions. Their significance was further expounded by books such as Martinez de Herrera's *The Wise Prince* followed by an explanation of the epigrams produced at Naples for the feast of St John (1631).

Nearly all Spanish writers used Bodin's idea of sovereignty, especially D. Tovar Valderrama (*Instituciones Politicas*, 1645). Nearly all allowed the king full authority over the lives and goods of his subjects, to break laws and customs, to dispense with them and to change them according to the necessities of government. Nearly all agreed that the king was the vicar of God, a god on earth, that he ought to be an example to his subjects and govern according to God's will for the glory of God and the common weal, respecting natural laws and the law of nations and ordinarily acting according to the laws which he had made. A royal officer ought not to execute a king's orders if they were against conscience, against God's commands and the teachings of the church. But they did not conceive of organs for limiting princely power, since sovereignty could not be limited. The limits came from the very structure of princely power and the natural order in which it was exercised; 'the crown's circumference was drawn with justice as its centre' (Saavedra Fajardo, *Idea of a Politic Christian Prince*, 1640). Thus the prince's education was a major political matter. He should be instructed always to make use of his council. If he was inadequate to the crushing tasks demanded of an absolute prince so that he had to make use of a favourite as his deputy, at least he should guard against favouritism. His subjects owed him obedience and love, whatever his personal merit, for he was the mystical symbol through whom the citizens had communion and through whom the individual thought and wills of society were harmonized.

The Spaniards sought in Tacitus natural rules for the governments of states and interpreted them in the light of Thomism. They distinguished between Machiavelli's false *raison d'état* and the true one, agreeable to divine law. By prayers and virtuous actions the king protected himself from political evil as from sin, but *raison d'état* allowed him to crush revolts without recourse to judicial process, since all means were justified in order to preserve order and authority. If the king became a tyrant he must be endured, as God's punishment for the people's sins, and not resisted: 'to kill the King is an execrable crime' (Quevedo, *Politica de Dios*, 1626). On these points all the authors agreed. Spanish political books were commonly read in France; many were printed at Rouen, or Paris, either in Spanish, or in Latin and French translations.

France was the kingdom where the king was most absolute and the doctrine of absolutism reached its height, while neothomist influence was more circumspect. Men of the robe, counsellors in the *Conseil du Roi*, like Cardin le Bret (*De la Souveraineté du Roi*, 1632), courtiers like the royal historiographer André du Chesne (*Les antiquités et recherches de la grandeur et majesté des Rois de France*, 1610), royal or seigneurial officers like Charles Loyseau (*Oeuvres*, 1610), agreed with Suarez and Bellarmine in seeing the state as a moral organism, a mystical body, part of the order and hierarchy of the universe, created by God. They were all disciples of Bodin and emphasized sovereignty more strongly than authors from other countries:

Sovereignty cannot be separated from the state; should this happen, there would no longer be a state. Sovereignty is the form which gives being to the state, the state and sovereignty, taken *in concreto* are synonyms and the state is so called, because sovereignty is the fulfilment and expression of that power whereby the state is necessarily ordained and established ... [Sovereignty] consists of absolute power ... perfect, complete in every respect ... and just as the crown cannot exist unless it is an unbroken circle, so sovereignty would not exist, if it lacks anything.

Thus the state and the sovereign who personifies it has absolute power. The king alone has power to legislate, to give privileges, to create offices, render justice, coin moneys, 'levy taxes without the consent of the Estates', since the prince's authority covers goods as well as persons and he can use them for the 'rightful service and needs of the people'. Thus wrote Loyseau in his *Traité des Seigneuries* and le Bret repeated it in different terms. These writers also insisted upon the divine and sacerdotal character of the king of France, especially at moments of crisis, such as the Day of Dupes, or the Fronde.

The Kings of France are Kings, elected and chosen by God, Kings after His own heart, who, thanks to the divinity that His finger has printed on their face, have the honour of being at the head of the kings of all Christendom. Kings are the living images of God ... like earthly divinities ... our great kings have never been considered simply as laymen, but as endowed both with priesthood and royalty ...

(du Chesne).

They recalled the episcopal function at the coronation with 'the heavenly liquid brought by an Angel in the Sainte-Ampoule at the baptism of Clovis' as well as the French kings' power to perform miracles, or to heal scrofula by their touch. Their healing powers brought thousands of sick from all over France as well as from all parts of Europe, to the jealousy of other kings. On 13 November 1625 the bishop of Chartres in the name of the assembly of the clergy declared 'That kings are ordained by God and that furthermore they themselves are gods'. No hand should be laid on the king and he must not even be criticized. Moreover *raison d'état* allowed them to demand an almost passive obedience in most cases. As le Bret put it:

To know whether obedience is due to commands which, although they seem unjust, have the welfare of the state as their constant object, as if the prince should command the killing of someone who was notoriously rebellious, factious and seditious. My opinion is that on such occasions one should obey without reservation . . . all such orders should be judged just, or unjust, according to the advantage or disadvantage that the state might receive from their execution . . . Is a man, whose conscience tells him that what the king orders him to do is unjust bound to obey? . . . He ought to follow the king's will not his own . . . If it is an occasion when urgent assistance is required for the common weal, resistance . . . would be pure disobedience. *Necessitas omnem legem frangit* . . .

Thus the French went much further in the direction of absolutism than the Spaniards.

However, these Frenchmen distinguished between absolutism and despotism and considered themselves free men protected by guarantees. There were the fundamental laws, of which the first was the Salic law 'written upon the hearts of Frenchmen . . . born with us . . . arising from nature itself' (Bignon). This ensured hereditary succession by male primogeniture, prevented elections, or the nomination of his successor by the king, and so avoided murders, vengeance and civil wars. This law bound the king who could not change it; without it there would have been no king. Next the king ought to respect natural law, especially property rights, personal liberty and the sacredness of contracts. But imprisonment by royal *lettres de cachet* did not seem to them to violate individual liberty, since the king was the supreme judge. Finally the king ought to respect God's commandments and to treat his subjects with the goodness and justice of God on pain of calamities in this world and of punishment in the next.

Most, but not all, Frenchmen accepted these views. In 1611 Turquet de Mayerne, a Protestant from a family of merchants and doctors who had become landowners and been ennobled, published the *Monarchie Aristo-Democratique*, dedicated to the States General of the United Netherlands. He advocated the disappearance of the ancient military nobility and that merchants and members of the liberal professions, *agripossesseurs*, should have the first place in the state, provide its officials and have sovereign powers. They would make a contract with the king who would swear to maintain each in his rank and possessions. Estates General, whose members were *agripossesseurs*, indirectly elected, would meet regularly, legislate, vote taxes and control their expenditure, make war, peace and alliances, appoint commissioners to supervise the administration, control the membership of the king's council, which would be reduced to a purely executive role, and finally would control the militia of armed bourgeois. The state would thus be the agent of the bourgeois class. The book was well received by Parisian *bourgeoisie*, but was suppressed by the king's council, though it was remembered again on the eve of the Fronde.

Other anti-absolutist views, stressing the fundamental laws, reappeared periodically during the minorities of Louis XIII and Louis XIV, especially during the Fronde (1648–53). The princes of the blood were prepared to accept sovereignty and *raison d'état*, provided they shared power with the king. They invoked 'the ancient constitution' and demanded a council composed of princes of the blood, the other princes and of the great officers of state, instead of one freely chosen by the king. Above all, they wanted the subordination of the robe and the exclusion of favourites, such as Richelieu or Mazarin, men devoted to the king and apt instruments of absolutism. During minorities they demanded that a council of magnates should exercise absolute power to the exclusion of women (Marie de Medici, Anne of Austria) and foreigners (Concini, Mazarin). The nobility as a whole was opposed to any conception of sovereignty and *raison d'état* and only demanded the summoning of the Estates General according to their petition of 28 February 1651, in order to preserve 'the franchises, honours, rights and immunities of our order and to re-establish ourselves in our former lustre'. They wanted to preserve feudal relics and to prevent the fulfilment of the state.

The Parlement of Paris, although merely a court of justice, in its decree of 21 May 1615, in the *Arrêt d'Union* of 13 May 1648, and in pamphlets during the Fronde, declared itself the king's true council, his 'throne', as heir of the old *curia regis* and of the Frankish assemblies. Thus the king needed its assent for all important acts of government; it claimed legislative power, the right to consider, amend, reject, and vote freely upon royal edicts and ordinances, without having their registration enforced by *lit de justice*. The Parlement even wished to have immediate knowledge of all state affairs, to summon at will the princes of the blood, the lay and ecclesiastical peers, the great officers of state, and the councillors of state to form the *curia regis* and a substitute for the Estates General. In 1652, during the civil war, the Parlement, as a substitute for the Estates General and as heir of the general assembly of the Franks which had conferred sovereignty on Pharamond (!), went so far as to claim the right to entrust the royal authority to whomsoever it wished and to make final decisions on all matters, since it was 'the depository and as it were the perpetual guardian of sovereign authority'. The Parlement aimed at judicial absolutism with the courts exercising sovereign power.

Others dreamed of transforming the kingdom into a *Ständestaat*. Claude Joly was the most celebrated of these. He was a canon of Notre Dame who had seen the German states for himself when attending the Congress of Münster. He used history and the fundamental laws to argue that the monarchy was contractual in his *Recueil de Maximes véritables et importants* in 1652. The peoples had set up kings, had made contracts with them and had granted them full power on condition that kings protected them and gave them justice. God ratified this contract and the prince's authority derived immediately from this. But it follows that royal power was 'limited and restricted', while the form of government should be aristocratic. The Estates General watched over the maintenance of the 'ancient customs, laws and ordinances' thus guaranteeing each man's intangible rights. The Estates would vote taxes and appoint commissioners and receivers to raise them, exclude evil councillors, and together with the king they would decide on war and peace. They would meet at regular intervals and between sessions their deputies would supervise the carrying out of their decisions. Judicial officers would no longer be royal nominees; existing officers would choose three candidates for each vacant place from whom the king would select one. Joly seems to have foreseen that the other royal officials would be accountable for their actions to the courts. Finally the Parlement would still verify all royal acts and with the other sovereign courts would form a commission to judge any breaches of the Estates General's acts by royal officials. Thus the executive power would be under the control of the judiciary. The king must govern without favourites and be his own first minister. He should do nothing without a council of wise men from which cardinals, bishops, and foreigners would be excluded; while foreigners would be excluded from all employment and benefices. The realization of these ideas was prevented by the anarchy of the Fronde, which emphasized the need for order and security and so assisted the triumph of absolutism.

Absolutism was also a problem in Sweden, where the Charter of 1612 had consolidated the *Ständestaat*, but Gustavus Adolphus was deeply influenced by the Lutheran conception of princely power. He also learnt the neo-Stoic ideas of Justus Lipsius from Daniel Heinsius, a professor at Leiden, who in 1618 became his councillor and historiographer, and from Johann Skytte. Lipsius was a Deist and does not mention Christ; for him religion consists of acting according to the will of God. Man functions in a community devised for the common good, the state. Monarchy is the most natural and reasonable form of state. The prince is above the people and ought to have an absolute power which should be patriarchal, having the welfare and prosperity of his subjects as its object. The prince should observe the law, and Lipsius protested against Bodin's formula *rex legibus solutus*. The prince ought always to listen to the advice of his council, but should make decisions himself. Lipsius agreed with Seneca that *necessitas omnem legem frangit*. Such prudent and moderate views suited Gustavus Adolphus. He respected constitutional forms and was ready to share sovereignty with the Estates, but also knew how to impose his policy on the four Estates of the Riksdag by presenting himself as the champion of Lutheranism and the fatherland against Poland and the emperor, and so achieved a patriarchal absolutism.

After 1625 he was much influenced by Grotius, who maintained that sovereignty belonged to the prince and that the people had no right to check or punish him, if he misused his authority (*De Jure Belli ac Pacis*, I, 3).

Queen Christina also surrounded herself with Netherlanders and Germans and was deeply influenced by neo-Stoicism, but she adopted the French theory of absolutism and tried to introduce it in practice. She was always convinced that an absolute sovereign was responsible to God alone, while the example of Richelieu and Mazarin convinced her that royal sovereign power needed to be joined with absolute spiritual authority to function effectively. In her act of abdication she reserved absolute sovereignty to herself over all the members of her court. She used this power when she herself accused and tried Monaldeschi and had him executed. But like Descartes, Corneille, Retz, and Louis XIV, she understood that to claim such sovereignty implied taking the ideal hero as a model. His freedom came from strict control of passions; acting on clear and distinct ideas he takes decisions from which he never retreats, whatever their consequences. The conquest of power by being perfect mistress of herself and an unswerving pursuit of her goal was her ideal. Probably she thought of her abdication as a means to this end, since freedom and victory over self provided authority of a higher order than did possession of a crown.

In the northern Netherlands problems of absolutism occurred in each province, for the provincial Estates were not truly sovereign in view of the conflicting privileges of towns and nobles. The union between the provinces was only a loose federation; any decision of the Estates General implied unanimity from deputies of the provincial Estates who were bound by strict mandate. In practice, any decision seemed to require a referendum involving some 1,200 persons. Many thought that the provincial Estates ought to be sovereign and such people, usually members of the urban oligarchies, found the theories of Althusius satisfactory. Many wanted a centralized sovereignty. The stadtholder, whose office was hereditary in the House of Orange, retained some of the attributes of sovereignty; Maurice of Nassau hoped to increase his power and so was led to ally with the Gomarists, who were strict Calvinists, against the Arminians, supporters of free will and toleration. Strict Calvinism favoured absolutism in a prince who was a good Calvinist and the existence of a sovereign power above the provincial estates in order to impose religious uniformity. The Arminians such as Oldenbarnevelt, the Grand Pensionary of Holland, asserted the sovereignty of the provincial Estates, since in practice this ensured Holland's preponderance in the States General. After the triumph of the Gomarists at the Synod of Dordrecht (1619), the execution of Oldenbarnevelt and the flight of Grotius, Maurice of Nassau named regents and chose the pensionary from a list of three candidates. His power was much greater, but he was very far from being an absolute prince. The problems of sovereignty and absolutism remained continuing issues within this federative republic. In the southern Netherlands neo-Stoic and neo-Thomist views were dominant, despite Jansenism, thanks to the University of Louvain.

In England between 1600 and 1640 the predominant notion was still that of a body of rights, possessed by corporations and individuals, according to their social function. The king possessed rights, guaranteed by 'fundamental laws' which were part of the common law. The king's power appeared to be primarily judicial, as did that of Parliament, the supreme court of the kingdom, whose role was to declare and apply already existing law rather than to make laws. Everyone spoke of these fundamental laws and took them for granted without explaining precisely what they were. James I recognized their existence and told Parliament in 1610 that the law had placed the crown on his head and that he was king by the common law of the realm. In *The Trew Law of Free Monarchies* he had written that the first and most fundamental law was the coronation oath which obliged the king to maintain the established religion, cherish good laws, preserve each man's privileges and liberties, and to seek the common weal. This he said in 1609 was primarily concerned with private property, *meum ac tuum*. Seneca's phrase, *ad reges potestas omnium pertinet, ad singulos proprietas*, was often cited. Sir Dudley Digges said at a conference of the Lords and Commons in 1628 concerning resistance to forced loans:

It is an undoubted and fundamental point of this so ancient a Law of England, that the subjects have a true property in their goods, lands and possessions. The law preserves as sacred this Meum and Tuum which is the Nurse of Industry and Mother of Courage; for, if no Property, no Care of defence. Without this Meum and Tuum, there can be neither Law nor Justice in a Kingdom; for this is the proper object of both.

This individual right of property extends to a man's own body and so produces personal freedom. Thus, 'Every free subject of this realm hath a fundamental propriety in his goods and a fundamental liberty of his person.' The fundamental laws naturally included those rights which were necessary to enable the king to govern: his absolute power, his prerogative, in certain matters. These were matters of state, cases of urgency or involving the being, welfare, or property of the state, thus including everything essentially concerned with foreign policy, war and peace, the army and navy, coinage, regulation of industry and supplies necessary for defence, public order and in case of necessity, any matter. Parliament had a duty to watch over the fundamental laws. It consisted of three Estates; traditionally these were the Lords spiritual and temporal and the Commons, though some already held the view, preponderant after 1642, that they were King, Lords and Commons. Parliament could not infringe the king's rights guaranteed by fundamental law for 'no Act of Parliament can bar a King of his Regality' (Sir John Finch).

Neither James I nor Charles I directly challenged these fundamental laws. In levying ship money Charles I claimed to be driven by necessity and thus had not violated the ordinary sacred rights of property. But they did seek to extend the scope of their absolute power and stressed fundamental principles of monarchy. James I said that 'Kings are justly called gods, they are God's lieutenants sitting upon his throne on earth'. In the sphere of their prerogative their powers are unlimited; as Samuel told the Jews, 'the king could take their sons as soldiers or servants and give away their fields and vineyards'. The people should obey the king's demands

in all things, except directly against God, as the commands of God's Minister, acknowledging him a Judge set by God over them, having power to judge them, but to be judged only by God to whom only he must give account of his judgement . . . praying to him as their protector, for his continuance if he be good; for his amendment if he be wicked; following and obeying his lawful commands, eschewing and flying his fury in his unlawful commands, without resistance, but by sobs and tears to God . . .

The Anglican clergy, including many Puritans, preached that monarchy was the best form of government, that the king's power came immediately from God, that the king was responsible for the safety of his kingdoms and was furnished with a discretionary power to this end which was absolute. Down to 1640, nearly everyone accepted such views, including leaders of the Parliamentary opposition: Pym in 1621 and Coryton in 1628 said, 'the King hath the power of God'. But men resisted any extension of absolute power, whether inspired by social changes in England, or by continental examples, or by any ideas of the school of natural law, or those of Bodin who was much read in England, or by those invoking *raison d'état.*

The boundaries between the king's rights and those of the subject were extremely vague. The opposition leaders could find nothing in the common law in 1610 which clearly forbade the king to take the property of his subjects by means of impositions on trade and nothing in 1628 which forbade him to imprison their persons. The law could be adapted to suit any case. Opposition became embittered in so far as the individual's rights no longer came to be considered as privileges arising from a particular situation, but as absolute rights, derived from general principles. On the king's side some of the clergy brought out the plenitude of the king's sovereign power, as did Dickinson in his sermon *The King's Right* (1619), Manwaring in two sermons in July 1627 told Charles I his sovereign will gave binding legal force to 'Royal Edicts concluded out of Reasons of State' and in 1614 W. Goodwin had declared that the king was *Ipse solutus legibus.* Some royal judges (Sir Thomas Fleming in Bate's Case, 1606; Sir John Davies in his treatise on impositions; Sir Robert

Heath in Darnel's Case, 1627; Sir John Banks, the Case of Ship Money, 1637) tried to extend the royal prerogative, especially in the direction of giving the king autonomous power to impose taxes. They wished to show that the common law was equivalent to divine law, to natural law and to the law of reason, which laid down the principles of monarchical rule, so that according to the common law 'Rex is Lex', and that the king could rule like an emperor, since *salus populi suprema lex*. Davies even argued that by natural law all things were common and that the king, by limiting the absolute power given him by the law of nations, had as an act of grace created private property, which remained fundamental, but was under positive law and subject to *raison d'état*.

The theorists and lawyers of the opposition followed the same procedure in an opposite direction, identifying the fundamental laws with natural law and the law of reason. Sir Edward Coke, in Bonham's Case, said: '. . . in many cases the common law will control acts of parliament and sometimes adjudge them to be utterly void: for when an act of parliament is against common right and reason, or repugnant, or impossible to be performed, the common law will control it and adjudge such an act to be void'. Natural law, reason and the common law agree that a man cannot be judge in his own case. Thus the College of Physicians was not competent to condemn Bonham. Chief Justice Hobart (Day *v.* Savadge) and Sir John Davies (*Le premier report des cases et matters en ley*, 1615) argued that the laws of nature are immutable and sacred, the touchstone of laws, identical with reason and the foundation of the common law, so that any Act of Parliament, or still more of the king alone, contrary to them, is void. For Coke the essence of the common law, as of all law, was reason, showing itself constantly in the life of a nation. The judges declared the law according to the dictates of reason. Coke also created a historical myth that the pure law of the Saxons, corrupted by the Norman Conquest, had begun to revive with Magna Carta and was now to be made the basis of the state by Parliament. Coke had been dismissed from the chief justiceship by James I in 1616, but became a member of the parliaments of the 1620s and a principal author of the Petition of Right. He wrote the *Institutes of the Laws of England* of which the first part appeared in 1628, the rest only being published in June 1642 by Parliament.

The opponents of Charles I constantly invoked fundamental law in this wide sense to show that property and liberty were absolute and inviolable rights. The difficulty was that the rival theorists pitted one set of absolute rights against another. Their impeachments accused Strafford, Laud, and Sir Robert Berkeley of having 'endeavoured to subvert the fundamental laws and established government of the realm of England'. In 1641 the Grand Remonstrance claimed all mischiefs were due to a '. . . pernicious design of subverting the fundamental laws and principles of government upon which the religion and justice of this kingdom are firmly established'. Charles I was condemned to death in 1649 for his 'wicked design to subvert the ancient and fundamental laws and liberties of this nation and in their place to introduce an arbitrary and tyrannical government'.

Puritanism played a large part in resistance to the crown, although until 1640 Puritan preachers expressed no very distinctive political views. But to many Puritans the king was not a hero, a living god, exalted above the subject masses. He was depraved, like all men, and might be inferior to those roused directly by God's grace to struggle against sin. God's elect were not necessarily the great of this world; the sign of election was experience of spiritual conflict, not worldly learning. They were saints, made kings and priests by justification, whose characteristic was to follow their consciences whatever the cost. A king who was not one of the saints was in a weak position. Some Puritans while maintaining the supremacy of faith and revelation gave great weight to reason and nature, claiming that the principles of the common law supported the doctrine of predestination (J. Preston, *The New Covenant*, 1629; *Life Eternal*, 1631); they insisted that obedience was due to God rather than the king, that God was the true king of England. As they were not free to follow their ideas of church order within the Anglican church, they were opposed to the bishops and so to the king. Puritan feeling helped to rouse opposition and was the motive force in the Long Parliament, when preaching was freed and many public fasts, accompanied by sermons, were ordained. The preachers applied to Charles I what the Bible said of wicked kings, repeated that human laws did not bind conscience and told members of Parliament that they were agents of God, replacing the king as his lieutenant. They recalled that government according to divine and natural law rested on a compact made by the people for satisfaction of their natural needs and was to be obeyed only as long as it observed that compact and God's commands.

After 1640 Parliament exercised an arbitrary, absolute and truly sovereign power of which the kings had only dreamed, helped by ideas of using sovereignty and *raison d'état* in the name of the people. Unable to condemn Strafford by due process of law, Parliament had invoked necessity and public safety. Similarly, in justifying their ordinance taking control of the militia from the king, they declared that Parliament was not only a court of judicature, but also 'a counsel to provide for the necessities, prevent the imminent dangers and preserve the public peace and safety of the kingdom and to declare the king's pleasure in those things that are requisite thereunto'. Parliament ruled absolutely, but refused to proclaim its sovereignty; though Henry Parker, secretary to the Parliamentary army, in his *Animadversions* (1642) asserted 'the sovereign power resides in both houses of Parliament, the king having no negative voice'; while William Prynne in *The Sovereign Power of Parliaments and*

Kingdoms (1643) saw kings as 'but servants to, not absolute lords over their kingdoms in whom the legislative power and authority resides'. An anonymous pamphleteer (*Touching the Fundamental Laws*) found the court of Parliament '. . . fundamental and paramount, comprehending law and equity, and being entrusted by the whole for the whole, is not therefore to be circumscribed by any other laws which have their being from it, nor it from them, but only by that law which at first gave it its being . . . *salus populi*'. Charles, in answering the declaration of 19 May 1642, was justified in complaining that the will of the majority at Westminster had displaced the law and was asserting an absolute and arbitrary power.

Puritans saw the history of the world as a struggle between Christ and anti-Christ for men's souls and identified the victory of Parliament with that of Christ. In setting up a presbyterian system of church government (1646), Parliament found its sovereignty challenged by Puritan dissidents. Puritan preachers had appealed to the claims of the individual conscience; some now held that any man could be saved if he would accept God's grace; others that as long as a man believed in God and the Bible, errors must be tolerated. The dissidents claimed liberty for tender consciences to group themselves freely in congregations and under ministers outside the presbyterian system. They were numerous in the New Model Army, where there were groups denying predestination, believing in the immediate and absolute effects of grace, in the religion of the Holy Spirit, rejecting the laws of all former dispensations, or expecting the second coming. The most extreme denied the magistrate any power in religion and demanded complete freedom of preaching and printing. All the dissidents feared that Parliament would impose religious uniformity and were ready to resist its claims to absolute authority. From 1646 a group whose revolutionary demands led their enemies to call them Levellers formed round Lilburne, Walwyn and Overton in London. Lilburne rebuked Parliament for refusing the people freedom in religion, the press and trade and so tyrannically violating the natural rights of Englishmen. He appealed once more to the fundamental laws, identified with the laws of God, nature and reason. Overton in 1646 declared all men equal. Nature revealed to each man's reason what was necessary for his good. Each had a natural right to property and liberty and was king, priest and prophet according to the order of nature. Members of Parliament were deputies of the people and could not violate individual rights, the just prerogatives of all mankind. Walwyn equated king and parliament, saying that for the Levellers 'it is all one to them who oppressed them'. Their political programme (*The Agreement of the People*) included biennial parliaments, equality before the law, the vote for all who were not paupers or servants, redistribution of seats in proportion to density of population, freedom to meet, speak, publish, and to petition Parliament upon any subject.

When Parliament attempted to rid itself of the New Model Army, the agitators elected by the troops adopted the Leveller programme, although Cromwell and Ireton considered that it threatened property rights. At the Putney Debates in 1647 Ireton said that if all men had the vote by 'the right of nature', then 'you must deny all property too'; for if 'a man hath an equal right with another to the choosing him that shall govern him— by the same right of nature he hath the same right in any goods he sees . . .' 'Here is the most fundamental part of the constitution of the kingdom, which if you take away, you take away all.' Ireton wished to limit the parliamentary franchise to those with 'a local, a permanent interest in the kingdom', freeholders, freemen of towns and gentry. Ireton and Cromwell did not believe that complete toleration, if this meant denying the magistrate any authority in religion, was possible. They found Lilburne's democratic method of defending natural rights unacceptable. Cromwell preferred something nearer to the traditional constitution and re-established discipline in the army. At the end of 1648 after some hesitation they broke finally with the Levellers and chose to accept the purged Parliament, the Rump, as the instrument of the godly. On 4 January 1649 the Rump resolved

that the People are, under God the Original of all just Power . . . that the Commons of England in Parliament assembled being chosen by, and representing, the People have the supreme Power in this Nation.. . That whatsoever is enacted, or declared for Law by the Commons, in Parliament assembled hath the Force of Law; and all the People of this Nation are concluded thereby, although the Consent . . . of King, or House of Peers be not had thereunto.

Ideas of sovereignty and *raison d'état* had triumphed.

Some supporters of the king turned arguments from fundamental laws against Parliament. Sir Robert Filmer in *Patriarcha or the Natural Power of Kings* (written before 1642) used natural law as revealed by scripture and history to justify royal absolutism as of patriarchal origin. The first government was Adam's over his family, followed by Noah's over his sons. Patriarchs had an absolute power which came from God, not from the votes of their children. Kings had the same absolute patriarchal power over their subjects that Noah had over his sons.

But the most formidable defender of absolutism was Hobbes. Before 1637 he had begun a general treatise on nature and man, founded on materialist and mechanistic principles. As a known defender of absolutism, he took refuge in France in 1640, where his *De Cive* was published in 1642. His masterpiece *Leviathan* was written in Paris, but published in 1651 in London, whither Hobbes returned, submitting to the Commonwealth. Hobbes did not believe that man was naturally a social animal. His natural state was war of 'everyone against everyone'. Men are approximately equal in ability and in hopes of attaining their ends. If one is stronger, the weaker can defeat him by ruses or by joining with others. In pursuit of 'their End (which is principally their own conservation . . .)

[they] endeavour to destroy or subdue one another'. In this state of war, nothing can be unjust, because there is no law, which needs a common power to keep all in awe; 'everything is his which getteth it and keepeth it by force; which is neither Propriety, nor Community; but Uncertainty'. Men wish to escape from this miserable state. Their reason, given them by God, shows them laws of nature, 'Justice, Equity, Modesty, Mercy and (in summe) doing to others as we would be done to', which would ensure peace. But men will only keep these laws when they can do so safely. 'Covenants without the Sword are but Words', so they must erect a common power to enforce obedience, reduce all their wills to one. This is more than consent, it is a covenant whereby each 'gives up my Right of governing myself, to this Man, or to this Assembly of men, on this condition, that thou give up thy Right to him and Authorise all his Actions in like manner'. This creates the state, 'that great Leviathan . . . to which we owe . . . our peace and defence', the essence of which is the exercise of sovereign power 'as great as possibly men can be imagined to make it'. The sovereign, whether a man or an assembly, has the right to raise troops, administer justice, make war and peace, legislate, appoint judges and officials and to forbid opinions and doctrines considered dangerous. Division of sovereign power, or belief in absolute individual rights, such as property rights, will destroy the state. Once conferred and established, sovereignty cannot be denied, limited, or repudiated. It can be exercised in three types of state: democracy, aristocracy, and monarchy, whose difference is not one of power, but of aptitude 'to produce the Peace and Security of the people'. The aptest is monarchy, provided it is absolute.

Hobbes had transformed the theory of contract and so influenced Locke and Rousseau. His work also had an immediate success. In France, Mersenne and Gassendi recommended *De Cive*, 'this rare work... of the incomparable M. Hobbes', to Sorbière. The first edition was soon exhausted, as was the second, published by Sorbière at the Hague in 1647. Sorbière published a French translation in 1649 which went through three editions that year. He also translated *De Corpore Politico*, publishing it in 1652.

Thus absolutism made considerable progress from 1610 to 1651, thanks to the influence of various embodiments of ideas of sovereignty and *raison d'état*. But there was a striking change in methods of argument. Suarez, Bellarmine, the neo-Thomists and their disciples, had mainly used the scholastic procedure of deduction starting from axioms provided by metaphysics and theology. Their politics was a science, because it was purely rational, a knowledge founded on essences and real causes. They used history simply to verify and confirm these results by experience. But there were others more in tune with the new philosophy, like Turquet de Mayerne and Loyseau in France, Alamos in Spain, or Hobbes in England, who used induction. From a knowledge of particular instances they devised categories including them and general laws governing them.

Many facts were obtained by historical studies, but many also by observing their own societies, as Turquet de Mayerne and Hobbes so strikingly did. They were also remarkable for being deeply concerned in the scientific movement of their time. Turquet de Mayerne, like the neo-Pythagoreans and the disciples of Archimedes of the sixteenth century and Galileo and the mechanists in the seventeenth, believed that mathematics was the key to nature. Hobbes held similar views; he had been a familiar of Bacon, was an admirer of Copernicus, Galileo and Harvey and was himself a mechanist. From 1634 to 1636 he associated with the leading mechanists, Mersenne, Descartes, Gassendi at Paris, and visited Galileo in Italy. He published a little treatise in 1637 in which he explained sensations as variations in movement and in 1646 a treatise on optics. For such men political science had a character different from that recognized by the neo-Thomists. It was a practical science which provided knowledge of how things happened and interacted and how they might be controlled; they were not concerned with the essence and formal causes of things. The word cause changed its meaning, the final causes which had dominated the constructions of Suarez and Bellarmine were eliminated, while efficient causes became simply varying arrangements of facts. Political science was transformed by the substitution of mechanistic for Aristotelian methods.

Suarez, Bellarmine and the neo-Thomists, as heirs of the biologist Aristotle, saw the state as an organism whose general character they grasped at first sight; men who by nature were social animals were forced to choose a body politic and were bound by the laws of its functioning. Thus the choice of a particular kind of body politic arose from consensus, not contract. But Turquet de Mayerne, and Hobbes were accustomed through application of mathematics to the natural sciences to abstracting simple material elements, to seeking their connections, preferably materially verifiable, measurable ones. Men were individuals whose egoistic concerns forced them to associate with each other, while making free use of the full scope of natural laws to form contracts. In the last resort everything in social and international relations depended upon contracts and conventions. Everything was a matter of convention, of adjusting mechanisms which might differ in themselves, yet produce the same results.

The neo-Thomists' practice produced a limited and finite number of political forms and categories which corresponded with the Aristotelian conception of a finite and limited cosmos with a fixed number of kinds and species. Although Hobbes retained the old classifications into monarchy, aristocracy and democracy, his approach in principle opened up unlimited possibilities of creating new political and social forms. This fitted in with the conception of the universe as heliocentric and infinite, held together solely by the uniformity of its laws. Political ideas were not merely linked to political, social and economic situations, but were a function of the whole of European civilization.

CHAPTER IV

THE SCIENTIFIC MOVEMENT AND ITS INFLUENCE 1610–50

NEARLY all Galileo Galilei's (1564–1642) intellectual contemporaries would have agreed with his dramatic declaration that in order to introduce a new philosophy 'it will be first necessary to new-mold the brains of men, and make them apt to distinguish truth from falsehood'.[1] They called for a revolution in thinking about nature that would still be far in advance of results at the mid-century, but no previous generation had had so much reason to believe that it had at last acquired a method which, by correcting its own errors, offered the certainty of discovering the one actual structure of the physical world. Older habits of erudition and speculation in natural philosophy were losing their appeal and were being replaced by the practice of systematic research. The promise and achievements of the enterprise gave fresh confidence to appeals for conditions making such research possible, for more adequate provision for natural science in the universities and in new institutions, and for money to be spent on science in the public interest.

To a large extent the new science was establishing itself on the margins of official learning and recognized professional activities. This is reflected in the diversity of the occupations and social origins of the men engaged in science and the conditions in which they carried out their scientific work. Central to the traditional profession of learning were those holding academic posts in the faculties of arts or of medicine in universities or in newer institutions such as the Collège de France in Paris and Gresham College in London. If we include the minor figures this remained the largest single group. Yet the list of scientists who had no full-time academic post is equally impressive. Some of these, for example Simon Stevin (1548–1620) and Johann Kepler (1571–1630), and Galileo in later life, were employed by governments or great patrons specifically for scientific work. A much larger number earned their living wholly or in part in professions related to science. Many of these were practising physicians like William Harvey (1578–1657), J. B. van Helmont (c.1580–c.1644) and Jean Rey (c.1582–c.1645). Some engaged in other 'learned' practical professions as engineers, architects, or surveyors, like Stevin, Cornelis Drebbel (1572–1634) and Gérard Desargues (1593–1662). Others, lower down in the hierarchy of learning, practised as surgeons or as apothe-

[1] Galileo, *Dialogo sopra i due massimi sistemi del mondo* I (1632), in *Opere*, ed. naz. Vol. 7 (Florence, 1897), p. 82; Thomas Salusbury, *Mathematical collections and translations* (London, 1661), p. 43.

caries like the chemist Rudolf Glauber (1604–70), as lens-grinders or as instrument makers like Joost Bürgi (1552–1632), or as teachers of 'practical mathematics' and other practical subjects outside the universities. But a great many of the scientists of the period owed their principal livelihood to wholly non-scientific sources. These included officials like Pierre Fermat (1601–65), conseilleur du Parlement de Toulouse, and Otto von Guericke (1602–68), mayor of Magdeburg; gentlemen of private means such as René Descartes (1596–1650), John Napier (1550–1617), Blaise Pascal (1623–62) and Nicolas Claude Fabri de Peiresc (1580–1637); and many clerics: regulars like the Jesuat Bonaventura Cavalieri (1598–1647) and the Jesuit Christoph Scheiner (1575–1650), and Marin Mersenne (1588–1648), a Minim friar; beneficed seculars like Pierre Gassendi (1592–1655); and Anglican country parsons like William Oughtred (1575–1660) and Jeremiah Horrox (1617–41).

Critics of the state of scientific learning in the early seventeenth century were largely in agreement in their diagnoses of its alleged ailments and their causes. The most systematic critic was Francis Bacon. In *The advancement of learning* (1695) and later in the *Novum organum* (1620) and in the preface to the *Instauratio magna* (1620–3), Bacon presented his diagnosis of present ills through an interpretation of the history of learning. He found only three societies in which, for short periods, the sciences had progressed: among the Greeks and the Romans in antiquity, and among the modern nations of western Europe. But even in those relatively favourable periods progress had faltered. In present times practitioners of the mechanical arts had fared best because of their close contact with practical experience, but they took no account of larger theoretical issues; by contrast, philosophers spinning out theoretical systems without reference to experimental facts had discovered nothing new. Bacon pointed out that each side lost by remaining ignorant of the other's problems; his own proposal for an experimental 'inquisition of nature'[1] was offered as a method of discovery that would provide both explanations of nature and a rational basis for technology. The failure of the theoretical sciences to search for new knowledge he traced back to the failure of the contemporary university system.

Contemporary scientists such as Descartes and Evangelista Torricelli (1608–47) likewise urged the extension of scientific studies in universities and the endowment of research. Criticism of the conservatism and pedantry of formal courses in the sciences became a commonplace of intellectual autobiographies of the period. Yet in spite of the criticisms of university education in science and in spite of the diversity in origins, training and occupations of the men engaged in scientific work, the leaders of the scientific movement who made the great original contributions of this period were without exception university graduates. However justified the complaints against academic conservatism, it was in fact the

---

[1] Francis Bacon, *Instauratio magna*, preface.

universities that produced the body of men educated to think at the abstract theoretical level where these contributions could be made. From the staple compulsory Aristotelian logic and natural philosophy of the arts course they learnt the elements of a theoretical scientific system, even though an outmoded one; those with the enterprise to go beyond this would introduce new theories making the common assumption with the old, that nature was explicable as a rational, discoverable, abstract system. Against such a background scientific innovation was intelligible, and intelligible at the most abstract theoretical level, even when not encouraged; the new philosophy made its appeal by offering a far more effective means of theoretical explanation. The other main form of scientific education available, a purely technical training in one of the skills for 'practitioners', provided no such preparation for thinking at this abstract level where the main scientific debates were taking place. The contributions made possible by such an untheoretical technical training might be indispensable for experimentation, but something more was needed to appreciate the critical bearing of an experiment on a scientific argument. It is significant that the critics of the universities were all themselves their products, and that it was the university 'philosophers' and not the practical 'mechanics' who pointed out the scientific interest of the empirical information, instruments and problems provided by contemporary technology. If graduates went outside the universities to 'practitioners' for experimental and practical skills, it was from their university education that they learnt the meaning of creating not merely a scientific technology but a 'new experimental philosophy'.

The innovators attempting to reform scientific education had to contend with an academic structure established in the medieval foundations and persisting generally in European universities, in spite of some concessions already made to new studies in literature and history. Non-experimental science had its traditional place in the mathematical quadrivium (arithmetic, music, geometry, astronomy, with some additions such as optics) and natural philosophy of the arts course, and in the course for a professional degree in the higher faculty of medicine. Formal instruction consisted traditionally of the exposition by 'lecture' and commentary of standard texts of Euclid, Ptolemy, Aristotle, Galen and in favourable circumstances more recent authors, together with disputations in which the student defended 'theses' provided by these texts. This system weighted even medical education overwhelmingly with book-learning; in all the years of the Cambridge course only three days were given to dissection and even so these had to be enforced under penalty. For the most part the innovators were on common ground with the conservatives in assuming that the primary function of a university was 'the virtuous education of youth'[1] in arts and the provision of good professional train-

[1] M. H. Curtis, *Oxford and Cambridge in transition, 1558–1642* (Oxford, 1959), p. 83.

ing in the higher faculties. The place of research in universities was to be a subject of the reforms of the nineteenth century: what the scientific reformers of the seventeenth century wanted was that universities should provide teaching for the new mathematical and experimental sciences that recognized their radical difference in content, aims and methods from the older studies and was appropriate to this different character.

By 1650, indeed for long afterwards, no university had yet made statutory changes on a scale that came near meeting the wishes of the reformers, but opportunities for the new scientific studies had been provided both publicly and privately in many universities and in some these exerted an increasing influence. Public provision for such studies had been and continued to be made through the establishment of new chairs, and through collections of mathematical, astronomical and physical instruments, chemical laboratories, and the anatomy theatres and botanical gardens which most of the larger universities possessed by 1650. The faculties of medicine were especially active in providing for their professional interest in anatomy, botany and chemistry. The new chairs in these subjects and in mathematics and natural philosophy helped to establish the sciences as independent disciplines and at the same time provided a livelihood for individuals whose researches contributed to the general advance of knowledge and made them famous in the republic of letters at large. In addition to these public provisions, private advantage was taken in teaching of the opportunity to introduce new content into the old form of the statutory curricula.

Conditions varied characteristically in different countries. Until the middle of the century the Italian universities retained their lead in offering the most professional scientific training. More than elsewhere the Italian cities provided in princely academies, the entourages of dukes and cardinals, religious houses, and the universities themselves an active scientific body of mathematicians, astronomers, experimenters, medical men and philosophers from which all could gain. The richer universities like Padua and Bologna could afford well-paid chairs in all the main scientific subjects—mathematics, astronomy, physics, anatomy, botany, surgery, medicine—and more than one specialized chair in some fields. The great medical school at Padua had brought the study of anatomy by dissection to a high degree of perfection and the distinguished succession of professors since Vesalius continued with the pupils of Hieronymo Fabrizio of Aquapendente (c.1553–1619), the great anatomical teacher of his day. Other pupils of Fabrizio had carried Paduan methods beyond the Alps to Basel, Leiden and Copenhagen; Harvey, greatest of them all, brought them to London. Also with a chair at Padua was Santorio Santorio (1561–1636), a pioneer of experimental medicine. As well as at Padua, teaching of anatomy by dissection was prescribed by statute and carried out systematically at Bologna, Pisa, the Sapienza in Rome, and

Pavia where Gasparo Aselli (1581–1626), discoverer of the lacteal vessels, held a chair. At Bologna worked the Jesuits Giovanni Battista Riccioli (1598–1671) and Francesco Maria Grimaldi (1618–63), both skilful experimenters in physics. Pisa especially cultivated the mathematical sciences and offered courses in applied mathematics and engineering; there also the mathematician Giovanni Alfonso Borelli (1608–79), coming to a chair at the same time as Marcello Malpighi (1628–94), developed his interest in physiology. Galileo's friend Benedetto Castelli (c.1577–1643) taught at Pisa and Rome; his most brilliant pupil, Torricelli, succeeded Galileo at Florence.

Outside Italy the universities in which the new sciences were most actively cultivated were those in the Netherlands. Courses in the mathematical sciences at Leiden were up to date, a good collection of 'mathematical instruments' was available and the mathematical professors included Willebrord Snell (1591–1626), but it was in the medical faculty that the university came to establish its reputation for scientific learning. Leiden and in less degree Utrecht came to rival the universities of north Italy in attracting foreign students. In spite of initial opposition it was in the Netherlands that the Cartesian system first took root, and from there it spread to the rest of Europe. The German universities, both Protestant and Catholic, although predominantly conservative, also took some steps to introduce the new science before the wars of religion put a temporary stop to progress. Marburg in 1609 established what was apparently the first European chair of chemistry. At Giessen there was a *laboratorium chymicum* in 1612 and the botanist Joachim Jung (1587–1657) held a chair of medicine. At Würzburg, under Jesuit control, new ideas on pathology were taught. Further anatomy theatres were built, for example at Freiburg (1620), Jena (1629) and Altdorf (1637). In neighbouring northern countries Caspar Bauhin (1550–1624), a graduate of Padua, had established the study of botany and anatomy through his double chair at Basel, and Thomas Bartholinus (1616–80) brought fame to the chair of anatomy at Copenhagen. At the other end of Europe the great university of Salamanca, which had taken a lead in the teaching of anatomy and of Copernican astronomy in the sixteenth century, seems to have lost its interest in science, but at the Casa de Contratación, the school of navigation in Seville, a good training in 'practical mathematics' could still be found.

Apart from Montpellier with its tradition of teaching in botany, anatomy, and medicine, in no great European country did the universities offer so little encouragement to the new philosophy as in France. Dominated by Paris, still by far the largest university in Europe, the French universities reacted conservatively on all sensitive issues whether in relation to philosophy, theology or respect for ancient authorities. The importance of the University of Paris in political and ecclesiastical affairs exposed it to strong outside pressure; its energies became absorbed in a double controversy over Jansenism and over Jesuit control. Philosophy remained strictly Aristotelian, and the university exercised its function as censor of books to condemn the new mechanistic philosophies of both Gassendi and Descartes as theologically subversive. No provision was made for teaching the new science in the arts faculty. Gassendi persuaded the Sorbonne not to condemn the Copernican hypothesis in 1631, but the medical faculty led by Guy Patin (1602–72) and the distinguished anatomist Jean Riolan (1580–1657) rejected Harvey's theory of the circulation of the blood and were to earn the satires of Molière and Boileau. Meanwhile the physicians of the faculty of medicine rigidly maintained the exclusion of the surgeons from a university education and kept tight control of all aspects of the medical profession. With the one exception of Montpellier the new science was given a place in French education almost entirely apart from the universities. Some courses were available at the Collège de France on anatomy and on mathematics, in which Gassendi and Gilles Personne de Roberval (1602–75) successively held the chair. Botany, and from 1648 chemistry, were taught at the new Jardin du Roi founded in 1636 with chairs of botany, anatomy and surgery. And among the Jesuit colleges physical science figured prominently in the teaching: thus at La Flèche Descartes gratefully records that he was not only introduced to ancient and modern mathematics and astronomy but learnt also of Galileo's newly invented telescope and its startling discoveries.

Besides Italy and the Netherlands, it was England whose universities gave most encouragement to the new science. In spite of the conservatism of their statutes some public provision had been made available through the regius chairs of medicine at Oxford and Cambridge, and Oxford acquired chairs of geometry and astronomy founded by Sir Henry Savile in 1619, a chair of natural philosophy founded by William Sedley in 1621, a 'Physick Garden' in 1622 and a readership in anatomy in 1624. Other foundations at both universities followed later in the century. Savile required his professor of geometry to read Archimedes and Apollonius as well as Euclid and to teach applied mathematics, including practical instruction in surveying, and his professor of astronomy to teach the Copernican theory and practical applications of astronomy, especially in geography and 'those parts of navigation depending on mathematics'.[1] Elected into the chair of geometry in 1649, John Wallis (1616–1707) introduced Descartes' analytical geometry and Cavalieri's method of indivisibles into his teaching. At Cambridge Francis Glisson (1597–1677) had by 1637 introduced Harvey's theory into his teaching as regius professor of physic. But it was through the tutorial system in the colleges that best advantage was taken of opportunities to introduce new scientific knowledge into the old statutory curricula. For a new class of

[1] Curtis, *Oxford and Cambridge in transition*, p. 117.

gentry entering the universities the desirability of learning was tested by utility and *virtù*. There were fellowships for medicine and for the mathematical sciences in various colleges. At Oxford a tutor in arts at Corpus Christi College, one Brian Twyne, left full notes showing that between 1605 and 1623 he was teaching his pupils 'practical' mathematical subjects, based on recent English works, similar to those laid down by Savile for his professors, and was expounding the astronomical theories of Copernicus, Kepler and Galileo as against Ptolemy. There is evidence of similar mathematical teaching in other colleges both at Oxford and at Cambridge, where distinguished men such as Oughtred, Henry Briggs (1561–1630) and Lawrence Rooke (1623–62) held fellowships and where the new astronomy was also expounded in comparison with the old.

Yet even accepting Sprat's claim that it was in the universities that natural philosophy in England 'has been principally cherish'd, and reviv'd',[1] the best professional scientific training in England was available not at Oxford or Cambridge but in London. Lectures open to the general public were given at Gresham College in geometry, astronomy and 'physic'. The geometry and astronomy were strongly related to practical problems, especially in navigation, and the professors, several of whom had previously taught in Oxford or Cambridge, were in close contact over many years with the Royal Navy and with instrument-makers and other mathematical practitioners. It was at Gresham College or nearby that there met from about 1645 the group which was to form the nucleus of the Royal Society. For the study of medicine many Englishmen still went to Italy or Holland, but in London serious training was provided by the Royal College of Physicians and, in surgery, at the College of Barber Surgeons. At the former Harvey as Lumleian Lecturer had from 1616 pioneered morbid and comparative anatomy and prepared for his demonstration of the circulation of the blood,[2] and at the latter Sir Charles Scarborough (1616–94) 'was the first who introduced Geometrical and Mechanical Speculations into Anatomy',[3] when lecturing on muscles. Christopher Wren had at one time acted as his demonstrator.

The main case of the scientific critics against the universities as teaching institutions was that even when in the most favourable circumstances they allowed new knowledge to be fitted somehow into old curricula and methods of instruction, they would adapt neither in such a way as to make a really congenial home for the new scientific enquiries. Too often

---

[1] Thomas Sprat, *The history of the Royal Society of London* (London, 1667), p. 328; critical ed. by J. I. Cope and H. W. Jones (London, 1959).

[2] Sir G. Keynes, *The life of William Harvey* (Oxford, 1966), pp. 84–111; cf. Sir G. N. Clark, *A history of the Royal College of Physicians*, Vol. I (Oxford, 1964).

[3] Charles Goodall, *The Royal College of Physicians of London...: and An Historical Account of the College's Proceedings against Empiricks...*, Epistle Dedicatory to latter (London, 1684); P. Allen, 'Medical education in seventeenth-century England', *Journal of the history of medicine*, Vol. I (1946), pp. 139–40.

the new disciplines had to be acquired outside the universities altogether. The result was that while the practitioner, whether 'learned' like the physician, the surveyor or the engineer, or 'unlearned' like the surgeon, the apothecary, the instrument-maker or the assayer, could learn his skill professionally by clinical experience or practical apprenticeship, the theoretician, the university-educated natural philosopher who was primarily responsible for the development of original scientific thought, usually had to bring himself abreast of new knowledge by private reading or tuition. Many Oxford and Cambridge men, including the future Savilian professors Seth Ward (1617–89), Wallis and Wren, learnt modern mathematics from Oughtred after he had left Cambridge for a country living, and the biographies of other leading scientists of this period show that throughout Europe a high proportion of them acquired an up-to-date mastery of science by similar means outside their formal university studies. The concentration of universities on teaching, leaving research as a private activity, left curricula out of contact with advancing knowledge and the spirit of enquiry, even where no theologically or otherwise sensitive issues were involved. Where such issues did arise a positive stand was taken against the new. Thus whereas new methods in mathematics and experimentation as such encountered no external opposition, criticism of Aristotle's physics or Galen's anatomy and physiology ran foul of a strong residue of academic humanist conservatism. Opposition to Copernican astronomy was largely academic until *De revolutionibus* was prohibited *donec corrigatur* by the Roman Congregation of the Index in 1616,[1] when the issue became an ecclesiastical one. After Galileo's condemnation in 1633 administrative measures in Catholic countries against Copernicanism became even more determined. Descartes' innovations in mathematics and optics were welcomed but his mechanistic physics and physiology were at first opposed, in Protestant Utrecht and Leiden as in Catholic Louvain and in Paris, because his doctrines were held to lead to atheism and to have theologically dangerous implications for the nature of the soul and for the eucharist.

The pursuit of original enquiry sprang from a wide variety of motives, ranging from the religious to the wholly utilitarian, that had only a limited place in the conception of their functions normally accepted in the seventeenth-century universities. The habit of research was cultivated almost entirely apart from teaching and when it came to receive organized recognition this was in institutions of a new kind, the scientific societies. Beginning as associations of men of similar interests either in universities, under great patrons or round some private figure, these societies aimed in the first place to meet the need for a means of communicating and discussing new knowledge more direct than was possible through the

---

[1] Galileo, *Opere*, ed. naz. Vol. 19 (1907), p. 323.

publication of books and through correspondence. They also met to perform experiments, but the need for endowment and apparatus for research, though expressed, was not provided for on any adequate scale before the end of the century. Like their literary predecessors on which they were modelled, the scientific societies cultivated a new kind of learning still neglected in the universities and placed the highest value on original skill.

A common pattern was for associations beginning informally to set down their customs later in formal rules governing activities and membership; later still some of these associations gave rise to officially recognized national academies. Beginning in Italy, a number of such societies passed through a transitory if active existence there during the sixteenth century. In 1603 a new society, the Accademia dei Lincei (the lynx being endowed with specially keen sight according to bestiary lore), was formed at Rome by Duke Federigo Cesi (1585–1630), a young man of eighteen, with three friends. Conceived on grandiose lines as a research institute on the model of a religious order or order of chivalry, it was reorganized in 1609 with an enlarged membership rising to over thirty and including Giambattista della Porta (c.1534–1615) and Galileo. For two decades it had an active life, supported by Cesi and meeting at his palace where there was a botanical garden, a cabinet of natural history and a library. Members studied botany and entomology; an ambitious description of plants and animals of Mexico was published; and it was in the academy that the term *microscopium* was coined for an instrument made for it by Galileo and first used for zoological investigations by another member, Francesco Stelluti (1577–1653). The academy also published Scheiner's and Galileo's letters on the sun-spots (1613) and Galileo's *Il Saggiatore* (1623). It survived a bitter quarrel that arose among the members over its continued support, encouraged especially by Galileo, of Copernican cosmology after its condemnation of 1616, but, as Cesi's death in 1630 was followed by Galileo's condemnation in 1633, the academy's activities became more and more difficult, and they ceased altogether in 1657. In the same year a new society, the Accademia del Cimento, began its short but successful life of one decade in Florence (see Vol. v in this series).

Following those in Italy, associations for scientific work were formed most actively in France, where Italian influence was most immediate. The earliest French associations grew up informally round private individuals and were kept in touch by correspondence as well as meetings. A good example of such an individual is Peiresc; Counsellor to the Parlement of Provence and in science an intelligent and well-informed dilettante, he became with Mersenne the chief link between French scientists and with others outside France in the early years of the century. The centralization of France gave prominence to Paris in intellectual as in other aspects of life and among Peiresc's correspondents were the principal men round whom the scientific life of the capital came to revolve. Intellectual circles in Paris were composed largely of men of independent means or of high professional position as lawyers, judges or counsellors of state, or doctors or clerics, who met in each others' houses to share common interests. The earliest of the private Parisian associations with scientific interests was the famous Cabinet, called first du Président de Thou, and later des frères Dupuy after the two sons of a counsellor to the Parlement of Paris who effectively organized its meetings in the Hôtel de Thou. More specifically scientific in character were the meetings held by Descartes in his lodgings about 1626. Other meetings with a rather different tone were organized by Théophraste Renaudot (1586–1653), a graduate in medicine at Montpellier, who between 1633 and 1642 arranged lectures and discussions on an inconsequential variety of topics ranging from medicine to popular morality at his Bureau d'Adresse, an organization offering an equally wide assortment of services including those of a free clinic and dispensary and an advertising agency. Renaudot's conférences are said to have attracted large crowds to the Maison du Grand Coq in the Ile de la Cité where they were held on Monday afternoons. But the most important of the early scientific associations in Paris was undoubtedly that formed by Mersenne about 1635. Educated by the Jesuits at La Flèche, Mersenne became a Minim friar and made his cell in the convent near Place Royale (now Place des Vosges) both a meeting-place for scientific discussions and experiments and, from 1620 to 1648, the centre of a vast and systematic scientific correspondence by which he maintained a flow of news of scientific discoveries and ideas between most of the leading scientists of the day.[1] His correspondents included Torricelli, Cavalieri, Descartes, Fermat, Gassendi, Desargues, Roberval, Pascal, Thomas Hobbes (1588–1679), Theodore Haak (1605–90), and many others from as far apart as Sweden, Poland, and the Levant. For Mersenne, the methods of the new science were of supreme value because they freed men's minds from error. A skilful experimenter himself, especially in acoustics, and a capable mathematician, he chose his group with discrimination to discuss problems and to perform experiments. The observations associated with Pascal concerning the void, including the famous experiment made in 1648 with a barometer on Puy-de-Dôme, arose out of the discussions in this group, at which visitors from abroad were welcomed. Descartes in Holland kept in touch with scientific news through Mersenne. In 1634, the year after Galileo's trial, Mersenne translated into French and published an early work by Galileo under the title *Les mécaniques de Galilée* and gave a summary account of his *Dialogo* and trial in *Les questions théologiques, physiques, morales et mathématiques*. After Mersenne's death in 1648 meetings of the same group

---

[1] *Correspondance du P. Marin Mersenne*, ed. C. de Waard, Vol. 1 (Paris, 1932), pp. xix–lv; edition continued from Vol. 7 (1962) by B. Rochot.

were carried on by others; but all such private associations were eclipsed by Colbert's foundation of a national Académie royale des Sciences in 1666.

Some sense of a scientific community not only in Paris but in France as a whole was created by contacts maintained between the capital and provinces. Du Thou's and Mersenne's groups especially kept in touch not only with Peiresc but also, for example, with local groups at Bordeaux and Périgord. Mersenne also kept in touch with scientific activity outside France, his relations with Italian and English scientists being especially close. One result of the exchanges of scientific correspondence that took place between Paris and London was to aid the flow of knowledge of English science and of Bacon's experimental philosophy into France, and of French mathematics and of Cartesian philosophy into England. Another was to bring English scientists into contact with the habit of forming associations, so that the group that met at Gresham College on 28 November 1660 to take the first formal step towards the founding of the Royal Society could describe their action as being 'according to the Manner in other Countryes, where there were voluntary associations of men into Academies for the advancement of various parts of learning'.[1]

The extent to which speculative proposals for a scientific institute such as those made in Bacon's *New Atlantis* (1627) or Abraham Cowley's suggestion for a philosophical college (1661) influenced the founders of the Royal Society is problematical. The event of material significance is that some of the persons present in 1660 had begun a few years before the mid-century to meet for scientific discussions and to make experiments. According to the only reports available from an eye-witness, in two accounts written long afterwards by John Wallis, a group including himself, John Wilkins (1614–72), Glisson and others began during the Civil War 'about the year 1645'[2] to hold informal weekly meetings at Gresham College or near by. In his second account Wallis suggested that the idea of the meetings may have been first proposed by Theodore Haak, a German resident in London who had some connection through Samuel Hartlib (d.1662) with Comenius' pansophic movement. But the activities at the meetings had no connection with this or any other such general scheme for human enlightenment. According to Wallis they met weekly

at a certain day and hour, under a certain Penalty, and a weekly Contribution for Charge of Experiments, with certain Rules agreed amongst us. Where (to avoid diversion to other discourses, and for some other reasons) we debarred all Discourses of Divinity, of State Affairs, and of News, (other than what concern'd our business of Philosophy) confining our selves to Philosophical Inquiries, and such as related

---

[1] D. McKie, 'The origins and foundation of the Royal Society of London', in *The Royal Society; its origins and founders*, ed. Sir H. Hartley (London, 1960), p. 1; cf. C. Webster, 'The origins of the Royal Society', in *History of Science*, ed. A. C. Crombie and M. A. Hoskin, Vol. 6 (Cambridge, 1967), pp. 106–28.

[2] John Wallis, *A defence of the Royal Society* (London, 1678), p. 7.

THE SCIENTIFIC MOVEMENT AND ITS INFLUENCE

thereunto; as Physick, Anatomy, Geometry, Astronomy, Navigation, Staticks, Mechanicks, and Natural Experiments.[1]

Haak himself in a letter written to Mersenne in 1648 mentions repeating an experiment with a tube of mercury (Torricelli's experiment) of which Mersenne had sent him news; it seems unlikely that he was referring to any other than Wallis's group. Thus it seems that from these early meetings a characteristic policy, to be continued later by the Royal Society, was adopted: to concentrate on natural science, exclude all other subjects, and perform experiments. This is not surprising when it is remembered that the meeting-place of this group was the most professional scientific institution in the country, and that professors at Gresham College were among its leading members (see Vol. v in this series).

The supreme achievement of the generation that first firmly established this new scientific philosophy, the generation of Galileo, Kepler, Bacon, Harvey and Descartes, was that instead of merely skirmishing like their predecessors within recognized conceptual frontiers or proposing programmes without precise enough specifications for their realization, they found an opening into the intelligibility of nature through which they successfully deployed a whole, systematic campaign. In essence the new 'physico-mathematical experimental learning',[2] 'the real, the mechanical, the experimental philosophy',[3] comprised three interconnected elements: a new conception of scientific research, a new conception of nature itself and hence of scientific explanation, and a new conception of the utility and power of scientific enquiry. Although considerably diversified by the content of the different sciences, in these elements the 'new philosophy' provided a common form shared widely enough to be seen as characterizing the whole scientific movement.

The distinctive new move made in scientific research was to look for the intelligibility of nature not in immediate observation but in an underlying mathematical and mechanical structure, and to seek by systematic and quantitative theoretical analysis and experimentation to discover the one actual structure of this real world. For Galileo and his contemporaries the basically Aristotelian physics still dominant at the beginning of the century was not only inaccurate but fundamentally misconceived. Their main criticisms of it were that it was explicitly qualitative and that its generalizations were too hastily formulated from immediate observation: essentially it was a classification of the immediately observed behaviour of different things, presented as manifestations of their qualitatively, irreducibly distinct 'natures' or principles of behaviour, and as such it

[1] *Ibid.* Cf. 'Dr. Wallis's Account of some Passages in his own Life', in *Peter Langtoft's Chronicle*, transcrib'd...by Thomas Hearne, Vol. I (Oxford, 1725), pp. clxi–clxii.
[2] M. Ornstein, *The rôle of scientific societies in the seventeenth century* (3rd ed. Chicago, 1938), p. 101.
[3] Robert Hooke, *Micrographia* (London, 1665), preface.

was incapable of becoming more than a mere classification. They saw in this system of explanations only an accidental provision for measurement, calculation and quantitative prediction, but these, by contrast, became the essential procedures by which nature as they conceived it must be investigated. For them, in Galileo's famous words:

Philosophy is written in this greatest book that is continuously open in front of our eyes (I mean the universe), but it cannot be understood unless one first learns to understand the language and to know the characters in which it is written. It is written in mathematical language and the characters are triangles, circles, and other geometrical figures, without which means it is impossible to understand humanly a word of it; without these, one is wandering hopelessly in a dark labyrinth . . .[1]

Once this was accepted the new physics came clearly into the light as a physics of what Galileo distinguished as the mathematical and mechanical 'primary and real properties', in contrast with Aristotle's physics of the immediately experienced 'secondary qualities'. As he concluded his discussion of what 'we call heat', the *locus classicus* of this distinction in modern literature:

I do not believe that for exciting in us tastes, smells, and sounds there are required in external bodies anything but sizes, shapes, numbers, and slow or fast movements; and I think that if ears, tongues and noses were taken away, shapes and numbers and motions would remain but not smells or tastes or sounds. These, I believe, are nothing but names, apart from the living animal, just as tickling and titillation are nothing but names if the armpits and the skin round the nose were removed.[2]

In thus establishing the methodological programme for the new physics explicitly as the search for the laws of nature as the laws of the primary properties and the processes lying behind the appearances they produced, the new scientific philosophy introduced a systematic change in the questions asked about nature and in the criteria for accepting the conclusions reached. Simply as an epistomological doctrine the mechanistic philosophy was of course not new, as Galileo and Kepler acknowledged in their different claims to be 'Platonists' and Gassendi recognized in setting out to restore the atomism of Democritus and Epicurus. The novelty of the 'new Philosophy' lay in the attempt made to use the success of quantitative mathematical and experimental analysis as the *only* criterion for accepting conclusions about the nature of things. In consequence much that was essential in the Aristotelian science of physics was not so much refuted as laid aside as answers to questions no longer thought relevant. In its place the mechanistic conception of natural laws as the stage machinery behind the spectacle of appearances implied that the discovery of a true science of nature depended upon the manipulative

---

[1] *Il Saggiatore*, question 6 (1623), in *Opere*, ed. naz. Vol. 6 (1896), p. 252.
[2] *Ibid.* question 48, p. 350; cf. A. C. Crombie, 'The primary properties and secondary qualities in Galileo Galilei's natural philosophy', in *Saggi su Galileo Galilei* (Florence, in press), *Galileo's natural philosophy: theories of science and the senses* (in press).

mathematical and experimental skills traditionally classified as mere *techne*, *ars*. These then became the essential methods of the new philosophy, which inevitably changed the model adopted for the whole universe as well as for its parts. In place of the organic model of the Aristotelian cosmos, with parts teleologically related to the whole, the universe became likened to a vast automaton. 'My aim in this', wrote Kepler (in cautiously abandoning one peculiar organic model of his own), 'is to show that the celestial machine is to be likened not to a kind of divine living being but rather to a clockwork . . . , in so far as nearly all the manifold movements are carried out by means of a single simple magnetic corporeal force, just as in a clockwork all motions come from a simple weight. Moreover I show how this physical conception is to be presented through calculation and geometry'.[1]

Actual scientific enquiry is a different activity from that of formulating scientific philosophy and method, and their influences on the course of history may differ widely, but the whole notion developed in the seventeenth century of science as a new philosophy, and not just a new technology, linked them closely together. With the exception of Bacon the chief writers on method also made important contributions to science, whether to the natural sciences like Galileo, Kepler, Descartes and Gassendi or to the social sciences and psychology like Hobbes. The logical and practical methods used for this new art of scientific enquiry were developed within inherited forms which set the initial problems both of how to proceed and of what to accept as a satisfactory conclusion. The ideal made explicit in cleanly mathematical sciences such as mechanics and astronomy and also in more experimental sciences such as optics was the 'Euclidean' form with which the Greeks had scored their greatest successes with these sciences. Kepler's *Dioptrice* (1611), Galileo's *Discorsi e dimostrazione matematiche intorno a due nuove scienze* (1638), as later Huygens' *Horologium oscillatorium* (1673) and Newton's *Principia mathematica* (1687), are only outstanding examples of scientific treatises presented (in Galileo's case within a dialogue) in this 'geometrical' form beginning with a set of 'first principles'—axioms, definitions, postulates and hypotheses—from which the experimental conclusions demonstrated are shown to follow. The problem was how to discover such principles, expressing the real causal relations between the primary properties, as satisfied the criterion that these speculations *a priori* must not conflict with experimental evidence'.[2] As the great optimist of the scientific movement, Descartes habitually wrote as if he had so far succeeded in discovering the true principles that the whole scientific programme was within sight of com-

[1] Kepler to Herwart von Hohenburg, 10 February 1605, *Gesammelte Werke*, Vol. 15, ed. M. Caspar (Munich, 1951), p. 146.
[2] Kepler to Herwart von Hohenburg, 12 July 1600, *Ges. Werke*, Vol. 14, ed. Caspar (1949), p. 130.

pletion; then, in Seth Ward's neat epitome, 'when the operations of nature shall be followed up to their staticall (and mechanicall) causes, the use of induction will cease, and syllogisme succeed in place of it'.[1] But Ward continued: 'in the interim we are to desire that men have patience not to lay aside induction before they have reason'.

Contemporary writers saw in this process of enquiry, whereby the observed world was first anatomized and then rationally reconstructed as a consequence of the principles so discovered, a definite logical sequence and structure to which Galileo and Castelli applied the name *metodo resolutivo e compositivo*, derived from sixteenth-century Pisan and Paduan logic, and Descartes (in whose method, despite his over-optimism, experiment played an essential part) applied the corresponding terms 'analysis and synthesis'. Even with subject matter not immediately open to a simple mathematical approach or to straight reduction to mechanisms, the leading sciences of the seventeenth century aimed at a similar *form* to this: idealized postulates or hypotheses with some mathematical or logical means of operating with them, whether that being postulated was the principle of inertia or Descartes' mechanistic models for optics or physiology or Harvey's hypothesis of the circulation of the blood. For contemporaries the novelty given to this form by the 'experimental philosophy' lay in the effectiveness of its clear procedures beginning with an *intellectual* dissection of a problem before one approached it experimentally. In the light of this *antecedent* theoretical dissection experimental situations could be devised, with essential factors varied one by one, in which nature could be *compelled* to answer questions not readily answered simply by observation. Bacon was only making a current view explicit when he declared that 'the secrets of nature reveal themselves more readily when tormented by art than when they go their own way'.[2]

In normal experience a science grows largely because one question leads to another, that is, through its content, rather than because some particular form of enquiry is put into operation. Nevertheless both the form and the conception of nature assumed in an enquiry establish general objectives that are effective especially in determining the criteria accepted for a satisfactory conclusion to the enquiry and for satisfactory scientific explanation. The common objective of those who explicitly discussed scientific method in the early seventeenth century, notably Bacon, Galileo and Descartes, was to show how to establish undeniable causal relationships between phenomena, the causes themselves being assumed to lie in the underlying abstract structure of the primary properties. Bacon made an original and very important contribution to the logic of such an enquiry by his systematic exposition of his method of 'exclusion' by negative instances in the *Novum organum* (1620), a name given to the

---

[1] Seth Ward, *Vindiciae academiarum* (Oxford, 1654), p. 25.
[2] *Novum organum*, I. 98.

work as an explicit challenge to Aristotle. Bacon's 'true and legitimate' induction began by collecting instances of a phenomenon (in his example heat) and classifying them into three tables which he called respectively tables of 'Essence and Presence', of 'Deviation or Absence in Proximity', and of 'Degrees or Comparison'. Induction consisted in the inspection of the tables and the rejection of a causal connection between phenomena which were not always present or absent together and did not vary concomitantly. In his example Bacon went on to show that motion 'is as the genus of which heat is the species', meaning that 'heat itself, or the essence of heat, is motion and nothing else',[1] a conclusion in keeping with the mechanical philosophy but which Bacon did not know how to develop scientifically. In the more mathematically tractable sciences the aim coming into focus, that correlations between phenomena should be expressed quantitatively as relations of functional dependence between cause and effect, at once made the discovery of concomitant variations—the subject of Bacon's third table—the essential criterion of a causal relationship. Thus, Galileo wrote, 'whenever a fixed and constant alteration is seen in the effect, there must be a fixed and constant alteration in the cause'.[2] These criteria for establishing causal connections brought into play all the characteristic practices that came to be part of experimental enquiry, especially the use of controls to isolate factors and, where the subject permitted, the measurement of concomitant changes in isolated factors varied one by one.

The contribution made by Descartes to the forms of enquiry and explanation used in seventeenth-century science was something different from that of either Bacon or Galileo. Descartes made his impact upon his contemporaries and established his lasting influence by publishing in the *Principia philosophiae* (1644) and other works something never attempted before or afterwards, a *complete* reduction (enriched by some genuine discoveries) of all forms of physical change to a single form, that of matter in motion. The basis of Descartes' reduction was his division of the created world into two mutually exclusive and collectively exhaustive essences or 'simple natures', extension and thought, and his conviction that his arguments to this conclusion were guaranteed by the perfection of God who would not deceive true reason. Since the whole world of matter was nothing but extension, with motion as its mode, existing in various stages of complexity, the laws of nature became for Descartes nothing more than the laws of motion. 'I have described', he wrote, 'the whole visible world as if it were simply a machine in which there was nothing to consider but the shape and movements [of its parts]'.[3]

[1] *Novum organum*, II. 20.   [2] *Dialogo*, IV, in *Opere*, ed. naz. Vol. 7, p. 471.
[3] *Principia philosophiae*, IV. 188, in *Oeuvres*, ed. C. Adam and P. Tannery, Vol. 8 (1) (Paris, 1905), p. 315 (Latin); Vol. 9 (2) (1904), p. 310 (French): the passage in square brackets occurs only in the French version (1647).

Descartes criticized Harvey as well as Galileo for not making this reduction and so for failing to show why things happened as well as how. It was a programme that led him into his worst mistakes, but also into reversing a normal Greek attitude to nature inherited in Aristotelian thought and so into making his most original contributions to methods of scientific discovery. In Aristotelian thought an absolute ontological distinction was made between artificial and natural bodies, whether naturally generated substances or living organisms, so that in principle no humanly constructed model could throw any real light on the nature of natural things. But Descartes' universal mechanism put him into a position to declare that there was no difference between machines and natural bodies except in the size of their parts.

And certainly there are no rules in mechanics that do not hold also in physics, of which mechanics forms a part or species, [so that all artificial things are at the same time natural]: for it is not less natural for a clock, made of these or those wheels, to indicate the hours, than for a tree which has sprung from this or that seed to produce a particular fruit. Accordingly, just as those who apply themselves to the consideration of automata, when they know the use of some machine and see some of its parts, easily infer from these the manner in which others which they have not seen are made, so, from the perceptible effects and parts of natural bodies, I have endeavoured to find out what are their imperceptible causes and parts.[1]

By his innovation of asserting the *identity* of the synthesized artificial construction with the natural product and of making this identification an instrument of scientific research, Descartes made himself the first great modern master of the hypothetical model. Models and analogies had been commonly used in science since Greek times. Descartes' reduction enabled him to make the fundamentally new move of making the principles of the mechanistic model the *only* principles operating in nature, thus bringing the objectives of the engineer into the search for the nature of things and throwing the entire world of matter open to the same form of scientific inquiry and explanation. The value of the Cartesian model, like that of any other theory advanced in anticipation of factual knowledge, was to raise questions of which otherwise no one would have thought, and the main issue, in any historical judgement of Descartes' role in the scientific movement, is not whether his conclusions were true but whether his questions were fruitful. In some sciences, especially in optics and physiology, they undoubtedly were.

The 'new philosophy' of Galileo and Kepler, Bacon and Descartes liberated the science of nature from old bonds, from the ontology of the qualitatively irreducible Aristotelian 'natures' and the perfection of circular motion, and brought about a submission to fact, however untidy,

[1] *Ibid.* IV. 203, in *Oeuvres*, Vol. 8(1), p. 326; Vol. 9 (2), pp. 321–2: the passage in square brackets occurs only in the French version.

and eventually a greater scruple over actual, observational as distinct from theoretical, mathematical accuracy. In consequence it brought about an increasing emphasis on precision, both in calculation and in closer observation and measurement, in the last augmenting the senses by 'a supplying of their infirmities with *Instruments*, and, as it were, the adding of *artificial Organs* to the natural'.[1] Indeed, if the conceptual organization of the new philosophy was to be made effective in scientific enquiry, adequate tools, both mathematical and observational, were an absolute necessity.

In this the task of the first half of the century was to reveal the power latent in such tools rather than to apply the tools to specific problems. Only after 1650 were the traditional scientific instruments and apparatus supplanted by inventions of the first half of the century. Especially where mass production was required it took time for the instrument makers to adapt themselves to the new techniques; and where the instruments were for practical use, in navigation, cartography, or chemistry, it took time for the practitioners to learn their use. Meanwhile aids to the senses in piercing the veil of nature had to be not only invented but also constructed by the scientists themselves, and their immediate impact was lessened by their rarity and by imperfections in their design. A form of compound microscope was in use about 1610 and Stelluti published a fine illustration of the structure of the bee in 1625, but it was not until Hooke's *Micrographia* (1665) that the new worlds to be discovered with this instrument were appreciated. Meanwhile the simple microscope in fact remained the more precise scientific tool, as Leeuwenhoek was to show. An air thermometer was devised by Galileo by 1603, and its use in medicine described by Santorio in 1612, but variations in air pressure combined with loss from evaporation to make these instruments unreliable, and it was many years before the thermometer became a serious scientific tool. The barometer, simplest to construct of all the tools, was significant for its part in the development of the theory of atmospheric pressure in the 1640s rather than as a source of observations. The isochronism of the pendulum had been established by Galileo. By early 1634 Mersenne demonstrated that its frequency was inversely proportional to the square root of its length,[2] and he and Riccioli used it to measure time in their experiments, but it was first incorporated into a mechanical clock by Christiaan Huygens (1629–95) about 1656.

The telescope, similarly, became a serious scientific tool only with the

---

[1] Hooke, *Micrographia*, preface.

[2] Mersenne, *Correspondance*, ed. de Waard, Vol. 4 (1955), pp. 81–2, 444–55; *Harmonicorum libri*, II, props. XXVI–XXIX (Paris, 1636), *Harmonie universelle...*, 'Traité des instrumens', I, prop. XX (Paris, 1636–7); A. C. Crombie, 'Mathematics, music and medical science', *Proceedings of the Twelfth International Congress of the History of Science; Paris, 1968* (Paris, in press) and forthcoming studies of Galileo and Mersenne; A. Koyré, *Metaphysics and measurement* (London, 1968), pp. 89–117.

work of John Flamsteed and others in the last decades of the century. But the brilliance with which Galileo exploited his early observations made the telescope the symbol of this movement towards 'artificial organs'. 'The present observations strip the decrees of former writers of authority,' he wrote, 'who if they had seen them, would have decided differently.'[1] It had been in 1609 that word had reached him from Holland that combinations of lenses had been used to make distant objects seem near, and he had needed only ten months to devise and construct his own telescopes, apply them to the stars, and announce his dramatic discoveries to a startled world. The Moon, he claimed in *Sidereus nuncius*[2], was not 'robed in a smooth and polished surface' but had mountains whose height he was actually able to measure; the Milky Way was composed of innumerable tiny stars; so-called 'nebulous' stars were similarly formed; and, most striking of all, the planet Jupiter, like the Earth on the Copernican view, had satellite moons, four in all. Similar observations were made in England during 1609 and 1610 by Thomas Harriot (1560–1621).[3]

At first these discoveries, and Galileo's announcement of spots on the surface of the Sun and of the Moon-like phases of Venus which followed in 1612, were widely doubted. How could mere combinations of lenses lead to truths unknown since the world began, especially as curved glass had been since Antiquity the means of producing illusions? But Galileo's claims aroused immediate and widespread interest and as they were confirmed by other astronomers it was realized how much new tools might do towards enlarging man's horizons, even though it was to be many years before telescopes were manufactured in quantity. Galileo himself hoped that eclipses of the satellites of Jupiter, being frequent, could be used to solve the problem of the determination of longitude at sea: tables would supply the times of these eclipses for a standard longitude. For this purpose a table for the first satellite was published annually from 1690 onwards, but even at this late date telescopes could be not adapted for use at sea, the long refractors proving unsteady and the specula of reflectors tarnishing rapidly.

New mathematical tools likewise proved their power only in the second half of the century, above all in Newton's *Principia* (1687). Only then was there developed a physics of broad application and mathematical in fact, not merely in intention as had been the case with Descartes' cosmology. Descartes himself, even when claiming to have reduced science to mathematics, had practised mathematics mainly for its intrinsic interest, and the same was true of his leading contemporaries. The great

[1] Third letter about the sun-spots (1612), in *Opere*, ed. naz. Vol. 5 (1895), p. 201.
[2] In *ibid*. Vol. 3 (1892), p. 59.
[3] S. P. Rigaud, *Supplement to Dr. Bradley's miscellaneous works: with an account of Harriot's astronomical papers* (Oxford, 1833), pp. 17–70; see the two papers by R. C. H. Tanner and J. V. Pepper, 'The study of Thomas Harriot's manuscripts', *History of science*, ed. A. C. Crombie and M. A. Hoskin, Vol. 6 (1967), pp. 1–40.

sixteenth-century printed editions of Archimedes, Apollonius, Hero and Pappus suggested problems and techniques some of which had originated in the context of physics and were later to prove of immense value in that field, but in the early seventeenth century these were studied for their own sake and with little reference to the development of science and still less to that of technology.

Logarithms provided the main exception. Here the stimulus came from the need to handle long computations in theoretical astronomy, and logarithms were frequently discussed in the context of trigonometry and spherical geometry. Their invention, by Bürgi and by Napier,[1] who published the first tables in 1614, was equivalent to the addition of many years to the life of an astronomer. Among those who published tables soon afterwards were Briggs and Edmund Gunter (1581–1626) of Gresham College, and Kepler; the popularity of these tables greatly accelerated the acceptance of Arabic numerals. The slide-rule, which is based on the same principle as logarithms, was developed gradually during the century from instruments devised by Gunter and Oughtred, and the nautical interests of the Gresham circle also led to the invention of mathematical instruments for use in navigation, although observations at sea were still too crude to warrant the use of sophisticated mathematical techniques. It was some time before either logarithms or the slide-rule came into general use, but meanwhile the tedium of long calculations led to the invention of various other devices, ranging from the elementary 'bones' of Napier to the cumbersome calculating machines of Pascal and Leibniz.

Logarithms aside, mathematicians worked at problems suggested by the Greek works or by the more arithmetical and algebraic tradition inherited from Arabic authors. Infinitesimals were studied in the context of area and centre-of-gravity problems first of all in Italy, notably by Cavalieri and Torricelli, and later in northern Europe by Fermat and Roberval and by the Belgian Jesuit mathematician Grégoire de Saint Vincent (1584–1667). The study of moving bodies also required the use of infinitesimals, for example in Kepler's derivation of his first two laws of planetary motion and in Galileo's treatment of concepts such as instantaneous velocity ultimately based on theoretical treatises written in fourteenth-century Oxford.

Analytical geometry was created by Fermat, who was stimulated by Pappus' account of a lost work of Apollonius, and by Descartes, whom a correspondent interested in a famous problem discussed by Pappus. Both men developed methods of determining tangents to curves, although it was not until the time of Newton that the close link between this problem and that of areas was appreciated. Fermat's work, often done at odd moments, was known to his contemporaries chiefly by report. Descartes

---

[1] *Mirifici logarithmorum canonis descriptio* (Edinburgh, 1614).

published his *Géométrie* in 1637 as the third essay illustrating his method of discovery, but his presentation was intentionally obscure and the originality of his thought in both algebra and geometry was revealed only through the efforts of later commentators. Less fortunate was the Lyonnaise architect and engineer Gérard Desargues. His projective geometry, although extended further by the precocious Blaise Pascal, went unnoticed in his controversy with Parisian artists and architects. Apart from Descartes, the principal contributors to algebra were Harriot and Oughtred, although an influential legacy from the sixteenth century was contained in the 1646 edition of the works of François Viète (1540–1603).

The 'new philosophy' found expression and justification in specific scientific achievements. The unshakable confidence of its adherents stemmed from its success in reorganizing three large areas of natural enquiry, each of which yielded a developed system of thought. The first of these areas was that of cosmology and the science of motion. Traditionally, the detailed study of the heavens concentrated on mathematical descriptions of the planetary motions rather than on their causes. Terrestrial physics, on the other hand, was concerned with the causes of movement; and since the world formed a cosmos analogous to a living body, particular motions were referred to this general pattern: natural motion brought an object closer to its place in the scheme of things, while violent motion imposed from without had the reverse effect.

The destruction of this outlook and its replacement by a new view of nature was mainly the work of three men, Galileo, Kepler and Descartes. Galileo laid the foundations of his contributions to physics early in his career, when he was professor of mathematics first at Pisa and then at Padua, but his main publications date from 1610, when he became chief philosopher and mathematician to the grand duke of Tuscany. His best-known work, which led to his condemnation and house arrest, bears the misleading title of *Dialogue on the two great world systems, the Ptolemaic and Copernican* (1632). While a young man, Galileo had been converted to the Copernican view that the Earth moves round the Sun, and he realized that the need was for a new physics that would explain why such a motion was imperceptible to us. It must be change of motion, rather than motion itself, that required a cause; for then a passenger on the moving Earth would be as unconscious of its steady motion as was a sailor on a calm day. But to transform the traditional view of motion demanded the creation of a new world system to replace the cosmos, and Galileo appreciated that such a fundamental change in outlook could not be forced on readers by particular experiments or observations. The *Dialogue*, therefore, was mainly an informal initiation into a new philosophy of nature in which motions no longer required a continuously acting cause. It is significant that for Galileo the world was still finite, so that indefinitely extended straight-line motion—the inertial motion of Newtonian physics—was automatically excluded. In conformity with this view of the world the motions that persisted (under ideal conditions) were circular: a spinning top, or a ball rolling on a smooth surface curving with the curvature of the Earth. Galileo failed to go one stage further and explain the movement of the ball as the result of a force restraining it from moving away from the Earth along a tangent line: for him heaviness remained an intrinsic property of matter, leading him to retain privileged places in the world, such as the centre of the Earth, about which bodies turned. Against this Descartes in *Le Monde* (published posthumously in 1664) and *Principia philosophiae* explained heaviness as a mere consequence of the motion of matter. Arguing that it followed from God's immutability that a body would persist in the state in which it was at any instant of time unless acted on by an external cause, and that only motion in a straight line existed at an instant, he concluded that it was this motion that would persist. This conception of motion was intimately associated with and led naturally to Descartes' view of space as infinite and without privileged places or directions, representing the final and complete break with the cosmos and its replacement by the universe of classical geometry.

But Galileo's conception of large-scale inertial motion as curved did not affect the discussion of free fall and the path of projectiles which he published in 1638. His ideas on this subject had been maturing for some forty years, and his law of free fall had already been announced in the *Dialogue*; published when its author had become blind, the *Discourses on two new sciences* was to be his last and greatest work. 'The suprahuman Archimedes', as Galileo described him,[1] had shown how to idealize statical problems in such a way that they were mathematically tractable while still relevant to the real world, and his methods had recently been applied to other questions in statics by Stevin, particularly to the equilibrium conditions of bodies on an inclined plane. A theory of moving bodies, on the other hand, had been developed by fourteenth-century writers, but although Galileo was to draw on their analyses and concepts, they had not succeeded in relating their results to the real world. It was Galileo who extended the Archimedean technique to the study of how projectiles move. Basing himself in the *Discourses* on the belief that nature acted in simple ways, he first demonstrated that under ideal conditions velocity in free fall was proportional to the time elapsed. This relation he transformed by mathematical argument into one between distance, which he could measure, and time; then by viewing free fall as a special case of rolling motion down an inclined plane, he arrived at a relationship between distance and relatively large intervals of time, which he could also measure. Finally he confirmed this relationship by experiments,

---

[1] *De motu*, in *Opere*, ed. naz. Vol. I (1890), p. 300.

although his account of their perfect success does not carry complete conviction.

For Galileo motions were no longer processes, as with Aristotle, that could interfere with each other. They might therefore be combined mathematically, and Galileo showed how uniform motion in a horizontal direction combined with accelerated motion in the vertical to give a parabolic path for projectiles, and proved many other similar theorems. The elementary character of his results is no index to the great importance of his book. He wrote himself :'what I think is more important, a passage and entrance will be opened to a most ample and excellent science, of which these our labours will be elements; into the more hidden recesses of which science more perspicacious minds than mine will penetrate'.[1]

By implying in the *Dialogue* that only two world systems deserved consideration, Galileo had deliberately closed his eyes to the existence of a third system which two decades before had replaced the Ptolemaic as the rallying point for those who believed the Earth to be at the centre. This was the one developed after 1584 by the great Danish observer Tycho Brahe. In it the relative motions of the planets were basically the same as for Copernicus; but it was the Earth that was absolutely at rest. This system retained many of the advantages of the Copernican while avoiding the scandal of a moving Earth. Tycho was only one of a number of astronomers who independently adopted similar systems, some allowing the Earth to spin daily and others having it wholly at rest; as late as 1625 the Oxford geographer Nathanael Carpenter (1589–1628)[2] was claiming the invention for himself. Unfortunately Galileo's strongest anti-Ptolemaic arguments, in particular the Moon-like phases of Venus, could be interpreted as support either for Copernicus or for Tycho. So, as he could not disprove Tycho, he sought to discredit him by presenting his system as a compromise unworthy of serious consideration, although after the condemnation of Copernicanism in 1616 Jesuit astronomers had adopted the Tychonic system to a man, and it was to command a considerable body of outside support until well into the second half of the century.

The most powerful arguments in favour of the heliocentric view were contained in Kepler's *Astronomia nova* [*New astronomy studied through causes, or celestial physics*, 1609]. In this epoch-making work Kepler finally broke with the age-old approach to planetary motions in terms of circles, by stating that the planets in fact moved in ellipses with the Sun at one focus—one single curve sufficing for each planet. His work was widely discussed among mathematical astronomers, including in England Harriot and Horrox and their respective friends, although it was ignored

---

[1] *Discorsi...*, III, in *ibid*. Vol. 8 (1898), p. 190. See the important critical edition of the *Discorsi* with extensive historical notes by A. Carugo and L. Geymonat (Turin, 1958).
[2] *Geography* (Oxford, 1625), p. 111.

by men like Galileo and Descartes who had no patience for the intricate calculations which Kepler delighted to inflict on his readers. But even more important than his results were the physical considerations that had guided him. The causes traditionally studied in terrestrial physics were now applied to the planets; and the world was to be thought of not as an organism, a cosmos, but as a machine actuated by a force residing in the Sun.

As so often with the products of a period of transition, the *Astronomia nova* was antiquated as well as prophetic. It taught that the Sun's force was required continually to maintain the planets in motion, for without it they would, in Aristotelian fashion, come to a halt. With Kepler's physics quickly superseded in this important particular, and with general uncertainty as to whether his laws of planetary motion were exact or mere approximations, planetary astronomy entered on a period of indecision which was resolved only in 1687 when Newton showed that all three Keplerian laws were consequences of his gravitational attraction.

If Descartes was unequal to the detailed study of planetary motion, he did give in his *Principia philosophiae* magisterial expression to the mathematical and mechanical vision of the world. The distribution of motion and the transference of motion, under laws 'derived not from the prejudices of the senses, but from the light of reason',[1] were to provide a complete account of the physical world, at least in so far as this did not depend upon the particular way in which God had chosen to distribute motion at the moment of Creation. Irrespective of this choice one could assert, by analogy with disturbances in pools of water, that in time matter must arrange itself in whirlpools or vortices, of which the solar system was an example; and one could plausibly explain many detailed properties of bodies such as the Earth which were carried round in these whirlpools. But for a discussion of the properties of an individual whirlpool it was necessary to abandon the deductive method and instead make hypotheses and test them by experiment.

The Cartesian synthesis was doomed to eventual failure because although mathematical in principle, in practice it had to be developed by verbal, non-mathematical discussion which could too easily be accommodated to almost any facts. The deductive approach, so powerful a tool when used in suitable circumstances and with discretion as in the hands of Galileo, was now employed without discrimination: even Descartes' laws of motion proved to be not merely false but mutually contradictory. And within his own lifetime his disciples had begun to gloss over the metaphysical basis to his physics which for him was fundamental. Yet his work with its serenely confident exposition of the mechanical philosophy marks the watershed between the anti-Aristotelian polemics of Galileo's writings and the positive application of the new approach characteristic

[1] *Princ. philos.*, III. I.

of science in the second half of the century. To the educated layman especially he offered for a wide range of phenomena explanations at last shorn of all mystery: gone for ever were the 'occult' forms and qualities of the Aristotelians. Other writers gave expression to the power of explanations through matter in motion: in particular Gassendi's Christianized version of Epicurean atomism provided for many a refreshing alternative to the cramping rigidity of Cartesianism. But it was Descartes who both systematized the mechanical philosophy and applied it plausibly on a massive scale to detailed problems taken from fields as far apart as cosmology and physiology.

The second large area of natural enquiry to be reorganized by the new philosophy was the experimental investigation of the mode of production of a series of inanimate physical phenomena within this range of contemporary interests. Although the new philosophy was mechanical in conception, paradoxically the actual science of mechanics depended too heavily on theoretical rather than experimental developments to be the exemplar for the mathematical and experimental method that exploited the power of the conception. This role was played rather by optics, which since Greek times had been the most advanced of the terrestrial sciences in combining experiment with mathematics. A new impetus came from Galileo's challenge to accepted ideas on the basis of evidence derived from a combination of lenses. Even Kepler, who had done so much to clarify the ancient confusion between the physics, physiology and psychology of vision (see below), seems to have hesitated before accepting the existence of satellites of Jupiter, but it was not long before the triumph of Galileo's primitive telescopes brought urgency to the study of lenses and in particular the law of refraction. Within a matter of months Kepler in his *Dioptrice* (1611) described an experimental study of refraction, and in spite of only partial success he was able to go on to explain many of the phenomena associated with lenses. He proposed an important improvement in the construction of the telescope which was quickly adopted.

The correct law, that the sines of the angles of incidence and of refraction are in a constant ratio depending on the media concerned, had been discovered about 1601 by Harriott in the course of a fundamental mathematical and experimental study of refraction carried out between 1597 and 1605.[1] Equipped with this law he made the first major advance since the

---

[1] J. Lohne, 'Thomas Harriott (1560–1621): the Tycho Brahe of optics', *Centaurus*, Vol. 6 (1959), pp. 113–21, 'The fair fame of Thomas Harriott', *ibid.* Vol. 8 (1963), pp. 69–84, 'Zur Geschichte des Brechungsgesetzes', *Sudhoffs Archiv für Geschichte der Medizin und der Naturwissenschaften*, Vol. 47 (1963), pp. 152–72, 'Regenbogen und Brechzahl', *ibid.* Vol. 49 (1965), pp. 401–15; cf. J. W. Shirley, 'An early experimental determination of Snell's law', *American Journal of Physics*, Vol. 19 (1951), pp. 507–8; Rigaud, *Supplement to Dr. Bradley's ...works*, p. 41.

fourteenth century by determining mathematically the behaviour of rays of sunlight in passing through globes of water to form a rainbow, and by measuring the dispersion into different colours of sunlight passed through a glass prism, and in water and other liquids. Neither Harriot nor Snell, who also arrived at the sine law of refraction probably not long before his death in 1626, published their results. Whether Descartes knew of their work is uncertain, although the physical derivation he gave in *La Dioptrique*, published in 1637 in illustration of his *Discours de la méthode*, is not very convincing. Fermat, in fact, while accepting Descartes' formulation of the law, later gave quite another physical derivation of it. In *Les Météores*, another essay appended to the *Discours*, Descartes like Harriot used the law to give a quantitative analysis of the formation of a rainbow and of the dispersion of colours, but he added an important physical explanation relating colour to a periodic speed, that of rotation of the corpuscles assumed in his theory of light. Some years later Johann Marcus Marci of Kronland (1595–1667), already the author of an original work on motion and the pendulum, published in Prague (1648) the further discovery that the colours formed by a prism passed unaltered through a second prism.

Another field of physics in which experiment combined with conceptual developments to open up vast new possibilities was pneumatics. In the *Discourses on two new sciences* Galileo mentioned what must have been common knowledge to those whose task it was to pump water out of mines, that there is a limit to the height through which water can be raised by suction. Isaac Beeckman (1588–1637) and Giovanni Battista Baliani (1582–1660) had attributed this phenomenon to the weight of the atmosphere, but it was Torricelli who hit upon the idea of experimenting with the heavier and more compact fluid mercury. In a letter written in 1644 Torricelli described what was to become a famous experiment, in which he filled a long tube with mercury, placed a finger over the open end and inverted the tube so that its mouth was submerged in a dish of mercury. When he removed his finger the level of mercury in the tube fell to about thirty inches, leaving what became known as the Torricellian vacuum. Torricelli explained his results by saying 'We live submerged at the bottom of an ocean of the element air, which by unquestioned experiments is known to have weight',[1] and he drew the conclusion that variations in the height of the mercury reflected variations in the air pressure. To Pascal, who learned of Torricelli's work from Mersenne, this suggested a simple but striking test for the hypothesis: the air pressure, and therefore the height of the mercury, should be less at the peak of a mountain than at its foot. In 1648 the experiment was successfully carried out

[1] Evangelista Torricelli, *Opere*, ed. G. Loria and G. Vassura, Vol. 3 (Faenza, 1919), p. 187; see Galileo, *Discorsi*, ed. Carugo and Geymonat, pp. 616–22; C. de Waard, *L'expérience barometrique* (Thouars, 1936) and W. E. K. Middleton, *The history of the barometer* (Baltimore, 1964).

on the Puy-de-Dôme by Florin Périer. Meanwhile von Guericke was developing at Magdeburg apparatus for withdrawing the air imprisoned between two tightly fitting hemispheres, and in 1654 he publicly demonstrated the powerful force which then united the two hemispheres: teams of horses could not separate them. These striking experiments drew attention to the unexpected opportunities for studying physical and physiological behaviour in the absence of air. The air pump became the first complex machine in laboratory use, it accustomed scientists to working with controlled and wholly artificial conditions, and the wealth of new information that resulted was proof again of the value of apparatus and instruments in extending the range of available evidence.

A number of problems in acoustics also began to give way when attacked by a combination of mathematics and experiment. Following the sixteenth-century work of Girolamo Fracastoro, Giovanni Battista Benedetti and Galileo's father Vincenzo Galilei, between 1614 and 1634 Beeckman, Descartes and Mersenne finally established the fundamental proposition that pitch is proportional to frequency of vibration and the laws relating pitch to the length, tension and specific gravity of vibrating strings and to similar quantities in pipes and percussion instruments, and so were able to give physical explanations of resonance, consonance and dissonance.[1] Mersenne published these results as well as further original work, including the law relating the frequency to the length of a pendulum and its application to the measurement of time, in his systematic treatises *Harmonicorum libri* (1636) and *Harmonie universelle, contenant la théorie et la pratique de la musique* (1636–7). In these and later works he also pioneered the scientific study of overtones, the measurement of the speed of sound which he showed to be independent of pitch and loudness, and the investigation of the medium of sound. He established that the intensity of sound varied, like that of light, inversely with the square of the distance from the source. Galileo published some similar results relating to vibrating strings and the pendulum in the *Discourses on two new sciences* (1638), and it was his discussion in this work of the vacuum in a suction pump that stimulated the experiments begun by Gasparo Berti probably shortly before 1642, and completed by Guericke and Robert Boyle, demonstrating conclusively that the medium of sound in the atmosphere is air.

In these fields of physical science, application of the mathematical and experimental method to problems interpreted through the mechanical philosophy proved immediately successful; elsewhere results were less fortunate. Magnetism, for example, had been the subject of an intensive investigation by William Gilbert (1540–1603), whose *De magnete* was

[1] C. V. Palisca, 'Scientific empiricism in musical thought', in *Seventeenth century science and the arts*, ed. H. H. Rhys (Princeton, 1961); Crombie, 'Mathematics, music and medical science' and forthcoming studies of Galileo and Mersenne.

published in 1600, and this was followed by other notable works such as the *Philosophica magnetica* (1629) of the Jesuit Niccolo Cabeo (1586–1650) and the monumental *Magnes* (1641) of another Jesuit Athanasius Kircher (1601–80). But although magnetic phenomena were becoming familiar, the nature of magnetism remained a profound mystery. It was Descartes[1] who removed much of the wonder surrounding it by giving a purely mechanical account of its action, but his explanation failed to achieve quantitative predictive power. The study of electricity, meanwhile, made little progress because methods of generating electricity were lacking and so there was limited evidence on which to theorize.

Chemistry, on the other hand, was embarrassed for the opposite reason. Thousands of years of metallurgical practice and alchemical theory and experiment had amassed a great variety of empirical knowledge, and to the normal human urge to understand were added the pressing require-ments of the physician, the druggist, the dyeworker, and many others. It was a daunting prospect, in the face of which many took refuge in hope-lessly inadequate theories which they made little attempt to support by experiment except by way of brief illustration. Interest still centred on reactions on heating. Apparatus was crude and fragile, and it was difficult both to maintain an adequate temperature and to prevent the heated vessels from shattering. Substances were seldom unadulterated, and those chiefly studied were organic and therefore complex. Under such condi-tions the interplay of mathematics and experiment would clearly have been impossible even if there had been an agreed interpretative scheme such as the mechanical philosophy, and the developments of lasting value that occurred were mainly at the levels of technique and natural history. Thus the German iatrochemist Glauber devised a method of preparing 'Glauber's salt', and obtained sal ammoniac from urine, common salt, soot and bulls' blood.

Chemical and alchemical theory meanwhile was divided between various schools, with the Aristotelian four elements and the three prin-ciples of Paracelsus predominant. At this level the most original con-tribution came from van Helmont, who taught that water was the basis of all substances. Air was for him chemically inert, but he obtained various gases which he regarded as air with impurities. By contrast some chemists, notably Daniel Sennert (1572–1637) and Joachim Jung, were already beginning to explain chemical reactions in terms of the motions of atoms, and in this they foreshadowed the work of Robert Boyle (1627–91) who was to bring chemical theory within the mechanical philosophy and so make chemistry a respected part of physics.

The third large field of natural philosophy in which the programmes of experimental and of mechanistic analysis combined to produce a radically

---

[1] *Princ. philos.*, IV. 144 ff.

new system of thought in this period was that defined by Galileo's phrase 'the animate and sensitive body'.[1] The philosophical assumption that the whole physical world, including living bodies, operated as a system of mechanics defined the problem as that of discovering the particular mechanisms concerned. Achievement was limited by the tools of research available: macroscopic anatomy, elementary knowledge of mechanics, geometrical optics and some other physical sciences, some elementary chemistry, simple instruments such as the scalpel and ligature, the lens, and the balance. In addition, the comparative method was revealed as a powerful instrument of research, both into the mechanisms of the body and into the rational ordering of living nature as a whole.

The outstanding physiological achievement of the period was the demonstration of the circulation of the blood by Harvey. Educated in medicine at Padua, Harvey used its methods. He has studied there for five years under the great comparative anatomist and embryologist Fabrizio, Galileo's colleague and personal physician and author of the first clear description of valves in the veins. Another of Galileo's colleagues, Santorio, systematically introduced quantitative methods into medicine, designing instruments to measure temperature and pulse-rate; in his *De medicina statica* (1614) he described a famous experiment in which he spent several days on a large balance weighing food and excrement in order to determine the material exchanges of the body. But it was Harvey who succeeded in using these methods to bring about a revolution in theory, first in the specific theory of the motion of the blood and then, because of the role of the blood in existing physiological systems, in physiological theory as a whole.

The Galenic physiology with which Harvey had to contend was based on the division of the body into three great independent systems: those of the veins, the arteries, and the (hollow) nerves. Venous blood carrying 'natural spirit' was supposed to be manufactured in the liver and to flow out in the veins from that organ, carrying nutriment to the whole body. Some of this blood entered the right side of the heart, whence, as it was shown in the sixteenth century, it went to the lungs and so to the left side of the heart. In the left ventricle this venous blood was endowed by the 'air' from the lungs with 'vital spirit' (the principle of life manifested as innate heat) and converted into arterial blood, which the arteries then distributed throughout the body. Some of this again was converted in the brain into 'animal spirit', the principle of sensation and voluntary movement which operated through the hollow nerves.

According to his own statement and the evidence of his manuscript notes for his lectures at the Royal College of Physicians, Harvey's doubts about the Galenic system for the blood and realization of its circulation developed in stages from over nine years before writing his *De motu*

[1] *Il Saggiatore*, question 48, in *Opere*, ed. naz. Vol. 6, pp. 348, 351.

cordis (1628).[1] In this work he set out the full argument, an elegant essay in fact if not in name in the Paduan logic of 'resolution and composition', establishing the essential propositions of his new theory. Galen had had an accurate knowledge of the anatomy of the heart and of the course of the blood through it as determined by its valves. But he thought that it was when the heart expanded that the arterial blood entered the aorta and the pulse occurred. Harvey showed that the heart pushed the blood out into the arteries when its *muscle contracted*, its structure allowing a flow through it in only one direction; later he compared it to a kind of force-pump. He showed by means of ligatures, puncturing of appropriate vessels, and observations on a variety of animals and embryos, that the blood could flow through the body also in only one direction, to the heart through the veins, whose valves prevented any return flow, and then out through the arteries. He calculated that the heart pumped through itself in an hour an amount of blood weighing more than the whole body. This amount could not be continuously manufactured in the liver, as the Galenic theory would have to suppose, and this led to the conclusion that the veins and arteries formed a *single* system through which the blood was propelled in a circle by the beat of the heart's muscle.

Apart from a lens with which he observed the flow of blood through a transparent shrimp and other small animals, Harvey used techniques that were familiar to Galen. His triumph was a triumph of thought and above all of the comparative as well as the quantitative methods. Thus he likened the practice of anatomists who based general conclusions on the examination only of the dead human body to 'those who, seeing the manner of Government in one Commonwealth, frame Politicks, or they who, knowing the nature of one piece of land, believe that they understand agriculture'[2]. By his comparative studies he was able to see the human (and mammalian) blood system as a special case within a general theory that included within its scope all the particular circulatory systems of different animals, with and without lungs and with and without red blood, and of embryos as well as adults. Gradually accepted by the younger generation in spite of opposition from the professional establishment, especially in the medical faculty in Paris, his new system put an end to Galen's general physiology and immediately raised a whole new range of physiological questions about the functions of the blood and of the lungs, liver and other organs. But perhaps his greatest contribution to future

---

[1] *The anatomical lectures: Prelectiones anatomie universalis, de musculis*, ed., with an intro., trans. and notes, by G. Whitteridge (Edinburgh and London, 1964), pp. xxv–xxix, xxxvii–li; cf. W. Pagel, *William Harvey's biological ideas* (Basel and N.Y., 1967); C. Webster, 'William Harvey's conception of the heart as a pump', *Bull. Hist. Med.*, Vol. 39 (1965), pp. 508–17.

[2] Harvey, *De motu cordis*, Chapter 6; earliest English translation, London, 1653. Descartes in his *Traité de l'homme* (1633; published posthumously in Latin, 1662, French, 1664) was one of the first to accept Harvey's theory of the circulation, but he held that the heart propelled the blood not by its muscular contraction but by heating it to vaporization so that it expanded.

biological thought was the example he gave of comparative experimental physiology.

As a study in intellectual behaviour, *De motu cordis* is a model of the intelligent control of ideas by experimental analysis, its author refusing to go beyond the organic structures he could see. Some of his contemporaries, viewing the operations of living things in the light of far more speculative schemes than his restrained Aristotelianism with its emphasis on the primacy of the heart, left their mark on the programme of enquiry by aiming to discover the more fundamental processes behind the visible. Each alternative scheme tried to extend a limited success into a universal principle of explanation. Van Helmont established one influential view by treating the living body as a system of chemical processes brought about by 'ferments' under the control of an immaterial principle, the 'archaeus'. Although hazardously speculative, van Helmont was a good experimenter; in addition to practising medicine he spent much of his time working in the laboratory which a wealthy marriage had allowed him to construct in his house in Louvain. To test his belief that the principle of all matter was water, he carried out a quantitative experiment similar to one described by Nicholas of Cusa, growing a tree in a pot for five years merely by watering it, and finding that at the end of that period the weight of the earth in the pot had scarcely altered.[1] The starting-point of his animal physiology was his study of digestions, where he demonstrated the acid 'fermentation' in the stomach and its neutralization by the bile. His view of the disease as an alien entity or 'archaeus' entering the body led him to become a pioneer in aetiology and morbid anatomy. The chemical view of physiology and medicine achieved a further success with François de la Boë (Sylvius, 1624–73), whose most valuable contribution was his explanation of digestion by the successive 'fermentations' of the food by the saliva, the pancreatic juice and the bile. In the field of therapy these chemical ideas came to dominate medical discussions for a time because of a furious debate, involving the French court itself, between the Galenists favouring vegetable drugs, the Paracelsists promoting the uses of inorganic drugs such as antimony and mercury, and other schools of thought.

The main alternative view, that the living body could be explained as a system not of chemical but of mechanical processes, originated principally from the successes of the mathematical and mechanical sciences in explaining sensory mechanisms and behaviour.[2] In his *Ad Vitellionem paralipomena* (1604) Kepler had made the first great discovery in modern physiology by showing how the eye, treated simply as an optical instru-

[1] Van Helmont's manuscripts were published posthumously with some additions by his son as *Ortus medicinae* (Amsterdam, 1648); see pp. 53, 109. An English translation appeared under the title *Oriatrike or, Physick Refined* (London, 1662).

[2] A. C. Crombie, 'The mechanistic hypothesis and the scientific study of vision', *Proceedings of the Royal Microscopical Society*, Vol. 2 (1967), pp. 3–112.

ment, focused the image of an object on to the retina. The immediate effect of this discovery was to allow further problems to be formulated for exact analysis, even if not immediately solved. Kepler himself in the *Dioptrice* (1611), Scheiner in his *Oculus* (1619) and *Rosa Ursina* (1630), Descartes in *La Dioptrique* (1637), and Mersenne in his *Universae . . . geometriae synopsis* (1644) and *L'optique et la catoptrique* (1651) brought current physiological optics to an advanced scientific stage by their exact, quantitative and frequently experimental investigations of long and short sight and the design of appropriate compensating lenses, visual acuity, accommodation, the formation of a single visual field with two eyes, the relation between direct and indirect vision, and numerous other phenomena. Mersenne, first in his *Harmonie universelle* and later in his *Cogitata physico-mathematica* (1644) and *Novarum observationum physico-mathematicarum tomus tres* (1647), embarked on a similar analysis of hearing. In the whole problem clear distinctions between the physiological and psychological aspects of sensation, and between conjecture and established fact, became possible and were often clearly made.

Yet the enquiry was committed from the start to giving an account of the mechanisms mediating not only each special sense but also the correlation of the stimuli from them into a consistent view of the external world and consistent behaviour in relation to it. This question was broached in different ways by Mersenne, Gassendi and Hobbes, but it was Descartes who carried it through to the point of producing a general mechanistic model for living things. 'I want you to consider', he wrote in his *Traité de l'homme*, 'that all these functions follow naturally in this machine simply from the arrangement of its parts, no more or less than do the movements of a clock, or other automata, from that of its weights and its wheels'.[1] By rigorously asking the same mechanistic question and allowing no others, by asking only what physical motions followed each preceding motion, beginning with the physical impressions of light and other material influences on the appropriate sense organs and carrying through to the consequential movements of the animal's muscles, he reduced the 'animate and sensitive body' to a system of built-in responses designed to preserve and propagate itself by pursuing the beneficial and avoiding the harmful aspects of the environment acting on it. The relations between the immaterial human soul and this bodily machine Descartes made the subject of his very interesting psychological essay, *Les passions de l'âme* (1649); all other living things were simply machines. The influence of these speculations on actual discovery was probably very small; discoveries were made rather by attacking limited problems as in the work of Harvey, in that on the sensory mechanisms, and later in that which G. A. Borelli published in his *De motu animalium* (1680). The significance of philosophical mechanism is rather that it made explicit the

[1] *Oeuvres*, Vol. 11 (1909), p. 202.

assumptions with which mathematicians and experimenters had already been working, providing a philosophical cosmology extending as far beyond physical science as psychology and the model for society described in Hobbes' *De cive* (1642), *Leviathan* (1651), *De corpore* (1655) and *De homine* (1657).

Beyond these investigations with a clear theoretical bearing, the steady accumulation of observations continued during this whole period to throw increasing light on the diversity of natural history. Collections of hitherto unknown plants were brought back from the Americas, Africa, India, and as far afield as China and the Philippines. In Europe itself experience with breeding plants under different conditions was developed through horticulture and agriculture and the establishment of botanical gardens, mainly with a medical interest. Publications on descriptive botany grew in number and with them the number of known species, which increased from about 500 recognized by Leonard Fuchs in 1542, to about 6,000 recognized by Caspar Bauhin in his *Prodromus theatri botanici* (1620), and then to about 18,000 recognized by John Ray in 1682. Bauhin, Jung and other botanists tried to keep up with this accumulation by devising ever more precise and diagnostic descriptions and comprehensive systems of classification. The continued study of anatomy, especially in Italy and England, brought about a similar increase in knowledge of animals, and in 1645 appeared the earliest comprehensive treatise on comparative anatomy, the *Zootomia Democritaea* (1645) of Marc Antonio Severino (1580–1656) of Naples. A remarkable feature of this work is Severino's recognition of unity of type based on man as the 'archetype', an idea which he tried to extend to the whole animal kingdom and even to plants. Further advances were made in comparative embryology, notably by Harvey in his *Exercitationes de generatione animalium* (1651), where the assertion, 'all animals whatever, even Viviparous also, nay man himself to be made of an Egge . . . just as the first conceptions of all Plants are certain seeds,'[1] was to lay down a fundamental principle to be established later by experiment. Knowledge of the earth's surface likewise accumulated. A theory of ocean currents was published by a French Jesuit explorer, George Fournier, in his *Hydrographie* (1643), and Descartes' brilliant conjectures, attempting to account for the geological history of the earth within the general mechanistic theory of the *Principia philosophiae*, projected this whole subject into the evolutionary discussions of a later period.

As in science, so in technology the application of mathematics was expected to usher in an age whose achievements would know no bounds; yet the technology of this period is related to that of the previous generation rather as the sculpture of the baroque is to that of the age of Michel-

[1] Exercitatio 1; cf. Exer. 62; earliest English translation, London, 1653.

angelo. The picture presented to us is of a somewhat overblown style: a growing ambition linked to an achievement that falls below even that of the sixteenth century. Mathematics applied to the arts and especially to machinery could, it was thought, compel Nature to deliver to the man who knew her secrets a Faustian capacity to achieve all his desires: his carriages would require no horses, his house would never lack light, the Moon itself was not beyond his reach. Most tempting of all was the promise of perpetual motion, that will-o'-the-wisp which obsessed so many of the imaginations of our period with the dream of infinite power, a chimera which enraptured them as much as Eldorado or the Philosopher's Stone. As Galileo observed:

I have seen the general run of mechanicians deceived in trying to apply machines to many operations impossible by their nature, of the success of which they have remained in error, while others have similarly been defrauded of the hope conceived from their promises. These deceptions seem to me to have their chief cause in the belief these craftsmen have had, and continually have, of being able to raise very great weights with a little force, as it were with their machines cheating nature, whose firmest instinct is rather that no resistance can be overcome by a force that is not more powerful than it . . . By the deception of so many princes and to their own shame, engineers of little comprehension go dreaming, applying themselves to impossible undertakings.[1]

Little books written mostly by amateurs, like *Thaumaturgus mathematicus* (1628) by Gaspar Ens and *Mathematicall magick* (1648) by John Wilkins, spread the good news. The titles are significant: fantasy played a large part in their conceptions, and where there was a scientific basis it was often an idea that had been long since exhausted. The perpetual motions of Jan van der Straet (Stradanus, 1536–1604) were being published long after 1650, and one of the first and most famous of these works, *Magia naturalis* (1558) by G. B. della Porta, appeared in a fine English version in 1658, a century after its original publication.

But if these dreams could only bring inevitable disappointment, progress in the more routine spheres of technology was little better. For this the reason often lay outside science. Just as today, a rapid advance could only be obtained by the investment, without hope of quick returns, of sums that were not in fact forthcoming. The more ambitious schemes, although using methods already long established, were also held up by slow communications and in consequence tardy and inefficient administration. Projects dragged on for decades, or were undertaken only many years after they had been first proposed. The Briare Canal, one of the first of the major French canals, connecting the Loing and Loire, took more than forty years to cover a hardly greater number of miles: begun some years before our period opens it was only completed a few years before its close. Plans for the draining of the fens, which occupied Cornelis

---

[1] Galileo, *Le mecaniche*, in *Opere*, ed. naz. Vol. 2 (1891), pp. 155, 158.

Vermuyden (*c.*1590–1677) much of the thirties and forties, had been laid down by Humphrey Bradley half a century before.

The machine of state, like those of industry, creaked slowly and inefficiently into action, when correspondence might take weeks to pass from a capital to its remoter provinces. Often the demands of the state, as for guns in time of war, had to be satisfied in quantity and without delay, and therefore by the traditional methods, leaving little scope for experimentation with new techniques. The plague of 1630–1 and the recurrent economic and political crises sapped initiative. Yet in the new and rising centre of economic progress in the North Sea—England and the Netherlands, and to a lesser extent north Germany and Scandinavia—repeated failures and delays did not prevent a growing optimism and belief in the possibility of indefinite technical improvement, if only science could be applied to the 'useful arts'.

Unfortunately the science that was in fact applied was often obsolete, a symptom of the gulf between academic and artisan that constituted a further barrier to technological advance. This of course did not apply to the virtuosi who were stimulated by the need to administer their estates and commercial interests. Edward Somerset (1601–67), second marquis of Worcester, employed a gun-founder to study inventions and make models of them, and in 1663 published *A century of the names and scantlings of such inventions, as at present I can call to mind to have tried and perfected.* Sir Nicholas Crisp (*c.* 1599–1666) rewarded inventors, actively encouraged the spread of their ideas, and himself devised a successful new method of making bricks. But the great majority of practical men had no contact with recent science. Galileo's masterly study of projectile motion in his *Discourses on two new sciences* showed that under idealized conditions a cannon-ball moved in a parabolic path, but for half a century afterwards the only books likely to fall into the hands of gunners continued to expound the doctrine taught by Tartaglia as long ago as 1537. Harriot's innumerable contributions to the desperate problem of accurate navigation began under his first patron Raleigh and went on after Raleigh's fall in 1603. Edward Wright (*c.*1558–1615), translator of Stevin's *Haven-finding art* and author of the famous *Certaine errors in navigation* (1599), until his death provided new tables and techniques in the use of charts and lectured annually on navigation on behalf of the East India Company. John Tapp (fl.1596–1631) and Briggs and Gunter of Gresham College continued this work, but how limited was their impact is shown by the republication in 1644 of *Pathway to perfect sayling* by Richard Polter, sometime Master of the King's Ships and typically conservative in outlook, whose book was hopelessly outdated when it first appeared in 1605. This preference shown by practical man for the traditional and tried techniques meant that the direction of influence was rather from technology to science: the difficulty of pumping mines clear of water, the repeated failures of apparatus in spite of the successes of small-scale models, the gunner's uncertainty over the correct elevation of his piece, all suggested problems that were given an autonomous existence within pure science rather than made occasions for science to aid technology.

Yet another obstacle to technological advance lay in the very nature of the new scientific ideas. The paradox whereby the complexity of the natural world must be idealized before it can be understood had been appreciated and accepted by the new philosophy both at the conceptual level and in controlled experiments. But it was altogether more difficult to take the next step and connect theory with the actual crudities of a primitive technology. Where the theory was classical the attempt to apply it was sometimes made. In innumerable contraptions gear was added to gear, lever to lever, in the fond expectation that, as with the idealized machines of mechanical theory, a small force would operate the whole. Where the theory was novel application was not even attempted. The range of a gun might be of great importance, but there was little use in applying Galileo's parabolas to a situation where not only was wind-resistance a major factor but powder, shot and bore all varied considerably; as Halley was to write, gunners 'loose all the Geometrical accuracy of their art from ye unfittness of ye boare to ye ball, & ye uncertain reverse of ye Gun, which is indeed verry hard to overcome'.[1]

Not surprisingly, then, the technological successes of the period were comparatively few. Dyeing improved strikingly, Cornelis Drebbel, that most fertile and ingenious of inventors, being partly responsible for a new scarlet dye that appeared about 1620. Complex machinery became popular with the spread of the knitting machine invented by William Lee in 1589. But the most significant developments were the result of a better understanding of the limitations of a mere multiplication of gears: the attempts to find new prime movers. To begin with there were efforts to expand the use of wind power which had proved so invaluable in draining the Netherlands. The first attempt at a land vehicle driven by an inanimate power was the Dutch sailing cart which tradition ascribes to Stevin. But it proved more a toy, a new game for Prince Maurice, than a generally useful means of transport.

More fertile for the future was the use of steam. Here too the first experiments were amusements more than anything, automata inspired by Hero of Alexandria. Hero's æolipile, in which a small boiler emitted a jet of steam from a narrow pipe, had been used in the Renaissance for reinforcing fires. Ens mentions a great many applications for the æolipile, most of them toys although he does include the driving of mills, and Giovanni Branca (1571–1640) in *Le machine* (1629) describes one to take the place of a jet of water in working a powder-mill. The idea has obvious

---

[1] Edmond Halley, 19 March 1700/1, in *Correspondence and papers*, ed. E. F. MacPike (Oxford, 1932), p. 168.

drawbacks and, like projects 'to drive up water by fire, not by drawing or sucking it upwards',[1] came to nothing. But it gave would-be improvers ideas, as did other failures of the period, and forced them to re-examine their theoretical foundations.

The period concluded then, despite the slow rate of progress, on a note of optimism and a sense of opening frontiers. There was a growing demand that this progress should be organized, the various useful arts studied with a view to their improvement, and scientific methods applied to the calculation of sounder technological theories. Philosophy and the useful arts were now to join hands to bring in an age of indefinite improvement, and both were to be brought under the shelter of national organizations. During this period these ideas had been put forward by somewhat eccentric individuals, at best by small groups. Their general adoption early in the second half of the century began a new era.

[1] Marquis of Worcester, *A century of . . . inventions*, No. 68.

CHAPTER V

CHANGES IN RELIGIOUS THOUGHT

THE first decades of the seventeenth century played a special role in the evolution of religious thought. They were neither the seedtime of new ideas about the relationship of God to man nor a time of the discarding of old beliefs, but rather the age in which some of the great issues of religious history were fought out anew. The chief concern of religious thought was one which had never lost interest since the beginnings of Christianity, that of man's free will and of his freedom to arrive at his own religious experiences. This problem was reflected in the controversies over free will and predestination which rent both Calvinism and Catholicism in our period. On another level, it was reflected in the quest for religious individualism against a religious orthodoxy which had become dominant in both Protestantism and Catholicism.

Under the impact of the theological quarrels which centred on these issues, the orthodox and their challengers, as well as those believing either in free will or predestination, took ever more radical positions. Thus some important ideas became re-emphasized. Rationalism penetrated to the very heart of religious thought, bringing the formulation of an explicit rational religion. This period also witnessed a growing trend towards deism and even unbelief. At the other end of the religious spectrum, religious individualism led to pietism and to a renewed mysticism. Beneath the issues raised by such religious thought coursed the piety of the ordinary people. We know almost nothing about this popular piety; yet it cannot be omitted from this account since modes of popular religious expression posed problems which theologians had to meet.

It will be useful to start with a discussion of Protestant religious orthodoxy. By the end of the sixteenth century both Lutheranism and Calvinism were revolutionary movements which had run their course. The Lutheran Reformation had begun with the 'pure' word of Scripture, but now Scripture was in danger of being replaced by officially enforced confessions of faith. The Book of Concordance of 1580 had become binding for two-thirds of German Protestantism. It included Luther's Catechism, the Confession of Augsburg, and the articles of the League of Schmalkalden. Contemporaries called the book a 'pope made out of paper', and it was indeed the Lutheran counterpart to the Canons of the Council of Trent. Everywhere there were attempts to define religious faith and to enforce the definitions. Luther himself became one sanctified, a 'last Elias'. Even the printers' mistakes in his works became a part of the new Holy Writ.

The impetus for orthodoxy was provided by the quest for order in an age when diversity of religious expression was regarded as' denial of religious truth. Every new form of religious worship, once it had established itself, sought to guard its own truth by excluding all others as heresy. At a time when toleration was thought to be the condoning of heresy or at best to be religious indifference, a surge towards orthodoxy was inevitable even in movements which themselves had once been regarded as heresies. Exceptions to this trend were found in those modes of religious expression—notably the Arminians and Socinians—which sought to widen the allowable within their own framework of thought.

In the sixteenth and seventeenth centuries the impetus towards orthodoxy was further strengthened by another traditional belief, that religious divergence was political treason. Religious disorder meant chaos, and chaos in turn meant dissolution of all established political and social order. This was not, however, merely the theory of conservatives who desired to preserve things as they were; a practical reason strengthened such belief. Throughout the history of Christianity in the West religious challenges to authority had been accompanied by political challenges. In Lutheranism there had been from the beginning an incipient conflict between religious individualism and the attempt to preserve order. It was order which won, even during Luther's lifetime, and the religious wars strengthened the feeling that political order and religious order were inexorably intertwined.

Lutheranism's equation of natural law with the Decalogue provided a strong rationale for the princes to regulate the faith, since the interpretation of natural law had always been a concern of rulers. Calvinists, like those of the Palatinate, were at one in this belief with the Lutherans. State control was spelled out in a series of 'church orders' issued throughout the sixteenth century. What started as the ordering of the outward manner of worship shaded over by the end of that century into the regulation of belief itself. This was a step which Luther had always opposed, yet confessions of faith triumphed throughout the Lutheran as well as the Calvinist world. The Anglican church followed this pattern. The Acts of Uniformity equated political loyalty with religious obedience. The Thirty-nine Articles went beyond outward conformity and attempted to order belief, although the lines were loosely drawn and some divergence of belief was allowed.

Though the enforcement machinery of such conformity varied, it tended to become vested in the powerful classes of the community. In Brandenburg the landlords enforced religious conformity and in England the justices of the peace were at times used for the same purpose. In towns, the gilds played an important part in effecting the religious conformity of their members. Calvinist Hesse used the nobility as well as the magistrates to oversee religious discipline. There was a tendency in Germany for ecclesiastical control to gravitate to the lowest authorities, the local squire and village council. However they were enforced, it was the ruler who laid down the regulations and decided upon the confession of faith for his territories.

In addition to defining belief, these regulations emphasized church attendance. Fines were often imposed on those who did not attend services or who were lax in taking communion. The regulations also significantly included a check on the morals of the community. Loose habits were taken to mean general political and social unreliability. Order had to be observed here as in all else. Once again there was a real base to the theory. As we shall see, the 'atheistic' movements of the century tended to be libertine. Moreover, in Germany the imperial police regulations of the fifteenth and sixteenth centuries gave an example to Protestant princes. They had condemned blasphemy, luxury, and drinking as evils which would bring upon the empire the wrath of God. Since drunkenness was the curse of Germany in our period, there was good practical reasoning behind such regulations. The *pater patriae*, the territorial ruler, had to guard his people. Because these vices led to hell, the citizens had to be protected from them as a part of religious conformity.

How effective were these regulations? Sometimes they were accompanied by cynicism. In Brandenburg the ministers were told to subscribe to the Book of Concordance but after that, could think and teach as they liked.[1] These sentiments remind one of that Elizabethan cynicism which emphasized subscription to Anglicanism chiefly as a matter of political loyalty. Even where there was less sophistication it seemed easier to make regulations than to enforce them. The Magdeburg visitation of 1656 tells us that there were no Bibles in the churches, that converts waited for years before having their children baptized, that preachers were not properly installed, and that weekday sermons had ceased in the country districts. Above all, popular piety went its own way, since it was difficult to harness its exuberance through regulations.

In the border regions between the faiths, Protestants streamed to Catholic festivities to obtain holy water blessed against sickness, to take part in religious processions, or to make merry at the inauguration of new churches. The triumphal entrance of the great Spanish saints Ignatius Loyola and Francis Xavier into Germany also affected Lutheran regions. Many a Lutheran living on the North Sea believed in Xavier as the protector against stormy seas, and as late as 1772 Protestants of Schwerin asked for Ignatius water to heal animal diseases. Similarly, the books of edification of the Spanish mystic Louis de Granada spread throughout Protestant lands. On this level, the baroque did not by-pass Protestant countries. Men everywhere delighted in a world which was not abstract

[1] I. P. Meyer, 'Der Konfessionszwang in den deutschen evangelischen landeskirchen des 16.–18. Jahrhunderts', *Zeitschrift der Geschichte der Niedersächsischen Kirche*, Vol. XXXIV (1929), p. 284.

but which stressed spectacles, feasts, and the imagination. Religion was a release from the drabness of daily life and from the many evil spirits and dangers that were menacing on all sides. If more often than not popular religious expression managed to circumvent the regulations of morals and belief, it was still true that such regulations were successful at times in controlling religious and political thought. Of the many antimonarchical systems of the century, none arose on Lutheran soil.

The acceptance of confessions of faith did not mean an end to theological argument; instead they gave it a different turn. Theologians now disputed not the fundamentals of faith but the words of the confessions. Such disputations, carried on both by Calvinist and Lutheran orthodoxy, were bound to be scholastic in tone, and the kind of argument which Luther had condemned when he talked about 'foolish Aristotle'. Significantly, one leading Lutheran now called the logic of Aristotle 'God's own logic'. Dialectics came into its own. Since no new dogmas could be formed, theologians became logicians. An important consequence of this Protestant scholasticism was the application of reason to religious debate. These theologians thought to prove the rightness of the confessions by the exercise of logic and reason. It seemed that in Lutheran orthodoxy the spirit of rationalism triumphed over the Bible.

If we search beyond the endless hair-splitting that these arguments involved, another unlooked-for consequence emerges. The very narrowness of theological speculation and its rationalist tendencies gave a fuller freedom to the development of natural sciences on Lutheran soil than elsewhere. A Lutheran prince furthered the publication of Copernicus' work and a Lutheran printer published it. Underlying this openness of Lutheranism to the natural sciences was Luther's own idea that heaven as the seat of God was not a fixed place in a geographical sense. This gave to the cosmos a kind of infinity which was able to assimilate more rapidly the great astronomical discoveries of the age. When Copernicus' ideas were taught, it was in Lutheran universities like that at Tübingen.[1]

These consequences of Lutheran orthodoxy were not apparent to contemporaries. The new scholasticism seemed stifling to them. It quite consciously excluded all those from religious discussions who were not qualified theologians, that is to say, ordained ministers. This assertion of the ministers' powers led one of them to state bluntly that only theologians could go to heaven. Such high claims came at the very time when ministers were declining in social status. The Thirty Years War had much to do with this decline, though such a development had haunted Lutheranism from the beginning. The ministers' material position was wretched; many preachers had to have a second profession as trader or craftsman, while in the countryside they tended in effect to become peasants. A basic abuse was the impropriation of the worldly goods of the churches, which were

---

[1] Werner Elert, *Morphologie des Lutherthums* (Munich, 1952), Vol. I, pp. 374 ff.

sometimes pawned or sold outright. This was a general evil of the century and was not confined to Lutheran regions. Rising prices in the second half of the century made bad conditions still worse. In Germany after 1633 there were frequent unsuccessful attempts to free the rural clergy from a condition in which the minister was often simply a 'Latinizing peasant'. This was not the fault of orthodoxy, but it demonstrated that even as religious thought became the monopoly of theologians and the minister's role was increasingly stressed, his status in society was deteriorating.

In the reactions against orthodoxy two different phenomena confront us. Initially there was a religious disorientation which led to a questioning of Christianity itself.[1] One German cobbler, for example, became in turn a Lutheran, a monk, a pietist, and a Catholic once more, only to end as a Jew, because for him the only certain fact was the existence of one God. Such a loss of religious moorings was manifest in all parts of Christianity. Less specifically, the second half of the century saw in the Lutheran regions a general decline in church attendance. In the end the trend towards deism and rationalism received an impetus through this religious disorientation.

Immediately, however, the second aspect of the reaction towards orthodoxy was more important. This reaction was linked to a deep-rooted trend of popular piety—that mysticism and chiliasm which Protestantism had combated from the beginning. Chiliasm, the expectation of the end of the world and the last judgement, fulfilled the deep need for hope among the lower classes but not among those classes only. It ran like a thread through much of the religious thought of the period. In Cromwell's England many radical sects lived in such expectation. In Germany as well as in Holland, chiliastic visions were frequent. These were spread by unlettered peasant preachers. One of their number proclaimed that 'misery and hate' were the lot of the peasant but the last judgement would obliterate them and redress human inequalities. Such preaching was also anti-clerical. In 1590 another successful peasant preacher told his audiences that hell was paved with ministers, and in it masters, intellectuals, and gamblers were chained together like the hounds of the devil. Enmity towards authority, the learned, and the preachers of the church were all one in this chiliastic thought. Such religious attitudes led to extremes. In Saxony in 1621 many peasants sold their lands in order to go to Zion in the expectation of Christ. This release from daily misery was not confined to German or Dutch peasants or to English Puritan radicals; the Jews also experienced the same phenomena. The appearance of the 'Pseudo Messiah' Sabbatai Zevi (1626–76) led many to sell their all in order to follow him to the Holy Land.

This ferment gave rise to one of the greatest figures in German religious thought, the Silesian cobbler Jakob Boehme (1575–1624). His chiliasm

[1] Leo Baeck, *Spinozas erste Einwirkung auf Deutschland* (Berlin, 1895), p. 61.

was drawn from the social misery of his native Silesia which he believed God could only have permitted because the last judgement was at hand. The church too was unimportant to Boehme as a preacher of the word. The true church was the 'invisible' church of the reborn. This belief made for tolerance, for it was unimportant whether or not one were a professed Christian as long as one strove towards God. Boehme, however, was no deist; in his thought, Christ was the salvation from death and sin, and the picture of Christ in the heart of man made it possible for him to unite with the Deity, to be reborn. God would realize himself in that human being who could become immune to carnal lusts. Religion thus became uniquely a matter of inward faith, of the soul.

Boehme was therefore symptomatic of another trend in seventeenth-century Christian thought which was coursing beneath the official orthodoxies. On the Catholic side at the same time, Francis de Sales spoke of a need to go beyond Christian institutions to Christian inspiration. The evangelism of the early Jansenists had much the same emphasis. But Francis de Sales and the Jansenists believed that the church and its sacraments were essential in Christian inspiration, while for Boehme God revealed himself not in the church but in and through nature. Through nature one might learn to understand Scripture, and Boehme hoped that the quarrels of the theologians would thereby be ended. Nature was at once good in her trees, stones, and flowers, and bad in her continuous ruthless struggle for existence. Life could be understood only through this contrast. What then was the relationship of all this to the reborn man? Only he could see the godliness of Nature, of God revealing himself. Just as God was above the good and evil in nature, so man had to overcome the dialectic of anxiety and freedom. 'In overcoming is joy', and only through suffering could the human spirit be conscious of itself.

Boehme's mysticism rejected predestination: it was man's own will, the working of Christ within him, which led to rebirth. Boehme's view of human nature was optimistic; man was essentially predisposed to good rather than evil. This voluntarism contrasted with the ideas of the Jansenist Blaise Pascal, who emphasized man's sinfulness. The Silesian cobbler had a kind of happiness not to be found in the tortured soul of the Parisian intellectual. The reborn viewed nature happily once he had overcome the dualism of good and evil. This emphasis upon nature was important; it was a part of the new feeling in the seventeenth century. The God of the Bible left the Word, now imprisoned in confessions, and emerged in nature to be recognized and worshipped.

We find identical ideas among the writings of the Rosicrucians (1614–16), although they also placed emphasis on alchemy, the stone of wisdom, and secret rituals. With them too, God was the God of nature, even if he was connected with it not through the human soul reborn but in the mysteries of alchemy. In England such extreme Puritan sects as the

Ranters had that same feeling for nature. They wished to live 'in unity with the creation'. They shared their ideas, in turn, with the learned and sophisticated Cambridge Platonists. This religious thought was connected with the neo-Platonic belief in a spiritual principle which illumined all the world. The emphasis on nature, bound up with mysticism here, could at the same time lead to an anti-Christian philosophy. Lucilio Vanini, a contemporary of Boehme, wrote of 'nature which is God'. His *Secrets of Nature* (1616) was called, not without reason, an introduction to the undevout life. Did he not cry out on the scaffold 'a miserable Jew [i.e. Christ] is the cause that I am here'? For Boehme, the Ranters and the Cambridge Platonists, God reflected himself in nature, but to Vanini and his group, nature herself was divine. Jakob Boehme's own mysticism, unlike orthodoxy, infused all of nature with Christianity and did not confine it to a narrow confessional base. Boehme's influence was widespread and in revolutionary England his writings were widely read.[1]

Piety, however, was not confined to such modes of expression. There was also an emerging pietism which sought to revive faith within the framework of orthodoxy. Johann Valentin Andreae constructed his *Christianopolis* (1619) as a place of refuge based upon virtue inculcated through education in the love of God. Such a piety also informed Johannes Arndt's *True Christianity* (1605), but here personal belief was emphasized: 'piety of the heart'. Religious creativity also found other outlets within accepted orthodoxy. The hymn, free from the confine of the letter of faith, provided a partial release. Paulus Gerhardt (1607–76) proved to be, after Luther, Protestantism's greatest hymnologist. In contrast with the dogmatic sermons of theologians, Gerhardt's hymns touched the mainstream of popular piety. They were songs of the cross and of consolation, written against the background of the Thirty Years War. Calvinism saw a similar attempt to revive piety within orthodoxy after the Synod of Dort through pietistic conventicles which were intended to serve as examples. These in turn were similar in purpose to the oratories founded as a part of the Catholic Reformation.

The reaction against orthodoxy, then, meant both religious disorientation and a deepening of personal faith. The contrast between this faith and orthodox thought can be seen in a typical orthodox funeral eulogy: the deceased, it said, never failed to attend church: he was always the first in church and the last to leave it; he was conscientious in taking the sacraments, in reading the Holy Scripture, and in leading a life of sobriety and moderation. There is nothing about inner piety, the linking of his soul to God; instead, church attendance had become the prime mark of the pious man.[2] Not only Lutheran orthodoxy preached such eulogies.

[1] Cf. Wilhelm Struck, *Der Einfluss Jakob Boehmes auf die Englische Literatur des 17 Jahrhunderts* (Berlin, 1936), p. 195.
[2] D. A. Tholuck, *Vorgeschichte des Rationalismus* (Berlin, 1862), Vol. II (pt. 2), p. 203.

In England also church attendance played a primary role in official religion, and in most Calvinist countries it was no different. Orthodoxy was the officially sanctioned religion in an age of increasing conformity. It was religious control in the age of sovereignty and mercantilism.

The problems of Lutheran orthodoxy were duplicated in Calvinism. Yet, despite such similarity, the relationship between these two chief branches of Protestantism was far from amicable. Characteristic was the Lutheran theologian who in 1621 attempted to prove that the Calvinists agreed in ninety-nine points with the Arians and Turks and that the Huguenot martyrs deserved their fate. Such feeling is easy to understand against the background of rivalry exacerbated by the Thirty Years War in which Lutheran princes preferred co-operation with the emperor to union with the Calvinists. The original Lutheran attack on the papacy was now partly deflected against the Calvinists and partly broadened to include them. The slogan 'keep us, Lord, close to your holy word, and put an end to the murdering Popes and Turks' was interpreted by one Lutheran preacher to include with the pope's name that of 'all our enemies', that is to say, the Anabaptists and the Calvinists. In spite of such polemics, the actual development of Calvinism and Lutheranism towards orthodoxy was very similar.

Calvinist princes also ordered their church. Even where the church took form as a presbytery, rulers promulgated orders for it and told the elders what to do. The church orders of Hesse in 1657 were an example of such commands to the supposedly elected officials of the church. The democratic element in the Calvinist church structure was vanishing. Calvin's successor at Geneva, Theodore Béza (1519–1605), stressed the function of the ministers. Calvin's biblical ordering of the Christian community was in Béza's hands centred on the religious aristocracy of preachers. Here, as in Lutheranism, the ministry trained as theologians became the pivots of the church. The increasingly authoritarian church organization was accompanied also by a series of confessions of faith: the Confessio Gallicana of 1559, Scotia of 1560, and the Heidelberg Catechism of 1563. In England, too, when the Presbyterians had a chance at power, they tried to impose the Westminster Confession of Faith in 1647.

These confessions differed as to the strictness of detail. The Helvetic Consensus of 1675 made the vowel points of Hebrew in Scripture a matter of regulation. The basic tenets of Calvinism and its view of Scripture were here codified into an official interpretation. It is important to realize that this Calvinist orthodoxy entailed a denial of free will on the part of a predestined man. The element of predestination emerged more sharply in Calvinist orthodoxy than in Calvin's own work. The Reformer's image of the world as the 'theatre of God' was taken to mean that God rigidly controlled his actors. Mankind was divided into the elect and the damned, and it was widely held that the 'saints' could not fall from grace. The gulf between the will of God and the actions freely taken by men was vast and unbridgeable. This was true even when these ideas were expressed with moderation as, for example, by the leader of Calvinist orthodoxy in Holland, Franciscus Gomarus (1563–1641), who asserted that no man taught that God absolutely decreed to cast man away without sin. As he did decree the end, however, so he decreed the means—that as he predestined man to death, so he predestined man to sin, the only way to death. Gomarus' statement to the Synod of Dort was echoed by the synod's canon that God chose certain individuals from the mass of fallen man for salvation while the rest of sinful mankind was doomed.

This orthodox thought had a great deal of appeal. It gave to Calvinism a faith in the cause of its elect which was echoed by that English Puritan who wrote: 'For who would not courageously fight that is beforehand assured of victory?' This piety had to reject any human tampering with the Divine. It was small wonder that the opponents of Calvinist orthodoxy believed that such emphasis upon God's will swamped all personal or scriptural religious experience. In the Netherlands, opposition to orthodoxy came into its own. A predominantly urban and commercial community with its emphasis on private initiative in trade found it rather difficult to understand the powerlessness of man before God. This statement needs qualification, however, for election could be and was equated with external success as a successful waging of war against sin. More important for the challenge to orthodoxy, however, was the humanist tradition of the Netherlands, the country of Erasmus and of the Christian Renaissance.

Arminianism has rightly been called a theological revival of humanism.[1] Jacobus Arminius (1560–1609), a professor at the University of Leiden, found himself unable to defend the orthodox Belgic Confession, though he had been brought up in orthodoxy and had been a student of Béza's. His chief opponent was Franciscus Gomarus, a Leiden colleague. What started as a dispute within the university soon became a debate dividing all Calvinism. Arminius sought to modify the doctrine of predestination, which had always been the Achilles heel of Calvinism. Together with his disciples he made the attack on predestination the basis for advocacy of a more general religious liberalism.

The controversy began in 1603 when Arminius accused Gomarus of making God the author of sin through stress on God's direct rule over man, allowing man no freedom. This accusation was a commonplace one against the predestinarians; it had been made forcefully by Cardinal Bellarmine against the earlier Calvinists. Gomarus in turn accused Arminius of reviving the Pelagian heresy by exalting the human element

[1] Hans Emil Weber, *Reformation, Orthodoxie und Rationalismus* (Gütersloh, 1951), Vol. I, p. 100.

in redemption so as to obscure the doctrine of grace given freely of God's own volition. Since the controversy between the Jesuits and the Jansenists also concerned the accusation of Pelagianism, we touch once more upon a general current of the century. A basic problem of Christian thought was involved; how to reconcile the sovereignty of God with the free will of man. Arminius believed that the human will had to co-operate freely with God in salvation. Free will thus became necessary for the reception of grace, and in this manner personal religious striving became the centre of religious experience. Arminius was especially concerned with the imprisonment of Scripture within the bounds of theological determinism; he tried to revive the centrality of the Holy Word by reasserting the principle of private judgement. Truth in religion was not something certain as orthodoxy professed, but something towards which man, guided by Scripture, had to strive by means of his free will.

Several important consequences follow from this doctrine. Since the decree of election applied only to those who repented, believed, and persevered in their individual striving, the elect were not a fixed religious élite. Election was thus fluid, and the saints could fall from grace while the reprobate could attain it. Moreover, the bitter quarrels of theologians were beside the point in a faith oriented to Scripture revitalized by private judgement. Doctrinal belief or theological creeds were not necessary to Christian communion. Arminians came to distinguish between fundamental and non-fundamental creeds. The only fundamentals were the language of Scripture and the creeds of the Apostles. Here was a latitudinarianism opposed to the 'vanity of dogmatizing'. A rational spirit was also in evidence. The Holy Word being central, Arminianism could only make good its arguments by biblical enquiry, and here it used a rational method. To Luther, reason was a whore, but for the Arminians reason was a revelation from God within which man's free will moved.

Arminius died in the early phase of this controversy. His successor as leader of the Arminians was Simon Episcopius (1583–1643), who led the movement through the critical phase of its development and formulated still more sharply the tenets of Arminianism. For him, the whole personality was destroyed if man lost free will. Moreover, doctrine should be reduced to its essentials. 'It is better to err concerning a truth that is nonessential, than so to misuse or correct views of it as to make it an occasion for dissension and odium.' Christ had died for all and made everyone's salvation possible, not just that of the elect. Before the Synod of Dort he reiterated the essence of Arminian belief: Scripture and solid reason would lead to the truth. Man's conscience should rest not on the vote of the multitude (the synod) but upon the strength of reason. Episcopius was a forceful leader, and upon hearing him the Englishman John Hales 'bade Calvin good-night'. Arminians also stressed personal piety and here Jan Uytenbogaert, with his practical bent, added impetus.

Personal piety was the highest good and could not be captured within the confines of a religious organization. The controversy became a concern for the whole of the Netherlands when in 1610 the Arminians presented the States of Holland with a Remonstrance setting forth their views. From that time on, they were called the 'Remonstrants'. The Remonstrance rejected the idea of election and predestination; challenged the concept that Christ died for the elect alone and the belief in irresistible grace, i.e. the exclusion of man's free will from co-operation with God; and rejected the idea that the elect could not fall from grace. The opponents of this Remonstrance, the Contra-Remonstrants, demanded the calling of a national synod.

The controversy meanwhile became enmeshed in politics. The advocate of Holland, Oldenbarneveldt, was friendly to the Arminians. As long as he dominated affairs, Oldenbarneveldt prevented the calling of a national synod which might be unfriendly to their position. His control was challenged by Maurice of Nassau, the stadtholder. The religious question became involved in the struggle for power between the stadtholder and the advocate. Maurice's opposition to the Remonstrants was political rather than religious, a part of his attempt to concentrate the executive power into his own hands.

Arminians were not hostile to a ruler's power, indeed more friendly to it than the orthodox. While the latter sought to safeguard the rights of the church by stressing the divine importance of its ecclesiastical organization, the former denied the existence of a separate ecclesiastical jurisdiction. As part of their emphasis on personal religious enquiry, the Arminians stressed the 'internal' nature of the church; in external ecclesiastical power the magistrate possessed his *imperium* directly from God, but spiritual life was inaccessible to this *imperium*. This last doctrine tempered the erastianism of the Arminians. The ruler's powers were seen to be incapable of persuading men of the truth in religion; thus, persecution was morally unjustifiable. Freedom of worship was a civil right. There was, however, in Arminian political thought no doctrine of resistance. Its greatest weakness lay in the assumption that the magistrate would be a Christian complying with the Arminian definition of his office.

Once Maurice had won his struggle with Oldenbarnevelt, he fell far short of the Arminian view of a Christian ruler. Not only was the National Synod called (1618) despite the Remonstrants and the State of Holland, but it was from the outset weighted against the Arminians. In his opening prayer the president of the synod praised Maurice as ' *verus et fortissimus heros*'. The Remonstrants were received as prisoners awaiting judgement. On the surface the synod had been called to revise confessions of faith, like the Heidelberg Catechism, but in reality it was committed to the confessions before any discussion occurred. A decision for orthodoxy was a foregone conclusion. Typically enough, however, while confirming predestination, election and irresistible grace, the synod failed to settle church–state relationships on a Calvinist basis. From the first it was forced to co-opt representatives of the state at its sessions. Maurice had not called the synod to lessen his own powers. His political purpose in calling Dort was reasserted when he threatened to treat all further meetings of Calvinist synods as disturbances of the peace.

The Synod of Dort was an impressive gathering of Calvinists from the Netherlands and from other countries as well. One hundred and five theologians attended; twenty-six were from abroad. James I of England played a large role throughout, supporting orthodoxy against the Remonstrants. This seemed strange for a king subsequently accused by Puritans of that very Arminianism which he had done his best to expunge. For James, however, any divergence from official orthodoxy was treason, whether it concerned the Puritans at home or the Arminians abroad. The lasting results of the synod must not be overlooked. Orthodoxy was reaffirmed. The Remonstrants, when they did return from exile, became merely a tolerated sect which was without official status. People took greater pains to preserve an orthodox demeanour since the church in the Netherlands interfered in the most personal matters. War was declared on those elements of popular piety which still clung to Catholic customs. Here we perceive the same phenomenon previously observed in Lutheran orthodoxy, the attempt to bring popular religious expression under control.

The synod did not succeed, however, in imposing the strict orthodoxy it had sought. The pretensions of the Calvinist ministers had led to an instinctive reaction against them on the part of the patriciates. The very decentralization of Dutch political life which Maurice could not overcome meant that anyone threatened with persecution could always find shelter somewhere under the authority and protection of the provinces sensitive about their special privileges. While in the southern Netherlands after 1618 theological considerations continued to play a major part in government, in the north, even after Dort, no one thought of consulting synods or theologians on political matters. Under such circumstances the Remonstrants' exile was brief. Amsterdam initiated a counter-revolution against orthodox ministers and after 1631 ignored the decree of the States General against the Arminians. Even before this date Arminians had started to return. Maurice died in 1625 and Prince Frederick Henry was more sympathetic to the Arminian cause. When a Remonstrant school and seminary was established at Amsterdam in 1632, Arminianism had once again found a home in the Netherlands.

During this struggle for existence, the elaboration of Arminian thought continued. The most important theorist in this stage of Arminian development was Hugo Grotius (1583–1645), who had been exiled after the Synod of Dort. He, too, stated the fundamentals of the Arminian faith.

Religion was something received by morally free men. The act of faith had nothing to do with being 'reborn', as mystics like Boehme had thought; rather, faith was a rational act of the will. God, he wrote in his *De Veritate religionis Christianae* (1627), had created man with liberty of action. Such liberty was not evil in itself but it might become the cause of something evil. To make God, through predestination, the author of evils of this kind was the highest wickedness. There was in Grotius, the Arminian of the second generation, an increasing emphasis on rationalism. For him the end of life included both the spiritual and the civil good, because man's happiness contained both. His viewpoint reflected not so much the paganism with which Grotius was subsequently charged, but a unitary view of the world: 'The universality of the end is correspondent to the universality of matter.' Since God dominated all, the Christian life also entailed leading a good life in society. This in turn contributed to Grotius' view of the state. If the state was a part of the totality of things, the two-kingdom theory of orthodox Calvinism had to be rejected. God, the author of unity, disposed all things in due order and the state was disposed under the final authority of the magistrate. Like Episcopius, Grotius believed religion to be an inward matter. The true invisible church was not the concern of authority, but the visible organized church was a part of society. It had no methods of law enforcement of its own; as opposed to the Calvinist form of discipline it depended upon the voluntary co-operation of individuals. The sovereignty in which Grotius believed was concerned with external actions alone.

Authoritarian though all this seems, in the end it facilitated the advent of toleration. While on its face Arminianism was well fitted for a state church, as James I and Archbishop Laud realized, Grotius believed that the essence of religion was authorized by God alone and subject to the will of no man. Though there were no real safeguards against the encroachment of the sovereign magistrate into the spiritual sphere in either Grotius or Episcopius, their emphasis on spiritual freedom, on ecclesiastical voluntarism, was important. They put forward ideas of toleration and of a free church within the state, without, however, menacing the actual power of the ruler. In an age when religious dissent was thought to be a threat to political order, we have here an important step towards making the doctrine of toleration politically respectable.

Arminianism was carried into the French Huguenot church by Moses Amyraut (1596–1664). However, the French church followed Dort and ordered its ministers to subscribe to its canons (1621). This, in turn, led to debate and dissension. While Grotius was refused communion by the chief Huguenot church of Paris, the issue was kept alive by Episcopius and Uytenbogaert, who both spent their exile in that city. In England Arminian ideas filtered into the state church, as the Puritan opposition never ceased to declare. To most of the latter, Anglicanism had fallen into 'an error that makes the grace of God lacky after the will of man'. Citing an equal emphasis on free will in Catholicism, Puritans regarded Arminians as 'spawns of the Papists'. Arminianism became a stick with which to beat the established church, but once that church had been defeated, Calvinist orthodoxy could not maintain itself either.

Arminianism raised within the Protestant fold the question of man's free will, just as Jansenism raised the problem for the Catholic church. Beyond that, Arminianism laid the foundation for an increasingly rational approach and method of enquiry into religious thought and experience. Like the reaction to Lutheran orthodoxy, it stressed piety and the Word of Scripture considered on the basis of personal experience rather than creeds. There were obviously many common concerns in the Christian thought of the century. If we pass to Catholicism, its orthodoxy and its challenge, this will become increasingly clear.

The Council of Trent formulated Catholic orthodoxy in the sixteenth century; the beginning of the seventeenth saw the further triumphant progress of the Catholic Reformation. The political victories of Emperor Ferdinand II, of Richelieu, and of John Sigismund in Poland, gave to Catholicism an *élan* which was augmented by the conversion of notables, like Queen Christina of Sweden. A Rome transformed by Bernini and Borromini reflected this feeling of triumph and power; *Roma triumphans* became a city designed for religious spectacles on a grand scale. Whatever the objections to this transformation of Rome were, whatever the actual setbacks of the Catholic Reformation at the Treaty of Westphalia, there was in this phase of that Reformation a delight in grandiose religious ceremonies and in liturgical colour and form.

The dramatic element in popular piety to which we have already referred was in tune with this impetus. No doubt the rulers in Catholic countries encouraged the peasants in pilgrimages and religious spectacles in order to deter them from Protestantism and to assuage their sad life. Their intentions were in tune with ancient popular needs. The miracle came to be central in this popular piety. Pictorial representations of the lives and, above all, the miracles of saints became common, especially in Germany. Moreover, chronicles were now kept, reporting miraculous healings and tales of wonders wrought by the patron saint of the town or village. In addition to patron saints, the beginning of the century saw an added emphasis on Spanish saints, especially Ignatius Loyola and Francis Xavier. The Jesuits furthered the introduction of their saints but the great popularity of Francis Xavier was due in part to another reason: through him the imagination of the people could follow into strange and exotic lands.

Power came to the foreground of the worship of saints. They were ruler types. Their power became power over the human spirit; earthly and heavenly power complemented themselves in their lives, reflecting Spanish realism and Spanish idealism.[1] The ever-present social hierarchy was reflected in the fact that the nobility was the chief beneficiary of the miracles performed by the saints.

Side by side with popular piety and the feeling of *Roma triumphans* was a deeper revival of Catholic piety, especially in France. Cardinal Pierre de Bérulle (1575–1629), Francis de Sales (1567–1622), and Vincent de Paul (1580–1660), all typified this new spirit. Bérulle's thought, like much of this Catholic piety, was deeply influenced by neo-Platonism. The universe for him was suffused by the divine. But Bérulle was also in the Augustinian tradition; his tragic view of life, his emphasis on redemption and the insufficiency of man links him to the later Jansenist movement. Personal sanctification was the centre of his thought. Such sanctification entailed a rigoristic moral attitude on the part of sinful man. Humanity had to be reminded of what it had forfeited with original sin. This went hand in hand with a moral protest against the growing luxury of the *Grand Siècle*. In 1611 Bérulle founded the Oratory in Paris on the model of that already founded by Philip Neri in Rome in 1564. These oratories were associations of secular priests, without specific vows, but under the authority of a 'superior general'. Their purpose was individual sanctification and the deepening of individual piety in order to bring people to Christ. The oratories were a creation of the revitalized piety of the Catholic Reformation; the orthodoxy of Trent did not lead to a stifling of such piety. There was, nevertheless, danger to orthodoxy in such oratories. Bérulle's oratory came under the suspicion of Jansenism, and in the next century many members actually joined the Jansenist movement.

We have already quoted Francis de Sales as saying that Christian inspiration must go beyond Christian institutions. De Sales revived the mystical piety in Catholicism which was so often threatened by extinction through undue emphasis on hierarchy and discipline. Love was his central theme. The love of man should tend naturally towards God but it needed God's grace to give effect to this natural inclination. The love of God was superior to earthly acts, for man could not add to God's perfection. As the eye could see a flower and immediately understand its beauty, so the soul by simple looking and sentiment could conceive God's truth in God's love. This was the vision which was called grace. Francis' thought, however, was not quietist; good works were the means of conversion and a part of the love towards man. Such love is an act of free determination in which man is sustained once he has united himself with God. For this the sacraments and the liturgy of the church are necessary. Piety, for the bishop of Geneva, was not something apart from this world but something to be practised within the context of daily life. Nor did it mean the ecstasies and castigations of an exaggerated popular piety; the contrary was the case. Man must avoid both despair and pharisaical

---

[1] Georg Schreiber, *Deutschland und Spanien* (Düsseldorf, 1936), p. 139.

security merely through rules. To do this, Francis de Sales presented a solution which impressed contemporaries as his greatest innovation; men had to choose a spiritual director who understood them better than they knew themselves, who should be blindly obeyed because God spoke through his mouth. This emphasis upon the spiritual director became the fashion in much of French society. However, the unquestioning devotion of the nuns of Port Royal to Saint Cryan was to go much beyond the usual devotion to the spiritual director of a convent. It came close to idolatry.

The religious thought of the bishop of Geneva was re-enforced by that of Vincent de Paul. What de Paul stressed was the abandonment of man to the love of God, an abandonment which to him consisted both in living at a high point of spiritual tension and in actualizing this through the practice of humble and solid virtues. For Vincent de Paul, charity became central, though it had also played an important role in the thought of Francis de Sales. These ideas were translated into practice when Vincent made it clear to the women of French society that their social status entailed, as a point of duty, leadership in charitable works. Thus de Paul founded the Daughters of Charity in 1629. Under the impact of such piety a whole segment of Paris society went mad over theology. In competition with the worldly salons at the court Madame Arcarie (1566–1618) established a centre for spiritual action at her Paris home. Francis de Sales and de Paul became the spiritual directors of many of the nobility. Such piety could easily escape the moderation upon which the two saints always insisted. Madame Arcarie spole about 'burning in God', about 'annihilating' herself before God. This kind of French society provided the setting for Jansenism. The emphasis on man's complete abandonment to the love of God could lead, and did lead with Jansenism, to a sharp revival of the doctrine of predestination. This was especially opposed to Jesuit theology, which was becoming the accepted mode of thought in the church.

The Jesuits entered fully into the spirit of *Roma triumphans;* indeed, they provided many of the ingredients which went into its making. Strict though their own discipline was, they were open to the new tendencies and ideas of the age. Their Church of Gesú in Rome was typical; it combined the architectural techniques of the Renaissance and the love for space and colour of the Catholic Reformation with the needs of the order. As the shock troops of the papacy, Jesuits stood in the midst of the political life of their times. They approached human nature from a practical point of view, and in doing so raised once more the problem of man's free will. Their thought thus led Catholicism into the same kind of controversy that we witnessed in Calvinism and the Arminians.

This controversy centred around the Jesuit interpretation of casuistry, the adjustment of the Christian framework of ethics to meet new situations and dangers. Such casuistry raised the question of how much free will man had to regulate his affairs and, subsequently, what the relationship of this free will was to man's salvation. In our period the ideas of the Spanish Jesuit Luis Molina (1535–1600) became the official doctrine of his order (1613). 'Do not', Molina wrote, 'insist so much upon the efficacy of grace that we grow in the midst of men the poisonous error which denies liberty.' To him there was a constant concurrence between man's will and God's in the quest for salvation, as if two men were pulling a barge ashore. God wanted to save all men, but the salvation of each man was in his own hands. God had foreknowledge of man's actions, to be sure, but he did not in any way ordain them. This theory gave ample room to the free will of man. It also emphasized the art of persuading the free man to use his liberty in the service of godliness, an art at which the Jesuits were adept. But how far could such persuasion go without becoming impious? The Jesuits were accused of making religion easy to attain and easy to observe.

The books of casuistry, which were meant for father confessors only, sought to deal with this problem. The most important were those of the Spaniard, Escobar y Mendoza (d. 1669), which went through countless editions and drew upon themselves the famed invective of Blaise Pascal. Escobar's theme was that the human in man would sometimes err and had to be excused. This contrasted with the Jansenist position that ignorance did not excuse sinning. Moreover, for Escobar, a right action could be judged, not by its object alone, but also by its purpose and the surrounding circumstances. If there were any uncertainty about an action, the father confessor had to be consulted. Indeed he became central in a situation where man's single acts did not tell the tale of eventual righteousness. Circumstances might well permit the use of mental reservations, and for this the Jesuits were constantly attacked by their enemies. Such reservations, however, were never outright lies but rather circumlocutions in extreme situations, and, for Escobar, circumlocutions which the hearer could easily notice. Despite all the attacks on Jesuit casuistry which accompanied Molinism in our period, their opponents also employed casuistry. The Puritan William Perkins' question as to how one could with good conscience use policy in the affairs of this life, confronted all religious thought. It was answered on all sides of the Reformation barrier in a way not too dissimilar to Escobar. Once more we touch upon a general current on the age. It was symbolized by Cardinal Richelieu, who ordered a textual comparison between Machiavelli and Scripture to be made, pointing out the similarities.

But what of the papacy? The Council of Trent had defined a papal centralism in the church by leaving future reforms to papal discretion. Nuncios appeared everywhere supplied with papal briefs, and permanent papal nunciatures were established in many countries. Such papal centralism led inevitably to reactions. The Gallican assertions of France put forward in the second half of the century were one reaction. In Germany the national-church element was represented by the territorial rulers seeking to diminish the rights of the church in their territories. The papacy itself fell increasingly under the influence of the secular powers. At the election of Pope Innocent X in 1644 the right of veto was exercised openly when Spain excluded one candidate from the election without bothering to give any reasons for this action.

After this episode, other local cardinals exercised vetoes by their nations at later papal elections and these wishes were observed. The papal protest on the Peace of Westphalia was typical of the contrast between papal centralism and the actual extent of papal power. Innocent X in his breve *Zelo domus dei*, 26 November 1648, complained that the emperor had given away things that were not his to give: the goods of the church to the heretics in perpetuity, freedom of worship to heretics, and a voice in the election of the emperor. It was a peace against all canon law, all councils, all concordats. This was a declaration by a pope much more conciliatory than his predecessor Urban VIII, who had consistently refused to recognize the Protestant powers as partners in any negotiations. It had been Urban's intransigence which largely ended papal influence on the course of events at a time when after many years of war a longing for peace emerged from sheer weariness.

The long reign of Urban VIII, Barberini (1623–44), brings out in sharp relief the problems of the papacy. Urban conceived the papacy in medieval terms. Since heretics and infidels were the enemy, he wanted to form a league of princes for war against the Turks. He saw himself as repeating the pontificate of the crusading Urban II. A part of this dream left its mark: the College of the Propaganda of the Faith stands as a monument to Urban's zeal. In a gesture meant to demonstrate the superiority of popes over rulers Urban had the remains of Countess Mathilda, heroine of Canossa, brought to Rome and entombed in St Peter's. Bernini's frieze on the tomb shows the humiliation of one emperor, perhaps to warn another. Urban's actions, however, were more often dictated by the interests of the papal states than by grandiose visions of a militant church. He fought a dreary war against those princes who held out against his power and he continued the struggle against Venice. On the international scene he gave his support to France, seeing a menace in Austrian predominance, despite the emperor's piety and leadership of the Catholic cause in Germany. These contradictions were inherent in the political position of the papacy.

But Urban, despite his ambitions for the church, was no doctrinal purist. He himself composed poetry and sonnets in Latin and Greek. Moreover, he received Galileo in six long audiences, and when Galileo came into doctrinal conflict with the Holy See, he treated him with the utmost consideration. Indeed, he could not bring himself to sign the document, ratified by the cardinals, which condemned Galileo's defiance of the church. Urban presented a mixture of medieval intransigence for the power of the church and an openness to new ideas in art, architecture, and scientific thought. He was the principal creator of the *Roma triumphans* of the baroque. As patron of Bernini and Borromini, he transformed Rome, making his capital a fit setting for the confident might and aspirations of the papacy. His inauguration of St Peter's Cathedral in 1626 symbolized the feeling of triumph in Rome; yet this feeling was not shared by many of Rome's citizens. Urban had to raise taxes on staples and had to strip the classical monuments for materials to aid Bernini's building programme. Both actions were unpopular, and the stripping of ancient monuments led to the famous quip: *Quod non fecerunt barbari fecerunt barberini* (1625). There was little gratitude for the new and grandiose city that was under construction. To the Romans it was expensive modernization.

Urban was the absolute ruler of Rome and of his states. Moreover, he still thought of the papacy as a dynastic institution, even if it was not hereditary. Nepotism remained an evil in the papacy, becoming especially grave under Urban's successor, Innocent X (1644–65). This pope found only one able member of his family to assist him and this was a woman. The presence of Donna Olympia at the papal court caused widespread scandal. It was, however, precisely in Innocent's reign that nepotism received a severe blow when the key office of secretary of state was put into the hands of a cardinal, where it has remained. Though more flexible in his political approaches than Urban, Pope Innocent was rigorous in dogma. There was good reason for this, since his pontificate faced the serious Jansenist threat to the unity of the church.

The Catholic church thus presented a varied front to the religious problems of the century. The new piety seemed to conflict with the Jesuit approach to religious thought and reform, while the papacy, concerned for the power and unity of the church, compromised with political realities and retained some of the abuses from an earlier age. In the end, papal centralism was to combine with the Jesuits against the Jansenist movement.

The origins of Jansenism trace to a dispute at the University of Louvain between the Jesuits and those who opposed their doctrine of free will. In opposition to the Jesuits, Cornelius Jansen, bishop of Ypres (1585–1638), emphasized a rigid determinism based upon the idea of predestination. For him the prime fact in the relationship between God and man was that man had fallen. Fallen man was powerless in the hands of God; without God's grace he could not perform any good works or deeds because through original sin man had fallen into the necessity of sinning. But God's free grace was given only to a very few, and for these elect such grace was irresistible. Jansen, who saw such ideas exemplified by Augustine, called his work the *Augustinus* (1640). Like Augustine, he accused his opponents of being Pelagians, just as Gomarus had accused Arminius of that ancient heresy. Through Jansen's friendship with Saint Cyran, these concepts became central in Jansenist theology.

From these ideas it became axiomatic for Jansenists that very few people went to heaven and then only by an exercise of God's mercy which could not be resisted when it came. Thus they viewed practically all of mankind as reprobates. The world had to be shunned if one were to live the religiously strenuous life which might merit election. As good works could only be accomplished by God's direct inspiration, every action had to be carefully scrutinized. With this they combined a stress on grace as an interior matter. However, the offices of the church were central to Jansenists, and about this there was no pseudo-Protestantism whatsoever. Because the mass was essential, temporary abstinence from communion— the great joy of being in God's presence—was thought to be a useful discipline for unworthy man. Such was Jansenist teaching, and as such, most of it was condensed into five propositions by the Sorbonne and condemned by Innocent X in the bull *Cum occasione* of 1650. Innocent rejected Jansenism's denial of human free will and its sombre, hopeless outlook on the role of man in the world.

The founder of Jansenism was not Jansen himself, but Jean du Vergier de Haurranne, the abbé of Saint Cyran (1581–1643). He started his career in anti-Protestant polemics in the shadow of the court. But his great opportunity came when, through diverse machinations, he displaced the previous spiritual director of the Convent of Port Royal in 1635. Port Royal des Champs, the original Jansenist convent outside Paris, was no ordinary religious house when the impact of Saint Cyran's ideas fell upon the nuns. It had been restored to the primitive Cistercian life by a young reforming abbess, Angélique Arnauld (1591–1661). Mère Angélique was a spiritual daughter of Francis de Sales and like Saint Cyran was closely linked with Bérulle's oratory. However, it was Saint Cyran who transformed the convent. Not only did he introduce an ever more Augustinian theology but he also gave Port Royal two auxiliary institutions which furthered its influence. The school, *la petite école*, was designed to match and rival Jesuit education. The second innovation comprised the *sociétaires*, men who without taking vows undertook a religious life under Saint Cyran's direction outside the convent walls. In this manner the movement was extended beyond the nuns and the leading controversialists became men like Antoine Arnauld and Blaise Pascal. At the height of the movement Port Royal contained only some 200 nuns, both in the original Port Royal des Champs and the Port Royal in Paris; yet despite its small size, the influence of the movement embraced wide circles of society. In a sense it was a family affair, and members of the important Arnauld family occupied leading positions in the movement.

Saint Cyran's influence was further increased by his supposed martyrdom when Richelieu had him imprisoned in 1638. The abbot had become involved in the dispute between the 'Catholic' (*dévot*) party at court and the policies of the cardinal. The *dévots* disapproved of Richelieu's alliance with the German Protestants, of his concept of 'reason of state' which they contrasted to Christian idealism. The abbot opposed the 'selfish' policies of Richelieu, and his imprisonment was part of the continuing struggle between the *dévots* and those who advocated the politics of reason of state and centralization. Louis XIV's opposition to Port Royal belongs in this setting: here was a coterie of important families whose religious attitudes opposed them to pragmatic royal policies.

Saint Cyran died in prison, but meanwhile he had read Jansenius and, in collaboration with Antoine Arnauld, written his Jansenist books. If Saint Cyran introduced such religious ideas into Port Royal, Mère Angélique combined these with great self-consciousness and a tendency to dramatize all situations. She was confident that her life and that of her nuns was THE life which brought grace. Self-righteousness, hand in hand with a rigid predestinarianism came to the fore. This serious outlook upon life produced a certain pomposity as evidenced in the letter of one solitary to his father: 'God has used you to put me into this world.'[1] It also produced a puritan attitude towards the world, though Port Royal had no monopoly of puritanism defined as a moral rigorism which is an ingredient of most religious revivals. Like the English Puritans, Jansenists opposed the theatre, gambling, indeed all mundane amusements. The world was, after all, evil. A Jansenist countess wrote that when servants commit faults against God, one should be strict to the point of being terrible, for terror would bring true repentance and deepen their spirit.

Jansenism was a genuine religious revival. Jansenists believed that ever since the time of the Fathers, the church had left the true path of theology. As time went on, however, Jansenists concentrated increasingly on controversy against the Jesuits or, indeed, against anyone who questioned their actions. Here the second generation shone: Antoine Arnauld (1612–94), Pierre Nicole (1625–95), and Blaise Pascal (1623–62).

The great Arnauld was, above all, a controversialist. His *De la fréquente communion* of 1643 was a reply to a broadsheet of an obscure cleric. His statement of the necessity of abstaining from communion from time to time in order to purify one's love for God was made in a huge folio volume full of patristic learning. Jansenist controversial writing was not directed to the market-place but to fellow-theologians. Yet the first edition of *De la fréquente communion* was sold out in one fortnight.

[1] Cf. R. A. Knox, *Enthusiasm* (Oxford, 1950), p. 186; see also account of Jansenism, pp. 176 ff.

Nevertheless, the quarrels had much the same tone as the theological quarrels in Lutheranism. Legalism also entered here, and Arnauld's distinction of 'fact 'and 'right' was typical. A question was raised of how the nuns could subscribe to the five propositions without repudiating what they held to be the doctrine of Augustine. They could do so by distinguishing the doctrine of Augustine, as interpreted by Jansen, from the propositions by the claim that in 'fact' these doctrines were not contained in the propositions and therefore by 'right' as a legal thing they could subscribe.

Blaise Pascal was also a controversialist. His *Provincial Letters* were a bitter attack upon the Jesuits. But Pascal was also more than this, as his *Pensées* (1670) show. That book reflected the spiritual climax of Jansenism precisely at a time when the movement was granted its last decade of relative peace from persecution. Pascal based himself upon the supernaturalism of Port Royal. Man for him was nothing before the infinite. He did not stop there, however; man was not a zero because he had the power of thought. This power man could employ to relate himself to the whole of the universe. Could man do this through his reason, through that geometrical spirit which represented the link between thought and space? Pascal rejected this view of man's capabilities; the former geometrician was wholly converted. Man could not comprehend the whole of that universe of which he was a part through the power of his own individual self. This great supernatural unity had to be grasped by intuition. The universe, then, could not be understood by man through his own reason. Thus there was a continual tension in man's thought between his desire to comprehend the whole universe through reason, to possess certainty, and his inability to do so. It was a tension that could not be resolved. Indeed, for Pascal, any certainty and, in consequence, security in religion was rejected. Man's soul and mind were torn between the attempt to comprehend the incomprehensible and the necessary failure of that attempt.

Man was not, however, entirely helpless; his thought did amount to something before the almighty universe of God. Man's thought could make him recognize his very powerlessness before God, his misery: 'The greatness of man is that he can recognize his misery, a tree cannot recognize its misery.' In this way man's thought could surpass his nothingness, and ' *l'homme dépasse infiniment l'homme*'. Pascal's view of man was dim but there was no smug self-satisfaction with election. Man was a tortured soul, torn between the capability of his thought and reason and the inability to comprehend the universe in that way. The end had to be an insight into man's own misery before God. The *Pensées* injected a note of pessimism into the Jansenist movement as Pascal renewed the stress on man's abandonment to God and his condition as a 'feeble reed'.

While Pascal was renewing the spiritual impetus in Jansenism, the persecution, though a bloodless one, of the movement had already begun.

Saint Cyran remained the only 'martyr' for the cause. Papal condemnation and the five propositions did not end the movement; eventually the nuns did subscribe, keeping the distinction between 'right' and 'fact' in mind. Even when the nuns were forced to subscribe without reservations in 1661, Jansenism continued into the next century.

The Jansenists remained a threat to Catholic orthodoxy. They posited an Augustinianism which ignored the tradition of the church since the Church Fathers. Their doctrines of grace, free will, and abstinence from communion could not be reconciled with the canons of Trent. This revival of piety differed from that in the Protestant countries. There orthodoxy was rigid and protest was channelled along the lines of free individual religious experience. Here orthodoxy was wedded to free will and the reaction was rigid and determinist. But Jansenism was not Protestant. Arnauld and Pascal regarded all Protestants as morally lax. While Protestantism had reduced the sacraments, Jansenists believed in the necessity of both external and internal religious action, with the latter providing the foundations for the former. Arnauld stressed that approbation of actions by God was co-existent with the approbations of actions by the church. But these orthodox sentiments did not mean that Jansenists were unwilling to defy the papacy. Their theology forced them to conceive of themselves as right and all their opponents as wrong.

Since the Jansenists had the support of many French bishops, they tended to regard the pope as *primus inter pares* among the episcopate, subordinate to general councils. It is not to be wondered at that Jansenism had a certain sympathy with Gallicanism. In their constant struggle with Rome they found a refuge in Gallican principles. But the Gallicanism of the Jansenists was not regalism but episcopalianism. Though they remained loyal to the crown during the Fronde, the increasing hostility of the monarchy against them left them no choice but to oppose royal encroachment upon religious matters. Despite all this, the Jansenists were social conservatives. Pascal believed that social hierarchy was a necessity, that all men wanted to dominate, but only some could. Starting from their view of sinful men, the Jansenists took a position in favour of political absolutism. For Arnauld, oppression was the only possible basis for political government among men. Pascal, who condemned any moral laxity whatsoever, had a cynical view of politics. Stratagem was justified to maintain the necessary power and order. Though casuistry was denied to ordinary mortals, it was not so condemned for the ruler. Despite their attacks upon Jesuit casuistry, even Pascal was forced to realize that Christian ethics had to bend when unregenerate man was confronted with political problems.

Jansenists, sure that theirs was the doctrine of Augustine in its purity, constituted a revival of Augustinian piety. Augustinianism, a strong force in the Reformation itself, now played a role in reasserting religious determinism as a challenge to doctrines of free will and man's power. Augustine had been the main opponent of Pelagius, and seventeenth-century men steeped in church history saw the ancient struggle repeated in their own time.

The Jansenists were not alone in reviving Augustinianism. The Puritans in England were akin to them in this struggle against established orthodoxy. Like Catholicism, the Anglican church was in the midst of a religious revival, here centred upon liturgy. A typical figure, Lancelot Andrewes (1555–1626), stressed the ceremonial ritual of the church, which for Puritans was close to the Catholic; he combined with ritual an appeal beyond Scripture to church history. Moreover, under increasing Puritan attacks, Anglican preaching stressed the divinely established authority of church and state. Archbishop Laud (1573–1645) clearly formulated and enforced the ideas behind this Anglican revival. On the one hand, he built new churches and talked about the 'beauty of holiness', while on the other, he held that the church had the right to decree ceremonies and to decide religious controversies. He was imbued with the image of an idealized medieval church which he also viewed as a social institution regulating the anti-social appetites of men. This also he attempted to re-create. The broad Arminian base which had influenced the church never vanished. Laud protected men like Chillingworth, and Andrewes demonstrated wise tolerance. Anglicanism continued to stress man's free will and to reject the pseudo-Augustinian definition of predestination.

This Anglican revival was curtailed by the victory of the Puritan opposition. Laud's intransigence was matched by Puritan hostility to a church, which not only had its Inquisition in the Court of High Commission but which was also a firm supporter of the unpopular monarchy. It was typical that Puritanism tended at first to take a negative position opposing the liturgy, the High Commission, and above all, the monarchy which Anglicans saw as of divine origin. Their attitude on social regulation was ambiguous. Some Puritans did not oppose governmental paternalism provided it was not exercised by the Stuart government, which they regarded as oppressive. Others followed that Puritan who opposed such regulations by citing the biblical story of Job: 'it was an old trick of the devil when he meant to take away Job's religion he begins at his goods'.[1] Such differing positions on the social question enabled Puritanism after 1640 to find a variety of allies, each with different grievances against the existing régime. Nevertheless, a basic core of belief common to most of Puritanism developed.

This belief centred in a hidden God who did not reveal himself wholly in his creation. The Bible was his declared will; behind this lay his secret will. God was a mysterious, threatening God, who hid that part of his will

[1] *The Proceedings and Debates of the House of Commons etc.* collected by Sir Thomas Crewe (London, 1707), p. 17.

from man which was not declared in Scripture. Predestinarianism accompanied such thought. The elect were surrounded by a depraved and evil world. Those regenerated were made so by God's free, irresistible grace. The emphasis was once more upon the fall of man in paradise, upon predestination, and upon election by irresistible grace. In this, Puritanism was close to the piety of the Jansenists.

However, the Puritans relegated church sacraments to a lesser place. They emphasized instead two things: man's conscience and literal biblicism. The latter emphasis was combined (in contrast to Jansenism) with disinterestedness in church history. All had to be supported by Scripture, the only revealed will of God. Such biblicism, however, meant the introduction of a certain rationalism into Puritan thought, for how was one to get at the 'matter' of Scripture? By and large, they adopted the logic of Petrus Ramus (1515–72) which had become linked to Calvinist orthodoxy on the continent and which was a formal method of reasoning. Part of the Puritan success was due to the fact that their sermons were scriptural and simply organized according to a Ramist pattern which the unlettered could follow. Their emphasis on conscience went back specifically to Calvin, who saw in it the mechanism through which God spoke to man. For Calvin a clear conscience had been the only sign of election; it was equally central in a Puritan thought which rejected any external aids to grace. As one Puritan defined it: 'The conscience of man . . . is man's judgment of himself according to the judgment of God of him.' This common core of Puritan thought, however, was not static.

From the end of the sixteenth century Puritans in England and Presbyterians in Scotland began to cast their theology into the form of covenants between God and man which they deduced from Scripture. Christ had introduced a 'covenant of grace', a covenant with man which made salvation possible for the regenerate. Hand in hand with the 'covenant of grace' went the 'covenant of works' which affected all mankind since the fall. It implied that all had pledged themselves to be obedient to God and to follow the leadership of those elect who had already attained to the covenant of grace. This covenant provided the reason for ecclesiastical discipline and the regulation of morals. The importance of covenant theology was twofold. It softened the orthodox view of God to one who out of his mercy covenanted with fallen man; secondly, this religious thought went beyond confessions of faith, like that of Dort, to deduce the covenants directly from Scripture. This development was not confined to Puritanism. In Leiden Johannes Cocceius (1603–69) systematized covenant theology in order to combat Protestant scholasticism in the name of a more biblical approach.

Not all Puritans accepted covenant theology; it was the more conservative who did so. Nor could such orthodoxy be introduced into England; the Westminster Assembly of Divines tried but failed. Many of

those who had fought the Civil War desired freedom from enforced dogmas. This desire affected church organization. The 'independents' did not
want organizational centralism to stifle their religious expression; instead,
they insisted on the self-sufficiency of each congregation. In theology the
ideal of predestination was accepted even by some radicals. Such men
thought that they were elect and on that basis they revived the idea of
prophecy, believing that as saints they had the right to prophesy on all
matters.

Religious individualism could feed on this piety if church discipline
was removed and the Ramian logic regulating scriptural interpretation
was disregarded. Self-consciousness of election combined with the gift of
prophecy became a human and present sainthood. John Saltmarsh
thought that as a saint he had rights beyond any ordinary man damned by
reprobation. Ludovic Muggleton conceived of himself as a prophet
chosen by God to elect and to damn his fellow-men. The distance was slight
from being chosen by God to salvation to becoming God's instrument in
choosing others. Predestination penetrated deep into Puritan thought.
Even a man like Robert Greville, Lord Brooke, imbued with platonism
and Christian stoicism, held fast to doctrines of election and reprobation.

The self-deification of radical Puritan groups also had those chiliastic
overtones which we saw exemplified in German popular piety. They
thought the judgement day was at hand. The political revolution was the
prelude to the second coming of Christ which would issue in the golden
age of the righteous. The notion became widespread that the English
nation would soon see the fulfilment of the prophecies of the Book of
Daniel about a coming fifth kingdom. The Fifth Monarchy men were the
specific sect which expressed these ideas but they affected a wide variety
of religious experience. Thus the 'particular Baptists' split from the
Baptist movement in upholding such chiliastic ideas and in the belief
that only the elect were to be saved.

Some of the religious radicals did modify exclusive ideas of election and
rejected the determinism of predestination. This was true of the Baptists,
a continuation of the more moderate strain of the Anabaptist movement
of the previous century. Menno Simons (1492–1559) had given them their
form of religious thought, one opposed to the chiliastic and excited
anabaptism connected with David Joris. The moderates believed in adult
baptism and held infant baptism to be worthless. Above all, they clung
to the idea of the church as a purely voluntary gathering of believers. Their
community was open to every man who could attain to 'active sainthood'.
All men could do so, if they repented and believed in the gospel, none
was irrevocably damned. The Baptists advocated complete toleration on
the basis of their beliefs. One early English Baptist proclaimed that as 'the
wind blows where it listeth, so is everyman that is born of the spirit'.

Emphasis on the 'Holy Spirit' was central to such Puritan radicalism, and at times, even to orthodox Puritan thought. For God was not only all-powerful, he was everywhere close at hand, working through man's conscience and through the 'Holy Spirit' in his heart. This 'Holy Spirit' or 'Inner Light' gave emotional certitude of salvation to those who recognized themselves to be of the holy community. It was this 'inner light' which George Fox (1624–91) stressed as the central realization of the Society of Friends, who were called 'Quakers' because they quaked in ecstasy before the Lord; however their radicalism was tempered by an emphasis upon the Scriptures in contrast to many radicals who tended to dissociate Scripture and the 'Holy Spirit'. The Quakers also stressed the sinfulness of man and the need to combat this by means of a simple and frugal life. The Society of Friends managed in this way to strip itself of the undisciplined excesses of religious individualism while maintaining the 'inner light' as the centre of their religious experience. Similarly the Baptists, with their tolerant and disciplined holy community, were able to avoid the chaotic individualism of the radical sects. It is significant that out of all the religious ferment of revolutionary England, the only sects to survive were those which managed to discipline turbulent and chaotic religious expression. Such radical religious manifestations were expressions of popular piety; lower-class membership predominated in the sects. They expressed, as did all popular piety, the undisciplined longing for a better world.

Free will and determinism were the two poles around which much of the religious thought of the century moved. To the partisans of free will must be attributed that development which is known as the rise of rational theology. Here the Socinians stood in the forefront, though their rationalism was limited by a revelation which was beyond human reason. If Puritanism and Jansenism have certain affinities, that of the Socinians was with the Arminian movement. The organization of the Socinian or Anti-Trinitarian church was an accomplished fact by the time our period opens. From humble origins, the much-persecuted sect had founded flourishing churches in both Poland and Transylvania. Although Socinianism was the least numerous group among the Protestants in Poland, none had more distinguished adherents. Their centre was the city of Rakow, which became a kind of New Jerusalem for the Socinians. Its presses issued their books; its church was their largest.

The early leader of the Anti-Trinitarians in Poland was an Italian, just as the movement had been fed by Italian leadership from its beginning. Faustus Socinus (1539–1604) established the dogma of the sect which bore his name. Scripture, Socinus believed, could not contain anything contrary to reason and good sense. Man's will was free and rational. Adam had transgressed because his senses dominated his reason but this transgression did not result in original sin. Christ saved mankind in the sense that he made man more perfect to choose the good freely. These ideas were incorporated into the Catechism of the Socinians, known, because of its place of origin, as the Rakovian Catechism (1605). Translated into every European language it spread their cause abroad. Free will was asserted because God's equity could not strip man of the will and power to act rightly. Sin was a voluntary act, for one sin like Adam's could not have deprived all humanity. Predestination was utterly false for it would make God unjust; this was the same argument as that of the Arminians. But what of Christ? Anti-Trinitarians or Unitarians, as they were also called, denied the Trinity and with it the 'Godhead' of Christ. None the less, the only way for mortal man to gain salvation was by knowledge of God and Christ. Since God was only one person, belief in the Trinity would, the Catechism held, destroy the unity of God. It was also a belief against reason and not warranted by Scripture. Christ was by his nature a true man, though not a mere man because he was miraculously born and he performed miracles, but he was the son of God and not a God himself. An important Socinian theologian thought that the Trinity might involve Christians in polytheism.

Socinians sought to reduce theology to a minimum since Holy Scripture was clear and explicit. Indeed, the Rakovian Catechism sought to deny that it was a confession of faith akin to those spreading throughout the Christian world. These catechisms were termed 'trumpets of discord'. Instead, the framers of the Rakovian Catechism, not wanting to bind the conscience, stated at once: 'Let every person enjoy the freedom of his own judgment in religion.' The school at Rakow contained within it different faiths; students were left a religious liberty unique in Europe. When for the first and only time a Unitarian king, John Sigismund, attained power in Transylvania, perfect equality was established between Catholic, Lutheran, Calvinist, and Unitarian faiths (1571) at a time when elsewhere such procedure would have been all but impossible.

Scripture and reason led the Socinians to this position of toleration because, as in Arminian thought, innate human reason governed the judgement of Scripture. Within this movement the rational stream of the Reformation had found a home from the beginning. It is not strange that the leaders of the movement numbered Episcopius and Grotius among their friends and correspondents. Socinianism did not have popular appeal. It demanded too critical an attitude, a too individual and rational approach to life. Its adherents were drawn from the noble and professional classes. The movement was one of an intellectual élite, dependent in Poland upon the support of about 1,000 of the nobility. When that support failed them, the Socinians were doomed. It did fail eventually, not only because of the Catholic reconquest of Poland but also because of Protestant disunity in the nation itself. Despite repeated Unitarian efforts the Calvinists would not align with Lutherans and neither would join with the Socinians against the increased menace of Catholicism. When Lutherans and Calvinists finally held a conference at Thorn in 1645, the Unitarians were pointedly excluded. Thus all fell together. The Swedish invasion of Poland led to the final Catholic conversion. John Casimir swore an oath to the Virgin to submit to her protection if Poland were to be saved, and in 1657 Poland was. John Casimir, however, could not have reconverted Poland if the nobility had not already deserted the Protestant cause. Here, in preparing the way, the Jesuits scored their greatest triumph of the century. In Transylvania also the end came. The Jesuits had again prepared the way and the process was completed when Transylvania came under Austrian rule in 1690. Only in a part of Hungary, protected by the Turks suspicious of Catholic Habsburg designs, did Unitarianism continue in the region of its erstwhile glory.

Exile was bitter. The other Protestants could expect welcome from governments loyal to their respective faiths. No such welcome awaited the Socinians from Poland or Transylvania. Their physical wanderings in the political desert were extensive but their ideas wandered with greater force. In Holland they influenced Arminian development. In England they came together once more with Arminianism to influence rational theology, though, like Anglicans and Catholics, they were excluded from the general toleration of Puritan England and their books were burned. While Socinianism and Arminianism provided one of the factors which went into the making of rational theology, there was also another impetus of great importance.

The penetration of rationalism into the heart of seventeenth-century religious thought was closely linked to the influence of classical thought. Stemming from the Renaissance, this had seen something of a revival in the early century. Platonism and stoicism in particular became influential. The Cambridge Platonists, like some of their Renaissance forerunners, believed that Plato derived his wisdom from Moses. In the great controversy between free will and determinism, Plato supported free will in opposition to Augustine as that century understood him. The idea of the good was for Plato the end and aim of knowledge, of all striving; in comprehending all beings it drew the world into unity. Eros, the spirit intermediate between the divine and human, worked against the doctrine of original evil and triumphed over it. No Augustinian eradication of the will was predicated; original nobility was not lost through contact with the senses. Man was his own master, united to the universe and God through the principle of love. Platonism thus forged a weapon against predestination. Reason and will were one in this platonic thought; reason signified not a mere logic or critical faculty but a capacity for man to attain the divine truth in a universe suffused by God. These ideas were taken up in particular by a group of men in England known as the Cambridge Platonists, whose religious approach was based on reason. As Benjamin Whichcote (1609–83) put it: nothing truly religious was irrational and nothing truly rational was irreligious. As this was so, religious questions could only be settled by free discussion.

There was no need for infallible guides. William Chillingworth (1602–44), for example, believed that men achieved different degrees of truth according to their endowments; it was the effort to find the truth that was important. Chillingworth was an Anglican who wanted to broaden the church rather than abandon it. Here the Arminianism of Anglicanism provided, together with platonic influences, the background for a tolerant latitudinarianism. Divine grace, however, was a necessity for all these men. It came to man through his reason: 'Reason discovers what is natural, and reason receives what is supernatural.' The essence of piety was the use of reason, but something else entered as well; an ethical principle held together the universe and thus men were compelled to lead a good life. John Smith (1616–52) defined divinity as divine life rather than divine science. A pure, good, and beautiful life could only exist in the Divine which was a reality.

All religions desired this good life, but in this case it was divorced from any dogma. There was no need for confessions, books of casuistry, or ecclesiastical discipline. The essence of rational theology can be simply stated: it divorced religion from enforced dogma or theology and made man his own master on the basis of his reason and ethical nature, but within the divine context. The Cambridge Platonists and their allies fought with equal vigour against the sects and against what they considered to be the barren materialism of Thomas Hobbes.

Stoic ideas also made themselves felt. The significance of stoicism lay in the bridge it formed between rational religion and deism, as well as unbelief. William du Vair (1556–1621) had tried to Christianize this stoicism, asserting that reason had to be used to overcome man's passion and aid him to live according to his true nature. God's universe here too, was suffused by the divine, but it was a universe whose laws were immutably fixed by God and which would never be changed. Neo-stoicism seemed to combine man's free will, in the need to overcome his passions, with a kind of general predestination. Such Christian stoicism thinly disguised two pagan ideas. The first was the stoic idea of resignation, of apathy, and to one writer Christ on the cross signified such a concept. The second, and more important, was the stoic idea of an inevitable destiny, here transformed into God's immutable providence. God was the captive of His own providence; He had created but did not create. These ideas led directly into deism. A typical work was the *Quatraine du Déiste* (1622), a poem which was widely read. In it God's whole involvement with the world was denied. How could a sovereign God have anything to do with a world which was so evil? How could a good God take notice of human sin? God, adored as a first cause only, removed from human concerns, allowed man freely to enjoy His creation.

The atheistic possibilities of such deism were demonstrated by Pierre Charron in his *Of Wisdom*, of 1601. With God so far removed, it was man's place to live according to his nature and his reason. Charron inveighed against men being good or bad because they were Christian; goodness and badness were things which man's own nature can clearly distinguish. The emphasis was brought from heaven to nature, because, for Charron, 'nature is God'. Religions that have miracles, saints, articles of faith and oracles were false to human nature. This 'nature which is God' could be elucidated through human reason. The removal of God from the world and apathy in the face of destiny meant an emphasis upon man's nature, his own ethical self-sufficiency. Atheism, implicit here, came into focus with the ideas of the French poet and courtier Théophile de Viau (1590–1626). If nature was God, it followed that it was not the divine, but passions which moved the soul. By omitting the tempering factor of human reason and by believing man's passion to be his natural expression, the way was opened for libertinism. The word libertine had been used in the previous century to denote those who thought themselves as free from the church and subject only to the Holy Spirit; but now the word was increasingly used for men like Théophile, who ridiculed Christianity on behalf of a naturalistic philosophy which allowed free reign to human passions. Their philosophy could easily become outright materialism; indeed, Théophile asserted that it was the elements, not God, which had created man.

In France such ideas became fashionable, contrasting with the revival of piety. With great exaggeration Father Mersenne in 1623 counted 50,000 such 'atheists' in Paris alone. However, not only France was involved, for Venice was the real fountainhead of such ideas. At its university of Padua, Cesare Cremonini (1550–1631) taught a naturalistic philosophy. A teacher of great fame, he held in Aristotle's sense that the soul was mortal and that God was not an efficient cause. His philosophy was taken up by the Venetian ruling classes, who were embattled with the papacy. The Academia degli Incogniti formed by the young aristocrats of the city reflected these ideas.[1] Anti-Christian in tone, it at times struck a note of nihilism and negation.

Two Italians gave to this unbelief a still wider currency. Thomas Campanella's *Atheismus triumphatus* of 1631 was in form a tract against atheism, but in reality its arguments were a support of that position. What governed this world were the blind forces of nature; man had to live according to his natural reason. The divine mysteries and Christ were rejected. Under platonic influences, however, Campanella kept a vague sort of religion as a force for the general good. This appeared as such in his famous Utopia, the *City of the Sun* (1623). Typically enough, however, the priests of this imaginary state occupied themselves with natural

[1] Cf. G. Spini, *Ricerca dei Libertini* (Rome, 1950), pp. 139 ff.

199

science and astrology, trying to make their prophecies more accurate. Christ was merely *primus inter pares* among important commanders, lawgivers, and scientists. Campanella, like other 'atheists', was influenced by Averroism, especially in the concept of religion as a mere law, perceiving the founders of religions not as divine but as lawgivers only. Moreover, the Averroist stress upon astrology had continued into this age as a kind of astrological determinism which had led one Florentine to write that Christ's death was not connected with the salvation of humanity, but with an unfavourable conjunction of the stars.

While Campanella was at times hesitant in his unbelief, there was no such hesitation in the thought of Lucilio Vanini (1585–1619). For him, man was a biological phenomenon whose character was formed not by the divine within him but by the material circumstances of his life. Nature and, through it, natural circumstances, represented the immutable decree of God. Christ and Moses were mere impostors; a pretence of divinity kept poor people in servitude. Religion was the opium of the people for most of these men long before Marx used that term. Vanini had a remarkable liberty of movement until he opened a successful school to teach his doctrine in Toulouse. Only then, in 1619, was he burnt as a heretic.

The frequent attacks on such atheism and deism during the first half of the century demonstrated the relative force of these ideas. Writers never tired of reiterating the existence of a body of men who did not believe in Christ, in the immortality of the soul, or in the Bible. To these men nature was the only and highest power. It became obvious, however, that this seventeenth-century unbelief destroyed Christianity only to erect a new authoritarianism: man chained to nature unable to escape a destiny in which an absent God refused to intervene. The element of free will meant living according to this nature, giving to man an ethical self-sufficiency which excluded the divine. Most of these men did believe in a God, however remote or powerless. There were some, however, who under the influence of Epicurean thought rejected even this belief. Thus, starting from a classical impetus, our period saw the rise of an important movement, anti-Christian in character, which went beyond rational religion to various forms of deism and unbelief.

Did the growing strength of such religious attitudes lead to toleration? The theory of toleration was embodied in rational religion and in the thought of those who stressed the 'Holy Spirit' working within man, but nowhere did such men have political power. Confessions of faith were enforced in Protestant lands and Catholicism had its Inquisition. Yet there were examples of practical toleration: Poland and Transylvania before re-Catholicization, the Netherlands, and revolutionary England. However, in the Netherlands such toleration was largely confined to the province of Holland; under the English Protectorate Socinians were excluded, while Anglicans and Catholics were only allowed to worship in private. There were also some other small islands of tolerance: Altona near Hamburg; Friedrichstadt in Schleswig-Holstein, Glueckstadt in Denmark. As in Amsterdam, all religions, including Jews, were encouraged to live side by side in these towns. The reason for these astounding phenomena was not theological, but economic. In every case toleration was desired to encourage trade and to found a flourishing and profitable commercial centre.

For all these examples, the important development may well have been a less tangible one. Persecution for heresy did grow less, burnings there still were, but fewer in number than before. Perhaps the growing penetration of religious rationalism was, in part, responsible for this latitudinarianism which we saw reflected in many of these movements. Perhaps also a growing religious indifference was responsible, which placed less value on religious conformity if political allegiance was preserved.

Several unifying threads have run through our analysis. The challenges to orthodoxy in this age are obvious. Many challengers managed to establish themselves and to gain a following. Religious diversity could not be stopped with the Protestant Reformation, though Protestant as well as Catholic orthodoxy tried to restrain it. The issue of free will against predestination occupied much of the religious thought of the age, involving as it did the great question of man's power over his own destiny. In this struggle rationalism played a principal part though it led, as we have seen, under the impetus of classical thought not only to rational religion but also to modes of deism and unbelief. Modern materialism and modern anti-Christian thought have their clearly defined beginnings here as movements in our age. The greater emphasis on nature was striking also, exemplified in Boehme's mysticism on the one side, and in Vanini's ideas on the other extreme. Yet the age was also that of the revival of piety. It gave to Catholicism two of its greatest saints, and Augustinianism was certainly one expression of this piety within Jansenism and in Puritanism. Beneath it all, on the level of popular piety, there was a sameness of expression, a traditionalism, re-emphasized by the hard times of a period of almost continuous war and rising prices. Chiliasm, mysticism, and an exuberance in religious expression typified the longing for a better world. The first part of the century settled none of these issues, just as it did not begin them. The change in our period was not so much the creation of something new, but the crystallization and definition of these trends of religious thought.

CHAPTER VI

MILITARY FORCES AND WARFARE 1610–48

For the military historian, the main feature of what is usually called the modern period is that it is dominated by the professional soldier, hired at home or abroad. In the early part of the period, troops were recruited abroad to serve for a limited period only: these were the mercenaries or 'hired troops' in the strict sense, of whom the purest example were the *Lansquenets*, troops completely unattached to any one state or government, who sold their services to the highest bidder on terms mutually agreed and laid down in a deed of engagement. Mercenaries, however, came to be replaced by troops of home origin, engaged by the state for an indefinite period of time and organized into regiments or companies which were permanent sections of the military forces; that is, by a standing or national professional army. In practice, such standing armies also comprised a varying number of foreigners, either grouped into separate regiments or spread among the various sections of the army. Naturally, the process of transition from the one method of raising an army to the other differed from country to country, but in general it can be said to have taken place in the first half of the seventeenth century. This was closely bound up with the development of the modern state and with the evolution of absolute monarchy, the most powerful weapon of which the standing army proved to be.

The use of hired troops can be traced far back into the Middle Ages and predominated from before the beginning of the sixteenth century. But, obviously, governments forced to take hired troops into their service could not close their eyes to the danger of entrusting their own and their subjects' interests to foreign adventurers, nor to the thieving, plundering, extortion and other outrages which made these bands the terror of friend and foe alike—not only in the field, but also after they had been disbanded. Then, too, not every ruler could afford the heavy cost of maintaining a hired army. Attempts were therefore made to find some other way of providing defence forces, and the obvious answer was a national militia, raised from among the home population. This was in line with the long-established practice of general conscription in the event of enemy invasion. Similar instances were found in the 'franc-archers' of Charles VII of France, in the civil guard on the Roman model which Machiavelli had built up in Florence in the early years of the sixteenth century, and in the 'legions' of Francis I.

In Germany particularly, where, after the failure of Charles V's policy real power had passed into the hands of the local princes, several wrestled with the problem of defence—and with good reason, for the animosity between Protestantism and the Counter-Reformation sharpened visibly about the end of the sixteenth century, and it became obvious that an armed clash would not be long in coming. And so in this period there were attempts throughout Germany to build up people's armies, referred to as the *Landesdefension* or *Landrettung*. Here, Bavaria (where Duke Maximilian, the energetic head of the Catholic League, founded in 1609, did much to help the cause) was the most prominent state, along with Brandenburg, Saxony, the Rhine Palatinate and Nassau. The *Landrettung* of Nassau is important because of the close ties between Count John the Elder—brother of William of Orange—and his son, John *de Middelste* [the Middle One], and the Dutch generals, Maurice and William Louis. Since the Peace of Augsburg (1555) there had, after all, been no opportunity in Germany of acquiring any practical knowledge or gaining any experience of modern warfare. We can therefore understand why the Nassau leaders turned to the Netherlands, then the military college of Europe. John of Nassau (*de Middelste*) was the chief intermediary for this purpose. He went on some of the most important campaigns undertaken by Prince Maurice and recorded the valuable experience he gained there in a number of military manuals [*krijgsboeken*], which form one of our chief sources of information about the reforms in the Nassau army. The manuscripts now lie in the state archives at Wiesbaden.

Great pains were taken with the *Landesdefension*, but they were doomed to failure. The causes were many. One of the first requirements for an army based on national service is a strong national feeling. This was entirely lacking in the countless patriarchally ruled states into which the German Empire was divided. Passive resistance rather than co-operation was to be expected from the 'subjects', good-natured peasants whose interests did not range far beyond local matters.

The extensive paperwork which national service inevitably involves was also under-estimated. The state administration at that time was unable to cope with the work, as it did not have enough well-trained and reliable officials. As far as the organization of the army was concerned, one of the weaknesses always encountered in a people's army of this kind, was the shortage of officers, that is to say, of an efficient corps of instructors. Moreover, the training period was too short, attendance poor and irregular, while months or even years might elapse without any exercises being held. The nobility looked upon the arming of the peasants with distrust: they were afraid there would be marauding and had not forgotten the Peasants' War. The townspeople, who had to provide the funds, showed little enthusiasm for a venture in which no one had any confidence. Admittedly the main purpose of the system was to provide protection against bands of plunderers, but the Thirty Years War demonstrated clearly enough that it could not achieve even this modest aim. The beginning of the Thirty Years War meant the end of the *Landrettung*. When, in 1620, Spinola and his experienced troops invaded the Palatinate, rapid collapse ensued, practically without a struggle.

One may ask whether the *Landrettung* left any positive gains. Of chief importance are the military writings it left, designed to advance the knowledge of warfare in line with modern ideas. The manuscripts of John of Nassau (*de Middelste*) have already been mentioned. In addition, he became very famous as the compiler of the first European drill-book, consisting of plates by Jacob de Gheyn, reproductions of which can still be found in countless books all over the world. He found a partner in George Frederick, the margrave of Baden-Durlach. Another was Johann Jacobi van Wallhausen, who published a series of books on the art of warfare and who may be regarded as the leading author on military matters at the time of the Thirty Years War. He was also the first head of the military college for sons of the nobility which John *de Middelste* had founded at Siegen in 1616. The aim of this establishment was to meet, by theoretical study, the need for practical experience of war, there being little opportunity of acquiring it, as there had been peace in the Netherlands since 1609. This military college, the first of its kind in Germany, was, however, to enjoy only a brief existence: the outbreak of the Thirty Years War was the probable reason why it had to close as early as 1619.

The failure of practically every experiment with a militia based on compulsory military service may be taken as proof that, given the political and social situation in Europe in the sixteenth and succeeding centuries, the professional army was the type of military force required. There was hardly a country at war which did not have to engage large or small numbers of foreign troops to supplement the home or 'national' army. Thus the United Netherlands continuously had regiments of English, Scottish, French, German and Walloon troops in their service. Spain fought her wars mainly with Italians, Burgundians, Walloons, Germans and Swiss. German mercenary cavalry [*reitres*] and infantry [*lansquenets*] were important in the French religious wars. During the Thirty Years War Walloon regiments served with commanders like Tilly and Bucquoi under Bavarian and imperial banners. Even Gustavus Adolphus had German and Scottish troops in the army with which he landed in Germany in 1630.

Provided they were paid regularly, hired troops can be generally said to have possessed one good quality, courage. In battles, sieges, and especially when storming cities and redoubts, they repeatedly showed a defiance of death, which is all the more remarkable as they were seldom, if ever, inspired by patriotic feelings. The hired soldier has often been regarded as a ready mutineer, but he mutinied almost always because of arrears in his pay. Moreover, he would never mutiny for higher pay, but because he received no pay at all. Discipline and regular pay went hand in hand. Under leaders with such forceful personalities as Maurice and Frederick Henry had, there was, for those days, excellent discipline in the Netherlands army. The most striking evidence for this is that the towns liked having a garrison, which in former times had been looked upon as a scourge. After all, a garrison brought a town money and trade, the city treasury benefited by higher excise revenues, while many citizens found it very profitable to let rooms and to receive a compensation for billeting. This was only true, however, if order and discipline were maintained; the terms of the deed of engagement laid down severe punishments for fighting and for mishandling people providing quarters; anyone even drawing a sword in the garrison did so on pain of death.

One of the main advantages of the professional army compared with the militia system was that it was a result of what people wanted. After the religious wars had come to an end, people did regard warfare as a matter for rulers and governments; a recruiting system which interfered as little as possible with social and economic life was consistent with this attitude. The professional army undoubtedly met this requirement and this was its main justification. As early as the third decade of the sixteenth century the states of Holland rejected the idea of recruiting a militia, considering 'that it was impolitic to set citizens or countryfolk against hirelings who had nothing to lose'. This was to be the prevailing opinion right up to the time of the French Revolution. The argument heard in favour of the hired army—that it did not withdraw any labour from the home market— sprang from the same line of thought. It was also considered no small advantage of such an army that it relieved society of its unemployed, of its vagrants and of elements likely to cause unrest and endanger the state, thereby undoubtedly performing a useful service to society. It is obvious as well that once war was over, or the threat of war had passed, block discharges became necessary, and a new problem arose for the solution of which society in those days had only primitive means at its disposal. Finally, there was this to be said for the hired army, that in poverty-stricken or poorly developed areas it could absorb the surplus population and be a welcome refuge in difficult times. It is not surprising, then, that severe winters, bad harvests and famine had a favourable effect on recruiting.

The fact that the hired army was a necessity in its day does not mean that the system had no disadvantages: there were, in fact, great disadvantages. First and foremost, the indispensable bond between army and people was lacking. The two existed side by side, with little mutual contact, respect or understanding, as two entirely separate entities within the state. The soldier served for pay, and once this pay had been found, the citizen had no further obligation towards the army. The mercenary, in his turn, had little or no interest in the cause for which he fought. This is why there were always deserters and turncoats; why, for instance, prisoners would sometimes go over to the enemy *en masse*; why mutiny and treachery were of great importance in the wars of the time. One should be careful, however, not to generalize too much about this. In those countries, like Gustavus Adolphus' Sweden and Cromwell's England, which had a mainly national army, and which, moreover, were fighting for some religious or political ideal, morale was definitely higher than when pay and booty were the sole motives. The same was true of those religious wars which really were struggles of faith, but not all religious wars were of this kind. For purely practical reasons, leaders had to be very tolerant. The notorious duke of Alva frequently used German Lutheran regiments with the Spanish troops operating in the Netherlands, whereas, elsewhere, supporters of the faith preached by the Lutheran chaplains were put to the sword. In Wallenstein's army Protestant officers were to be found right up to the highest ranks, and as far as the rank and file were concerned, we know for certain that their faith was never recorded when they were enlisted. All one can say is that, very broadly speaking, both Protestant and Catholic countries recruited their forces in districts where their own faith was predominant. It was to be expected that the terms of the deed of engagement reflected the attitude of the state or official church, and as some of these deeds made attendance at religious service compulsory (the Swedish ones of 1621 and 1632; the Danish one of 1635; and the English one of 1585, among others), this meant that soldiers would be forced to practise a religion or take part in services different from their own. It is likely that the terms of the deed were not applied too strictly in this instance. In the Dutch deed of 1590, there were, it is true, threats of severe punishments for swearing and for disrespectful treatment of servants of the church [*kerken dienaers*], but attendance at church services was not made compulsory. Contemporary historians were generally agreed that officers and men did not lead very religious lives. Swearing and blaspheming in particular, which carried such severe punishments (in the Netherlands, for example, piercing of the tongue with a red-hot dagger), seem to have been prevalent, along with drunkenness and whoring, not to mention other offences. Military life apparently fostered licence rather than piety, and this was certainly one of the reasons for the army's bad reputation in most countries.

The chief victims of the 'other offences' were the people living in the country. From the very first days of its existence, the mercenary army was a two-edged sword. The homeland often had to suffer as severely as, if not more than, the enemy territory. And in later periods too, the chronicles of war are accompanied by a sombre tale of murder and arson, plundering, extortion and robbery. The countless edicts published to curb all these enormities had little effect. To some extent, the lack of funds with which almost all the warring rulers had to contend was the source of these evils too. It was, in fact, a very common practice simply to 'quarter' troops whose pay could not be found in country areas and let them fend for themselves, the countryfolk having to shoulder the burden.

During the Dutch war of liberation, the Spanish side resorted to this method with troops whose pay was in arrears by two years or more and whose demands for food and drink knew no bounds. The Spanish soldiers acted in similar fashion, but then on their own authority, during the many mutinies—again the result of irregular payment—which hampered and sometimes completely paralysed military operations. They sent their officers packing and chose an *eletto* which, supported and supervised by a sort of soldiers' council, laid down the duties, observing very strict discipline, maintained by barbarous punishments. The duties consisted in collecting food and forage by means of a levy on the surrounding villages; for this purpose threatening letters were circulated, the purport of which was sometimes made quite clear by scorch-marks on the corners. Here again, it was the home territory that had to foot the bill. If the *escadron* submitted once more to government authority, which never happened unless it was paid off and granted an amnesty, the *eletto* would receive a sum of money to enable it to seek its fortune abroad.

Columns on the march were also a plague, not only because the soldiers and the women, boys and horses following in their train had to be provided with food and shelter, with hay, straw and carts and anything else they might require, but also because troops on the march were usually accompanied by bands of marauders who looted and pillaged on their own account. In this, the role of the partisans was very important. Partisans were small bands of soldiers which would set out, with or without a commander, on short expeditions or on reconnaissance. Their good knowledge of the region frequently enabled them to penetrate deep into enemy territory, showing great adroitness and daring. Nevertheless, it was difficult to draw a line between such 'expeditions' and looting raids. In the northern Netherlands it was therefore stipulated that, to claim the right to be treated as prisoners of war, members of a 'party' must be at least twenty-five in number, and under the command of an officer.

A country which suffered particularly was Germany during the Thirty Years War; most of all from the swarms of wives, whores, boys, children, drivers and servants which followed the army together with hundreds of waggons and herds of cattle, and which, at the end of every march, spread across the countryside like a plague of locusts. While on the march the armies must have resembled a mass migration, increasingly so as the war proceeded. As early as 1617, however, in his *Krijghskonst te Voet* [*The Art of Infantry Warfare*], Van Wallhausen estimates that there were at least 4,000 'whores, boys and bawdy-waggons' to 3,000 German soldiers. It was the task of the *Rumormeister* and the *Hurenweibel* to maintain law and order among this rabble. The longer the army remained in one place, the wider the area stripped clean. The worst feature of all was the atrocious tortures inflicted to discover where food and valuables had been hidden. The armies which Wallenstein recruited with his own means in 1625 and succeeding years had a particularly lamentable record.

It goes without saying that the actual aim of the war did not make the slightest difference to the situation. Officers as well as ordinary soldiers assembled from all corners of Europe at the sound of the recruiting drum. The men who slew Wallenstein at Eger in 1634 were partly Scottish Protestants, partly Irish Catholics. It was inevitable that the army-camps developed their own type of language—a crude professional slang—which gave rise to a host of the most outlandish corruptions, such as 'leutenampt' for 'lieutenant'; it has left its traces in many modern languages. The international composition of these armies certainly helps to explain why we find similar military terms used all over the world today, such as the names for army units and ranks.

The way in which the state obtained its mercenaries is typical of the—as yet—primitive structure of its government. In those days, the state organized as little as possible itself, leaving as much as possible to private initiative. The head of state could acquire soldiers in two ways: by recruiting at home or abroad, or by employing one or more of the corps of foreign troops already existing. In the latter case, a contract or 'capitulation' was signed with the government concerned, containing details of the mutual financial and other commitments, as well as of the conditions on which the troops might be used. An advantage of this procedure was that trained soldiers were obtained and recruitment expenses avoided. In the former case, recruitment was put in the hands of a general who was popular among the soldiers and who had sufficient funds to pay the cost of recruiting and arming the troops, and, sometimes, to advance their first month's pay as well. Conditions were laid down in a special 'commission' [*commissie* or *Bestallung*]. The general, in turn, commissioned colonels or captains to take charge of recruiting. The large towns were favourite recruiting centres. The men who came forward were ordered to attend at the place-of-muster or drill-ground on a given day; at the same time they were paid a sum as muster money. At the assembly-point they were enrolled by muster-commissioners, provided, where necessary, with weapons, the cost of these being deducted from their pay, and divided into sections. The subordinate commanders were appointed, the colours handed out with a show of ceremony, the articles of war read out; the oath of allegiance was sworn to the king or whoever was hiring the soldiers, who promised to protect the colours and obey the articles of war. With this, the regiment existed officially, and, having received the first month's pay, it was ready to march off to its destination.

The advocates of the national militia did not fail to point out the great disadvantages of this system. First, there were the high costs incurred before the troops had even caught sight of the enemy; the muster-money had to be paid, and weapons bought and transported; the recruiting staff's travelling and subsistence expenses had to be met, and above all there was the cost of providing for the recruits at the place-of-muster. Every day spent there cost a considerable sum of money and this was particularly felt if there were delays in mustering. If payment was not forthcoming, the soldiers were forced to provide for themselves by plundering until they finally made off for good—a frequent occurrence—so that all the expense had been in vain, which sometimes even benefited the enemy. The same happened when the enemy attacked the place-of-muster, often on neutral ground, dispersing the troops that had been recruited and seizing their weapons. It is not surprising that a number of the recruits disappeared without trace after receiving the 'king's shilling'. Finally, the discharging of mercenary troops often involved difficulties. Arrears of pay had then to be paid, besides money for the journey back home, if the mercenaries were to be dissuaded from remaining in the country as vagabonds or joining the enemy. With the treasuries of the warring princes usually all but empty, troops could often neither be paid nor discharged. This was the situation in the Netherlands, when, on the occasion of the famous siege of Bois-le-Duc, the republic had altogether no less than 120,000 men under arms, a great many of whom had to be discharged after the campaign. This was carried out quite successfully, although with great difficulty, leaving in the end some 6,000 men, for whom no better solution could be found than to let them spend the winter in the neutral territories of Cleves, Mark and Berg, at the expense of the local inhabitants.

Newly recruited regiments, entirely lacking in discipline, cohesion and training, were naturally no match for old experienced soldiers. The very reason for the defeats which the Netherlands suffered in the field at the beginning of the Eighty Years War was that they had to go to war with scratch regiments of newly recruited German auxiliaries. This explains the clause in the Dutch deed of engagement, which reads: 'Anyone demanding money when our forces are marching on the enemy or setting off to make any kind of attack will forfeit his life, without appeal to mercy.'

It is general knowledge that the armies were made up of the scum of the nations. Dislike of regular work, the prospect of booty, a craving for adventure, debts, the desire to keep out of the hands of the law, these were the principal reasons for answering the call of the recruiting drum. George Gascoigne, an English captain who was a poet of the English Renaissance, divided those who earned their living by soldiering into three categories, to which he gave the allegorical names of 'Haughty Harte', 'Greedy Minde' and 'Miser'; that is to say, those eager for fame and honour, those out for money and booty, and those driven by poverty and need, extravagance or crime. If it seems surprising that so many young men preferred a soldier's life to the workshop or the plough, it must be remembered that living conditions were unfavourable, hours of work long and wages low in town and countryside, and this is probably where the explanation lies. Countrymen were said to make the better soldiers.

Of course, the situation was not the same in every army. In the Spanish infantry, for instance, many sons of the lower nobility—*hidalgos*—served as ordinary soldiers, though with a batman and a horse for marches, which they left behind with the baggage during battle. In France, a large part of the cavalry consisted of volunteer noblemen; these must be distinguished from members of the *arrière-ban*, service in which was, in theory, still compulsory for all vassals, but which had already largely fallen into decay by the sixteenth century. In the southern Netherlands the nobility was strongly represented in the *Benden van Ordonnantie*. There was a curious development in Germany. Here the lance had already gone out of use by the early sixteenth century even, and had been replaced by two pistols. Unlike the lance, the pistols could also be used by batmen and servants, who were accordingly incorporated into the large, unwieldy squadrons of the day, the nobleman being paid according to the number of mounted retainers he had. The German cavalry [*reitres*] played an important part, particularly in the French religious wars. Owing to their custom of not polishing their armour, but painting it black instead—a practical measure—they became known as the 'Black Cavalry'.

There was no proper course of training for officers. As we saw, the military academy at Siegen enjoyed only a brief existence. Those destined for careers as officers joined a company as 'noblemen', 'cadets' or 'captain's bodyguards', and had to climb the ladder. Others began their careers as volunteers in a general's or colonel's retinue; then there were those who obtained commissions as lieutenants or ensigns by favour or purchase, often at the expense of others who had a better claim to the rank. Most officers ended their careers with the rank of captain; or sometimes as captains-of-the-guard or adjutants in a fortress or redoubt. Colonels and lieutenant-colonels who had worked their way up from the ranks were not unknown, but this was usually referred to as exceptional. There was no more question of a fixed rule for pensions than there was for promotion. They were granted to ordinary soldiers, non-commissioned officers and officers' widows, by way of exception only, and on request.

Educationally, the officers of the sixteenth and seventeenth centuries could naturally not compete with the officers of today. Only a few had been to a university, either at home or abroad, or undertook any serious study. Furthermore, the situation varied from country to country. It is especially worth noting that several English officers who fought in the Netherlands against Spain became known as scientists or artists or recorded their experience of the war in books. Most celebrated of them all was Sir Philip Sidney, who was fatally wounded at Zutphen: as well as being a distinguished poet, he was a man of great erudition and refinement. But there were others too, among them George Gascoigne (who was mentioned above), Ben Jonson, Thomas Churchyard, John Weymouth, Roger Williams, Francis Markham and his brother, Gervase.

In the south of Europe, especially in Spain and France, there seem to have been more officers with an academic education than in the north. The military literature of the south, to which the Renaissance had come so much earlier than to the north, is proof of this; it was unrivalled by anything published on the subject in Germany or the Netherlands. Works such as those by Mendoza, Coloma, Ufano and Melzo—to name but a few—are outstanding for their clarity, objective presentation and erudition. Many revealed a more than superficial knowledge of the classics. Military writings in the north were very often left in manuscript form, so that no enemy power could benefit by them. The works of John *de Middelste*, for example, were not printed. Nevertheless, important works appeared in the Netherlands and Germany on fortress engineering and on artillery, the technical subjects proper, the experts on which were not regarded as soldiers.

For a long time the prejudice against reading remained fairly common among officers, this giving all military reformers much to contend with. It was said that warfare could not be learned from books. It must be admitted that many authors encouraged this conservatism by embellishing their works with battle formations of the strangest kind, entirely devoid of practical value, in order to give them a 'learned' appearance.

A characteristic difference between the officer corps of former times and that of today is that the higher-ranking officers, up to the very highest ranks, each had a company, either in their own or in another regiment. These companies were under the command of a 'lieutenant-captain'. In addition, the higher-ranking officers held numerous other posts, which carried high salaries, one of which was that of fortress-governor. But a company in itself was considered well worth having, since all manner of other emoluments, official and unofficial, went with the salary. The main thing, however, was to ensure that there were many more soldiers on the muster-roll than were actually present. All sorts of ruses were therefore invented to mislead the muster-commissioner—the captain's sworn enemy—on the day of the muster, with the company-clerk in particular lending his powerful support. The idea was to have all those who had died, deserted or been discharged since the last muster reported as present and fit for duty at the new muster. This was done by substituting soldiers from another company, townspeople, peasants, or any others willing to offer their services, in return for a small consideration, in the place of the absent troops. Such persons were known as *passevolanten*. They are often confused with the *mortepaien* or 'dummy names' of the system whereby the captain received pay for a few more men than the number shown on the muster-roll; in effect, this was like awarding him an extra allowance for some reason or other.

The records tell us that captains had other advantages too. If a soldier died or deserted, his weapons became the captain's property; if he was discharged he had to forfeit, in the captain's favour, most of what the latter still owed him; a fifth or sixth of all booty went to the captain; and finally, he made something on the soldier's clothing. On occasions, troops were paid in cloth, more being deducted from their ordinary pay for this than was right and proper. In the Netherlands, the number of troops actually serving was sometimes estimated to be three-quarters of the nominal strength, even lower for some companies. Attempts to remedy these abuses by direct payment to the men were always frustrated by those who had something to lose. Since this state of affairs was common knowledge outside the army too, it obviously deterred citizens from making financial sacrifices for the military forces, while the popularity and prestige of the army greatly declined as a result of all this corruption.

Something which had a far-reaching effect on the armies of the time was the absence of barracks. When not in the field, the soldier was in billets. The provider of these quarters received a certain sum in payment, known as 'service money'. The soldier paid for his own meals, and, if he was married, for those of his wife and children as well. It is a mystery how a soldier ever managed to keep a family on the pay he received. The wife probably earned something too, by washing, cleaning, spinning or by doing some similar type of work. Apart from drill and target practice, both of which were infrequent at first, the only duty in the garrison was keeping the watch. In the summer, many soldiers worked for farmers or practised some craft or other, much to the annoyance of the urban gilds. They found others who were willing to do their sentry-duty for them, and paid them for it; in this way, these people too, who were known as 'paid sentries', were able to earn a little extra. The town authorities were not very well disposed to the wives and children of soldiers. If, at the end of a campaign, a soldier went to live in a garrison other than the one where his wife and children were staying, a strict ban was imposed on letting rooms or sleeping accommodation to these unfortunate people, and sometimes they were expelled from the town without more ado.

Basically at least, the armies of the sixteenth and seventeenth centuries were all organized in much the same way. For example, in an English infantry company of 150 men (the normal complement), there were, besides the captain, a lieutenant, an ensign, two sergeants, two drummers, a surgeon, a chaplain, a gunner and a clerk. There were also six corporals, each in charge of a section of the company and responsible for training recruits. A number of noblemen were assigned to each company. The strength of the companies varied considerably: in the Netherlands it was usually 113 or 150 in the seventeenth century, and in Germany 300. In other countries, in addition to those already mentioned for England, there were a number of other ranks: that of *landspassaat*, corresponding approximately with that of corporal; that of *capitaine d'armes*, for the company armourer; and in the United Netherlands, France, and Germany respectively, those of *adelborst*, *cadet* and *Gefreyter*, all referring to what may be called prospective officers. In Germany and Sweden, there was also a *Führer*, who carried the colours when the company was on the march, but not when it was in the field, and finally, in the Netherlands and Germany, the captain's bodyguard. Ranks below those of lieutenant and ensign were appointed by the captain; but for a long time all members of the company staff, including for example, the drummers and the surgeon, were called 'officers'. In England and the Dutch Republic all officers down to and including the ensign held the commission or warrant of the king or whoever else was paying them. This explains why corporals, sergeants and certain others below the rank of second-lieutenant in the British army are still called non-commissioned officers.

The only permanent unit above a company was a regiment. The number of companies in a regiment varied considerably. In 1635, there were 582 companies of infantry spread over 33 regiments in the Dutch Republican army, the number of companies per regiment varying between 9 and 30. They included four English regiments, two of 17, one of 18 and one of 23 companies (9,550 men in all), and 3 Scottish regiments, each of 10 companies (3,870 men). The colonel's company was always larger than the others. In addition to the colonel, the regimental staff consisted of the lieutenant-colonel, the sergeant-major, the quartermaster and the provost. In some countries it was quite a long time before permanent regiments with a permanent staff were formed. The Spanish Tercios were very old regiments, while in France the regiments known as *les Vieux*, which went back to Francis I's legions (Picardie, Piémont, Navarre and Champagne), had existed since the middle of the sixteenth century. Henri IV added a few more, known as *les Petits Vieux*. It was not until 1623 that the first permanent regiment was formed in the Netherlands. Until that year the practice had been to amalgamate a number of companies under a colonel for one campaign as a temporary measure, since there was no permanent staff. Foreign troops in the service of the states, on the other hand, were organized into permanent regiments. The first English regiment was Humphrey Gilbert's, which fought in Zeeland in 1572; its men were probably the original 'Buffs'.

For many years the States' cavalry also had no regiments except when in the field. It was not until 1635 that it was organized into four standards, companies or 'cornets'. In the field, the regiments were led by a major, since the colonel almost always held other posts which kept him elsewhere. Sometimes, too, as a favour, a very young person or even a child would be appointed colonel. That officers could hold a command in the cavalry and the infantry at one and the same time was another evil that could never be rooted out entirely.

As early as the end of the sixteenth century, an important reform had taken place in the cavalry: the lance had been abolished. There was much discussion about the advantages and disadvantages of the lance compared with the cuirassier's pistol. The ultimate reason for the disappearance of the lance (it was to return two centuries later) was that it made heavy demands on both rider and horse, demands which it became increasingly difficult to meet in the new age. And so the knightly weapon *par excellence* disappeared from the armouries of France in 1594 and from those of the Dutch Republic in 1596. Apparently, it remained in use longer in other countries. As late as the Battle of Marston Moor (1644) a unit of lancers 400 strong was successfully deployed by the parliamentarian army.

Meanwhile, various countries had found it necessary to introduce troops of a type midway between the infantry and the cavalry. These were the dragoons. Before this, there had been no better ways of moving foot soldiers rapidly from one place to another than to carry them in waggons or mount them behind cavalrymen. Horses had even been taken from arquebusiers to transport troops. Mounted infantrymen were used in France as early as the religious wars; the origin of their name '*dragons*' remains obscure. They were armed and fought as infantrymen, the horse being for them not a weapon, but simply a means of conveyance. In the Netherlands it was not until 1606 that the first companies of dragoons were formed. Of cavalry proper, there were only two kinds: cuirassiers, the heavy cavalry, and arquebusiers, the light cavalry. The former were armed with a sword and two pistols, the latter with a carbine, a pistol and a sword.

In the seventeenth century there was a general tendency towards uniformity in weapons. Thus the double-handled broadsword went out of use, as did the shield (buckler) of the captain's bodyguard. The halberd was retained only as an emblem of rank for sergeants, the partisan (long-handled spear) for captains and lieutenants. Weapons no longer serviceable in the field, including ones like the *morgenstern* [mace] and the storming flail, found their way to the fort lumber-rooms.

Armour remained unaltered for the time being. Cuirassiers wore a complete suit of plate armour, except that below the knee the leg was protected by a boot only; they wore a helmet with either a visor or bars. The left hand only was protected by a steel glove. The breastplate, backplate and helmet had to be proof against pistol-fire. The arquebusiers, known also as carabineers or 'bandoleer-horsemen', wore a helmet open at the front, their only other protection being breastplates and backplates. In the course of the Thirty Years War, an entirely new and highly practical type of helmet was introduced from the East; it came to be widely used, and was worn, for example, by the cavalry in England during the Civil War. The helmet consisted of a metal skull, to which were attached a horizontal rain-flap with an opening for an adjustable nose-guard, a strong, reliable neck-guard and cheek-flaps with apertures for the ears. The pikemen, also known as 'double-pay men' on account of the high pay they received, who were the backbone of the battle-formation, were protected by a morion, breastplate and backplate, gorget and by guards of steel covering part of their arms and legs [*besagues* and *tasses*]. In addition they carried a 13-ft pike and a dagger. The musketeers and unmounted arquebusiers wore either a hat or a morion. Using $\frac{1}{12}$ lb. bullets, the musket had a range of between 220 and 270 yards. The powder was carried in leather-lined tin canisters attached to a bandoleer; the arquebusiers, however, used powder-flasks.

In the first half of the seventeenth century there were still no uniforms proper. It was always a simple matter, therefore, for partisans or soldiers taking towns by surprise to pretend they belonged to the other side. The absence of uniforms made all kinds of stratagems possible, but also encouraged numerous abuses, desertion, of course, being the main one. Sashes, sword-knots and cockades of a given colour were used to distinguish one side from the other. Other means employed were battle-tokens of foliage, cloth or bunches of straw attached to the headgear, and a pre-arranged battle-cry. Companies with all their men dressed in uniforms of the same colour existed quite early, but this would be because the captain or colonel had bought cloth of one colour, not because a general order had been given. The first general order regulating the colour of uniforms came with the introduction of the New Model Army in England in 1645, when red was the colour prescribed for all troops. This was to remain the colour worn by British troops right up to the First World War.

By tradition the infantry, especially the pikemen, who represented the real strength of any force, were drawn up in the battle-field in three or four rectangular masses, referred to as battalions, squadrons, *hopen* (Dutch) or *Gewalthaufen* (German). They were usually twice as deep as they were broad. The artillery and musketeers either stood, in deep formation like the infantry, on the four corners or on the wings of the squadron, or in a few ranks all the way round the outside. In the cavalry, the lancers originally fought *en haie* in the medieval manner, but after the pistol had become their main weapon, they too adopted the rectangular formation, with squadrons of 500 to 1,000 men. During an engagement, the artillery and musketeers fought in small groups as skirmishers, seeking cover among or behind the pikemen in the event of a cavalry charge. The cavalry's usual method of fighting was the *caracole*; this meant that they fired rank by rank, the rank which had just fired closing up behind the squadron and reloading.

The disadvantage of deep, unwieldy formations was that they were difficult to move and, more especially, that only the outer ranks (in the case of the pikemen no more than the first five ranks, according to estimates) could take a direct part in the fighting. Besides, once it was engaged in man-to-man combat, a battalion or squadron, whatever its size, was highly vulnerable to attack from another quarter. These considerations above all led the stadtholders of Nassau to adopt a new battle-formation, with which the name of Prince Maurice is associated. Its special features were: battalions no bigger than one regiment (500 to 1,000 men); cavalry squadrons no bigger than one company (c. 100 horse); battalions drawn up in ten ranks, cavalry squadrons in five; the entire force in three lines; the cavalry on the wings, except for a few squadrons held in reserve. The artillery and musketeers stood on the left and right of the pikemen and, with them, comprised one squadron. Firing took place rank by rank, the rank which had just fired moving to the back, via gaps left open for the purpose, and reloading. This allowed continuous fire to be maintained. This new battle-formation proved its superiority at Nieuwpoort in 1600. This would not have been possible without first-class troops. The ten-rank formation was a venture at the time and the firing in particular obviously called for much practice and a high standard of discipline. This standard was obtained by the reintroduction of drill exercises on the model of the Ancients, as described in the works of classical writers such as Aelianus Tacticus, Leo VI (the Wise) and Polybius. An intensive study was made of these works, with the help of Latin translations. The work of scholars such as Justus Lipsius, professor at Leiden and later at Louvain, under whom Prince Maurice studied for eighteen months and whose De Militia Romana went through eleven editions, was of great assistance; and particularly that of the versatile scholar Simon Stevin, whom Maurice, quite justifiably, refers to as his guide and mentor. It is difficult to over-estimate the importance of this drill, which was the main feature of the Nassau army reform. Its value far exceeded its direct, tactical use in the battle-field: the eventual aim was to create a type of soldier entirely different from the soldier of the time, who was still moulded in the mercenary tradition. Maurice and his nephew and brother-in-law, William Louis, undoubtedly had great difficulty in overcoming initial resistance. Eventually, however, the drill was not only accepted in the Netherlands, but was adopted sooner or later by all European powers and is now in use all over the world.

Maurice gave much attention to siegecraft and fortress engineering, intervening personally in these matters. As far as the artillery, bridge-building, the supply-train and encampment were concerned, here, too, a reorganization took place which was unsurpassed in any other country and met requirements for many years. It was in this period that nobles and soldiers from numerous countries visited the Netherlands to study 'modern' warfare, with the aim of returning home and building on the foundations laid there.

As can be expected, it was mainly the Protestant powers which strove to reform their military systems on Nassau lines, Sweden being the first to organize its army as the Netherlands had done. Charles of Södermann-land, later Charles IX, had already made some attempt at army reform in Sweden, but with little effect as, being poor, the country could not find the necessary funds. The intermediary was John *de Middelste*, mentioned earlier as the organizer of the Nassau national militia and of the *Landrettung* in the Palatinate. In 1601 and 1602 he fought as commander-in-chief of the Swedish troops against the Poles in Livonia, his services being highly appreciated. There can be little doubt that knowledge of the new methods of warfare was greatly increased in Sweden as a result of the period he spent in command of these troops, short though it may have been. In 1608 Jacob de la Gardie, a former general in Prince Maurice's army, was entrusted with the military education of the young Gustavus Adolphus, who was then fifteen years old. Like the Nassaus, the heir to the Swedish throne, who had a great talent for languages, made a thorough study of the classical authors on the art of war. Records mention that he read the works of Aelianus, Frontinus and Vegetius, as well as Lipsius' celebrated *De Militia Romana* and his *Poliorceticon* which deals with siegecraft.

It is therefore little wonder that, when in 1611 he ascended the throne at the age of seventeen, Gustavus Adolphus concentrated all his efforts on improving the army and that—even though it was only because of his great respect for Prince Maurice—he took the Dutch system as his model. It was not, however, a question of mere slavish imitation, but of further development based on the Dutch reforms. Indeed, the situation, particularly as regards the method of recruiting, was entirely different in Sweden. The Netherlands possessed an international army of mercenaries; although its core was Dutch, most of the troops were foreigners from a variety of countries. Sweden, on the other hand, was the first country in Europe to possess an entirely national army, recruited on the basis of compulsory service, and stationed in regimental districts, corresponding with the ancient rural provinces, where martial qualities were fostered by strong local patriotism. In this country, where feudalism had failed to make the same inroads as in the other countries of Europe, fighting spirit was not the monopoly of a particular social class or profession, but a quality possessed by an entire nation of robust peasants. It was an inheritance from Germanic times.

Piety, enthusiasm for the Protestant cause: loyalty to a king who was a member of the courageous Vasa family: these were the foundations on which Gustavus Adolphus was able to build a strict discipline. Experience gained in the Polish and Russian wars forged the army into an efficient instrument of war; in addition, there were the tactical and technical changes demanded by the times.

In the infantry, a lighter type of musket was introduced, so that the forked rest could be dispensed with; thus greater mobility and a faster rate of fire were achieved. The firelock was no longer needed; this weapon had already disappeared from armoury orders in the Netherlands by 1623. An important change resulting from the increase in the rate of fire was that it became possible to reduce the number of ranks in a battalion. These were reduced from ten to six and, if necessary, this number could be reduced to three by doubling the rate of fire. Otherwise the battalions were drawn up in the same way as those under Maurice's command with the pikemen in the centre, musketeers on each side, and with gaps to facilitate rank-by-rank firing. It became possible to shorten the length of the pike, which still remained indispensable for warding off cavalry charges. While, in Maurice's army, the most frequent ratio of pikes to firearms was 5 : 6, the new type of company which the Swedish king introduced in about 1621 had 54 pikes to 72 firearms, a small proportionate reduction. A natural result of the increased fire-power was that it became more and more common for troops to be drawn up in lines. Since there was a danger of the infantry therefore becoming split up into too many weak battalions, the king introduced the brigade unit, with four battalions to the brigade. Thus a unit now existed which could match the very powerful squadrons still in use on the Spanish–German side, while at the same time the troops became more manoeuvrable.

Fire-power was increased not only in the infantry, but also in the artillery. Until this time, artillery had played a major role in sieges, but only a very minor one on the battle-field. Gustavus Adolphus created the first real field artillery. This was regimental artillery, consisting of light three-pounders, two—later three—per battalion. The ammunition used appears to have been grapeshot, but it would be wrong to under-estimate the effect of the bullets on the serried ranks of the time. In the army with which the king crossed over to Germany in 1630, there were 81 three-pounders of this kind, in addition to 24 twenty-five-pounders (siege artillery) and 25 mortars.

Pieces of artillery very famous during this period were the 'leather cannons'. They were invented by a certain Eberhard, of Zürich, and were taken across to Sweden by the Austrian general Wurmprandt. Their composition long remained a mystery, and in recent times X-ray techniques have been used to reveal the secrets of the sole surviving example. Only the outer casing was of leather. The rest of the cannon consisted of an iron core, reinforced by a system of coiled wire and rope, iron strips, a wooden filling and linen wrapping. It was an attempt to manufacture a piece of field artillery lighter than the usual type. A number of these cannons were successfully used in the war against Poland between 1627 and 1629. They were never, however, used on a wide scale, probably because of their intricate construction and the difficult manufacturing process involved. A man who did much to help build the Swedish artillery was Louis de Geer, a great merchant, industrialist and financier, and the founder of the Swedish iron and armaments industry. He was on intimate terms with Gustavus Adolphus. Although his importance is perhaps greater for the economic than for the military historian, this does not diminish the relevance of his work for the latter.

Gustavus Adolphus also improved the cavalry: his main achievement was to abolish the *caracole*. During the charge only the front rank was allowed to fire, from the shortest distance, after which the cavalry engaged the enemy hand-to-hand with sword and pistols.

As in Sweden, the military situation in England was also rather special, for the task of defending the homeland was entrusted to the trained bands, a sort of national militia. Thus military power was not in the king's hands, which is why absolute monarchy never obtained a footing in England. The few troops maintained by the king as palace guards, and engaged in policing duties in Ireland and along the Scottish border were inadequate for war on an extensive scale. The national militia comprised all male residents from fifteen to sixty years of age and was organized according to the Statute of Winchester of 1285. Two statutes of Mary's reign and later administrative efforts had brought this venerable institution up to date to some extent, but no radical change was involved. One of the remarkable features of this situation was that the crown in fact had no right whatsoever to compel its subjects to serve overseas, or even outside their own country, except in the event of enemy invasion. In practice, however, this was disregarded. Thus the troops which were sent overseas consisted partly of recruited volunteers, the rest being militia conscripts. In the militia, a distinction was made between trained men—those who had received some sort of training—and untrained men; since the former were considered indispensable for the defence of the country, the others were preferred for service overseas. The selection, arming and mustering of the conscripts was the task of the lord lieutenant of the county. Here, again, there were two categories: substantial citizens, who tried by every possible means to avoid the highly unpopular service in the militia, and the 'rogues and vagabonds' (the unemployed and the tramps), who were simply pressed into service. This brief summary gives some idea of the military value of these overseas contingents, especially when it is borne in mind that a sea journey of any length was enough in itself to cause the loss of many men and horses. The expedition to Cadiz in 1625 was one notorious case in point. In the Netherlands, the English had the reputation of being courageous soldiers in the field, who found it difficult, however, to adapt themselves to the food, climate and way of life of foreign lands. The names of Vere, Morgan, Norris and Cecil are sufficient reminder of the valour shown by the English on countless occasions in the Eighty Years War.

In England, the impetus for the setting up of a standing army cast in the new mould did not come until the Civil War. In the nobility and gentry, inspired by the virtues of chivalry and honour, lay the strength of the Royalist army; above all else, they provided an excellent cavalry. On the parliamentary side, on the other hand, support came from many of the cities, the ports and, above all, from London, the commercial metropolis, and from part of the gentry. Provided the resources thus available were used properly, there could be no doubt of final victory. In this respect the Civil War in England bears some resemblance to the American Civil War.

At first there was chaos on both sides. Each county waged its own war and the struggle seemed to be disintegrating into a series of minor operations, sieges in particular. Admittedly, there were no true strongholds in the country, but then neither side had reliable siege artillery. The Parliamentarians, who were commanded by a parliamentary committee, made the further mistake of constantly setting up new regiments and allowing the old ones to disintegrate; so it was not surprising that the initial advantage lay with the Royalists who had an excellent cavalry general in Prince Rupert of the Rhine. At the Battle of Edgehill (October 1642), the Roundheads were driven north, but Charles did not consider himself strong enough to advance upon London. Later attempts to do so also failed, and Charles' headquarters continued to be at Oxford. In July 1643 the Cavaliers took Bristol, the country's second city, by storm: this was to be their last great success. The intervention of the Scots, after they had signed the Covenant with the Parliamentarians in September of the same year, in effect decided the war against the king, and his defeat was certain after the battles at Marston Moor (July 1644) and Naseby (June 1645). On both occasions the Roundheads owed their victory to the magnificent charges of Oliver Cromwell and his Ironsides.

It is general knowledge how Cromwell succeeded in inspiring the Parliamentarian army with a religious fervour bordering on fanaticism, which was at one and the same time a source of relentless energy, iron discipline and sober living. These qualities fashioned a military force unique in history. Cromwell's remarkable achievement was all the more astonishing as he was not, in fact, the commander-in-chief, but merely the lieutenant-general of the cavalry.

The new army, known by historians as the New Model Army, was given concrete shape in the New Model Ordinance which passed the Commons in January 1645 and the Lords in February of the same year. It has rightly been called 'a body of Bible warriors'. Both Dutch and Swedish influences were reflected in its organization, English officers having served in the Swedish army and in the Dutch army under Prince Frederick Henry. The infantry was divided into 12 regiments, each with 1200 men in 10 companies—two-thirds musketeers to one-third pikemen. The cavalry consisted of 11 regiments, each with 6 squadrons of 100 horsemen, armed as cuirassiers, with a sword, two pistols, helmet, breastplate and backplate. As elsewhere, however, about the middle of the century, the helmet and suit of armour were replaced by a hat and jerkin of buffalo hide. The New Model Army also had a regiment of dragoons of 1,000 men which were divided into 10 companies and armed like musketeers. They were usually drawn up in ranks of ten, one rank sometimes looking after the horses of the other nine. The artillery, which had so far been the Cinderella of the forces, was put on a firm basis; each cannon was served by a gunner who had two men to help him. Two regiments of 'firelocks' and two of infantry were specially detailed to escort the artillery. The records tell us that artillerymen and pioneers had a bad reputation, particularly for their foul language. Apparently, they were not regarded as soldiers, any more than the engineers and the baggage-train men were.

Some idea of the composition of the headquarters staff can be obtained from the following list of the main appointments: commander-in-chief or 'captain-general' (Sir Thomas Fairfax); chief of staff (Major-General Skippon); a commissioner-general for the muster, another for provisions and another for forage; a wagonmaster-general; a scoutmaster-general (cf. French *Maitre de Guet*); eight paymasters; a solicitor-general; two doctors of medicine; an apothecary; a chaplain; a secretary of the war council with two clerks; and two adjutants.

In addition, there was a general staff for the infantry, for the cavalry and for the baggage-train, under a major-general (Skippon), a lieutenant-general (Oliver Cromwell) and a lieutenant-general of the artillery (Hammond) respectively.

The artillery had an inspector, a master-gunner of the field, a superintendent of ammunition and a superintendent of the draughthorse. There was also an engineer-general with four engineers under him and, finally, a captain of the pioneers. What is nowadays known as the engineers did not, therefore, exist as a separate army department.

While England, in 1660, after fifteen years of military dictatorship, returned to constitutional monarchy, France had an absolute monarchy after the end of the Fronde in 1653. From the death of Henri IV until 1653, the internal political history of France was an uninterrupted succession of civil wars, risings and court intrigues which formed the background to the resistance of the nobility to the growing despotism of the throne. France's foreign affairs during this period were dominated by the traditional struggle against the Spanish-Habsburg alliance, which was continued after the Peace of Münster until as late as 1659, against a Spain falling deeper and deeper into decline. Of the few battles in this conflict, that at Rocroi (1643) is of military-historical importance, as the defeat there of the Spaniards under De Melo is usually regarded as marking the end of the superiority of the Spanish infantry after a century and a half of dominance. All the same, according to reports of the fighting, the Spanish infantry gave a good account of itself. It was at this battle that the great Condé won his first laurels.

The construction of fortifications occupies an important place in the development of warcraft. About the middle of the sixteenth century nearly every town still had its medieval walls with their gateways and moat. With the increased use of cannons, new fortifications were added here and there, principally to defend the gateways, while the towers in the walls were converted into round bastions and rebuilt to accommodate cannons. New fortifications were constructed on the Italian model, with high earth walls, retaining walls (revetments) and small bastions. During the Dutch war of liberation against Spain the need to modernize fortifications became urgent, but because of the lack of funds, the watery nature of the terrain and the softness of the ground in many places, the heavy, expensive revetments were dispensed with, earth walls having to suffice. Such walls could withstand bombardment by the solid cannon balls of the time, in contrast to stone walls which, when they collapsed, also filled in the moat. The moats (or ditches), which were deep, broad and marshy, gave sufficient protection against storming; there were palisades to thwart surprise attacks. When it froze, the ditches were hacked open and water was poured over the walls. The walls being very thick, there was a large 'blind angle', which meant that the defence of a town was entirely dependent on flanking fire from cannons and muskets. The bastions or bulwarks were used for this purpose, the attack being largely concentrated on them.

In the moat, there were very often smaller defence works called ravelins, and, on the other side, there was a covered way with a glacis; moreover, important strongholds and forts on the frontier also had *demi-lunes* and hornworks. The result was an elaborate system of defences, care always being taken to see that each defence-work could be covered by flanking fire from a distance of 220 to 250 yards—the range of a musket. Thus, all distances and angles were interrelated; the task of calculating these, and of marking out the terrain, was that of the engineers, who therefore needed a sound knowledge of arithmetic and surveying.

The Old-Dutch type of fortress engineering which developed in this way had great influence elsewhere in Europe, principally in the Protestant countries and where strongholds were situated in low-lying marshy terrain. Dutch engineers frequently served with foreign armies or were consulted by foreign rulers. There was evidence of their activity in the fortifications of Berlin, Hamburg, Bremen, Danzig, Neisse and even as far afield as Rostov and Terki in Russia.

Improvements in siegecraft kept pace with advances in fortress engineering. Sieges became slower and more methodical, and called for more artillery. While Prince Maurice, for instance, besieged Groenlo in

1595 with 16 pieces of artillery, and in 1597 with 14, in 1627, Frederick Henry used 80 pieces including 15 mortars. Again, while Maurice used 22 pieces when besieging Bois-le-Duc in 1601—unsuccessfully, it is true—in 1629 Frederick Henry took the city with 116 cannon, not counting the mortars. During the siege of Hulst in 1645, more projectiles were fired in one month than during the entire seven months of the siege of Haarlem in 1573.

If there was a possibility that relief would be brought to a besieged town or fort, a wide circumvallation was built, almost a fortress in itself. Within this line the besieging forces set up three camps or 'quarters', from which, under cover of artillery fire, zig-zag trenches were dug towards the bastion or front being attacked. The covered-way was usually taken only after a hard struggle. Then, however, came the most difficult phase of the operation, the crossing of the moat. For this, a dam had to be constructed, across which a gallery (proof against cannon and musket fire, was built. Once the foot of the wall had been reached, usually, after the requisite mine-galleries had been dug out, an attempt was made to blow it up. Both of these tasks were always given to experienced sappers or professional miners. It sometimes required weeks of struggle underground before the breach could be stormed. Often, however, the defender did not allow things to reach this extreme, but capitulated in order to avoid the slaughter and plundering which, according to the rules of war, inevitably followed upon capture by storm; and also to obtain favourable conditions. And so, in the course of time, a remarkable change took place: as sieges became more methodical, the main defence was shifted to the covered-way. This situation was very different from that during the religious wars.

Of the countries of eastern Europe, Poland and Turkey[1] deserve particular attention. In both countries, there was clearly an intimate connection between the organization of the army and the political and social structure. In Poland, a country with a weak central government, the army was in a state of acute disruption. Lithuania had its own army, separate from Poland's. Apart from the state army, there were the private troops which all manner of potentates—such as secular and ecclesiastical leaders and nobles—as well as the free cities, maintained at their own expense. The state army consisted of two entirely different kinds of troops: first, those levied by feudal summons; and secondly, the professional soldiers of the standing army which was the nucleus of the defence forces and comprised both Polish and foreign troops, especially Germans. In addition, there were the Cossacks, who formed an important element of the national army in the south-east of the country; and in times of extreme need, a peasant reserve could be called up. The main section of the army was the cavalry, of which there were three types: heavy, medium and

---

[1] For Turkey, see Vol. III in this series, Chapter XI; and below, Chapter XX.

light. The light cavalry was unarmoured and consisted of Wallachians and Tartars. The infantry was of little account, compared with the very strong cavalry.

A few words on the method of waging war: although strategy was based on a few main principles of a general nature, the manner in which these principles were applied depended very largely on factors which, in the course of time, were subject to change. Thus the long duration of most wars must be attributed mainly to the custom of halting operations in the winter (which always gave the weaker side an opportunity to recoup its losses), and to the fact that wars consisted principally of sieges. In the Dutch war of liberation, for instance, not a single battle was fought after the Battle of Neiuwpoort in 1600; in the Franco-Spanish War (1635–59), too, the battles were few; in the Thirty Years War and in the Civil War in England, however, they again became comparatively more frequent. It can be generally said that sieges were more, and field campaigns less important than they are today. War was more territorial in character. Indeed, a field army seldom set out with the express aim of searching out and destroying the enemy army; on the contrary, it was used chiefly to besiege and relieve strongholds, mainly towns. The towns were the seats of trade, industry and government; they controlled the roads and—even more important—the waterways and river-crossings, and served as operational bases; from some border strongholds, vast areas were laid under contribution. The field armies were not large enough to undertake other operations while conducting a siege of any appreciable size. The campaigning season (from April to October) therefore soon passed with the taking of one or two fortresses.

In conclusion, a comparison of the military situation in the year the Peace of Münster was signed with that at the beginning of the seventeenth century reveals many similarities, but also a number of important changes. Not only did armies increase considerably in size during this period, as a result of the states' greater financial resources, but a general modernization took place. Armaments, as we have seen, were adapted to the needs of the time. In the artillery, modernization took the form of a much larger number of pieces, standardization based on a small number of calibres, progress in the manufacture of pieces, particularly of bronze and 'metal' pieces, and the frequent use of bombs fired from mortars. Developments in fortress engineering have already been discussed, as have the new tactics and battle-order.

The fundamental change, however, was that in the seventeenth century an army was forged which was different from that of the sixteenth century. The hired army made way for a standing national army of professional soldiers, or at least an army with a national core, an army meeting the requirements of increasingly centralized government. Discipline in the new army was stricter, its standard being maintained in peacetime by drill and exercises: it moulded a new type of soldier. The remaining traces of the days of the *lansquenet* disappeared: the nomination of the subordinate commanders by the troops at the recruiting stage, the dispensation of justice by the council of soldiers gathered in a ring, the holding of meetings by the soldiers on their own authority, were abolished for good; even religious congregations were strictly forbidden, unless expressly ordered. The deed of engagement, originally a form of contract, was replaced by a penal code. The ferocity and bitterness of the religious wars belonged to the past; the prisoner-of-war now bought his freedom for the fixed price of one month's wages; and officers on opposing sides now regarded each other as colleagues and exchanged courtesies, when the occasion arose. These were all signs of the arrival of a new age, and a new spirit in the armies of western Europe.

CHAPTER VII

SEA-POWER

CHANGES in the distribution of sea-power among the states of Europe affected large areas outside Europe more directly than ever before. For Europe's sea communications had encompassed the world. Besides the regular trans-Atlantic routes, little-frequented ones went across the Pacific to the Philippines and from the East Indies to Macao, Formosa and Japan. Commercial exchanges with Europe might require a cycle of as long as five years, quantities were minute, in some of these cases only one ship a year reached the final destination, but a regular pattern of trade existed. Originally the Portuguese had established themselves in the East thanks to a margin of technical superiority in sea-fighting, but by the late sixteenth century they were accustomed to peaceful trading in almost unarmed ships. After 1600 both they and the native traders were to suffer from the competition and incursions of heavily armed Dutch and English ships. In particular the heavier armament, superior organization and better seamanship of the Dutch East India Company enabled them to establish a commercial supremacy in Indonesia by 1650, despite prolonged and sometimes effective resistance by the Portuguese and others. Europeans did not control the trade of the Indian Ocean or Indonesia, even the Dutch never held a completely effective monopoly of the spice trade. Nevertheless they dominated important and profitable trades, because ultimately their naval power was greater than that of the native states. If Iberian power was eclipsed in the East, their monopoly of trans-Atlantic trade, still virtually intact in 1600, was also broken. By 1621 over half the carrying trade of Brazil was in Dutch hands, by the 1650s the Dutch and English were permanently established in the Caribbean and were establishing treaty rights in Brazilian and Portuguese trade.

Distribution of sea-power was itself changed by changing distribution of trade and also by technical developments in shipbuilding and the conduct of war. Heavily armed ships from north-western Europe began to dominate the trade and warfare of the Mediterranean. The traditional galleys were still used in war, but together with sailing ships which more and more dominated the battles. By the 1650s the battle-fleets of the English and the Dutch were dominated by specialized fighting ships with two or three gun-decks, designed for inboard-loading and for increasingly heavy and controlled broadside fire, which in turn involved the gradual adoption of line-ahead formations. There was increasing professionalization of naval officers, though in wartime seamen from the merchant marine were essential to man the fleets which still also included merchant ships. Naval strategy turned more than ever on the protection and destruction of trade, and sea-power as always depended upon both trading and fighting fleets. But the maintenance of a fighting fleet was more expensive than ever before, requiring a larger permanent organization which could design, build and maintain specialized ships, unsuitable for trade. In 1639 before the Battle of the Downs Tromp's strength had been trebled in a matter of weeks by fitting out merchant ships. Before 1642 hired merchantmen had usually made up more than half the numbers of English fleets. Their proportion in the Parliamentary fleets during the Civil War was much smaller; in the Dutch war Blake wished to keep it down to a fifth and in fact it seldom exceeded a third.[1] After 1653 hired merchantmen might still play a decisive part in the war between Venice and the Turks but not in wars between great naval powers.

By the 1650s the distribution of sea-power had changed decisively. In 1600 the Iberian kingdoms might still claim to be the greatest maritime power, their merchant fleet was second only to the Dutch and their combined naval strength greater than that of either the Dutch or the English. Even in the 1620s Spain was the strongest naval power in the Mediterranean and in the Atlantic and could hopefully plan to challenge the Dutch in their home waters. The Habsburgs could even dream of dominating the Baltic in alliance with a revivified Hanseatic League. By 1659 Spain was weaker in both the Atlantic and the Mediterranean than England or Holland and was soon to be outstripped by France. The technical changes of the period seem to have largely passed Spain by. In the 1630s the English and Dutch built the *Sovereign* and the *Aemilia*, prototypes of the heavy and medium ships of the future battle lines.[2] The Spaniards still built relatively undergunned galleons, just as they failed to adopt newer types of fishing vessels and cargo carriers, although they were more receptive to the Dunkirkers' example in developing fast frigates. Spain's fleets were chronically short of gunners and seamen so that their ability to fight and even to survive the ordinary hazards of the sea were both impaired. Matters were even worse for the Portuguese on the Cape route, since they persisted in using unwieldy carracks of 1,000 tons[3] or more, though well aware smaller ships would be more seaworthy. They then persistently overloaded and overcrowded them, despite regulations to the contrary and a shortage of seamen. Losses from shipwreck increased in the late sixteenth century and continued to be heavy until 1650, afterwards the rate dropped steeply; from 1590 to 1635 some 220 sailings from

[1] A. H. Taylor, 'Galleon into ship of the line', *Mariner's Mirror*, Vol. XLIV (1958), pp. 267–84.
[2] J. E. Elias, *De Vlootbouw in Nederland . . . 1596–1655* (Amsterdam, 1933), pp. 61–3.
[3] Estimates of tonnage throughout are approximations, concealing divergent measures. One last has been taken to equal two tons.

Lisbon resulted in the loss of thirty-four ships, while some 130 from India lost thirty-three.[1]

The decline of Iberian sea-power did not happen because statesmen were blind to its importance, though the general contempt for sailors and their profession found in both Spain and Portugal may have contributed to it.[2] As with so many problems which beset Spain, the need to maintain her power at sea was understood and analysed, but the resources for effective action were lacking. To renew the war against the Dutch Spain had to accept continental commitments and communications, sending troops and money from north Italy overland to the Netherlands. To secure these communications Spain had to subsidize and assist allies in the empire whom she could neither control nor afford. Spain's maritime resources had to be concentrated on keeping her Atlantic communications open for her treasure-fleets and the western Mediterranean safe for the transfer of funds and troops to Genoa for Milan, Germany and Flanders. The failure to continue the land campaign against the Dutch with real success after the capture of Breda (1625) meant that the risk of the Dutch wearing down Spain's Atlantic communications by the organized attacks of the West India Company increased. To counter this pressure Olivares wanted to erode Dutch sea-power by destroying her trade. Like his predecessors he would have liked to close the Straits of Gibraltar to the Dutch and English, but there was no real prospect of establishing an effective blockade. Hopes of a potentially much more decisive counter-stroke caused the revival of projects for attacking the Dutch in the most vital area of their maritime and commercial hegemony, the Baltic. In 1624 Olivares proposed to found a company with Flemish and Hanseatic participation which would have a monopoly of Iberian trade with the rest of Europe, thus undermining the *entrepôt* trade of Amsterdam as well as providing a fleet of twenty-four ships to challenge the Dutch from bases in East Friesland. After 1626 this last objective was changed and the fleet was to be based in the Baltic in order to harry Dutch trade there. Sigismund III of Poland had long wished to build up a fleet and was anxious to ally himself with Madrid, but none of the Hanseatic towns would entertain the project for fear of offending the Dutch. In 1628 the arrival of Wallenstein on the Baltic coast roused fresh hopes, but he refused to accept Madrid's terms for subsidizing a fleet. He was determined to keep complete control of it himself and to use it against the Danes rather than the Dutch. The Spanish envoys did buy some ships from the Hanse, but in 1629, to the fury of Sigismund, they were sent to Flanders. The main result of these projects was to disillusion Sigismund

[1] M. Godinho, cited by P. Chaunu in *Studi in Onore di A. Fanfani* (Milan, 1962), Vol. IV, pp. 247–8, notes 61–2; C. R. Boxer (ed.), *The Tragic History of the Sea*, Hakluyt Soc., Ser. II, Vol. CXII (1959), pp. 1–30.

[2] *Ibid.* p. 11. This also seems to have been a feature of Venetian society.

about Habsburg plans and promises and to encourage him to make his truce with Sweden.[1] The only real damage to Dutch trade was done by the Dunkirkers. They seldom had more than thirty ships at sea at one time, but the admiralty records show that from 1626 to 1634 they captured 1,499 ships, sank another 336 (two-thirds or more may have been Dutch), and sold booty for £1,139,000 sterling, while losing fifteen royal ships and 105 privateers to the enemy. From the late 1630s the Dutch blockade may have been more effective in reducing losses, but it was never more than partially effective.[2]

Although Spain beat off the first Dutch attacks on Brazil and the English attack on Cadiz, her Atlantic power suffered a great disaster when Piet Heyn captured and destroyed the treasure-fleet at Matanzas in Cuba in 1628. This not only financed the West India Company's successful conquests in Brazil, but also destroyed about a third of the ships employed in Seville's Atlantic trade. Between 1623 and 1636 the company took or destroyed 547 ships worth some 5,500,000 *gulden*.[3] Spain made a last great effort to reconquer northern Brazil in 1638, when twenty-six galleons and twenty other ships were sent from Lisbon in September, later reinforced at Bahia to a total of eighteen Spanish and twelve Portuguese galleons, thirty-four armed merchantmen and twenty-three small ships. This armada was frustrated by unfavourable weather and irresolute command and was scattered by the Dutch in January 1640 without achieving anything.[4] This final failure to protect Brazil and the Caribbean from the Dutch was overshadowed by Tromp's annihilation of the last Spanish fleet to challenge Dutch sea-power in the Channel at the Battle of the Downs in October 1639.

This Spanish effort was a last desperate gamble by planners who had lost touch with the realities of both Dutch and Spanish sea-power. Both before and after 1639 troops were taken to and from Flanders by sea, but this was done by taking risks and evading the Dutch, not by challenging them to battle. The fall of Breisach in 1638 and the consequent closing of the land route doubtless made some attempt at reinforcement by sea essential in 1639, while the French fleet's incursions against the Biscayan ports also needed checking. But it was reckless to scrape together all available ships from the Mediterranean and the Atlantic and then instruct the admiral, Oquendo, when encumbered with the transport of 10,000 troops, to give battle if he met the Dutch, and stake everything on

---

[1] A. Gindely, *Die maritime Pläne der Habsburger . . . 1627–9* (Vienna, 1890); Rafael Rodeñas Vilar, 'Un Gran Proyecto anti-Holandes en tiempo de Felipe IV', *Hispania*, pp. xxii (1962), pp. 543–58; *La Politica Europea de España durante la Guerra de Treinta Años (1624–30)* (Madrid, 1967), pp. 113–47.

[2] H. Malo, *Les Corsaires Dunkerquois et Jean Bart* (1912), Vol. I, pp. 314–20, 333–4, 342–7.

[3] J. de Laet, *Iaerlyck Verhael . . .*, ed. Naber and Warnsinck (Hague, 1937), Vol. IV, pp. 282–5.

[4] C. R. Boxer, *The Dutch in Brazil 1624–1654* (Oxford, 1957), pp. 89–94.

destroying their fleet. Of the seventy-odd ships which sailed from Corunna some thirty had been hired from foreigners (from Ragusa, Lübeck and Hamburg, apart from at least eight English transports). In all there were some fifty warships, as usual short of gunners and seamen; Tromp with twenty-four ships established such a decisive superiority in sailing and gunnery that he drove the Spaniards to take refuge off the English coast. In the final attack the Dutch had superior numbers, but the Spaniards mostly ran their ships aground without a fight, losing forty-three ships and 6,000 men. Ironically most of the troops and treasure did reach Dunkirk along with the only efficient part of the fleet, the original Dunkirk squadron; a result which could have been achieved without destroying a large part of Spain's navy and all its reputation.[1]

The composition and fate of Oquendo's armada is only one symptom of Spain's declining sea-power. The trend of Seville's trans-Atlantic trade suggests even more serious structural changes; comparing 1616–20 with 1646–50 the tonnage employed had decreased by about half. In the later period only some forty per cent of the ships were Spanish built, roughly the same number were American built, while some seventeen per cent came from northern Europe; before 1610 most of the ships used had been built in northern Spain.[2] In the late sixteenth century ships from northern Spain had predominated in the fisheries off Newfoundland; their share declined rapidly in the seventeenth century and was insignificant by 1650, as was their share in Spain's European trade. The main source of Spain's maritime strength had begun to fail even before being subjected to further stress by war. Dr Andrews has recently suggested that this failure was due to the Elizabethan war against Spain's shipping.[3] Although this never seriously interfered with the trans-Atlantic routes, by forcing Spain to concentrate all her resources on protecting them, it left shipping on shorter and coastal routes, especially on the approaches to Galician and Biscayan ports, unprotected against privateers. The losses in ships and seamen were certainly serious and, whether or not it decisively undermined Spain's sea-power, it may well have contributed to the decline of her northern ports, along with shortages of timber.

When the revolts of Catalonia and Portugal followed less than a year after Oquendo's defeat, it might have seemed dubious whether Spain could defend her own coasts. Luckily France, her nearest enemy, was not strong enough at sea to exploit the situation. Richelieu had been at pains to build up the French navy but he started from scratch; in the 1620s the crown had to hire foreign ships against La Rochelle, in 1635 there was a Channel fleet of some thirty-five sizeable ships, though many of them were

---

[1] C. R. Boxer, *The Journal of M.T. Tromp* (Cambridge, 1930), introduction, pp. 1–67.
[2] [H. and] P. Chaunu, *Séville et l'Atlantique 1504–1650* (Paris, 1955–9), Vol. VIII, 2, ii, pp. 1428–9, 1566, 1621–2, 1878; Vol. VI, Pt I, pp. 166–7, Table 12 E.
[3] K. R. Andrews, *Elizabethan Privateering* (Cambridge, 1964), pp. 224–6. Spain and Portugal lost about 1,000 ships to the English.

foreign-built and the Mediterranean fleet had been increased from thirteen to twenty-two galleys. By concentrating her resources, especially those of the royal squadron from Dunkirk, first in Biscay, then in the western Mediterranean Spain held the French in check. French strength in the Channel declined after 1642 and Spain was able to concentrate more effectively in the Mediterranean so that the French were usually outnumbered. Despite much hard fighting in the 1640s they were never able to get command of the sea, or seriously interrupt Spanish communications. Spain's superiority at sea helped her to reconquer Catalonia and prevented the French establishing themselves in Tuscany and exploiting the revolt of Naples. Consciousness of France's growing naval inferiority to Spain after 1648 made Mazarin the more anxious to secure either a Dutch or an English alliance.

By the 1650s the decline of Spain and the failure to achieve a lasting revival of the French navy meant that the relative preponderance of the Dutch and English was greater and affected a greater geographical area than had been true of leading sea-powers in the past. There were now purely local balances of power between the states bordering each of Europe's inner seas, the Baltic and the Mediterranean, but these ultimately depended upon the new powers of Atlantic Europe. The most striking local changes were in the Baltic. There Denmark had long been the dominant naval power, but Gustavus Adolphus built up the Swedish navy to protect his communications and control the Prussian ports. After his death its growth continued and in 1644 it decisively shook Denmark's supremacy, though both sides also hired Dutch ships. Local supremacy passed to Sweden and Charles X wished to convert this into an absolute control of the Baltic, which would have been fatal to Dutch commercial hegemony. From 1649 the Dutch supported the Danes and in 1658 their fleet defeated Charles' ambitions.[1] The English were always jealous of Dutch power in the Baltic, but it was also against their interest to allow any local power absolute control. Thus in 1659 the local balance of power was dictated by the Dutch and English fleets' ability to keep the area open to their influence.

In the western Mediterranean, as we have seen, Spain was still able to enforce her interests against her local rivals. In the eastern Mediterranean the Turks had been at war with Venice for control of Crete since 1645. In the first years of the war the Turkish fleets consisted almost entirely of galleys and the mixed fleets of the Venetians were more successful. In the 1650s the Turks used mixed fleets, but they suffered a severe defeat off the Dardanelles in 1656, losing forty-six ships and forty-seven galleys. However, the Venetians were unable to maintain an effective blockade of the Dardanelles and they never established command of the Aegean for any considerable period, while the effort of maintaining fleets there contri-

---

[1] See Vol. v in this series, pp. 286–7, 519–22.

buted to the final eclipse of Venice as a commercial and maritime power. If either the English or the Dutch put their naval strength, or even part of it, into the Mediterranean they could outclass any of the local powers. All they needed, as Blake and De Ruyter showed, was the use of ports which local rivalries could be relied on to provide.

But the local balance of maritime trade had changed long before the mid-seventeenth century. In the long period of official truce between Spain and the Turks after 1580, Dutch and English ships entered the Mediterranean in increasing numbers. They not only dominated the trade between the Mediterranean and north-west Europe, but also captured an ever-increasing share of trade within the Mediterranean. They introduced a new type of ship, known there as the *berton*, and a new phase of warfare. The *berton* was smaller, but more heavily armed and built, faster and more manoeuvrable than the Mediterranean argosies which were similar to the Portuguese carracks. Around 1600 the northerners engaged in both trade and piracy, as opportunity offered, making the sea unsafe for native shipping. After about 1604 northerners who specialized exclusively in piracy began to appear. They mostly operated from Tripoli, Tunis, Algiers and Sallee and they taught the Muslims there to use *bertons*. Before 1620 their pupils had become so apt that the golden age of the Barbary corsairs began, at its height they may have had 150 ships. They raided throughout the Mediterranean and into the Atlantic as far as Cape Verde, Iceland, the Azores and the Great Banks, though they usually concentrated on the approaches to the Straits and the Channel. But even after the first generation of northern captains had gone, piracy was not an exclusively Muslim enterprise; the dukes of Savoy and Tuscany provided bases for privateers at Villefranche and Leghorn, while the knights of Malta and San Stefano took prizes indiscriminately. In these conditions only heavily armed ships, like those of the English Levant Company, could trade safely and the worst sufferers were native traders, especially the Venetians. Venice not only provided the richest prizes in the Levant, but was often unable to protect her shipping in the Adriatic from the local pirates, the Uscocchi. Piracy helped to weaken Venice and to make her increasingly dependent on northern shipping.[1]

The amount of shipping using the port of Venice increased from 1587 to 1609, but the proportion of foreign-owned and -built ships also grew. By the early 1620s the total volume was barely half that of 1607–9 and the decline continued; interrupted during the 1630s, it became very steep during the Cretan war and the relative share of foreign shipping probably increased. The main reason for hiring foreign ships was that they were better able to protect themselves.[2] Venice had to hire Dutch and English

---

[1] A. Tenenti, *Venezia e i corsari 1588–1615* (Bari, 1961).
[2] F. C. Lane, 'Le Trafic Maritime de Venise' in *Quatrième Colloque d'Histoire Maritime, Les Sources de l'Histoire Maritime*, ed. M. Mollat (Paris, 1962), pp. 12–14, 28.

ships to meet the challenge of Osuna, the Viceroy of Naples, in the Adriatic in 1617–18. Both sides in the Cretan war made extensive use of foreign-built and -hired ships. Of course the northerners were not immune to piracy; from 1617 to 1625 the Algerines took some 200 Dutch ships.[1] But the northerners increased their trade, while that of Venice declined, and in the long run they were more successful in forcing the Barbary states to respect their flags. In the mid-1650s the English and Dutch had squadrons in the Mediterranean partly for this purpose. England made treaties with Sallee, Algiers and Tunis from 1655 to 1658. After the English squadron withdrew in 1658 there were difficulties, but after 1661 the treaties were observed.

If only well-armed ships could usually trade securely in the Mediterranean, conditions in the North Sea and Baltic were different. The main cargoes of the Baltic and Scandinavian trades were bulky ones, grain, timber, salt, wine and fish. The Dutch had long dominated these trades and by the last years of the sixteenth century had developed a type of cargo carrier, the *fluit*, which perpetuated their domination. This was a slow, lightly built, virtually unarmed ship, with a long keel, bluff bows and a relatively flat bottom, needing only a small crew to manage its relatively small area of sails. Its cheap building and running costs meant cheap freight rates which ensured Dutch supremacy in the carrying trades so that in 1669 Colbert enviously guessed that they owned three-quarters of Europe's total tonnage. The Dutch themselves in 1636 estimated that they had 1,050 ships trading to the Baltic, Norway and south-west France averaging a hundred lasts, 250 ships (of 120–50 lasts) in the Mediterranean and Archangel trades, 450 of 20 to 40 lasts in the Channel and North Sea as well as 2,000 fishing busses and 300 ships in the extra-European trades. This would suggest a total of 4,500 to 4,800 ships with a tonnage of 600,000 to 700,000, four or five times that of England.[2] The basic Dutch trades were very vulnerable to the Dunkirkers so that they flourished most in peacetime. In war they were checked by losses which meant high insurance and freight rates. With the Peace of Westphalia trade boomed and the customs figures suggest that from 1648 to 1651 it reached a level which was possibly never surpassed in the seventeenth century,[3] while Dutch shipping threatened to eliminate all rivals from the Baltic, North Sea and Atlantic trades.

This triumphant position was partly founded on the eclipse of the Hanseatic towns' ability to assert any effective power, either collectively or individually. Their share of Baltic trade had declined in the sixteenth

[1] K. Heeringa, *Bronnen Tot de Geschiedenis van den Levantschen Handel*, Vol. II (The Hague, 1910), p. 1042, note 451.
[2] J. E. Elias, *Het Voorspel van den Eersten Engelschen Oorlog* (The Hague, 1920), Vol. I, pp. 61–2.
[3] J. G. van Dillen in *Algemene Geschiedenis der Nederlanden*, Vol. VII (Utrecht, 1954), pp. 312–51.

century. About 1600 they had about 1,000 ships amounting to some 90,000 tons, about one-third belonging to Hamburg (7,000 lasts) and Lübeck (8,000 lasts). Lübeck's fleet was still growing in the early seventeenth century;[1] its first *fluit* was built in 1618[2] and its shipbuilding only declined decisively after 1648. Hamburg's fleet doubled to about 14,000 lasts between 1600 and 1650. But the shipping of Danzig declined, as did that of Wismar, Rostock and Stralsund. These last had been heavily involved in trade to Norway which after 1625 was completely dominated by the Dutch and Danes. Hamburg and to a lesser extent Lübeck were able to increase their trade to southern Europe after 1621. Although Hamburg sustained a flourishing *entrepôt* trade, it was dominated by foreign merchants, while after 1648 Sweden levied tolls of 350,000 thalers a year on the other Hanseatic towns, a revenue approaching that of the Sound tolls.[3] Thus Lübeck's and the Hanse's rejection of Spain's offers in 1628 lost them their last dubious chance of reversing their decline at the expense of the Dutch. The decline of Iberian sea-power meant increasing exploitation by foreign merchants. First Cromwell forced Portugal to grant privileges to English merchants both there and in the Brazil trade. Spain later tacitly acquiesced in the exploitation of her trade by Dutch, English and French merchants. The failure of the Hanseatic towns to find effective allies and their inability to mobilize naval power condemned them to exploitation by Sweden, under which only Hamburg prospered, having 277 ships (42,000 tons) by 1672.

If by 1650 the Hanseatic towns were powerless to avoid exploitation by the victors at Westphalia, the English were not. Their reply to the Dutch was war.

English shipbuilders had never attempted to imitate the *fluit*. Their typical product was the 'defensible' ship of sixty tons and upwards more heavily built, with finer lines, faster, needing a larger crew and carrying a number of guns proportionate to its size. Even colliers in the Newcastle trade conformed to this type, so that foreign ships dominated in the export of coal. Such ships were very suitable for dangerous Mediterranean waters and for privateering, but in most other trades they could not compete with the Dutch in peacetime. Nevertheless the tonnage of English shipping had probably doubled between 1582 and 1624 but the opportunity provided by the Dutch being at war after 1621 was spoilt initially by England also being involved in war from 1625 to 1629. England lost some 300 ships amounting to well over 20,000 tons and may have taken rather more prizes herself. In 1629 England's total tonnage was 115,000 and it may have risen to about 140,000 by 1640.[4] Until then the

---

[1] W. Vogel, 'Zur Grosse der europäischen Handelsflotten...' in *Festschrift... Dietrich Schäfer*, ed. A. Hofmeister (Jena, 1915), pp. 283–301.
[2] W. Vogel, *Die Deutschen als Seefahrer* (Hamburg, 1949), p. 118.   [3] *Ibid.* p. 125.
[4] R. Davis, *The Rise of the English Shipping Industry* (London, 1962), pp. 7, 10–11, 15, 315. I have estimated the tonnage lost from several MSS. of the report to the Commons in

greatest expansion since 1600, apart from the Mediterranean and the coastal coal trades, was in the Newfoundland fisheries which came to be dominated by the English. In the early 1630s the East India Company had 9,000–10,000 tons of shipping.[1] If the Dutch dominated the North Sea fisheries, the English held their own to a greater extent off Iceland and in whaling off Spitzbergen. After 1640 direct English exploitation of all these fisheries declined. To compete successfully even for the carrying trade of their own ports, English ships needed either government protection or the advantages of neutrality when the Dutch were at war.

The Civil War obviously hindered trade and shipping, but it increased England's naval strength. From 1642 to 1647 Parliament sent thirty to forty warships to sea every summer and kept a winter-guard of some twenty ships, so that the fleet was more continuously manned than ever before. Then the Commonwealth expanded the fleet from 1649 to 1651 and forty-one new ships were added, almost doubling it. The ships were used to pursue the ships which had joined the Royalists in 1648, to secure the trans-Atlantic colonies and enforce respect for the Commonwealth's flag in European waters. These efforts meant long voyages to Portugal, the Mediterranean and America. The French not only assisted the Royalists, but also placed an embargo on English cloth. This produced an embargo on French wines and silk in 1649. Both sides proceeded to seizures of goods and ships. Convoys were needed for English ships in the Mediterranean and the Dutch became the neutral carriers of Anglo-French trade. The Navigation Act, searches of Dutch ships for French goods and exaction of salutes all annoyed the Dutch. By February 1652 the States General, alarmed by the growth of the English fleet, resolved to fit out 150 ships in addition to the 76 already available. The expansion of the English fleet continued even after the end of the Dutch war; from 1650 to 1656 80 new ships were built and many prizes added to it. In 1625 the navy had about 30 ships, in 1640 about 40, in 1651 about 95 and in 1660 about 140.[2] Probably many fewer large merchant ships were built in the 1650s compared with the 1630s, so that the naval building may only have made up this difference.

Although Dutch resources in shipbuilding and seamen were so much greater, their ability to transform them into effective naval power was limited. The fact that they had far more trade to protect and that Britain

June 1628. R. G. Marsden estimated the number of prize sentences 1625–30 as at least 600, *E.H.R.* Vol. xxv (1910), p. 256. The crown received £217,468 from French goods, reprisal goods and wrecks and £20,131 from tenths of Admiralty, B. M. Harleian MS. 3796, fo. 36.

[1] Estimated from K. N. Chaudhuri, *The English East India Company 1600–1640* (1965), Appendix B.

[2] Numbers built and strengths calculated from R. C. Anderson, *English Men-of-War 1509–1649, English Ships 1649–1702*, Soc. for Nautical Research Occasional Publications, Nos. 7, 5 (1959, 1935).

235   9-2

lay across the vital routes nourishing their Baltic trade were severe handicaps. Their naval administration suffered from decentralization among five boards of admiralty and from friction between the provinces. The English had more very large ships and in general their ships were more heavily built and armed with heavier guns. They were also quicker to see the advantage of line-ahead formations and made greater efforts to found their battle tactics upon them. All these factors helped to give them the balance of advantage in the whole series of battles. The English attempt to blockade the Dutch coast in 1653 was not completely successful, but the Channel was closed to Dutch shipping from February 1653. The Dutch economy depended on the sea far more than the English and for the first time they were fighting an enemy whose naval strength was ultimately more effective. The truth of this can be seen not by claiming the last battle off the Texel as a decisive English victory—both sides could have put powerful fleets to sea again in 1654, if they had not chosen to make peace—but in the fact that the war was disastrous for Dutch trade. The English took between 1,000 and 1,700 Dutch prizes (a figure nearer the lower one seems more likely) and lost few of their own ships. The English having failed to build economical cargo carriers had now captured them in abundance. They appeared to have checked the growth of Dutch trade which had been so evident after 1647 and had acquired the means to survive in the carrying trade; it is probable 'that between 1654 and 1675 foreign built ships were never less than a third of the total tonnage in English ownership . . .'.[1]

The immediate consequences of the effective mobilization of so much naval power were not altogether happy for English trade. Despite the Navigation Act, English trade to the Baltic remained depressed and the Dutch continued to carry a large part of English colonial trade. One of the reasons for undertaking the Western Design against the Spanish Indies was that Cromwell's council were mostly anxious to find a use for the large navy which had been created and hoped the venture would pay for itself, as the Dutch West India Company had done in its heyday. The resulting war with Spain demonstrated the greatness of English sea-power, since Spain's Atlantic communications were far more effectively cut than they had ever been by the Dutch. But the gains were disappointing; instead of delivering a death blow to the Spanish Empire, Jamaica was captured; Blake destroyed the silver fleet, but failed to capture the treasure. English sea-power commanded the approaches to Spain, but the Dutch as neutral carriers monopolized Spanish trade, while the English suffered severely from privateering. Anti-Cromwellian propaganda put the loss as high as 1,800 ships, more probably about 1,000 were lost as against some 400 captured by the English; in three months, May to July 1656, the Dunkirkers claimed to have taken over 100 English ships.

[1] Davis, *Rise of the English Shipping Industry*, pp. 51–2.

Cromwell's acquisition of Dunkirk not only removed a real threat to English shipping, but also reinforced the command of the Channel, already asserted in the Dutch war. By 1659 an equilibrium existed; if Dutch naval and commercial power still dominated the Sound, they had to respect English interests there; if the English dominated the Straits of Dover more completely than before, the Commonwealth's hopes of mobilizing naval power to destroy or capture Dutch commercial supremacy and the Protectorate's dreams of using it to destroy the Spanish Empire in America had both proved equally illusory. Nevertheless England was enabled to share naval, though not as yet commercial, hegemony with the Dutch and to assert her power and interests in the Atlantic, the Mediterranean and the Baltic. Temporarily England might even claim to be the strongest naval power in Europe, though this would be challenged again by both the Dutch and the French. Her achievement had altered the balance of power in Europe and was part of the process whereby power was being concentrated in north-western Europe at the expense of the Iberian and Mediterranean states.

If England had become one of the two greatest naval powers by 1660, in terms of merchant shipping her relative position is less clear, but despite losses in the Spanish war the total may have been about 200,000 tons. In 1664 French shipping, including fishing boats, amounted to about 130,000 tons. This total was probably little larger than it had been about 1570,[1] when it was perhaps twice as great as that of England. The total of the German ports had probably fallen slightly since 1600, when it was about 120,000 tons;[2] that of Spain and Venice must have declined drastically. The years 1600–60 seemed to show men such as Colbert and Downing that the prosperity of trade and shipping depended more closely than ever on possession of effective naval power. The changes in the tactics and in organization of armies between 1560 and 1660 were so considerable that they have been held to amount to a military revolution. For sixteenth-century lansquenets war had been a seasonal occupation, for the soldiers of the Thirty Years War it was a full-time one. By 1650 many states were heavily in debt to tax-farmers and military *entrepreneurs*, but the future did not belong to *entrepreneurs*, such as Wallenstein, Bernard of Saxe-Weimar, or Charles IV of Lorraine, who raised whole armies. As the organization of armies became more elaborate, so they came more and more completely under the control of the state. In France Le Tellier had endeavoured since 1643 to reform military administration and to give the crown real control over its officers and regiments, though he did not begin to achieve anything appreciable until after the peace of 1659, when royal control grew rapidly. Taxes continued to be farmed out to contractors, but not armies and regiments. As long as naval power

---

[1] Vogel, *Festschrift . . . Dietrich Schäfer*, ed. Hofmeister, pp. 329, 331.
[2] Vogel, *Die Deutschen als Seefahrer*, p. 111.

could be farmed out to *entrepreneurs* such as the West India Company and as long as hired merchant ships were a major part of battle-fleets, direct and continuous control by the state was restricted. While privateering remains an obvious exception, the growth of professionalism and specialization in naval forces in the 1650s can be seen as part of a general process in which states were beginning to exercise much more rigorous and effective control over their armed forces.

CHAPTER VIII

DRAMA AND SOCIETY

THE first half of the seventeenth century marks an important stage in the development of European drama. Inevitably greater heights were attained in one country than in another. In England Shakespeare was only the greatest among an extraordinary galaxy of talented playwrights active in this period, and if the years between his withdrawal from the stage and the closing of the London theatres by Parliament in 1642 are generally regarded as a period of decline, it was none the less an age of intense dramatic activity which bore within it the seeds of future developments. In Spain another summit of dramatic achievement was reached in the plays of Lope de Vega and his contemporaries, and this great age of the Spanish theatre was prolonged into the second half of the century by the works of Calderón.

Although in our period Italy produced no outstanding playwrights, not only did it continue to influence the drama of other European countries through the Commedia dell'Arte; it created the new genre of the opera which was gradually to spread to other lands, and in the sphere of theatre architecture, machinery and scenery it showed the way to the whole of Europe. In France the opening decades of the century form a strange contrast with the extraordinary flowering of drama in the age of Corneille, Molière and Racine from about 1630 to 1680: it was only with the triumphant success of *Le Cid* (1637) that France began to rival England and Spain in the drama. In Germany, where the backwardness of drama was still further increased by the ravages of the Thirty Years War, the main impetus towards theatrical activity came at first from abroad and it was only at the very end of our period, with Andreas Gryphius, that a native drama of any note began to emerge.

Although the tendency to transfer the term 'baroque' from the history of art to that of drama and of literature in general continues to spread from country to country, the fact remains that, however important outside influences may have been, the drama of each country developed on national lines. If the drama of England and France had certain things in common at the beginning of the century, the two countries were to develop in a very different manner. For all its influence abroad, Spanish drama, with its intensely spiritual side, revealed particularly in its Corpus Christi plays [*autos sacramentales*] which were developed out of medieval religious drama, followed its own native pattern. Each nation, with its own traditions and social and political conditions, evolved its own types of drama, however much it might owe to the theatre of other countries.

239

Even so, considering the difficulties of travel, there was an extraordinary amount of coming and going by companies of actors in search of an audience. If Italian actors do not seem to have carried their improvised comedy as far afield as they had done in the second half of the sixteenth century, they made several lengthy sojourns at the French court under both Henri IV and Louis XIII, and were frequently called upon to entertain the Habsburg emperors. Spanish actors, while they chiefly performed outside Spain in their country's possessions in Italy and the Netherlands, occasionally found their way to Paris and once, in the reign of Charles I, even to London. As French drama grew in stature, French actors made their mark in both Holland and the Spanish Netherlands, while at rarer intervals they found their way across the Channel to London and to the courts of James I and Charles I. English actors in their turn visited the continent. Although their last recorded visit to the French court took place in 1604, they were long to continue their wanderings through Holland and especially Germany, entertaining the courts of princes and princelings as well as the citizens of the great commercial centres.

Inevitably the travels abroad of these strolling players combined with the diffusion of the printed play to influence in some degree the drama of the different countries. The Commedia dell'Arte continued in our period to exercise a wide influence, both in the German-speaking countries and in France where the comedy of Molière is rooted in this popular drama. The *comedia* of Spain offered a model to the struggling drama of Germany, and from about 1630 onwards stimulated the development of both comedy and tragi-comedy in France; Corneille's first masterpiece, *Le Cid*, like his later comedy, *Le Menteur*, was an adaptation of a Spanish play. Although Shakespeare and English drama in general were virtually unknown in these years over the greater part of Europe, in Germany English strolling players, who were gradually absorbed into the national life by the addition of native actors and the use of the German language, helped to bring to life a native drama with their crude adaptations of English plays.

The professional actor, whose existence one takes for granted, now emerges as a distinct social type. Performances by amateurs, especially by schoolboys and students, gradually ceased to have their old importance, at any rate so far as drama in the vernacular was concerned, although even at the end of our period, in a backward country like Germany, the plays of Gryphius were mostly performed by schoolboys. In countries where the drama had begun to flourish earlier—in Italy, Spain, England and even France—the professional actor had established himself before 1600, but the growing popularity of drama made his position more assured, while even in Germany, largely under the influence of foreign strolling players, particularly English, the professional actor slowly began to emerge.

Even in those countries where the drama was most highly developed and where many actors had risen above the status of impoverished strolling players, their status was not on the whole a high one, although it varied from country to country according to social and religious conditions. In England the Puritan tradition had always been hostile to the purveyors of such a lewd art as drama; and if in Catholic Italy the actor enjoyed more esteem, in Catholic France the church set him beyond the pale and denied him the sacraments, while middle-class opinion tended to despise so immoral and often so precarious a calling. The place of women in the profession varied from country to country. In Italy and Spain actresses had long been admired members of the profession, and in France, where they had not been numerous before 1600, they gradually came into their own in our period. In England, on the other hand, and in Germany too, they were virtually unknown; female parts continued to be played by boys or men, and the presence of women on the stage was a cause for horror.

When a visiting French company gave a performance at a London theatre in 1629, the presence of actresses on the stage was one of the reasons for the hostility of a contemporary who wrote: 'Last daye certaine vagrant French players, who had beene expelled from their owne contrey, *and those women*, did attempt, thereby giving just offence to all vertuous and well-disposed persons in this town, to act a certain lascivious and unchaste comedye, in the French tonge at the Blackfryers.' Not without some exaggeration perhaps, he thus describes their reception: 'Glad I am to saye they were hissed, hooted, and pippin-pelted from the stage.'[1] The scandal caused in Puritan circles by the appearance of Charles I's French queen in a court performance of a pastoral play in 1633 coincided with the publication of William Prynne's *Histriomastix* where in the index, under the heading *Women-Actors, notorious whores*, he wrote: 'S.Paul prohibites women to speak publikely in the Church . . . And dare then any Christian women be so more than whorishly impudent, as to act, to speak publikely on a Stage (perchance in mans apparell, and cut haire, here proved sinfull and abominable) in the presence of sundry men and women?' The savage punishment meted out to Prynne was intended as a warning to those who meddled with the royal pleasures among which, as we shall see, various forms of dramatic entertainments played a prominent part.

Social and political conditions in this and the previous age brought about a very different development of the theatre in the various countries of Europe. Although Italy led the way in most spheres, its drama lacked the central focus provided by the capital of a large, unified country. There the drama evolved in a piecemeal fashion at the courts of a series

[1] G. E. Bentley, *The Jacobean and Caroline Stage. Dramatic Companies and Players* (2 vols. Oxford, 1941), Vol. I, p. 25.

of small states, particularly those of northern Italy, such as Florence, Mantua or Parma. Such playhouses as were constructed were for the entertainment of the prince and his court, though occasionally spectators from outside that narrow circle might be admitted; a famous playhouse like the Teatro Farnese at Parma, built in 1618, was, of course, a court theatre. Permanent theatres, open to the public in return for payment, developed late, and then through the emergence of opera; it was only in 1637 that the first public theatre was constructed in Italy. This was at Venice and was for use as an opera house. Eight years later Evelyn wrote in his diary:

We went to the Opera which are Comedies & other plays represented in Recitative Music by the most excellent Musitians vocal & Instrumental, together with variety of Seeanes painted & contrived with no lesse art of Perspective, and Machines, for flying in the aire & other wonderfull notions. So taken together it is doubtlesse one of the most magnificent & expensfull diversions the Wit of Men can invent.[1]

A similar dispersal of dramatic activity was inevitably also found in the German-speaking countries. There were no public theatres, and such dramatic performances as were given took place at the court of the emperor or of the princes, in schools and in great commercial cities like Frankfurt. Once again there was no common centre for the development of the theatre such as was provided by the capitals of such centralized countries as England, Spain or France.

In London the first playhouse, named the Theatre, dated from 1576. Between that date and the closing of the theatres in 1642 a considerable number of playhouses were built or rebuilt, among them the so-called 'private' theatres which were differentiated from the 'public' theatres by being indoor buildings, smaller and considerably more expensive. Looking back to the flourishing state of drama in London before the civil wars, a writer of the end of the century declared:

Before the wars, there were in being all these play-houses at the same time. The Black-friars and Globe on the Bank-side, a winter and summer House, belonging to the same Company, called the King's Servants; the Cockpit or Phoenix, in Drury Lane, called the Queen's Servants; the Private House in Salisbury Court, called the Prince's Servants; the Fortune near Whitecross Street, and the Red Bull at the upper end of St. John's Street.[2]

Just as there were curious, if quite accidental resemblances between the material set-up in the 'public' theatres of London and the theatres of Madrid, so there too public playhouses go back to the last quarter of the sixteenth century: the Corral de la Cruz dating from 1579 and the Corral del Principe from 1582. Yet Madrid did not play quite the preponderant role in the theatrical life of Spain that London did in that of England.

---

[1] *Diary*, ed. E. S. de Beer (6 vols., Oxford, 1955), Vol. II, pp. 449–50.
[2] James Wright, *Historia Histrionica* (1699), reprinted in Dodsley's *Old English Plays*, ed. W. C. Hazlitt (London, 1876), Vol. XV, pp. 406–7.

If English provincial towns were by no means deprived of theatrical performances, since there were more or less frequent visits from companies of strolling players, in Spain where Madrid had only recently been elevated to the status of capital, provincial towns like Seville or Valencia played a part denied to towns of the same size in England or France, Again, despite the popularity of the drama in Madrid, the number of permanent theatres was never so great as in London and in our period it never rose beyond the two founded in the sixteenth century.

It is true that in France, during the first two decades of the seventeenth century, a provincial town like Rouen would seem to have been at least as important as Paris as a theatrical centre. The only permanent theatre in the capital, the Hôtel de Bourgogne, was hired out to a succession of French companies, with at intervals Italian, Spanish and even English actors; to begin with none of the French companies could find enough support to establish itself permanently in the capital and had soon to return to touring in the provinces or go abroad. However, as time passed, Paris, by far the largest city in France, the seat of the government and court, gradually came to exert its influence in the world of the theatre. By 1630 the Comédiens du Roi were permanently established at the Hôtel de Bourgogne, and a second company had settled in Paris, eventually putting up a new building, the Théâtre du Marais. Even so, the attempt of the young Molière in the 1640s to set up a third theatrical company in Paris soon ended in failure, and from 1645 onwards he and his companions were compelled to spend thirteen years touring the provinces.

Although in our period the principal developments inevitably took place in the field of vernacular drama, drama in Latin must not be left completely out of account. In Catholic countries, from Spain to Poland, the teaching orders, and more especially the Jesuits, deliberately used the dramatic performances given in their schools for both educational and propaganda purposes. Most of their plays, though by no means all, were written in Latin, but even so they were not designed exclusively for a learned audience. If the elegant language in which they were written appealed to the connoisseur, the great stress on scenic effects, on music and dancing, and even on comic interludes, was designed to interest much wider circles, from the members of the court and the aristocracy of both sexes to bourgeois and even plebeian spectators. Inevitably the plays performed in the different countries reflected to some degree tendencies in local vernacular drama, but at the same time, particularly in the theatrically backward German-speaking countries, they influenced the development of the drama, including opera, particularly through their relatively advanced technique in the use of scenery, costume and spectacle.

What sort of spectators frequented the public theatres for which men like Shakespeare or Corneille or Lope de Vega wrote is a fascinating question, but one which it is by no means easy to answer, despite its importance for an interpretation of the historical significance of their plays. Only too often labels such as 'aristocratic' or 'plebeian' are attached by historians to the audiences of the age without much preliminary investigation of the available facts; and if an attempt is made to assemble the scattered contemporary documents which bear on this question, they are often interpreted in too narrow a spirit, without reference to long-term trends in the theatre of the country under discussion and without comparisons with conditions in neighbouring countries in the same period.

Unfortunately our information about Paris theatre audiences in the first two or three decades of the seventeenth century is extremely meagre. Given the poorness of such plays of the time as have survived, this is not an unmitigated misfortune, but it does make it difficult for us to assess the long-term trend in changes in the composition of audiences and to link on to the much more definite information which we possess for the age of Corneille, Molière and Racine. Our almost total ignorance of what Paris theatre audiences were like in the opening decades of the century has left the field clear for the over-simplified view that the aesthetic and moral crudity of French drama in that period was due to the preponderantly plebeian audiences which lacked the refining influence of the aristocracy, of the learned and especially of respectable women.

The information at our disposal for these decades does not do more than enable us to qualify this view by pointing to fragments of evidence which indicate that the aristocracy—even the king and his court—did on occasion frequent the Hôtel de Bourgogne; and that not only did writers and other middle-class spectators find their way to this place of perdition, but that the ban imposed by some modern historians of the theatre on the attendance of respectable women does not seem (any more than in London at the same date) to have been by any means strictly observed. The presence of Henri IV's queen and the ladies of the court at the Hôtel de Bourgogne is attested.

No doubt it is possible that when, about 1630, the theatre became more popular in Paris and began to produce plays of a greater aesthetic and moral refinement, the audience did become less plebeian; but it is also possible that this improvement was the result less of changes in the social composition of the audience than of the growing refinement of taste which was brought about in these years among the upper classes of society by the development of the *salons* and of social life.

Fortunately we can discuss the question of Paris theatre audiences in the period after 1630 on a firm foundation of documents, fragmentary and at times tantalizingly incomplete, it is true, but still sufficiently clear for our purpose. Despite a multitude of contemporary references to the presence of *le peuple* in the theatres of Paris during the rest of the century, it is clear that in contemporary usage the word, when it did not simply mean 'audience', generally implied 'those who were not of noble birth', as in the expression *la cour et le peuple*. Most of the spectators below noble rank appear to have been solid bourgeois like merchants or lawyers or else writers or aspiring writers and in general people of some education. Undoubtedly in the days of Corneille, Molière and Racine the middle-class section of the audience was already extremely important, especially as the part of the theatre which it mainly frequented—the *parterre* [pit]—generally contained at least half the audience. On the other hand, given the thoroughly aristocratic nature of French society in that age, the noble-men and their womenfolk played a very important part in the Paris theatres of our period. Theatre prices rose steeply in the course of the century, and the high cost of the best seats—particularly the first row of boxes and, as the custom established itself towards the middle of the century, the seats on the stage—made the spectators with blue blood or money increasingly important from the box-office point of view. Scattered remarks of contemporary playwrights and critics make it clear that the importance of the aristocratic section of the audience was fully recognized, even if, owing to their numbers, the spectators in the pit, who were all men, could have a great influence on the success or failure of new plays.

The size and composition of London theatre audiences in this period—inevitably with special reference to those of Shakespeare—have been studied in much greater detail than those of any continental country. Although the evidence is fragmentary and at times contradictory, there seems to be broad agreement about the long-term trend in changes in the audience during these years. It is generally accepted that in the flourishing days of Elizabethan drama and especially in the years when Shakespeare was engaged both in acting and in writing plays, 'public' theatres like the Globe (built in 1599 and rebuilt after a fire in 1613) took in all classes of the community from the 'penny stinkards' who stood in the pit to the noblemen who sat in the galleries, in the rather mysterious 'lord's room' or—as was seen to be the case in the Paris theatres—on the stage.

Whether therefore the gatherers of the publique or private Play-house stand to receive the afternoones rent, [wrote Dekker in *The Gulls Hornebooke* (1609),] let our Gallant (having paid it) presently advance himselfe up to the Throne of the Stage . . . On the very Rushes where the Commedy is to daunce, yea and under the state of *Cambises* himselfe must our fetherd Estridge like a peece of Ordnance be planted valiantly (because impudently) beating downe the mewes and hisses of the opposed rascality.[1]

Among the spectators in the galleries were a fair proportion of women—respectable women as well as those who were less respectable.

Even in Shakespeare's day, however, there was a difference between the 'public' and the so-called 'private' theatres. In the former, where the male spectators in the pit were exposed to all the variety of English weather,

[1] E. K. Chambers, *The Elizabethan Stage* (4 vols. Oxford, 1923), Vol. IV, p. 366.

admission was undoubtedly cheap, at any rate to that part of the house. Indeed the author of the most detailed study of early seventeenth-century London theatre audiences goes so far as to declare that 'audiences were composed largely of shopkeepers and craftsmen' and even that 'it was predominantly a working class audience'.[1] Although this is going far beyond the available evidence and under-estimating the importance, especially in the society of the day, of the aristocratic spectators, the lawyers, merchants, and the other representatives, male and female, of the leisured classes, it does seem established that the 'public' theatres of Shakespeare's day attracted an audience drawn from all ranks of society.

A much more restricted audience was inevitably attracted to the so-called 'private' theatres because of their smaller size and much higher charges. Whereas in Shakespeare's day a penny secured admission to the pit of the Globe or other 'public' theatres, sixpence was the minimum charge in the more select 'private' theatres which were completely protected from the weather. In a poem prefixed to a play published in the 1630s (by this time all theatre prices had risen somewhat) we read of the thrifty bourgeois who has blundered into one of the 'private' theatres and soon regrets having parted with a shilling for a seat there:

> I will hasten to the money Box
> And take my shilling out again, for now
> I have considered that it is too much;
> I'll go to th' Bull, or Fortune, and there see
> A Play for two pense, with a Jig to boot.[2]

Before the Civil War the Fortune and the Red Bull, we are assured by a writer at the end of the century,[3] were 'mostly frequented by citizens, and the meaner sort of people'.

In considering this problem it must be remembered that in 1609 the company of actors to which Shakespeare belonged added to its 'public' theatre, the Globe, which it henceforth used only in the summer months, the 'private' theatre of the Blackfriars which from that time onwards was a far more lucrative proposition. Thus already in Shakespeare's day there was developing a move away from the sort of audience which embraced spectators drawn from all social classes, towards two rather different types of theatre—the one attracting a more select audience, drawn from the more aristocratic and wealthy sections of society, from the court, the gentry, the professional classes, and the other appealing to the middle classes and the lower orders.

The eventual outcome of this long evolution was that, when public performances could at last begin again in London at the Restoration, the smaller number of theatres available (there were never more than two

---

[1] A. Harbage, *Shakespeare's Audience* (New York, 1941), pp. 64, 90.
[2] *Ibid.* pp. 64–5.
[3] James Wright in his *Historia Histrionica*, p. 407.

and for a period there was only one) were virtually monopolized by the court and its hangers-on, and that both middle class and plebeian spectators were not catered for at all. Thus in little more than half a century London theatre audiences changed completely. In the age of Shakespeare they were drawn from all classes of society, from nobleman to artisan; in the age of Dryden and Congreve they came from a somewhat raffish élite.

It is possible that an evolution in the same direction took place in Paris theatres in our period but, as we have seen, our almost total ignorance of what went on in the Paris theatrical world in the opening decades of the century makes discussion of this point difficult. It is, however, certain that even after the theatre became much more fashionable round about 1630, the solid bourgeois section of the audience in the pit retained considerable importance, one which was recognized by the flattery addressed to such spectators by Molière, among others, in the 1660s. It seems reasonably clear that no such drastic transformation took place in Paris as occurred in London, from a 'universal' audience to one drawn from only a narrow section of society.

The theatres of Madrid seem to have continued throughout our period to attract spectators from all sections of the community. Philip IV, who had a passion for the theatre and for actresses, even had a special box [aposento] in one of the two public theatres, though he went incognito. The clergy too, whose attitude to drama was not as hostile as that of French clerics in the seventeenth century, had seats set aside for them in the theatre; while the most distinguished spectators, male and female, followed the play from the grated windows of the houses round the courtyard where the stage was set up, and an area at the back was reserved for women of more modest means, the pit, in which most of the spectators stood, was, as in Paris, reserved for men. Its occupants had a very considerable influence on the fate of a new play, applauding or showing disapproval in the most vigorous fashion. The autos sacramentales, performed by professional actors, also appealed to a wide range of spectators. They were performed first at the royal palace and then before the members of the royal council and the municipality of Madrid before being given on portable stages for the general public in the squares of the capital. From 1648 onwards the autos were also performed in the public theatres.

The crude adaptations of English plays performed in Germany in our period, at first in English and by English actors and then gradually in German and with an admixture of German actors, are frequently considered to reflect the crude taste of the masses in the German cities through which these companies passed. In the process the plays of Shakespeare and his contemporaries certainly underwent a drastic transformation. Prose replaced verse, all poetic passages were eliminated, the maximum amount of dramatic tension was aroused and the spectator was treated to processions, drums and trumpets, along with music, songs and comic interludes. Yet to attribute this transformation purely to the influence of the plebeian spectators who flocked to such entertainments is surely wrong. Not only did town councils attend in a body the performances given in their honour by the newly arrived actors, but from the beginning the *Englische Komödianten* enjoyed the patronage of courts all over Germany. While it is true that opera rather than drama was the main theatrical entertainment of German princes and princelings in our period, they were far from despising the offerings of the professional actors. Their companies would be made welcome at court and passed on with commendations to other prospective patrons, whether princes or town councils.

Since we are here concerned with the age of absolute or would-be absolute rulers, it is important to enquire a little more closely into the interest in drama taken by the ruler and his court. Contrary to what was once believed, there is every reason to think that in the opening decades of the century the French court did take some interest in the theatre. If, during the earlier years of the century, it is easier to find information about ballets being performed at court than about plays, that does not mean that no professional actors made their appearance at the court of Henri IV or of the young Louis XIII. We have evidence of visits to the court by French actors during Henri's reign, and both he and his Italian wife, Marie de Medici, had Italian companies fetched across the Alps for their own entertainment at court and incidentally for that of their subjects at the Hôtel de Bourgogne. Before and after his accession the young Louis XIII was taken on several occasions to see performances at this theatre, while both French and Italian actors frequently appeared before the court. In one particularly active period, between November 1612 and February 1614, we have records of at least seventy-six performances by French actors and fifty-seven by Italians.

If, when he grew older, Louis XIII did not show anything like as much interest in the theatre as his son in his prime was to do, he and his queen, Anne of Austria, by no means ignored the drama and what was going on in the theatrical world. It is true, however, that Richelieu's role as a patron of the drama was much more important. The first evidence which we have of his connection with the theatre goes back to 1629, and right down to his death in 1642 that interest was sustained. Not only did he give pensions to playwrights and thus encourage a much greater output in plays; he also took an interest in the composition and performance of the works of his protégés. He inspired the production of a number of plays which were performed in the Palais Cardinal (later the Palais Royal) before members of the royal family and the court. To the smaller theatre which he had there he added in due course a larger one.

This second theatre, which was opened early in 1641 with a performance of a spectacular tragicomedy, *Mirame*, written under his guidance by one of his favourite playwrights, was technically a great advance on any such building available in Paris down to that date. In it was performed, a few weeks before the cardinal's death, a political play, *Europe*, which defended his foreign policy and in the composition of which he was alleged by contemporaries to have had a considerable part. After his death and that of Louis XIII soon after, the regent, Anne of Austria, continued to interest herself in the theatre; even her period of mourning did not prevent her from attending court performances in secret. All this laid a foundation for the part which her son, Louis XIV, was to play as a patron of the drama in all its forms until in his old age his piety made him develop scruples about attending plays.

In England, in our period, down to the Civil Wars, the court showed an increasing interest in drama. While Elizabeth was far from scorning theatrical entertainments, the records of court performances which we possess show that these were relatively few in number and concentrated generally in one period of the year, between Christmas and the beginning of Lent. The accession of James I brought about a considerable change, as he, his queen and other members of the royal family showed considerably more interest in the drama than Elizabeth had done. On James' accession the company to which Shakespeare belonged, the Lord Chamberlain's Men, became the King's Men; down to her death in 1619 the queen, Anne of Denmark, gave her name to another London company, formerly known as the Earl of Worcester's Men. Their sons also had companies named after them. The number of court performances increased significantly, particularly those given by the favoured company of the King's Men; whereas for the last ten years of Elizabeth's reign the average number of their performances at court was only three, the average figure for the next ten years rose to thirteen, with great profit to their purse.

With Charles I and his French queen who, as we have seen, did not disdain on occasion to mount the boards herself for private performances at court, the royal preoccupation with all forms of drama increased still further. Professional companies were summoned to court more frequently than ever before. The king's interest went so far as make him go through the manuscript of one play and restore certain expressions removed by the censor; on more than one occasion Charles appears to have furnished the playwright with his plot. In the epilogue of one of these plays the author addresses the king thus:

> If what hath been presented to your sense
> You do approve, thank your own influence;
> Which moving in the story that you told
> Infus'd new heat into a brain grown cold ...

It was, however, his queen who showed the livelier enthusiasm for the drama.

The sixteen-year-old Henrietta Maria brought with her from the French court an interest in the ballet and in dramatic performances. Shortly after her arrival in England a foreign envoy reported the following entertainment in which the young queen took part:

On the day of carnival, for which Tuesday was set aside, she acted in a beautiful pastoral of her own composition, assisted by twelve of her ladies whom she had trained since Christmas. The pastoral succeeded admirably; not only in the decorations and changes of scenery, but also in the acting and recitation of the ladies—Her Majesty surpassing all the others. The performance was conducted as privately as possible, inasmuch as it is an unusual thing in this country to see the Queen upon a stage; the audience consequently was limited to a few of the nobility, expressly invited, no others being admitted.[1]

Seven years later, in 1633, Henrietta's appearance, in the part of Queen Bellesa, in a court performance of Montague's pastoral play, *The Shepherd's Paradise*, coincided with Prynne's brutal onslaught on the stage. The queen was also the patron of one of the London companies of actors —Queen Henrietta's Men—and she is also known to have attended public performances given by the King's Men at the Blackfriars Theatre. Again, when Floridor's company came over from Paris during the winter of 1634–5, she did her best to make their visit a success. This royal interest in the theatre was certainly to have an important effect on drama.

In Italy, as we have seen, the courts were inevitably the centre of dramatic activity as they had been in the sixteenth century. The patronage of Mantua was important for the development of the Commedia dell'Arte, and opera first developed in Florence and other courts before finding its chief centre in Venice. In Spain Philip III, unlike his father, showed some interest in the theatre, having both secular plays and *autos* performed in the royal palaces. With his successor, Philip IV, who came to the throne in 1621 and reigned until 1665, the drama was a veritable passion. Though politically his reign was marked by Spain's defeat at the hands of France, it coincided with a great flowering of Spanish drama in which the king played a part. As a child he had taken part in amateur performances at court, and not only did he and his queen (Henrietta Maria's elder sister) attend vast numbers of theatrical performances in their palaces; he is even said to have written several plays himself. At first court performances mostly took place in the royal palace in Madrid or in the gardens at Aranjuez, but from 1632 onwards many were given at the new royal residence of Buen Retiro on the outskirts of Madrid, where the first performance of many of Calderón's plays was to take place. Here were a great variety of theatres—in the open air as well as the indoor Coliseo

[1] *Historical Manuscripts Commission*, Eleventh Report (London, 1887), Appendix, Part I, p. 47.

de las Comédias, a splendid building erected in 1640. It was designed by an Italian architect and equipped with all manner of up-to-date devices to produce the most startling spectacular effects.

In German-speaking territories it was the Austrian Habsburgs, in close contact through successive marriages with the Italian courts, who led the way in the development of drama, even though it was only in 1652 that a court theatre was constructed at the Hofburg. This, the work once again of an Italian architect, was equipped with the very latest stage devices. In Austria and throughout the rest of the empire there were large numbers of courts, large and small, which played their part in the development of the drama, whether by taking on companies of strolling players or by offering other dramatic entertainments.

The performance of plays was by no means the only form of theatrical entertainment indulged in by the courts of Europe in our period. In France, for instance, in the opening decades of the century the royal family and courtiers seem to have been more interested in ballet than in drama in the narrow sense. Although the ballet did not reach its highest point until the reign of Louis XIV, this form of entertainment was extremely popular during the reigns of Henri IV and Louis XIII; the courtiers, headed by the king himself, delighted to take part in such performances, which ranged from relatively modest entertainments (*ballets-mascarades*), often with a strong farce-like, grotesque element, to a great spectacle like *Le Ballet de la Prospérité des Armes de la France*, performed before the king in Richelieu's palace in 1641.

In England the allied entertainment of the masque reached its high point at the courts of James I and Charles I. Two names are always associated with these performances—those of Ben Jonson who for some twenty-five years provided the words, and of Inigo Jones who furnished the elaborate settings and spectacular effects, based largely on Italian models, until the Civil Wars put an end to all such court entertainments. The dancing, the splendid costumes and scenery, varied by the addition of a rudimentary plot and the grotesque characters of the 'anti-masque', provided sumptuous spectacles for the king and court.

Italy, which had been the home of the ballet and the masque, also developed during these years in its courts the new genre of the opera. The first opera was performed at Florence in 1597, and the earliest opera of which the music has survived—*Euridice*, with text by Rinuccini and two separate musical settings—was performed there in 1600 for the wedding of Henri IV of France and Marie de Medici. Monteverdi, whose first operas were performed at the court of the dukes of Mantua, moved to Venice in 1613. There the new genre ceased to be a purely court entertainment, and the establishment of the first opera house in 1637 heralded an extraordinary development of opera in the republic in the second half of the century, when many other Italian cities also set up their own opera houses. The later operas of Monteverdi, produced shortly before his death in 1643, marked the final step in the establishment of modern opera.

From Italy the new genre spread rapidly to the courts of Austria and southern Germany; performances at Salzburg are recorded as early as 1618, although Vienna was quickly to become the centre of its development. Italian operas remained extremely influential in German-speaking territories, but attempts were soon made to produce German libretti and music, beginning with Martin Opitz' adaptation of a work by Rinuccini, which was first performed at Torgau for a princely marriage in 1627.

The purposes of these court entertainments, whether they offered ballets, masques, operas or plays, were no doubt varied. In the words of the preface to one of Davenant's masques they were given by 'princes of sweet and humane natures' in order to 'recreate their spirits wasted in grave affairs of State, and for the entertainment of their nobility, ladies, and court'. They also served to impress a wider public (for attendance at many of such entertainments as masques and ballets was not rigorously confined to the court circle) with the greatness and splendour of the ruler, be he duke, king or emperor—or principal minister, like Richelieu. Occasionally they might be made to serve a more precise propaganda purpose. The *comédie héroïque*, *Europe*, which Richelieu had performed in the Palais Cardinal a few weeks before his death, had originally been composed several years earlier to defend his foreign policy and particularly the war against Spain.

Its aim, the preface tells us, was to depict 'l'ambition des Espagnols pour se rendre maîtres de l'Europe et la protection que lui donne le Roi avec ses alliés pour la garantir de servitude'. The prologue of the play, spoken by Peace, announces her return to the world:

> Assez ont brillé par les champs
> Les casques emplumés et les glaives tranchants.
> Assez la triste horreur a régné dans le monde.
> O vous, invincibles guerriers,
> A qui tout a cédé sur la terre et dans l'onde
> Venez vous reposer dessous mes oliviers.

In the play the courageous warrior, Francion (France), is chosen by Europe as her knight to defend her against the schemes of the dark-skinned villain, Ibère (Spain). It is the ambition of Spain, Francion explains to Europe, which has compelled France to enter the war:

> Quoi! j'attendrais de voir mes voisins terrassés,
> Et qu'Ibère, enrichi du bien des oppressés,
> Glorieux de leur perte et riant de leurs larmes,
> Jusque dans mes états osât porter ses armes! . . .
> J'ai droit de m'opposer à son injuste effort.
> L'innocent et le faible ont en moi leur support . .
> Enfin il faut la guerre, et j'y suis emporté,
> Non par ambition, mais par nécessité.

The evil designs of Spain are denounced in words put into the mouth of
Ibère: . . . . Pour mon ambition
> J'immole honneur, parents, respect, religion.
> Au besoin, pour avoir l'autorité suprême,
> J'immolerais encore une part de moi-même.
> Je veux placer mon trône au-dessus de cent rois,
> Par le mépris du sang, par le mépris des lois . . .
> Un empire m'est tout, le reste ne m'est rien.

The conclusion of this *comédie héroïque* is, of course, a happy one.
Francion compels Ibère to renounce his dream of adding the conquest
of Europe to that of America, and the play leaves the spectator with the
hope of French victories bringing about a negotiated peace between
France and Spain.

The same sort of political allegory is found in the masques performed
just previously to this at the court of Charles I as the clouds heralding the
Civil War grew thicker. Indeed, the stock ending for the masques performed at Whitehall in this period was the disappearance of the clouds,
'leaving behind' as in Carew's *Coelum Britannicum* (1634), 'nothing but
a serene sky'—the symbol of the disappearance of opposition to the royal
will. Particularly striking from this point of view are Davenant's *Britannia
Triumphans* (1638) and, the last masque given before the Civil War, his
Salmacida Spolia (1640). In their elaborate Inigo Jones settings, with
Charles and Henrietta leading the dancers in their splendid costumes,
these masques view all the political discords of the times from the angle
of the ruler.

In the first, Britanocles (Charles) is presented as 'the glory of the western
world' who 'hath by his wisdom, valour and piety, not only vindicated
his own, but far distant seas, infested with pirates'—a roundabout way
of defending the hated ship-money against the opposition of Imposture.
Imposture and Merlin, the magician, are driven out by Bellerophon at the
approach of Britanocles:

> Away! Fame, still obedient unto fate,
> This happy hour is call'd to celebrate
> Britanocles, and those that in this Isle
> The old with modern virtues reconcile.
> Away! Fame's universal voice I hear,
>
> [a trumpet within]
> 'Tis fit you vanish quite when they appear.

Britanocles' entry is announced thus by the chorus:

> Britanocles, the great and good appears,
> His person fills our eyes, his name our ears,
> His virtue every drooping spirit cheers!

At this point the masquers dance their entry and address their praises to
the queen, after which Galatea, riding in the sea on a dolphin, renews the
praise of Britanocles.

The subject of *Salmacida Spolia* is set forth by the author in these terms:

Discord, a malicious fury, appears in a storm, and by the invocation of malignant spirits, proper to her evil use, having already put most of the world into disorder, endeavours to disturb these parts, envying the blessings and tranquillity we have long enjoyed.

These incantations are expressed by those spirits in an Antimasque: who on a sudden are surprised, and stopt in their motion by a secret power, whose wisdom they tremble at, and depart as foreknowing that Wisdom will change all their malicious hope of these disorders into a sudden calm, which after their departure is prepared by a disperst harmony of music.

This secret Wisdom, in the person of the King attended by his nobles, and under the name of Philogenes or Lover of his people, hath his appearance prepared by a Chorus, representing the beloved people, and is instantly discovered, environed with those nobles in the throne of Honour.

Then the Queen, personating the chief heroine, with her martial ladies, is sent down from Heaven by Pallas as a reward of his prudence, for reducing the threat'ning storm into the following calm.

Verses like these are addressed to the king by 'the chorus of the beloved people' when he appears seated on the throne of honour:

> If it be kingly to outlast
>   Those storms the people's giddy fury raise,
> Till like fantastic winds themselves they waste,
>   The wisdom of that patience is thy praise . . .
> Since strength of virtues gained you Honour's throne.
>   Accept our wonder, and enjoy our praise!
> He's fit to govern there, and rule alone,
>   Whom inward helps, not outward force doth raise.

While the chorus was singing this song, the queen, once again pregnant, descended with her 'martial ladies' from the heavens in a cloud 'in a transparent brightness of thin exhalations, such as the gods are feigned to descend in'. After the two dances, 'the chorus below filled all the whole scene with apparitions and harmony', in a song addressed to Charles and Henrietta, which contains the following verse:

> All that are harsh, all that are rude,
> Are by your harmony subdu'd;
> Yet so into obedience wrought,
> As if not forc'd to it, but taught.

The events of the remainder of the decade were to show up the complete unreality of this world of make-believe.

The overwhelming majority of the straight plays of the period—comedies, tragedies, tragi-comedies, pastoral plays and the like (not forgetting the farces)—seem to have been performed quite indifferently at court or on the public stage; for the most part they received their first performance in the public theatres. Clearly the audiences in the public playhouses— more or less restricted in their social composition according to the country concerned—were always decidedly more mixed than were the relatively 'select' groups of spectators who attended a performance given at court before the king and the royal family. It must not, however, be imagined that the audience at court was completely different from that of the public theatres. If at court the members of the aristocracy inevitably made up the great majority of the spectators, they also provided a respectable part of the audiences of the public theatres—not only numerically and financially, but also in a much wider sense, given the social setting of the time in which the aristocracy enjoyed an importance difficult for us to imagine today.

Even in countries like England or Spain where the audience, especially in the opening years of the century, seems to have embraced representatives of most sections of the community, plays might pass straight from the public stage to performances in the royal palaces. In any case, it was not as if, as is sometimes imagined, the king and his courtiers had a peculiarly refined taste, raised far above that of the vulgar plebs in the public theatres. Farce was popular at the French court under Henri IV: in the rare glimpses which we have of him in the theatre we see him being entertained by French or Italian farce-actors. The farce tradition persisted at court in ballet as well as in comedy, right through the next reign into that of the Sun-King. It is well known, for instance, that when in 1658 Molière's company returned from the provinces and made its first appearance in Paris at the Louvre before the king and court, it was not his company's performance in a tragedy of Corneille which made an impression on this audience, but the little farce which rounded off the proceedings.

Sometimes two strands may be seen in the drama of the age, particularly where, as in England, there was a definite trend towards a splitting up of the once universal audience into the more plebeian spectators of the 'public' theatres and the more aristocratic audiences of the so-called 'private' theatres, which were both smaller and more expensive. On the one hand, one finds certain types of play which owed their appeal to middle class and plebeian spectators to their treatment of scenes from the life of their equals; while, on the other hand, we find in the last decade or two before the closing of the London theatres in 1642 a trend towards the types of drama which were finally to emerge in the Restoration period, after a period of incubation during the years when public performances of plays were banned.

We find, for instance, in the tragedies and tragicomedies of Beaumont and Fletcher, Shakespeare's successors as the chief playwrights for the King's Men, installed from 1609 onwards for most of the year at the 'private' house of the Blackfriars, a foretaste of the drama of the Restoration period. Their comedies of manners and those of writers like Middleton and Shirley portray, in a manner close to that of Restoration comedy, the world of fashionable society and at the same time pour scorn on the middle classes. There is a great gap between plays like these and the picture of the middle and lower ranks of society presented by such earlier comedies as Dekker's *Shoemaker's Holiday* or Heywood's *A Woman Killed with Kindness*.

Closer to contemporary European fashions in drama stand romantic comedies or tragicomedies of this period like Shirley's *The Wedding*, or the vogue, especially great at the court of Charles I, for pastoral plays which, taking their source in Italy, had achieved some popularity in France, where Racan in his *Bergeries* (performed *c.*1620) produced the outstanding play of this type. The elaborate conventions of the pastoral, whether in drama or the novel, were more calculated to win the approval of a sophisticated court or preponderantly aristocratic audience than that of a wider circle of spectators. Fletcher's *Faithful Shepherdess*, written in the first decade of the century, found greatest favour when, in the 1630s, it was given for Twelfth Night before Charles and Henrietta; we have already seen what scandal was caused during the previous season by the queen's appearance in another pastoral play, Walter Montague's *Shepherd's Paradise*. One of the most significant developments in the English theatre during the 1630s was the emergence of the so-called Cavalier drama, the work not of professional writers, but of courtiers like Montague, a gentleman of the privy-chamber to the king, or Sir John Suckling, who is still remembered as a poet. To the same world belonged William Davenant who, although the son of an Oxford vintner, succeeded in securing entry to the court through his plays and masques, and was made poet laureate in 1638. After being knighted during the Civil War for his services to the Royalist cause, he revived dramatic performances in London in 1656 with, among other works, *The Siege of Rhodes*, the first English opera, and at the Restoration secured one of the two theatres in the capital, thus forming a link between the early and the later Stuart stage.

Nowhere on the continent was the trend towards two relatively clearly differentiated types of drama, the one inclining towards the middle class and the plebeian, and the other to the court and the aristocracy, so clearly visible as in England. Yet even in this country one broad type or series of types of play might please all audiences, whatever the social rank of the spectators. The important thing for the playwright, then as now, was to catch the spirit of his age and country as it was reflected in the tastes and outlook of such spectators as could be attracted to a play. However popular the theatre may have been in any given European town or city, it could never attract more than a minority of the adult inhabitants. Even when theatregoing was a habit not confined to the upper classes, there was still a strong prejudice among the middle classes against the public theatre as an entertainment, not only in Puritan London, but in Catholic Paris.

Under certain circumstances the same plays might very well be seen by both king and cobbler, although probably in very different surroundings; but even so, given the society of the day with its worship of rank, the choice of theme and its treatment would make more concessions to the tastes and interests of the upper classes than to those of the masses.

It was, for instance, an accepted theory that while tragedy deals with the misfortunes of the illustrious, comedy portrays the adventures of characters drawn from the middle or lower ranks of society. With rare exceptions the tragedy of the age is concerned with such highly placed personages as the prince of Denmark or the Emperor Augustus, while comedy brings on the stage private persons of less account. The European vogue of tragicomedy tended to portray, against a confusing background of romantic adventures, personages of birth involved in situations bordering on the tragic, but ending after all happily.

Theatre audiences of the time were not merely composed of noblemen and commoners; there was another division—that between the learned and the unlearned. The learned also helped to colour the drama of the age, though very variously according to country. Everywhere the great majority of plays were written by men of some education, brought up at least in the grammar school or its continental equivalent and given a nodding acquaintance with Latin, if not with Greek. Often they wore their learning, such as it was, very lightly, though it generally sufficed to enable them to make use of the drama as well as of the mythology of the ancient world in the writing of their plays. The great majority had their eye on box-office success and the payment of the next month's rent or even of the next meal, rather than on providing an exhibition of their learning. Playwriting was still a miserably paid profession; receipts from actors and publishers were seldom more than a mere pittance, and writers who lacked private means (as most playwrights certainly did) were driven to seek the patronage of kings and princes, ministers and tax-farmers, great noblemen and ladies, a state of affairs to which the obsequious flattery of the flowery dedications usual in this period bears eloquent witness. It was to please both a wider audience of potential theatregoers and a narrow circle of patrons that playwrights strove, rather than to show off their learning, which in the circumstances of the day meant their knowledge of the ancient tongues and literatures.

In England or Spain the famous rules of drama, inherited by many devious routes from Aristotle and other ancient writers, left next to no mark on the drama of the period. In Germany the more learned *Schuldrama*, as distinct from the crude offerings of the strolling players, was performed in grammar schools to a more or less cultured audience; in the 1620s and 1630s Martin Opitz urged writers to seek their models in the Ancients, the French and Italians. Italy was, of course, the home of the rules which the humanists of the previous century had derived from the ancients; but most Italian playwrights of our age (Cicognini is the best known of them), while paying lip-service to the rules, were more concerned to produce popular plays.

The France of this period offers extraordinary contrasts in this field. Corneille was later to confess that when in 1630 he began his long and prolific career as a playwright, he had not even heard of the rules. Yet at the very moment he began to write a revolutionary transformation was taking place in French drama. Partly under Italian influence the rules— not only the famous unities but the rules of verisimilitude [*vraisemblance*] and the proprieties [*bienséances*]—were being slowly imposed by the learned, against the resistance of those who stood for the freer drama of the earlier decades of the century. It was in vain that they claimed for the dramatist the right, indeed the duty, to keep himself free from such entanglements which could only restrict his freedom to give the spectator the variety of action and setting which he wanted. In the two decades between 1630 and 1650 the rules were imposed on French drama with, to some extent, the encouragement of aristocratic patrons, including Richelieu himself, although it is nonsense to see in his support for the rules yet another aspect of his desire to fasten an iron control over the whole of the life of France.

Yet although the rules triumphed in France to a degree unparalleled in any other European country and gradually effected a complete revolution in drama, eliminating step by step both the pastoral play and then the immensely popular tragicomedy from the stage, it would be an utter mistake to imagine that the result was a learned drama, written for an intellectual élite. Comedy, as distinct from farce, only really began to develop in France in the 1630s; but it always enjoyed a fair degree of freedom from the rules, as can be seen in many of the comedies of Molière later in the century. Although the rules always weighed more heavily on tragedy from its beginnings with Mairet's *Sophonisbe* (1634) down to its unlamented demise nearly two centuries later, none the less it reflected the outlook and tastes, not of a narrow intellectual élite, but of the fairly broad cross-section of the population of Paris which frequented the theatre, and more especially the interests of the upper-class section of the audience, female as well as male. If the love theme was to occupy a central position in tragedy only after the middle of the century in such illustrious works as Racine's *Andromaque* or *Phédre*, already it almost invariably occupied an important secondary place, whether as the driving force behind the conspirators in Corneille's *Cinna* or in rivalry with the religious theme of a martyr-play like *Polyeucte*. What is more, the typical political tragedy of the 1630s and 1640s reflected something of the restless ambition and desire for self-assertion which went into the nobility's perpetual conspiracies against Richelieu or the tragic farce of the civil wars of the Fronde.

In these forty or fifty years to which we are driven to return by the masterpieces of Shakespeare, Lope de Vega, Calderón and Corneille we find, as we move from country to country, an infinitely varied interaction between drama and society. Everywhere the small world of the theatre reflected to some degree what was going on in the world outside. Now dominated by the court, now appealing to the broader masses, drama and the allied arts of the masque, the ballet and opera mirrored the aspirations, the fears and sufferings of an age of international wars and civil strife, or else provided escape from the cares and anxieties of everyday life in a profusion of splendour, mingled characteristically with the exaggerated and the grotesque.

CHAPTER IX

SPAIN AND EUROPE 1598–1621

WHEN Philip II's long reign came to a close, his Mediterranean policy had largely succeeded. He had defeated the Turks and closed his grip on Italy. But his northern policy had failed. He had not defeated the Dutch 'rebels'. The vast enterprises into which he had been tempted by the hope of quicker victory had been disastrous. His treasury was empty. And now the favourable conjuncture which had lasted so long, and which he had hoped to exploit, was over. For most of his reign Phillip II had profited by the division and anarchy of France. But by 1598 that was past: the new Bourbon dynasty was firmly established and could not even be rejected as heretical. In his last year, therefore, Philip II came to terms with reality. Since the Netherlands would not yield to him, he ostentatiously devolved his authority over them to an 'independent' sovereign, his own safely Spaniolized son-in-law, the Archduke Albert; and he allowed this sovereign to negotiate, in his name, peace with France.

Thus the dying Philip II laid down the policy which his son Philip III should follow. Through the Archduke Albert he was to continue the northern struggle. The 'rebels' in the Netherlands were to be crushed. The war with heretical England, however disastrous, should be continued: after all, the succession to the English throne was still open and Elizabeth's death, when it came, would offer a great opportunity. But on the landward side the archduke should be undistracted. There was no point in continuing the war with France. For practical purposes France must be neutralized. Ideally—this at least was the papal ideal—France might even combine with Spain against the heretics of both England and Holland. Unfortunately neither of these last hopes was realized. France would not join the crusade against England and Holland, and even in peace it continued to distract the effort of Spain. The policy laid down by Philip II was made impossible for Philip III, not least by the mere presence of a re-united France, a restored French monarchy.

How distracting this presence could be is clear from a glance at the map. Spain's war in the Netherlands depended absolutely on communications. Originally the normal route had been by sea, from Laredo or Coruña to Flushing, but by 1580 Dutch and English 'pirates' had made this route impossible, and as long as Spain was at war with Holland and England it would remain impossible. Therefore all supplies of men, material and money now had to reach Flanders by land. From Barcelona or Naples they sailed to Genoa, assembled in the Duchy of Milan, and passed through the Alps and down the Rhine to Franche-Comté and Luxembourg. In the 1580s this had been easy enough. The Alpine passes might be narrow, the Spanish stepping-stones small and scattered: but the Spanish monopoly of power made the difference. The duke of Savoy, the Catholic cantons of Switzerland, the princes and bishops of the Rhine, lacking an alternative patron, had all accepted the power and pensions of Spain. Little local difficulties, as in Cologne, had been easily settled. But now it was not so easy. With the revival of France, an alternative patron was in sight. The vital land route was exposed to a new force, its local rulers to a new temptation. Franche-Comté and Alsace could be invaded, Lorraine and Savoy reduced. Local difficulties might become international difficulties. So a sudden electric tremor was felt along the string of petty states which hitherto had quietly transmitted the Spanish forces along the eastern borders of France.

Nor was the threat confined to the land-route north of the Alps. The revival of France threatened the Spanish monopoly even in its securest stronghold. In Spain itself the hated Moriscos were believed to be encouraged not only from Constantinople but from Paris. That view was perhaps somewhat extravagant. But there could be no doubt about the effects of French revival in what had previously seemed the firmest part of the Spanish empire, Italy. Throughout the reign of Philip II, Italy had been entirely and apparently happily subjected to Spain. The popes, at least after the death of Pius V, had been wholly dependent upon Spain. The duke of Savoy owed his throne to Spain. The grand duke of Tuscany had been a Spanish client. Both Genoa (anyway tied to Spain by finance) and Venice, though now proverbially neutral, had relied on Spanish patronage to keep their colonies: Corsica in constant rebellion against Genoese rule, Cyprus and Crete exposed to Turkish attack. And then there were a dozen variations of *ragion di stato* whereby Spain could manage the Italian princes: marriage into Spanish regal or vice-regal families; commands in Spanish armies; offices in Milan, Naples, Sicily; the lure of Spanish pensions; the pressure of Spanish garrisons as in Piacenza or the Tuscan *presidii*. By such means all Italy had been, or seemed, little more than a single, docile Spanish protectorate throughout the reign of Philip II.

And yet, beneath the surface, what hatred of Spain was everywhere apparent! The princes and their courts might be loyal to their makers and preservers, and their philosophers and clergy—a Botero, an Ammirato, and the Jesuit *claque*—might praise the new system of government; but the heirs of the Renaissance and the voice of the people clamoured insistently for freedom, and sometimes even princes listened to that voice. Of course, in the reign of Philip II, they did not obey it. How could they? Spain was irresistible. But suppose another great power were to patronize them? Leo X, after all, had driven the French out of Italy by bringing in the Spaniards. What if France were to revive and another Italian ruler were to call in, once again, the French? By 1595 the power of France had revived. In 1600, by the Treaty of Lyon, Henri IV obtained from Savoy the marquisate of Saluzzo, the gateway to Italy, and could come in.

Thus, after 1595, the same electric tremor which shocked or galvanized the Rhineland electors and Alpine sentinels was felt, in different strength, throughout Italy. Venice would turn openly to Henri IV, and would soon win European fame, and become the Catholic hero of Protestantism, by its resistance to both Rome and Spain. Ferdinand I of Tuscany, whose father and brother had gained so little from the jealous protection of Spain, would marry a French princess, support France in war, and defend the local Italian lords against Spanish garrisons. A little later Charles Emmanuel of Savoy, who had begun his career as a Spanish client and had married the daughter of Philip II in the fond hopes of a royal throne, would begin his long and turbulent career of seeking thrones as the client of France, or the champion of Italian independence. By 1608 he would be weaving conspiracies in Parma and Modena. Even the duke of Mantua, fearing for his detached and exposed marquisate of Montferrat, even Genoa, treasuring the relics of its independence, sometimes wavered towards France or at least towards Tuscany, as a possible guarantor of Italian liberties. And the same refreshing thrill was felt, of course, in the greatest of all Italian courts, the court of Rome.

The popes of Rome were doubly tied to Spain. They were therefore, at times, doubly resentful. Both as Italian princes and as rulers of Catholic Christendom they resented their loss of independence. No doubt Rome had gained something by Spanish power, even in religion. It was thanks to Spanish (or Portuguese) arms and patronage that Catholicism had been spread in Asia and America, that Protestantism had been stayed in Europe. But Spanish patronage had its price. The popes had deeply resented the heavy royal control over the church in Spain, in Portugal, and more particularly—since it was nearer home—in Naples. Moreover, Catholicism was not always the same in Spain as in Italy, and Italian popes became increasingly impatient of Spanish dictation in religion as in politics. While gladly relying on Spanish arms, they lamented the temporary lack of any great Catholic ruler to balance against the house of Habsburg. Now, in the 1590s, Clement VIII saw his chance. In the name of Catholicism Philip II was seeking to impose his daughter on the throne, first of France, then of England. To avoid this, Clement had sought rather to convert the native claimants, James VI of Scotland and Henri of Navarre. If he had failed in England, he had succeeded in France. Undeterred by the intrigues of the Spanish ambassador and his clique among the cardinals, in 1595 he had solemnly absolved the returned prodigal Henri IV, and all Rome had been lit up in honour of this triumph of the faith. Ten years later Henri IV returned the compliment: in 1605 he ordered salvos and illuminations throughout France to celebrate the election of 'the French Pope', Leo XI. In those days of illumination, Spain, it seemed, was in eclipse: it had lost its temporal monopoly of the Catholic church in Europe.

For all these reasons the revival of France under Henri IV is of great importance in the history both of Spain and Europe. Though outwardly at peace, in fact Henri IV was a constant menace to Philip III throughout his scattered empire; and this menace, combined with Spain's financial weakness, make it impossible for the feeble successor of Philip II to continue, even on a reduced scale, his northern wars. It is no accident that the period of Henri IV's reign in France is the period, in Spanish history, of *las Pazes*, the successive conclusions of those long, exhausting wars.

Philip III and his all-powerful minister, the duke of Lerma, are sometimes described as peace-loving. It is true they made peace. It is true that, once made, they were reluctant to break it. It is true that, though they connived at some of the aggressive acts of Spanish officials abroad, they refused to be committed by them, and thus preserved the general peace. But this love of peace was not positive or pure: it sprang from a combination of indolence and hateful necessity. In fact, when we look at the documents, we see that the court of Spain made its peace-treaties with the utmost reluctance. Though the will-power of Philip II was gone, his successors were still imprisoned by his spirit. Again and again, we catch the echoes of his voice: the war against England is so holy, *tan de Dios*, that it must go on, whatever the cost; the king will never, never, consent to diminution of his title; he would rather lose all his kingdoms, and his life also, than be 'a king of heretics'. It is the voice of ancient pride, obstinate bigotry, the voice of the clergy and confessors who ruled both king and Council of State, of the *cristianos viejos* throughout Spain. Even in bankruptcy and defeat, even in dearth and plague, it was hard for a lifeless court to resist that voice, and for a long time Lerma continued to echo it. The initiative in resisting it came not from him but from the theatre of war itself, from the man who had already negotiated the peace with France, the archduke Albert. Theoretically independent, in fact jealously controlled from Spain, in this one respect the archduke contrived to impose his will. Though entirely Spanish in his outlook, entirely Catholic in his convictions, he at least studied the interests of his new subjects, and he deserves to be remembered as the maker of all the three treaties which ended the disastrous wars of Philip II.

After France, the next enemy to detach was England. Peace with England was logical. By 1598 the war had lost its purpose. Originally designed as a short, successful, diversionary war in order to end the revolt of the Netherlands, it had now proved long, meaningless and disastrous. Fortunately England too was weary of it, and in that year both sides felt their way towards peace. In 1600 a general peace-conference was arranged at Boulogne. Unfortunately it came to nothing. When it met, the Spaniards suddenly made impossible claims, and it was broken off. The reason was clear enough. Once again, even at its nadir, the court of Spain had been seduced by hopes of a miracle: a miracle promised by plausible voices from the bogs of Ireland and the exiled Jesuits of England.

So for another four years the war dragged on while a Spanish expedition was sent to Ireland and a Spanish queen was offered to England. Ireland, after all, was in open revolt: who could say whether Spanish help might not turn the scale? And if the Spaniards had a base in Ireland, the rest (said Fr Persons and his friends) would be easy. The Spanish infanta's only rival for the English throne was the king of Scots. But the king of Scots was the candidate of the earl of Essex, and Sir Robert Cecil, who held all power in England, would never allow him to prevail. Therefore all that was necessary was to keep up the war, stand firm in Ireland, rely on the Jesuits in England, and wait for Queen Elizabeth to die. It seemed too simple. And besides, thought King Philip, if the infanta were queen of England, she and her husband could be made to give that improper sovereignty of the Netherlands, which he had always resented, back to Spain.

In fact, as so often, the court of Spain had miscalculated and, as always, the English Jesuits were wrong. The expedition to Ireland in 1601 was two years too late and landed in the wrong place: in Kinsale, where the revolt had already been crushed. The prospect of a Spanish queen of England caused Henri IV and the French cardinals to protest in Rome; the pope refused to support the project; and the English Jesuits, for pressing it, were disowned by the English lay Catholics and secular priests, already disgusted by their 'holier than thou' attitude. Meanwhile all the conditions of success disappeared. Within a few months the Spaniards had been driven out of Ireland, and, while Queen Elizabeth was still alive, Essex was dead, and Cecil could therefore commit himself to the Scottish succession. In March 1603, when the Ulster rebels surrendered unconditionally and James VI was proclaimed king of England unopposed, the last hope and purpose of the war had finally disappeared. Even Spain could do nothing but accept the facts, and the peace which the new king of England hastened personally to offer. After all, as king of Scotland, James had never been at war with Spain; and anyway, he added privately, he liked neither the Dutch nor their cause.

Even so, it was not Lerma but the archduke who made the first move. Without waiting for Spanish approval, he sent an emissary to Scotland to congratulate the new king, and an ambassador to England after him. The English Jesuits still protested that now was the time for a *coup*, that the king of Spain had only to appear sword in hand to obtain all his desires; but the archduke's emissaries insisted that all could be had much more cheaply— £50,000 to the Howard family would fix anything. And in effect thus it was

done. The Spaniards complained bitterly of the archduke's show of independence, but soon they had to follow his example. Early in 1604 the
constable of Castile came to London as Spanish ambassador explicitly
empowered to treat of peace, and in August the Treaty of London was
signed. It ended hostilities while leaving other questions prudently vague.
James would have included the Dutch in the treaty, but they refused all
terms. The treaty was almost equally disliked by Puritans in England and
Catholics in Spain; but it inaugurated a period of great prosperity in
England. To Spain it gave new opportunities, if only they could be
exploited.

One such opportunity was to settle, at last, the problem of the Netherlands. Unfortunately, this proved no easier now that France and England
had been quieted than it had been forty years ago, before they had been
roused. Protestant critics of the English treaty complained that by it, the
United Netherlands had been 'deserted' and left to face Spanish power
alone; but in fact this was hardly so. English and Scottish regiments continued to serve in the Netherlands as volunteers and trade was uninterrupted. Moreover, thanks to their growing economic strength, their
superiority at sea, and the reorganization of their armed forces by Maurice
of Nassau, the Dutch were perfectly capable—in spite of the loss of
Ostend in 1604—of holding their own and wearing down the Spanish
forces. So successfully did they do so that within five years the Court of
Spain was obliged to make its third surrender to reality and consider
peace with 'the rebels'.

Once again, the initiative did not come from Spain but from the archduke. The Spanish government might feel the financial strain of the war,
but the archduke saw every day the economic misery of the people with
which he now identified himself. If the country were ever to flourish again,
he insisted, peace must be made: and peace entailed the recognition of
the rebels and the withdrawal of the Spanish army. But such a peace was
not yet acceptable to Spain. The Spanish court absolutely refused to
recognize either heresy or rebellion and it would not consider withdrawing
the Spanish army which now seemed almost as necessary to control the
archduke as to fight the Dutch. The independence of the archduke in these
matters was strongly resented. It was said that he listened only to 'the
greatest enemies of the greatness of Your Majesty'—that is, to his Belgian
councillors; and he was regularly and bluntly reminded of his true position: that, although officially declared an independent sovereign, he
really owed his authority to Spanish power and Spanish money, and that
if he ignored Spanish wishes he would be deposed and his provinces
subjected once again to direct military rule.

In fact, in 1604, the Spanish government took steps to discipline the
insubordinate archduke. It had already twice considered his deposition;

now it decided to deprive him of his military authority and impose upon him an independent commander who should take his orders direct from Spain. It is ironical that the man thus sent to supplant him was in fact to become the archduke's greatest ally in his struggle against a suicidal war. For in the contest over the appointment the archduke contrived to get rid of an uncongenial Spanish officer and secure the nomination of an Italian whose services he had learned to value. This was Ambrogio Spinola who had come to Flanders as a volunteer, at his own expense, and had just saved the archduke's reputation by his brilliant capture of Ostend. The court of Spain appointed Spinola, who was to prove the greatest military commander of his generation, a worthy successor to Alexander Farnese; but it did not forget the purpose of his appointment. In 1606 Spinola received from Philip III a series of secret instructions for use in the event of the infanta's death. By these, he was to ensure that all power was taken out of the archduke's hands, and the archduke himself, if necessary, arrested and imprisoned in the fortress of Antwerp. In fact Spinola would never have to use these powers. In fact the infanta would survive the archduke, and Spinola, though trusted by Spain, would become for the rest of his life the firm ally of both sovereigns, a constant advocate of peace in the Netherlands against the war party in Spain. Thus the attempt to weaken the archduke by depriving him of his army in the end strengthened him, by giving him a loyal and powerful ally who made that army doubly effective in his service.

From 1605 onwards the archduke and Spinola constantly pressed for peace. Their position was expressed clearly. Either the court of Spain must make effective, aggressive war, and supply the cost of such a war, or it must make peace; half measures were useless. 'If your Majesty could assure the regular despatch, for a given time, of 300,000 ducats a month', Spinola wrote to Philip III in 1607, 'we could continue operations with some hope of reducing the pride of the rebels. But such an effort is beyond the resources of Spain. Therefore there is only one course to take: to end this long and costly war.' Two months later, on his own authority, the archduke concluded an armistice with the Dutch, undertaking to recognize their independence and sovereignty for the duration of the truce. The Spanish government was furious, refused to ratify the truce, and once again threatened to depose the archduke. But the fury had to pass. From now on, fighting ceased in the Netherlands. Philip III, supported by his confessors in Spain, continued to cry out that nothing could be more disastrous than such a truce and that neither financial need nor any other cause would force him to abandon the cause of God. But it made no difference. Spinola, as the archduke's representative, sat at The Hague negotiating for peace with the Dutch, under the mediation of England and France. In 1608 there were renewed protests from Spain, and renewed talk of deposing the archduke; but the archduke was firm. He had now converted not only Spinola, who had been sent to control his person, but also the Dominican confessor who had been sent to control his conscience, and who now came as his emissary to Spain to echo his views. 300,000 ducats a month, declared Fr Brizuela, were essential for war. Otherwise there must be peace. Half-measures would not recover Holland, they would only lead to the loss of Belgium; 'and you must consider that if the obedient provinces are lost, the Catholic religion, which, as you know, is now well established and accepted there, will be lost too; and we well know what grief that would cause his Majesty'.

In the end, the archduke forced the truce on Spain, while on the Dutch side Oldenbarnevelt forced it upon the extremists behind him: the military nobility and gentry, the preachers, the privateers. It was a truce, not a peace, and was to last twelve years. By it the military stalemate was recognized and, as with England, under vague forms of words the enemies of Spain contrived to surrender nothing. To Spain, the advantage was merely respite: respite for twelve years from the crippling financial burden of the last generation. Once again the question was, how would that respite be used?

Thus at last, in 1609, the disastrous legacy of Philip II had been cleared off. Philip III was at peace with both England and the Netherlands. It was not a moment too soon. For in that very year a new danger threatened to set off a new European war on that sensitive, exposed nerve of the Spanish Empire, the Rhineland route from Milan to Flanders. In 1608 the elector of the Palatinate had drawn the German Protestant princes into alliance in the Evangelical Union. In 1609 the elector of Bavaria had replied by forming the Catholic League. The Evangelical Union looked for support to Henri IV of France; the Catholic League had been largely created by the Spanish ambassador to the emperor, Balthasar de Zúñiga, the constant advocate of a forward policy throughout Europe. Now, in 1609, these forces were set dangerously in motion by a succession-crisis in the duchy of Jülich-Cleves on the Lower Rhine. The reigning Catholic duke had died and his Protestant kinsmen quickly seized the inheritance. The emperor claimed the right to decide and sent the Archduke Leopold to occupy the duchy. One episode, in that combustible area, quickly led to another: it seemed as if the Cologne war of 1583 was to be repeated. But this time there was a difference. This time French power was able to intervene; and Henri IV made it clear that he was going to intervene.

Precisely what Henri IV's plans were we cannot now say. The Spanish government made heavy mirth over the amorous episode in the struggle: Henri's pursuit of the fugitive Princesse de Condé, the 'new Helen' who was to launch a new war of nations. Sully, in his *Memoirs*, decently buried this detail behind a vast political enterprise. He ascribed to Henri IV a 'Grand Design', entailing the destruction and division of the whole

Spanish Empire. Later historians have demolished that too-systematic thesis. But it is certain that Henri IV—on however limited a front—intended to renew the old, direct struggle between France and Spain. He was already in treaty with the Protestant princes of Germany. Now, early in 1610, he turned to Italy and concluded, with Charles Emmanuel of Savoy, the Treaty of Brussolo, by which the forces of Savoy were to be launched against Milan. He was thus ready for action against Spain both in the Rhineland and in Italy. Then, in May 1610, he prepared to strike. He declared his queen, Marie de Médici, regent of France in his absence, caused her to be crowned, and prepared to lead his army to the Rhine. Before he could leave Paris he was dead, murdered in his coach by the dagger of Ravaillac. With that blow, the whole pattern of European politics was changed.

Whether Spanish gold or Spanish agents had inspired Ravaillac or not, his feat was an incomparable service to Spain. Olivares afterwards counted it as one of the saving miracles of the House of Habsburg. For in effect, for the next decade, it destroyed the new power of France which, during the last decade, had forced Spain into retreat in Europe. Henri IV's Grand Design, whatever it was, collapsed. The years which followed his reign were like those which had preceded it. The France of Marie de Médici, like the France of Catherine de Médici, was held to ransom by the great nobles, and both at court and among the great nobles the Spanish ambassador, Iñigo de Cárdenas, with his pensions and promises and patronage, easily built up a party. He forced the resignation and demanded the imprisonment of Sully. He patronized the Jesuits and the *dévôts*. Père Coton, the Jesuit confessor, and the papal nuncio were his closest allies. And having secured, or at least discovered, a government entirely in the Spanish interest, he consolidated the alliance by means of a double marriage treaty. In 1611 it was agreed that the young king of France and the heir to the crown of Spain should each marry the other's sister; and in the following years the marriages duly took place, in France and Spain, in scenes of costly splendour which seemed to immortalize the final concord of the Catholic crowns.

Betrayed from above, the lesser clients of Henri IV quickly made their peace, happy if the new government of France sweetened the terms of their surrender. The governor of Milan soon brought Savoy to reason. Isolated and defeated, Charles Emmanuel was obliged to send his son to Madrid with abject apologies and a written, though unsigned, profession of homage to Spain. Soon Spinola would as easily settle the affairs of Jülich-Cleves: an excursion into the Palatinate, in 1614, re-established Spanish patronage there and elsewhere. Meanwhile the princes of Italy withdrew from exposed positions. Pope Paul V, though elected with French support, had already become a Spanish client; now Venice made its peace with him. Tuscany under a new *fainéant* grand duke sank comfortably back into Spanish tutelage. The dukes of Mantua and Modena hastily forgot their half-hatched anti-Spanish conspiracies. Instead of European war, the year of 1610 began an age of European peace. And it was *Pax Hispanica*. Defeated in France, defeated against England, defeated in the Netherlands, it was nevertheless Spain—the Spain of Philip III and Lerma—which was, or seemed, thanks to a series of surrenders and an assassin's knife, the sole and universal victor of Europe.

Flattery, pensions, an open-handed ambassador, royal marriage: such was the technique of Spain in France. But why only in France? After 1610 it was applied in England too, and hardly less successfully. Till 1610, in spite of the peace of 1604, James I of England had continued the methods and ministers of Queen Elizabeth. But in 1610 he emancipated himself, first from Parliament, then from his inherited Elizabethan ministers. The reign of the Howards, pro-Spanish and crypto-Catholic, began. The memory of Queen Elizabeth was suppressed, the memory of Mary Queen of Scots revived. The body of Mary—the agent and martyr of Rome and Spain—was even brought in pomp from Fotheringhay to Westminster Abbey. In 1613, by marrying his daughter to the Calvinist Elector Palatine, James paid a last tribute to the old policy; but in the same year he began a longer and more serious treaty to marry his heir to a Spanish infanta. For the next ten years, while one infanta tied France to Spain, another was dangled before the English Court. In England, as in France, a skilful ambassador flattered the court, distributed bribes, appealed to the *snobisme* of crowned heads and courtiers, and held up, as a shining model, Spanish gravity, Spanish government, Spanish discipline. And here as there, the treatment worked—indeed, its success here was even greater. If Cárdenas, in France, dismissed Sully from power, Gondomar, in England, would send Sir Walter Raleigh to the block.

So the *Pax Hispanica* was established in Europe. It was a paradoxical peace, for the universal victor was the power which had been universally defeated. Economically, peace was more necessary to Spain than to any of its enemies. And yet there could be no doubt that in the decade after 1610 Philip III seemed 'monarch of the world', more powerful through peace than his father had been through war. Critics both in Spain and in Europe might realize that his monarchy rested on precarious foundations, but outwardly its strength was imposing. It might have withdrawn from a few provinces, but its total extent was now greater than ever. It might have lost all its wars, but its *tercios* were still invincible. It might be bankrupt, but it always had money for pageants and pensions. Kings and ministers, cardinals and bishops throughout Europe were its pensionaries—even firm Protestant statesmen like the earl of Salisbury and Maurice of Nassau featured on its payroll. And thanks to its alliance with the church, and particularly with the Jesuits, it enjoyed genuine ideological and social support even in independent or politically hostile countries.

This indeed was the essence of the *Pax Hispanica*, its strength and its weakness. It was not merely a set of political alliances: it was an international social system—static perhaps, parasitic perhaps, but deeply involved in social interests everywhere. Spain at war might be the enemy of the free states of Europe, but Spain at peace was the ally and example of a whole social class, and moreover of a possessing social class, within all those states. That social class was the class of princes and their courts—administrators, courtiers, officers, and the great merchants and state clergy who depended on them. Since the Jesuits, in Catholic countries, had become the teachers and consolidators of this class, the Jesuits were the natural allies of Spain. Wherever Spain triumphed, the Jesuits followed; wherever the Jesuits were admitted, a pro-Spanish party was created. Moreover (and herein lay the strength of the Spanish system), this class was everywhere growing in wealth and numbers. It was the European ruling class, a freemasonry, an 'establishment'.

Of course this social division was a source of weakness too. The *Pax Hispanica* of Philip III was like the *Pax Austriaca* of Metternich. It was essentially defensive. For in all the countries of Europe the princely courts were becoming a social and economic burden, and opposition to them was growing. If there was a freemasonry of the 'court', there was also a freemasonry of the 'country', of the gentry and lesser merchants who did not profit from the establishment, and who might enlist, above or below them, at different times, other allies: discontented politicians, special groups interested in war or privateering, or mutinous, overtaxed consumers. This freemasonry of 'the country' can be found, with only trivial differences, in many lands. Where Spain and the Counter-Reformation had triumphed, it was stifled; but in England, in Venice, in France, in Holland it was articulate, even powerful. And it had a recognizable ideology. It was conservative, with a conscious, positive conservatism, for the 'court' was a mushroom beside the ancient institutions which it had overtopped; it was nationalist, for it opposed an international system; it was puritan, for the court lived by ostentatious consumption; and since the court ultimately looked to Spanish power or example, it was anti-Spanish.

How completely the *Pax Hispanica* was identified with the princely 'establishment' of the time can be seen if we compare the 'country' parties of both Catholic and Protestant lands and then look at the areas of direct Spanish rule. The programme of the *giovani* in Venice—the lesser nobles and merchants, ready for maritime aggression in the Mediterranean—is hardly different from that of the English puritan 'country party' with its allies the West Indian privateers, demanding maritime aggression in the Atlantic, or from the Dutch Orangists with their allies, the exiled Flemings who would create the Dutch West India Company, the organ of oceanic aggression even in time of peace. All these parties were, in some sense, 'puritan'. They were also nationalist and anti-Spanish. On the other hand the ruling classes in all three countries—the court and city in Jacobean London, the 'arminian' merchant oligarchies in Holland, the 'old' nobility of land and finance in Venice—profited by the present system, accepted, to some extent, the patronage of Spain, and were accused, in consequence, of 'appeasement' and popery. Finally, in the countries of direct Spanish rule the full effects of the *Pax Hispanica* could be seen. In Italy, in Flanders, in Spain itself we see the growth of officialdom and clericalism; the fiscal oppression and consequent flight of capital; the transformation of municipal into bureaucratic institutions; the switch of 'bourgeois' wealth from trade into office or land (the basis of office); the competition—and the market—in titles of nobility; and, in consequence of this switch, the decay of industry and increase of 'official' expenditure in lavish building or mere consumption. On top of all this was the most obvious, most loudly denounced, of all burdens: the constant pressure of huge Spanish armies, here migrant, there billeted, but always predatory. When we remember that the Spanish Empire in Europe included Flanders and Italy and much of the Rhineland between them, and that the towns of these areas had hitherto been the commercial, industrial and intellectual centres of Europe, and when we look at these areas under Spanish rule and find them everywhere dominated by rural landlords and urban officers, we may measure some of the social changes which, if not caused, were at least favoured by Spanish patronage and Spanish rule.

In the areas of direct rule the *Pax Hispanica* was successfully applied. We see it at its most extreme in Spain itself, where emigration to America and the expulsion of both Jewish *entrepreneurs* and Morisco labourers still further weakened the productive classes while an inflated court lived largely on foreign tribute. We see it at its most oppressive in Italy, where the original vigour of the Counter-Reformation was largely spent and its message, from a new spiritual adventure, had become little more than the propaganda of a crushing social system. We see it at its best in Flanders, where the challenge of material desolation, and the proximity of triumphant heresy, evoked, for a time, the positive, constructive spirit of the Counter-Reformation.

Flanders indeed, the Flanders of the archdukes, was the shop-window of the Counter-Reformation in northern Europe. There the old society had been dissolved by the war. The great cosmopolitan *entrepreneurs* who had made Antwerp the economic capital of Europe had largely emigrated to Amsterdam, Hamburg, Frankfurt and the Baltic towns. The craftsmen of the industrial towns had often gone with them. The old democratic structure of the cities was broken. The States General were forbidden to meet. But out of the ruins of the old urban freedom the new bureaucracy, intellectually formed by the Jesuits, was gradually creating a new form of society. Industry, destroyed in the towns, was revived on a rural basis. There was even some rural prosperity. The towns, or some of them, were compensated for their losses by becoming centres of consumption dependent on the new, lavish, resident court. And the physical gaps in them left by long years of war and iconoclasm were filled by new baroque churches and palaces whose building, for a time, absorbed labour and distributed wealth and whose decoration gave full employment to the greatest genius of the Flemish Counter-Reformation, Peter Paul Rubens.

Nevertheless, even in Flanders the voice of protest was heard. In 1615 the city of Antwerp sought to recover some of its old prosperity by drawing to it the English cloth-staple from Middelburg. The English of course were heretics but they promised to be discreet and, on those terms, Belgian theologians supported the project. Why then should they not come? But the Spaniards saw one insuperable reason. What was profit, they asked, compared with spiritual danger? Had not King Philip expelled the Moriscos from Spain 'without counting the gains they had brought him'? So Antwerp was silenced. But four years later there was an urban revolt in Brussels. It was a revolt not of city aldermen, the great merchants converted by office and loans into government officials, but of the lesser merchants organized in the merchant gilds. The Spaniards recognized their enemy. 'Sire,' wrote an official to the king, 'this bourgeoisie is proud and impudent, and this town has always been at the head of all revolts . . . If you do not take steps to chastise and break it now, while the stick is in your hand, it may be that, when you wish to do so, it will be too late.'

In Italy, though the spirit was spent, the general pattern was similar. The Spanish viceroys satisfied their distant masters with public *donativos* and private bribes, and governed much as they pleased. They defended the frontiers—Naples and Sicily against the Turks, Milan against Savoy; smothered the economy of their provinces under top-heavy, predatory courts; and paid the cost by raising the taxes on industry and transferring lands, titles and jurisdictions to a growing local baronage. The highest titles, especially in the kingdom of Naples, went to Genoese financiers, the mainstay of the system. Most of these Spanish viceroys owed their posts to kinship with Lerma. Some of them were patrons of art and letters —though often in the spirit of the Roman Verres: their palaces, both in Italy and in Spain, were stuffed with the spoils of empire, and the duke of Osuna, it was noted, left Sicily with twice as much luggage as he had brought in. Occasionally they sought to correct the financial and administrative dropsy which was inseparable from the system: Lerma's son-in-law, the count of Lemos, did this in Naples, thanks to the services of a

Portuguese Jew. But Lemos was an exception: in general the viceroys allowed the process to proceed unchecked. In this way growing official patronage could be used to silence some at least of the critics.

But outside the charmed circle they were not silenced. Voices were always being raised against the foreign bureaucracy which had extinguished the old city republics and ruined the old industry and commerce. Among the critics were poets like Marino and Tassoni, political writers like Boccalini and Sarpi. Many of their protests, like Boccalini's *Pietra del Paragone*, were not published by their authors. Others, like the famous *Filippiche*, directed this time against Philip III, were anonymous. But sometimes a particular combination of circumstances—a popular revolt here, a princely challenge there—gave them means of public expression. The misery of Calabria was the occasion of the messianic revolt in 1601 which brought the Dominican friar, Tomaso Campanella, to torture and prison; the firmness of Venice under interdict gave Paolo Sarpi his opportunity; the ambitions of Charles Emmanuel of Savoy released a spate of anti-Spanish works. And in fact, thanks to the ancient mercantile traditions of Venice and the random pugnacity of Savoy, it was in Italy, in these years, that the *Pax Hispanica* was most frequently disturbed, and the forces which would destroy it most clearly shown.

The constant opponent of the whole Spanish system in Italy was the mercantile republic of Venice, the only republic which, by 1610, had not yet yielded to Spanish pressure. Betrayed after the common victory of Lepanto, Venice, under the lead of the new 'puritan' generation which had broken through the old oligarchy, had recognized Spain as the enemy without, the Counter-Reformation as the enemy within. In 1597 its ambassador at Rome had contrived to break Philip II's project of a league of Italian princes which (since he was himself one of them) would have legalized a disguised Spanish protectorate over all Italy. Between 1605 and 1609 the republic had stood firm against the pope and the Jesuits. But meanwhile the pressure of Spain had not slackened and Venice felt it on all sides. By land the threat came from the duchy of Milan, under direct Spanish rule, and from the Tyrol, now governed by the most Spaniolized of the Austrian Habsburgs, the Archduke Ferdinand of Styria. By sea, the same archduke overlooked the base of the Adriatic from Trieste and Carniola, and the Spanish viceroy of Naples overlooked its mouth from Apulia. It happened that, in the reign of Philip III, these three positions, Milan, Styria and Naples, were all commanded by masterful and aggressive men.

The pressure came first from Milan. From 1600 to 1610, the count of Fuentes, as governor of Milan, had used despotic authority to extend Spanish power and ensure Spanish communications. He had renewed Philip II's treaty to ensure the passage of troops through the Catholic cantons of Switzerland. He had built a fortress, the *fuerte de Fuentes*, to command the even more vital route which linked Milan with the Tyrol, the Spanish with the Austrian Habsburgs. This route passed through the Valtelline, a valley whose Catholic population was subject to the Protestant Swiss canton of the Grisons. To improve sea-communications with Spain and Naples Fuentes had annexed or forced into vassalage a series of petty lordships along the Ligurian coast: Piombino, Finale, Monaco. He had also annexed Parma, Modena and Mirandola by force, seized Lunigiana (commanding the inland route to Tuscany), and foreshadowed Louis XIV's *réunions* by summoning independent princes to Milan to account for alleged usurpations. And in the time of the Venetian Interdict he had not hesitated to offer military force to the pope to crush the religious obstinacy of the republic.

Fortunately, the republic was able to survive these threats. Without breaking its own traditional neutrality, it was able to rely on an accidental ally in north Italy. This was the irrepressible disturber of the Spanish peace, Charles Emmanuel of Savoy.

Charles Emmanuel's excuse for making war on Spain was a claim to the duchy of Montferrat, a detached possession of the duke of Mantua. On the death of the duke of Mantua in 1612, Charles Emmanuel sought to detach it politically as well as geographically. It was, he pointed out, a *feudo femminile*. Spain dissented; but Charles Emmanuel was not deterred. Ignoring all protests, refusing all mediation, he sent back his collar of the Golden Fleece, expelled the Spanish ambassador, and seized most of the duchy. In spite of successive defeats and occasional treaties, he remained in arms for five years, against two successive governors of Milan. In this he was sustained by the enthusiasm of Italian patriots, by open military support from the Huguenot governor of Dauphiné, the duc de Lesdiguières (who paid as little heed to his government as the Spanish viceroys did to theirs), and by secret subsidies from Venice.

But if Venice avoided a direct military confrontation with Spain in the West, it was soon indirectly involved in the East. This involvement began with the war against the Uskoks: Bosnian and Albanian pirates who, with the encouragement of their overlord, the Archduke Ferdinand of Styria, issued from Segna (Senj), on the Dalmatian coast, to prey on Venetian commerce in the Adriatic. By 1613, having disposed of their domestic enemies, the pope and the Jesuits, the Venetians had turned their attention to this external nuisance, and made war on the Uskoks. But one conflict soon led to another, and by 1615 Venice found itself at war with the archduke on land as well as with the Uskoks by sea. The rest of Europe recognized both the archduke and the Uskoks as Spanish agents and acted accordingly: by 1617 there was a general resort of the enemies of Spain to the Italian front. Dutch Protestant troops under Maurice of Nassau fought for Venice on the Isonzo; English troops were invited to join them; the ambassador of Savoy in London sought to divert Sir Walter Raleigh from Guiana to Genoa. On the other side the Spanish ambassador in Vienna, the Spanish governor of Milan, and the Spanish viceroy of Naples contemplated open intervention not only against Savoy, the open enemy of Spain, but against Venice. Venice, they agreed, was the secret source and inspiration of all the enemies of Spain in the Mediterranean. Venice, said the Spanish ambassador, the marquis of Bedmar, 'has always sought to harm and depress the name of Spain'. Fortunately, he added, it was now weak, a mere shadow of itself. With his network of agents and his corrosive pensions he was ready to undermine it within; and the new viceroy of Naples, the duke of Osuna, was ready to strike from without. He had already set out to break the Venetian control of the Adriatic; he had allied himself with the troublesome Uskoks; and now he had a fleet poised at Brindisi, flying his personal flag, awaiting the sign. 'If they resist', he wrote to Bedmar, 'I shall deal with them once and for all'; he was prepared to strike 'in spite of the world, in spite of the king, in spite of God'; and in spite too of the relatively unimportant fact that, in 1617–18, by the treaties of Madrid and Wiener Neustadt, both Savoy and Venice had made peace with both Spain and the archduke.

In fact Venice acted first. On 18 May 1618 its inhabitants awoke to find the corpses of two of Osuna's supposed agents hanging on the public gibbet, upside-down, with the limbs broken, signifying treason. Five days later a third corpse was exposed, mutilated by torture. No explanation was given, but it was clearly advertised that the republic had acted just in time. Bedmar, after an attack on his palace, fled from Milan without waiting for orders from his government. Osuna was burnt in effigy. So was his most trusted agent, the Spanish poet and satirist Francisco de Quevedo, who himself escaped from Venice immediately after the incident but never explained the mystery of his presence there. It was not the first time that Quevedo had made such an escape. In 1613 he had similarly escaped from Nice where Osuna had employed him in a plot to seize that town for Spain. From this parallel it was difficult not to draw certain conclusions.

The reality of 'the Spanish conspiracy' has often been doubted. Possibly there was no precise plan. The complicity of Osuna and Bedmar cannot be demonstrated. But there can be no doubt that both were contemplating a *coup* against Venice even if the particular episode illustrated the suspicion they incurred rather than the plans they had laid.[1] Osuna in particular

---

[1] The true facts of 'the Spanish conspiracy' are still contested. The latest authority, Giorgio Spini, 'La congiura degli spagnoli contro Venezia del 1618', *Archivio Storico Italiano* (1949–50), shows, from the Spanish archives, that neither Osuna nor Bedmar was committed to the particular projects revealed by captured spies and conspirators in Venice; and from this he concludes 'che di congiura spagnola contro Venezia non è possibile parlare in alcuna maniera, neppure nel senso più limitato'. But this merely absolves them from complicity in one particular project. It remains certain that both Bedmar and Osuna envisaged

aroused the deepest suspicions. Though a brilliant sea-captain and naval organizer, who had delivered some notable blows at the Turks, he was irresponsible, even disastrous, as a governor. He destroyed the administrative work of his predecessor in Naples, courted popularity by ostentatious demagogy, and ruined the province by his arbitrary rapacity. His reign has been described, by a modern historian of Naples, as beginning 'the worst period of the Spanish viceroyalty'. After the Venetian fiasco he was recalled to Madrid in 1620, accused—no doubt falsely—of seeking to make himself independent king of Naples, and died in prison. Meanwhile, thanks to the quiescence of the Great Powers the Spanish conspiracy had had no sequel. It illustrated the international tension, but it was not this episode that was to break the Spanish peace.

The tension, however, remained and other incidents were soon to follow. Osuna was not the only fire-eating viceroy, nor Bedmar the only conspiratorial ambassador. In fact, by 1618, though the Spanish government remained quiescent, its European officials were everywhere demanding and sometimes enforcing an aggressive, forward policy. If Bedmar and Osuna were frustrated in Venice, Gondomar was successful in England. It was in 1618 that he achieved his most spectacular success: the execution of Sir Walter Raleigh for invading the king of Spain's monopoly in America. On the other hand in Bohemia the equally aggressive policy of successive Spanish ambassadors met a spectacular check. The very month in which the Spanish conspiracy was announced in Venice saw an equally dramatic episode in Bohemian history: the Defenestration of Prague.

Bohemia had long been an advanced post of Spanish power and diplomacy. Prague had been the capital of the Emperor Rudolf II, and the centre of all the intrigues concerning the succession to his throne. Even after the capital of the empire had moved to Vienna, Bohemia retained its importance: for whoever was elected as next king of Bohemia would probably hold the casting vote in the election of the next emperor. At present both crowns were safely on the same Habsburg head, but in the

some such *coup*, and it was the knowledge of such ambitions which generated the hysterical fear of conspiracy in Venice. In their private correspondence and conversations, Osuna and Bedmar made no secret of their plans: see, for instance, Osuna's letters in *Collección de Documentos Inéditos*, Vol. XLIV, and the documents concerning Bedmar printed in I. Raulich, 'Una relazione del marchese di Bedmar sui Veneziani', *Nuovo Archivio Veneto* (1898); P. Negri, 'La politica veneta contro gli Uscocchi in relazione alla congiura di 1618', *ibid.* (1909), pp. 370–84; and Lamberto Chiarelli, 'Il marchese di Bedmar e i suoi confidenti', *Archivio Veneto-Tridentino* (1925). How far Osuna and Bedmar were actually prepared to go is of course another matter, and one which, in the absence of any record of the Venetian investigation, is perhaps insoluble. After the *débacle*, Osuna and Bedmar naturally posed as injured innocents. Their protests have been repeated by most Spanish historians, but not by the best qualified among them, Cesareo Fernandez Duro, who regretfully but emphatically dissents. See his *El gran Duque de Osuna y su Marina* (Madrid, 1885) and *Armada Española*, Vol. III (Madrid, 1897), p. 349.

childlessness of the Austrian Habsburgs the future was far from certain. If the Bohemian Diet should elect the wrong king, and the empire, in consequence, pass into the wrong hands, the effect in the Spanish Empire would be serious; for the emperor was lord of numerous fiefs in Italy, controlled the Tyrolean passes, and had rights throughout the Rhineland, including the sovereignty of Alsace. Thus the future of the crown of Bohemia was an essential Spanish interest, and from the time of Philip II onward the Spanish ambassadors in Prague had laboured to build up a strong Spanish and Catholic party. Throughout the reign of Philip III this party was headed by the chancellor of Bohemia, Zdenek Lobkovic. From 1608 till 1617 the Spanish ambassador to the empire was one of the most masterful of Spanish statesmen, Balthasar de Zúñiga; in 1617 Zúñiga was succeeded by an even more forceful official, the count of Oñate. Under the weak emperors Rudolf and Matthias these men exercised decisive influence both in Prague and in Vienna.

The ultimate aim of Zúñiga and Oñate was to ensure the succession of a safely Spaniolized member of the Habsburg family to the crown of Bohemia and the empire. In the uncertainties of the time they sometimes thought of solving the problem by advancing Philip III's own claims; but as neither Philip nor Lerma welcomed such a prospect, they preferred to surrender these claims to a reliable Austrian Habsburg in exchange for solid assets. The reliable Habsburg proposed was, of course, their constant ally the Archduke Ferdinand. The solid assets suggested were Alsace, an essential stage on the route to Flanders; the Tyrol, which linked Italy with Germany and provided an alternative route to the north; and the imperial fiefs in Italy. In spite of the apathy of Madrid, Zúñiga had already made progress with these plans when he returned to Spain in 1617. His successor Oñate completed them, in that year, by negotiations culminating in a secret treaty signed at the Archduke Ferdinand's residence, Graz. As a result of these negotiations the Emperor Matthias designated Ferdinand as his heir; to avoid uncertainty, the Bohemian estates, brilliantly managed by Lobkovic, pre-elected Ferdinand to be their king on the death of Matthias; and Ferdinand paid for Philip III's renunciation of his claims by the promise of Alsace and the Tyrol to be given to Spain in full sovereignty. Thus in 1617 the Spanish party had won a complete triumph in Bohemia and the empire, had secured both for the future, and incidentally had guaranteed Spanish communications in Europe.

Unfortunately this paper triumph was too good to last. In May 1618 the Protestant nobility of Bohemia struck back. They threw the hispanophil Catholic ministers out of the window of the Hradžany Palace and set up a revolutionary government whose first act was to expel those constant allies of Spain, the Jesuits. Having gone so far, it was essential to go further. To consolidate their position the revolutionary noblemen needed a revolutionary king: they could not possibly accept the pre-elected *pro-*

tégé of Spain, the Archduke Ferdinand. They therefore looked around for a sufficiently radical candidate; and their eyes lit on the boldest Calvinist prince, the leader, or figurehead, of the Evangelical Union, Frederick V, Elector Palatine.

The effect of this sudden and dramatic *coup* in Bohemia was instantly felt throughout Europe. All the enemies of Spain were roused. Two months later the Protestant party in the Valtelline murdered their Catholic enemies, whom they accused of 'Hispanismus', seized control of the pass, and so cut Milan off from the Tyrol. As the same time, Savoy and Venice made a formal alliance against future aggression. In August Maurice of Nassau, the leader of the war party in Holland, overthrew, arrested and would afterwards judicially murder the Advocate Oldenbarnevelt, the maker of the Truce of 1609, which he was now accused of seeking to prolong by appeasement of popery and Spain. Next year Venice and Holland joined in a defensive alliance explicitly directed against Spain. Meanwhile, in Spain, Lerma himself was at last driven from power by his domestic enemies. It seemed as if the *Pax Hispanica* was over.

In fact it was not yet over. In fact it might still have been preserved. As yet, none of the great powers who preserved it wished to see it broken. Even when the Emperor Matthias had died and the Elector Palatine had accepted the throne of Bohemia, the cause of peace was not yet lost; for two days later the Archduke Ferdinand, at Frankfurt, as yet unaware of his deposition, helped to elect himself emperor. Thus the empire at least was safe. The Treaty of Graz would stand. All that was lost was Bohemia. But Bohemia in itself was not a direct Spanish interest; the successors of Lerma had no wish to reverse his policy; James I of England refused to support his usurping son-in-law; French mediation kept both the Catholic League and the Evangelical Union neutral. The storm was stayed.

In fact, once the empire had been secured for the Habsburgs, the Bohemian adventure might even prove an asset to Spain. It opened local opportunities, supplied local excuses. In 1620, while the Elector Palatine was being crowned in his new capital, Spinola again marched from Flanders into the Palatinate and thus neutralized another danger-spot on the Rhineland route. At the same time the governor of Milan carried out a successful *coup* in the Valtelline. Under his patronage the Catholic party in the valley suddenly rose and in the *Sacro Macello* [the Holy Butchery], massacred their Protestant rulers and placed the vital corridor, for a time, under Spanish protection. The Bohemian affair itself would soon be locally liquidated. The Battle of the White Mountain would drive the usurper from Prague. Then there would be a general settlement. The *Pax Hispanica* could be restored, and with advantage to Spain.

Why was it not restored? When we ask that question, we are obliged to turn away from events to persons. The logic of events did not require a general war, but the new Spanish rulers, the men who were creating these events, did. The old Spanish rulers, the men of Madrid, did not create the events, nor did they want war. Philip III and Lerma, having swallowed the bitter pill of *las Pazes*, wished to keep the peace from which, incidentally, they profited. Lerma's successors also wished to keep it: they were profiting from it too. The other European great powers who guaranteed the peace, England and France, also did not wish to disturb it. But the Spaniards in Europe—the Osunas, the Bedmars, the Ferias, the Zúñigas, the Oñates—thought differently. They were convinced that the Spanish peace had already failed and they looked forward to 1621, when the truce of 1609 would run out and war could be resumed. That was why they were pressing on all fronts, provoking incidents, forcing action. They wished to be ready to deliver the knock-out blow. By 1621 they must be poised for action on all fronts. Italy, the reservoir of Spanish armies, must be securely held. Venice, the focus of heresy and discontent in Italy, the southern ally of Holland, must be crushed. The Valtelline must be controlled, the Rhineland guaranteed, the danger from the Palatinate eliminated. Then, when the truce lapsed, the northern war could be launched and the Netherlands reconquered, this time for good.

In 1617, when Lerma fell from power, this 'war party' won its first victory. It was not that the new junta in Madrid, a mere court faction, was on their side. It was because in that year Balthasar de Zúñiga returned from Germany to Madrid and sat, as their spokesman, on the Council of State. Next year the truculent Bedmar, expelled from Venice, appeared as ambassador in Brussels to overrule the Archduke Albert. And then, in 1621, the year when the truce expired, the archduke expired too. With his death, the sovereignty of Flanders returned to Madrid. But it did not return to the pacific Philip III. In the same year he also died, and on his death the advocates of war, kept hitherto on the periphery, closed finally upon the centre of power. Balthasar de Zúñiga dictated policy; and Balthasar de Zúñiga had a nephew who shared his views, followed his lead, and absolutely controlled his pupil, the young King Philip IV. This nephew was Gaspar de Guzmán, the future count-duke of Olivares, who would seek to renew, in the Netherlands and in France, even in the Baltic and against England, the most grandiose ambitions of Philip II.

Why did the viceroys and governors of 1618, the policy-makers of 1621, regard the *Pax Hispanica* as a failure? Had they, among the wealth of Flanders and Italy, forgotten the poverty and bankruptcy of Spain? Were they insensitive to all reasons but force? We cannot say this. They included able men, and at the Council of State they heard, and uttered, reasoned views. Their view was that the Netherlands Truce of 1609—perhaps even the English peace of 1604—though they had seemed so necessary at the time and had opened up an age of peaceful Spanish supremacy, had in fact been a terrible mistake. Philip II had been right. The war should have been fought to a finish.

For who had really gained by *las Pazes*? One after another the Spanish statesmen expressed their views. In interpretation at least they were unanimous. In the years of peace Spain, in spite of its superficial magnificence, had sunk still further into poverty and torpor. In the same years the Dutch, in spite of their odious heresy and indecent institutions, had become the richest, most dynamic people in Europe. In 1620 Carlos Coloma, the governor of Cambrai, wrote a memorandum on the subject. When the truce had been made, he declared, the Spaniards had supposed that peace would relieve their treasury and gradually dissolve the spirit and polity of the Dutch. But had any of these things in fact happened? They had not. On the contrary, the Dutch had made covert war on Spain in Venice and Germany, had captured the trade of East and West Indies, and had built up in twelve years an empire such as had cost the Portuguese and Spaniards 120 years. Amsterdam, forty years ago 'an almost unknown village', had become a world-city eclipsing Genoa for wealth, Lisbon for merchandise, Venice for situation. 'I conclude', wrote Coloma, 'that if in twelve years of peace they have undertaken and achieved all this, we can easily see what they will do if we give them more time . . . If the truce is continued, we shall condemn ourselves to suffer at once all the evils of peace and all the dangers of war.' In Madrid the same view was expressed in the Council of State by Balthasar de Zúñiga. 'If the republic of these rebels goes on as it is', he said, 'we shall succeed in losing, first the two Indies, then the rest of Flanders, then the states of Italy, and finally Spain itself.' If seemed to him as if the Spaniards had shed their blood only to fill the veins of subject nations: 'we have left our own country deserted and sterile in order to populate and fertilize the countries which we have conquered.' Therefore, these men argued, the disastrous truce must be ended, or at least only continued if the Dutch were effectively excluded from the East and West Indies, if they re-opened the Scheldt, and if they gave up 'their ill-founded liberty'. As that was hardly likely, let there be war. If the social and political system of the Spanish Empire were to be preserved, the social and political system of the Netherlands must be destroyed. Amsterdam, like Venice, must be annihilated.

But why had Spain lost the peace? Was it not precisely because it had used the peace only to consolidate such a system? In other words, was it not because the system itself had failed? A greater man than Zúñiga or Coloma had already pointed that moral. In 1616 Gondomar, at the height of his success in England—a success which consisted in keeping England at peace—had set out his views at length in a secret despatch to the court of Spain. The burden of the despatch was that the Spanish government was losing the peace and that unless better use was made of the peace, 'I consider that war would be much better for the Catholic religion and for the state and monarchy of Spain'. For by means of the peace the English were increasing their trade and wealth and at the same time ceasing to do very little of what they did in war. They were becoming rich at the expense of Spain which, for all its mines, was now the poorest country in Europe, bringing gold and silver from overseas 'only to distribute them among all the nations of the world whose ships wait to carry it home'. If Spain wished to profit by the peace, Gondomar insisted that it adopt a new and positive policy. It was not enough merely to draw breath and meanwhile to maintain, in repose, a static, aristocratic, bureaucratic system. A radical change was necessary. The government must invest in commerce, encourage shipping, found trading companies, abolish inland tolls, give honour, status and public facilities to merchants: in short, adopt a complete mercantilist policy. If this were done wealth might be restored to Spain, shipping would be increased, and sea-power would give ultimate victory: 'for the world today is such that whosoever rules the sea, rules the land also'. But if this were not done, then the proper course was war, and war now: for time was not on the side of those who sat still. King Philip must send 'invincible Armadas to conquer this kingdom'. After all, Gondomar went on, the conquest of England was easy (Osuna thought the conquest of Venice, Coloma the conquest of Holland easy). Only winds and waves could hinder it. Had it not been for winds and waves, Philip II would soon have achieved it in '88. History showed that every invader who had landed in England had conquered it: the Romans, the Saxons, the Danes, the Normans. Therefore (since expeditions to England and Ireland had misfired) a fleet should be sent to Scotland; in eight days from the first battle on English soil, London 'the arsenal for all the enemies of God and Spain' would fall; and 'England being won, the King our Lord will be true monarch of the world: for till then we risk the loss of the East and West Indies and cannot hope to reduce Holland; but thereafter all is ours and the rest is easy'.

In the midst of these fantasies, these nostalgic dreams of the *Empresa de Inglaterra*, Gondomar had touched the heart of the problem. If Spain was to win the peace, it must undergo a radical, even a structural change. If it was not prepared for such a change, the empire could only be preserved by using force, while its force was superior, to crush its enemies, and to crush them at their head. Gondomar's prescription of force differed from that of Zúñiga and Coloma. Castilians, landsmen, whose services had been on the continent of Europe, they urged the conquest of Holland by land. Their minds dwelt on Italy, the Valtelline, Alsace, the Palatinate: the essential land-route. England they would have kept neutral: their policy was that of the duke of Alba in the 1560s. Gondomar, a Galician from the Atlantic coast, familiar with the sea, serving in England, believed in sea-power. He would have conquered England in order to recover sea-power and open up the sea-route again: his policy was that of Philip II in the 1580s. But these were merely tactical differences: the ultimate objective, now as then, was the same: through peace or through war, by land or by sea, this way or that, the Carthage on the Zuider Zee must be destroyed.

So, in 1621, the matter was debated in Madrid. At first, we are told, the advocates of a forward policy found themselves in a minority. No doubt the poverty of the crown was more obvious to officials in Madrid that it had been in spendthrift embassies and viceregal palaces abroad. But soon the balance was turned. It was turned by the representatives of the East and West India trades, the Councils of Portugal and of the Indies. These men were only too well aware of Dutch expansion during the truce, and now they agreed with Zúñiga and Coloma: the heart of Holland should be destroyed by land in order to loosen its tentacles at sea. So they threw their weight on his side and turned the scale. The diplomatic conjuncture, after all, was favourable. France and England, for the moment, would not stir. A quick campaign would do it. The only protests came—as they would long continue to come—from Belgium, sacrificed on the altar of Spanish imperialism. But who now cared about Belgium? On 3 July 1621 the archduke died with the truce he had made, and none heeded his last feeble protest, 'even if all Europe is destined to be subject to one monarch, that time is not yet'.[1]

Thus, in the end, the truce was not renewed, and Spain found itself, once again, at war with 'the rebels' in the north. The diplomatic conjuncture was favourable. The two branches of the House of Habsburg were united in action as they had never been in the reign of Philip II. It seemed that, this time, the final blow would be struck. In fact, the merging of two wars—the war of Bohemia and the war of the Netherlands—was to engender the worst of all European wars hitherto: the Thirty Years War in which the European supremacy of Spain would finally founder.

[1] Spanish resentment at the economic consequences of the truce can be seen in several documents printed in H. Lonchay and J. Cuvelier, *Correspondance de la Court d'Espagne sur les Affaires des Pays Bas, 1598–1700*, Vol. 1 (Brussels), e.g. Nos. 1375, 1466, 1488; Coloma's views are given in two papers of 1620 and 1621 printed in A. Rodriquez Villa, *Ambrosio Spínola, Primer Marqués de los Balbases* (Madrid, 1904), pp. 342–8, 382 ff. The opinions of Zuñiga are quoted in J. Carrera Pujal, *Historia de la Economia Española* (Barcelona, 1943), Vol. 1, 485 f. Gondomar's despatch of 1616 is printed in Pascual Gayangos, *Cinco Cartas Politico-Literarias de . . . Gondomar* (Madrid, 1869).

CHAPTER X

THE STATE OF GERMANY (to 1618)

GERMANY in the early seventeenth century was a land of contrasts. It was a great and on the whole a prosperous country, even if it no longer led Europe in either mining or industrial technique or in financial expertise. In political structure, it was 'the Roman empire of the German nation'—briefly, the German Reich—at whose apex was enthroned the Kaiser Rudolf II (1576–1612), the senior representative of the Austrian branch of the Habsburg arch-house. In 1606 his envoys had concluded at Sitvatorok in Hungary a peace with the Turkish sultan doubly unprecedented, alike in its terms and its duration. Further territories had to be ceded to the Turk, but the Christian prince was for the first time admitted by the Muslim as a monarch of equal status, and over half a century elapsed before formal war was resumed between them. Although the chronic threat of Turkish invasion did not immediately disappear, the internecine struggles which were soon to devastate much of central Europe were in fact conducted without interference from the infidel. Yet despite the aura of partly successful achievement that might in retrospect seem to surround the Sitvatorok agreement, it had been made only because Turkish government was as incapable as the Austrian. The plight of the Habsburgs in Germany was never so desperate as in the early seventeenth century. The kaiser was an elderly and half-demented recluse, the Reich constitution was being eroded almost to the point of disappearance, political and religious antagonisms within Germany had been mounting towards the point of crisis for a generation and more, while the lack of a firm central government was a grave disadvantage to the economic development of the country and made it possible for foreign armies to prey upon the inhabitants in frontier regions. In this chapter, the main topics will be considered one by one—first, the family difficulties of the ruling dynasty, then the political and religious problems which were causing the breakdown of the Reich constitution, and lastly the condition of German industry and trade.

A major weakness of the Austrian Habsburgs lay in the division of their patrimony between various members of the family—the fruit of improvident partitioning in previous generations. Tyrol, Vorarlberg and the Swabian lands were administered by the Archduke Maximilian, while his cousin the Archduke Ferdinand independently ruled Styria, Carinthia and Carniola. Kaiser Rudolf, who resided at Prague, was represented at Vienna by his brother the Archduke Matthias. Rudolf was now secluded in the Hradžany Palace, increasingly remote from political realities and subject to hallucinations and to long bouts of melancholy during which he was unwilling either to transact public business or delegate his authority to others. From 1600, he was seen by few people other than his domestic servants—creatures who might be bribed to induce him at a favourable moment to signify his will, to sign a document or even to grant an audience. Since 1594, he had ceased to attend meetings of the Reichstag. His devotion to the Catholic cause was complete, though owing to the irregularities of his private life he went—in great trepidation—to confession at Easter only, and he no longer cared even for Jesuits. He was at loggerheads with all his nearest relatives. He envied his cousin of Spain for his wealth and power. He had fallen out with his brothers, of whom three had survived—Matthias, Maximilian and Albrecht. Matthias he distrusted as obvious (though unrecognized) claimant to the succession and therefore a possible supplanter; Albrecht he never forgave for marrying the Spanish infanta for whose hand he had himself irresolutely negotiated for some twenty years. As none of the four brothers had any legitimate children, the ultimate succession was likely to pass to the young Archduke Ferdinand of Styria. But much was to happen before this reunion of the Habsburg lands.

The family bickerings that came near to wrecking the future of the Austrian dynasty may in their immediate origins be traced to the series of events that led up to the conclusion of the Sitvatorok treaty. In 1604, Rudolf had provoked a rebellion in Hungary by an ill-timed disclosure of his intention to uproot heresy there. Under the leadership of Stephen Bocskay, the Magyars rose to defend their liberties; before long, Hungarian forces with their Turkish and Tartar contingents were under the walls of Vienna and the invasion of Austria and Moravia seemed imminent. The news of disaster brought upon the kaiser a renewed fit of his distemper: he withdrew completely from contact with the outside world and allowed public business to come to a standstill. Four of the archdukes, including Matthias and Ferdinand, thereupon met in family conclave and combined to force Rudolf in the following year to delegate to Matthias all his authority in Hungary, and a little later, full power to conclude a peace with the Turks. The indispensable preliminary for this was to win over the defiant Hungarian leaders; this in turn involved the grant to Hungary of distasteful concessions that included complete toleration to both Lutheranism and Calvinism, together with enlarged constitutional liberties, a recognition of Transylvanian autonomy and of Bocskay as prince of Transylvania. Matthias with great reluctance agreed to these conditions, the Hungarians were won over and the Turks, deserted by their essential allies and encumbered by commitments elsewhere, soon agreed to the peace. Such limited realism as Matthias had displayed in making the Hungarian agreement and the Turkish treaty was however incomprehensible to the kaiser, who brooded on the unrighteousness of the concessions. There was a grave danger that some sudden assertion of his will might upset the peace and bring all into question again. Yet only disaster could be expected from a reopening of the war, and it was evident that a further restraint must be put upon the political authority of Rudolf. At another family conclave the archdukes, with the encouragement of Melchior Khlesl, Bishop of Vienna, agreed that Matthias should be recognized as head of the family and that the practical exercise of power in Bohemia and Austria should be transferred to him, Rudolf retaining the title only of kaiser.

High responsibilities were thus falling upon Matthias, an elderly man of mediocre ability who had not yet shed personal ambitions. It was in any case a difficult task for him to respect the frontier between obedience to the family behest and the infliction of damage on long-term dynastic interests. The latter were ill-served by the method now employed by Matthias to lever himself into power—the invocation of the Estates of the various provinces, who profited by the struggle between Rudolf and Matthias to assert their own privileges. The details of the conflict are related elsewhere in this volume. When in May 1611 Matthias was formally recognized as the supplanter of his brother by coronation at Prague as king of Bohemia, his authority was chiefly honorific. In Austria, still more in Hungary and above all in the lands of the Bohemian crown, power had passed to the nobles, a class permeated by heresy, whose ascendancy endangered the liberties of the peasants and the towns. They were in close touch with the Protestant princes of the Reich, who were interested and hopeful spectators of the fratricidal struggle. The Calvinists especially welcomed the apparent crumbling of the chief Catholic monarchy within the Reich. In January 1612 Rudolf died, still plotting revenge against his enemies, real and imaginary, and Matthias was formally elected kaiser.

The feeble rule of Matthias, kaiser from 1612 to 1619, was a tense and unstable period for the Reich and for the Austrian Habsburg patrimony, and the deluge began before his death. In all his territories the Estates had the upper hand, and even in Austria his authority was circumscribed. Reverses at the hands of the prince of Transylvania and of the Republic of Venice underlined Habsburg weakness. Matthias himself was no gloomy solitary like his brother. He loved company, hunting and music, but he had no taste for business, the conduct of which fell chiefly into the hands of Bishop Khlesl—cardinal from 1616. Khlesl was now an old man; in his prime he had been the champion of the Counter-Reformation in Austria, but now, partly because he saw that an inflexible policy would invite final disaster to the Habsburg dynasty, still the keystone of the Catholic cause, and partly perhaps with an eye to the maintenance of his own position in politics, he was prepared to act the statesman and compromise with the Protestants. For the inflamed politics of the Reich, this had some momentary significance. But at home, the conciliatory line favoured by Khlesl brought him into disfavour with the younger members of the arch-house—notably the heir, Ferdinand of Styria, whose influence in the government grew steadily. The likelihood of children being born to Matthias decreased year by year, and accordingly the problem of the succession ultimately came to dominate the scene. The chief external obstacle to the smooth passage of the Archduke Ferdinand to power lay in the claims of the king of Spain, whose continued goodwill and support were indispensable. Philip III was, through his mother, a grandson of Kaiser Maximilian II, while Ferdinand was no more than a nephew. A Spanish claim was therefore put forward in 1613 to the Bohemian and Hungarian thrones, or alternatively in compensation to Tyrol and the hereditary lands in Swabia and Alsace. Ferdinand finally bought off his cousin in 1617 by a secret agreement, in which he promised the cession of family possessions in south-west Germany and of certain imperial rights in Italy. Internally, there were initial obstructions from Khlesl, on the grounds that the succession of such a partisan would embitter the relations between Protestant and Catholic in Germany: but the real problem lay in the attitude of the Estates of the various Habsburg lands. The complicated manœuvres needed to secure their assent were still not completed in 1618 when diplomacy was overtaken by events. A revolution had broken out in Bohemia.

Events in Germany did not wait upon the settlement of the family disputes of the arch-house. Throughout the reign of Rudolf II the Reich constitution was under severe strain, and its component organs were ceasing to discharge their functions. The troubles in the Rhineland reflected the feebleness of the executive.[1] A further ominous development was the maiming of the Reich chamber tribunal, the supreme organ of imperial justice. Its competence was admitted by all, and although there were manifest defects in its working it had some claim to be regarded as impartial. But from 1588 onwards the regular annual review of its verdicts by an appellate commission [*Visitationskommission*] appointed by the Reichstag had lapsed. Disappointed litigants were thus free to bring their grievances before the Reichstag itself, where politics alone counted. The 1594 and 1597 Reichstags had both concerned themselves with this situation, and the latter allotted to its interim committee [*Deputationstag*] the task not only of resuscitating the appellate commission and thus restoring to the chamber tribunal some semblance of impartial authority, but also of judging the outstanding appeals. Foremost among these was the highly delicate problem of adjudicating the legal position with regard to four religious houses in south-west Germany that a generation or so earlier had been secularized by lay neighbours [*Vierklosterstreit*]. Their fate, by implication, involved the fate of many other secularizations that had taken place since 1552. The committee was torn by its regard for strict legality which

[1] See Vol. III in this series, Chapter x.

dictated a confirmation of the verdicts of the chamber tribunal that the houses must be restored to religion, and the conflicting confessional partisanship of its members. In the end, the more extreme Protestants in 1601 withdrew from the committee, which thereupon adjourned without reaching any decision. Only the Calvinist leaders saw any cause for pleasure in this final breakdown of the effort to mend the machinery of Reich justice. Henceforth, however learned the chamber tribunal might be, there was no hope of earning general respect and acceptance for its verdicts. Somewhat paradoxically, the sinking of its fortunes helped to strengthen the rival jurisdiction of the Reich court council, which was under the control of the kaiser: in the controversies that raged over Aachen, Strasbourg and Donauwörth, its voice alone was heard. But its competence was flatly rejected by the Protestants.

From the undoing of the Reich supreme law court to the paralysis of its legislature was not a long step. Rudolf II was no lover of Reichstags; he did not convene one until 1582. But the renewal of the Turkish war in 1593 made it impossible to avoid this disagreeable necessity, and accordingly there were meetings of the Reichstag in 1594, 1597, 1603 and 1608. Unhappily, the business of these gatherings was apt to boil down to the twin topics of voting the subsidies requested by the kaiser to enable him to keep the Turks at bay, and the ventilation of the grievances felt by one religious party against the other. After 1594 the kaiser no longer appeared in person, and the princely habit of sending proxies developed, so that each assembly was less and less a meeting-place for the German ruling class and more and more a catalyst for inflaming controversial issues in politics and religion. In 1594 and 1597 the subsidies were granted, but on the latter occasion the Calvinist leaders—the 'corresponding princes'— refused to accept liability to pay taxes they had not personally voted. In 1603, for local reasons, they were more disposed to comply with the imperial request for aid, but after an harmonious beginning the session ran into violent storms as soon as the problem of Reich justice and the ancillary matter of the verdict of the chamber tribunal in the cases of the four religious houses was raised. No decision could be reached, and the assembly came to an end with confessional antagonism sharpened. The Protestants were in a permanent minority, and the Calvinists now took the logical but catastrophic course of denying the competence of a majority vote either in Reichstag or appellate commission: they demanded parity of representation. It is one of the many ironies of German history in this period that the chief of the corresponding princes responsible for this momentous fracturing of the Reich constitution should have been the Elector Palatine Frederick IV (1583–1610), a drunken young Nimrod, lavish in his court expenditure and lazily content to have his policy executed for him by a circle of narrow-minded and pedantic councillors.

The next Reichstag, in 1608, opened with the Protestants in full alarm at the manifest intentions of the kaiser in Hungary, the progress of the Spanish troops in the Netherlands and their misdeeds in the Rhineland, capped by the sudden news of the Bavarian intervention in the free city of Donauwörth a few weeks earlier.[1] Tempers were short, and the Protestants were challenged over the central issue of their acquisitions since the religious deadline of 1552. In the contentious and stormy atmosphere thus generated, no constructive business was possible. The moderate Lutherans, led by electoral Saxony, for a time actually took their stand beside the palatine and other Calvinist fire-eaters, but in the end it was the latter alone who disrupted the assembly by their abrupt departure. The legislature thereupon broke up without the usual formalities and courtesies. After this disaster, there might seem to be faint hope of fruitful achievement from any subsequent assembly. Nevertheless in 1613 Khlesl, in pursuit of his policy of compromise, persuaded the Kaiser Matthias to summon another meeting. It was not quite so forlorn a venture as might at first sight appear, for both the Catholic League and the Protestant Union, the contending confessional organizations, were beset by financial and political difficulties. Khlesl hoped by conciliatory moves to revive the constitutional organs of the Reich, to bring the contending factions together, to unite them for common aims and finally to induce them to dissolve their military formations. But the aged prelate lacked experience of Reich politics. He was personally distrusted by the duke of Bavaria, and he failed to soften the Calvinist leaders. The old issues, more burning than ever, soon stalked the stage—Reich justice, the four religious houses, the Donauwörth episode and so forth—and claim was met by counter-claim. The Catholic and Lutheran leaders finally agreed to vote the kaiser a subsidy, against which the corresponding princes promptly protested. The Reichstag was dissolved with no hopes answered. More than a quarter of a century was to elapse before its successor met.

Since the religious peace had been framed in 1555, the antagonism of Catholic and heretic had in each generation grown more definite, while the course of German history had abundantly illustrated the weaknesses of the compromise—the only partly effective principle of 'ecclesiastical reservation', the hollowness of the imperial assurance that Lutherans might continue to practise their faith in church lands, the precarious situation of minorities in the free cities and the defiant establishment of Calvinism in various principalities. Yet virtually no German prince was ready to face the incalculable consequences of unloosing a religious war, though the Electors Palatine had become the traditional leaders of a militant group of Calvinist extremists and their cousins the dukes of Bavaria had come to the fore as champions of the Catholic cause. It is a commentary on the

[1] See Vol. III.

strength of dynastic links that these two branches of the Wittelsbach family remained on personally friendly terms. Meanwhile, with the break-up of the 1608 Reichstag the confessional rift in Reich politics reached a new depth. The Calvinists were baffled and provoked by the solid Catholic majority in the legislature. They also had their eyes fixed, with mingled hopes and fears, on the startling developments in the hereditary Habsburg lands to the east. But it was the seizure of the free and Lutheran city of Donauwörth by the duke of Bavaria—acting nominally on behalf of the kaiser—that gave them the most violent proof of the vigour of Antichrist. In the summer of 1608 and under the patronage of the Elector Palatine, the Calvinist princes with some Lutheran allies—chiefly from Swabia, where Bavarian power was feared—founded the Union for the Defence of Evangelical Religion, a military alliance. Its general was Prince Christian of Anhalt, who had seen service in the French wars and was now the right-hand man of the Elector Palatine and his lieutenant in the upper Palatinate. This move was answered in little more than a year by the formation of the Catholic League—essentially a confederation of the three spiritual electors, whose lands lay along or near the Rhine, with the duke of Bavaria and his allies further south and east. Both union and league were financed by contributions levied in the manner of Reich taxes and kept in a central war chest. The army of the league was under Bavarian leadership. In view of the tension in Germany, the formation of the league had been observed with misgivings at Rome, and old Bishop Julius of Würzburg, who united the virtues of a model Catholic prelate with a great deal of worldly wisdom, hesitated much before joining it.

A long pre-history attaches to both these confessional alliances. Reich problems for many generations had been formulated in numberless assem-blies and committees, from meetings of the Reichstag or of the electoral princes down to the local circle assemblies or the less formal gatherings of neighbouring princes, and in the ruling class the habit of confederation was ingrained. There were various local alliances to maintain the peace for example, the Landsberg League, a Swabian association comprising both Catholics and Lutherans, which existed during the later sixteenth century under the presidency of the duke of Bavaria. In the reign of Charles V there had been the religious alignment of the Schmalkaldic League, and protestant unity had been resuscitated by the Torgau Alliance in 1591. Duke Wilhelm V of Bavaria had in 1583 come near to organizing a great Catholic union. What made the founding of the Evangelical Union and the Catholic League at this moment so ominous was not only their mili-tary emphasis but also their connections with foreign powers and, even more sinister, the domestic political context. This was now dominated by the breakdown of the Reich constitution. Law court and legislature had crumbled, imperial authority had evaporated, and whether there would ever be another kaiser seemed unsure. Electoral Saxony, in its habitual role of mediator between the extremists of either side, was powerless to prevent the princes from rallying to opposing standards.

How close to the brink of general war the Reich had travelled became clear with the death in 1609 of the mad duke of Jülich-Cleves. The largest secular territory in north-west Germany, recently rescued for Catholicism, was left with no agreed heir.[1] The chief claimants were the elector of Brandenburg and the palatine count of Neuburg, both Lutheran, who were quick to lay hands on the principality. Soon the whole Reich was astir, union and league preparing to act, and even the threat of Habsburg intervention taking shape. In a matter of months there was the further menace of French invasion, for Henri IV was not prepared to allow the Habsburg grip on the lower Rhine to be tightened. Catastrophe was averted only by the assassination of the French king and the death a little later of the Elector Palatine: only active diplomacy helped to restrain the hotheads. Subsequently, the conversion of the two 'possessing princes'— Brandenburg to Calvinism and Neuburg to Catholicism—did not prevent an agreement in 1614 to partition the disputed inheritance. The settlement was much later made permanent. But the whole episode illustrated how slender was the thread on which rested the peace of Germany.

While the edifice of German political stability was thus tottering towards collapse, one formidable prince kept a clear head—Duke Maximilian of Bavaria (1597–1651). During his long reign he was the most significant political figure within the Reich. His duchy though not very large was compact and administered with a close-fisted efficiency. It was not weakened by any disunity in religion. Maximilian had been carefully educated, under Jesuit auspices, but although a very pious man he was by no means priest-ridden. Within his duchy, the church dovetailed neatly into the secular administration; its personnel was appointed and controlled by the ducal government, while attendance at Mass was compulsory and before each Easter every Bavarian had to secure a certificate to prove that he had gone to confession. Indeed, such was the zeal of Maximilian for the salvation of his subjects that early in his reign he tried to institute a system of public guardians of morality, beside which the efforts of the English Puritans a little later look piecemeal and amateur. In Reich politics, he naturally condemned heresy, but in other ways he was a stout conservative. He disliked the presence of foreign troops on German soil as much as any Protestant, and he championed the prescriptive rights of the princely oligarchy. For the office of kaiser he had a genuine reverence. He took care to remain on good terms with the Habsburgs and to avoid becoming embroiled in their family disagreements, though this did not inhibit him, when in 1602 Rudolf was being pressed to name an heir, from toying with the notion of securing the imperial dignity for himself. The Catholic League was his special creation, and it soon helped to fortify his leading position among

---

[1] See Vol. III.

the princes of southern Germany. But it required careful nursing. Its members were apt to fall into arrear with their contributions for the military chest. Worse, after the accession of Matthias, Bishop Khlesl tried to dilute it into a constitutional confederation under Habsburg patronage by procuring the admittance of the faithful but Lutheran elector of Saxony as well as of Austria. For such a merely political alliance, Maximilian had no taste, and he was too much of a realist not to be aware of the divergences of interest between himself and his Austrian cousins. He accordingly withdrew from the enlarged body in 1616, and set about refounding the religious league as a smaller military confederation of Bavaria and some of her Catholic neighbours. This reformed league was a more modest organization than its predecessor, but it was more flexible and more tightly knit.

While German politics thus plunged fatally towards violence, the economic life of the country was by no means so unpromising. Of course there were unfavourable aspects. Chief among them was the impracticability of following the economic policy which in the calmer days of Ferdinand I and Maximilian II the Reichstag had begun to adumbrate. The coinage statutes of 1559 and 1566, which had been among its major legislative achievements, were generally flouted, the worst offenders being members of the Habsburg arch-house itself; German trade suffered accordingly from the lack of a good standard currency. Another discouragement to economic life lay in the enforced departure, from Protestant and Catholic areas alike, of religious dissidents.[1] Tolls were rising both within and across the frontiers of the Reich, and levies on commerce in transit being more systematically exacted, though it is not clear how far these burdens were increasing out of proportion to the rising price level. But there is no doubt about the clogging of traffic and the insecurity of goods on the lower Rhine from 1568 onwards, as a result of the fighting in the Netherlands, and the readjustment of trade routes eastwards to the Elbe was not easy. The Rhine valley suffered more from plundering by foreign soldiery than any other part of Germany in the generation or so preceding the Thirty Years War, especially during the Cologne conflict in the eighties and in the subsequent struggles for the control of the duchy of Jülich-Cleve. The city of Cologne lost much of its trade at this time. Among international events, the sack of Antwerp by Spanish troops in 1576 caused great damage to German firms, and the extinction of the world-wide market there was a disaster for the German mercantile and financial houses that had dominated it. Augsburg and other southern cities also suffered when most of their banking houses went out of business in the

[1] E.g. the departure of the mining *entrepreneur* Hans Steinberger, a Lutheran, from Tyrol c. 1570—J. Kallbrunner, 'Hans Steinberger', *Vierteljahrschrift für Sozial— und Wirtschafts-geschichte*, Vol. XXVII (1934), p. 2.

later sixteenth century. The eclipse of these merchant princes did not however permanently injure the prosperity of the city, though the mining enterprises they had sponsored often languished. Germany ceased to be a major producer of silver, and although the mining of copper was still an important source of revenue for the Austrian Habsburgs and the electors of Saxony, Germans no longer led the world in metallurgy. In short, they had lost their primacy in European finance and technology.

Yet there are other aspects to be considered. The German economy had not ceased to adjust itself to changing business trends, less favourable as they may have become. The Rhineland apart, Germany on the eve of the Thirty Years War still prospered, though there was naturally a great variety of conditions. Population was growing: rural colonization, both internally and along the eastern marches, was yet in progress. In some industries, as gild restraints were jettisoned, production was increasing— for instance, in the glass manufacture of Hesse and Thuringia. Ruthless and short-sighted as the princes mostly seemed in Reich politics, some at least were scrupulous and intelligent rulers at home—Bishop Julius of Würzburg, Dukes Christopher and Ludwig of Württemberg, or Archduke Ferdinand of Tyrol are examples of such. The rise in the consumption of alcoholic drinks established for the much-taxed duchy of Bavaria can indicate only an increase in well-being. In parts of south-western Germany the peasants had never been so well off as in the generation before the Thirty Years War. Some cities were flourishing as never before. Frankfurt-am-Main, to take an outstanding example, benefited greatly, like Amsterdam and Genoa, by the arrival of refugees from Antwerp. Many of these were Jews, but there were also other Netherlanders and Italians, who all contributed to give their new home that peculiar stamp as a financial and cosmopolitan centre, the home of luxury and elegance, that it was to retain for centuries to come. Frankfurt in the early seventeenth century was in process of rapid growth both in wealth and size. The foundation of the exchange in 1585 betokened that the city was succeeding Antwerp as the chief money-market within the Reich. Its merchants dealt in all the luxuries of the age, from jewellery and gold and silver plate to Italian silks and satins and the drugs and spices of the east. Its bookshops were the most famous in Europe. The March and September fairs of Frankfurt were never so opulent as during the period 1560–1630: Thomas Coryat of Somerset, visiting the autumn fair in 1608, noted that 'the riches I observed at this Mart were infinite' and that the wealth of the goldsmiths in particular 'was incredible'.[1]

But while the flourishing condition of Frankfurt bore witness to the busy trade of western Germany, there were even more striking developments to the east. In the lands north of Bohemia, settled in still comparatively recent times, there existed a broad border zone, able to exchange its cruder products

---

[1] T. Coryat, *Coryat's Crudities*, Vol. II (Glasgow, 1905), p. 290.

and its raw materials for the traditional manufactures of the west and even in some measure to fulfil the economic functions of the 'frontier' that was so significant an element in American history down to the end of the nineteenth century. The heart of the German economy was moving away from Swabia and the Rhineland towards these newer regions. The progress of agriculture and of the linen industry in eastern Germany had some remarkable features to its credit, and these developments lent a fresh impetus to the trade of the German coastal cities, especially Hamburg.

The German linen manufacture, like the English woollen cloth trade, is one of the classic industries of Europe, with its origins far back in the remote past. Linen cloth was made in many parts of Germany, but the chief exporting areas at the end of the Middle Ages were the Westphalian region in the north-west and the upper Danube and Lech valleys, from Ulm to Augsburg. Throughout the sixteenth century, Westphalian linens were being sent to Scandinavia, the Netherlands and England, where Osnabrück webs had a special renown. Swabian linens were consumed chiefly in Mediterranean countries, but with the overseas discoveries from the fifteenth century onwards they were further re-exported to tropical and colonial lands, and supply fell short of demand. The merchants of Augsburg and Ulm sought to supplement their local products by the purchase of linens made further afield, and so came to act as distributors of the coarser and cheaper products of Saxony, Lusatia and Silesia. North, east and even south of the Erzgebirge, the linen manufacture in the sixteenth century was thus stimulated into higher and finer productivity. This was especially true of the little industrial towns of Saxony and Lusatia: in Silesia, where urban life was feeble, the towns were not strong enough to prevent linen-making from taking deeper root in the countryside, to the profit of the landed nobles. For the linens produced in this whole region of Germany, the foremost outlet was traditionally at the Leipzig fairs. But as the century progressed, the channels of trade altered. The merchants most concerned with the buying of webs ceased to be preponderantly natives of Ulm and Augsburg, and tended more and more to operate from Nuremberg. These Nuremberg firms by 1600 were distributing great quantities of linen cloth to consumers at Venice, Milan and elsewhere in northern Italy, either directly or by sale at the periodic fairs of Bolzano. There was an important colony of German merchants at Genoa, whose main business was the shipment of goods from their homeland to southern Italy, Sicily, Spain and Portugal. In the last decade or so of the sixteenth century, linens displaced copper as the leading item of this Genoese traffic. A lively trade in German linens was maintained there until the spread of warfare in central Germany interrupted it in the sixteen-twenties.

The Nuremberg merchants did not monopolize the sale of Saxon and Lusatian and Silesian linens at the fairs of Leipzig, Bolzano and Frankfurt-am Main. From the last quarter of the sixteenth century they were being concurrently purchased by English and Dutch merchants, who not only attended the Leipzig fairs in large numbers but also established their own direct contacts with the manufacturers at various centres in the industrial area—the English for instance had a special headquarters at Görlitz, though they also made use of the distributing centre at Nuremberg. They outclassed as buyers the Dutch, who were more intent on the purchase of yarn for their own weavers at home. The English were Merchants Adventurers or their emissaries, often coming from their 'factory' at Emden, Stade or Hamburg, and their arrival at these remote Saxon and Lusatian towns at the foot of the Erzgebirge was an unplanned by-product of the dispersal of the commerce once centralized at Antwerp. Their presence serves to illustrate how within a couple of generations a quiet domestic manufacture had been transformed into one of the great exporting industries of northern Europe. The weavers of Lusatia and Saxony learnt to produce finer webs and to adapt these to current market demands; sales were organized in bulk through little town gilds formed for this purpose. It was the policy of these gilds to restrict the number of weavers admitted to mastership, but in fact these rose steadily and reached their maximum in the decade 1615–25. The flourishing linen industry was thus an important element in the general prosperity experienced in Saxony during the half-century before the outbreak of the Thirty Years War, and it helped to offset the closing of the silver mines of the Erzgebirge owing to the influx of cheaper American metal.

Nuremberg drew much benefit from its new role as distributing centre for east German linens. It was one of the important free cities of the Reich, and ruled an extensive tract of countryside beyond its well-fortified walls. Its rulers avoided the extremes of religious antagonism, and it remained the centre of a trade network that extended from Italy to the Netherlands, from Danzig to Lyon. The economic mainstay of the city lay traditionally in metallurgical products, and the interests of its leading families were in mining. As has already been mentioned, German mining was in difficulties during the later sixteenth century—there was not only the competition of American silver, but also the need for sinking shafts deeper and deeper, with the extra outlay of capital this necessitated. The threatened decline of Nuremberg was averted by the linen trade. The men who ran it were not connected with the conservative patrician families of the city—the Welsers, Imhofs and the like. These latter clung to their customary business: they were complaining of immigrant Italians in 1571, they were administering the city finances clumsily, and many of them retired from active trade before the end of the century. The traffic in linens was handled by new pioneering firms, sometimes of Swabian origin, who contracted with the town gilds of Saxony and Lusatia for their webs, checked and re-sorted the latter upon delivery, and perhaps arranged for them to be dyed and finished before distributing them to their far-flung markets. The trade-marks of the better firms were a valuable guarantee of quality—for example, the famous business of Viatis and Peller, that flourished for a century and a half and kept its selling agents in all the more important linen markets from Linz to Seville. The Nuremberg patriciate for long kept at arm's length the second-class citizens who ran such firms. But their exploitation of east German products—furs and leather as well as linens—enabled the wealth of the city to be maintained, though on a new basis, down to the upheavals of the Thirty Years War.

The richest merchant of Nuremberg—and probably of Germany—at the outbreak of the struggle was Bartolomäus Viatis, founder of the firm already mentioned. His remarkable career in many ways personified the tendencies that were remoulding the economy of the country. Characteristically enough, he was not by origin a German: he was born in 1538 at Venice, where his father had migrated from an Alpine valley above Bergamo. But he came early in life to Nuremberg as an apprentice to a local merchant, and although he served his employer subsequently for four years as a factor at Lyon, he acclimatized himself to German ways even to the point of remaining a pious Lutheran. He may well have set himself up as an independent merchant by the time-honoured method of marrying the widow of his recently deceased master; certainly, the basis of his fortune was securely laid when in 1590 he entered upon his partnership with Martin Peller. His fortune lay in trading: the purchase and sale of commodities. There was, first, the ancient and now resuscitated traffic in spices and luxury textiles bought at Venice; Viatis marketed them not only at Frankfurt, Leipzig and Nuremberg, but also in Poland and Russia, where Nuremberg manufactures also had an outlet. But far more important were the linens he systematically procured from the town gilds of Saxony and its neighbours—he had annual contracts with about fifty of these bodies. The linens were mostly dyed at Nuremberg, where the firm had an efficient central organization, and then despatched to Italy and Spain. The contrast with the Swabian financiers of a generation or two earlier at once catches the eye. Viatis did not deal in mines or metals, and he steered clear, as far as possible, of pure finance and banking. Such loans as he allowed were granted with an eye to the advantage of his trade. It was efficient method and a flair for organization that made him rich. As he thus rejected the opportunities as well as the snares of court finance, it is not surprising that his fortune never approached that of the Fuggers at their zenith: but since it was not sunk in dubious loans to defaulting princes it was to that extent more solidly based. Despite his wealth, and his prominent share in the foundation of the Nuremberg Exchange Bank in 1621, Viatis at his death ten years later remained outside the select ranks of the city patriciate.

There were many other wealthy merchants in Germany ready to engage in the brave venture of lending money to princes. There was, for instance, Johann von Bodeck, the earliest outstanding merchant of Frankfurt, son of a migrant from Antwerp, whose interests covered all sorts of activities, from mining, smelting, money-changing and banking to the despatch in all directions of both European and tropical goods, and who kept agents at Venice, Seville, Amsterdam and Hamburg. Even more in the Fugger tradition was Lazarus Henckel, born in Upper Hungary, who received his business training in southern Germany. He came to Vienna as factor for an Ulm firm in 1579 and established himself there permanently two years later. The basis of his fortune was laid by the sale of kerseys—presumably from England—that he bought at Nuremberg and sold in Austria and further east: the troops fighting for the Habsburgs were clad in them. Wine, scythes and knives were other commodities that he despatched eastwards. In the opposite direction, he was clever enough to foster—before the outbreak of the Turkish war—a great traffic in cattle from Transylvania and the middle and lower Danube valley for consumption in Austria and southern Germany: in 1590 alone he sent at least 5,000 beasts to Vienna. Speculation on the exchanges and lending to the kaiser were already familiar to him; but his greatest opportunities came with the war in 1593, which brought him virtually to the position of banker to the imperial government. He underwrote loans raised by the kaiser in Germany, transmitted subsidies to Sigismund Bathory and other allies, and gave his help in the payment of troops in the field—far outpacing other merchants of Vienna in these services. After 1600 his situation grew precarious, with the increasing inattention of the kaiser, the political setbacks to the Habsburg cause and the longer delays of the imperial treasury. The nadir of his fortunes was reached after the rebellion of Bocskay in 1604, when his trade with Transylvania was cut off, his Hungarian estates passed out of his control and the Neusohl copper mines, once leased to the Fuggers and recently acquired by him, lay in enemy hands. But the profitable sale of Italian and tropical luxuries to the court continued, his properties accumulated, the tide finally turned and he died a wealthy landowner and founder of the noble house of von Donnersmarck.

No less striking than the progress of the German linen industry was the development of agriculture in the northern European plain, including its German portion. No doubt the general increase of inhabitants throughout Germany during the sixteenth century, especially the towns, had something to do with this. But the increase in population over much of the rest of Europe, which made it impossible for many Atlantic and Mediterranean regions to supply themselves locally with sufficient corn, was even more important. First among these importing areas was the northern part of the

Netherlands. The Dutch were already having to fetch Baltic corn to provide themselves with both bread and beer in the later Middle Ages, and they were soon carrying it as far as Iberian harbours. In the 1580s, the food shortage in the Mediterranean became sufficiently acute to impel some of the Italian princes to seek to import northern corn by sea. The Baltic region was now established as the major granary of Europe, and the consequent impact on agricultural conditions in north-east Germany was profound.

The greatest beneficiary from the increasing demand for north German corn was the landed nobility, which was not hampered by any scruples about soiling its hands in commerce. In Holstein, the nobles seized their opportunities at an early stage; the never-distant coastline and the many harbours enabled them to convert their estates into large-scale business enterprises, employing their serfs to produce not only grain, wool, butter, cheese and horses, but even to go to sea and catch herrings for them to market. They owned their own ships and despatched their cargoes to the Netherlands, England and as far afield as Spain. Peter Rantzau, whose family took the lead in foreign trade, arranged in the 1580s with the grand duke of Tuscany for the shipment of corn to feed his subjects. Before the end of the sixteenth century, some of the Holstein nobles had in addition established industries on their estates, using for their manufactures the copper and iron that they imported from Sweden or southern Germany. Local markets were now available for them at Hamburg and Lübeck, but they developed their own money exchange at Kiel, where many of them owned town houses with special privileges. This enabled some of the richest families to complete a well-known pattern of evolution and emerge as specialists in high finance, lending money in the seventeenth century to the crowns of northern Europe.

The peculiar geographical situation of Holstein gave its landowners special opportunities, and it was not until the middle of the sixteenth century that their neighbours in Mecklenburg, Pomerania, Brandenburg and elsewhere were tempted by the rising price of corn to extend crop-raising on their estates so as to increase the surplus available for sale. This involved far-reaching changes in agricultural organization and in the social order. In western Germany the normal unit of agricultural production was, as in the English midlands and much of France, the open-field village community, where the peasants possessed variable rights in their holdings and usually could not be ejected at the order of the landlord [Grundherrschaft]. In Tyrol, Vorarlberg and parts of Swabia, their conditions were by contemporary European standards very favourable. In Baden and one or two other territories, they had risen before 1600 almost to the status of co-proprietors with strictly limited obligations that could be—and sometimes were—remitted in return for a money payment. But as a general rule, the further east the less secure was the peasant. The German villages east of the Elbe had mostly been founded in the Middle Ages by free colonists, but forces had long been at work to depress the position of the villagers, and in the first half of the sixteenth century the tendency had been to tie them to the soil. From the last quarter of the fifteenth century corn prices had gradually been rising. From c. 1550, the rate outstripped the current inflation of the general price level, owing doubtless to the rapid expansion of the international corn market. Hence a strong temptation for the landlord to build up his demesne farm—the beginning of a policy whose logical end was the ultimate consolidation of the unit of agrarian production into a single unified undertaking, run by the officials appointed by the landlord, with the peasants reduced to the position of landless or virtually landless labourers [Gutsherrschaft].

The later sixteenth century accordingly witnessed over much of north-east Germany a marked propensity on the part of the landowners first to enlarge their demesne farms at the expense of the peasant holdings, and subsequently to abolish the latter entirely and organize the estate as a single business unit. There were various obstacles in the way of this policy, and the process was nothing like complete until the devastations of the Thirty Years War had enabled the landlords, whether by force or by law or by a mixture of both, to clear their estates of the remaining smallholding peasants. The major obstacle was the fact that the German peasant, unlike his Polish neighbour, still had legal rights and could not be arbitrarily evicted from his holding. Enclosure had to be piecemeal and gradual; sometimes by purchase from the tenant, sometimes by escheat, sometimes by direct forfeiture. Much turned on the interpretation of the local territorial law. A crucial factor was the policy of the electors of Brandenburg, the dukes of Pomerania and other princes, who in the half-century before the Thirty Years War whether through weakness or self-interest did not oppose their nobles but allowed the law to be amended bit by bit in the direction they required. North-east Germany thus joined Poland and the lands east of the Baltic in provisioning Spain and the Mediterranean, and there is no reason to doubt that there was a significant increase of agricultural output and still more of exports. But while the townsman of Seville, Florence or Venice was thus provided with his daily bread, the effects of this enclosing movement on the producer were socially retrograde. The peasant lost not only his land but his liberty, becoming the chattel of his landlord, who was also his judge and his employer. It is not surprising that the traveller Fynes Moryson, writing in the early seventeenth century, should have considered that the poor people in the districts nearest to Denmark and Poland were 'more oppressed than anywhere else throughout Germany'.[1] The political repercussions of this evolution were apparent from the middle of the seven-

---

[1] Fynes Moryson, An Itinerary, Vol. IV (Glasgow, 1908), p. 331.

teenth century onwards. They were visible especially in the rise of the Hohenzollern electorate, whose sovereigns naturally enough based their administration upon an alliance with the most experienced business class in their dominions—not, as in western Europe, the townsfolk, but the landlords who ran their estates for profit.

By the beginning of the seventeenth century the Hanseatic League was moribund. The rise of the Dutch Republic, with its exclusive commercial policy, had cut off Cologne and the other inland members from easy communication by water with the seaports of the Netherlands, and the organization that once had reached from Novgorod to London had now for all practical purposes shrunk to a loose *entente* between Lübeck, Danzig, Hamburg and Bremen. The commercial interests of these cities were by no means identical, and they conducted their foreign policies like independent republics. Apart from these remaining Hanse ports, there were other important coastal towns that did not possess even the formal link of membership of the league—Emden, for instance, or Stade or Elbing. The rivalries of all the German ports, whether members of the Hanseatic League or not, had been exacerbated in the later sixteenth century by their competition to secure the settlement of the English merchants with their valued imports of cloth, tin and lead, and no attempts either to persuade them to sink their differences and present a united front, or to procure the active support of the distant Reich government, had ever met with more than fleeting and incomplete success. Yet despite the jealousies and enmities of the German seaports, it is safe to say that their harbours had never been so busy as they now were in the opening years of the seventeenth century, though there had been a great change in the pattern of trade since the hey-day of the Hanse 300 years earlier. Hansard merchants were no longer predominant in the countries of northern Europe; most of the long-range shipping in German ports was now Dutch, and English and other foreign ships were also regular visitors. These strangers came chiefly in quest of essential commodities. Although it was possible to procure timber and other naval stores from Norway and Archangel, supplies were available in greater quantity and variety from the Baltic. There was also corn, whether German or Polish, to be shipped for transport westwards and southwards. German linens, as has already been explained, were another great export, as were copper, iron and brass. The English still reckoned Germany as their best market for woollen cloth.

Yet the predominance of foreigners did not amount to a monopoly. A good deal of trade remained in German hands and was carried in German ships. For this, the political situation was partly responsible: especially the fact that Spain, and therefore also Portugal, was at war with the Dutch until 1609 and again from 1621, and with the English until

1604. The state of war did not mean a complete cessation of Dutch or even English traffic with the Peninsula, though it undoubtedly limited it and drove it into circuitous and underhand channels. For Dutch shipowners, one obvious expedient was to transfer their vessels to the flag of some German seaport, a course of action that led in particular to an enormous but somewhat spurious increase in the shipping of Emden. From the Spanish side, the alternative to the usual course of buying Baltic products fetched by the Dutch was to encourage ships from Hamburg, Danzig or some other German port to bring them. Thus, from the 1570s onwards, there was a great expansion of German–Peninsular trade, very welcome to both parties. Spain direly needed timber and corn, while the return cargoes included bullion from America as well as tropical produce that would formerly have gone to Antwerp. As the German ships were manned by Lutheran sailors, special favour was required to permit their entry into Spanish ports: this was an uneasy point until in 1607 a wide agreement was reached, embodying large concessions to the Hansards, who on their side undertook not to convey Dutch goods. There thus came into existence a curious Hispano-Hanse maritime association based upon commercial ties but with a political aspect that was illustrated by the Hanse backing for King Sigismund Vasa of Sweden and Poland. German seaports throve on the Peninsular trade—hundreds of their ships were involved—and German consuls were maintained in the chief Iberian ports. The nastiest threat to this traffic sprang at first from the enmity of the English and the Dutch, who were not ready to tolerate the supply of food and munitions to their enemy. Hanseatic shipping therefore shunned the Channel and risked the Atlantic route past the Hebrides—though this did not save a German fleet of some sixty sail from capture by Drake off the mouth of the Tagus in 1589. Even this catastrophe did not deter the Hansards from plying so profitable a trade. It continued to flourish into the seventeenth century, and the Germans lost little business during the twelve years of truce, 1609–21, between Spain and the Dutch.

The overseas trade of the German coastal cities was not limited to the Peninsula or even to the Old World in the later sixteenth century. Although it was not Spanish policy to allow foreigners to participate directly in traffic with America, the Portuguese were for a time more liberal, and German merchants resident at Lisbon were able to trade with Brazil and the Portuguese islands in the Atlantic. From at least 1587, there are indications that some Germans were actually engaging in a three-cornered intercourse from Lisbon to Brazil that enabled cargoes of sugar to be carried direct to Germany. This direct sailing came to an end in 1602—in all probability there had never been much of it. Although a few German ships did subsequently visit Brazil from Portugal, the trade with the Portuguese settlements in America was henceforth conducted through non-German intermediaries at Lisbon.

More significant than the few and short-lived contacts with Brazil was the opening of direct communication by sea between the north German cities and the Mediterranean. This was not an expansion of the Peninsular trade, but sprang from the shortage of corn in Italy in the 1580s. The first northerners to trade direct with Italy in the later sixteenth century had been the English and the Dutch, but their ships were liable to seizure by the Spaniards, and the Germans were therefore safer carriers. The grand duke of Tuscany and the Republic of Venice were followed by the pope and the duke of Mantua in sending envoys to Hamburg and Danzig to open up a supply of northern corn. Cereals were accordingly being delivered by German ships to Italian ports from 1590 onwards. The Venetians found by experiment that it was cheaper and safer to import corn by sea than transport it overland. A profitable traffic thus began: grain prices soon responded by sharp rises and freight charges increased even more. At first the corn was sent chiefly to Leghorn, where the Grand Duke Francesco of Tuscany was himself the importer. On his personal order, cargoes were shipped from Hamburg, Lübeck and Danzig. But Leghorn was the haunt of the English and the Dutch, and the Germans soon found it more convenient to deliver their foodstuffs at Genoa. Here the ruling oligarchy of the republic wisely left the corn trade open and from 1595 provided a free warehouse for it, so that it was possible to land shiploads here without awaiting a specific order. Further west, German ships were also provisioning Marseille. The policy of Venice was far more jealous than that of Tuscany or Genoa, and at first only Danzigers were welcomed: they remained predominant even after the relaxation of the regulations in 1610. Although the worst years of food shortage in Italy were over by 1593, the north German trade continued on a broader basis; metals and metalwares, shipbuilding materials and linens were carried as well as corn. In return the Germans brought home wines, spices, fruits and oil. The produce of the Greek islands in Venetian possession was fetched by Danzigers. Further east, trade with Turkish lands was impossible before 1606, since legally the Germans were subjects of the kaiser, who until that date was at war with the sultan. It was a significant example of the disadvantage of belonging to the Reich.

The development of the southern traffic in corn and naval materials, and especially the opening of the Venetian trade, helped Danzig to stave off any decline and indeed to maintain great prosperity in the later sixteenth and early seventeenth centuries. An epoch of extensive rebuilding, especially in the centre of the city, reflected the wealth of Danzig as the corn staple of the Baltic. But the chief beneficiary of the new commercial trends was Hamburg, whose rise to a place among the very greatest ports of Europe demands some examination. Hamburg no doubt owed its spectacular fortune in the first place to its site at the mouth of the Elbe, a navigable river less impeded by tolls than the Oder, and less harassed by war and politics than the Rhine. Its patricians showed much skill in fending off the threats of successive kings of Denmark to the freedom of traffic on their river, though these were never so deadly as the pretensions of the kings of Poland and Sweden to control the navigation of the Vistula and thus the essential trade artery of Danzig. Their first efforts to develop a commerce independent of that of other Hanse cities involved, in the mid-sixteenth century, the expansion of the Iceland trade and the finishing of English woollen cloths imported from Antwerp. Then in 1567 the Hamburg senate managed to lure the English Merchant Adventurers to fix their cloth mart in the city. This not only meant more business for the dyers and cloth-finishers, but also attracted other merchants with their wares, for example the dealers in Hungarian copper and north German linens. Although the English settlement was very profitable to the city it lasted only for ten years. It was disliked by the government of Spain, a customer whom the senate was unwilling to offend, and it was a standing provocation to Danzig and the other sister cities of the Hanse, who resented the refusal of the English government to restore their privileges at London. These latter subsequently mobilized the antique machinery of the Hanseatic League in a final effort to secure the backing of Reichstag and kaiser for the expulsion of the English from the soil of the Reich. After this had failed, the merchants of Hamburg welcomed back the English settlement in 1611, this time for nearly two centuries. By now, Spanish opposition had also vanished, since England and Spain had made peace in 1604.

There had been a trading connection between the north German ports and Portugal since the later Middle Ages, but it was only with the up-heaval in the Netherlands in the 1570s that Hamburg began to traffic to any mentionable extent with Spain. Various fragments of the commercial heritage of Antwerp, now in process of disintegration, were attracted to the mouth of the Elbe. By 1580 or so the Welser firm was importing pepper, sugar and other goods from the Peninsula through Hamburg instead of Antwerp, and for a period of rather less than twenty years Hamburg became a major European staple for East India produce. The contractors who in 1591 agreed with the Portuguese crown to sell pepper in Lisbon (they were a powerful consortium that included both Fuggers and Welsers) disposed of most of their supplies at Hamburg. The city did not however inherit the monopoly that Antwerp in its great days had enjoyed. The oriental traffic at Lisbon was precarious and intermittent, and not all the spices arriving there were shipped to the Elbe. Further, the weakness of the Portuguese in the Indian Ocean had led in the later sixteenth century to a revival of the rival Levantine trade route via Alexandria to Venice. The conquest of the East Indies by the Dutch in the early seventeenth century in any case brought to an end this episode in the commercial history of Hamburg, which from then on had to procure its pepper and spices from the Netherlands. But the Peninsular trade remained. More than any other German city, Hamburg now provided the essential link between the Baltic and southern Europe. It was a distributing centre for all sorts of southern and tropical commodities, from salt and wine to sugar, brazil-wood and even tobacco. In addition, there were dangerous though profitable sidelines in the re-export of English lead and tin and the clandestine shipment of arms and munitions. The primacy of Hamburg among the German trading cities reached beyond the Peninsula to the Atlantic islands and the Mediterranean; at Venice alone, as already mentioned, the Danzigers were specially privileged. But great risks always attended this whole southward traffic. Even when the Dutch and English had ceased to wage war on the king of Spain, there was danger from the Barbary corsairs, who in the early seventeenth century were entering upon a new and bolder phase of the operations.

The remarkable expansion of the trade of Hamburg in the later six-teenth and early seventeenth centuries brought with it new occupations, industries and financial techniques. New enterprises included salt and sugar refineries, while among other industries shipbuilding and such ancillary crafts as ropemaking occupied a prominent place. Sometimes there were generous windfalls of profit: we have it on the word of one Hamburg merchant that the Italian requests for corn in the 1590s caused the price to rise by 30%, while freight charges were put up by 70%. The expanding wealth and the financial maturity of the city were illustrated by the growth of bill-broking and by the foundation in 1619 of the Hamburg Exchange Bank. Much was due to the presence of immigrant merchants, who had brought with them their skill and their capital; the sums initially handled by the bank provide full confirmation of the extent of their investment. By this time, the nucleus of indigenous merchants of wealth was outnumbered in the pursuit of foreign trade by the newcomers. Some came from Nuremberg, Augsburg or elsewhere in southern Germany, or even from Italy. But a much more important contingent consisted of refugees from the Netherlands, especially Antwerp. Some of these were native Dutchmen or Brabanters, but many were Marranos of Portuguese extraction, who by the local law were permitted from 1612 onwards to throw off the mask and openly admit to their Jewish faith. They were however apt to be cautious and slow to do this, since they mostly had relatives remaining in the Peninsula whom they were afraid to incriminate. With these, they kept their trade contacts and also maintained touch with Marrano colonies in many other ports, from Constantinople to Pernambuco. Such were the men who directed the large mercantile fleet of small but up-to-date ships that flew the Hamburg flag, and who by the early seven-teenth century had enabled Hamburg to become a major purveyor to the Peninsula of the essential materials of the north, and to function as a vital junction in the new pattern of trade that was linking London and the

Netherlands with the German and Baltic market on the one hand and the Peninsular and Mediterranean traffic on the other.

German historians have not paid much attention to the study of their national history in the epoch before the outbreak of the Thirty Years War.[1] It was an age when the feeble scions of a cosmopolitan dynasty reigned ineffectively over a nation cleft by deep religious antagonisms; when German political weakness was illustrated by the final decay of the Hanseatic League, the unchecked violation of the western frontier by French and Spanish troops, and the growth of a separatist nationalism among the Dutch and the Swiss; and when foreign influences overlaid German art, literature and even language. Intellectual life found its chief expression in the drab controversies of theology; simple folk were left a prey to all sorts of superstition, including witch-hunting of the cruellest sort. Sensibility coarsened, we are told, and morality loosened. We certainly know that the buoyant population of the countryside helped to cause overcrowding in the towns, where the real wages of artisans and other humble folk were falling and reached a depth unsurpassed for centuries in the years immediately after 1600. In the external field, Germans failed to take any appreciable part in the enterprises which were opening up new parts of the world to European settlement and exploitation. Yet it would be unfair to judge an almost land-locked country by this last criterion. The foregoing pages contain plenty of evidence to illustrate the abounding economic vitality of Germany before 1618, from the thriving traffic of Hamburg and Danzig to the hum of commerce at Frankfurt-am-Main, Nuremberg and Leipzig. In a different sphere, the generation that saw the building, for example, of the Rathaus at Augsburg or of such impressive churches as the Michaelskirche at Munich or the Marienkirche at Wolfenbüttel was capable of high achievement in architecture. There were some celebrated artists and craftsmen at work in Germany in the age before the Thirty Years War, and signs of an incipient revival of the native spirit.[2] Foreign visitors judged the Germans to be honest and industrious, even if somewhat addicted to tippling.

There was no tragic inevitability with regard to the approaching catastrophe. But there was a failure—a failure of the governing class, of the princes who produced no statesman capable of seeing effectively beyond the prejudices of religion or the dynastic rivalries of his forefathers. It was rulers with a local, not to say parochial, outlook who determined the destiny of their country. No doubt some responsibility lay on the degenerate shoulders of Rudolf II: but regionalism and even separatism were embedded in the cumbrous mechanism of the Reich constitution and it is more than doubtful whether its collapse could have been averted or even

---

[1] A glance, for instance, at the titles of the contributions to the *Historische Zeitschrift* during the last half-century serves abundantly to illustrate this.

[2] G. Dehio, *Geschichte der deutschen Kunst*, Vol. III (2nd ed. Berlin and Leipzig, 1931,) p. 182.

much delayed by a kaiser less miserable. The classes that marched in the van of economic progress—the merchants of the northern ports, the landowners of the north-eastern principalities, the *entrepreneurs* of Nuremberg and Frankfurt—had little or no voice in the government of the country. They lived in a different world from the blinkered magnates who dominated the Reichstag, and it is perhaps hardly surprising that its sessions should have provided occasions for princely strife rather than constructive legislation. Of the enforcement of the national ideal and of a statesmanship that should transcend local or sectarian ambitions there could be no possibility—save in the universally dreaded release of widespread war.

CHAPTER XI

THE THIRTY YEARS WAR

I

IN the early years of the seventeenth century, the Holy Roman Empire of the German people had the misfortune to be the centre of intense internal and international rivalries. The authority of the emperor, Diet and imperial courts had broken down, and there could be no settlement by peaceful means of conflicting claims to territory and title. Protestant princes feared the loss of church lands secularized after 1552; the return to the Roman Catholic church of bishoprics, abbeys, cloisters and countless parishes also meant the enforced re-Catholicization of the populations involved. Since the Donauwörth affair of 1608, not even an imperial city could feel safe in the worship of its choice. The very existence of a defensive Protestant Union confronted by an armed Catholic League was a menace to peace. While the great majority of German princes were peace-loving, sometimes at the risk of their security, a few were ready to seize any opportunity to increase their territories and to enhance their prestige.

If there was danger of chaos and civil war, foreign entanglements posed an even greater threat. England and the United Provinces (the Dutch) were members of the Protestant Union. The marriage of the Elector Palatine of the Rhine to the daughter of James I added to England's interest in Germany. In the north there were further foreign involvements. The king of Denmark was also duke of Holstein, a prince of the empire with claims on secularized bishoprics. His ambition to control the Baltic coast was, in turn, challenged by the king of Sweden. Most important was the close co-operation of Habsburg emperor and Habsburg king of Spain. Any increase of their power in the empire meant absolutist government and the suppression of Protestantism.

Two major issues dominated European international politics: French ambition to break the ring of Habsburg territories surrounding their state, and the preparations by Spain to reconquer the United Provinces. They were interrelated, and both involved the empire. To reach the Netherlands by land, Spain sought a secure passageway from her Italian possessions through the Swiss Valtelline valley and down the Rhine. This posed a further threat to France. A vigorous French anti-Habsburg policy was, however, postponed until the rise of Richelieu. The Dutch had won a respite by the conclusion of a twelve-year truce in 1609, but a renewal of hostilities by Spain was certain. Before the expiration of the truce, a revolt in Bohemia against Habsburg rule and Catholic domination precipitated the series of wars known as the Thirty Years War.

The German and international situations made it possible for the war to spread from Bohemia to Germany, and to involve England, Spain, the United Provinces, Denmark, Sweden, northern Italy, and France. As the war continued, its character changed. Religious issues, so prominent in the early years, declined, and power politics, never absent, finally predominated.

It is customary to divide the war into the following sections: the Bohemian revolt and the conquest of the Palatinate, 1618–23; the Danish period, 1624–9; the Swedish period, 1630–4; and the French period, 1635–48. The negotiations leading to the peace of Westphalia were carried on from 1644 to 1648.

Since 1526 the Habsburgs had ruled Bohemia and the adjoining associated territories of Moravia, Silesia and Lusatia. These lands furnished large revenues, while Bohemia was of particular political significance, for its king was one of the seven princes who elected the emperor. For this reason it was important to ensure the kingship of Bohemia as a means to the acquisition of the imperial title.

Bohemians had legitimate grievances against their Habsburg king; but the ingredients for a successful revolt were lacking, namely, a common ideal, leadership and military strength. Instead, Bohemia was torn by dissension and suspicion. The great majority of the population were peasants whose old 'liberties' were being suppressed by a landlord aristocracy. There were numerous towns, of which the capital, Prague, had the proudest history; but the *bourgeoisie* were taxed ruthlessly, their political rights were curtailed by both king and aristocracy, and trade and industry were largely dominated by foreigners. Power was in the hands of a small group of great noble landowners. The knights, the lesser landowners, were being absorbed into the nobility or, if economically weak, were forced to become stewards for the magnates or lesser government officials. Theoretically, at least, there was political representation in the Diet, a tri-cameral body of nobles, knights and cities; and yet, only about 20,000 of a total population of some 2,000,000 had full political rights. A revolution which promised satisfaction to oppressed peasants and dissatisfied burghers would have had some chance of success. There was no such programme. Instead, the initiative was taken by a strong chancellor, Count Lobkowitz, a Catholic, who since the close of the sixteenth century was pushing towards the creation of a centralized absolutist state at the expense of the Diet, and particularly at the expense of the nobility.

Traditionally, religion should have been the common ideal which drew together the various elements of Bohemian society. But the religious situation had changed in the two centuries since the days of John Hus. The disciples of the great Bohemian reformer had won the right to take communion in both kinds, the wine as well as the wafer, and therefore called themselves, Utraquists. With the introduction of Lutheranism and then Calvinism, the great majority of the population, including the nobility, had turned truly Protestant, although they retained the name of Utraquist in order to maintain official recognition. Lacking, however, was the strong fighting spirit of the old Hussites, at the very time that it was most needed to combat the Habsburg policy of re-Catholicization. By the beginning of the seventeenth century, the forces of the Counter-Reformation headed by the Jesuits and backed by the Catholic hierarchy had made considerable political headway. The predominance of the nobility was now seriously threatened not only by the programme of centralization, but by the supplanting of Protestant high officials with Catholics.

In 1609 the Protestant majority won a temporary victory by forcing the ruling king and emperor Rudolf II to grant the so-called Letter of Majesty. This edict, approved by the Diet, recognized liberty of worship to members of the reformed Bohemian church, and guaranteed the church properties of both Protestants and Catholics. Moreover, Protestants lacking a place of worship in royal cities or on royal domains were permitted to build churches.

The Letter of Majesty was anathema to the Catholic extremists, yet neither Rudolf, nor his brother Matthias who succeeded him as king in 1611 and emperor in 1612, favoured a war of religion. The situation changed radically when the Habsburg princes chose Archduke Ferdinand of Styria to succeed his cousin, the childless Matthias. The Habsburg king of Spain was won over to this decision by the promise of the Austrian Habsburg fiefs in Alsace. These were of the utmost importance as links in the road for the passage of Spanish troops from Italy to the Netherlands. To the Bohemian Protestants the selection of Ferdinand was indeed ominous, for the archduke was an enthusiastic pupil of the Jesuits who had ruthlessly rooted out heresy in his domains. Nevertheless, in 1617 Ferdinand was 'accepted' as king-designate by almost unanimous consent of the three estates. By tacit recognition of the hereditary character of the kingship, the Diet threw away a golden opportunity to assert Bohemian independence. Perhaps there was no other choice. No great native leader rose to seize the crown or to establish a republic. Nor did there appear to be a foreign candidate to the throne acceptable to the Diet.

Before his return to Vienna after Ferdinand's coronation, Matthias appointed ten deputy governors to rule in his absence. The membership of this group is an indication of the growing strength of a belligerent Catholic party. Seven were Catholics, and of their number, significantly, were two noblemen, William Slawata and Jaroslav Martinitz, who had refused to sign the Letter of Majesty. The religious settlement had indeed never been upheld, and the cases of two towns, Klostergrab and Braunau, precipitated the crisis. On the pleas that they were not royal lands but church properties, the ecclesiastical authorities refused permission to build Protestant churches in these towns. Matthias supported this position, and the deputy governors ordered the imprisonment of a number of recalcitrant Braunau burghers.

By the Letter of Majesty a committee of defensors had been authorized to protect Protestant rights, and the defensors now called for a meeting of delegates from the whole kingdom which met in Prague on 21 May 1618. Two days later the deputies surged into the royal palace and hurled the unpopular Slawata and Martinitz, together with an inoffensive secretary, from a window. The defenestration, a Bohemian custom in times of rebellion, was intended to kill the victims, but all three escaped with their lives. To the Catholics this was a miracle, and a contemporary print shows the drop of about 46 feet eased by the support of angels, while the rebels declared that the three men were saved by falling on a heap of rubbish.

A provisional government of thirty directors was elected by the estates, and an army of 16,000 men was voted to be commanded by Heinrich Matthias, Count Thurn. Everything depended on the army, and the revolutionary government failed miserably to give it support. The landowners and cities, who were held responsible for the soldiers' pay, shirked their responsibility. In consequence, Thurn's force was miserably equipped, poorly fed and mutinous. Short of an efficient professional army, the only alternative would have been to rouse the peasantry against the foreign enemy. That this was possible is proved by the acts of sabotage committed by peasants against the invading imperialists. The nobility could not be expected to lead a popular revolt; but the failure to do so turned the peasantry against the marauding soldiers of their own nation. Lack of common ideals and inspired leadership, and deeply rooted social cleavages were evident from the very beginning of the revolt.

Despite the efforts of three important German princes, Frederick of the Palatinate, John George of Saxony and Maximilian of Bavaria, to arrange a settlement, the Bohemian uprising could not be localized. The king of Spain, influenced by family solidarity and the promise of the Alsatian fiefs, sent an army from Flanders across Germany to aid Ferdinand. The Bohemians in turn were aided by Charles Emanuel, Duke of Savoy, an old enemy of the Habsburgs, who offered a mercenary force under the command of a well-known professional soldier, Count Mansfeld. Ernst von Mansfeld, who looms so large in the early years of the war, was the illegitimate son of a minor German prince. His sole aim in life was to carve out for himself an independent principality, and he was willing to fight under any flag to accomplish this purpose. He seldom had sufficient pay for his soldiers, who therefore roamed the countryside for food and booty. His name became a byword for ruthless cruelty to the helpless peasantry. In the immediate circumstances, the *condottiere* was effective. He prevented the destruction of Thurn's amateur conscript soldiers and captured the city of Pilsen, one of the two Catholic cities in the country. Neither side had sufficient strength to strike a decisive blow.

Whether the Bohemians would carry a revolt to its logical conclusion by unseating their Habsburg ruler was at first uncertain. A small group of nobles favoured this solution, and sought a candidate strong enough to maintain his crown. The duke of Savoy expressed an interest both in the Bohemian kingship and in the imperial succession. His Catholicism and military weakness militated against him. The Lutheran elector of Saxony would have been the favourite candidate, but he was tied to the Habsburg by sentiment, and he abhorred rebellion against constituted authority. He would certainly have refused the offer. Finally, there was the youthful Frederick V, Elector Palatine of the Rhine. Much seemed to be in his favour.[1] As head of the Protestant Union, he could presumably enlist German support. As the son-in-law of James I, he could hope for funds and armies from England. The Dutch should favour him, for he would oppose their greatest enemies, the Habsburgs. As for Frederick himself, he was not a declared candidate for the Bohemian throne. Sincerely concerned for the Protestant cause in Bohemia, he wished only to aid the rebels so that they could negotiate from strength. For this reason he sponsored Mansfeld's army, and appealed to the duke of Savoy for further support. Also he sought, unsuccessfully, to place the Protestant Union on a war footing.

The chief proponent of Frederick's candidature was Prince Christian of Anhalt, his most trusted adviser, and administrator of the Upper Palatinate. Christian and his friends, the princes of Ansbach, Württemberg and Baden-Durlach, and Camerarius, Frederick's chancellor, were convinced that there was a papal-Habsburg plot to conquer Europe in the name of the Catholic Church. Bohemia was but the latest proof of this design. To meet the threat it was necessary to form a great coalition of German Protestant states, England and the Dutch Netherlands. France, as the hereditary Habsburg foe, was also expected to join, even though it was a Catholic state. To obtain the Bohemian crown for Frederick would not only deprive the Habsburg of a prosperous province and the electoral vote, but would strike a decisive blow for Protestantism against the Catholic menace. While a few Bohemian leaders and Frederick's chief adviser were secretly planning his future, Frederick does not seem to have been informed until November. His first reaction to the proposal was surprise and fearful hesitation. In a letter to the Bohemians he promised to support their cause, yet modestly disclaimed any desire for the crown. At the same time he thought it necessary to prepare for possible eventualities, and particularly to sound out England and the Dutch.

---

[1] For a good account of Frederick V and his advisers during the period of the Bohemian crisis, see J. G. Weiss, 'Die Vorgeschichte des bömischen Abenteuers Friedrichs V. von der Pfalz,' in *Zeitschrift für die Geschichte des Oberrheins*, New Series, Vol. 53 (1939–40), pp. 383–492.

The death of the Emperor Matthias on 20 March 1619 brought the related problems of the Bohemian and imperial crowns to a head. The extremist party in Prague urged the deposition of Ferdinand and the election of a new king, and an electoral meeting for the election of an emperor was called for July. Ferdinand had no doubt of the issue. Fortified by religious conviction strengthened by Jesuit schooling, he was certain of his hereditary right to the Bohemian throne, of his election as emperor, and of his mission to Catholicize his subjects. Ferdinand's calm assurance was put to severe test immediately after the death of Matthias. Silesia had already joined the Bohemians. Now Moravia, Lusatia and Upper Austria revolted against their Habsburg overlord. In June, Thurn led his army to the very gates of Vienna where Ferdinand was in residence, and he was saved only at the last moment by the arrival of a small cavalry force under the command of his brother Leopold. Further reinforcements for Ferdinand, and frantic calls from Prague that the imperial armies in Bohemia were being strengthened, forced Thurn to withdraw. In any case, he was not prepared to conduct a siege. Ferdinand's position was further improved by Mansfeld's defeat on 10 June near the village of Sablat, where all but fifteen of his 3,000 men were killed or captured. It was the first Habsburg victory.

Meantime, while Frederick and Anhalt had won some German support for the Bohemian cause at the Protestant Union's June meeting at Heilbronn, it was not sufficient to influence the course of events. A loan was made to Bohemia, and an army of 15,000 men was to be raised to protect the members of the union, and to prevent the passage of troops going to the aid of Ferdinand. Repeated attempts to win English support failed, for King James, although expressing sympathy for the Bohemian Protestants, made it clear that his chief interest was to keep the peace. As for his son-in-law's interest in the Bohemian throne, it would be necessary first of all to determine whether the kingdom was indeed elective.

Under these circumstances, favourable for Ferdinand, unfavourable for Frederick, the two elections were held almost simultaneously. On 28 August, Ferdinand II was chosen as emperor at the electoral meeting held in Frankfurt. Following his instructions, the Palatine delegate first made the useless gesture of voting for Duke Maximilian of Bavaria, and then made the election unanimous for Ferdinand.

When Frederick heard that the Bohemian estates had finally determined to dethrone their king, he said to Anhalt: 'I never thought that it would come to this. This is a risky business; now I believe that the Bohemians will want to elect a new King. My God! If they elect me, what should I do?' To which Anhalt replied: 'My lord, in such a case time will bring advice!'[1] Indeed, Anhalt, much as he wished to make his master a king, now recoiled from precipitous action. It would be necessary first to make

---

[1] Weiss, 'Die Vorgeschichte . . .', *Zeitschrift für die Geschichte des Oberrheins*, p. 456.

certain of adequate support, especially from England. An ambassador was therefore again despatched to James to find out if he would assist his son-in-law in the case that he accepted the Bohemian crown. There was little time to bring advice, for on 26 August, two days before Ferdinand's election as emperor, the Bohemian estates deposed him as king, and elected Frederick almost unanimously.

Frederick was faced with a fateful decision. He first wrote to his ambassador in England that he would wait for his father-in-law's answer before deciding. He then attended a meeting of the Protestant Union at Rothenburg whose members wished him luck, though only three princes, Ansbach, Baden-Durlach and Anhalt, advised acceptance of the crown. Towards the end of September Frederick called upon his council for advice. The councillors had already sent Frederick a memorial, listing the reasons for and against acceptance. There were fourteen points against and six in favour, and certainly the negative ones are the most impressive. In brief, the councillors warned that the Bohemian venture was beyond the resources of the Palatinate, that it could not succeed without aid from England and the Dutch, and that their assistance must be assured before an answer could be given to the Bohemians. In the discussions at the council table, most of the members insisted that it was necessary at least to await the king of England's reply. Since this had been Frederick's original position, the councillors must have been shocked and surprised to find that Frederick had already made up his mind. He declared that he had been called by God to rule Bohemia, and that he would accept the crown in God's name. There can be little doubt that Frederick sincerely believed that he was God's instrument to further the cause of Protestantism. It is equally true that his decision was foolhardy. Without outside assistance the Bohemians would be conquered by Spanish or imperial arms. Moreover, intervention by Frederick without military support from foreign powers could only invite Spanish invasion of the Palatinate, and the interference of German princes, particularly of the duke of Bavaria, who could benefit by Frederick's downfall. The Holy Roman Empire was in delicate equilibrium, and any aggressive move made by a German prince would upset the balance. Frederick made the first move, and transformed a rebellion in Bohemia into a German, and inevitably, into an international war.

The new king of Bohemia and his charming, vivacious wife Elizabeth had no such forebodings when they made their triumphant entry into Prague on the last day of October 1619. As hopes for outside aid melted away, there was, however, little cause for rejoicing. The Protestant Union promised to protect the Palatinate, but would not be drawn into the Bohemian venture. The elector of Saxony refused to attend a meeting of Protestant German princes suggested by Anhalt. More important still was the attitude of foreign powers who were counted upon for assistance.

King James, peace-loving, shocked by rebellion, and pursuing a Spanish marriage for his heir, refused to support his son-in-law. Instead, he informed the sovereigns of Europe that he had had no previous knowledge of Frederick's election, nor would he recognize it. It was his intention, he announced, to join with the king of France 'to pacify the present broils that are on foot in Germany'. The Dutch, much as they feared a Spanish invasion of the Palatinate, felt that they could not protect it without support from England and the Protestant Union. The Scandinavian powers, although sympathetic, were busy with their own concerns: Christian IV of Denmark in a commercial dispute with Hamburg, Gustavus Adolphus of Sweden in the perennial conflict with Poland. The duke of Savoy, now that he had been cheated, or so he pretended, of both the Bohemian and imperial crowns, withdrew his support of Mansfeld. Another prince, Bethlen Gabor of Transylvania, had taken advantage of Ferdinand's difficulties, invaded Hungary, and even reached Vienna, when a revolt in his own lands forced a retreat. It might have been expected that France would oppose the Habsburgs; but Richelieu was not yet in control, and the ministers of Louis XIII thought it sufficient to send an embassy to arrange an armistice between the Catholic League and the Protestant Union. This came to pass at Ulm on 3 July 1620, when each party agreed to respect the territories of the other. The French believed that the agreement would ensure the protection of the Palatinate by the union, but in this belief they were to be sadly mistaken.

While Frederick was steadily losing ground, Ferdinand was gaining in strength. On 8 October 1619, the day before Frederick left Heidelberg for Prague, Duke Maximilian of Bavaria signed an agreement with the emperor. Of all the German princes, Maximilian was the ablest. Like Ferdinand, he was a pupil of the Jesuits and a devoted son of the church. Unlike Ferdinand, he was a hardworking administrator and possessor of, the only efficient German army. His position as leader of the Catholic League was, therefore, much more than a formality. To win his support, Ferdinand promised Maximilian full control of the armies which were to quell the Bohemian revolt, the possession of conquered lands as a pledge for his expenses, and Frederick's electoral title. In his own eyes, Maximilian was assisting his overlord to put down a revolt of heretical subjects. It can also be argued that he seized this opportunity to deprive a Calvinist prince of an electoral title; but apart from the fact that the emperor had no right to make him the promise of the electorate, this demand was certain to aggravate the German political situation when it became known.

Another recruit to the imperial cause was John George of Saxony. Religious considerations here too played a role for, as a fanatical Lutheran, John George hated the elevation of a Calvinistic prince in Bohemia. He also stipulated that as the price of his help, the emperor should guarantee Lutheranism in Bohemia and the secularized church lands in the two

Saxon Circles. Not forgetting himself, John George demanded the province of Lusatia in payment for his help.

While the net was being drawn around Frederick in Bohemia, his patrimony was in the greatest danger. The rulers of the Spanish Netherlands, the Habsburg Archduke Albert and his wife, the Spanish Infanta Isabella (known collectively as 'the Archdukes') were forced by Madrid reluctantly to plan the reconquest of the Dutch, and a well-trained army under the capable General Spinola was preparing to take the offensive. In these preparations the Palatinate played an important part, for it was the one substantial strip of territory blocking the march of troops from the Spanish-held lands in northern Italy to the Netherlands. The chief obstacle to an attack on the Palatinate would be English support for Frederick, and English neutrality was now assured by the Spanish ambassador in London, Count Gondomar, whose influence over King James was notorious. As soon as Gondomar informed Madrid of his success, Spinola was given his marching orders. In September 1621 he crossed the Rhine. The only opposition in the Palatinate was a volunteer army of 2,000 Englishmen under the command of the experienced soldier Sir Horace Vere, and a small force from the Protestant Union which soon withdrew its support.

Meantime, Frederick's Bohemian venture was coming to an end. Maximilian of Bavaria brought into the field the polyglot mercenary army of the Catholic League commanded by the able Count Tilly, a Fleming whose monkish character, according to his enemies, was marred only by an inordinate love of sweetmeats. In July 1620 the army crossed into Austria, devastated the countryside, and crushed the resistance of the anti-Habsburg Austrian Estates. Joined with an imperial force, the troops of the Catholic League invaded Bohemia at the end of September, and a few days later the elector of Saxony swept into Lusatia. Outnumbered, Mansfeld was forced to remain inactive in Pilsen, while Tilly's armies, although severely reduced by disease, marched toward Prague.

Early on the morning of 8 November 1620 Christian of Anhalt, in command of the Bohemian army numbering about 16,000, took a stand on the White Hill, a plateau overlooking the city. The Bohemians had the advantage of position and, though inferior in numbers, might have repulsed the enemy, which opened a surprise attack on the hill as the sun cleared the early morning mist. But, mutinous for lack of pay, Anhalt's conscripts were overwhelmed by better-trained and well-led soldiers, and those who survived fled back towards the city. Here, Frederick and his queen were entertaining two English ambassadors, convinced that the enemy was too weak to attack. The burghers, who had lost all confidence in the new government, closed the gates on the fleeing soldiers, which made impossible any defence of the city. Frederick, on Anhalt's advice, escaped with his family, and made his way to Brandenburg. He was never again to see either of his capitals, Heidelberg or Prague. The fugitive monarch was henceforth known as the 'Winter King', an epithet bestowed by Jesuits who prophesied that his reign would last only a winter —the rule of an additional summer made no practical difference.

After the Battle of the White Hill, Prague was given over to the victorious soldiers who were permitted to pillage the 'rebels'. On 21 June 1621, after summary trials, twenty-seven leaders of the revolt were executed. Only a few escaped, most noteworthy being Christian of Anhalt, who fled to Sweden and then made his abject peace with the emperor; and Count Thurn, who spent many years of exile in vain intrigues against the victorious Habsburg. The landed estates of nobles and knights accused of rebellion were confiscated, and sold or presented by the emperor to his generals and to his favourite officials. Thus, nearly one-half the land of the kingdom changed hands, and a foreign nobility, German, Austrian, Italian and Spanish, supplanted the old, with the exception of a few native Catholic families who vastly increased their holdings. The wealth of the towns declined when the government devalued the currency. The peasants, already the chief sufferers at the hands of marauding soldiers, were ground down by ever-increasing services demanded by their aristocratic landowners. Ferdinand was pleased with the results of his victory. The work of Count Lobkowitz was completed by the establishment of a hereditary monarchy and the destruction of an independent nobility. The Letter of Majesty was repudiated, the Jesuits were recalled, and the process of forced re-Catholicization was so successful that Protestantism was permanently uprooted not only in Bohemia but in Austria, Moravia and Silesia. Lusatia, in the hands of the elector of Saxony, alone escaped.

With the conquest of Bohemia, and the Palatinate at the mercy of Spinola's troops, it might be thought that the war would end. But the ambitions of the chief actors in the political drama made any peaceful solution impossible. Frederick stubbornly refused to make a formal submission to the emperor, and was heartened by a promise of support from Prince Maurice, the Dutch leader, who gave the Palatine family refuge at the Hague. The emperor, in order to repossess Upper Austria, held in pawn by Maximilian of Bavaria for his war expenses, was prepared to hand over Palatine lands to the duke. Besides, Ferdinand had promised him the electorate. As a first step, Frederick was put to the ban. After satisfying his chief German ally, Ferdinand could look forward to the continuation of hostilities which would lead to the spread of his faith and of his power in the empire.

The emperor's ambitions were furthered by the accession of Philip IV on the death of his father, Philip III, in March 1621. The Spanish government was bankrupt and corrupt, while a preposterous system of taxation and a ruinous fiscal policy stifled the country's economic activities. Nevertheless, during the next twenty years the Count of Olivares, Philip IV's chief adviser, vigorously pursued the traditional Spanish policies: the suppression of heresy and the furtherance of Habsburg hegemony.

The Protestant Union, frightened by Spinola's troops, dissolved in May 1621, and such opposition as remained played into the hands of Spain, the emperor and the duke of Bavaria. After the Battle of the White Hill, Mansfeld moved his troops from Bohemia into the neighbouring Upper Palatinate, and planned an invasion of the lost kingdom in Frederick's name. Maximilian of Bavaria, well satisfied with the emperor's secret promises, marched his army to meet Mansfeld, and on 2 October 1621, in return for a large bribe, extracted an agreement from the *condottiere* that he would cease to fight for Frederick. Mansfeld callously broke his word, and a fortnight later appeared with his army in the Lower Palatinate, where the English troops were holding out in three beleaguered towns. Mansfeld's treachery gave Maximilian an excuse to despatch his troops under Tilly's command to the Lower Palatinate. Mansfeld withdrew to Alsace, where his troops spread typhus and devastated the countryside for food and booty.

Two more princes appeared to perpetuate the war, the Margrave George Frederick of Baden-Durlach and Prince Christian of Brunswick. The margrave, a man in his sixties, was a devout Lutheran who had read through the Bible fifty-eight times, and had also composed a great compilation of his readings in military history. He had been one of the few princes of the Protestant Union who advocated strong military measures in defence of the Protestant cause. Now his little principality was endangered by the presence of Spanish troops in the neighbouring Palatinate, and he determined to take action. In the autumn of 1621 he raised an army of 11,000 men. Simultaneously Christian of Brunswick gathered a force of about the same strength. Five years before, at the age of eighteen, he had been installed as administrator of the important northern bishopric of Halberstädt through the influence of his brother, the reigning duke of Brunswick-Wolfenbüttel. Hatred of Catholics and love of warfare were his passions, and posing as a knight-errant, he wore in his hat the glove of his cousin, Elizabeth of Bohemia. He vowed that he would regain the Palatinate for her. Christian's high spirits and dashing cavalry charges soon won for him the title of the 'mad Halberstädter'.

If the three armies of Mansfeld, Baden and Brunswick could have been joined they would have created a serious menace to the troops of Tilly and the Spaniards. Frederick, with his usual optimism, joined Mansfeld, now back in the Palatinate; but the three commanders did not succeed in restoring his hereditary lands. George Frederick was defeated by Tilly and the Spanish general Cordoba while attempting to cross the Neckar at Wimpfen on 6 May 1622, and the shattered margrave gave up in despair. Christian, bringing sorely needed money extracted from bishoprics and villages, was intercepted at Höchst on the Main (20 June). In spite of severe losses he managed to join Mansfeld; but now there was a change of plans. Mansfeld refused to risk his army in the face of a stronger enemy, and after first retreating into Alsace and then Lorraine, induced Christian to march north with him to assist the hard-pressed Dutch. Since the end of the Twelve Year Truce in April 1621, Prince Maurice could do no more than carry on defensive warfare, and he was no doubt pleased when the arrival of the riff-raff Mansfeld–Brunswick army in October 1622 enabled him to save the fortress of Bergen-op-Zoom from capture.

Frederick, sorely disappointed by the failure of his military adventure and sickened by the burning of villages and the pillage of peasantry, had left the army during the retreat into Alsace. Making his way first to Sedan for a visit with his uncle, the duke of Bouillon, and then back to The Hague, Frederick heard of the subjugation of his native land by Spain and Bavaria. Heidelberg fell in September 1622, Sir Horace Vere surrendered Mannheim in November, and the last of the English troops marched out of Frankenthal in April 1623. Warfare and disease had ravaged the once prosperous land. As the English ambassador wrote from besieged Frankenthal in 1622: 'It grieves me to behold the waste and ruin of so many towns, boroughs and villages which were lately rich and prosperous, and to hear of the intolerable oppression and rapine committed upon the poor people that are left, by the soldiers as well of our own army as that of the enemies.'[1] Adding to this material misery, Maximilian was now free to expel Protestant ministers, and to introduce Catholic worship in the churches. As a final indignity, he shipped the valuable library of Heidelberg's university to the Vatican where most of it remains to this day.

Maximilian needed only the title of elector to make his victory complete, and the emperor was ready to fulfil his promise. Ferdinand first called an advisory council of princes. The electors, with the addition of an archbishop, a bishop, the duke of Bavaria and three Protestant princes, were invited to attend the meeting at Regensburg. Of the Protestants, only the landgrave of Hesse-Darmstadt appeared in person, and then only to further his claim to a disputed territory. The electors of Saxony and Brandenburg, shocked by the suppression of Protestantism in the Austrian hereditary lands, expressed their disapproval by sending representatives. Only the elector of Cologne, Maximilian's brother, and of course Maximilian advocated the transference of Frederick's electorate. Despite the almost unanimous opposition of his advisers, Ferdinand had his way, and on 25 February 1623 Maximilian was solemnly invested as an elector of the Holy Roman Empire. Two concessions of little practical value were

[1] Chichester to Calvert, 10/20 July 1622. Public Record Office, S.P. German States, XXVI, f. 75.

made: Maximilian was to hold the electorate for life, and at his death other claimants to the title, including Frederick's heirs, would be considered. The Regensburg meeting was a victory for Maximilian; but it was an even greater victory for Ferdinand, whose power, based on the army of the Catholic League, could not be contested.

With the submission of Bohemia and the hereditary lands to the emperor, and the subjugation of the Palatinate by Spain and Bavaria, there was again the possibility that the German war could come to an end. But peace faded with the growing danger that war would engulf northern Protestant Germany, where important secularized church lands were at stake. As early as 1620, in order to win the support of the elector of Saxony in the Bohemian war, the Catholic League and the emperor had agreed not to interfere with these lands as long as their possessors remained loyal to the emperor. This agreement of Mülhausen was now in jeopardy. In 1623 the Lower Saxon Circle was invaded by Tilly in pursuit of Christian of Brunswick. The princes of the circle, after a half-hearted attempt to defend themselves, submitted to this breach of their neutrality. After the defeat of the 'mad Halberstädter' at Stadtlohn (6 August), Tilly's troops remained quartered in the southern portion of the circle.

The secularized lands were endangered not only by direct attack. Overawed by the proximity of Tilly's troops, the chapter of Osnabrück in Westphalia, hitherto Protestant, elected a Catholic as bishop, the brother moreover of Maximilian's chief councillor. The emperor already had his eye on the bishoprics of Halberstadt and Magdeburg for his second son, sees claimed also by a son of Christian IV of Denmark. When Christian approached the emperor to sanction his son's claim to Halberstadt, he was not only rebuffed. Relying on the letter of the law, Ferdinand demanded the return to the Roman Catholic church of certain churches, lands and cloisters secularized since 1552. Among them was a church in the bishopric of Halberstadt.

Northern Germany was defenceless, a prey to the emperor's demands which could be enforced by Tilly's army.

Except for the Dutch, the year 1624 opened with armed opposition to the Habsburgs at a standstill. This was only a lull, for preparations were under way to challenge the successes of emperor, Spain and Catholic League.

In France, the king's ministers were reversing a pro-Spanish policy. The immediate issue was control of the Valtelline, the strategic valley which furnished the passageway for Spanish troops and money from northern Italy to both Austria and the Netherlands. The valley was inhabited by Catholic communities over which suzerainty was claimed by the Protestant League of the Grisons. In 1620, after a bloody revolt of the Catholic Valtelliners against the Grisons, Spain stepped in as protector of her co-religionists, and took control of the all-important pass. Two attempts by the Grisons in 1622 to recover the valley ended in disaster. They were forced to renounce their suzerainty over the Valtelline in favour of Spain, and a portion of the Grisons was seized by Austria.

Alarmed by these Austro-Spanish victories, France signed a treaty with Venice and Savoy in February 1623 for the recovery of the Valtelline. Pope Gregory XV, equally alarmed by the prospect of war spreading in Italy, agreed to sequester the disputed territory and despatched papal troops to take over the fortified places. The French agreed to this arrangement on condition that the sequestration should come to an end in four months' time, and that the forts should be razed. Gregory XV died in July 1623 and was succeeded by Urban VIII. The new pope. although a staunch opponent of Habsburg dominance, could not, while under Spanish pressure, remove his troops on the expiration of the four-months' period. The Valtelline, to all intents and purposes, still remained under Spanish control.

Even more startling reversals of French foreign policy were a treaty with the Dutch signed on 10 June 1624, and the negotiations for a marriage between Henrietta Maria, the king's sister, and Charles, heir to the English throne.

Cardinal Richelieu, who had been admitted to the king's council in April 1624 and who became chief minister in August, subscribed fully to the anti-Habsburg policy which he inherited. Although a more pious Catholic than Henri IV, he was a true disciple of the great king. The cardinal's aims were simple: unity within the state, and strengthening the state to combat the encirclement of France by Spain. Any means were admissible to accomplish the ends, and Protestant allies were as acceptable as Catholic. When asked his advice about the Dutch alliance he replied that it would be understood in Rome, for 'in Rome, more than in any other place in the world, affairs are judged as much by the criteria of power and interest as by ecclesiastical argument'.[1] But the immediate objective was still the Valtelline, which Richelieu considered 'importantissime'.[2] In July 1624, he made an agreement with Savoy and Venice to intervene.

In England, too, an aggressive foreign policy supplanted pacific negotiations. King James turned over the making of policy to his favourite, the duke of Buckingham, a man with grandiose plans, but with mediocre ability to put them into execution. The powerful favourite and his intimate friend Prince Charles, soon to begin his unfortunate reign, were deeply chagrined by the failure of the Spanish marriage plan. It was not only a personal affront; the possibility of recovering the Palatinate with Spanish aid was for ever gone, and France was therefore to take the

[1] J. H. Mariejol, in E. Lavisse, *Histoire de France, depuis les origines jusqu'à la revolution* (1911), VI, pt II, p. 227.
[2] G. Pagès, *La Guerre de Trente Ans* (1939), p. 106.

place of Spain both in marriage and in the reconquest of the lost land. Additional allies were of course needed. Besides the Dutch, who could be relied upon, it was proposed to bring Denmark, Sweden, Venice, Savoy and German princes into the great anti-Habsburg coalition. For this purpose ambassadors were despatched to the continent in the spring of 1624.

The hope of cementing a firm Anglo-French alliance to regain the Palatinate by a marriage alliance proved to be a bitter disappointment. France was interested in Italy, England in Germany, and the result of this divergence is illustrated by the ill-fated Mansfeld expedition.

In the spring and summer of 1624, Mansfeld, temporarily without an army, travelled back and forth between France, England, and the United Provinces seeking an employer. Finally, in November, James I, spurred on by Buckingham, gave his consent to levy 12,000 conscripts for Mansfeld, and agreed to pay £20,000 monthly for their upkeep. The French promised 2,000 cavalry. But when the news arrived that a French army had expelled the papal troops from the Valtelline, Richelieu lost interest in the expedition. It was suggested that Mansfeld be used for the relief of Breda, besieged by Spinola's troops. He would not, however, be permitted to land in France, for that would involve open war with Spain. Richelieu was not yet prepared for this drastic step, and would not be for many years. James I, on the other hand, to his dying day refused permission to use Mansfeld's army against Spain for the relief of Breda. When the troops finally arrived on the Dutch coast in February 1625, Prince Maurice at first refused them permission to land. Cooped up in the cold ships, eating foul food, and drinking contaminated water, thousands died and the bodies washed ashore spread pestilence throughout Brabant. Not more than 7,000 men disembarked, and when the death of King James released them from the prohibition to assist in the relief of Breda, it was too late. The city fell on 25 May, a great Spanish victory made memorable by the celebrated canvas of Velasquez. The Mansfeld expedition was a sorry prelude to a coalition intended to contain Habsburg ambitions.

A Huguenot revolt in January 1625 made French co-operation even more remote, and now the success of the anti-Habsburg league depended on the English negotiations with Denmark, Sweden and the German Protestant princes.

The king of Denmark, Christian IV, and the king of Sweden, Gustavus Adolphus, had certain traits in common. Both were energetic, physically vigorous, brave, and ambitious for the extension of the territory and power of their states. Both had hitherto been successful in foreign affairs. Christian maintained a strong position in the western Baltic by control of the Sound where he collected lucrative tolls, and besides held secularized bishoprics, through his sons, in Germany. Gustavus Adolphus by wars against Poland and Russia had won territories in the eastern Baltic.

Both were firm Lutherans, and wished to act as the saviours of German Protestantism. Here the resemblances end. In military affairs the king of Sweden was a genius, the king of Denmark a talented amateur. Gustavus Adolphus had built a strong native army. Christian had a militia which could be used only for home defence, and he would be forced to rely upon foreign mercenaries in an offensive war. Above all, Gustavus Adolphus was that rare combination of man of action and careful planner, while Christian's ambitions were not matched by the ability to devise means for their accomplishment.

The difference between the two monarchs is clearly revealed in the plans presented to England for the invasion of Germany. Gustavus insisted that an army of 50,000 men would be required, of which he would furnish 16,000, the remainder to be provided by his allies. To guard against possible attack from Denmark or Poland he asked for a fleet of seventeen vessels to be added to eight of his own. As bases for the disembarkation of troops and for magazines of munitions and food, the cities of Wismar and Bremen should be placed at his disposal. England, Sweden, and the allied German princes were each to pay one-third of the expenses of the war; but the conduct of the war must be entirely under his control. Nor would Gustavus stir a step until four months' pay was in his hands. Finally, he gave warning that if his offer were not acceptable he was resolved to renew the war with Poland, which was temporarily suspended by a truce. No wonder that James, when confronted by the Swedish demands in January 1625, exclaimed: 'I am not so great and rich a prince as to be able to do so much. I am only the king of two poor little islands!'[1] Christian of Denmark's plan was much more to his taste.

When Christian was first approached in July 1624 he gave a cautious reply, and remarked that one could never be assured that England wished to do anything until one had seen an English army in the heart of Germany. Late in January 1625, after much hesitation, Christian proposed that an army of 30,000 should be raised. England's contribution would be 6,000 foot and 1,000 horse at a cost of £170,000 or £180,000 a year. The fact that Christian, unlike his Swedish competitor, did not demand payment in advance must have weighed heavily in his favour. On the last day of February, James accepted the Danish offer. Gustavus, when asked what he would do if the leadership of the projected army were given to another, replied: 'Nothing.' At the expiration of the truce, he renewed his war against Poland.

Christian had good reasons for entering the war. His son had in 1623 been elected bishop of Verden, and he sought to gain for him in addition the wealthy sees of Halberstadt, Osnabrück, Paderborn, and Bremen. The archbishopric of Bremen alone would give control of the mouths of the Elbe and Weser rivers. These grandiose plans would be upset if Tilly

[1] S. R. Gardiner, *History of England*, Vol. v, pp. 297–8.

conquered the Lower Saxon Circle, and made the bishoprics secure for the Catholic church. The chief influence in the king of Denmark's decision was, however, the possible intervention of Gustavus Adolphus. To permit Sweden to take the leadership in defence of the threatened north German lands would have meant the loss to Denmark of its dominant position in the western Baltic. Yet to plunge into war without adequate military and financial support was as foolhardy as Frederick's acceptance of the Bohemian throne. English assurances, as Christian himself had said, were surely not enough; nor were 30,000 soldiers sufficient. He had high hopes of French support, but no definite agreement had been reached.

Christian was soon to see the consequences of his rash decision. The death of King James in April 1625 speeded the conclusion of the Anglo-Danish alliance, and Charles I promised Christian £30,000 monthly until the English army was sent to Germany. A first payment of £46,000 proved also to be the last, for Parliament refused to grant the necessary funds. Christian was, to be sure, elected head of the Lower Saxon Circle. With the assistance of Mansfeld, Christian of Brunswick and Duke Ernest of Saxe-Weimar, he recruited about 34,000 men. But the plan for the great anti-Habsburg league failed miserably. Gustavus Adolphus had withdrawn, and with him his brother-in-law, the elector of Brandenburg, who had hitherto been willing to lend his support. The elector of Saxony categorically refused to fight against the emperor. Even members of the Lower Saxon Circle continued negotiations with the emperor in the hope of maintaining their neutrality. The Treaty of The Hague signed on 9 December 1625, by England, Denmark and the United Provinces was the sole result of the feverish attempts to form a league of all Habsburg enemies, both Catholic and Protestant. Most disappointing was the failure of French support. A serious Huguenot revolt forced Richelieu to withdraw his troops from the Valtelline, and the treaty of Monzon signed in May 1626 reopened the valley to Spain.

While Christian's hopes were failing, his enemy's strength was increasing. For the first time, a large well-equipped army raised in the name of the emperor appeared in the field. The commander was Albrecht von Waldstein, commonly known as Wallenstein. So many books have been written about him that it is difficult to estimate his aims and achievements. He seems to have been a mass of contradictions: a loyal servant of the emperor and a traitor, a soldier who sought peace, a Bohemian patriot and a good German, a man of powerful will and ambition with strange periods of inactivity. He showed all these characteristics at one time or another in the course of his spectacular career.

Wallenstein came of a noble Bohemian family, was educated first as a Protestant, then by the Jesuits, and ended by believing in astrology and in himself. Both a professional soldier and an enterprising businessman, Wallenstein took full advantage of the Bohemian revolt. He served the emperor and at the same time became the greatest landowner and probably the wealthiest man in the kingdom. Military success brought credit with bankers who loaned money for the purchase of land, some of them the confiscated estates of the Bohemian nobility. With increasing wealth, Wallenstein made loans to the emperor, always in financial distress, and Ferdinand in turn repaid him in lands and dignities. By 1623 Wallenstein possessed a block of territory comprising some 2,000 square miles in the north-east corner of Bohemia. He was appointed governor of the kingdom, quartermaster-general of the troops, and created prince of Friedland.

In the spring of 1625, Wallenstein offered not only to raise an imperial force of 20,000 men, but undertook to advance the money necessary to recruit the army. The offer was accepted, and in July he was made commander-in-chief of all imperial forces and raised to the dignity of duke, the highest title in the emperor's gift. In order to equip, pay and feed his army, Wallenstein formed what amounted to a partnership with Hans de Witte, the great international banker and merchant of Prague.[1] De Witte advanced the needed money, and acted as supply agent and shipper for military supplies. The farms of the Friedland duchy were one of the chief sources for provisioning the army. The greatest difficulty was financial. Little could be obtained from the emperor, and Wallenstein therefore resorted to 'contributions' for the repayment of de Witte's loans and of his own outlays. 'Contributions' was the euphemistic term applied to the forced payments exacted from townsmen and peasants by the colonels of the invading army. Judged by imperial law, these forced contributions were clearly illegal; but at least prompt pay made less likely the customary atrocious activities of the soldiery. This army was remarkable in another respect: officers were appointed and promoted for merit, and not according to social rank or religious faith. Many were indeed Protestants.

On 28 July 1625, three days after Wallenstein received his final commission, Tilly crossed the Weser 'in the name of God and His Holy Mother'. This marks the beginning of the Danish war. The first opposition came from the enraged Brunswick peasantry and from hostile towns which closed their gates on the invading army. In return, the maddened soldiers took vengeance by plundering and burning towns and villages, and murdering helpless civilians. Even Tilly, forgetful of his motto, remarked that the peasants deserved these horrors. There were no military encounters. Christian of Denmark was seriously injured by a fall from the ramparts of Hameln and his army withdrew northwards to Verden. Tilly did not feel strong enough to pursue.

Early in September Wallenstein marched his army of 20,000 men out

[1] For a detailed study of de Witte's relations with Wallenstein see A. Ernstberger, 'Hans de Witte, Finanzmann Wallansteins', *Vierteljahrschrift für Sozial- und Wirtschaftsgeschichte*, Suppl. 38 (1954).

of Bohemia. He had no intention of joining Tilly in an attack on the Danish army. His immediate objective was the occupation of the bishoprics of Halberstadt and Magdeburg, earmarked for the fourteen-year-old son of the emperor. Here winter quarters were set up for the raw recruits, while the colonels collected huge contributions from the near-by cities. As a defensive measure, Wallenstein fortified the Dessau bridge on the Elbe to prevent Mansfeld or the duke of Brunswick from crossing into Silesia.

There was nothing to fear from Brunswick, who failed to raise an adequate army. Diseased in body and dejected, the ferocious chivalric prince died at the early age of twenty-eight. But Wallenstein had correctly guessed Mansfeld's intentions. He appeared at the head of 12,000 men to storm the bridge of Dessau, and Wallenstein rushed his best troops to meet the attack. On 25 April 1626 Mansfeld was repulsed with the loss of one-third of his troops and retreated into neutral Brandenburg. In July he was again on the move, to join Bethlen Gabor of Transylvania who was threatening to make one of his periodic attacks on the emperor. Wallenstein went into pursuit leaving behind eight regiments to strengthen Tilly. This was indeed necessary, for Christian of Denmark planned to attack the army of the Catholic League in Wallenstein's absence. Instead, because of the Wallenstein reinforcements, the king was now forced to retreat northwards. On 27 August, Tilly caught up with him at the village of Lutter. The Danish army was routed in spite of Christian's reckless courage, and its remnants took refuge in Stade near the estuary of the Elbe.

Meantime, Wallenstein with an army of 30,000 followed Mansfeld into Hungary where he joined Bethlen Gabor. Neither the wily prince of Transylvania nor Wallenstein was anxious for battle, and after skirmishes a truce was arranged in October. It had not been a glorious campaign. Hundreds of miles from his base of supplies, the imperial commander-in-chief had lost half of his army by disease, starvation and desertion. The chief objective had, however, been achieved: the career of Mansfeld was at an end. Bethlen Gabor had no further use for him, and the unlucky soldier of fortune set out on his last journey, perhaps with Venice as his goal. He fell ill, and on 25 November died in the hills near Serajevo.

Step by step the emperor and the elector of Bavaria suppressed the little resistance that opposed them, and consolidated their gains. In 1626 a fierce peasant uprising in Upper Austria against Bavarian and Catholic rule was ruthlessly suppressed. The following year Ferdinand promulgated a new constitution for Bohemia which made the monarchy hereditary and gave him the power of all official appointments. Protestants in the kingdom had the choice of conversion or exile. Wallenstein dispersed the last of Mansfeld's troops in Silesia, and in 1627 only the king of Denmark was still in arms.

Christian's position after the battle of Lutter was desperate. England promised an army of 10,000 men, which diminished to about half that number. The troops were to be paid by the pawning of a royal jewel valued at £100,000, a sum which was never realized, instead of the £600,000 owed by the treaty of The Hague. 'Let God and the world judge', the king wrote to England, 'whether this be answerable or Christian-like dealing.'[1]

In fact, just at the time when the king of Denmark's need was greatest, Buckingham's inept foreign policy threw France into alliance with Spain against England. The breach with France, and Buckingham's unsuccessful attempt to relieve the Huguenots at La Rochelle in the summer of 1627, made it impossible for England to support Christian.

When Tilly and Wallenstein joined forces on the Elbe in September 1627, the Danish forces were vastly outnumbered. The only important battle was fought at Heiligenhafen on 23 September, where the imperialists defeated an 8,000-man army commanded by the margrave of Baden-Durlach. Christian fled to Holstein and in October crossed over to the island of Fünen. Holstein, Schleswig and Jutland were overrun by the enemy, and the king retained only his island possessions and three fortified towns on the mainland.

In the flush of victory, Wallenstein thought of a great crusade against the Turks; but a more immediate objective claimed his attention: the control of the northern seas. As early as 1624, Spain's chief minister, Olivares, had proposed a treaty with the Hanseatic cities. In return for trade concessions in the Indies, the cities would serve as Habsburg naval bases. The project was actively discussed in 1626, and now with Denmark's defeat, it was revived. Meanwhile, Wallenstein extended his conquests on the Baltic coast. Mecklenburg was occupied, and the native dukes expelled from their territory. Pomerania was next in line, and its ruling prince was forced to admit imperial troops. In April 1628 Wallenstein could add to his titles, General of the North and Baltic Seas [*General der ozeanischen und baltischen Meeres*]. Unexpected opposition, however, came from the Hanseatic cities. They were suspicious of Habsburg, especially of Spanish, domination, and refused to furnish the fleet essential for a general of the seas. Wismar was seized; but this was not enough, for Wallenstein realized that the chief obstacle to the control of the Baltic would come from Sweden. It was therefore necessary to secure the whole of the Pomeranian coast, and here the port of Stralsund refused to submit to imperial occupation.

Gustavus Adolphus had watched Denmark's defeat with great anxiety. While still deeply engaged in the war against Poland, it was also clearly evident to the king that the spread of imperial power in north Germany

[1] 'Statement by the King of Denmark', 26 February/8 March 1627, Public Record Office State Papers Denmark, VIII, f. 14.

threatened both Sweden's security and the very existence of German Protestantism. The old rivalry with Denmark was no longer an issue, and on 8 May 1628 Gustavus Adolphus signed a three-year alliance with Christian IV. It was none too soon, for three weeks before the signing of the treaty, Wallenstein's General Arnim began the siege of Stralsund. Without the arrival of Danish and Swedish troops the town could not have held out. In July, Wallenstein took charge of the siege, swearing that he would capture the port 'though it were bound with chains to Heaven'. Not heavenly chains, but Wallenstein's lack of a fleet, and foreign troops saved Stralsund. The besiegers withdrew in August, and the town was garrisoned by a Scottish regiment in Swedish service under the command of Alexander Leslie, later famous in England's great Civil War. By a treaty signed on 12 September 1628, Stralsund became the first German ally of Gustavus Adolphus, who was convinced that it was only a matter of time before he would find it necessary to launch a full-scale invasion of Germany.

The siege of Stralsund was scarcely lifted when the king of Denmark made a final effort to retrieve his fortunes. He landed on the Pomeranian coast, seized Wolgast and prepared to invade Mecklenburg. Wallenstein marched to meet him, and on 2 September the Danish army was destroyed. Christian fled back to his islands and sued for peace. The attempt of Gustavus Adolphus to hold him to the recently concluded alliance failed. The Peace of Lübeck, signed on 7 June 1629, was not too harsh. The German bishoprics, for which the king had entered the war, were renounced, and Christian retained his hereditary lands.

It is not surprising that Emperor Ferdinand thought that the time had come to use his military preponderance for the benefit of the Catholic church. His position had, in fact, not changed since 1608, when as imperial delegate he demanded that all church lands seized by Protestants since 1552 should be restored. On 6 March 1629 Ferdinand, his religious fervour encouraged by his Jesuit confessor Lamormain, issued the Edict of Restitution. By its provisions, all ecclesiastical properties taken over by Protestants were to be returned to the Catholic church. The transfers were to be entrusted to imperial commissioners from whom there was to be no appeal, and in their decisions they were to confine themselves simply to the question whether church properties had been seized by Protestants before or after 1552. Approval was given to the expulsion of Protestants from the territories of Catholic rulers. Only Lutherans were given legal recognition, which meant the exclusion of Calvinists. A few days after the promulgation of the edict, commissioners were appointed with the right to call in imperial troops for the enforcement of their decisions.

The edict changed the map of northern Germany. Before the victories of Gustavus Adolphus turned back the Catholic tide, five bishoprics, about thirty imperial and Hanseatic cities, nearly one hundred convents, and an incalculable number of parishes were recovered. Thousands of Protestants were subject to expulsion or forcible conversion by their new rulers.

The edict not only deprived Protestant princes of lands, and subjects of their religion and homes. It destroyed the unity of the Catholic party. Pope Urban VIII demanded that the imperial commissioners be replaced by his own representatives. The religious orders fought each other for the spoils. Above all, a serious breach was opened between the princes of the Catholic League, headed by Maximilian of Bavaria, and the emperor. To Catholic princes, no less than to Protestant, the absolutist rule of an emperor by decree, rather than through the constitutional channel of a diet, was a serious threat to their power. Moreover, Ferdinand and Maximilian were in direct conflict. The emperor sought the installation of his younger son, the Archduke Leopold William, as bishop of Magdeburg as well as bishop of Halberstadt, Hildesheim and Bremen. Maximilian claimed Halberstadt for his brother, the archbishop of Cologne, and Bremen for another Bavarian prince. The Catholic princes gave way to Habsburg claims on Magdeburg and Halberstadt with great reluctance.

Of equal importance to the edict as a divisive factor in the empire was Wallenstein. Jealousy, fear and hatred of Wallenstein had been growing since his appointment as commander-in-chief. Obviously there were great nobles in Prague and Vienna who were jealous of his wealth and rank. German princes were not only jealous but fearful when, in March 1628, the emperor bestowed on him the title of duke of Mecklenburg to replace the exiled native rulers. This was an act which could have only one meaning: the absolute power of an emperor to make and break the highest in the land. Even the transfer of the Palatinate electorate and lands to Maximilian of Bavaria paled in comparison. Maximilian was a German prince, while Wallenstein was a mere Bohemian nobleman. There were besides continual and bitter complaints from both Catholic and Protestant princes of the contributions and exactions for the imperial army, which at times exceeded 100,000 men. Wallenstein had dared even to occupy large portions of Brandenburg and Pomerania despite the protests of their rulers. To Catholics it was evident that he was not enthusiastic in the enforcement of the edict except in so far as it strengthened imperial power. It was noted that there was no interference with Protestant worship in the duchy of Mecklenburg, and the many Protestant officers in the imperial army offered further proof that Wallenstein had no interest in the furtherance of the Catholic faith. His enemies circulated wild rumours that he had sought the Danish crown, and that he now aimed at an elector's title or even the imperial throne. But undoubtedly the chief reason for the fear and hatred of Wallenstein was the belief, not without justification, that he was attempting to establish an imperial despotism. His own words, spoken in outbursts of temper, could be quoted against him: 'He would teach the electors manners; they must be dependent on the emperor, not the emperor on them.' And again: 'I am accustomed to serve the house of Austria and not to be harassed by Bavarian servitude.'

While the empire was torn by internal dissension, the foreign situation became threatening. With the surrender of the Huguenot stronghold of La Rochelle in October 1628, and the Peace of Alais in the following year, Richelieu was free to renew his campaign against the Habsburgs. His foreign policy is clearly stated in the memorandum which he presented to Louis XIII in January 1629. There was both a long-range and an immediate programme. In the future it would be necessary to open doors into the neighbouring states. Metz should be fortified, and if possible, French power should advance to Strasbourg in order to acquire an entry into Germany. Time, discretion, and careful and covert conduct would be needed to achieve these ends. Richelieu's fixed aim, as he explained it to his master, was to arrest 'the progress of Spain', and a particular occasion was presented in Italy where the Gonzaga duke of Mantua and Montferrat died in December 1627 without a direct heir. Louis XIII, in alliance with Venice, defended the claim of Charles of Nevers, a prince more French than Italian, while Spain in alliance with the duke of Savoy supported another branch of the Gonzaga family. The two provinces were of military importance for they contained the fortresses of Casale and Mantua.

The Mantuan war which ensued marks a turning point in the fortunes of Spain, and tied up imperial troops in Italy, soon to be desperately needed in Germany. Richelieu's action in the Mantuan affair proved to be the first permanent check to Habsburg power since the beginning of the Thirty Years War, and the first in a series of Spanish disasters.

Without a declaration of war against Spain, Louis XIII crossed the Alps in March 1629, and defeated the Savoyard army. This victory forced the Spanish army to raise the siege of Casale. The intervention of the emperor, who maintained that Mantua as an imperial fief was subject to his jurisdiction, forced Richelieu into further activity. In the summer of 1629, a portion of Wallenstein's army under the command of Collalto marched through the Valtelline pass and besieged Mantua, while the veteran Spinola invested Casale. In the dead of winter, Richelieu himself leading, the troops crossed the Alps, and in March 1630 captured the fortress of Pinerolo. In June Louis XIII conquered Savoy, but Mantua fell to the imperialist army in the following month.

While concentrating on military efforts in Italy, Richelieu had not neglected the northern theatres of war. The Treaty of Altmark (26 September 1629) mediated by the French ambassador Charnacé, provided for a six-year truce between Sweden and Poland. This freed Gustavus Adolphus for the invasion of Germany. In June 1630 France and the United Provinces concluded a seven-year alliance, which provided the Dutch a yearly subsidy of a million *livres*. Dutch successes in the summer and autumn of 1630 amply repaid this assistance.

On 3 July 1630 the emperor presented a memorial to a meeting of the Electoral College at Regensburg requesting assistance for the Dutch and Italian wars, and protection against the threatened invasion of the king of Sweden. Three days later, Gustavus Adolphus landed on the Pomeranian coast, a momentous event which caused little excitement in Regensburg. As might be expected, the representatives of the Protestant electors of Saxony and Brandenburg (they refused to attend the meeting in person) made vigorous protests against the Edict of Restitution. The Catholic electors joined the emperor in rejecting these remonstrances, but there was no further co-operation between them. A solid front was presented against Ferdinand's plans to involve the empire in the Dutch and Italian wars which could only be to the advantage of Spain. As for Sweden, a solemn letter was despatched by the electors to Gustavus Adolphus asking him to withdraw his troops. Nor would they listen to the emperor's plea for the election of his eldest son as king of the Romans, a title which recognized succession to the imperial throne. The electors were interested only in curbing the emperor's power, and this they believed could be accomplished by the reduction of the imperial army and the dismissal of Wallenstein.

The revolt of the electors against the emperor was further complicated by Richelieu's intrigues. He sent an ambassador to Regensburg, accompanied by his intimate adviser the Capuchin monk Father Joseph, popularly known as his Grey Eminence, to negotiate an Italian peace, and to strengthen the opposition against the emperor. One of the electors, the archbishop of Trier, was favourable to France, and Richelieu hoped to win over Maximilian of Bavaria.

Faced with such determined resistance to his plans, and fearful of the Franco-Bavarian negotiations, Ferdinand agreed, on 13 August 1630, to dismiss Wallenstein. The general retired to his estates in Bohemia, no doubt confident that his services would again be required.

The emperor and the French ambassador now reached an agreement on the Italian war. It provided for the recognition of the duke of Nevers as ruler of Mantua and Montferrat. In return, France was forbidden to assist the enemies of the emperor. The French ambassador had, however, exceeded his instructions, and Richelieu repudiated the agreement. The Treaty of Cherasco, finally signed in March 1631, recognized the duke of Nevers, but did not tie Richelieu's hands.

While a large imperial army fought in Italy, and the electors still further weakened the military power of Germany, Gustavus Adolphus was consolidating his position in Pomerania. A new period of the war was beginning. Politically, the country was hopelessly and dangerously divided. The rulers of Germany, who could not manage their own affairs, were to have them managed by Sweden and France.

II

Gustavus Adolphus was thirty-five years old when he landed at Peene-münde on 6 July 1630. His military campaigns, ending two years later at Lützen, changed the course of the Thirty Years War and the course of European history. In partnership with his friend and constant adviser, the Chancellor Oxenstierna, he saved German Protestantism and made Sweden a great power. The king's administrative and military abilities were inspired by the righteousness of his cause. In the fight for this sacred cause, there could be only friend or foe. Shortly after the landing, he had a stormy meeting with the elector of Brandenburg's ambassadors who pleaded for neutrality. The king replied:

I tell you frankly, I will not listen to talk about neutrality. His Excellency [i.e. the elector] must be either friend or foe . . . If his Excellency wishes to hold with God, good; he is on my side. If, however, he wishes to hold with the Devil, then in truth he must fight against me. There cannot be a third way that is certain . . . [As for neutrality] it is nothing but rubbish which the wind raises and carries away. What is neutrality anyway? I do not undertsand it.[1]

To Gustavus Adolphus, the security of the realm and the protection of Protestantism were inseparable. The Polish wars were fought not only to prevent his cousin King Sigismund from making good a dynastic claim to the Swedish crown, but to stop a Catholic ally of the Habsburgs from extending the conquests of the Counter-Reformation. Both Gustavus Adolphus and Oxenstierna were outraged by the pusillanimity of the German Protestant princes in the opening years of the Thirty Years War, and yet as early as 1620 the chancellor realized that intervention in Germany might at some future time be necessary. The failure of the negotiations for a powerful Protestant alliance in 1624 threw the king back into the Polish war, which he considered a diversion in the Protestant interest. The extension of his operations into Prussia in 1626, and the relief of Stralsund brought him closer to the German war. With the defeat of Denmark and the ever-increasing imperial and Catholic predominance, the decision to invade Germany could no longer be postponed. The two guiding principles of Gustavus Adolphus, Sweden's security and the Protestant cause, coincided.[2]

Before his landing in Pomerania, the king made strenuous efforts to obtain the support of the German Protestant princes, especially the elec-

---

[1] J. Paul, *Gustaf Adolf*, Vol. II (1930), pp. 180-1.
[2] For Sweden and Gustavus Adolphus before 1630, see Chapter XIII below. Michael Roberts in *Gustavus Adolphus, a History of Sweden 1611–1632* (2 Vols. 1953, 1958), gives a brilliant account of the king's reign.

tors of Brandenburg and Saxony, but without success. John George of Saxony made it clear that if Sweden invaded Germany, he would remain loyal to the emperor. George William of Brandenburg, even though Gustavus was his brother-in-law, sought only a peace which would guarantee his lands from further invasion, and attempted to act as mediator between Sweden and the emperor. Richelieu sought an alliance during the winter and spring of 1629–30, but the negotiations broke down. The cardinal's policy was to build an anti-Habsburg league based on Bavaria, while the king insisted on the headship of the league, and equality with France. Thus Sweden entered the war with only one ally, the city of Stralsund.

There were, however, compensating circumstances. As has been pointed out, there was disunity in the ranks of the enemy, and their greatest general, Wallenstein, had been dismissed, to be replaced by the septuagenarian Tilly. The imperial forces in Germany, about 40,000 strong, although overwhelmingly superior to the small invading Swedish army of 14,000, were widely scattered. An imperial army of 55,000 was tied up in Italy. The army of the Catholic League, dispersed from west of the Elbe to the Rhine, was in poor fighting condition. Gustavus Adolphus therefore had no difficulty in establishing a bridgehead and by August the greater part of Pomerania was in Swedish hands. The important city of Magdeburg declared for Sweden, opening up the possibility of a campaign on the Elbe, and Gustavus Adolphus sent a distinguished officer, Dietrich von Falkenberg, to take command of Magdeburg's defence. But there were no further revolts in favour of the invader, while the difficulties of obtaining adequate military supplies, reinforcements, food, and cash for the payment of the soldiers, slowed up further military advances. Finally, on Christmas Day 1630,[1] Gustavus Adolphus won a striking victory by storming Greifenhagen, followed by the capture of Gartz, and a chase of the imperialists across the Pomeranian border as far as Küstrin in Brandenburg. The king established headquarters at Bärwalde in his brother-in-law's territory. He was now in a stronger position to negotiate for alliances.

The aid of allies was indeed indispensable as the king's practical programme unfolded. It was necessary, he realized, to acquire German lands, both for Sweden's security (*assecuratio*), and as compensation for the great sacrifices imposed by the war (*satisfactio*). But he was still unable to budge the electors of Brandenburg and Saxony from their neutrality. The most that John George of Saxony would do was to call a conference of German Protestant princes and cities to meet in Leipzig in February 1631.

More successful were the renewal of the negotiations with France which had broken down in the previous spring. A five-year treaty of alliance was signed at Bärwalde on 23 January 1631. The terms of the

---

[1] Old style: 4 January 1631 in the new calendar.

treaty were a defeat of Richelieu's diplomacy, and a victory for the king. The cardinal hoped to break Habsburg power in Germany by a coalition of Sweden, Bavaria and Protestant German states. An anti-Habsburg league should fight the battles of France in Germany. Instead, the Treaty of Bärwalde provided Gustavus Adolphus with much-needed financial assistance (400,000 *reich* dollars annually, and 120,000 for the year 1630), without tying his hands. Richelieu protected his co-religionists by a clause in the treaty which permitted Catholic worship in any Catholic territories conquered by Sweden. In an agreement signed five days after the treaty, Gustavus Adolphus also promised to respect the neutrality of Bavaria and the Catholic League, provided that they remained 'sincerely' neutral. Inasmuch as the king could interpret this sincerity in the broadest sense, any direct or indirect attack by Maximilian of Bavaria on a Swedish ally or friend could be considered a breach of neutrality. Gustavus Adolphus received French support without losing independence of action, and Richelieu was powerless to influence his decisions.

German aid for Sweden depended on the Leipzig conference whose proceedings dragged on from February to April 1631. The results were meagre. John George of Saxony, who dominated the conference, still hoped that the mere threat of opposition would induce the emperor to modify the Edict of Restitution, and to prohibit the incursions of imperial armies into Protestant territories, especially into his own. The convention, to be sure, agreed to raise a defensive army of 40,000; but it was to be locally divided and commanded, and could be called into action only by order of the elector of Saxony. The convention of Leipzig was a blow to the Swedish king's hope for German support, and a subject of derision to his enemies.

Meantime, neither Gustavus Adolphus nor Tilly had the military preponderance necessary for a decisive victory. Both, moreover, awaited the outcome of the Leipzig conference. The immediate stake was Magdeburg, since November 1630 besieged by Count Pappenheim, the fiery Bavarian cavalry officer. Gustavus Adolphus had given repeated assurances of protection to the beleaguered city, and until April 1631 it appeared to him that it could be saved by diversionary tactics. But now the combined forces of Tilly and Pappenheim, twice the size of the Swedish army, threatened the city. It could be saved only by immediate relief, and this was delayed by the two Protestant electors. Gustavus Adolphus needed a line of retreat in case of failure, and he finally forced George William to grant him the fortress of Spandau and the use of Küstrin for this purpose. The Saxon elector, however, refused permission to march through his territories, the shortest way to the city, or to support him with troops. In desperation, Gustavus Adolphus nevertheless prepared to go to the relief of Magdeburg, when the news reached him that the city had fallen on 20 May. The destruction of Magdeburg by assault and fire, and the death of some 20,000 inhabitants, is the greatest single tragedy of the war. Tilly had won the campaign at a terrible loss to the reputation of his cause.

Magdeburg had both political and military consequences. Gustavus Adolphus gave up all hope of a militant German league headed by Saxony. The king's long-term plan was to form a strong German Protestant league under the leadership of Sweden, and meantime he made alliances with individual princes who would agree to accept Swedish control. Of these alliances, the most fruitful were with Bernard of Saxe-Weimar, who now began a brilliant military career in the Swedish service, and with the Landgrave William of Hesse. The landgrave, a gifted soldier and statesman, became the staunchest Swedish ally in Germany.

Nor did Magdeburg stop the king's military advance. The disaster forced him into action to prevent Tilly from pushing him back to the Pomeranian coast. Another factor which made speed a necessity was the release of imperial troops in northern Italy after the signing of the Peace of Cherasco. The first steps in the recovery of the military initiative were the storming of Greifswald, the last imperial stronghold in Pomerania, and the conquest of Mecklenburg where the exiled dukes were restored. While his generals Tott and Baner were engaged in these campaigns, the king moved the main body of his troops from Spandau to the Elbe. At Werben he set up a strong system of trenches and breastworks which effectively blocked the imperialists. Tilly's retreat after fierce skirmishing (6–7 August) was an important pyschological as well as a military defeat for the hitherto uniformly successful general.

Checked by Gustavus Adolphus, the old veteran turned his attention to Saxony. At the end of August he was joined by the long-awaited imperial troops from Italy. Threatened by this formidable army on his northern frontier, the elector of Saxony was finally forced into the Swedish camp. When Tilly ordered John George not only to cease the recruitment of an army, but threatened him with the loss of his secularized lands, the elector realized that Swedish aid was indispensable. While Gustavus Adolphus prepared to give this support by moving his army toward Saxony, he at the same time attempted to bind the elector by a firm alliance. But even now, when the imperialists had invaded his lands, John George refused to commit himself irrevocably to the Swedish cause. The alliance, concluded on 12 September, satisfied neither party. Forced to accept Swedish aid, the elector insisted that future operations must be planned by agreement between the two parties, and he would accept Swedish directions only 'as far as possible'.

On 15 September the Swedish and Saxon armies joined at Düben, about twenty-five miles north of Leipzig, which on this same day was occupied by Tilly. Gustavus Adolphus, John George, and Tilly as well, were ready to risk a battle, and on 17 September the armies clashed at Breitenfeld near Leipzig. The king had the numerical superiority, 24,000 of his own men, and 18,000 Saxons, while Tilly's army numbered about 35,000. Compared to the enemy, the Swedes were a ragged lot; as Adler Salvius, the Swedish diplomat, reported to the council in Stockholm:

Ragged, tattered and dirty were our men (from the continued labours of this last year) beside the glittering, gilded and plume-decked imperialists. Our Swedish and Finnish nags looked but puny, next to their great German chargers. Our peasant lads made no brave show upon the field, when set against the hawk-nosed and mustachio'd veterans of Tilly.[1]

Despite the flight of the Saxons early in the battle, Gustavus Adolphus won an overwhelming victory after five hours of desperate fighting. His superior tactics and the discipline of his troops overwhelmed the imperialists who suffered some 20,000 casualties, and lost 3,000 men by capture. The Swedish losses were only about 2,100. The great cavalry leader Pappenheim had met his match. Tilly, wounded, fled beyond the Weser. The victory of Breitenfeld was celebrated throughout Protestant Europe, and even in Moscow. In popular German verse the king of Sweden was compared to the Old Testament heroes Joshua, Gideon, David and Judas Maccabaeus, to Alexander the Great and the Emperor Theodosius. He was the 'Lion of the North' sent by God to save the righteous.

There were now three possibilities open to Gustavus Adolphus: a pursuit of Tilly, a drive toward Vienna, or toward the Rhine. The first, perhaps mistakenly, was scarcely considered, and its rejection gave Tilly the opportunity to rebuild his army. The king decided to march through Thuringia and Franconia (the 'Priests Alley' as it was called, for here lay the rich ecclesiastical territories), and so on to the Rhine. This developed into a great strategic plan to establish a strong position in the west, then to move south and east for the final conquest of Bavaria and Austria. Meantime, the Saxon army was to hold Silesia and Lusatia, thus acting as a hinge for the huge enveloping movement. Gustavus Adolphus could scarcely have envisaged this mighty plan when he landed at Peenemünde. To assure the security of Sweden and the safety of Protestantism, it was now considered necessary to conquer the whole of Germany and the emperor's homeland!

At the end of September the Swedish army started on its triumphal march to the west. Two weeks later Gustavus Adolphus entered the episcopal city of Würzburg where he remained for a month, setting up an administration for Franconia, and welcoming the Protestant estates, princes and cities now willing to ally with the conqueror. Frankfurt-am-Main, the ancient capital of the empire, was entered on 27 November. Crossing the Rhine at Oppenheim, where strong Spanish resistance was overcome, the army marched north along the river to Mainz which capitulated on 22 December. The elector, in precedence the first of German princes, fled to Cologne.

[1] Roberts, *Gustavus Adolphus*, Vol. II, p. 537.

The march to the Rhine was, however, most displeasing to Richelieu. In pursuance of his long-range programme to obtain entries into neighbouring states, he acquired the fortress of Pinerolo by surreptitious purchase from the duke of Savoy. This flagrant breach of the Treaty of Cherasco furnished the necessary entry into Italy, and the cardinal could turn his attention to the eastern frontier of France. But now he was faced not only by the old enemy, Spain, but by the new ally, Sweden. His objective, therefore, was to prevent Gustavus Adolphus, by diplomacy and by threats, from obtaining permanent bridge-heads on the Rhine. At the same time he continued his attempts to detach Bavaria and the Catholic League from the emperor. A truce between Bavaria and Sweden was, in fact, arranged by Richelieu; but it broke down when Pappenheim, on Maximilian's orders, continued military operations in the Lower Saxon Circle. As for the Catholic League, it collapsed when the Swedes overran the ecclesiastical territories, and when one of its members, the elector of Trier, signed a treaty of neutrality with both France and Sweden. By the terms of the Trier treaty, Richelieu gained the rights to occupy the Rhine fortresses of Ehrenbreitstein and Philipsburg. Ehrenbreitstein was occupied in June 1632, and by arrangement with Sweden, Coblenz was also handed over to France. Spanish troops were ejected from Trier itself. Richelieu thereby gained his coveted entries into Germany. The attempt to build a German anti-Habsburg alliance based on Bavaria, and dominated by France, had, however, again failed. Richelieu's aim to remove Swedish power from the left bank of the Rhine had, moreover, strained the alliance with Gustavus Adolphus to the breaking point. When the French ambassadors foolishly threatened that their king was ready to march with 40,000 men, Gustavus Adolphus angrily retorted: 'Your king has no need of so many men in order to beat me. Had it depended on mere numbers, it had not been I who beat the emperor, but he me. Let your king go where he will; but let him have a care not to cross the path of my armies, or he may look for a *rencontre* with me.'[1] The Treaty of Bärwalde continued in force; but henceforth Richelieu and Gustavus Adolphus were unfriendly allies.

Relations with France were only one of many difficult problems facing Gustavus Adolphus in the winter of 1631–2. The organization and rule of the large conquered areas, relations with the Protestant German princes, religious policy, military affairs, and above all, the recruitment and supply of the armies necessary for the final victory, all these matters demanded the constant attention of the king. Until January 1632, when he was joined by Oxenstierna, the harassed monarch had the sole responsibility, and even then the few available Swedish administrators could scarcely cope with the situation. Mainz became the capital of an administration for the conquered territories, while German princes, assisted by

---

[1] Roberts, *Gustavus Adolphus*, Vol. II, p. 587.

Swedish agents, acted as governors in the local areas. Fundamentally, it was a system of controlled exploitation to raise taxes for military purposes and, though harsh, it was not unbearable. To be sure, the soldiery sometimes got out of hand, ravaged the countryside and committed atrocities, despite a strict disciplinary code and royal anger.

In religious matters, Gustavus Adolphus showed remarkable toleration. Catholic church lands were confiscated and handed over to high officials and military officers, both German and Swedish, as compensation for their services; but to the surprise of the Catholic inhabitants, their worship was permitted. The king also saw to the protection of his own Lutheran faith. When the exiled Frederick V of the Palatinate arrived in Mainz in high hopes for the restoration of his hereditary lands, Gustavus Adolphus insisted that there must be toleration for Lutherans in the Calvinist Palatinate.

The king's military difficulties arose in those regions which were too distant to control directly. If he had pursued the enemy's army after the Battle of Breitenfeld some of these difficulties could have been avoided. Pappenheim, with a force far inferior to the Swedish forces in the area, pinned down thousands of much-needed soldiers in the Lower Saxon Circle. The greatest danger lay in the eastern front, assigned to the elector of Saxony.

The commander of the Saxon army was Hans George von Arnim, a pious Protestant Brandenburger who changed masters on principle. He had served with distinction under Wallenstein; but the Edict of Restitution induced him to desert the emperor, and to enter the Saxon service. He was, however, no friend of Sweden, and acted on his own judgement of military and political situations. In November 1631 he invaded Bohemia and entered Prague, in direct contradiction to the strategic plan of Gustavus Adolphus which called for a holding position for the Saxon army in Lusatia and Silesia. The invasion of Bohemia endangered the whole eastern front, if the emperor could increase his military strength. That strength was indeed forthcoming with the revival of imperial power wielded by Wallenstein.

The emperor's first reaction to the Battle of Breitenfeld had been so fearful that he considered flight to Italy. With the consent of his spiritual advisers, he was ready to make unusual concessions to save his crowns and lands: suspension of the Edict of Restitution, return of the northern bishoprics to the Protestant possessors, and temporary possession of ecclesiastical lands by the electors of Brandenburg and Saxony. Ferdinand quickly recovered his customary optimism, and determined to raise a large imperial army to repulse the heretical invader. On 10 December Wallenstein agreed to return as commander-in-chief, and in April 1632 he received not only complete military authority, but the right to negotiate with the enemy. The duke of Friedland had guessed correctly when he was dismissed in August 1630—his services would again be required.

Wallenstein's activities during the period of his enforced retirement had been of a peculiar nature. Ostensibly, he withdrew completely from public life, even to the extent of refusing to supply food from his great estates for Tilly's army. At the same time, he carried on secret and complicated intrigues with the emperor's enemies. Since early in 1631, a group of exiled Bohemian nobles, headed by Adam Terzka, Wallenstein's brother-in-law, were in touch with Bohemian officers serving in the Swedish army. Of these officers, the most conspicuous was Count Thurn, one of the leaders of the ill-fated Bohemian revolt. Their objective was the establishment of an independent Bohemia with Swedish support and under Wallenstein's leadership. To the great surprise of Gustavus Adolphus, Wallenstein, in July 1631, asked the king to supply a force, 10,000 to 12,000 men, to be commanded by Thurn. The proposal was accepted, and Gustavus Adolphus also promised to appoint Wallenstein as viceroy of Bohemia, until Frederick V's restoration. So Wallenstein appears at this period of his life as a Bohemian patriot and a traitor to the emperor. After the victory of Breitenfeld, Gustavus Adolphus and Wallenstein had less need of each other. The king was in the full tide of success, while the duke of Friedland, because of this success, could look forward with some confidence to his re-employment by the emperor.

Wallenstein's negotiations with Gustavus Adolphus were replaced by strange dealings with his former companion-in-arms, Arnim. Although Wallenstein had already signified a willingness to resume command of the imperial armies, he informed Arnim that Prague would not be defended. Relations between the two were put on a different footing when the emperor empowered Wallenstein to negotiate with Arnim in the furtherance of a general peace. They met at the end of November 1631 and the negotiations were continued until May 1632, with the connivance of the Saxon elector. Wallenstein could therefore be considered a man of peace, although it is more likely that he was merely attempting to wean Saxony away from the Swedish alliance.

Gustavus Adolphus was already alarmed by the Saxon intrigues of which he got wind, and by Pappenheim's successes. Now came the news that Tilly had defeated the Swedish army commanded by Horn, and had invested Bamberg. Immediate action seemed necessary, and in March 1632 the king left Mainz with an army of 13,000 men in pursuit of Tilly who retreated east to the Upper Palatinate. Before his military preparations were completed Gustavus now embarked on the conquest of Bavaria, the first step in the campaign which he hoped would lead to final victory. But he was 90,000 men short of the 210,000 planned for the destruction of his foes.

The Danube was crossed at Donauwörth on 8 April. The following day, the main army was augmented by the arrival of reinforcements, so that the total strength came to 22,500 infantry and 15,000 cavalry. Opposed were not more than 22,000 troops commanded by Tilly. Maximilian of Bavaria, fearful and depressed by the Swedish advance, called for aid from Wallenstein, and meantime Tilly placed his army on the east bank of the River Lech, the western boundary of Bavaria. Against the advice of his council of war, Gustavus Adolphus determined to storm the strong enemy position. On 15 April the infantry crossed the river by the use of a huge floating barge, while the point of attack was hidden by a barrage of cannon fire and the smoke of burning straw. Meantime, the cavalry crossed at both ends of the main crossing-point and closed in on the flanks of Tilly's army. It was a spectacular victory. Maximilian led his beaten troops back to the fortified city of Ingolstadt. The old veteran Tilly, wounded in the battle, died two weeks later, attended by a famous surgeon sent by Gustavus Adolphus. Bavaria was deliberately devastated and its peasants slaughtered, partly to weaken the enemy, but also in a terrible spirit of revenge for the ravaging of the Protestant north.

The king's master plan to proceed from the conquest of Bavaria to a campaign down the Danube into Austria, was, however, ruined by the news from Bohemia. On 21 May Arnim held his last conference with Wallenstein. Fully prepared to use his new army if his proposals were rejected, the imperial generalissimo made the most extravagant promises: cancellation of the Edict of Restitution, religious toleration, and the restoration of Germany to the conditions of 1618. With the remark that these proposals were 'bacon to catch the mouse', the elector of Saxony broke off the negotiations, and called on Gustavus Adolphus for assistance against Wallenstein's threatened attack.

Greatly disturbed by the possible collapse of the eastern front, Gustavus Adolphus promised his support to John George. Before moving north, he could not, however, resist the temptation to capture Munich, which fell on 16 May. The king was accompanied by Frederick V, jubilant to enter the capital of the enemy who had deprived him of the Bohemian crown and electoral title.

Wallenstein acted quickly after the rejection of his peace proposals. He entered Prague on 25 May, and the Saxon army retreated from Bohemia. Early in June Gustavus Adolphus recrossed the Danube on the way to Nuremberg. This marked a great strategic victory for Wallenstein. The king had hoped that by campaigning on the Danube, Wallenstein would be forced to give up his pressure on Saxony. Instead, Wallenstein had upset the king's timetable and forced him into a defensive position.

Despite the serious military setback, Gustavus Adolphus optimistically outlined his plans for the future of Germany to a committee of Nuremberg burghers. He projected two alliances, a military league to win the war, and a political league to keep the peace. All the German Protestant estates and cities would, it was hoped, join these alliances to be headed by Sweden. The political league did not, however, contemplate the end of the empire; it would be a state within the state [*corpus in corpore*], with its own army and legislature. There was much contemporary speculation about Gustavus Adolphus himself becoming emperor; but there is no evidence to support these rumours. Sweden's own demands were based on Grotius, the king's favourite political theorist. On the principle that the conqueror enjoyed the rights of sovereignty, Gustavus Adolphus claimed, in theory at least, that Sweden had complete control over all conquered territory, whether Protestant or Catholic. In practice, this could mean that Catholic lands would be used as pawns in a final peace treaty, while war contributions could meanwhile be collected in Protestant as well as in Catholic states. One territory, Pomerania, was specifically mentioned as an imperial fief to be retained by Sweden, an arrangement which would make the Swedish monarch a prince of the empire. This was the programme of Gustavus Adolphus, a programme to ensure security for German Protestantism and for Sweden, and to provide compensation for his country's war efforts.

It was not until the end of June that the king realized that Wallenstein, after making a juncture with Maximilian's army, was heading not for Saxony but for Nuremberg, with a force vastly superior to his own. To meet this danger, the king built fortifications around the city walls, and sent out orders for reinforcements. Wallenstein did not dare to attack the king's strong position, and he was thus cheated of a victory while his army counted some 48,000 to the enemy's 20,000. About three miles from the city he built his own strongly fortified camp. At one end stood an old fortress known as the Alte Veste. Here Wallenstein waited to starve out the Swedish army.

Gustavus Adolphus put Oxenstierna in charge of gathering the relief forces, and although the operation took two months, the chancellor accomplished his mission with consummate skill. At the end of August he joined the king, with about 30,000 men. Now that Gustavus Adolphus had a slight superiority over the enemy, he decided to attack the Alte Veste. In the mistaken belief that Wallenstein was in retreat with the main body of his troops, the attack was made on 3 September, and was repulsed. For the first time, the two famous commanders had met in combat, and for the first time since his landing in Germany, the ever-victorious 'Lion of the North' had been checked in battle.

The repulse at the Alte Veste was more than a lost battle; it demoralized the Swedish army and it was a strategic disaster. During the following fortnight the army lost one-third of its strength by desertion and by disease. Unable to draw Wallenstein out of his impregnable camp, the king was forced to withdraw from Nuremberg on 18 September. Three days later, the imperial general destroyed his camp and marched north. Wallenstein had the initiative, and the king's plans depended on the general's moves. Gustavus Adolphus attempted to draw Wallenstein into open battle by a campaign on the Danube; but was forced to hurry north when his lifeline to the Baltic seemed endangered by the deteriorating military position in the Lower Saxon Circle.

Meantime, Wallenstein invaded Saxony, entered Leipzig (2 October), and prepared to winter in the electorate. Joined by a contingent from Bavaria and by Pappenheim, recalled from his successful Lower Saxon campaign, he now commanded about 19,000 men. The king, still uncertain of his enemy's plans, built a strong camp at Naumburg on the Saale river only a few miles from the imperialist outposts, and waited for news and reinforcements. The news which he heard on 14 November was much to his liking. Wallenstein was dispersing his army in winter quarters, in the belief that there was no immediate danger of attack. Pappenheim's troops, including 3,000 horse, were stationed in Halle, 35 miles from imperialist headquarters. 'Now in very truth I believe', the king is said to have exclaimed, 'that God has delivered him into my hands.'[1]

Early in the morning of 15 November, Gustavus Adolphus started out on his last march, hoping to surprise Wallenstein before Pappenheim could return. The Swedish army comprised 12,800 men and 6,200 horse, about the size of Wallenstein's army, but its inferior in cavalry. The element of surprise was destroyed by an unexpected encounter with an advance contingent of imperialists, and Wallenstein was able to rally his forces. By a prearranged signal, three cannon shots fired at headquarters brought the scattered units together at the town of Lützen, about fifteen miles west of Leipzig. Pappenheim was ordered to return at once and Wallenstein spent the night of 15–16 November putting his army into battle array. On its right was the castle of Lützen and windmills where he placed his artillery. The left wing was weak, to be strengthened by Pappenheim's cavalry when it arrived.

Luck was against the king. On the morning of 16 November a thick mist held up the attack on the left wing until eleven o'clock. An hour later Pappenheim arrived in time to prevent the certain defeat of the imperialists. But the great cavalry leader was mortally wounded in the counterattack, the left flank crumbled, and once more Swedish victory seemed assured when the mist again descended. Meantime, the Swedish left commanded by Bernard of Weimar was in serious difficulty, and before Pappenheim's arrival, the king started to go to his assistance. Leading a cavalry charge, he was struck by a musket-ball which shattered his left arm. Carried away from his men, he was shot in the back, fell from his horse and was killed by a shot through the head.

Bernard of Weimar turned defeat into victory by a desperate successful attack on the imperialist right wing, and at nightfall Wallenstein withdrew

[1] Roberts, *Gustavus Adolphus*, Vol. ii, p. 748.

his troops to Leipzig. The Swedes lost between 5,000 and 6,000 men, the imperialists even more. Lützen was also a strategic victory, for the Swedish army had not been cut off from the Baltic sea, while Wallenstein was forced finally to retreat back to Bohemia.

No military victory could compensate for the loss of Gustavus Adolphus. He saved German Protestantism, and made Sweden a great power: to him the two were intertwined. No other leader would again combine idealism with statecraft and military genius. The last sixteen years of the war were dominated by power politics and secular aims.

One more death should be noted. A fortnight after Lützen, Frederick V, whose acceptance of the Bohemian crown precipitated the German war, died of the plague in Metz, a broken man at the age of thirty-six.

Christina, the heiress to the Swedish throne, was only six years old when her father died, and the government was now in the hands of the royal council acting as regents. The councillors in Stockholm were glad to turn over full responsibility for the war to Chancellor Oxenstierna, who considered himself the executor of the late king's plans. The chancellor and the councillors at home were agreed on two points: Pomerania must be permanently held by Sweden, and the war must be paid for by Germans. Oxenstierna's first concern was therefore to ensure continued military support and funds from the German Protestant states.

As might be expected, John George of Saxony, never happy with the Swedish alliance, hoped to seize the leadership of the Protestant party, and to arrange either a general peace, or a separate peace with the emperor. Oxenstierna quickly blocked the elector's bid for leadership by calling a meeting of the four circles of south-western Germany, Franconia, Swabia, Upper Rhine, and Lower Rhine.

The deputies of the four circles met at Heilbronn on 18 March 1633, and after a month of negotiation the League of Heilbronn was signed on 23 April. Oxenstierna was made director of the alliance, but a consultative council of ten was also created of which seven were to be chosen by the estates of the circles and three by Sweden. Besides, instead of the sole rule of Swedish governors, each circle would be administered by a council of four, one of whose members would be a Swede. The chancellor could not obtain more than a promise of 2,400,000 imperial dollars for the army, a quarter of his original demand. As can be seen, Sweden's influence had been weakened by the king's death; but even so, the Heilbronn Alliance might have formed the nucleus of an Evangelical Union as it had been planned by Gustavus Adolphus, provided that Sweden could command sufficient military strength.

One political decision made by the new alliance sought to rectify a wrong committed in the early years of the war. The Palatinate was restored to Frederick's heir, Charles Lewis, and during his minority the 'Winter King's' brother, Louis Philip, was installed as administrator.

Oxenstierna also succeeded in renewing the subsidy treaty with France, and at the same time foiled Richelieu's attempts to take advantage of the Swedish king's death. The cardinal hoped to dominate the anti-Habsburg party by forming an alliance with Saxony and Sweden, and clearly showed his interest in the Rhine region by laying claims to Alsatian towns and the river bridge-heads of Philippsburg and Breisach. The old plan to neutralize and protect the German Catholic states was again revived; but the opposition of both Oxenstierna and his Heilbronn allies, and Saxony's unwillingness to ally with France, ruined the cardinal's plans, and he was forced to content himself with the renewal of the Bärwalde treaty which was signed on 19 April 1633.

One more serious problem faced Oxenstierna: the control of the army. A consummate diplomat, the chancellor did not have the experience necessary to assume military command in the field. The jealousy existing between the chief generals, the Swedes Horn and Baner, and the Germans William of Hesse-Cassel and Bernard of Saxe-Weimar, however, made it impossible to appoint a commander-in-chief. Bernard, younger scion of a Saxon house, with a great reputation as a soldier at the age of twenty-nine, was moreover ambitious to found a principality. Oxenstierna was forced to grant him the 'dukedom of Franconia', comprising the bishop-rics of Würzburg and Bamberg, to be held as a fief of the Swedish crown. This was the largest bribe paid to a general; but the army could be held together only by grants of estates to lesser officers, while mutiny in the ranks was quelled by the partial payment of arrears in pay.

While Oxenstierna was consolidating his position, his enemies were preparing to renew hostilities. New vigour was infused into the Habsburg family coalition by the rise of two younger men, the Infant Ferdinand, brother of Philip IV of Spain, and the emperor's son Archduke Ferdinand, crowned king of Hungary and of Bohemia, and future emperor. The Infant Ferdinand, still in his twenties, had been trained for the church and received the cardinal's hat, so that he was commonly known as the cardinal-infant. In 1632 he succeeded the aged Archduchess Isabella as governor of the Netherlands. Worldly, politically ambitious, a close student of war, he discarded the cardinal's robes for a coat of mail, and became the ardent leader of Spain's plans for the reconquest of the United Provinces. The cardinal-infant's chief ally in Vienna was the Archduke Ferdinand, usually called by his title of king of Hungary. At the time of Wallenstein's dismissal he had tried in vain to obtain command of the imperial armies, and failed again when the general was recalled.

The king of Hungary became one of Wallenstein's chief enemies in Vienna, and he was now joined by the Spanish ambassador, who was aroused by the general's refusal to co-operate in the war against the Dutch. The plan, which Wallenstein opposed, was to send an imperial army to the Rhine which would join forces with a Spanish army coming

342

up from Italy under the command of the cardinal-infant. On his way north to fight the Dutch, he hoped to clear the Rhine country of French and Swedish troops.

Meanwhile a Swedish army under Horn threatened Breisach, the key city on the Rhine whose fall would jeopardize the cardinal-infant's campaign. Regensburg fell to Bernard of Saxe-Weimar on 14 November 1633. The Bavarian peasantry revolted, driven to desperation by marauding troops and poor harvests. Wallenstein's inactivity in the face of these disasters, as well as his mysterious plotting, made it increasingly clear to the statesmen of Vienna and Madrid that the general stood in the way of an all-out war against the foes of the house of Habsburg.

There can be no doubt that after Lützen Wallenstein degenerated both in mind and in body. Following the defeat, he ordered the arrest and execution of thirteen officers and five soldiers for cowardly conduct, a vindictive procedure which lost him his popularity in the army. Stories circulated of his peculiarities and cruelty: accustomed to the sound of gun and cannon, he could not bear the jingling of spurs, the barking of dogs, the crowing of cocks, or loud speaking. He ordered the hanging of a servant for waking him from sleep.

Much more serious were Wallenstein's dealings with the enemy, some known, some suspected, and others still shrouded in mystery. Although the general spoke much of peace, the methods by which he hoped to achieve peace laid him open to the charge of treachery. The negotiations with the elector of Saxony and his general Arnim, and with the Bohemian exiles continued. To detach Saxony from the enemy camp would certainly aid the emperor; but the secret meetings with the Bohemian exiles could only be interpreted as treasonable. Thurn, Kinsky and Terzka, representatives of the fallen Bohemian nobility, still hoped to expel the Habsburg ruler, and if they succeeded, who but Wallenstein would be king? Substance was given to the general's partiality for the Bohemian rebels when he released Thurn after capturing him in Silesia. The secret negotiations with Sweden, broken off in 1631, were renewed. Richelieu, through his ambassadors in Germany, was in touch with Kinsky who spoke of Wallenstein's willingness to desert the Habsburg cause. So the Friedlander plotted for kingship, peace, and revenge for his dismissal in 1630. But no one line of action was followed with energy and consistency. Reliance on astrology, fits of depression, and an ailing body overwhelmed the practical man of affairs and military strategist.

The emperor moved slowly to counter the general's moves. In August, he assured himself of the loyalty of Wallenstein's chief lieutenants, particularly Piccolomini and Gallas. Henceforth Piccolomini kept the emperor informed of his commander-in-chief's doings. The court clique opposed to the general meantime lent their support to pamphlets which openly attacked him.

Wallenstein played into the hands of his enemies. On 12 January 1634 he called a meeting of his officers who signed a document known as the 'Pilsen Revers', in which they pledged their loyalty and swore never to separate from him. The emperor and even Wallenstein's friends at court were now finally convinced that treason was being plotted. On 24 January the emperor signed a patent which was sent secretly to Piccolomini, Gallas, and Maximilian of Bavaria. It ordered the dismissal of Wallenstein and his seizure dead or alive. The order was not made public until 18 February.

Deserted by all but a handful of officers and a small number of troops, Wallenstein sent out desperate calls for help to Bernard of Weimar and to Arnim. Then, carried in a litter, he made his way to Eger near the Saxon border, still hoping for succour. Colonel Butler, an Irish Catholic, was ordered by Piccolomini to carry out the emperor's wishes. Two Scotch Protestants, Leslie and Gordon, commanders of the Eger garrison, joined Butler, together with three Irishmen, another Scot, an Italian and a Spaniard. On the evening of 25 February the conspirators invited Terzka, Kinsky, and two officers faithful to Wallenstein to a banquet at the castle. At a given signal the guests were murdered. Wallenstein, ill in his quarters on the market square, was killed by the Irishman, Captain Devereux.

The execution, or murder, of Wallenstein and his accomplices brought unity to the Habsburg armies. The king of Hungary was granted his long-desired wish for supreme command, with Gallas as his chief lieutenant. It was otherwise with Sweden and her allies. While his general Arnim invaded Bohemia, the elector of Saxony began peace negotiations with the emperor. The elector of Brandenburg, fearful of Oxenstierna's demand for Pomerania, was unreliable. Despite the chancellor's strenuous efforts to strengthen his army, the Heilbronn League lagged in its support, and even diminished its financial contributions.

On the military front, the divided Swedish armies of Marshal Horn and Duke Bernard were slow in joining to defend Ratisbon, which fell to King Ferdinand and Gallas on 22 July 1634. On 16 August they crossed the Danube, laid siege to Nördlingen, held by a small Swedish force, and awaited the arrival of the cardinal-infant who was marching up from the Black Forest. There was no longer a Wallenstein to impede the co-operation of imperial and Spanish armies. Horn and Bernard hastened to relieve Nördlingen, but were too late to block the cardinal-infant's arrival with 15,000 trained Spanish troops. The Habsburg troops now numbered 39,000 men, about one-third more than their enemy. In spite of this numerical inferiority, the Swedish commanders determined to risk a battle, and attacked on 6 September. After five hours of fierce fighting, distinguished by the bravery of the Spanish infantry, the Habsburg cousins won a great victory. Horn was captured, and Bernard barely escaped with about 14,000 men. The rest of the Swedish armies were killed or captured.

The Battle of Nördlingen was as decisive as the battles of the White Hill and Breitenfeld, both in military and political consequences. With the exception of a few cities, the conquests of Gustavus Adolphus in southern Germany, all the way to the Rhine, the Necker and the Main were lost. The political and religious conditions as they had existed before 1631 were largely restored. Nördlingen and the subsequent imperial successes led to the weakening and final dissolution of the Heilbronn League, to the Peace of Prague, and to the official entry of France into the war.

Since March 1634 John George of Saxony had been negotiating for peace with the emperor. In November they made a preliminary agreement, a truce was arranged in February 1635, and on 30 May the Peace of Prague was signed. Both elector and emperor made concessions. On the all-important question of church lands, the determining year was fixed at 1627. Lands held at that time were to be retained for forty years, and meantime disputes were to be adjudicated by the imperial court composed of Catholic and Protestant members in equal number. This suspension of the Edict of Restitution troubled the emperor, and was opposed by Lamormain: but Ferdinand's conscience was salved when the majority of his spiritual advisers gave their approval. Calvinists were not specifically excluded from the treaty, for that would have shut out the elector of Brandenburg; and yet, Calvinism was not recognized. There was no general amnesty. The heir of Frederick V was still deprived of his electorate and lands, an arrangement which satisfied Maximilian of Bavaria. The treaty was open to all belligerents, including Sweden, whose withdrawal from Germany would be purchased by monetary compensation contributed by the Protestant estates.

While the Peace of Prague was being negotiated an English ambassador, the earl of Arundel, was travelling across Germany on a vain mission to the emperor on behalf of the luckless Palatine family. Only four years before, Robert Monro, a Scottish officer in the victorious army of Gustavus Adolphus, was so delighted with what he saw in the march from Frankfurt to Würzburg that he wrote: 'no country in Europe is comparable unto Germany, for fertility, riches, corn and wine, traffic by land, pleasant cities, fair buildings, rare orchards, woods and planting, civility as well in the country as in the cities'.[1] Now William Crowne, a member of Arundel's suite, made his notes on the state of the country, and the contrast with Monro's report is indeed striking. From Cologne, the ambassador and his train were towed up the Rhine 'by many villages pillaged and shot down'. In Bacharach 'the poor people are found dead with grass in their mouths'. In Rudesheim, the ambassador 'gave some

---

[1] Robert Monro, *His Expedition with the Worthy Scots Regiment (called Mac-Keyes Regiment)* (London, 1637), part II, p. 89.

relief to the poor which were almost starved as it appeared by the violence they used to get it from one another'. At Mentz, the ambassador found it necessary to stay on ship-board for his meals, for there was no food to be had in the city. Starving people pushed each other into the river in their eagerness to obtain food sent from the ship to relieve their hunger. From Cologne to Frankfurt 'all the towns, villages and castles be battered, pillaged or burned'. Passing up the Main through Würzburg, the ambassadorial party arrived at Neustadt 'which hath been a fair city, though now burned miserably, here we saw poor children sitting at their doors almost starved to death'. Travelling through the Upper Palatinate, the Englishmen had dinner at a village 'which hath been pillaged eight-and-twenty times in two years and twice in one day and they have there no water but that which they save when it raineth'. Reaching the Danube, they continued the journey by boat to Linz, still meeting with ruined villages, and with people seeking relief.[1]

Small wonder that the eligible princes and cities hastened to sign the Peace of Prague. The Heilbronn League was dead, and only Bernard of Weimar and William of Hesse refused to lay down their arms. But the treaty did not bring true peace to the empire. The choice of the year 1627 as the determining date for the possession of church lands meant defeat and despair for the Protestants of southern Germany. Nor did the war end. Sweden fought on for territorial 'satisfaction', and France became a formal belligerent.

Richelieu had never deviated from the objectives of his foreign policy: to stop the 'progress' of Spain, and to obtain 'entries' into the territories of neighbouring states. He had long foreseen that the time would come when unofficial war must give way to open war. After the disaster of Nördlingen, the combined power of Spain and Austria threatened France on its eastern frontier, and to meet this danger French troops took over the Alsatian cities which had been captured by the Swedes. Lorraine too was occupied, for its trouble-making Duke Charles had openly joined the Habsburgs.

The appearance of the imperial armies on the Rhine, the threat to Lorraine, and finally a Spanish raid on Trier, whose elector was carried off as prisoner, forced Richelieu to take further action. On 8 February 1635 he arranged a treaty with the Dutch which provided for the joint conquest of the Spanish Netherlands. On 28 April he concluded a new alliance with Sweden. On 19 May a herald of arms, standing in the great square of Brussels, proclaimed that the king of France declared war against the king of Spain and against the cardinal-infant, ruler of the

[1] William Crowne, *A True Relation of all the remarkable places and passages observed in the travels of the right honorable Thomas Lord Howard, Earle of Arundell and Surry ... 1636* (London, 1637), pp. 5–17.

Netherlands. The king of France was at war with the emperor as well, although he was not named. From 1635 to the conclusion of the final peace, the Thirty Years War was predominantly a struggle for power between the Habsburgs and France in alliance with Sweden.

France, as Richelieu himself knew, was ill-prepared for war. Despite the country's large population, and greater wealth than any other state of its day, the government suffered the usual seventeenth-century financial difficulties. There was not enough money to keep up an efficient standing army even in times of peace, and when at war, the problems posed in providing pay and supplies for a great army were immeasurably increased. In 1635 the French forces had neither adequate training nor organization, and there were no officers of marked ability.

Besides the Dutch, who would, in any case, be available only for a war in the Netherlands, Richelieu could count on only two small German armies commanded by William of Hesse and by Bernard of Weimar. These the cardinal took into French pay. To compensate for the loss of his duchy of Franconia, now overrun by the imperialists, Bernard was granted the landgravate of Alsace and the county of Hagenau. As for Sweden, her chief concern was to maintain her hold on Pomerania. Until March 1637, with the death of Duke Bogislav XIV without issue, Oxenstierna had some hope of making a separate peace with the emperor which would acknowledge Sweden's claim to the duchy. The chancellor did not, therefore, wish to tie himself too closely to France. On the other hand, in accordance with a provision of the peace of Prague, Sweden's refusal to withdraw from Germany brought the elector of Saxony into war against his former ally. The elector of Brandenburg followed Saxony's example.

While the Habsburgs grew stronger, Richelieu, inadequately prepared, planned to attack Spain simultaneously in the Netherlands and in Italy. The results were disastrous. After defeating the Spaniards near Liège, the French army, lacking pay and provisions, disintegrated. In Italy, a treaty with the dukes of Savoy and of Parma (11 July) to conquer Milan, was followed by a short fruitless campaign.

In the summer of 1636 the combined forces of Spain and the emperor took the offensive against France. Reinforced by the Bavarian cavalry of the distinguished officer Johann von Werth, the cardinal-infant advanced into Picardy, while the imperialist general Gallas occupied Franche-Comté and invaded Burgundy. On 14 August 1636 the cardinal-infant's army seized the fortress of Corbie near Amiens, and Werth advanced to Compiègne. Paris was in imminent danger, mobs rioted, and it was believed in court circles that Richelieu would fall from power. The firmness of Richelieu, and of Louis XIII who joined his army as commander, quieted the city. Gallas was checked by a French garrison at Saint-Jean-de-Losne, which won for the town the name of Saint-Jean-Belle-Defense.

Neither was the cardinal-infant able to follow up his initial advantage, for the difficulty of provisioning the army made a further advance impossible. Louis XIII recaptured Corbie, and the enemy armies retreated from French soil.

Meanwhile the Swedes, after a brave start, barely held on in northern Germany. The Swedish marshals Baner and Torstensson defeated a Saxon army, reinforced by imperial troops, at Wittstock in Brandenburg on 4 October 1636. Brandenburg was overrun, and the Swedes penetrated as far as Leipzig and Erfurt. But in the following year Gallas, with superior numbers, forced the Swedish army back into Pomerania.

The death of the emperor in February 1637, and the accession of the king of Hungary as Ferdinand III, made little difference in the conduct of the war. The new emperor was as pious as his father but less bigoted, so that religious considerations would be less likely to stand in the way of peace.

The strengthening of their military power became the immediate objectives of both Oxenstierna and Richelieu. The chancellor had returned to Stockholm in July 1636, leaving the conduct of the war in the hands of his generals, while ensuring financial support and recruits for the Swedish armies. Before his departure from Germany, Oxenstierna with the assistance of Richelieu also renewed the truce with Poland (Treaty of Stuhmsdorf, September 1635) which released soldiers for the German war. The native Swedish forces (they numbered about 74,000 men at the end of the war) were, however, used mainly for garrison duty and for the defence of the homeland. Increasingly, Sweden's battles were fought by German mercenaries supported, as they had been in the days of Gustavus Adolphus, by Germany.

After the initial defeats of the French armies, Richelieu worked indefatigably to reorganize the military establishment, to supply food, pay and munitions for the armies, and to raise the number of effectives. At the same time he encouraged the rise of vigorous young commanders, particularly the vicomte de Turenne and the duc d'Enghien, a prince of the blood and later prince de Condé. That the cardinal's efforts were successful is proved by the mounting success of the French armies.

At least as important for the future, France and Sweden made a firm three-year alliance, the Treaty of Hamburg, signed on 15 March 1638. This co-operation was made possible by Oxenstierna's withdrawal of claims on Rhine territory, and was made necessary when the chancellor failed to obtain Pomerania by agreement with the emperor. The treaty provided for a declaration of war by France on the emperor, and for the rejection of any separate truce of treaty with the enemy. France promised Sweden an annual subsidy of one million *livres*.

Even before the signing of the treaty, the struggle for the control of the Rhine had begun. On 3 March 1638, at Rheinfelden, a few miles east of

Basel, Bernard of Wiemar defeated an imperial army supported by Werth's famous Bavarian cavalry. Werth himself was captured and remained in captivity until 1642. Marching down the Rhine, Bernard reached Breisach where he was joined by a French army commanded by Marshal Turenne. After a long siege, the strategic town capitulated on 17 December. All Alsace could now be occupied. Following his brilliant military successes, Bernard claimed Alsace as a German principality, a claim rejected by Richelieu, and the bitter dispute was ended only by the duke's death in July 1639.

During the Rhine campaign the imperialists were severely handicapped by the lack of Spanish support. On 10 October the Dutch, under the leadership of Prince Frederick Henry, re-captured Breda, which had been held by Spain since Spinola's famous siege in 1625. The cardinal-infant required all his strength to prevent further Dutch gains. The fall of Breisach was an even greater blow than the loss of Breda. It cut the Rhine route for Spanish troops marching from Milan to the Netherlands and into Germany. In October 1639 the sea route to Flanders was also severed when the Dutch admiral Tromp destroyed a great Spanish fleet in the Downs near Dover. In 1640 the very existence of the Spanish monarchy was threatened. Catalonia revolted and elected Louis XIII as duke of Barcelona. The Portuguese threw off their allegiance and elected their own king of the native house of Braganza. The Austrian branch of the house of Habsburg, which had hitherto depended so much on aid from the Spanish branch, now found itself saddled with a weak ally calling for help which was not available. Olivares, exponent of Spain's survival as a world power, was in despair. In desperation he sought to continue secret peace negotiations with Richelieu which had begun as early as 1636. In the earlier years, the cardinal had shown some interest in reaching an accommodation with his rival. Now, French successes on the field of battle made him less amenable, and the negotiations came to nothing.[1]

Meanwhile, the Swedish army under Baner's command, although not as successful as the French on the Rhine, harassed the imperialists and Saxons. In January 1639 the Saxons were driven back to Dresden, and in May, after defeating an imperialist army near Chemnitz, in Saxony, Baner reached Prague. Unable to capture the city, he devastated northern Bohemia. The year 1640 seemed about to fulfil one of the chief purposes of the Habsburg treaty, namely, the co-operation of the French and Swedish armies. Baner appeared at Erfurt in May, where he was joined by French, Hessian, and Brunswick forces. But the imperialists under Piccolomini refused battle, and the allies parted. The campaign ended in a stalemate.

Defeated on the Rhine, his empire overrun by Swedish and French armies, deprived of Spanish aid, Ferdinand III called an imperial Diet,

[1] For details of these complicated negotiations see A. Leman, *Richelieu et Olivares* (1938).

the first to meet since 1608. Perhaps, if he could obtain the full support of the empire's representatives, the war could be fought to a favourable conclusion. The Diet was opened at Ratisbon on 13 September 1640. In the early sittings, the delegates were sympathetic to Ferdinand, even though he made the Peace of Prague the basis for a settlement of the empire's affairs. The death in December of George William, Elector of Brandenburg, and the accession of his twenty-year-old son Frederick William, upset the emperor's calculations. The young prince, later known as the Great Elector, was the very opposite of his weak father. He dismissed the Catholic pro-Habsburg chief minister Schwarzenberg, and immediately took measures to free his lands from the marauding bands of soldiery. He then dropped a bombshell on the Diet when he instructed his delegate at Ratisbon to proclaim that the Peace of Prague was an unsatisfactory basis for a settlement. In July 1641 he signed a truce with Sweden, another serious blow to the emperor. Inspired by Brandenburg, the opposition to Ferdinand grew, and when the Diet ended its sessions in October 1641, he had neither obtained sufficient funds to replace the dwindling Spanish subsidies, nor maintained his leadership in the empire. Undoubtedly and understandably, the predominant sentiment at the Diet was for peace, rather than for war, and there now seemed to be some prospect of ending hostilities.

In 1635, and again in 1638, Pope Urban VIII had made abortive attempts to act as mediator for peace. Then, from 1638 to 1641 there were sporadic meetings in Hamburg between French, Swedish and imperial ambassadors which finally led to a preliminary treaty which was signed on 25 December 1641. By its provisions two simultaneous peace conferences were to be opened, one at Münster where the emperor would negotiate with France and its allies under the mediation of the pope and Venice, the other at Osnabrück where the emperor would treat with Sweden under the mediation of Denmark. The preliminary treaty was accepted by Louis XIII in February 1642, and by the emperor in July; but the real work of the congress did not begin until two years later. There was no provision for a cessation of arms, and the diplomats employed delaying tactics as they waited for favourable military news to strengthen their bargaining powers.

In 1641 Richelieu renewed the alliance with Sweden, and during the following year French arms were particularly successful. Taking advantage of Spain's weakness, troops occupied Artois in the north, and Roussillon in the south. When Richelieu died on 4 December 1642 he had accomplished his work. Those very territories and strategic positions which would be acquired by treaty in 1648 and 1659 were in French possession: Breisach to control the Rhine, Pinerolo the entry into Italy, Alsace, Artois and Roussillon.

Louis XIII appointed Cardinal Mazarin, Richelieu's own choice, as his successor. When the king died on 14 May 1643, the subtle Italian became the sole director of foreign affairs in the name of the Queen-Regent Anne of Austria and the boy king Louis XIV. The first great military victory of the new reign was won by Enghien on 19 May at Rocroy on the border of the Spanish Netherlands. The flower of the Spanish infantry was decimated, a defeat on land as striking as the famous defeat on sea of the Armada in 1588.

After Rocroy, the emperor gave up all hope of further support from Spain, and in the last five years of the war his military strength was gradually whittled away. He was, moreover, handicapped by a lack of efficient military commanders. The old veteran Piccolomini was the only one of any ability. Had it not been for the Bavarian generals Mercy and Werth, defeat would have come earlier, and Mercy, the abler of the two, was killed in battle in 1645. In comparison, the French marshal Turenne was a great strategist, and if Enghien sometime fought battles that cost more than they were worth, he at least won them. The Swedes, after Baner's death in 1641, were ably led by Torstensson, trained in the army of Gustavus Adolphus, and after 1646 by Wrangel. There were, however, great difficulties in the way of obtaining final victory. Armies were raised, campaigns planned, and battles were fought; but the victor was usually unable to follow up his advantage for lack of provisions in a devastated countryside. Nor was it any longer possible, as in the days of Wallenstein and Gustavus Adolphus, to levy 'contributions' on wealthy cities, for the wealth was gone.

In 1644 Werth and Mercy were strong enough to mount an offensive in the Rhine country, where they captured Freiburg and threatened Breisach. Enghien and Turenne fought the Bavarian-imperialist army in a bloody three-day battle near Freiburg (4, 5 and 9 August) which ended in the retreat of Mercy, who could no longer feed his troops. The French were then able to occupy the left bank of the Rhine as far as Mainz. A year later, on 3 August 1645, Enghien and Turenne won the second battle of Nördlingen, in which Mercy was killed; again the victors could not maintain their position, and withdrew to Alsace. On the eastern front, Torstensson's experience was a similar one. He defeated a Bavarian-imperialist army at Jankau in Bohemia (5 March 1645), and in April came within thirty miles of Vienna; but he was forced to retreat back to Bohemia.

The emperor's position was finally made untenable by the loss of Saxony, the defeat of Bavaria, the annihilation of the Spanish army in the Netherlands, and the imminent fall of Prague. A Swedish invasion of Saxony induced the elector of Saxony to sign a truce in September 1645. In July 1646 Turenne and Wrangel invaded Bavaria; and although the electorate was protected by Werth, the country was so miserably devastated by both friend and foe that Maximilian agreed to a truce on 14 March 1647. In the following September he broke the truce, but in vain.

On 17 May 1648, at Zusmarshausen near Augsburg, Wrangel and Turenne defeated the Bavarian-imperialist forces, and Bavaria was again overrun. At Lens, on 20 August, Enghien's army shattered the forces of Archduke Leopold, the emperor's brother, now governor of the Spanish Netherlands. In July a Swedish army besieged Prague, which held out for three months until the signing of the peace treaties. Ironically, the city of the famous 'defenestration', no longer Protestant and rebellious, fought to the end for its Catholic Habsburg ruler. These successive blows forced Ferdinand III to agree to peace, even though it meant deserting his ally the king of Spain.

Peace was made at Münster and Osnabrück by a truly European congress at which all the powers were represented save England, Poland, Russia and Turkey. It was a cumbersome peace conference, for the emperor treated with France and her allies at Münster, and with Sweden and her allies at Osnabrück. The two little Westphalian cities were thirty miles apart and there was the constant necessity of communication between the two sets of delegates. At Münster, the papal nuncio Chigi, later Pope Alexander VII, and the Venetian Contarini, acted as mediators. There was no mediator at Osnabrück. The smouldering enmity between Denmark and Sweden, which broke out into open war from 1643 to 1645, made it impossible for Denmark to undertake this role.

Six months were spent verifying credentials and the powers of the delegates, and quarrelling over procedure, before the meeting at Münster was officially opened on 4 December 1644 by a solemn mass and procession. The French and Swedish ambassadors at once insisted that they could not make peace with the emperor alone, and that the estates of the empire must therefore be seated at the conference tables. Another eight months dragged on before the emperor made this important concession. Now the congress would settle not only peace between the emperor and his enemies, but would also determine the internal affairs of the empire. This decision also further complicated the work of the congress. The representatives of the Protestant estates gathered at Osnabrück where Sweden served as their leader, while the Catholics went to Münster as clients either of France or of the emperor. Moreover, the Catholic and Protestant estates acted as two sections of an imperial Diet which would be forced to agree on all questions. The estates took no part in the negotiations with the foreign powers. They requested only that no German lands should be alienated, a futile gesture, and that the settlement should be submitted to them for ratification. Count Trautmansdorff, the emperor's intimate adviser, therefore had the difficult task of satisfying the demands of France and Sweden. The chief negotiators for France were the experienced diplomats d'Avaux and Servien, and for Sweden Axel Oxenstierna, the chancellor's son, and the much abler Adler Salvius.

France and Sweden did not stand alone in the negotiations which now took place. Maximilian of Bavaria supported France, in return for help in the retention of his electoral title and Palatinate lands. The emperor supported Sweden in the demand for Pomerania at the expense of Brandenburg as the price for a general peace.

France and Sweden waited on the course of the war to put themselves in the best bargaining position, and it was not until 7 January 1646 that they gave the details of their claims. The Swedes demanded Silesia from the emperor, Pomerania from Brandenburg, Wismar, and the bishoprics of Bremen and Verden. The French claimed the full sovereignty of Metz, Toul, Verdun, Alsace, Breisach, Philippsburg, the Breisgau, and the so-called 'four forest cities'[1] on the Rhine east of Basel.

On 13 September a preliminary agreement was reached between Trautmansdorff and the French ambassadors which granted France all her demands but the Breisgau and the 'four forest cities'. Alsace, however, posed a difficult problem which was not cleared up even in the final peace treaty. The territory, divided into Upper and Lower Alsace, was not a political unit, but rather a conglomeration of ancient rights and holdings, and free cities. In upper Alsace a Habsburg archduke, the emperor's nephew, held the title of landgrave, and besides possessed certain definite small areas. With the title of landvogt a Habsburg prince had ill-defined rights, particularly over ten free cities known as 'the Decapole'. These did not include Strasbourg and Mülhausen which were practically independent. There were also ecclesiastical principalities, and possessions of German princes, owing allegiance directly to the emperor.

It was, therefore, no simple matter to arrange the transference of Alsace to France, and the treaty is obscure and contradictory. According to the text of the final treaty, the House of Austria cedes to the king of France the landgravate of Upper and Lower Alsace in full sovereignty; but the bishop of Strasbourg was landgrave of Lower Alsace. In another article of the treaty the ten towns of the Decapole, certain monasteries, and the nobility of Lower Alsace are to retain the same privileges which they had previously enjoyed in relation to the empire. The king of France renounces territorial sovereignty over these territories; but then a clause is added which states that this does not mean that full sovereignty is denied to the king of France! Both Trautmansdorff and the French ambassador Servien wished to bring the negotiations to a conclusion, and it appears that they were willing to leave these contradictions in the treaty for the sake of reaching an agreement. Besides, Mazarin might have hoped that by not breaking all connections between some of the Alsatian territories and cities with the empire, France could claim a seat in the Diet. In this peculiar fashion France gained a foothold in Alsace. The population spoke a German dialect, and German historians have be-

[1] Waldshut, Laufenburg, Säkingen and Rhinefelden.

353

moaned the seizure of a land German in culture. It should, however, be pointed out that in the seventeenth century, and in the following century as well, territories were divided up without reference to the wishes of the inhabitants. There is also no doubt that the Alsatians became loyal Frenchmen.

The problem of satisfying Sweden was also difficult, for Sweden demanded Pomerania, a duchy to which the elector of Brandenburg had an undoubted legal claim when Duke Bogislav XIV died in 1637 without issue. Sweden's demand, and the emperor's willingness to appease Sweden by the grant of the duchy, or at least a part of it, met with the elector's fierce opposition. The impasse was finally broken by the joint threat of the emperor and the Swedish ambassadors that if he did not agree to a division of Pomerania, he would be deprived of the whole duchy. When the Swedes again demanded all Pomerania, d'Avaux stepped in on behalf of Brandenburg, for France had no desire to see her ally become too strong a power. Despite this intervention, Sweden achieved the hold on the southern shore of the Baltic which had been one of the chief aims of Gustavus Adolphus. By a convention signed on 7 September 1647, Sweden received, as fiefs of the empire, western Pomerania including the mouth of the River Oder and Stettin, and the islands of Rügen, Usedom and Wollin. In return for giving up eastern Pomerania, the Swedes obtained the secularized bishoprics of Bremen and Verden by which they controlled the rivers Weser and Elbe, and the port of Wismar. In compensation for the loss of western Pomerania, Frederick William received the secularized bishoprics of Halberstadt and Minden, as well as the expectancy of the archbishopric of Magdeburg on the death of the Saxon administrator. The elector of Brandenburg, thanks to French intervention, had done very well, for he was now, next to the Habsburgs, the ruler of the largest territory in the empire.

While France and Sweden were receiving their 'satisfaction', the internal affairs of the empire were under discussion. In these negotiations, the two foreign powers took a prominent part, for both held that their kings had entered the war against the emperor for the protection of the 'liberties' of the German princes. Besides, Sweden acted as the champion of German Protestantism. The French even attempted to prevent the continuance of the Habsburg hold on the imperial title. They failed, but so drastic a solution was made unnecessary by a clause in the Münster treaty which determined the practical independence of the German princes. Henceforth, the princes had 'territorial superiority in all matters ecclesiastical as well as political'. They had the right to conclude treaties both between themselves and with foreign powers. To be sure, they were under the obligation not to make any treaties directed against the empire or against the emperor, an obligation easily evaded. The old 'liberties' of the prince were thus transformed into sovereignty, even though this word was not used.

The princes were further strengthened by making the Diet innocuous. When religious issues were discussed, the Diet would henceforth divide into two bodies, Catholic and Protestant, and differences would be resolved not by majority vote, but by 'amicable agreement'. A unanimous vote was moreover necessary on all questions which divided the diet. Inevitably this meant that the Diet would sit perpetually without ever accomplishing anything of importance.

The 'Westphalian constitution' of the empire contained nothing new. It only verified and strengthened the power of the territorial princes, and put an official end to any possibility of the unification of Germany by the emperor. It remained the fundamental constitutional law of the empire until its dissolution a century and a half later.

The solutions found for the religious problem and the associated problem of ecclesiastical territories were essentially a broadening and a clarification of the Peace of Augsburg. For the first time Calvinism was officially recognized. This by no means meant toleration, for Protestant sects, other than the Lutheran and Calvinist, were still illegal. The year 1624 was made the determining date for the holding of church properties. This concession favoured the Protestants, for the year 1627, fixed by the Peace of Prague, came after the reconquest of secularized lands following the defeat of Christian IV of Denmark. The 'ecclesiastical reservation', strongly opposed by the Protestant princes ever since the Peace of Augsburg, was accepted with the provision that when either a Protestant or a Catholic changed his faith he would be forced to resign. In cases where the chapter of the cathedral was divided between Catholics and Protestants, the numbers of each would remain the same. By these measures, the holding of ecclesiastical lands would be fixed as they were in the year 1624. Another controversy was settled by giving the lay holders of bishoprics, called administrators, seats in the Diet.

The right of the prince to determine the religion of his subjects, already granted by the Peace of Augsburg, was again admitted in the clause which gave them 'territorial superiority in all matters ecclesiastical as well as political'. Some restrictions were, however, placed on the prince. If he changed his faith, he could not interfere with the religion of his subjects. Rights of public worship by dissidents as they existed in 1624, whether by law or by custom, were to be respected. The clauses concerning dissidents who were not legally protected are ambiguous. There is a grant of private worship, and a plea for toleration, but the prince also has the right of expulsion. Those expelled would be given five years to settle their affairs, and to take their property with them. With a few exceptions in Silesia and in Lower Austria, the emperor refused, however, to make any concessions to his Protestant subjects in the hereditary Habsburg lands.

The year 1618 was fixed as the date of restitution and amnesty. This meant particularly the restoration of the princes excluded by the Peace of Prague: the duke of Württemberg, the landgravine of Hesse-Cassel, widow of William V, and the margrave of Baden-Durlach. A special arrangement was made for Charles Lewis, the heir of Frederick V, the unfortunate 'Winter King'. It was impossible to deprive Maximilian of Bavaria of his electoral title, and an eighth electorate was therefore created for Charles Lewis. Maximilian moreover retained the Upper Palatinate, while the Lower Palatinate was restored to Charles Lewis.

Here again the emperor refused to be bound by the general law, for to go back to the year 1618 would have completely upset the great confiscations in Bohemia and in Austria after the battle of the White Hill. Ferdinand therefore declared that there would be complete restitution in his domains only to those who had taken up arms against the emperor after 1630.

By the spring of 1648 peace seemed to be in sight, but there were still outstanding difficulties to be overcome. The French delegates insisted on the emperor's neutrality in the war between France and Spain, a demand vigorously rejected by Ferdinand. This question became even more important when, on 30 January 1648, Spain and the United Provinces of the Netherlands signed a peace treaty. To the French, the withdrawal from the war of their staunchest ally against Spain made the emperor's neutrality all the more necessary. France wished also to exclude the duke of Lorraine from the peace treaty, in the hope of incorporating his duchy in the French monarchy. Finally, the Swedes demanded the payment of the huge sum of twenty million imperial dollars to pay off their armies.

These last obstacles to peace were overcome after months of wrangling. The disputes could finally be settled because both Mazarin and the emperor found it necessary to end hostilities, while Sweden could not continue the war without French assistance. Mazarin needed military forces at home to cope with the Fronde. Ferdinand's intransigence was overcome by military defeats. The chief German princes, Catholic as well as Protestant, also brought pressure to bear on the emperor to give up his ties with Spain. In the words of the Brandenburger delegate, the German people and lands must not be forced to endure the further horrors of war 'until Spain and France finished their game'. The elector of Mainz demanded the exclusion of all 'exotic' interests, especially those of Spain. Maximilian of Bavaria fully agreed with his fellow electors. Compromises were finally made. The emperor agreed to neutrality in the current war between Spain and France. In future wars between the two powers, individual German princes, including the emperor, were entitled to assist either belligerent power. The problem of Lorraine was postponed to later negotiation. Sweden's demand for twenty million imperial dollars was reduced to five million.

On 24 October 1648 the plenipotentiaries of France, Sweden, the emperor and the estates of the empire signed the treaties of Münster and

Osnabrück, commonly known as the Peace of Westphalia. A popular ballad tells of the ringing of church bells and the lighting of bonfires when the postilion from Münster rode through the land to proclaim the end of thirty years of suffering.

Indeed, scarcely a region had been spared the sufferings inflicted by invading armies and undisciplined bands of marauding soldiers, and even more by starvation and pestilence. There are many contemporary accounts of atrocities, some no doubt exaggerated to attract popular attention. The engravings of the Lorraine artist Callot give the most graphic picture of burning peasant houses and tortured peasants. There are not sufficiently accurate statistics to calculate the loss of life and the material damages. A modern historian has estimated that the population of Germany sank 40% in the countryside, and 33% in the cities.[1] The material damages of war, at least until the present time, have been quickly repaired, and the Thirty Years War was no exception. The peasants rebuilt their houses and again tilled their fields, commercial activities were resumed and the population increased rapidly. It has been estimated that the population of Germany in 1750 was 75% higher than at the end of the war.[2] A more lasting effect of the war is to be seen in the increase of serfdom in eastern Germany. The noble landowners needed labour for their huge estates, and overcame the difficulties of a decreased labour supply by binding the peasants to the soil, a process which had, to be sure, begun long before the war.

Some of the political consequences of the peace for Germany have already been mentioned, particularly the impotence of the emperor and the diet, and the independence of the princes. For the future, this meant that the emperors would turn their attention to the hereditary Habsburg possessions in the east, while the few powerful princes established states which could compete in the European state system. The elector of Brandenburg became the most successful in this competition. The old controversies which combined territorial and religious interests were for ever settled.

In its international aspect, the Peace of Westphalia marked the victory of France and Sweden over the Austrian Habsburg. The territorial gains of the two powers proved, however, to be of unequal importance. The Swedish conquests on the Baltic were soon lost to the growing power of Brandenburg-Prussia, while the French hold on the Rhine was maintained. Richelieu's work was not yet completed. The task of stopping the 'progress' of Spain was continued until the Treaty of the Pyrenees of 1659.

The Thirty Years War is the last European war in which religious motivation played a role, and Gustavus Adolphus was the last great

[1] Günther Franz, *Der dreissigjährige Krieg und das deutsche Volk* (2nd ed. Jena, 1943), p. 53.
[2] *Ibid.* p. 54.

statesman who equated religion and power politics. His ally, Richelieu, on the other hand, furthered the notion that the interest of the state formed the basis for political and military actions. This attitude was strengthened when Catholics as well as Protestants ignored the pope's solemn protest against the clauses of the peace treaties which were injurious to the Catholic church. The claim of a supranational religious authority to interfere in affairs of state was rejected.

Until the days of the French Revolution, the Peace of Westphalia was considered to be the basis of the European state system. The recognition of the independence of two states, the United Provinces of the Netherlands and of the Swiss Confederation, could give some sanction to the belief that only a European congress could ratify the creation or extinction of states. Many years later, Edmund Burke protested that the partition of Poland was a breach of the Westphalian treaties. The Treaty of Utrecht of 1713 was considered to be a rectification of the Peace of Westphalia. One final conclusion can be drawn. The Thirty Years War and the peace which ended it prevented the establishment of Habsburg hegemony, and prepared the way for the aggressions of Louis XIV. In this sense the Thirty Years War may be called the beginning of modern power politics. It brought into being a new awareness of the danger involved in the domination of Europe by any one power, a danger which could be met only by concerted diplomatic action, or if necessary by war.

CHAPTER XII

THE LOW COUNTRIES

THE truce of 1609 which for the time being terminated Spain's attempts to reconquer the northern Netherlands was in fact a defeat of the southern Netherlands, although the Archduke Albert and his principal minister Spinola had done so much to bring it about. It was a defeat because until further notice the independence of the rebel provinces was recognized and the split in the seventeen provinces confirmed. The period now starting is indeed one of growing estrangement between the two parts of the old Burgundian state. In 1609 the northern republic had not yet reached its full territorial extent. The parts of Brabant, Limburg and Flanders which were finally to belong to it were conquered only after 1621. But in principle this northern state was already by 1609 what it continued to be until the French Revolution. Already in these early years of the seventeenth century it was getting used to its status of sovereign independence and was adopting the character of a nation. In the southern provinces a parallel development took place. Religious, social, economic and political contrasts seemed inevitably to lead to the growth of two different, indeed hostile national feelings.

This should not, of course, be exaggerated. The national factor did not yet possess much influence. Far more important was religion. When studying the attitude of the Jesuits who had such a predominant importance in the history of the southern Netherlands and of the Calvinists in the north who had comparatively much less influence but nevertheless set their seal upon Dutch political and social life, it is evident that both these groups in this period had not yet given up the idea that the north and south fundamentally formed a unity; they even sought to restore it. But they wanted this reunification to be brought about on their own conditions only, that is to say, through the establishment of exclusive supremacy of their own particular creed in both parts of the Netherlands. Since this obviously could not be achieved by either group, both were by the sheer force of circumstances driven back into their own provinces. There their influence was unchallenged or, if they were Calvinists, at any rate considerable. As the hope of reconquering the other part faded both Jesuits and Calvinists developed a rather resigned hatred of the other group, now regarded as irretrievably corrupted, and as a complete stranger. The stupendous polemics of Jesuits against Calvinists and vice versa (an immense literature in Latin and Dutch) which passionately contrasted heretical Holland and popish Belgium, helped to break the national unity of the religiously divided Netherlands.

A characteristic instance of this process of drifting apart of two groups of provinces which had been brought into close contact by political events and, partly, by the common language was the divergence in the historical interpretation of the revolt of the Netherlands. Two contrasting myths were developed. In the north the struggle for liberty of religion and for national independence was described in a series of major historical works: by Grotius, in his beautiful Latin, or by the Renaissance poet P. C. Hooft, in a vigorous Dutch inspired by Tacitus, full of delightful innovations. In the south, on the contrary, the writers considered reckless pursuit of gain, ambition, criminal lust to be the motives of the revolt. William 'the Silent', praised as the *pater patriae* in the north, was in the south an egoistic, ambitious tyrant whereas Philip II, in the eyes of Belgian authors a prince distinguished by his careful love of his subjects, remained for the northern historians and pamphleteers the personification of evil. So the most recent past lost its character of common history and was made to fit into two hostile mythologies. North and south seemed to become an antithesis of widely diverging principles. The north, a maritime power, governed by a *bourgeoisie* and its commercial interests, looked fundamentally different from the continental south with its Spanish court at Brussels, its Jesuits, its loyalty to the monarchy, its nobility growing in number and social importance.

There is, however, some danger in overstressing these differences. For although the north developed at an amazing pace into the leading commercial power of Europe it is (as we shall see) by no means certain that the economy of the south declined. The tendencies, moreover, which made the southern Netherlands into a society dominated by a court and a nobility were not altogether absent in the northern republic. It is significant that precisely at the moment when the archducal court at Brussels withered away after Isabella's death in 1633, Stadholder Frederick Henry was building up at The Hague a court life and a regal style which, had not the regents and a series of unpredictable events prevented their development, might well have transformed the character of Dutch society. A comparison of the development of the political institutions in both parts of the old Burgundian Netherlands would also suggest the need of caution. In the southern Netherlands the traditional structure, with its complicated pattern of local rights and privileges which Charles V had been unable or unwilling completely to destroy, was preserved, although the spirit running through the central government was more absolutist than ever before. In the northern provinces only the names and the forms of the old institutions were maintained, while they acquired new contents. Both in the south and the north, however, federalism, provincial autonomy, local particularism remained the leading principles of everyday political life. And if southern monarchism is, in a general way, to be contrasted with northern republicanism we should, on the other hand, overlook neither

the monarchical tendencies apparent in Frederick Henry's stadholdership
nor the remarkable fact that the main trend of Dutch political theory
remained, throughout this period, monarchical. During several decades
in the early seventeenth century professors of Leiden, Utrecht and
Groningen universities taught their pupils that monarchy was the oldest
and the best form of government. The endlessly repeated Calvinist
doctrines of the sixteenth century, moreover, seemed to take for granted
a limited monarchy in which the States as representatives of the people
were by no means the sovereigns but only the protectors of the old constitution. A truly republican political ideology was not developed in the
northern Netherlands before the 1650s.

The state which had come into existence in the north was not built
according to any constitutional programme nor was it felt or recognized
by its inhabitants as a new, revolutionary creation. Yet it obviously was.
When Grotius tried to prove in his book *De Antiquitate et Statu Reipubli-
cae Batavicae* (1610) that Holland's government had fundamentally always
been what it was in his own time, he completely misinterpreted history.
Although traditional institutions were preserved their meaning and function were transformed with the result that a political system emerged
which created great and often very critical amazement in contemporary
Europe. It seemed so unworkable a mixture of all forms of government
and so devoid of any leading organizational principle that its near collapse
was confidently predicted. It did not collapse, of course, and its supple-
ness, though often causing dangerous uncertainties, proved on the whole
more beneficial for the stability of the nation than did the contemporary
absolute monarchies for theirs. It should, moreover, be noted that within
this structure it was possible during the early seventeenth century to build
upon the ruins left by the revolt a very coherent and efficient system of
local government and local or provincial jurisdiction. This work was
directed or commented on by a school of jurists who, thanks to their
humanistic outlook, not only participated in the rapid development of
their science in its international context but often even acquired a leading
position among their colleagues in north-west Europe.

The federation of the northern Netherlands was based on the Union of
Utrecht of 1579. This was not a constitution but an alliance made by some
provinces in order to carry out a number of specific purposes, in the first
place the continuation of the war against Spain which the States General
representing the whole of the seventeen provinces did not pursue with
sufficient determination. The course of events consolidated this alliance
and detached from it those provinces which eventually formed no part
of the northern republic. The Union of Utrecht became in this way the
nucleus of what might be called the Dutch state (although the usual expression was the Republic of the United Netherlands) as it was the only formal
bond which held the provinces together. The central organ of this union

was the States General. Not the entire territory of the Dutch Republic was represented in this assembly. Gelderland, Holland, Zeeland, Utrecht, Friesland, Overijssel and Groningen sent delegates to the States General but Drente (indeed a backward and unimportant province) was not represented in the central government although it had a sort of provincial States of its own. The slices of Flanders, Brabant and Limburg which finally were appended to the republic did not possess any kind of regional representation or administration and were governed by the States General as conquered territories with complete disrespect of their traditions and wishes.

Each of the seven provinces sent as many representatives to the States General as it wanted or as the limited space of the meeting room at The Hague permitted. But each possessed only one vote and the representatives were bound to vote as instructed by the States of their respective provinces. In important matters there was no question of outvoting the minority since unanimity of the seven sovereigns was required for taking a decision binding on each of them. The States General met every day, even on Sundays, for a couple of hours. Their importance was considerable. They acted as the representative of the union, conducted foreign affairs, controlled defence and the federal taxes which were apportioned among the provinces according to a strict scheme. Holland paid about 58 % (half of which was contributed by Amsterdam), Overijssel not quite 4 %.

Another federal institution was the Council of State, no longer as in the old days an advisory body to the ruler but a committee of about twenty-five persons in which the seven provinces were represented and which was entrusted with much military, financial and other business. It was perhaps better equipped for acting as the central government than the States General because its proceedings were not hampered to such a degree by the principle of provincial sovereignty. Yet this very fact caused the States General to leave only minor questions for it to deal with, although by its instruction of 1588 it was designed to be the central executive of the union. The Chamber of Accounts of the Generality did not possess much power either. It is significant that there was a federal mint chamber exercising some control over the mints of the various provinces but no federal mint.

Although the fleet lay under the control of the States General and the admiral-general, the daily direction of naval affairs was referred to the so-called Admiralty Colleges. These five colleges (three in Holland, one each in Zeeland and Friesland), the members of which were appointed by the States General on the recommendation of the provinces, provided for maritime defence including the collection of the taxes for this purpose (the *Convooien* and *Licenten*, in fact import and export duties). The trading companies also depended on the authority of the States General because these had the right to grant monopolies. Yet the actual direction for example of the East India Company consisted of the so-called chambers, local administrative bodies which exercised supervision on company affairs. Membership of these chambers was lucrative and as the government of the towns in which they were established took care of the appointments they were exclusively composed of members of the group of municipal regents. The body of seventeen members [*De Heeren Zeventien*], representing these local chambers, acted as central administration. It should be clear from this survey that the federal government only possessed a severely limited authority. There was no federal court of justice, no federal church government, no federal internal administration in general. Provincial sovereignty was carefully respected and it was difficult for any of the federal organs to encroach upon provincial rights. If in practice the republic possessed a far greater unity than this federal system would seem to allow this was due to the overwhelming power of the province of Holland. For it was Holland which provided the money, the ships, the leading ideas and the leading statesmen.

Holland's system of government was rather complicated. Legally sovereignty resided undoubtedly in the States. But there was some discussion about the way in which they had acquired it. Because it was often and officially stated that they acted as the representatives of popular sovereignty it might perhaps be concluded that ultimately the members of the States, as a personification of the people, possessed sovereignty individually rather than corporately. For these members were indeed supposed to be the people themselves. There were nineteen of them; one vote belonged to the nobility, eighteen votes belonged to the towns (it should be noted that The Hague had no vote). In important matters unanimity was required. The States met four times a year for a few weeks. The daily work was done by a standing committee of ten members appointed for three years. As the urban delegations to the States were composed of men belonging to the urban regent families it is clear that provincial government was largely in control of this small group. The States of the other six provinces were composed in totally different ways. Those of Gelderland, for instance, were in fact only the joint meeting of representatives of the three parts into which the province was divided and which each sent two deputations, one of the nobility and one of the towns. It is easy to see that the nobility played an incomparably more important part here than in Holland. The States of Utrecht were composed of three 'members'. Besides the nobility and the towns the chapters (which were of course no longer Roman Catholic but which, unlike the other institutions of the Catholic church in the republic, had not been abolished), also sent a deputation; the other two 'members' however had the right to elect the deputation of the 'first member' out of the body of Protestant canons. It was a highly anomalous situation which led to much friction.

The main characteristic of the States of Friesland, to mention still another example, was the predominance of the rural interests. The whole organization of the Friesland States, moreover, was remarkable because, unlike the other provinces, representation was more than mere theory here. The thirty groups of villages [*grietenijen*] into which the province was divided, had the right to appoint members of the States; they were elected by the owners of houses to which the right of voting was attached. The members of the States, appointed for one year—besides the rural representatives there were the deputies of eleven towns—were true plenipotentiaries. There was no need in Friesland to refer matters back to the constituents. The States really exercised sovereignty on behalf of a fairly large electorate. It should however be added that because of much corruption and highly oligarchic practices this government lost its democratic character during the seventeenth and eighteenth centuries.

Holland's most important official was the land's advocate, whose title was changed after 1618 into council pensionary (foreign contemporaries preferred to use the term grand pensionary to distinguish him from the legal advisers of many of the towns equally called pensionaries). Thanks to the cumulation of duties with which he was charged he was able to exercise great influence in all the various spheres of provincial and federal government. He acted as chairman of the States of Holland and of their committees and as the leader of the Holland deputation to the States General; he carried on the correspondence of the republic with the Dutch ambassadors abroad and received their communications, while the official despatches they sent to the Greffier of the States General were merely formal. And through his knowledge of all current affairs, though officially only a paid servant of the States of Holland, he sometimes wielded decisive power not only in his own province but in the whole republic. Much, however, depended on his own capacities and energy. At no time were either the States of Holland or the States General really subject to him. Nor was there any possibility of the office developing into a more or less permanent presidency of the union. It was personal qualities which enabled some of its incumbents to assume the role of leading statesman of a republic which sometimes needed this leadership but which was never willing permanently to adapt its institutions to what was ultimately regarded as an anomaly.

The position of the Stadholder was still more complicated. As he was appointed by the States of the various provinces his was legally a provincial function dependent on the sovereign will of his principals. Several elements, however, bestowed on the incumbent of the office a far higher status. The dignity derived great importance from the fact that in Holland, Zeeland and most of the other provinces only the princes of Orange, heirs to the immensely popular tradition of William the Silent, were appointed as stadholders (whereas in Friesland and sometimes also in Groningen

and Drente the office was held by the counts of Nassau). Moreover, thanks
to his being stadholder in various provinces at the same time the prince of
Orange, though not a member of the States General, naturally participated in the making of federal policies. As he also often held the functions
of captain-general and admiral-general of the union his activities were,
in fact, never confined to merely provincial matters. The stadholdership
itself included several truly sovereign rights which had formerly belonged
to the stadholders of Burgundian times who often acted as the substitutes,
the *locum tenentes*, of the distant sovereign. The stadholders of the republic
possessed the right of electing urban magistrates and appointing several
provincial officials. They equally had the right of granting pardon or
remission of penalties. Often the stadholdership was regarded by contemporaries as the monarchical element in a state with a mixed constitution. This was certainly an inaccurate way of describing the structure of
the republic but it had the merit of indicating that notwithstanding the
legal supremacy of the States actual practice as well as its theoretical
rationalization needed the help of different powers and conceptions. From
a sociological point of view it is clear that the presence of this princely
tradition helped to mitigate the absolute character of the ruling oligarchy,
though it should be added that the princes of Orange were rarely willing
and never able to supersede the Holland plutocracy—from whom they and
the republic ultimately received the money they needed and the directives
motivating their policies.

It would, indeed, have been disastrous for the republic as a whole if
Holland's power had been eliminated. For Holland was the mainspring
of all Dutch activity whether commercial, industrial or cultural. There is
perhaps no other example in history of a complete and highly original
civilization springing up in so short a time on so small a territory. It is, of
course, true that the conditions necessary for its development were
already beginning to be fulfilled a century before when the Amsterdam or
the Holland staple market started functioning. It is also true that the
newly won independence imbued the inhabitants with self-reliance and
optimism and prompted them to find their own forms in all the spheres in
which they moved. National or patriotic pride made them transform the
vernacular into a rich and precise language to be used as easily in literature
as in science. The University of Leiden rapidly acquired international
fame and certainly owed much of its resilience to the inspiring force of
Protestantism and the lack of medieval tradition which enabled it to break
through the old curriculum. It should, moreover, not be forgotten that the
many thousands of Calvinist south-Netherlanders who found refuge in the
north (totalling, according to a modern estimate, 60,000) contributed their
fortunes, their skill, knowledge and dynamism to the development of
Dutch economy and civilization. But all this makes the phenomenon of
this small people (the population of Holland, half of the total population

of the Republic, amounted to not yet 700,000) unexpectedly rising to such a height hardly less unaccountable an event.

The growth that is most easy to measure is economic growth, though we do not possess enough data to provide our description with an adequate statistical basis. The mechanism of the staple market was no innovation of this period; but it was refined and elaborated. No doubt Amsterdam derived inestimable benefit from the fact that since 1585 Antwerp was cut off from the sea. Yet the differences between the Brabant market in the sixteenth century specializing in small and expensive merchandise and largely dependent on foreign freightage as well as capital and the much more varied Holland staple based on its own immense merchant fleet and it own capital are obvious. The removal of the staple in western Europe from Antwerp to Amsterdam is symbolized by the building of the Amsterdam Exchange in 1611. The development of the central goods market in Holland created the urgent necessity of improving the monetary situation. By bringing money exchange under municipal control and opening the possibility for a transfer system the discount banks in Amsterdam (1609), Middelburg (1616), Delft (1621) and Rotterdam (1635) tried to meet this need. It is remarkable that the Bank of Amsterdam soon started granting credit, although this went against the original intention.

Amsterdam grew rapidly. About 1600 it had perhaps 50,000 inhabitants; about 1620 the figure rose to 100,000, about 1650 to 200,000. In 1610 the work of extending the city boundaries and the construction of the three famous concentric canals with their elegant houses was started. At the same time large warehouses sprang up where the staple goods, above all grains, could be stored, early examples of highly satisfying aesthetic utility building. No firm figures illustrating the expansion of trade are available. But we know that in the 1640s it reached its climax and that throughout the whole period Amsterdam left the other growing towns of Holland far behind. We also know the rapidity with which enormous amounts of assets were gathered by some Amsterdam families and the amazingly quick rise of foreigners on the social ladder. Banningh Cocq, the central figure of Rembrandt's *Night Watch* (he died in 1655) was the son of a poor German who started his career in Amsterdam as a beggar, made a fortune and contracted a very successful marriage. The son rose to the rank of knight and burgomaster. These upstart families, eager to acquire titles of nobility (as there was in the Dutch Republic no authority which could ennoble them they asked for favours of foreign princes) soon adapted themselves to the humanistic culture of the universities, and though few of them may have been able to write Latin they all exaggerated their pride by adopting the classicist prejudices concerning the lower orders and democracy.

The nucleus of the *entrepôt* business continued to be the Baltic trade. The most important articles transported to the Baltic were salt, herring, wine and colonial products. In addition to cereals, wood and wooden products which formed the bulk of their homeward cargoes and for which they found a large market in western and southern Europe, the Dutch ships carried iron and copper. On their outward voyages they sailed partly in ballast, loaded with the Dutch bricks with which the Baltic countries built their Renaissance architecture. It is clear that one of the essential tasks of Dutch statesmanship was to keep the Sound open. During this period also trade to Norway in ships specially equipped for transporting timber and to Archangel increased. The Dutch merchants began to be successful in competing with the English Muscovy trade. It is equally characteristic that France and the French colonies, in matters of trade and shipping largely dependent on Holland, had to tolerate Dutch trading-posts often to the detriment of their own population. Trading with the enemy continued to be a fundamental element of Dutch economy. Not only did the Holland merchants after 1621 go on trading to the southern Netherlands and Spain, but probably this trade actually increased because Amsterdam had during the previous years become the centre of the traffic in weapons and ammunition. It is ironic that even the hated Dunkirk privateers, who waged so unrelenting a war against the Dutch, sometimes were provided with ammunition by the Dutch themselves, notwithstanding a sharp prohibition by the States General but with the connivance of the Amsterdam admiralty.

It was a long way from these more or less tolerated activities to the actual privateering business in the Mediterranean though there are indications that Dutch patricians did not always shrink from financing it. More important was the ocean-going trade of the East India and West India Companies, not however because during these years it already formed an essential part of the Dutch economy but because it led to new developments in the field of commercial organization and to the foundation of what later became a Dutch colonial empire. The East India Company of 1602 owed its existence to the initiative of the grand pensionary of Holland, Oldenbarnevelt, who realized that the numerous companies trading to the East, now unnecessarily weakening each other, would in the long run be unable to carry on their struggle with Portugal if they did not collaborate. In comparison with these older companies the new elements of the organization of 1602 (essentially a federation of them) were twofold. It was, in the first place, designed to be permanent whereas formerly the merchants merely pooled capital to finance a single journey. All the inhabitants of the republic, moreover, were free to buy shares in the new company. This was the motive for the States General to grant the company the monopoly of Dutch trade in the area east of the Cape of Good Hope. Thanks to the enormous capital of 6,500,000 *guilders* brought together in 1602 and the concentration of ships and armed forces now made possible, the Dutch position in the East Indies was considerably strengthened. Yet the profits were small during the first decades. Dividends could be paid but seldom (1610/11: $162\frac{1}{2}$%; 1619: $37\frac{1}{2}$%; 1623: 25%). Only from 1634 was it possible annually to pay a dividend fluctuating between $12\frac{1}{2}$% and 50%. By that time the capital stock which in 1602 had been shared by all classes of the population was already concentrated in the hands of relatively few capitalists.

The West India Company had a less satisfactory development. Its immediate purpose was totally different from that of the East India Company. The fact alone that it was founded only in 1621, after the end of the truce, although it had been under discussion for many years, indicates that its essential function was to wage war against Spain. It enjoyed the support of the orthodox Calvinist war party, but throughout its history the less orthodox patricians felt sceptical or even hostile towards the company, and though it achieved useful results in its piratical war against Spain (as for example the capture of the Spanish Silver Fleet in 1628) lack of money and indifference towards the establishment of colonies rampant among the regents prevented its developing to an instrument of lasting importance.

Colonial trade, it has already been said, was of secondary importance within the framework of Dutch economy. The tonnage of the fleet trading to the East Indies amounted to no more than 0·2% of the total Dutch merchant fleet. Industry was in comparison a considerably more essential element of Dutch economic life. There was however, generally speaking, a fundamental weakness inherent to Dutch industry (as well as to the Dutch staple) because industry, instead of providing the staple with Dutch products, was largely dependent on the staple. Finishing or merely improving semi-manufactured articles imported from abroad was its main activity. There were notable exceptions. In some fields industry indeed worked up the raw material and produced the finished article itself. The textile manufacture of Leiden, for example, developed rapidly during the early seventeenth century thanks to the introduction of some mechanization and of industrial capitalism, but on the whole such industries as the sugar refineries, the tobacco factories, the sawmills, the cloth-dressing and the whitelead works were most typical of Dutch industrial enterprise. Another important branch of Dutch economy was fishing. It is worth noting that herring fishing was organized in a system which later became characteristic for the mechanism of the whole staple market: a group of ship-owners ('the first hand') took care of the supply of the products and a group of capitalist wholesale dealers ('the second hand') brought them on the market. Agriculture, finally, was of only limited importance but the abundance of available capital made it possible to start the expensive and very risky work of reclaiming the numerous lakes of Holland.

The social structure of the various provinces of the republic showed striking differences. In Friesland it was the gentlemen-farmers, in Gelder-land and Overijssel the noblemen, in Holland the urban patricians who formed the ruling class. The most important feature in the growth of Dutch society was the formation of the group of urban patricians, of *bourgeois gentilshommes* who, though belonging to and indeed acting as the 'regents' of the towns, gradually withdrew from business. This development was as yet only in an early stage and it was not completed before the end of the seventeenth century. Nevertheless the tendency was clear for the urban plutocrats to form a semi-noble, aristocratic governing class sometimes not shrinking back from taking advantage of government with the same ruthlessness with which former generations had enriched themselves in trade. But despite many examples of corruption, narrow class egoism and shortsighted pride, on the whole this government by unsalaried and legally unprivileged regents worked fairly efficiently. It is perhaps symptomatic that so few social disturbances were really directed against the governing class. The substantial and petty *bourgeoisie*, though rigidly excluded from the ruling oligarchy, generally seem to have accepted their position. It is not surprising that the mass of the people whose poverty increased in these years of growing prosperity (the price revolution and other factors may explain this phenomenon) did not put forward any workable plans of social and political reorganization. But in what way must the absence of any major social conflict—there are, how-ever, examples of local riots often caused by the heavy indirect taxation—be explained? Does confidence in the government or rather lack of docu-ments or lack of research account for this? In this connection the advanced forms of private charity organized by the patricians and of the work-houses or the houses of correction organized by the urban governments and imitated throughout Europe should be taken into consideration by the historian trying to assess the benefits due to this peculiar oligarchy.

How do the form of government and the economic development of the southern Netherlands compare with this? The political system of the southern provinces is often described as tempered absolutism and the south Netherlanders were proud of being governed as subjects, not as inhabitants of conquered territory. They were indeed perfectly justified in contrasting the despotic government by the States General of the slices of Brabant and Flanders belonging to the republic with the civil government prevailing in those parts of these provinces which were ruled by Brussels. They also took it for granted that the government of the southern Nether-lands was less absolute than that of Spain. The provincial States con-tinued to exercise the right to vote benevolences and subsidies; local law was preserved notwithstanding the legislative activity of the central government. As far as internal government in the southern Netherlands was concerned, the Spanish crown carefully kept up the principle that only a personal union linked the provinces with the Spanish Empire. Even in the international field it was made clear that the state of the southern Netherlands was supposed to continue the sovereign state of the Burgundians. The governors of the southern Netherlands were represented abroad by their own ambassadors and foreign ambassadors were accredited to the Brussels court.

It is difficult to decide how far legal forms reflected actual practice. From different points of view different interpretations concerning the relative autonomy or the relative dependence of the southern Netherlands are possible. Studying the situation on the plane of local government and jurisdiction, of church government, of intellectual life in general, nothing can be found but autochthonous elements bearing the responsibilities and spreading the directive ideas. The fact that the privileges were newly established (the gilds reorganized themselves more rigidly); the phenomenon of a rural nobility which thanks to the ambition felt by rich patricians to be ennobled, grew in number without becoming a court nobility (for after 1633 there was no court life of any importance) or possessing valuable tax privileges, assumed a great position in local and provincial government; the appeal of the Jesuits, relatively more numerous and influential than anywhere in Europe (the order had in 1630 about 1,700 members in the southern Netherlands as against about 2,200 in France, 2,300 in Germany, 3,000 in Spain); all this can perhaps be explained by the circumstances which deprived this society of the possibility of urban expansion and made it into an outpost of the Counter-Reformation, but it is by no means to be regarded as a Spanish import. A different picture, however, presents itself when the policies of the central government are taken into consideration. The part played by the Archdukes Albert and Isabella who from 1598 to 1621 were in theory the sovereigns of the southern Netherlands—after Albert's death sovereignty reverted to the Spanish crown—or that of the governors succeeding them, the large number of Spanish officials working at the Brussels court and the stiffness of the ruling etiquette, the role of the southern Netherlands in international politics or the sad history of the States General in 1632 (we shall describe it later) indicate so overwhelming a measure of Spanish influence that but for some short moments no real autonomy seems to have existed.

A general judgement on the economic development of the south needs to be equally cautious. There can be no doubt that compared with the enormous expansion of the north and (as far as this expansion was due to the closure of the Scheldt) precisely in consequence of the great achievements of the republic, economic growth in the south was slow and restricted. But was there, on the whole, absolute decline? In some fields this seems undeniable. It is true that the closure of the Scheldt, though excluding Antwerp and the old Flemish towns from direct openings to the sea, did not prevent their trading to Zeeland and Holland. It is equally true that thanks to the important trade it continued to carry on along overland routes Antwerp was by no means an exhausted and dead city; yet the central, radiating force which had distinguished it before 1585 was broken. Also for Bruges and Ghent, already in the sixteenth century no longer the important industrial and trading towns of the Middle Ages, it was extremely hard to achieve some measure of recovery. But there was, on the other hand, so much activity and expansion in agriculture as well as in rural industry that it is better to describe the development of this economy as a renewal and a transformation rather than a decline. On the whole the early seventeenth century presents the picture of recovery. The disasters of the sixteenth century were gradually overcome and new solutions were being found for the difficulties of the present.

The society of the southern Netherlands makes the impression of being very homogeneous. It was Roman Catholic. Thanks to the emigration of the most convinced Protestant minorities, to the astounding energy displayed by bishops and priests in preaching and education, to their suffocating censorship and the extreme care with which everything in the life of the south Netherlanders from birth to death was given the seal of the church; thanks, finally, to the close collaboration of the civil and the ecclesiastical authorities, the Counter-Reformation achieved a complete success. Heresy disappeared, not through force (the bloody *placcaten* of Charles V and Philip II though not abolished were no longer applied and there was no question of persecutions) but through making it impossible for those who refused strict outward conformity to Roman Catholicism to find a place in this society. The whole civilization of these years seems to be organized in the service of the triumphant religious ideal. How vigorous and lively that could be is shown by Rubens and his school whose genius, however, possibly makes us forget too much of the tensions and the counter-currents which were not altogether absent. But on the whole the south formed until Rubens' death in 1640 undoubtedly an impressive intellectual unity and, as such, a sharp contrast with the northern republic where theological and political disruptive forces seemed to confirm the often repeated prophecy that as soon as it would no longer be united by the war with Spain, this state would irretrievably disintegrate.

It was in the first place religious disputes which shook the northern provinces when, after having signed the truce, they had the opportunity to concentrate on them. In the reformed church tensions became apparent that after a lapse of only a few years came to dominate the political situation. Gomarus, professor of theology at Leiden University—he was born at Bruges in 1563—opened shortly after 1600 an attack on the dogmatic views of his nearest colleague Arminius who was three years his elder, reproaching him for deviating from the Calvinistic tenets especially those concerning predestination. This is not the place to examine these doctrinal disputes.[1] The question which has to be put here is in what way they became involved with the purely political contrasts in the republic. There is indeed reason for astonishment here. For though these discussions could only be regarded as fundamental by those who were directly concerned and who tried to push the arguments of their adversaries to their last consequences in order to combat them the more easily, they did in fact nearly bring about a civil war. How was this possible? It was not because so many people were involved. The conflict was entirely confined to Holland as the Arminians hardly got any support outside this province. Within Holland the groups were small; probably only a very tiny majority of the Holland population belonged to the reformed church at all and among its members many felt indifferent about these incomprehensibly complicated theological issues.

The government tried in 1607 and 1609 without success to bring about a reconciliation. In 1610 the Arminians, aware that their minority position was becoming untenable, addressed to the States of Holland a request for protection couched in a document called Remonstrance (hence they were called Remonstrants). The Grand Pensionary Oldenbarnevelt was probably informed beforehand of this step; he might even have suggested it. The majority of the States responded favourably to the Remonstrance. By no means all the urban patricians were Calvinists. Most of them did not belong to the reformed church but were either Mennonites, Lutherans, Roman Catholics or religiously indifferent. Few only were attracted by Gomarus' severity. Among these few were some leading families in Amsterdam. Most regents, however, reacted to the conflicts in the church with feelings of amazement and fear. One thing was obvious to them: it was intolerable that the majority in the church should drive a minority into the wilderness, closing the official church to people with slightly diverging ideas and increasing the already considerable number of sects. After many fruitless attempts to find a solution the States decided to intervene. By a resolution supported by the majority (but what legal validity did such a non-unanimous decision possess?) the ministers of the church were forbidden to deal with the doctrinal points in question and more or less advised to accept an intermediate point of view on predestination and salvation (1614). The Gomarists, now commonly called the Contra-Remonstrants, refused to submit to this arbitrary ruling with the result that they were driven out of those towns where the urban administrations were in favour of Arminianism. This happened, for example, in Rotterdam where no less a man than Hugo Grotius, fervent adherent of Oldenbarnevelt's religious policy, acted as pensionary.

In Amsterdam, however, the burgomasters supported the Gomarists, partly because of the genuine convictions of some of the leading men in

[1] See above Chapter v, pp. 176–81.

the town council but for the other part because of their aversion to Oldenbarnevelt's policies in general, Oldenbarnevelt having in 1609 forced through the conclusion of the truce in the face of Amsterdam's vehement opposition. Amsterdam had at that time been supported by Stadholder Maurice. It was perhaps only natural for him now to act once again as a supporter of Amsterdam's cause and to side with the Gomarists. He took his decision in July 1617. A month later, Oldenbarnevelt answered with a resolution backed by the majority in the States, by which the towns were advised to engage troops of their own for the preservation of order. The commanders of the regular army were ordered to co-operate with the States of the province or the administrations of the towns where they lay in garrison, notwithstanding any orders to the contrary. This meant that the States withdrew the army stationed in Holland from the authority of the captain-general, Stadholder Maurice, if he refused to support them.

In this way the religious disputes developed into a conflict between two political parties, each provided with a kind of political programme. This was a development quite unforeseen by Gomarus, when he objected to Arminius' supposed latitudinarianism. On the one hand was the party of Oldenbarnevelt, supported by the majority in the States of Holland, that is, by the majority of the urban administrations. They defended the right of the secular government to control the church, they rejected the suggestion frequently made of summoning a national, that is inter-provincial, synod and they seemed to claim that they could deprive the captain-general of the exercise of his authority as far as provincial troops were concerned. It was therefore—or so it seemed—erastianism, latitudinarianism and provincialism which they were defending. The other group, supported by Maurice, by Amsterdam and some other Holland towns, by all the other provinces and the majority of the States General, stood or proclaimed to stand for the opposite: severe orthodoxy, the right of the church to decide about its own dogma, submission of the provinces to the wishes and the authority of the majority in the States General. Much however in all this was mere appearance. Principles, no doubt, were involved, but old resentments, obstinacy, constitutional uncertainties help to explain the tragedy. From a strictly legal point of view both opponents were able to refer to law and precedent so that both, in their blind pursuit of what they regarded as right, exaggerated views equally defensible.

In fact the conflict was more than anything else a conflict between two rival, personal powers: that of Oldenbarnevelt and that of Maurice, both supported by small groups of adherents. It had taken many years before this position was reached. As soon as it was arrived at the result could be predicted. Maurice had the best cards: the army, the immensely powerful city of Amsterdam, the large majority of the States General. Tactfully and slowly preparing his charges as though he were leading a military campaign, he isolated Oldenbarnevelt's party. Then, supported by the States General, he had its leaders put into prison: Oldenbarnevelt himself and, among others, Hugo Grotius (1618). His party confirmed its victory by means of what might be called two lawsuits. An extraordinary tribunal sentenced Oldenbarnevelt to death (on 13 May 1619 the great man was executed) and some of his collaborators, among them Grotius, to imprisonment for life. The famous national as well as international Synod of Dordrecht condemned the Remonstrant doctrine in the presence of the élite of Calvinistic scholarship and drove its adherents out of the church and the country (1619). If the practice of those times is taken into consideration both sets of sentences, although obviously partisan, seem from a formal point of view unobjectionable.

The result of these conflicts determined the history of the republic for the next thirty years but it did not fundamentally change its course. Prince Maurice, now in possession of nearly unlimited power, did not frame a new, more workable constitution. He was a soldier rather than a statesman and his personal ambitions (he had contracted a morganatic marriage) did not include dynastic glory. He did not even make a determined effort to break the power of the urban aristocracies in Holland, though some of them remained Remonstrant. During the years that immediately followed the government of Amsterdam was gradually taken away from the Contra-Remonstrant leaders, and the town which had helped to undermine Oldenbarnevelt's authority pursued in face of the stadholder an independent and self-willed policy. The victory of the Gomarists of 1619 was no more lasting than Maurice's successes. The leaders of the Remonstrants were driven away but not beaten. Their doctrine increasingly developed in an anti-Calvinistic direction and it got so much hold of large groups of the regents and the intellectuals as to become a dominating element in Dutch civilization. In the 1620s the Remonstrants were able once more openly to preach their doctrine. In 1630 they founded a church in Amsterdam and in 1632 a semi-academic institution, the Athenaeum Illustre. The vitality of the church of Dordrecht was not strengthened by the stiffening of its doctrine and its discipline.

Maurice's only political act of importance after 1619 was his decision not to allow an extension of the truce in 1621. But the war against Spain and the southern Netherlands which was consequently resumed (in fact against the will of Archduke Albert) became another disappointment for him. Financial difficulties, uncertainties in his foreign policy, military setbacks and a Spanish offensive overshadowed his last years. One month after his death in April 1625 the important town of Breda was captured by the Spaniards. His brother Frederick Henry, who was pressed by the dying stadholder to marry Amalia of Solms for the sake of perpetuating the dynasty, took over a heavily charged inheritance when he was appointed to all the functions held by his predecessor. Yet his time of office (1625–47) became one of the most brilliant periods in the history of the republic.

In many respects Frederick Henry resumed the ideals and the political style of his father William the Silent rather than those of his brother Maurice. He was religiously tolerant; he was possessed by the ambition to reconquer the southern Netherlands and especially Antwerp (we shall later study its frustration) and more clearly than Maurice he strove after a position raising him above the status of a mere civil servant and general. He succeeded indeed in becoming the actual leader not only of the army but of the whole Dutch domestic and foreign policy. The federal organs of the union, the Council of State and the States General, were made dependent on him. From 1630 onwards foreign affairs were administered by a standing committee of the States General to which he managed to get appointed only those men who were prepared to follow his directives. No longer did the grand pensionary (after 1636 the office was held by the docile Jacob Cats whose glory is founded on his abilities as an indefatigable versifier) dominate the republic and the centre of possible opposition to the new state of affairs seemed to be eliminated. The prince and his wife took delight in displaying their semi-royal position by building up a fashionable court at The Hague; though it drew numerous international visitors, it stood outside Dutch life in general.

About 1640 Frederick Henry reached the pinnacle of his power. The remaining years until his death in 1647 witnessed a gradual but inexorable decline. This was due to different sets of factors, of which the most important was the resistance springing up against the triumphant achievements of his personal policies. In 1641 his son William II was married to Charles I's daughter Mary. Consequently Frederick Henry embraced the Stuart cause and one of the preoccupations of his later years was to make the republic support the English Royalists. But the province of Holland was not prepared to let itself be drawn into a war which only could be a maritime war against the Parliamentary party including London, the merchant fleet and the navy. In 1643 the States of various provinces, among them those of Holland, refused further to collaborate in the government by the standing committee of the States General. It was therefore matters of foreign policy which undermined Frederick Henry's so carefully built up, semi-monarchical position. However, the general character of his foreign policy can only be properly understood after an analysis of the history of the southern Netherlands during the years 1621–48.

The homogeneity of the southern Netherlands during this great and creative period was apparently so complete that the tensions which arose seem only superficial disturbances. Yet about 1640 the intellectual unity of the country broke up. And during the years when this cultural crisis was slowly maturing, political conflicts occurred which were not without significance.

The year 1621 had made remarkably little impression upon the southern Netherlands although it was of such incomparable importance for the country. The experiment begun in 1598, when the southern Netherlands were made a formally independent state governed by the archdukes, ended in failure. Albert died in 1621 without issue. Sovereignty reverted to the Spanish king. Albert's widow, Isabella, carried on the government of the southern Netherlands until her death in 1633, but she was an old, disillusioned lady in deep sorrow, quite unable to check the gathering momentum of Spanish influence. Albert had lived just long enough to witness the breakdown of another experiment. In April 1621 the truce came to an end and once again the war which he knew would be disastrous was resumed. But he was too weak to resist the Spanish king, Philip IV, who had in March 1621 succeeded his father and who was completely dominated by his minister Olivares, an ambitious man who wanted to revive the most ambitious Spanish traditions. The Dutch Republic, moreover, also preferred to resume the struggle.

After 1621 power in the southern Netherlands belonged in fact to the Marquis of Bedmar, Cardinal de la Cueva, who had in 1618 come to Brussels as Spanish ambassador. It was he who directed the work of the two extraordinary juntas—a Spanish and a Belgian one—which governed the country over the head of old institutions like the Council of State. Resistance to this system was slow in developing. But in 1629 Belgian dislike of the new régime was so strong that Isabella felt obliged to give in and to withdraw her support from Bedmar. For some time to come the situation looked dangerous. After the initial Spanish successes Frederick Henry's genius turned the fortunes of war. In 1629 he took Bois-le-Duc. The finances of the southern Netherlands were in a most miserable condition. It was apparently beyond Isabella's power any longer to meet her liabilities by increasingly inadequate expedients; she even pawned her jewels. But although Bedmar's successor, the marquis of Aytona, radically altered the system and restored the Council of State, he could not prevent indignation and defeatism from growing rampant. The conclusion of peace was, in fact, the only possible solution of the problems that beset the masters of the southern Netherlands. Isabella had seen this for long and her general, Spinola, fully agreed with her. When he found in 1627 that Madrid was not prepared either to provide the necessary funds or to start on a peace policy, he refused any longer to remain in command of the army.

The crisis which shook the southern Netherlands dominated Isabella's last years. She did not see the end of it but when she died (December 1633) the desperate weakness of the opposition against the Spanish régime had become apparent. In 1632 the so-called conspiracy of some young magnates failed miserably. Their intentions are not altogether clear. They probably wanted with French aid to overthrow Spanish authority. But these haughty and incompetent aristocrats found no support among the masses of the population nor were they capable of determined action. General attention was directed elsewhere. Against Philip IV's will Isabella had decided to call the States General, which had not met since 1600. They had but one task: to negotiate a peace with the Dutch Republic. When these negotiations (they will be discussed later) broke down, Philip IV ordered the States to disperse (18 June 1634). Obviously the southern Netherlands—in fact one immense army camp—were unable to thrust their will upon the Spaniards.

After 1634 the Spaniards recovered their authority thanks to the labours of Aytona and the staunch royalist Antwerper, Pieter Roose, president of the secret council at Brussels. The Cardinal-Infant Ferdinand, Philip IV's brother, became governor-general. He was an excellent soldier but a poor statesman and after Aytona's death in 1635 it was, ironically, Roose's lot to further the Hispanization of the southern Netherlands. Ferdinand's death in 1641 inaugurated a period of clumsy emergency measures which was only terminated in 1647 by the appointment of Leopold William, a brother of the Emperor Ferdinand III, as governor. But Belgian dependence on Spain was now so complete that in 1648 he took no part in making the peace which put an end to the meaningless, exhausting war. And we shall see that this peace was just as catastrophic for the southern Netherlands as had been the war.

Just as in the political life of the country conflicting tendencies lay behind the brilliant façade of the Counter-Reformation, so the baroque civilization possessed its conflicts and fissures. The year 1640 is memorable in the cultural history of the southern Netherlands. It was the year of Rubens' death. It was also the year of publication of two important books: the *Imago Primi Saeculi Societatis Jesu* in which Belgian Jesuits described the triumphs of the first century of their order (and it was not by accident that Belgians wrote this proud survey) and the *Augustinus* by Cornelius Jansenius (the bishop of Ypres, originating from Holland, who had died in 1638)—an extremely controversial work already in 1643 condemned by the papal bull *In Eminenti*. The disputes which arose about Jansenius' theses—his emphasis on the decisive role of God's mercy, his moral rigorism, his mystical tendencies and his preference of national ecclesiastical autonomy to Roman centralization—do not belong to the period here under review. But it is remarkable that this book, in a way a protest against Counter-Reformatory optimism, immediately found influential supporters in Belgium, made the famous University of Louvain, for so long a stronghold of Rome, turn against Rome, and drew the attention of the clerical and secular intellectuals who had become interested in the most modern philosophical development, Cartesianism.

The powerful art of Rubens and his school, the promise of rich theological and philosophical discussion cannot take away the impression that the early seventeenth-century civilization of the southern Netherlands was one-sided. Erudition was mainly historical and the study of history produced compilations and critical investigation of material rather than historiography; a good example is the monumental *Acta Sanctorum* of which the first volumes appeared in 1643. Literature, however, whether in Flemish or in French, withered away. Here the contrast with the surprisingly rapid development in the northern provinces is striking. The separation of south and north deprived the language of Flanders and Brabant, in the Middle Ages the best medium for literary expression in all the Netherlands, of the vitality which could have made it grow to the clarity, the richness and the delicacy of northern Dutch. It is this struggle between north and south which calls for attention because the war of 1621–48, in some respects a civil war, was of such crucial importance for the development of both countries.

The international position of the republic was determined by tradition and by the course taken by the revolt. Spain was the enemy; France the ally. According to a treaty of 1624 France supported the States General with subsidies and the republic provided France with ships—ships which were used (with permission of the States but to the indignation of the Dutch Protestants) at the siege of La Rochelle, the fortress of the Huguenots. Yet French support during these years was relatively unimportant. Until 1625 the Spaniards achieved surprising military successes but soon after that date their offensive power became exhausted. It is significant that already in 1628 Philip IV declared himself prepared to grant the republic peace with preservation of its sovereignty but requiring the Dutch (in vain of course) to recognize the Spanish king as their eternal protector and to improve the lot of the Roman Catholics. Tentative negotiations, however, continued to accompany the military operations. But although Philip IV reduced his pretensions, the war which neither Holland, nor Brussels, nor Spain really wanted to continue, could not easily be terminated. The extremely complicated international situation as well as hesitations and contradictory tendencies among the belligerents rendered a rapid solution impossible.

The great fact in the first decade of the war was the capture of the important city of Bois-le-Duc in Brabant by Frederick Henry (1629). Thanks to this feat he carried the war to the provinces south of the big rivers. The character of the struggle changed. From 1621 to 1629 the Dutch were defending their small territory against the Spaniards, now they penetrated southward. This complicated their policies, for suddenly the conquest of the southern Netherlands became a practical possibility. The relations between north and south, which the truce of 1609 seemed to have defined by recognizing for the time being both parts of the Burgundian Netherlands as independent countries, once again became an acute problem. The reaction in the southern Netherlands was vehement, as we have already seen. But immediately a grave disappointment was in store for those who hoped for a southern revolt—for Frederick Henry did not exclude this possibility from his plans. The influence of the orthodox Calvinists on the policies of the republic prevented the stadholder from granting religious freedom to the Roman Catholics in Bois-le-Duc. Voetius himself, the formidable leader of the Gomarists, soon a professor of Utrecht University, a man of encyclopaedic knowledge and strict dogmatism, came to Frederick Henry's army camp to point out the commander's duty. A religious revolution took place in the homogeneously Roman Catholic town.

The year 1630 went by without important decisions being taken. But in 1631 tension in the southern Netherlands grew. Count van den Bergh, the native commander-in-chief of the southern Netherlands and a first cousin to Frederick Henry, was relieved from his function and replaced by a Spanish general. In conjunction with another personality of considerable influence, the president of the Council of Finances at Brussels, the count of Warfusée, he entered upon secret negotiations with the States General at The Hague. Their plans are not quite clear, but so much is certain: that they wanted in the case of a general uprising in the southern Netherlands —an uprising which they were trying to start—French help for the Walloon and Dutch support for the Flemish-speaking provinces. In May 1632, before Frederick Henry began his summer campaign, the States General issued a proclamation addressed to the southern Netherlands summoning them 'to liberate themselves from the heavy and intolerable yoke of the Spaniards . . . and to join themselves unto these United Provinces' and promising the preservation of their privileges as well as the right publicly to exercise the Roman Catholic religion. Frederick Henry's campaign started successfully. He took Venlo and Roermond in Upper Gelderland and, after a siege of more than two months, Maastricht (August 1632). But then nothing happened. The French king had given no effective support whatever to the plans of the Walloon nobility. The Flemish-speaking provinces did not stir. And Frederick Henry, who was expected rapidly to march on Brabant, stayed cautiously near Maastricht.

We have already seen that Isabella called the States General of the southern Netherlands, allowing them to negotiate with the States General of the northern Netherlands. In December 1632 the negotiations started at The Hague; they lasted a year. But they were meaningless from the very beginning. In December 1632 the military situation was fundamentally different from the position during the summer months. At that time not only Frederick Henry but also Gustavus Adolphus' army in Germany had pressed the Spaniards hard. But Frederick Henry did not exploit his victories and Gustavus Adolphus was killed in the Battle of Lützen (November 1632). The south Netherlands representatives finally did not negotiate in The Hague as persons wanting to join the Dutch Republic or to build up, with northern aid, a state independent of Spain, but as spokesmen of the Spanish king. The possibility of north and south collaborating on the basis of religious peace and with the aim of founding either one united state or an independent state had not materialized. It is extremely difficult to assess how real this possibility may have been. But so much is certain: although the northern Netherlands had shown interest in this co-operation, formidable obstacles soon became apparent. The religious question weighed heavily with the Contra-Remonstrants in the north as well as with the Roman Catholics in the south. In Holland, moreover, and especially in Amsterdam, it was being realized that the freedom of the southern Netherlands, whatever form it might take, would inevitably entail the opening of the Scheldt. And was not the prosperity of Holland dependent precisely on the Scheldt remaining closed?

After 1633 Dutch policy towards the southern Netherlands changed once again. This is very clear from the treaty with France concluded, after long negotiations in 1635. Originally this was an initiative of the French, who saw Dutch war-weariness growing to alarming proportions. But finally the States General took over the initiative and persuaded Richelieu by means of a tempting project at last to abandon French neutrality and to declare war on Spain. The project concerned the southern Netherlands. In fact it was no longer expected that they would liberate themselves. In the case of their being indeed incapable of rising spontaneously France and the republic agreed jointly to conquer them. France was promised the right to occupy the Walloon provinces and Flanders (consequently Flemish-speaking areas including such towns as Ghent and Bruges!) whereas the republic would acquire Brabant. From the point of view of international power-politics this treaty meant a success for the republic. Thanks to its ruthless attitude towards the southern Netherlands it obtained precious French help in the war against Spain. There was, however, one dangerous concession the Dutch had been forced to make; they had agreed with France not to conclude peace otherwise than 'jointly and by common consent'.

This alteration of Dutch policy concerning the southern Netherlands did not imply a real turn of Dutch international policy in general. Also after 1635 the Dutch took care lest their war with Spain should be absorbed into the Thirty Years War—a characteristic proof of their refusal to pursue power-politics in the grand style. And if the French had really relied upon a rapid conquest of the southern Netherlands they must have been greatly disappointed. The joint Franco-Dutch campaign of

1635 started successfully but ended in disaster. The campaigns of the following years did not produce any more important results. In 1637 Frederick Henry recaptured Breda, but Venlo and Roermond were lost. An attack on Antwerp in 1638 failed. At sea the Dutch gained an important victory in 1639 when the Dutch fleet under Tromp beat a strong Spanish fleet in English home waters. But the land war brought no victory during the early 1640s. Frederick Henry, prematurely ageing, was no longer capable of vigorous enterprise. At the same time his dynastic schemes and his loyalty to the Stuarts were undermining his position in Holland where resistance to the whole tendency of his foreign policy was stimulated by the fear which his semi-monarchical status and ambitions inspired.

Gradually in Holland a well-defined peace party, strongly opposed to the stadholder, came into being. Meanwhile the great peace congress at Münster and Osnabrück, intended to terminate the Thirty Years War, had opened in 1643. It took several years before the Dutch statesmen, paralysed by their immensely complex system of government as well as by their equally complicated internal conflicts, were able to determine their own course of action. Only in January 1646 Dutch ambassadors left for Westphalia, to find there a highly peculiar situation. For in fact only one obstacle blocked the road to an immediate Spanish–Dutch peace: the Franco-Dutch alliance. France was not prepared to make peace with Spain and according to the treaty of 1635, renewed in 1644, the Dutch were not allowed to act independently in this matter. Consequently there was no need for the Spanish diplomatists to persuade the Dutch of the necessity of at last concluding peace; their preoccupation was to make it possible for their enemy to violate his agreement with France. In the republic Holland was perfectly willing immediately to reach a final settlement with Spain. Zeeland, however, which got more than any other province out of the piracy practised by the West India Company, wanted to continue the war. Frederick Henry himself, who notwithstanding all his disappointments still hoped to conquer Antwerp and who knew that peace would in no case be advantageous to him personally, supported the war party until shortly before his death in 1647. Despite all this resistance Holland had its way. On 30 January 1648 at last the Dutch Republic made peace with Spain at Münster. This was clearly a violation of the treaty with France, a violation, however, which from the Dutch point of view was justifiable because the only alternative was carrying on the aimless war till the French would be good enough to terminate it.

The Peace of Münster repeated and extended the settlement of 1609. It meant a triumph for the republic, now recognized and feared as a sovereign great power. The republic kept the slices of Flanders, Brabant and Limburg which it had conquered but it did not acquire Upper Gelderland. Spanish efforts to obtain religious liberty for these homogeneously Roman Catholic territories failed. During the whole *Ancien Régime* these regions were to be arbitrarily governed as conquered territory by the States General. The peace confirmed the humiliation of the southern Netherlands. Brabant and Flanders lost valuable parts of their territory. The Scheldt was kept closed. The northern provinces, quite aware of their cynical egoism, continued their policy of crippling the prosperity of the southern Netherlands. The north was not only the victor in the war against Spain but also in the civil war which for so long had raged in the Netherlands.

In March 1647 Frederick Henry died. In the 1630s his son William II, born in 1626, had been secured the succession to all his offices. The three years during which he indeed performed the traditional functions of the princes of Orange form an extremely peculiar period in the history of the republic. William II, a brilliant but badly educated and frivolous man, tried to pursue his father's policies. However, they were rendered out of date by recent events and it was reckless to resume them. Already in November 1648 William II informed Mazarin—whose blunders were at that time bringing about the Fronde—of his unwillingness to resign himself to the Peace of Münster. Apparently his purpose was to start a new war against Spain on France's side and, having forced Philip IV to conclude peace rapidly with Louis XIV, to intervene in conjunction with France in the English Civil War on behalf of the Stuarts. Fundamentally such a plan was perhaps not altogether fantastic in the extremely complicated and adventurous international politics of those years. But there is little doubt that William II was mistaken in his assessment of French politics as well as of his own position in the republic. He seems to have thought that French help would enable him to perpetrate a *coup d'état* directed against Holland and intended to force the recalcitrant province to come into line. Yet even if this had met with complete success, it is difficult to see how he could, in the end, have obliged Holland to finance his adventures. His own position, moreover, would have come to depend on French help with the result that Dutch policies would have had to obey French orders. It is clear that William II's dynastic policies meant a most dangerous and prejudicial overstraining of Dutch forces.

William II of course did not publicly propagate his ultimate aims. For his more moderate policies, which seemed to go along the lines laid down by Frederick Henry, he easily found supporters among the groups of people traditionally hostile to the preponderance of the province of Holland. The contrasts which had existed during the truce came once again to the fore. Some Contra-Remonstrant ministers and those parts of the population which listened to their word, the army, most of the provinces and consequently the States General were prepared to support, on behalf of union and religion, William II's fight against Holland with its latitudinarian regents and its concentration on the interests of commerce and shipping. Holland's position was stronger however than that of Oldenbarnevelt thirty years before, for Amsterdam which had already resisted Frederick Henry now had the lead in the opposition to William II. It is improbable that the so-called Orangist party would have been willing to accept William II's wilder schemes. In fact it hardly was a party at all. The only sentiment which kept the component groups of the party together was aversion to the province of Holland. During the whole course of the seventeenth century this aversion did at certain moments when great decisions were to be taken unite large portions of the population, but never was the Orangist party capable of putting forward a positive social or political programme intended to break the power of the oligarchy, to improve the organization of government and to alter the direction of Dutch foreign policy. Although the prince of Orange could rely on the unswerving loyalty of certain specific groups, the struggles which he pursued remained his personal affair and the conflicts dividing the republic did not develop into civil wars.

The conflict which broke out in 1649 is proof of this. It was brought about by a discussion on the reduction of the army. In June 1648 the States General reduced the size of the army from 55,000 to 32,000 men, thus saving 3,000,000 *guilders* yearly. This was most welcome since the republic was deeply in debt; Holland alone owed 140,000,000 *guilders* at 5%. But when Holland wanted in 1649 to reduce the army further the prince of Orange and, thanks to his influence, the States General, refused. Tension grew in 1650. After long but useless negotiations Holland cut the knot and informed on 4 June 1650 a certain number of commanders of companies paid out of Holland's contribution to the States General that they could no longer expect to receive their pay. On 5 June William II appeared before the States General and had himself ordered to prevent disturbances by all means considered necessary by him. The authority which he acquired in this way amounted in fact to dictatorial power and is comparable to that bestowed on his uncle Maurice in 1618. From 8 to 27 June William II, accompanied by an impressive suite of noblemen and army officers, made a journey to the various towns of Holland, but he could not persuade the majority among them to obey his orders. By the end of July he imprisoned six Holland regents, among them the father of the later grand pensionary, John de Witt. On the same day he made his troops march on Amsterdam but the town was warned in time and closed its gates. On 3 August 1650 a compromise was reached. The troops withdrew but Amsterdam dismissed some of its regents and promised not to obstruct William II's policies in the States of Holland. The six prisoners were set free. It is not quite clear why Amsterdam did not take further action as it was becoming apparent that even the States General did not approve of the prince's aggression. This unwillingness of the States

General to follow the prince any longer was explicitly expressed in their refusal to support William II when he at last tried to bring about the alteration of Dutch foreign policy for which he had for so long striven. They left no doubt that notwithstanding Amsterdam's humiliation they were not prepared—any more than the States of Holland—to declare war on Spain and revolutionary England. But suddenly after an illness of ten days, William II died of the smallpox (6 November 1650). Did he take secret plans with him into his death? Were there still real possibilities for his projects to be carried out? We know nothing about it. The only thing we know is that for two decades to come his so-called party had no power and but little influence. When in November 1650 the spectre of a new war vanished the men who came into power hoped at last to enjoy peacefully the achievements of half a century of hard efforts and tremendous decisions.

CHAPTER XIII

SWEDEN AND THE BALTIC 1611-54

I N the first half of the seventeenth century two states established themselves for the first time as great powers. The one was the United Netherlands; the other, Sweden. The period of their greatness was almost equal, and for both it was brief; each expanded into an empire of sorts; and each, perhaps, reached its zenith about the year 1660.

As far as Sweden was concerned, this rise to greatness was certainly unexpected. At the opening of the century it would have seemed doubtful whether the country could maintain its independence, and most improbable that it should ever become the leading power in the north. With the waning of the political ascendancy of the Hanse towns in the sixteenth century, that position appeared likely to fall either to Denmark or to Poland. There had, indeed, been a moment, in the 1560s and 1570s, when it looked at least possible that Muscovy might emerge as a formidable challenger: in the political convulsions which followed the collapse of the Livonian state of the Order of the Knights of the Sword, Moscow for a time won great successes, and the tsars came near to securing an extensive coastline on the Baltic; but the anarchy of the Troublous Times postponed for more than half a century any resumption of the plans of Ivan IV. The major portion of the lands of the knights fell to Poland; while Sweden maintained a precarious hold upon Reval and the northern coastlands of Estonia. It was the first of Sweden's overseas possessions, a nucleus around which other possessions would gather, and the need to defend it led Sweden step by step to ever deeper commitments in the politics of this region; but if it turned out to be in fact the springboard for imperial expansion, this was a development probably unforeseen in Stockholm, and certainly unlooked-for in Europe: in the years around 1605 it must have seemed much more likely that Estonia would soon be reunited to Polish Livonia. There was, indeed, a further possibility: the possibility that the rivalry for the control of these lands might be resolved by the renewal of that personal union of Sweden with Poland which had lasted from 1592 to 1599. It was always possible, and occasionally it appeared probable, that Sigismund III might still recover his hereditary kingdom of Sweden, and dislodge his usurping uncle, Charles IX. The papacy, the Jesuits, and the Habsburgs all earnestly hoped so: a Sweden re-converted to Catholicism, a Spanish base in Gothenburg (convenient for attacks on Dutch shipping) were advantages worth some effort to secure.

From the point of view of Sweden's traditional policies, however,

Poland was a new, and almost an accidental, enemy. It is true that their quarrel was not simply dynastic or religious, the mere consequence of the disputes provoked by Sigismund's rule; for over Estonia neither side could compromise. But the real danger to Sweden in the east was not Polish, but Muscovite: Muscovy had for a century and a quarter impended menacingly over Swedish Finland; and fear of Muscovy's expansion to the west was deeply ingrained in the minds of Swedish rulers. And apart from this defensive determination to press back the Muscovite, Swedish kings had latterly developed an ambition to gather into Swedish hands the trade between Muscovy and western Europe, and so to channel it that Dutch or Hanse or English merchants must do their business at Swedish-controlled *entrepôts*, and thus enrich with their dues the meagre revenues of the Swedish crown. Certainly no Swedish ruler could contemplate with equanimity the conquest or absorption of Muscovy into the Polish-Lithuanian realm, and the consequent reinforcement of Russian barbarism by Polish technical skill; nor could Charles IX stand idly by if Sigismund seemed likely to possess himself of the back door to Finland. When, therefore, Sigismund began to manoeuvre for the election of himself or his son Ladislas as tsar,[1] Charles was dragged into the confusion of the Troublous Times, and as a Russian partisan fared almost as ill as in his open war against Sigismund in Livonia.

If Russia was the perennial enemy in the east, Denmark was the historic foe in the west. In 1611 it was still less than a century since Gustavus Vasa had broken the old Scandinavian union: Sweden's final emergence as an independent state dates from 1523. The Danish monarchs of the later sixteenth century were not prepared to accept that verdict as final. When belligerently inclined, they were still prone to display in their coat of arms the three crowns of Sweden; and in the context of the times this implied a more precise political programme than (for instance) the retention of the French lilies in the arms of England. The southern provinces of the Scandinavian peninsula—Blekinge, Skåne, Halland— were still part of Denmark, separated from independent Sweden by a frontier that took no account either of geography or of economics; and the Danish kings had some justification for feeling that the dissolution of the Scandinavian union was a political aberration from the natural order of things. Certainly the two countries were more closely bound to each other, even yet, than to any non-Scandinavian state. Similarity of language and institutions, identity of religion, aristocracies ramifying on either side of the border, a dim feeling of the separateness of 'The North' from the rest of Europe—these things drew them together, even while political interests divided them; so that their relationship oscillated violently between feud and fellowship, alliance and war. They had their own precisely formulated devices for settling their disputes by peaceful

[1] See below, Chapter XIX, Pt. I.

means. They permitted freedom of trade between each others' subjects. Already they upheld for each other—and denied to the rest of the world— the *jus classis immitendae*, the right to maintain a fleet of war within the Baltic sea. And, not least important, the kings of Denmark exempted Swedish ships and goods from payment of dues on passage through the Sound.

The Sound dues were among the most important financial assets of the Danish crown. They were, indeed, properly the private revenues of the king; but he used them to maintain a navy which at the beginning of the seventeenth century was probably one of the best and most modern in Europe. But they were more than this: they were the signs of political pretensions which the navy existed to make good. The kings of Denmark claimed a *dominium maris Balthici*, a vague sovereignty over the waters of the Baltic; and in the Sound, at least, they were able to assert that claim effectively. For both sides of the Sound were Danish territory; and Christian IV could maintain that the Sound was no more than a stream flowing through Danish lands: in no sense to be regarded as an international waterway. In that claim the Hanse had perforce to acquiesce; and though the English first, and the Dutch afterwards, found a way to Russia's back door at Archangel, the great bulk of their trade to north-east Europe must pass the Sound also. It was certainly an advantage to Sweden, therefore, to be exempt from the Sound dues, even though her mercantile marine was still negligible, and even though she possessed, in Älvsborg, a west-coast port lying outside the Baltic altogether. But the Danish claim to *dominium maris* could not be admitted in Stockholm; and the strategic handicaps of Sweden's position with regard to Denmark were such that it was unlikely that they would be suffered indefinitely. Sea-communication between Sweden's east and west coasts was possible only by Denmark's favour; Sweden's solitary window to the Atlantic, at Älvsborg, was so hemmed in by Danish and Norwegian territory to south and north that it could easily be blocked, and in wartime could hardly be defended; Denmark's outlying islands—Bornholm, Gotland, Ösel—were strung out eastwards across the Baltic, cutting across the main Swedish trade-routes to the Hanse towns.

It was these fundamental causes of disagreement which underlay the recurrent crises in Swedish-Danish relations. In Charles IX's time they assumed special forms: a Swedish insistence on excluding Danish ships from Riga, which Charles was blockading; Swedish concessions to west-coast merchants which Christian IV considered to be an infringement of his sovereign rights; above all, a provocative forward policy in the Arctic, designed by Charles to put him in possession of an Atlantic port near the modern Narvik, with the hope of collecting toll from Dutch mariners *en route* to Archangel. Christian IV, on his side, revived the controversy over the Three Crowns, and skilfully used Swedish pinpricks to carry a reluctant council with him into a declaration of war in 1611. His objective was not merely victory, but reconquest; and if he succeeded, he might well make *dominium maris Balthici* a reality. It was not a prospect which was much relished in Amsterdam.

Thus it happened that when Gustavus Adolphus succeeded Charles IX in 1611, he inherited from his father three wars—against Denmark, against Poland, and in Russia—and small prospect of success in any of them. The dynastic quarrel with Sigismund III, indeed, was for the moment languishing, at least on the Livonian front; but that was only because the struggle had been transferred to Muscovy. There, Charles had been aiding the boyars' tsar, Basil Shuiskij, against the attempts of Ladislas to secure the crown—a political speculation which ended disastrously when the Poles routed Basil and his Swedish allies at Klushino in 1610. This catastrophe, which was followed by Basil's enforced abdication, had constrained Charles to consent to the candidature of his younger son, Charles Philip, as the best remaining hope of countering the menace of a Polish tsar. And for a moment, at the end of 1612 and the beginning of 1613, there seemed a real chance that this move might be successful: Charles Philip was adopted by Pozharskij and the Second National Rising as their candidate; and if he had made a timeous appearance he would probably have been elected. But the election of Michael Romanov in February 1613, and the consequent elimination of both Swedish and Polish candidates, was by no means the end of the affair, either for Poland or for Sweden. Both Gustavus Adolphus and Sigismund felt that the opportunity presented by Russia's weakness must not be let slip: if they could not impose their candidates, they could at least use the occasion for extorting territorial concessions. Sigismund coveted Smoleńsk and much of White Russia; Gustavus Adolphus sought to safeguard Sweden from a Muscovite irruption into the Baltic by acquiring territory which would provide a firm land-bridge between Finland and Estonia, would shut off Moscow from the sea, and would buttress Sweden's position against future Polish attacks. And he may have hoped too, as some of his predecessors had hoped, that territorial gains here would put him in a stronger position to tap—perhaps to control—the trade between Muscovy and the West. This hope, if it existed, proved chimerical: there were too many end-ports for merchants to choose from. But in other respects both Sweden, and to a lesser extent Poland, were successful in getting what they wanted. The Treaty of Stolbova, concluded between Sweden and Russia in 1617, was justly regarded by Gustavus as a major success: the tsar ceded Ingria and Kexholm; the second stone of Sweden's Baltic empire was laid; Moscow was thrust back from the sea; and the emergence of Russia as a Baltic power was deferred for nearly a hundred years. Two years later, by the Truce of Deulino (1619) Sigismund gained large strips of land on his eastern frontier, including Smolensk. Thereafter the perennial feud between Poland and Muscovy was for a time damped down; but it was by no means extinguished. Obviously Sweden's interest was to foment it; and obviously it must now be Sweden's policy to keep on good terms with the tsar. The Peace of Stolbova was accordingly followed by a period of nearly forty years of cordial relations between Stockholm and Moscow; and when in 1632 the Russian attack on Poland was renewed, it was launched with Sweden's connivance and goodwill. Already, perhaps, it was beginning to be clear that Polish-Russian hostility was one of the preconditions for Sweden's existence as a great power.

Meanwhile, Gustavus Adolphus had been defending himself with difficulty against the assaults of Christian IV. The so-called War of Kalmar (1611-13) went very badly for Sweden. The Danes captured Kalmar; and what was worse, they captured Älvsborg, and so shut off Sweden from direct access to the Atlantic. The Swedish navy proved incompetent; the Swedish army, inadequate. Gustavus was forced in 1613 to accept the peace of Knäred, which provided for Älvsborg's retention by Denmark pending the payment of an indemnity so large that there seemed little prospect of its being raised within the stipulated time. But though Gustavus had thus been defeated and humiliated, in a longer view the loser was Christian IV. For the peace left Sweden still independent; and never again would Denmark find so favourable an opportunity to revive the Scandinavian union. The extent of Denmark's military and naval success, moreover, alarmed mercantile interests in the west: to the Dutch, in particular, Sweden began to appear as a necessary counterweight to Danish arrogance. The Wendish towns of the Hanse viewed the question in the same light. Christian IV had dynastic interests and ambitions in north Germany, as well as in the Baltic; and for much of his reign he made unnecessary difficulties for himself by his attempts to obtain secularized bishoprics in the area for one or other of his sons. It was a policy which brought him many enemies, and in the coming struggle for Baltic supremacy it acted as an appreciable handicap. It was felt by many Protestants, moreover, that Christian was not as much concerned for the cause of religion as he ought to be: just at this time he was showing a disquieting inclination to friendship with Spain. He and Gustavus were the only Lutheran kings in Europe; and in a decade when a religious war in Germany appeared imminent, it was natural that German Lutherans should look to Denmark for possible aid and comfort. But Christian seemed preoccupied with secular ambitions, and indisposed to subordinate them to the interests of the evangelical cause. Gustavus was at least more tactful and sympathetic. It was true that his father, Charles IX, had in his day been suspected of Calvinist leanings; and the Vasas had certainly close dynastic links with the Calvinist dynasties of Hesse and the Palatinate. But it was perhaps an advantage thus to have a foothold in each of the two Protestant camps; and it was certainly an advantage even greater, that nobody could suspect Gustavus of territorial ambitions in Germany. The combined effect of all these considerations was that though Christian won the war against Sweden, he lost the peace. Gustavus was able to conclude an alliance with the Dutch in 1614; the war indemnity was paid off, and Älvsborg redeemed (in 1619) by Dutch financial assistance; Gustavus scored what seemed at the time to be a significant political success by his marriage with Maria Eleonora of Brandenburg in 1620. His relations with leading German Protestants were good; and when in 1617 the war with Poland—which had latterly been put into cold storage by a succession of truces—revived for a season, he had some success in persuading his friends that the dynastic feud with Sigismund was but an aspect of the general struggle of Protestants everywhere against the Counter-Reformation.

By 1620, when the first great disasters fell upon German Protestantism, there could be no doubt that Sweden had made a remarkable recovery from the desperate position in which she had found herself in 1611. The events of the next few years made this very plain. Gustavus seized the occasion of Poland's preoccupation with a Turkish invasion[1] to renew the war in Livonia; and in 1621 he startled Europe, and alarmed Christian IV, by his capture of the great trading city of Riga. It was, indeed, an event of some importance. The Swedish possession of Estonia had not been a matter of much concern to the mercantile world: Swedish attempts to constrain the trade to Novgorod or Pskov to go by way of Narva or Reval had never had much success; and even after the Treaty of Stolbova, when the tsar's rival port of Ivangorod passed into Swedish hands, the situation was not much altered. But Riga was one of the great cities of the Baltic, and one-third of Poland's exports had passed through it. It was also a great fortress; and its capture revealed a startling transformation in Sweden's military efficiency, as compared with the lamentable weakness of 1611–13. The event therefore made a considerable impression on contemporaries; and that impression was reinforced by what followed. In successive campaigns Gustavus overran much of Livonia; and in January 1626 a remarkable victory at Wallhof seemed to make these conquests sufficiently secure for him to risk transferring the main theatre of war to Polish Prussia and the valley of the Vistula: he calculated that the resulting disruption of Polish grain exports would force Sigismund to accept terms upon which a lasting settlement could be based. Two years earlier, in 1624, a sharp crisis in his relations with Christian IV had been resolved by an agreement in which it was Denmark that made all the concessions, and Sweden that took all the gains. This too was a significant development. In 1624 Christian had not dared to risk a war: Sweden was already too powerful, the Danish army and finances too weak. Gustavus' victories in Livonia, remote and obscure as they were, an-

---

[1] See below, Chapter XIX, Pt. I.

nounced the arrival of a new and considerable military power; and the invasion of Prussia in 1626 gave ample opportunity to confirm this fact at closer range.

In these altered circumstances, Sweden came to be regarded not merely as a necessary counterpoise to Denmark in the Baltic, but as a real alternative to Denmark in the calculations of Protestant strategy: Ludwig Camerarius, for instance, soon perceived that Gustavus, rather than Christian IV, must be the sword of any effective Protestant league. It took time and tribulation to convince other Protestant leaders of this: the League of The Hague (1625) chose Christian rather than Gustavus to lead it, merely because Christian offered help on easier conditions. But by 1625 it was plain enough that to existing causes of friction between Sweden and Denmark had now been added another—competition for the position of director and commander of the evangelical coalition. Christian, sore at the diplomatic reverse of 1624, embittered by the disasters that followed his defeat at Lutter (1626), certainly viewed Gustavus' successes in Prussia with a jealous eye; and only extreme need was likely to persuade him to political collaboration with his rival. But in fact the pressure of events forced him to swallow his pride. The whole of Jutland was overrun by imperial troops.[1] The fall of Stralsund was imminent. Sigismund III's creation of a fleet seemed to imply a real danger that Poland might become the third naval power in the Baltic. There was no doubt that Olivares and Ferdinand II had designs for the foundation of a Habsburg navy in the Mecklenburg ports; and when Sigismund agreed to transfer his squadron to Wismar, it appeared likely that the two projects might coalesce. By 1628 the League of The Hague was politically bankrupt, ruined by the feebleness of England, the preoccupations of the Dutch, the timidity of Brandenburg, and the necessary caution of Richelieu. Faced with the threat of Wallenstein's violation of the *jus classis immitendae*, the Scandinavian monarchies were constrained into a brief alliance, whose main effect (and it was no small one) was to have saved Stralsund. In that alliance there could be no doubt (however galling it might be to Christian) that Sweden was the stronger partner. But there could be no doubt either that Christian hoped to use the alliance in order to extract tolerable peace terms from his victorious enemies. Wallenstein was ready enough to oblige him: it was the emperor's interest to be lenient, if thereby he could detach Denmark from Sweden. In 1629, therefore, Christian made all haste to desert his ally, and accepted at Lübeck terms of peace which were indeed astonishingly moderate. And Denmark thereupon withdrew into a neutrality which to Swedish eyes appeared increasingly malevolent; and by doing so left Sweden indisputably the leading power in the north, and the only prospective deliverer of German Protestantism.

---

[1] See above, Chapter XI, pp. 325–6.

At the time of the peace of Lübeck, however, it was by no means certain that Gustavus would be able or willing to stand forth as the Protestant champion. His war with Poland still dragged on; and the economic sanctions which its transference to the Vistula had been designed to apply seemed to have no other effect than to produce strong irritation in the Dutch. He could not interfere in Germany until a peace or a long truce gave him security on the side of Poland. He considered his war with Sigismund as essentially defensive; and if as it progressed it brought ever-greater stretches of Baltic coastline into his hands, they were occupied as a means of constraining the enemy to peace, and in order to deny the use of their ports to the infant Polish fleet, lest they become the bases for an invasion of Sweden. In return for a renunciation of Sigismund's claims upon the Swedish throne, and a firm peace, Gustavus would have been willing to retrocede almost all his conquests: certainly he had not hitherto proceeded with any plan in mind for the creation of a Baltic empire, or the systematic control of all the rivers emptying themselves into that sea. In so far as he was barring the way to a re-catholicization of Sweden—which, it was arguable, would necessarily follow Sigismund's restoration—he could represent his war to be an aspect of the general European struggle; but in truth it was a national struggle too. Yet intervention in Germany, if it came, would represent a new direction for Swedish policy, which had concerned itself very little with German politics in the past. It might well engage the country's efforts for objects far removed from the narrow world of Baltic affairs; and to some Swedes it seemed that if such a venture were undertaken Sweden's own interests might be postponed to others that were foreign to her, or prejudiced for the sake of that vague notion 'the Protestant cause'—while the old enemy Denmark (whose burnt fingers might well serve as a warning) waited for a Swedish disaster, or Swedish exhaustion, to resume her former supremacy in the north.

Gustavus Adolphus thought otherwise. He convinced himself (and skilful propaganda convinced his people) that an imperialist occupation of Mecklenburg and Pomerania would imply direct danger to Sweden, since the combined Polish and imperial fleets, if left undisturbed, might one day be powerful enough to ferry over a legitimist invasion. Thus the Protestant cause became Sweden's cause too; and the north German coastland became a Swedish interest: 'better prevent than be prevented'. And at this point, in September 1629, the diplomacy of Richelieu (who already cherished the illusion that he could make Gustavus his tool) succeeded in arranging a truce between Sweden and Poland at Altmark. Its effect was to transfer to Swedish control, for the next six years, a number of places of great commercial importance: among others, Memel, Pillau and Elbing; and to secure to Sweden the right to levy tolls at these places for so long as the truce should last. As a result of this provision, between

1629 and 1635 every port of any consequence on the southern shore of the Baltic, from the Neva to the Pregel, was in Swedish hands. Danzig, indeed, had resisted Gustavus' attacks, and was obstinately loyal to Poland; but a treaty supplementary to that of Altmark ensured to Sweden a share of the tolls levied at Danzig also. It might be supposed, on the face of it, that these arrangements represent one further step in the king's plans for the creation of a Baltic empire, a new stage in a long-term scheme of expansion. But in fact they were nothing of the sort. They were the accidental result of a compromise proposed by George William of Brandenburg, in a desperate effort to save the negotiations from deadlock.

The conclusion of the truce liberated Gustavus from an imbroglio which had become of secondary importance. At the moment when Christian IV turned his back on Germany in despair, Gustavus was free to address himself to the great question of the hour, free to pursue the victorious career in Germany which ended at Lützen. But, once again, there lay no far-reaching political project behind the intervention in Germany: the acquisition of extensive tracts of territory there was no part of the king's original scheme, still less any involvement in German domestic politics. Stralsund (which already had a Swedish garrison) he intended to retain as a defensive outpost, until the emergency should be at an end; and since Wismar was the base of the nascent imperial navy, it might be politic to secure that too. But his real aim was security from invasion; and if the pursuit of that aim led him far from Sweden's frontiers, that was no part of the plan with which he embarked: his object rather was so to animate the German Protestants that they should be able in future to take care of themselves. The expansion of the Swedish Empire, in Germany as in the Baltic, was in the beginning unplanned, and in a sense it was as much the result of accident as of design.

Nevertheless, whether planned or no, the Swedish Empire became a reality before the Thirty Years War was over, and it may well be asked how Sweden was able to acquire it, and subsequently to maintain it. In comparison with Denmark, for instance, Sweden was sparsely populated, backward, and poor: the court and capital of Gustavus Adolphus compared unfavourably, in point of wealth, luxury and taste, with the court and capital of Christian IV; and the Danish aristocracy lived more fashionably, and probably more expensively, than their Swedish cousins. The revenues of Gustavus Adolphus were modest, by English standards; and though they might have sufficed in peacetime to meet the running costs of a highly personal monarchy and a still-rudimentary civil administration, they were obviously unequal to the financing of massive military operations sustained over many years beyond the seas. The fiscal system was in any case unsuited to provide resources on this scale, since a great part of the royal revenues was still paid in kind; and though some of it could be allotted to crown servants by way of wages, and some could be eaten by a voracious and peripatetic court, it was not convenient for the payment of armies operating abroad. Sweden had, indeed, rich mineral resources; but hitherto her rulers had lacked the requisite capital for their proper exploitation.

The reign of Gustavus Adolphus brought important changes in these matters. In an effort to convert revenues in kind into cash, the king began to sell or pawn the royal domains, or the income that came from them. New direct and indirect taxes were levied, payable in coin; and some of them were paid by the nobility, despite their privilege of exemption from all ordinary taxation. A more important measure was the systematic attempt to induce foreign capitalists to come to Sweden, and to invest in Swedish mining and industry. The attempt was remarkably successful: Gustavus succeeded in attracting, in the person of Louis de Geer, one of the ablest of Dutch *entrepreneurs;* and de Geer was only the most famous of many financiers and armourers who came from the Netherlands or Germany, followed or accompanied by trained workmen or specialist technicians. They came the more readily, because the opportunities were really great: cheap fuel, low labour costs, and abundant waterpower—to say nothing of lavish privileges dangled by Gustavus as bait—gave the promise of competitive prices; and the deposits of ore were exceptionally rich and extensive. The Flemish immigrants, though their numbers were counted in hundreds only, did much to transform Swedish industry. They brought new manufacturing processes to old industries, and new subsidiary industries (brass-founding and large-scale arms-manufacture, for instance) in association with the old. It was in the iron and armaments industries, perhaps, that their influence was most marked; and by 1630 this latter had so far developed that Sweden was virtually self-supporting, and had even begun the export of cannon. In regard to copper, their contribution was rather to the technique of marketing and mining: the great copper mine at Falun remained in the hands of the small miners, and did not pass into those of the new capitalists. Nevertheless, until the middle of the century, copper was even more important to the Swedish finances than iron. The accident of war had produced a situation in which the main European competitors in the production of copper were either put out of action by hostilities, or cut off from their main markets. Until the mid-twenties (when Spain abruptly ceased to mint vellon coins) it was a sellers' market for copper, and the price rose sharply; and though it fell thereafter, Sweden for many years had a virtual monopoly of supply save for a distant threat from Japan. Every effort was made (not always wisely or successfully) to exploit this situation to the utmost. The income from copper, and the booming arms industry, gave Sweden two assets which were denied to Christian IV; for Denmark was a wholly agricultural country, and the foreign market for her products underwent no such favourable conjuncture as was the case for Swedish copper.

Christian had, indeed, the revenue from the Sound dues; but by 1630 it seemed likely that Sweden might draw not much less from tolls of her own. During the closing years of the war in Prussia, the Swedish navy had begun to enforce the collection of high duties at the ports of the southern Baltic which were under Gustavus' control. It was one of the most important provisions of the truce of Altmark that their collection at the Prussian ports was sanctioned for the duration of the truce; while separate treaties with Brandenburg, Kurland and Danzig not only gave Sweden a share in the tolls which they levied, but also ensured that they should not undercut Swedish-controlled ports by conceding lower rates. As Gustavus' armies conquered the coasts of Pomerania and Mecklenburg, in 1630 and 1631, the same system of 'licences' (the term was borrowed, by false analogy, from the Dutch, in the vain hope of parrying Dutch objections) was applied there; so that by the time Gustavus fell at Lützen there was scarcely a port, from Wismar to Ivangorod, from which the Swedish crown did not derive what was in normal years a very large revenue.[1]

The 'licences', indeed, were not less important to Swedish finances than the state monopoly of the sale of copper. And to these two sources of income was soon added a third, in the form of French subsidies, the payment of which (at the rate of 400,000 *riksdaler* a year) was one of the terms of the Franco-Swedish treaty concluded at Bärwalde, in January 1631. After Gustavus' death, and especially after 1638, the subsidies became of prime importance; but in Gustavus' time, though they were undeniably useful, they were of minor consequence only, without much effect on policy or strategy. The difference is to be explained by the fact that Swedish war finances balanced or failed to balance according to the ability or inability of the Swedish armies to live on the country. While Gustavus was alive, his extraordinary military successes made this comparatively easy: vast areas of Germany were in the occupation either of Sweden or of her allies; much of the country was still unravaged; and it was perfectly reasonable to think in terms of maintaining armies of 150,000 men. Ten years after Lützen, the position was radically altered. Germany had been plundered and devastated from end to end; the area under Swedish control had at times shrunk to the merest wisp of Pomeranian coastland; an army of 15,000 or 20,000 men was as much as a prudent commander would expect to be able to feed—and that only if they were not kept together in one place for any length of time. In these circumstances, the French subsidies might make all the difference between a spirited offensive and open mutiny. But from about 1632 one financial

[1] One other source of supply may have had a temporary importance, especially in 1630. This derived from the permission given by the Russian government to buy grain at very advantageous prices (free of the internal duty levied on other foreign merchants). For a time, at least, this concession may have enabled Sweden to sell grain on the Amsterdam market at a considerable profit.

14-2

principle was accepted by all Swedish statesmen and generals as axiomatic: whoever paid for the German war, it must not be Sweden. The heaviest burden of war expenditure, therefore, fell upon the Swedish taxpayer before, and not after, Breitenfeld. The finances of the German armies were kept quite distinct from the domestic finances; and though the Swedish exchequer defrayed the cost of the navy, and of the home garrisons, the German armies must finance themselves elsewhere—from well-timed sales of copper in Amsterdam, from tolls extorted from the outraged Dutch, from loans in Hamburg on the personal security of Swedish agents, or against the next instalment of Richelieu's subsidies, or, finally, from heavy ransoms levied on captured cities or occupied enemy lands. The remarkable measure of success with which this principle was applied does much to explain how the cost of the creation of the Swedish Empire was sustained.

It is obvious, however, that wars are not won with money only, nor empires acquired by contriving a corner in copper. Sweden's rise to greatness came as the consequence of military successes, and those successes were themselves the consequence of a sound system of military organization and administration, better tactics than the enemy, and the accident that in two generations Sweden produced an unprecedented constellation of great generals. Gustavus Adolphus himself was included by Napoleon in his brief list of the great commanders, and few will be found to dispute that verdict; but Baner and Torstensson, in their several ways, were not by much his inferiors, and each had achievements to his credit of a type that Gustavus did not attempt. And after them came Charles X, who was certainly no ordinary commander. But the victories they won were not merely the product of their genius: they were based on reforms which together had made the Swedish armies for a time the best in Europe. These reforms were essentially the work of Gustavus Adolphus, and most of them were carried through in the years between 1617 and 1630. They based the Swedish army on a properly organized system of conscription, each regiment being assigned to a particular province; they assimilated the administrative to the tactical unit; and they thoroughly trained the forces in a drill designed for the battle-field rather than for the parade-ground. Gustavus adopted many of the tactical principles of Maurice of Orange: his armies, for instance, fought in line, rather than in the deep formations of the Spanish *tercios*. But he designed his formations, as Maurice had not done, for offensive purposes, and gave them the necessary power to attack with success. He rehabilitated the pike (for the last time) as an offensive weapon. He exploited the salvo to give increased concentrations of fire. He armed his infantry with light two-pounder guns which could be freely moved in battle to give support to pikemen and musketeers. Under the influence of the Polish examples which he had observed in the Livonian wars he restored the cavalry to its true function, forgotten in most western armies, of breaking the enemy by impact, rather than firing ineffectively at him with short-range pistols. In both infantry and cavalry he contrived that the shock of intense fire should pave the way for, and alternate with, the shock of mass-impact. His field artillery was of unprecedented mobility; and retained its superiority in this respect until its achievements culminated in Torstensson's great victory at Jankow in 1645. Gustavus proved, in fact, what contemporaries had refused to credit, that a native conscript army could be trained to be better than an army of hired professionals. The vast demands of the German war made it necessary to supplement the purely Swedish and Finnish troops by large levies of German and Scottish mercenaries: before Gustavus fell the mercenary regiments were already in a majority, and by the end of the war the Swedish field-armies were usually overwhelmingly non-Swedish in origin, for it was felt prudent to husband native resources, and politic to put them to garrison key fortresses which they could be relied upon to defend to the last. But the mercenaries learned the Swedish methods under Swedish commanders soon enough. And indeed, Sweden's enemies were not long in attempting to imitate them too.

These were important factors in the Swedish successes; yet it is permissible to think that Sweden's greatness might have been more difficult to achieve without some other assets of a less material kind. One such asset was certainly religious uniformity. Despite occasional lapses to Catholicism by scholars and clerics who had assimilated dangerous ideas at foreign universities (and whose conversion was sometimes associated with political activities as Sigismund's agents), despite too a grudging tolerance accorded to the handful of immigrant Calvinist workmen and *entrepreneurs*, Sweden was a solidly Lutheran country; and, as in Spain, a monolithic religious structure gave strength in an age of religious strife. A foreign policy in which obvious national interest went hand in hand with championship of the Protestant cause was therefore understood and approved by the nation at large; and despite the heavy sacrifices of manpower, it was on the whole accepted as inevitable and right, at least so long as the great king was alive. Gustavus could appeal to the Diet for moral support, for endorsement of his policies, or for supplies of men and money, in the justified confidence that they shared his outlook, and were ready to shoulder burdens in order to carry his policy into effect, since in general it was their policy too. It happened, moreover, that the severe internal tension which had marked the reign of Charles IX had since 1611 been greatly relaxed as a result of the joint efforts of Gustavus and his chancellor, Axel Oxenstierna. The constitutional struggle between king and aristocracy, which had been raging with varying degrees of intensity for the previous half-century, was in Gustavus' time followed by a period of harmony and mutual trust; while the social struggle which was to reach a crisis in 1650 and again in 1680 was still in the background. One result of this state of affairs was that the nobility under the stress of war proved ready to forgo its privileges and tax-exemptions to an extent which would hardly have been tolerated by the aristocracy of Denmark. There were, indeed, periodical riots and distur-bances, arising from local abuses or local distress; but on the whole it may be said that the Sweden which intervened in Germany was a nation of remarkable unity of temper and purpose; and the absence of any major crisis at home, in the last decade of Gustavus' reign, was certainly a factor which contributed to the success of Swedish arms.

The victories of Gustavus transformed Sweden within the space of two years from the leading power in the Baltic into one of the two or three leading powers in Europe. As long as Gustavus lived it was he, not Riche-lieu, that was the dominant partner in the alliance with France. Swedish diplomacy suddenly extended its scope, to match the new position which the king was winning: intrigues with the Tatar khan or with the Greek patriarch, negotiations with George Rákóczy of Transylvania, liaison with the revolted Protestants of the Habsburg hereditary lands. Swedish armies roughly jostled their French allies for control of strongpoints in Alsace; Swedish recruiting agents tried in vain to compromise the neut-rality of the Swiss; and the Roman Catholic world feared for a moment that the new Goths might emulate their forefathers and strike south-wards across the Alps for Rome itself. At the head of a coalition of German Protestant princes, Gustavus and his armies effectively occupied half Germany. His war-aims expanded with success: from an *assecuratio*[1] at first conceived as a territorial outpost on the Pomeranian shore, into a Germanic league (with himself as *caput*) which should provide a political security of a semi-permanent character. And just as in the course of time *assecuratio* changed its nature, so *satisfactio*[2] developed from a simple claim to an indemnity for the expenses of a rescue-expedition into the demand for a cession of territory as a reward for services rendered. Military success, in fact, tempted an appetite which had not hitherto been particularly sharp: by the time of Lützen Gustavus had accustomed himself to the idea of Sweden as a German power. His servants and allies canvassed the possibility of his election as emperor; while he himself was thinking of modifications in the constitution of the *Reich*. In the last year of his life he was putting forward plans for a joint Russo-Swedish campaign against Poland, of which the objective was to be the partition of that country, and the incorporation of the Ukraine into Russia. The imperialist age of Swedish history had come with a rush; and soon Axel Oxenstierna would be debating the expediency of pro-viding the new Swedish Empire with a second capital—a northern Byzantium—at Narva; while Salvius would urge the transference of

[1] See above, Chapter XI. [2] *Ibid.*

the Swedish foreign office to Hamburg. Nor would it seem inappropriate that the chancellor of so great a monarchy should aspire to the electorate of Mainz, as a dignity commensurate with the political power and personal prestige which he commanded.

This great enlargement of the horizons of Swedish policy had obvious effects upon the balance of forces within the Baltic. The German venture, after all, had implied only the postponement of a final settlement of the long controversies with Denmark and Poland. There was more than one moment, even in the last two years of the king's life, when the danger of a stab in the back from Denmark seemed so imminent that he seriously debated the expediency of a preventive war. When Sigismund III died in 1632, Gustavus sought to confuse Polish politics, and make trouble for the Polish Vasas, by putting himself forward as a candidate for the vacant throne; and when the news of Lützen reached Warsaw, Ladislas IV did not allow his genuine admiration for the dead king to prevent him from asserting his hereditary claim to the crown of Sweden. Against each of these dangers—from Poland or from Denmark—the victories in Germany gave increased security. The occupation of the ports of Pomerania and Mecklenburg put Sweden in a strong position in the rear of Denmark and on the flank of Poland; while Swedish armies and Swedish allies in the Lower Saxon Circle did much to neutralize Christian's attempts to meddle in north Germany. The occupation of Pomerania, it is true, brought difficulties; for George William of Brandenburg had strong claims to the succession to Pomerania when the reigning duke, Bogislav XIV, should die. Relations between Gustavus and his brother-in-law in Berlin had been strained since 1626, when Sweden had violated the neutrality of George William's duchy of Prussia; and the king's expressed intention of retaining Pomerania for himself made them worse: the hostility of Brandenburg was to prove one of the most fateful legacies bequeathed by Gustavus to his successors. Yet in 1632, and for some years afterwards, it seemed that the problem might be resolved by a marriage between Queen Christina and the electoral prince. Such a marriage opened up the prospect of a great new northern state, straddling the Baltic, overtopping all possible competitors in that sea, able to assert—in Saxony's despite—a permanent leadership of German Protestantism, and (who could tell?) even to aspire to the imperial crown itself.

To Axel Oxenstierna, as he took up Gustavus' task in the years after Lützen, Swedish power in Germany seemed in fact to be the basis for Swedish domination in the Baltic. Already, within a year or two of Gustavus' death, there were those in the council in Stockholm—and even among the regents—who began to be uneasy at the implications of imperial expansion: 'the branches spread outwards, but the tree dies at the heart'. Oxenstierna had no such qualms. He frankly accepted his country's imperial destiny; he had no idea of curtailing Swedish pretensions in

Germany unless he were forced to do so; and he hoped to exploit the position which his master's victories had won to settle in Sweden's favour the outstanding quarrels with her Baltic neighbours. Gustavus' plan for a Protestant union under Swedish leadership took shape in 1633 as the League of Heilbronn; there was no bating of Sweden's demands for *assecuratio* and *satisfactio;* and though Gustavus' death made a renewal of the French alliance necessary, Oxenstierna at first showed few signs of softening the intransigent attitude which the king had always adopted towards France.

The disasters of the years 1634 and 1635, however, made it very difficult to stick to this programme.[1] The catastrophe at Nördlingen (27 August 1634) put an end to the hope of carrying out Gustavus' grand strategic plan of ending the war quickly by an encircling attack upon the heart of Habsburg power; and by forcing the League of Heilbronn to run for shelter to France it made nonsense of the idea of a Swedish-controlled evangelical union as a standing *assecuratio*. The terms upon which Richelieu now offered alliance were such that Oxenstierna would not accept them; indeed, relations with France grew so strained that Richelieu seriously considered ordering the seizure of Oxenstierna's person. The union with France was broken; and the subsidies stopped. South Germany seemed for ever lost as a quartering-area for Swedish armies; the north German Protestant princes—whom Oxenstierna had never managed to cajole into a meek acceptance of his leadership—were moving fast towards peace with the emperor. In 1635 they made it, at Prague; and one after another Sweden's former allies and clients accepted the Prague terms. Some, like John George of Saxony, or George William of Brandenburg a little later, became open enemies. Henceforward Sweden's position in Germany rested on no basis of kindness of feeling or community of ideals; it rested on naked force. And force now seemed wanting. The Swedish armies found themselves engaged in a desperate attempt to hang on to the Pomeranian coastlands, fighting against numerical odds in supply-areas which, as they grew narrower and narrower, were less and less able to provide the troops with the contributions which they required. The old enemy Denmark was offering a mediation which Oxenstierna was rightly chary of accepting. In 1635 Swedish fortunes in Germany sank to their lowest ebb. Oxenstierna was driven to a vain effort to buy off Brandenburg's hostility by offers to hand over Pomerania when the war was over; he was for a time almost a prisoner of his own mutinous troops in Magdeburg; he was even reduced to making a humiliating appeal to the emperor to open direct negotiations for peace—an appeal which Ferdinand contemptuously ignored. The peace-party at home became vocal; and Oxenstierna had to endure sharp censures from his co-regents in Stockholm. And at this juncture, when the position

---

[1] See above, Chapter XI.

in Germany was at its worst, the Truce of Altmark ran out, and Sweden faced a renewal of the war with Poland. Something not far short of panic in the home government, a disastrous indiscretion which allowed their minimum terms to leak out, and the bungling of the Swedish negotiators, enabled French mediation to patch up an arrangement with Poland at Stuhmsdorf in 1635. The truce was indeed extended for a further twenty-six years; but Sweden paid a heavy price for the respite: evacuation of her holdings in Prussia and, worst of all, an end to the Swedish 'licences' at the Prussian ports. The news came near to breaking Oxenstierna's courage. At the moment when the armies in Germany were least able to make war support war, when the resources of French sub-sidies were no longer available, a great part of the income from tolls was cut off: in 1634 the 'licences' had yielded some 800,000 *rdr.* (or double the amount of French subsidies); in 1637 the figure had fallen to 250,000 *rdr.*

The crisis was surmounted. The Truce of Stuhmsdorf made possible the transfer of 10,000 troops from Prussia to Germany, and so enabled Baner to take the offensive against the Saxons; and his classic victory at Wittstock in 1636 did much to restore the prestige of Swedish arms. Poland and Brandenburg did not (as they might have done) destroy the whole structure of the Swedish toll-system by lowering the rates at their own ports: necessity or greed prevailed over policy. Oxenstierna, returning to Sweden in the summer of 1636, took the government into his strong and capable hands and infused fresh spirit into a regency which had latterly been inclined to be defeatist. It was clear to him that without the financial support of France the war could not long be carried on; but it was equally clear that he must not bind himself to France if by his diplomacy and Baner's victories he could get out of Germany on reasonable terms. The revival of Sweden's fortunes in the year of Wittstock made this at least a possibility: it needed Baner's celebrated (but disastrous) retreat from Torgau in 1637 to persuade Oxenstierna that the French alliance was not to be evaded. It was concluded, at Hamburg, in February 1638; the subsidies began to flow again; and in 1639 their effect was duly seen when Baner was victorious at Chemnitz. In June 1641 the treaty of Ham-burg was renewed, this time for the duration of the war, and the amount of annual subsidy raised to 480,000 *rdr.*—a figure about equal to one-third of Sweden's domestic revenue. The renewal did not come a moment too soon. Baner's death in March had been followed by a crisis of discipline which very nearly led to the complete disintegration of the Swedish forces in Germany; for the mercenary colonels demanded a settlement of the arrears due to them, and the government in Stockholm, uncertain of the outcome of the negotiations with France, had been forced to raise money by the sale of crown lands. The resumed influx of French money made it possible for this emergency, too, to be surmounted; it paved the way for Torstensson's victory at Breitenfeld in October 1642;

and that victory in turn produced 150,000 *rdr.* for the war-chest, paid by the city of Leipzig to buy off a Swedish attack. Once Richelieu's subsidies had primed the pump, the financial machinery of war began to operate with something of its old automatic ease: Torstensson and Wrangel were able to move into the Habsburg hereditary lands, and stay there for long periods; and henceforward until the end of the war they could claim, with more truth than at any time since Nördlingen, that *bellum se ipsum alit.*

The crisis of the thirties had not gone unobserved by Christian IV. He had neither the resources, nor perhaps the wish, for overt hostilities with his neighbour, but he was very ready to add to Sweden's embarrassments. His proffers of mediation in Germany were intended to do that; and also to recover for himself, if possible, some of the political influence which he had forfeited in 1629. Towards the end of the thirties and in the early forties he was engaged in obscure intrigues with England and Spain, with Brandenburg and Poland and Russia, out of which he hoped that an anti-Swedish coalition might be born. One result of these manœuvres was that the great fleet which Spain sent to the Channel in 1639 had, as its secondary objective, an attack on Gothenburg; and it might have gone on to make the attempt, if the Dutch had not destroyed it in the Downs. The Swedish regency considered that the aid and comfort given by Christian to Gustavus Adolphus' widow, when she made a hurried and clandestine departure from Sweden in 1640, was a provocation; and when Christian began once again to collect tolls off Ruden (as he had earlier done, in 1630 and 1631) that was felt to be a provocation too. There was no doubt, either, that Christian had played some part in exacerbating the crisis which convulsed the Swedish army after Baner's death, by offers to take discontented colonels into his service. Oxenstierna expressed a general feeling when he said in 1639 that Christian had 'repeatedly chucked us under the chin to see if our teeth are firm in our heads.' The Danish maritime pretensions were not abated; and in the Sound itself Christian was exercising his admitted rights in a fashion which was felt to be oppressive and capricious.

In the years between 1629 and 1639 the Sound dues were varied eight times: and their general tendency was to grow heavier. This drew upon Denmark the ill-will of the Dutch, who contended (probably incorrectly) that as far as they were concerned the level of the Sound dues had been for ever fixed by the treaty of Speyer in 1544. They were by very much the largest users of the Sound; and many of their skippers met Christian's exactions by sailing under Swedish colours, since Swedish ships and goods were exempt from toll. Christian tried by more stringent visitations to check this fraud, and inevitably there were 'incidents' with genuine Swedish ships and cargoes. Moreover, the emergence of Sweden's Baltic empire posed an important problem of interpretation: were ships and goods from Swedish-occupied ports on the continent—from Wismar, Stralsund, Stettin, Pillau, Riga—to be entitled to exemption from the toll? It is not surprising that Christian IV should have felt that the extension of Sweden's territory could not be permitted to carry this consequence, nor that Sweden should have felt the imposition of toll on ships from these ports to be vexatious. Ten years earlier, the Dutch had directed their protests mainly against the Swedish 'licences'; by the beginning of the 1640s, when the Prussian tolls were no longer in Swedish hands, and when the whole mercantile community was suffering from Danish exactions, they were drawn by common grievances to Sweden's side. In 1640 they concluded with Sweden an alliance for the maintenance of freedom of trade in the Baltic, which in effect was an alliance with a point against Denmark.

It was under cover of this alliance, and with the tacit goodwill of the Dutch, that Oxenstierna sent Torstensson to attack Jutland, without a declaration of war, at the close of 1643. The surprise was complete, the initial successes great; and though the later course of the war did not quite fulfil the promise of the beginning, Sweden was able to impose very hard terms of peace at Brömsebro in 1645. Christian IV was forced to cede the Norwegian provinces of Jämtland and Härjedalen (both of which lay on the Swedish side of the mountains, and geographically and ecclesiastically could be considered part of Sweden), together with the islands of Gotland and Ösel; while the secularized bishoprics of Bremen and Verden, which had been the property of Christian's second son, Frederick (afterwards Frederick III), were left in Swedish occupation. Exemption from the Sound dues was henceforward to be accorded to Swedish ships from all ports in Swedish possession. And, most important of all, as a guarantee of this exemption Denmark was to hand over Halland for thirty years, with the stipulation that Sweden should be entitled to territorial compensation upon its retrocession. This was a mere form of words devised to soften the blow to Christian's pride; for everybody knew that the cession was intended to be permanent. It represented a portentous alteration in the political geography of the Baltic. The transference of Halland to Sweden meant that the Sound was no longer controlled by a single power, since the two sides of the narrows were now in different hands. It destroyed for ever the Danish theory that passage through the Sound was a *transitus* through Danish dominions. And in another aspect it marked the first step towards that expansion of Sweden to her natural frontiers which was to be the permanent achievement of Charles X.

The Danish war showed very plainly that the rulers of Sweden had now passed the stage at which an empire is acquired by accident, or by force of circumstance. The aggression against Denmark was deliberately planned— it had been predicted as early as 1640 by the Danish ambassador in Stockholm—and it was popular with the nation, as the German war no longer was. In the intoxication of early success there were some who talked of annexing the whole of Denmark. For such men Brömsebro was a disappointment: the work was half-done; and some day Skåne and Blekinge must be Swedish too. Yet even this result, unsatisfactory as it might appear to the Swedes, could hardly have been achieved without Dutch aid. The Dutch had at first been officially neutral, and for a time even acted as mediators; until in the last stage of the peace negotiations they had thrown off the mask and applied unscrupulous pressure to Denmark to extort concessions for themselves. Dutch merchantmen had passed through the Sound without paying toll; a Dutch fleet had cruised in Danish waters to protect them; and Dutch warships and a Dutch admiral, chartered for the Swedish service by Louis de Geer, had given Sweden the crushing naval superiority which really decided the issue. The Swedish Empire was by nature a maritime empire: without command of the sea it could hardly hope permanently to maintain itself. Oxenstierna fully appreciated this. The blow to Danish naval power inflicted by the annihilating victory of Femern in 1645 gave Sweden a temporary naval superiority so great that the government could afford in 1647 to sell warships to France, or dispose of them in settlement of the claims of its creditors. But Charles XI's war[1] would show that only constant naval ascendancy could guarantee Sweden against a Danish *revanche;* and on the whole it may be doubted whether the Swedish fleet was ever consistently powerful enough to make the Swedish Empire really secure.

Naval strength was the more necessary, because by 1645 the mercantile marine was beginning a period of fairly rapid expansion. Hitherto Swedish ships had played only an insignificant part in Swedish commerce: the main carriers, as everywhere in the Baltic, had been the Dutch. But already in 1645 the Swedish government had introduced a system of graduated duties designed to encourage the use of Swedish bottoms and to stimulate the enterprise of Swedish shippers; and it was significant that the peace of Brömsebro contained a clause abrogating the old freedom of trade between Sweden and Denmark: Sweden wished now to be able to discriminate against the foreigner. At the end of the thirties there had been discussions with the Dutch about the possibility of making Gothenburg the staple for Eastland products, and plans for a canal through Sweden which should enable skippers to evade the Sound. Such projects were evidences of a renewed determination that Sweden should have her share of the trade between east and west; and another sign of the times was the establishment in 1651 of a new government department, the College of Commerce, with an instruction drafted by Axel Oxenstierna himself. And the growth of Swedish shipping, and the efforts of the government to foster it, were in the nature of the case a challenge to the

---

[1] See Vol. v in this series, Chapter xxii.

commercial ascendancy enjoyed in the Baltic by Sweden's recent allies the Dutch.

The peace of Brömsebro was followed by a diplomatic revolution in the Baltic, just as the peace of Knäred had been, thirty years before; but this time it was in the reverse direction. It was now Sweden that appeared truculent and insatiable, while Danish diplomacy adroitly exploited its opportunities, and made political capital out of weakness and defeat. Mazarin had not relished Oxenstierna's use of French subsidies for an attack on Denmark. It was not in France's interest that Sweden should allow her attention to be distracted from Germany at a moment when the terms of peace which could be extorted at the Congress of Westphalia were so directly related to military success or failure. Mazarin, therefore, had offered mediation in the north; and to his ambassador, de Thuillerie, fell the main credit for arranging the Peace of Brömsebro. But the war was hardly over before Mazarin realized, and realized with misgiving, how the situation in the Baltic was changing. It was not now so much a matter of ensuring 'the tranquillity of the North' (as the diplomats of the next century would have phrased it) in order that every effort might be concentrated against the Habsburgs. It was a question rather of ensuring that the north should not be dominated by a single overmighty power. Danish diplomats—and especially Christian IV's able and unscrupulous son-in-law, Korfits Ulfeld—harped persistently on this string; and soon after the peace they had their reward. In November 1645 France signed a treaty of alliance with Denmark. It was to last for six years; and by its terms French ships were granted the same rates for the Sound dues as had been accorded to the Dutch, while Denmark was promised diplomatic support for her efforts to recover Bremen and Verden for Prince Frederick. And thus began a policy, destined to be pursued by so many French statesmen in the course of the next hundred years—a policy of trying to run the two Scandinavian powers in double harness, and be the ally of both at once, flattering each in turn with nicely graded evidences of French goodwill, and restraining both (as far as possible) from beginning hostilities; a policy expensive in the article of subsidies, and doubtful in the returns it yielded. In 1645, at all events, it was a policy that came too early: the smart of defeat was too keenly felt in Denmark to be assuaged by French plasters. A decade later Mazarin would be driven to make choice between Denmark and Sweden; and political tradition, as well as present interest, would lead him to choose Sweden. But for the moment the Franco-Danish alliance seemed the first significant indication of changing times.

It was soon followed by others. The Swedish triumph had evoked similar misgivings in Oxenstierna's Dutch accomplices. At Brömsebro their plenipotentiaries, once they had abandoned the pretence of mediation, confined themselves rigorously to blackmailing Denmark for their own advantage: to Sweden's territorial demands they gave little or no support. The alliance with Sweden was indeed renewed immediately afterwards; but relations were far from cordial. In order, as the Dutch alleged, to cover the cost of their naval activities in the Sound, their fleet was levying a toll (the so-called *veilgeld*) on vessels going into the Baltic, and not only was this imposed upon the ships of their ally Sweden, but it was levied at double rates on ships to German and Livonian ports in Swedish possession. It was not until a full year after the conclusion of peace that Swedish protests and reprisals obtained the cessation of this imposition. The Dutch were beginning to be alarmed at the measures taken to protect Swedish monopoly companies, and at the expansion of the Swedish mercantile marine, which was in fact proceeding so fast that by the middle of the next decade almost all Swedish exports would be carried in Swedish ships. In short, the state of Swedish-Dutch relations in 1646 offered an opportunity for a statesman who might be concerned to separate the two powers. This opportunity Korfitz Ulfeld adroitly seized. In February 1647 he was able to sign a treaty with Their High Mightinesses which settled outstanding claims from the period of the recent war; and in September 1649 he brought off a remarkable diplomatic *coup* by concluding two further treaties with them. One was a treaty of alliance and mutual aid; the other—the so-called Redemption Treaty—was a financial agreement, whereby the United Provinces bound themselves to pay Denmark 140,000 *rdr.* a year in return for the exemption of Dutch ships from the Sound dues.

Economically, the Redemption Treaty was an excellent bargain for Denmark, and the Dutch were glad enough to be allowed to cancel the arrangement (by the so-called Rescission Treaty) in 1653. Politically it was even more advantageous. It secured Denmark against further Swedish aggression. It virtually ended the Dutch alliance with Sweden. It seemed to ensure that the balance of power in the Baltic would not be tilted further in Sweden's favour. And almost inevitably it led to a further deterioration of Sweden's relations with the Dutch; for in order to compensate themselves for the annual payment to Denmark, the States General now proceeded to levy a duty, not only on the Dutch skippers who were now relieved of the Sound dues, but on all ships engaged in the Baltic trade that might put into Dutch ports. This, as the Swedes complained, was in effect to transfer the Sound dues to Dutch waters, and so to destroy the exemption from those dues which Swedish ships had so long enjoyed. And when to this provocation is added, that the Dutch had given diplomatic support to Denmark at Westphalia over Bremen and Verden, and that they had sympathized with Brandenburg in the bitter controversy over Pomerania, then it is clear that by 1650 the brief period of Swedish-Dutch friendship was quite over. Dutch feeling in the fifties would be decidedly hostile to Sweden; and in 1659 and 1660 De Witt and Mazarin would collaborate to impose a settlement on Scandinavia which was entirely in the spirit of Dutch policy.

If in the Baltic French statesmen were now showing signs of a disposition to hedge, in Germany (as Mazarin realized) the Franco-Swedish alliance was still indispensable to both partners. There were moments, it is true, of intense irritation, when the military or diplomatic collaboration appeared about to break down, and the one ally or the other for a time threatened to strike a bargain with the enemy; but on the whole the alliance held firm. This solidarity, in the field and at Westphalia, explains the magnitude of the gains made by each at the peace. In the closing years of the war, Sweden's essential aims were, first, Pomerania; and, secondly, an indemnity large enough to permit the disbandment of the mercenary armies. Peace without indemnity would be ruinous; for, lacking the French subsidies, Sweden could neither keep her troops nor dismiss them. Peace without Pomerania would be disgraceful; for in Pomerania were now conflated the last vestiges of *satisfactio* and *assecuratio*. But in addition to these two indispensables, the Swedish diplomats fought hard for indemnity to Sweden's most faithful German ally, Hesse-Cassel; and did their best to obtain reasonable guarantees for those Protestant states who had been excluded from the benefits of the Peace of Prague. Religious feeling still counted for a good deal at Westphalia; and the fire of the Protestant cause was not yet quite extinguished. How long it would survive the ending of hostilities was perhaps another matter.

The terms which Sweden ultimately obtained at the peace did, on the whole, satisfy these demands. After long haggling, an indemnity of five million *rdr.* was secured for the 'contentment of the soldiery'—a sum which the ravaged lands of Germany found great difficulty in raising—and by 1650 it was possible to bring back the army to a peacetime footing. The landgrave of Hesse-Cassel obtained his indemnity too; the Calvinist states were put on an equality with the Lutherans; and Sweden could feel that she had done her duty by her friends in Germany. It proved impossible, indeed, to obtain the whole of Pomerania (though both Oxenstierna and Christina in the final stages believed that it could have been got, if the negotiators had shown a little more firmness); but eastern Pomerania—impoverished, unfertile, with a single third-rate port at Kolberg—was no great loss: all that was worth having of Pomerania lay west of the Oder, and all of it became Swedish. Stettin itself, with all the Oder-mouths, passed into Swedish hands. In 1653, after protracted and embittered negotiations, the great elector was compelled, in order to obtain the evacuation of the Swedish troops from his half of Pomerania, to accept a very disadvantageous frontier, and to concede to the Swedes a half-share in the tolls—such as they were—levied in eastern Pomeranian ports. In addition, Sweden not only obtained at Westphalia the cession of the Mecklenburg towns of Wismar and Warnemünde, but continued (in defiance of legality) to take toll at other Mecklenburg ports also. And, finally, the secularized bishoprics of Bremen and Verden, which had been in Swedish occupation since the Danish war, were now formally transferred to Swedish ownership.

By the Peace of Westphalia Sweden emerged, in law as well as in fact, as a German power. Queen Christina became, in virtue of her German possessions, a member of no less than three circles of the empire. Henceforth Sweden had a permanent seat in the Diet: permanent, because the emperor granted the Pomeranian fief not to Christina and her heirs, but to the Swedish crown. The great rivers of north Germany were now under Swedish control; the trade from Silesia down the Oder could be milked at Stettin (hence the great elector's construction of the Hohenzollern canal, in the sixties, to circumvent this obstacle); a substantial proportion of the war-time system of 'licences' remained intact; and the threat to Denmark from Wismar was now reinforced from Bremen, which Per Brahe rightly pronounced to be 'a bridle for the Jute.' The gains at Westphalia, therefore, though they might seem to risk involving Sweden for many years to come in eccentric questions of German politics, were welcomed at home as a strengthening of her position against her most dangerous Baltic rival. It was not apparent, in 1650, that the Swedish dominions were already too extensive to be adequately defended. Swedish statesmen did not as yet realize that the favourable financial conjunctures of the years from 1631 to 1648 were unlikely to recur, nor appreciate how difficult it might prove to maintain a straggling empire from Sweden's own resources. It was expected that Sweden would resume, after the peace, her historic role of leader and champion of German—indeed, of European—Protestantism against the Habsburgs and the papacy; and old Oxenstierna, like many others of his generation, would have wished that it should be so. Together with France, Sweden was joint guarantor of the Westphalian settlement; and that settlement had among other things given new security and a new status to evangelical Germany. But this expectation ignored the implications of Sweden's membership of the Germanic body, and forgot that she had thereby inevitably acquired a share of that same particularist selfishness which Gustavus Adolphus in his day had so loudly condemned. Like electoral Saxony, or the Brunswick dukes, Sweden had now her own petty ambitions and private quarrels in Germany, for the realization or prosecution of which she needed the goodwill of the emperor. So, for example, in regard to Brandenburg; so in regard to Bremen and Verden. For Bremen and Verden Queen Christina still lacked that imperial investiture which would make her possession of these territories legally unassailable; and the city of Bremen in 1654 forcibly resisted Sweden's attempts to destroy its status as an immediate vassal of the emperor. Christina, moreover, like many another German ruler, had personal and dynastic problems, and hoped to solve them more easily with the emperor as a friend rather than as an enemy: her intended abdication, and her conversion to Catholicism, both drew her to the side of Ferdinand III. In the early fifties, therefore, Europe saw with astonishment a sharp veering of Swedish foreign policy towards friendship with Austria and Spain; and the Swedish representative at the imperial Diet even supported the election of Ferdinand IV as king of the Romans in 1653. It may be doubted whether, after 1650, there was in any case sufficient Protestant solidarity in Germany, and still less sufficient goodwill towards Sweden, for any revival of Gustavus' *corpus evangelicorum* to be conceivable: Sweden's bullyings of Brandenburg and Bremen had made the most deplorable impression among her former well-wishers. The day for a foreign policy of Oxenstierna's type was passing, if it had not already passed; and Salvius and the new men perceived this. But this implied no obstacle to Sweden's entering into combinations with other German states to maintain particular interests, or safeguard the public peace, or oppose imperial pretensions—combinations in which religion would be a secondary, if not an insignificant, element. The League of Hildesheim, with Hesse-Cassel and the Brunswick dukes (1652), matched the analogous efforts of John Philip von Schönborn of Mainz to organize the Rhineland states for mutual protection against the unamenable armies of Charles of Lorraine; and the fusion of these two initiatives, under French guidance, would produce the completely undenominational League of the Rhine. And the coalition which was formed to fight Charles X in 1658 would include (besides Catholic Poland and Austria) Lutheran Denmark, Calvinist Brandenburg, and Orthodox Muscovy.

In August 1654 Axel Oxenstierna died at the age of seventy-one. It was nearly fifty years since he had entered the public service; it was forty-five since his admission to the council; and he had held the office of chancellor in unbroken tenure since 1612. His working life had thus covered the whole astonishing chain of events by which Sweden became a great power; and few, certainly, had done more to forge that chain than he. He had been the chief negotiator for Sweden of the humiliating Peace of Knäred; and thirty-two years later he had had the satisfaction of being the chief negotiator of the triumphant Peace of Brömsebro. He had lived long enough to see Denmark depressed into a position of inferiority, and he would willingly have seen her weakened still further: to the end of his life he retained his full share of that national hatred for 'the Jute' which the sufferings of the War of Kalmar had so strongly reinforced. Over the other arch-enemy, Poland, there had been no such clear victory to establish, despite the successes of the twenties, and nothing better than a long truce to be had: a determined effort by Mazarin to arrange a settlement in 1651 had come to a stop before the unshakable refusal of John Casimir to renounce his hereditary claim to Sweden. Yet though some of the old problems were thus unresolved, and though Denmark was by no means finished with, Oxenstierna's death does mark an epoch. The age of expansion—based on especially favourable financial and military circumstances, and the close identity of Swedish national interests with the general interests of Protestantism in Europe—was at an end; from about 1650 Swedish copper production began to show a progressive decline, and Oxenstierna's financial policy of converting crown lands and revenues into cash was seen to have reached its limit of safety, if it had not passed it; Swedish advances in the art of war had become more or less common form; the Protestant cause was already little more than a memory or a dream. The reign of Charles X was to be—as the fifties in so many countries were—a transitional period, leading to the very different world of Louis XIV. And though in Charles' time the process of expansion continued and reached its limit, it was only in the matter of the completion of Sweden's geographical unity that his military exploits made a lasting effect. Already in the fifties it was possible to discern the emergence of dangers and problems different from those with which Oxenstierna had been familiar; and there are some grounds for thinking that Charles X perceived this. The inexpiable offence of the seizure of western Pomerania was to make Brandenburg Sweden's most dangerous enemy in the immediate future; and the great elector was to devote his life to the effort to undo that wrong. The catastrophes of 'the Deluge'[1] not only removed Poland as a serious challenger in the Baltic (at Oliva in 1660 the Polish Vasas finally abjured the crown of Sweden) but created a vacuum of power which sooner or later Muscovy would be able to fill. It was already plain that Sweden need not hope to rest undisturbed upon her arms, in placid enjoyment of her territorial booty. The empire would have to be defended, if it were to be held; and defence would somehow have to be paid for. Henceforward, in peace no less than in war, Sweden would be, characteristically, a subsidy-hunting power.

[1] See below, Chapter XIX, Pt. I.

CHAPTER XIV

INTERNATIONAL RELATIONS AND THE ROLE OF FRANCE 1648–60

THE evolution of international relations dominates the entire history of the period between the Peace of Westphalia (1648) and the Treaties of the Pyrenees (1659) and of Oliva (1660). These few years saw the termination of the Thirty Years War, of the war between France and Spain and of the war in the north. But, apart from some territorial adjustments arising from the Treaty of the Pyrenees, these conflicts appear to be of minor interest; they did not transform the map of Europe. The appearance is misleading, for this short period, when the first indications of French supremacy emerged to view, witnessed a change in the relations between the European powers. It saw the end of the Franco-Swedish axis which had dominated the history of the Thirty Years War, the final downfall of Spain and the decline of Sweden and Poland, the entrance of Russia into European politics and the rise to power of the little state of Brandenburg. Finally, with the first Anglo-Dutch War, came the confident assertion of English sea-power in an alliance—albeit episodic—with France. The shifting of power, the emergence of new forces or rather of new ambitions, the breakdown of the old European equilibrium which was everywhere in a state of collapse—these are the themes it is proposed to elucidate, taking as a guiding thread the policy of France which gives unity to the whole.

Although it brought peace in Europe, peace in Germany and a constitutional charter, the achievement of the Peace of Westphalia remained incomplete. It had provided a lasting solution to some of the problems from which it stemmed, notably to the religious question on the basis of a reciprocal tolerance between the Catholic, Lutheran and Calvinist faiths; it also assured the exercise of territorial sovereignty to princes and cities; finally, it gave the victorious states substantial 'satisfactions': yet it was, above all else, a 'potentiality', calling for careful surveillance by France if all its rewards were to be reaped.

The immediate military result was certainly achieved. '[We must] fortify ourselves in Metz and advance, if possible, as far as Strasbourg, to secure an entry into Germany', Richelieu had written in 1629 in his *Avis au Roi*. He was concerned to destroy the power of the House of Austria by preventing the strategic and political union of the two branches of the Habsburgs, in Vienna and Madrid. Did not the publicist Fancan remark at the time: 'If Germany is lost, France cannot survive'? In the 'satisfaction' obtained by France, the two landgraviates of Alsace and the Sundgau were less important than the fortress of Breisach on the right bank of the Rhine. As an 'open gateway to the Empire' Breisach had replaced Strasbourg, which was not to become French until 1681. A former possession of the archdukes, Breisach lay across the road from the Low Countries to Italy which, for Spain, remained a road carrying missionaries, treasure and *tercios* rather than merchants. An equally important provision, instigated by the French, was the guarantee of the contracting powers, in particular of France and Sweden. These powers had the right to be represented by an ambassador at the Diet, to form themselves by alliances into a party within the empire and, finally, to intervene in its affairs in defence of the 'German liberties' whose affirmation sealed the emperor's impotence and destroyed his dream of religious and political unity.

This outcome appeared satisfactory; but it had now to be consolidated and there was another side to the picture. Despite the skill of the French negotiators, the German princes came to feel certain misgivings about an alliance or protection which, though disinterested in theory, was in practice concerned with territorial advantages. Again, though the emperor was defeated and his ambitions stood condemned, he was not deprived of all authority in Germany. He shared legislative power with the Diet; he commanded an important following and continued to figure as the hereditary defender of the Catholic faith against Protestantism; he remained suzerain of all the estates of the empire and, through his patrimonial dominions, the enemy of the Turks—the kingdom of Hungary was but a narrow strip of territory bordering Ottoman Hungary. The emperor's prestige on the Rhine was to depend upon his success on the Danube. Finally, the decline of the emperor encouraged the rise of the princes. The Treaty of Westphalia empowered them to conduct an independent foreign policy and to conclude any alliances they pleased. A newcomer, Brandenburg, appeared on the political scene: treated by the Swedes with scant respect, she was obliged to leave them not only Stralsund, 'the German Calais', but also the mouth of the Oder and Stettin, contenting herself with the eastern extremity of Pomerania, burdened by Swedish customs dues, with the reversion of Magdeburg and with the territories of Camin, Halberstadt and Minden. But these last were thrice as valuable as the lost province and joined together the ancient possessions of the Hohenzollerns. Frederick William, now the most important of the Protestant electors, 'with more lands and revenues than the two most powerful kings of the North had possessed thirty years earlier', improved his position through the play of European politics and endowed his country with a fine army.

Since 1635, when France declared war on Spain, a European conflict had been grafted on to the German war. There were, in fact, two separate wars which frequently became confused. Each theatre of operations, whether in the Low Countries, the Iberian Peninsula, or Italy, had its own laws and its intrinsic development. The conflict in the Low Countries, which first arose with the revolt of the former Spanish provinces against Philip II, had moved towards the establishment of two separate territorial, religious and political régimes: in the north, the Protestant and republican United Provinces; in the south, the provinces which remained Catholic and Spanish. Though in 1635 the alliance concluded between the France of Richelieu and the United Provinces had envisaged the possible division of the Spanish Netherlands between their two neighbours, the situation had changed by 1648. The capture of Dunkirk by the duc d'Enghien on 11 October 1646, an exploit celebrated by Voiture and Corneille, as well as Sarrazin, Mademoiselle de Scudéry and Balzac, had alarmed the United Provinces, who viewed the French advance into Flanders with some anxiety. They were afraid of being confronted by a powerful and victorious nation carrying all before it. They also feared the commercial rivalry of Dunkirk, a mighty naval arsenal, the haunt of pirates and the scourge of the French coast. At the same time, arising from the projected marriage between the young king and the infanta of Spain who was to bring the Belgian provinces as dowry, the idea was abroad that Spain might exchange these provinces for Catalonia. All these reasons had led the United Provinces to break the alliance which formerly linked them to France. On 30 January 1648 they signed a separate peace with Spain which transformed the truce of 1609 into a definitive treaty and marked the capitulation of Spain in the spheres of politics, religion and, above all, commerce. Mutual freedom of trade was granted in Europe, without opening the Spanish colonies to the Dutch; Spain recognized the closing of the mouths of the Scheldt; Antwerp was sacrificed for the benefit of Amsterdam. This separate peace, sought by Spain, who was anxious to devote all her strength to the struggle with France, and desired by financial and mercantile circles in Holland and Zeeland, had a twofold result. On the one hand, by confirming the role of the United Provinces as a great colonial and sea power, it led them into conflict with England, where Cromwell had seized power after the fall of Charles I; on the other hand, it raised the territorial problem of the Spanish Netherlands, closely linked to the destiny of Spain, condemned to economic strangulation, in the grip of clerical despotism and coveted by France. But 1648 did not see the last moves in the game. The arrival of the Archduke Leopold William, brother of the Emperor Ferdinand III and appointed governor-general of the Spanish Netherlands in 1647, led to an appreciable recovery of Spanish authority. The Battle of Lens, won by Condé on 20 August 1648 with the help of German troops brought in by Erlach, the governor of Breisach, re-established the situation in favour of France, but in a manner more spectacular than decisive.

Two problems less pressing for France, but agonizing for Spain, were those of Portugal and Catalonia. Portugal, linked unwillingly to the destiny of Spain since 1581, had revolted in 1640. Despite the opposition of the Dutch who were anxious to continue exploiting Brazil, Richelieu had concluded an alliance with John IV. This alliance, which remained largely a dead letter, had the effect of paralysing Spain at sea and of retaining Spanish troops in the Peninsula. The struggle was not to end until 1668 with Portuguese independence. In Catalonia, where the Cortes in revolt against Olivares had appealed to France, the French government saw a pawn or an object for eventual barter with Spain and a means of waging war with Philip IV on the frontiers of the provinces of Valencia and Aragon. Perpignan had capitulated on 19 September 1642, but the difficulties of climate and terrain, together with the lack of men and money, had led, despite the efforts of Pierre de Marca as visitor-general, to the inaction of La Motte-Houdancourt and to the failures of Harcourt and Condé himself before Lerida. The appointment of the cardinal of Santa Cecilia, formerly Michel Mazarin, as viceroy of Catalonia was merely an interlude. On 13 July 1648 Schomberg, who had reorganized the army, took Tortosa, a success which accompanied that of Condé in the north.

Finally, Italy with her anarchic constitution, a mere geographical expression, remained a notorious sphere of war and intrigue, where French and Spanish factions were at grips. Though Spain had political control of the two Sicilies and the Milanese, France still held in Pinerolo, which belonged to the duke of Savoy, a door opening into the peninsula; she also controlled, like two advanced posts against the House of Austria, Casale and Mantua, the most important strongholds in the Po valley. On 1 September 1647 Francis d'Este, Duke of Modena, had signed an offensive and defensive alliance with the king. But, although an expedition in October 1646 had led to the capture of Piombino on the coast and of Porto Longone on the Island of Elba, the invasion of the duchy of Milan by Prince Thomas of Savoy and the duke of Modena was a failure. In Rome, whose support was necessary for the success of French plans, the result was no better. The election of Innocent X in 1644, in spite of Mazarin's opposition, was significant: 'the whole court', he wrote, 'and the *parlements* of the kingdom believe that we have now a Spanish Pope'. His hope of obtaining a cardinal's hat for his brother Michel was now less bright, and the long-cherished dream of a league of Italian states united against the common oppressor was shattered. There remained the question of Naples, whose chequered history was entirely characteristic of this highly coloured period; her population was restive under the Spanish yoke. Mazarin had hopes of installing there a member of the House of Savoy, Prince Thomas. In the draft treaty which he prepared with the latter Mazarin provided that, if the elder branch of the House of Savoy should die out and Prince Thomas, already king of Naples, became duke of Savoy and sovereign of Piedmont, he would cede to France Savoy and the county of Nice, 'everything on this side of the mountains bordering France'. These fine hopes were not realized. The revolt led by Tommaso Aniello (Masaniello) broke out in Naples. It was followed by the proclamation of the republic on 24 October 1647, and by the arrival of the Duc de Guise—an exponent of kid-glove warfare. Mazarin's policy of delaying until 'the fruit is ripe and the Neapolitans themselves ask for the help of France', coupled with internal rivalries, facilitated the return of the kingdom of the two Sicilies to Spain, on 6 April 1648.

If peace was to be securely established in Germany and the war against Spain pursued on the various fronts, the French government needed unity, firmness and a stable policy. These it entirely lacked, in appearance at least. There is a striking contrast between the broad sweep of the international scene, with war everywhere except on the Rhine, and the paltry intrigues which disturbed France. The death of Louis XIII had been followed by a minority. A child, Louis XIV; a woman, the Spanish-born regent, Anne of Austria, who had been granted full sovereign powers by the Parlement; a foreigner, Cardinal Mazarin, chosen as chief minister by Louis XIII and retained by the regent—these were the protagonists in the drama in progress at court. They had to grapple with problems arising from shortage of money, opposition in the Parlement, intrigues of the nobles and unrest in the provinces.

As early as the beginning of 1647, the Venetian ambassador had drawn attention to the chaos in financial administration: 'Such are the methods in practice in the confused state of financial administration that the king has never a penny in his purse.' Financial difficulties delayed the ending of the war; the lack of funds encouraged the desertion of the troops, disgruntled at not receiving their promised pay in due time. Once a battle was won, the army halted or disbanded for lack of money. The horrors of war grew apace, and the soldiers lived on the country. Taking advantage of the fiscal situation, the opposition in the Parlement attempted to call in question the whole organization of the kingdom.[1]

To what extent had these opposition groups, active until 1654 and adding a veritable civil war to the foreign war, a foreign policy different from that of the government? They were in general much given to proposing the ideal of peace as an alternative to the war. Some, for reasons of political and religious opinion recalling the choice which Louis XIII had to make between Richelieu and Marillac, favoured a separate peace with Spain. The duchesse de Chevreuse, and Châteauneuf, a man who had suffered at Richelieu's hands, hoped to put an end to an impious war 'in which brother and sister contend, and Catholics take up arms against Catholics to the advantage of the Protestant powers'. They wanted to abandon the alliances contracted in the reigns of Henri IV and Louis XIII, to adopt a Catholic policy and to sign a peace based on a *status quo*

---

[1] See below, Chapter XVI, pp. 496-9.

favourable to Spain. The majority, however, wanted an end of the war for reasons of internal politics. After thirteen years of conflict, the peace party drew into its ranks all those who had smarted under the demands of Richelieu and suffered by the prolongation of the war: the provincial nobles humiliated in the previous reign, the legal middle class whose distrust and resentment were expressed by Guy Patin, and finally, the masses in Paris and the provinces who, though still loyal to the monarchy, accused Richelieu's successor of opposing peace with Spain in 1648 and took up in unison the current slogan: 'Away with Mazarin!'

Cardinal Mazarin remained the mainspring of home and foreign affairs, which were closely interlocked. At a time when Frenchmen gave themselves over entirely to the preoccupations of the moment, expressed in outbursts, sometimes reasoned like those of the Parlement, sometimes sparking spontaneously from the throng like the reactions of the people on the Day of the Barricades, this Italian, who became a naturalized Frenchman in 1639 and a cardinal in 1641 (he received the biretta from Louis XIII on 25 February 1642), showed an acute awareness of the greatness of France and reverted, though with other methods, to the policy of Richelieu. He was the man for the hour, for this period when diplomacy and war went hand in hand. His faults are well known: the passion for money which led him to confuse the state coffers with his private purse: the love for his family, for the nieces he dowered and married into the highest aristocracy, or for his brother Michel, made cardinal of Santa Cecilia and viceroy of Catalonia; his genius for intrigue, so much in evidence in his *Carnets*, which justify the epigram of La Rochefoucauld, a good judge of the human heart, that 'he was a man of limited vision, even in his greatest schemes'. He remained pre-eminently a diplomat who moved with relish in the network of alliances, who knew his Europe, the general interests of the powers and particular appetites of their rulers, who discerned all men's weaknesses, which he used, and even abused, in the belief that every man has his price. In this way, he pursued his task through the troubled atmosphere of the Fronde and the Mazarinades from 1648 to 1653, finding his most effective support in the regent, who was anxious to convey the heritage of monarchy intact to her son. Though economically—despite the popular outcry—the burden of the war was not crushing, politically the continuing struggle encouraged the development of the institutions of absolute power and aroused opposition of various kinds. The conflicting policies proposed by the different camps reveal Mazarin's terrible loneliness. Frenchmen were incapable of understanding that a foreigner—that 'rascally Sicilian', as the duc d'Orléans called him—could excel them in discerning, beyond the tribulations of the moment, the permanent interests of the country. Mazarin's first concern was to safeguard the benefits conferred by the Peace of Westphalia, to consolidate the situation now obtaining in Germany by using the guarantee accorded to France and Sweden. In the short term also, he strove to secure strong frontiers for France, particularly in the north and east. In a letter dated 20 January 1646 he wrote:

The acquisition of the Spanish Netherlands would provide an impregnable bulwark for the city of Paris; it might then truly be called the heart of France, and would stand in the safest place in the kingdom. Our borders would have been extended as far as Holland, and, on the German side, a quarter from which there is also much to be feared, as far as the Rhine, by the retention of Lorraine and Alsace and the possession of Luxemburg and the County of Burgundy.

The war against Spain was less an end in itself than a means of safe-guarding the influence of the monarchy in Europe. In the long term, bold investments were made in the future—in the Spanish succession, for example. In less skilful hands they were to lead to the mistakes of the end of the reign. With these basic themes there were blended, in mid-century, new interests arising from the commercial revolution and the discovery of new continents in the preceding century. War was impending between England and Holland, not for political supremacy—now no longer an objective—but for control of the seas and colonial trade; there was also a struggle in the north for control of the Baltic, where the ambitions of Scandinavia, Poland, Brandenburg and Russia were in conflict. Here once again, Mazarin made his choice: unlike Richelieu, he was neither a sailor nor an economist. He was to use external wars as a source of indis-pensable alliances, or as a theatre in which to intervene as arbiter. Under his government, from 1648 to 1661, the choice of the monarchy was for France as a European power, with territorial and political pretensions.

It would be tedious to enter into the chronological details of events. Each problem on the international scene impinged upon the next, might have moments of quiescence, of unforeseen resurgence, of swift develop-ment, according to the internal situation in each state. Four questions appear to call for examination, in terms of the role played by France: relations with the empire, relations with the maritime powers, the conduct and conclusion of the war with Spain, and France's intervention in the war in the north. The tireless diplomatic activity of Mazarin forms the close weft of international relations.

Once the German war was over, there immediately arose the problems of the peace. Some were pressing and concerned the carrying out of the Treaties of Münster and Osnabrück; others, perhaps more important, but less urgent, raised the question of France's future policy in the empire. The first stage was the evacuation of the German towns by allied garrisons and armies. The solidarity of the victors was now put to the test. Circum-stances were not favourable for France. The loyalty of Turenne, whose prestige was still high in Germany, was wavering; Harcourt, the governor of Alsace, was intriguing at Breisach, which he wanted to make the capital of a buffer state between France and the empire; the ten free imperial towns of Alsace were unwilling to ascribe more than a restricted meaning to the term 'protection' and claimed to owe allegiance only to the empire. 'From every quarter', wrote Vautorte, the French envoy in Nürnberg, to Mazarin in 1649, 'there come complaints against France.' This was a galling situation for the conqueror, arraigned and impotently watching the manœuvres of Austria. It was useless to attempt, as Mazarin wished, to obtain recognition of the cession of Alsace as an imperial fief instead of in full sovereignty. A curious paradox, explained by Mazarin's desire to see the king of France seated in the Diet of Ratisbon as landgrave of Alsace. This claim, already advanced in 1646, met with the same resistance in 1653: 'I have sure proof', declared Vautorte, 'that the Emperor, and those of the Estates which share his views, are opposed to Alsace becoming an Estate of the Empire.' In the three bishoprics, held by France as vicar-general of the empire since 1552, the king's full sovereignty had been recognized by the Treaty of Münster. How far did this sovereignty extend? The plenipotentiaries claimed that it covered 'the temporal dependencies of the bishops as well as the places within their spiritual jurisdiction'. It should be noted that, after 1679, this interpretation was to authorize the procedures of the Chambre de Réunion of the Parlement of Metz.

The end of the Fronde and the arrival of La Ferté's army in Alsace reversed the situation. The Estates dropped their complaints, but the plan for holding Alsace as a fief was not broached again, nor was the reform of the imperial institution brought about at Ratisbon. At Münster, Mazarin had tried to set the democracy of the towns up against the aristocracy of the electors and the oligarchy of the princes. He described the towns as then being 'the most important [force] in Germany . . . it is principally they who have the money, the lands and the munitions of war . . .'. This was an interesting theory, but no longer valid: the towns emerged from the Thirty Years War as a group lacking both unity and a corporate existence. It was only the great territorial princes who could, if not oppose the emperor, at least manœuvre skilfully enough to obtain a following which had confidence in them. France urgently needed to find an alternative policy in the empire. The defence of German liberties, so attractive to the Valois and Richelieu, seemed like an outworn slogan at a time when no one threatened them. Sweden claimed to lead the Protestant states, the most dynamic element in the empire, but Brandenburg, confronted by the elector of Saxony at the head of the evangelical community owing allegiance to Austria, also aspired to the leadership. France's policy could not fail to be based upon dynastic, federative and interconfessional considerations.

Mazarin remained, above all, intent upon depriving the Habsburgs of the imperial crown. It had become customary to elect the emperor's eldest son king of the Romans during his father's lifetime. This was how the

Habsburgs had succeeded, over the centuries, in monopolizing the imperial crown. The legitimacy of the procedure had often been challenged, and France and Sweden had secured the insertion in the peace treaties of a clause providing that the election of a king of the Romans would not be permissible during the emperor's lifetime, except in case of necessity. France would have liked to add the following provision, which was not adopted: *ne ex familia Imperatorum regnantium Rex eligatur*. But the value of written agreements depends entirely upon the strength of those who enforce them. On 31 May 1653, taking advantage of the decline in French prestige and the disunity of the victors, Ferdinand III succeeded in having his son, Ferdinand IV, elected king of the Romans at Augsburg; he was crowned at Ratisbon on 18 June. But Ferdinand IV died on 9 July 1654, and his brother Leopold, only fourteen years old, could not immediately succeed him. On 2 April 1657 the emperor followed his son to the grave, and there now ensued a veritable interregnum. The time seemed ripe to wrest the imperial crown from the Habsburgs, and the electoral horse-dealing began. 'The Electors', said the instructions sent by the French government to its ambassadors at the Diet of Election, Marshal de Gramont and Lionne, 'have a unique opportunity of showing all Europe that the Imperial dignity is not the patrimony of a single house and in the gift of the council of Spain, as it has been until now, but does in fact depend upon their votes.' Now came the search for a suitable candidate. The French court would doubtless have been delighted to see the choice of the electors fall upon the young king, the heir of Charlemagne, now potential heir to the throne of the Caesars! If need be, they would have married him to a German princess, either a Catholic or a convert from Protestantism! Mazarin, who did not *a priori* exclude any stratagem, was ready to make the necessary financial sacrifices. But there was swift opposition to such a plan, which was never officially avowed. There remained two possible candidates: Ferdinand Maria, elector of Bavaria, son of Maximilian the Great who had died in 1651, and husband of Louis XIV's cousin, the spirited Henriette Adelaide of Savoy; and Philip William, count of Neuburg, who had a fine palace at Dusseldorf and had aspired to the hand of a French princess. But, while agreeing that the powers of the future emperor should be limited, the majority of the electors still supported the retention of the crown by the House of Habsburg; they believed that the elevation of a new house to the imperial throne would inevitably lead to civil war and foreign oppression. The election of Leopold, king of Bohemia, took place at Frankfurt on 18 July 1658; he had all the votes, including his own. He was crowned on 1 August, under the title of Leopold I, at the age of eighteen. Even before the election, Mazarin had been striving to confine his power behind a double barrier, formed by the juridical restraints of the capitulation and the political restraints of the League of the Rhine.

A normal though illegal procedure, emanating from electors anxious for safeguards against the master they were setting over themselves, the capitulation imposed upon Leopold I reflected rather the prevailing pre-occupations in the field of foreign affairs than the defence of the privileges of the electoral body. Its foundations lay in an international act, the Treaty of Münster, which had become, on the same footing as the Golden Bull, part of the constitution of the empire. French armies were then threatening Flanders, reputed to be the bulwark of the empire, and the Milanese, its historic centre. Yet articles 13 and 14 of the capitulation forbade the emperor to give any help whatever to Spain. This provision was in accordance with the wishes both of the Germans and of Louis XIV. 'No nation is more abhorred in the Empire than the Spanish nation', wrote the Venetian ambassador. By an additional provision, the emperor and his Austro-German house were assured of French neutrality, but the princes and Estates were left complete freedom to seek French help in the event of aggression. Finally, the emperor undertook to encourage the restoration of peace between Spain and France, 'principally within the confines of the Circles and patrimonies of the Empire'. This part of the test reflected an attempt at mediation by the archbishops of Mainz and Cologne. The Spanish ambassador, Peñaranda, at first reticent, intimated on 23 July 1658 his master's desire to see the formation of 'an assembly in the Pyrenees, on the common frontier' to discuss the peace. This was the first step towards the treaty which, in the following year, was to bring peace to western Europe.

Mazarin was anxious to strengthen French influence in the empire. The attempt, in 1649, to achieve an *entente* with the emperor, by the projected marriage of Ferdinand III and Mademoiselle de Montpensier, had failed: Spain had raised obstacles, and the court in Vienna had actually proposed that 'France should substitute Breisach and Alsace for the possessions of Mademoiselle, in order to deliver them into the hands of the Emperor'. Leopold I did not notify the king of France of his election; the king did not recognize him and avoided 'styling him Emperor in public documents, as if unaware of the existence of such a personage'. Imperial aid continued to flow to the Spaniards in Italy. Mazarin organized the defence of the region of the Rhine on the basis of the Treaty of Münster and the existing agreements. Already in 1651, the spiritual electors had formed a league for their common defence; they had been joined by the Bishop of Münster and the count of Neuburg. On the Protestant side, a similar league had been formed by the king of Sweden as duke of Bremen and Verden and overlord of Wismar, the three dukes of Brunswick-Lüneburg and the landgrave of Hesse-Cassel. Repudiating exclusive confessional alignments, John Philip von Schönborn, arch-chancellor of the empire and elector of Mainz, known as 'the Solomon of the North', undertook the task of welding the two leagues together, for the protection of the common fatherland and the maintenance of peace. Mazarin, attracted by the idea of uniting the two faiths in a single political body, kept a watchful eye on this project, which would have been embarrassing had the emperor been 'of French making', as was to be the case in 1742, but seemed admirable after the election of Leopold I. Difficulties arose because it was impossible to bring in both Sweden and Brandenburg, who were hostile to one another. Sweden was included on account of her German possessions, and Brandenburg was provisionally excluded. The treaty, concluded for three years, was signed at Frankfurt on 14 August 1658 by the representatives of Sweden, the bishop of Münster, the count of Neuburg and the electors of Cologne, Trier and Mainz. On 15 August, Gramont and Lionne signed on behalf of France. The king formed a defensive alliance with the confederated electors and princes, on the basis of the Peace of Westphalia. The Franco-Spanish war remained outside its scope, but the signatories were to close their territories to the passage of troops 'sent to Flanders or, elsewhere, against the Most Christian King and his allies'. The king undertook 'not to bear arms against Germany; to recognise the freedom of the electors and princes to remain loyal to the Empire, to their fatherland and to the Emperor; and to place at the disposal of the League both infantry and cavalry, with the appropriate number of cannons'. In return he laid claim to their help in defending the possessions he had obtained from the Treaty of Münster.

This was a success for French diplomacy which must be recorded, but not unduly acclaimed. We are far from the suspicions of the conference at Nürnberg or the Diet of Ratisbon; Mazarin had been able to win the confidence of the German princes. Personal relations were at the root of the agreement: the courtesy of the chief minister, his shrewdness in eliciting the views of John Philip von Schönborn and, even more, in heeding them. His careful handling of his allies was more than the adoption of a correct attitude; it amounted to a veritable policy, or rather a 'style', which was to be absent from the diplomacy of Louis XIV after the death of Mazarin's disciple Lionne. On the Rhenish side, John Philip had no illusions, but he had managed to arm the league with the spearhead which it lacked, in the form of men and money. The League of the Rhine was a memorable phase in Franco-German relations, when there was mutual confidence in a community of interests and in a common will to peace: a meeting of two minds, a conjunction of two necessities, a symbol of religious tolerance and reciprocal understanding, it was founded upon the Treaty of Münster and stood for the established order. The league would not be a party to any and every policy, as Louis XIV was to discover. Its strength was revealed in the episode of the 'translation': angered at finding that the meeting-place of the ordinary deputation coincided with that of the council of the alliance, the emperor decided to transfer the former to Nürnberg. John Philip, supported by France, opposed this move. The tussle was doubtless of minor importance, but it served to confirm that there was henceforward a legal force in Germany, distinct from that of the territorial princes, capable of resisting Austria.

At the close of the period the scene of anxiety shifted; it was no longer a question of internal struggles and legal intrigues, but of the defence of the empire. In the spring of 1660 the Turks had defeated Rákóczy at Klausenburg and invaded Transylvania. They were threatening the empire which now sought a protector: was this to be Leopold I or Louis XIV?

Considerations of foreign policy explain the relations which Mazarin deemed it expedient to maintain with the sea powers. The need to loosen the Spanish vice compelled France to secure alliances with them, or at least to be assured of their neutrality. Richelieu had already, with mixed results, prepared the way by instructing Blainville, appointed ambassador in London in 1625, to seek an alliance with England, and to approach the envoys of the United Provinces 'who have', he declared, 'the same interests and the same enemies as ourselves and whose independence we have applauded and assisted'. The aim was 'to counterbalance the might of Spain which, on various religious pretexts, had so increased . . . that she was lording it over Europe and subjugating the Empire . . .'. Though the separate treaty of 1648 with Spain, concluded by the United Provinces in spite of their alliance of 1635 with France, had cast a shadow over Franco-Dutch relations, there were no such obstacles between France and England. The indispensable English alliance remained a fundamental aim of Mazarin's policy. To achieve it he was to surmount the difficulties and make the necessary sacrifices.

First, there were political difficulties, arising from the successive changes of government in England. On 30 January 1649 Charles I, the uncle of Louis XIV, had been beheaded in London, whereupon France had given refuge to Charles II. The Commonwealth's insistence that recognition must precede any negotiations raised a moral rather than a legal problem. For Mazarin it was less a matter of overcoming his own scruples—he had very few in this domain—than of conciliating public opinion. The emergence of Cromwell, to whom he was instinctively drawn, and the strength of the Protectorate reassured him. Spain had set the example: His Most Catholic Majesty had been the first to recognize the Commonwealth of England.

There were also economic difficulties, connected with the attacks by Prince Rupert's privateers on French merchant shipping in the Mediterranean and Atlantic. In the summer of 1649 a customs war broke out between England and France. The Declaration of Saint-Germain had prohibited the importation into France of English cloth. England retaliated by refusing to admit French beaver hats, scarlet dyes and haberdashery; the prohibition was later extended to red and white wines and woollen and silk cloth. To the allegation that they could not do without the wines, the English replied 'that men grow accustomed to all things; that, contrary to the general expectation, they were managing well enough without a king, and would also be quite able to dispense with French wines'. On 9 October 1651 England passed the Navigation Act, which came into force on 1 December of the same year. This warlike measure against Holland emphasizes the important expansion, between 1580 and 1640, of overseas trade—involving English ships—a trade centred upon the exporting of textiles and the importing of iron, timber and wool.

Finally, there were religious difficulties. Cromwell set himself up as the defender of European Protestantism. He wished to protect the French Protestants—whereupon Mazarin proved to him that they lived peacefully under the protection of the law—and he fulminated against the duke of Savoy's persecution of the Vaudois. In response to these representations, the Most Christian King interceded with the duke on behalf of the victims.

These difficulties did not appear insuperable to Mazarin who, already in 1652, had entered upon talks with Cromwell. He had need of England for his Scottish and Irish recruits, for the books and pictures which he bought from the Royal collections, on show at Somerset House; above all, he wished to prevent her from falling into the arms of Spain, which dangled the magnificent bait of trade with the Indies.

At first, until the beginning of 1653, relations were cool. Spain pursued her negotiations in London. In January 1652, her ambassador, Cardenas, proposed an agreement whereby Dunkirk, Gravelines and Calais were to be captured by armies of the two countries, and Calais then handed over to England. At Dunkirk, besieged by the Spaniards since September 1651, the governor, d'Estrades, was visited by an English envoy, Fitzjames, seeking an accommodation which would save the fortress. Mazarin would gladly have acquiesced, but the negotiations failed. A French fleet, sent to the aid of Dunkirk, was seized by the English fleet commanded by Blake. This was a reprisal for privateering; the crews were released, but the vessels were retained. On 16 September 1652 Dunkirk capitulated to the Archduke Leopold, Gravelines having surrendered on 19 May. The Spanish threat increased; Barcelona and Casale had fallen. Civil war was raging, with Condé in command of the enemy forces. By 1650 Mazarin was already convinced that, as he wrote in his *Carnets*, 'it is important to establish close relations with England or, if this cannot be brought about, with the States of Holland'.

At first it seemed that the second alternative would be the easier to achieve. The Anglo-Dutch War was at its height. In October 1653 the French envoy, Chanut, was sent to convince the States General that the king of France, while not wishing to take up arms against England, would welcome an invitation to act as 'mediator and arbiter'. The Dutch were asked to reject Cromwell's 'specious' proposal for the union of Great

Britain and the United Provinces in a single republic, on the grounds that 'this coalition of the two Republics would be a leonine partnership which would devour their liberty'. Mazarin attempted to secure the inclusion of France in the Anglo-Dutch treaty, but he met with refusal. Though the provinces of Friesland and Groningen voted in favour, that of Holland, at the instance of De Witt, expressed categorical opposition: 'their bark is too small to tow such a great vessel as France'. On 6 April 1654 the peace was signed between England and the United Provinces.

In England, Cromwell was now Protector, having taken the oath on 16 December 1653. The time seemed ripe for an understanding between the two statesmen. Mazarin's instructions of 16 July 1654 to the president de Bordeaux recalled the common aim—the defeat of Spain—and specified the conditions for an agreement: an annual subsidy of 1,500,000 *livres* and 8,000 men to help recapture Dunkirk which would be handed over to England. Any conquests which might be made in the West Indies were to be retained by the conqueror. On 3 November 1655 the president de Bordeaux signed at Westminster a commercial treaty in French and Latin; it was of modest scope, but excluded the possibility of a *rapprochement* between England and Spain: 'There will henceforth be a lasting peace, friendship, association and alliance between the Kingdom of France and the Republic of England, Scotland and Ireland.' Hostile actions at sea came to an end; outstanding questions were to be settled by arbitration, with the Republic of Hamburg as referee. War with Spain was made inevitable by Penn's attack on Santo Domingo and the seizure of Jamaica. On 23 March 1657 Sir William Lockhart, sent to France as ambassador, signed in Paris with Brienne and Lionne a closer alliance, which was renewed the following year and had a specific objective: the two countries were to attempt 'some spectacular feat of arms' in order to force peace upon Spain. Charles II, having fled to Brussels, had now rallied to the side of Spain, who had promised substantial assistance for the reconquest of his kingdom. On 14 June 1658 Turenne, after investing Dunkirk, defeated Don Juan of Austria, Condé and the duke of York (later James II) at the Battle of the Dunes. Dunkirk capitulated on 24 June and, in accordance with the terms of the treaty, was handed over to the English, who appointed Lockhart as governor. Mazarin's enemies exploited this cession, alleging that, in spite of the precautions taken, the Catholic faith was in peril in a stronghold delivered to the heretics by a prince of the church!

On 3 September 1658 the Protector died, and there followed a short period of political instability in England. The alliance was maintained with Richard Cromwell, but when, on 8 May 1660, the monarchy was publicly proclaimed in London and Charles II returned to power, relations with France were far from cordial. The president de Bordeaux, who had negotiated the Treaty of Westminster and thus forced the exiled king to leave France, was obliged to leave London. Neither Charles II nor Mazarin wished for a break. A friendly welcome was given to Ruvigny, leader of the French Protestants, whose visit preceded the sending of an official mission under the comte de Soissons, husband of Olympe Mancini. Charles II did not allow his mother, Henrietta Maria of France, to interfere in the government and refused to fall in with her plan for a marriage between himself and Hortense Mancini, a plan to which Mazarin was also opposed. Anxious to keep Charles as their ally and, at the same time, to help Portugal, which had been abandoned at the peace, the French government encouraged his marriage to Catharine of Braganza, who brought her royal spouse Tangier, the key to the Mediterranean, and Bombay. On 31 March 1661 Louis XIV's brother, the duc d'Anjou, later the duc d'Orléans, married Henrietta of England, who was destined to play an important part in maintaining the alliance between the two kingdoms. In 1662, Charles II was to sell Dunkirk to Louis XIV.

Peace had been preserved with the United Provinces, in spite of a threatened break provoked by Ruyter's capture of two French vessels in the Mediterranean. The States General had supported French mediation in the north. The Treaty of London, signed on 6 August 1661, settled the war which had broken out between Portugal and the United Provinces after the rising in Brazil in 1654. The Dutch were to sign an alliance with France on 27 April 1662.

Thus, despite differing systems of government and unforeseen events, Mazarin's cherished dream of an alliance between France and the sea powers was realized. His final advice to Louis XIV, as reported to Charles II, is alleged to have been 'to create a community of interests between the two states [France and England], so far as should be humanly possible'. To Mazarin their interests appeared complementary. But how long were they to remain so?

In spite of the various conflicting events on the European scene, in both the diplomatic and military spheres, the war against Spain was the real hub of international relations. Its evolution was itself a function of the internal evolution of France. There were two phases: the first, lasting until 1654, was a period of defeat for France, when Spain, allied to the Frondeurs, won back some of her advantages; the second was a period of recovery for France, when she took the offensive on the various fronts; in both periods negotiation and war went hand in hand.

After 1648 came a series of defeats on both land and sea. In Italy the Spaniards took Casale, the Tuscan strongholds and Porto Longone; in Spain they seized Barcelona; finally, in the Low Countries, they reoccupied Ypres, Gravelines, Mardyk, Dunkirk and Rocroi (1653). In these circumstances Mazarin, twice forced into exile, showed admirable tenacity. He gradually succeeded in re-establishing the internal situation; in

August 1653 the royal army entered Bordeaux. On the eastern front, a bold winter campaign (October to November 1653) led to the recapture of Sainte-Menehould. Harcourt, the governor of Breisach, threatened by La Ferté's armies and won over by Mazarin's offers, surrendered the fortress. But these local successes were not decisive. Despite the king's coronation at Rheims, Mazarin's enemies had not disarmed. Condé was sending envoys to London to win over Cromwell; Bordeaux rallied to Spain; Arras was besieged. At this time two diplomacies were claiming to speak for the king and France: the one, directed against Mazarin, reverted to the idea of an immediate peace with Spain; the other, inspired by the cardinal, relied upon the coming victories to induce Spain to make an honourable peace.

Following upon these setbacks, the siege and capture of Arras in 1654, in a struggle between Turenne and Condé, marked the beginning of French recovery. In Catalonia, Conti held Cerdagne and Conflans for France. Spain had profited by the Fronde to consolidate her domination of Italy, robbing France of the support of the dukes of Modena and Mantua. As early as 1653, however, Mazarin sent the *lieutenant général* du Plessis Bezançon on a journey through the peninsula to conciliate the princes and counter Spanish influence in Mantua, Modena, Florence and Venice. A fresh expedition was sent to Naples in 1655, in spite of unhappy memories of the affair of 1647; entrusted to the duc de Guise, it miscarried and confirmed Spanish control of the kingdom of Naples.

In Rome the situation was complex, owing to the impact of internal political events on the attitude of the Holy See to France. Relations between Mazarin and Innocent X, who was sympathetic to the Spanish faction, were far from cordial. They had been embittered by the pope's reception of Cardinal de Retz. On the death of his uncle, the archbishop of Paris, on 21 March 1654, the coadjutor, imprisoned for his intrigues during the Fronde, had relinquished the archbishopric in return for financial compensation. He was transferred to the prison at Nantes, but escaped and fled to Rome, where Innocent X gave him the cardinal's hat. The pope's death, in the midst of the affair, raised a twofold problem: how to bring about the election of a pope sympathetic to France, and how to ensure that he should adopt, in regard to Retz, a policy acceptable to the French government. After a conclave lasting for eighty days, France waived her objection to Cardinal Chigi, who became Pope Alexander VII. Despite the accusations of Jansenism hurled at the fugitive prelate—was it not the period of the *Lettres Provinciales*?—Alexander VII, though under pressure from Lionne, showed prudence and moderation; he was not disposed to condemn Retz, but persuaded him, in December 1655, to place the administration of the diocese of Paris in the hands of a vicar-general. When he soon afterwards withdrew the powers he had delegated to the vicar-general, Retz deeply offended the peacemaking pope. He was obliged to leave Rome and thereafter shared the life of those wanderers through Europe so beloved of the period. Like Charles IV of Lorraine, Christina of Sweden, or Condé, they come on to the stage of history, play their part, and disappear. The antagonism to Rome engendered by this episode was the prelude to the incidents which, in the second half of the century, were to bring Louis XIV and the Holy See into conflict.

The Retz affair was but one example of the struggle in progress between French and Spanish influences in the courts of Europe. Though there was not always, as in Rome, a 'flying squadron' to decide the final outcome, there were frequently strange alliances of sympathies and interests. Negotiations followed the successive phases of the war. At first they seemed no more than a continuation of the talks at Münster, broken off by the Spaniards in their pleasure at the defection of the Dutch. In February 1649 Peñaranda, the plenipotentiary of Philip IV, demanded from Vautorte, sent as envoy to Brussels, the return to Spain of the French conquests. The court in Madrid hoped to profit by the internal dissensions in France and sent the archduke two mandates, one to treat with the king and the other to treat with the Parlement of Paris. The Treaty of Rueil, signed on 12 March 1649, foiled these subtle calculations. In 1656 serious negotiations began; order had been restored in France and the Treaty of Westminster now allied her with England. By choosing this moment to treat with Spain, Mazarin would avoid having to cede Dunkirk—still to be recaptured—to the English. Lionne arrived in Madrid on 4 July and met Philip IV's minister, Don Luis de Haro. Three groups of questions were discussed: first, which of the French conquests were to be retained and which ought to be relinquished, in what form and within what limits; next, the guarantees to be given to the allies, Portugal, Catalonia and the dukes of Lorraine, Modena and Mantua; finally, the interests of Condé, allied to Spain by the private treaty of 6 November 1651. This last question led to a breakdown in the talks, for the Spanish government demanded the restoration of Condé's possessions, offices and dignities. The French government agreed to restore possessions, but not offices. Condé's success in raising the siege of Valenciennes, at the head of the Spanish army on the night of 15–16 July, increased Philip IV's demands. Lionne left Madrid in September and the French government signed the Treaty of Paris with England. On 25 June 1658, after the Battle of the Dunes, Dunkirk capitulated. The campaign of 1658 was disastrous for Spain: she was defeated in Flanders, threatened in the Milanese by the duke of Modena, and routed by the Portuguese near Elvas in Alemtejo. To humble the pride of Philip IV, Mazarin pretended to be negotiating, at Lyons, a marriage between the young king and Margaret of Savoy, daughter of Christina of France and sister of the electress of Bavaria. Pimentelli was thereupon sent from Madrid to offer the French court both peace and the infanta.

Twofold negotiations ensued; at first political and territorial, and later dynastic. The first treaty, signed in Paris on 4 June 1659, reverted in substance to the dispositions made in the Madrid conversations. Of her conquests, France retained Artois, Roussillon and part of Cerdagne. Spain relinquished the rights she had held in Alsace (from the treaty concluded by Oñate in 1617). Various strongholds in Luxembourg, Hainault and Flanders were handed over to France. On the other hand, France restored to Spain a large number of strongholds in Catalonia, Italy and Flanders. On the subject of the allies, discussion was brief. Mazarin undertook, by a clause in the secret articles of the treaty, not to support Portugal if, within three months, she had not made peace with Spain. An amnesty was stipulated for the Catalans. The arrangements made at Cherasco were ratified in regard to the House of Mantua. The question of Condé's return to France was settled to the satisfaction of both parties. Heavy sacrifices were demanded of the duke of Lorraine, now released after imprisonment by the Spaniards in Toledo since 1655: he was required to cede the duchy of Bar and Clermont in Argonne, and to allow French armies the right of passage through his duchy to Alsace. The duke refused these conditions. By a new treaty, signed 28 February 1661, he regained his estates, but remained under French suzerainty.

The dynastic aspect of the negotiations had its element of romance in the young king's infatuation with Marie Mancini, an obstacle overcome by reasons of state. The question of rights to the Spanish succession had been changed since 1656 by the birth of another infante. Don Luis de Haro, demanding complete renunciation, prevailed over Mazarin who would have liked to retain the infanta's right in regard to the Low Countries and Franche-Comté. Her renunciation was to be conditional upon the payment of a dowry of 500,000 gold crowns.

The 124 articles of the Treaty of the Pyrenees were signed by the two ministers on 7 November 1659. On 9 June 1660 Don Luis de Haro, as proxy for the king of Spain, introduced the infanta Maria Teresa, and on 26 August the young couple and the court returned to Paris. Though it brought a happy ending to twenty-five years of war, the peace gave rise to recriminations; the most celebrated protest was Saint-Evremond's pamphlet. Why did the cardinal abandon his original ambition, the complete conquest of the Spanish Netherlands, on the threshold of a campaign which promised to be easy? This is a delicate psychological problem to which we can only suggest possible solutions. Was it the secret and earnest desire of Anne of Austria, the possibility of securing the Spanish inheritance, fear of the Austro-Spanish alliance, or the exhaustion of a France threatened by famine? In fact, the conquest of the Spanish Netherlands would have been neither swift nor easy, and would have meant a war of some length. Northern Europe was in turmoil and the time had come for France to intervene in the wars encircling the Baltic. Also, the

Turks were still threatening Venice. The Treaty of the Pyrenees, coupled with the marriage contract, represented a shift in activity from the territorial and military to the dynastic and diplomatic spheres, and though it confirmed the victory of France, it left the door open for many conflicts.

Article 101 of the Treaty of the Pyrenees provided for the joint intervention of France and Spain to obtain 'a swift and satisfactory settlement' for the powers engaged in the war in the north.

After the conclusion of the peace, the Franco-Swedish alliance had survived only in a very limited form. The great Franco-Swedish period, which dominated the first half of the century, had closed with the abdication of Christina. When Charles X ascended the throne of Sweden, other political groupings were formed in the course of the wars. The new king, fiery, bellicose and envious of the laurels of Gustavus Adolphus, was less concerned with the observance in Germany of the provisions of the Peace of Westphalia than 'to sow discord in the Empire' in order to consolidate his control of the Baltic. He precipitated Sweden into a series of wars of an extreme complexity owing to the interventions and *volte-faces* of neighbouring powers, but in which it is possible to distinguish two main orientations, involving Poland and Denmark.

At the time of Queen Christina's abdication John Casimir, king of Poland, also of the House of Vasa but of the Catholic branch, protested against the accession of Charles X. The latter took advantage of Poland's trouble with the Czar Alexis, who had responded to the appeal of the rebellious Cossacks, to send his army to Warsaw and later to Cracow. John Casimir fled to Silesia. When Charles X began upon the conquest of Prussia, Poland revolted against his occupation, for religious as well as political reasons. Frederick William, elector of Brandenburg, then allied himself to Sweden. By the Treaty of Königsberg (7 January 1656) he broke the bond of homage uniting him to Poland in respect of the duchy of Prussia and, despite the anger of the Dutch, declared that he held his duchy from the king of Sweden, the new king of Poland. The Treaty of Marienburg (15 June 1656) prescribed the aid which the elector and the king were to give one another and outlined a first partition of Poland. The allies re-entered Warsaw, which Charles X had been forced to abandon but, owing to the size of the country and the extreme mobility of the Polish cavalry, military victory was slow to materialize. A new treaty signed at Labiau (10-20 November 1656) put an end to Swedish suzerainty in Prussia.

The second act of the war was heralded by a reorientation and the entry of Denmark into the struggle. Relations between Denmark and Sweden had not been good. In 1645 Christian IV had been obliged by the Peace of Brömsebro to make various concessions to Sweden: exemption from all passage dues and right of search in the Sound and the Belts and on the

Elbe; the cession of two Norwegian provinces, of the island of Gotland in the middle of the Baltic and the island of Oesel at the entrance to the Gulf of Riga. Taking advantage of Charles X's departure for Poland, Christian IV's successor, his second son Frederick III, laid hands upon the duchy of Holstein-Gottorp, which belonged to Duke Frederick, the father-in-law of the Swedish monarch. Angered by this aggression, Charles X crossed the Belts over the ice in January 1658 and laid siege to Copenhagen. Peace was signed at Roeskilde on 28 February, Sweden retaining the provinces of Halland, Scania and Bleking, and half the customs dues from the Sound. Dissatisfied with this treaty, Charles returned five months later to besiege Copenhagen, with the intention of establishing himself in Scania and closing the passages of the Sound. The reaction of the Dutch, who had no wish to see Sweden dominate the Baltic, was prompt: a fleet of thirty-five vessels relieved Copenhagen. Charles X's position became critical, for a coalition against Sweden emerged from the conjunction of the war with Denmark and the war with Poland.

After an unfortunate attempt at intervention in support of Charles X by Rákóczy, prince of Transylvania, a vassal of the Turks who aspired to the throne of Poland, the last act of the war was marked by the entrance of Austria upon the scene. By the treaty of 1 December 1656, the emperor, who had promised the Poles 4,000 men, attempted to detach the elector of Brandenburg from his alliance with Charles X. By the Treaty of Wehlau (24 September 1657), John Casimir conceded the sovereignty of Prussia to Frederick William and freed the Prussian towns and nobles from their oath of allegiance, swearing an eternal alliance between Prussia and Poland. He also ceded to Brandenburg the town of Elbing, greatly to the annoyance of Danzig and the Prussian nobility. The Treaty of Bromberg (8 November) completed these arrangements; at Berlin, Austria, Brandenburg and Poland concluded an offensive treaty against Sweden (February 1658).

Despite the distraction of the war with Spain, Mazarin had continued to keep a very careful watch on events in the north. He remained faithful to the policy of close alliances which had imposed the Peace of Westphalia on the empire; as early as 1655, the French ambassadors d'Avaugour and de Lumbres attempted to restore peace between the kings of Sweden and Poland, each equally the friend of France. On 24 February 1656 Louis XIV signed a treaty of alliance, including a guarantee, with Brandenburg; Mazarin was at that time less concerned with the Baltic than with the empire, where the imperial election was pending. The various attempts at mediation failed. When, after Warsaw had fallen for the second time, d'Avaugour and de Lumbres waited upon John Casimir, the Poles refused to 'abandon Prussia for which they had fought for three hundred years' and to treat with the elector of Brandenburg, 'a recreant vassal'. At this very moment, in Königsberg, the elector was receiving from a

Russian ambassador the demand that he should agree to declare himself the vassal of the czar in respect of Prussia.

These manœuvres came to nothing on account of conflicting ambitions, swift changes in the situation, the impetuous nature of Charles X, the duplicity of Frederick William and the difficulties which beset France. The alliance with England enabled Mazarin to intervene. In February 1659, by the Treaty of London, France and England undertook to restore peace in the north on the basis of the Treaty of Roeskilde, slightly modified in favour of the Danes and the Dutch. The belligerents were given six weeks to accept the mediation, with which Holland reluctantly associated herself; when this period had elapsed, action was to be taken. Charles X refused the offers of the mediators; Ruyter defeated the Swedes at Nyborg (24 November 1659). For his part, the elector of Brandenburg joined forces with the Austrians, invaded Swedish Pomerania and laid siege to Stettin. But on 7 November the Treaty of the Pyrenees was signed, and Mazarin informed Frederick William that Sweden was to retain Pomerania. The League of the Rhine threatened to intervene in support of Sweden; the Turks, who had punished the fickleness of Rákóczy, protested against the entry of Austrian garrisons into certain fortresses on the Hungarian frontier; the czar was once again threatening Warsaw.

A double congress opened in 1660, with the western powers as mediators. At Copenhagen, under the direction of the Chevalier de Terlon who had replaced d'Avaugour, were Sweden and Denmark, with the representatives of England and Holland; in the monastery of Oliva, near Danzig, Sweden, Poland and Brandenburg met under the presidency of de Lumbres. A double treaty concluded a conflict which had flared up in many successive forms. The Treaty of Copenhagen (27 May-6 June 1660) confirmed the terms of the Treaty of Roeskilde: Sweden retained the three southern provinces of the Peninsula; the provisions excluding foreign warships from the Baltic were abrogated. At Oliva the mediator had a hard struggle to reconcile the interests of the three rival powers. The death of Charles X on 13 February 1660 made an agreement easier. On 3 May the last difficulties raised by Brandenburg, concerning Elbing and the Pomeranian customs dues, were swept away. Poland renounced her claim to the crown of Sweden; Livonia was partitioned, the northern half going to Sweden and the southern half to Poland; Sweden relinquished Polish Prussia and Kurland; Brandenburg evacuated Pomerania. Circumstances had favoured the peacemaking efforts of the king of France, who was declared guarantor of the articles concerning the interests of the various powers. The Czar Alexis, to whom Louis XIV had sent as envoy a certain Desminières, having in December 1659 concluded with Sweden, at Valiessar near Narva, a three years' truce which left him Dorpat, finally signed the Peace of Kardis (July 1661), by which he renounced all his conquests in Livonia. He was to be more fortunate with Poland, for when he signed with her the Truce of Andrusovo (1667) he retained part of the Ukraine or Little Russia, namely the left bank of the Dnieper, Kiev on the right bank, and Smolensk—the first victories of the Muscovite Empire in the face of the barrier in the east formed by Sweden, Poland and Turkey, all traditional allies of France.

When Mazarin died, on 9 March 1661, a certain number of the problems which arose in European relations after the Peace of Westphalia had been resolved. First, the great duel between France and Spain for continental ascendancy was now over. Spain was moribund. Her decadence which began in the reign of Philip II, had been sealed by the Treaty of the Pyrenees. Under Louis XIV the process of dismemberment was to continue, and her very monarchy, as the result of marriages it was unable to avoid, was to fall into the hands of a French dynasty. The decadence of Spain was accompanied by decadence, though of a different order, in the Holy Roman Empire. The concept of the empire as Austrian, absolutist and Catholic, which the reforms of Maximilian, on the one hand, and the aggressive tactics of Ferdinand II, on the other, had tried to impose on the German lands, was now finally dead. The end of the imperial dream was accompanied by the disintegration of Germany. The country split up into several hundred autonomous states, each jealous of its independence. In these conditions of general anarchy, Mazarin had been able to take full advantage of the provisions of the Treaty of Münster, but the League of the Rhine, a conservative body and an obstacle to any return of imperial authority, remained a fragile creation which required careful handling.

Too much stress is laid on the divisions in Germany during this period. It is not sufficiently realized that there existed at the time what might be called a feeling of nationhood; this declared itself, during the imperial election of 1658, in favour of the Habsburg of Vienna. After 1660 a distinction must, of course, be made between the history of the empire and that of Austria. But, while the strength of the Habsburgs lay chiefly in the territorial importance of their possessions, the value of the title of emperor must not be underestimated. Though it did not raise its holder above other sovereigns, this title did designate him as the indispensable bulwark against the Turkish menace and as the defender of Christendom. Now, with regard to Turkey, the position of France was ambiguous. Since 1645 the Venetians had been struggling against the Turkish invasion of Crete. Mazarin secretly supported the republic and the French ambassador was imprisoned in Constantinople. Blondel's mission of 1658 was a failure. At this time we are again aware of the contradictions in French policy in the Levant, which prevailed from the sixteenth century until the end of the *Ancien Régime*. The Most Christian King, who in 1649 had proclaimed himself the defender of the Maronites, not daring to make either a friend or an enemy of the Turk, never reaped the full benefit of either the capitulations or the crusade. For Mazarin, the Turks were only a pawn in the game of maintaining a balance of power in the Mediterranean and the East, a counterweight to the might of the Habsburgs of Vienna and Madrid.

In 1648 the alliance between France and Sweden was the keystone of the European system established by the Treaties of Westphalia. These agreements had made the northern state into a German power, playing in the empire the role later to devolve upon Brandenburg—that of the natural enemy of Austria, the leader of the Protestant party in Germany, disposing of considerable material power and of a seasoned army always ready for action. But by 1659 the alliance with France was no more than a façade. Preferring to adopt an independent policy, Charles X had attempted to wrest from Denmark and Poland the provinces required to complete the Swedish encirclement of the Baltic. Though the war in the north had, thanks to French mediation, maintained the *status quo ante bellum*, it had at the same time confirmed the new hierarchy of the powers: to confront a declining Sweden and a Poland now given over to anarchy and a prey to the policy of partition which was to reach its climax in the eighteenth century, there emerged two new powers—Brandenburg and Russia. Though Frederick William had been obliged to yield on the territorial question—over the acquisition of Pomerania—he had triumphed on the question of sovereignty in Prussia. It had, admittedly, been laid down that if the male line of descent from the elector should die out, Prussia would again become a Polish fief; admittedly, the privileges of the Prussian nobles and towns were still guaranteed by Poland; but the principle had been established. There remained but a step from here to the crown, and Fehrbellin was to make that step possible. French diplomats had been astounded when, in the instrument of peace in 1648, Queen Christina had caused the name of the grand duke of Muscovy to be included among those of her allies. The French court knew little about the court of 'the barbarous Emperor with the light eyes'. When a Russian embassy visited Paris in 1654, Louis XIV had spoken of his distress at the war between the czar and Poland and had offered to mediate between the two powers. In the north, where the struggle for supremacy had begun, France, the general peacemaker, had acted as arbiter, pending the fulfilment of the plans of Colbert, who was eager to supplant the Dutch in the Baltic trade, 'the most profitable trade of all'.

It was, in fact, the modifications caused in the European equilibrium by the actions of the sea powers which proved the more important. These powers were less concerned with territorial gains than with the development of their colonial establishments, quite as common a cause of war as European possessions. 'Trade is a war for money', as Colbert, the faithful servant of Mazarin, was soon to remark, and money is the sinews of war. It has often been suggested that the United Provinces were in decline from 1660. This is untrue. They remained a great power, thanks to their naval, colonial and banking strength. They were, nevertheless, to meet the fate which had befallen Venice a century and a half earlier. While maintaining their key positions—losing Brazil, but gaining Malacca, Ceylon and the Cape from Portugal—they yielded before the upsurge of British commerce. The death of Cromwell, the incompetence and retirement of his son Richard and the recurrence of internal disputes, admittedly led to the brief eclipse of England, an eclipse which perhaps chiefly accounts for French supremacy at this time. But after 1668, and above all after 1688, the recovery of England was to challenge Louis XIV's policy of strength and prestige.

From the middle of the century there were signs, beneath their apparent friendship, of the opposition between the two powers. The one, turned towards the continent, fascinated by the mirage of the Spanish inheritance, involved in the empire by the League of the Rhine, faithful to the disappointing Swedish alliance; the other, looking towards the open seas, in pursuance of a policy which was still symbolized by the Navigation Act of 1651 and had in Jamaica, as well as Bombay and Tangier, laid the foundations of her future greatness. It is in this context that the Anglo-Dutch war of 1654 assumes a vital importance. Cromwell's dilemma was clear: the choice lay between the federation desired for reasons of religion —and destruction. There was direct opposition, in both scope and significance, between this naval and colonial war, looking to the future, and the Franco-Spanish war, the events in Germany and, to a lesser extent, the war in the north. Thanks to Mazarin's intelligent handling of affairs, the foundations of French continental supremacy had been laid but, even more clearly, there now emerged to view, strengthened by popular support and surviving the hazards of the Restoration, the guiding principles and future objectives of British policy in the world.

CHAPTER XV

THE SPANISH PENINSULA 1598–1648[1]

ASPAIN without Philip II was difficult to imagine. For forty years every sudden alteration in the affairs of Europe had somehow seemed connected with the man who sat alone at his desk in the Escurial, surrounded by mountains of paper. 'When he goes', a Spanish noble had remarked a year before his death, 'we shall find ourselves on another stage, and all the characters in the play will be different.'[2] In the event, not only was the cast changed, but the play itself turned to tragedy. The king died on 13 September 1598, leaving an aimless son and an empty treasury. In 1596, for the third time in his reign, the crown had repudiated its debts to the bankers. Financial exhaustion made peace essential: peace with France in 1598 and with England in 1604. As Spain slowly abandoned its militant imperialism, and the glorious pageant of notable victories slipped quietly from the memory, the grim reality could no longer be ignored. The nation which, for the extent of its empire and the reputation of its arms, ranked as the greatest power in the world, was visibly in a state of ruin, and its ruin demanded explanation. At once came a spate of books, questioning, analysing, suggesting remedies. All were devoted to explaining the paradox of Spain: the paradox that it was poor because it was rich, that it had gold and silver in abundance and yet it had none.

The very number of schemes and projects suggested a deep anxiety about the condition of Spain. The years 1598 to 1621 were pre-eminently years of national introspection, the first of those recurrent moments in modern Spanish history when the country turns inward upon itself in an agony of self-appraisal. They were years not only of crisis but also of the awareness of crisis—of a sharpened sense of impending catastrophe. The tragedy of Philip III's reign lay in the failure of the government to match the words of the *arbitristas*—the economic writers—with corresponding action. Court and *arbitristas* might have been living in different worlds. But the contrast between a heedless court and anxious *arbitristas* was only one among the many contrasts and paradoxes which gave to the reign of Philip III its distinctive character: the contrast between the ostentatious extravagance of a handful of aristocrats and the famine that haunted the people; between the fervour of popular religion and the corruption of moral standards; the paradox of the flowering of the arts in the autumn

---

[1] The typescript of this chapter was completed in the summer of 1959.
[2] Duque de Feria to Thomas Fitzherbert, 28 February 1597. Archive of the archbishopric of Westminster, MS E.2, f. 15.

and winter of Spain's economic life. In the words of González de Cellorigo, Spain had become 'a republic of the bewitched, living outside the natural order of things';[1] a republic whose creation and whose symbol was Don Quixote.

While the mood was to change, there was no breaking the enchantment. Where the first twenty years of the seventeenth century were passive years of governmental inactivity and national self-preoccupation, the following twenty were to be years of renewed energy and action. In the field of administration, lethargy gave way to feverish activity; after more than a decade of pacifism, the aggressive imperialism of Philip II's later years again became the order of the day. Some of the lessons of the *arbitristas* were taken to heart, and attempts were made to correct the more glaring defects in the economic and constitutional structure of the state, while simultaneously restoring it to the position of European predominance it had enjoyed in its prime. But too much was attempted, and not enough achieved. The conde duque de Olivares, striving to attain what perhaps was unattainable, drove his country too hard. After 1640 it was no more than a broken relic of its former self, a defeated, disintegrating country compelled by its own weakness to seek peace in 1648 with its most persistent and dangerous enemies, the Dutch. In the space of fifty years, the world empire of Philip II had sunk to the level of a second-rate power.

The reasons for this drastic alteration, the specific importance to be attached to each of the circumstances surrounding Spain's collapse, have long ranked among the most disputed of historical questions, raising as they do the perennially absorbing problem of the rise and fall of empires. The idea of 'decline' was inherent in the cyclical concept of history favoured by the seventeenth century. States, like human beings, reached their peaks and then declined in accordance with those inflexible laws that governed the life of all living organisms. Of this universal process the 'decline of Spain' provided a classic example. But a purely determinist explanation was neither fully satisfying nor universally acceptable. It was tempting to search for specific causes of decline, and the explanations of these varied with the preconceptions of different ages and nations. Inside Spain, from as early as 1600, the causes of the country's decline [*declinación*] were being passionately discussed, while, outside the Peninsula, a 'Protestant' explanation was gradually taking shape. As the prosperity of the United Provinces came to be attributed in particular to their policy of religious toleration, so Englishmen and Dutchmen of the seventeenth century came to regard Roman Catholicism as incompatible with commercial success, and seized upon Spain as the proof of their thesis. Their views were to find wide acceptance in the world of the Enlightenment. To Protestants and rationalists of the eighteenth and nineteenth

---

[1] Martín González de Cellorigo, *Memorial de la Política necessaria y útil restauración a la República de España* (Valladolid, 1600), p. 25.

centuries, the decline was primarily to be explained by the intellectual and religious history of Habsburg Spain; it was the outcome of the suppression of free enquiry by the Spanish Inquisition, of Spain's cultural isolation, and of that religious obscurantism which drove the industrious Moriscos from the Iberian Peninsula. In the twentieth century, these predominantly religious explanations have been relegated to the background, in favour of a closer concentration on purely economic conditions; on the inherent weaknesses of Spanish trade and industry, on the fiscal policies of the crown and on the effects of the price revolution.

Although the modern emphasis on Spanish economic conditions has produced valuable work, it has been restricted in its scope. Under the influence of Hamilton's pioneering study,[1] the greatest attention has been devoted to problems of trade, finance and coinage, and little more is known than was known fifty years ago about conditions of land tenure and cultivation, or about population changes or the economic circumstances of individual classes of society. Until these subjects are examined in detail, the current 'economic' interpretation will remain incomplete and distorted. At the same time, the very concentration on certain aspects of Spain's economic misfortunes has helped to encourage the assumption that Spanish conditions were unique, and has prompted a search for their origins in the dubious realm of supposedly unchanging national characteristics. But if, as seems possible, the first half of the seventeenth century was a period of economic crisis not only for Spain but for most of Europe, the alleged characteristics of Spain in decline may neither be necessarily confined to the Iberian Peninsula, nor be attributable solely to the Spanish temperament. The 'idleness' to which the seventeenth-century Spaniard was considered particularly prone, is often seen simply as a failing in the national character. But idleness was a feature also of English and French society in the same period and, allowing for variations of emphasis from nation to nation, it might more correctly be regarded in all three countries as the consequence rather than the cause of a backward economy: the inevitable outcome of the inability of a predominantly agrarian society to offer its population adequate or regular employment.

Yet even if Spanish conditions prove on closer examination to have more in common with conditions in other contemporary societies than is sometimes allowed, there is no escaping the fact that in the seventeenth century Spain's international power declined. The country which dominated Europe in the reign of Philip II fell into a secondary rank among the European states in the reign of his grandson. But how far does this loss of international status reflect the economic 'decline of Spain'? The Spanish peninsula was not a single economic or administrative unit, but

[1] Earl J. Hamilton, 'The Decline of Spain', *Economic History Review*, Vol. VIII (1938), and *American Treasure and the Price Revolution in Spain, 1501–1650* (Cambridge, Mass., 1934).

a complex of kingdoms and territories: Castile, Aragon, Valencia, Catalonia, Navarre, Vizcaya, Galicia and Portugal. Spain is often equated
automatically with Castile, but many of these regions of the peninsula
were separated from Castile by different economies and monetary systems,
different forms of government, and even different languages. The rhythm
of life varied from one to the other. Agricultural decline in central Castile
was perfectly compatible with agricultural prosperity in the east of
Catalonia, monetary stability in Portugal or Valencia with violent fluctuations in the coinage of Castile. If large tracts of the economic history
of Castile have been neglected, the life of the other Iberian kingdoms
during the seventeenth century has almost been forgotten. Enquiry into
the administrative and economic conditions of the various regions may
represent the most enlightening of all new approaches to the problems of
seventeenth-century Spain, in so far as it is likely to show that the 'decline
of Spain' consists of two connected, but not identical, processes: the
ending of Spain's predominance in Europe, and the ending of Castile's
predominance in Spain.

Spanish power in the later sixteenth century had primarily been Castilian power. Many of the best troops fighting for the king of Spain on
foreign battle-fields were Castilian; the officials who governed the Spanish
Empire were Castilian; the capital of the empire was located in the heart
of Castile, and the crown's revenues were provided largely by Castilian
taxpayers and by the mines of an America which belonged to Castile by
right of conquest. The resulting dependence of the Habsburgs on Castile
naturally gave the Castilians an advantage over the other nationalities
ruled by the dynasty, and helped to accelerate the transformation of the
Spanish into a Castilian Empire. The other dominions of the king of
Spain, and especially the realms and territories within the Iberian Peninsula, were uneasily aware of this transformation: 'the King is Castilian
and nothing else, and that is how he appears to the other kingdoms'.[1]
But however much they might grumble at Castile's predominance, it
was too firmly established in the sixteenth century to be effectively
challenged. Castile's primacy derived from the vitality of a population
which far outnumbered that of the other kingdoms of Spain; from its
fiscal resources, greater and more easily exploited; and from its monopoly
of the trade and wealth of the New World. As long as it could keep these
assets, Castile would remain the natural head of the Spanish monarchy.
The years 1590 to 1620 were to prove crucial for the future of the Spanish
Empire precisely because they saw a drastic diminution of each of these
three assets. During the sixteenth century the sharp rise in food prices

[1] In order to save space, no references will be given to the MS sources of quotations
which are to be found in the author's *The Revolt of the Catalans; a Study in the Decline
of Spain (1598–1640)* (Cambridge, 1963).

and Castile's increasing dependence on supplies of foreign grain suggest that, in spite of losses through emigration, foreign military service and entry into the church, the population of Castile had been increasing faster than the capacity of Castilian agriculture to feed it. In a country where the sheep industry was officially favoured at the expense of arable farming, and where the yield of the soil was restricted by lack of irrigation schemes and by poor methods of cultivation, this swollen rural population naturally drifted to the towns for work and sustenance. A population tightly packed into a few large towns was terribly exposed to disease. In 1599 and 1600 famine and plague swept across Castile and Andalusia, and ravaged the land. This great plague of 1599, with its long, dreary aftermath, was a catastrophic event in the history of Castile. While exact figures do not exist, the epidemic may have claimed some half a million victims. Its ravages brought the demographic upsurge of the sixteenth century to a sharp halt, and left Castile with a population of around six million, as compared with one million in Portugal and one million in the crown of Aragon.

The decline in population inevitably affected Castile's capacity to meet the fiscal demands of the crown. A village called Villatoro reported that only eighty inhabitants had survived out of a population of over 300. In response to the village's request for tax relief, the Council of Finance agreed to reduce by 15,000 *maravedis* a year for two years, the annual quota of 135,000 *maravedis* which it paid in the *alcabala*.[1] While the example may not be typical, the inadequacy of the tax reduction in relation to the village's loss of inhabitants gives some indication of the crown's reliance on the fiscal contributions of Castile. While the other kingdoms of the peninsula were shielded by their Cortes from excessive fiscal demands, the Cortes of Castile had proved to be too weak to resist the insistent requests of a king who lived on Castilian soil. Philip II had therefore been able to place a heavy financial burden on a country whose economic life was naturally precarious. The production of wool, on which Castile's economy traditionally rested, had suffered since the middle of the sixteenth century from a decrease in the number of migratory flocks which had not been counterbalanced by the growth of sedentary grazing. Agricultural production had proved insufficient to meet the country's needs. Industry, crippled by high prices, the lack of capital investment and the restrictive practices of the gilds, had found it hard to meet the competition of cheaper foreign goods. Now, with the plague, there came an acute shortage of labour, reflected in a 30 per cent rise in Castilian wages in the next three years. This rise in wages coincided with the return of European peace, which stimulated competition for international markets. It is doubtful whether Castilian industry ever really recovered from the

[1] *Consulta* of Council of Finance, 27 August 1601. A(rchivo) G(eneral de) S(imancas) Hacienda, leg(ajo) 409, no. 222.

setback it suffered at this moment. High labour costs combined with the loss of foreign markets to ruin native industries, until by the middle of the seventeenth century even the great traditional cloth centres, like Toledo and Segovia, had fallen into decay.

The collapse of urban industries in Castile left Castilian markets wide open to foreign manufactures. Their increasing importation worsened an already adverse balance of trade. Traditionally the trade deficit was made up with the silver that came to Seville from America, but the stream was gradually beginning to run dry. In 1597 Spanish merchants began for the first time to realize that the American market was overstocked.[1] Although the record year for Seville's trade with America was to be 1608, and the trade figures fluctuated around a high level until 1620, the whole pattern of Spain's commerce with the New World was changing in the reign of Philip III, to the detriment of the national economy. As Mexico developed its industries, and Peru its agriculture, the colonies' dependence on the traditional products of the mother country diminished. There was less demand in America for the Spanish cloth, and for the wine, oil, and flour which had bulked so large in the trans-Atlantic shipments of the sixteenth century. Instead of the traditional Spanish goods, the ships that set out from Seville carried an increasingly large proportion of foreign products; so large, indeed, that Sancho de Moncada, writing in 1619, believed that nine-tenths of the American trade was by now in foreign hands. This fateful loss of the American market undermined the confidence and credit of the merchants of Seville, and still further reduced the chances of industrial revival in Castile. Less American silver was now entering Castile; less was coming into Spanish hands, and there was less to bridge the widening gulf between Castile's imports and exports.

With a declining population, diminished national wealth, and decreasing revenues from the Indies, the foundations of Castile's primacy were crumbling in the years between 1590 and 1620. Beneath a surface which, to all outward appearances, remained the same, the character of the Spanish Empire was changing. Castile, which for so long had taken the lead, was growing weary. It still asserted its absolute superiority over all the other parts of the Peninsula and Empire, and would continue to do so with increasing determination; but the solid backing for its claim was far less apparent in the seventeenth century than it had been before. It is this which makes the opening years of the seventeenth century a decisive moment in the fortunes of the Spanish Empire. It was primarily the period of Castile's decline; of an absolute decline in wealth, population and productivity from the level attained in the mid-sixteenth century, and a relative decline in comparison with some other parts of the Iberian

[1] See the detailed study of American trade by H. and P. Chaunu, *Séville et l'Atlantique* (Paris, 1955–9), especially Vol. VIII,2,ii, for this and later comments.

THE SPANISH PENINSULA 1598-1648

Peninsula. Where, under Charles V and Philip II, the central kingdom
of the Peninsula, Castile, had been strong, and the peripheral kingdoms
weak, some of those kingdoms in the first decades of the seventeenth
century escaped certain of the worst misfortunes that afflicted Castile,
and consequently improved their relative standing within the Peninsula.
As a result, Spain was faced with a period of delicate adjustments, since
Castile's absolute political preponderance was no longer accompanied
by the overwhelming economic preponderance it had enjoyed in the
sixteenth century.

The adjustments would never have been easy, but the crown's financial
problems made them immeasurably harder. The extravagant enterprises
of Philip II's later years, leading to the bankruptcy of 1596, had involved
the crown in heavy debts. Not only did it owe an enormous sum of
accrued debts to the bankers, but an investigation of the royal finances in
October 1598 suggested that the annual deficit would still be as high as
1,600,000 ducats in 1601 and succeeding years.[1] This figure must be seen
in the light of an annual expenditure of some 9,000,000 ducats in the
opening years of Philip III's reign. During these years, the ministers in
charge of the crown's finances had to work with the knowledge that only
three major sources of income remained to them, now that most of the
crown's traditional supplies had been mortgaged to the bankers in perpetuity, and the secular revenues of all the king's European possessions
other than Castile were consumed on the spot. These three major sources
of income consisted of the taxes paid by Castile, the dues collected from
ecclesiastics and laymen in the various kingdoms of the monarchy by
papal authorization, and the annual supply of silver brought by the
treasure-fleet. Their nominal annual yield was as follows:[2]

	ducats
Taxes paid by Castile	
Alcabala (10% tax on sales)	2,800,000
Millones (tax on articles of consumption)	3,000,000
Servicios (voted by Cortes)	400,000
	6,200,000
Dues collected by papal concession	
Cruzada	912,000
Subsidio	420,000
Excusado	271,000
	1,603,000
Treasure-fleet	2,000,000

In reality, the crown received nothing like so large a sum each year as
these figures suggest, since some of the taxes were already pledged to the
bankers two or three years in advance. As an indication of the crown's

[1] *Relación* of 21 October 1598. AGS Hacienda, leg. 380, no. 1.
[2] These figures are taken from various papers of the Council of Finance in AGS Hacienda
for the years 1598–1607, and must be treated as rough estimates.

real annual revenues they are therefore misleading. Their value lies in their revelation of the relative contribution made to the crown's finances by each of its remaining sources of supply. In particular, they show how great was the crown's dependence on the assistance of Castile. But Castile's depopulation and its economic prostration meant that its contributions were increasingly uncertain: by 1606, for example, the *millones* yielded less than 2½ million ducats.

At the same time the crown's supplies of American silver were also beginning to fall, probably because of declining production in the mines, and the withholding of larger sums by the viceroys in America for their own needs. In 1598 the treasure-fleet had brought 3,347,000 ducats. This was an exceptional figure, and 2,000,000 ducats was nearer the average during the first years of the new century. The figure fell to some 1,800,000 in the middle of the second decade, and the fleets of 1619, 1620 and 1621 brought only some 800,000 ducats each. There was a recovery after these unusually poor years, but between 1621 and 1640 1,500,000 ducats represented a very good year, and not more than a million ducats a year could be expected with any degree of confidence.

It is against this sombre background of the slump in silver supplies from America and the diminishing fiscal returns from Castile that the crisis of Spanish imperialism between 1600 and 1640 must be seen. Confronted by the vast debts of its predecessor, a large annual deficit, and the threatened failure of traditional revenues, Philip III's régime would either have to make a drastic cut in expenditure, or find and exploit alternative sources of supply. A reduction of expenditure would entail the further retreat of Spanish imperialism, and the renunciation of spending habits that were deeply engrained, but the exploitation of new sources of supply offered still more obvious difficulties. For political as well as economic reasons it would be inadvisable to impose any new direct taxes on Castile. Perhaps more money could be obtained from the king's other dominions, and especially from those within the Spanish peninsula.

Kingdoms like Aragon and Valencia did not pay the two heaviest taxes paid by Castile, the *millones* and the *alcabala*, and their Cortes, unlike those of Castile, were summoned infrequently and voted subsidies at irregular intervals. A memorandum presented to Philip III at the beginning of his reign dwelt at some length on this fiscal anomaly: 'in all other states, all the parts contribute to the maintenance and greatness of the head, as is only just . . . But in ours it is the head which does the work and sustains the other members.'[1] In other words, Castile, the head of the monarchy, had for too long borne the full weight of the burden imposed on the country by Habsburg imperialism, and could legitimately expect the other kingdoms to offer more effective help. It was easy, however, for those who argued like this to overlook something which the other king-

[1] Alamos de Barrientos, *L'Art de Gouverner*, ed. Guardia (Paris, 1867), p. 67.

doms could never forget: that if Castile contributed more than the rest to the preservation of Spain's Empire, it also enjoyed the most lucrative offices in that empire, and a preponderant role in the formulation of policy.

These conflicting points of view contained the seeds of an angry dialogue which was to develop during the coming decades between a Castile desperate for help and realms which felt themselves under no obligation to pay for the defence of an empire in which they had no share. The very existence of this dialogue suggested that far more was involved than a simple fiscal problem in any attempt on the part of the crown to spread taxes more evenly over the Peninsula. Such an attempt would raise the whole question of the constitutional structure of the monarchy; of the relation of the various kingdoms to Castile and to their king. Since they were notoriously sensitive to any governmental action which threatened their traditional laws and constitutions, attempts to reorganize long-standing fiscal arrangements would need the most cautious diplomacy. Yet the crown was heavily in debt, and Castile in urgent need of relief. If, as was not impossible, the constitutional obstacles to the achievement of greater fiscal parity between the various kingdoms were too formidable to be hastily brushed aside, alternative means of relief must quickly be found. Otherwise the precarious fiscal foundations of Habsburg imperialism were in danger of collapsing beneath the strain.

Those who hoped for bold fiscal and constitutional measures from the new régime were rapidly disillusioned. Philip III himself was a nonentity. Personally incapable of governing, he set the pattern for his seventeenth-century successors by placing his confidence in a single minister entrusted with all the important affairs of state. The presence of this omnicompetent minister, known as the *privado* or favourite, was to cast a long shadow over the government of Spain throughout the century, and perplex a nation which, by instinct and tradition, expected its kings to be kings.

The *privado* of Philip III's choice was a well-intentioned but indolent Valencian aristocrat, the marqués de Denia, soon to be created duque de Lerma. Nothing in Lerma's character would have led his acquaintances to expect in him a capacity for ruthless action, and in his twenty years of personal rule he never deceived expectation. This, as he himself was fully aware, was the explanation of his survival. He was a prisoner in a gilded cage, the pawn of a small group of Castilian and Andalusian magnates. He lived, and knew that he lived, upon the sufferance of about thirty-two grandees, the inner circle of a Castilian aristocracy of some 120 dukes, marquises and counts. A study of these powerful territorial magnates is yet to be made, but there are signs that they enjoyed increasing political influence during the reign of Philip III. Excluded from the inner councils of the realm by Charles V and Philip II, great magnates like the duques del Infantado had preferred to hold a court of their own in the isolated grandeur of their family seat, rather than humble themselves in constant attendance upon an ungrateful monarch. On the death of Philip II their long years in the wilderness came to an end. Attracted by the alluring prospects of entry into a world of political influence and lucrative offices hitherto denied them, they moved to Madrid, thereby contributing both to the magnificence of court life and to the troubles of Lerma. Afraid of offending the powerful interests that surrounded him, he found that the best means of retaining power was to refrain from exercising it, and contented himself with a lavish bestowal of patronage on friends, relations and potential rivals alike.

A minister with such limited abilities and such heavy obligations to those around him was not the man to undertake radical reforms. Crown expenditure continued at a fantastically high level. There was never enough money either to pay the troops regularly, or to meet the daily expenses of the royal households. In his determination to escape the unpopularity of imposing new taxes or extending existing ones to social groups and geographical regions at present exempt, Lerma fell back upon what appeared to be more painless methods of increasing the crown's revenues, such as the sale of offices and privileges of nobility, and the alienation of royal jurisdictions. The inadequacy of these measures compelled him to have recourse also to the manipulation of the coinage. In 1599 a *vellón* coinage of pure copper was authorized. In 1603 this was returned to the mints to be stamped at double its face value. Although the Cortes in 1607 made their vote of taxes conditional on the suspension of *vellón* production, it was resumed in 1617 and continued, with interruptions, until 1626.

Lerma introduced his fiscal experiments into a country which was just beginning to draw breath after the long price rise of the sixteenth century. Between about 1600 and 1615 the Castilian price level was stationary, and the premium on silver in terms of *vellón* stood at about 4 per cent. Although inflation during these years was still relatively insignificant, the increasing circulation of *vellón* in Castile added to the economic advantages already enjoyed by the nations of northern Europe in their trade with Spain. The *vellón* was largely minted from Swedish copper, sold at high prices on the *bourse* at Amsterdam. The purchase of copper itself constituted a drain on Castilian silver, but the loss was inevitably increased by the practice indulged by the Dutch and their agents along the Spanish coast of introducing counterfeit coins into Castile and taking silver in exchange. The influx of these smuggled coins, and the growing quantity of legal *vellón* in circulation, eventually played havoc with Castilian prices. The fall in real prices, which began about 1620, was concealed by the rapid inflation of Castile's debased coinage. The premium on silver reached nearly 50 per cent in 1626. In the following years inflation, alternating with sudden deflationary measures, caused Castilian prices to fluctuate violently, and put Castile's economy at a grave disadvantage both to that of other regions of the Peninsula and of other parts of Europe.

The relief that debasement brought to the royal finances was short-lived. Lerma was lavish in the granting of offices, pensions and privileges; his confidants, adventurers like Don Pedro Franqueza and Don Rodrigo Calderón, used their positions to accumulate vast personal fortunes out of public funds; and the court, which at Lerma's behest was transferred at great expense from Madrid to Valladolid in 1601 and remained there till 1606, displayed a degree of ostentation remarkable even for that age of court magnificence.

While the régime's inability to curb expenditure prevented any reduction of Castile's taxes, the inadequacy of the existing taxes to meet the annual deficit compelled a resort to credit which placed a growing strain on the crown's bankers. By the summer of 1607 they were professing themselves unable to make further advances, and in November of that year the crown was forced by the stringency of credit to default on its obligations and announce a total suspension of payments. It was the repetition of an old story; but this time, instead of a period of twenty years between one royal bankruptcy and the next, the gap was reduced to ten.

Although, as always, a settlement was finally reached with the bankers, the royal accounts remained sadly unbalanced. The sum available for the year 1608 was expected to be 6,410,104 ducats (of which 2,241,942 ducats had come from the Indies). The expected expenditure until the end of October 1608, excluding the inevitable extraordinary expenses in Flanders, Italy and elsewhere, was calculated as 7,272,173 ducats:

	ducats
Pay for the Flanders army	2,000,000
Pay for frontier guards and garrisons	794,063
Atlantic fleet	650,000
Troops of the guard	200,000
Arms manufacture	100,000
Ambassadorial expenses	100,000
Ordinary expenses of royal households	620,000
Two years pay for servants of royal households, in part payment for three years' arrears	200,180
Mediterranean fleet and Genoa squadron	400,000
Arrears payable to bankers	1,000,000
Urgent outstanding expenses	250,000
Sundry lesser expenses	957,930
	7,272,173

This implied a deficit of 862,069 ducats, in addition to outstanding obligations to the bankers and general arrears which indebted the crown to the extent of more than 7,000,000 ducats, 'the exact figure not being given since its liquidation will be impossible without long delays and difficulties'.[1]

[1] *Consulta* and *relaciones*, 22 December 1607. AGS Hacienda, leg. 536, no. 405.

There seemed only one way of escape. The war in Flanders had been slowly grinding to a halt, as scarcity of money reduced the Spanish armies to defensive warfare. At the end of 1606 the first tentative moves were made towards the negotiation of a truce with the Dutch, but questions of prestige made progress slow. The bankruptcy of 1607, however, showed that a settlement in Flanders was essential. Lerma seems to have handled his more bellicose colleagues with skill, but it was sheer financial necessity which finally produced the Twelve Years Truce signed with the Dutch in April 1609. The majority of the king's ministers accepted it with reluctance. According to one of them, writing a few years afterwards: 'The truce in Flanders was considered an indispensable measure because of the shortage of money.'[1]

However unenthusiastic the reception accorded to a truce made with heretics and rebels, Spain was at last at peace with all the world. The return of peace did not, however, bring the expected advantages. Even if expenditure on the army in Flanders could now be halved, new emergencies were always occurring to absorb any money saved on military expenditure in the Netherlands. It also became clear that the Dutch stood to gain even more from peace than war. Already before the truce they had broken into the Caribbean and had started to make inroads into Portugal's Far Eastern Empire; and they had long been supplying Spain itself, either legally or under cover of Hamburg flags, with manufactures from northern Europe and with grain and naval stores from the Baltic. The coming of peace removed the last obstacles from their path. Northern products carried in Dutch vessels flooded into Spain, either for home consumption or for export to the New World. Since Spain could not offer in exchange sufficient goods to provide a full cargo for the return journey, the balance was made up in American silver.

The constant loss of silver to foreign countries, the domination of Spain's economic life by foreign merchants, and the unsatisfactory character of a trade which exchanged native raw materials for foreign manufactures, caused deep concern among the *arbitristas*. In their opinion the sole cure for Castile's troubles lay in the encouragement of native industry and agriculture. But how was this to be done? Although each had his own special remedy, leading *arbitristas* like Sancho de Moncada, Fernández Navarrete, Lisón y Biedma, were generally agreed on both the diagnosis and the principal features of the cure. They applied themselves in particular to two points: Spain's economic relations with the outside world, and the necessity for a programme of internal reform. Almost without exception the *arbitristas* when considering the first of these points advocated protectionist measures. It was essential to break the hold of foreign merchants and bankers on Spain's economic life, and

[1] Don Fernando Carrillo to king, 17 June 1616. AGS Hacienda, leg. 536, no. 162.

to forbid the import of foreign goods. Once the country ceased to be dependent on foreigners, there was a real chance of economic revival. But such a revival demanded a radical programme of internal reforms. The root causes of Spain's troubles were diagnosed by the *arbitristas* as the high rate of taxation, the love of luxury, the pursuit of idleness, and the diversion of the population into economically unproductive occupations. They saw at the heart of their country a vast court, a monstrous tumour swelling larger and larger, and relentlessly consuming the life of the nation. The court and the swollen bureaucracy were crying out for reform. Let the king reduce the size and expenditure of the royal households; let him forbid the prodigious expenditure of his wealthy subjects on costly jewels, clothes and buildings; let him call a halt to the lavish outpouring of gifts and favours at the expense of a bankrupt royal treasury; let him stop the sale of offices, send back the nobles to their estates, and clear the court of the hordes of servants and suitors which infested it. Let him reform the thirty-two universities and four thousand grammar schools, the breeding grounds of scribes, tax-collectors, and government officials, and forbid new foundations of colleges and convents. Finally, let him give special privileges and tax concessions to labourers and married men, so that the fields might be brought back to cultivation, and the countryside be repopulated.

The spur to this ambitious programme of reform was a hatred which was not confined to Spaniards: the hatred of the vast, extravagant, inefficient apparatus of government which in Spain, as in other nations of western Europe, was growing more expensive and more powerful until it threatened to squeeze all the life out of the nation. But a large bureaucracy and a parasitic court were not to be reformed out of existence by the stroke of a pen. In advocating their reforms of Spanish government and society, the *arbitristas* were in effect challenging the most powerful forces in Spain. On one side they were confronted by the inertia of the masses; on the other by the vested interests of the powerful oligarchy of landowners, churchmen, office-holders and courtiers determined to preserve the established order.

This established order drew its strength from the social organization of Castile and from the administrative processes developed under Habsburg government. The complexity of the task awaiting anyone willing to challenge its customary practices can be seen from the character of Spanish taxation and the fate of seventeenth-century attempts at its reform. The operation of the Spanish tax system in the early seventeenth century could be criticized on the double count of social injustice and economic inefficiency. It contained at least two striking anomalies. Within Spain, Castile paid much more proportionately in taxes than the other kingdoms of the Peninsula; and within Castile itself the more impoverished classes of society paid incomparably more than the rich.

The duque de Lerma, after the failure of a half-hearted attempt to extend the *millones* to Vizcaya, decided to leave the first of these fiscal anomalies severely alone. He showed himself no more courageous in his approach to the tax structure within Castile, although it was visibly operating to the prejudice of the more industrious sections of the community.

Unassisted by the other kingdoms, Castile was expected to provide over six million ducats a year in taxes for the crown. Evenly distributed, this would have come to about a ducat a year for every man, woman and child in the kingdom, at a time when a Castilian labourer's annual income was about eighty ducats. But the distribution was extremely uneven, and methods of collection created the maximum inconvenience. *Hidalgos*, who probably accounted for some 10 per cent of the population, were exempt from the *servicios* voted by the Cortes, and the wealthy had methods of escaping payment of the *alcabala* and the *millones* which were not available to the poor who bought retail. 'There is extreme inequality between the contributions of the poor and the rich', declared a would-be reformer of the tax system, who calculated that, in a poor man's daily expenditure of 30 *maravedis* (there being 375 *maravedis* to the ducat), 4 went in the *alcabala* and the *millones*.[1]

Lerma's government did nothing to redistribute contributions on a more equitable basis, and was unwilling or unable to use tax concessions to stimulate economic activity. Many powerful interests would have been antagonized by a thorough fiscal reorganization, even if this had been administratively possible, and the poor had no friends in high places to speak for them. Nominally this was the duty of the Cortes of Castile, but by the seventeenth century the *procuradores* of the Cortes represented little more than the interests of the exclusive municipal oligarchies from which they were drawn. As *hidalgos* they did not pay the *servicios* which they voted, and their own social background aligned them with those groups in Castilian society interested in the continuation of the present system. By placing the bulk of the taxes on essential articles of consumption, this system automatically discriminated against agricultural workers and artisans, who found themselves at the tax-collector's mercy.

Foreign travellers in seventeenth-century Castile ascribed much of its misery and depopulation to its peculiar tax system. They saw nothing but desert: a monotonous, boulder-strewn landscape, with here and there a half-deserted village. Although the value of their testimony is to some extent reduced by their unfamiliarity with methods of cultivation in a countryside more reminiscent of Africa than of Europe, many of their comments can be confirmed from other sources. A Castilian village was easy prey, with few means of natural defence. It was exposed not only to the unwelcome attention of the quartermaster and the recruiting sergeant,

[1] *Actas de las Cortes de Castilla*, Vol. 39, p. 142.

but also to the depredations of the tax-collector, and to the exactions of powerful nobles who encroached on the common lands, pressed hard for their feudal dues and passed the taxes for which they were liable on to the shoulders of their vassals. When a village was oppressed in this way, it was compelled to have recourse to loans, often with disastrous consequences. In the little village of Sanzoles, for example, a succession of bad harvests prevented the villagers from paying the annual interest on the *censo* or rent-charge with which they had raised their loan. As the arrears mounted, the creditors moved in and seized their property. Eventually, out of ninety householders no more than forty were said to remain.[1] This was the story of many villages. Rural life had become so insecure that many villagers abandoned their homes for the shelter of some town which offered better protection against an endless succession of fiscal demands.

On the one hand, Castile was a land of deserted villages, abandoned by peasants who had run into debt as a result of bad harvests, ceaseless fiscal exactions and the fixing by government decree of artificially low prices for agricultural products. On the other hand, it was a land of vast latifundia, in the inalienable possession of the church or of great aristocratic families uninterested in the improvement of their estates. If agriculture were ever to recover, it seemed that absentee landlordism must first be abolished. In a *consulta* of September 1609 Lerma's government attempted to tackle the problem of rural depopulation by suggesting that absentee landlords leave the court and return to their estates. This, it was hoped, would encourage their vassals to remain on the land. But the measure was inadequate and totally ineffectual. The whole fiscal and social structure of the country was such that towns and court proved irresistible magnets to a population which could find neither adequate security nor remunerative employment in the countryside.

Although the movement of the rural population to the towns might have provided cheap labour for industry, an industrial revival depended upon the availability both of personal enterprise and capital resources. Here again, Castile found itself prejudiced by methods of government finance which had given birth to a highly organized system of credit. The crown's persistent need for money had led to the wide circulation of *juros* or government bonds yielding a fixed annuity. These *juros*, together with *censos*, were bought by all those with money to spare or to save— by government officials, by members of the powerful municipal oligarchies, by wealthy middlemen in the villages, and by convents and pious foundations anxious to invest their funds. The result was the creation in Castile of a vast *rentier* class living comfortably off its yearly dues. The investment habits of this class diverted large sums of money from channels which might have enriched the nation's economic life. According to the Council of Finance, *censos* and *juros* offered better interest rates

---

[1] *Consulta* of Council of Finance, 25 March 1607. AGS Hacienda, leg. 473.

than those to be gained from investment in trade, agriculture or industry, and as long as this continued, there was no hope of reviving the Castilian economy.[1]

If this striking statement by the Council of Finance is correct, or accurately reflects contemporary opinion, at least some of the backwardness of economic enterprise in Castile can be satisfactorily explained. A detailed study of the social and economic consequences of the *censos* and *juros* would in any event be extremely valuable, since the opportunities which they provided for the safe investment of capital may help to account for one of the most remarkable features of seventeenth-century Castilian society: the complete absence of a vigorous urban class actively engaged in commercial and industrial enterprises. Such a class had in fact existed in Castilian towns like Burgos and Medina del Campo during the first half of the sixteenth century, but by the seventeenth it was gone, and its place in the Castilian economy had been taken by well-established communities of foreign merchants who dominated the commercial life of a passive society. Its disappearance left an obvious gap. According to González de Cellorigo in 1600:

Our republic has come to be an extreme contrast of rich and poor, and there is no means of adjusting them one to another. Our condition is one in which there are rich who loll at ease or poor who beg, and we lack people of the middle sort, whom neither wealth nor poverty prevents from pursuing the rightful kind of business enjoined by Natural Law.[2]

'People of the middle sort', with the enterprise and the resources to invest in trade or industry might one day, as in the Netherlands or England, have succeeded in transforming a society dominated by a traditional outlook and traditional habits. In their absence, Castilian society stood still. Church and aristocracy, the two most influential forces in medieval Castile, were, if possible, more powerful in the seventeenth century than they had been in the fifteenth. Already in possession of some 95 per cent of the soil of Castile at the start of the sixteenth century, they had continued to accumulate lands, the church by acquisition of lands in mortmain, the great magnates by establishing *mayorazgos* [entails] and building up vast entailed estates.

Church and aristocracy were therefore admirably placed for the continued propagation of their traditional ideals. These ideals, martial and crusading, were already deeply engrained in a society which for many centuries had devoted its energies to the waging of a Holy War against the Moors, and they acquired further life and prestige from the miraculous discovery of America. The persistence of these ideals into the sixteenth century helped to perpetuate in Castile a social outlook ill-equipped to cope with the economic problems which the acquisition of

[1] *Consulta* of Council of Finance, 3 September 1617. AGS Hacienda, leg. 547, no. 58.
[2] *Memorial de la Política*, p. 54.

empire brought in its train. It was natural to disregard the dictates of financial prudence when one could rely upon an annual shower of American silver to replenish the national coffers. Equally, it was hard for a nation imbued with aristocratic and religious ideals to abandon its traditional contempt for manual labour.

It was, of course, true that the contempt for manual labour was far from being an exclusively Castilian characteristic. Castile only shared a common European ideal of nobility and the impoverished Castilian *hidalgos* who haunted the court in pursuit of royal favour and scorned to work for a living differed little from the *hobereaux* of France and the gentry of England. Castile seems to have been remarkable less for any great originality in its national ideals than for the tenacity with which they were held, and for the way in which the political, social and economic circumstances of the age conspired to favour them. If manual labour and economic enterprise were at a discount in a society which glorified the ideals of church and aristocracy, the harsh realities of seventeenth-century Castilian life worked to the same end. The proportion of *hidalgos* to the rest of the population was very high, especially in north Castile; the laws of landownership and inheritance kept the land market tight, and left the control of the soil in the hands of a class of powerful land-owners uninterested in agrarian improvements; chronic underemployment in an ill-organized agrarian economy made idleness inevitable; sudden monetary changes, an arbitrary tax system, and the profits to be gained from the purchase of *censos* and *juros* removed all incentive to financial enterprise; and if church, army and a parasitic bureaucracy absorbed a considerable proportion of the population into economically unproductive occupations, the economy itself was incapable of providing alternative outlets.

The exaltation of military and religious ideals therefore to some extent made a virtue of necessity, but it also helped to create a climate little conducive to fundamental changes in social and economic attitudes. The aristocracy naturally set a pattern of life which the rest of the nation aspired to imitate.

The natives of these kingdoms, each in his own sphere and station, desire honour and estimation above everything else,

wrote a minister of the crown in 1641.

Each tries to advance himself, and so all apply themselves to those jobs which are held in the highest esteem. This is apparent in the fact that no son follows in his father's footsteps. The shoemaker's son abhors that particular calling; the merchant's son wants to be a *caballero*, and the same is true of all the rest.[1]

This craze for *hidalguía*, for a title of nobility, dominated the social aspirations of the inhabitants of Castile. Anyone who became rich would

---

[1] Paper by José González. AGS Guerra Antigua, leg. 1378.

acquire land, buy a title, found a *mayorazgo*. His younger sons, like those of the aristocracy, would join the army, or be sent to the university as the first step towards a career in the bureaucracy or the church. Salamanca and Alcalá, although they had lost the intellectual vigour which distinguished them in the sixteenth century, swarmed with students who saw in a university education and in the recommendation of their college the sole hope of future employment. There were too many students, too many lawyers, too many clergy. Yet however great the number of posts, there were always more candidates. The councils in Madrid were bombarded with petitions for *mercedes* or favours, for pensions and offices. The search for jobs was the disease of the age.

The unsuccessful joined the great army of the idle, which was swollen by recruits from above and below. The penurious student and the displaced peasant travelled the same road. Fiscal oppression, poor harvests, bad trade could turn the artisan or the peasant of today into a pauper tomorrow; it was easier, and in the long run no more unprofitable, to live in idleness and trust to native wit and the charity of the church. The beggar, the vagabond, the *pícaro*, living on their wits, constantly on the move, defeated one day, triumphant the next, were the symbols of Philip III's Castile. Round the corner lay the miracle—or the disillusionment. The contemporary addiction to games of chance was particularly suited to a nation which, almost as a matter of course, had come to stake all that it had on the fall of a single card.

This predominantly medieval society, uneasily poised between an exalted concept of its own high mission and an increasingly bitter sense of disillusionment, was fickle and easily swayed. Sometimes an appeal to traditional values provoked no more than a shrug of the shoulders. At others it could whip the nation into a sudden frenzy of almost mystical fervour, as Lerma's government discovered when it found itself undertaking the most drastic action of its inglorious career: the expulsion of the Moriscos.

It was natural that the advocates of expulsion should make a bid for the widest possible popular support by presenting their case in terms of the national ideal. The Moriscos, they proclaimed, must be driven from the Peninsula because, as infidels, their continued presence constituted a grave offence in the sight of God and was liable to call down His justified wrath upon the heads of the Faithful. Their expulsion would be at once an act of national expiation and of renewed dedication to the formidable tasks that still awaited the chosen nation of Castile. Although this was the most publicized argument for expulsion, there were others of equal or greater cogency. Ever since the Granada revolt of 1568–70, the Moriscos presented a complex and possibly insoluble problem. They formed a widely scattered racial minority which Spain had failed to assimilate.

THE SPANISH PENINSULA 1598-1648

The Moriscos driven from Granada spread northwards into the towns and villages of Castile, to create a rootless and potentially revolutionary element in Castilian life. The rootlessness of the predominantly town-dwelling Castilian Moriscos differentiated them from their brethren in the kingdom of Valencia, who enjoyed an acknowledged position in the economic structure and agrarian life of the realm. But the very cohesion of the Valencian Moriscos seemed as threatening in its way as the dispersion of the Granada Moriscos through Castile. Sporadic efforts made in the sixteenth century to woo them from their traditional customs and religious practices had proved fruitless. They continued, as New Christians, to form a close-knit racial community which the Old Christians of Valencia proved unable to absorb.

Madrid could never forget that there existed in Spain a community bound by ties of kinship and religion to the national enemy, the Turk. Fears of a Morisco rising in conjunction with a Turkish invasion were never far away, and as late as 1601 arms were distributed in Valencia against a possible attempt at revolution by these 'domestic enemies'.[1] However ill-founded these fears may have been, many were ready to magnify them. Certain groups would have been well pleased to see the last of the Moriscos. Landowners without Morisco labour on their estates were jealous of their more fortunate neighbours; those, like Lerma himself, who had estates near the coast, were haunted by forebodings of an invasion from the sea timed to coincide with a revolt on land; and many owners of lands occupied by the Moriscos in return for small fixed rents would have been glad to recover the direct use of their properties. Above all, the lower orders of Valencian society, whose numbers had been swollen by the population increase of the sixteenth century, were hungry for the land at present occupied by Morisco communities. There was, therefore, a genuine popular movement in Valencia against the Moriscos. The same was true of Castile where, during the last thirty years of the sixteenth century, the Moriscos had made a corner in many of the humbler trades, as small craftsmen, carriers and muleteers, and had become unpopular for working too hard, spending too little and breeding too fast. These combined Castilian and Valencian popular movements, reinforced by arguments at higher levels about religious unity and national security, and abetted by certain influential groups, eventually carried the day. Lerma's ministry, yielding to the pressure of an excited public opinion, decided that total expulsion was the only solution to an intractable problem and, by decrees of 1609 and 1610, ordered the Moriscos of Castile, Valencia, Catalonia and Aragon to leave the country forthwith.

The expulsion of the Moriscos has given rise to much controversy. For long it was considered one of the principal causes of the 'decline of Spain' until Hamilton, observing that Valencian prices and wages showed

[1] Conde de Benavente to king, 22 December 1601. AGS Estado, leg. 190.

no marked change after the expulsion had occurred, concluded that it cannot have possessed the economic importance generally attributed to it. This conclusion has recently been subjected to several criticisms and qualifications.[1] The points at issue are the number of Moriscos expelled, their economic role in the community before the expulsion, and the effects of the expulsion on the general level of prosperity. As far as numbers are concerned, it is now clear from the investigations of M. Lapeyre that Hamilton's figure of 100,000 was a serious under-estimate. A figure of some 275,000 would be much nearer the mark. The geographical distribution of these 275,000, in round numbers, is as follows:

Valencia	117,000
Catalonia	4,000
Aragon	61,000
Castile, La Mancha, Extremadura	45,000
Murcia	14,000
Andalusia	30,000
Granada	2,000

the exact figures for the last three regions probably being a few thousand above the actual figures given.

If Hamilton's figures have not stood up to the test of later investigations, his views on the economic activities of the Moriscos before their expulsion, and his low estimate of their status, have, on the other hand, been generally confirmed. The Valencian Moriscos were not, on the whole, very wealthy members of the community. Most of them were carriers and hawkers, or labourers on seigneurial estates; they traded only on a small scale, and their participation in the textile industry did not rival that of the Old Christians. They were not, therefore, a dynamic economic group, and it has yet to be proved that their expulsion deprived Spain either of technical inventiveness or of vigorous commercial enterprise. Their value to the country's agrarian life is, however, less easily assessed. Hamilton's thesis, that the impact of the expulsion on both wages and prices was negligible, deserves more careful scrutiny than it has so far received. No conclusions on this subject can be really satisfactory until a detailed study has been made of the neglected problem of the resettlement of the deserted areas by Valencian Old Christians and by colonists from neighbouring regions. But since so many Moriscos worked in the fields, and Hamilton provides no wage figures for agricultural labourers in Valencia, he can hardly be said to have substantiated his claim that wages were unaffected. As for prices, the failure of certain products to rise in price may well be explained by the decreased demand after a quarter of Valencia's population had disappeared. In any event, the in-

---

[1] See J. Reglá, 'La Expulsión de los Moriscos y sus consecuencias', *Hispania*, Vol. 13 (1953); the articles on the Valencian Moriscos by Tulio Halperín Donghi in *Cuadernos de Historia de España* (1955), pp. 23–4, and in *Annales*, Vol. II (1956); and, for statistics, Henri Lapeyre, *Géographie de l'Espagne Morisque* (Paris, 1959).

ference from price statistics that the expulsion had little effect on agriculture is not borne out by recent work on Valencian land values after
1609. During the sixteenth century, in Valencia as elsewhere in Spain,
those who acquired a small amount of capital would commonly invest it
in *censales*: loans on the security of the borrower's land, and paying fixed
annual interest from its yield. The nobles in particular had borrowed
large sums, the interest on which they paid from the incomes of estates
worked by their Morisco vassals. Immediately these vassals were expelled,
they found extreme difficulty in continuing the payment of interest at the
agreed rates, since the income from their estates had disastrously slumped.
This tends to counteract the evidence drawn from prices and wages, and
suggests that the impact of the expulsion on the life and economy of
Valencia, was, after all, sharp. It was made sharper still by the policy
adopted by Lerma's government. Inundated by complaints from nobles
who were harassed by angry creditors and saw themselves threatened
with ruin, it eventually yielded to their pressure and greatly reduced the
rate of interest payable on the *censales*. This action shifted much of the loss
from the nobles to their creditors, drawn from the middle and poorer
classes of Valencian society, who had invested their money in *censales*
and now found their annual incomes much diminished. The Lerma
régime had again conformed to its traditional practice of favouring the
privileged at the expense of the less privileged. All classes of Valencian
society suffered from the expulsion, but the nobles, who had stood to
suffer most, escaped more lightly from the general wreckage than those
other groups which had few friends at court.

At least for Valencia, then, the expulsion of the Moriscos was an
economic disaster. The sudden loss of one quarter of the population,
accompanied by an inevitable dislocation of the country's economic and
social structure, would take long to repair. For Castile, however, the
economic consequences of the expulsion are more difficult to gauge,
Since Valencia's economy was not integrated with that of Castile, the
expulsion of the Valencian Moriscos seriously affected Castile's future
only in so far as it reduced the wealth of a kingdom on which the crown
would one day make heavy fiscal demands. Long after the Moriscos had
gone, the Valencians would continue to make their departure an excuse
for their inability to vote the king larger subsidies. But the crown of
Castile had also lost some 90,000 Moriscos of its own. If their place in
Castilian society was not comparable to that occupied by their brethren
in Valencian society, this does not necessarily warrant the conclusion that
the economic effect of their departure was insignificant. The disappearance
of Morisco artisans and craftsmen must have played its part in prolonging
the labour crisis begun by the plague of 1599, although only local studies
could show how far the continuation of the crisis can be specifically
attributed to the expulsion. In the light of what is known about the chosen

fields of activity of the Castilian Moriscos, the effects of the expulsion are more likely to have been felt in the towns than in the country, but with considerable variations from town to town. Seville in particular was hard hit. A twelfth of its population was Morisco and, as the great emporium of trade with the New World, it relied heavily on Morisco labour for carrying and lading and other essential services. The loss of this labour force added one more to the many grave problems which were already beginning to overwhelm Seville, and which would culminate in the 1640s in the dislocation of Spain's Atlantic trading system.

But in the mood of euphoria created by the expulsion of the Moriscos, it was easy to discount the unpleasant testimony of facts and figures. Everything else paled before the one dominant consideration that a long-standing irritant, and a cause of national shame, had at last been successfully banished from the Castilian body politic. Beside this notable achievement, any possible economic consequences seemed of minor importance. After centuries of struggle, Castile's crusade had at last been completed, and pure religion established through the length and breadth of Spain.

It was perhaps ironical that the régime which had achieved the long-desired religious unity of the Peninsula should have shown itself singularly indifferent to its continuing constitutional and administrative disunity. 'Aragon, Valencia, Catalonia and Navarre devote all their energies to preserving their many privileges, and are content', reported the Venetian ambassador.[1] Lerma was quite prepared to gratify their more reasonable wishes, so long as this would keep them quiet, and his policy towards them was compounded at once of flattery and neglect. Except for an extended visit to Lerma's native province of Valencia, Philip III's visits to his other dominions in Spain were fleeting, and brought neither satisfaction to the majority of their inhabitants nor any real financial relief to Castile. During the twenty-three years of his reign, he summoned and attended personally the Cortes of Catalonia once, in 1599, and obtained a subsidy of 1,100,000 ducats in return for large concessions; those of Valencia once, in 1604, where the subsidy of 400,000 ducats was all spent in gifts and bribes; and those of Portugal, convened to take the oath of allegiance to his son, once also, in 1619.

Even if the reign was unusually favourable to the particularism of the peninsular kingdoms, they showed little gratitude to a régime which paid them only the most casual attention. Lerma not only failed to further the unity and co-operation of the different states within the Spanish peninsula, but came very close to abdicating all his responsibilities towards them. Between 1600 and 1615 Catalonia, overrun by bandits, drifted towards anarchy; but Lerma appeared to be totally unconcerned. 'Here

[1] N. Barozzi and G. Berchet, *Relazioni degli Stati Europei* (Venice, 1856), Series I: Spagna, Vol. I, p. 321.

it's all a matter of gaming, hunting and comedies, and no one will be bothered with anything', complained an angry Catalan sent by the city of Barcelona on an important mission to Madrid. At a time when the apparatus of government appeared to be constantly growing, government itself was ceasing to exist. A passive, negative régime, incapable of taking decisions, and almost unaware of the decisions to be taken, was squandering one by one the precious years of respite.

Lerma at last fell from power in October 1618, a victim of the palace intrigues of his own son, the duque de Uceda. A fitting epitaph on his government was written anonymously in 1640: 'Although in the reign of Philip III there was universal peace, and long-established evils should have been set right, nothing was done either in the Indies or inside Spain, and the Crown's finances were given no relief.'[1] A heavy responsibility lies with Lerma himself, the half-willing prisoner of social groups and forces which he had neither the inclination nor the energy to defy. His downfall, however, altered little. The change of favourites brought no change of policy; the son proved no more energetic a minister than the father. But the crown's finances were in such straits, and the exhaustion of Castile so patent, that pressure for reform was becoming irresistible. The Council of Finance, in memorandum after memorandum, insisted on the necessity of curbing royal expenditure and the liberal distribution of *mercedes*. The Council of Castile, in its famous *consulta* of 1 February 1619, pressed for greater economy and for the lightening of Castile's intolerable burden of taxation. As an analysis of Castile's troubles, the document added nothing to the reiterated conclusions of the *arbitristas*, but it was important as the first attempt by a council to examine as a group the many fiscal and economic problems which has for so long been ignored.

The introduction of the reforms recommended in this *consulta* required more political courage than that possessed by Uceda, but the days of the new ministry were numbered. Philip III died suddenly on 31 March 1621. With the new king came new favourites, Don Balthasar de Zúñiga and his nephew, the conde de Olivares. The change of ministers was generally acclaimed as bringing hope of reform; when the news reached Barcelona a Catalan lawyer wrote in his private diary that a new dawn had broken.

Philip IV himself, with more intelligence but no more strength of character than his father, hardly represented a very inspiring herald for a new dawn, but in the conde de Olivares he had chosen a favourite of a very different calibre from the favourites of Philip III. Olivares, who became sole *privado* on the death of Zúñiga in 1622 and remained in power for over twenty years, was, as a man and a minister, the antithesis of Lerma. He was hard, dynamic, puritanical. As a member of the Andalusian aristocracy he had no need, unlike Lerma, to ingratiate himself

---

[1] *Súplica de la . . . Ciudad de Tortosa* (Tortosa, 1640), fo. 95.

with the great families of Castile. No personal considerations would be allowed to stand in the way of that restoration of Spain which he considered himself called upon to accomplish. In his intense nationalism, in his desire for a thorough reformation, and in his disgust with the old ministers and their policies, Olivares, who was only thirty-four at the time of his advent to power, represented the hopes and ideals of the new generation in Castile. But he also possessed, perhaps in a heightened degree, the failings of the age; above all, its expectation of the miracle, its willingness to embark upon great enterprises without first calculating sufficiently the possibilities of success. One of the Venetian ambassadors wrote of him: 'He loves novelties, allowing his lively mind to pursue chimeras, and to hit upon impossible designs as easy of achievement. For this reason he is desolated by misfortunes; the difficulties proposed to him at the beginning he brushes aside, and all his resolutions rush him towards the precipice.'[1]

Formidable problems awaited him. The Council of Finance was constantly submitting the most gloomy reports on the crown's revenues. The *alcabalas* and royal rents in Castile were sold or mortgaged to such a degree that their redemption would cost 350,000 ducats more than their value; the proceeds of *cruzada*, *excusado* and *servicios* had been assigned up to 1625 to pay for royal expenditure before 1621; the collection of the *millones* was so defective that the bankers could never count on receiving the sums promised them; and 'the treasure fleets have brought such small sums in recent years that, unless there is an improvement, they will be of very little assistance'. The only means of meeting the deficit on the anticipated expenditure of 1621 was to manufacture more *vellón* coins, and this was done on as large a scale as the limited quantity of available copper permitted.[2]

The Council of Finance was working on the assumption that Spain would remain at peace. But in April 1621 the twelve-year truce with the Dutch was due to expire, and unless it were renewed, the council would have to find large additional sums of money for the army and the fleet. The question of whether or not the truce should be prolonged was debated in both Brussels and Madrid. Although the condition of Flanders and the state of the crown's finances suggested the desirability of prolongation, it was finally decided that the war with the Dutch should be resumed. The exact circumstances in which this decision was taken are not yet known, but it seems probable that Zúñiga and Olivares were primarily influenced by the long chronicle of Dutch overseas successes since 1609. Under cover of the truce, the Dutch had penetrated into the Spanish and Portuguese preserves of the Indian and Pacific Oceans. This entailed not

[1] Barozzi and Berchet, *Relazioni...*, Vol. I, p. 650.
[2] This, and the following information on the financial situation in 1621, is from AGS Hacienda, leg. 573, fos. 11, 172 and 303.

only the loss of lucrative trades, but a weakening of the ties of interest that bound Portugal to the crown of Spain. Philip IV's ministers could not afford to overlook Portugal's reaction to Spain's failure to protect its overseas territories; nor could they overlook the heavy expenditure in recent years on relief expeditions, of which the latest, a costly fleet for the Philippines, had been totally destroyed by a storm off Cadiz in January 1620. By 1621 there seemed much to be said for attacking the trouble at its source. A well-organized military and naval campaign against the United Provinces would keep the Dutch occupied at home, put an end to their incursions into Spanish and Portuguese waters, destroy their trade, and perhaps finally bring their fifty-year revolt to an end.[1]

While these arguments had much to commend them, they displayed an optimism about Spain's capacity for war which was not supported by the available information about Castile's economy and the royal finances. A return to war meant the recruiting of new armies, for which Castile would have difficulty in finding the men. It meant also a considerable increase in the size and efficiency of Spain's long-neglected fleet. Certain ministers had pressed vigorously for this during the reign of Philip III, in the belief that the preservation of Spain's Empire depended principally on the strengthening of its naval power. Olivares shared these views, but at this stage a naval revival was likely to be difficult. As soon as the truce expired, the Dutch put an embargo on all naval stores for Spain, and effectively crippled the shipbuilding industry in a country where wood was scarce and where techniques of naval construction had been allowed to lag behind those employed in the dockyards of northern Europe.

Above all, a resumption of the war with the Netherlands meant more money. During the truce, the annual expenditure on the forces stationed in Flanders had stood at about $1\frac{1}{2}$ million ducats. As soon as war broke out again in 1621, this figure rose to $3\frac{1}{2}$ million ducats, bringing the total expenditure for the year to well over 8,000,000. It was asking much of the Council of Finance to find an annual figure of this order, and it was not long before Olivares himself came to take a hand in negotiating the crown's yearly *asiento* or contract with the Genoese bankers. His bullying and bludgeoning of the Imbreas, the Spínolas and the Stratas had the desired results: sooner or later an *asiento* was agreed. But the price paid was fantastically high, and it was principally paid by Castile.

The last twenty years of Spain's international power are only understandable in terms of this relentless pressure of fiscal necessity, never abating after the resumption in 1621 of the war with the Dutch. The twelve years' breathing-space provided by the truce of 1609 was gone, squandered by a prodigal ministry. When a reforming régime came at last, it came too late, since reform could be carried out only to the dis-

[1] There is a vigorous exposition of some of these points in a paper by Don Carlos Coloma, printed in Antonio Rodríguez Villa, *Ambrosio Spínola* (Madrid, 1904), pp. 382-92.

rupting accompaniment of an intolerably expensive war. In this lay the tragedy of Olivares' government. War, while making long-delayed reforms indispensable, created conditions which made their fulfilment impossible. The history of Olivares' government is littered with good intentions frustrated by the insatiable demands of war.

Olivares began his ministerial career by attempting to make a clean break with the past. While Lerma had taken care to ensure his own survival by investing in a cardinal's hat, his unfortunate creature, Don Rodrigo Calderón, was sent to the scaffold. A vast investigation was begun into the personal fortunes of Calderón's colleagues and of all ministers who had held office since 1603. The list of favours and pensions distributed by the king was mercilessly cut. A special junta was established for the 'reformation of manners', and in February 1623 the government issued its famous reforming decrees.[1] They constituted an almost exact replica of the *arbitristas*' demands for the axing of the Castilian bureaucracy and the curbing of court extravagance. The number of municipal offices in Castile was to be reduced to one-third; restrictions were imposed on extravagant clothes and jewellery and, more effectively, the king's personal example led to the substitution of the austere *golilla* for the elaborate ruff; the court was to be cleared of suppliants and suitors, the nobles were to return to their estates and many grammar schools were to be closed.

It took little time to discover that sweeping reforms of this nature were more easily decreed than effected. Not even an assault from within the citadel could make much headway against personal interests and against the established practice of many generations. The imposing superstructure of court and bureaucracy stood fast while the storm harmlessly blew itself out. The economy campaign was forgotten in the festivities celebrating the unexpected visit of the prince of Wales in March 1623; the order for the reduction of municipal offices was withdrawn in 1626 at the request of a Cortes speaking in the interests of municipal governments threatened with heavy financial loss.

Only in the sphere of administrative reorganization did Olivares meet with any real success. In an attempt to rescue government from the cumbrous machinery of the conciliar system, he came to place more and more reliance on special or permanent juntas, staffed with his own friends and relations and a select group of officials in whom he could place his trust. These were the men of the new régime, men like José González and Jerónimo de Villanueva, personally devoted to Olivares and to the realization of his ideals. By working through small juntas, some of which he attended personally, Olivares obtained a much tighter control of the administrative machine than would otherwise have been possible. One after

[1] A. González Palencia, *La Junta de Reformación* (Valladolid, 1932), Document LXVI.

another the routine-bound councils saw their powers clipped by the creation of some new junta: juntas for fleets and garrisons and mines, for the Military Orders and for the administration of new taxes. Even the Council of State, the supreme organ of government under Philip III, lost much of its power to a special *Junta de Ejecución*, which was to become the effective policy-making body in the last years of the Olivares régime. But government under Olivares was essentially a one-man affair. The councils and juntas continued to meet and produce their *consultas*, but it was Olivares who took the decisions.

Imbued with the ideals of the *arbitristas* he was particularly concerned to salvage Castile's economy. He shared their views on the need for protectionist measures to encourage national development, and he showed considerable anxiety over the technical backwardness of Spain in such matters as the construction of canals. He proposed that trading companies should be established with royal encouragement, and that honours should be conferred upon merchants to destroy the traditional disrepute in which trade was held. He devised or approved schemes for the encouragement of foreign settlers, for the establishment of a state bank, and for the relief of the lesser nobles, whose plight preoccupied him as much as the plight of their colleagues preoccupied Richelieu in France.

Scarcely one of these plans was realized. An India Company was indeed founded at Lisbon, but it survived only a short time, and was principally useful as establishing a mutually advantageous alliance between the Spanish crown and a number of wealthy Portuguese businessmen. Otherwise, Olivares' schemes, like those of Richelieu, were shelved or forgotten as the overwhelming problems of war and finance came to dominate every aspect of the nation's life. The armies must be paid, new fleets must be built, and this could only be done if the crown's revenues were substantially increased. But how could they be increased without imposing fresh burdens on the long-suffering taxpayers of Castile? It was clear to Olivares, as it had long been clear to the *arbitristas*, that the time had come for a complete reappraisal of Spain's system of taxation.

Since the beginning Philip III's reign, when Alamos de Barrientos had commented on the strange character of an empire in which the principal kingdom was expected to subsidize the rest,[1] the disparity between the fiscal contributions of Castile and the other realms and territories had provoked a series of angry complaints in Castile. At a time when Castile, with its prostrate economy, was paying over six million ducats a year in taxes, it was surely reasonable to demand some sacrifice from the king's other realms. 'The kingdoms of Aragon, Valencia and Catalonia contribute nothing to His Majesty's expenses outside their own territory', complained the president of the Council of Finance in 1618. 'In fact', he

---

[1] See above, p. 442.

continued, 'money has to be sent from Castile to pay for their garrisons', and the same was true also of Navarre, Milan, Naples, Sardinia and Sicily. Admittedly the king had obtained something at the beginning of his reign from Portugal, through customs dues, freight charges and pepper imports, but this income had dwindled away, and Castile was now maintaining the Portuguese fleet and the troops stationed on Portuguese soil.

It was significant that the Council of Finance's urgent requests for financial assistance from the other kingdoms should have coincided with a period of intensified Castilian nationalism, which itself was very probably a natural response to Castile's misfortunes. While the *arbitristas* campaigned against the domination of Castile's economy by foreign merchants, certain sections of the Castilian aristocracy showed a renewed antagonism to the semi-autonomous government of the king's other territories. In Catalonia, for example, the Castilian duque de Alcalá, viceroy from 1619 to 1622, treated the principality's laws and privileges with a contempt which convinced the Catalans that the government in Madrid was conspiring to abolish their contractual form of government. In the Council of State, the duque del Infantado and Don Pedro de Toledo commented bitterly on Portugal's exemption from the taxes levied on Castile, while preparations were made to wrest from the Portuguese their monopoly of lucrative overseas trades and to restrict the activities of Portuguese merchants who had infiltrated into Castile's American possessions since the Union of Castile and Portugal in 1580.

It was against this background of xenophobia and of revived Castilian nationalism that Olivares set himself to solve the problems created by the fiscal and constitutional peculiarities of the Spanish monarchy. These problems appeared at their most acute in the question of imperial defence. It was difficult and costly to defend an empire of widely scattered territories, and it seemed unreasonable to Olivares and his colleagues that Castile, in its present state, should be expected to provide both the men and the money to defend territories which raised not a finger to defend themselves. The time had come to consider radical changes in the structure and organization of the Spanish Empire, so that the fiscal burden should be more evenly distributed and the kingdoms should come to each other's help in time of need.

The plan devised by Olivares for the future of the Spanish Empire was presented to the king in the form of a long, secret memorandum written in 1624.[1] To Olivares, as to other European statesmen of his generation, unity implied uniformity. All the kingdoms of the Spanish monarchy must be integrated and reduced to a single legal and administrative unit.

---

[1] *Instrucción que dió el Conde Duque a Felipe IV*, B(ritish) M(useum) Egerton MS 347, fos. 249–90. The only complete printed version of this important text is an eighteenth-century one, wrongly ascribed to Philip IV's tutor, in A. Valladares, *Semanario Erudito* (Madrid, 1787–91), Vol. XI, pp. 161–224.

The most important thing in Your Majesty's Monarchy is for you to become King of Spain; by this, I mean that your Majesty should not be content with being King of Portugal, Aragon and Valencia and Count of Barcelona, but should secretly plan and work to reduce these kingdoms of which Spain is composed to the style and laws of Castile.

These words in themselves would seem to place Olivares among the extreme Castilian nationalists, but other parts of the text show that he sympathized with the various territories in many of their grievances and was anxious to remove them. Since they complained that they never saw their king, he would in future live in each of his kingdoms in turn. Since they felt themselves excluded from the benefits of empire, the Castilian monopoly of offices and honours would be abolished, and imperial posts be thrown open to all. In future it would be a Spanish, not a Castilian, Empire: an empire ruled, it is true, by the laws of Castile but an empire in which posts would be open to everyone, irrespective of nationality. Customs barriers between the kingdoms would be removed, intermarriage among their nationals encouraged. The empire of Olivares' dreams was to be an integrated empire in the fullest sense; a constitutional, economic and racial whole.

Since the integration of the Spanish Empire by these means could only be achieved by degrees, Olivares prepared a second, short-term plan, known as the Union of Arms.[1] The union was to be made by the creation of a common reserve of 140,000 men, supplied and maintained by all the states within the Spanish monarchy in fixed proportions:

	paid men
Catalonia	16,000
Aragon	10,000
Valencia	6,000
Castile and the Indies	44,000
Portugal	16,000
Naples	16,000
Sicily	6,000
Milan	8,000
Flanders	12,000
Mediterranean and Atlantic Islands	6,000

The king, drawing on this reserve, would send the seventh part of it, or 20,000 infantry and 4,000 cavalry, to the help of any territory which was attacked. This, according to Olivares, was 'the sole cure for all the ills that can arise: namely that, as loyal vassals we all unite . . .'.

In devising these plans for a closer measure of co-operation between the realms of the monarchy, Olivares showed himself the first ruler of Spain to formulate a coherent policy for the empire's future development. His plans, if successful, might perhaps bring some relief to Castile; but, whether successful or not, any attempt to put them into practice would entail great changes in the relationship between the king and his non-

[1] The printed version of this plan, as presented to the Cortes of the crown of Aragon, is in BM Additional MS 13,997, fs. 11-16.

Castilian subjects. Each kingdom of the Peninsula had always maintained that the king was primarily *its* king, and only accidentally the ruler of other territories. Taking shelter behind this fiction, the kingdoms had for long revolved in orbits of their own, ostentatiously oblivious of the king's wider obligations. But the fiction was wearing thin. Henceforth every action taken by Olivares for the relief of Castile would have its repercussions among the other kingdoms, and they in the days to come would find themselves inexorably drawn into the orbit of Castile.

In November 1625 the English attacked Cadiz. This foolhardy attack occurred at a convenient moment for Olivares since it provided the requisite note of urgency for the launching of his plan for the Union of Arms. In the opening months of 1626 the king and Olivares laid the plan personally before the three Cortes of Aragon, Valencia and Catalonia. It was coldly received. The traditional fears of Castile's intentions had been aroused during the first years of the new régime, and rumours had for some time been circulating that Olivares planned to introduce *un rey, una ley, una moneda* [one king, one law, one coinage]. Not one of the three Cortes was willing to raise troops for compulsory service beyond the provincial frontiers. Each suspected a scheme which demanded large sacrifices, and the abandonment of cherished privileges, in return for the most hypothetical advantages. Of what interest was the fate of Flanders to Catalonia, or that of Milan to Aragon? These arguments reflected that long-standing isolation of the different kingdoms which had effectively prevented the growth of any tradition of mutual assistance on which Olivares could begin to build. The resistance proved too strong to allow any rapid settlement of the Union of Arms, and Olivares had to content himself with more conventional forms of help. From Valencia and Aragon he at least obtained money, if not men: 1,800,000 ducats from the Valencian Cortes over a period of fifteen years, and sufficient money from the Cortes of Aragon to maintain 2,000 men, if possible Aragonese volunteers, for the same period. The Catalan Cortes, however, were adjourned after a series of sharp clashes without having voted either men or money. Olivares returned to Madrid disappointed, but still confident of final success.

The setback of 1626 meant that Castile would continue to provide most of the men and money required for the king's foreign enterprises: for the wars in Germany, the expeditions to relieve Brazil, and the unfortunate Mantuan War of 1628–31. Castile was ill equipped to meet these heavy commitments. A series of bad harvests was accompanied by an exceptionally sharp rise in prices between 1625 and 1627, to which the government responded in August 1628 by a deflationary decree reducing the tale of *vellón* by 50 per cent. During this period of acute monetary instability, the crown finances underwent another crisis. On this occasion Olivares secured the help of a group of Portuguese businessmen, whom he skilfully played off against the Genoese bankers. On 31 January 1627, twenty years after its last bankruptcy, the crown was once again able to repudiate its debts. But the repudiation brought only temporary relief: the treasure-fleet of 1628 fell into the hands of the Dutch, and the *servicios* voted by the Castilian Cortes, although raised in 1626 by two million ducats a year, were in fact yielding only half a million.

It was essential to find new sources of revenue, and this could only be done by casting the fiscal net more widely. Since an irremovable social stigma was attached to direct taxation by the crown, Olivares fell back on a host of ingenious devices for indirect taxation, which would allow him to mulct those groups in Castilian society enjoying special fiscal advantages or immunities. In 1631 he introduced a tax known as the *media anata*, appropriating to the crown half the first year's income from all new appointments, and also a tax on salt which provoked a serious rising in Vizcaya; in 1632 he secured papal consent to a special grant from the clergy and appropriated a year's income from the wealthy archbishopric of Toledo; in 1635 he confiscated half the yield of all *juros* held by natives, and the entire yield of those belonging to foreigners—a device imitated in whole or in part almost every year thereafter; in 1637 he imposed a profitable tax on the sale of paper, and seized 478,000 ducats in American silver belonging to private individuals, compensating the unfortunate owners with *juros;* two years later, oblivious to the consequences for Seville and the American trade, he confiscated a further 1,000,000 ducats in the same manner. All these special fiscal devices were introduced over and above both the direct taxes voted in increasing quantities by the Cortes, and the more timeworn methods of raising money, like the sale of crown rents, titles and offices. But even they did not exhaust the conde duque's repertoire. He revived the old feudal obligations of the aristocracy, so that the *hidalgos* found themselves serving in the army at their own expense, while the magnates were expected to raise and maintain complete infantry companies. He endlessly exhorted nobles and ecclesiastics, town councils and cathedral chapters to offer money either in the form of loans, or as 'voluntary' gifts or *donativos* to meet some special emergency. The collectors would go from door to door demanding contributions not only from the head of the house but also from his wife, children and servants, carefully grading the demands according to the estimated wealth of the victims.

These various fiscal stratagems had social and political consequences of profound importance for Castile. The rapid growth of indirect forms of taxation under the government of Olivares blurred the sharp line that had once divided the *pechero*—the ordinary taxpayer—from those who traditionally enjoyed special consideration for reasons of social prestige. The clergy were now groaning beneath the unprecedented weight of their taxes. Many *hidalgos* of moderate means were ruined, while the great magnates, although saved from financial disaster by the inalienability of their estates, were mulcted of enormous sums: by 1640 the crown was said to have obtained 900,000 ducats from the Duque de Arcos alone. His ruthless treatment of the great and privileged brought down upon the head of Olivares the most bitter personal hatred. Bombarded with an endless succession of demands, the nobles, one by one, retired from Madrid to their estates, in self-imposed or compulsory exile from a court dominated by a favourite who treated his equals with arrogance and dismissed their protests with contempt.

While the conde duque never allowed himself to be deterred by aristocratic or popular antagonism, he was passionately concerned to alleviate the sufferings of his beloved Castile. This, he believed, could only be achieved by pressing on with the Union of Arms. Since Catalonia had failed to vote a subsidy in the Cortes of 1626 and had indeed voted no taxes to the crown since the Cortes of 1599, it was singled out for early attention. The Catalan Cortes were convened again in the spring of 1632. News had reached Madrid that ships of the treasure-fleet had been lost in a storm, and the conde duque hoped for a grant of three million ducats from the Catalans to cover the reported loss. He had chosen an unfortunate moment. After their experiences in 1626 the Catalans would in any event have been unwilling to loosen their purse strings, but their reluctance was increased by recent economic misfortunes. Between 1629 and 1632 corn prices had reached famine level, the plague raging in the south of France had penetrated into northern Catalonia, and the principality's Mediterranean trade was at a standstill. Hardly had the Cortes met when a clash on a question of ceremonial between the city of Barcelona and Philip IV's brother, the *cardenal infante*, brought them to a sudden halt. Neither threats nor blandishments could make Barcelona waive its claims. Once again, in 1632 as in 1626, the Catalan Cortes had failed to vote money to their king.

Olivares expressed his anger by resorting to a series of dubious devices for obtaining money from Barcelona, which only served to deepen the antipathy between the Catalans and the Castilians, and presaged the fateful events in Catalonia at the end of the decade. From the outbreak of the war between Spain and France in May 1635, the history of the Spanish peninsula comes to be dominated by the deteriorating relationship on one side between Castile and Catalonia, and on the other between Castile and Portugal. To Madrid, both provinces presented a similar problem. Both, when viewed from a stricken Castile, had the air of privileged, prosperous undertaxed lands, far removed from the din and disruption of war. Neither had offered any material assistance to the crown or Castile at a time of desperate need. The Portuguese had stood aloof while Castile prepared the relief expeditions of 1634 and 1635 for the recovery of Portugal's own possessions in Brazil. The Catalans had failed on two different occasions to vote a service to the king; they neither provided, nor paid, the troops which defended their own frontiers with France, nor did they even contribute enough to meet the expenses of a viceregal government whose annual income was only half that enjoyed by the city of Barcelona. No Catalan troops fought in the German wars, or could be used for the invasion of France. In Olivares' words, the Catalans showed themselves to be 'entirely separate from the rest of the Monarchy, useless for service, and in a state little befitting the dignity and power of His Majesty'.

To both the east and the west of the Peninsula, therefore, Olivares found himself saddled with territories whose reluctance to co-operate in the task of common defence had disappointed all his hopes of closer union among the dominions of the king. Yet the Union of Arms had never seemed more necessary than now. With the coming of war with France, the anticipated expenditure for 1635 had risen to over 11,000,000 ducats. Spain was engaged in a battle to the death, for which Castile alone could never provide sufficient money or men. The resources of both Catalonia and Portugal must be mobilized.

Any successful exploitation of the wealth of Portugal was likely to require the preliminary establishment of a more effective administration in Lisbon. The forms of government introduced by the union of 1580 had given little satisfaction either to Madrid or to Portugal itself; nor was any real improvement effected in 1621 when the viceroyalty of Philip III's reign was replaced by an administration of governors. Hoping to end the constant dissension in Lisbon and to allay Portuguese complaints of royal neglect, Olivares in December 1634 sent out Princess Margaret of Savoy to govern Portugal. But since she was accompanied by Castilian advisers the new government was quick to divide itself into two opposing camps of Castilians and Portuguese, and proved to be even less satisfactory than its predecessors.

Princess Margaret had instructions to introduce into Portugal a fixed annual levy of 500,000 *cruzados* for the country's defence and the recovery of its lost possessions. The new taxes imposed for this purpose created considerable discontent among a populace which had always disliked the union with Castile. The fact that the money was to be used on a fleet being equipped for the relief of Brazil did nothing to reconcile people to payment and in 1637 riots broke out in Evora and other towns. French hopes that the Evora riots would turn into a general revolution were, however, to be disappointed. The popular movement, although abetted by a discontented clergy, had no hope of success without the adherence of the duke of Braganza and of the aristocracy. Braganza was naturally cautious, the aristocracy was faction-ridden, and Olivares was able to bring the disorders to an end by a judicious combination of threats of armed force and a show of leniency.

While the Portuguese risings of 1637 alarmed Madrid, they also convinced the conde duque that Portugal must not be left in its present condition, 'so separate and divided from the rest of the Monarchy . . . with which it refuses to conform'. He therefore summoned to Madrid various influential Portuguese to discuss questions affecting the government of Portugal and the recovery of its empire. Almost at once, however, the Portuguese question was pushed into the background by the still more urgent problem of Catalonia.

The principality of Catalonia, unlike Portugal, occupied a vital strategic position in the war against France. It was an essential base for operations against the French, but in 1636 Olivares had been compelled to abandon plans for an invasion of France from Catalonia partly because of uncertainty over how the Catalans would react. He had on occasions contemplated the use of force against them, only to desist because the time seemed inopportune and the advantages doubtful. His dilemma was aggravated by their behaviour in 1637 and 1638. In the first of these years French troops crossed into northern Catalonia, but the Catalans' contribution to the defence of their own province was belated and ineffective. In 1638 the French invaded Guipúzcoa, and Catalonia alone among the Levantine kingdoms of the Peninsula failed to send troops to the aid of the defending army.

Angered by the recalcitrance of a province which he regarded as the most prosperous in the peninsula, Olivares determined that the Catalans should be made to concern themselves 'as up to now they have apparently not been concerned, with the general affairs of the Monarchy and of these kingdoms'. By choosing Roussillon as his theatre of operations for the campaign of 1639 against the French, he hoped to involve Catalonia's population and financial resources in a war from which the principality had so far stood aside. During the summer and autumn of 1639 the ministers of the viceregal government in Catalonia, under strong pressure from Madrid, harried the principality remorselessly for men and provisions to be sent to the front. When the French finally surrendered the fortress of Salces in January 1640, Olivares had achieved his object of involving the Catalans in Spain's wars, but only at the expense of creating in Catalonia an intense bitterness against his government and against Castile. During February and March of 1640, when the troops which had been fighting in Roussillon were billeted in the principality for the winter season, this bitterness turned to smouldering revolt. In his anxiety to make the most of the wealth which he attributed to the principality, Olivares insisted on the maintenance of the troops by the native population. The Catalan peasantry took its stand on the very specific laws of Catalonia relating to billeting, and refused to comply with the royal orders. Underpaid and underfed, the soldiers either ran wild or deserted. One clash between soldiers and peasants followed another until, by the late spring of 1640, all northern Catalonia was in a state of revolt, and the last trained army of the king in the Spanish peninsula found itself threatened with destruction at the hands of an irate peasantry.

Olivares almost certainly did not intend, as has sometimes been alleged, to employ the billeted army to destroy at a blow the laws and liberties of Catalonia. But he did plan to use this occasion to compel the Catalans to offer troops for service abroad, and to play a part in the war commensurate with their presumed resources. These resources were calculated on the assumption that the population of Catalonia was over 1,000,000. It was in fact under 400,000. Nor was Catalonia as prosperous as a hard-pressed Madrid believed: Catalan trade had suffered severely from the war with France. It was true that agriculture in parts of Catalonia was flourishing, and the coinage was stable, but this did not make the principality a source of unbounded wealth. It did, on the other hand, strengthen the Catalans in their determination to resist exploitation by a country with an impoverished economy and a notoriously unstable currency, for the sake of a cause which in no way interested them. If the Catalans now defied the orders of a viceroy who had become the puppet of Madrid, it was fundamentally because they had no wish to suffer the fate of Castile.

It was only towards the end of May 1640, after an armed force of Catalans had penetrated into Barcelona and released from prison a deputy arrested on the orders of Madrid, that Olivares awoke to the gravity of events in Catalonia. Relying largely for Catalan affairs on the advice of Jerónimo de Villanueva, the protonotario of the crown of Aragon, the conde duque had pursued towards Catalonia a policy based on the conviction that the Catalans had evaded their obligations to their King, and should be compelled to co-operate with the other kingdoms of the monarchy. Now that this policy had driven the Catalans not to co-operate but to rebel, it must hastily be abandoned. A revolution in a region bordering on France would be highly inconvenient at a time when the struggle with Richelieu was nearing its climax, and all the available troops were fully engaged in war with the French. But Olivares' attempts at conciliation came too late. The rebellion in Catalonia was gathering a momentum of its own. Under the energetic leadership of Pau Claris, the Catalan *Diputació*[1] had made its first approaches to the French. On 7 June 1640 riots in Barcelona culminated in the murder of the viceroy, the conde de Santa Coloma. Neither *Diputació*, aristocracy nor municipal authorities were able to restrain the armed gangs which passed from town to town carrying revolution in their wake. When, in late July, the revolt reached the indispensable port of Tortosa, Olivares was compelled to

[1] The traditional standing commission of six entrusted with the task of seeing that the ruler's contractual obligations to the principality were observed.

abandon all hope of conciliation. There was now no alternative to armed intervention—if ever he could find the troops to intervene. 'And my heart admits of no consolation that we are entering an action in which, if our army kills, it kills a vassal of His Majesty, and, if they kill, they kill a vassal and a soldier.'

By the autumn of 1640, therefore, civil war had come to Spain. Since Catalonia was deeply divided by social feuds, its revolt might have been crushed fairly soon, but for the assistance rendered by the French, and the grossly incompetent leadership of the Castilian invading army. The troops of the marqués de los Vélez were defeated outside the walls of Barcelona in January 1641, and there was no army ready to take their place, for on 1 December 1640 Portugal also had come out in revolt.

Portugal's motives for revolution were similar to those of Catalonia, although its immediate grounds for discontent were less. Olivares' attention had been concentrated on the Catalans during the past two years, and the Portuguese had suffered none of that daily harrying by royal ministers which had done so much to aggravate the principality. No large army had been billeted in Portugal, and no war had been fought along its frontiers. But the events in Catalonia encouraged the Portuguese to end a union with Castile which no longer held any attractions, and the conde duque's plan to use the Portuguese nobility in his war against the Catalans made it essential to act with speed. When the duke of Braganza declared himself willing to accept the throne of an independent Portugal as King John IV, there was no further impediment to a movement which enjoyed the sympathies of the mass of the Portuguese, and which no Castilian troops were present to prevent.

The existence of two simultaneous revolts within the Spanish peninsula meant the end of all Olivares' hopes and ambitions. From the end of 1640 Spain and Spain's international power were visibly crumbling. The crown's difficulties in obtaining credit were now acute. The Portuguese Revolution administered one more blow to the confidence and the prospects of the business community of Seville, already faced with the grave problems of a contracting American trade and subjected to all the vagaries of a short-sighted governmental policy, which interfered arbitrarily with the flow of commerce and appropriated at will the private capital of merchants in the name of public necessity. Between 1639 and 1641 Seville's trade was foundering, and the Spanish-American economic system, which had for so long helped to sustain the wildly extravagant foreign adventures of the Spanish Habsburgs, was in process of rapid dissolution. With Seville on the edge of bankruptcy, and the government driven to new inflationary measures, the years 1641 and 1642 were years of frantic price rise in Castile, the premium on silver reaching 120 per cent, until a drastic deflationary scare in September 1642 brought prices tumbling down.

The general discontent with Olivares' government was now no longer concealed. A plot was discovered in the autumn of 1641 which would have made the duque de Medina Sidonia king of an independent Andalusia. Medina Sidonia declared in his confession that the aims of the conspiracy had included the relief of the country from its burdensome taxes, the removal of the conde duque from the control of government, and the restoration of the nobles' Estate in the Cortes of Castile. This was a clear signal that, after twenty years of sullen acquiescence in the government of the conde duque, the great aristocrats of Castile and Andalusia were beginning to stir. The obvious failure of Olivares' policies, and his own increasing signs of mental instability, gave them their long-awaited opportunity. Nobles like the conde de Castrillo, one of the few who had dared to disagree openly with Olivares at the time of his greatness, brought heavy pressure to bear on the king. Finally, on 17 January 1643, Philip IV gave Olivares leave to retire to his estates. His fall from power came only a few months after the death of Richelieu. In Spain, as in France, an epoch had ended.

Little is known about the government of Spain in the period that followed the fall of Olivares, but it would appear to have been a time of aristocratic reaction after the long years of darkness. The control of administration passed into the hands of Don Luis de Haro, the conde duque's nephew, who governed with more circumspection and more attention to the wishes of the aristocracy than his uncle. The twenty years nightmare of the Olivares régime was over. The juntas were abolished, the nobles returned to Madrid. But there was little now that any government could do. The loss of Spain's fleet at the Downs in 1639 and the defeat of the Spanish infantry at Rocroi in 1643 already portended the collapse of Spain's international power. The army's advance into Catalonia was slow and expensive; Portugal was consolidating itself as an independent state, and Spain's Italian possessions were showing signs of restlessness. In 1647 the harvests in Andalusia, New Castile and Valencia were among the worst of the century, and famine was followed, as in 1599, by plague: a devastating epidemic which claimed in 1649 half the population of Seville. The age was ending, as it had begun, in demographic disaster.

Without resources, its credit shattered by bankruptcy in 1647, Haro's government, like that of Lerma forty years before, had no choice but to seek peace with the Dutch. The Peace of Münster brought it precious relief. Its foreign commitments further reduced by the civil wars in France, the régime could now set about recovering something of what Olivares had lost. It was fortunate in that the Catalans' will and capacity to resist were being undermined both by the ravages of the plague, and by internal dissensions and feuds with the French. In October 1652, after a terrible siege, the city of Barcelona surrendered to the royal army, and the principality returned to allegiance to Philip IV on the understanding that its laws and liberties were left inviolate.

It was now the turn of Portugal, but this was a different matter. Better placed by geography than Catalonia, and enjoying both the protection of England and the wealth of Brazil, Portugal was able to preserve its new-found independence against the Spanish attack. The war dragged on, against Portugal as against France; and Castile, as always, bore the brunt of the burden.

Spain's defeats in the 1640s, following upon the revolutions of Catalonia and Portugal, and the palace revolt of the aristocracy, marked the end of an age in which Spain had dominated the affairs of Europe. Olivares' imperialism had represented a return to the imperialism of Philip II, but his reserves of money and manpower were less than Philip's, and his task was proportionately harder. The negligence of Lerma, and Olivares' own failure to carry out the reform programme of the *arbitristas*, had condemned him to look beyond the frontiers of an exhausted Castile for the military and financial assistance he required.

In appealing to the other Peninsular kingdoms, however, Olivares had found himself hopelessly handicapped by the policies of his predecessors. The reaction of the Catalans and the Portuguese to Olivares' demands constitutes a striking commentary on the failure of Spain's sixteenth-century rulers to establish any form of unity among the various kingdoms of which Spain was composed. Catalonia and Portugal revolted against the Olivares régime for essentially similar reasons. Neither their historical traditions nor their economic interests bound them sufficiently close to Castile to make them willing to associate themselves voluntarily with it in a common enterprise. The populace and lower clergy of both countries were instinctively anti-Castilian; their aristocracies saw themselves deprived of the opportunity to obtain offices and honours by the permanent absenteeism of their king; their urban and mercantile classes were increasingly alienated from Castile by the fiscal demands of the conde duque, who had exacted large gifts and loans from the cities of Barcelona and Lisbon. Both countries were afraid that alien forms of government would be imposed upon them, and that they would be sucked into the economic system of a depressed Castile. This was a profoundly unattractive prospect. Catalonia, barricaded behind a stable currency, was still hypnotized by the commercial possibilities of a Mediterranean region whose wealth was slowly ebbing away. Portugal, after the loss of its Far Eastern Empire, had directed its gaze across the Atlantic to the New World. The vitality of some of the Portuguese coastal towns in the first half of the seventeenth century suggested that its hopes were not misplaced, but the gradual exclusion of Portuguese merchants from Castile's American possessions after 1620 made it clear that the economic advantages to be derived from a Castilian-Portuguese union were by now exhausted. None of the Portuguese merchant class in 1640, with the exception of a few crown financiers, had much to gain from a continued association with Castile. The future lay with Portuguese Brazil, which the king of Spain had shown himself too weak to defend. Militarily, as well as economically, the union with Castile had outlasted its value.

Since the unity of Spain had not grown organically, and contained no form of economic or other attraction for the peripheral kingdoms after about 1620, Olivares could only hope to impose it by threats and force. It was too late to convince the Portuguese and Catalans that a close association of the kingdoms of Spain could bring them any real advantages. In the Union of Arms they could see no more than a plan for common impoverishment. Rather than submit, they broke away from allegiance to Philip IV, and Castile discovered that it was no longer strong enough to force them back into the fold. The disintegration of Spain therefore followed as the natural consequence of the decline of a Castile which insisted on retaining and extending its hegemony over the Iberian Peninsula, while no longer possessing sufficient strength for the task.

Yet even if Olivares' schemes for a closer union had succeeded, it is doubtful whether it would have brought the immediate benefits for which he hoped. In his desperate desire to alleviate the sufferings of Castile, he had come to exaggerate the economic resources of the other kingdoms, and the extent to which they might prove of benefit to the crown. But there was about this an irony in keeping with the history of Castile's imperial career. In the sixteenth century Castile had relied upon miraculous benefits from the El Dorado of America; in the seventeenth, it came to expect no less miraculous benefits from the El Dorado of the Spanish periphery. The failure of one miracle demanded the working of another; and, as the grounds for hope were less, so the act of faith was greater. A Lerma had replaced a Philip II, and an Olivares a Lerma, but nothing had changed. Seventeenth-century Castile remained a 'republic of the bewitched, living outside the natural order of things', hoping against hope for the miracle that never occurred. Under the last kings of the House of Austria it died as it had lived, the victim of its own illusions, a Quixote to the last.

CHAPTER XVI

FRENCH INSTITUTIONS AND SOCIETY
1610–61

At the death of Henri IV, his son Louis XIII was not yet nine years old. Kings of France came of age at thirteen and a day, so a regency was necessary. On 15 May 1610 the young king, from his *lit de justice* in the Parlement of Paris, appointed his mother, Marie de Medici, regent, according to his father's wishes. Periods of regency were always difficult for France and seemed to threaten the kingdom's dissolution. Jurists, political theorists and members of the government had a clear concept of the state,[1] not shared by others, least of all by the nobility. They preferred a simpler concept of greater emotional force, loyalty between man and man, inherited from the feudal or remoter past. With the king dead and a child on the throne, it seemed as if every man had regained complete freedom, as if laws no longer existed, as if social obligations, society and the state had died with the king. On hearing of Ravaillac's attack, some nobles took to their fortified chateaux, while others roamed the countryside in bands, plundering, holding men to ransom and seizing the money in the royal coffers. The princes and magnates summoned their followers. In town and country tumult and sedition were rife.

The princes and magnates dreamed of regaining the independence they had enjoyed under Hugues Capet, both in their own domains and in the provincial governorships to which they were appointed by the king (which sometimes became hereditary), and in the apanages granted by the king to the princes and princesses of the royal blood and to queens-dowager. Princes and magnates made use of the division of society into 'vertical' groups of men bound by ties of loyalty. These cut across the other social divisions into orders (clergy, nobility and third estate); into the corporations (universities, companies of officers, ecclesiastical corporations and trade gilds); and into provinces, towns and peasant communities. Each prince and magnate had 'clients', their devoted followers, who had 'given' themselves to a lord to serve him, with arms, counsel, skill or money in all his enterprises—even those against the king or the state. In return they enjoyed his confidence, his friendship, his protection (from the law if need be) his help in securing places at court, commissions in the army, or offices, in making advantageous matches, in gaining ecclesiastical preferment for younger sons and in every sort of social advancement. This system was not strictly speaking feudal, for these

---

[1] See above, Chapter III.

henchmen were not usually given fiefs, nor were they bound to their lord by virtue of holding fiefs. It was based on personal ties reminiscent of commendation. These ties were often strengthened by marriage, for mutual obligations of service and protection were most important within families, which resembled clans in their zeal to win social advantages for their members. Once a member of a family had arrived, he had to bear in mind his cousins to the nth degree. Marriage to the seventh cousin of a magnate carried with it loyalty to the lord and assurance of his protection. A noble sought the hand of a distant relative of Richelieu and was accepted; a few months later, Richelieu married the girl off to another, but offered the younger sister to the gentleman, who replied that it was all one to him: 'I am marrying your Eminence'. These *dévoués* came primarily from the lesser nobility or gentry. But the nobility provided the dominant social ideals to which the king's legal and financial officers, whether members of the sovereign courts or lesser officers, merchants and bourgeois rentiers, municipal oligarchs, all aspired. The gentry in their turn had their own followers, while gentlemen, officers, merchants, bourgeois were all owners of land and seigneurial jurisdictions and employed some country dwellers. They regarded the peasants as their 'men'; thanks to the protection they gave against the royal tax collectors and soldiers, they were very powerful in the countryside. In the towns the magistrates and the royal officers (charged with the regulation of crafts and trades, wages and conditions of work) had so much prestige that they were often followed by the shopkeepers and workers. Princes and magnates naturally had even greater influence. In provinces of which they were governors they appointed to posts such as governorships of towns or fortresses; in apanages, they appointed fiscal and judicial officers. Within their governorships, apanages and domains, the gentry felt themselves to be the magnates' vassals, the more so as some of their fiefs depended on the magnates' fiefs. Consequently, when the princes or magnates gave the signal for revolt, whole provinces rose, and the rebels could count on help from strongholds, towns and the royal coffers.

Revolts by the aristocrats were well received by the discontented provincial gentry, who had often been impoverished by the wars of religion. Their way of life was also ruinous, for to live nobly meant avoiding any profitable activity and much spending on luxuries, presents, feasts, marriages, religious benefactions, on service with the army and at court. Few of the gentry took full advantage of their lands by making the effort to sell grain, cattle and fleeces, as they were entitled to do without derogation. Most of the gentry fell into debt and eventually sold their lands to merchants from the towns, to royal officers, or even to large farmers. Most small or middling fiefs were in the hands of bourgeois or peasants and only the larger fiefs remained in noble hands. In much of the country the feudal system no longer had any meaning and the services attaching to a fief were not performed; in many places such as the regions south of Paris, around Beauvais or Lyons, the proper recipient of such services was not even known. The gentry were also discontented at their exclusion in practice from most offices. They overlooked their general ignorance, to which there were few exceptions so that their handwriting was generally childlike and their spelling phonetic. They blamed the sale of offices and the Paulette or *droit annuel*, a sort of insurance premium, which enabled the holder of an office, or his family, to dispose of the office freely in the event of his sudden death provided the tax had been paid. As a result many offices remained in the same families and their rising prices could only be afforded by officers and merchants.

This picture would need modifications for each region. The rural gentry seem to have been particularly weak in regions where capitalism and trade were most advanced, such as the Beauvaisis, where the class would have died out but for the influx into its ranks of officials and merchants, eager for social advancement. They bought fiefs and were ennobled by letters patent, or by buying offices of royal secretaries, or by repute acquired by three or four generations of living nobly. The nobility survived, but the noble families changed, and the newcomers' outlook was different. The nobility of the Beauvaisis, ruined by the wars of religion, then partly renewed by new families, took no part in the revolts against Richelieu, or in the Fronde.

Elsewhere, for instance in Brittany, Auvergne, Limousin, Quercy and Perigord, the position of the gentry was relatively better, and ties of manorial subjection and feudal homage were stronger. The gentry were more conscious of their obligations to the great families and of their own seigneurial authority over their peasants, to whom they often behaved like tyrants. Almost throughout this period in Auvergne, the marquis de Canillac, like the king, imposed direct and indirect taxes on the peasants and abused his judicial authority by imprisoning unfortunate wretches for trifles, or for no reason, in order to force them to buy their freedom. The Canillacs even dominated the city of Clermont and reduced the king's envoys to despair. There were many other nobles who levied unlawful taxes, imposed *corvées* unjustly and misappropriated the church's tithes.

Royal taxes cut into seigneurial dues when harvests were bad or below average and led nobles to incite their peasants against royal taxation and to attack royal agents. The worst and most frequent revolts were in the provinces where nobles were preponderant.

Fortunately for the king, the gentry did not form organized bodies, or an estate in practice. In certain provinces, such as Auvergne, a syndic of the nobility survived, but the king's consent was necessary for any nomination and its functions must have been only honorific. At the States General of 1614 and during the Fronde, when delegates of the nobility met, the gentry's activities only echoed those of the magnates and princes, lacking any real independence.

The gentry declined, for its military and knightly ideals and its anxiety not to lose caste excluded its members from capitalist commerce. This was the life of the ports—Rouen, Nantes, La Rochelle, Bordeaux, Marseilles; of the cities at crossroads—Lyons, Toulouse, Poitiers, Paris; of towns in the midst of fertile plains with good communications, such as Amiens, Beauvais, Noyon, Soissons. Their merchants and officers dominated considerable surrounding areas both economically and socially. Beauvais may be taken as an example. It has received little attention hitherto, it was not one of the leading industrial or trading towns, so its example is all the more revealing.[1] There a handful of great merchants controlled the whole textile industry. They bought wool from the regions of Noyon, Soissons, Brie, the Beauce, and even from Spain, via Rouen; flax and linen for bleaching from Mayenne, Laval, and Chateau-Gontier, and also from Arras, Tournai and Courtrai in the Spanish Netherlands. They controlled the weaving and processing of textiles in the town and its region, producing fine woollen cloth, comparable according to contemporary evidence with that of Florence until the 'open' war with Spain in 1635, when they turned to hard-wearing serges. They sold their woollens and linen throughout northern France through Rouen and Dieppe to Spain and America and in the Spanish Netherlands before 1635. Thereafter they looked increasingly to Lyons and through Lyons to the East and the Mediterranean. They felt responsible for the livelihood of a vast number of people and in fact gave employment to several thousand persons in Beauvais. These belonged to many categories including the clothier with several looms and weavers, spinners and combers, or the man with one loom, as well as mere day labourers. Many ancillary trades, such as dyers, fullers, shearers, were also employed by clothiers and others. The only ones who were independent of the big merchants were a tiny number of merchant drapers [marchands drapiers drapants] who might have anything from six to twenty looms and all the other equipment needed for finishing the cloth (except fulling and dyeing). They sold directly on the markets of Troyes and Paris, without their goods passing through the hands of the great merchants. Thousands of peasants on the plateau to the north of Beauvais were dependent on the town's merchants. Labourers, who accounted for two-thirds of the village population, wove serge or linen for them in winter. A few owned their own looms and sold their cloth unfinished, but most were given their equipment and raw materials by agents of the merchants and worked for wages, though each might own a cottage and a garden or a field. Throughout the region, women and girls spun wool for Beauvais, Amiens,

[1] See Pierre Goubert, *Familles marchandes sous l'Ancien Régime: Les Danse et la Motte de Beauvais* (SEVPEN, Paris, 1959); and *Beauvais et le Beauvaisis de 1600 à 1730* (Paris, 1960).

Paris, Flanders, Holland and England. The agents of the merchants in the country were often peasants, owning some thirty acres, a couple of horses and a plough, who often served as carriers for textiles and other products. The entire plain owed its living to the merchants of Beauvais. The upper classes were also interested in their activities, for it was from them that the merchants obtained part of their capital, by loans at a fixed interest; the Danse and La Motte families illustrate this.

Moreover, even isolated farming regions with which communication was difficult could be centres of long-distance trade. The parishes of the *Election* of Brive only produced a tenth of the grain they needed. They obtained additional supplies from Quercy, Perigord, Auvergne, and paid for them with money received from the sale of wines at Limoges and of cattle at Bordeaux. Almost the whole of France was involved in a trading economy, and sometimes in commercial capitalism.

Trade might be a family pursuit for two or three generations, but the position of merchant was not the ultimate ideal of this class. The trader bought fiefs and manors, his daughters entered convents or made marriages with officers or minor nobles, his sons might become priests, monks, canons or officers. Then the head of the family would one day give up trade, buy an office in a *Bailliage* or *Election* and become receiver-general of the feudal dues of an abbey. The new officer's son would buy an office conferring nobility, such as that of king's secretary, or councillor of the Parlement of Paris or Rouen, and he would take a title from one of his properties. The son of this new noble might enter the army, buy a company and gain recognition as a true noble. The family would then begin to ruin itself by living in the way fitted to its station, until it had to sell its lands and was replaced by another family. Rise, success, decline and fall covered some five to seven generations in most cases. By 1789 the greater part of the French nobility consisted of families who had begun to rise during our period.

A good example of an officer is Toussaint-Foy, an *élu*,[1] whose fortune was dispersed after his death, in 1660 and 1661. He left 171,000 *livres*. His office accounted for about 6% of this sum—10,000 *livres*—lands and seigneuries at farm 55%, and stocks of foodstuffs 9%. He was receiver-general of the feudal dues of the bishopric-county of Beauvais, of two abbeys and a priory, and possessed 565 quarters of wheat and 229 casks of wine, and had rented five houses in Beauvais to store them. Prices leapt between 1660 and 1662. Wheat, which had cost 27 *livres* in June 1660, rose to 38 *livres* in August and to 42 *livres* in October. Toussaint-Foy had 1,030 obligations owing him, worth 23,113 *livres*, mainly from peasants. 603 were acquired between 1647 and 1653 during the rise in prices during the Fronde. Thanks to a thousand other obligations he had

[1] [The *élection* had a tribunal of some 20 *élus;* it judged cases arising from the *taille* and other taxes and supervised assessment and collection.]

acquired many mortgaged parcels of land and built up seven domains from 1646 to 1657.

Not all the officers were men of culture. Many were mere administrators, whose library consisted of a few works of devotion and some law manuals, but often by the third generation such families produced humanists, jurists and theologians. George le Boucher, of the *Election* of Beauvais, had in his library in 1652: Isocrates, Plato, Plutarch, Cicero, Livy, Seneca, Gregory of Tours, Robert Etienne, Lorenzo Valla, Calvin, the *Satyre Ménippée*, Olivier de Serres, Cardin Le Bret, Jansenius, Antoine Arnauld, 72 folio and 411 quarto volumes and a mass of pamphlets and tracts.

The example of Toussaint-Foy demonstrates another aspect of the domination of town over country: the feudal dues and the debts of the peasants. In years of bad harvest, high prices gave the merchants and officials who received grain in payment of feudal rents a larger profit than in good years, whilst the peasants starved. The structure of society killed some and enriched others. In bad years the small farmer had to borrow to meet all his expenses—food, seed, taxes and dues, from the bigger farmer, often the collector of tithes and dues, or from the merchant or officer who was the local seigneur. The peasant mortgaged his land and was not able to meet his payments until eventually his creditor sold the property. To the peasant it seemed a process of spoliation. In 1664–5, during the special judicial enquiry [*Grand Jours*] in Auvergne, the local peasants thought that the royal commissioners were going to return the lands which they had had to alienate to the seigneurs.

Merchants and officials controlled the municipal institutions, becoming *échevins*, consuls and mayors [members of municipal corporations]. In many towns either the king nominated the mayor, or else the royal officers exercised a close control over the election of the town's magistrates and their activities. In Beauvais the royal officials had much less influence, in spite of the nearness of Paris. The city corporation was elected by an electoral body on which the lower-class textile workers had ten votes and the merchants and officers twenty-one. As a result, from 1600 to 1655, 84 *échevins* out of 116 were merchants and all the mayors except two. The commune saw to the upkeep of the ramparts, defence, allocation of taxes, and had some powers of *police*.[1] The bishop of Beauvais, a count and peer of France, possessed the main judicial authority from which there was the right of appeal to the Parlement of Paris, and the major powers of *police*. The royal *Bailliage* only concerned itself with royal cases, and the *Election* only supervised the division of taxes and fiscal disputes. The local authorities held the workers' lives in their hands. The bishop's *bailli* fixed wages at a low level, which fluctuated

---

[1] [*Police* included many functions wider than the modern meaning, such as regulation of wages, prices, weights and measures, food supplies and holidays.]

slightly and dropped in times of crisis, when prices rose. The worker's life was hard and he was often without bread. At the time of very poor harvests accompanied by epidemics—the time of 'mortalities'—the workers were the worst hit, especially from 1630 to 1632, from 1648 to 1653, from 1660 to 1662. In the poorest quarters of Beauvais the expectation of life was eighteen years. The workers' attitude to the authorities and other social groups was changeable. In times of increasing prices of food there were uprisings against employers and magistrates, which were repressed by the bourgeois militia, of three privileged companies. When the king's demands on the town, or the duties on cloth became too heavy, bourgeois and workers were united against them. In many towns traders and officials incited the workers to revolt and made no attempt to check the disorders. When threatened by foreign invasion, Beauvais again became united. The bourgeois armed and drilled the workers, who formed four companies, commanded by merchant drapers. This happened in 1636, the year of Corbie, several times during the Fronde, notably against the princes in 1652 and again in 1657, when there was an incursion by Spanish cavalry.

In the country 'mortalities' might carry off a third of the population. Day labourers were the main victims, and with the death of many craftsmen there were long economic crises. The 'mortalities' of 1630–2, 1648–53 and 1660–2 had lasting consequences; their effects were cumulative producing destitution and fear of lack of men and resources. Bands of vagabonds descended on the towns and there were peasant risings. Such disturbances were not serious in the Beauvaisis, because both gentry and nobles remained loyal to the king. Indeed it should be noted that revolts mainly occurred if the overlords (gentry, officials, merchants) stirred the peasants up against the various agents of the royal treasury, and a rebellion often began with the murder of some tax-collector.

The king's government was never confronted with a united opposition, although seigneurs, nobles, merchants and officers had a common cause in opposing the king's financial demands which in wartime adversely affected returns from rents and feudal dues. The king, however, had his own loyal followers, his *dévoués* and could rely on them. The nobles despised the bourgeois, who in turn envied them. The officials of the *Bailliages* and of the *Presidiaux* [local royal courts], who were not nobles, were jealous of the officers of the sovereign courts, especially those of the Parlements, who were ennobled by their offices; the *élus* were hostile to the *Tresoriers de France*.[1] Peasants and workers were lacking in class consciousness, towns and provinces were concerned only with their own privileges. What Frenchmen had in common with each other, their social ideals and reasons for living, were all embodied in the

[1] [The *Tresoriers* were more recently created offices, forming the *bureau des finances* which supervised the *élus* and other fiscal officers in each *généralité*.]

king. All oppositions wished to return to outmoded political and social systems, incompatible with the independence and very existence of the kingdom, and with the fuller development of individual self-expression. The king and his supporters, by their efforts to build up the state, represented forces of progress and the future.

Marie de Medici kept the ministers and councils of Henri IV. The main decisions were taken in a secret council, whose members were Villeroi, the secretary of state, Jeannin, president of the Paris Parlement and Sillery, the chancellor of France, but the real government was in the hands of a court clique; the Jesuit Coton, Henri IV's confessor, Ubaldini the papal nuncio, Leonora Galigaï, lady-in-waiting to the Queen, and her husband, the Florentine Concini, who was one of those favourites now more numerous in Europe, because the demands of absolutism were too heavy for many kings. Henri IV's old companion, Sully, resigned on 26 January 1611.

The queen-regent was a foreigner, the king was a child; the new government was content with a policy of peace and alliance with Spain, confirmed by the marriage of Louis XIII to the eldest Spanish infanta, Anne of Austria (Treaty of Fontainebleau, 20 April 1611). In domestic affairs, Marie de Medici wisely made the magnates lead a life of continual celebrations at court and showered bounty on them. Even so, they muttered that the time of kings had passed and that the time of the princes and magnates had come. Their demands were unceasing and finally they revolted. In February 1614 the princes, Condé, Mayenne, Nevers, Bouillon and Longueville, retired to the provinces of which they were governors, raised armies and forced the summoning of the States General. The regent took Louis XIII on a tour of the provinces and the sight of the young king on horseback aroused the enthusiasm of the people. Further, the king was declared to be of age on 2 October 1614. Loyalty to the monarchy revived and the elections were unfavourable to the princes' faction.

The States General met in Paris on 27 October 1614, but were rendered powerless by their divisions. The majority of the Third Estate consisted of officers. The nobles demanded the abolition of the Paulette or *droit annuel*, whereupon the Third Estate demanded the abolition of pensions. Harsh words were exchanged. The *lieutenant-civil*,[1] Henri de Mesmes, had said that 'the three Orders were three brothers, children of a common mother; France'. At this certain gentlemen asserted 'that they had no wish for the children of cobblers and shoemakers to call them brothers, and that there were as many differences between them as between master and servant'. The Third Estate also quarrelled with the Clergy. They wished it proclaimed that the king derived his power directly from God

---

[1] [Chief officer of the civil court at the Chatelet, also responsible for police of Paris.]

and that the pope had no power to depose him; while the Clergy rejected this. The Government dissolved the States General and the representatives went home (February–March 1615). They did not meet again until 1789.

However, the government considered it desirable to announce a reduction in pensions and the abolition of sale of offices. The sovereign courts were also active; on 28 March 1615 the Parlement of Paris decided to summon the princes, dukes, peers and great officers of the crown to consider 'the king's service, the relief of his subjects and the good of his state'. The Parlement was attempting on its own initiative to revive the *curia regis*, or even the assemblies of the Frankish nation, and to intervene freely in affairs of the state. This would have meant the king's permanent subordination to two aristocracies, the nobilities of the Sword and Robe, an aristocratic government, or at least a sort of *Ständestaat*.[1] But the king held himself responsible 'to God alone and to his conscience' and 'as the sovereign power of the Prince is a reflection or lustre of the omnipotence of God, so the power of the officers is a reflection of the absolute power of the prince'. He commanded Parlement to desist. At the same time, 13 May 1615, he deferred the abolition of the sale of offices and allowed officers to retain the Paulette. The sovereign courts calmed down and began to hunt for a way to save their faces. By a decree of 23 May 1615 the princes were declared guilty of *lèse-majesté*.

The ministers were now old men, 'greybeards'. They made peace at Loudun (3 May 1616). Condé and his supporters received large sums of money and Condé became head of the council. He was preparing to assume power and to change the constitution to his advantage. Concini replaced the ministers by energetic men devoted to the royal cause, Barbin, the queen-mother's *intendant*, being controller of finances; Mangot, the first president of the Parlement of Provence, chancellor and Richelieu, bishop of Luçon, secretary of state for foreign affairs (November 1616). The new ministers threw Condé in the Bastille and three royal armies marched against the rebellious princes. A council of dispatches was set up to deal with reports from the provinces, a sort of ministry of the interior, charged with the restoration of law and order. Many *intendants* were sent to the provinces, often with very wide powers, such as judging cases in place of the usual officers, deciding all administrative matters and supervising towns and communes. The council alone had authority over the *intendants* and when the *intendants* came into conflict with the Parlements, the council annulled the latter's decrees. Thanks to these commissioners, the king was no longer dependent on officers who owned their posts. Richelieu negotiated with the German Protestants, who were friendly with the duc de Bouillon and prevented the rebels from raising troops in the empire. He also claimed for Louis XIII the role of arbiter of Christendom.

[1] See above, Chapter III.

This truly monarchical policy was advocated by Concini, but Louis XIII, kept out of affairs and pushed on one side, hated his mother's favourite. With his own favourite, Charles d'Albert de Luynes, he decided to remove him. As the fount of justice, the king could pass sentence of death independently of the courts; *raison d'etat* provided further justification. Vitry, the captain of the guard, was entrusted with the execution of the sentence. On 24 April 1617 Concini was shot down at the entrance to the Louvre. Nobles crowded round Louis XIII, shouting 'Vive le Roi'. Louis XIII recalled the former ministers and Marie de Medici was exiled to Blois. The removal of Concini saved the princes from complete defeat and from unconditional surrender.

Louis XIII felt a great affection for Luynes, making him a duke and peer and entrusting all power to him. But the favourite was undistinguished and he put the kingdom in jeopardy. To satisfy public opinion and above all the officers, he summoned a great assembly of notables to reform the kingdom. In it the officers of the sovereign courts were put on an equal footing with the nobles and as a result of its proposals, a great edict was drawn up in 1618. It limited the powers of the council over the sovereign courts and of the *intendants* over the provinces, but was never strictly applied. Luynes enriched his family and friends, and joined forces with Lesdiguières, Condé and Guise: as a result, the other great nobles in 1620 seceded to their provincial governorships. Mayenne and d'Épernon went to Guyenne and Saintonge and Longueville to Normandy where he made contact with the queen-mother. The government was obliged to restore the Paulette to the officers (it had been suppressed in 1618) to regain their support and won an easy victory at Ponts-de-Cé (August 1620). Luynes embarked on a vast Catholic campaign, supported the Emperor Ferdinand II, helping him to win the battle of the White Hill, and allowed Spain to occupy the Valtelline, contrary to France's real interests. He attempted to restore Catholicism in Béarn and promulgated the Union of Béarn and Navarre, the former personal possessions of Henri IV (1620), with the French crown. The Protestants rose; Luynes as constable besieged Montauban without success and died soon after of purple fever (1621).

Louis XIII was twenty-one and dreamt of greatness and absolute power. When he had reduced the Protestant town of Saint-Jean-d'Angély on 25 June 1621, he had refused to discuss terms with his rebellious subjects. They had been obliged to beg for mercy, which he was then pleased to grant; thus adopting a policy usually attributed to Richelieu. With Luynes out of the way, he began to reform his council in 1622. Although brave, honourable, scrupulous in his religious duties and with a highly developed understanding of the state, Louis lacked political ability. He was not able to restore the foreign situation and left the initiative with the Habsburgs. In home affairs, he could not overcome the Protestant opposition (Peace of Montpellier, 18 October 1622). He regarded the work of Catholic reform demanded by a large section of public opinion as inadequate. Under the influence of St Francis de Sales (*Traité de l'amour de Dieu* (1616) 'a wave of mysticism swept through the élite of French Catholicism'. Prayer was the means of reforming the religious orders. The clergy were often too ignorant and coarse to make good priests; Bourdoise had formed the Community of Saint Nicholas du Chardonnet in 1612, while on 11 November 1611 Bérulle had founded the French Oratory which influenced Vincent de Paul. At the same time libertinism was rife, from 1623–1625 its leading representative being the poet Théophile de Viau, whose collection of obscene verse, the *Parnasse Satyrique*, appeared in 1623. All the young nobles at court followed him. Mersenne thought that there were 50,000 atheists in Paris. The devout were alarmed and called for a strong government to repress libertinism and to give effective support to the 'Catholic Renaissance'.

In turn, Louis XIII tried Condé, the Brûlarts and La Vieuville as ministers. All of them failed when faced with the inconsistent policy of fighting in defence of orthodoxy at home, while attacking the Habsburgs abroad, who claimed to be the champions of orthodoxy. By now Louis XIII was reconciled with his mother who had her favourite, Richelieu, made a cardinal (5 September 1622). Louis was distrustful of him, but the cardinal suggested, via the queen-mother, prospects of glory and the means of achieving greatness for the monarchy. On 29 April 1624 he was admitted to the council and on 13 August, under pressure of public opinion, Louis made him its head, for the defeat of heresy and the House of Austria.

Louis XIII was a conscientious king who knew his limitations. He chose Richelieu from among those who alarmed him to be the instrument for executing his will in return for Louis' unfailing support. The bonds of fidelity were strengthened by the genuine friendship between these two men, both Catholics and both soldiers. Richelieu was a man of action: ambitious, authoritarian, and he gave the hesitant king confidence and the strength to assert his will. By word of mouth and by a profusion of notes and memoranda he explained to the king in minute detail carefully balanced reasons for and against every decision, but it was the king who finally decided. 'These two men devoted themselves entirely to the welfare of France and sacrificed all to *raison d'état*.'

Until 1630 Richelieu was not the absolute master of the council whose members included Marillac, keeper of the seals (1626), the cardinal de la Rochefoucauld, the chancellor d'Aligre, and Schomberg. These men were devoted to the queen-mother, and were more concerned with internal reforms and the struggle against heresy than with opposition to the House of Austria. In 1625, therefore, Richelieu put forward far-reaching plans for reforms, aristocratic in trend: the suppression of the

Paulette and sale of offices and a balance between the three estates in the king's council (though the higher clergy came mainly from the nobility). Richelieu wished to return to a less absolute monarchy, to governing by a great council, with the restoration of the old hierarchies; the magistrates ranking below the old nobility were to be secure in power and social position and so he suppressed many *intendants*. He attacked the propaganda of heretics and libertines, limited the number of printers, forbade private persons to have printing presses and allowed printers outside Paris and Lyons to print nothing but Books of Hours, catechisms, and doctoral theses (1626).

Seeing the need to check the Habsburgs' progress towards hegemony, which would have been followed by a renewal of the conflict between the papacy and the empire, he attacked their lines of communication in the Valtelline and Genoa and subsidized their Dutch and German enemies. As he turned against the Catholic powers, the Protestants chose to rebel at La Rochelle, in the Cevennes and in Upper Languedoc, under the prince de Soubise and Duke Henri de Rohan. Meanwhile the Catholic faction, the queen-mother, d'Aligre and Marillac, advised by Father Bérulle, called for peace with the Habsburgs to leave them free to crush heresy in Europe. The king's brother, Gaston d'Orléans, the Vendômes, bastards of Henri IV, the comte de Soissons, the duc de Longueville and the duchesse de Chevreuse began to plot against the king and Richelieu, while the Spaniards, informed by Anne of Austria, lent their support. Richelieu had to give up his plans against the Habsburgs and come to terms with the Huguenots (5 February 1626) and the Spaniards (Treaty of Monçon, May 1626). This showed Richelieu the necessity of sacrificing everything to secure the king's absolute authority. Louis XIII had one of the conspirators, the marquis de Chalais, beheaded in August 1626, banished Madame de Chevreuse and put aside Anne of Austria. The great nobles were quiescent for a while. The prince de Condé rallied to Richelieu, who abandoned his plans for the nobility, and made it his main concern to appease the high robe and the bourgeois officers. He convened an assembly of notables (1626–7), with a majority of members of the sovereign courts. They protested at the actions of the *intendants* and evocation of cases from the ordinary courts by the royal council; on these points Richelieu was unhelpful, but he dropped his plans for abolishing the Paulette and sale of offices and for balancing the three orders in the council. They went home appeased.

The king's council was divided into several sections, in theory it was one body and its members came mainly from the high robe; the king governed through men who in the eyes of nobles were mere 'bourgeois'. In 1630 the last of a series of decrees completed the reorganization of the council. The king in his Cabinet Council with one or more ministers decided the most important matters which were approved by the *Conseil d'en haut*, comprising the ministers of state, the first minister, the chancellor or keeper of the seals, the superintendent of finances and the secretary of state for foreign affairs. This council was mainly concerned with general policy, but also with anything detrimental to the other councils or concerning public security. It assumed increasing control of finance. The ministers were granted a patent, entered in 'possession' of their 'functions', taking the title of minister after being 'installed'. There were several clerks under their control—their 'servants'. They now received a salary and expenses from the king; real ministers were emerging.

The other councils, concerned with administration and not with general policy, began to form a corps of administrators. The career of André d'Ormesson was typical. After being *maître des requêtes* and therefore *rapporteur* to the council [preparing legal, judicial and other business] he later received his patent and took the oath in April 1615. Before taking up his duties, he was *intendant* in Champagne, and subsequently entered the Council of State and the Privy Council as *quadrimestre* serving three months a year, in 1626. After acting as commissioner to the Estates of Brittany, he was made *semestre* (serving six months a year) in January 1633. He was then promoted and sat on the Council of Finance as well as on the others. In April 1635 he was granted the patent of Councillor-in-Ordinary.

An effort was made to preserve the council's archives in the Louvre, but records were badly kept and the ministers and secretaries of state retained their own papers. Numerous temporary or permanent commissions of councillors prepared the business of the councils. It was from the councils that the king drew most of his commissioners and *intendants*. The king's power depended on ready supplies of bullion. Richelieu therefore proposed to the enthusiastic notables a mercantilist programme which he pursued at least until 1630. In March 1626 he assumed the title of 'Grand Master, Chief and Superintendent General of Commerce and Navigation'. He wished the French to produce and export as much as possible and to buy as few foreign manufactures as possible. Duties were to be removed on imported raw materials and greatly increased on finished goods imported and raw materials exported. He dreamed of making France 'the common warehouse of all the trade of the world' by a Navigation Act and by linking the Sâone and the Loire by means of a canal to avoid the Straits of Gibraltar. He tried to raise trade in the public esteem. The Ordinance of 1629, drawn up by Marillac, allowed nobles to engage in maritime trade without derogation, and ennobled shipowners and merchants of long standing. Richelieu wished to obtain silk and dyes for the textile industry direct from their countries of origin, cutting out the Dutch middlemen. From 1626 to 1628 emissaries, among them des Hayes de Courmenin, bargained with the Barbary pirates, the Sultan and the Bedouins to reopen the Mediterranean–Euphrates route to India and Persia and so damage the Anglo-Dutch trade routes by sea.

This failed and he then attempted to open up a route through the Baltic, the Neva, the Volga, the Caspian and Persia. In 1629 des Hayes de Cour-menin obtained from Denmark a reduction in tariffs in the Sound and the czar gave permission to trade at Archangel, Novgorod, Pskov, and Moscow, with the proviso that the French should obtain Asian produce through Russian traders. Twenty French vessels reached Russia in 1630 and seventy-two in 1631, then war checked trade.

For Atlantic trade Richelieu would have liked to cut a canal from Paris to Rouen, making Paris a sea-port. He dreamed of Canada becoming a 'New France'. He wished to open the Northwest Passage to China with its silk and spices. He set up trading companies; Morbihan (1626), Nacelle de Saint-Pierre fleur de Lysée (1627) and New France (1628). But the war paralysed these attempts.

The royal power was incompatible with the existence of a Protestant state in France. The Protestants were organized in a way not anticipated by the Edict of Nantes, with a general assembly, provincial assemblies, eight military departments, strongholds, a standing army and com-mander-in-chief. A Protestant and a Catholic state united by the king implied a political dualism, the kind of federalism which inspired aristo-cratic movements. The religious party (*dévots*) and its leader Bérulle, a cardinal since 1627, incited Richelieu to attack the leading Protestant town, La Rochelle, the main port in the kingdom, through which they could maintain contact with England and Holland. The time was oppor-tune. The Protestants were growing lukewarm; they were casting doubt on predestination and free-will. Their religion, from being a life in God was becoming a mass of rules and regulations. Among the nobles conversions to Catholicism were numerous. The duc de Lesdiguières turned Catholic and was made constable and given the Order of the Holy Ghost. The duc de la Trémoille became a Catholic just as the siege of La Rochelle began. The Protestants held important financial posts at court and many judicial offices in the south of the kingdom, even whole *présidials*. They were attached to their offices, whose value was increased by the Paulette. They shared the bourgeois mentality of the officers: their legalism, pru-dence, taste for order, love for hierarchy. In the Protestant towns, officials and traders held the monopoly of the municipal offices and feared popular risings. They also feared the dictatorship of the duc de Rohan during a civil war. They desired peace and order.

In 1627 the inhabitants of La Rochelle revolted, instigated by England. Only a small number of southern Protestants followed them. The duke of Buckingham landed on the Ile de Ré, but in November Louis XIII and Richelieu forced the withdrawal of the English and, to stop them relieving the town by sea, Richelieu built a large mole bristling with cannon. The English fleet was repulsed on 11 May 1628 and the starving town surrendered after a heroic resistance: the king entered it on 1 November.

The war continued in the south, but the English came to terms at Suze, 24 April 1629. Rohan signed a military alliance with the king of Spain (3 May) but it was in vain, and the plight of the Protestants was desperate. The king refused to treat with his subjects, but on 28 June 1629, by the Grace of Alais, the rising was forgiven and the Edict of Nantes reaffirmed, but the edict alone: all the fortifications of the rebels were razed, the Protestant organization broken up and the duc de Rohan was obliged to go into exile. The Protestant state ceased to exist.

Meanwhile the council was endeavouring to introduce reforms. The Chancellor de Marillac presented a first list in January 1629. These limited the power of the high robe by the suppression of the sale of offices in the royal households and in the army, by restricting the power of remonstrance of the Parlements, which could only delay edicts for two months and by legalizing the position of the *intendants*. Richelieu announced the council's intention not to renew the Paulette, granted for nine years, when it expired in a year's time. 'The Parlements were enraged and the situation of the kingdom became revolutionary'. After the fall of La Rochelle the king had had to intervene in Italy against the Habsburgs and taxation had to be increased. From 1626 to 1628 there was a sharp drop in agricultural prices causing difficulties for farmers. After 1628 a succession of bad harvests caused grain prices to shoot up and famine was accompanied by epidemics of 'plague'—the great 'mortality' of 1630–2. There had already been popular disturbances in 1627 and 1628. The royal officers, burdened with forced loans and capital payments for increased salaries, did nothing or secretly connived at disturbances. In 1629 and 1630 even the sovereign courts openly rebelled, broke open the royal coffers, seized their arrears of salaries and incited the people to plunder the army grain stores or to attack the *intendants*. Armed risings by peasants and craftsmen grew in number and seriousness. It was impossible to wage war and reform the kingdom simultaneously. Richelieu offered the king the 'great choice'. Louis XIII could follow the religious party (*dévots*), Marillac and the queen-mother, make peace with Spain, decide to wipe out heresy in his realm, respect the rightful possessions and liberties of his subjects and try to make his people happy. Richelieu pointed out that it was not possible to achieve conversions by force, that the safety of the kingdom and the independence of the country were the greatest of all goods and that the Habsburg threat had to be removed before reforms could be considered. The king followed Richelieu and (21 May 1629) appointed him 'principal Minister of State'. In April 1630 he took the decisive step by refusing to yield Pinerolo the gateway to Italy, therefore opting for a long war against the Habsburgs and giving up 'all thought of rest, economy and re-ordering of the domestic affairs of the kingdom'. At first he waged a hidden war by supporting the enemies of the Habsburgs—the United Provinces and Gustavus Adolphus—and by attacking lines of communication; then after the defeat of the Swedes at Nördlingen he embarked on 'open' war with Spain and the empire.

Marie de Medici was shocked by Richelieu and made several attempts to secure his dismissal. On 10 November 1630, during a painful scene between herself, the king and the minister, she thought she had succeeded. On 11 November the courtiers hastened to her and loaded her with compliments, but the king assured Richelieu of his trust in him, and next day the news came that Marillac had been arrested and Richelieu was all-powerful. After this 'Day of Dupes' Marie was obliged to go into exile for the last time and Gaston d'Orléans retired to his apanage to foment rebellion. The king declared his brother's accomplices guilty of *lèse-majesté*, but the Parlement of Paris refused to register the declaration and so authorized rebellion. The king banished some officers of the Parlement and forbade it to meddle in affairs of state, but also abandoned the ordinance of 1629, restored the Paulette to office-holders and maintained the sale of offices. The sovereign courts deserted the rebels and registered the fiscal edicts. Gaston d'Orléans incited Henri de Montmorency, governor of Languedoc, to revolt: they were defeated at Castelnaudary (1 September 1632). Henri was beheaded and Gaston fled to Brussels, married Marguerite of Lorraine, the sister of the duke, an enemy of France, and was a continual source of difficulties. Attempts were made to have the marriage annulled but eventually (8 October 1634) Gaston yielded and returned to France.

Richelieu had had his hands free since 1630. The main task of the reign was to be the struggle against the Habsburgs. This drove Louis XIII and Richelieu to dictatorship for war with arbitrary, centralized, egalitarian government which unintentionally began revolutionary changes. The solution of two problems guided all the government's actions: those of finance and of national morale and intelligence with the enemy.

The sovereign courts delayed the ratification of financial measures by presenting seven or eight remonstrances on fiscal edicts. In order to break this resistance and to end their refusal to grant essential credits, the king gave the council power over the courts in his absence. From 1632 the council had power to annul, on its sole authority, any decree of the courts conflicting with the public interest or the crown's authority. Moreover, by an edict of 21 February 1641 the king finally reduced the number of remonstrances to two before registration in financial matters, while they could only be made after registration in matters of state. He restricted the courts to their judicial functions: 'You have been established only to judge between Master Peter and Master John . . . and if you continue your ventures, I shall clip your nails so close that you will repent it.'

In the provinces the king was dissatisfied with his financial officers.

He complained that they showed excessive respect for legal forms. The treasurers of France refused to sanction the levying of taxes when the edicts had not been verified by the sovereign courts and were able to do so because they formed companies, empowered to make remonstrances. Further, these officers, who regarded the offices they owned primarily as dignities giving them a position in the society of the time, were held to be negligent and indolent. In 1634 the *intendant* de Vertamont found some officers at Bordeaux who could give him no information on the taxable value of parishes and who had made no changes in the assessments of the *taille* for sixty years. It was said that the *élus* under-assessed taxes on parishes where their friends, relations or superiors had lands or houses or farmers, and overburdened the rest. They looked the other way when the rich and influential taxpayers, the 'cocks of the parish' or nobles' farmers, were spared and the poorest were crushed. The taxes, being levied on those unable to pay, could not be collected. The nobles, seigneurs and officers took the inhabitants into their strongholds when the bailiffs arrived, guarding goods, crops and cattle from distraint and driving off the revenue officials if need be with firearms. Incited by seigneurs and nobles whole parishes rose. The royal judges made no effort to punish the guilty, but helped to cover their escape and to conceal them. In order to increase the income from taxation, to ease the lot of the 'weakest and most helpless' and prevent revolts, after 1633 the government made increasing use of commissioners sent to the provinces to assess taxes more equitably between the parishes and between individual taxpayers. These tasks were for preference entrusted to *maîtres de requêtes* and to *intendants* of justice, police and finances, who had new financial powers in addition to their other powers. Their missions were temporary and local. Whenever necessary the *intendants* performed the functions of the treasurers of France, *élus* or *assesseurs-collecteurs* [parish assessors and collectors of *taille*], while exercising general supervision over all the officers and the whole population. These missions became increasingly frequent and finally the decree of 22 August 1642 and the declaration of 16 April 1643 transferred all the duties of the financial officers as well as those of ordinary jurisdictions in financial matters to the *intendants*: they were given wide powers to punish the recalcitrant. The 'companies' of financial officers remained, but their functions became merely formal and the *intendant* was empowered to ignore them in certain circumstances, so that they lost their power of remonstrance and resistance. They provided the *intendant* with a reserve of men from whom he could choose experts loyal to the king. It was an expedient, but the war made it last and turned it into an institution.[1]

[1] See Roland Mousnier, 'Etat et Commissaire. Recherches sur la création des intendants des provinces (1634–48)', *Forschungen zu Staat und Verfassung, Festgabe für Fritz Hartung* (Berlin, 1958).

To keep up the morale of the nation, Louis XIII and Richelieu made extensive use of political surveillance. In addition to the reports sent to Richelieu, the Chancellor Séguier and the secretaries of state by commissioners, *intendants*, the king's advocates and by secret agents in all the companies of officers and municipal corporations, Richelieu had had his spies and emissaries everywhere. Every morning at his *lever*, the governor of the Bastille and master of posts, and the *lieutenant-criminel* [chief officer of the criminal court] told him of the rumours of Paris and the behaviour of the prisoners. The *intendants* were ordered to prepare cases against enemies of the state. Isaac de Laffemas, the 'Cardinal's hangman', was notorious for his ability to build a case of *lèse-majesté* on the slightest evidence and to extract confessions. Judgement was passed by a commission of the council which often condemned on presumption of guilt. For the king, the cardinal and the council all agreed that with conspiracies it was almost impossible to obtain rigorous proof and that it would be fatal to wait on events. The government made more use of preventive detention of unlimited duration than of extraordinary courts. Men were imprisoned by *Lettre de cachet* alone and the Bastille was bursting with illustrious prisoners: the comte de Crammaing, the Maréchal Bassompierre and Baradas, who, surprisingly, was one of Louis XIII's favourites. Louis XIII and Richelieu appreciated that it was impossible to control the kingdom by force alone and tried various methods of propaganda to influence public opinion and win its support. They made use of the press. Pamphleteers such as Fancan, Pelletier, Ferrier and Sancy defended royal policy, as did the academicians Hay du Chastelet, Jean Sichon, and Sirmond. After 1631 Théophraste Renaudot published a weekly, the *Gazette*, a sort of official journal: Richelieu sent him news and Louis XIII wrote articles. The *Mercure Français* gave the official history of France and Europe.

Louis XIII and Richelieu were in favour of classical art, with its aesthetic of unity and hierarchy, as against the baroque, embodying diversity. Moreover the lead given to the nation by the king and his minister, the feeling of belonging to a great nation in the process of making the old humanist dream of Gallic hegemony come true were an inspiration, and numerous major works of art appeared from 1630 to 1642 (Corneille, Descartes, Poussin, Philippe de Champaigne, etc.). Richelieu nationalized a group of men and letters, became its protector, augmented it with councillors of state and made it into the Académie Française, whose task was to provide him with polemicists and to make the French language and its literature the first in Europe. The academicians envisaged the time when the French language, carried forward by French arms, would become the tongue of the whole civilized world. It was the desire for glory which led the king and his minister to build the Pavillon de l'Horloge at the Louvre (Le Mercier), the Sorbonne church (1635–42), the Chateau de Rueil, the Chateau de Richelieu and a sort of Versailles, also the work of Le Mercier, the town of Richelieu. In 1641 the king set up an academy or royal college there. Richelieu gave it an encyclopaedic syllabus which anticipated that of the central schools of the revolution.

Richelieu would have liked to control Catholicism. He improved the recruitment of bishops; as abbot of Cluny (1629), of Cîteaux (1637) and administrator of Chezal-Benoit, he reformed the Benedictine monasteries. He tried to give effect to the canons of the Council of Trent. Monks were obliged to recognize their subjection to the diocesan bishop. He would have liked the pope to make him patriarch of the Gauls, but it was not to be and the religious movement passed him by almost entirely—the mystics, the Oratory, St Vincent de Paul, the Company of the Blessed Sacrament (a secret society set up in 1629) and the foundations by nobles or high robe of charitable organizations. The whole of this minor 'Renaissance' of Catholicism passed him by and indeed the majority of the religious party (dévots) were among his adversaries. Among these were Caussin, the king's Jesuit confessor, exiled in 1637, the followers of Bérulle and the first Jansenists, including Saint-Cyran, whom he imprisoned at Vincennes. After 1635 Saint-Cyran's influence at the monastery of Port Royal grew enormously. From 1637 laymen, the 'messieurs', began to gather around Port Royal des Champs and Saint-Cyran was able to form a sort of party from his prison.

Richelieu was not able to prevent numerous revolts. Taxation was too heavy. He had been obliged to increase the taille from 17,000,000 to 69,000,000 livres, to multiply indirect taxation in order to make the rich contribute and to burden officers both with creations of offices which lessened the importance of existing offices and with forced loans never to be repaid. In 1633 the income from the sale of offices provided 52 per cent of the receipts, but loans also had to be raised from financial officials, financiers and tax farmers to whom royal demesne and future tax receipts were pledged. These taxes and the fortunes made by financiers enabled Richelieu's enemies, aristocrats, officials, dévots, to rouse discontent by pamphlets, remonstrances and rumours and to stir up revolts against taxes and the king. In Paris the journeymen of the gilds rose in 1633; at Lyons the populace plundered the customs offices (1633, 1642). At Rouen the rope-makers and paper-makers attacked the office of the tax-farmer (1634), the textile workers pillaged the office of the treasurers of France and stormed the house of Nicholas le Tellier, receiver-general of the gabelle, in 1639. In the country the 'croquants' (mainly peasants) rose in Limousin, Poitou, Angoûmois, Gascony, Perigord, hacked a tax collector to pieces and dismembered a surgeon whom they mistook for a revenue official (1636). The 'Va-nu-pieds' [barefoot ones] rose in Normandy in areas where the government wished to introduce the gabelle (1639). The king's armies had to be sent everywhere and there were some real battles (La Sauvetet d'Eymet, June 1637). The Chancellor Séguier himself went to Rouen to attend to the execution of the rebels, to suspend the Parlement and the *Cour des Aides* [appeal court for fiscal cases] and to abolish the positions of mayor and *échevin*, as these officers had not acted with sufficient severity.

Meanwhile the king's health was deteriorating and he gave Richelieu more and more freedom of action. The latter surrounded the king with his own men, Father Joseph, the 'grey Eminence' (d.1638), Superintendent Bullion (d. 1640), the secretaries of state, Claude and Leon Bouthillier, Séguier and the Neapolitan Jules Mazarin. Richelieu had formed a retinue of loyal followers who had sworn to be faithful to him and who received appointments everywhere. The king was alarmed to see his captains leave him and pass into the cardinal's service. He foresaw the time when he would not be able to command obedience in his kingdom except through Richelieu and his men. The cardinal was founding a dynasty: he made his relations marshals of France, generals of galleys, governors, dukes and peers. He made one of his nieces duchesse d'Aiguillon: another married the duc d'Enghien and became a princess of the blood. He owned fortresses which he left to his heirs, at Brouage and Le Havre; he had a company of infantry and another of gentlemen. He took precedence over princes of the blood and began to behave like a mayor of the palace of late Merovingian times.

If Cinq-Mars had been content with attempting to have the cardinal killed, without plotting with the duc d'Orléans and the duc de Bouillon and without negotiating with Spain for the support of Spanish troops in return for restoring French conquests, Louis XIII might not have put him to death (12 September 1642). Richelieu, worn out, died on 4 December 1642. At the king's death (14 May 1643) he had gained Artois, Roussillon and Alsace. Spain and the empire had been defeated and negotiations for peace had begun. The king of France was regarded as 'one of the greatest monarchs in the world' and he was convinced that with his minister he had preserved the independence of France, liberty and the balance of power in Europe.

Louis XIV was four years old, having been born on 5 September 1638. Louis XIII, suspicious of Anne of Austria, had regulated the regency by a declaration of 20 April 1643. He was unable to prohibit the queen from becoming regent, the duc d'Orleans lieutenant-general of the kingdom, and Condé head of the council, but he also appointed four irremovable councillors, all Richelieu's men: Cardinal Mazarin, as chief minister, Séguier, the chancellor, Bouthillier, superintendent of finances, and the latter's son, Chavigny. All decisions required a majority vote. Unfortunately this declaration was unconstitutional. As soon as the king was dead, his successor assumed the royal powers in full and could not be bound by any act of his predecessor. The queen took advantage of this. On 19 May 1643 Louis XIV held a *lit de justice* in the Parlement to make his mother regent with full freedom to constitute the council as she wished and without being bound by the majority. Anne of Austria kept her favourite, Cardinal Mazarin, as first minister, but a good many Frenchmen despised this upstart foreigner. The troubles began again, as during every royal minority, but were graver than in 1610. After the 'harsh Richelieu' who, in de Retz's words, 'had blasted men rather than governed them', after the hard and implacable Louis XIII, everyone relaxed and many thought themselves dispensed from obedience. All the exiles returned and, led by Mme de Chevreuse, intrigued against Mazarin, who imprisoned the duc de Beaufort in Vincennes and exiled the 'Cabale des Importants' (September 1643) but agitation continued. The queen was obliged to provide the magnates with endless festivities and to admit a large number of nobles to the Council of State so that its efficiency was impaired. Séguier lamented that 'each day saw a new Councillor of State . . . it was like the aftermath of a shipwreck, with bits of wreckage washed up on the shore every day . . . all confusion and disorder'. The king's minority, disturbances and risings helped to prolong the war against the emperor until 1648 and against Spain until 1659, while the war worsened financial difficulties and in turn aggravated domestic disorders.

After the death of Louis XIII, resistance to taxation increased. Seigneurs and nobles were constantly inflaming the peasants against taxes and gave an example by driving the agents of the tax-farmers from their lands by force of arms, encouraging their peasants to do the same, spreading false rumours about the restoration or abolition of taxes and hiding the rebels, even if guilty of murder, with the support of the bourgeois magistrates. The *intendants'* reports to Séguier leave no doubt that it was not the poorest or most heavily taxed parishes which rebelled, but those where the gentry stirred up trouble, with a view to increasing their own rents in money and in kind. Such was the case in Normandy, Touraine and Limousin—where M. and Mme. de Pompadour excited the peasants of fifty or sixty parishes belonging to them to uprising—in Auvergne, Angoûmois, Aunis, Saintonge, Poitou and Perigord in 1644. From 1643 to 1644 there were continual peasant risings in the west, the centre and the south, the northern and eastern limits of the risings passing through Normandy, Berry, Auvergne and the Dauphiné. The peasants refused to pay their taxes, drove out the tax collectors, threatened the financial officials, seized several chateaux and threatened towns, at the instigation of the nobles.[1]

The royal officers endeavoured to guarantee the safety of the rebels,

[1] See R. Mousnier, 'Recherches sur les soulèvements populaires en France avant la Fronde', *Revue d'Histoire Moderne et Contemporaine*, Vol. v (1958).

intervening against the *intendants* and hiding the guilty. The Parlement of Rouen quashed a judgement given by the *intendant* de la Potherye, forbade the *lieutenants-criminéls* from acting and made it impossible for anyone to be arrested (June 1643). The *Cour des Aides* of Paris on 21 July 1643 verified the royal declaration of 16 April on the financial powers of the *intendants*. The court endeavoured to subordinate the *intendants* to it by obliging them to submit their commissions for registration and possible modification. They attempted to assert the principle that the royal commissioner—an instrument of absolutism—was subordinate to the ordinary courts, the guardian of the old laws and established customs. The *Cour des Aides* amended the declaration so as to maintain the traditional role of the treasurers of France and the *élus* and to protect seigneurs and nobles.[1]

The government was obliged to have recourse again and again to the tax-farmers and financiers [*traitants et partisans*], who were granted in return the right to collect the *taille*, to sell offices, to farm domains and to levy an incredible number of taxes. The tax-farmers demanded that the taxes should be assessed promptly and that their agents should be backed by decrees of the *intendants*, summary justice and armed force. The government therefore employed an increasing number of *intendants;* thirty or thirty-five performed most of the duties of [the treasurers of France and *élus* throughout the country. They used regiments of cavalry and infantry, passing through or quartered in their districts, or raised special troops, fusiliers or carabineers, to crush resistance and raise taxes. They marched in, besieged the rebels, hanged the most guilty and were accused by their adversaries of 'ruining parishes and desolating provinces more surely than if they had been enemy troops'.

The action of the council and the *intendants* affected the officers so that their honour and their pockets both suffered; for apart from their salaries they also received fees or a percentage of receipts, according to their duties. They also complained about the excessive sums levied on them and the multiplying of offices. The treasurers of France claimed that on the death of Henri IV, there were ten of them to each *bureau des finances*, while in 1648 the number was twenty-five and the market price of their offices had fallen by two-thirds. Moreover they had paid the king over 30 million *livres* for increased salaries, taxes and dues. The *élus* claimed to have disbursed over 200 million *livres* since 1624, including 60 millions since 1640 'for confirmations of an imaginary right or of a fictitious supplement'. Since 1640 the government in desperation had cut salaries and dues, first a cut of a quarter's salary for the *élus*, whose salaries were whittled down to nothing by 1647, depriving

[1] Mousnier, 'Recherches sur la création des intendants des provinces', *Forschungen zu Staat . . .*

them of three-quarters of the dues for which they had paid such vast sums. The treasurers of France, officers of *Bailliages*, *Sénéchaussées* and *Présidiaux* were all subjected to the same levies.[1] This had the unexpected result that posts became increasingly hereditary, fixed within one family. The officers assessed the value of their posts by reckoning all they had paid out for increases in salaries and allocations of dues: there were twenty to fifty in the lifetime of an officer. Their valuation of the offices became so high that they were impossible to sell, for the market price was much lower. This was common after 1635 and particularly towards 1648. Families were thus forced to keep offices, which were more in the nature of a burden and which by preventing any purchases of higher offices blocked any rise in social status.[2]

It is not surprising that the Fronde began in 1648 with a revolt of public servants. The Parlement was for ever raising and dashing hopes by its remonstrances. It argued that the war concerned the king alone and was prolonged only by the will of the government. This was the more readily believed, since Mazarin had more than once boasted that peace was in his hands. The Parlement held that the financial deficit was caused by the speculations of financiers and the extravagance of the court and asserted that economies would balance the budget. Its opposition increased in 1648 over the renewal of the authorization to pay the Paulette,[3] granted for periods of nine years, which had expired on 31 December 1647. The government renewed it on 30 April 1648, but kept back four years' salaries from the officers. The Parlement was exempt from this deduction, but it associated itself with the other sovereign courts. The Decree of Union, 13 May 1648, decided that deputies should be elected by the four sovereign companies of Paris, to meet in the Chambre Saint Louis, to discuss the reform of the state. The treasurers of France and the *élus* joined the movement, the latter having formed a syndicate in 1641, while the treasurers had been organized in an association since 1599 for the defence of their professional interests, with two representatives at Paris. After May 1648 most of the *bureaux des finances* had a delegate at Paris, where they formed a permanent assembly. On 30 June the Chambre Saint Louis proposed the recall of the *intendants* and all royal commissioners, abolition of the farming of the *taille* and its reduction by a quarter; the restoration of the old financial officers to their full functions and powers and a ban on the creation of new offices. New fiscal edicts should be registered by the courts only after free votes and discussion, while the taxes should be levied by the sovereign courts. Imprisonment of anyone for more than twenty-four hours, without

[1] See F. Mousnier, 'Recherches sur les Syndicats d'officiers pendant la Fronde', *XVIIᵉ Siècle*, Nos. 42–3 (1959).
[2] P. Goubert, 'Les officiers royaux des Présidiaux, Bailliages et Elections', *ibid*.
[3] See above, p. 476.

interrogation and being delivered to his rightful judges was forbidden. Thus control of administration and political life, the sinews of government, would have been transferred to the sovereign courts and in particular to the Parlement of Paris, which claimed to be the true king's council, an epitome of the States General, the descendant of Frankish popular assemblies, the representative of the kingdom.

The example of Paris was followed in the provinces; Parlements, companies of officers and towns rebelled in many places. In July 1648 the government was forced to give the proposals of the Chambre Saint Louis legal force by edict. After the victory of Condé at Lens the council decided on the arrest of the main leader of the Parlement, Broussel. On 26, 27 and 28 August 1648 Paris rose in his support.

The barricades forced the government to release Broussel and to reaffirm on 22 October 1648 the constitution of the Chambre Saint Louis. The *intendants* were only to be kept to supervise army matters in six frontier provinces: Languedoc, Provence, Lyonnais, Burgundy, Champagne and Picardy.

The people lit bonfires in many places anticipating a general remission of taxes. The Treaties of Westphalia passed by unremarked, but the court summoned Condé and his troops, fled from Paris and civil war began, called the 'Fronde' after the name of a children's game (5–6 January 1649). Passions were roused against the favourites around the king who engrossed absolute power, betrayed and sold the people, above all against Mazarin. Hence demands that the Parlement should appoint and dismiss the members of the Council of State, which should abide by majority decisions, and that government by a chief minister and his clients should cease.

The civil war coincided with a great 'mortality' (1648–53) resulting from bad harvests and a calamitous rise in the price of grain. The food crisis was followed in many places by crisis in textile industries whose sales collapsed. The political disturbances erupted before this crisis. The continual passage of troops, pillage, arson, taxes and dues levied by rebels as well as by king's men, all helped to make the economic situation worse and to increase disorder. In the country men were reduced to eating earth, husks, rags, even to gnawing their own hands and arms. Unburied corpses infected the air, the 'plague' ravaged the starving people and France was depopulated. At Verdun-sur-le-Doubs in Burgundy there were 86 births and 72 deaths in 1648, but 37 births and 224 deaths in 1652. The economy was in chaos. Twenty to thirty years later, under the personal government of Louis XIV, there was a decrease in marriages and births due to the coming of age of the depleted generation of children born during the Fronde.

The government could not defeat Paris and the parliamentary Fronde ended in March 1649 with the Peace of Rueil. The declaration of October

1648 was confirmed. Then Condé, as a victorious general and a prince of the blood, demanded honours, offices and money for himself and his men. He was arrested with the princes de Conti and de Longueville (January 1650), and the princes' Fronde began. Mme de Longueville raised Normandy and the princesse de Condé Guyenne and Bordeaux. The Spaniards invaded France and threatened Paris. The princes' supporters asserted that the fundamental laws of the state prevented the queen-mother from being made regent and demanded that a council of princes, great officers of state and members of magnate families, should exercise power during the king's minority. They accused Mazarin of holding the king prisoner and of ruling France as a tyrant. Bordeaux however had to yield in October and the Spaniards were defeated at Rethel, 15 December. In the provinces the government went on employing various commissioners, *maîtres de requêtes*, councillors of state and officers of the *Cour des Aides*. In Champagne, in 1650, Pagès was simultaneously *intendant* of justice, police and finance for the army in Champagne and *maître des requêtes* on tour, which empowered him to supervise all royal officers, while as commissioner-general for troops' victualling he had wide powers in financial matters.

However, Mazarin had been able to arrest the princes by making promises to the other nobles. When he did not keep his word, all the magnates united against him and he had to flee (6–7 February 1651). During that year the *intendants* disappeared and other commissioners became less numerous. The nobles demanded the summoning of the States General and the delegates were elected, but never met. The rebels again quarrelled among themselves. The Parlement did not want the States General. Condé broke with the other magnates and had to flee Paris in September and at the same time the king was declared of age. Condé formed an alliance with Spain and was declared a rebel and traitor. The war was carried into his own governorship of Guyenne and the royal army repulsed the prince.

Mazarin thought it possible to return in December 1651, with an army recruited in Germany. Many Frenchmen loathed him: carters styled a vicious horse *bougre de Mazarin*. The union of malcontents, Gaston d'Orléans, Condé and the Parlement was revived. What was more, there were casuists to argue that the prince's revolt was justified by natural law, for he had taken arms in self-defence and it would be right to support him. His appeal to Spain was justified, for as he was waging war he was entitled to exploit the stratagems of war. The Spaniards were not the real enemies, for it was 'Mazarin's cabal' which prevented peace! Condé found allies in the Parlement of Bordeaux, the town council and the democratic faction of the city, '*L'Ormée*'. These last wished to come to terms with the English and the Spaniards. General war broke out anew in the terrible year 1652. From February to July there were military operations all round Paris and the monarchy was saved by a handful of faithful (*dévoué*) captains. The royal forces were victorious at Blénau and Etampes. After the arrival and prudent withdrawal of the duc de Lorraine in June and the battle of the Porte-Saint-Antoine (1 July), the princes were besieged in Paris. The revolution of 4 July saw the formation of an insurgent government, with Broussel as head of the municipality of Paris, Orléans as lieutenant-general of the kingdom and Condé as commander-in-chief of the insurgent armies. During this year the most extreme political projects for replacing the king and organizing a *Ständestaat* were produced.[1] The princes proved incompetent and only concerned with selfish interests. In addition to the divisions within the aristocracy and the hostility of the Parlement to the States General, there were struggles between the various officers. The treasurers of France opposed the *élus*, the chambers of accounts [*chambres des comptes*] and the *Cours des Aides*. Each company sought to increase its importance at the expense of its rivals and nothing constructive emerged from rebellion and opposition, instead the kingdom was disintegrating. In the Soissonnais whole villages put themselves under the protection of nobles and seigneurs, offering rents or voluntary submission to *banalités* in order to escape the exactions of the troops. Even in areas near Paris, such as Beauce, the royal courts may have ceased to function. The civil wars revived features of the ninth and tenth centuries, due to Norman, Hungarian and Moslem invasions, producing a spread of commendation, a growth of seigneurial and feudal power built on the ruin of the state. The members of the council alleged that the treasurers of France and the *élus* had made the collection of taxes even more chaotic and that the people now regretted the *intendants*. Clearly there was general weariness and in August 1652 Mazarin went into exile to clear the way for the rebels to submit; Paris was reconciled with the king. Broussel was obliged to resign, Paris refused supplies to the troops of Condé and the duc de Lorraine and they decamped on 13 October. The king returned on 21 October to an accompaniment of splendid but expensive celebrations. In February 1653 Mazarin returned; on 3 August Bordeaux surrendered and the Fronde was over. The state had been saved, but was still tottering. The civil war and the economic crisis had plunged the country into appalling poverty. The Company of the Blessed Sacrament engaged in the struggle against famine; its most active members were Jansenists (the duc de Liancourt and the magistrate Charles Maignart de Bernières). Its best auxiliaries were the Ladies of Charity and Vincent de Paul and his missionaries, whose travels round the country discovered those in need of help. The company diminished the hardships, but after 1653 internal disputes between the Jansenists and their enemies made it less effective.

---

[1] See above, Chapter III, pp. 121–2.

The peasants and workers were the hardest hit. On the other hand there were profiteers, among them the great merchants, textile manufacturers, who had found a profitable outlet for their goods by supplying the troops or by finding foreign markets. More fortunate were the landowners, merchants or officers, who made loans to peasants in need and acquired their lands strip by strip in cancellation of their debts. The period of the Fronde apparently saw a large-scale transfer of land from peasant to bourgeois hands in many regions. But the biggest profits were made by tax-farmers and financiers. 'The fine air of their town and country houses, the beauty of their parks, the dignity of their furnishings, the glitter of their clothes and jewels, all this splendour of gold dazzled and corrupted the nobility and the magistracy ... France at this time was really a plutocracy ...' (Lavisse). Their protector and partner was Fouquet, the *surintendant des finances*. In the process of financing the state by endless expedients he inextricably confounded his personal fortune with his official balances. His house at Saint-Mandé was a source of wonder, while his chateau at Vaux-le-Vicomte, with decorations by Le Nôtre, Le Brun and Poussin excelled even the Versailles of Louis XIV as a work of art. His collections, drawn from all over the world, had an Arabian Nights air. He kept open table, was the patron of writers such as Corneille, Scarron and La Fontaine and was highly successful with the ladies. The salons of his wife and his mistress, Mme du Plessis-Bellières, were prominent in society. 'He was the Maecenas of France during the childhood of Augustus.' His motto was *Quo non ascendet* and the ceiling of his library was decorated with an eagle with wings outstretched. As well as *surintendant*, he was the *procureur-général* of the king to the Parlement and had founded a dynasty and a following among the nobility and the clergy. In 1658 he bought Belle-Isle-en-Mer which he converted into a fortress. His friends called him 'The Future'. He had conceived the main parts of Colbert's programme and was preparing plans for civil war.

The government was slow in regaining its authority. From the end of 1653, the *intendants* gradually returned to the provinces, but the government had to proceed with caution. The instructions for Le Febure, the councillor of state sent as *intendant* to Dauphine on 19 November 1654 were typical; the title 'Intendant of Justice, Police and Finances in the said Province' was crossed out and replaced by the title 'Intendant of Justice, Police and Finances for the Troops who shall be in the said Province'. He had also been empowered to make contracts for supplying the troops and audit their accounts in place of the treasurers of France. These instructions were also struck out and replaced by authorization to join in making the contracts and to check the accounts of expenses. Ordinances reforming the councils and edicts for restoring order among officers, promulgated in 1655, had to be reissued in 1657, as they had never been put into effect. The Parlements went on fighting the council, issuing judgements contradicting those of the council, forbidding execution of its decrees and condemning those who took cases to the Council of State.

The government had to fight Jansenism, 'warmed-up Calvinism', whose expansion in France dates from the publication of the *Fréquente Communion* by Antoine Arnauld, a disciple of Saint-Cyran (1643). On 1 July 1649 Nicholas Cornet, a syndic, asked the faculty of theology at Paris to condemn five propositions on grace drawn from the *Augustinus* of Jansenius. The advice of the pope was sought and he condemned the propositions in the Bull *Cum Occasione* (31 May 1653). The Jansenists admitted that the five propositions were erroneous, but claimed that in fact they were not in Jansenius and had not been condemned in the meaning used by him. The pope declared that he had condemned the five propositions as being in Jansenius and according to his usage (September 1654). The government ordered that the Brief was to be executed throughout the kingdom (May 1655). At this, the Jansenists called upon Pascal with his *Lettres Provinciales* (23 January 1656 to 24 March 1657), but even so the assembly of the French clergy condemned the Jansenist heresy (1–2 September 1656). After 1655 the government closed the *petites écoles* of the Jansenists and in September 1660 the *Provinciales* were burnt by the public executioner. In February 1661, at the king's command, the assembly of the clergy drew up a formulary condemning the five propositions to be signed by all ecclesiastics. The superiors of Port Royal de Paris and Port Royal des Champs were obliged to send their novices and postulants away and the 'Messieurs' scattered.

The king was obliged to fight against heresy by his coronation oath. Port Royal was a refuge of disillusioned Frondeurs and seemed a centre of plots. The pessimism of the Jansenists was contrary to the ideal concept of the Hero, one of the foundations of absolute monarchy. The Company of the Blessed Sacrament began to be cornered; Anne of Austria had revealed the secret to Mazarin who was appalled by it. The company also endangered its position by excess of zeal which went so far as arbitrary confinement. In 1660 it was denounced in pamphlets. A police trap failed, but the Parlement forbade all assemblies without the express permission of the king.

Mazarin had completed the work of Louis XIII and Richelieu. After the Peace of the Pyrenees (1659), of Copenhagen and Oliva (1660), Europe was at peace; France was the greatest power and the arbiter of the European states. Like Richelieu, Mazarin had founded a dynasty and a clientele. His nieces married the greatest in the land. He was all-powerful and allowed no one to be seated in his apartments, not even the chancellor. Louis XIV allowed the old minister to enjoy the fruits of office and he was able to leave his vast and ill-gotten fortune to his family, when he died on 9 March 1661. The Fronde had taught Louis XIV that Frenchmen wished to see their king governing alone without a first minister, or favourites, without foreigners, without a cardinal. A few hours after the death of Mazarin, the president of the assembly of the clergy asked the king to whom he should refer in future for decisions on affairs. 'To me, my Lord Archbishop', Louis XIV replied.

CHAPTER XVII

THE HABSBURG LANDS 1618-57

AT the beginning of the seventeenth century the states of the House of Habsburg stretched from the Vosges to the Carpathians. This vast domain lacked organic and political unity. In the west it began with fiefs scattered through southern Germany and continued eastwards with a group of compact but distinct principalities from Vorarlberg onwards. It included a great variety of geographical regions and climates and a diversity of peoples. Through it ran the Danube, rightly portrayed as the king of European rivers on Bernini's great fountain in the Piazza Navona in Rome. It ran through Habsburg territory from the bishopric of Passau to the Turkish frontier not far below Pressburg. Across it ferries and bridges linked the southern Alpine region with the Bohemian and Moravian plateaux, but the Danube was not yet the principal artery of a political complex. The Moldau (Vltava), separated from the Danube valley by a mountain ridge, flowed north through Bohemia to join the Elbe at Mělník, linking the region with the river system of northern Germany.

These states belonged to one family and had one suzerain, but as a result of family compacts, as in Styria and the Tyrol, for administrative convenience as in Alsace, or to avoid the threat of secessions, cadet branches governed several of these countries. Moreover, the important kingdom of Hungary, whose lands by tradition and law were indivisible and inviolable, was split into three regions. In practice, the Habsburgs ruled over only a narrow strip of Croatia, the plain between the Drava and the Danube and the mountains of Upper Hungary. Pressburg had inherited the position of capital from Buda, now in Turkish hands. Transylvania was an autonomous principality governed by a Hungarian noble, a vassal of both the emperor and the sultan, but more effectively subjected to the latter. In thinking of these states in the light of their later history we might be tempted to see them either as a great central European power or a chaotic agglomeration. More objectively we can see not only many features inherited from the Middle Ages, but also much that was new.

There were profound and important economic changes and religious upheavals in progress, while the political activity of the princes, by turns hesitant and resolute, showed a strange amalgam of Roman and Germanic law and Italian statecraft. Medieval traditions survived in each of these regions, all preserved customs strongly cherished by its inhabitants, however ignorant in other respects. Longstanding compacts were everywhere the basis of some form of association between the sovereign *Landesfürst* and the people, or rather those enjoying privileges (privileges here being a matter of guarantees rather than exemptions), who were represented by Diets or Estates. Yet there were new developments as a result of the accidents which had brought each of these territories into the hands of the Habsburgs.

The dynasty had two guiding ideas, complementary rather than contradictory: their entrenchment in certain regions where the prince's role as fount of justice won the lasting affection and confidence of the people and the desire to control these isolated forces for a common end. Within three generations these ideas created a family tradition. By 1600 traditional institutions peculiar to each region are found by the side of princely institutions common to the whole, some of which were also common to the empire.

Surveying their domains from west to east, we come first to their fiefs and rights in Alsace—at the foot of the Vosges. Across the Rhine, in the Black Forest, lay Breisgau, and the scattered territories in Württemberg; all forming a single government—Vorderösterreich. This was important for its strategic position, controlling military and trade routes, and because it kept many German feudal lords directly under the Habsburgs. Beyond Lake Constance and Vorarlberg lay the county of Tyrol with the seat of government of Upper Austria at Innsbruck. Then came the Alpine duchies of Styria, Carinthia and Carniola, the county of Gorizia and the margraviate of Istria, which were linked, oddly but advantageously, with the region, divided to the south by the River Enns, where the last foothills of the Alps meet the Danubian plain. Here Maximilian had set up the capital of Lower Austria (Austria above the Enns was distinguished from Austria below the Enns—modern Upper and Lower Austria, with Linz and Vienna as capitals—and from Central Austria, consisting of the Alpine duchies, erected into a principality for the cadet branch of Styria).

In each of these lands power was shared between the estates and the sovereign. The composition of the *Landtag* reflected the social order: the prelates, the nobility of lords and knights, in either one or two curias, the clergy and the towns. Even the peasant communities sent delegates; but this representation was based on status rather than on counting heads. The nobles and the clergy could sit individually, but the towns and markets of the Tyrol and the districts of Vorarlberg nominated deputies, bound by strict instructions, and Vienna and eighteen other towns shared a single vote in the *Landtag* of Austria below the Enns. During the sessions the prince or his representative proposed taxes and considered petitions and grievances, but in each territory the prince also had his own government. An officer chosen and appointed by him, the *Landeshauptmann* or *Landesmarschall*, his resident representative, saw to the carrying out of decrees and supervised general security. This officer had to be of the native-born nobility: a noble born elsewhere, though subject to the same prince, was ineligible. The supreme judicial authority of the country was vested in the *Landrecht*, acting in the name of the prince. This was a court of appeal for the seigniorial courts, and a court of first instance for the privileged. The *Landrecht* sat several times a year, under the *Landeshauptmann*. The revenues of the prince's domain, customs and taxes granted by the estates, were administered by a supreme chamber where the prince maintained a legal representative. As a result of this, Ensisheim, Innsbruck, Vienna, Linz and Graz gradually assumed the position of minor administrative capitals. These Austrian lands kept their character of medieval German principalities, but for a hundred years the prince had been centralizing the administration, stimulating economic activity, and establishing and supervising markets, gilds and trade. Prince and subjects began to develop some common interests transcending purely local ones.

The kingdoms of Bohemia and Hungary were a different world. Their territories were more extensive and they had historic constitutions, granted by their former dynasties. Bohemia was the only kingdom within the empire and its king was the first lay elector. The crown of St Wenceslas included the kingdom and its associated territories: Eger or Cheb, Elbogen or Loket, Glatz or Kladsko, the margraviate of Moravia and the duchies of Silesia and Lusatia, styled 'the kingdom and the incorporated lands'. In each land power was vested in the king and the estates (lords, knights and towns) who also took part in choosing the monarch. It was only with the sanction of the diet of Bohemia that the king exercised his royal authority, whether he was elected or merely accepted from the reigning dynasty, and he swore to respect the constitution. The Diet enjoyed unlimited legislative power, but the king had to execute the laws. Taxes on noble or peasant property had to be voted by the Diet, but the king supervised fiefs, controlled coinage, customs, dues from royal cities and administration of mines and forests and so was able to take the initiative in economic matters. Supreme justice reposed in the king, and judicial and administrative affairs were often confused, as often happened in contemporary Europe. Disputes over the prerogatives of king and estates were frequent. Nevertheless, the great officials of the realm, the burgrave of Prague, the grand master of the court, the grand marshal, the grand chamberlain, the justiciar, and the burgrave of Karlov-Tyn, custodian of the crown and the old charters, all held office for life and were responsible to both the king and the estates, as did the local officials, the circle captains (a lord and a knight in each circle). Without modifying the constitution and the reservation of office to natives of the realm, the emperor-kings consolidated their rights and exercised them more effectively, aiming at good government rather than absolutism, though the one led to the other. For example, the royal towns which had made an alliance with the elector of Saxony in 1547 were now under the control of royal judges (the captains of the three towns of Prague)[1] and subjected to a perpetual tax on each barrel of beer. A royal appeal tribunal had been set up in Prague and it increased the autonomy of the kingdom by unifying the administration of justice and by banning henceforth appeals to external jurisdictions even within the empire. General administration had been reorganized on Austrian models in the chancery of Bohemia, the president of which, though not the first officer in dignity, became the most powerful in fact, as both head of the royal service and representative of the estates; he was chosen by the king from a list of the royal council (consisting of the great officers and the principal judges). He could claim to have a hand in all matters requiring the use of the royal seal. A lieutenancy council performed the king's functions when he was absent from the kingdom. The same drive towards centralization and royal control was found in Moravia and Silesia, but it was carried through more effectively in the margraviate than in the twenty principalities of Silesia where the feudal powers still stood firm and influenced the general *Landtag*.

The constitution of Hungary, which was not a part of the empire, was even more strongly particularistic. The *Opus Tripartitum* of Verböczi at the beginning of the sixteenth century had settled the characteristics of the constitution. The crown of St Stephen was recognized as the head of a mystical body of which the estates formed the members. Only the coronation ceremony could give the elected king the authority to rule. An uncrowned king was no true king. The country was divided into *comitatji* and the numerous nobility jealously preserved its privileges and assemblies, binding its deputies to the Diet with strict instructions from which no deviation was allowed. In the seventeenth century this Diet comprised two chambers or tables. The first, of magnates, sat under the presidency of the Elector Palatine, the king's representative, himself a sort of viceroy and delegate of the tables. Its members were the diocesan bishops, the high dignitaries of the court, the governors of the *comitatji* and the members of the upper hereditary nobility. The table of the Estates was composed of delegates of the *comitatji*, deputies of the royal towns, noble members of the royal council, protonotaries, royal judges, and representatives of various religious corporations. Its president was a royal judge, the primate.

What merits attention is not so much the constitution as the circumstances which made it nearly unworkable. Since the disaster at Mohačs, disputes over the succession in Hungary and the contested elections between Ferdinand and Zapolya had favoured the Turkish advance. Again, Transylvania was ruled by autonomous princes elected from among the privileged Hungarians of the region by the Diet of Transylvania

[1] Prague comprised three administrative divisions: the old town, the new town and the little quarter on the other side of the river.

on which three nations (juridical not ethnic bodies) were represented: the Nobles or Hungarians, the Siculi and the Saxons. The Hungarian noble who ruled over Transylvania was a more national figure than the German sovereign at Vienna, and constituted a permanent threat to the Habsburgs, who were obliged to respect Hungarian privileges in the part of the kingdom still in their power, buying support and restraining their use of the centralized agencies legally under royal control. It is sometimes held to be a weakness that certain provinces were bestowed, either for life or with rights of succession to cadet archdukes, but this had always been Habsburg practice. It was a convenient means of governing very large domains and it advanced the interests of the dynasty. The revolts against the Emperor Rudolf by his brothers and nephews were attributable in the main to their fear that he would put his own comfort before the defence of his own and the dynasty's rights, for the prince, though highly intelligent, was neurotic and loathed his royal responsibilities. Close relations were maintained with the Spanish branch. Family marriages and the agreements of Graz in 1617 over the succession to a childless Emperor show a tenacious family solidarity and a desire to keep the imperial crown in the family.

Thus the king of Bohemia and Hungary was also the *Landesfürst* of many Austrian lands, and was at the same time the Holy Roman Emperor, around whom some centralized institutions were beginning to develop, such as the *Hofrat,* a council modelled on the *Reichshofrat.* Its members were nobles and jurists, all imperial subjects, and its authority extended over the Austrian lands and the empire, though soon restricted in practice to cases affecting fiefs and the direct dependants of the empire —princes and cities. One section, the secret council [*Geheime Rat*] became a permanent council of state for general policy. It consisted of dignitaries, nobles and jurists, chosen for their knowledge of particular problems, including members of the governments of Bohemia and Hungary. The imperial chancery was the supreme appeal court and court of registration; its arch-chancellor was the archbishop of Mainz who chose his own vice-chancellor, necessarily a jurist. Finally the court chamber [*Hofkammer*], consisting of a president, auditors and councillors, was concerned with the interests of the ruling house throughout its domains and the empire. It administered those royal revenues, not dealt with by the regional chambers, and exercised some control over those chambers; it also controlled the collection of imperial contributions and extraordinary taxes. This cumbersome administrative machine belonging to the emperors, not the empire, co-ordinated the work of the regional governments rather than directed them. It made each country aware that it was part of a power greater than itself and that the existence of a common sovereign committed them to common interests and policies. There was however no real absolutism which would have needed an active sovereign and a small but effective bureaucracy. These collegial courts, often sharing the same councillors who were also frequently dignitaries and councillors in their own countries, were painfully slow-moving by nature. They were useful for securing some uniformity of policy and action within the system, but they could not give any effective unity to the whole.

Historians have traditionally laid much stress on the different characteristics of the inhabitants of the Habsburg lands, on their diverse racial origins and on their different languages which accentuated differences. In the seventeenth century, belonging to the same country and acceptance of the same laws were much more important than any feeling of racial or linguistic solidarity. Germans, Slavs or Magyars were much more conscious of being Tyroleans, Austrians, Styrians, Bohemians, Moravians or Hungarians. Recent ethnological research has shown that the various physical types in central Europe have a long history and that in the seventeenth century such racial groups were intermingled. A Czech ethnologist, Henry Matiegka, has examined numerous seventeenth- and eighteenth century skeletons from the cemeteries of Prague and the countryside. Out of 25 skeletons in the Cemetery of St Nicholas, 12 (48%) belonged to the nordic or subnordic type, which was predominant in northern Germany in the Middle Ages; 6 (24%) were of the Alpine type most numerous in central Europe, and 7 (28%) of the Dinaric type which originated in the Balkan Peninsula. Seventeen skeletons from the Cemetery of St Charles Borromeo showed 5 (29·4%) of nordic type; 5 of Alpine type and 7 (41·2%) of Dinaric type. Out of 25 skeletons from the country, 9 (36%) were nordic or subnordic, 11 (44%) were Alpine, and 5 (20%) Dinaric. Such mixtures within single national or social groups prove that there is no question here of alleged racial characteristics. Language was a more important factor than physical characteristics. Men were Czech, German or Croat, primarily because they spoke those languages. In Bohemia, knowledge of Czech gave access to a body of literature, religious, hagiographical and political. Czech and German speakers were conscious of profound differences between them, which might lead to choices with far-reaching consequences for an individual's life. Choice of language might result from specific social activities or might depend on circumstances. The towns with their numerous traders and craftsmen of German origin and speech formed centres of germanization for newcomers from the country, in both Bohemia and Hungary. The phenomenon was also common in mining regions, where those in charge of operations were often foreigners. In rural areas the language spoken by the lord had some influence on the region's linguistic destiny, but sometimes the lord adopted the language of his vassals. On the whole the rural areas tended to preserve their local idiom, but in the seventeenth century the linguistic map was not firmly fixed, and changes from one group to another were more common than has subsequently been believed. Above all, the mental attitudes of the time, with each group protected by its privileges, did not conceive of linguistic unity as essential for a state, nor did they conceive of undying racial enmities underlying differences of language. Hungary gives the most striking example of this variety, with its Croats, Magyars, highlanders of Upper Hungary, speaking Slovak dialects related to Czech (literary Czech having been adopted by the upper classes) and the Transylvanians including German and Magyar elements. Latin remained the language of government, a common means of expression, standing above all these linguistic groups.

Economic and social developments and religious differences which cut across social groups were more important in determining the course of events than linguistic and national differences. These developments cannot be fully understood without some reference to population statistics. The inhabitants of the empire numbered some 20,000,000 at the beginning of the seventeenth century. The notable studies of Otto Placht on Bohemia give the figure of 4,000,000 for the whole kingdom, a density of 34·5 per square kilometre, one of the highest in Europe at the time. The population of Bohemia alone is put at 1,700,000. Thus the kingdom provided a much larger number of subjects than any other single territory of the empire. Size of population however was not everything; although it played a part in the success or failure of a policy, it was of less account to rule a densely populated kingdom than to exploit its resources effectively, and effective power depended mainly on the good administration of the state's resources. Towns were numerous in the Habsburg domains, though this status was legal rather than economic or demographic in origin. They included large urban agglomerations which derived their importance from the strategic and trade routes on which they stood. Such were Linz and Vienna, possibly the largest city in the empire if the figure of 60,000 inhabitants is accepted. Prague, however, must have had a population of 60,000 or 70,000. None of these figures is as reliable as modern statistics but they may be taken as very close to reality and allow a reasonable estimate of the importance of these regions.

From the beginning of the sixteenth century, major changes had been taking place in organization of production and in working conditions. The rise in prices, the discoveries and the growth of trade all had repercussions in the Habsburg lands. In the traditional economic pattern the land of an estate was adequate for the needs of those who worked it, providing food and clothing and enough cash to pay taxes and buy a few essentials. For many families this pattern continued, but in addition a new system of production for sale emerged. This required the creation of workshops and some concentration of industry and labour. In administrative and trading centres the population grew and new towns sprang up for the mining of iron-ore in Styria, and precious metals in Bohemia and Hungary. Given the competition of American silver, despite the formal ban on its importation, production could only be undertaken by those with considerable resources and enterprise. Recently the increased construction of artificial lakes in southern Bohemia, from the early sixteenth century, by rich landowners to their profit has been studied. There is some analogy with the effects today of building dams for electric power. Many of these lakes covered 50,000 square yards, but some, as at Wittingau and Třeboň, were ten times as large. Noble demesne and peasant holdings alike were flooded; the peasants seem to have been compensated with land elsewhere on the estates. The labour for these enterprises was provided either by the tenants, who were obliged to work for their lord, or by hired hands. Once the lakes were ready, more employment was provided. The lakes had to be stocked with spawn, fished and the catch transported. For this rafts were used, plying up and down the rivers hauling baskets in which the fish were kept fresh. The markets of Prague, Linz and Vienna were supplied with carp and pike which competed seriously with the dried herrings and salted fish from the North Sea. Figures show that at the end of the century the revenue from fish was three times as great as the former income from feudal rents and leases in Krumlov, Rožmberk and Třeboň. The lakes of Bohemia remain a special case. Of more general interest and importance is the change in agricultural production. It was in the interest of the noble proprietor with reasonably extensive lands to revise the conditions of tenure, to increase the area of his demesne continually by the purchase of peasant lands and to use the *corvée* as an essential means for its exploitation. The old money rent had been rendered insignificant by devaluation and the rise in prices. The great estate became more important, on account of its size and economic viability. The effective exploitation of the great estate, consisting of farms and share-croppers' holdings, where peasant smallholdings were found side by side with land directly controlled by the lord, required a large labour force and vigilant administration. Hence the detailed rules given to stewards when they took office, telling them how to supervise work in the fields.

This extension of demesnes occurred in all the Habsburg states, often by imitation, as when the commission of 1571 which visited the royal domains borrowed its instructions from a Hungarian administrator. The group of landowners which profited most from the opportunity to enlarge their estates was the upper nobility. There was however nothing to prevent knights from doing the same, for status was not determined by the extent of possessions, and the king (with agreement from the estates) was continually promoting men from the lower to the higher rank. On the other hand, it was hardly possible to reach the upper nobility without wealth, and that rank was associated with holding important offices which in various ways provided large revenues. Historians, whether democratic or marxist, know most about great lords and great estates, because they are better documented. However small estates and the knightly class survived in the sixteenth century. This class remained the largest and benefited from rising prices and from increased agricultural production; as always, some were more fortunate than others. Above all, it must be emphasized that the old feudal institutions remained.

Recently definitions of feudalism have been much discussed. Some see it as essentially a question of military obligations, of ties between man and man, symbolized by the grant of lands and the payment of dues in money or kind, which lost its meaning with the decline in the value of money over the years. But feudalism also meant the overlord's right—whether usurped or not—to administer justice and to police his lands, which implied the levying of tolls on roads and waterways. Moreover, in the case of lands granted in perpetuity or leased by the lord, contractual obligations bound the vassals to various duties (hence the *corvée*) and particularly forbade them and their descendants to leave the estate. These feudal rights carried duties with them: the lord had to protect his vassals, by giving them refuge in time of war, and by the guardianship of widows and orphans. These features, with local variations, are found throughout Europe in the seventeenth century. One cause of this is that work on the land, under prevailing methods of cultivation—which have been modified and improved over the centuries rather than entirely changed—involves landholders in patriarchal and family associations, which have not always disappeared under modern conditions of free individual ownership. However that may be, the expansion of great estates in central Europe took place within the framework and traditions of the feudal system. Some historians seek to reject the term 'feudalism', preferring to use the term capitalism for this phase; others speak of a 'new feudalism'; but all are obliged to concede that the extension of great estates took place in the social framework inherited from feudalism and that this contributed to increasing landowners' privileges and to further restrictions on the independence of those working the land.

Henceforth the seigneurial estate was organized as a little state. The number of administrative officials varied with the importance of the estate. An officer, styled the administrator or captain, exercised general supervision. Under him was the burgrave, later to be charged with economic administration. One or more secretaries kept the registers of receipts and expenses. Separate accounts were later kept for each form of production— lakes, woods, brewing, milling. Around 1600 the Rožmberk estates at Krumlov were controlled by twelve officers and fourteen secretaries. In each part of the domain the bailiffs had to keep daily accounts. The impression given is of a little private state, with perhaps several thousand subjects. Unfortunately, too little is known of the rights reserved at this period by the officers of the realm and of their interventions in seigneurial lands.

Presumably not all the great estates were well managed. This often depended on whether the master was present or whether the officials were competent. The crown lands had the best reputation and they served as a model for many private estates. The king could dispose of his estates and of escheated lands and he occasionally gave some to his followers as a reward. The crown peasants dwelling on these lands became subject to a new master. Crown peasants were one thing, free peasants another. The latter were found in many regions, direct dependants of the king as supreme head of states and not as a landlord. There was a danger of confusing the two classes. Rudolf II wished to bestow a score of them, holdings and men, on the lord of Rožmberk. The protests of the peasants and the proofs of their inalienable independence given by charters produced a decision by the royal judges which reversed the royal act as illegal: this throws some light on the limits of absolutism in Bohemia at this time.

The liberty of the peasants, which remained very much alive in some countries—for example the Tyrol—was increasingly threatened by the advance of the great estates. Historians disagree as to whether personal servitude [*Leibeigenschaft* or *člověčenství*] existed in Bohemia or whether the peasants' freedom of movement was restricted merely by a ban on leaving the estate without written permission. During the seventeenth century decrees repeatedly asserted the lord's right to demand the return of peasants who had left the estate, and forbade employers, whether in towns or on other estates, to hire peasants from other estates freely. It has not been demonstrated that these measures exclusively reflect the concern of the great landowners to keep their labour force. The knights as owners of medium and small estates were equally concerned as they had fewer workers at their disposal.

The status of the peasants was complex. Some had hereditary holdings and were said to be established; others, not established, were in the position of tenants; all were subject to seigneurial justice and control. In each class there was a hierarchy based on wealth, ranging from the husbandman working fifty acres to the smallholders, journeymen, woodcutters and charcoal-burners. During the slack times of the farming year, many peasants found work in the towns; in busier times, the great estates hired harvesters and it became impossible to keep a check on permits to move. The mobility of the peasants—which some lords found advantageous—was easier to control where the estates had a large and watchful administration.

It should not be thought that the country dweller lived only by working the land; many followed a trade. A survey of the occupations of 234 youths on a great estate in southern Bohemia in 1607 revealed that 98 were apprenticed to the trades of baker, carpenter, shoemaker, smith, draper, painter, dyer, tailor, potter, butcher, furrier, cooper, fuller, mason and glass painter. In 1612, the parish priest of Jiřetin (northern Bohemia) urged his parishioners to thank God for giving them, if not rich corn-fields, vineyards, or mines, at least the means of growing flax and weaving cloth, which attracted many foreigners and enabled every father of a Christian family, artisan or farmworker, to provide his family with bread.

The lords had won for the towns on their estates the same rights as the royal cities. They established markets, and won the right to monopolies. In particular, after 1517, when the privilege of brewing beer, claimed by the towns as their exclusive right, was extended to the nobles, the land-owners reserved the right to sell the beer produced in their breweries throughout their domains in town and country alike. Hence the saying: 'Sheep, beer and fish make the Bohemian nobles rich'. From 1578 to 1615 there was a sharp rise in the price of beer, and a small number of noble families acquired great economic power. Even so, if there were 340 great estates in Bohemia held by the king, the clergy and the lords, there were an equally large number of estates of over 35 households held by members of the knightly class. This parity of numbers does not necessarily indicate that power was equally divided, but it might suggest that the progress of the great estate would cause friction between neighbouring social groups.

As far as the towns are concerned, the royal cities showed a decline in population and activity, whilst the seigniorial towns advanced, as though the protection of the economic system of the estate afforded greater security and advantages, but this advance was not as yet very marked. The situation of Prague seems unusual. The city was not as busy as Nurem-berg or Leipzig, lying apart from the main flow of trade and producing only one major export, felt hats; but it retained its importance because it was the centre of distribution for the merchandise of the entire kingdom, and because the presence of the court ensured a market for fine cloth, jewels, furnishings and good wines. Merchandise flowed through Prague in transit for Nuremberg: iron from Bohemia and Austria, farm produce and cattle from Hungary, Poland and Austria, cloth from northern Bohemia. Its trade figures account for about two-thirds of the country's commerce. Inevitably Vienna suffered as a result, though that city remained thriving and populous within its defensive system. Linz was the great international market in the Habsburg lands, followed by Krems. At the beginning of the century, the German traders of the empire had lost their predomi-nance in Prague to the Jews (the richest inhabitant of the city was the Jew Meyzl, loaded with privileges by Rudolf II) and to Italians such as the Pestalozzi or Heracles de Novi.

Religious questions exerted a greater influence on opinion than econo-mic matters and indeed economic conditions were complicated by religion. The conflict of interests, and the social divisions which led to hostility between large and small estates, between lords and peasants, between the royal cities and the nobility did not coincide with religious divisions; both Catholics and Protestants were found in every group and even within one family. The most serious cause of conflict was that in all Habsburg lands the majority were Protestants, while an active and powerful minority had returned to the Catholic fold. In Alsace and Lower Austria and the Alpine duchies, in Bohemia, Moravia and Silesia and Hungary, Protestantism held its ground in spite of Jesuit campaigns and all attempts to win men back to Rome. In Hungary, the Estates had obliged King Mathias to recognize the privileges of the Protestant churches. In Bohemia in 1609 the Diet had obtained in the Letter of Majesty one of the most liberal charters ever granted to a country of many creeds.

The Bohemian Evangelical Church, professing the Confession of 1609, had received the widest guarantees for their religion and their church buildings. Magistrates—the *defensores fidei*—had been appointed to see that these guarantees were observed. Lords were forbidden to force their subjects to change their religion; it might be thought that this measure would have been advantageous to Catholic peasants of a Protestant lord, but it was mainly directed against Catholic lords. The Roman Curia had long been convinced that the Counter-Reformation could only become effective with the support of the ruling classes of the empire and its territories. It also seemed essential that the most important posts should be given to Catholics; if Protestants were to retain or regain key posts, the reconquest would never be more than superficial. Since Charles V the Habsburg emperors had been lukewarm or passive in their Catholicism compared with the militancy of the Spanish branch. The Emperor Mathias was old, childless and timid, but his cousin Ferdinand was a militant Catholic whose rule in his duchy of Styria had followed the example of the Counter-Reformation in Bavaria.[1] In 1617 Ferdinand was recognized as king of Bohemia, thanks to the Chancellor Lobkowicz, who skilfully handled the uncommitted members of the Estates.

The Thirty Years War had many longstanding causes and brought into play all the economic, social and political problems of contemporary Europe. But its immediate cause was whether Ferdinand could be successfully barred from securing the full Habsburg inheritance before the death of Mathias. Even if the Defenestration of Prague was the work of a small group of plotters or the result of the exuberance of a few hotheads, the resistance of the Protestants of Bohemia, using the affairs of Grab and Brunnau as pretexts, can only be explained in terms of the anxiety caused by the election of Ferdinand. It was not a question of economic interests, of threats of absolutism, nor even of the ancient laws of the realm. There was a man to be crushed and the first issue in the struggle was the religion whose fortunes that man embodied.

[1] See Chapter x, p. 290.

In the event it was not the imperial crown, but his power in Austria and Hungary which Ferdinand seemed most likely to lose as a result of the revolt in Bohemia in the spring of 1618. When Mathias died in 1619, Ferdinand was refused entry into Bohemia and his election of 1617 was declared null and void by the Estates. Soon afterwards the Elector Palatine, Frederick V, was elected king of Bohemia in Ferdinand's place. Meanwhile Ferdinand was elected emperor with the support of the Palatine ambassadors.[1] By the summer of 1619 the crisis was no longer confined to Bohemia. The House of Austria still kept the imperial crown, but the political system which had supported it and had guaranteed its perpetual succession to the empire was shattered and slipping from its grasp.

The Estates had everywhere regained the advantage over the king or *Landesfürst*, and imposed their ideas of government. In July 1619 a general Diet of the kingdom of Bohemia inaugurated a confederation of the various lands under the crown of St Wenceslas. The summoning of such a Diet was itself a triumph of common interests over local differences. The Letter of Majesty and the Protestant privileges were re-established as fundamental laws. The principle of election to the throne was reasserted unequivocally and the prince's authority was again subjected to the close supervision of the Estates. Thus, when Frederick V assumed the crown of Bohemia, he inherited a power far more limited than that enjoyed by his Habsburg predecessors. The Estates entrusted important duties to the *defensores fidei* elected by them. These *defensores* had the permanent duty of watching over the maintenance of privileges and the observance of the laws. They met in council to consider the general situation and to allocate the funds needed for the common defence. In August 1619 delegates of the Estates of Upper and Lower Austria sought membership of the confederation. The act passed in Austria made no mention of *defensores*, but laid down that each of the confederate states could appeal to the others in case of need. The necessary decisions would then be made collectively. Every five years, a general congress would meet to consider disputes between the members, and to complete the charter of confederation by adding new articles as needed. Early in 1620 the Estates of the kingdom of Hungary joined the confederation. Further, in Upper Austria, at Linz, Erasmus von Tschernembl, a Protestant lord who had always favoured an alliance of the nobles against the sovereign, called in question the rights of Ferdinand under the pretext that he was not the nearest male relative of the late *Landesfürst*. According to laws of inheritance and the constitutional law of the country, the throne should have passed to the last surviving brother of the Emperor Mathias, the Archduke Albert, regent of the Low Countries. The Archduke Albert rejected this solution which was contrary to the family compacts. Thus the rights of the dynasty were in

[1] See Chapter XI, pp. 310–11.

conflict with those of the old local constitutions. It was all very well for Ferdinand of Styria to be emperor; most of the states of his House were slipping from his grasp and he had no alternative but to win them back by force.

The nobility was everywhere asserting its rights and privileges against those of the sovereign. The system of 1619 has been variously assessed by historians. As against the absolutism of the prince, it was based on the privileges of the Orders. This confederation between neighbouring countries, approved by the legal representatives of the various political and privileged orders of the countries, claimed that it defended religious liberties, and proclaimed this as a general principle (though failing to apply it when the Jesuits were banished from Bohemia for ever). This corresponded to a Protestant ideal: to them, subdivision into small units as in the United Provinces and Switzerland seemed the most suitable form of government. At that date, certain French Huguenot circles had the idea of introducing the system into France. Many historians have taken the view that the régime of 1619 was the most liberal of all and that it even contained the seeds of republican and democratic liberties; but these considerations carry less conviction to those modern historians who are primarily concerned with economic and social problems. In their view, whether the political system gave power to prince and council or to magnates and diets, the social order remained the same feudal and seigneurial one. The question which exercised nineteenth-century historians —which of the two systems, centralized monarchy or oligarchical confederation, was the best ground for the general advance of society and the emancipation of the population—is thus brushed aside. In both cases political and social power was in the hands of a privileged landowning minority.

The election of Frederick V in Bohemia was in the hands of the Diet, that is to say of the same men who two years earlier had voted for Ferdinand. Only those regarded as avowed supporters of Austria were excluded from the voting, such as the Chancellor Lobkowicz and William of Slawata, who in any case had both fled to Austria. For a year, the new king's government worked smoothly and in principle equitably towards his subjects, whatever their religion. In a letter to Louis XIII Frederick boasted that the least of his subjects enjoyed freedom of religion and conscience. Such was the spirit at least of the Letter of Majesty. The people of Bohemia rallied to the new prince, whatever their creed or nationality. The Catholics however were naturally suspicious of a Protestant king and hoped for the return of the House of Austria, while some few Protestants, among them Zerotin, the Moravian noble and former friend of Henri IV of France, remained loyal to the Habsburgs. Thus the whole nation seemed implicated in the revolt and to share the guilt, so that a terrible punishment could be anticipated.

The course of the war between Frederick and Ferdinand has been described elsewhere.[1] It is appropriate to recall here that, in the opinion of recent historians, the sacrifices which resistance on a national scale would have necessitated were never accepted in Bohemia, either by the aristocracy or the commercial middle class of Prague, where the largest liquid fortunes were to be found, or by the people in town or country. Peasant revolts, the features of which have not been sufficiently studied, broke out on many estates. No convincing argument has yet been advanced to confirm the hypothesis that a *levée en masse* might have been obtained by social reforms freeing the peasants from their obligations to their lords.

At all events, both the imperial armies and Frederick V's foreign levies committed such depredations that the people desired only peace. This disillusionment was reinforced by the inactivity of the European powers. Bohemia and its allies were left isolated and were defeated at the White Hill, 8 November 1620. Just as the Defenestration of Prague (23 May 1618) had precipitated the latent crisis in the states of the House of Austria, the victory of the White Hill—an episode in a religious rather than a political war—made a revival of the Habsburg fortunes certain and, though the ultimate result of the struggle remained doubtful, its conduct was made easier because internal order was restored.

In the evolution of what may be called the Austrian system, the crisis of 1618–20 was of the greatest importance. In political and human terms the balance of forces was modified for several centuries and there were important indirect effects on the economic future of the country. According to the notions of the time a king had a right and even a duty to punish his rebellious subjects. Severe measures could therefore be anticipated. Ferdinand's attitude, however, alarmed even those who did not blame him for inflicting punishment. They soon saw that he was looking beyond domestic politics, and was developing ambitions to dominate all Germany and to establish a Habsburg preponderance in Europe together with Spain, now resuming the war in the Netherlands.

Bohemia had hitherto occupied a privileged position in the Austrian system, as much on account of its intrinsic importance as because of its status as a kingdom and because the emperors had dwelt in its territories. Ferdinand favoured Graz as capital and wished to be buried there, but he could not govern his states from such an out-of-the-way city, and Vienna assumed the position of capital. Pressburg, the capital of royal Hungary, was very near Vienna. These cities were more exposed than Prague to any renewed Turkish offensive. It is true that as the war dragged on Prague became the focus for the Protestant armies of Germany and Sweden, from which they attacked the states of the emperor himself, but this danger did not arise before 1630. Ferdinand felt bitter towards

[1] Chapter XI: 'The Thirty Years War.'

Prague as the centre of the revolt, and the dynasty's lasting aversion to the ancient kingdom influenced its future as much as constitutional changes. Despite appearances, this aversion hindered the process of centralization and unification which might have taken place in central Europe to the advantage of the victorious dynasty.

It was often asserted in the nineteenth century—and still sometimes today—that the emperor, a German prince, vented his personal hatred on the Czech people, that he deprived them of all their rights, forbade them to speak their language, put all the leading nobles to death, despoiled families of their possessions, converted the people to Catholicism by force and set up one of the most cruel and tyrannical régimes ever known in Europe. This account is highly exaggerated and still worse shows a complete failure to understand what was possible in the seventeenth century. An example was made of those implicated in the government of Frederick V. A special commission was set up under the country's new governor, Charles of Lichtenstein, and twenty-seven men were condemned to death: they were executed in Prague Square on 21 June 1621. They included three members of the lords, Slik, Budovec and Harant; seven knights, Cernin being one, and seventeen burghers including the German doctor Jessen, the rector of the university. Such severity was excessive, but the Czech nobility was hardly destroyed by the loss of ten of its number. In Moravia, where the government was entrusted to Cardinal Dietrichstein, there were no executions. Silesia and Lusatia benefited from an amnesty because of the protection of the elector of Saxony who could not be treated lightly. On the other hand, in Bohemia and Moravia, all who had collaborated with the revolutionary government of 1618, either by providing subsidies or by petitioning it, were subjected to various penalties. Their property was confiscated wholly or partially; but even in the latter case it was sold by the royal chamber which then repaid the price of the unforfeited remainder. In this form the operation was absurd, because the punishment affected too many, so that the process of pacification was delayed, and because the vast amount of land glutted the market and declined in value. Furthermore, in keeping with prevailing economic conditions most of the possessions sold were direct or indirect security for debts which the former owner could no longer honour and which in principle the chamber agreed to settle. In consequence there was an upheaval of fortunes throughout the country and the royal treasury ran into debt. The effective power of the king was compromised and that of some individuals underwent a sudden and scandalous increase. The main victims were the Protestant knights whose estates were too small for them to be left with anything in the event of partial confiscation. The main beneficiaries were the great Catholic landowners who were able to expand and consolidate their estates by acquisitions, and officers of the imperial army to whom the sovereign was in debt. Even the richest had to borrow to pay for their acquisitions, but sums owed by the treasury could be used towards purchases and the liberality of the sovereign sometimes led to remission of part of the price. Adam of Valdstejn the grand master of the court paid only 20,000 Rhenish ducats out of a purchase price of 260,000 ducats for the estate of Houska, confiscated from the Berka family; the emperor made him a present of the rest. His nephew, Albert of Valdstejn, who had remained loyal to the emperor, paid 150,000 ducats for the estate of Friedland in northern Bohemia, confiscated from the Raedern family, and later consolidated it by new acquisitions. The wife of the Chancellor Lobkowicz was highly intelligent and took prompt advantage of opportunities so that she and her husband became the richest landowners in the country. The Slawata family remained at Jindrichuv-Hradec, but the emperor gave the nearby estate of Krumlov, a crown possession, to Eggenberg, an Austrian councillor. This was an exceptional instance though often cited to show that the emperor was introducing a foreign nobility into the country. In fact it was rather the Czech Catholic nobility which profited from the first confiscation. Thirteen years later a second confiscation took place. Wallenstein had extended the duchy of Friedland to the size of a small state. After his dismissal and death, his possessions were confiscated and shared out, though a portion was left to his family. By then the imperial army, reinforced thanks to his efforts, included many foreign officers to whom the emperor was in debt. He rewarded them with huge bounties, such as the gift of the Friedland estates to Gallas. This led to an influx of foreign landowners into the kingdom; most were given lands in Bohemia, but many sold their property. A great German family of the empire, the Schwarzenbergs, received extensive estates in southern Bohemia by inheritance, succeeding the Eggenbergs. By 1650 the aristocracy of the kingdom was certainly very different from what it had been before the war. The indigenous element was still in the majority, with three-fifths (60,000) of the 107,000 peasant properties in noble hands, but two-fifths (44,000) were in the hands of newcomers. These figures do not explain everything. After so many upheavals attitudes and traditions had changed.

In 1627 Ferdinand by his sole authority altered the constitution of Bohemia. The throne was made hereditary in the reigning family, even in the female line. The king, by his coronation oath, undertook not to permit any alienation of territory and to respect the ancient liberties, but Catholicism was the only permitted religion and the Letter of Majesty was abolished.[1] A first chamber of prelates was added to the Diet, which retained the right to vote taxation, and this constituted the main limitation of the king's power.[2] Officials were henceforth nominated by the

[1] The original document of the Letter of Majesty was slashed twice with a dagger. It is preserved in this state in the Czech National Archives at Prague.
[2] See also Vol. v in this series, p. 476.

king and bound to him by an oath of personal loyalty. In consequence they no longer bore the title of officers of the kingdom of Bohemia, but that of royal officers in the kingdom of Bohemia. The constitution was promulgated in German, the prince's language, but there was no legal restriction on the use of Czech. Linguistic and nationalistic persecutions were not a feature of seventeenth-century politics; what mattered was to be loyal to the prince.

It did not seem essential as yet to pursue centralization and create a single state which would abolish the traditional liberties of each country. The system set up after 1620 marks a retreat from the attempt to form a central European confederation stimulated by the revolution. The only link between the states was the person of the sovereign, and nothing seemed more likely to inspire and guarantee loyalty than religious unity, produced by practising membership of the Roman Church. Such a result could not be achieved easily and in certain lands the measures adopted to achieve peace prevented its realization. The elector of Saxony had contributed to the imperial victory and to please him, Silesia and Lusatia had been spared repressive action. In Silesia the Letter of Majesty was confirmed, and the province became the centre of refuge for Protestants and the centre of moral resistance to political actions which elsewhere were destroying the traditional Evangelical cult.

The prince of Transylvania, Bethlen Gabor, had supported the revolution, joined the confederation and threatened Vienna. More prompt and determined assistance on his part might have changed the course of events. By the Peace of Nikolsburg in 1622, several Slovakian *comitatji* had to be ceded to him and Transylvania remained a stronghold for the Protestant Hungarian nobility. In Turkish Hungary conditions were the same for Protestants and Catholics.

In Upper Austria, where Maximilian of Bavaria was regent, the Protestants were tenacious. As late as 1626 there was a peasant revolt because their preachers had been expelled and an attempt made to force them to pay tithes to the Catholic clergy. They demanded the restoration of their religion wherever it had been practised forty or fifty years earlier, and also demanded the right to build new churches and schools. For these purposes they sought the return to the Protestant Estates of their former revenues and confiscated properties.

In Bohemia many Catholic lords did not hurry to drive Protestant officials from their lands, as this would have been against their own interests. The restoration of Catholicism was far from easy, but it involved more than tortures, executions and burning Bibles and Protestant books in Czech, though these are not simply the fantasies of polemicists. The two most effective instruments of the Counter-Reformation were education and preaching. Colleges and universities were reorganized in order to educate the nobility and to recruit clergy—hence the presence of pupils from the common people. In Prague the university, founded in 1348 by Charles IV, was amalgamated with the Jesuit Academy under the name of the Charles Ferdinand University. In Alsace, the University of Molsheim was in Jesuit hands and the religious orders with the support of the arch-dukes worked to combat the influence of the Protestant middle-class in the towns. Colmar returned to the Catholic faith.[1]

In western Hungary, where the law of 1608 had maintained Protestant privileges and forbidden religious orders to hold property, Cardinal Pazmanny, archbishop of Esztergom, founded a university at Nagy-Sombath (Tyrnau-Trnava) in 1635 and fostered the establishment of houses of Jesuits at Pressburg, Ödenburg, Raab, Varasdin, Agram, Trentschin and Neusohl. Minds and hearts were to be won above all by sermons and the splendour of the ritual. The cardinal, himself an orator and humanist, preached dazzling and eloquent sermons.

Thus as a result of Ferdinand's victories in Bohemia, rivalry between Reform and Counter-Reform continued in those Habsburg states which offered the greatest chances of success to Catholicism. A generation later an educated and devoted priesthood was to be recruited from the people, but for the present the religious orders' help was indispensable. In Prague the Carmelites were given the church built by the German traders of Mala Strana after the Letter of Majesty. The former Protestant church was dedicated to Our Lady of Victories and a statue of the Infant Jesus of Spanish origin was placed there. However, most church building was undertaken at Vienna: the churches of the Capuchins (1622), of the Dominicans (1631) and of the Jesuits (1627). The two latter had beautiful façades, adorned with pilasters and volutes, architectural innovations based on Roman models. Vienna, in addition to being the seat of the court and government, was also a Catholic city, a reflection of the sovereign and his suite, the centre from which the enterprise of reconversion spread through the various Habsburg states and through the empire itself. By asking their subjects to identify loyalty to their dynasty with acceptance of Catholicism, the Habsburgs bound themselves so closely to the church that any harm suffered by the one seemed to shake the other. This funda-mental feature of the Austrian system lasted until modern times.

The period from the White Hill to the Diet of Ratisbon (1630), was remarkably favourable to the emperor, but this good fortune could not last. Conditions changed after 1630; he was checked by the German princes, alarmed at his success. Ferdinand made the mistake of giving up the chief source of his power, Wallenstein's army. As a result his govern-ment underwent a succession of trials which continued after his death in 1637. This new phase of the war, from 1630 to the Peace of Westphalia (1648), was one of the most difficult for the House of Austria and ended

---

[1] G. Livet, *L'Intendance d'Alsace sous Louis XIV*, p. 25.

for ever the prospects promised by the earlier victories. Alsace was virtually lost when, to avoid the horrors of war, the Alsatian towns placed themselves under the protection first of Sweden and then of France. Transylvanian Hungary, whose Prince Rakoczi was the ally of Brandenburg and then of Sweden, renewed the struggle for religious and political privileges and was a constant threat to the eastern flank of the Austrian possessions. The inhabitants of royal Hungary were thus in a permanent state of unrest. Lastly, and more important, Bohemia and Moravia became the invasion route for the northern armies marching on Vienna and were constantly disturbed by the passage of troops (1631–4, 1639–41, 1645–8). Their exactions were much harsher than in the earlier part of the war.

The production of the great estates, formed after the revolt, had soon reached a high level. A completely new side of Wallenstein has been revealed by recent historiography: in a few years, he had ensured order and progress in his duchy of Friedland, just as he had tried to stop pillage in the conquered German lands and to establish reasonable government in Mecklenburg. After his defection, the lands which he had so successfully developed in northern Bohemia appropriately suffered most from invasion and were soon ruined. The Treaty of Prague (1635) with the imperial electors raised hopes briefly, but it cost Austria dear. In spite of the royal oath that Bohemia should lose none of its territory, the elector of Saxony gained the province of Lusatia where Slav peoples, Swabians, lived surrounded by Germans. Thus the emperor agreed to a reduction in his power both in his personal states and in the empire and a general peace seemed imminent. Markets revived, the price of land rose and public order was nearly re-established when the struggle began again with increased bitterness. Trade was at a standstill in the towns, while the countryside suffered the vicissitudes of good and bad harvests and the requisitions of imperial and foreign armies. The fate of the peasants was more intimately bound up with the lord than ever. He alone could wrest a safe conduct from the emperor, soften the demands of the invader, or charitably direct the armies to some neighbouring estate. Sometimes it was no longer clear who the lord was. The exiles, returning in the wake of the Swedish armies, declared their intention of resuming control of the estates confiscated by the emperor. Estates such as those of the Slawatas in southern Bohemia which remained continuously in the same hands were fortunate.

The sovereign no longer exercised his authority. As a result of devaluation, the imperial government in Vienna found itself unable to pay for the war effort from taxation and ordinary revenues; it had to rely on military *entrepreneurs* and mercenaries whose loyalty was dictated by self-interest as Wallenstein and Bernard of Saxe-Weimar had shown. It was a time of anarchy and hand-to-mouth existence. The results of these dark years can only be assessed by considering the results of the war and the way in which the reconstruction of administration and the individual lands was attempted.

In 1645 the Peace of Linz with Prince Rakoczi suspended hostilities on the eastern front, but by it the emperor was obliged to grant his adversary further Hungarian *comitatji*, and to confirm Protestant privileges in royal Hungary. Here again his authority was strikingly circumscribed. In 1648 came the Peace of Westphalia, with France, Sweden and their allies. The news that it had been signed halted Königsmark's Swedish troops, who had held Mala Strana for several months, at the bridge into Prague, but the last foreign detachments did not leave the kingdom until 1650. The Peace of Westphalia sacrificed Habsburg rights and possessions in Alsace to France and especially weakened the power of the emperor within the empire. The possibility of the Habsburgs securing a hold on Germany and gradually turning the empire into a hereditary kingdom was averted for ever. German liberties were safeguarded against Habsburg absolutism, whether or not the danger had been as great as the propaganda of the Habsburgs' enemies had contended. Although Czech exiles (e.g. Komensky) begged the Swedes not to sign the peace until the internal affairs of the kingdom had been settled, the Treaties of Westphalia made no stipulations about the emperor's personal possessions. Consequently Ferdinand III's power extended over a vast area from the Rhine to the Carpathians, and from the Oder Valley to the Adriatic, one of the largest geographical units in Europe, the potential basis of a large modern state. It was not yet possible to impose a common policy on these neighbouring countries, to co-ordinate their economies or their attitudes, or to subject them to the will of the prince. The first task was to rebuild the ruins: not only abandoned houses, smoke-blackened castles, or thriving little cities turned into dead towns; the population was also in ruins. The figures are still subject to revision and dispute, but the overall results are reasonably accurate. On the eve of the war Bohemia had been the most populous of the Habsburg states: in 1648 it was the most ravaged. A census of taxable properties in 1654 revealed that out of 155,000 households known before the war, only 123,000 remained. Statisticians have recently analysed these summary conclusions, including the inhabitants and properties outside the census, assessing the numbers of a household in the country and evaluating the fiscal unit in the towns. The masterly studies of Otto Placht show that between 1615 and 1650 the population of Bohemia fell from 1,700,000 to 930,000, a drop of nearly 50%, while the population of Moravia had fallen by a third (30%). The population of Prague numbered some 40,000 and the other royal cities some 65,000. This decline of the ancient cities was a striking feature of the new state of affairs. Prague was passing through a period of decline and stagnation; the religious authorities requested the civil government to close the markets, as Protestant traders from Germany might spread propaganda for their religion. The majority of the population lived in the provinces: 145,000 in the seigneurial towns and 580,000 in the country.[1] Families were smaller than before the war, averaging about 3·6 instead of 6 in the towns and 4 instead of 9 in the country. Military operations were not directly responsible for this decline, but they led to widespread famine to which the weaker—the old, expectant mothers, children under fifteen, the newly born—fell an easy prey. The birth-rate declined, especially among the poorer peasants, and the proportion of people aged over fifty dropped. At the end of the war, the population of Bohemia consisted in the main of country dwellers (among whom may be numbered the inhabitants of some of the royal and seigneurial towns) born and brought up during the war and with no recollection of a free and happy land. Indeed few if any could remember such a time: they naturally loathed war, having experienced only its horrors, but the war constantly returned, brought by foreigners, while the emperor seemed to represent the old order and the promise of peace. The Bohemian students of the Charles Ferdinand University defended the Charles Bridge against the Swedes in 1648, fighting for something their grandfathers had tried to destroy. It is not possible to estimate the proportion of Germans and Czechs, or of Catholics and Protestants in the country. The Protestant element had certainly not disappeared, for in spite of imperial proscriptions, Protestant administrators continued to be found on the estates. In addition there were still too few Catholic clergy to accomplish the tasks of conversion, education and parochial duties for which they were needed. However, the leading figures of the Czech Counter-Reformation were coming to maturity. The Jesuits Bridel and Bohuslav Balbin, the first a preacher and professor, the second a historian and philologist renowned for his defence of the Czech language, were born in 1619 and 1621 respectively.

The ravages of war had not affected the whole country, but in the regions which had suffered, reconstruction of farming and agriculture was especially difficult for landowners unless they were very wealthy. Both the old families of the knightly order and the foreign families who had received small properties from the emperor (such as the Tyrolean family of Spaur at Houska, north Bohemia) were unable to support themselves and were obliged to sell their lands at unfavourable prices, while large estates, whatever their origin, were in an advantageous position. They already predominated in the southern regions by-passed by the war, with the vast possessions of the Eggenbergs (5,400 households), the Slawatas (3,569) and the Bucquoys (3,100). After the war this became the pattern for the country's economy. The estates, usually well run, were expanded, sometimes field by field, by purchasing lands which poor

---

[1] These figures are given by Otto Placht, p. 116, *Lidnatost a Společenska Skladba Českého Státu v. 16–18 stoleti* (Prague, 1957). The precise figures are: Prague, over 40,000; royal cities, 64,814; seigniorial towns, 145,560; rural population, 581,050.

peasants or impoverished nobles were obliged to sell and which were farmed directly by the lord's agents. The state revenue suffered, for noble lands exempt from taxation (dominical) were confused with servile lands (rustical) which should have been taxed. On these farms and on the lord's demesne the peasants' *corvée* provided labour. The various grades of tenants were all obliged to provide equipment or time and labour for so many days a week, husbandmen, smallholders, journeymen and tenants alike, and the *corvée* became the chief economic feature of this system. However, the lords did not derive their main income from agriculture; administration of justice, taxes on sales and legacies and above all the monopolies of beer, wool, meat and skins sold to the inhabitants of the seigneurial towns often brought in as much as, or more than the income from the land. Apart from the *corvée* the main feature of the régime was the paternal authority of the lord on his estates. The inhabitants, including even prosperous townspeople—brewers, dyers, clothiers—could neither marry, nor inherit, nor sell their property, nor apprentice their children without the permission of the lord or his officers. They were not allowed to move or to leave the estate: if they attempted to do so they could be sent back. The lord was legal guardian of orphans: he administered their property and required work from them in return; this was later extended to all young vassals, who were obliged to serve the orphan years. This revival of feudalism was not confined to Bohemia, but was also found in Hungary, where the minor nobility preserved their privileges alongside the upper nobility, and also to a lesser extent in Innerösterreich.

This system maintained the wealth and influence of a minority of a few hundred families from which a small number of magnates emerged: the families of Lobkowicz, Slawata (succeeded by Cernin); Eggenberg (succeeded by Schwarzenberg), Gallas and Colloredo; Dietrichstein, Lichtenstein and Kaunitz in Moravia. Many were anxious to run their estates well and, as far as the law allowed, to behave justly and humanely towards the inhabitants. 'An estate where justice is observed and respected', William of Slawata told his son in 1634, 'is by its essence in a better condition than the others; more men and more profit can be expected from it.' Of course such generous and wise rule primarily benefited the lord, but the connection between his wealth and the material and moral well-being of his subjects was the heart of the system and was its justification. Today land is held in so little esteem that it is not easy to understand this desire of families to run their estates well. They were proud if the estate was enlarged, if its production increased, if religious foundations were set up and if it was embellished by chapels and castles; they wished to hand it on to the following generation in better condition. The *paterna monita* of the prince of Schwarzenberg, at the beginning of the eighteenth century bear witness to this. The character of the lord and even more that of his steward were of vital concern to subjects and vassals, peasants and townsmen alike. The administrators of the estates who rose from the people were all the more pitiless to the peasants. The closed character of the estate made marriages between near neighbours or relations inevitable, and peasant dynasties established themselves more tenaciously than the noble families themselves. In the years immediately following the Thirty Years War, the basis was laid of a way of life which lasted, though not without accidents, disturbances and abuses, until the crisis of 1848 in the Austrian lands. Many features survived after this date in Austria-Hungary and even in its successor states. The war had strengthened and accentuated a development first heralded in the sixteenth century and which might have been expected to disappear during the crisis. It may be asked whether a system which gave such power to the aristocracy favoured the authority of the sovereign. He remained the supreme judge to whom vassals could appeal against the exactions of their overlord. He also controlled general policy, in peace or war, for which he asked the Diets to vote taxes, the officers of state were nominated by him and bound to him by oath. In practice however it appears that seigneurial authority was a barrier between sovereign and people. The great lords of Bohemia, Austria and royal Hungary were the sovereign's direct dependants. They served him, as members of his councils, of the chanceries of his various states and as diplomatic representatives. They were eager to receive feudal honours from him (the imperial titles of duke, count and baron, unknown in the ancient customs of the kingdoms) and the Order of the Golden Fleece, which enjoyed the greatest prestige of all. Nevertheless their personal loyalty, regarded as an adequate safeguard, and their authority over their vassals combined to check the sovereign from any process of unification comparable to that undertaken by the kings of France at this time through their bourgeois officials. The Habsburg sovereign, circumscribed by his hieratic prestige and by his attendant magnates, could not exercise the absolute authority which he was recognized as possessing in principle.

Short of a new revolution, such as that unsuccessfully attempted by Joseph II, he was unable to break down the profusion of feudal sub-divisions or to unite disparate human groups into one nation. Even so, Vienna and the court formed a centre to which the aristocracies of the various states were drawn and where they made matrimonial alliances. They developed into a single group united by their common interests and ready to adopt German, the language of the Habsburgs, as their common tongue. Thus the aristocracy gave up its regional characteristics and became Austrian. The change was neither rapid nor complete and this slow development is explained by the conditions of landownership. The nature of the lord's local authority, the time he spent on his lands, or both, so as to make use of the dues paid in kind and to live more cheaply than at Vienna, and from inclination to enjoy the comforts of his residences and the pleasures of the chase, both maintained or revived regional characteristics which he would have lost at court. The Czech language kept its hold. In 1634 William of Slawata expressed his regret that it was losing its purity and becoming full of germanisms. His son Adam established a foundation at the Church of the Assumption at Jindřichův-Hradec (Neuhaus) in 1652 for the preaching of sermons in Czech because the inhabitants were traditionally attached to that language. The high proportion of foreigners settled in Bohemia in the middle of the century (in the upper nobility there were 58 Bohemian families, including about 30 at least recently promoted from the order of knights, as against 95 of foreign origin) and the decline of the lesser nobility, the knights—still vigorous in Hungary—accounts for the spread of German as the current language. Foreigners of Italian or Belgian origin (Piccolomini, Bucquoy) adopted German more readily than Czech which was regarded as difficult, strange and archaic. Sometimes the nobility expressed Bohemian sentiments in German; in 1679 Humprecht Cernin advised his son travelling abroad to remember to communicate on the Feast of St Wenceslas, so as to honour the protector of the kingdom, as a good Bohemian. An Austrian system was emerging, for the hereditary king of Bohemia now lived in Vienna, to which the chancery had been moved, and the feudal régime was consolidated to the advantage of the German-speaking Austrian or foreign aristocracy (still enjoying the *Incolate*). Everywhere national traditions survived and preserved regional awareness. Even the Catholic faith, though maintained to some extent by force as well as by persuasion in the old Hussite lands, helped to foster this regional—almost separatist—spirit. An imperial decree ordered the restoration of calvaries and statues damaged during the wars. The lord attended to this on his estate. The statues of St Wenceslas, St Ludmilla and St Guy reappeared, reviving the attachment of medieval Bohemia to the protectors of the race. Devotion to the Virgin was the principal mark of loyalty to the Roman Church favoured by the men of the Counter-Reformation, but the restoration of the shrines of the Virgin and the traditional places of pilgrimage revived the veneration of the traditional Czech Madonnas: the Virgin of Svata Hora, of Stara Boleslav, of Zlata Koruna, of Haindorf. A new bond was formed between the land of Bohemia with its forests, lakes and hills and the half-forgotten and disputed religion which was rediscovering its holy places; it expressed itself in charming works of baroque art. This was not against the general policy of the House of Austria, nor was it likely to disrupt the feudal system or the *corvée*. But among the masses spiritual and moral values were preserved and fostered, which later events brought to fruition; they were the main cause of what has been inaccurately termed the 'reawakening' of a nation which had never fallen asleep. In the mid-seventeenth century only the seeds were there, but they must be recognized, if subsequent events are to be understood. This patriarchal peasant system may have unintentionally maintained national individuality better than a centralized system, with a more advanced and industrialized economy, in which the unity of the Austrian peoples would have been rapidly achieved by the mixing of regional groups.

The return of peace made possible the building or rebuilding of churches and of country and town houses for the nobility. Gradually the increasing numbers and prosperity of the population led to an increasing taste for building—particularly ornate building—in the Austrian lands. At the beginning of the century, Italian influences were already making themselves felt in Vienna and Prague, replacing the influence of the German Renaissance. In 1611 the Emperor Mathias commissioned a new portico for the entrance to Hradcany from the workshops of Scamozzi. Architects came mainly from north Italy—Milan and Venice—or at least adopted the style of that region. Some years later the religious orders began to model their churches on the Roman Counter-Reformation style: façades of two storeys (Dominicans of Vienna), or three (University of Vienna, Discalced Carmelites of Leopoldstadt) divided by mouldings of pilasters, with volutes linking each storey, the whole topped by a triangular pediment. The walls were decorated with niches and statues and the central portico would be crowned by a niche or decorated with pyramids (Our Lady of Victories, Prague). The towers of the old Gothic churches were not abandoned. They reappeared, short and squat on the Schottenkirche in Vienna (1652). As for the interior, the sanctuary was skilfully modernized with a new reredos and with plaster medallions or figures. There was still not enough money, nor were there enough craftsmen to permit many such renovations. Until the middle of the century, the sovereigns themselves lived in gloomy medieval dwellings—both the Hradcany at Prague, where in spite of some work over successive generations the old castle remained in use; and the Hofburg at Vienna, of which only one wing had been rebuilt at the end of the sixteenth century (Amalienburg). Similarly the nobles were still content with their old fortresses—Krumlov, Rozmberk, Friedland, Kost—though some of the richest had improved them by the addition of galleries on inner courtyards in the Florentine manner.

Wallenstein was the first to embark on a course of magnificence. He bought a whole quarter of Mala Strana to build a palace which still presented a stern front to the street, but with a loggia on the garden side, the Sala Terrena, recalling the Lanzi of Florence and the Te palace at Mantua, with its three arches supported by pairs of Doric columns: while inside, a delicate profusion of plasterwork over vault and walls, framed paintings. In all the apartments, the hall and the chapel, there were works of art—German and Italian Renaissance paintings, tapestries, plate. In the gardens the walls were masked by false grottoes, the aviary was full of exotic birds, the avenues were flanked by the bronzes of the Flemish sculptor Adrian de Vries. This was still an isolated example, despoiled of some of its treasures by the marauding armies, when peace returned, but a tradition had been established. The idea spread that each estate should have a palatial residence and that the glory of a noble family was confirmed by the beauty of its houses. Throughout the Austrian lands from 1680 to 1740 a whole artistic ethos, an independent form of the baroque, can be observed in the splendour of the church ritual and of sacred and secular music, in the luxury of the noble houses, in the feasts and banquets of the hunt, in the eagerness to own fine horses reared and selected in the studs of Bohemia and Hungary. These Slav, German and Hungarian lands fell under the influence of Italy. Latin thought and taste refined sensibilities and led to an enduring preference for form and grace rather than ideas and action. At the same time the high proportion of peasants in the society and the life of the great estates preserved some patriarchal features which tempered social distinctions and awakened in some aspirations for *douceur de vivre* after half a century of suffering and horrors.

Hereditary transmission of the crown was further confirmed by the custom of crowning the princes destined to succeed to the kingdom of Bohemia or Hungary in their father's lifetime. Ferdinand II took this course with his son Ferdinand III, who bore the title of king of Hungary when he precipitated the fall of Wallenstein and took his place as commander of the armies. Ferdinand III, austere and religious like his father, was the victor of Nordlingen and the most military-minded emperor of the seventeenth century. By his first marriage with his cousin Maria-Anna, daughter of the king of Spain, and sister of Anne of Austria, queen of France, he had two sons. The elder, Ferdinand IV, was brought up to rule and elected king of the Romans, while the second, Leopold, less robust and devoted to music, seemed destined for the church.

Ferdinand IV, however, died prematurely in 1654 aged 21, and the imperial succession had not been settled when the emperor himself died in 1657, aged barely 50. In 1650, bereaved of his second wife, his cousin Maria Leopoldina of Tyrol, he had married the daughter of the duke of Mantua, the Princess Eleonora who came from a court and city celebrated for their artistic traditions. She further extended Italian influence in Vienna. Neither Ferdinand II nor Ferdinand III was a nonentity; both had high conceptions of their responsibilities, but they were not statesmen. Constantly struggling against external difficulties, they were never in a position to study the problems of their own states or to prepare major reforms. Their frontiers were never entirely free from danger. In 1656, the renewal of the northern war between Brandenburg, Sweden and Poland against which George Rakoczi launched an offensive, threatened a general conflagration.

In such circumstances they were resigned to an outmoded and ponderous system. The imperial agencies were confused with and juxtaposed to those of the government of their own states and those peculiar to each state. Everything depended in the last analysis on personal loyalty to the emperor. Absolute legal masters in some countries (though not by any means in Hungary) and thought to be capable of becoming absolute overlords in the empire, they enjoyed in fact the trappings rather than the realities of power. A military victory had re-established their authority in 1620, another had confirmed it in 1634 and it had survived later changes in fortune. In 1648 they had yet preserved the potentiality of becoming a great power. They relied on a spiritual force—religion—but more effectively on the clergy of their states; a vigorous and disciplined society of bishops and secular and regular priests. They had made a tacit pact with another society, the aristocracy, relying on them to govern and control the people. Thus two forces, the church and the nobility, which were to be conspicuous in modern Austria, were already vital in the middle of the seventeenth century, but the army and the bureaucracy were still absent. The emperors had soldiers at their disposal, but in accordance with the traditional system of recruitment they still lacked an effective standing army, which began to develop after 1680. Meanwhile the Turkish threat was still at the gates of Pressburg and Vienna, the route to the east was blocked and the monarchy could not properly be called Danubian.

Nevertheless the term Austrian can reasonably be applied to this block of states. The dynasty was only important in international affairs because of power derived from the demographic and economic resources of these territories. The former legal power of the Estates was, at least in Bohemia and Austria, curtailed. But force of arms, outside help and empiricism, rather than any coherent political theory, had led to this result. Everything was bent towards obedience, but the sovereign did not exercise the plenitude of his powers over his peoples, either in person or through his agents. Amid the details and complexities of the administrative system he was not in direct control, nor could he direct the forces which would develop with the return of peace. Feudalism survived everywhere, taking on a new life within a commercial and capitalist economy.

At a time when absolutism was becoming effective in other European countries, secondary powers which had been subdued elsewhere continued to dominate the social system in Austria. If they repressed the spirit of revolt they also curbed, to their own advantage, the spirit of enterprise and limited the prince's authority. Austria was a system possessing elements of power and greatness, but it was far from being a modern state. It remained an association of peoples without the means to form a united nation.

CHAPTER XVIII

THE FALL OF THE STUART MONARCHY

THE development of political life and government in England since 1300 had been considerably affected by foreign war and to a lesser extent by domestic conflicts. English kings had been both attackers and defenders, defending their French inheritance and their northern border, asserting claims over Wales, Ireland, Scotland and France. From Edward I's conquest of Wales to Henry V's of France, attack and conquest had predominated. These claims were never clearly renounced by any of the Tudors and were asserted at enormous cost by Henry VIII. Part of that cost was the strength of movements of protest and rebellion 1525–54 which were broader in geographical and social characteristics than the disorders before Henry VII. The cost of trying to match effectively the scale of continental warfare in Charles V's time had profoundly affected English governments by 1559. Thereafter they were more than ever limited to a basically defensive policy, however much their subjects hankered after memories of past glories. From 1570 to 1639 England had its longest period of domestic peace since 1066 and, unlike the nearly comparable period 1330–80, was only engaged in foreign wars for just over a third of the time. One of the most important symptoms of political crisis under the Stuarts was their inability to pursue an effective foreign policy. This impotence saved England from direct participation in the Thirty Years War and at the same time helped to produce the Civil War.

Nevertheless the scale of the Elizabethan war effort had important consequences. The debts Elizabeth left were comparatively small, because she had kept to the tradition set by Henry VIII of selling crown land rather than meeting the full cost of war by taxation. The more serious effects were on government and governed. War was accompanied by profiteering and corruption, which was scarcely novel, though it has been argued that corruption and self-seeking in high places grew greater. This could have been a result of the crown's steadily decreasing direct resources for rewarding its servants, one symptom of which was the increasing number of grants of patents of monopoly as rewards leading to violent attacks on them in the Commons in 1601. More serious long-term symptoms were the steady decline in the yield of the lay subsidy (from £137,000 in 1559 to £71,000 in 1603) during a period of inflation and the acknowledged fact that it fell increasingly heavily on the poorer and spared the wealthier landowners. But the decline was also partly due to the fact that a large part of the costs of war was met by local levies.

From 1588 to 1599 thousands of men in the trained bands were being drilled six or more times a year. The rates levied to pay for arms, training and maintenance in crisis years for a town or county might be four times the yield of a subsidy. Both local élites and the government exploited the situation. The well-to-do increasingly evaded their obligations in personal service and cash, though greater landowners often did provide onerous voluntary services. The government increasingly commandeered arms, paid for by local rates, to equip troops sent overseas. Opportunities for favours and outright corruption were increasingly exploited. A contemporary wrote:

[When] the payment of subsidies, the service of musters and other common charges of this our time were not usual, the harm of retainments was not then so thoroughly seen . . . as now it is. There is nothing more usual than to retain the wealthiest yeomanry and others by forbearing them wholly, or charging them lightly to make recompense of their service, by robbing of the king's coffers or defrauding him and the realm of that help which they might bring, if they were equally burdened as their neighbours.

At the same time there was a general tendency for places of power and profit to be concentrated in fewer hands. The militia was administered after the 1580s by much smaller groups, whether commissioners or deputy lieutenants, than earlier. The numbers of commissioners for the subsidies fell, special commissioners for recusancy offences, or other business, were chosen from the J.P.s. The membership of all these usually came from one small group of notables. The crown had long accepted or fostered the growth of oligarchy in municipal government, but the importance of favour in county government was greater than ever. Both at the centre and locally the groups enjoying prestige and profit seemed to be growing smaller, while the numbers excluded grew larger.

Thus the war gave increased opportunities for patronage, faction and corruption in the country as well as at court. Although organization for war certainly increased the central supervision of local affairs in the short run, it did not provide new or permanent means of increasing the government's power, as had happened in Castile and was to happen in France. Much of the war effort depended directly on local resources, or in the naval war on private ones which the government employed, but could not fully control. Once peace came the militia organization became eventually a focus for local discontents and grievances against central authority, a testimony to its weakness rather than to its strength. Once visible threats of invasion and of domestic emergencies had gone, there was increased questioning of the scope and basis of the crown's emergency powers.

By 1603 desire for peace was general and strong. James was doubly welcomed as a bringer of peace, since many had feared a disputed succession. His own preconceptions were flatteringly confirmed, for he genuinely saw himself as an international peacemaker, while his succession defied Henry VIII's statutorily conferred power to determine the succession by his will and vindicated the most practical claims of indefeasible divine hereditary right. He also came as the expected bringer of 'a better time' to English puritans, whose advent was the 'day which the Lord hath made'.

James was the experienced ruler of a country where to survive and exercise some authority were major achievements of kingcraft. Physically timorous and unprepossessing, he had shown determination and ability to choose effective ministers. His own high opinion of his intellectual abilities was not entirely unjustified. But time would show that in his new kingdom he lacked not perception but persistence and application. His growing habits of self-flattery and self-indulgence mattered less in his intellectual pursuits, where he chose competent collaborators to do the donkey work in his later years.[1] But he failed to apply the same solution effectively to the problems of English government. There he could appreciate good advice, but seldom accepted the postponement of immediate satisfactions, whether in verbal victories, bestowing favours, or hours spent hunting, for the sake of future strength. Increasingly the captive of his homosexual tastes, he finally sacrificed his own preferences to those of Buckingham. He was in a sense corrupted by the magnificence and ceremonious ostentation of the court which was one of the Tudors' major achievements and which so impressed foreign observers. In mitigation it should be said that kings were not generally expected to show the obsessive dedication to paperwork of a Philip II and that James suffered from a painful and disabling disease (possibly porphyria) whose attacks became increasingly frequent and severe after 1610.[2]

These infirmities were not apparent in 1603. The welcoming crowds looked for bounty and a new dispensation. Such hopes always marked the beginning of a new reign, but they were stronger and more urgent now. James was ready to see himself as the uniter of crowns and creeds, bringing judgements of Solomon to cure his subjects' conflicts. After the poverty of Scotland, means for bounty seemed limitless and he never digested Elizabeth's saying 'no prince's revenues be so great that they are able to satisfy the insatiable cupidity of men'.

The desire to end the war was undoubtedly strong, but this could not solve the crown's financial problems and would increase its political ones, as vested interests in the war had grown up. Apart from contractors supplying the forces, there was heavy investment in privateering. Although this gave opportunities to West Country captains, the largest ships and profits belonged to great London merchants like Bayning. The war probably increased their domination of the country's trade still further

[1] See above, Chapter III, pp. 105–8 for his European reputation as a controversialist.
[2] I. Macalpine and others, *Porphyria—A Royal Malady* (1968), pp. 26–33.

and certainly increased their ability to gain privileges and favours from a harassed government. Both were bitterly resented by the outports who wished to ensure that these gains were not perpetuated in any peace.

In peacetime general prosperity depended upon industry and trade to a greater extent than in any country outside the Netherlands. Overseas trade was dominated by woollen textiles (some three-quarters of the total value of exports). Although the home market for cloth may have been bigger and agriculture was the basic sector of the economy, a serious slump in cloth exports produced unemployment, credit difficulties, falling rents and widespread discontent. Landowners in the Commons recognized an interdependence between industry, overseas trade and rents of land. The main export was of unfinished cloth to the Netherlands and was the monopoly of the Merchant Adventurers, a regulated company dominated by great London merchants, who thus seemed to control the fortune of much of the country. The importance and narrowness of the Merchant Adventurers' market was a limiting factor in English foreign policy and a longstanding ambition had been to diversify the markets for cloth. Peace might provide opportunities for this, while the outports rallied behind the slogan of free trade in the hope of reducing London's domination through privileged companies.

Some merchants might want freer overseas trade, without attacking economic regulation in general. The crown had always in theory possessed wide powers of regulation, generally thought necessary to preserve order. Thus it controlled middlemen, forbade forestalling and regrating, tried to regulate prices in times of scarcity and found itself responsible for regulations concerning wages, apprenticeship, the poor, standards of cloth production, encouraging fishing by fast days, or discouraging imports of luxuries by sumptuary laws. Much regulation was based on statutes, but some was based on grants by the crown to companies or individuals ostensibly to encourage or reform branches of trade, or particular industries. Such grants were often monopolies with powers of search or inspection, or they might be licences or dispensations from statutes, such as those prohibiting the export of unfinished cloth. Thus statutory and prerogative power were mingled, complementing and contradicting each other, not so much for the profit of the crown, or at the behest of its policies, but rather for those of pressure groups and their intermediaries at court. In emergencies, such as bad harvests, the privy council might be active, trying to ensure that local authorities controlled grain supplies, regulated prices, or relieved the poor, but enforcement of most economic regulation was left to interested parties or common informers, who claimed the penalties provided in statutes. Professional informers (often the agents of Londoners) could live by forcing offenders to compound by threats of prosecution or by starting prosecutions. Sometimes the crown granted individuals power to dispense from penalties in statutes. Thus informing on penal statutes was a major grievance, even to those who wanted effective enforcement of economic regulation.

If the emergency powers of the crown to preserve order were wide and ill-defined, a number of tacit conventions had grown up which restricted its freedom in fiscal policy. Since the mid-sixteenth century debasement had never been used as a fiscal device; though considered a couple of times before 1640, it was felt to be politically impossible. Since Henry VII's time offices had been sold, but the profits almost always went to other office-holders, not to the crown. Both the Commons and crown before 1642 accepted the view that to reform the system of direct taxation by introducing excises was also politically impossible. Thus the only revenue which could be readily increased was that from customs. Apart from the constitutional issues as to whether this could be done by prerogative power, there was the fiscal limitation that duties had to be kept low to avoid smuggling and discontent. To pursue effective protectionist policies by abolishing export duties and imposing high import duties on manufactures would have involved sacrificing certainty in yield which the crown could not afford.

War and the queen's old age had not caused the postponement of all efforts at reform. Attempts to improve the educational standards of the clergy, procedures in Chancery, Star Chamber and other courts and put statutory limitations on informers made some progress. Even these modest efforts offended some vested interests, but many men wanted much greater and often contradictory changes, any of which would upset even more interests.

This was especially true of the church, where the wealth, status and education of most of the rural parochial clergy had probably risen during Elizabeth's reign. As the country parson was usually an active farmer, this may have enhanced him in the eyes of some of his neighbours, or encouraged the jealousies of others. The improvement in education necessary for 'a godly preaching ministry', like other long-sought improvements, seemed to make some problems worse. The more graduates, the more of the poorer livings they held; the output of clergy from the universities doubled or perhaps tripled between 1560 and 1600 and continued to rise. Some graduates might have to be content to be curates, others held pluralities. After 1600 the number of pluralities increased in some dioceses. Another response was the endowing of lectureships (for weekly or more frequent sermons) by laymen and towns. Their increasing numbers after 1600 threatened the traditional order and authorities of the church, while providing Puritan corporations and patrons with opportunities for propagating their views, which were the greater since lectureships were often relatively well paid. Thus, as in other cases, an improvement which everyone desired in principle, in practice seemed to call either for more sweeping changes, or repressive measures to preserve the old order.

Abuses attacked in the Reformation Parliament still seemed as vexatious as ever. Bishops now defended pluralism as a practical means of ensuring an adequate living for educated men. The promised reform of canon law and the church courts had never taken place. Their procedures remained dilatory and ineffective, their officials often corrupt; when high commission provided more effective sanctions its legality might be challenged. Complaints came both from those who wanted an effective godly discipline and those who resented clerical pretensions and power. These latter can be seen as the heirs of medieval anti-clericalism, or as pioneers of modern secularism, or more immediately as the defenders of their own selfish interests; over 40 per cent of rectories were impropriated to laymen. Such sentiments also helped the Commons to pass bills on four occasions between 1604 and 1629 making clergy with cure of souls ineligible for commissions of the peace. Constructive reformers including both the subscribers to the Millenary Petition at James' accession and their opponents such as Bancroft, Robert Cecil or Thomas Egerton agreed on the desirability of taxing impropriate tithes in lay hands; the Commons of the 1604 Parliament rejected such proposals.

If the greatest and most immediate expectations of reform were in the church, James again could not hope to satisfy all expectations, which were equally high among both Puritans and Catholics. Between 1580 and 1604 the number of families of Catholic gentry in Yorkshire had risen by 60 per cent to include nearly a third of all gentry families. This trend fed Catholic expectations and confirmed the Puritans' view of the Elizabethan church's failure to evangelize 'the dark corners of the land'. The Puritans seemed to have real grounds for hope and were encouraged by James' chaplain. Their movement was not exclusively clerical, nor were their lay supporters confined to prosperous landowners and townsmen. Many ministers claimed that they omitted to wear surplices, or perform prescribed ceremonies, especially the use of the cross in baptism, not because they held them to be against the law of God, but because their congregations, or most of them, would leave. Almost everyone agreed in abhorring separation from a national church, few regarded episcopal government as unscriptural, just as very few bishops recognized non-episcopal ordination and church government as ungodly. As yet few acknowledged deep doctrinal differences, however much they disputed about ceremonies, discipline and the priorities demanded by preaching and evangelism.

Whitgift, the archbishop of Canterbury, and Bancroft who succeeded him in 1604, were against any conference with the Puritans whom, like Elizabeth, they regarded as presbyterian conspirators against church and state. But at least four bishops favoured accommodation with the moderate Puritans, as Grindal had done. Whitgift was overruled by James, who nominated Puritan spokesmen for the Hampton Court Conference

(January 1604). They were moderates, but received instructions from a conclave of delegates; this represented many areas and did include some believers in divinely ordained presbyterianism. The instructions were conspicuously moderate, except for claiming the surplice and ring in marriage were unlawful. They concentrated on asking for union of small parishes, redemption of impropriate tithe to ensure a preaching ministry, revision of the Prayer Book and the Thirty-nine Articles and some participation by the lower clergy in ordination and discipline, while acknowledging episcopal authority. Some minor concessions were agreed of which some found their way into the Canons of 1604 and the Prayer Book, but most were ignored by the bishops and forgotten by James, despite his instructions for their execution. These included abolishing the power of chancellors and other lay officials to excommunicate, and means to plant preachers in Ireland, Wales and the North. The moderation of the Puritan spokesmen may have made James feel they could be ignored.

Bancroft was left free to pursue his campaign for complete conformity which resulted in the deprivation of some ninety clergy and strong efforts to defend them in the Commons. But this triumph was somewhat illusory, many of the deprived finding their way back into livings or lectureships. Anglicanism continued to accommodate many clergy who used only part of the ceremonies, prayer book, or vestments and still hoped for reform in the spirit of Grindal. The conference's failure perhaps had more serious effects on the Puritan movement, since it was never again to unite effectively behind a moderate programme. Hampton Court was the real birthplace of Independency.[1] However this may be, it certainly ensured that crown, Parliament and common lawyers became involved in quarrels over the nature of the royal supremacy and ecclesiastical jurisdiction as a result of the Canons of 1604. The practical objectives of reform which many of the clergy and laity accepted were effectively obstructed.

If there was much dislike of clerical pretensions to wealth, power and precedence over the laity, going back to before the Reformation, there was also another longstanding tradition of resentment at the pretensions and profits of the lawyers. This expressed itself in demands for control of fees in legal proceedings and of the number of attorneys, for simplification or codification of the law and in general for cheap and speedy justice. Not all lawyers were hostile to reforms but those which professionals attempted (such as Egerton's in Chancery) often seemed to produce fresh grievances. The fact that England never received Roman law and the procedural changes this entailed meant the survival of lay judges (especially the J.P.s) and juries of trial and presentment. On the continent professional jurists were usually judges in local courts, whether royal, seigneurial, or public. The lack of concepts such as the French crown's

[1] P. Collinson, *The Elizabethan Puritan Movement* (1967), pp. 464–7.

justice retenue and powers of evocation restricted the crown's ability to interfere formally with procedures of courts and to create new jurisdictions. The crown could and did influence judges by dismissing them, but the revival of the House of Lords in the 1620s as the supreme court of common law was a denial of the crown's judicial supremacy.

Nevertheless the common law courts at Westminster began to exercise greater powers of supervision by the late sixteenth century. They did this mainly by the process of defining the privileges of their own and other courts. In asserting a supremacy over other courts, the selfish interests of common lawyers and judges in maintaining the business and fees of their courts were certainly important. This involved them in attacks on the courts of Admiralty and High Commission which did use civil and canon law, but it is a mistake to think of the common law in conflict with or threatened by other systems of law. Chancery, Star Chamber, the Councils of the Marches and the North used procedures derived from the common law, their pleaders and many of their judges were common lawyers, though all had some reliance on lay opinion. Disputes between common law judges and Chancery did occur, but their usual relationship was co-operative, especially in asserting the subordination of the provincial courts and of Admiralty and Requests. The Star Chamber largely exemplified co-operation between chancellor and judges and was not seriously challenged, even by Coke. However, this process of definition did lead to conflict over the privy council's functions and the king's personal judicial powers.

From the point of view of litigants the results of these efforts are more obscure. In tightening their procedural rules, Chancery and other courts tried to prevent vexatious litigants pursuing vendettas simultaneously in several courts. But increasing formality of process in Chancery, or Star Chamber, also gave opportunites for delay. Down to the 1570s many cases (perhaps most) were sent to local commissioners for arbitration or settlement by Star Chamber, Chancery, Requests and the privy council. While Chancery still did this on a large scale in the 1590s, Star Chamber had ceased to do so and the activity of Requests and the privy council declined after 1599. It is likely, but not certain, that as process in Chancery grew more formal fewer cases went to commissioners. It is certain that in most manorial courts civil litigation shrank steadily after 1600, and their discretion was checked by the frequent settlement of manorial customs by Chancery. Custom ceased to be flexible and changing as it had been in the thirteenth century; immemorial binding custom was a discovery of the sixteenth century. Fuller reporting of cases, stricter interpretation of statutes increased the courts' tendency to bind themselves by precedents. By 1600 the justices of assizes monopolized criminal justice to a greater extent than ever before. Local gentry no longer delivered gaols and quarter sessions had been ordered not to try serious crimes, while the assize judges were expected to exercise close supervision over local administration.

The privy council not only directed local administration, but tried to supervise administration of justice. It reinforced execution of process, ordered juries to be changed and courts to speed judgement. This often involved prohibitions from other courts against cases in Requests and Admiralty. Although it refused to hear cases begun in other courts, it explicitly asserted its right to hear cases not so begun, and hear complaints about courts. After protests by the judges more cases were dismissed to the common law courts from 1589. Apart from appointing arbitrators, or commissioners, to end cases, much of the council's legal activity was concerned with debtors and creditors. Commissioners for poor debtors were appointed, creditors were forced to accept compositions and prevented from pursuing the full rigour of process at common law. The sanctions were imprisonment of creditors by order of commissions or privy councillors. This led to release of prisoners by writs of *habeas corpus* and a protest by all the judges in 1591. Later commissions had no power to arrest and general commissions ceased after 1603. Nevertheless similar means to relieve individual debtors were used by the council, on the king's personal authority and by bills of conformity in Chancery which were stopped after attacks in Parliament in 1621.

The harshness of the law to poor debtors was a constant theme of law reformers throughout the seventeenth century. Yet attempts to relieve them raised important questions about the crown's power to interfere with proceedings and judgements of the courts and to imprison men without showing causes recognized by the common law. The king's personal responsibility for administering justice revived rather than diminished after 1603. Down to at least 1616 hundreds of cases came before the king by petition and show 'constant ... intervention ... in all kinds of private litigation with summary action under the king's personal authority on a very large number of personal cases appropriate for ordinary trial'.[1] Abuses by influence and favouritism were possible and even likely. But this was also a last stronghold of the traditional basis of much English justice, enforceable arbitration, and the king was still a source of arbitration for the poor as well as the powerful. As oligarchy grew stronger in local government and factions more entrenched there and at court, such a system was likely to produce more dissatisfaction than ever. It was also endangered by the central courts' growth in power and formalism. Men of all ranks feared that a system of technicalities, exploited by professional lawyers and fee-hungry officials, was obliterating any hope that justice could be cheap, speedy and based on generally accepted notions of equity. Coke's common law which is 'perfect reason

[1] J. P. Dawson, 'The Privy Council and Private Law in the Tudor and Stuart Periods', *Michigan Law Review*, Vol. XLVIII (1950), pp. 393–428, 627–55.

which commands those things proper and necessary and which prohibits contrary things' might seem sympathetic to such aspirations. But Coke's reason is artificial: 'gotten by long study . . . and not of every man's natural reason . . .', so that the common law refined by generations of learned lawyers is 'grown to such a perfection for the government of this realm' that it is superior to the private reason of individuals, whether kings or subjects. In the long run the crown was blamed for failing to control the system, though its ability to do so was often weakened by professional lawyers in Parliament and elsewhere seeking to define its prerogatives. The supreme expression of this was Coke's view, developed in the 1620s, that Parliament was the summit of the common law, though its voice was to be that of professional lawyers, bound by precedents of artificial reason, interpreting Magna Carta, to control both crown and Parliament.

Now it is true that the political nation spoke the same language of politics, based on common assumptions about the ancient constitution. Conflicts in Parliament about the crown's religious, fiscal and foreign policies occurred throughout Elizabeth's reign, not only in its last years. Recently these facts have been taken to show that such conflicts toppled the Stuarts because of their incompetence and extravagance and that there were no deeper problems with which Elizabeth and her councillors could not have coped. Obviously there is some truth in this, but this common language expressed agreement over vague and ambiguous generalities, such as the complementary character of prerogative and parliamentary privilege and subjects' rights, or the existence of fundamental laws. Everyone agreed the crown had emergency powers, the difficulty was in agreeing on their scope and the occasions on which they could properly be used. Most immediate precedents, if not always much immediate political wisdom, were on the side of the crown. Agreement often proved to be about inessentials, on many actual issues new demands and unwillingness to compromise were characteristic of the Commons' leaders.

The rickety theoretical foundations of this agreement are illustrated by the problem of conquest. As the ancient constitution was agreed to be immemorial, the Norman conquest had to be treated as a non-event; any suggestion that parliamentary institutions, privileges, or laws had specific origins in the will of later kings seemed to threaten the whole constitutional position of parliament. James himself disliked claims based on conquest, as diplomatically he wanted to recognize the United Provinces as a legitimate state and to resist any Spanish claims arising from attempts to conquer them or England. It needed civil war, before the myth of the ancient constitution inherited from the Saxons could be subjected temporarily to rational criticism. Any conflict was dangerous, not only because of the presumption that harmony was the pre-ordained outcome of the constitution, but because arguments were based on searches for precedents which might further undermine the whole precarious structure of agreement on fundamentals. James' hostility to the Society of Antiquaries was on the mistaken grounds that their researches could only produce precedents against his prerogative, but critical historical researches, such as Spelman's, might subvert the whole accepted order of things. Men were inured to sudden death and uncontrollable extremes of pain in ways beyond our imagining. They saw society as subject to various divine plans, not as the result of evolutionary process. Social and political changes might be the product of human sin, some had millennial expectations of destruction and transformation, but the idea of conflict as part of a continuing process of relatively peaceful and ultimately fruitful change was absent: toleration might be expedient; very few accepted it as an essential basis for society. The observation that everyone (except a few high-flying clergy) used the same political language applies to the polemicists of the first Civil War. This might persuade us that the Civil War was consciously fought about narrow issues as a result of misunderstanding, but not that this vocabulary demonstrates the lack of conflicts serious enough for shedding blood.

In parliamentary politics behaviour and conflicts can be classified in terms of court and country, terms in use by the 1620s. But it is misleading to envisage two monolithic blocks, however much the convenience of static analysis in terms of office-holding and connections may encourage this. In fact there were always factions at court and conflicts within the privy council, liable to seek allies in the Commons to discredit and attack their rivals. Thus a spokesman who attacked the policy of a dominant minister or group endorsed by the crown was not necessarily cutting himself off from connections with the court or hopes of office. This was clearly so in 1610, 1614, 1624 and even 1626. The effective political nation was small in numbers, so that its leaders were personally known to each other and at least formally to the king. For many who were not courtiers or officials came occasionally to court. M.P.s did see themselves as representatives who had to explain themselves and their doings to quarter sessions, municipal corporations and especially to meetings to assess subsidies. This public opinion was that of small groups, of those with weight in local affairs, themselves divided by rivalries and factions.

The claim that the constitution rightly understood must produce harmony, though clearly untrue historically, exacerbated political feeling; when disharmony and deadlock manifestly prevailed, scapegoats had to be found. Conflicts under Elizabeth were frequently denied by the Commons' leaders, while defenders of the *status quo* could deny the need for reforms. While it is doubtful whether the Commons contained conscious seekers of revolutionary changes, from James I onwards there were men such as Ellesmere, who feared such changes would happen, or Bacon who thought wholesale legal and intellectual reform and reconstruction were needed. Even the leader of the pro-Spanish Howard faction, Henry earl of Northampton, had his programme of reforms for stabilizing society. He wanted the revocation of all grants of arms since 1568, their restriction to gentlemen of blood or merit, and strong measures to suppress duelling. Whether or not they were practicable, useful, or desirable, the Millenary Petition, the unenacted bills passed by the Commons of 1604, James' Union with Scotland, the Great Contract, Bancroft's further programme of reforms, or Sir Henry Neville's legislative programme of 1614, would have produced substantial changes in both the constitution and social relationships, if any of them had been accomplished. The failure of the Stuart monarchy is partly the history of its failure to accomplish any reforms, even where there was substantial agreement that something needed doing. Elizabeth had always been hostile to ecclesiastical reforms, including those of her own bishops. The view that there were no really new problems, other than those created by Stuart incompetence, no consciousness of need for reform for any other reason, does not seem to be demonstrated by the first ten years of James' reign. There was perhaps more general desire for change and reform among the political nation then and less fear of chaos and disorder resulting than in 1640. Because men spoke the same political language and believed in a basically unchanging constitution, it does not follow that they did not desire reforms which would in fact have involved political and social changes.

It has also been argued that profound social and economic changes made political conflicts inevitably sharper and finally broke the monarchy. The monarchy and the existing order stood for regulation and exploitation of economically progressive elements; businesslike landowners, industrialists, merchants, or the middling sort, wishing to maximize profits, were hindered by tillage laws, monopolies, chartered companies, regulation of prices, or attempts to set the poor on work. These propertied groups eventually found economic freedom in the Interregnum and had contributed most to the Commons' opposition before 1642. These economic and social freedoms largely survived the political and religious restoration of 1660 and were finally secured in 1688. Another more social interpretation asserts that a decisive part was played by a crisis in the affairs of the peerage. 'For a time this group lost its hold upon the nation and thus allowed political and social initiative to fall into the hands of the squirearchy.'[1] By 1603 the peerage had lost a great part of the lands it had owned in 1558, had ceased to constitute a majority of the greater landowners and was losing its political and military power and prestige. Although it was very successful after 1603 in increasing its income from land and other sources, this further weakened its prestige and

[1] L. Stone, *The Crisis of the Aristocracy* (Oxford, 1965), p. 13.

power with other groups and identified it more completely with court corruption. It traded 'respect and loyalty for cash' which was spent 'on pleasure rather than power,'[1] making possible a naked struggle for power, although most of the peers supported the king in 1642.

While no one would deny that economic and social changes occurred, it is not clear that they were qualitatively so decisive as either of these explanations require. The first view exaggerates the amount of economic and social *laissez-faire* achieved by 1660, while what was achieved was more the result of accident than of conscious design. As to the 'crisis of the aristocracy', even if Professor Stone has correctly diagnosed the peers' economic position in 1603, his assumptions seem to exaggerate the extent and character of their political power and social prestige in 1558. It is unlikely that they were then 'a reasonable majority grouping of the greater landowners'; if they were not in 1603, this does not imply a radical change in the social landscape, so that a whole generation lacked familiar landmarks. There is evidence that peers' incomes in aggregate rose faster than prices down to 1641, but that this was at the expense of their political power and social prestige is highly disputable.

Thus the ending of the war and the coming of a new king heightened demand for solutions to old problems and created new ones. These certainly reflected changing conditions, but it is not clear that structural economic and social changes were inaugurating a new era. Doubtless it is a distortion to see the Commons as inexorably, if unconsciously, pursuing their privileges along a road which inevitably led to a total usurpation of sovereignty. But if there was no struggle for sovereignty in 1604, it does not follow that a patient and co-operative country was goaded to intransigence by a corrupt and feckless court. The Commons' attitude to the crown's discretionary powers is illustrated by two uncontroversial minor measures in the first session of James' first parliament.

An act regulating the tanning and leather trades included an ingenious proviso that any grant dispensing with any provision of the act would automatically repeal that provision (1 James I c.22, cl.51). This was presumably inspired by memories of Dyer's patent for dispensing offences under the 1563 act now repealed. On the second day of business and the first on which bills were considered, a bill repealing all previous statutes of apparel was rejected by 125 votes to 75 at its first reading when debate or division was 'not usually admitted without some extraordinary Conceit of Mischief...'. The mischief was the power given the king to regulate apparel by proclamation, though Elizabeth had in effect revised the old statutes by proclamation. The Commons then produced a bill restricting the use of cloth of gold or silver to the royal family, which the Lords rejected. A third bill, which allowed their use by peers, misliked by the Commons, passed because it repealed the earlier acts. James

[1] *Ibid.* p. 164.

vetoed it, but allowed the repeal of the acts: yet a bill of apparel passed the Commons in 1621, others were read in 1626 and 1628. There was general agreement that such regulations were necessary, yet disagreements about how to revise them effectively left no regulations at all. In the1620s an agreed measure was probably still possible, but wider conflicts left no time for its enactment.

On the matter of wider theoretical import, the Commons of this first parliament undoubtedly challenged the way Elizabeth had interpreted and exercised her powers. The most serious challenge was to her concept of the royal supremacy in religion. The Commons denied that king and clergy alone could legislate in ecclesiastical affairs and held the Canons of 1604 '. . . in prejudice and impeachment . . . of the lawes, statutes and free customs of the realm . . .'. In 1606 a bill invalidating canons and church ordinances made during the last ten years, or in future, without parliamentary consent passed the Commons and was read twice in the Lords. Another bill to limit the crown's power to dispense from penal statutes reached the same stage.

Lord Chancellor Ellesmere, reviewing this first parliament after its dissolution in 1610, found that while the power of king and Lords had declined, that of the Commons 'hath grown big and audacious . . . it will not cease (if it be not stayed in time) until it break out into democracy'. He pointed to their unprecedented and successful claims of privilege in deciding disputed elections and returns of members and interfering with process of the courts. Despite not being a court of record, they had attempted to review judgements and to examine Sir Stephen Proctor for misdemeanours in his office as collector of fines on penal statutes. They attacked prerogative and equity courts and High Commission, as well as denying the king's right to impose customs duties without parliamentary consent.[1]

Ellesmere was right that the demands of the Commons had grown, but he omits to mention the unprecedented financial demands and difficulties of the crown. James had inherited debts and war expenses, as well as ministers, notably Robert Cecil (secretary and master of the wards, later earl of Salisbury) and Thomas Sackville, earl of Dorset (lord treasurer), who knew how to profit from office. Dorset told Parliament in 1606 James' ordinary expenses were £80,000 a year greater than Elizabeth's, owing to his wife and family. His detailed account of royal expenses, putting the debt at £735,000, aided by a reminder that the charges of the militia had ceased and by the reaction to the Gunpowder Plot, produced a grant of £453,000 to be paid over four years. Salisbury succeeded Dorset in 1608 and sold crown land (ironically much of it impropriate tithe) for some £411,000, but as ordinary expenditure continued to grow, there was a debt of £280,000 in 1610. Salisbury wished

---

[1] *Proceedings in Parliament 1610*, ed. E. R. Foster (1966), Vol. I, pp. 276–83.

to increase ordinary revenue and limit the king's bounty. Unfortunately, like his predecessors and successors, he never believed that such limitations should apply to his own profits and this always provided scope for rival factions to attack both inside and outside the court. All ministers had to treat royal favourites and their exploitation of the king circumspectly.

In 1609 most of the crown lands were entailed so that they could not be granted without consent of a number of privy councillors and James undertook not to grant pensions or favours at the expense of revenue. Meanwhile Salisbury had imposed new customs duties and was improving the yield of crown lands. In 1610 he staked everything on the Great Contract. In return for abolishing the court of wards and purveyance, for regulating fees, codifying penal statutes and preventing abuses by informers, the Commons were to grant £200,000 a year revenue and a supply of £600,000 to pay off debt, strengthen the navy and provide a reserve. After much bargaining during which James agreed to remove some of the new impositions and that in future they could only be imposed with parliamentary consent, the Commons promised £200,000 a year and a grant of £100,000. During recess the Commons consulted their counties and James heeded the warning of Salisbury's enemies about the loss of patronage involved; both raised their terms; attacks were renewed more violently on impositions, the clergy and the Scots, and ensured the dissolution of the first parliament. The contract ruined Salisbury's influence with James and ensured the triumph of his enemies even before he died in 1612.

Whether it would ever have really solved the financial problem— already in 1607 Hoskyns had claimed 'whatsoever wee give, wee cannot give that (which) may suffice'—it could certainly have altered the constitution. Already members were calling for the summoning of Parliament at regular intervals, and there would have been a permanent direct tax for the first time which the crown would have been tempted to increase in emergencies. Both Dorset and Salisbury taught the Commons the strength of their position by giving details of the crown's financial weakness, without offering a constructive legislative programme. James' own cherished plan for union had been rejected. The contract's failure also meant failure to tackle the longstanding problems about fees, informers and penal statutes and to settle the question of impositions. James had also contemplated far-reaching law reforms, codification and proceedings in English. The attempt to provide a constructive programme in 1614 failed, thanks to James' vacillations, and the question of impositions. Another dissolution was partly engineered by the Howard faction at court. Their supremacy meant years of increasing corruption. Attempts at parliamentary solutions had failed and left a legacy of increasing debt, worsening credit and scepticism about royal promises of economy and the motives of ministers which further impaired prospects of agreement.

Yet if James had died in 1614, despite further sales of crown land and debts of £600,000, his reign might have seemed one of real achievements. He had made peace with Spain and seemed established as Europe's mediator. His mediation had secured the Truce of 1609 in the Netherlands and the settlement of the Clèves-Julich dispute in 1612. He had married his daughter to the Elector Palatine, the leader of militant Calvinism, and hoped to marry his son to a daughter of Philip III, the leader of militant Catholicism. Yet in reality these successes had depended on the hostility between France and Spain and their consequent need to court England. The assassination of Henri IV prevented a war over Jülich-Cleves, in which James had been willing to assist and which would have made understanding with Parliament essential. It also ensured France's drift into passive or co-operative policies towards Spain, when James' financial weakness made it less possible for him to pursue an independent policy effectively. Nevertheless he was the first king to rule effectively throughout Ireland, which remained a serious burden on government finance, though there was at last some prospect this would cease. Irish society was being transformed after the wholesale destruction by war and famine by the imposition of English law, institutions and settlement. His authority over the Scots nobles and church was greater than ever before. He could claim to have strengthened the church of England by protecting the bishops from their critics and their lands from the lay exploitation they had suffered under Elizabeth, while reaffirming the authority of Convocation and High Commission. Minor compromises and reforms had been made; Abbot, Bancroft's successor, was a moderate. Once the crisis about subscription was over, moderate Puritans and some of the more extreme ones found ways of accommodating themselves within the church.

James could also claim to have maintained order among the courts, he had effectively protected the church courts and Chancery from the prohibitions of the common law courts. He had restored the authority of the Council of the Marches after limiting it in 1606. In these cases he had listened to lengthy arguments from both sides. The judges and the Commons had refused to accept the High Commission's powers to imprison and use *ex officio* procedures, though the commission's validity had been recognized by the judges in 1591. James did not accept all the bishop's demands and promised reforms; the judges were forced to accept new letters patent in 1611. These restricted and defined the arbitrary powers of the commission to imprison and fine, limited its discretion and allowed appeals. As after Hampton Court, not all the reforms promised were implemented. Yet wordy and pedagogic as James was, he was accessible to the Commons of his first parliament. He was at pains to deny explicitly any claim to legislate, or levy direct taxes, without parliamentary consent, just as he had been willing to renounce his power to levy impositions. To some extent the outports had won concessions to their fears of domination by London. The general free trade bill of 1604 had failed, but trade to France and Spain had been declared free by Parliament; although a French company was later chartered, the privy Council consistently consulted the outports about its scope. Some obsolete statutes had been repealed and an act attempting to restrict the number of attorneys was passed.

Bacon complained that Salisbury had taught the Commons to haggle with the king and to take the initiative in legislative reform. After failing to regain this initiative in 1614, James was constrained to a period of expedients, which exhausted his credit and increasingly restricted his freedom of action, both at home and abroad. Some expedients were futile but relatively harmless, such as the attempt to raise a benevolence. Others had more serious consequences, such as sales of honours, grants of monopolies and Cockayne's project. James had dubbed nearly 1,000 knights in his first year and thereafter sale of knighthoods was a regular means of rewarding courtiers. In 1611 the order of baronets was created,their sale brought £101,000 to the exchequer down to 1619. From 1615 peerages were sold, down to 1628 some 30 English and 40 Irish and Scots ones for perhaps £350,000. The crown may have got £150,000, but most went to courtiers, especially to George Villiers, the new favourite from 1616, later created duke of Buckingham.[1] Sale of offices, such as the mastership of the wards, became more blatant, though again most of the profits went to the favourite and his clients. The court seemed more than ever a synonym for corruption. The sale of honours increased tensions and divisions in a society which was ideally conceived as a stable hierarchy, and where living individuals were jealous of rights to precedence. Sale of office and of honours came to be grouped together with older grievances about excessive fees. On fees a commission in 1611 and another in 1623, following more intensive parliamentary agitation, achieved nothing.

In 1604 the government had not accepted the case against the Merchant Adventurers, when their enemies had a majority in the Commons, yet in 1614 Alderman Cockayne got their privileges abolished by promising to procure the finishing of white cloth in England and additional revenue of £47,000. As the most important part of the cloth exports was unfinished, this would vitally affect the country's prosperity. Cockayne's real objective seems to have been to share the export of undressed cloth between his associates and the old adventurers rather than seriously to create a cloth-finishing industry. The old adventurers refused to recognize the new company's privileges; the consequent lack of capital and disorganization of exports helped the growth of foreign industries. The

[1] Some money which did go to the crown did not go through the exchequer and so cannot be traced.

export of old draperies had reached a peak in 1614, and never achieved this level again. This was not due solely to the project, but to drastic debasements in Germany and Poland from 1616 which tended to price English cloth out of these markets, followed by a depression in international trade after 1620. In 1617 the old adventurers bought back their privileges for some £80,000 which was recovered by imposts (imprest money) on cloth exported which was also burdened by the crown with new praetermitted customs. It was easy and not totally unreasonable to blame the depression of the cloth industry and its repercussions throughout the economy on the crown's disastrous policies, though Cockayne's project had been blessed by Coke himself. The situation was the more humiliating because English trade and shipping had lagged so far behind the Dutch in the years of truce, except perhaps in the Mediterranean. Dutch ships were capturing carrying trade from English ports. From 1610 onwards there were demands for navigation acts and a whole literature of warning and imitation about the Dutch. From being clients the Dutch had become all too successful rivals.

By 1618 the royal debt was £900,000. In 1617 the crown's credit was so bad it could only borrow by forcing London to guarantee the loan; as the crown defaulted on both interest and repayment, James' credit there was exhausted for the rest of his reign. The Howard faction's supremacy completed the ruin of the royal finances, and had added the moral corruption of the Essex divorce and the Overbury murder to the venality of court life. The new favourite George Villiers, eventually created duke of Buckingham, was wooed by those with programmes of reform and self-advancement—notably Coke, Bacon and Cranfield. Even the hoped-for dowry from the Spanish match could not have met the debts, still less stopped the deficit, so Buckingham came to power as the patron of reformers. Reform was the weapon which would destroy the Howards.

Buckingham's most important hatchet man was Lionel Cranfield, who had the qualifications needed to carry out plans for retrenchment. The first was that of the sub-committee of the privy council investigating the household. By 1620 substantial economies and improvements were achieved there, in the navy, the ordnance and the wardrobe. Cranfield, their chief executant, had combined a profit of £7,000 a year for himself and a saving of £22,000 for the king as master of the wardrobe. These efforts saved some £87,000 a year and increased revenues (mainly from customs) by £37,000. But the debt and royal credit were unchanged and nothing had been done to cut pensions; grants of monopolies and favours to Buckingham and his relatives had increased, as had the expenses of foreign policy thanks to the Elector Palatine's involvement in Bohemia.

As lord admiral, Buckingham did repair the decay achieved by the Howards and built up the navy. The decisive work was done by commissioners down to 1623, but Buckingham concerned himself effectively with naval administration. From 1618 the crown made as many paternalistic efforts as after 1629. It tried to deal with the adverse balance of trade by enforcing prohibitions on the export of bullion and the statutes of employment. It tried to deal with abundant harvests by encouraging export of grain and the setting up of county magazines and with bad harvests by regulating prices and markets. Much was vitiated by considerations of fiscal or personal gain, most obviously in the granting of monopolies, or the commissions to pardon conversion of arable or dispense with apprenticeship. After 1620, unlike the 1630s, real efforts were made to consult opinion and some workable compromise did seem to be emerging. This was first undermined by war and the resulting fiscal and political crises, and was finally undone in the years of personal rule.

It can be argued that only determined retrenchment could ever improve the crown's position enough for it to meet Parliament with any confidence. Clearly this would exclude Buckingham and his clients and an expensive foreign policy, but, even without them, increases in ordinary revenue were needed to maintain credit, a strong navy and reasonable diplomatic activity. The only substantial increases possible were in customs' revenue, whose legality continued to be challenged. Even without the crisis in foreign policy some new modus would have had to be worked out with Parliament.

As Spain was invading the Lower Palatinate and Bavaria the Upper, Parliament was called to finance the demands of foreign policy. When it met in January 1621 Frederick had been driven out of Bohemia. James could point to considerable achievements in administrative reform and Bacon was ready with a programme of legal reforms. Unfortunately serious tactical mistakes had already been made. Bacon had wished to anticipate complaints by withdrawing patents of monopoly, especially vexatious ones belonging to Villiers' connections, but he was overruled by the privy council, including Coke. Coke had hoped for the treasurership and was passed over in favour of Montagu (later earl of Manchester) who had previously supplanted him as chief justice. Grievances were pressed as soon as the Commons met, but they granted £160,000 quickly on promises of co-operation in reforms of the law, informers and trade grievances. The crown needed £500,000 for the Palatinate, but the grant was freely given with an implication that more would be forthcoming. The Commons turned to monopolies, especially those involving Buckingham's relatives. They wished to punish monopolists themselves, but were persuaded by precedents to have Mompesson and Michell judged and condemned by the Lords. Steered by Coke and Cranfield into enquiring who had approved the grants as referees, the Commons accused Lord Chancellor Bacon, refused to leave his judgement to James, so that he was condemned and made incapable of holding office by the Lords. This revival of impeachment was perhaps the most important constitutional development of the reign, while more immediately the enthusiastic preparing of accusations against officials of ecclesiastical courts hastened the prorogation. Sir Thomas Wentworth denied to his fellow Yorkshiremen meeting to assess the subsidy 'that we have given away your money and made no laws', promised the king would give 'free and speedy passage for whatever we might require of reformation . . . ' especially against common informers, '. . . your traffic with foreign parts (shall) flourish with increase'.

Dissension among the councillors had destroyed Bacon and drove Coke further into opposition when Cranfield became lord treasurer. Buckingham hesitated between co-operating with the Commons and seeking a dissolution, becoming more hostile as the enquiries pressed nearer to him and his brother. But not only vacillation at court hindered legislation; in May the Commons were invited to pass twelve bills, including ones about informers, export of wool and Sabbath observance, but preferred to debate the depression and outports' grievances. Cranfield promised action; after the adjournment proclamations withdrew many of the patents attacked, allowed free internal trade in wool and Welsh cloth and the outports freedom to export new draperies. Another had abolished bills of conformity without creditors' consent, until Parliament took further action.

Unfortunately these concessions coincided with the arrest and questioning of members for their conduct in Parliament. This and Bavaria's conquest of the Upper Palatinate ensured the thwarting of reforming bills when Parliament resumed in November. The Commons now wanted to pass bills, including one against monopolies, but would not give priority to supply as they wished to ensure another meeting in February. The king did not wish them to debate foreign policy or the Spanish match. In so far as there was some hope Spain might force the emperor to restore Frederick to the Palatinate, James was not wholly unreasonable. Elizabeth had denied her parliaments' right to discuss foreign policy uninvited. But in asserting his prerogative James tactlessly denied that Parliament's privileges were 'your ancient and undoubted birthright and inheritance', but 'derived from the grace and permission of our ancestors and us'. Even members like Wentworth with no great interest in foreign policy were roused and the Commons excitedly passed a Protestation, asserting their privilege of free speech was unrestricted and all their privileges were 'the birthright and inheritance of the subjects of England'. This ensured prorogation without supply or legislation, followed by dissolution.

As lord treasurer, Cranfield, now earl of Middlesex, had no immediate solution for the financial problem, except the old one of the Spanish marriage. Given the Commons' demands for full enforcement of the recusancy laws, this was incompatible with parliamentary supply. The dowry would pay off debts, restore credit and end the need for extraordinary expenses by restoring Frederick. The big economies by administrative reform had been achieved by 1621, though Cranfield applied himself to supervising reform of Irish government. Customs yields could not be increased appreciably during a depression. Cranfield refused to sell crown lands. They were so encumbered with long leases their yield could not be increased (it actually fell 1619–24), so his wisdom is questionable. This left attempts to curb James' extravagance and Buckingham's perquisites, politically the rasher, since Cranfield's profits from office had grown from £4,100 p.a. in 1618 to £20,000 in 1624, while his income from rents had grown from £1,500 in 1614, when he ceased to be a merchant, to £7,100.[1] Buckingham grew more hostile and he and Charles were taking decisions instead of James. Their journey to Madrid to pursue the Spanish match was against James' wishes, as was their decision after their return to attack Spain and to summon Parliament.

While James was being dragged into ruinous foreign policies and Cranfield was adding to his enemies by his share in dissolving the Virginia Company, more constructive efforts were going on. In 1621 a committee of trade was appointed and in 1622 another to investigate the decay of the cloth trade, followed by a standing commission on trade, under Manchester. This commission had a wide membership; it carefully considered the views of many interests, problems referred to it by the privy council and most important of all recommendations of the Commons' committee of trade in 1624. The result was a number of informed and acceptable compromises on economic policy.

This is only one aspect of the co-operation achieved with Parliament in 1624, though the least ephemeral one. Buckingham persuaded James to accept an immediate vote of £300,000 and to wait till a later session for further supply. The bills considered in 1621 were now enacted, including those limiting common informers, monopolies, prescriptive title to land by the crown, reforming legal procedures and repealing many obsolete statutes. It was the first body of legislation since 1610. Despite James, Buckingham and the Commons co-operated to impeach and condemn Middlesex. They proved little in the way of bribery, his real offence was the enmity of Buckingham and the Southampton-Sandys faction in the Virginia Company. His fall demonstrated how powerful impeachment was, provided Lords and Commons were in agreement. Once again the positive and negative powers of the Commons had been enhanced by court factions.

The Commons acted in ways that pointed towards either considerable changes or serious conflicts, as their procedures against patents of mono-

---

[1] M. Prestwich, *Cranfield, Politics and Profits under the Early Stuarts* (1966), pp. 123, 131, 253–4, 419–20.

poly show. Their committees summoned patentees and their servants, examined them and other witnesses, called in patents and condemned them as illegal in content or execution, or as inconvenient. Although their examinations were not on oath, they were exercising functions, hitherto belonging to the privy council, the law officers and the courts. As the Lords refused to condemn existing grants in the statute of monopolies, the Commons presented them to the king as illegal.[1] James objected to their condemnations and seizures of letters patent, 'For the Lawfullness of Pattents I must relye upon my lerned Counsell and my Judges, but if there falle out any Inconvenience in the Exeqution you may complaine ... but I am the Judge', but a final answer was deferred till the next session. The Commons still held impositions illegal, though this was most strongly pressed by members hostile to war, like Wentworth. They again turned to religion and prepared to impeach the bishop of Norwich for suppressing preaching. James was correct in seeing all these as innovations encroaching the prerogative, just as the monopolies act was the first statutory limitation of it. Yet there were new potentialities for co-operation as well as conflict 1620-5. The commissions and special committees, first adumbrated by Bacon for law reform, proved their worth on economic matters. Even the treasurers appointed by the Commons to receive the 1624 subsidies and the Council of War, had they been encouraged to report to Parliament, might have built up confidence.

Contrary to a commonly held view co-operation proved easier in economic than in other policies. The Commons in 1621 and 1624 heard new demands for a free trade bill; their committee of trade examined the Merchant Adventurers' charter and evidence from them and others. It was resolved that the adventurers' monopoly should apply only to white cloth with free trade in coloured and mingled cloths and kerseys in addition to new draperies. They also demanded abolition of the adventurers' imprest dues and unrestricted entry to the company. The commission of trade accepted these recommendations—except that imprest was reduced by a third and confined to white cloth—and others for the prohibition of foreign tobacco imports and continued prohibition of export of wool. Demands for the total abolition of imprest and the praetermitted customs continued in the next two parliaments, but the worst grievances of the outports were met. The commission also concerned itself with regulating the cloth industry including the new draperies; charters for thirty-two county corporations including J.P.s and with powers to raise stocks were prepared in 1625. Their issue was interrupted by James' death which also ended the commission, and they were finally abandoned on account of the war.

[1] E. R. Foster, 'The Procedure of the House of Commons against Patents and Monopolies 1621-4', in *Conflict in Stuart England*, ed. W. A. Aikin and B. D. Henning (1960), pp. 59-85.

Buckingham's foreign policy made continued co-operation with the Commons impossible; over-ruling James he accepted toleration of Catholics as a condition for a French alliance and marriage. As even those who had doubts about the war had supported enforcement of the recusancy laws, this made the promised meeting of Parliament impossible. Prorogations continued until James' death dissolved it. Thus reply to grievances, further supply and legislation had to wait thirteen months till a new parliament met in June 1625, after waiting in plague-stricken London for a month.

The death of James worsened political tempers. Although over-ruled on major matters and wary of concessions to Parliament in 1624, James was widely believed to be preparing to check Buckingham's domination. This was perhaps wishful thinking, but it underlines the new reign's reversal of the normal expectations of new alignments in making Buckingham's power even greater. Experienced magnates and courtiers like the earls of Arundel and Pembroke found this intolerable. Even among his clients Lord Keeper Williams, Sir John Eliot, Sir Nathaniel Rich and William Coryton began to doubt his leadership. Many like Abbot or Cranfield remembered his ingratitude, others like the Howards and Mansell had been disgraced by him. Even those who wanted war with Spain resented the increased efficiency in controlling privateering and in collecting the lord admiral's and the crown's dues from prizes.[1] Buckingham never achieved any military, diplomatic or naval successes which might have provided some popularity.

If those who attacked him contributed something to his failures, Buckingham's foreign and parliamentary policies were equally irresponsible. When the Commons at last met they received no specific demand for supply or explanation of policy and had to wait a fortnight for an answer for their petition of grievances of 1624. In the absence of any official request, they hastily voted £140,000 at Sir Robert Phelips' suggestion. As the answer to the 1624 petition was unsatisfactory about praetermitted customs and impositions, tonnage and poundage (the basic customs duties) were only voted for one year instead of for Charles' life, as had been customary since 1485. Buckingham ignored Williams' and Eliot's advice to proceed cautiously, offer concessions and leave supply till a winter session. Parliament was adjourned for three weeks to Oxford. There Buckingham took full responsibility for the fleet which was preparing and for the continental alliances whose extent and some of whose cost was at last revealed. The Commons' leaders demanded enforcement of the recusancy laws, settling of impositions, enquiry into sale of honours and offices, into fees and royal revenues. The general implication was of some new deal which would reduce Buckingham's monopoly and exploitation of power, though he was not directly attacked until the last few days.

---

[1] See above, Chapter VII, p. 234.

Some like Wentworth did not want war, but to '. . . carry some good bills down with us to his people'. Others wanted war with Spain, but no continental entanglements. Most resented threats of adjournment. Some, particularly Sir Robert Mansell, whose spectacular corruption as treasurer of the navy had led to his dismissal by Buckingham, had selfish motives. The opposition showed no understanding of the need to sustain the government's credit by firm promises of future supply. The only concession was a promise to enforce the recusancy laws, thus breaking the treaty with France. Buckingham dissolved Parliament for attacking him and refusing supply; he had offended his most important ally, yet by hiring ships to her which were used against La Rochelle gave another weapon to his enemies.

To make up for the lack of preparation for their first parliament, Charles and Buckingham excluded from their second, summoned for February 1626, Phelips, Wentworth, Coke and three other leaders by making them sheriffs. Meanwhile Mansfield and the Cadiz expedition had failed and the French alliance was foundering. Disasters like this made attempts to silence critics of the war futile, but no attempt was made to conciliate magnates like Pembroke with followers in both Houses. In religion, apart from enforcing the recusancy laws, the Commons were allowed to pursue their attack on Montague's Arminian writings in a way not countenanced in 1625. The Commons complained of increase of papists, ill guarding of the seas, plurality of offices in one man's hand, sale of honours and judicial offices, impositions, use of English ships against La Rochelle and the misuse of the 1624 subsidies for projects not intended by Parliament. They promised to vote three subsidies when their grievances were redressed. Direct personal attack on Buckingham was evaded, but Charles' reply was to demand an immediate and larger supply on pain of dissolution. Through Buckingham he then retracted and offered to appoint a committee of both Houses to 'take the view of his estate'. This might have won co-operation in 1625, but now, urged on by Buckingham's former client Sir John Eliot, the Commons impeached the duke. The charges included the hastening of James' death and must have mortally offended Charles. He dissolved Parliament rather than receive a remonstrance demanding Buckingham's dismissal, but was not deterred from declaring war on France.

A constitutional deadlock had resulted from the Commons' pressing their newly won right to question and accuse the king's servants against one whom the king was determined to defend. The new importance of the old maxim that kings cannot command unlawful things and Pym's appeal to fundamental law raised problems which could disrupt the traditional constitution, but the political crisis which produced them was not necessarily insoluble. With a little more luck at Ré and more concessions to men like Pembroke and Warwick, or to men like Digges,

Wentworth, or Phelips with whom the court was still in communication, a political settlement might be found. Buckingham, unlike Charles, did eventually show some capacity for political self-preservation.

But immediately the crisis did lead to invocation of the crown's emergency powers which to many seemed to endanger the traditional frame of government. The levying of the forced loan was a real cause for alarm. It was a loan only in name and was in fact a demand for five subsidies without parliamentary consent to be collected in the unprecedentedly short time of three months. The judges refused to endorse its legality and Lord Chief Justice Crew was dismissed. Abbot was suspended for refusing to license a sermon by Sibthorpe defending the loan. Though there was opposition, most of the £300,000 was collected, though more slowly than planned. The minority like Wentworth who refused and were imprisoned raised important issues of consent and individual rights leading from the Five Knights Case to the Petition of Right and the Habeas Corpus Amendment Act. Most acquiesced, comforting themselves with Charles' promise it would not be used as a precedent. But the immediate question was whether a new system of prerogative expedients might not appear.

In the event neither side was prepared for a confrontation outside the traditional concepts. The crown considered in detail debasing the coinage, levying ship money on inland counties, hiring foreign mercenaries and raising an excise only to abandon each of them. The final decision was for conciliation and a new parliament. The resisters to the loan were released, though even in confinement some like Wentworth had been in touch with the court.

Some of the most difficult and longstanding problems arose from the militia and raising troops for foreign service. The Elizabethan militia had depended on assessments of the act of 1558, revised by prerogative. The act was repealed in 1604 so that when training was revived in 1612 the assessments rested solely on the prerogative. To the long-resented rates for paying the muster masters were added ones for re-equipment with modern weapons. From 1618 the privy council was concerned to punish the recalcitrant, demand uniformity of equipment and provide new training orders. But the really vigorous attempt to reform the militia began immediately after Charles' accession, including efforts to strengthen the horse, provided by the gentry and freeholders, culminating in a scheme for regional musters in 1628, reluctantly abandoned after Parliament met. These growing burdens may have fallen more heavily on the gentry than the Elizabethan ones.

But the greatest grievances arose from pressing, billeting and disciplining troops for foreign service, whose immediate burdens fell heaviest on the poor. Billeting was potentially the most dangerous, since it might be used to overawe districts and in practice the long delays in payment

DECLINE OF SPAIN AND THE THIRTY YEARS WAR

made it a form of local indirect taxation. Commissions of martial law to prevent desertions and plundering were regarded as an invasion of common law rights. Yet martial law had been used against civilian rioters in late Elizabethan times, and power to use it at discretion against riots and unlawful assemblies was regularly included in the commissions of lieutenancy, while some grants of commissions of martial law had been at the request of local authorities under Charles. The commissions were often joined with ones of *oyer* and *terminer:* in Hampshire, the only place where their proceedings have been studied, there were no summary executions. Soldiers were imprisoned, then tried at assizes, quarter sessions, or commissions of *oyer* and *terminer*. The commissioners of martial law also administered billeting which led to some confusion of jurisdictions, with civilians being summoned as witnesses or given orders. Martial law was a grievance, because it emphasized the vagueness of the crown's emergency powers and was another means of attacking the already unpopular powers of lieutenancy,[1] but it was not used as it was in Ireland. In 1627 it was less of a real menace than the threats to impress humble refusers of the loan or to send gentry to serve with embassies at their own expense.

When Parliament met in March 1628, most of the Commons' leaders had just been released from confinement after refusing the loan. They seemed very aware that the future nature of government was at stake, and probably agreed to redress grievances before seeking for their authors. Charles in his opening speech offered no concessions, only demands for supply, if these failed there were other means 'which God hath put into my hands'. Later a programme for a mainly naval war from the Baltic to Spain and for building twenty warships a year was presented, but aroused little response. Conciliation came from Buckingham; he had been given a mediatory role unsuccessfully before, but in 1628 he showed more patience and tactical skill in the Lords, though the report of his desire for more frequent parliaments was ill received by the Commons. There Wentworth was the leading figure in the first weeks; they agreed to vote five subsidies, but that the grant should go hand in hand with remedying their grievances about the forced loan, billeting, martial law, imprisonment without cause shown. Their aim was a bill of rights declaring all these illegal and providing penalties for any future transgressors.

Charles refused to accept any new law and the Lords wanted a compromise. When Sir Dudley Digges suggested a Petition of Right to declare the law, a conception already found in the 1624 petition of grievances, he got no support; but eventually it seemed preferable to a bare confirmation of Magna Carta and other statutes which was all Charles offered. The

[1] L. Boynton, 'Martial Law and the Petition of Right', *E.H.R.* Vol. 79 (1964), pp. 255–84.

Lords after hesitating accepted the Commons' text without substantial change, but Charles refused to record his formal assent. This produced an attack by Eliot on Buckingham, and at the insistence of both houses Charles gave his assent to make the petition a matter of record. The Commons passed the subsidy bill and produced a remonstrance attacking Buckingham and naming Neile and Laud as promoters of innovation in religion. This was rejected and they turned to tonnage and poundage. They apparently intended a detailed revision of duties which would still give Charles the equivalent of his present revenue including impositions. This required more time than Charles would give, as he feared pursuit of the remonstrance. The Commons wanted an adjournment during which Digges and Rich proposed commissioners including members should sit to produce a detailed customs bill to be enacted in October.[1] Charles insisted on prorogation and the Commons claimed that the levying of tonnage and poundage and impositions was 'a Breach of the Fundamental Liberties of this Kingdom' and contrary to the Petition of Right. Charles plausibly answered that the petition was not intended to trench on his prerogative and its interpretation belonged to the judges, but less reasonably claimed tonnage and poundage by prerogative right.

Though the issues raised by the petition had long-term constitutional significance, despite its lack of any immediate effect, the inquisitorial activities of the Commons were perhaps more immediately important. They continued to condemn patents, ordered that Hull should be free to fish off Greenland, despite the Muscovy Company's charter, they collected figures about shipping losses and investigated abuses in the stannaries. Manwaring was impeached, and disabled from holding any office by the Lords for his sermons asserting the king's power to levy taxes in 1627. Perhaps as remarkable was the case of Mr Burgess of Witney; examined by the committee of religion for scandalous preaching and catechizing on the testimony of his parishioners, and a motion prepared that he should make public recantation and submit to the House.[2] The Commons' tendency to supplement or encroach on the crown's executive and judicial functions and its supremacy in religion were not just theoretical pretensions.

Charles' unwillingness to make concessions might still really seem proof of the influence of evil counsellors to Eliot, but the fiction was wearing out. In fact Buckingham was the more pliant. From late May his tactics were more conciliatory; he was reconciled with Bishop Williams, Arundel and Abbot; he met complaints of his pluralism by giving up the wardenship of the Cinque Ports. Weston was made lord treasurer and under his patronage Wentworth was reconciled to the court, made a baron and promised the presidency of the Council of the North. Buckingham

[1] Warwickshire County Record Office, Newdegate Diary, 24 June.
[2] B. M. Stowe MS 366, fos. 137v, 193.

also hoped to limit his commitments by making peace with France, but he was determined first to relieve La Rochelle and get terms for the Huguenots. His assassination by Felton, an officer disappointed by lack of promotion and arrears of pay, leaves the question of what he might have done. His desire to redeem his reputation in war would presumably have made him readier with concessions to Parliament in return for supply than Charles was after the failure to relieve La Rochelle. Unquestionably his death meant a change in Charles' conduct of affairs. But the immediate and bitterest facts were Felton's assertion that he was inspired by the Commons' remonstrance and the acclamation that he and his act enjoyed.

Meanwhile many merchants refused to pay tonnage and poundage and their goods were seized. Parliament was prorogued from October to January, but Weston tried conciliation. The exchequer refused to judge the king's right to tonnage and poundage, referring it to Parliament, but equally refused to release the merchants' goods. A declaration forbidding disputation about interpretation of the Thirty-nine Articles was issued and Abbot was readmitted to the privy council. Against this Charles made Montague a bishop, though withdrawing his book *Apello Caesarem*, but he over-rode Parliament's sentence by pardoning Manwaring and giving him a rich living, adding pardons to Montague and Sibthorpe. Charles' efforts at religious peace may have been sincere, but were unperceptive.

His declaration by invoking Convocation and High Commission as the only authorities for settling religious questions raised the question of Parliament's relationship to the royal supremacy which had been relatively dormant since 1610. As the new session opened without a royal speech, the Commons were freer to devote themselves to religion and the seizures of the merchants' goods, especially Rolle's, which were held to be a breach of privilege since he was an M.P. Charles belatedly urged them to grant tonnage and poundage, denying he had claimed it by prerogative, but the House was deep in questions concerning Rolle's privilege, the pardons to Manwaring and the rest and the spread of Arminianism. The resolutions of Pym's sub-committee on religion show determination to censure Arminianism, defend Calvinist orthodoxy and uproot the favourers of innovations, though they also urge Parliament to consider means for maintaining a godly minister in every parish. The deadlock on tonnage and poundage caused an adjournment for a week of private negotiations with the Commons' leaders. All we know for certain is that they failed.[1] On 2 March the House met again and refused

[1] The Venetian ambassador believed this was because Charles refused their demand to condemn and punish the customers as they 'had acted by his special command' and he would not 'establish a precedent by virtue of which none would obey him again', *Cal. State Papers Venetian*, 1628–9, pp. 579–80.

to accept the Speaker's order from the king to adjourn. They passed resolutions condemning payment of tonnage and poundage without Parliament's consent, innovation in religion and countenancing of popery. Eliot and eight others were arrested and after some debate in the council Parliament was dissolved.

The Venetian ambassador thought Charles well pleased at this, but not all his councillors were. Moreover the Commons debate of 2 March shows that some who supported the resolutions disapproved of Eliot's tactics. He denounced Weston as another Buckingham and the author of evil counsel and present grievances. But Digges, Littleton and Clement Coke demanded proof before naming councillors, Phelips thought Weston would clear himself; Clarendon later blamed Weston for urging dissolution to save himself, when he could have triumphed over an impeachment. Several leading figures of the Commons, Digges, Littleton, Noy, Phelips, were reconciled with the court after the dissolution. Sir Simonds D'Ewes, a strong Puritan and defender of parliamentary privilege, blamed the dissolution on 'fiery spirits' in the Commons who 'were very faulty and cannot be excused'. Yet by 1638 D'Ewes was seriously considering emigrating to New England, while thousands had actually done so.

Yet Charles enjoyed more positive support in 1629 than 1626, if only because he was making peace. His direction of government has not had enough detailed study for precise judgements of his responsibility, but he never gave his undivided confidence to any servant after Buckingham. Chronically unsure of himself, he was obstinate in his ultimate intentions, yet a canvasser of contradictory tactical advice without discriminating among its authors so that he 'often changed his own opinion for a worse' (Clarendon) and 'they who at night have pulled off his doublet... divested him of the resolution of the preceding day'. He had a genius for making concessions too late, and behaved in the long run as though the purity of his private devotions absolved him from public honesty. If on the scaffold 'he nothing common did or mean', on his throne he too often acted differently, showing a petty vindictiveness towards those in his power which pursued Eliot beyond his grave. Tender-hearted about executing criminals, he was not a man of blood, save in his steady expectation that men should be willing to die for the justice of his causes.

His attitude to Parliament differed from his father's. Eliot at first found the briefness of his speeches a refreshing change. This was probably dictated by an impediment in speaking, but Charles often took little pains to explain himself by the mouths of others. His tone was peremptory. James too had threatened adjournments and dissolutions, but he was often willing to confer and explain. Charles more often simply demanded that they trust his word. In 1628 the Commons were perturbed by the belief that Charles thought the forced loan had been paid willingly.

Certainly he seemed deliberately to choose to do things by prerogative, especially in Scotland, when James, while fond of the theory, might be more politic in the act. If James might have made a better professor than a king, Charles might have made a better connoisseur and patron of painting and architecture, an unscandalous and uxorious Beckford. Capable of choosing loyal gentlemen of the bedchamber, he was less capable of discrimination about the loyalty and honesty of his councillors.

Along with debts Charles inherited lost opportunities from his father, one of the most serious being the failure to settle impositions. This might still have been done in 1625 or even 1628, if Charles had allowed time to work out a bargain or compromise. Instead of trying to review the customs duties in the interests of trade, both sides became entangled in legal technicalities over tonnage and poundage and argued extreme cases. A settlement of impositions might only have led to embroilment over the royal supremacy. Certainly the Commons' range of enquiry and determination to question all royal servants grew. When Pym in 1626 said 'we sitt heere as law makers as councillors and as judges' this is how Commons' committees wished to act. But in religion moderates could also find common ground in promoting preaching, repressing Catholics, or in the bill of 1628 allowing liberty to hear sermons in other parishes. The antiquarianism of the Commons' leaders search for dubious precedents is tedious, unhistorical and often perverse, but in one respect it was realistic. The fourteenth century's frequency rather than Tudor infrequency of parliaments was more appropriate, if Parliament was to survive.

The breach of 1629 meant that all customs revenues now rested on the prerogative and the merchants' attempts to resist soon ceased. But the failure to put militia assessments and powers of lieutenancy on a statutory basis had more damaging consequences. It hindered reform of the militia, fed local disputes and in a crisis made deputy lieutenants reluctant to act. Court and country may have become more polarized in the absence of a forum where factions and individuals could interact. Such contacts did not cease but they were more confined to individuals acting in a local context. The process of consultation was more random and was only institutionalized at assizes. There were plenty of occasions for local opinion and factions to form, but fewer opportunities for reaching the central government, a greater sense of being governed. Presumably because of the war little constructive work had been done since 1624. Moderates in 1629 did not see that a period of personal rule had begun, but the acceptability of prerogative government would depend on its ability to provide at least some of the reforms which parliamentary stalemates had seemingly prevented.

Charles' Parliaments had frequently urged general consideration of the royal finances. The return of peace made this possible, and some historians have claimed that relative solvency was achieved. War and diplomacy had cost over £2 million, lands and woods were sold for £651,000. Crown lands were conveyed to the corporation of London in settlement of £350,000, nearly half of which was capital and interest of the loan of 1617. This was repaid last and was still not fully paid in 1642, so the credit of crown and corporation remained poor. From 1630 fines on those who were not knighted of £40 a year or more from land—a right not used since the mid-sixteenth century—raised £174,500. Thus debt was reduced to £1,164,000 in 1635, but the old problems of increasing ordinary revenue and decreasing expenditure remained.

Ordinary revenue averaged £618,000 p.a. 1631–5 and showed little increase, but the average 1636–41 was £899,000. The main increase was from customs, yielding about £500,000 in 1640 against £300,000 in 1635. This was achieved by increasing official valuations of goods and by new impositions, helped by a greater volume of trade. Most of the other increases came from the wards, the soap monopoly and the mint. But 60% of the ordinary revenue was anticipated in 1635 and the proportion remained high so that the crown had little cash available and became more dependent than ever on advances provided by the customs' farmers. A principal reason for this was the failure of attempts to reform the spending departments, especially the royal households, whose expenditure continued to rise, diet alone cost £107,000 in 1640 (the king's cost 60% more than in 1617).

This epitomizes the best of the personal rule, good intentions and poor results; the worst was that no policy was persisted in except in hope of fiscal gain, while fiscal expedients and personal interests of courtiers reduced the execution of policy to incoherence. Despite increasing revenue, lack of cash and credit and rising expenditure provided constant pressure to seek new projects. Despite later parliamentary assertions, every expedient was arguably legal, however much the intention of the law was defied. Thus the proviso in the statute of monopolies for the privileges of corporations was used to grant monopolies to companies instead of individuals. As before profits went mostly to the projectors, only the soap monopoly after years of campaigning by Laud yielded an appreciable revenue to the crown (£33,000). Charles, like other contemporary rulers, constantly appealed to emergency powers and necessities of state, but unlike them pursued an entirely pacific foreign policy.

Some efforts were made to deal with public grievances. Parliament repeatedly complained about sale of honours and these ceased after Buckingham's death. A new commission of fees was appointed in 1627, it laboured long and repetitiously till 1640, investigating multitudes of offices and fees. Its achievements were that the crown profited by selling officers pardons for their irregularities and asserted its right to sell some offices, formerly sold by other officers. The crown gained some £35,000, offended many officers and disappointed its subjects. An apparently ineffective effort to limit the number of attorneys and solicitors was made by the privy council and judges. The commission for poor debtors of 1630 had much weaker powers than its Elizabethan predecessors, but it was more discreet in that it tried to ensure co-operation with the common law courts. Indeed action with the approval of the judges was characteristic of the personal rule and necessarily limited its attempts at legal reforms. While the Council of the North under Wentworth was given power to check prohibitions by common law courts, the Council of the Marches found its jurisdiction over fornication, which provided an essential part of its revenue, undermined by Laud.

Monopolies were not the only instance of earlier agreements being undone. In 1634 the free trade in cloths other than white cloths agreed in 1624[1] ended with the restoration of the Merchant Adventurers' monopoly of exporting cloth to the Netherlands and Germany. The adventurers were being pressed to pay heavier dues to the duchess of Richmond for her licence to export white cloths and the 1634 proclamation may have been their price. In 1640 the then licensee, the Duke of Richmond and Lennox, unable to get his terms, seized the adventurers' cloth shipments with the crown's help. Attempts by Wither, a failed adventurer, under a royal commission inspired by the adventurers to enforce regulation of cloth and put down market spinners in Wiltshire and neighbouring counties produced successful resistance from J.P.s, who were willing to enforce inspection themselves, but not to suppress yarn dealers. Yet in 1640 a royal commission on the cloth industry, with Wither among its members, proposed suppression of market spinners and regulation of the cloth industry by companies which, unlike those of the 1625 scheme, excluded J.P.s. If the adventurers' monopoly was restored, that of the East India Company was broken by the Courteen Association, whose sleeping partner and contact man was Endymion Porter, gentleman of the bedchamber, despite Charles' promises to the company 'as a Christian king' that no damage was intended to it.

The notion that whatever vexes men of property must favour the poor and social justice appeals to sentimental authoritarians of right and left. Certainly Charles vexed landowners with commissions of depopulation, revival of the Forest Laws and the higher prices and harsher terms for selling wardships after 1634.[2] But the commissions of depopulation for all their professions of preventing such enclosures became a means to sell licences to confirm them. Charles ignored his own precepts when he disafforested lands and sold them, disregarding common rights enjoyed by customary tenants and others. James was less hypocritical when in

---

[1] See above, p. 552.
[2] *Sales of Wards in Somerset*, ed. M. J. Hawkins, Somerset Record Soc., Vol. 67 (1965), pp. xxi–xxiii.

1618 he set up a commission to sell pardons for enclosure; at least one of those who bought a pardon was still fined by Charles I's commissioners. Similarly the earl of Salisbury had to compound for disafforesting lands for which his father had already been pardoned. The revival of the Forest Laws extended forest bounds beyond those settled under Edward I in order to force landowners to compound for disafforestation. This produced some £39,000[1] and annoyed scores of gentry and peers.

The best claims for the government's paternalism rest on the policies and results for poor relief of the Book of Orders of 1630. The book was immediately a response to the dearth of 1630–1, as the machinery of the Elizabethan Poor Laws was normally used for such emergencies rather than to provide permanent parochial relief. In ordinary times the main provision for the poor came from private charity, from individuals and from endowments, such as almshouses. The book probably owed most to Manchester, little to Wentworth or Laud, and was partly based on his brother's experience as a Northamptonshire J.P. Professor Jordan concludes from a regional survey of surviving parochial accounts that the council's 'efforts were without any substantial consequence at all' and that the 1,200 returns it obtained from J.P.s were largely worthless.[2] Against this, Professor Barnes claims that in Somerset 'throughout the 1630's the content of the Book was effectively translated into reality',[3] though his evidence is the records of the J.P.s. rather than the parishes. Certainly the lord keeper's charge in 1638 complained of general neglect of the book, but it seems likely that there was increased activity in repressing vagabonds, dealing with alehouses and apprenticing pauper children. The book may also have stimulated the effective organization of petty sessions.

If there was reinvigoration of local administration in the early 1630s, it soon produced its own undoing. For the extension of Ship Money to the inland counties in 1635 and its establishment as a regular tax put the burdens on the sheriffs, J.P.s and constables. In Somerset what proved fatal was not appeals to fundamental law and precedent, but interminable disputes about rating, fed by local jealousies, which swamped the J.P.s sessions. If Somerset is representative, local administration was becoming as hopelessly overburdened as the king's finances. In 1637 some eighty J.P.s were removed from the commissions of twenty-one counties, presumably because they were unwilling to serve. 'Had not war put a virtual end to county government, it is possible the dwindling number of magistrates would have crippled it.'[4]

Serious resistance to Ship Money only developed in 1640 after its

---

[1] P. A. J. Pettit, 'Charles I and the Forest Laws in Northamptonshire', *Northamptonshire Past and Present*, Vol. III (1961), pp. 54–62.

[2] W. K. Jordan, *Philanthropy in England 1480–1660* (1959), pp. 128–42.

[3] T. G. Barnes, *Somerset 1625–1640* (1961), chapter VII and p. 196.

[4] *Ibid.* pp. 301–6.

denunciation in Parliament. The charges for the militia had long been debated and met increasing opposition earlier. As the rates varied between different areas they seemed inequitable, quite apart from the question of authority for raising them. Some counties now pressed men for the trained bands, raising further legal problems. The main challenge to the deputy lieutenants was refusal to pay assessment, especially for the muster masters. The council failed to deal effectively with refusers, 'have gone with so tender a foot in those Businesses of Lieutenancy that it hath almost lost that Power to the Crown' (Wentworth). As a final touch of farce the lieutenancy was harassed by Laudian injunctions which treated the traditional mustering in churchyards as sacrilege.

This is a trivial but public illustration of why many without being fervent Puritans found Laud an innovator. Already in 1626 new instructions for High Commission undid most of the restrictions of 1611, restored its unlimited visitatorial powers and complete discretion in using *ex officio* procedures. It is true that James had issued instructions for silencing controversies, controlling lecturers and more rigorous censorship, but Charles and Laud tried to achieve a much greater degree of uniformity in both England and Scotland.

The English church exemplified the balances and tensions of political life. In so far as it was comprehensive, this was not the result of pursuit of an ideal *via media*. Lay patronage, the privileges of nobles and corporations sheltered Puritan clergy. Successive archbishops of York had relied on Puritan preachers' zeal against papists, encouraged the West Riding Exercises, many of whose preachers had no cure of souls, and turned a blind eye towards tendencies towards congregationalism in some of the chapelries. Enthusiasts and selfseekers might join to promote a godly discipline which would increase lay participation or might despoil the church. Royal and episcopal authority held such forces in check, along with radicals who denied the lawfulness of tithes. But if grateful or sycophantic clergy, like Manwaring, cried up royal authority too far, or if others yearning for a more independent authority cried up episcopacy by divine right, they raised fears of clerical domination. As the church became less comprehensive under Charles it seemed to be overthrowing established traditions and vested interests. The moving of communion tables, placing them permanently altarwise at the east ends of chancels behind rails where communicants received the elements, instead of kneeling round three sides of the table, was a breach of established tradition. No theology, or even literacy, was needed for anyone finding his parish church refurnished according to Laud's injunctions to detect innovation. The tearing down of wrongly placed pews, the deploring of the spoliation of the church, securing of increased tithe rates in London, attempts to obtain augmentations from impropriators, the silencing of lecturers for not wearing surplices, or not reading the full liturgy, were all to promote decency and order. To the owners of pews and tithes, to those who contributed to lecturers' stipends or levies for refurnishing churches, who preferred sermons to services, it all seemed a counter-reformation against which interest and conscience were powerfully united.

Not all the bishops and fewer of the clergy were enthusiastic Laudians, many churches remained unchanged, but there is evidence of greater strictness in several dioceses after Laud's metropolitical visitation (begun 1634). Silencing of lecturers and afternoon sermons and sanctions against those going to churches outside their parish increased. The translation of Neile to York in 1632 had striking results. He was vigorous in enforcing refurnishing of churches; the exercises ceased. At his first visitation forty-six ministers were presented for Puritan offences, the previous maximum had been six. Perhaps the muddled comprehension of Abbot was doomed and the Commons' attacks on Harsnet, Neile and Laud forced them to rely on Charles' supremacy. If so, it was impolitic to insist on uniformity in non-essentials, to use the Book of Sports (enjoining lawful games on Sundays) as a shibboleth for detecting moderates in postures of disobedience. Abbot had persuaded James not to insist on its public reading. While it is true that strict Sabbatarianism was a recent development, the book conflicted with traditions exemplified in the Homilies. Still more unwise was the use of Star Chamber against the bishops' critics and the martyrizing of Leighton, Prynne, Bastwick, Burton and Lilburne. Charles fed fears of popery by refusing Laud's request to suppress Catholic proselytizing at Henrietta Maria's court. His predilection for bishops as councillors was resented even by courtiers, particularly his making Juxon of London the first episcopal treasurer since 1470.

In Ireland, where the church was crippled by encroachments and faced a Catholic hierarchy effectively reorganized in the 1620's and growing Presbyterianism among the Ulster Scots, the need for reform was more urgent. Wentworth went there as lord deputy in 1633. He set himself to recover the church's endowments which had been especially exploited by the Protestant 'New English' who dominated Irish administration, and to assert ancient crown titles to huge areas owned by the Catholic 'Old English' (traditionally supporters of the crown) as well as by the 'mere Irish'. This was to be the prelude to large-scale plantations, especially in Connaught, to secure permanent royal revenues and a firm basis for Protestant rule. Although Wentworth used traditional means of intimidation of Irish governments, he used them against 'New English' magnates and officials and 'Old English', not exclusively against the mere Irish. He was also unusually successful in exploiting the Irish Parliament, playing off Protestants against Catholics to get an unprecedentedly large subsidy, extend the scope of the court of wards and leave the crown free to pursue its claims to land. Wentworth was so confident of his management that he intended to keep Parliament on session longer, but Charles insisted on a dissolution. Although Wentworth's own religion had been mildly Puritan, Laud became his principal ally at court and his ecclesiastical instrument in Ireland was the Laudian Bramhall, not the more Calvinistic primate, Usher.

Wentworth's rule in Ireland seemed the only example of vigorous sustained and effective action in the 1630s. He doubled Irish revenues, bringing them to £80,000 a year, and made considerable profits for himself. For the first time the Irish government was financially self-supporting and the prospects of its contributing to English resources seemed good. Wentworth's will-power and self-confidence made him a gambler who, unlike Charles' other servants, was prepared to risk his own profits, fortune and eventually his life in service of the crown and his own ambition. In Ireland he had offended so many interests and individuals that peace was essential for his policies to succeed, just as it was for the rickety finances and contradictory expedients of the English government. The death blow came from Scotland.

If James' legacy in England was one of lack of credit and confidence, in Scotland it was of relatively effective government. Royal justice was comparatively ineffectual in Scotland, thanks to the crown's poverty and the power of the nobility through heritable jurisdictions and their followers. Attempts to introduce justices of the peace in 1609 and 1634 were ineffective; probably the kirk sessions were an enduring force in local government.[1] Their superintendence by bishops, High Commission and privy council was the surest basis of James' authority. The procedure adopted in 1621 gave the bishops a decisive part in securing royal domination of the committee of the articles which controlled Parliament. Charles soon called all in question by theoretical claims and impolitic actions. Absence of the court from Scotland tended to produce resentments like those of the nobilities of the other Iberian kingdoms against Castile. Charles was as much personally concerned with governing Scotland as his father, and after Buckingham's death the Scots Hamilton and Lennox were treated as intimates, but they were near-aliens to the resident nobility, some of whom spent longer in France than England.

Charles' revocation of 1625 rescinded grants of crown property since 1540 and all dispositions of ecclesiastical property. James had erected twenty-one abbeys into hereditary temporal lordships, as the complement to restoring the estate of bishops. Church lands were later confirmed to their grantees, but the crown kept the right to redeem their feudal superiorities, though as yet it could not afford to do this to any appreciable extent. Machinery for the valuation and commutation of tithes, provision of minimum stipends and an annuity to the crown was a genuine reform which lasted. But the revocation alarmed all holders of church

[1] G. Donaldson, *Scotland James V to James VII* (1965), pp. 224-6.

property, the more so as Charles also revoked some hereditary sheriff-ships and other noble offices, had regular annual direct taxes granted for the first time, and put increased burdens on Edinburgh. The bishops' attendance and importance in the privy council grew considerably after 1630. The parliament of 1633 showed unprecedentedly strong opposition, but the crown's control was unbroken and it confirmed an act of 1609 empowering the king to prescribe apparel. Charles proceeded to break with tradition by prescribing the wearing of surplices by ministers. Attempts at protest outside Parliament by supplication led to Lord Balmerino's condemnation for treason.

Charles seemed more determined to rely on his prerogative in Scotland than in England. In promulgating canons in 1636 and commanding the use of the new Prayer Book in 1637, he defied the general view that changes in the church must be ratified by a general assembly. The Prayer Book was largely the work of less moderate Scottish bishops, but Charles was responsible for retaining numerous saints' days in the calendar, chapters from the Apocrypha and a rubric providing for communion at a table set altarwise. Spalding believed that the riots which greeted the book's inauguration in Edinburgh were the result of a conspiracy by the nobility against the bishops. Organized petitions denounced the book and the bishops as councillors. Delegates of the petitioners formed 'the Tables' and forced the bishops to withdraw from the council. In February 1638 the National Covenant was drawn up, denouncing popery, the canons, the Prayer Book; appealing to statutes and the coronation oath, it pledged its signatories to disregard recent changes until allowed in free assemblies and parliaments.

The covenant can be interpreted as constitutional and conservative, seeking a return to a moderate episcopalian régime, and some signed in that sense. But the importance of the bishops in government meant that their exclusion involved radical constitutional changes (the notion of free parliaments was new) which could be secured by abolishing episcopacy. As a covenant it appealed to conceptions of federal theology,[1] to pre-reformation traditions of the Scots as a chosen race and to the idea of God's covenant with the nation preached by Presbyterian dissenters under James. Many now saw the covenant as a divine commission to complete the reformation in Scotland and England, save continental Protestantism and destroy Rome so that, as Johnston of Wariston said later, 'Until King Jesus be set down on his throne with his scepter in his hand, I do not expect God's peace . . .'.[2]

Throughout Charles helped on the work by his constancy in giving 'nothing in time'. As the leaders armed and the council had lost control,

[1] See Chapter v, p. 193.
[2] S. A. Burrell, 'The Apocalyptic Vision of the Early Covenanters', *Scottish Hist. Review*, Vol. 43 (1964), pp. 1–24, 20–1; I. B. Cowan, 'The Covenanters', *ibid.* Vol. 47 (1968), pp. 35–42.

Charles suspended the canons and Prayer Book and summoned an assembly to Glasgow. The covenanters packed the assembly by excluding ministers and by the unprecedented inclusion of lay elders, while Charles told his commissioner, Hamilton, 'to flatter them with what hopes you please so you engage me not against my grounds . . . until I be ready to suppress them'. Ignoring Hamiltons' dissolution, the assembly deposed the bishops and annulled the canons. A majority of the nobility and gentry had taken over the church in defiance of the king and many clergy; next, with the help of the towns, they organized an army to defend themselves.

Charles tried to attack and demonstrated his deluded ignorance of his situation in both Scotland and England. All the local dissensions, grievances and legal doubts about the militia ensured its ineffectiveness. The navy was helpless without bases in Scotland. What forces he had could not be kept in being for lack of money, appeals for a loan from London and for voluntary contributions failed, despite the revocation of a large number of monopolies. Hamilton urged compromise and Charles reluctantly made peace (June 1639). He agreed that church and state should be settled by assembly and Parliament summoned for August. Neither side kept faith; the Covenanters did not effectively disarm, Charles confirmed the abolition of episcopacy, believing that the bishops' absence would invalidate the proceedings of both assembly and Parliament. He had decided to try conquest again, while the assembly declared episcopacy contrary to the law of God and Parliament destroyed the crown's control of the committee of articles. Scotland had embarked on constitutional and religious revolution, but conservative doubts were gathering strength.

Charles now made Wentworth one of his inner ring of councillors. They discussed extraordinary ways of raising money, but Hamilton, Wentworth and Laud demanded a parliament. Charles seems to have regarded this a means to strengthen an ultimate appeal to his emergency powers, for he insisted on a pledge from the privy council that 'if the Parliament should prove . . . untoward . . .' they would assist him in extraordinary ways. A loan of £300,000 was raised immediately from councillors and officials. Wentworth (now created earl of Strafford) crossed to Ireland, obtained a vote of four subsidies from the Irish Parliament and arranged to raise a new army of 8,000 foot before returning to England. The English Parliament met (13 April) and the lord keeper demanded immediate supply without offering any concessions, except to acknowledge the need for a parliamentary grant of tonnage and poundage. As Convocation's commission included power to make canons, the whole question of Parliament's relationship to the royal supremacy was again revived.

The Short Parliament's failure now seems inevitable and was probably expected by Charles. It is not clear that Strafford or even the Commons saw this. Pym in a two-hour speech rehearsed the grievances of 1629 adding under propriety of goods, ship money, monopolies, military charges, denounced the responsibility of the judges and the bishops' claims that their authority was *iure divino*, and demanded annual parliaments. The Commons were determined to pursue their grievances, but the Lords voted that supply be given priority by 52 to 25 and rejected the Commons' subsequent protest by 60 to 25. This might be seen as a court manoeuvre to provoke a breach between the Houses and justify a dissolution. But at Strafford's insistence Charles agreed to concede the illegality of Ship Money, but rejected his advice to trust the Commons' affections for supply; he agreed instead to ask for eight subsidies instead of the twelve proposed by Secretary Vane, then apparently changed his mind. Vane asked for twelve subsidies and refused any compromise; even so one observer thought they might have been voted, until some members demanded the inclusion of military charges with Ship Money.[1] Charles was determined to dissolve, on Vane's assurance that no supply was possible. Strafford agreed and the privy council voted the dissolution with only two dissentients (5 May).

If supply had been voted, full investigation of grievances had been promised in a later session, so that at best Charles would have conquered Scotland, while awaiting an investigation of his rule by the Commons. The moment Charles had anticipated had come, perhaps he imagined he could repeat the forced loan of 1626, but the privy council's promises of full support proved of little worth. Charles overruled Laud and insisted that Convocation should continue to sit in order to vote supply and canons embodying Laud's innovations, thus ensuring a united attack by any future parliament. Only Strafford and to some extent Cottington were prepared to invoke the full emergency powers of the crown. Even so threats failed to raise any appreciable amount of money, negotiations to obtain troops and money from Spain were fruitless. When the Irish Parliament met again in June the Old and New English allied to attack Stafford's policies and reduce the subsidies. In England men pressed for service rioted, destroyed enclosures and altar rails, on their way to the north, where the army's commanders had already despaired. When the Scots invaded, they took Newcastle and Durham easily and, though the Yorkshire trained bands rallied to Charles, he still lacked money to continue the war. A great council of peers was summoned to York, but was only willing to guarantee a cessation with the Scots and a loan from London on condition of calling Parliament. The Scots referred themselves for a final peace to this Parliament and until then their presence costing £850 a day guaranteed its continuation.

Factions at court became more deadly, looking for ways to conciliate parliament by sacrificing their rivals. Holland, Vane and Cottington all

[1] B. M. MS Harley 4931, fo. 48.

patronized by the queen saved themselves, as did Hamilton, thanks to the Scots. All were hostile in varying degrees to Strafford, who had not meant to attend Parliament. After it met Charles summoned him, promising to protect him. On Strafford's arrival, his enemies at court warned the Commons' leaders that he intended to accuse members of both Houses of treason with the Scots. Laud thought there was such a plan and the warning made Pym procure an immediate vote for Strafford's impeachment for treason. The Lords accepted this, although the Commons had not had time to prepare full charges, and Strafford was arrested. His fate became the main political issue for the next six months.

By December Laud, Lord Keeper Finch and six judges had been impeached, charges against two bishops were preparing. Finch and Secretary Windebank had fled abroad. Many grievances were being considered, but the most important piece of legislation was the Triennial Act (February 1641) inspired by that of the Scots Parliament of June 1640, which provided machinery for the summoning of Parliament every three years, irrespective of the king's will. The only impeachment actively pursued was Strafford's and the attempt to prove constructive treason and alteration of government failed, partly because the evidence from Ireland was unsatisfactory and because the evidence of advising Charles to levy war on his subjects was not only dubious, but involved the king's personal responsibility. If making a division between king and people was treason, what of the twelve peers who had denounced Charles' rule in August 1640? The political reasons for Strafford's execution were that he had invoked the crown's full emergency powers in 1640 and was an object of army plots in 1641; the reason of state of Essex's 'Stone dead hath no fellow' was forced on Charles by riots which threatened Charles' courtiers and queen. But the Lords in passing the Bill of Attainder and ignoring Charles' pleas were guided by the judges' view that alteration of government was treason, not that Strafford had constructively compassed the king's death.[1] This helped to reconcile law and political reality, but the fact remained that Charles had been coerced. Strafford offered himself to the scaffold as a sacrifice to that unity which was the foundation of all order, yet his presence there exposed the fiction. Everyone agreed that without this unity there would be chaos, which duly came. Was this because Charles' critics were determined to subvert government's fundamental laws, or because Charles was, or because a mixed constitution was self-destructive in trying sacrilegiously to share out sovereign power, or because a new distribution of property made it unworkable?

All these explanations were offered by contemporaries. Clearly by September 1641, the monarchy which James inherited had been drastically changed and we must lastly, generally and even more selectively consider

[1] C. Russell, 'Theory of Treason in the Trial of Stafford', *E.H.R.* Vol. 80 (1965), pp. 30–50.

why these changes led to civil war and the effects it had and failed to have on English society and government. First the Long Parliament's achievements had been based on agreement between the Houses, so that by September Ship Money, High Commission, Star Chamber, the Council of the North, the king's discretion in summoning parliament, his right to impositions and to dissolve the Long Parliament without its own consent had been abolished, peace had been made with the Scots and the army disbanded.

Like the Covenanters, some leaders of the Parliament had millennial aspirations. They saw themselves called not only to punish evils, but to complete a final reformation in church and state. Pym and others had long patronized Hartlib and hoped to invite Comenius to England to promote Protestant unity and educational reforms. An invitation was sent in the name of Parliament and finally in September Comenius arrived. His plans for a complete system of education on Baconian lines and for the conversion of the Jews as a prelude to the imminent last age of enlightenment were frustrated by the renewed political crisis.[1]

At a more mundane level attempts to enable king and Parliament to work together so that further encroachment on the executive would be unnecessary failed. The chief instrument was to have been Bedford who was to have become lord treasurer, accompanied into office by his followers including Pym. These hopes were wrecked by Bedford's failure to persuade Pym to spare Strafford's life, and by Bedford's sudden death. Although Bedford, Essex and others were made privy councillors, or given office, this made things worse, as Charles continued to take so much of his advice from outside his council. Hence the demand of both houses that Charles should remove from him all councillors who had divided him from his people and appoint ones in whom they could confide.

The differences between the Houses were strongest in church government. Everyone had been united in denouncing innovations and clerical pretensions; differences arose as to the reforms needed. The Lords would exclude the clergy from all secular offices, but not from their House, as the Commons wished. The Commons then turned to a bill to abolish the office of bishop, voted that episcopal lands, except for impropriations, should go to the crown, that dean and chapter lands should go to promote education and augment poor livings, and that ecclesiastical jurisdiction should be exercised by lay commissioners. There was a strong movement for abolishing episcopacy in London and some support in the Commons, but many who voted for these resolutions wanted a primitive episcopacy. The Lords guided by Bishop Williams produced a bill to moderate episcopacy by joining twelve clerical assistants in ordination and jurisdiction and providing a fund from the revenues of bishops,

[1] H. R. Trevor-Roper, 'Three Foreigners: The Philosophers of the Puritan Revolution', in *Religion, the Reformation and Social Change* (1967), pp. 237-93.

chapters and colleges to buy in impropriations. Both Williams and Pym were patrons of Comenius, but it is not entirely clear that his cloudy plans could have reconciled these contradictions. Charles might have stomached Williams' plan, but not the Commons.

Moreover, outside Parliament it was not only Londoners but some of the clergy who had a covenanting exaltation. Many of the sermons to Parliament showed a willingness to see Parliament as an instrument for speedy reformation, but rejected the Erastianism of moderate Anglicans. Surprisingly Prynne, who had been a martyr for moderate episcopacy, rejecting episcopacy by divine right as destructive of the constitution, in 1641 was converted by his zeal for moral reformation to presbyterianism by divine right, rejecting Williams.[1] Others, perhaps a majority, viewed these questions very much in a social and political context. Thus Sir Thomas Aston argued that Presbyterianism might be suitable for Scotland where 'the Nobility and Gentry having absolute power over their tenants, shall ever bear sway in the Church', but as this is not so in England the commoners in electing elders would 'exclude both Nobility and Gentry . . . our Communalty depend upon Lawes, not Lords.' But Nathaniel Fiennes objected to episcopacy as incompatible with English forms of government which are 'aristocraticall and placed in many and not in one', as in parliament, assizes and commissions of peace, such interests should not be excluded from church government. But increasing numbers also believed that there was a scriptural model of church government which properly presented would command acceptance. Hence the summoning of an assembly of divines was both a way of postponing clashes between different aims inside and outside Parliament, while sustaining faith that unity and reformation were attainable. The plan for the assembly was included in the Grand Remonstrance and nominations began in February 1642.

Meanwhile Charles' insistence on visiting Scotland alarmed Parliament, which rightly suspected him of seeking allies against them. He found none and had to allow Parliament there to nominate officers of state. But he was beginning to see allies in England. Petitions were being organized to support episcopacy and the Prayer Book in a number of counties; the lord mayor and aldermen of London, alarmed for their oligarchic commercial and municipal interests by the leadership of the city's Puritan M.P.s and ministers over the populace, were rallying to him. But earlier intrigues in Ireland now came home to roost with the Irish rebellion which was to precipitate the civil war. The Irish claimed to have Charles I's commission to fight for his just prerogative and were joined by the 'Old English', traditionally loyal to the crown, who denounced the English Parliament's claims and policies towards Ireland.

Although Charles had not issued the commission, he had started, but

[1] W. M. Lamont, *Marginal Prynne* (1963), pp. 77–84.

not pursued, negotiations to use the Irish and 'Old English' which influenced the rebels' timing and tactics.[1] Their professions and the earlier English army plots made it impossible for Pym to trust Charles with an army against the Irish. Pym attempted to rally opinion by the Grand Remonstrance, most of which recited the grievances before 1640 on which everyone agreed, ending with demands for counsellors in whom Parliament could confide, dismissable at Parliament's discretion, as a condition of aid to Ireland, and exclusion of bishops from the Lords; but it was only carried by 159 to 148 (20 November). Hyde opposed it because of its violent language, mistrust of Charles and failure to seek support from the Lords. The breach with the Lords was emphasized by preventing the bishop's attendance by riots whose instigators also defeated leading members of London's common council at the December elections. Having acquired moderate supporters, Charles followed extreme counsels. First he reunited Lords and Commons by demanding registration of a protest by the bishops that proceedings were invalid without them. Next his attempt to impeach and arrest Pym and four other members ensured their uniting with the new forces in London. Charles' appeal to the common council to deliver them was as vain as his appeal to the speaker. A committee of safety, appointed by the common council, took over control of the city and its militia from the royalist mayor and moderate aldermen whose resistance produced the impeachment of the mayor and recorder. Having ensured the impotence of his moderate supporters, Charles took refuge in the country and conceded the bishops' exclusion from Parliament. He refused to give up control of the militia and the war began on this issue.

Cromwell's view that religion was not at first the thing contended for is often applauded as though it were a profound analysis. It is true, partly because Charles in both Scotland and England was readier to make tactical concessions about religion than about his prerogative, but ultimately he believed his supremacy and his prerogative were indissoluble. In 1646 he wrote '... if the pulpits teach not obedience (which will never be if Presbyterian government be absolutely established) the king will have but small comfort of the militia ...'. Moderates made a party for Charles, partly because they wanted moderate church reforms, necessity made him heed them and allow them to write his manifestoes. Pym rightly doubted the permanence of his conversion. Sir Edward Walker, Hobbes and Newcastle believed moderates on both sides agreed in fearing Charles' use of a complete victory. While his followers fought for what Parliament had enacted with his constrained consent and Charles may have died for it, what he fought for was shrouded. by his evasions, his past actions and his multiplicity of counsels.

[1] R. Dunlop, 'The Forged Commission of 1641', *E.H.R.* Vol. 2 (1887), pp. 527–33. A. Clarke, *The Old English in Ireland 1625–42* (1966), pp. 220–34.

Not all moderates, however attached to the ancient constitution, saw Parliament's claims as usurpations. Some like D'Ewes gave the establishment of religion 'in power and puritie among us . . . that all might know their duty to God and the King . . .' priority. Most Royalists execrated 'lordly prelacy' and many wanted reformation, but the primitive 'moderated' episcopacy of Dering and Du Moulin was not acceptable to Royalists like Sir Thomas Aston and many clergy whom Dering complained 'had rather the Kingdom should be blown up than . . . the King . . . forbear to hear the blowing of Organs'. The Royalists defended a balanced constitution and most of the Prayer Book and deprecated further constitutional change. Most Parliamentarians claimed to be defending the constitution against change, but even the most moderate favoured some change in religion, though represented as a return to primitive truths.

If no one defended the personal rule, the great majority of the propertied wished to stay out of the war. London may be an exception, but even here a count of wealth rather than heads might have shown a majority of neutrals. It has been argued that the drive to fight for Parliament came from below, but even in London it was organized by men of wealth and standing, though mainly outside the dominant oligarchy of great merchants, customs farmers and aldermen who ruled before December 1641. Elsewhere there were popular movements; in some towns, such as South Molton, the townspeople prevented local gentry from proclaiming the king's commission of array; in Staffordshire the Moorlanders rose for Parliament with little help from the gentry, but were unable to achieve anything without them. At all levels the determination of comparatively few was needed to start the war and decisive leadership came mainly from the landowners. Clarendon considered 'it had been utterly impossible' for Parliament 'to have raised an army then if the earl of Essex had not consented to be general . . .'. The earl of Warwick was responsible for bringing over the navy to Parliament. Thus if only some thirty-odd peers stayed with Parliament while some forty joined the king by August 1642, about half the peers of 1640 eventually actively supported the king and a quarter Parliament; in 1642 many were passive.

Generally speaking in most areas a passive or neutralist majority was forced to choose sides. Thus the strength of neutralism and royalism is hard to gauge in London, which was under Parliament's control from the start. Kent does not fit the often asserted claim that the economically advanced south and east were parliamentary; it was controlled by London; but most of the established gentry were moderate Royalists, though few were active. In Cornwall which became a Royalist stronghold initially 'the prime of those persons that were most conversant in the government by commission of the peace' were Parliamentarians. The exceptions are Suffolk where the leading families were solidly Parliamentary and Wales where the gentry was solidly Royalist, while both lacked declared neutralists. Sometimes families took opposite sides as they had been rivals for generations, as Greys and Hastings had been in Leicestershire. Some, choosing on principle or under pressure, brought with them individual jealousies which disrupted their own sides. Even the recusants, though a majority supported Charles, included an appreciable number who were passive and tried to avoid committing themselves to him.

Control of the seas meant that Parliament held nearly all the port towns. But the ruling groups of some towns wished to avoid involvement as much as possible, as at Bristol and Newcastle, while at King's Lynn most of them supported a Royalist rising. Parliament got considerable popular support in the textile areas of Lancashire and the West Riding, though in Manchester and Leeds the leading men held back; local conditions did not favour such caution in the East Anglian areas. The clothiers of Wiltshire were predominantly neutralist; though their Somerset neighbour, the wealthy John Ash, was an active Parliamentarian, he asked for the earls of Bedford and Pembroke to bring aid 'for though the Countrie people be stout and resolved, yet we are not able to maintain the cause . . . without expert men that can lead and advise us'.

Clarendon believed that not only most of the nobility but most of the gentry, especially those of wealth and standing, were Royalist. This last was true of the second Civil War, but for the first it seems more comparable to the claims of Parliamentary propaganda that Royalist nobles 'gather unto them the decayed gentry of several countrys who . . . conceive civil war to be the best way suddenly to raise their fortunes equall to their descents . . .'. So far studies of M.P.s and county divisions have not shown that either side had a monopoly of rising or declining gentry, or even of capitalists. The Royalist M.P.s median age was eleven years younger than the Parliamentarians which may suggest that those with most experience of Charles and politics trusted him least. Some believe that the gentry rallied to the king because of fear of social disorders. Admittedly since 1640 there were probably more riots against enclosures, more resentment about tithes and there were frequent riots in London. Each side accused the other of promoting popular anarchy and then provided grounds for this by ordering tenants to refuse rents to landlords who recognized their opponents. In the summer of 1643 fears of popular disorders were invoked by Pym and by the parliamentary peace party as a reason both for sacrifices to win the war and for making peace. Clearly this consideration might move men in quite different directions.

The situation was revolutionary in 1642 because men failed to find ways to avoid settling their disputes by force. The longer the war continued the more often negotiations failed, the more the moderates on both sides were blamed, the more complete victory seemed the only solution. The tactics of middle of the road leadership, pursued by Pym and St John since 1641, of postponing any clear commitments on forms of church government meant that victory was sought for quite contradictory reasons. The middle group needed victory because it did not trust Charles, it did not trust the peace party to make a satisfactory peace, or the radicals to keep enough support to win the war. As Charles never really recognized defeat, it was impossible for moderate terms to be won without destroying the constitution.

But it is also worth considering how each side chose to see themselves and their opponents in general. Lord Robartes at Essex's installation declared '. . . the liberty of the subject . . . ought to be maintained that we may not be converted into a Country of Peasants and slaves as France is, where the King . . . doth . . . squeeze his subjects like so many oranges . . . who would not adventure life for . . . the Protestant Religion which is in danger now to be changed into Popery . . .'. If Parliamentarians saw Royalists promoting popery and wooden shoes under a king, bewitched by evil councillors, Royalists saw them as Anabaptists, sectaries, iconoclasts, dedicated to destroying social and religious order. This propaganda seemed verified by the many papists fighting for Charles and by the behaviour of some Parliamentarians. Essex's troops in Worcester Cathedral 'eased themselves in the Font and upon the Communion Table, calling to them that chearfully looked on to name the child and sign it with the sign of the Cross'.[1] These doubtless were 'the ruder sort of soldiers' whose society the pious Londoner Nehemiah Wharton avoided and who deprived him of his pillage. For Wharton the march from London was a providential succession of torn surplices and service books, sustained by venison cooked with fuel from altar rails, and Worcester (still an important cloth town) 'so vile and the country so base papisticall and atheisticall and abominable, that it resembles Sodom and is the very emblem of Gomorrah . . .'.[2]

Both sides conducted the war by methods which most of them had previously denounced. They used martial law against civilians and soldiers; they used free quarter and pressed men to fight. They raised forced loans, military contributions and excises and confiscated and pillaged their opponents' property.

The reasons for Parliament's victory seem overwhelming in retrospect. Control of the sea and London's wealth and credit were the basis for a relatively effective system of administration, in which county committees and sub-committees, responsible to committees of Parliament, or appointed by Parliament, organized local resources, but also were accountable to a remarkable though imperfect extent for the moneys raised and spent.[3] These resources were eventually concentrated behind an effective striking

[1] T. Carte, *A Collection of Original Letters*, Vol. I (1739), p. 15.
[2] *Archaeologia* (1853), pp. 311–34.
[3] D. H. Pennington, 'The Accounts of the Kingdom 1642–9', *Essays in the Economic and Social History of Tudor and Stuart England*, ed. F. J. Fisher (1961).

force, which acted independently of regional and local concerns, the New Model Army. While the fervour of many of its officers and troopers is undoubted, its foot consisted mainly of pressed men, another tribute to effective local administration. Against this, Charles had few ports— Newcastle, Chester, Bristol, those of Cornwall and South Wales; the textile areas under his control still depended on London's trade and credit. His forces and administration were fragmented and further weakened by local and personal rivalries. Central administrative and strategic control diminished and with it the ability to maintain an effective field army. But these contrasts only became true in the long run.

For at least the first year of the war, the king was comparatively well supplied. His forces were first raised mainly by voluntary contributions of men and money and then sustained by contributions from occupied counties (fifteen counties were supposed to raise £540,000 a year). The Council of War supplied some general direction and organization. But from 1644 its effectiveness and authority declined; as always Charles was unwilling to delegate his authority or to abide by the council's decisions, when sought. Royalist commissions acted much more independently in their localities and there is little sign of any effective accountability to Oxford, except for the counties adjacent to Oxford. The Royalist excise only seems to have worked at all in some towns such as Bristol and Chester. The strategic direction of the war became more incoherent as a result of rivalries centring on Rupert and Digby. By January 1645 the contribution system had broken down even in Oxfordshire, while the setting up of a council for the prince of Wales in the west further fragmented the Royalist war effort.[1]

Parliament's success after 1643 in enforcing collection of excises and assessments over wider areas through its committees and the king's decreasing ability to control the exactions of local commanders produced a resurgence of local efforts to protect themselves from both sides. The Clubmen's movement has been too little studied to be fully understood,[2] their strength was in the country people. In the winter of 1644–5 movements against the Royalists in Worcestershire, Shropshire and Herefordshire were put down. The movement in Wiltshire and Dorset was strongly organized; one Dorset petition asked for a return to religion of the purest times under Elizabeth and James with no consciences to be troubled by indifferent ceremonies. Here and in Sussex they demanded a return to traditional county government through quarter sessions. The Sussex petition also attacks the county committee's arbitrary actions and un-

[1] I. Roy, 'The Royalist Council of War 1642–6', *Bull. Inst. Hist. Res.* Vol. 35 (1962), pp. 150–68; J. Engberg, 'Royalist finances during the Civil War', *Scandinavian Ec. Hist. Rev.* Vol. 14 (1966), pp. 73–96.
[2] The only, but excellent, general survey is in B. S. Manning's unpublished Oxford D.Phil. thesis, 'Neutrals and Neutralism in the English Civil War 1642–6' (1957), pp. 405–65.

audited accounts. Such petitions were doubtless written by gentry and clergy, but there was widespread support from Somerset to Sussex. Fairfax made some concessions in July in Dorset, before breaking them in August 1645. Resistance to their exactions helped to defeat the Royalists in the west.

The Clubmen not only demonstrated the power of the New Model Army, but the extent to which Parliament was out of touch with local feelings. Parliament's own county committees held that the New Model abrogated 'the ends and purposes' of their Eastern Association and ignored the needs and burdens of the counties, complaining that coat and conduct money was not paid out of the monthly assessments.[1] County committees dominated by a militant local leader, such as Sir William Brereton in Staffordshire or Sir Anthony Weldon in Kent, meant the eclipse of many established families and opportunities for new men by 1645, or earlier. This trend culminated in the exclusion of the ruling families of 1640 in Kent and Wales after 1648, though in Wales the old families began to emerge again under the Protectorate. The same emergence took place in Northamptonshire, Wiltshire and Norfolk, though the original ruling families had never been so totally excluded. These last counties may be typical, where Suffolk whose ruling groups were little disturbed throughout is almost certainly not.

This alienation between the local communities and the managers of the Parliamentary war effort was well under way before the war ended and was part of the process whereby the moderates on both sides became helpless. In Parliament the middle party, led first by Pym and then St John, had bought Scots' intervention without committing themselves to more than abolishing episcopacy. Instead of winning the war that intervention destroyed the Covenanters' unity and faith in their destiny, and undermined the middle party. Most of these continued to support Essex as commander rather than Waller, the war party's hero. The establishment of the Committee of Both Kingdoms was not a complete defeat for Essex and a victory for the war party, but a compromise with the middle group. A decisive shift came in late 1644 when Essex joined the peace party and the Scots. This led St John to support the formation of the New Model.[2] An essential part of Pym's strength had come from London, but in the long run the New Model drastically reduced the direct military power of London's rulers, while its religious aims were irreconcilable with theirs. Immediately the New Model's victories united Commons and city behind the Propositions of Newcastle, but eventually the middle party had to choose between their old allies in London and the army; St John and many others chose the army.

[1] *Suffolk and the Great Rebellion*, ed. A. Everitt, Suffolk Record Soc., Vol. 3 (1960), pp. 85–6.
[2] V. Pearl, 'Oliver St John and the "middle group" in the Long Parliament', *E.H.R.* Vol. 81 (1966), pp. 490–519.

THE FALL OF THE STUART MONARCHY

One of the Newcastle Propositions was the confirmation of Parliament's religious settlement. Despite the protests of the assembly of divines this was a 'lame Erastian Presbytery' with appeals from the censures of the presbyteries to a Parliamentary committee, though this was a considerable concession from the Commons' original desire to have ecclesiastical jurisdiction exercised by lay commissions. In fact the reluctance of the divines and the Commons' delays produced the settlement too late. The Independent (congregationalist) ministers had originally been willing to accept accommodation within a national Presbyterian system, but in 1644 this was thwarted by the Scots. When it was offered them in 1645, the Independents demanded toleration 'for every way not scandalous'. Although they believed congregationalism was divinely ordained, they now allied themselves with the sects which were strong in the New Model. The Baptists have been claimed as believing in toleration on broader grounds than self-preservation, but neither their writings then, nor the intolerance of Baptist officers and ministers in power in Ireland under Fleetwood confirm this. The Independents wanted a national church and publicly maintained ministry and power for the magistrate to suppress some beliefs, such as popery, unitarianism or familism. There were many arguments against toleration, all stressed its incompatibility with a national church and demanded control of mechanic preachers. Many of the examples of excess were taken from the army's lay preachers.

If the demand for toleration was a matter of tactics for most Independents and sectaries, its radical social implications may be unfamiliar. Many sectaries and some independents objected to paying tithes for a variety of reasons. Given the amount of lay impropriation this seemed to attack property rights. But more serious was the threat of toleration to the basis of society, the family (taken to include servants and sometimes non-resident adult sons). Here paternal authority was supposed to be supreme, but it would be destroyed if servants, sons, daughters, even wives claimed liberty to worship differently. Disruption of domestic piety would be the greater, since some sects discouraged their members from intercourse with non-members. Neither Parliament nor assembly had ever intended to allow the freedom of printing or speaking which had occurred since 1642 especially in religion. Conversion and the freedom of the spirit did in fact divide many families more bitterly than the war itself. That war had been fought to defeat the ungodly and blasphemers, how could they be kept in order except by the discipline of a national church which was also the only means of evangelizing the dark corners of the land?

Apart from Roger Williams' demand for complete separation of church and state, the only demands for full toleration had been those which gave priority to civil peace. These included pamphlets by Walwyn, Overton and

Lilburne. By 1646 John Lilburne had challenged both Lords and Commons, claiming to criticize members in seeking redress of his personal grievances and in virtue of fundamental rights which the power and privileges of Parliament could not override. He denied that the Lords had any juris-diction over commoners and was imprisoned as a result. From the Tower he continued his publications, becoming the most well-known leader of those their enemies called Levellers.[1]

Lilburne became more prominent when the Commons' majority lost control of the army in 1647. It had ignored the religious interests of many soldiers by being prepared to impose Presbyterian uniformity; it tried to disband the New Model without settling its arrears of pay or guaranteeing indemnity, hoping to get most of its men to re-enlist to conquer Ireland. Like Charles, the Commons were blinded to the realities of power by their own legal theories. The army's petitions of protest were rejected, as so many others had been, but the army mutinied and drove out the officers who accepted Parliament's demands. The privates elected agitators who were in touch with Lilburne and other Levellers. There were three successive bad harvests after 1646 along with depression in overseas trade so that distress and discontent were widespread, feeding the Leveller movement in London.

The officers' programme, the Heads of the Proposals, included re-distribution of parliamentary seats, reform of the law and tithes, abolition of coercive ecclesiastical jurisdiction and penalties for not attending church, removal of the excise from necessities and its eventual abolition. Neither Parliament, the Levellers, nor Charles, found this acceptable. The army leaders took custody of Charles, broke the power of the agitators, defeated the old alliance between the Commons' majority and the city, only to find a second civil war. Charles, confident that his enemies' divisions would ensure his triumph, preferred to ally himself with a faction in Scotland and the Commons' majority; the royalists found themselves fighting to establish Presbyterianism for three years. Despite wider support than ever before, including most of the navy, Charles' supporters were defeated piecemeal.

Some of the army leaders were determined to try Charles, some wished to dissolve Parliament, as did Lilburne who had supported the army during the war. The Army Council under Ireton's guidance accepted the principle of an Agreement of the People and a wide franchise but, powerfully supported by the Independent clergy, they refused full tolera-tion, including papists and episcopalians, and kept some authority for the state in religion. Because of this and because the agreement was to be submitted to Parliament, now purged by Pride, Lilburne denounced it, but not all his associates inside and outside the army agreed. Lilburne is often criticized for lacking political realism, or more fashionably for

[1] See above, Chapter III, p. 128 for a brief account of their programme.

accepting property rights; he was prepared to compromise on tithe and the franchise, but not on toleration, or on trusting any group or assembly with unlimited power. In fact by giving priority to trying Charles the army found themselves prisoners of the Rump's leadership. After Charles' execution they were fully occupied in defeating Lilburne's attempts to influence the army and then in conquering Ireland and Scotland. The Commonwealth's sea-power built up for defensive reasons involved them in war with the Dutch.[1] But the officers did not forget their declarations.

By 1648 the dominant figure among them was Cromwell, of whom many interpretations are possible and none is definitive. A plausible one is that he acted without any consistency, moved by the spirit and by circumstances; sympathizing with millennial aspirations in 1653, conservative defender of the traditional constitution in 1658. But it is arguable that some of his aims were constant. He wanted a national church, a publicly maintained ministry and a minimum of confessional definition. Tithe must be kept until another form of maintenance was found. Genuinely tolerant, he did not believe there was only one divine model of worship and discipline; prelatists and papists had tacit freedom to worship privately. He wanted to reform the law and bring it nearer to scripture. Unlike some Puritans he did not wish to reimpose the Mosaic code, although he invoked it when he attacked the use of capital punishment for theft. One of his chief grievances against the Rump and probably against the Nominated Parliament was their failure to enact the bills prepared by Hales' committee. These included simplifying conveyancing, county registries for transactions concerning land, regulations of lawyers' and official fees and of admission and conduct of attorneys, decentralization of much civil litigation to county courts under a judge from Westminster and five nominees of the J.P.s, and provision for speedy hearing of appeals. As Protector, Cromwell reformed Chancery on the committee's lines and under his patronage William Shepherd prepared schemes to codify the law, merge equity and common law and supervise judges by assessors. The church was to be comprehensive and not coercive and the state was to regulate litigation and lawyers according to the county communities' notions of justice.

Cromwell was less concerned about means, seemingly little involved in his son-in-law Ireton's paper constitutions. Ready to purge the Long Parliament before Pride did, he lost patience with the Rump later than most of the officers. In 1657 he saw himself with some exaggeration as the officers' 'drudge upon all occasions', dissolving the Rump and pursuing expedients from the Nominated Parliament to the major-generals, without satisfying themselves or the country. In 1658 he dissolved the second Protectorate Parliament, purged the army and could have taken the crown, had he lived longer, though his intentions are not known. The

[1] See above, Chapter vii, pp. 235–6.

kingship party's Humble Petition and Advice ended with a promise to join in reforming the law, but Whitelocke and other lawyers of that party had wrecked the attempt to reform Chancery. Perhaps if Cromwell could have regained the trust of the gentry he could have defeated the lawyers. His church settlement did work, though Owen and other Independent clergy attacked it after allying with the Republicans in 1657. Baxter's Association movement was successful in getting agreement on ordaining ministers, but it also raised the question of ministers' authority to exclude men from the sacraments. In the event Cromwell's death destroyed any hope of settlement without restoring Charles II, the most unexpected result of which was the restoration of the Anglican structure of 1641.

Although Parliamentary Presbyterianism was never implemented, the Assembly's Prayer Book was generally used by Independents and by that majority (perhaps 70%) of beneficed Anglicans who had accepted the new dispensation. Serious efforts were made to augment livings; tithe reserved from the sales of bishops and capitular lands and some £11,300 from Royalist compositions provided a fund of perhaps £80,000–90,000 a year. By 1655 338 augmentations had been made; the Restoration ended the most serious effort to provide an adequately paid parochial clergy before the nineteenth century. What survived was a *de facto* Parliamentary supremacy, founded not on reforming the church, but on ending comprehension.

If law reform ceased, it has been claimed that the old tradition of economic regulation and social paternalism ended and the Commonwealth saw the beginning of industrial *laissez-faire*. But the standing committee for advancing and regulating trade echoed the 1620s that more regulation through corporations was necessary; in 1656 the great Somerset clothier Ash agreed 'our manufactures are lost and snatched away into Holland for want of regulation'. In 1650 the Norwich weavers were incorporated by Parliament with powers over all Norfolk. Leeds failed to get a similar corporation for the West Riding, because of local jealousies as it had failed with the crown before 1640, when the privy council were trying to encourage regulation in Norwich. The character and machinery of poor relief was not transformed. In the counties studied by Professor Jordan the amount raised increased in the 1640s and 1650s. In Warwickshire the JPs dealt with an average of thirty-seven poor relief cases a year in the 1650s against fourteen in the 1630s and increased the rates of dole. The Commonwealth and still more the Protectorate favoured industrial regulation, like earlier régimes they were distracted from doing as much about it as expert opinion demanded. The Navigation Act of 1651 reflected new power and self-confidence; earlier proposals had not been pursued for fear of Dutch reprisals. Regulation of overseas trade was more than ever Parliament's concern, a complement to the struggle for complete control of the customs. An improved Navigation Act was passed at the Restoration and the book of rates was included in the Act granting the customs.

Some have held that there were significant permanent transfers of land due to sales by Royalists to pay the compounding fines imposed by Parliament and to the confiscation and sale of other Royalists' estates after 1648; these and the sales of church and crown lands created new landowning families, many of whom survived 1660. Sales of church and crown property may have brought some windfall profits, but the lands were let on comparatively long leases and were not open to much immediate exploitation, though tenants often bought their holdings to safeguard their future. Other purchasers paid more cash in order to get some return on earlier loans now heavily discounted by the government's bad credit. Most Royalists recovered their confiscated estates. Compounding fines realized £1.3 million, but 'at least half of this—and probably a great deal more—was raised by borrowing'. The fines caused landowners who were already heavily in debt in 1642 to sell land, even then sales were often delayed until after 1660. Impoverishment and heavy taxation caused lasting bitterness and some attempts to exploit estates more effectively. Lawyers obligingly developed forms of strict settlement and mortgage, enabling landowners to create unbreakable entails and borrow more easily,[1] and ended the uncertainty about the validity and effects of earlier settlements, when law reformers inclined to encourage partible inheritance.

Although Parliament was singularly unsuccessful in managing its debts, it did reshape taxation effectively. The excise became a permanent tax mainly on beer and spirits, though the general excises on the Dutch model were too unpopular to continue. The assessment was meant to fall on landowners' incomes and was the model for the later land tax. Its apparent permanence inspired the Humble Petition and Advice's demand that no part of the ordinary revenue should be raised by a land tax.

A tragic and lasting legacy was the settlement of Ireland. Catholics in 1641 held about three-fifths of the land and in 1665 about one-fifth, having lost their political influence in towns and their control of trade. A contingent of new planters, including many Cromwellian soldiers, had been added to the 'New English'; any hope of converting the Irish had gone, but their hope of overthrowing the settlement continued. Cromwell's policies in Scotland of abolishing heritable jurisdictions and feudal tenures, reforming law and local government and attempting greater toleration, were more novel and radical than his Irish ones. In 1661 all legislation since 1633 was repealed and of the Covenanters' achieve-

---

[1] H. J. Habakkuk, 'Public Finance and Sale of Confiscated Property during the Interregnum', *Ec. Hist. Rev.* Vol. 15 (1962–3), pp. 70–88; 'Landowners and the Civil War', *ibid.* Vol. 18 (1965), pp. 130–51.

ments virtually only the excise and the land tax remained, whereas in England most of the legislation before 1642 survived.

There the lasting negative legacies were fear of government through a standing army and of the exercise of executive power by Parliament or its committees. More immediately the considerable number of men from outside and beneath the established ruling groups in counties and many towns who had reached positions of power meant that the dispossessed and slighted were determined to seek revenge and to re-establish the old local order more firmly. Successful attempts at structural reforms of law, church and most aspects of government seemed to be frustrated by the complexities of English society and politics. The things which conservative or radical gentry reformers, or those of the middling sort wanted, seemed only to be attainable across the Atlantic: Erastian parochial Anglicanism with the Prayer Book but without the real presence of bishops in Virginia; codification of the law and laws agreeable to the word of God along with the rule of the godly in Massachusetts; the prevalence and recognition of partible inheritance there and in Plymouth and Connecticut; the setting up of popular government and toleration by agreement in Rhode Island.

CHAPTER XIX

THE ENDING OF POLISH EXPANSION AND THE SURVIVAL OF RUSSIA

I. POLAND–LITHUANIA 1609–48

IN the first half of the seventeenth century the kingdom of Poland–Lithuania was still the most important Power in the Slav world. With an area of over 375,000 square miles (in 1618) and a population of some 8 to 9,000,000, it was smaller than Muscovite Russia, but compensated for this inferiority by its greater political and military strength. From the standpoint of its national composition, Poland was not homogeneous. The Poles themselves, the largest group, comprised less than half the total population. After them came eastern Slavs (White Russians, Ukrainians), followed at a considerable distance by non-Slavic nationalities, amongst whom the most important groups were the Lithuanians, Germans and Jews.

Formally at least, the constitutional structure of the Polish state remained by and large unchanged during this period. As in the sixteenth century, political power lay with the king and the Diet [*Sejm*], which consisted of two houses, the Senate and the Chamber of Deputies [*izba poselska*]. The Diet, as is well known, was a parliament of nobles. The Senate was composed exclusively of high-ranking ecclesiastical and lay dignitaries, that is 'magnates', or members of the upper aristocracy; whilst in the Chamber of Deputies there sat, apart from some deputies of the urban population, few representatives of the lesser nobles, the *szlachta* or gentry, who constituted about one-tenth of the population. The peasants, who comprised the overwhelming bulk of the population, exercised no political influence whatsoever. Already in the sixteenth century they had to a large extent forfeited their legal rights and had become entirely dependent upon landed proprietors from the nobility.

The Diet's most important function was to share in the work of legislation, but its powers of control over the administration were also of considerable significance. Its strength lay in the fact that no taxes or dues could be levied without its consent. The balance of power between king and Diet had tilted appreciably in the latter's favour during the course of the sixteenth century, particularly after the extinction of the Jagellon dynasty in 1572. At the beginning of the sixteenth century the king had still possessed great legislative, executive and judicial authority; but one hundred years later his powers in all these spheres had been substantially curtailed. Originally, for instance, he could summon the Diet at his own

585

discretion; but from the 1570s onwards he was obliged, by the *Articuli Heinriciani*, to convoke it for a regular session once every two years. These articles also prevented him from deciding questions of war or peace, or summoning a general levy of gentry, without the consent of the *Sejm*. As the influence of the Diet grew, so did that of the chief dignitaries (e.g. the hetmans and the grand chancellor) in the field of foreign policy. The scope of the sovereign's jurisdiction was severely limited by the establishment of the Crown Tribunal for the Kingdom of Poland (1578) and of a similar institution for Lithuania three years later. These tribunals, composed of members elected by the nobility at the local diets [*sejmiki*], acted as the highest judicial instance in all cases concerning those belonging to the noble class. The limitations imposed upon the royal power were emphasized by the recognition, in the *Articuli Heinriciani*, of the nobles' right in certain circumstances to offer opposition to the king. By the end of the sixteenth century there was no doubt that the Diet was in a stronger position than the sovereign. This development was closely connected with the transition from hereditary to free elective monarchy after the extinction of the Jagellons; for the nobility felt it necessary to exercise stricter control over a king who had been elected and was of foreign origin.

The dynastic policy pursued by the first two kings of Poland from the house of Vasa (Sigismund III, 1587–1632; Władysław IV, 1632–48) served to encourage the ambitions of the *szlachta* and the tension between them and the crown. The few resolutions concerning the constitution passed by the Diet during the first half of the seventeenth century led to further limitations upon the royal power, and in part also to an extension of the Diet's sphere of competence. A resolution of 1607 established in practice the standing senatorial commission [*senatorowie rezydenci*], foreshadowed in the *Articuli Heinriciani*, to exercise control over the king; since the commission's decisions were subject to approval by the *Sejm*, the latter also secured for itself a share in this supervisory function. The king had to submit to restrictions even in his private affairs. In 1631 members of the ruling dynasty were forbidden to acquire hereditary estates; ten years later the reigning monarch was forbidden to travel abroad without the Diet's consent. The king's authority suffered further encroachment from the hetmans, who played an increasingly important part in affairs of state. From the end of the sixteenth century onwards the grand hetman of Poland [*hetman wielki koronny*], who had command of the army in the king's absence, was appointed for life, and thus won for himself a position of independence *vis-à-vis* the monarch. He soon began to wield considerable influence upon the conduct of foreign policy; it was he who largely controlled diplomatic relations with Turkey, the Crimean Tartars, Moldavia, Wallachia and Transylvania. The extent to which the grand hetman could interfere in matters of foreign policy can be gauged from the actions of Stanisław Żołkiewski, who when still only 'field hetman' (a subordinate of the grand hetman) attempted to pursue an independent policy towards Moscow. The grand hetman was undoubtedly the most powerful secular dignitary in Poland, and was even spoken of as a 'rival' of the king.

Whilst the monarchy continued to decline, the Diet succeeded to some degree in extending its powers. It obtained the right to confer noble rank and indigenous status. At the same time the local assemblies [sejmiki] of nobles in the palatinates [województwa], and in part those in the districts and the territories [ziemie], also grew in importance. This tendency toward decentralization of power was particularly marked in the field of taxation. From 1613 onwards the Diet generally only fixed the quota which each palatinate had to provide, leaving it to the local assembly to make the actual assessments. In the 1640s the Diet even empowered local assemblies to vote taxes quite independently, thereby enabling the palatinates to build up their own treasuries [skarby wojewódzkie], and to become financially autonomous. This in turn enabled them to recruit their own armed forces, the so-called 'district troops', or żołnierz powiatowy. These innovations brought about not only a diminution of royal power, but a weakening of the central government as such.

Less obvious, since they were not expressed in legislative form, but of greater importance for the constitutional development of Poland–Lithuania, were the social changes taking place within the politically dominant noble class. During the seventeenth century the lesser nobility became largely dependent upon the magnates, members of the great families who owned vast estates and filled the highest offices in the state. This enabled the magnates to obtain sufficient support at meetings of the local assemblies, and at the Diet itself, to exert a decisive influence upon their proceedings. After the collapse of Zebrzydowski's revolt (1606–7), a rising of the szlachta directed against Sigismund III, the magnates acquired a position of hegemony over the entire nobility. Basing their power upon their landed properties and their private armies, they often indulged in high-handed intervention in political matters, and even in foreign relations, as will be discussed shortly. This accession of political strength to the magnates undoubtedly did more to weaken the Polish state than the decentralization of the financial system. This was most clearly shown by the great part which the magnates played in the increasingly frequent 'confederations', leagues formed by nobles, generally for the purpose of promoting sectional interests.

During these years the monarchy made only half-hearted attempts to counterbalance the ambitions of the nobility by strengthening the authority of the crown. After Zebrzydowski's revolt Sigismund III refrained for a long time from any efforts at all in this direction. It was only in the last years of his reign (1630–2) that he endeavoured, without success, to win the support of the Diet and the local assemblies for a reform of the procedure adopted to elect a new sovereign, in the hope of assuming the succession of one of his own sons. Władysław IV toyed throughout his reign with the idea of consolidating his position *vis-à-vis* the nobility. The best known of his schemes is his establishment of an order of chivalry on the Spanish model, the 'Order of the Immaculate Conception of the Virgin Mary', which he hoped would constitute a dependable bulwark for the monarchy within the noble class. But the nobles reacted coolly to the idea, and all Władysław's plans collapsed. For the same reasons the military reform which he introduced achieved only limited success. The general levy of gentry was already beginning to lose its former importance, and was only rarely summoned. In the last decades of the sixteenth century mercenary troops had been formed on the western model, but they proved inadequate and soon fell into decay. Władysław IV now sought to emulate the example of other European rulers by forming a powerful army of mercenaries dependent entirely upon the sovereign. But the realization of this plan was frustrated by the nobility, and except in time of war Władysław had to be content with the few thousand hired soldiers that had been available to his predecessors.

Thus the political order that was now developing in Poland-Lithuania was the reverse of that now generally coming into being in the rest of Europe. Whereas in most European states the absolutist régime, or at least the central government, consolidated its position more firmly, in Poland-Lithuania the monarchy was still further weakened, and even the efficacy of the other central institutions undermined. One result of Poland's deviation from the general European pattern was that now, in contrast to the sixteenth century, she frequently met with criticism in the West.

The Polish economy still remained predominantly agricultural. The most significant development in this field was the great expansion of grain production (chiefly rye, whilst wheat, barley and oats were much less important), which had begun in the previous century. This was made possible by an extension of the sown area, which took place mainly in the area of the Ukraine, since in the central districts of the country all suitable land had long since been brought under cultivation. The growth of grain production was accompanied by a decline in livestock-breeding, especially marked in central and western Poland. Both these developments were connected with the transition by the larger proprietors from tenant-farming to the practice of farming their estates on their own account, mainly with serf labour. The landowners concentrated upon growing grain, whilst the peasants devoted themselves mainly to livestock-breeding. The more the peasants were obliged to perform compulsory labour-services on the farms, the less they were able to tend their cattle. The widespread use of serf labour on the landowners' estates was only feasible because the peasants had now lost all legal rights *vis-à-vis* their masters.

In handicrafts, unlike agriculture, there were no notable developments;

and this applied also to such modest industries as Poland possessed at this time. The most important enterprises were in Little Poland, and were concerned with the mining of salt, lead and iron and the working of metal. There were as yet no independent industrialists, and the whole system of industrial production was closely bound up with large-scale landowning. Until the middle of the century output was on the increase, but it went almost exclusively to satisfy the domestic market.

Poland's exports consisted primarily of agricultural produce, with grain, for obvious reasons, taking pride of place. It was now that this trade, carried on mainly through Danzig with England and the Netherlands, reached its climax. Other important exports were cattle and hides, despatched by overland routes to Germany and neighbouring countries. Next to agricultural produce in importance came the wealth derived from Poland's rich forests, such as timber, tar and potash; these, like grain, were mainly exported to England and the Netherlands via the Baltic ports. The total value of Polish exports far exceeded that of imports, which comprised chiefly such commodities as textiles, metals and metal goods, and fish. By and large Poland's economic development during this period was not unfavourable. This was particularly true in the commercial field, but from this progress the Polish middle class derived little advantage— largely because the state continued to pursue a commercial and tariff policy which served the interests of the nobility alone.

In ecclesiastical affairs two developments were of decisive importance: the triumph of the Counter-Reformation at the turn of the century, and the Union of Brest in 1596.

The first of these developments found clearest expression in the renunciation of Protestantism by the Polish and Lithuanian nobles, which had begun in the 1560s and reached its climax at the turn of the century. This movement received a strong impetus after the failure of Zebrzydowski's revolt, in which the rebels endorsed some of the demands put forward by the non-Catholic 'dissidents'. Of the influential aristocratic families only a few, such as the Leszczyńskis in Greater Poland and a branch of the Radziwiłłs in Lithuania, remained loyal—for a time—to the cause of the Reformation. This sealed the fate of Protestantism amongst those who were dependent upon the nobility. The peasants had in any case generally shown little enthusiasm for the new creed. In the towns the Protestant ranks thinned under renewed Catholic pressure. In the 1610s and 1620s there took place in such towns as Cracow, Vilno, Poznań and Lublin major disturbances directed against Protestant elements, in the course of which their churches and prayer-houses were destroyed. Cracow no longer had a Protestant church at all after 1593. Another measure employed was to deprive the dissidents of the right to hold municipal office. It was only amongst the Germans of western Poland, especially in the towns of Danzig, Toruń (Thorn) and Elbląg

(Elbing), that the Protestants preserved their strength. Their position improved under Władysław IV, who was less concerned to advance the cause of the Counter-Reformation than to moderate the bitterness of the conflict between the rival creeds. He ensured that those who participated in religious strife were severely punished. In 1645, with the aim of calming the passions that had been aroused, he sponsored the inter-denominational debate (*colloquium charitativum*) of Toruń (Thorn), in which Catholic and Protestant spokesmen took part; it did not, however, achieve any concrete results. At the same time measures continued to be taken against the Socinians and other radical groups. The more moderate treatment of the dissidents in Poland after the death of Sigismund III did not lead to a revival of Protestantism: its power had already been broken by the triumphant Counter-Reformation. The outcome of the religious struggle in Poland was that the overwhelming majority of Poles recognized the authority of Rome.

The success which the Catholic church attained in Poland-Lithuania would doubtless have been impossible had it not been reinvigorated from within. The main role in this reinvigoration was played by the Jesuits, who now experienced their 'golden age'. The leadership of the church passed into the hands of militant elements. Since the Jesuits obtained almost complete control over education, they were able to extend their influence far beyond the immediate ecclesiastical sphere, and to inspire wide sections of the population with the spirit of the Counter-Reformation. The favour and protection afforded to the Catholic church by the state, especially under Sigismund III, known as 'the Polish Philip II', gave it a position of supremacy *vis-à-vis* the other confessions which it was to maintain undiminished so long as Poland continued to exist as an independent state. Poland became the champion of Catholicism in eastern Europe, although the struggle was fought more energetically by Sigismund III than by his successor. The more tolerant attitude which Władysław displayed towards the dissidents led to coolness between Poland and the Vatican, and even to a temporary breach of diplomatic relations. Later Polish rulers returned to the policy of energetic promotion of the Catholic cause.

Much the most important religious problem, and one which had important consequences upon both the internal evolution and the foreign policy of the Polish-Lithuanian state, was that of relations with the Orthodox church, which had a strong following amongst the White Russian and Ukrainian minorities in the eastern part of the country. The decision of the Synod of Brest (1596) to unite the Orthodox and Roman Catholic churches in Poland-Lithuania was not acceptable to the whole Orthodox community, and a split ensued. A struggle developed between supporters and opponents of the union, in which neither group won a decisive victory. The opponents of the union found themselves in dire straits since all

Orthodox bishops except one, the bishop of Lwów, joined it; but on the other hand the number of 'Uniates' (as adherents of the union were called) rose only very slowly, at least until the 1620s. In White Russia the situation changed after the murder in 1623 by ecclesiastical opponents of Archbishop Josephat of Połock (Polotsk), an energetic champion of the union—an act of violence which swung opinion in favour of the Uniates. Eventually their supporters obtained a majority amongst the White Russians, but the Orthodox church continued to command a considerable following, especially in the Ukrainian areas of the Polish-Lithuanian kingdom. It found its most active adherents among the gentry and lower clergy of the south-eastern districts (Galicia, Volhynia, Kiev), the townspeople of Kiev and, from the early 1620s onwards, the Dnieper Cossacks. An important part in defending the Orthodox tradition was played by the numerous 'brotherhoods' [*bratstva*], which sprang up in the Ukraine and White Russia during the latter half of the sixteenth century. The members of these societies considered it one of their most important tasks to raise the moral and intellectual level of the Orthodox clergy. The Orthodox also had their allies: in the Diet, for example, they and the Protestants made common cause. In general the Orthodox church was in such a strong position that its right to exist had to be acknowledged even by such a zealous advocate of Catholicism as Sigismund III. In 1609 the *Sejm* prescribed that Orthodox clergy should not be deprived of their offices or livings on any pretext, and that disputes between Uniates and Orthodox should be settled by a joint tribunal. A Diet resolution of 1618 assured the Orthodox the right to hold religious services. But Sigismund III stubbornly refused to concede their main demand, to be allowed to re-establish their own episcopal hierarchy.

It was in these circumstances that the Orthodox took the step of re-establishing their hierarchy illegally, with the aid of the patriarchs of Constantinople and Moscow (and probably also the Russian tsar), as well as the Dnieper Cossacks, who were in close contact with the Orthodox clergy of Kiev. In 1618 Patriarch Theophanes of Jerusalem, with the sanction of the patriarch of Constantinople, made his way to Muscovite Russia, where he remained until early in 1620. At the same time a Cossack mission arrived in Moscow, and it was probably during their visit that the crucial negotiations were held on this question. In 1620, after the Poles had been defeated by the Turks at Ţuţora (September), Theophanes consecrated one metropolitan bishop and one archbishop, without the knowledge of the king or the Polish authorities; the consecration of four more bishops followed early in 1621. This move was made in the confidence that it would have the support of the brotherhoods and the monks, and a certain amount of military protection from the Cossacks. Although King Sigismund III refused to legalize the new hierarchy, he was in no position to annul the action that had been taken.

The ecclesiastical situation that now developed in the eastern territories was not regarded as durable either by the Uniates or by the government. Several attempts were therefore made during the 1620s to effect a reconciliation between the Uniates and the Orthodox, and to reunite them within the framework of a single church. Plans in this spirit were discussed from 1623 onwards, largely on the initiative of the Uniates. But these endeavours also had the backing of the king and the senators, who feared that the religious conflict in south-eastern Poland, coupled with the Cossack question, might well lead to serious political consequences. Although the higher Orthodox clergy were ready to enter into negotiations, the idea of a new union met with opposition on the part of the Cossacks— as well as the papal Curia. The difficulties that accumulated were so great that the joint synod of Uniates and Orthodox, called by Sigismund III for October 1629 in Lwów, did not come about at all. Under Cossack pressure the Orthodox bishops were obliged to refrain from sending any official representatives to the meeting. So long as Sigismund III was on the throne, the problem of the relations between the Orthodox church and the state thus remained unsettled.

Under his successor the situation was rapidly normalized. In 1633 Petr Mogila, who had been appointed metropolitan of Kiev the previous year, was confirmed in his office by Władysław IV. At about the same time the king also recognized the Orthodox bishops of Mogilev-Mstislavl' and Łuck (Lutsk), and in 1635 the bishop of Przemyśl. In addition to these Orthodox bishoprics there existed one other, at Lwów, which had never been in Uniate hands. The Orthodox church in Poland-Lithuania now disposed of one metropolitanate and four bishoprics, and acquired a recognized legal status alongside the Uniate church. Under these circumstances it was almost a foregone conclusion that the king should go on to grant the non-Uniates religious liberty, which he did at his Coronation Diet.

During the reign of Władysław IV the position of the Orthodox thus noticeably improved. There was now undoubtedly greater tranquillity in the eastern districts of the country. In the first decades of the century the antagonism between Uniates and Orthodox had not been entirely free from violence (the first instance of this being the attack upon the Uniate metropolitan Potej in 1609). This, together with the resistance offered by Sigismund III and the secular authorities to the restoration of the Orthodox bishoprics, had led to the Orthodox minority establishing contact with Moscow, thereby giving the religious tension a pronounced political flavour. But the legalization of the hierarchy now strengthened the hand of those elements in the Orthodox community who sought to remain loyal to the Polish state. The Orthodox educational system now began to show itself receptive to Polish cultural influence, although there were still continual disputes between Orthodox and Uniates over posses-

sion of land, church buildings and schools. Their most important grievance was that they did not enjoy genuine equality of rights with the
Catholics and Uniates. The Orthodox church therefore still constituted
an element of uncertainty, especially in south-eastern Poland, as was to
become evident in 1648, when Khmelnitsky's rising broke out.

On the whole the internal situation in Poland during these years was
more favourable than in many other countries of Europe. Though there
was tension between the crown and the nobility, there was no civil war;
nor was there a prolonged war of religion, but only a number of isolated
violent incidents between the adherents of rival faiths. The country's
economy was making progress. But the peacefulness of the domestic scene
between 1609 and 1648 ought not to obscure the fact that it was precisely
at this time that Poland began to lag behind the rest of Europe.

This is clearly shown by developments in the cultural field. Whereas in
the sixteenth century religious and intellectual movements in other European countries had had a strong appeal for members of the upper classes
in Poland and Lithuania, they now evoked only a feeble response. This
change was due, at least in part, to the control exercised at this time by the
Jesuits over the Polish educational system. The ties with the rest of Europe
weakened. Young men now travelled abroad less frequently, and in Poland
itself foreign books became a rarity. In many spheres of intellectual
and cultural life there was stagnation. Cracow University, for example,
turned away from humanism and prescribed a narrow scholasticism.
But in some fields, such as poetry or historiography, this was still
the end of a 'golden age'. With his *Chronica gestorum in Europa singularium* Bishop Piasecki (d. 1649) continued the tradition of the great
fifteenth-century Polish chroniclers, and brought it to a worthy climax.

As Poland's ties with the West weakened, so her attention came to be
focused more than ever upon the east. This was particularly true of the
gentry, who during the seventeenth century did much to colonize the
south-eastern districts, and thus also to extend the influence of Polish
culture beyond the borders of what was ethnically Polish territory. In the
Ukraine this was manifested most impressively in the work of the Kiev
Academy, founded by Petr Mogila in 1631. These achievements in the
east must be taken into account when assessing Polish cultural development during this period.

In foreign policy, too, this increased concern with eastern problems
was clearly evident. The troubles which broke out in Muscovite Russia
after the extinction of the old dynasty in 1598 attracted the attention of
the Polish nobility and of the king. At first individual magnates intervened on their own initiative, but later King Sigismund III also decided
to join in the struggle for power in the tsardom of Moscow.

Sigismund's objective was to win the Russian throne for himself. Polish
rule in Moscow would facilitate the newly-launched Polish drive for

expansion to the east. But at the same time he sought to extend Polish territory at Russia's expense: Moscow was to be forced to return the districts of Smolensk and Chernigov, ceded to her by the Jagellons in the early sixteenth century, which were once again to be incorporated into the Polish-Lithuanian state. Sigismund's expansionist ambitions were not merely political and military: as a stout upholder of the Counter-Reformation, he nurtured the hope of opening up Moscow to Catholic influence. Finally, he was motivated by purely personal and dynastic considerations: Moscow could serve as a base for an offensive against Sweden, whereby he might win back the throne of his ancestors. Characteristically, Sigismund decided to intervene in Russia at the moment when Charles IX, his rival on the Swedish throne, had entered into an alliance with Tsar Vasily Shuisky.

It was inevitable that, on religious grounds alone, Sigismund's plans should meet with strong opposition amongst the fervently Orthodox population of Moscow. For this reason the commander of the Polish forces in Russia, field hetman Stanisław Żółkiewski, sought to pursue a more subtle policy which took account of the political and religious outlook of the Russian upper class. He advocated that Sigismund's son Władysław, rather than the king himself, should be put forward as a candidate for the tsardom, and that the rights of the Orthodox church should not be infringed. Presented in this form, the idea of a union between Poland-Lithuania and Moscow found considerable support amongst the Russian boyars. In August 1610, when Żółkiewski appeared with his army before the gates of Moscow, they accordingly concluded with him an agreement for the election of Władysław as tsar. This agreement incorporated the assurances desired by the boyars regarding the inviolability of the Orthodox church, and the Muscovite political and social order in general. The pact seemed likely to succeed, for, prompted by the boyars, a section of the Russian population swore an oath of allegiance to Władysław, and militarily the Poles were now in a strong position in the country. In July 1610 Żółkiewski had won a resounding victory over a Muscovite army, reinforced by Swedish troops, at Klushino (about 120 miles north-east of Smolensk) which freed the way to Moscow; and early in October the boyars allowed the capital, including the Kremlin, to be occupied by Polish forces.

It is a debatable question whether Poland, for all these military and political successes, would have been able to carry through the plan of union with Moscow in the face of Swedish opposition as well as the resistance offered by those sections of the Russian population which contested the policy of the boyars. Before this problem demanded attention, the policy of union was wrecked by the actions of Sigismund III. With the support of a group of senators, he insisted that he himself, and not Władysław, should accede to the Russian throne, although he had already given his consent to his son's accession—apparently not in earnest—in an undertaking given to a group of boyars in February 1610. In view of the king's attitude, the agreement between Żółkiewski and the Moscow boyars lapsed, and a breach inevitably ensued. The capture of Smolensk (June 1611) revealed clearly the Poles' annexationist designs; and this, together with the harsh repressive measures employed by the Polish troops occupying Moscow, generated amongst the Russian population a religious and national movement, directed primarily against the Poles. A popular levy was formed which marched on Moscow, and in the autumn of 1612 forced the Polish garrison in the city to capitulate. The election of Michael Romanov as tsar early in 1613 finally destroyed the chances of a Polish succession in Moscow.

This was an accomplished fact, which could not be altered by King Sigismund's belated readiness, in the years that followed, to give up his claim to the Russian throne in favour of his son. In 1617–18 Władysław undertook another campaign in the hope of bringing Moscow under Polish rule, but the attempt failed. Moscow had now regained a measure of internal stability, and a continuation of hostilities promised little hope of success; furthermore, in south-eastern Poland there was trouble with the Turks and Tartars. The campaign was therefore abandoned, and an armistice concluded at Deulino (December 1618). This brought Poland-Lithuania an appreciable accession of territory, for Moscow was obliged to cede the districts of Smolensk, Starodub, Novgorod-Seversk and Chernigov. This represented a considerable success for Poland, which now had more territory than at any time since the dawn of the modern era, but this gain was vitiated by the acute antagonism between Poland and Russia that resulted from Sigismund's policy. Henceforward a vehemently anti-Polish feeling was prevalent in all sections of Russian society.

When Sigismund III died (23 April 1632), Moscow took advantage of the interregnum to try to undo the settlement of 1618, which had still left intact Władysław's claim to the Russian tsardom. In the autumn of 1632 Russian troops crossed the border and occupied several districts, but failed to take their main objective, the city of Smolensk. Peace was concluded on the River Polyanovka, near Vyaz'ma, in June 1634. The territorial terms restored the *status quo* (except for the district of Serpeysk, which was returned to Moscow); Władysław gave up his pretensions to the Russian throne. On the whole, Poland-Lithuania had undoubtedly succeeded in maintaining her position *vis-à-vis* Moscow; nevertheless the balance of power was now unmistakably beginning to tilt to the advantage of Russia. This development did not pose a threat until the middle of the century: in the years immediately following, indeed, there was even a certain *rapprochement* between Poland and Russian in the face of the common danger from the Turks and Tartars. It was only after Poland had been enfeebled by the Cossack rising of 1648 that Moscow had the opportunity to displace her from her position of supremacy in eastern Europe.

This shows the significance of the developments in south-eastern Poland for her foreign policy. Poland's position along the lower Dnieper and Dniester was governed by several factors: by her relations with Turkey, by the attitude of the sultan's vassals, the Crimean Tartars, and in particular by the attitude of the Dnieper Cossacks, who lived in this area. Since the sixteenth century it had been one of the cardinal principles of Polish foreign policy to avoid a military conflict with the Porte. It was only in Moldavia that Turkish and Polish interests clashed directly. Poland had old claims to sovereignty over this area, which she generally refrained from pressing, although the Polish magnates resident in the south-eastern districts would often intervene in Moldavian affairs on their own initiative. A more important cause of tension in Polish-Turkish relations were the attacks made on Polish territory by the Tartars, and the unauthorized raids undertaken against the Turks by the Cossacks, which became more and more frequent from the latter half of the sixteenth century onwards.

The Cossack system that existed in the south-east of the Polish-Lithuanian kingdom came into being during the sixteenth century as a means of defence against the Tartar hordes; it was, indeed, as Macůrek has shown, a by-product of their proximity. Most of the Cossacks were Ukrainians, although until the turn of the century there was also a considerable number of Polish *szlachta* amongst them. The disappearance of the latter element from the Cossack bands resulted from the fact that the Polish gentry formed the spearhead of the advancing wave of Polish colonization in the south-eastern palatinates. By the early seventeenth century an acute antagonism was developing between the Cossacks on one hand and, on the other, the Polish or Polonized gentry of these territories, and thus also the Polish state. The state exercised control over only a small section of the Cossacks, the so-called 'registered' Cossacks. The remainder retired to the lower Dnieper, and came to be known, from the location of their fortified strongpoint below the Dnieper rapids(*porogy*), as Zaporog Cossacks. Here they successfully asserted their independence against the Polish authorities. Between 1613 and 1620, in their 'heroic age', they took particularly vigorous action against the Tartars and Turks, even crossing the Black Sea to carry out daring raids upon the Turkish towns on the northern coast of Anatolia.

Since these attacks were made from territory which was at least nominally Polish, they led to considerable tension between that country and the Porte, and in 1617 almost to war. Actual hostilities were delayed until the Deulino armistice freed Poland from her preoccupations in Russia, and the Turks had concluded peace with Persia. The clash that took place in 1620 was the first direct encounter between Poland and Turkey since the battle of Varna in 1444. One of the factors that brought the conflict about was King Sigismund's policy in the opening phase of the Thirty Years War: he allowed the Habsburgs to recruit in Poland bands of irregulars, the so-called *Lisowczycy*, who late in 1619 helped to parry the attack upon Upper Hungary by the sultan's vassal, Prince Bethlen Gabor of Transylvania. But the principal cause of the war was not Sigismund's cautious support for the emperor, but the continuing militancy of the Cossacks. The Polish commander, Grand Hetman Żółkiewski, attempted to forestall the anticipated Turkish attack by advancing into Moldavia, but in September and October 1620 suffered catastrophic defeats at Țuțora on the Pruth and Mogilev on the Dniester. In the following year a Polish army, aided by Cossack elements, succeeded in halting the Turkish advance near Khotin (Chocim). It was there, in October 1621, that the war was terminated on the basis of a return to the *status quo*. To have beaten off an attack by the strongest European military power of the day was undoubtedly a notable achievement. For more than a decade the internal struggles at the Porte and the resumption of the war between Turkey and Persia safeguarded Poland from another Ottoman attack. It was not until the early 1630s, when she was again involved in a struggle with Moscow, that the Turks made another attempt upon the south-eastern borderlands (1633). It was successfully repulsed, and peace was restored in the following year.

But although Poland could defend this area against the Turks, she was unable to control it effectively or establish ordered conditions. It was still exposed to Tartar attack, and the Cossack question remained unsolved.

The continual Tartar raids upon the south-eastern palatinates could be eliminated only by subjugating the Crimean Tartars and the other Tartar hordes that roamed the western shore of the Black Sea. But Poland was no more able to undertake such action than Muscovite Russia. In 1628–9 the Dnieper Cossacks intervened in the Tartars' internal feuds and in this way attempted to bring the Crimea under their influence, but without success. Conquest of the Tartars would have been feasible only in the event of a decisive Polish victory over the suzerain Power, the Ottoman Empire. Towards the end of his life Władysław IV did contemplate a major attack upon the Turks, but the other Powers whose support he had hoped to obtain held back, and so did the *Sejm*. Thus for various reasons the Tartars were not confronted with effective counter-measures, and throughout the first half of the seventeenth century south-eastern Poland was still exposed to their raids. Some contemporary observers considered that the extent of this evil could have been diminished if the *szlachta* of the south-eastern districts had constituted a more efficient military force.

The second problem was still more important. The Cossack community had become more powerful than was compatible with the interests of the Polish state. In 1625 and 1630 they revolted, and severe measures of repression were taken against them. But these did not suffice to make the Zaporog Cossacks bow to the authority of the state. On the contrary, it was now that the antagonism between the Cossacks and the central government was becoming intensified by the religious issue. From the 1620s onwards the Cossacks came to regard themselves as defenders of the Orthodox faith against the attempts of Polish Catholics to promote ecclesiastical union. After the Cossack insurrection of 1637–8 the Polish state summoned up the determination to take energetic action against both the Zaporog and the registered Cossacks, which brought a decade of relative calm. In this era of 'golden peace' Polish colonists, led by a few magnate families, and in particular the Wiśnowieckis, rapidly extended their authority in the lands beyond the Dnieper. But some of the Zaporog Cossacks remained beyond the government's reach, and even the measures of 1638–9 (which included, for example, the rebuilding of the strong fort of Kodak on the Dnieper) did not serve to subdue the Cossacks completely. Being mainly of peasant origin, the Cossacks came to develop a burning hatred for the gentry and magnates whom they identified with Polish rule. Early in 1648, led by Bohdan Khmel'nitsky, the Cossacks rose in a great revolt. This insurrection revealed the true character of the situation in the south-eastern districts: in part of this area Polish rule was so precarious that it collapsed, never to be restored.

These wellnigh incessant conflicts with the Tartars and Cossacks were a great drain on the resources of the Polish state. Indeed, the situation in the south-eastern territories was to have fateful consequences for Poland. In the 1650s the struggle against the Cossacks triggered off a succession of prolonged and burdensome wars which did much to bring about Poland's decline as a European Power.

Poland's preoccupations with eastern problems during the first two decades of the seventeenth century meant that she had in general to confine herself to defensive action in the north, where she faced the Swedish drive for control of the Baltic. During the previous period there had developed a certain rivalry between the two countries over Livonia, which formed part of the wider breach between Catholic and Protestant Europe. But the tension only became dangerously acute as a result of the conflict within the Vasa dynasty, which from 1587 onwards ruled in Poland as well as Sweden. Sigismund III (1587–1632), the first Vasa to occupy the Polish throne, was recognized as king of Sweden in 1592 on the death of his father, John III, but seven years later was deposed by the Swedish Diet on the grounds that he resided permanently in Poland, and in 1604 his uncle, Charles of Södermanland, acceded to the Swedish throne as Charles IX. Sigismund, however, refused to reconcile himself to the loss of his hereditary rights. The dynastic struggle which thus developed was to weigh heavily upon relations between the two countries until the peace of Oliva in 1660. In the early years of the century it gave rise to fighting in Livonia. Under Charles IX's successor, his son Gustavus Adolphus, the war received a new impetus, and came to be waged on a far more extensive scale than hitherto. Sweden had now become a formidable military power, and her new king set himself far-reaching political objectives: control of the whole southern coast of the Baltic, from Ingria to northern Germany. However, the Polish nobility continued to regard the conflict between the two sovereigns as an essentially dynastic matter, and it was not until Livonia had been lost that they gave more resolute support to Sigismund in his struggle against Sweden. At this time it was not in the interests of the dominant class in Polish society to engage in a struggle for the Baltic; instead the nobles, as we have seen, had their eyes fixed upon the east.

As soon as the Peace of Stolbovo in February 1617 put an end to the hostilities between Sweden and Moscow, Gustavus Adolphus launched his attack upon Sigismund. In the summer of that year his troops marched into Livonia. Poland still had her hands tied by Władysław's campaign in Russia, and was alarmed at the threat of an attack by the Turks and Tartars. In 1618, faced with this trying military and diplomatic situation, Sigismund thought it wiser to agree to an armistice, even at the price of ceding some territory in Livonia. Three years later the Swedish king resumed his Livonian offensive. Once again Poland was preoccupied elsewhere, for the war with Turkey was still in progress. In September 1621 Riga fell, and in 1625 the Swedes occupied the rest of Livonia. During the intervening years the Poles had had a favourable opportunity to counter-attack; but the Diet had refused the necessary funds, and the chance had been missed.

In 1626, as a result of this success, Gustavus Adolphus could proceed with an attack upon Royal Prussia (West Prussia). Now even the central districts of Poland were exposed to the threat of Swedish attack. This dangerous turn of events impelled the Diet to grant the sum required to augment the size of the Polish army. But although this time Poland was not hampered by campaigns against other external enemies, Sigismund failed to repel the Swedish attack. In July Gustavus Adolphus landed at Pillau and from there penetrated into the northern part of Warmia (Ermland) and the Vistula–Nogat delta. Except for Danzig, the whole coastline was under his control. Nor could the Polish armies prevent the Swedes from registering further successes. In 1628 they threatened Grudziądz (Graudenz) and Toruń (Thorn); by the early months of 1629, after the Polish defeat of Górzno, a Swedish drive into central Poland had come within the bounds of possibility. The threat was averted only by the arrival of a relief corps despatched by Wallenstein.

Neither of the belligerent Powers, however, was able to score a decisive victory. The Poles only accepted aid from the emperor with some hesitation, since they feared possible imperial claims to west Prussia, and the gentry, who looked askance at Sigismund's policy, were pressing for negotiations with the Swedes. Gustavus Adolphus, for his part, was anxious to shift his attention as soon as possible to the German theatre of hostilities. Both France and England were deeply interested in obtaining effective Swedish intervention in Germany, and it was through their mediation that the six-year armistice of Altmark (near Malborg [Marienburg]) came about in September 1629. This agreement gave the Swedes all Livonia except a few districts in the south-east; in Royal Prussia they won possession of all the ports apart from Danzig and Puck (Putzig), and in the dukedom of Prussia (East Prussia) almost the entire coastline except for Koenigsberg. The treaty was a severe blow to Poland; yet the Diet ratified it without turning a hair.

The difficulties in which the Swedes found themselves in Germany after the death of Gustavus Adolphus afforded Poland a chance to effect a revision of the settlement of 1629. Negotiations held during 1635 led to the Treaty of Stuhmsdorf, which provided for a twenty-six year armistice. Poland regained what she had lost in Prussia, but in Livonia had to sanction a continuation of the territorial *status quo*. Nothing was said in the terms of this agreement about the dynastic conflict, and Władysław maintained his claim to the Swedish crown. The Polish nobles, however, had little or no sympathy with his ambitions, and refused to contemplate a war with Sweden for the reconquest of Livonia. Consequently no further developments took place in Polish-Swedish relations during the remaining phases of the Thirty Years War.

The struggle with Sweden, which with a few intermissions had lasted throughout the first three decades of the century, weakened Poland's position both directly, through the loss of Livonia, and indirectly, by consolidating the rule of the Brandenburg Hohenzollerns in the dukedom of Prussia. Already in 1611 the elector of Brandenburg, John Sigismund, had secured from the Polish king and Diet recognition of his claim to inherit the fief of Prussia. This ensured that Prussia should pass to the Brandenburg branch of the Hohenzollern dynasty, and in 1618, on the death of the weak-minded Albert Frederick, the last duke of the Prussian line, he was succeeded by John Sigismund. When he died the following year the fief passed, in conformity with a previous agreement, to the new elector of Brandenburg, George William—although only after some delay, for it was not until September 1621 that he was granted title to his fief. It was impossible for Poland to prevent his succession, even if she had wanted to do so, since she was preoccupied with the Swedes in Livonia, and the new elector had gained the support of the Prussian Estates. When George William died in 1640, Poland offered no opposition to the succession of the great elector, who secured his fief in October 1641. By and large the relations between Poland and the dukedom of Prussia show that in Poland the ruling class had no lasting interest in the struggle for Baltic supremacy. In the 1640s Poland even disbanded the small navy which she had begun to build during the two preceding decades, and both the harbours that had been constructed for it, Kazimierzowo and Włady-sławowo, were allowed to fall into decay.

Poland's attitude towards the course of events in central and western Europe was largely determined by the alliance between the Polish Vasas and the Habsburgs. This carried on a tradition dating back to the days of the Jagellons, for since the early sixteenth century Poland had maintained peaceful relations with Austria, thus ensuring tranquillity along her western border. The alliance of 1613 came about naturally, as a result of the common opposition of both signatories to Sweden and the Ottoman Empire. Although it contained no explicit military obligations, it sufficed to keep Poland well disposed towards the Habsburg camp throughout the Thirty Years War. During the early phases of this struggle the pro-Austrian policy pursued by the Polish king was not devoid of military significance. As already mentioned, the *Lisowczycy* recruited in Poland by the Habsburgs rendered useful service against Prince Bethlen Gabor of Transylvania. Subsequently these irregular troops were employed by the emperor in Bohemia and in other theatres of war. But towards the end of the 1620s the Poles themselves were so hard pressed by Gustavus Adolphus that they had to request the emperor for military support.

Sigismund's successor continued the policy of the Austrian alliance. The treaty of 1613 was renewed in 1633, and in March 1637 relations with the Habsburgs were further strengthened by the conclusion of a purely dynastic compact, sealed by Władysław's marriage to the Arch-duchess Cecilie Renate, a daughter of Ferdinand II. But despite the Austrian alliance Poland did not take an active part in the Thirty Years War. Władysław sought to mediate between the belligerents, but his efforts were totally unsuccessful, for Poland had ceased to be a significant factor in the struggle for power in central Europe. This remained the case even after Władysław's *rapprochement* with France, which found expression in the king's marriage in 1645 to a French princess, Louise Marie of Gonzaga-Nevers. (His first wife, Cecilie Renate, had died the previous year.)

Taken as a whole, during the first half of the seventeenth century Poland's international position deteriorated significantly, despite the successes achieved in the struggle against Moscow and the repulse of the Turks. Not only the dangerous situation in the south-east, but also the growth of Swedish power, presented major threats to Poland's existence. It was Sweden which, with France, emerged as the victor in the Thirty Years War; and the outcome of this struggle, though strictly speaking not an actual defeat for Poland, did represent a weakening of her position. The international developments of these years paved the way for Poland's decline, which set in after the middle of the seventeenth century.

2. RUSSIA 1613–45

During the reign of Michael Feodorovich (1613–45), first tsar of the Romanov dynasty, Russia made a slow and painful recovery from the devastation wrought by the 'Time of Troubles'. The peasants and Cossacks who had risen in revolt against the encroachment of serfdom lacked the ability to construct a new social order. After years of anarchy and civil war the country was exhausted; political passions were subsiding, and there was a general desire for a return to normality and order. Foreign intervention had stimulated national sentiment, expressed most forcibly in the successes of the popular levy [*opolcheniye*], which in the course of 1612 split the rebel Cossack forces, regained possession of the capital, and established a shadowy authority over most of the country. But the problems it faced were formidable in the extreme: Moscow lay in ruins; Novgorod and the north-west were occupied by the Swedes, and along the western border Polish armies were active; bands of fugitive peasants, Cossacks and Tartars freely roamed the countryside, burning and pillaging; over wide areas trade was at a standstill, and villages lay desolate and empty, silent witnesses to the cataclysmic violence of the storm that had swept over Russia. The Troubles had cost some two and a half million lives.

In January 1613 a national assembly [*Zemsky Sobor*] met to elect a new tsar. Apart from the peasantry, all social groups were represented. As was to be expected, the gathering was dominated by those elements most prominent in the *opolcheniye:* provincial serving men, townspeople and Cossacks. But considerable influence was also exerted surreptitiously by the clergy and such of the aristocratic boyars whose political reputation permitted them to be present. The debates were prolonged and acrimonious. A decision had first to be taken with regard to the Polish and Swedish candidates. Władysław's belated expedition to Moscow (October 1612) had finally destroyed any chance he still possessed of acceding to the throne of the tsars by popular consent. Prince Charles Philip of Sweden was less unpopular, but the Swedish court delayed his departure for Russia, and this proved fatal to his cause. The new tsar had thus to be a born Russian. But there was no obviously suitable candidate among the senior boyar families, many of which were compromised by their collaboration with the Poles. Attention gradually focused upon the sixteen-year-old Michael Romanov. The role played by his father in the Troubles[1]

---

[1] Michael's father, Feodor Nikitich Romanov, was a nephew by marriage of Ivan Grozny. Under Boris Godunov the family had been persecuted, and Feodor Romanov forced to take vows as a monk (Filaret). During Shuisky's reign he had accepted service with the second pretender as his patriarch. After participating in the events leading to Shuisky's overthrow (1610), he had headed the Russian delegation sent to Smoleńsk to negotiate the accession of Władysław. Here his stubborn refusal to accept Polish terms had led to his imprisonment, which was destined to last until 1619.

made the family popular with Cossacks as well as with serving men, and the genealogical connection with the old dynasty was close enough to satisfy legitimist sentiment. Michael's youth and inexperience told rather in his favour: personally uncommitted to any faction, he could serve as a symbol of reconciliation and national unity. On 21 February (O.S.) he was proclaimed tsar.

Michael showed an understandable reluctance to assume the burdens of office. The idea of an elected ruler accorded ill with Muscovite traditions, and it seemed uncertain whether his subjects, whose intellectual horizons had been broadened by recent events, would willingly submit to his authority, and pay him the almost religious veneration granted to hereditary sovereigns. His first actions revealed an acute anxiety to strengthen his authority *vis-à-vis* the provisional government and the *Sobor*. But fortunately for the new dynasty these apprehensions proved exaggerated. The clergy assiduously spread the view that the tsar owed his crown to divine intervention, and was responsible to God alone. The upsurge of popular initiative expressed in the *opolcheniye* was not sustained; tradition reasserted itself, and Russian society relapsed into its old passivity. The national unity briefly achieved at the *Sobor* vanished almost immediately, and the various social groups abandoned themselves to the pursuit of their respective sectional interests. The men who suddenly found themselves thrust to the forefront of Russian political life did not attempt to consolidate their new position in constitutional form,[1] but hastened to divest themselves of their responsibilities.

The *Sobor* remained in existence during the early years of the reign, but it was apparently less representative, and certainly less authoritative, than it was in 1613. It collaborated with the government in issuing some (but not all) decrees, appeals and exhortations, but exercised no independent initiative. In effect it served as camouflage: the government exploited its moral authority to render more palatable unpopular decisions taken elsewhere. Power in these years lay with a clique of boyars, most of whom were related to the new dynasty, assisted by powerful officials—'ignorant youths' and 'ravenous wolves', as they were termed by a contemporary Dutch observer, 'all of whom without distinction rob and ruin the people'. Patriots who had served in the *opolcheniye* were ousted in favour of men with dubious records. Michael himself, a colourless personality, exercised no authority, and the new régime acquired an unenviable reputation for corruption and maladministration. It was incapable of dealing effectively with the many urgent questions with which it was confronted.

[1] The once prevalent view that Michael's powers were limited on his accession by agreement with the boyars is not supported by the available evidence. It may be considered a rationalization of popular discontent at governmental practices during the early years of the reign. The most that can be said is that the tsar may have given some informal promise not to abuse his power by engaging in personal feuds.

Of these the most pressing was the need for revenue. The treasury was empty, but the claims upon its resources limitless. The cadastral survey, the basis of taxation in normal times, had been rendered totally unrealistic by devastation and depopulation. It was nevertheless pressed into service, with the result that those communities which still had a minimum of resources were reduced to the general level of misery. Petitions for reassessment poured in, but the government shrank from a fundamental reform, and resorted instead to such desperate expedients as forced loans and 'fifth moneys' (levied arbitrarily upon capital as well as income), the burden of which fell chiefly upon the hard-pressed townspeople. The landowners, on the other hand, often succeeded in evading their fiscal obligations by securing favourable reassessments, bribing the local surveyors to grant them exemption and to confirm their rights to land they had illegally appropriated. There now occurred a general scramble for property, in which the wealthiest elements—*sil'nye lyudi* (literally, 'strong men'), as they came to be called—were naturally the most successful. The area under private landownership greatly increased, especially in the centre and south, and a great many estates changed hands. The government was in no position to control this process, and in fact assisted it by making lavish grants to the gentry of crown estates, and more particularly of 'black' (i.e. peasant)[1] land. Never was the loyalty of the serving men more essential than now, when Russia's national integrity was at stake.

Early in 1614 Moscow regained control of the lower Volga from the rebel Cossack leader Zarutsky, who had retired with his small force to Astrakhan. The last embers of the Time of Troubles were now extinguished, although some years elapsed before the government could finally suppress the ubiquitous bandit gangs, often several thousand strong, that terrorized much of the country. Even the far north was not spared. In the vast forests concealment was no problem, and the troops sent in pursuit were cumbersome in manœuvre and unreliable. Sometimes bandits disposed of foreign bases and support: in 1615–16 the Polish guerrilla chief Lisowski entered Russian territory, swept around Moscow, leaving a trail of destruction behind him, and returned almost unscathed to Polish soil.

Fortunately for Russia, her two western adversaries were themselves at loggerheads, and could be engaged singly. The rejection of Charles Philip's candidature left the small Swedish occupation force in Novgorod in an exposed position. The local population harboured autonomist sympathies, but were not separatist. Refusing Gustavus Adolphus' demand that they should swear allegiance to him, they secretly established contact with Moscow; reprisals by the occupying authorities stimulated the spirit of resistance. In 1615 the Swedish king landed in Russia and laid siege to Pskov, but the inhabitants of the ancient city offered a stout defence.

[1] See below, pp. 607, 617.

England, keenly conscious of her commercial interests in Russia, responded to Tsar Michael's plea for aid by despatching Sir John Merrick to facilitate a mediated settlement. Negotiations, punctuated by intermittent warfare, dragged on throughout 1616, until in February of the following year peace was signed at Stolbovo, a village near Lake Ladoga. Sweden, recognizing the inevitable, surrendered her claim to the Russian crown and (in return for an indemnity) to Novgorod, but retained the Ingrian fortresses, thus cutting Russia off from direct access to the Baltic. Henceforward, until the days of Peter the Great, Archangel was Russia's only port. Stolbovo was a bitter pill, but in her present state of exhaustion Russia could not hope for better terms, and she desperately needed peace to face a new threat of invasion by her principal enemy, Poland.

Władysław refused to admit that the situation in Russia had changed with Michael's accession, and believed that a show of strength would suffice to win the throne for himself. However, the Diet would not sanction a bold stroke on his part whilst Poland was preoccupied with more dangerous neighbours, Turkey and Sweden. The emperor, too, urged peace with Russia, and sent a representative to mediate in the talks held on the border in 1615. The conference broke down largely because both Russia and Poland, for reasons of strategy and prestige, insisted on possession of the key city of Smolensk, which a Russian army had just tried in vain to recapture. Inconclusive frontier skirmishing followed until, in the autumn of 1617, Władysław succeeded in mounting a rather half-hearted invasion of Russia. Though he had only limited forces at his command, his appearance seemed to hypnotize Moscow into immobility. The government feared that active defensive measures, necessitating further sacrifices from the exhausted population, would stimulate opposition. Vyaz'ma surrendered without resistance, and Władysław, after wintering in Russia, was allowed to continue his languid advance eastwards. Whilst he invested Mozhaisk, 20,000 Dnieper Cossacks swept up to his assistance, and in the last days of September he appeared before the gates of Moscow. An attempt to take the city by surprise failed. Despite the weakness of Russian resistance, it was plain that the country had no desire for Polish rule. The approach of winter and mutinous outbreaks on both sides induced the two combatants to terminate a campaign from which neither derived glory or advantage.

In December 1618 an armistice was signed at Deulino, north-west of Moscow, to last fourteen years. Russia ceded Smolensk and a broad belt of territory along her western border. Unlike Stolbovo, Deulino did not lead to an enduring settlement. Władysław's refusal to surrender his claim to the throne made a resumption of hostilities inevitable. But for the present, at least, a valuable breathing-space had been gained. Moreover, the Poles had lost their greatest opportunity: never again would their armies penetrate into the heart of Russia.

The exchange of prisoners agreed upon at Deulino enabled Filaret to return to Moscow (June 1619). Almost immediately he was installed as patriarch. The head of the Russian church traditionally enjoyed considerable authority in secular matters; as father of the tsar, Filaret's position was naturally one of exceptional power. In theory, Russia now became a dyarchy, with Michael and his father as joint and equal sovereigns. In practice Filaret, whose strong personality completely eclipsed that of his weak-willed son, was now the absolute master of Russia, and his authority remained supreme and unchallenged until his death in 1633. His position somewhat resembled that of Richelieu; but he differed from his great contemporary in the source of his ideas. Filaret had no sympathy with the Latin or semi-secularized culture of the West, but looked for inspiration to the Byzantine traditions of the Russian past. Upbringing and temperament had not endowed him with breadth of vision. His aim was to restore rather than to reform: to patch up the shattered framework of Russian society and, by steering an impartial course between competing pressures, to establish the autocracy upon a new pinnacle of eminence. Under his firm hand government policy, whilst it did not change direction, acquired a new consistency and sense of purpose.

The implementation of Filaret's programme necessitated the centralization and systematization of the administrative apparatus. The court reverted to the elaborate semi-religious ceremonial of former times, with hundreds of nobles waiting upon the tsar. Filaret's own court, which rivalled that of the tsar in Oriental splendour, was also a centre of political life. Informal gatherings held here, attended by favoured members of all the articulate classes, served to keep the ruling group in touch with the popular mood. The *Zemsky Sobor* thus became superfluous. The Council [*Duma*] of Boyars likewise wielded little power. Filaret ruled through the bureaucracy: the most important offices [*prikazy*] were headed by his intimate associates, including even the so-called 'investigating' [*sysknye*] offices which, to assuage popular discontent, were established expressly to check abuses by the 'strong men'. The arbitrariness of the Muscovite administration was legendary. The work of government was largely carried on in response to petitions; in taking decisions, the authorities paid more heed to the wealth and influence of the supplicant than to the merits of his plea or to abstract principles of justice. Officials were ignorant of the laws, which were chaotic and contradictory. Filaret ordered each *prikaz* to maintain a register of legislation relevant to its field of competence, but did not attempt to codify the law—let alone to separate judicial from administrative procedure. At the provincial level, each district [*uyezd*] was now normally governed by a 'commander' [*voyevoda*] with full military and civil power. He received no salary, but was expected to maintain himself by 'gifts' from the local population. This allowed the *voyevody* ample scope for every conceivable abuse, particularly in the remoter areas. In 1627, in an effort to control them, the government decreed the general introduction of elected *gubnye starosty*;[1] but in practice these popular representatives degenerated into submissive agents of the 'commanders'. The elected authorities of the peasant communities also declined in importance, particularly on private estates, where the landowner wielded absolute power. Elsewhere, they served as convenient instruments for raising taxes: if a community defaulted, the elder and his electors were held responsible, and were mercilessly beaten by government agents until they paid.

Fiscal matters were still the main preoccupation of this powerful bureaucratic instrument. Within a few days of Filaret's return a nation-wide survey was ordered of land and other sources of wealth, with the aim of reconstructing the cadastre, stopping tax evasion, and making possible an equitable redistribution of fiscal burdens. But the survey did not embrace monasteries and other holders of charters of privileges, whose ancient rights were now confirmed (although in most cases on a less generous scale). Moreover, the surveyors were not properly guided or controlled, and were generally unfit to perform their complex and delicate task. The few who conscientiously attempted to obey their instructions, and to describe matters as they found them truthfully and fearlessly, found their efforts frustrated by the absence of uniform criteria of assessment: thus, for example, towns at an approximately equivalent standard of prosperity might be taxed at grossly different rates. In the face of obstruction by landowners, who refused to allow surveyors to check the veracity of their declarations, the government made an important concession: in areas where private landowning was general, surveyors were told not to attempt an assessment of actual resources, but to content themselves with the purely mechanical task of registering the number of peasant households; a group of households of specified size was henceforward to constitute a taxable unit. The landowners subsequently (1631–2) pressed for a reduction in the norms fixed; and since this was a moment of national emergency, the government again gave way.

There now emerged a clear distinction between, on the one hand, the townspeople and 'black' peasants, subject to heavy direct taxation and, on the other hand, the privately owned peasants, who generally paid less tax, but rendered dues to their landowners. This differentiation (which was geographical as well as social) had the effect of making the survey virtually useless for revenue-raising purposes. The results of this vast operation failed to justify the efforts expended, and the government again had to rely mainly upon sources of income other than direct taxation, which were necessarily less predictable and less equitable. Of these

[1] Authorities with jurisdiction over criminal matters (especially banditry), chosen by the entire population of the *uyezd* from amongst the local gentry. They had existed in some areas since the days of Ivan Grozny.

the most important (apart from the ruinous 'fifths', again levied twice during the war years 1632–4) were internal customs duties and the spirits monopoly. The state taverns, often farmed out annually to concessionaires who undertook to provide a fixed sum in advance, proved highly profitable to the treasury, but most injurious to popular well-being, and were largely to blame for the extensive drunkenness that was one of the conspicuous features of the Muscovite social scene. The state also intermittently monopolized trade in certain commodities, much to the detriment of private commerce.

The cadastral survey had military as well as fiscal aims: to bring order into the chaos that reigned in the ownership of landed property—for the heart of the Russian army was still the primitive cavalry force mobilized by the gentry, who in return for compulsory service were granted estates on conditional tenure [*pomestya*]. The government sought to ensure that all landowners were registered for service, and that holdings corresponded as closely as possible to official entitlements. Where necessary, excess land was confiscated and re-allocated, and landless gentry allotted new estates. But in the central districts the reserves of 'black' land were now virtually exhausted, and in 1627 grants of court land were suspended, ostensibly for the same reason; the extensive possessions of the church enjoyed the powerful protection of Patriarch Filaret. The only alternative was to encourage the gentry to make better use of their existing land or to extend the area of cultivation. Tentative steps were taken in this direction, but with disappointing results. The *pomestye* system itself hindered the gentry from acquiring a more rational economic outlook: engaged in service for long periods, they regarded their estates less as homes than as means of rapid enrichment. The government, therefore, whilst maintaining strictly the principle of obligatory service, allowed *pomestye*-holders to strengthen their property rights. In certain circumstances *pomestya* could be occupied by the widows or children of deceased or incapacitated serving men, and could be exchanged or given as dowries—though not, of course, bought or sold. This was possible only in the case of estates in full ownership [*votchiny*]. But many *pomestye*-holders succeeded in obtaining such land, by purchase or even by direct government grant.

These measures helped to improve the social status of the gentry, but their soldierly qualities remained alarmingly low. They received virtually no training, and the same was true of the infantry [*strel'tsy*], who between campaigns eked out a modest living as traders and artisans. Yet the need for efficient and properly equipped troops was obvious. In 1630 the government began to form regiments on the western model, recruited locally but officered by mercenaries engaged in the Protestant countries of northern Europe; by 1632 such units comprised one-third of Russia's military effectives. A still more radical, and unjustifiably extravagant, innovation was the hiring of a 5,000-strong contingent of foreign infantry-men (1631). Orders were placed in England and elsewhere for equipment and munitions; in Moscow itself cannon were cast, and at Tula A. Vinnius, a Dutchman, founded an arms works, the first tender shoot of Russian industry.

The object of this military consolidation was a war with Poland, the prospect of which dominated Moscow's foreign policy during Filaret's supremacy. Across the border the Russian-speaking Orthodox population seethed with discontent, and the Dnieper Cossacks in particular were developing a strong religious and national consciousness. But Filaret was cautious about utilizing this potentially most effective weapon, and received coolly the idea, mooted by emissaries from Kiev, that the Ukraine (as it was later known) might accept the tsar's protection. Moscow hesitated to provoke her powerful neighbour by intervening in her internal affairs, though she welcomed an opportunity of exploiting her external difficulties. In 1621, when Poland, reeling after her defeat at Ţuţora, was under simultaneous attack from north and south, Filaret expressed interest in a Turkish plan for concerted operations, and called a *Zemsky Sobor*, which obediently endorsed the idea of war. However, the Poles' resounding victory at Khotin, and the subsequent cessation of hostilities against both Turkey and Sweden, transformed the inter-national situation and compelled Russia to renounce her plans.

Fortunately for her this rashness went unpunished. Filaret now moved more circumspectly, endeavouring to strengthen links with other non-Catholic Powers. Merrick's diplomacy had increased Russia's regard for England, and the idea of an alliance, which dated back to the days of Ivan Grozny, was raised by successive envoys to London. In 1623 James I unexpectedly signed the draft of a treaty, but to Moscow's chagrin it never came into force. The interests of the two countries were too far apart: whilst Russia sought political support, England was mainly concerned to maintain her extensive commercial privileges. Moscow's initiatives met with much the same response in the Netherlands, which had now displaced England in the White Sea trade.

Of all the northern countries Sweden, as Russia's nearest Protestant neighbour and the enemy of Poland, was best placed to be her ally. But memories of the intervention were still fresh, and although Gustavus Adolphus, who recognized the advantages of Russian support in realizing his designs, twice proposed the conclusion of a defensive alliance, the offers were rejected. Nevertheless, relations remained close, and in 1631 Sweden became the first country to establish permanent diplomatic representation in Moscow. In return for supplies of grain and saltpetre, Gustavus Adolphus facilitated the recruitment of mercenaries for service in Russia. Filaret even agreed to a somewhat unrealistic scheme whereby Russia was to finance an attack on Poland from the west by an international contingent under Swedish command, to synchronize with the Russian attack from the east. Had the plan taken effect, it would have involved Russia in the general European conflagration, from which distance and religious differences had hitherto kept her aloof. But Lützen intervened, and Swedish-Russian amity lapsed.

Filaret had even less success in gaining the co-operation of Poland's other constant enemy, Turkey. In 1627 the Turkish envoy gave a verbal promise of military assistance, but this was not considered binding at the Porte. For most Ottoman functionaries the war in Asia had priority over the conflict with Poland. Turkey could only welcome a Russo-Polish conflict, which would weaken both combatants, and had no reason to lighten Moscow's task. Moreover, both the warring European camps, for opposite reasons, wished to prevent a Turkish attack on Poland, and brought their influence to bear in Constantinople.

Russia was thus diplomatically ill prepared for the conflict upon which she now embarked. The prospect of an interregnum upon the death of Sigismund III (April 1632) encouraged her to attack before the Deulino armistice expired. An army of 32,000 men was assembled and placed under the command of M. B. Shein. Its advance was delayed until the autumn by a Crimean Tartar raid, but by the end of the year the principal towns ceded in 1618 had fallen into Russian hands—except Smolensk, to which Shein laid siege. Having held the city against the Poles twenty-one years before, he had an exaggerated respect for its defences, and acted in desultory fashion. The guerrilla movement which sprang up locally showed more spirit, but the conservative-minded military command, fearing a resurgence of social conflict, treated its leaders as dangerous rebels. The Russian invasion served to consolidate Polish opinion behind the new king, Władysław IV, who marched to the relief of beleaguered Smolensk, and in October 1633 even succeeded in encircling Shein's vastly superior forces. By timely concessions Władysław had ensured the support of the Dnieper Cossacks, who had been disillusioned by Moscow's failure to come to their aid during their recent revolt and tactless encroachments into their territory by the invading armies. The morale of the Russian troops, already low, deteriorated further when the Crimean Tartars, encouraged by the Poles, launched a major attack upon the undefended southern borderlands. The gentry deserted en masse for their estates, and the reinforcements which Shein had been promised had to be diverted. Disease was rife amongst his men, and his foreign officers, aggrieved by their hardships and the military reverses, showed signs of disloyalty. Ceding to their pressure, Shein accepted an armistice (February 1634) whereby his remaining 8,000 men were permitted to retire, after laying down their arms and standards at Władysław's feet.

Discontent was widespread at the conduct and outcome of the war and the added burdens it had imposed. Filaret had died (October 1633), and the ruling group of boyars, amongst whom the war had never been popular, sought a scapegoat. Shein had aroused their jealousy by his overbearing manner, and as the only member of Filaret's circle of intimates not related to the dynasty, his position was particularly exposed. Accused of treason, he was tried in secret and executed. But responsibility for the *débâcle* lay rather with the government, for having blundered so recklessly into war. In central Europe there was now a lull in the fighting, and in the Balkans the anticipated major Turkish offensive failed to materialize. The Smolensk war proved that Moscow was not yet strong enough to prevail over Poland in isolation, and without support from internal dissident elements.

But though the war had been lost, the ensuing peace, signed on the River Polyanovka in May 1634, brought Russia significant gains. The territorial *status quo* was restored, but was rendered palatable by the acquisition (against financial compensation) of the district of Serpeysk. More important, Władysław finally surrendered his claim to the throne, thus making it possible to normalize Russo-Polish relations. Although Moscow refused to contemplate a fundamental re-orientation of policy, remaining unmoved by Polish suggestions of a constitutional union, she now permitted local collaboration against marauding Tartars. Prejudice died hard, but it was becoming increasingly clear that hostility towards Poland undermined Russia's security in the south, and it was to this quarter that her rulers now belatedly turned their attention.

Russia was still very inadequately protected against the age-old menace of Tartar attack.[1] The main bulk of her army was normally concentrated immediately south of Moscow for the defence of the capital, whilst the scattered Russian settlements further south were guarded by a thin network of military outposts. During the first twenty years of Michael's reign the border defences were neglected, partly from lack of means, and partly because Moscow assiduously cultivated the friendship of the Crimean khan, Djanibek, by making humiliating annual payments of tribute (euphemistically termed 'gifts'). Until the early 1630s a tolerable peace prevailed, chiefly because the Tartars were preoccupied with raids on Poland and factional struggles. The situation then changed, as a result of several factors: the inability of the ageing Djanibek to restrain his followers, a succession of droughts, the conclusion of peace between Turkey and Poland, and tension with Moscow over Cossack raids and the amount of tribute; finally, the further thinning of the border garrisons in connection with the Smolensk war presented the Tartars with a

[1] During the first half of the seventeenth century Moscow lost an estimated total of 200,000 men, women and children as a result of Tartar raids. The Tartars of the Crimea, nomadic cattle-raisers, supplemented their meagre income by raiding neighbouring states for captives and selling them on the slave-markets of the Orient. Though formally a vassal of the sultan, the Crimean khan in fact pursued a largely independent policy; so also did the individual clan chieftains, since the authority of the khan was seldom absolute.

tempting target. The raids of 1632–4, which materially affected the outcome of the war, were followed by others, mainly by Nogai Tartars.[1]

This serious threat made it imperative to strengthen the defences. No change, however, was made in basic strategy: the army command remained excessively centralized and unenterprising in battle, whilst the gentry cavalry were no match for the highly mobile invaders. But the trickle of colonists southwards perceptibly thickened, and many new garrison towns sprang up, particularly in the upper reaches of the Don and its tributaries. An important role was also assigned to the Cossacks settled along the lower Don. These free military communities, composed mainly of fugitives from Muscovite oppression, enjoyed in effect autonomous status. In return for a promise to serve as directed, they received an annual grant of money and supplies. They had demonstrated their power in the Troubles, and the government had no desire to antagonize them. Its attitude was one of cold calculation: whilst exploiting their strategic potentialities to the utmost, it took no risks on their behalf, especially where Turkey was concerned. When the Turks protested at the frequent Cossack raids, Moscow denied all responsibility, sent the Cossacks sharp reprimands, and even took measures of reprisal. The Cossacks, for their part, considered themselves true patriots, but had no illusions about the self-interest which animated official policy. They were quick to resent any sign of Russo-Turkish *rapprochement*, which threatened to extinguish their precarious liberties. The fact that envoys between the two countries passed through their territory gave them a lever with which to exert pressure upon Moscow.

In 1637 the Cossacks, on their own initiative, seized the formidable Turkish fortress of Azov and executed the Turkish envoy to Moscow, whom they had detained. This threatened to provoke the war which Russia had consistently striven to avert. Hurriedly despatching an envoy to placate the Turks, Russia prepared for the inevitable retaliatory Tartar raids. But to her good fortune both Turks and Tartars were involved elsewhere, and the Cossacks were given time to consolidate their victory. Not until 1641 could Sultan Ibrahim launch the long-expected major offensive. The Cossacks, though outnumbered fifteen to one, resisted with legendary bravery, and eventually forced the Turkish armies to retire. Aware that their heavy losses made it impossible for them to repeat this spectacular success, the Cossacks then offered their prize to the tsar.

This unparalleled opportunity confronted Moscow with a painful dilemma: acquisition of Azov would radically transform Russia's international position, but would involve her in a dangerous war, without

---

[1] The Great Nogai horde, which normally roamed the steppes east of the Volga, had reverted to Muscovite sovereignty in 1616. But in 1634, pressed by the Kalmyks further east and the Don Cossacks, they moved westwards, linking up territorially with the Crimeans and the autonomous Lesser Nogais in the Azov area in a formidable concentration of power. In 1639 the *status quo* was restored.

allies, against the whole might of the Ottoman Empire. At a *Zemsky Sobor*, called to discuss the question, the spokesmen of most groups, whilst dutifully promising the tsar their support, called loudly for the relief of their manifold grievances. A major war, it seemed, might well result in a new Time of Troubles. A Turkish envoy warned sharply of the risks involved; commissioners sent to Azov reported that the fortifications were in ruins. Reluctantly, Moscow ordered the Cossacks to withdraw (April 1642).

Peace had thus been preserved—but at a price. The Cossacks were subjected to reprisals, in which Moscow meekly concurred, by the reinforced Turkish garrison in Azov. The Tartars interpreted the evacuation as a sign of weakness, and resumed their attacks on a heavier scale; in 1643 and 1644 their raids were prompted directly by Turkey, concerned at evidence of a Russo-Polish *rapprochement*. The long columns of captives wending their way across the steppe into slavery were the most eloquent testimony to Russia's continued inability, despite thirty years of slow recovery, to safeguard her essential security.

A similar weakness, and apparent unwillingness to face up to her national and international responsibilities, characterized Russia's relations with other European Powers during Michael's last years. Moscow seemed to lapse deliberately into a self-sufficient isolation; the atmosphere was one of inertia and stagnation. The closer relations with Protestant countries encouraged under Filaret were now discountenanced: embassies arrived infrequently, and were despatched still more rarely; attempts were made to expel the Swedish resident. Russia's misgivings at the growth of Swedish power caused her to look somewhat more benignly upon Denmark. Prince Valdemar was selected as a fitting consort for the tsar's daughter, Irina. Induced, much against his will, to come to Moscow on the express promise that his Protestant faith would be respected, Valdemar was soon bidden to accept conversion to Orthodoxy. Unmoved by threats or entreaties, he refused, and was kept confined under guard. Diplomatic intervention had no effect, and it was only after Michael's death (June 1645) that he was released. The reasons for this curious affair, and for Moscow's generally reserved attitude towards the West, must be sought in the religious and cultural crisis in which the country was now deeply embroiled.

The Time of Troubles had profound psychological repercussions upon the Russian people. On the one hand, revulsion against anarchy and foreign domination strengthened the spirit, characteristic of Muscovite Russia, of stubborn adherence to national and ecclesiastical tradition; on the other hand, the sudden sweeping away of familiar landmarks undermined the proud belief that 'Holy Russia', as the only land in which true Orthodox piety survived, enjoyed special divine favour and protection. Men who sought to explain the problems raised by the great convulsion began to break free from the intellectual shackles imposed by obscurantism and bigotry, and to make use of their powers of reason and imagination. The spirit of free enquiry was stimulated by increased contact with foreigners. By the end of Michael's reign Moscow had a vigorous community, over one thousand strong, of western (mainly Protestant) merchants, artisans and soldiers. In court circles in particular there were a number of Russians who, though otherwise outwardly conformist, readily adopted western fashions in dress and manners—and thus, inescapably, also in ideas. Under the influence of Socinian teachings a prominant nobleman, I. A. Khvorostinin, questioned theological dogmas, spoke of the tsar as a despot, and complained of the intellectual barrenness of Muscovy in contrast to the West. He planned to flee abroad, but was betrayed, characteristically enough, by his unenlightened serfs—although, as he claimed, he had treated them with consideration. Khvorostinin died before finding a new creed to replace the one he had forsaken; in his egoism, superficial dandyism, and over-eager acceptance of everything foreign, he anticipated a cultural type familiar to eighteenth-century Russia.

Such developments naturally alarmed the influential but chauvinistic church hierarchy, which urged the government to restrict opportunities for Russians to mix with 'accursed foreign heretics'. An edict of 1643 ordered some of the Protestant churches in Moscow to be demolished. Such half-measures were clearly inadequate; but the government, appreciating that *raison d'état* necessitated acquisition of western techniques, had no desire to seal off the country hermetically from the outside world. The more intelligent churchmen realized that heresy could only be countered effectively by the spread of knowledge: but for this task the Russian church was singularly ill equipped. Learning was traditionally regarded with disfavour, as tainted with the sin of rationalism: true knowledge was acquired by faith, and in particular by strict observance of ancient rituals, sanctified by centuries of usage. Furthermore, it could no longer be concealed that the liturgical books abounded in errors, so that the rites of the Russian church no longer corresponded to those followed elsewhere in the Orthodox world. But even the slightest attempt to amend them raised the gravest issues. Owing to the exaggerated significance attached to ritual, correction implied an assumption that the Russian church, instead of being a model of purity, had fallen into heresy, and should seek guidance from the scholars of Kiev[1] or Constantinople, who had long been suspected of having succumbed to Latin influences.

Modest efforts at liturgical reform, initiated in 1616 by Dionysius, the

---

[1] Kiev was now the centre of a religious renaissance amongst the Orthodox population of Poland-Lithuania, who from 1620 had an episcopate of their own, subordinate to Constantinople. With its theological college at Kiev (reformed by Petr Mohila in 1631 as an Academy) and a rudimentary school system, western Russia was culturally far advanced by comparison with Moscow, where there were no regular schools at all.

saintly abbot of the Trinity Monastery, were frustrated by the traditional-ists. Dionysius was accused of heresy and imprisoned, but was liberated by Filaret on his accession as patriarch. Filaret's chief preoccupation was to tighten church discipline and impose strict conformity in matters of doctrine by excluding foreign influences. *Emigré* Orthodox clergy from western Russia who settled in Moscow had to undergo re-baptism, and their lives were closely supervised. Books by western Russian churchmen were carefully examined for any sign of heresy, and some were publicly burnt—although, since insufficient locally printed works were available, they nevertheless circulated in manuscript form. During Filaret's patriar-chate the work of correction proceeded at snail's pace, but after his death western Russian influences increased, and a number of works were published which often contained innovations in ritual.

Thus the seeds were being sown of the great Schism [*Raskol*] that was to split the Russian church, and Russian society, a few years after Michael's death. Nationalistic resentment against foreign influences and sentimental adherence to traditional ritual practices were two charac-teristic features of the outlook of the *raskol'niki*, although their dissent was in fact more profound. The 'zealots' [*revniteli*], as the leaders of the future *raskol* were known at this stage, sought to bring about a wholesale regeneration of the religious and moral life of the country. The proverbial piety of the Orthodox Muscovite was in truth a shallow formality. Scarcely anywhere else in Europe was there such widespread brutality and cruelty, such coarseness in manners and moral laxity. The priests set a poor example, and enjoyed little respect: too ignorant to preach, they performed the prescribed ritual as if by rote. In the churches the atmo-sphere was irreverent in the extreme. Against all these abuses the con-science-stricken 'zealots', led by a vocal parish priest, I. Neronov, campaigned with a spiritual fervour little to the taste of ecclesiastical officialdom. The hierarchy had become increasingly bureaucratized. The great prelates lived in a world of pomp and luxury, intent on maintaining the extensive privileges accorded them by the state. With few exceptions they were incapable of satisfying the aspirations of ordinary believers, for whom the 'zealots' naturally held a strong attraction.

As in the West, religious dissent was to a large degree a means of expressing popular discontent at oppressive social and economic condi-tions. In Russia the masses lived for the most part in abject poverty, and the Troubles had shown that the prevailing attitude of fatalistic resigna-tion was compatible with violent explosive outbursts. Development of productive resources and accumulation of wealth were hindered by unfavourable natural conditions, and more especially by the inexhaustible demands of the state. The government narrow-mindedly concerned itself only with satisfying immediate fiscal and military requirements, regard-less of the economic consequences. Such economic progress as was registered during Michael's reign occurred largely in spite of (or, at least, as an incidental by-product of) the actions of authority. The establishment of the Tula arms works was characteristic in this respect. Modest attempts to manufacture products (glass, paper, etc.) for the domestic market met with little success. Russia's vast mineral riches remained virtually untouched.

Trade could not develop on an extensive scale so long as each village or estate tended to constitute an almost self-contained unit. The towns, with their bazaar-type markets, bore an Oriental aspect: except for Moscow, which could boast a population of 200,000, they were small, and closely connected to the countryside. They enjoyed no special rights or privileges. The commercial classes were numerically weak and their social status low. The wealthiest elements were siphoned off as state employees; the remainder laboured under the burden of heavy taxation and service obligations. Credit was difficult to obtain; interest rates were extremely high, and debts were exacted with the cudgel and the knout. Merchants were tempting prey for rapacious local officials, who could, for example, arbitrarily seize their property with little fear of legal consequences. Moreover, they suffered from the effects of competition from the state, with its various commercial privileges and monopolies, from the *strel'tsy* and other serving men, and from the inhabitants of tax-exempt settlements [*slobody*] established by powerful landowners. And finally, they faced competition from the more enterprising and experienced western merchants who had acquired almost complete control of foreign trade, the most lucrative branch of Russian commerce.

In Russia's exports furs and other forest products occupied a predominant place. The fabulous natural wealth of Siberia led to a development of considerable political, as well as economic, significance: Russian acquisition of enormous territories in northern Asia. This was largely a spontaneous process. Lured by the prospect of easy profit, trappers, traders, Cossacks and serving men penetrated swiftly eastwards, overwhelming the almost defenceless natives and establishing Russian rule by means of strategically located forts and blockhouses. The founding of Krasnoyarsk (1628) completed the subjugation of the Yenisey region; during the 1630s the Lena river-system was brought under control, and in 1639 a small detachment reached the shores of the Pacific near Okhotsk. Four years later an expedition explored Trans-Baikalia, sailing down the River Amur to its mouth. Intermittent contact was established with China. Russian colonial policy was in practice characterized by a singular ruthlessness. Furs, levied as tribute [*yasak*] upon the natives, often at extortionate rates, or as tithes upon Russian traders, flowed back to Moscow in a swelling stream, forming a sizeable element in state revenue and the basis of many private fortunes.

But the overwhelming majority of Russia's inhabitants derived their livelihood from agriculture. As the population began to recover after the holocaust of the Troubles, so the area under cultivation expanded. Surveys of certain estates in the Moscow region in the 1620s and 1640s showed a doubling or trebling of the number of peasant households. The fertile black earth of the northern steppe was slowly being brought under the plough. But agricultural techniques remained as primitive as ever, and there was little if any increase in productivity. The well-being of a peasant community depended not only on natural economic factors but also on its juridical status. Most peasants now lived on estates belonging to the court, the church, or to private landowners. The chief exception were the 'black' peasants[1] of the northern forests who, despite higher taxation, were better off than most other categories.

The court peasants and those of some large landowners, ecclesiastical and lay, also enjoyed certain material advantages over peasants belonging to provincial gentry. But by and large the economic position and juridical status of all dependent peasants now deteriorated markedly. The devastation caused by the Troubles intensified their need for loans (in money, seed, stock or implements), which only the landowners could supply. In return for such loans (and often, indeed, even without them) peasants would contract to pay dues [*obrok*] in money or produce, or to perform labour-service [*barshchina*] in the landlords' fields. Generally no time-limit was specified, and peasants undertook that neither they nor their descendants would leave the estate, thus becoming serfs [*krepostnye*], bound in perpetuity to the owner of the land they worked. Juridically and economically inferior to the serfs were those peasants known as *bobyli*,[2] who were exempted from tax on account of their poverty, and household servants, etc., who were usually not peasants but slaves [*kholopy*]. Full slavery was now fairly rare, but debt-slavery [*kabal'noye kholopstvo*] was widespread. Here again the debts were often fictitious: hunger drove men of all classes to sacrifice their liberty in order to survive.

The state did not normally intervene in relations between master and serf. The landowner was free to demand such dues as he thought fit, although the scale of these impositions obviously affected the peasants' capacity to pay tax. Instead, the state merely held the landowner responsible for the prompt collection of revenue. This greatly enhanced his powers over his peasants. In judicial matters, too, his authority was almost absolute: only the most serious crimes (treason, murder, banditry)

---

[1] 'Black' [*chernososhnye*] peasants paid tax directly to state agencies, not through a landowner. These were now the sole survivors of the era when most of the land had been in peasant tenure. They paid rent [*obrok*] to the state, which in theory owned their land, although it did not normally attempt to regulate the peasants' economic activities. But they were liable to be compulsorily transferred to other areas, and it was in this way that there grew up another category of 'black' peasants, the 'free ploughmen' [*volnye khlebopashtsy*] in Siberia where, however, agriculture was not extensively practised.

[2] *Bobyli* generally had no land of their own; but many other categories of dependants, not all impoverished, became classified as *bobyli*, so that the term lacks precision.

617

were dealt with by the tsar's officials. Indicative of the spirit of Muscovite legislation is an order of 1628 that provincial gentry unable to pay their debts might send their serfs to Moscow to be cudgelled in their stead. In the eyes of the law, the serf was no longer a human being, but a mere chattel.

Though they had no legal means of redress, the peasants still had one effective weapon: they could exploit the prevailing acute shortage of labour by fleeing, either to other landowners, or to the freer atmosphere of the southern border. Geography facilitated this passive, but traditional, means of resisting oppression. The main theme in Russian social history during this period is the fierce and unedifying struggle by certain interested groups to close this loophole, and so make bondage comprehensive and absolute.

Since exploitation was most intense on smaller and poorer estates, it was the provincial gentry who suffered most from these flights. The great boyars and monasteries, on the other hand, were able to attract fugitives by offering larger loans and better conditions. Generally peasants changed masters on their own initiative, but some of the more enterprising and ruthless landowners resorted to fraud and violence. On many large estates enjoying fiscal privileges there sprang up the *slobody* already mentioned: centres of handicrafts and trade, inhabited by fugitives, especially artisans from the towns, the so-called *zakladchiki*.[1] These men, though personally dependent upon their creditors, were 'white', i.e. not liable to tax, and could thus compete favourably with members of the 'black' communities from which they had fled; some of them actually continued to live in the towns, but paid no tax. The *zakladchiki* aroused intense resentment amongst the townspeople, who had to pay tax on behalf of these privileged competitors so long as they were still officially registered as members of the community. The interests of the provincial gentry and townspeople thus coincided: both had grievances against the wealthier landowners, and welcomed the idea that fugitives should be forcibly returned to their original place of residence.

The state had a certain natural sympathy with their viewpoint, in so far as flights undermined the strength of the taxpayers and serving men. But the church and boyars exerted considerable influence, particularly under Filaret, whose policy of manœuvring between competing pressures in effect worked to their advantage. Some boyars had over 3,000 peasant households, and many monasteries even more. The Trinity Monastery retained all its ancient privileges, and as a special concession was granted a nine-year limit for the return of fugitives, whereas for all other landowners the limit was fixed at five years from the date of flight. Great landowners were sometimes afforded official assistance in locating runaways, whilst others, who had to rely upon their own efforts, had little hope of enforcing a fugitive's return.

[1] Literally, 'pledged persons' (*zaklad* = pledge).

After Filaret's death the state lost its self-assurance and was more responsive to extraneous pressure. The gentry had now improved their economic position and were readier than they had been twenty years earlier to further their social aims by political action on a national scale. An opportunity for organization was presented by the annual mobilizations for border defence: 20,000 armed men constituted a force which even the most autocratic régime could not afford to ignore. In 1637, in response to their pressure, the time-limit on the return of fugitives was raised from five years to nine, better provision made for hearing lawsuits against powerful proprietors, and high-ranking nobles prohibited from acquiring land in the southern border region. The townspeople also won concessions: whereas efforts to return *zakladchiki* had previously petered out in bureaucratic delay and intrigue, now large numbers of them were re-integrated into their former communities. In 1641 the provincial gentry demonstrated noisily in support of their demands, which included the total abolition of restrictions upon the return of fugitives. This tension formed the background to their unco-operative attitude over the question of Azov. The government, whilst not conceding their demands in full, extended the time-limit from nine years to ten (fifteen for peasants seized by force), and took various other steps, such as annulling slavery contracts concluded by serving men. The way was prepared for the events of 1648–9, when serious riots, in which gentry and townspeople participated, led to the significant social gains enshrined in the Code [*Ulozheniye*] of Tsar Alexis: liquidation of the *slobody*, control of ecclesiastical landowning, ascription of peasants to their present owners and, finally, abolition of limitations on the return of fugitives.

Flight was still a practicable possibility—but henceforward the overwhelming majority of Russians had to endure the heavy yoke of serfdom. Society was now moulded in the form it was to retain for the next two centuries. All classes had their specific obligations to the omnipotent absolutist-bureaucratic state. This system was to be perfected and modernized by Alexis, Peter and Catherine the Great. But much of the groundwork was laid in the reign of the unassuming Michael Feodorovich. It was the heavy price which the Russian people paid for recovery from collapse and slow progress towards the position of a Great Power.

CHAPTER XX

THE OTTOMAN EMPIRE 1617–48

O N the death of Sultan Ahmed I in 1617 the problem of the succession to the throne assumed a particular importance. The Ottoman custom had been that the sons of a reigning sultan should be sent out, while still young, to rule over provinces in Asia Minor. A prince thus sent out with the rank of *sanjaq begi*, that is, governor of a *sanjaq* or province, would now receive, under the guidance of the dignitaries composing his household and of the officials controlling the local administration, a long and elaborate education in the '*adet-i 'othmaniyye*—the *mores* and the culture distinctive of the Ottomans. It was an education which embraced language and literature, physical training and the practice of arms and which inculcated, moreover, a close and practical knowledge of how the empire was run—in short, an education designed to fit a prince for the responsibilities of rule, if ever he should come to the throne.

At the same time it had been the custom of the Ottomans that a new sultan should order forthwith the execution of all his brothers and their male children. The pressures imposed on princes of the blood through the operation of this 'law of fratricide' were acute. Aware that to win the throne or to die was the ultimate choice offered to them, the princes strove with all the means at their command to strengthen their resources in expectation of the evil hour which would mark the death of their father. Each of them sought to create in his particular province a nucleus of armed force and, in addition, to establish at the Porte, amongst the high dignitaries and the troops of the imperial household,[1] a faction committed to his cause.

To the influence of these factors must be ascribed in no small degree the sustained excellence of the Ottoman sultans before and including Süleyman the Magnificent. The experience acquired in the government of a province was invaluable as a preparation for the throne. The 'law of fratricide'—whatever judgement be made of it on moral grounds—had at least one beneficial effect: it exerted a psychological pressure which tended to drive the princes towards the development of all their personal capacities in the face of the mortal threat hanging over them.

The accidents of birth and death within the imperial house brought about now a less favourable situation. Of the male children of Selim II (1566–74) one alone, the future Murad III, and of Murad III (1574–95) again one son only, the future Mehemmed III, attained an age suitable

---

[1] Cf. Vol. III in this series, pp. 347–8.

for their assignment to a province in Asia Minor. Mehemmed III (1595–1603) was destined indeed to be the last prince sent out to act as a *sanjaq begi*.

The 'law of fratricide' was also to fall into desuetude. It had served to limit the dangers of dynastic conflict and of political fragmentation at a time when, in the fourteenth and fifteenth centuries, the Ottoman state, then rising towards greatness, was beset with numerous difficulties. These dangers receded, however, into remoteness after the long consolidation carried out during the reign of Mehemmed II (1451–81). Henceforward the 'law of fratricide' acted more to the detriment than to the benefit of the Ottoman state, as the violent rivalries over the succession to the throne made clear in 1481–2, 1511–13 and above all in 1553–61. A western source of this time declares that in 1574 Murad III, on ascending the throne, enforced the 'law' against the wishes of the mufti, who stressed the fact that of the brothers of Murad none was old enough to be a danger to the empire. This account reflects perhaps uncertainties present in official circles at Istanbul over the wisdom of continuing a usage which, it could be argued, had outlived its original purpose and value.

The year 1595 witnessed the most dire example of fratricide in the annals of the imperial house. Mehemmed III, on his accession to the throne, ordered the execution of his brothers, nineteen of them in all. This grim event, however, was to be the last enforcement of the old 'law of fratricide'. The death of Mehemmed III in 1603 confronted the great dignitaries at the Porte with a situation unparalleled heretofore. The dead sultan left two sons—Ahmed, then almost fourteen years of age, and Mustafa, about two years younger than Ahmed. As the elder of the princes Ahmed now came to the throne, but there was no order for the execution of Mustafa. Ahmed, as yet, was childless. If Mustafa were done to death and if Ahmed should die before he had a son, the House of 'Osman would be extinct. Mustafa, therefore, was allowed to live. He was confined in the imperial palace and did not go out to govern a province in Asia Minor. The birth, in 1604, of 'Osman, the eldest son of Ahmed I, brought no change in the situation. Sultan Ahmed was still a mere youth and the death rate amongst infants was high. To execute Mustafa was not in fact feasible, unless and until there existed an heir to the throne who had survived through the years of childhood.

The death of Ahmed I in 1617 made Mustafa the eldest prince of the imperial line—the only prince of adult years—and as such he was raised to the throne. Mustafa I, however, was a man of feeble intellect. His brief reign of about three months (1617–18) revealed his unfitness to rule. He was now removed in favour of 'Osman, the eldest son of Ahmed I. On the deposition of 'Osman II in 1622 Mustafa became sultan once more, reigning for some fifteen months (1622–23), until his incompetence brought about his deposition for the second time. Thereafter, of the remaining sons of Ahmed I, Murad IV (1623–40), who left no male heir, and Ibrahim (1640–8), held the throne in succession.

The particular sequence of birth and death within the imperial house had created a new situation. The sending out of princes to appointments as *sanjaq begi* in Asia Minor was now at an end. The 'law of fratricide', too, ceased to be operative. Henceforward the princes would spend their lives in the seclusion of the palace, until and if the course of events should call them to be sultan. In fact, a new principle had come to govern the succession to the throne—the throne passed now, in descending order of age, from one prince to another within a given generation, until that generation was exhausted, and then fell to the eldest surviving prince of the next generation. Brother followed brother on the throne—and not the son in succession to the father. On the death of Sultan Ibrahim the throne went to his sons in the order of their age—to Mehemmed IV (1648–87), to Süleyman II (1687–91) and to Ahmed II (1691–5). Only on the death of Ahmed II did it go to a son of Mehemmed IV, to Mustafa II (1695–1703).

These changes worked to the disadvantage of the Ottoman state. The system prevailing before the reign of Ahmed I had done much to ensure that a series of able sultans should stand at the head of affairs. No such favourable judgement can be made for the new mode of procedure, which condemned the princes, in general, to long years of idle and enervating confinement within the palace walls—to a life, in short, which failed to prepare them for the responsibilities of power and, indeed, tended to undermine the capacities innate in them. It was still possible that a prince who came young to the throne might develop into a capable sultan. The House of 'Osman could even now produce a vigorous and ruthless monarch like Murad IV—but Sultan Murad was to be henceforth the exception rather than the rule.

On a government highly centralized the accession to the throne of sultans incompetent to rule well had perforce a most adverse effect. The sultan was the source of power within the state, his will set the machine of government in motion. If he did not define and direct the exercise of power, there were others—the great dignitaries of the central régime—who would do it for him, seeking at the same time to manipulate him to their own advantage.

The period here under review can be described, not unjustly, as one of rule by courtiers and officials—a period of intrigue, of shifting alliances and of spasmodic violence at the centre of affairs. Of great importance were the women of the harem, and in particular the Walide Sultan (the mother of the prince on the throne) and the Khasseki Sultans (the consorts who had borne the sultan a child). Often their influence was wielded through the *Kîzlar Aghasî*, the chief of the black eunuchs, who controlled the administration of the harem. Their rivalries on behalf of their children, their private and personal access to the sultan, their forging of bonds between themselves and the high officials of the government—all these factors had a marked effect on the conduct of state affairs. A notable example can be found in the years 1617–23, which saw three Walide Sultans involved in the conflict around the throne: the mothers of Mustafa I, of 'Osman II and of Murad IV.

There was faction and intrigue, too, amongst the officials of the central régime, especially amongst the viziers, the number of whom was to rise as high as nine. These dignitaries, striving to attain the highest office in the empire, the grand vizierate, often aligned themselves with other elements engaged in the quest for power. Some of them had received in marriage princesses of the imperial house. These exalted ladies, endowed as of right with access to the intimate circle around the sultan, often counted for much in the advancement of their husbands.

To the factors mentioned thus far must be added here the *'ulema*, the men learned in the *Shari'a*, the Sacred Law of Islam. The *'ulema*, as the guardians of the Sacred Law, enjoyed great influence and prestige. Now, in these years of confusion, that influence was sometimes used to legitimize the course of events or to further the interest of a given cause—as, for example, in 1648, when the mufti issued a *fetwa* or legal pronouncement approving the execution of Sultan Ibrahim.

A further element in the complex picture is to be found in the troops of the central government—above all, the janissaries and also the sipahis of the Porte, the mounted regiments of the imperial household.[1] These forces, swollen in numbers and far less disciplined now than of old, rose in revolt from time to time, either of their own volition in quest of increased remuneration, donatives and other privileges or as a result of instigation emanating from one or other of the rival factions amongst the high dignitaries.

The intrigues and feuds surrounding the throne were especially virulent and bitter in the years following the death of Ahmed I in 1617. Mustafa, the brother of Ahmed, as the eldest of the Ottoman princes, now became sultan. His unfitness to rule soon led, however, to his deposition in 1618, a number of the great officials—amongst them the *Kizlar Aghasi*, the chief of the black eunuchs, and the mufti, Es'ad Efendi—reaching an agreement with Mah-Firuze, the mother of 'Osman, to bring her son to the throne. The new sultan ,'Osman II, then about fourteen years of age, was too young and inexperienced to dominate the situation before him. He failed, moreover, to retain favour with the troops of the central régime—a disadvantage arising in no small degree from the ill-success of the campaign that he conducted against Poland in 1621.[2]

The position of the sultan became precarious indeed when it was

[1] Cf. Vol. III in this series, pp. 347–8.　　　　[2] See below, p. 636.

known that he intended to make a pilgrimage to Mecca. Suspicion grew amongst the janissaries and the sipahis of the Porte that the pilgrimage was a stratagem concealing designs hostile to themselves—that 'Osman II, escaping from Istanbul to the provinces, meant to use the armed strength available there as an instrument to curb their own pre-eminence and indiscipline. On 18 May 1622 the troops rose in revolt, demanding the lives of the dignitaries held to be most influential with the sultan, amongst them the grand vizier, Dilawar Pasha. Members of the *ulema* submitted these demands to 'Osman II, but the sultan was loath to yield and hesitated too long before sending Dilawar Pasha to his death. The rebels, meanwhile, broke into the imperial palace and, freeing Mustafa, the brother of Ahmed I, from his confinement, acclaimed him as their master. Some of the janissaries consulted with the mother of Mustafa about the appointments to be made and it was in fact her son-in-law, the Bosnian Da'ud Pasha, who now became grand vizier. The faction committed to the cause of Mustafa and of his mother, the Walide Sultan, could not feel secure while 'Osman II was still alive. Their uneasiness was well grounded, since some of the rebels wished to spare 'Osman, hoping no doubt to make use of him for their own ends at some future date. Da'ud Pasha had recourse, therefore, to the last extreme measure—on 20 May 1622 'Osman II was strangled in the prison of Yedi Kule at Istanbul.

The second reign of Sultan Mustafa was a time of confusion, during which the troops of the imperial household dominated the course of events. Da'ud Pasha, in 1623, lost his life in the fluctuation of intrigue and violence around the throne. The unbridled conduct of the troops—with the janissaries and the sipahis of the Porte often at odds amongst themselves—was at its worst in 1623 during the grand vizierate of Mere Hüseyn. It was now becoming difficult to achieve even the indispensable minimum of government. A 'revolt' of the *ulema* led, however, to the fall of Mere Hüseyn and also to the deposition, for the second time, of Sultan Mustafa—an event which was the essential prerequisite of a return to some degree of order.

The new sultan, Murad IV, was a son of Ahmed I. His accession to the throne did not mean that the rule of courtiers and officials was at an end. Murad, when he became sultan, had not yet completed his twelfth year. He was to remain for some time yet little more than a tool in the hands of his mother, Kösem, and of the dignitaries aligned with or against her according to the circumstances of the moment. Moreover, from time to time, indiscipline amongst the janissaries and the sipahis of the Porte still flared out into open violence. The intrigues of Rejeb Pasha in 1626 constituted, it would seem, one of the factors responsible for a new turmoil which, despite all that Sultan Murad and the Walide Sultan could do, brought death to a loyal and trusted vizier—the eunuch Gurji Mehemmed Pasha, who was ninety-six years old, had served under

Sultan Süleyman and now, in the judgement of the English ambassador at Istanbul, Sir Thomas Roe, was still 'the most able and only wise man in this state'.[1]

More violent still was the spasm of revolt which occurred in 1631–2. The animosities dividing some of the most prominent amongst the great dignitaries—Khusrew Pasha and Rejeb Pasha as against Hafîz Ahmed Pasha and Mustafa Pasha—awoke once more the fires of revolt. Murad IV, with his own life in danger, had to sacrifice Hafîz Ahmed to the anger of the soldiers. His reaction to this moment of humiliation was prompt and vigorous. Convinced that Khusrew Pasha was responsible in no small measure for the renewal of violence, he gave orders for his execution. A further paroxysm of revolt ensued, in the course of which the sultan suffered a second humiliation, even more intimate and personal, in the death of his friend Musa. For some two months the janissaries and the sipahis of the Porte gave free rein to their licence and indiscipline at Istanbul. Murad IV waited until the time was opportune and then struck hard, removing from the scene Rejeb Pasha, whom he considered to be one of the most active personalities behind the recent troubles. The execution of Rejeb Pasha was carried out on 18 May 1632—a date which saw the sultan liberated once and for all from the tutelage of the great officials and which marked the real beginning of his reign. He had grown to manhood in a world of danger and duress. His character was tempered to the hardness of steel in the harsh and bitter experiences of his youth. A ferocious and inexorable resolve to be the master in his own house would henceforth dominate his actions. It is not surprising that in the eight years of life remaining to him he was to become perhaps the most feared and terrible of all the Ottoman sultans.

The long turbulence which followed the death of Ahmed I was not due to the spirit of intrigue and faction alone. One factor contributing towards the murder of 'Osman II was, as noted earlier, the belief current among the janissaries and the sipahis of the Porte, that under the guise of a pilgrimage to Mecca, he meant to set in motion a scheme contrived for their ultimate ruin. The main proponent of this scheme, according to the correspondence of Sir Thomas Roe, was Dilawar Pasha, raised to the grand vizierate at the time of the Polish campaign in 1621 and destined to lose his life in the revolt of 1622—a resolute man, who won over 'Osman II, in the words of Sir Thomas, to 'a brave and well-grounded designe and of great consequence for the renewing of this decayed empire'[2]—a project for raising in the provinces of Asia Minor and Syria forces powerful enough to give the sultan control over the troops of the central régime. A scheme so daring reflected, in the mere fact of its formu-

[1] Cf. J. W. Zinkeisen, *Geschichte des osmanischen Reiches*, Vol. IV (Gotha, 1856), p. 48, note 2.

[2] Cf. Zinkeisen, *Geschichte des osmanischen Reiches*, Vol. III (Gotha, 1855), p.745, note 1.

lation, the existence of a particular and grave situation confronting the Ottomans.

The wars against Persia (1578–90) and against Austria (1593–1606) imposed on the Ottomans the need to increase greatly their regiments of infantry equipped with firearms and their technical services (e.g. armourers, artillerists, engineers, etc.)—to increase in fact the paid troops of the imperial household. The forces of the central régime, amongst them the janissaries and the sipahis of the Porte, had been recruited thus far from Christian captives of war and from the child tribute levied on the Christian subjects of the sultan—from human material non-Muslim and non-Turkish in origin. These sources of recruitment did not suffice to meet the new circumstances of war. The Ottomans had, therefore, to incorporate in the regiments of the household—or at least to assimilate in status to those troops—recruits drawn from the Muslim-born population of the empire. One consequence of this radical change was a decline in the discipline of the janissaries and the sipahis of the Porte.[1]

This change came, moreover, at a time when the Ottoman government was faced with serious financial difficulties. The tide of conquest was far less rapid and the campaigns much less lucrative than before. Warfare in the Caucasus area and on the middle Danube had become inordinately expensive. Now, with the paid troops of the central régime vastly swollen in number, the strain on the revenues of the state was still more insistent and severe. To find the enormous sums required of it the government had recourse to expedients like the manipulation of the coinage or the reservation to itself of lands belonging to the fief system in the provinces, these lands being then transformed into tax farms [*muqata'a*] and leased out to tax contractors [*mültezim*]. It also raised additional revenues known as '*awariḍ-i diwaniyye* [levies of the Diwan or Council of State]—taxes imposed formerly to meet exceptional needs, usually of a military character, but now exacted as a regular contribution, and at a rate which increased steadily throughout these years. These factors—allied to other causes, amongst them the pressure of a rising population on resources—combined to bring about a marked inflation unfavourable to all classes enjoying a fixed income and, in particular, to the paid soldiers of the sultan. Inflation was indeed a powerful force driving them to indiscipline and to a reiterated demand for new emoluments and donatives—a demand which had behind it the ultimate sanction of revolt. So frequent and excessive did their claims become that Sir Thomas Roe felt justified in writing that 'the Turkish emperor is now but the Janizaries treasurer'[2]

Of the personnel—officials and soldiers—belonging to the imperial household no small proportion had come to be located in Asia Minor. The process began on a considerable scale as a response to the dangerous

---

[1] Cf. Vol. III in this series, pp. 352, 356–7, 360–1, 365–6.
[2] Cf. Zinkeisen, *Geschichte* . . . , Vol. III, p. 745, note I.

tensions visible there during the conflict over the succession to the throne between Selim and Bayezid, the sons of Sultan Süleyman, in the years 1559–61. It was intensified thereafter when the paid forces of the central régime grew more numerous as a result of the great wars against Persia and Austria. The government at Istanbul, finding it difficult to meet the new and burdensome demands on its revenue, assigned to the janissaries and to the sipahis of the Porte offices and emoluments in the administration of the provinces. These troops, in the course of time, bade fair to dominate the provincial scene and to divert a large measure of its local resources to their own advantage. Their penetration into the world of the provinces was to call forth, however, a long and violent reaction.

The sultan had at his command a numerous and influential class of 'feudal' horsemen, known in general as sipahis and established in most, though not in all the regions of the empire. The sipahi held a fief of small [*timar*] or of large [*zi'amet*] yield per annum. No title to the land itself was vested in him—he received no more than the usufruct of the land constituting his fief, that is, the right to take from the population living on it certain dues in cash and in kind. Good service would raise him from a fief of lower to one of higher yield. Out of the revenues thus granted to him the sipahi maintained himself as an efficient soldier. He came to war, moreover, with a retinue which increased in size with the importance of his fief—and this retinue he had to furnish in arms and equipment from the resources made available to him.[1]

To the 'feudal' horsemen—above all in Asia Minor, where the number of small fiefs was large—the changing circumstances of warfare had been unwelcome. The profit to be won in war against Persia and Austria was diminishing, the risk of serious loss much heightened for the individual sipahi in respect of supplies, arms and beasts of burden, so arduous were the long campaigns. To make good the loss was now, in view of the current inflation, more difficult and expensive than before. Warfare, in short, beyond Lake Van or on the middle Danube had become an unrewarding business for the sipahis endowed with a small fief. At the same time the retention in government hands or the lease as *muqata'a* of lands hitherto included in the fief system led to confusion, to a lessened prospect of advancement and to disaffection amongst the 'feudal' horsemen.

A further cause of unrest in Asia Minor was the growth of the population—a growth more rapid than the bringing of new land into cultivation. This imbalance and the resultant pressure on the means of subsistence led to the rise of a surplus element, largely of peasant origin, landless and unemployed. Their number was swollen with the accession of men whom various factors had driven from the soil, for example, the effect of inflation, the fiscal demands of a government straitened in its

[1] Cf. Vol. III in this series, pp. 348–50.

resources, the exploitation of the tax-farmers and also the exactions of sipahis reduced to narrow circumstances.

Of this unattached and vagrant class—known as *levendat*—a large proportion became soldiers in the service of the state. The central régime, under the altered conditions of warfare, was obliged to expand its armed forces, hitherto, in general, of non-Muslim and non-Turkish provenance. Now it had to allow recruitment from amongst the Muslim-born subjects of the sultan. It was the human material of the *levendat* which made this expansion possible. Soldiers drawn from this source fought on the frontier as volunteers [*gönüllü*], acted as fortress guards [*mustahfîz*] or served as troops bearing the designation of *sarïja* or *sekban*—troops sometimes assimilated in status to the regiments of the imperial household or else hired as mercenaries for one or more campaigns.

The *levendat* also found employment in the provinces of the empire. With the fief system falling into disorder under the harsh stresses of a warfare expensive to sustain, ill-suited to the capacities of horsemen and demanding above all the use of firearms, the authorities at Istanbul countenanced yet another departure from the old modes of action. The provincial governors began to recruit large retinues, infantry as well as cavalry, composed of *sarïja* and *sekban* levies from the *levendat* of Asia Minor. To maintain these troops the pashas raised in the towns and villages a tax called the *sekban aqçesi*. This recruitment was to be carried so far that the *sarïja* and the *sekban* became the most numerous element in the armed strength of the provinces and, indeed, a main element also in the imperial armies assembled for the great campaigns.

The use of the *levendat* as soldiers was of grave consequence for Asia Minor. Warfare, whether in Armenia and Adharbayjan or on the Danube and the Tisza, was laborious and hard. At times, regiments of the *sarïja* and the *sekban* might abandon a campaign rather than endure the severities of war. There were intervals also when some of the *levendat* soldiers would be out of service. The end of hostilities in 1590 against Persia and in 1606 against Austria saw a reflux, to Asia Minor, of *sarïja* and *sekban* troops bereft of employment. Of serious effect, too, was the fact that Ottoman control over the lands won from the shah in 1578–90 collapsed before the Persian counter-offensive of 1603–7. This collapse meant the return westward of thousands of *levendat* now without an assured occupation.

Of this numerous *soldatesca* no small proportion took to brigandage and revolt as a means of livelihood, acting at times in co-operation with discontented members of the sipahi class and with nomads of Turkish and Kurdish descent. These rebel elements, known in their new guise as *jelali*, exacted from the villages and towns a contribution called *qurban aqçesi*, [i.e. protection tax]. The *jelalis* plundered much of Asia Minor between 1596 and 1610. It was in fact a time of hydra-headed rebellion, and of a kind unusually dangerous, the *jelali* bands consisting, for the most part, of *sarija* and *sekban* trained in the great wars, expert in the use of firearms and strengthened with a measure of assistance from another class adept in the arts of war—the 'feudal' sipahis.

The Grand Vizier Kuyuju Murad Pasha crushed this wave of revolt in Asia Minor during the years 1607-10, but armed repression was no more than a brief palliative and the basic causes of the unrest continued to operate as before. The government at Istanbul sought to overcome the internal difficulties confronting it. Under Ahmed I (1603-17) a new *qanun-name* or code of regulations was issued, together with several edicts relating to specific matters of reform. The main objectives in view were to reduce in number the troops and officials belonging to the imperial household, to end the intervention of the janissaries and the sipahis of the Porte in the conduct of affairs and to protect the provinces from the ills afflicting them in recent years.

To the advocates of reform some prospect of amelioration seemed to lie in the divergence of interest visible between the personnel of the central régime and the forces gathered around the provincial governors. The 'men of the Sultan' demanded for themselves assignments of revenue and offices of profit and privilege in the local administrations. This development was inimical to the aims of the *sarija* and *sekban* levies enrolled in the service of the pashas—levies which saw in the resources of the provincial world the means to their own well-being and advantage. It is against a perspective of this order that the death of 'Osman II should be set. The more responsible dignitaries at Istanbul, aware of the need to restore efficient rule, proposed that the sultan should move to the provinces and create there, out of the *sarija* and the *sekban* experienced in war, a powerful counterpoise to the janissaries and the sipahis of the Porte. This scheme, in 1622, brought death to the Grand Vizier Dilawar Pasha and to 'Osman II himself.[1] It also brought to the fore the antagonism separating the *levendat* of the provincial régimes from the troops and officials of the imperial household.

Amongst the *sarija* and the *sekban* in Asia Minor the events of 1622 gave rise to a bitter reaction, soon to be expressed in the great revolt (1622-8) of Abaza Mehemmed, the beglerbeg of Erzurum. Abaza Mehemmed, in 1622, drove out the janissaries stationed at Erzurum and then, with large numbers of the *levendat*, the 'feudal' sipahis and the nomadic tribesmen gathering around his banners, reduced to his own control much of eastern and central Asia Minor, killing off the 'men of the Sultan' wherever he encountered them. Although defeated in 1624 not far from Kayseri, Abaza Mehemmed was still able, in 1627, to repulse the forces which the then grand vizier, Khalil Pasha, directed against him at Erzurum. It was not until the following year that he surrendered at

[1] See above, pp. 623-4.

last to the Grand Vizier Khusrew Pasha. Too powerful still amongst the *sarija* and the *sekban* to be punished with death, Abaza Mehemmed was sent to an appointment far from the region where his influence was so strong—he became now the beglerbeg of Bosnia on the north-western frontier of the empire. His removal to Europe did not mean that the 'time of troubles' in Asia Minor was over. The old grounds of disaffection and tumult remained active. Their stubborn and enduring vigour would be demonstrated on a number of occasions in the future—for instance, the revolt, in 1647, of Varvar 'Ali Pasha; the career of Ibşir Mustafa Pasha, a nephew of Abaza Mehemmed and, for a short interval, grand vizier in 1654–5; and the insurrection of Abaza Hasan Pasha in 1658.

Of the difficulties facing the Ottoman government after 1617 not the least onerous was a new war against Persia. Shah 'Abbas I (1587–1629), in the years 1603–7, had recovered the territories ceded to the Ottomans in 1590. A peace made in 1612 gave formal recognition to the success of the Persians. Further hostilities in 1615–18 led to the confirmation of the settlement reached in 1612. Conflict was to break out once more in 1623, the main theatre of operations being now Iraq.

The northern and central regions of Iraq had been conquered from Persia and incorporated into the Ottoman Empire during the years 1534–5; the southern areas, and in particular Basra, came under Ottoman control in 1546–7. The population of Iraq was of mixed racial origin, embracing elements of Arab, Persian, Turkish and Kurdish descent. It was, moreover, a population divided in its religious allegiance. Kurdistan and the northern territories followed, in large degree, the Sunni or orthodox Muslim faith; central and southern Iraq contained numerous adherents of the most notable of the Muslim heterodoxies, Shi'i Islam, which was the official creed of Persia. Over some areas Ottoman rule was precarious and uncertain—over Basra, vulnerable to attack from Persia or from the marsh Arabs located in the Shatt al-'Arab; over the desert lands, known as al-Ahsa, along the north-western shore of the Persian Gulf; and over various border zones often in dispute with Persia—in the regions of Khuzistan, Luristan and Shahrizur. The Ottomans had also to deal with the Arab tribes inhabiting the deserts to the west of Iraq —tribes able to threaten the caravan routes leading from Basra to Aleppo and ever prone to encroach on the settled areas, whenever the administration at Baghdad was involved in difficulties or rested in the hands of men not equal to the circumstances of the moment. Iraq was, in short, a frontier province complex in character and troublesome to rule.

Ottoman control in Iraq began to weaken in the time of Mehemmed III (1595–1603) and Ahmed I (1603–17). A little before or a little after 1600— the exact date is not clear—Basra fell under the domination of local dynasts known as the House of Afrasiyab. At Baghdad the Ottoman garrison troops stationed there in the reign of Sultan Süleyman had evolved into an entrenched social class composed mostly of local recruits and responsive, above all, to the aspirations of its own dignitaries. One of the regimental officers, a certain Muhammad ibn Ahmad al-Tawil, was able to assert an effective control over Baghdad during the years 1604–7. A situation much more dangerous for the Ottomans arose, however, in 1621–3.

An officer of the janissaries, by name Bakr Subashī [i.e. Bakr, the chief of police] created for himself a faction so strong amongst the troops of Baghdad that from about 1619 onwards he was the most important figure in the town—far more influential, in fact, than the pasha. Opposed to Bakr Subashī was the faction of Muhammad Qanbar, the officer in charge of the soldiers called '*Azeban*. In 1621 the strife between the two factions broke out into violent conflict as a result of which Bakr Subashī became the master of Baghdad, his rival Muhammad Qanbar being now done to death. Bakr sought to obtain from Istanbul a formal recognition of himself as pasha of Baghdad—but without success. The Porte ordered Hafîz Ahmed, the governor of Diyar Bakr, to reduce Baghdad to obedience. At this juncture of affairs Bakr Subashī turned for aid to Shah 'Abbas of Persia. The shah at once sent a force to relieve Baghdad. Hafîz Ahmed, with a Persian intervention imminent, acceded to the demands of Bakr and withdrew his troops, while Bakr, having secured recognition from the Ottoman authorities, renounced his now unwelcome allies from Persia. The Persians, however, besieged Baghdad and took it with the assistance of Muhammad, the son of Bakr, who wanted to govern the town himself. Bakr Subashī was executed and the Sunni Muslims of Baghdad subjected to a fierce persecution at the hands of the Shi'i forces of the shah.

These events marked the beginning, in 1623, of a war which was to last until 1639. Hafîz Ahmed Pasha, as grand vizier, made a determined attempt to wrest Baghdad from the Persians in 1625–6. A lack of sufficient artillery contributed much to the failure of his siege operations. Moreover, an army of relief under the command of Shah 'Abbas beleaguered the Ottomans in their own lines and entrenchments. Hafîz Ahmed, with his situation precarious and with discontent rife amongst his men, was obliged at last to raise the siege and withdraw to Mosul. Not until 1629 did the Ottomans concentrate their forces for another major campaign in Iraq. The winter of 1629–30 was, however, exceptionally long and severe. Snow, rain and floods made operations in central Iraq almost impossible. The Ottoman grand vizier, Khusrew Pasha, decided therefore to undertake a campaign in the march-lands of Shahrizur. After routing the Persians at the Battle of Mihriban, Khusrew Pasha took and sacked Hamadan in the summer of 1630 and then, in the autumn of that year, led his troops to a new siege of Baghdad—a siege abandoned in November 1630 after a fruitless assault, the Ottomans retiring once again to Mosul.

The years following the campaign of 1630 witnessed a further out-break of factional violence at Istanbul and, in 1632, the emergence of Murad IV as sultan in fact as well as in name. Sultan Murad, before the renewal of operations against Persia, resolved to eliminate a possible source of danger in Syria. The Ottomans had never sought to exert a direct and immediate control over the Lebanon—a region which afforded a sure refuge in its mountain fastnesses to the ethnic and religious minorities established there in earlier times—the Druzes and the Maronites. The tribesmen of the Lebanon, after the Ottoman conquest of Syria in 1516, remained free to pursue, high in the mountains, their own purposes and feuds, provided that the Ottoman hold on the routes and cities of Syria was not called into question.

One Druze chieftain, Fakhr al-Din II, of the House of Ma'n, began in 1590 to consolidate and extend his influence—an endeavour so successful that it was to make him the master of the Lebanon. His efforts to win control over the northern reaches of the land, Kisrawan and the adjacent littoral, brought him into conflict with the Ottoman administration at Tripoli, while his attempts to move southward into the areas of Hawran, 'Ajlun and Nabulus threatened the pilgrimage route leading to the Hijaz and alarmed the Ottoman authorities at Damascus. A number of factors worked, however, in favour of Fakhr al-Din. At Istanbul his agents used bribes to forestall measures hostile to him. Moreover, the Ottoman officials in Syria had, in general, only a brief tenure of appointment—a fact which made it difficult for them to set in motion a long-term resistance to the Druze amir.

In 1613 the local opponents of Fakhr al-Din aligned themselves with Hafîz Ahmed Pasha, the beglerbeg of Damascus. Hafîz Ahmed, strengthened by reinforcements and by the co-operation of a naval squadron sailing off the coast of the Lebanon, now moved against the Ma'nid chieftain. Fakhr al-Din fled to Europe, where he remained for five years under the protection of Cosimo II, the grand duke of Tuscany, and later of Philip III, the king of Spain. He was able, in 1618, to secure from the Ottomans permission to return to the Lebanon. Once more Fakhr al-Din began to extend his influence both northward into Kisrawan and southward to 'Ajlun, Nabulus and Safad, all of which the government at Istanbul, in 1622, entrusted to his nominees. At 'Anjarr in 1625 the Druze amir defeated his local enemies and the beglerbeg of Damascus, who had made common cause against him. Fakhr al-Din was to dominate the Lebanon thereafter for some ten years. His power rested on his Druze adherents—but even more on a strong force of mercenaries. To support these troops, to maintain the forts guarding his territories and to provide the funds dispensed in his name at Istanbul Fakhr al-Din needed a large revenue. He obtained it through the increase of the lands under his control, but also through the efficient exploitation of the economic resources available to him. His efforts to promote a new growth of trade at Beirut and Sidon met with considerable success. An agreement that he made with Cosimo II in 1608 brought into his service Italian merchants, engineers and agricultural experts. At the same time he favoured the cause of religious toleration, extending a welcome to Christian missionaries from Europe, to Kurdish elements from the region of Aleppo and to the Maronites, some of whom settled in the southern Lebanon and helped to improve the condition of agriculture there.

The power of Fakhr al-Din rested, however, as much on the confusion rife at Istanbul as on his own abilities. In 1632 Sultan Murad assumed control of the imperial government. Murad IV was eager to launch a new offensive against Persia and reluctant, therefore, to allow the continued existence of a strong régime in the Lebanon—a régime which was of doubtful allegiance and which might seek to turn to its further advantage in Syria a renewed and major involvement of the Ottomans in the eastern war. Küçük Ahmed Pasha, the beglerbeg of Damascus, strengthened with large reinforcements, moved against Fakhr al-Din in 1634. The Ma'nid amir, beaten in the field, was captured in 1635 and sent to Istanbul where, in April of that year, he was executed on the suspicion that his influence stood behind the still active unrest in the Lebanon.

The war with Persia now entered into its last phase. Sultan Murad took the Persian fortress of Erivan after a short siege (July–August 1635) and then advanced towards Tabriz, which fell to him in September 1635. As on earlier campaigns into Adharbayjan, the Ottomans found that the Persians had adhered to their usual tactics of retreat—harassing the columns of the enemy, lengthening his lines of communication and sweeping the land clean of supplies. The sultan, with no prospect of a decisive result before him, abandoned Tabriz and retired westward into Asia Minor. By December 1635 he was once more at Istanbul. It was at the moment of his arrival there that the Persians appeared before the walls of Erivan. After a stubborn resistance the Ottoman garrison surrendered the fortress in April 1636. The events at Erivan in 1635–6 demonstrated a truth long since manifest—that, in war against Persia, there would be no enduring success for the Ottomans save through the permanent occupation of wide territories beyond their eastern frontier, a solution which was difficult to achieve and expensive to maintain, as the great conflict of 1578–90 had made clear.

Sultan Murad now turned his attention to Iraq. The years 1636–8 saw elaborate preparations in progress for a new campaign, this time with Baghdad as the main objective. On 8 May 1638 the sultan left Üsküdar and, on 15 November, began the siege of Baghdad. A fierce assault on 24 December was decisive. The Persian commander yielded the town on the following day. Some of the garrison continued to resist, however, despite the capitulation. A conflict of extreme violence ensued, in the course of which most of the Persians lost their lives. Murad IV set out on the return march to Istanbul in January 1639, leaving the Grand Vizier, Kemankeş Qara Mustafa Pasha, to conduct negotiations with the representatives of Shah Safi. A settlement was reached at Zuhab, near Qasr-i Şirin, in May 1639. This peace brought to an end the long contention between the Ottomans and the Persians begun in the time of Sultan Selim I (d. 1520) and Shah Isma'il (d.1524). Erivan and the adjacent territories would remain under Persian control, while Iraq was to be Ottoman. The peace terms also included measures for a demarcation of the frontier separating the Ottoman Empire from Persia— and, in fact, along a line which, at least in relation to the modern states of Iraq and Iran, has endured without serious modification until the present day. Sultan Murad did not long survive his triumphant return to Istanbul in June 1639. He died on 9 February 1640.

Amid the intrigue and violence surrounding the throne in the years after 1617 there were men able and willing to exercise power in a responsible manner, 'strong men' like Dilawar Pasha (d.1622) or Gurji Mehemmed Pasha (d.1626). Influential, too, were those officials—for instance, Koçu Beg, the author of the famous *Risale* [i.e. *Treatise*]—who analysed the reasons and explained the remedies for the troubles which beset the Ottoman state.[1] It is here among the dignitaries and soldiers intent on the restoration of efficient rule that Murad IV must be numbered, above all during the years (1632–40) of his personal control over the conduct of affairs.

To the extirpation of disobedience and revolt within the empire Sultan Murad brought a shrewd intelligence, an indefatigable resolution—and a pitiless severity. The intrigue and violence encompassing his youth did much to fashion the man that he was to become. All went down before him in a ferocious and unending sequence of executions. Vengeance, he is reputed to have said, never grows old, it only grows grey![2] In the judgement of the Venetian bailo at Istanbul, Alvise Contarini, no sultan ever attained a more absolute domination of the empire. The great physical strength of Murad, his skill in the use of arms and his vivid, though sombre character made a deep—and, for his purposes, a valuable —impression on the soldiers of the imperial household. These same qualities won for him also much favour amongst the *sarīja* and *sekban* levies and, in addition, amongst the populace of Istanbul, that is, with forces which might act as a counterpoise to the indiscipline hitherto so frequent in the janissaries and the sipahis of the Porte. Contarini observed

[1] Cf. Vol. III in this series, pp. 350–2.
[2] Cf. J. von Hammer, *Histoire de l'Empire Ottoman*, trans. J.-J. Hellert, Vol. IX (Paris, 1837), p. 389, note 3: 'Solea dire che non invecchiano mai le vendette benche incanutissero'.

of the sultan that he was unwearied in his application to business and eager to be well informed on all matters.[1] An elaborate 'espionage system' gave him news about events and opinions both in the provinces and amongst the people of Istanbul. It also enabled him to maintain a close surveillance over the troops of the central régime. Of relevance here are the measures that he took to restrict the use of tobacco, coffee and wine —at the establishments selling these commodities the soldiers often met and, in talk amongst themselves, magnified discontent into sedition. Sultan Murad, through means of this kind and through the fear that his implacable temper called forth, was able to restore discipline and order in the regiments belonging to the imperial household —able to reduce the troops in number, to eject the least welcome elements among them and to eradicate some of the worst abuses. A similar programme was carried out in the provinces, where much was done to reorganize the 'feudal' system and to recover fiefs which had fallen into illegal or incompetent hands. At the same time Murad IV set in train the preparation of an 'Adalet-name, a 'Book of Justice' containing measures for the protection of the peasants.

The labour of reform was long, complicated—and also expensive. Moreover, the war against Persia demanded a large expenditure of revenue. It was not accidental that the sultan had, amongst his contemporaries, a reputation for excessive avarice—'avarizia per ecesso' in the words of Alvise Contarini.[2] Of Murad IV it was said that what he did not do for cash he would do neither for prayer nor intercession, neither for justice nor law.[3] A verdict of this kind reflects the determination of the sultan to fill the coffers of the state. An abundant treasure was one of the surest means to the achievement of his aims. It was also a safeguard for his own person, since he was able, with the ample funds at his command, to ensure the regular payment—and thus the allegiance—of his armed forces. An efficient collection of revenue, measures to guide the resulting yield into the hands of the government and out of the hands of officials and tax-farmers, the use of confiscation as a further and rich source of income—such methods led to a success so great that one Venetian of this time, Pietro Foscarini, described Murad IV as the richest of all the Ottoman Sultans.[4] The years of his effective rule, with their remarkable combination of sober policy and wise management, of fierce energy and also of signal cruelty, stemmed for a while the disorders

[1] Cf. N. Barozzi and G. Berchet, *Le Relazioni degli Stati Europei lette al Senato nel secolo decimosettimo*, Fifth Series: *Turkey*, Pt I (Venice, 1871), p. 368: 'applicatissimo al governo, vago di saper tutto'.

[2] Cf. Barozzi and Berchet, *ibid.* p. 367.

[3] Cf. Hammer, *Histoire . . .*, Vol. IX, p. 421: 'quello che per il denaro non fa, non lo fa per preghiere, non per intercessione, non per giustizia, non lo fa per legge'.

[4] Cf. N. Jorga, *Geschichte des osmanischen Reiches*, Vol. III (Gotha, 1910), p. 463, note 2: 'È il più ricco di tutti i principi che sono stati della Casa ottomana.'

within the empire. But their duration was all too brief and it was not long before the work had to be done again.

The Ottomans, since the death of Ahmed I in 1617, had been involved in no major conflict with the states of Christendom. There was, however, a short war against Poland in 1620–1. Along the march-lands dividing the Polish and the Ottoman territories the raiding of Cossacks from the Ukraine and of Tatars from the Crimea was a source of continuing friction. The Cossacks also sailed down the rivers, the Dnieper and the Dniester for instance, and ventured out into the Black Sea, plundering Sinope in 1614 and Anchialos in 1621.[1] A further cause of unrest was the intervention of Poland, from time to time, in the affairs of Moldavia, seeking to establish on the throne of this small Christian state dependent on the sultan a vaivoda favourable to Polish interests. There had been in 1616 a brief outburst of hostilities, in the course of which the Ottoman frontier begs of the Danube line inflicted a severe defeat on a Polish-Cossack force operating in Moldavia. These hostilities ended in 1617 with the Peace of Buzsa, which laid it down that Poland was not to interfere in matters relating to the government of Moldavia and that measures should be taken, on the one side as on the other, to hinder the incursions of the Cossacks and the Tatars.

The peace was soon to be broken. Gratiani, the vaivoda of Moldavia, being deposed from office in 1620 on the order of 'Osman II, sought and secured aid from Poland. At Ţuţora, near Iaşi, the Danube begs, reinforced by a numerous contingent of Tatars, routed the Polish–Moldavian forces in September 1620. It was now that Sultan 'Osman resolved to undertake a major offensive against Poland—and this in opposition to the advice of the more moderate amongst the high dignitaries of the Porte and in spite of the fact that a Polish ambassador was bringing proposals for the renewal of the peace. The march northward to the Danube in the late spring of 1621 was slow and difficult because of the bad weather. After crossing the Danube at Isaqça, the Ottomans moved towards Chocim, which was not reached, however, until August 1621. The Poles held a fortified encampment on the banks of the Dniester. A first Ottoman attack met with some success, but the subsequent assaults, five in number, ended in failure. The cold and the rain presaging the onset of winter and the growing lack of supplies now brought the campaign to a close. Sultan 'Osman was obliged to make peace with Poland in October 1621, and on terms which constituted in fact a reaffirmation of the agreement made in 1617.

As for relations between Vienna and Istanbul—the involvement of Austria in the Thirty Years War (1618–48) and of the Ottoman Empire

---

[1] The Cossacks even penetrated into the Bosphorus and, in 1625, plundered Yeniköy, a suburb of Istanbul. In 1637 Azov, at the mouth of the River Don, fell to them and remained in their hands until 1642, when the Ottomans sent a strong force to drive them out of the town.

in the long conflict with Persia (1623–39) meant that neither side could envisage a serious confrontation on the Danube. The *kleinkrieg* between Christian marcher lord and Ottoman ghazi along the frontier continued unabated as heretofore. None the less, the Peace of Zsitva-Torok, negotiated in 1606, was confirmed, with some modification of detail, at Neuhäusel in 1608, at Vienna in 1615, at Gyarmath in 1625, at Szön in 1627 and again at Szön in 1642—confirmed after long discussion to achieve the dismantling, in Hungary, of the small forts [*palanka*] sometimes erected in contravention of the articles of peace and to ascertain the dependence—on the Christian or the Muslim state—and also the taxation status of the villages adjacent to the great fortresses like Erlau, Kanizsa or Stuhlweissenburg, which were now under Ottoman rule.

The old idea of the Crusade, though shorn of compulsive force, was still not without effect in Europe. To the realization once more of this idea the men of the Counter-Reformation gave much time and effort. These years saw the unfolding of numerous designs for the invasion of the Ottoman Empire—designs centred on such 'claimants' to the Ottoman territories as the duc de Nevers (descended from one of the last Palaeologi) or the '*gran principe ottomano*', Yahya, reputed to be a son of Sultan Mehemmed III (1595–1603). Numerous, too, were the schemes for exploiting the possibilities of local resistance to Ottoman rule within the Balkans, above all in regions which had never come under the full and direct control of the Porte, for instance, the district of Maina in the Morea and also Albania and Montenegro. A good example of such schemes can be found in a project submitted to the Diet of Ratisbon in 1640, envisaging an advance into Albania and the capture of important fortresses like Kroja and Skutari, a mass rising of the Christians and the occupation of the strategic routes through Serbia in order to hinder the arrival of Ottoman relief forces from Bosnia and the lands along the middle Danube, and then, to crown these efforts, a 'break-out' eastwards and a rapid march on Istanbul. There was in fact small prospect of success for an enterprise of this kind. The states of western and central Europe, dedicated to the pursuit of their own ambitions and involved, most of them, in the Thirty Years War, had neither the will nor the means to embark on a design so grandiose and so dubious. As to the 'resistance' in the Balkans against Ottoman rule—the stress laid, in these projects of invasion, on areas like Maina and Albania is sufficient to underline the character and limitations of that 'resistance'. It reflected far more a readiness to defend local traditions and modes of life than a zeal for general insurrection in the name of a 'crusade'.

A more practical approach was available, however, to the forces of the Counter-Reformation. The Peace of Vienna (1615) contained a clause permitting the Jesuits to maintain their own establishments and churches within the Ottoman Empire. A little later, in 1622, the foundation at

Rome of the Congregatio de Propaganda Fide strengthened the activities of the Catholic church in the eastern lands. Moreover, the interest which Father Joseph, the agent of Cardinal Richelieu, showed in the work of the Congregatio led him to organize a Capuchin mission to Istanbul. The Jesuits and the Capuchins had the support of the Catholic ambassadors at the Porte—a fact which caused the Ottomans to view the two orders with some suspicion and to see in their religious endeavours a cloak for political ambitions emanating from Rome, Paris and Vienna. To the dignitaries of the Greek Orthodox church the arrival of the Catholic orders was unwelcome and resistance to them soon became concentrated around the person of Lukaris, the patriarch of Constantinople, a known and respected champion of the Greek religion, language and culture. On the side of the patriarch and his adherents stood the ambassadors of Protestant England and Holland, in opposition to the representatives of Catholicism.

The Jesuits and the Capuchins, in pursuit of their religious calling, devoted much time and effort to education. It was now that under the guidance of the two orders young Greeks, usually of good birth, went in considerable numbers to be educated at Catholic centres of learning in Rome, Padua and Venice—now, too, that with the approval of the anti-Catholic forces mustered around the patriarch young Greeks studied at Protestant centres of learning in Germany and in England. The year 1627 saw the arrival in Istanbul, from London, of a printing press for the publication of religious literature written in Greek and intended for distribution amongst the adherents of the Orthodox faith. The Jesuits induced the Ottomans to seize the press, whereupon the printer, Nikodemos Metaxas, took refuge at the house of the English ambassador, Sir Thomas Roe. A vigorous protest from Sir Thomas, who had much influence at the Porte, led now to the banishment of the Jesuits from the empire. After Roe's departure for England in 1628 the Jesuits returned to Istanbul, careful henceforth to act with greater circumspection than before and in directions less apt to awaken the distrust of the Ottoman authorities.

The Peace of Zuhab in 1639[1] left the Porte free to turn its attention elsewhere. Soon it became involved in a new and formidable war, this time against Venice and for possession of the island of Crete. Along the eastern shore of the Adriatic, on the borders of the enclaves still under Venetian rule, there was often friction between the Ottoman frontier warriors and the mercenaries—Albanian, Greek and Cretan—in the service of the Signoria. At sea the situation was still more uncertain. Here the maritime forces of Venice came into conflict with the corsairs of Algiers, Tunis and Tripoli.

A moment of crisis had occurred in the summer of 1638, when a

[1] See above, p. 634.

squadron from Tunis, commanded by a well-known renegade, 'Ali Piccenino, sailed into the Straits of Otranto, raided the coast of Apulia and then captured a Venetian ship off Cattaro. The Signoria ordered Marino Capello, cruising at that time in the waters of Crete, to deal with the corsairs. Piccenino found refuge under the guns of the Ottoman fortress at Valona. Capello, after a blockade of Valona lasting about a month, entered the harbour, bombarded the town and made off with the corsair vessels. Murad IV, with the Persian war still in progress, restrained his anger and agreed to negotiate. The affair ended peacefully when, in 1639, Venice paid 250,000 *sequins* as compensation for the ships taken by Capello.

A further source of tension was to be found in the militant religious Orders of Christendom—the Knights of Saint Stephen and the Knights of Saint John at Malta. Around the orders there hung, in pious Christian eyes, an aura of splendour deriving from long-maintained conflict with the Muslim infidel. To the Muslims the Knights of Saint Stephen and Saint John—not less than the corsairs of North Africa to the Christians— were pirates greatly to be feared because of their raids at sea and along the shores of the Levant. The activities of Malta, to an especial degree, envenomed the relations existing between the Ottoman Empire and the Christian states. Even in Europe itself, as a report from France written in 1627 made clear, the view was gaining ground that the orders had outlived their usefulness. Venice, in general, regarded with disfavour the depredations of the knights, which were sometimes indiscriminate at the expense of friend and foe alike, and discouraged her subjects from serving with the orders. The Signoria found it impossible, however, to close to the knights the harbours in Crete and in the other islands and mainland territories under her control.

A Maltese squadron in September 1644, near Rhodes, encountered a number of Ottoman vessels laden with a rich cargo. The knights captured these ships after a stiff fight and then sailed with their plunder to Crete. This episode sufficed to bring to the fore the faction hostile to Venice amongst the dignitaries at the Porte. The winter of 1644–5 saw the Ottomans engaged in elaborate preparations for war—preparations which included the building of ships, the casting of guns and the gathering of munitions and supplies in the harbours of the Morea and along the western coast of Asia Minor. On 30 April 1645 the Ottoman fleet sailed for Crete, moving first to Chios and then to Navarino. Ottoman troops, transported from Navarino, landed in Crete on 23–4 June 1645, some distance to the west of Canea.

The Porte had now committed itself to an arduous war—and against no mean foe. Crete would not become Ottoman until 1669. The fact that Venice was able to bear the expense of so long a conflict underlines the richness of the resources still at her command. The decline of Venice is not to be dated from the conquests of the Portuguese around the shores of the Indian Ocean after 1498. Those conquests disrupted for a time, but did not end the flow of spices and other eastern commodities from India through the lands of Islam to the Mediterranean world. The transit trade across Egypt and Syria soon recovered its former amplitude. Not till the arrival in the Indian Ocean—and also in the Mediterranean— of powers stronger than the Portuguese, i.e. the English and the Dutch, was the balance altered decisively in favour of the sea route to Europe via the Cape of Good Hope. By the second quarter of the seventeenth century the two Protestant states had won a preponderance in the spice trade from the East and a large share, too, in the local traffic of the Mediterranean itself. Venice was able, none the less, to offset in no small degree the consequences of this change in her situation. She strove, and with success, to retain some of her commerce to and from the Levant and to extend her trading activities in the regions behind the eastern shore of the Adriatic. The readiness of the Signoria to grant concessions in respect of tolls, customs and labour dues brought numerous Dutch and English ships to Venice and thus enriched the finances of the state. Moreover, the government and the citizens of Venice began now to exploit more than ever before the abundant resources, agricultural and industrial, of the *Terra Firma*, that is, of the north Italian lands under their control. It was from measures of this order, much more than from the expedients usual in a time of crisis (donations, the sale of titles, new taxes and the like) that Venice drew the means to defend Crete so well against the Ottomans.

The balance of success, during the first campaigns of the war, inclined towards the armies of the sultan. The rule of the Signoria in Crete amounted to little more than the domination, often harsh and intolerant, of a small class of soldiers, officials and administrators, Italian and Roman Catholic in culture and religion, over a population Greek Orthodox in faith and Greek in speech and tradition. There was no prospect that the people of Crete would rise *en masse* in defence of Venetian rule over the island. Canea fell to the Ottomans in August 1645. Retimo surrendered to them in November 1646. The able soldier Hüseyn Pasha, in command of the Ottoman forces since September 1646, blockaded Candia in the summer of 1647 and began a formal siege of the fortress in April 1648. Of the naval operations in progress at this time it will suffice to mention that the Venetians, in 1645, sailed from Zante to Patras, bombarding and plundering the town; also that their fleet, in 1646–8, penetrated deep into the Aegean Sea, but failed to achieve a major success. There was fighting, too, in Dalmatia, where the Ottomans took Novigrad in 1646. An Ottoman attempt, in 1647, to capture Sebenico ended in defeat and the Venetians thereafter occupied a number of important fortresses, including Dernis, Knin and Klis, in 1647–8.

By 1648 the main lines of the war had become clear. Some areas of conflict would have only a local significance. On the Dalmatian front Venice used her command of the sea to reinforce a stubborn defence against Ottoman incursions into the Adriatic littoral. Moreover, the attempts of the Signoria to awaken resistance to the Ottomans, for instance amongst the Mainotes of the Morea in 1653 and in 1659, achieved only a limited result.

The Ottomans had to overcome Venetian naval pressure in the waters of the Aegean Sea. Of no less importance was their need to maintain as an effective force the army fighting in Crete—a task which involved the large-scale movement of men and supplies from southern Greece and from Asia Minor. To meet this continuing need the Ottomans organized 'convoy campaigns' at sea, employed also numerous small vessels which slipped out of the harbours in the Morea and on the coast of Asia Minor and, in addition, hired or impressed into their service foreign ships, notably of English and Dutch origin.

Venice was to centre her defensive effort in Crete on the maintenance of one great fortified base, Candia—a course of action which enabled her to concentrate her troops on the island in a manner at once economical and effective and, through her fleet, to reinforce them at will. As long as Candia remained unconquered, Crete was not yet Ottoman. The offensive operations of Venice would be carried out at sea. To cut off the flow of men and munitions to Hüseyn Pasha was to reduce the Ottoman army in Crete to desperation. The Venetians directed the most massive of their naval campaigns to the fulfilment of this aim, that is, sought to crush the Ottoman battle fleet in a major action or else to blockade the mouth of the Dardanelles and even penetrate, if possible, through the straits into the Sea of Marmara—a threat so dangerous that the Ottomans, during the earlier years of the war, fortified the Dardanelles anew. Although well and resolutely led by captains like Lazaro Mocenigo and Francesco Morosini, the Venetian fleet was not able to realize this programme. One reason for its failure to win a decisive success was the fact that the Ottomans had an alternative concentration area at their command—the 'canal of Chios', between that island and the coast of Asia Minor, where ships, reinforcements and supplies could be brought together for transport to Crete. The naval resources of the Signoria did not suffice for a firm blockade both of the Dardanelles and of the waters around Chios.

It was in 1654-6 that Venice made her supreme challenge at sea. A great battle off the Dardanelles in June 1656 shattered the Ottoman fleet and enabled the Venetians to seize the islands of Lemnos and Tenedos close to the mouth of the straits. The Ottomans, with a rapid and astonishing deployment of their rich resources, now built a new fleet and, in 1657, used it to regain Tenedos in September and Lemnos in November of that year. The war would in fact continue, with intervals of relative calm, until at last the Porte, under the guidance of the Grand Vizier Ahmed Köprülü, made a vast effort to bring the conflict to an end. Candia, in the course of a long defence begun in 1648, had been transformed into an almost impregnable fortress. Ahmed Köprülü, after a siege which lasted more than two and a quarter years and was perhaps the greatest feat of arms of the age, took Candia in 1669. Venice now accepted the peace terms offered to her. The war was over and Crete, henceforth, a province of the Ottoman Empire.

The firm rule which Murad IV had achieved remained in force for a little while after his death in 1640—that is, during the administration of the last of his grand viziers, Kemankeş Qara Mustafa Pasha, who was to hold the office from 1638 to 1644. Qara Mustafa was faithful to the precepts and practice of Sultan Murad. He sought to reduce in number the janissaries and the sipahis of the Porte. At the same time he was careful to ensure that the troops were paid well and regularly. He set himself, therefore, to reform the coinage, to introduce a more effective and just assessment of taxation and, by these means, to have at his command a full treasury. Qara Mustafa, however, was a grand vizier and not a sultan. Under the eccentric Ibrahim (1640–8) intrigue and faction grew once again to formidable proportions. The rigorous control of Qara Mustafa and his promptitude to punish wrong-doing awakened resentments against him—of the Walide Sultan Kösem, the mother of Ibrahim; of the vizier Sultanzade Mehemmed Pasha; also of the Silahdar Yusuf, who was the favourite, and of Hüseyn Efendi, who was the khoja of Sultan Ibrahim. These powerful figures conspired successfully to bring about the fall of the grand vizier. In 1644 the sultan gave the order for the execution of Qara Mustafa.

The rule of courtiers and officials, faction around the throne, the mismanagement of the state revenues, renewed turbulence amongst the troops of the central régime—all the evils so strong before 1632 now, after 1644, dominated the scene once again and with undiminished force. There was also a marked revival of *jelali* dissidence in Asia Minor under such men as Varvar 'Ali Pasha, Ibşir Mustafa Pasha and Abaza Hasan Pasha during the years 1644–58.[1] A revolt of the janissaries and the sipahis of the Porte in August 1648 led to the deposition and death of Sultan Ibrahim, whose ineptitudes and extravagance had earned for him the distrust of the soldiers and dignitaries belonging to the imperial household. The rivalries between the old Walide Kösem, the mother of Ibrahim, and the new Walide Turkhan, the mother of the young Mehemmed IV (1648–87) and their respective adherents called forth, in 1651, a new outburst of violence, in the course of which Kösem, a potent influence behind the throne during the reign of her sons, Murad IV and Ibrahim,

[1] See above, p. 630.

642

was done to death. An end had to be made to the sequence of intrigue, rebellion and murder. The Venetians, now at the summit of their naval offensive, were threatening in earnest a 'breakthrough' from the Aegean Sea into the Sea of Marmara. With the destruction of the Ottoman fleet in June 1656 a return to order was imperative. It was at this time of crisis that Mehemmed Köprülü came to the grand vizierate. The restoration of efficient rule was swift and sure. His tenure of office (1656–61) and still more the tenure (1661–76) of his son Ahmed Köprülü gave to the Ottoman Empire a further, though brief interval of glittering, but illusive splendour.

CHAPTER XXI

EUROPE AND ASIA

A T the close of the sixteenth century the Portuguese Empire in Asia, the *Estado da India*, had reached a climax of prosperity. The state balance-sheet showed that expenditure upon the salaries of officials, the stipends of the clergy and the upkeep of guard fleets and garrisons was much more than met by income from customs dues and land revenues. Everyone knew, moreover, that the recorded salaries of captains and factors, weighmen and clerks were more than matched by their income from perquisites, graft and extortion. For the soldier and the sailor life between campaigns might be hard, but he could hope for a prize or sack and, if deserving or fortunate, for a minor office or grant of land. The state had encouraged European colonization by the grant of estates to the *casados*, the married men available for local military service, in Goa, in the new conquests northwards to Damão and now in Ceylon. Furthermore, everyone, high or low, lay or cleric, who could raise the capital busily engaged in trade. The crown was only interested in a small number of monopoly products, pepper, cinnamon and the finer spices, destined for Europe and in such grand lines of trade as Goa to Mozambique, or to Malacca and Macau. There was ample scope for local licensed trade and, since control was lax, for infringement of monopoly too. Finally many Portuguese merchants, shipmasters and soldiers of fortune, whose activities might shade through commerce to piracy, were to be found in parts of Asia not under jurisdiction of the crown. Western India was fully administered, the east coast settlements of Negapatam and São Thomé were only loosely linked with Goa, but the rising settlements at Hugli in Bengal, and in Arakan and further round the bay were quite independent. Throughout Indonesia other pockets of Portuguese were to be found— a handful at Grisee [Gresik] in Java, another twenty or thirty families in Macassar, yet others, mercenaries and merchants on the south-east Asian mainland and among the off-shore islands of the China coast. All these contributed to the network of inter-Asian trade carried on by the Portuguese, often in close co-operation with Asian merchants and financiers. It was the profits of their trade, together with the customs receipts of Ormuz, Diu, Goa, Cochin and Malacca, the *entrepôts* whither the trade winds and Portuguese naval power directed the movements of Asian merchants, which ensured the continued prosperity of the *Estado da India*.

As the century ended the Malabar pepper lands were disturbed by a rash war and an earlier successful revolt in the spice-providing Moluccas had only partly been made good through the complex net of private trade.

But trade between Macau and Japan, with its offshoot of illegal trade to Spanish Manila, continued to flourish. Customs receipts at Malacca were rising and both its old enemies Johore and Achin were seeking peace. In Ceylon, Portuguese control of the lowlands with their valuable cinnamon and arecanut had been restored, and the captain-general Azevedo closely besieged the last independent Sinhalese kingdom, inland Kandy. In India the growth of the Mughal Empire, now advancing on the Deccan, roused alarm, but the peace and unity it imposed on all north India from Sind and Gujarat to Bengal were good for trade. There was a further compensation, too, in better relations with Golkonda and Bijapur, two kingdoms which as late as 1570 had come close to destroying Goa, but which now sought a common front against the Mughal danger. Westward, in the Persian Gulf, three Portuguese victories had ended the Ottoman naval threat from Basra and the Red Sea, a threat further diminished by the rise of the Safavid dynasty in Persia. The energy and enterprise of Shah Abbas might one day endanger Portuguese Ormuz, but for the moment his fostering of trade was all to its advantage. Finally, in East Africa Arab risings on the coast had been totally suppressed while inland the decline of the Monomotapa Empire raised hopes of a Portuguese advance up the Zambesi.

The crown trade between Asia and Europe, let out in contract to various European consortia, had run into difficulties from the 1570s onward. Antwerp was lost as a distribution centre; a revival of the old Levant routes cut the profit margins on pepper and spices; there were heavy losses of Indiamen to privateers and through poor fitting-out and overloading. The link between Lisbon and Goa was thus weak, for there were neither the funds nor the ships to permit any massive reinforcement of the *Estado da India*. Much depended therefore upon the resources which could be mustered and deployed within the *Estado* itself. Almost to the end of the sixteenth century these seemed sufficient. The main bases from East Africa to China, though manned by less than 7,000 native-born Portuguese, held firm. Similarly a handful of carracks, supplemented by smaller craft, were able to keep open the main lines of trade within the area and in the Indian Ocean and Malacca Straits to impose a system of *cartazes* or licences, which reduced competition, and compelled Asian traders to pay toll at Portuguese ports. Even such powerful states as Golkonda, Bijapur and the Mughal Empire submitted to the *cartaz* system. The element of compulsion in such a licensing system and in the fortification of the trading posts the Portuguese secured had been a new phenomenon when they first reached Asia. By the end of the century, however, the Portuguese had been absorbed into the state system of Asia. Familiarity had lessened offence, and deft manipulation of Asian rivalries prevented any united resistance. Moreover the Portuguese made no serious attempt to exclude Asians from whole areas of trade, and even in western India where they were strongest, infractions of the few monopolies the crown asserted were regularly winked at. Portuguese individuals actively co-operated with Asian merchants, entering into trading partnerships with them, giving out goods on commenda, either captaining or freighting their ships. Indians carried Portuguese goods to hostile Aden, Portuguese smuggled the goods of Indians into Cochin under cover of their privileges. The Dutch governor-general van Diemen later commented, 'Most of the Portuguese in India look upon this region as their fatherland, and think no more about Portugal. They drive little or no trade thither, but content themselves with the port-to-port trade of Asia, just as if they were natives thereof and had no other country.' Perhaps for this reason they were often received with more friendliness than later European arrivals. The Portuguese alike because of their naval power and their usefulness as trading partners had thus established a stable-seeming position in Asia. And then, in 1596, the whole balance was radically disturbed by the appearance of Dutch ships in Asian waters.

The Dutch role of distributors of Asian goods from Lisbon throughout northern Europe—a role they were outgrowing—had for some years been threatened by Spanish policy. They had therefore pushed their trade into the Mediterranean and Levant, ventured to West Africa, and vainly sought a northern route to China. Philip's seizure of all Dutch shipping in Portuguese ports, and the ending of their connived-at commerce, led them in 1595 to make their first voyage east round the Cape. Armed with West African experience, and the detailed information about the *Estado da India* secured from Goa and Lisbon by Linschoten and Houtman, they struck out for the Sunda Straits and the Javanese port of Bantam. This was an excellent base for the pepper and spice trades. Moreover, as Brouwer discovered in 1611, by using the south-east trade winds from the Cape it could be reached without touching the Portuguese strongholds astride the monsoon sailing routes.

The first voyage established that the route east was feasible and safe, a series of provincial companies quickly appeared to exploit the breakthrough, and within seven years no less than sixty-five ships sailed east. Initial instructions were to concentrate on profitable trade, to avoid Portuguese territory, and to use force only in self-defence. However, the Portuguese showed no intention of allowing the intruders to go unmolested. The viceroy from Goa put diplomatic pressure on Asian rulers to secure the closure of their ports to Dutch shipping. As a result Achin, anxious for aid against Johore, rebuffed three successive Dutch fleets, the Christian chiefs on Banda attacked them, and by 1601 both Bantam and Ternate had been half persuaded to repel the rebel, piratical Dutch. Nothing loth, Dutch commanders responded with counter-violence, joining in an Amboinese attack upon Portuguese Lei Timor, besieging their fort on Tidore, and in 1602 seizing the *Santa Catarina*, 'the greatest and richest carrack which ever sailed from China'. The viceroy's reply was to despatch all available forces under the veteran Andre Furtado da Mendonça. He threatened Achin, besieged Bantam, and strengthened the Portuguese garrison on Amboina, destroying the Dutch fort and visiting with fire and sword such villages as had traded with the enemy. He went on to reinforce Tidore, to drive the Dutch from Ternate and to install a Portuguese garrison there.

Such Portuguese determination, the formation of an English East India Company late in 1600, and the arrival of French ships in Asian waters drove the Dutch to prepare more thoroughly for conflict by the creation in 1602 of the United East India Company, the V.O.C. Three of the ten Voor-Compagnie had already amalgamated, for the danger of forcing prices up in the east and down in Europe was early apparent. But the union of 1602 had a wider aim than the giving of central direction to dispersed commercial effort: it was to create a military instrument with which to counter Iberian hostility and to secure for the Dutch that monopoly of the spice trade without which the burden of military expenditure could not be sustained. Oldenbarnevelt, the advocate of Holland, who engineered the union, had toyed with the idea of a state system of forts and fleets in the east. When instead a union of private companies was formed it was armed with all the powers of a state—the right to make treaties with native rulers, to build forts, to hold territory in full sovereignty, to raise troops and to appoint the necessary governors and military and judicial officers. The structure of the United Company was federal: the previously existing companies of Amsterdam, Hoorn, Enkhuizen, Rotterdam, Delft and Middelburg were incorporated as chambers of the new company, responsible for fitting out ships and financing individual voyages. But the over-all direction of the company, entrusted to seventeen delegates from the chambers, the famous 'Heeren XVII', was nevertheless strongly centralized. The seventeen were responsible for the size and distribution of the annual investment, for the sale of return cargoes, and for supervising the raising of funds; the debts of the company were a joint responsibility. The province of Holland, providing eight directors and over half the capital, was able to give a strong lead within the seventeen. Since the system of election to the directorate placed authority permanently in the hands of men who were powers in their towns and provinces and closely linked with the government, the Heeren XVII acquired such authority as enabled them to disregard the wishes of shareholders and to make the company an arm of the state in the fight for national independence.[1]

[1] In their struggle with King Philip, the Dutch shrewdly concentrated their attacks upon the overseas possessions of his Portuguese rather than his Spanish crown. Their few assaults on Spanish territories were singularly unsuccessful.

The United Company, commanding great resources, proceeded to send out twenty-seven ships in its first two voyages, armed with instructions as much military as commercial. In view of the 'improper and violent means' used by the Iberians, the fleets were to inflict all possible damage on the enemy. Accordingly, offensive alliances were signed with the zamorin of Calicut, the king of Kandy and the sultan of Johore. Steven van der Hagen took the Portuguese base on Amboina, built a Dutch fort, and secured from the Amboinese chiefs both an oath of fealty to the States General and the monopoly of their cloves and then followed up this blow to Portuguese prestige and authority by taking their fort on Tidore. Dutch ships visited Sumatra, Java, Borneo and Celebes as well as the Moluccas, everywhere furnishing arms and encouraging attack upon the Portuguese. As Matias de Nova mourned, 'In less than a year was lost that which a century of Spanish and Portuguese valour had conquered.'

The Dutch had swept the eastern seas, inflicting heavy losses on Portuguese shipping, but they lacked the strength to take a firm grip on land, especially as officers and crews protested against the directors' secret orders committing them to fighting ashore. This Dutch weakness was exploited by the Spaniards in Manila who, having sought and received aid from New Mexico, proceeded to occupy Ternate and retake Tidore. The Dutch regained eastern Ternate and with difficulty held it, but they failed completely when they broadened their attack to include the main Portuguese land bases. They had succeeded in Indonesian waters against Portuguese private traders and their Asian partners, but Matelieff's four-month siege of Malacca in 1605, Caerden's six-week siege of Mozambique in 1607, and Verhoeven's cruise against Mozambique, Goa and Malacca in 1608 with a particularly powerful fleet all failed. In each case heavy damage was inflicted on the Portuguese at sea—Matelieff destroyed a fleet led by the viceroy in person—but the fortresses held, a continuing threat to Dutch achievements.

The wider attacks from 1605 onwards had been prompted by the desire to snatch success before the Twelve Year Truce negotiated between Spain and the Netherlands came into force in 1609. Since the truce was never observed beyond the equator they served only to distract attention from the main objective, the islands of Banda and the Moluccas. Verhoeven and his successors, instructed 'to strive after winning these islands for the Company either by treaty or by force', tried both methods. At Banda the chiefs agreed to a trade monopoly but refused a fort, whereupon the Dutch landed in force, built their fort and compelled the chiefs to swear fealty and sign away the monopoly of their mace and nutmeg production. In Amboina the similar agreement, signed in 1603, was renewed. In Ternate a new treaty was concluded with the king, two new forts were built and the Spanish fort on Batjan was taken. By the end of 1609 the Dutch

had established trade from Bantam to the Moluccas and northwards to
Achin, Siam and Borneo and to Japan, where two ships despatched to
Nagasaki were well received, the Dutch being granted imperial protection
and freedom of trade.

The Dutch by treaty or force laid claim to a monopoly of cloves,
nutmeg and mace, and looked forward hopefully to an eventual pepper
monopoly. But before such monopolies could be made effective several
problems had still to be solved. First a more stable, effective administration was needed than that which government by the annual fleet commanders supplied. Secondly, though organized Portuguese resistance in
Indonesia had been broken and the Spanish counter-thrust contained,
there were still the English and many Asian competitors to be eliminated
before prices could be controlled. And thirdly, trade must be diversified.
The Dutch had begun by following Lisbon's example of sending out large
consignments of silver. But what was appropriate to trade in India, the
sink of precious metals, was much less suitable for trade in Java and the
Moluccas where Indian cottons and foodstuffs formed the most profitable
media of exchange; moreover, as trade expanded sufficient European
silver became harder to secure. The Dutch and English had both to learn
what the Portuguese had earlier discovered, that Asian trade must be
driven with the profits of inter-Asian trade, and European silver supplemented with Asian gold and silver.

The administrative problem was tackled by the appointment in 1609
of Pieter Both not as admiral responsible for one voyage only, but as
governor-general in charge of all the company's possessions in the East,
supported by a council of five. Here was the answer to the complaints of
such allies as Johore that Dutch commanders, after persuading them into
alliances against the Portuguese, sailed away leaving them to their fate.
But the Dutch, having appointed their viceroy, still lacked a Goa. Pieter
Both, constantly on the move in the Moluccas, could draw little support
from his widely scattered council. A permanent base was sought therefore, either at Johore or Malacca which commanded the Coromandel
cloth trade, the pepper of east Sumatra and the China trade, or at
Bantam or Jakarta, the supply points for the Moluccas. Jan Pietersz
Coen, director of Bantam and Jakarta, was left to choose. While still
undecided, he was driven to fortify the Jakarta factory by clashes with the
English in Bantam, the growing hostility of its regent and rumours of a
general Javanese conspiracy. When in 1618 the new fortifications successfully resisted attack by the English and the regents of Bantam and Jakarta,
it was decided that the long-sought headquarters had been found. Jakarta,
rechristened Batavia, became thenceforth the focus of all Dutch trade and
administration.

The elimination of competitors was not so quickly achieved. It was one
thing for the seventeen to instruct their governor-general that 'the com-

merce of the Moluccas, Amboina and Banda should belong to the Company, and that no other nation in the world should have the least part', but quite another, with overstrained forces, to achieve that happy end. The Spanish were contained in Ternate, and since there was little demand for spices in the Philippines and Americas and no profit in shipping them to Europe, it was only as suppliers to Macau and Malacca that they proved a nuisance. The English, however, were more serious rivals. After the collapse of Antwerp, English merchants had pushed further afield in search of spices and eastern commodities, first in the Russia Company with its Volga voyages to Persia and then in the Levant Company, tapping at Aleppo the large supplies which escaped Portuguese control. But by 1599 Dutch activities were threatening these Levant supplies: 'if our spices be not brought from Aleppo as in time past, into England . . . our Company shall not be able to defray half of their charges'. The answer was to form the East India Company in 1600 as the spice arm of the Levant Company. The first two English fleets went straight for Indonesia, and if subsequent voyages included the Red Sea and India this was initially only to secure cottons for the purchase of spices at Bantam. Throughout the first half of the seventeenth century pepper and spices were to be much the largest item in the English Company's sales.

However, by the time the English reached Banda and Amboina in search of nutmeg and cloves the Dutch had already made fifteen voyages and secured an exclusive treaty with the Amboinese. Shortly after Henry Middleton reached Banda in 1605, the Dutch arrived, took the Portuguese fort and stopped English trade. Middleton sailed on to Tidore and was well received—and again the Dutch arrived, ousted the Portuguese and by agreement with the sultan excluded the English. Only with the islanders of Ai and Run were the English able to secure a trade agreement, elsewhere though the people wished to trade the English were excluded. The English reply was to encourage smuggling and to foment and support native resistance to the Dutch. Conferences at London and The Hague in 1613 and 1615 failed to ease the tension and meanwhile in Asia the English had extended their bitter competition by opening factories in Sumatra, Java, Borneo and Macassar, and in Siam and Japan. By 1615 open conflict had developed between the two companies in the East. In 1615–16 the Dutch, ignoring English rights, took the factory and island of Pulo Ai; in 1617 they attacked Run; in 1618 Coen, newly appointed governor-general, prepared to crush the English before their support could lead to any general native rising against the scattered Dutch forces. He was backed by the express orders of Prince Maurice and the seventeen to expel all foreigners, friends or foes in Europe, from the Spice Islands. In November 1618, however, Jourdain, the English president at Bantam struck first, attacking Dutch shipping at Jakarta and besieging their new fortifications in co-operation with the Bantam regent. But distrust between the allies saved the garrison and Jourdain dispersed his fleet to collect cargoes. Coen, returning from the Moluccas with sixteen ships, snapped up the English in detail; his elimination of the English seemed achieved.

Then came news of an agreement in Europe between King James and the States General for co-operation between the two companies. Both would supply ten warships for attacks upon the Portuguese and Spaniards, both would share the spices, half the pepper and one-third the finer spices going to the English. Coen and his council were furious at this respite to the English and proceeded to ignore its provisions by conquering the Bandas and Run. The English also failed to fulfil their commitments: their total profits between 1613 and 1621 had been less than 90 per cent, they had lost eleven ships to the Dutch in one year, and now they were dragged into costly operations against Spanish and Portuguese possessions, in Dutch interests rather than their own. By 1622 it was clear that their share in a spice trade cut back by war would not cover their expenditure under the agreement. In 1622 President Fursland closed the factories on Ternate, and in January 1623 his orders went out, on Dutch ships, to abandon the Bandas and Amboina. Then on 27 February 1623 occurred the still inexplicable 'Massacre of Amboina' when Towerson and nine other Englishmen were beheaded on Amboina, charged with plotting to overthrow the Dutch garrison. The massacre marked the end of any Anglo-Dutch co-operation and any English attempt to enter directly into the spice trade.

Coen could now turn to two other aspects of his monopoly policy, the regulation of spice production and the elimination of all those Asian intermediaries who competed in the port-to-port trade and acted as suppliers of spices to the English, Portuguese and Danes. The Dutch had repeated the early Portuguese error of trying not only to monopolize purchases but to push prices down. The producers, tied by forced agreements to the Dutch, either rebelled or turned to wholesale smuggling. The seventeen insisted on buying spices cheap and selling cottons and rice dear. And when Councillor Steven van der Hagen pointed out that the Portuguese, paying more for cloves and permitting free trade in foodstuffs, had made handsomer profits than the company, they replied by issuing instructions for rooting out Asian traders, and when spice production fell heavily, for exterminating the recalcitrant growers. Coen actively supported their views. In 1621 he sailed to crush the Bandanese, long in revolt against Dutch demands. Hundreds were shipped as slaves to Batavia, thousands starved to death in the mountains, while the men of Run were rounded up and killed. Ceram suffered a like fate. The nutmeg lands were then parcelled out to Dutch settlers—Coen approved of Portuguese colonizing methods—to be worked by slaves. For cloves

Amboina and the Uliassers were later chosen as the sole producing areas, and control was sought through the destruction of unwanted plantations, enforcement of low-price delivery contracts and naval patrols against smugglers. From 1636 there were serious insurrections until opposition was cowed by laying waste most of Hitu. The pursuit of similar policies in the more powerful kingdoms of the northern Moluccas led to a mass rising in 1646 which endangered the whole Dutch position, but this too was quelled by mass destruction of clove and sago plantations and the deportation of populations.

Forcible control of production was supplemented by action against Asian competitors. When the Dutch reached Indonesia they found, for example, an active trade at the port of Grisee in Java, with some sixty junks a year sailing with food to Banda and returning with nutmeg and mace. Chinese junks also called to revictual and to exchange silks and porcelains for sandalwood and deerskins. There were also many resident Portuguese and Chinese merchants giving out cottons and copper cash in commenda to Grisee junk masters sailing to the Spice Islands, and a busy trade with Malacca either in Portuguese craft or on junks hired from the king himself. This trade the Dutch destroyed, first by seizing Portuguese shipping, then by demanding that the Malacca trade be abandoned. The king was ordered to abandon his trade with Banda, and when he refused both the Grisee and Chinese junks were seized.

As Portuguese control of the Moluccas weakened in the late sixteenth century, the kingdom of Macassar in Celebes had become another important market for spices and the source of food supplies to the Portuguese in Solor and Timor. After the early Dutch successes many Portuguese settled in Macassar, selling cottons against nutmeg and cloves brought in by Bandanese, Javans and Malays. Both they and the sultan regularly sent junks to Malacca. After 1624 the English used Macassar as their main source of smuggled spices, particularly cloves from Amboina and Ceram where the sultan's influence was strong. The Danish Company, established in 1616, also conducted an active trade between their Tranquebar settlement in eastern India and Macassar. In 1635 the Danes and English shipped some 400,000 lb. of cloves to Europe, nearly three times as much as the Dutch secured, while in eastern India the Danish competition drove prices down from twenty *pagodas* a *maund* in 1631 to four in 1639. From 1616 therefore the Dutch were at open war with Macassar, seizing their junks in the Moluccas while Macassar supported the people's opposition in Amboina and Solor. In 1641, however, the conquest of Malacca released Dutch forces for the Moluccas and in 1642 a large Macassar fleet sailing to aid a revolt in Ceram was destroyed. The back of Macassar's resistance was broken, though conflict dragged on until 1669, and the Dutch monopoly of the finer spices was largely achieved. The immediate cost of monopoly had been extremely high. War had absorbed capital urgently needed for the expansion and diversification of Dutch Asian trade. In the 1620s the Moluccas lost a hundred thousand florins a year, and in the 1630s the loss in Amboina and Banda was little less. The reward came in the 1670s when spices yielded a steady profit of over 1,000 per cent.

The Dutch also vigorously attempted to master the trade in Indonesian pepper. The pepper which had reached Europe before 1600, either via the Levant or round the Cape, was mainly Indian, from the Malabar coast. Indonesian pepper, though widely grown, went to Asian markets. It was this pepper which the Dutch put on the European market as much the largest item in their exports from Batavia and their sales in the Netherlands.

Their main competitors in Indonesia were the English, whose early voyages were directed to the pepper ports of Achin, Jambi and Bantam and whose first returns included over 1,000,000 lb of pepper. They could not be driven out by force, for the powerful rulers of Java and Sumatra would not brook violence in their ports. The Dutch therefore tried to break the less heavily capitalized English by underselling them. The first decade was indeed difficult for London because the combined Dutch and English supplies, plus the traditional Portuguese imports, glutted Europe. But in 1609 King James forbade any pepper imports but the company's, recognizing that 'a free and generall libertie...would be an occasion to overlay the trade, and strangers would of purpose vent their spices at small rates, thereby to enforce our owne subjects to desist from trading'. With their home market thus secured the London Company was able to go ahead with the creation of a network of export centres at Hamburg, Danzig, Amsterdam and Lisbon, at Leghorn, Venice, Naples and Constantinople. By 1615 prices had recovered and imports were reaching 1,500,000 lb. a year, and the offspring of the Levant Company was selling pepper worth £209,623 in Italy and Turkey. The naval disasters of 1618 in Indonesian waters, the general depression of 1620 and the burden of joint operations with the Dutch until 1623 caused a temporary financial crisis, but this storm once weathered pepper exports again rose sharply. After 1626 exports to the Levant in several years topped the million mark, while in the late forties when profit margins were narrowing, total English imports reached a record 3,000,000 lb a year.[1]

The Dutch, though dominant in the European pepper markets, thus signally failed to break their English rivals. Against their Asian competitors, however, they were more successful. When they first reached Bantam they found that this Muslim sultanate had a growing population of foreign traders, Gujarati, Arab and Chinese with Portuguese and Japanese from Malacca. The Gujaratis brought cottons to trade for pepper, some of which was then sold to Chinese junks for Chinese wares. Though their

[1] See K. N. Chaudhuri, *The English East India Company* (Cass, 1965).

trade was not large they had the support of the port master and admiral, both Indians. The Malacca and Malay merchants brought in more cottons for sale against pepper and supplies for Malacca. The Chinese were represented both by resident merchants, important middlemen in the pepper and cloth trades, and by those who came yearly from China to exchange silks, porcelain, musk and copper cash for pepper, spices and sandalwood. When the Europeans arrived with silver they increased their silk imports. They too were well represented in the sultan's council and administration. In 1598 when the Gujaratis shipped 3,000 and the Dutch 9,000 bags of pepper they shipped 18,000.

Dutch attempts to secure the bulk of the Bantam pepper were resisted, both by the port master who sought to safeguard Gujarati interests and by the Chinese who won the sultan's support. The Dutch complained bitterly about such curbs upon their purchases, coupled as they were to rising prices. The regent complained equally of Dutch and English gang-warfare in Bantam and of the forcible exclusion of two French ships by the Dutch in 1617. Coen, then director, replied first by attempting to bribe the port master and then by seizing pepper from Chinese junks, on the grounds that his advances to the resident Chinese had not been repaid in the promised pepper, which they assembled. Though censured by the seventeen for actions 'beyond all the limits of justice', Coen repeated his seizures in 1619. Riots followed in Bantam, the regent forbade advances to the Chinese, and when Coen persisted in violence he banned all sales to the Dutch. The Dutch then withdrew to Batavia, fortified it, beat off a joint English–Bantamese attack as already recounted, and proceeded to blockade Bantam. Pepper prices there tumbled, the Chinese deserted the port, and Bantam never fully recovered.

The Chinese and other traders then moved to Jambi, a rising pepper port in eastern Sumatra. Here again resident Chinese acted as assemblers of the pepper brought down from the interior, and overseas Chinese became its principal purchasers. Both the Dutch and English established factories at Jambi. When the Chinese middlemen, though working on Dutch advances, refused to accept prices lower than their compatriots offered, the Dutch again resorted to violence. The Chinese junks abandoned the trade. Similar violence was used at Japara in Java. Coen's demand for a monopoly of trade here led to an attack on the Dutch factory in 1618. In 1620 Coen sacked Japara, destroyed the English factory, ordered all Gujaratis to be killed, and carried off many Chinese to Batavia. Before the end of the decade the only pepper port at which the Chinese could still freely trade was Banjarmasin in Borneo.

The Dutch by their strength at sea, by the magnitude of their purchases of pepper—perhaps half to two-thirds of the Indonesian crop—and of rice, and by manipulation of local rivalries, imposed their terms on the smaller coastal trading kingdoms in Java and Sumatra. But there were larger Powers, themselves expansionist, which refused to be so used. They were strengthened in their resistance by the ties of a common religion, Islam. Through Achin, the chief port for trade or pilgrimage to the Red Sea, political ties were maintained with Ottoman Turkey, Mecca and the Muslim powers in India, and through Achin Muslim scholars and mystics passed to Java and beyond. Their influence can be seen in the preaching of Islam with which Macassar coupled its expansion in the Lesser Sundas, in the *jihad* waged by Mataram against Hindu Bali, in the Bantam regent's refusal to sign a truce with *kafir* Batavia, and their anti-European propaganda throughout the archipelago. Macassar, as has been seen, was a dangerous commercial threat. Mataram, in central Java, became a military danger. Sultan Agung took Tuban in 1619, Grisee in 1622, Sukadana in Borneo and Surabaya in 1625. He then assumed the title of Susuhunan and demanded Dutch recognition of his suzerainty of all Java. When this was refused two heavy attacks were launched against Batavia in 1628 and 1629. Both failed for lack of supplies, but the influence of Mataram still spread: Palambang in Sumatra paid homage, the independence of Jambi was threatened, closer relations were cultivated with the Portuguese. Only on the fall of Malacca, the alternative to Batavia as an outlet for Mataram rice, and the death of Sultan Agung in 1646 did the Dutch secure a peace treaty with Mataram.

With Achin, the dominant power in north Sumatra, relations were even trickier, for while the sultan was a bitter enemy to Portuguese Malacca, he was also expanding his control over pepper-producing areas in a way scarcely palatable to the Dutch and was at war with their ally Johore. When the Dutch first arrived a weakened Achin was seeking a rapprochement with Malacca and the Dutch were rebuffed. But the Portuguese overplayed their hand and Achin turned to the Dutch. Achinese envoys went to Holland and in 1607 the sultan entered into an offensive alliance and granted the Dutch freedom from customs dues and the exclusion of other Europeans.

Meanwhile the Dutch had also responded to the appeals of Johore for common action against Malacca, and in 1606 the two mounted the great siege which was only broken by the arrival of the Viceroy D. Martim Afonso de Castro. But the alliance proved less rewarding than expected, for since the annual fleets of the Dutch could not give sustained protection, the Johore sultan in 1609 made peace with Malacca, though continuing trade with the Dutch. The alliance also became embarrassing when Sultan Iskandar Muda of Achin set about expanding his kingdom at the expense of Johore, and the other Malay kingdoms in eastern Sumatra. The pepper country of west Sumatra was already his, and by 1623 he had crossed the Malay Straits and taken Quedda, Perak and Johore, and had pushed down eastern Sumatra and threatened Jambi. Achin was within sight of mastery of the Malacca Straits and the pepper trade of Sumatra, to which it allowed European access only under licence. When the Malay rulers of eastern Sumatra led by Jambi now united their forces, the Dutch decided to join them in opposing any further Achinese advance.

The decision was a delicate one, for in safeguarding their trade in Jambi, Indragiri and Palembang of Coromandel cloth against pepper, benzoin, wax and honey, they risked losing the pepper trade with Achin. Indeed, when an Achinese fleet appeared off Jambi in 1624 the Dutch broke their promise of aid to Jambi rather than incur the enmity of Achin. This double-dealing, repeated in 1627, led the Jambi sultan to raise duties on Dutch pepper to $22\frac{1}{2}\%$. The Dutch thereupon shifted to Indragiri, which was attacked in 1632 by Achin, and to Palembang where they did little better since it was closely tied to Mataram and Malacca by the trade in rice against cottons. The awkward balancing act continued, the Dutch trading at both Achinese and Malay pepper ports, half-heartedly encouraging Achinese assaults on Malacca, while seeking to maintain in existence the balancing power of Johore. The problem was only solved by the death of Iskandar Muda in 1639 and the accession of weak successors. In 1641 the Dutch took Malacca, and in 1649 by treaty incorporated Achin and its pepper ports in their monopoly system.

The intense effort to master the pepper and spice trade merely reflects the overriding importance of these commodities in the pattern of Dutch trade. In the years 1619–21 on the books of Batavia they formed 74% by value of the cargoes shipped home, and in 1648–50 some 68% and, though these last three years had seen pepper prices falling, some 57% of the sale proceeds in the Netherlands. It must be remembered also that pepper and spices were a major commodity in Dutch inter-Asian trade, and equally that much of that trade was developed to sustain and facilitate the trade in spices. If Dutch factors were sent in 1601 to Gujarat and in 1605 to Coromandel, it was because the one was the main source of cottons for Sumatra and the other for Java and the Spice Islands, cottons with which pepper and spices could most easily be obtained.

The first Dutch Coromandel settlements were made at Masulipatam and Petapoli, under agreements of 1606 with the sultanate of Golkonda, these being areas noted for printed cloth for the Moluccas. In 1608 further factories were opened to the south in the territory of the Hindu ruler of Gingi and in 1610 at Pulicat in the Vijayanagar kingdom. For some years, however, trade was hampered by the Portuguese at Negapatam and São Thomé, well-established customers in treaty relation with Golkonda, and able to bring considerable diplomatic pressure to bear at the various courts. The Dutch were welcome customers, but their attacks on Portuguese shipping in which Indian interests were often involved, their inadequate capital, and their failure to provide European and Asian goods of the quality supplied by the experienced Portuguese caused considerable difficulty. Nevertheless these troubles, and the sack of Pulicat by the Portuguese in 1612, when a great effort was made to prevent the Dutch establishing themselves in the vital trade in cottons, were weathered. In 1613 some 17,000 pieces of Coromandel cloth were shipped to Indonesia, in 1619 some 83,000, and as Dutch control of the Spice Islands grew and the order was issued to buy spices only with cottons and rice so as to conserve silver for other markets, purchases increased still further. In the 1630s, when a regular blockade of Malacca was instituted, more markets once occupied by the Portuguese were absorbed, completely so when the fortress fell in 1641. Dutch purchases were now impressive, for cotton piece-goods had become the most important item in their inter-Asian trade, while smaller supplies of coarser fabrics were sent to Europe for re-export to the West Indies. Of the later 8,000 pieces were purchased in 1620 and 40,000 or more in 1650.

The Dutch would have liked to monopolize the Coromandel cloth market, but cottons had always been the staple of what van Leur[1] has called the 'peddling trade' of Asia, and in many areas the Dutch could not compete with small Indian merchants working on low margins. In Arakan, Burma, Achin and the overland trade to Siam the Dutch abandoned the attempt, nor could they prevent Indian trade with Malacca, Jambi, Bantam and Macassar. From the 1630s the Dutch did attempt to impose a *cartaz* system, but under the stimulus of increasing European demand and rising prices many powerful Coromandel officials such as Mir Jumla entered the trade on a large scale—as did several Malay rulers and the sultan of Achin. When in 1647 Batavia refused *cartazes* to Achin, Malaya and further east in an attempt to exclude competition, the Bijapur, Golkonda and Tanjore rulers reacted so threateningly and many great nobles so openly flouted Dutch authority that the measure had hurriedly to be abandoned. The attempt to pre-empt supplies by doubling purchases in the 1630s and redoubling them in 1640s also failed. Despite striking increases in the capital furnished to the Coromandel factories, control of the market continued to elude the Dutch.

The second centre for Indian cottons was Gujarat, but though their merchants had reached Surat by 1602 the Dutch decided to buy Gujarati cottons at higher prices in Achin rather than face a major clash with the entrenched Portuguese.[2] In 1614, however, an invitation from the Mughal emperor, at war with the Portuguese, led them to open a factory at Surat. In the twenties, as more capital became available, new factories were opened inland and cottons were shipped in useful but never large quantities to Sumatra and by way of Europe to Brazil and the West

---

[1] J. C. van Leur, *Indonesian Trade and European Influence in the Indonesian Archipelago between 1500 and about 1630* (The Hague, 1962).

[2] The Portuguese had an active trade with Mughal Gujarat and commanded the seaward approaches with forts at Diu and Damão.

Indies. In Gujarat and Coromandel the cottons bought for the Spice Islands were paid for partly with spices, though in both areas demand proved inelastic and on Coromandel the Danes from Macassar offered sharp competition. Pricing the spices needed nice judgement; in Surat the demand for cloves fell by two-thirds because of the high prices fixed by the Dutch, and smuggling by Indian merchants increased. On the other hand, when mace was offered cheaply in 1653 Asian and European rivals bought it at Surat and shipped it to the Levant and Europe, undercutting Dutch consignments to Europe.

Dutch participation in the trade in Indian cottons strengthened their control over Indonesian trade and yielded steady and useful profits. But to Coen this was only a beginning. His vision was of a Dutch commercial empire, as wide as the *Estado da India*, using Dutch settlers like the Portuguese *casados* to conduct the port-to-port trade, self-sustaining so that the trade to Europe might be driven with the gains of trade and the ordinary revenues of the Dutch possessions. Indian cottons, Persian silk, Japanese copper and from China gold, silks and porcelain—all should be welded into one system of trade with Batavia as its hub. He pressed continuously for more money to prosecute these designs and to match the capital deployed by the Iberian Powers. He campaigned again on his return to the Netherlands in 1623: if the seventeen could not furnish the capital required, then open the Dutch East to private enterprise, to the capital of free merchants who should manage the inter-Asian trade and open trade with China, the richest mine the Iberians possessed.

The use of colonists, free merchants, was tried. But when they were given land they proved unenterprising; when allowed to trade they became embarrassing competitors of the company and a cover for the private trade of the company's officials. Since the company would not surrender the whole port-to-port trade to them it was driven by stages so to circumscribe the goods in which they might trade as to make nonsense of Coen's vision. The attempt to open trade with China also failed. Dutch seizure of the Macau–Nagasaki carrack in 1603 confirmed Portuguese statements that the newcomers were pirates, so that approaches to the Canton and Chincheo authorities were rejected. The Dutch intimidation of Chinese junks trading for pepper in Bantam, Jambi and Japara was followed from 1618 by persistent attacks upon Chinese shipping to Manila, designed to break Spanish powers of resistance in the Philippines. Conditions were therefore scarcely auspicious when in 1621 the seventeen ordered Coen to try trade with China again. In 1622 Coen duly sent eleven heavily manned ships against Macau, still an open city. The crushing defeat inflicted on the expedition by the Portuguese citizens and their slaves was followed by Chinese imperial orders to Canton to exclude the Dutch and aid the Portuguese. The Dutch thereupon tried to force the door open, seizing some sixty junks and blockading the coast. 'This trade has been sought with friendship for too long', Coen wrote: but neither his efforts, nor those of Brouwer in 1633 to compel trade succeeded. Driven from the coast and then from the Pescadores by the Chinese, a Dutch base was at last found in south-west Formosa, whence a flourishing trade with Amoy was built up. Spanish expeditions from Manila which established two forts on Formosa never proved a serious danger, and in 1642 both forts were taken by the Dutch. From Formosa a flourishing trade was built up in Chinese sugar. Shipments rose to over a 1,000,000 lb. a year in the 1630s, declined in the 1640s under competition from Dutch Brazil, but flared up again when the Portuguese revolted in Pernambuco in 1645, disrupting Brazilian supplies. There was also a trade in silks, porcelain and cinnamon, much of it directed, as was sugar, to the Asian port-to-port trade.

Once the Dutch had established their indirect trade with China from Formosa they were in a position to supplant the Portuguese in the extremely valuable trade with Japan. The latter had long enjoyed something of a monopoly of the trade between Japan and China, though under the Shogun Tokugawa Iyeyasu (1600–16), there was encouragement of Japanese merchant shipping and a renewal of Chinese traffic with Japan. But the Portuguese had been missionaries as well as merchants and their success in securing converts, welcome while the shoguns were breaking the political power of the Japanese Buddhist orders, came to be looked upon with suspicion thereafter. Their converts, some 300,000 by 1600, were mainly made in feudal lordships of suspect loyalty. The arrival of Spanish missionaries increased distrust, for accusations were rashly flung between the orders and the known political function of conversion in the Philippines led to fear of subversion in Japan. When the Dutch offered to take over the Portuguese role of intermediaries in the China trade, the shoguns were ready to expel the Portuguese and suppress Japanese Christianity. The Dutch reached Japan in 1601 and were welcomed. But they failed to live up to their promise to supply all the goods brought by the Portuguese and in their attacks upon Portuguese and native shipping seemed pirates rather than merchants. Only after their establishment on Formosa were they able to procure Chinese silks and gold to add to Coromandel ray skins, Siam deer skins, and pepper and spices. When in 1637 a peasant revolt in Shimambara turned into a Christian rising against the shogun the Portuguese were expelled. (This despite the fact that the great merchant and banking families of Kyushu had invested heavily in the Macau trade.) The Dutch now stepped into the Portuguese shoes. Through Formosa they shipped Japanese silver and Chinese gold to the whole of Dutch Asia. From 1640 to 1649 no less than 15,000,000 florins-worth of silver was exported from Japan, very much more than shipments from the Netherlands. Since silver was also remitted to Batavia from Persia and Surat and gold from Macassar, the Moluccas and Jambi, it is clear that by 1650 that

Asiatic self-sufficiency of which Coen had dreamed was approaching realization, in respect of the precious metals at least.

The English East India Company may be thought of as the poor man's version of the Dutch United Company, starting with the same plans, but diverging from them under pressure from its wealthier, state-backed rival and the pinch of poverty. Its first objective had been the spices formerly secured by the Levant Company but now threatened by Dutch trade round the Cape. As has been seen, the already established Dutch were able to maintain their commercial lead, and by political manœuvre and straightforward violence to exclude the English from direct trade to the Spice Islands by 1619. The experience of 1619–23, when co-operation with the Dutch was tried, merely confirmed that the London Company lacked the financial resources and quality of organization needed to break into the Far East against well-entrenched Dutch and Iberian competition. In 1623 the English factories in Japan, Siam and the Spice Islands were all abandoned.[1] In the pepper trade, however, the English were able to maintain an important share, sufficient to prevent Dutch control of European markets.[2] Pepper remained the largest single item in their returns, a staple commodity for which a network of outlets was created in northern Europe, the Mediterranean and the Levant, from the firm base of a protected home market.

The company soon realized that a direct trade for pepper with bullion and a singularly inappropriate supply of English goods was inefficient, and that for a glutted European market more diversified returns were needed. The third fleet, of 1607, was directed, therefore, to the Red Sea and Gujarat to procure cottons and was supplied with a pinnace to explore Coromandel, where the Dutch were known to be trading. In 1608 the *Hector* reached Surat where Hawkins, a Levant merchant who spoke Turki, was put ashore to seek from the Mughals capitulations such as the Ottomans granted. He achieved some personal success at court, but the Jesuits there denounced the English as pirates, while Gujarat officials afraid of interruption to the extensive Portuguese trade and of reprisals at sea also opposed admission of the English. Unsupported by any further English fleet Hawkins left in 1611. Merchant envoys sent to court by the fleets of 1612, 1613 and 1614 made little better impression and the Emperor Jahangir prepared to exclude the English altogether. Then the Portuguese, seeking to force the pace, seized Mughal shipping. A savage war followed. While it was in progress, four English ships at Surat were attacked by the Viceroy D. Jeronimo de Azevedo—and completely

[1] During their ten years in Japan the English never opened a trade with China. They were thus denied access to the lucrative bullion trade between Japan and China, to their great disadvantage.

[2] After a truce in Asia had been negotiated in 1635 between the English president and Portuguese viceroy, the English also had access to Goa and the Malabar pepper markets.

defeated him. Sir Thomas Roe, arriving at this juncture as a properly accredited English ambassador, was able to exploit the Mughal reaction against the Portuguese and the English naval victory to secure adequate terms for a permanent English trade in Gujarat. From Surat a net of inland factories was quickly thrown out and the trade in cottons for Sumatra, to which the main pepper trade shifted, was opened up. The value of cotton piece-goods was soon experienced—at Tiku and Priaman in 1612 the English factors had found it paid to buy cottons from Gujarati merchants there rather than buy pepper directly with reals—and as late as 1627 the president in Batavia was still rubbing in the lesson that throughout Indonesia cloth was wanted, not coin, 'clothing being of use but coin, save a little for ornaments, being buried in the ground . . .'. The varieties of cotton had to be right of course, Surat goods for Achin, Broach for Priaman.

The Gujarat factors also experimented with various goods for Europe. Indigo was known from the Levant trade to be a prime commodity, whether the fine quality Biana indigo from the Punjab or the coarser, cheaper Gujarat indigo, and until the 1620s indigo formed as much as seven-eighths of some homeward cargoes. (Coromandel indigo was tried but thought inferior, though the Dutch shipped it in quantity.) English shipments reached 150 to 200 tons a year, and large-scale re-exporting was soon under way, notably to the Levant. In the 1630s the trade levelled off, for the Dutch bought largely and once the change from woad and American logwood had taken place demand proved inelastic. The Gujarat famine of 1630 also damaged the trade, while in the late 1640s West Indian all but ousted Indian indigo.

Two other introductions, saltpetre and sugar, provided helpful but marginal additions to English cargoes, saltpetre being useful as ballast; neither grew to any great importance until Bengal and Bihar were tapped in the 1650s. A far more important innovation was the creation of a market for Indian cottons in Europe. Cottons overland had never competed with European linen, while Portuguese and Dutch shipments had mainly been re-exported to Africa and Brazil. In 1609 the Surat factors suggested calicoes for sheets and Coromandel dyed cloths for quilts and hangings. Soon sample consignments were on the way, and a very deliberate effort was made to create a market in Europe: as the directors said in 1623, 'calicoes are a commodity whereof the use is not generally known, the vent must be forced and trial made into all parts'. The 5,000 pieces of 1613 became 100,000 by 1620 and 221,500 in 1625, say two and a half million yards. Advance was then checked by the Gujarat famine, for the inefficient Coromandel factories could not make good the loss, and up-country purchases at Agra and even Lucknow, and in Sind did not entirely restore the situation. At the end of the period, however, Coromandel supplies did become important, and with the opening of Bengal in the 1650s the advance was vigorously resumed.

The English also had high hopes of one other commodity, Persian silk. This was a royal monopoly, and the shah had for some years been considering a diversion of the trade from the Ottoman-held Levant routes to the Portuguese at Ormuz. The Spanish authorities exchanged several embassies with Persia, whom they were anxious to embroil with the Ottoman enemy, but they showed little enthusiasm for the silk trade, too vast for their merchants to conduct. But the arrival of the English opened another possibility to the shah. In 1617 a first English voyage was made from Surat to the Persian Gulf and by 1619 a factory was fully established at Jask. The factors were soon planning to divert the whole silk trade through the Gulf: after spices, indigo and cotton, now silk would pass from being a Levant to an East India Company trade. In 1619, on receiving a letter from King James, the shah finally made up his mind. In 1622 the Persians besieged the Portuguese fort on Kishin. Joined there by an English fleet, they moved on to tackle Ormuz which fell to the allies on 3 May 1623. This was a major disaster for the Portuguese. Despite savage raiding up and down the Gulf, and notable naval battles with both English and Dutch in the 1630s, they never restored their dominance, though they continued to trade at Muscat and Basra.

The English discussed with the Dutch plans for diverting the whole silk output, 6,000 bales a year, round the Cape. This was beyond their resources for it would have required an annual investment of over half a million sterling. But from the fall of Ormuz both companies were sufficiently active to damage seriously the old Levant trade in silk. The Dutch with their greater capital resources and ready supply of spices secured the larger share of the silk (they were probably better served by their agents with the shah too), for the English had some difficulty in finding cargoes for Persia. But though once Portuguese pressure had eased the Dutch tried to drive the English out by heavy buying, the English held on. When the 1630 Gujarat famine reduced indigo and cotton supplies they too increased their purchases, and by 1640 English shipments of Persian silk exceeded those of the Dutch who, being on strained terms with the shah, switched to Chinese silk. The silk trade did not answer all English hopes, but it filled an awkward gap after 1630—in 1641 half the cargo from Surat consisted of Persian silk—and Persia also proved the most useful Asian market for the sale of English goods. The Persian trade had another, incidental value; ships waiting at Surat or on the Coromandel coast for cargoes to be assembled for Europe were able to carry Indian goods and merchants to the Gulf and back, earning both freight and local goodwill.

Russia also conducted an active trade in Persian silk. Direct trade across the Caspian to the silk province of Gilan began after Ivan IV's conquest of Astrakhan in 1555, and was fostered by both tsar and shah, united in their enmity to the Ottomans. It began as an aside to diplomatic missions and developed into a regular caravan trade conducted by the treasury to the exclusion of private merchants. Raw and boiled silk, damasks, satins and velvets formed the bulk of the imports by the state, while Indian and Persian merchants brought in silk sashes and handkerchiefs and carpets. Indian cottons found no market by this route, however, for the Dutch brought them more cheaply by sea to the Netherlands and so to Russia by the White Sea route. There was also some trade with Khiva and Bukhara and after 1646 there were Russian efforts to open direct trade with India.

The principal Russian export to Persia and central Asia was furs, handled like the silk by a state department in Moscow. The furs were obtained as tribute from the tribes of Siberia, as tithe from private fur traders and, in the case of the valuable sables and black fox, by purchase. At the opening of the seventeenth century they were collected between the Urals and the Ob and Irtysh rivers, but as these hunting grounds were exhausted new territories were opened to the east. By 1628 the Yenisey and Tunguska basins had been reached, by 1640 the Lena, and in 1643 prospectors reached the Amur and travelled down it to the Pacific. The advance of nearly 3,000 miles had taken only fifty years, for the pattern of great rivers linked by easy portages made it simpler to press east than to work the headwaters of the rivers. With the arrival at the Amur, rich in furs and grain, the stage was set for Russian conflict with China, the first major power encountered in the whole landward sweep across Asia.

The advance was initially made by Cossacks and infantry under state direction, and thereafter by trappers and traders pushing out into the wilds like Canadian *coureurs des bois*. Behind the trappers and Cossacks came the state, demarcating tribal districts, and setting up fortified head-quarter towns under *voyevodas* charged with collecting the fur tribute from the tribes. In the wilder areas subordinate blockhouses were established where hostages were held and furs assembled. A separate body of customs officials collected the tithe from private trappers and issued the tax certificates which passed the consignments through the posts westwards to Moscow. The tribute and tithe furs were despatched annually from district headquarters to Moscow where the treasury merchants sorted them and arranged for their sale, either retail or wholesale. Some of the furs were used in payment of salaries, the Russian economy being only partially monetized, others as gifts to embassies and to church dignitaries, and others in the silk trade with Persia. Other furs were exported by the Dutch and English trading via Archangel, a rapidly growing port, through the Swedish staples on the Baltic, and by the highland route through Smolensk to the fur centre of Leipzig.

During the first half of the seventeenth century Russia had come to control all northern Asia and the Dutch, from Batavia and Malacca, to control the trade of the Indonesian Archipelago and the sea routes eastwards to Japan. The English Company, though under-capitalized and still without any permanent jointstock, without steady state support and even exposed by royal action to the licensed rivalry of Courteen's Association, had nevertheless created a viable trading system centred upon India. The Spaniards in the Philippines had successfully held their ground there and in Ternate. Even the Danish trade between Tranquebar and Macassar survived. The one Power which steadily and irretrievably lost ground was the Portuguese.

For the Portuguese the half century was one of desperate expedients and agonizing choices as they sought to defend the whole sprawling territorial and commercial structure of the *Estado da India*. Against Asiatic rivals they had with some difficulty held their own, but for dealing with European opponents, whose coming also activated latent Asian enmities, their resources were inadequate. They could expect few reinforcements of men, money or ships from Europe, for Portugal had to produce cannon fodder for Spanish armies, try vainly to hold West Africa, and at great cost defend the line of coastal settlements in Brazil.[1] In the East they had to make do with existing and local resources, improving their organization and choosing how best to deploy them.

At home, the creation in 1604 of a Council of India, headed by an ex-viceroy, with responsibility for all Indian affairs except the despatch of fleets and purchase of pepper which remained with the Treasury Council, did much to speed and invigorate decision, notably in the timely preparation of fleets. It was a misfortune that the jealousy of the duke of Lerma and the Treasury Council led to its dissolution of 1614. There was also an overhaul of the administration and personnel of the India House. In India the independent powers of the Goa municipality were curbed, and the conde de Redondo, going out in 1618, carried lengthy instructions for tightening administration and streamlining correspondence. In both Goa and Ceylon elaborate new land registers were prepared so as to maximize revenues and steps were taken to ensure that *casados* maintained the required cavalry and musketeers. In such ways administrative efficiency was improved.

In the military field the most important reforms were the raising of a militia in 1622, captains being appointed to train both the European and native inhabitants, and to exercise them regularly. The regular troops were also organized on the lines of the Spanish *tercios*. A serious effort was made to provide for the scientific fortification of the main settlements by the grant of profits from crown voyages, a tax upon cities, and the despatch of a trained engineer with Flanders experience, Antonio Pinto da Fonseca. Some care was also taken to ensure that commands, granted as reward, were occupied by competent rather than merely deserving men,

---

[1] It is noteworthy that whereas in 1638 a fleet of 41 ships with 5,000 troops was assembled for the relief of Brazil, only a handful of ships and 500 men were sent to hard-pressed India during the viceroyalty of Pero da Silva, 1636–9.

though reliance was still placed on noble blood rather than sheer technical skill.

These, however, were defensive measures; to expel the Dutch and English intruders ships were needed capable of hunting theirs down. Initially shipbuilding and repair was left to contractors whose interest it was to build a few, over-large, under-gunned merchantmen rather than larger numbers of easily manned, easily handled 450-tonners capable of facing Dutch ships which were, as Queyroz put it. 'suitable for the purpose of trade, pillage or war'. The reform came, thanks to the representations of João Pereira Corte Real and Viceroy Linhares, but came too late. The fleets from Lisbon were too small, and mainly intended for a round voyage, to permit the building-up of a fighting force at Malacca. Some galleons were built in western India, admirable ships, but Lisbon's orders to build more were never accompanied by funds, and those of the *Estado* being based on customs dues steadily dwindled. The imposition of special taxes, borrowings from the charitable foundation, the Misericordia, the auction of public offices in 1614, the creation of a new monopoly of Ceylon cinnamon never supplied funds adequate to the need. Moreover there was divided counsel about whether to use available funds on galleons or upon the undecked, oared vessels long successfully used against Asian enemies. Even so experienced a commander as Andre Furtado da Mendonça plumped for oared ships; it was years before disastrous experience showed the folly of pitting such ships and boarding tactics against the heavy Dutch artillery. A temporary answer was found in abandoning the carrack for routes east of Goa in favour of swift, light-draught galliots. From 1618 this saved the Macau–Nagasaki trade, but the Dutch were soon building pinnaces to counter such tactics, while their tall ships blockaded Goa from 1621 to 1623, in conjunction with the English; sealed off the Malacca Straits from 1630 to 1641; and from 1636 for eight seasons blockaded Goa again—'a grip upon the heart itself'.

Meagre resources of men and material were misspent on technically inefficient instruments. They were also wasted by being spent in driblets in the attempt to hold everything Portuguese. This was partly a matter of pride, but the fact that the Portuguese were settlers, not temporary company employees, also made it more difficult to accept the loss of territory which had become an Asian home. Money continued to be spent therefore on numerous forts and settlements, often of little military value and profitable to individuals rather than to the state. 'Experience has shown us', wrote Ribeiro, 'that these three colonies (Ormuz, Goa and Malacca) should suffice us, and all the forts and settlements that we make we draw from these strong points . . .' Nevertheless the Indian authorities continued to prepare to seize Dutch Pulicat, to engage in war with the petty rulers of Malabar, even to launch plans for new conquests up the Zambesi. Strategic indecision is seen most clearly, however, in the failure to choose between the defence of Malacca and the south and the conquest of Ceylon. By 1601 the Portuguese were masters of the Ceylon lowlands and poised for the clinching blow against Kandy; they were also preparing to deal with Achin and to despatch a fleet capable of expelling the Dutch from the south. A choice was required, but none was made. The request that one carrack of Lisbon troops be earmarked for Ceylon was refused, only 340 Portuguese were sent from Goa, and in 1603, when a bare ten miles from Kandy, Azevedo's 800 Portuguese and 300 *topazes* were driven into disastrous retreat. The half-measure was enough, however, to starve the fleet sent to Malacca of reinforcements so that, unsupported for three years, it fell back exhausted from the defences of Ternate. In 1611, 1617, 1627 and 1638 Portuguese forces reached Kandy, a noose of forts was drawn round the kingdom, its territories were devastated by raids, its eastern seaboard was occupied and fortified. But at no time were sufficient troops supplied from Lisbon or Goa to hold what had been won, nor sufficient resources made available to ensure the loyalty of the Sinhalese troops. Meanwhile Malacca, its trade and revenues dwindling, received sufficient reinforcements to survive Achinese attack and Dutch blockade, but never enough to reimpose control upon the Straits and the sea routes eastward.[1] This Portuguese dilemma was exploited to the end by the Dutch. While already blockading Goa, van Diemen in 1637 ordered an attack on Ceylon in alliance with the Kandian ruler as preparation for a final push against Malacca. The move provoked a forestalling attack on Kandy by Diego de Melo which ended at Gannoruwa in the destruction of the whole Portuguese force. Batticaloa, Trincomalee and Negombo fell to the Dutch in 1639 and 1640, but more important still Malacca fell after a five-month siege in January 1641. Despite the respite given by the ill-observed ten-year truce signed in 1641 between the Netherlands and D. João IV of Portugal, the Portuguese were unable to prevent the loss of Ceylon in 1656—and of their Malabar settlements in the following decade. By grasping at too much they lost all.

Within some sixty years the *Estado da India* was thus destroyed as an imperial structure, reduced to some East African footholds, Goa and the western Indian settlements, Timor and Macau. The Spanish Philippines fared better, retaining their outlying position in the Moluccas and decisively throwing back Dutch attacks on the Philippines themselves. But for Portuguese and Spaniards alike the first half of the seventeenth century had involved an immense, unproductive outpouring of men and materials, which failed nevertheless to prevent loss of trade and territory. Yet throughout the period the Iberians continued to devote a considerable

---

[1] It is to be remembered, of course, that the choice was not limited to either Ceylon or Malacca. There was also the Persian and English threat to Ormuz to be coped with. Here also, too little and too late led to disaster, with the fall of Ormuz in 1623.

proportion of their manpower and resources, not to defence but to missionary endeavour. Chaunu has persuasively argued that Don Quixote and Saint Teresa were of more account to the Spanish crown than the balance of payments of the Philippines, upon whose maintenance perhaps 15 per cent of Spanish American revenues were expended.[1] Expenditure on the church in the *Estado* was equally heavy. Foreign observers were always struck by the number of clergy and churches in Portuguese India, while officials, notably the Viceroy Linhares, became increasingly critical of the burden. Complaint brought no change of policy, however, and as Iberian power declined the claim to rights of patronage became the more jealous in face of papal pressure to deploy French, Italian or German missionaries in Asia.

The best defence of such claims to patronage was that missionary success was still being achieved. In the early seventeenth century mission stations were pushed up the Zambesi from Mozambique, one Jesuit became patriarch of Abyssinia and another archbishop of the Syrian Christian church in India. In north India Jahangir succeeded Akbar as Mughal emperor without any diminution of support for the Jesuit mission at his court, while in China the year 1600 saw the establishment of the first Christian missionaries at Peking. Two years earlier, in Japan, the death of Hideyoshi had ended a burst of persecution, and permitted an active resumption of missionary work which was to carry the number of converts made towards the 300,000 mark. Not all these achievements proved lasting. Over-zealousness brought failure in Abyssinia and south India, while in the Mughal north, despite Jahangir's intellectual and aesthetic interest, the Jesuits achieved no imperial conversion and had to be content with a diplomatic role. In Japan, too, the change of ruler brought no lasting relief. The shoguns, having broken the independent power of the great Buddhist sects, were unwilling to allow the development of Christian communities, strong particularly in the lands of the Outside Lords, and looking for leadership beyond Japan. They were increasingly suspicious of the political designs of the Spaniards, and after the coming of the Dutch and English were less commercially dependent on Macau and Manila, the more so as there was a vigorous state-sponsored expansion of Japanese shipping throughout south-east Asia under Iyeyasu and his immediate successors. In 1616 a new ban was placed upon missionaries, and there was increasingly severe and brutal persecution of them and their flocks from the Nagasaki martyrdoms in 1622 until the crushing of the popular revolt at Shimambara in Kyushu in 1638. The Christian community under Japanese leadership proved remarkably tenacious, but the closing of Japan in 1639 made any further European aid impossible.

In China hope remained, for at Peking the learning of the Jesuits secured their official recognition and the conversion of important scholars

---

[1] P. Chaunu, *Les Philippines et le Pacifique des Ibériques*, pp. 267–8.

and officials. And while the family of the last Ming emperor, driven into exile, was being baptized, other Jesuits were obtaining office under the incoming Manchu dynasty. The cultural importance of this post at court has been widely noted, but it also provided the prestige under cover of which Portuguese and other Jesuits, and Dominicans and Franciscans from the Philippines were able to make widespread gains in the provinces. The Jesuit mission in China was also responsible for a major experiment in mission methods, the presentation of Christianity without a European garb. Ricci, the first head of the Peking mission, literally shed his black habit in favour of a Confucian scholar's robes, he would have adapted the pagoda to Christian uses, he allowed his converts to share in family worship of their ancestors and public honouring of Confucius, he used terms taken from the Chinese classics as names for God. In Japan, that most sympathetic of all provinces, the Jesuits adopted a similar approach, making use of Buddhist terms for God, heaven and religion. And drawing upon the Chinese model, the Jesuit Roberto de Nobili at Madura, in the heart of south India, made the still greater experiment of presenting himself as a *sannyasi* and Christianity in a Hindu dress. He lived austerely, a vegetarian dressed in the ochre robes of an ascetic, teaching in Tamil, drawing his illustrations from the classic Sanscrit texts, keeping company with Brahmins, avoiding both outcastes and Europeans. All three experiments, the Chinese and Indian especially, were responses to the problem of making Christianity acceptable to people with high cultures of their own, and without benefit of either the bribery of commerce or the coercive force of arms. The experiments had but a limited success, though they caused immense controversy within the missionary orders and the church. There was considerable doubt even among the Jesuits in China, not resolved by a conference in 1628, while Dominicans and Franciscans from the Philippines secured the condemnation of Jesuit accommodation first in Manila, and then in 1643 in Rome. In India Nobili's provincial and the archbishop of the newly created south Indian see were both ready to approve of the experiment and to defend it from the early missionary experience of the church in Europe, but many Portuguese Jesuits, who combined patriotism with faith, denounced conversion which was religious but not political. The Jesuit visitor Pimenta condemned Nobili in 1610, and the primate de Sa secured a further condemnation in 1619 at a conference in Goa. Ultimately, however, explanation directed to Rome secured guarded papal approval which allowed both experiments to continue until the end of the century.[1]

The importance of the Madura or Chinese missions was intellectual, for the problem they raised is still perhaps unsolved. Their rewards moreover were not in numbers, but in an understanding which permitted an exposition to Europe of the main elements of great Asian civilizations.

[1] See Vol. v in this series, Chapter XVII.

There were three mission fields, however, which yielded more conventional triumphs. In Portuguese India, though a decline in church building reflected the straitened circumstances of the state, and some of the older orders like the Franciscans were accused of greed and disciplinary disorders, new missions, Augustinian, Theatine, Oratorian and Carmelite injected fresh vigour, while increased concern for language, with the production of grammars, dictionaries, catechisms and devotional works made teaching more effective. In Ceylon as in India the power of the state was used to harass the unbeliever and reward the convert. But the resistance of the strong Catholic communities from Galle to Negombo and in the Jaffna peninsula to Dutch attempts at conversion in the second half of the century testifies to the quality of Portuguese mission work, especially in the education of the young, to their zeal and numbers, and to the continuing pastoral care of the Goan clergy. To similar factors must likewise be ascribed the rapid progress in the Philippines. By the beginning of the period nearly 500 missionaries had entered the Philippines, and the assignment of particular regions to the various orders encouraged the learning of the local dialects. Schools were started early, followed by colleges for higher studies, both for boys and girls, and Dominican and Jesuit universities in 1611 and 1623, together with printing presses. Though the Dutch blockade between 1618 and 1628 and renewed attacks after their conquest of Malacca imposed a heavy burden on the Filipinos, the process of Christianization continued and by 1650 had reached virtually the whole lowland population.

Against these missionary efforts and results of the Iberian Powers, the English in this period could set nothing and the Dutch but scant success. At home Protestantism was still engaged in arduous combat with domestic Catholicism and the forces of the Counter-Reformation. There were few men to spare for overseas endeavour, and as yet no missionary instruments comparable to the Jesuits or the Propaganda. Where Spain and Portugal sent out hundreds, the Dutch sent out tens, the English ones and twos. Moreover, where the Portuguese took all Ceylon, the Spaniards the Philippines as their field, the English looked no further than to the spiritual needs of their ships and factories, and the Dutch in the main to the basically political task of turning their Asian Catholic subjects into loyal members of the Reformed Church. Their *predikants* were servants of the company, posted where it chose and accorded only a very modest status—the lay readers were positively despised—yet expected to make head against powerful orders of dedicated men permanently supported in the mission field. Only on the animists of Formosa and the completely isolated Roman Catholics of Amboina was any wide or lasting impact made.[1]

As is perhaps to be expected the influence of the Dutch in Asia was

[1] See C. R. Boxer, *The Dutch Seaborne Empire, 1600–1800* (London, 1965), pp. 132–54.

political and commercial, not religious—except in the negative sense that they inspired a vigorous Islamic reaction in the Indonesian world, and undid the work of Catholic missionaries. The Portuguese discovery of the Cape route initially reduced the prosperity of Egypt and Venice, their fleets and *cartaz* system displaced some Muslim merchant-shipmasters of the Indian Ocean, though not the Muslim traders ashore who assembled goods for shipment, their customs houses laid new tolls upon the traditional monsoon routes of Asia: they modified but did not overthrow. The Spaniards with their majestic Pacific voyages opened a New World route and a new trade in American silver against Chinese silks and porcelain. The Dutch achievement lay somewhere in between. With the English they certainly ended the Levant trade in pepper, spices and indigo, and directed to the Cape route some of the cottons and silks which had passed by Aleppo and Alexandria. Revolts in Ottoman Syria, Baghdad and the Yemen mark the impoverishment this caused. The Dutch discovery of the 'roaring forties' route to the Sunda Straits likewise by-passed older monsoon *entrepots*, cut costs, and incidentally revealed the existence of Australia and New Guinea. But their most drastic innovation was certainly the imposition of an absolute monopoly of Moluccan spices with a consequent disruption of the whole pattern of Indonesian seaborne trade. The political readjustments the Portuguese imposed on Malabar were here repeated on a far larger scale.

More generally the coming of new European Powers, itself the sign of economic expansion and vigour, enlarged markets in the West for old staples like pepper and spices, so that Sumatran pepper was added to the traditional supplies from Malabar. There was also a notable increase in the export of coarse cottons for Africa and Brazil, 'nigger cloths' and slave clouts, while the English pioneered quite new markets for finer cottons to be used in European dress. This was paralleled by the growth of the trade in silk, not only traditional Persian and Chinese but also, after the 1640s, Bengali too. These were positive gains though they involved no radical change in the mode of production. The creation of a more unified world economy did bring losses and readjustments—Indian indigo succumbed to West Indian, Japanese had to struggle with Swedish copper for markets, or Bengal and Chinese sugar with the produce of Javanese plantations—but increased demand and competition raised payments to the Asian producer while lowering prices to European and Near Eastern consumers. There are some signs, too, of changes in Asian commercial organization, as in the emergence of rudimentary joint-stock forms in India.

Lastly the northern Europeans initiated a change in attitude towards Asian peoples and states of some significance. The Portugese began from the position that to those outside the Christian fold no duties were owed, and that with Muslims the natural relationship was war. They early accepted, however, that trade agreements with Muslims were licit, and by the seventeenth century had long been in regular political relationship with Muslim Golkonda and Bijapur as with Hindu Vijayanagar too. Historians like Couto and Bocarro made clear their acceptance of Asian kingdoms into the comity of nations. Ecclesiastical councils in Goa and Manila denounced any attempt at forcible conversion and demanded good treatment of subject people. The crown also made it clear that in the state's eyes the convert enjoyed full citizenship, whatever social colour bar might operate. And though most regular orders, however zealous for Asian souls, recruited only Europeans, the Jesuits at least admitted both Japanese and Chinese and, late and reluctantly, Indians, too.

The Dutch and English began with a pragmatic acceptance of the full sovereignty of Asian kingdoms and sought formal relations with the Achinese or Mughals on the lines of the capitulation system of the Porte. Hugo Grotius writing as counsel to the V.O.C. stressed in his *Mare Librum*, published in 1608, that Asian states 'now have, and always have had their own Kings, their own governments, their own laws and their own legal systems'. It was on their sovereignty that he rested his rejection of Portuguese claims based on papal decrees, arguing from Aquinas that 'Christians . . . cannot deprive infidels of their civil power and sovereignty merely on the grounds that they are infidels'.[1] As late as 1650 the seventeen were still stressing that here in Asia were 'free nations, where we find laws and do not have to bring them'. But whereas experience had mellowed the Portuguese it harshened the Dutch. Their *predikants* came to abominate the blackhearted Muslim, their merchants any who would not sell cheap and buy dear. The Dutch attempted therefore not only to secure a monopoly of spices, but to secure it at low prices fixed by themselves. To achieve this the seventeen in 1612 accepted Brouwer's memorandum on the destruction of Asian shipping and trade, and in 1613 ordered Reynst to curb Dutch private trade. When Reael and his council argued that Asian traders had a part to play, and that the spice producers must have their share of profit too, he was removed and Coen installed. His massacres of the islanders, his violence against Chinese and Gujarati traders, his battles with the English made them blench, but not draw back. To English queries about *Mare Librum* in the Moluccas Grotius could only reply that 'contract extinguished the liberty of the law of nations'. If *predikants* demurred at the uprooting of peoples they were sharply called to heel. Liberal voices such as Reael's or Steven van der Hagen's went unheeded. The new colonial era was ushered in to Coen's dictum: 'There is nothing in the world that gives one a better right than power and force added to right.'[2]

[1] See C. H. Alexandrowicz, *An Introduction to the Law of Nations in the East Indies* (Oxford, 1967), Chapter III.
[2] Boxer, *The Dutch Seaborne Empire*, pp. 98–9.

CHAPTER XXII

THE EUROPEAN NATIONS AND THE ATLANTIC

NINETY years after the discovery of America 'we of England could never have the grace to set fast footing in such fertill and temperate places, as are left as yet unpossessed' by the 'Spaniards and Portingales'. The Dutch too, still absorbed in their struggle for independence, had got no further than organized defiance of the Spanish trade monopoly. Their East India Company in 1609, as Pieter Both was ordered to acquire 'a convenient place and, for our contentment, a fort which shall serve as a rendezvous for our whole Indian Navigation', was still feeling its way towards unified control. More intent on trade than on possession of land, they had not yet staked a claim in the West. The French also, seeking fish and furs rather than colonies, had as yet but the most tenuous hold even on the lower St Lawrence. No country's colonies bore comparison with the Spanish settlements in the Caribbean and on the Spanish Main, or the Portuguese in the Atlantic islands and Brazil; and though the English and Dutch controlled an increasing share of the East Indies trade, and the English and French maintained two or three hundred ships on the Grand Banks of Newfoundland, Habsburg predominance had not been seriously challenged. But a challenging thesis had been formulated.

England had taken formal possession of 'Virginia'—the whole of eastern America from 30° northwards—and Raleigh's Roanoke voyage had also seen the use of a jointstock organization which distributed the costs of establishing colonies among merchants and speculators. The Roanoke venture, moreover, was a definite attempt at settlement, and that purpose was then transferred from Virginia to Guiana (as it had previously been transferred from 'Norumbega' to Virginia). True, Raleigh's voyages of 1595 and 1596, and even of 1617, made little mark; but a formal English title was established when in 1609 Robert Harcourt annexed all of Guiana between the Orinoco and the Amazon, and Thomas Roe's settlers in the Amazon delta survived from 1611 to 1617. The Elizabethans had 'disputed the Atlantic with Spain' and had won their place in it. In so doing, they stated, and vindicated, a claim that 'prescription without possession availeth nothing'. Where the Spaniards had not actually settled, the English (or any other power) might claim by right of first discovery or of actual possession. Though not accepted in the treaty with Spain of 1604, the English case was strongly put; and it was not withdrawn.

French and Dutch rebuttals of the Habsburg claim were equally clear;

but the lead lay with the English, and their interest was turning to the central coastal area of the vast district which the Elizabethans had called Virginia. In 1603 Bartholomew Gilbert, searching for survivors from Roanoke, landed in Chesapeake Bay; and though he was killed there, in 1605 an expedition sponsored by the earl of Southampton 'happened into' Pemaquid River and was delighted at the fertility of the land. At the same time Bartholomew Gosnold coasted down from Newfoundland, naming Cape Cod as he came, the Bristol Merchant Venturers sent two voyages under Martin Pring, and the East India Company sent to Greenland and (probably) to Labrador in search of a Northwest Passage. In 1606 these interests resulted in a royal charter for a Virginia Company. This grant, covering the whole area from 34° to 45°, gave all the land between 34° and 41° to a London 'colony' while the land between 38° and 45° went to a 'colony' to be organized in Plymouth and other western cities. The land between 38° and 41°, common to both of these 'colonies', was to be a neutral zone and neither company (for that was what the 'colonies' in the grant were) was to establish a colony within a hundred miles of any settlement by the other. Both Virginia companies were to be under a Council of Virginia, resident in England, with subordinate councils to manage separate colonies as these were created.

The purpose was clearly to establish colonies; but the petitioners who had secured the charter included a group of London merchants and several bodies of West Country merchants, as well as nobles and gentry who were primarily anxious to colonize. So trade was closely regulated. The settlers were to be supplied with necessities from England by a series of joint-stock voyages, the goods to be kept in a common warehouse and then distributed by a 'cape-merchant' acting on behalf of the investors; and (as in all such companies in England) the investors alone were called 'adventurers', the emigrants being 'planters'. For return cargoes the process would work in reverse, the cape-merchant shipping the colonial produce to England, to be disposed of for the adventurers.

The business of finding settlers remained with the Council for Virginia, which accomplished little; and the merchants profited so little that by 1609 a new charter, and a new approach to Virginia, was demanded. Something had indeed been accomplished. The Plymouth Company had sent out Henry Challons in 1606; designed for north Virginia, he was captured by Spaniards in the West Indies. The Bristol merchants then organized a survey of the coast, and in 1607 Sir Ferdinando Gorges set up a short-lived colony on Kennebec River. But the West Country merchants then turned to the Newfoundland fisheries rather than to Virginia. The London Company, in the meantime, had sent out Christopher Newport, who in April 1607 established Jamestown in Chesapeake Bay—the first enduring British settlement in Virginia. But the site was low-lying and malarial; disease, starvation and Indian raids reduced the settlers to about fifty by September 1607, and the council was at odds with the settlers. Jamestown was saved by John Smith, a soldier of fortune who had even been imprisoned by the first president, Edward Wingfield, but who was made president in September 1608. Smith curbed the settlers' obsession with gold-seeking, started voyages to explore inland, made peace with the Indians, and organized the construction and defence of Jamestown. But despite reinforcements only about fifty people remained by the autumn of 1608.

At this juncture James I, and Sir Edwin Sandys at court and in parliament, stood good friends to the Virginia Company. A new charter, granted in May 1609, defined Virginia as lying two hundred miles north and south from Point Comfort and extending 'from Sea to Sea', and granted all this land and the islands off the coast to a unified London Company on a joint-stock basis. Shares, valued at £12 10s. each, were bought enthusiastically. Planters were to receive one share for each person whom they transported, but control lay in London, where the council of the company appointed Lord Delaware 'absolute governor' and sent nine ships under Sir George Somers and Sir Thomas Gates to reinforce Jamestown. This expedition gave Britain her claim to the Bermudas, where Gates and Somers were wrecked; it also finally established the colony at Jamestown, for seven of the ships brought about four hundred new settlers in August 1609. Yet while Gates and Somers were wintering in Bermuda Jamestown was going through its 'starving time' and the sixty survivors who welcomed Gates in May 1610 insisted on embarking for England. John Smith, hurt in an explosion, had gone home already and the colony was only continued because the homeward-bound ships met Delaware in the mouth of James River, bringing his commission as governor, three ships, and supplies and reinforcements.

Delaware returned to England in 1611, but he held his position as governor until 1618. His deputies, Sir Thomas Dale and Sir Thomas Gates, ably managed the colony, while another charter, of 1612, granted the Bermuda islands and gave the stockholders power to appoint the governor and council of Virginia and to make laws provided they were not contrary to those of England. The laws already promulgated were then codified (known henceforth as 'Dale's Laws'), with strict regulation of economic and social life, including a veto on trade with Indians. Farming for the common stock gave place to individual land-holding in 1614, and the resultant industry and enterprise stabilized and invigorated the whole colony.

The Dutch and French were as convinced as the English that the power of Spain depended on wealth got from the New World; and to challenge that power both were ready to defy Spanish ownership. In fact, the Dutch had won away the wealth of the East Indies trade both from the Portuguese discoverers and from their Habsburg successors; for when the spices had been brought home 'the great rich purses of the Antwerpians ... ingrossed them all into their own hands'. Similarly, Spain was equally powerless to prevent the wealth in American gold and silver from creating inflation at home, and to forbid its transfer to other lands.

But though the wealth of the New World may indeed have been no source of strength for Spain, other powers found Spain's strength always formidable, and their own efforts at trade and settlement always in danger. The Dutch in particular, dependent on their *entrepôt* trade, were seriously threatened when they were excluded from the Iberian ports to which the eastern spices were brought. They moved into the eastern trade themselves, and having co-ordinated their local *Direkties* into a comprehensive state-sponsored Dutch East India Company in 1601, they sent the Londoner Henry Hudson on an exploring voyage in 1609. His object in 1609, as in two previous voyages in the service of the English Muscovy Company, was to find a passage to the East by way of Greenland and the north-west. But when baffled by ice off Nova Zembla he crossed the Atlantic to seek the passage along the American coast. Working on a report, derived from Verezzano, of a great western sea close behind the coast of Virginia, Hudson also knew that John Smith (with whom he was in correspondence) had proved that no passage existed near Jamestown. Hudson worked south from Penobscot Bay to Delaware River, whose volume showed that the western sea could not lie near the coast; so he turned north, and then north-west up Hudson River until stopped by shoal water in the Catskill mountains. The land was 'the finest for cultivation that I ever in my life set foot upon'; but the passage to the East was as remote as ever.

The Dutch therefore planned a further voyage in which Hudson might discover the passage, leaving on one side the possibilities of colonization which he had revealed. The English also were avidly interested in eastern trade and a Northwest Passage. So, when Hudson had landed at Dartmouth on his return from America, the English forbade him to depart for Holland, and in 1610 some members of the English Muscovy Company sent him on his last tragic voyage, to Hudson Bay. Though Hudson's voyage of 1609 was not followed up, the Dutch had nevertheless acquired a claim to a central part of the north American Atlantic coast and its hinterland.

The French also maintained that effective occupation was necessary to give title to lands in the New World, and their constant voyages to the Grand Banks of Newfoundland trained numbers of seamen who accepted the crossing of the Atlantic as a commonplace, to be undertaken without any particular preparation or acclaim. Moreover Tadoussac, at the mouth of the Saguenay River, had early become a rendezvous at which French fisherman and traders met Indians (especially the Montagnais from the north) and got furs in great quantities. Such furs made the younger Hakluyt's mouth water, and he included a fur trade among the benefits to be secured by colonization.

By 1609 Samuel de Champlain had voyaged up the St Lawrence to the Lachine Rapids above Montreal, he had collected Indian tales of the Western Sea (Lake Huron), of Lake Erie and Lake Ontario, he had tried settlement on the coast of Maine and in Acadia, and had explored down the coast to Massachusetts Bay and Cape Cod. Always seeking a route to the west, he devoted himself to the St Lawrence, and in 1608 he and his patron de Monts secured a fur monopoly for a single year on condition of establishing a colony inland. Prudently fraternizing with the traders at Tadoussac, they pushed on up river, built their small fort at Quebec, and spent the winter there, troubled with scurvy. Then, journeying further up river in the summer of 1609, perhaps in search of the Western Sea, perhaps to offset the end of his brief monopoly by taking trade to the Indians 'in their habitations', Champlain met the Hurons, a great trading tribe of Iroquois origin but committed to endless war with the Iroquois confederacy of the Five Nations. With the Hurons, as previously with the Algonquins, Champlain concluded an alliance; and as they set out on the warpath he and two more Frenchmen went with them, by Richelieu River to Lake Champlain and so south to Lake George. There at a point near the site of the future Fort Ticonderoga, they met the Mohawks, one of the Iroquois nations, and the Frenchmen intervened in the battle with their arquebuses and, against all the odds, brought victory to the Hurons, a notable victory, which hardened the pattern of French Indian alliances, by shedding of blood and attendance at tortures, into hostility to the Iroquois.

Though Quebec in 1609 was indeed a minute post, and there were only about a hundred settlers in all Canada, Frenchmen were already familiar with the land, their policy was clear, and their ambitions had been aroused. Champlain had journeyed south by inland waterways to the back of the New England coast, and Frenchmen had spread westwards and southwards from the St Lawrence in swift forays. Travelling in company with Indians, they sought the Western Sea—and furs and fur-trading Indians—and their voyages were bound to cut across English moves westwards from the coast. The English, moreover, had just entered into an alliance with the Iroquois Confederacy to whose defeat Champlain had so markedly contributed; for as the reinforcements of 1609 came to Jamestown John Smith was peacefully buying land from the Iroquois.

Although in the period 1609–10 English, French, and Dutch appeared equally alive to the possibilities of North America, with Champlain at the back of the Adirondacks, Hudson in Dutch employ sailing up to the

Catskills, and the newly charted Virginia Company stabilizing Jamestown and exploring Chesapeake Bay, it was the English who first moved forward with serious purpose. In the colonies of Iberian origin which had arisen in the century and a half since the Age of the Discoveries, the heavy work of agriculture was not performed by Europeans, and trade was not the business of the settlers but was in the hands of great corporations. Representative cross-sections of the European countries had not moved overseas until England began the emigration of balanced communities, of both men and women, who intended to work for their livings, clearly distinct from the earlier shipments of unaccompanied males, unused to work because they were gentry, or malefactors, or soldiery.

Virginia set the pattern; so vigorous was Virginia by 1613 that the colonists sent their ships north under Samuel Argall to destroy the French settlement at Port Royal. He took many of the settlers and their priests prisoners, and on his way back to the Chesapeake he also compelled the Dutch on Manhattan Island to haul down their flag. By the time Argall became governor (in 1617) Virginia boasted 350 inhabitants, including sixty women and children—a small but balanced community spreading north from Jamestown to York River, with tobacco grown for export, and with mixed crops grown for consumption. Stockholders, however, were getting little profit, and the company was by 1616 split into a 'court party' which favoured royal supremacy and authoritative government, and a 'country party' which favoured the extension of democracy. Sir Edwin Sandys and the earl of Southampton in 1618 secured control for the 'country party' advocating emigration, land grants for subsistence crops, less tobacco, and legislation by consent. A 'great charter of privileges, orders, and Lawes', granted in 1618, gave the settlers a right to elect the first colonial legislature, which met, on a single-chamber basis, in 1619. Local matters, relations with the Indians, religious observances, decorous conduct, and subsistence crops were discussed, and Dale's Laws were revoked, settlers were given the freedoms which they would have enjoyed in England, and a hundred acres were granted to each freeman who had paid his own passage out, with a second hundred acres if he was also a stockholder in the company. Other grants of land were made to individuals and syndicates within the company, which thus became something of a land-development corporation though it still had the duty of stimulating emigration. The balance of the community was levelled to some extent when in 1619 the company shipped out ninety maidens as wives for the bachelor colonists; and a new feature was introduced when Dutch shippers brought negroes in the same year.

Virginia was far from completely democratic; grants of private land stimulated enterprise but exaggerated inequalities, and tobacco as an export crop upset its economic balance. Between 1617 and 1619 tobacco exports rose from 20,000 lb. to over 60,000 lb, and the colonists, despite an import duty, flooded the English market and provoked a quota limit of 50,000 lb.—which drove them to ship to Holland. The 'Tobacco contract' then ordered Virginia's tobacco to be shipped to England only, gave a monopoly of the English market, and thus restricted both colony and metropolis so that each should supply the needs of the other within an imperial economy.

Notwithstanding the tobacco crisis of 1619–21, emigration to Virginia continued, stimulated by uneasy conditions in England and diversifying society as occasional artisans and merchants emigrated. Tobacco remained the great attraction, land the measure of social status. Though by 1629 tobacco did not normally pay production costs, the quantity steadily increased, from 500,000 lb. exported in 1628 to 4,000,000 in 1640. The immigrants did not all prosper, or remain in Virginia; and many died. Though 3,000 arrived in the period between 1621 and 1624, population only totalled 1,275 in 1624. Yet the colony was on its feet, immigrants arrived steadily, and about 1,000 a year came as indentured servants, contracted to serve from four to seven years under the plantation-owner who paid their passage. Vagrants, convicts, and sometimes 'naughty women' were also shipped out, and Virginian society early began to develop along 'plantation' lines, with considerable estates worked by hired or compulsory labour as the basis for an oligarchic community dependent on a single export staple.

Though malaria and mismanagement retarded growth, virgin soil was in demand and plantations spread through the tidewater area and then slowly inland, with small planters and time-expired servants dependent on wealthy planters in many ways, often for the use of stages and quays to load tobacco, or as middlemen to market or purchase the crop. The resultant encroachments on Indian lands almost brought ruin when in 1622 the Indians attacked the settlements along James River, killing the cattle, destroying a new ironworks, and killing about 350 settlers. The colonists adopted a policy of destroying the Indians' corn and driving them away from the settlements; and they still pushed outwards in search of good tobacco land, maintaining an uneasy peace until 1644, when again the Indians rose, and again were severely defeated.

Though Virginia survived, and even flourished, feuds, and dissatisfaction with the company, made royal intervention easy, and after a judicial enquiry the charter was annulled in 1624. The company was in fact almost insolvent and could not properly support the colony; and though the royal government which followed, from 1624 to 1642, had many defects, at least it left the company to act merely as a trading concern, without responsibility for government. Lands not yet granted away were given out on generous terms, and abolition of the cape-merchant and company-supplies brought new vigour to the economic life of the colony. With prosperity went constitutional development, and as their governor became a royal nominee, with a nominated council, the Virginians in 1629 again secured the grant of their General Assembly. This, with adult male franchise for elections to the lower House of Burgesses (soon modified by a property qualification), was a great vindication of democracy. It was secured at the cost of a tobacco monopoly, granted by the Virginia assembly, which gave Charles I revenue for his impending war with France. Here was a colony which could make a significant contribution to war expenses and to the economic and political balance of the mother-country. The colony, rising to about 5,000 people by 1635, was largely oligarchic; but it was neither royalist nor aristocratic; it would make its contribution on its own terms.

The annulment of the Virginia Company's charter made possible the establishment of Maryland, a proprietary colony owned by Lord Baltimore. George Calvert, first holder of that title, after earlier experiments tried to establish a colony at Avalon in Newfoundland in 1623; but French opposition, religious difficulties consequent on his conversion to Roman Catholicism in 1625, and the raw climate led him to seek some 'warmer climate of this New World'. Virginia attracted him, and despite opposition he secured the unoccupied land between Chesapeake and Delaware Bays by royal grant in 1632. But George Calvert having died, the second lord was given propriety of the soil, with the right to govern modelled on the palatinate jurisdiction of the bishop of Durham. He had power to make laws, appoint officials, coin money, grant titles of nobility, exercise jurisdiction and make war and peace. The token payment to the crown of two Indian arrows was supplemented by a fifth of any gold or silver ores, settlers were always to be guaranteed the same rights as Englishmen, laws must be consistent with those of England, and the proprietor must owe allegiance to the king.

Though the western boundary of Maryland was fixed, from the sources of the Potomac to the Atlantic, and Maryland clearly had no sea-to-sea claim, the other boundaries were uncertain, and disputes with Virginia soon developed, beginning with that over Kent Island in Chesapeake Bay. But much careful thought went into this colony. Religious disputes were to be avoided, good relations were to be maintained with Virginia, 1,000 acres were to be given to anyone who brought out five working men, with less in proportion down to heads of families who got a hundred acres for themselves and their wives and fifty for each child. Provisions and implements were supplied, trained artificers were attracted, and the first two ships, arriving in 1634, brought some twenty gentlemen, mostly Roman Catholics, over two hundred artisans, mostly Protestants, and three Jesuits priests. After a first settlement on an island in the river, the colony moved to the well-chosen site of St Mary's, overlooking the Potomac. But the proprietor's plans were not all fulfilled. Religious toleration in itself roused opposition; for the Jesuits took offence when in 1637 Baltimore declared that the Roman Catholic church must be subject to the law; they began to plan for a separate régime, bought land eagerly, and were forbidden to hold more land than was necessary for their support. Puritans, in the meantime, had entered Maryland in considerable numbers, often by re-migration from Virginia, and finding the Roman Catholic bias unacceptable, had begun to work for a more popular constitution. The charter to Baltimore provided for legislation with the advice, consent and approbation, of the freemen or their deputies, but the exact status of the freemen in the legislative process was vague, and the first assemblies in 1635 and 1638 were small and appointed by the proprietor; they nevertheless rejected a code of laws proposed by Baltimore and, fortified by popular election in 1639, vindicated their right to initiate laws instead of merely 'passing upon them'. Thereafter assemblies were sometimes elective, sometimes not; but the governor and his council, nominated by Baltimore, sat with the freemen and dominated them.

In 1644 the Maryland Puritans, assisted from Virginia, broke into open revolt, drove their governor into exile and secured the appointment of a recent immigrant from Virginia, William Stone. Helped by Virginian Royalists, Baltimore reasserted his authority, but he accepted the Puritan régime and even made half the members of the governor's council Protestants. Religious toleration was nevertheless maintained, and in 1649 Baltimore secured a Toleration Act which, while forbidding blasphemy and maintaining the divinity of Jesus Christ, granted free exercise of all forms of Christian worship. But religious persecution continued in Maryland despite the Toleration Act; and in 1650 Baltimore was forced to accept a bicameral legislature in which the popular representatives were separate from his nominees.

Yet Protestant sectarians could find a refuge there, and the soil and climate gave them many advantages. Navigable water in the tidewater area made transport to Europe cheap and easy, wheat and subsistence farming soon gave way to tobacco, the early semi-feudal manors were replaced by plantations, and the free householders yielded to indentured servants, and then to negro slaves, on the plantations. When in the 1640s grants of free land to immigrants were diminished, and the tidewater lands were taken up by large estates, small men and time-expired servants spread into the hinterland, where good land was still to be got. The new pattern of settlement reflected religious cleavages with the Roman Catholics making St Mary's their centre and the Protestants concentrating round Annapolis. But, subject to the limitations of its proprietary constitution, Maryland offered a unique blend of economic prospects and religious freedom. So by 1650 the colony was firmly rooted and boasted a population of about 8,000, most of them prosperous agriculturists.

While tobacco culture gave Virginia and Maryland an export staple, many hoped that furs and fish would provide a basis for settlement to the north. From such hopes sprang the New England colonies. The name had come into use when in 1614 John Smith, sent back to America by Sir Ferdinando Gorges, surveyed the coast from Penobscot River to Cape Cod; he described the area as 'New England', and returned with a reliable map and reports of the fertility of the territory which led Gorges to secure the foundation of a 'Council for New England', established at Plymouth in 1620. This was a joint-stock company for colonizing, its members mostly aristocratic adventurers who had no intention of emigrating, or even of financing and organizing settlement. Having secured the grant of all lands, from sea to sea, with a monopoly of trade and fishing, between 40° and 48° North, they sub-allocated these rights on condition of the setting up of colonies. Surveys were non-existent and the same land was sometimes granted several times; the grants included the allocation to a New England Company of a considerable area in the locality of the later state of Massachusetts, and of what was later to be Maine and New Hampshire (the land between the Kennebec and Merrimac) to Ferdinando Gorges and John Mason, who in 1629 allocated the land to the south and west (New Hampshire) to Mason and that from the Kennebec to the Piscataqua (Maine) to Gorges. Their boundaries with the New England Company's grant were uncertain, but their two territories were sparsely settled, so no great problem arose. Poor soil and long winters contributed to the slow development of these lands, but uncertainty of title and the attractions of Massachusetts were at least equally important.

Massachusetts owed much to the example of Virginia, and to the existence of organizations for government, finance and even of shipping, which facilitated the mechanics of emigration. But it revealed a new and compelling desire to emigrate. The Thirty Years War undoubtedly upset the export-market for English woollens; but that market had already been uncertain for over a century. The constitutional struggle in England, also, without doubt made men seek a quiet home elsewhere—and Englishmen habitually moved in search of work and of land in a way which made them a far from static population. These things, though not new, achieved a new importance as the state churches of the seventeenth century became increasingly intolerant. True, there was an air of tolerance abroad. But it was a tolerance enshrined in *cujius regio eijus religio*, the tolerance of Sully as he wrote that 'there is nothing in all respects so pernicious as a liberty in belief . . . and there would be no hardship in obliging all [a state's] inhabitants, either to conform—or quit the country'.

This doctrine brought numbers of Dutch, and later Huguenot, refugees to England; and in 1608–9 it carried from Scrooby and Austerfield some three or four hundred English Separatists to reside, first at Amsterdam and then at Leiden. Small farmers and artisans for the most part, they found that to join the Dutch gilds they must first 'lose their name of English'; and, nationalism apart, there was a strong corporate spirit in them. Having migrated as a body, with their pastor, they did not wish to merge with their Dutch neighbours; but it was difficult to preserve their identity, especially as their children grew up. America seemed to offer a home where they might preserve both their English character and their independent churchmanship, and by 1617 the decision to cross the Atlantic had been taken. Having explored the possibilities of settling in the lands claimed as New Netherland, the Separatists eventually agreed with the holder of a grant of land under the English Virginia Company. They secured a grant of land south of the fortieth parallel but at such distance from Jamestown that they should form a distinct body, and accepting James' vague statement that he would not molest them as adequate guarantee for freedom of worship, they organized a joint-stock company to finance their voyage. The 'planters' were to get one £10 share each, while 'adventurers' promised to raise £7,000, to be repaid from the common stock into which all produce from the colony was to be paid, the common stock to be dissolved after seven years. After much hard bargaining, during which many withdrew, the Separatists then chartered a small ship to bring them to England, and then on to America. The adventurers were also concerned to transport another, larger, group of English dissidents, and their agreements almost amounted to an arrangement to transport a couple of shiploads of indentured servants to America, bound for seven years in return for their passages.

Events emphasized this aspect when in September 1620 the *Mayflower* sailed from Plymouth with a mere thirty-five Separatists from Leiden, but with sixty-six emigrants (not all of them 'Saints') from London and Southampton. She made land in late November at Cape Cod, far north of any land ascribed to the Virginia Company and in territory allocated to the Council for New England. Since that council habitually sub-allocated its lands, this mattered little; but the 'Pilgrim Fathers' had no title to their soil. The Leiden contingent, however, had a strong corporate spirit, and the Pilgrims forthwith combined into a body politic, to make laws and constitutions for a colony. Landing on the heels of a smallpox outbreak which had decimated the Indians, they found stores of corn on which they subsisted while they explored the Cape Cod area and decided to remove across Stuart Bay to Plymouth. There they built a common house and divided the town land by lot, each householder building his own house and bachelors being required to live with some family. Agricultural land was farmed in common and, helped by friendly Indians, the Pilgrims got through their first winter. But their strong individualism, the vigour of their family lives, and shortage of food, soon led to the abandonment of common landholding.

This change was put in hand by Governor Bradford against the advice of the London adventurers; it produced greatly improved work, but in 1624 the adventurers withdrew their support, though they still had claims on the trade of the settlement, which was beginning to prosper, with furs to supplement its agriculture. Accordingly in 1627 a syndicate of settlers, led by their governor, undertook to buy out the adventurers, paying £1,800 by annual instalments of £200 and recompensing themselves by a monopoly of the fur trade for six years. The communal system was then completely abolished, cattle were imported, trade begun with other settlements, and there was even a corn surplus for export to England. Population grew from 300 in 1630 to 3,000 in 1640, new towns sprang up, and as the Pilgrims secured a grant of their land from the Council for New England (at first, in general terms, in 1621, and then with specific boundaries, giving title north to the Kennebec River, in 1639) the colony expanded. By 1637 it had outrun the Mayflower Compact with its General Court where all freemen assented to laws, and elected the governor and his councillors. So the practice of sending representatives from outlying districts, adopted in 1636, was confirmed in the 'Fundamentals of Plymouth' in 1639.

The Pilgrims had shown that the New England area could trade furs, and could support an agricultural population in much the same conditions as those of northern Europe. They had shown too that North America could offer a refuge for dissenters. Plymouth was therefore followed by several attempts to establish colonies, including two expeditions to Weymouth (one under Sir Ferdinando Gorges' son) and one ribald attempt at a refuge from the restraints of English life, at Mount Wollaston. Little was accomplished, but New England was becoming better known and better appreciated.

Among others, a group of merchants from Dorchester in 1623 set up a small fishing post at St Ann, which later moved to Salem. The Dorchester merchants sought a grant from the Council for New England but that body, in 1628, sent John Endecott, an intransigent dissenter, to take over the post; and Endecott concluded that a satisfactory settlement needed an autonomous grant. Accordingly, in March 1629, Endecott and twenty-five others, probably supported by the earl of Warwick, were incorporated by royal charter as the 'Governor and Company of Massachusetts-bay in New England' and given all the land, from sea to sea, within a line running from just north of the Merrimac River and a line running three miles south of Charles River—land which had already been granted to the Council for New England. Although the Massachusetts Bay Company's charter contained no special religious clauses, it did not specify that control must rest with the adventurers (or their committee) in England. Consequently the company could take power to control its affairs to America, and this possibility was developed when a predominantly Puritan group bought control and, in 1629, elected John Winthrop as governor.

Winthrop, lord of the manor of Groton, Suffolk, a graduate of Cambridge University, was a considerable man in his locality, but by 1629 was oppressed both by his own debts and by certainty that the wrath of God must fall on England. New England would offer means to depart from the corruptions of the English church without separating from that church; the 'elect', destined for salvation, could there find a refuge. So in 1629 Winthrop and other educated and respected eastern counties Puritans formulated the 'Cambridge Agreement', promising to take themselves and their whole families to New England provided they were able to take with them 'the whole Government, together with the patent' for their colony, 'to remain with us and others which shall inhabit upon the said Plantation'. These were men of substance, planning to take their servants with them and help neighbouring yeomen and artisans, determined to set up a community in which the same sort of educational opportunities as they had enjoyed should be available, in which trade as well as agriculture should flourish, and in which they might possess civic rights which England denied them, without interference in their religious lives. The charter of the Massachusetts Bay Company was ideal for their purpose, and was in fact taken to America by the first emigrants, organized by the company.

Winthrop himself led the first convoy of four ships in March 1630; by the end of the year seventeen ships had sailed, carrying over 2,000 emigrants. Such a movement by men who had capital equipment for settlement (stock, ploughs, seed and labour) naturally spread rapidly over the land. The settlers took over Salem and spread through the Boston area, setting up subsidiary communities. But although there were wealthy men among them, the Massachusetts settlers did not develop anything like plantation agriculture. Their model was the English mixed farm, and the soil of New England lent itself to this purpose, and to the development of urban and trading communities as counterparts to such an agriculture. The rivers were comparatively short, of little value as highways to transport the settlers' produce to the coast if they spread out in the hinterland; and excellent harbours gave access to ocean-going shipping and encouraged a commercial and industrial development which was alien to Virginia and which made towns and township meetings vitally important in New England. So, although the Massachusetts settlers rapidly covered the land in and around Boston, they did not penetrate westwards; rather, they faced to the sea and developed shipbuilding, lumbering, sea-fishing, and maritime trade as essential parts of their economy.

After a setback caused by hardships and high mortality, the 'Great Migration' of English Puritans gathered way in 1633 and continued for a decade during which about 20,000 people sailed for Massachusetts. By the time the Civil War broke out, despite deaths, re-emigration, and further emigration to other colonies, twenty-two towns had been established, and the population of Massachusetts was about 16,000. By that time at least sixty-five preachers had moved into the colony, many of them graduates of Cambridge, all imbued with some form of Calvinism, accepting the clergy as the authority from whom the civil officers should take their tone, and ultimately their instructions. Under John Cotton, a former Fellow of Emmanuel College, Cambridge, the 'Puritan Pope of the Massachusetts commonwealth', convinced that God had never ordained democracy as a fit government for either church or commonwealth, Massachusetts turned its back on democracy and became a theocratic oligarchy. First, however, the colony had to secure its position, and when Charles obtained a court order quashing the charter he met delays and defiance, which caused him to let things be. So the colony survived both the challenge of royal authority and a challenge in 1639 by Sir Ferdinando Gorges and the Council for New England. Rule apparently rested with a General Court, consisting of the 'freemen' of the colony and empowered to elect the governor and his assistants. But the 'freemen' were the stockholders of the company, and in 1630 these numbered only twelve; and they soon dropped to eight. The unenfranchised in 1631 secured a compromise by which citizenship rested, not on stock in the company, but on church membership. Yet the governor and his assistants had still to be elected from among the stockholders, assistants were elected for life, and they and the governor alone could make laws. The triumph of oligarchy was mitigated by the admission of over a hundred new freemen, but the great majority of the settlers were left outside the franchise and were not even admitted to the electoral roll because they were not (and for the most part did not wish to be) members of the Puritan congregations. For, of the 20,000 who migrated to Massachusetts during the first decade, less than 4,000 were members of a congregation. In theory the churches were merely purified versions of the established church of England, but in practice they were congregations of the 'elect' and each member must give some proof that he was among those who would be saved. Church membership became a privilege bestowed by priest and congregation, and the resultant oligarchy led both to a reform movement within Massachusetts and to re-emigration from that colony.

A tax for the fortification of Boston soon evoked protests from Watertown and other outlying settlements, who vindicated their right to send deputies to consult about taxation. Then, in 1634, Winthrop was forced to produce the charter, which revealed that the assistants should be elected annually and had no power to make laws; the towns asserted a claim to send deputies to the General Court, the right of all freemen to attend, or even to send proxies to, the meetings in May at which elections were made, to the ballot and annual elections. But although many small victories were gained over the oligarchy, there were still only 300 freemen in 1640 and the oligarchy had ensured that within the General Court all measures must have a majority both of the deputies from the towns and of the assistants, considered as separate bodies. In effect this gave a bicameral General Court and gave the assistants a veto over the deputies. Matters came to a head in 1644 when the legislature was formally split into two Houses, each with a veto over the other. This left the way open for power to pass either to the deputies or to the assistants; and Massachusetts remained in the grip of a small minority of clergy and conservative laymen. In church affairs each congregation managed itself and elected its own pastor; but admission to a congregation was highly selective, and from 1634 onwards no new congregation could be formed without approval of both church and state.

Town meetings, however, admitted many to the franchise who were not entitled to vote in the General Court of the colony: even 'cottagers' who were not landowners attended meetings although they could not vote, and management of local affairs soon slipped into the hands of these meetings, where local officials were elected (including justices of the peace and constables) and a body of overseers developed to manage the day-to-day affairs of the towns. Massachusetts, even so, was unacceptable to many. The powers of the assistants were too great; and since the only law administered was the common law of England, as adapted to circumstances by the magistrates, the deputies demanded a written code in 1636, and again in 1637. But they were unsuccessful until 1641, when the *Body of Liberties* was adopted, with trial by jury, and punishment only according to the law. But the death penalty might still be inflicted for blasphemy and witchcraft, and the liberties ensured guaranteed freedom from arbitrary punishment rather than active participation in government. When the *Body of Liberties* was revised in 1648, to become the *Laws and Liberties of Massachusetts*, the new code gave non-freemen the right to attend town meetings, courts and councils, and to present petitions; but they still could not vote, and although Massachusetts had a vigorous coherence as a colonial society, self-supporting and self-reliant, it clearly had grave limitations and was subject to ever-growing criticism.

Among the critics stood Roger Williams, once of Pembroke College, Cambridge, a man of sound scholarship, blameless life and uncompromising views. He had emigrated in 1631, and since Massachusetts insisted that its church was not separated from the church of England and Williams refused to officiate to 'an unseparated people', he moved from Boston to Salem, then to the Pilgrims at Plymouth, and then back to Salem despite protests from the General Court of Massachusetts. For him, church and state should be separate, each with its own tasks and discipline. He supported private judgement in religion, and legal equality for all sects, but he rejected that union of church and state upon which the establishment of Massachusetts was based. He was on even more tender ground in denouncing the Massachusetts Company's claim to lands which, he maintained, belonged to the Indians. Williams was inevitably censured, and being unrepentant was required to leave the colony in October 1635. In England his doctrines would have cost him dear, but before he could be shipped home he fled from Salem, tried to found a community on Naragansett Bay and then bought from the Naragansett Indians the land on which, in 1636, he founded the town of Providence, based on a covenant in which religious liberty was accepted and church and state were separate. Providence had no charter, and no legal title to its territory. Yet it soon grew into a community of hardworking agriculturists who produced surpluses for sale, and attracted others who sought a like freedom.

By 1644 there were four separate communities at Naragansett Bay, on Rhode Island, all with different beliefs but all determined on a liberty of conscience which Massachusetts denied, and all bound to the separation of church and state. First came Anne Hutchinson from Boston, banished because, being a woman, she meddled with religious matters, teaching that personal belief was more important than formalized observances, and grace than good works. Despite the friendly atmosphere of Boston her banishment was inevitable after she had admitted that her only justification was direct revelation from God; and she, her husband and their supporters, followed Williams to Rhode Island in 1639, to buy land from the Indians and found the community of Portsmouth. Within a year her strongest supporter, William Coddington, seceded and set up a rival community at Newport, at the southern end of Rhode Island. Then, in 1643, another principal supporter of the Hutchinsons, Samuel Gorton, set up his independent community at Warwick. Anne Hutchinson left Portsmouth in that year on the death of her husband, going to Long Island and then to Eastchester (where she was murdered by Indians). But the three early settlements of Providence, Portsmouth and Newport had already drawn together, in fear of Massachusetts, fear of Indians, and broad tolerance and sympathy; and Williams had gone to England, to secure a parliamentary charter in 1644 for the 'Providence Plantations'. Empowered to set up a civil government, they agreed in 1647 that representatives from the towns should form a General Court, but the town meetings could initiate legislation, and referendum could veto proposals from the General Court.

Much more truly democratic than Massachusetts, this federation (to which Warwick was speedily admitted) was too individualistic to be stable, even with Roger Williams as its first governor. Harried by both Massachusetts and Plymouth, each claiming its lands despite the purchase from Indians, Rhode Island was known as 'Rogue's Island', for not all religious refugees proved reliable citizens. But it was tolerant and prosperous, it survived the Civil War and got its charter renewed at the

Restoration, and it retained a homogeneous urban character and expanded slowly since most of the citizens were city-bred and the great harbours of Naragansett Bay helped commerce grow.

While Massachusetts had thrown off the Rhode Island towns as a democratic offshoot, the Pilgrim Fathers had sent an expedition in 1632 to explore Connecticut River and set up a trading post in 1633 on the site of the later town of Windsor. A fur trade was their object, but the soil proved fertile, and a group of English gentry claimed the land under the grant to the Council for New England and in 1635 sent John Winthrop Junior to set up Saybrook on Long Island Sound—for Lord Saye and Sele, and Lord Brooke, were the chief backers. Massachusetts, also interested, only set up a minute outpost at Wethersfield until in 1636 the congregation of Newtown secured permission from the General Court to move to the valley of the Connecticut since land for cattle was already scarce. But the Newtown pastor, Thomas Hooker, though an orthodox Puritan, was opposed to the Massachusetts oligarchy and sought government by consent of the governed. The Newtown congregation moved to Hartford, Connecticut, over a hundred strong, with their cattle and their household goods, other congregations followed their example, and within a year Watertown had sponsored Wethersfield, Dorchester had set up Windsor despite the claims of Plymouth, and Roxbury was responsible for Springfield. The General Court of Massachusetts insisted that the Connecticut congregations must continue under that colony, but a compromise was reached in which Massachusetts was only to appoint commissioners for the new towns for one year. By May 1637 there were some 400 citizens in the four 'river towns', and though Springfield turned out to be within the rightful bounds of Massachusetts, Windsor, Hartford and Wethersfield united to convene a General Court to carry on a provisional government which lasted until in 1639 the Fundamental Orders of Connecticut were drawn up, with a governor and a General Court on the normal colonial model, but with no criterion of church membership in the franchise, and no reference to the king. Authority came only from the people, and there was a limit on the tenure of the governor; but he had to belong to an approved congregation, the franchise was limited to 'all that are admitted Inhabitants of the severall Townes', and even under Hooker not half the men were admitted as freemen. Connecticut was no extreme democracy. It was, however, far less oligarchic than Massachusetts and, with its fertile land and with Long Island Sound at its disposal, it throve with both agriculture and trade to attract settlers.

The numbers in Connecticut are not quite certain, but it is clear that the towns were growing fast. Despite divergencies they were dominated by a common Puritanism, and they were tied to Massachusetts by a common frontier against the Indians. Official English policy was 'not to drive the Indians from their habitations by violence ... but to harbour our people so neere to them in places where they inhabitt that they may teach them by their christian and civill conversation how to live holyly towards God and wisely according to reason and justice', and migrants were instructed to ingratiate themselves with the Indians, and in particular not to abuse their women or mock at their nakedness. Consequently Indian relations in the northern colonies had on the whole been satisfactory and there had been no great movement to drive out the settlers.

But in 1636 the Naragansetts murdered a Massachusetts trader, and Massachusetts ordered the notorious John Endecott to slaughter the Naragansetts on Block Island, bring the women and children to Boston, and go on to avenge a Virginian trader who had been killed by the Pequots. Endecott destroyed the Naragansett villages, disregarded the protests of the governor of Saybrook, and sailed up Thames River to slaughter the Pequots. He then returned to Boston, leaving the Pequots united in anger with the Naragansetts. Only Roger Williams preserved the Connecticut settlers; he persuaded the Naragansetts to make their peace, to send an embassy to Boston, and to desert the Pequots, who attacked Saybrook and ravaged Connecticut. Massachusetts standing aloof, in May 1638 Connecticut organized its own militia; then Plymouth, and even Massachusetts, sent to help against the common danger. Under John Mason and John Underhill, with Naragansett allies, the colonists' force surrounded the great Pequot village on what is now Pequot Hill and burned it and all in it, shooting down those who tried to escape. About 400 Pequots fell in this 'sweet sacrifice', which was followed by other overwhelming victories. The Mohawks, like the Naragansetts, turned against the Pequots, and while the men were killed, the boys were taken as slaves to the West Indies and the women and girls as slaves to Massachusetts—for Indians captured in a just war were deemed forfeit in their lives and persons.

The savage Pequot War enabled Connecticut to expand more rapidly than might otherwise have been possible, and it gave the diverse English colonies an uneasy unity. John Mason, who led the Connecticut troops, for example, had claims to land which later came to be New Hampshire, where settlement was slow until in 1637–8 the intolerance in Massachusetts which had led to settlement in Rhode Island and Connecticut drove John Wheelwright and over thirty supporters of Anne Hutchinson to set up the town of Exeter. Other settlements followed; and the Massachusetts Bay Company maintained its claims and took over the territories in 1641 (to rule them until 1679, when New Hampshire became a separate and royal colony). The New Hampshire settlements did not federate, largely because they were under no great threat from Indians, yet they felt involved in the Indian relations of other colonies, and John Mason's activities in Connecticut revealed the common problems of the English colonies and gave an appearance of unity which affected other European powers at least as much as it impressed the Indians.

In the meantime, in Maine, small farming and fishing villages had indeed arisen, but no self-governing community was founded before 1649. But two extreme Puritans, Theophilus Eaton and John Davenport, brought a community of prosperous trading-folk, chiefly from London, to Boston in 1637 and, deciding that even Massachusetts showed laxity in doctrine, removed to Long Island Sound. There, in 1638, they founded New Haven. Buying land from the Indians, they set up a Bible Commonwealth which in adherence to the scriptures, subordination to the clergy, and oligarchic intolerance, outran even Massachusetts. Eaton held office till his death in 1658, and his followers led the advance of the English into Long Island and southern Connecticut. Over a dozen towns sprang up—Guildford, Milford, Stamford, Southwold, Fairfield, Greenwich, Southampton, Easthampton, Gravesend, Westchester and Hempstead—and in 1643 New Haven, Guildford, Stamford and Milford formed a federal government, tied to the scriptures and to church membership but with a general court of representatives from the towns. The magistrates were required to observe 'the judicial laws of God' as delivered to Moses. New Haven had no charter, and no title to lands by allocation from any company or colony. Its neighbours claimed its lands, and it was especially at feud with Connecticut (which secured its annexation in 1662, when Connecticut got a charter from Charles II); but it enjoyed quiet development, and it was among the four colonies which formed the New England Confederation in 1643.

The formation of the 'United Colonies of New England' derived from Connecticut's fears of Pequot vengeance and from realization that England, distracted by the Civil War, could neither discipline nor protect the colonies. But Indians were not the only danger; the Dutch and French were equally menacing. 'The French continually encroach and arm the natives for civil war, who kill and steal when they can', wrote the governor of Massachusetts in 1636. But the Dutch possessed the rivers, and the harbours at the mouths of the Hudson and Connecticut, which were the keys to English trade, co-ordination and expansion. After Henry Hudson's voyage of 1609 the trade in furs had attracted a few Dutch adventurers to Manhattan but such attention as the republican party, dominant in Holland, could give to colonial rivalry went to the East India Company. Agricultural settlement in America found few supporters, and the claim which Hudson had conferred on the Dutch was neglected. William Usselincx however, a refugee from Flanders and one of the greatest merchants of Amsterdam, in 1614 came forward with proposals for a West India Company. Dutch merchants on Manhattan were still few in numbers but they were driving a lucrative trade, and when Samuel Argall on his return from Acadia in 1613 made them haul down the Dutch flag he stimulated them to secure from the Estates General the Ordinance of 1614, which gave a monopoly for six years of new trades to be opened up by discovery. Definite proposals for a West India Company were again defeated, largely because they entailed hostilities with Spain; but Dutch explorers sailed through Long Island Sound, on north to Cape Cod, up Connecticut River to the site of Hartford, and past the south shore of Long Island to Delaware River and so inland.

This exploration was followed by a charter to the United New Netherland Company, conferring ownership of all land between the North River (the Hudson) at 45° and the South River (the Delaware). Seeking furs rather than agricultural land, the New Netherland Company pushed inland, set up its small Fort Nassau, moved the site to Albany and there, in 1618, agreed to supply arms to the Iroquois (who still smarted from their experience with Champlain), in return for which the Iroquois would bring their fur trade to the Dutch. The New Netherland Company failed to get its monopoly of trade renewed, but the Iroquois alliance brought so much peltry that ideas of settlement developed, and the round-the-world voyage of Lemaire, coinciding with the predominance of Maurice of Nassau and the Orange party, brought willingness to create a West India Company, and to challenge Spain if necessary. At one time there seemed to be a probability that the Pilgrims might settle under the New Netherland Company, but while the Estates General were working out details for a company which would be responsible for a colony the Pilgrims sailed under English auspices.

To complicate matters, the Virginia Company also claimed Manhattan and the Hudson River territory. Since war with Spain seemed imminent, the Dutch were not anxious to quarrel with England, yet the Dutch West India Company, chartered in June 1621, with control over Dutch navigation and trade on the coasts of America between the Straits of Magellan and Newfoundland, was given power to appoint governors and other officials, to administer justice, build forts, and make treaties with barbarous chiefs. It also had to defend its territories and to maintain (though not to provide) twenty warships. Control lay in the College of Nineteen, which ostensibly collated the views of five local *Direkties* but in fact soon came to be dominated by Amsterdam. On a joint-stock basis the company was ready for action by June 1623. In the meantime the Englishman Thomas Dermer, sent by the Plymouth Virginia Company, had in 1620 called and told the Dutchmen that Manhattan belonged to England. Then, in 1621, when James had granted all land between the 40th and the 48th parallels to the Council for New England, the English ambassador at The Hague informed the Dutch that they were trespassing on English land at the mouth of the Hudson River.

As diplomatic discussions continued, Dutch traders spread from Man-

hattan to Connecticut River and Naragansett Bay, and their West India
Company, appointing a director for 'New Belgium', turned to settlement
with a shipload of emigrants in 1623. A French ship, about to set up a post
on Manhattan, was sent away (without bloodshed), the Dutch put a few
men ashore there, and then, with the rest, reinforced their post at Albany,
then called Fort Orange. Other parties went to Delaware River, to build
near the site of the present city of Philadelphia, others built Fort Good
Hope near the site of Hartford on the Connecticut, and others settled at
Wallabout Bay on Long Island. The West India Company had taken
effective possession of its lands; and the English appeared to accept the
position when in 1625 one of the ships taking reinforcements was stopped
in Plymouth until the privy council declared that she might proceed. The
threat of war with Spain again produced settlement; in fact Charles even
made a Dutch alliance despite the treatment of the English East India
Company at Amboyna and elsewhere.

New Netherland was therefore safe from English molestation, and so
remained until England had gone through her Civil War; and when Peter
Minuit became governor in 1626 the Dutch colony began to consolidate
itself. First came the formal purchase of Manhattan from the Indians,
and New Amsterdam arose as a city centred round a fort, with about 300
inhabitants by 1628, but with no town meeting or anything comparable;
laws were made in Amsterdam and administered by a council nominated
from Amsterdam and empowered also to make local regulations. The
governor's authority, however, did not extend to the outposts, and in
1626 the garrison at Fort Orange took the war-path with the Mohegans
against the Mohawks. This almost wrecked Dutch policy, but the Mohawks were nevertheless persuaded to renew their alliance, and Minuit
called in the garrisons at Fort Orange, at Fort Nassau on the Delaware,
and on the Connecticut. But although Dutch settlers were concentrated,
traders continued to roam, using their ships to search the coast and to
penetrate up rivers in search of furs. So doing, they came in contact with
the Pilgrims of Plymouth. Yet once more common hostility to Spain kept
the rivalry peaceful, for Spain's treasure-fleets were being disrupted and
her commerce destroyed by the ships of the West India Company under
the command of Piet Heyn. The Dutch moreover could legally trade with
England and her dependencies under the Treaty of Southampton, and the
New England colonies found a market for their agricultural surpluses
among the Dutch settlers and traders.

But Dutch agriculturists were not emigrating. To encourage them, in
1629 the West India Company issued its charter of 'Privileges and
Exemptions' by which any *patroon*, who within four years took fifty
emigrants to New Netherland, should receive a grant of land which would
make him virtually a lord of the manor, with jurisdiction and a lien on the
labour of his men. In return for providing stock and implements he was

entitled to a proportion of the increase of their farms. All trade to Europe must go through New Amsterdam and pay dues there; but except for furs the *patroons* were free to buy and sell in America, and even to trade with the English and French colonies. New Amsterdam was to be reinforced and made defensible, and provision was made for a pastor and a school-master. Although there was still little peasant emigration, would-be landed gentry found this charter attractive, and shiploads of cattle and of indentured servants arrived as the *patroons* spread to Hoboken and Staten Island and up the Hudson; attempts on the Delaware were ill-supported, and none was made at this time on the Connecticut. Even so, the *patroons* were more interested in trade than in farming and they turned to the fur trade, and sometimes to whaling, so easily that in 1632 Governor Minuit was recalled for partiality to them. His ship was driven into an English port by bad weather and was there seized for trading against the charter of the Council for New England—an incident which emphasized the contradictory English and Dutch claims but which brought no solution since the two governments were still anxious to maintain friendly relations.

Minuit's successor, Van Twiller, was not a man of great purpose; but at the start of his régime the Dutch, buying lands on both sides of Connecticut River, completed their Fort Good Hope on the site of the present city of Hartford despite protests from Massachusetts and from Plymouth. The Pilgrims established a fort in the Windsor area and rein-stated in their lands a band of Indians who had been expelled by the Pequots, and so set the Pequots murdering and robbing till the Dutch intervened, when the Pequots sought alliance with Boston, surrendering their Connecticut lands to the English! Dutch and English were then near to blows in America, but the English were too numerous, and the Estates General and the West India Company were too heavily com-mitted elsewhere. So the English pushed into Connecticut, Saybrook guarded the mouth of Connecticut River and cut off Fort Good Hope from New Amsterdam, the English built Hartford alongside Fort Good Hope, and the Pilgrims' post near Windsor was strengthened and taken over by Dorchester.

Apart from other considerations which forbade an outright clash, the Dutch were still traders rather than settlers, not greatly concerned with title to lands though in 1639 they opposed an English grant to the earl of Stirling of Long Island, rich in small shells for making *wampum*, the currency of the fur trade, and drove the English to the eastern part of the island where they built the small town of Southampton. They also prevented a Virginian attempt to take over their Fort Nassau on the Delaware. Despite such incidents New Amsterdam became the *entrepôt* for much of the trade of the New England colonies; cattle and supplies came from Holland for English purchasers, and a lively trade in local produce, in salt, tobacco and grain, also ran from Manhattan to Boston, Salem and other New England ports. Dutch merchants throve; but, while the English colonies steadily increased, the population of Manhattan slightly declined in the period 1633–8. The Estates General therefore pressed the West India Company to stabilize its colony, and in 1638 William Kieft arrived to supersede Van Twiller as governor.

Kieft, a man of restless energy, reduced his council to one nominee (a Huguenot refugee) and ruled absolutely, proscribing the illicit fur trade and uttering a series of proclamations against evil conduct. But so far was he from inducing immigration that the *patroons* even sought convicts and vagabonds as indentured labourers. The Estates General offered the alternative bait of greater freedom; in 1638 the West India Company's monopoly of trade was abandoned, manufactures were set free, and the same rights were accorded to aliens as to Dutchmen. Free transport and generous land-grants were designed to attract immigrants, who were to get land, stocked by the company, on arrival. After six years they were to return the equivalent of the stock provided, keeping the increase and paying, throughout, a reasonable rent.

Under these incentives New Netherland saw a great growth in numbers; and the immigrants included Huguenots and Englishmen, and English colonists from Virginia and Massachusetts. All must take an oath of loyalty, but no distinction was made against aliens. Even so, the Dutch colony showed no growth comparable to the English colonies, and New Haven and Connecticut between them seemed likely to take possession of Long Island under the noses of the Dutch.

The two régimes were brought into contact when Kieft, alarmed at the spread of the English settlements, bought land near Greenwich from the Indians and made the English settlers acknowledge Dutch sovereignty. Despite their alliance with the Iroquois, the Dutch had hitherto managed to maintain friendly relations with the Algonquins, to which tribe the Indians of the Connecticut and Delaware valleys belonged, though they went by a variety of names such as Raritans, Manhattans, or Tappans. But expansion, under the *patroons*, embittered Indian relations. Within range of their main posts the West India Company forbade the trade of firearms to Indians; consequently the near-at-hands Algonquins could not get arms whereas the more distant Mohawks and other Iroquois secured a steady supply. Hostility burst into flame in 1641; petty pilfering led to murder of the Staten Island Indians, who retaliated in a bloodthirsty massacre. A vengeance-murder of a Dutch trader at New Amsterdam then brought outright war; and in order to get co-operation Kieft accepted an elected Council of Twelve Men—a concession soon evaded. Nevertheless population increased, and English refugees from Massachusetts (including Anne Hutchinson) came in such numbers that an English secretary was appointed; pressure upon Indian lands, disputes, even murders, followed, and in 1643 the Dutch massacred over a hundred Algonquins seeking refuge on their lands from the Mohawks. A general Indian rising threatened, and not until John Underhill came from Massachusetts to repeat his tactics of the Pequot War, surrounding and exterminating the Indian warriors in night attacks, was a sort of peace restored to the Dutch frontier in 1644.

These troubles forced Director Kieft to call a Council of Eight Men in 1643; five were Dutch, one German and two English; but real authority remained centred in Europe although the West India Company, fully extended in Brazil, was unable to help New Netherland. In his need the director overruled the eight men and set excise duties on beer and spirits, provoking argument as to whether he derived his authority from the company or from the Estates General, whether the settlers were responsible for defence and administration, whether they should pay taxes or could, in fact, afford to pay. The eight men eventually appealed to the Estates General and succeeded in getting the arbitrary Kieft replaced by Pieter Stuyvesant, former governor of Curaçao. Stuyvesant was instructed to work with a vice-director and a treasurer to help him. But it was May 1647 before he arrived in Manhattan, and in the meantime the settlers concluded a solemn peace with the Algonquins, while Kieft quarrelled endlessly with the leaders of both church and populace. Stuyvesant intended to govern 'as a father his children, for the advantage of the chartered West India Company, and these burghers, and this land', and he vetoed an inquest into the conduct of Kieft, continued the unpopular duties on wines and spirits, and even laid taxes on the fur trade. To win over the settlers he in 1647 set up a Board of Nine Men. But they were to be chosen by the director and his council, albeit from a panel elected by popular vote, they were only to act when called upon, and after the first election subsequent appointments would be by co-optation. Stuyvesant was therefore able to maintain power in his own hands, at least in New Amsterdam and on Long Island.

But further afield the *patroons* were able to defy him. In particular Killian Van Rensselaer, *patroon* of Rensselaerwyck, far up the Hudson River, with a fur trade to supplement agricultural wealth, defied Stuyvesant's ban on trading arms to Indians, and even controlled other traders to Fort Orange. As young Johannes Van Rensselaer succeeded in 1646, Stuyvesant sent troops to destroy houses outside the fortifications of Orange, and by 1650 he forced the *patroon* to renounce his claims to independence. This, however, merely added to Stuyvesant's troubles; for the Nine Men, despite Stuyvesant's manipulations, retained their democratic character, and now found a redoubtable leader in Adrian Van der Donck, who came from Rensselaerwyck and, buying an estate, made himself a 'young lord' (a *Jonkheer*, hence his estate was called 'Jonkers'). An advocate of the Supreme Court of Holland and a doctor of laws of

Leiden University, Van der Donck organized an appeal to Holland by the Nine Men with such effect that Stuyvesant was compelled to allow him to take home the petition, asking for the end of company rule, a municipal government for New Amsterdam, and settled boundaries with Indians and with white neighbours. Though Van der Donck stirred up a new enthusiasm when he presented his petition at The Hague, by 1650 the total population of New Netherland was still but 2,000, of whom over 800 lived in New Amsterdam; moreover the West India Company was too highly privileged for the settlers to assume self-government as the English colonies had done, and the polyglot population of the colony showed a stronger trading element and a correspondingly weaker attachment to the soil than the English did.

Yet the Dutch were fully exploiting the weaknesses of Spain, moving steadily forward to an independence finally vindicated at Westphalia while the Dutch East India Company took the trade of the East in possession, and the West India Company won universal respect both by plundering the Spanish and Portuguese colonies and by diverting the produce of English and French settlements to Amsterdam. This was achieved by commercial and maritime competence rather than by open warfare (though periods of war gave additional opportunities), but it roused the other powers to conscious imitation of Dutch methods, and conscious denial of their claims. They moulded their policies with the deliberate intent to keep Dutch merchants from carrying off the profits, and strength, which could be got from colonial development. Hence the Navigation Policy into which the mercantilists of the next generation fell, on the basis of exclusive trade—the *pacte coloniale*.

Its great achievements did not prevent the West India Company from failing as the costs of war in Brazil outran even its enormous revenues. For New Netherland was so sited that it incurred hostility from English and French neighbours. English hostility, inevitable since control over the maritime trade of the English colonies was impossible as long as shipmasters from New Amsterdam would help Boston, Philadelphia, or Charlestown to evade the rules, did not emerge until the second half of the seventeenth century. But the fur trade, the Indian alliances and the river system by which the fur trade worked, entailed early rivalry between Dutch and French. It was fortunate for the Dutch that the English colonies then stood neutral, for the English were stronger and more numerous while the French in Canada were if anything weaker in numbers than the Dutch, and they were if anything less purposefully supported from Europe.

The French nevertheless showed vigour and imagination, and their leaders almost compensated for their small numbers. It was certainly impossible for New Netherland to expect French support, example, or even tolerance, for French projects made this impracticable. In France also the urge to exploit North America had come from merchants, rather than from settlers seeking homesteads. But whereas Dutch, and much of English, settlement was confined to the Atlantic seaboard, the French pressed constantly inland. Their Atlantic colony of Acadia continued small and impoverished, for though it was refounded in 1614 the English granted the land to Sir William Alexander, later earl of Stirling, in 1622, and sent an expedition to found a colony of Nova Scotia there; this failed in 1623. But Quebec and Trois Rivières absorbed such enterprise as France, emerging from her Wars of Religion, could spare. For although Champlain could win support at court, the merchants of La Rochelle, Brest and the Breton ports, exploiting the fur trade of the lower St Lawrence, resented a company, with its monopoly, its noble patronage and its plans for emigration. Under Sully's influence, moreover, attention was directed to France's internal economy and to the Mediterranean and Levant trades; lands north of 40° offered little hope of profit, and though grants of privilege could indeed be got, there was little genuine support. Yet Champlain was geographer royal, encouraged by powerful nobles; his constant companion was the Breton merchant François du Pont-gravé, and the great merchant William de Caen was tempted by a mono-poly of the fur trade. Moreover, Champlain's search for the 'western sea' accorded well with that 'greedy penetration of the continent in pursuit of beaver' which led the French so far and so fast into the interior of Canada.

Until 1613 Champlain, with no monopoly of the fur trade, and beset by rivals who traded at Tadoussac, had not yet gone west of the rapids at Lachine, above Montreal. But then, inspired by a spurious account of Hudson Bay (where Henry Hudson was, nevertheless, engaged on his last voyage of discovery), and backed by the powerful prince de Condé, he set off by canoe up the Ottawa River, through Lac des Chats, to the Algon-quins' encampments near Lac des Alumettes. Frustrated in his major purpose, Champlain had yet opened up the Ottawa River route, leading westwards without the southern dip by way of Lake Ontario, Niagara Falls and Lake Erie, bordering on hostile Iroquois territories. Reports of his discoveries secured a renewal of Condé's monopoly, reorganization of their company, and reinforcement in 1615 by four members of the re-formed Franciscan Recollect order whom Champlain had interested in Canada.

The Iroquois, by 1615, acting as the outriders of the Dutch traders at Manhattan and Orange, were even ambushing the Algonquins up the Ottawa River. In face of such a threat Champlain was cautious; but the missionaries hardly paused at Quebec before embarking on a mission to the Hurons, and Champlain followed, by Ottawa River and Mattawa River to Lake Nipissing and then down French River to the Huron settlements on Georgian Bay. There he spent the winter, after an abortive attack on an Iroquois post at Lake Onondaga, south-east of Lake Ontario. His journey to Huronia was in itself a great achievement, but Champlain was unable to explore northwards to get accurate information about Lake Superior, Lake Michigan and their outlets, or to follow the Lake Erie and Lake Ontario route back to Lachine. The assassination of Henri IV, and renewed civil war, cut off help from France, and by 1622 there were still only about a hundred Frenchmen in Canada, and Quebec was but a fortified outpost of sixty-five men. In 1614 Champlain had formed his own group to sub-let the fur trade from Condé, and this continued when Condé's charter was withdrawn in 1620; and when the duc de Montmorenci secured a new patent, with the duty of maintaining the Recollect missions and encouraging emigration, Champlain settled at Quebec as a benevolent and experienced governor. Richelieu then, in 1627, cancelled all previous grants and set up a comprehensive Compagnie de la Nouvelle France (organized and known as the Compagnie des Cent Associés) with a perpetual monopoly of the fur trade, full sovereignty over the territory, and a monopoly of all trade save fishing for the next fifteen years, with the duty of organizing settlement so long as only French Roman Catholics were admitted.

It was unfortunate for Canada that at this juncture the three brothers David, Lewis and Thomas Kirke, supported by London merchants, secured a charter as a Canada Company, in 1627, to take possession of Canada and the St Lawrence fur trade, while Charles also renewed the charter to the earl of Stirling's Nova Scotia Company. The first reinforcements sent to Canada by Richelieu in 1628 were captured at sea by David Kirke, and in 1629 he took Quebec itself, made Champlain a prisoner and brought the furs to England. Meanwhile the Nova Scotia Company, working with the Kirkes, planted an English colony of about seventy men in Acadia.

The Compagnie de la Nouvelle France, incapable of defending its possessions, was strongly opposed by the traders whom it dispossessed, especially by William de Caen, who had bought the fur concession from the Compagnie de Montmorenci, bought it again from the Compagnie de la Nouvelle France, and who sued in England for the furs which Kirke had brought to London. So, even when the Treaty of St Germain, in 1632, restored the captured territories to France, and Champlain took office in Quebec again, the Cent Associés who ran the Compagnie de la Nouvelle France could not re-establish the trade, or organize emigration in adequate numbers. Yet such colonists as came were mostly sturdy peasants, and by Richelieu's death, in 1635, Trois Rivières was a township, Fort Richelieu had been built, and something of genuine agricultural settlement had been achieved by a system of *seigneurage*. Land-hungry and would-be-noble immigrants could secure a *seigneurie*, lying back from the river in strip cultivation, with a title of nobility, in return for bringing the land into cultivation and shipping out a quota of labour. Even this bait, reminiscent of the Dutch *patroons* and of the baronetcies offered in Nova Scotia, was inadequate. By 1643 the French colony still had no more than 300 settlers, dependent on the fur trade and on European food and supplies, at the mercy of their Indian allies and enemies, dreading the long Canadian winter, and dominated by the Compagnie de la Nouvelle France.

The *seigneurs* had failed to bring out the colonists. But the French colony received a great impetus when in 1625 an intrepid band of Jesuit missionaries arrived. The Jesuits found both an ally and an enemy in the fur trader; for the fur trade condemned the Indian to a wandering life in which Christian habits were sure to lapse, while the arms, the spirits, and the finery brought by trade made the Indian dangerous and irresponsible. Yet in the *coureurs de bois*, the traders capable of travelling and living with Indians, the missionaries found guides, companions and interpreters, who greatly assisted them in their work. One of Champlain's *coureurs*, Étienne Brulé, had already travelled along the north shore of Lake Huron towards Sault Ste Marie and the entrance to Lake Superior; he perhaps actually travelled on Lake Superior and he certainly brought back accounts of it. The route from Lake Ontario to Lake Huron by way of Niagara Falls, Lake Erie, and Lake St Clair had also been probed, and the French knew that this route went through lands dominated by the Iroquois and increasingly subject to the Iroquois desire to drain furs down to the Dutch and British traders of the Hudson and the Delaware. Huronia, the area south from Ottawa River, was the focus of this trade rivalry, as of French plans for western exploration; it was also the great field for Jesuit endeavour. There, remote from the Atlantic, Indians might be converted and even segregated from the vices brought by contact with Europeans.

French attachment to the Hurons, partly economic, partly missionary, and partly personal, necessarily challenged the Iroquois policy of dominating the approaches to Huronia, a policy which would starve Canada's fur trade and would counteract Jesuit influence. The Jesuits went so far as to conduct missions to the Iroquois; they thereby embarked on an adventure of travel, suffering, torture and martyrdom, unequalled in modern history. But they accomplished little, though they even penetrated to the Iroquois villages on Hudson River. Of the *coureurs* one at least, Jean Nicolet, penetrated from Lake Huron through the Straits of Mackinac into Lake Michigan, then westwards to Green Bay and out towards the upper waters of the Mississippi, and gathered rumours of a great lake and of rivers running north from that lake to the sea. Yet the fur-route by Lake Ontario and the upper St Lawrence remained under threat. By 1637 the Iroquois were astride the St Lawrence, raiding the

Huron canoes as they took furs to Quebec. They could only be overcome by depriving them of Dutch help.

Richelieu therefore, in allocating men and money in 1641 to fight the Iroquois, accepted the necessity to drive the Dutch from the valley of the Hudson, and even from Manhattan itself. He died at the end of 1642, and Canada never got the support necessary for such a policy. Yet enthusiasm in France was real, and when in 1641 the Society of Notre Dame de Montreal was formed it was inspired by both religious and secular desire to reinforce Quebec and Trois Rivières by a third city, sixty miles up-river from Quebec, in the heart of the Indian country. There, in May 1642, Montreal was established with sixty settlers on an island in the St Lawrence. The island had been granted to the Seminary of St Sulpicius, and the priests even nominated the governor. This was a 'holy city', communal in its life, a Christian bulwark against Indian savagery. But it marked the renewal of Iroquois attacks, which rose to a peak by 1648.

In the early stages the Iroquois' threat gave an impetus towards self-dependence and self-rule. Despite Iroquois interruptions the annual fur-returns increased, so that it seemed that if the incubus of a great company were removed local dealers might drive a profitable trade; and their incentive would be great since their furs must pay for their annual shipments of supplies. Accordingly in 1645 a group of colonists formed a Compagnie des Habitants, sub-contracted the fur trade from the Compagnie de la Nouvelle France, and made such profits that in 1647 the generality of the *habitants* protested against the monopoly and secured freedom to trade with Indians. But all still had to bring their furs to the company's warehouse within specified times, to sell them there at specified prices for the company to ship to Europe and to bring back the European goods which were needed.

The company was therefore in much the same position as the 'cape-merchant' in the early English experiments, particularly in the Plymouth colony. The *habitants*, moreover, had attained self-government in ways which were reminiscent of developments elsewhere. In 1647 the authority of the governor was delegated to a council of three, of whom the other members would be the governor of Montreal and the superior of the Jesuits (or the bishop if one should be appointed); and in 1648 this council was extended to include two or three syndics from Quebec, Montreal and Trois Rivières. This advance was offset by half of the furs being taken to pay for administration and defence; and the Iroquois intensified their ambushes of the fur-laden canoes going down to the French settlements, raiding in 1648 into the Huron villages near Georgian Bay, completing the dispersal of the Hurons, torturing to death their Jesuit missionaries in 1649, and closing in round Montreal and Quebec. By 1652 the French fur trade was at a standstill.

The Beavers are left in peace and in the place of their repose; the Huron fleets no longer come down to trade; the Algonquins are depopulated; and the more distant nations are withdrawing still farther, fearing the fire of the Iroquois. For a year, the warehouse at Montreal has not bought a single Beaver-skin from the savages. At Three Rivers, the little revenue that has accrued has been used to fortify the place, the enemy being expected there. In Quebec warehouse there is nothing but poverty.

The French colony did not founder, for the *habitants* had already developed virtues all their own. They seemed little likely to achieve primacy in North America, but they were, in their own way, more at home in the north than were the English, settled, prosperous and almost independent though the English were. Between English and French, dominated by neither, in 1648 the Dutch still held New Amsterdam and Hudson River, strong in the alliance of the Iroquois, who in a very real sense still controlled the destinies of the European colonies.

In north America the Iberian Powers had done nothing to substantiate their claims, and were not concerned to vindicate them. In the West Indian islands also there were valuable areas in which the Spaniards had attempted little or nothing, but there a challenge could not go unanswered, for to Spain, as to her enemies, the West Indies lay 'in the very belly of all commerce'. Yet Spain left unoccupied a fringe of outer islands (the Lesser Antilles) from which English, French, and Dutch ships conducted trade with the Spanish colonists in spite of regulations. In particular the Dutch began to exploit the vast salt-pans of Venezuela and to bring out cargoes of European goods in the ships which carried home the salt. English settlements on the mainland came to nothing although much interest was aroused; Charles Leigh failed in Guiana in 1604–6—his survivors were rescued by Dutch shippers—and Robert Harcourt failed in 1609–18—his survivors joined the Dutch to settle at Essequibo. North's Amazon Company in 1620, and Raleigh's attempt of 1617–19, both suffered because James I withdrew support in deference to Spain, and movements from these areas to St Lucia and Grenada also failed.

The interloping powers were little concerned to set up colonies in the Caribbean; their approach was still that of Hawkins and Drake, aimed at trade. But trade in defiance of Spain easily developed into *piraterie à l'aimable,* and the bullion collected at the focal points of Cartagena, Nombre de Dios and Panama was vulnerable both before it was shipped and as it went for Spain, convoyed though it was in powerful *flotas.* For the *flota* must break from the Caribbean into the Atlantic either northwards through the Florida Channel, or southwards through the Windward Isles, or perhaps by a middle course through the Windward Passage between Puerto Rico and Haiti. So the Bahamas were well sited to prey on the Florida Channel, the little island of Tortuga off the north coast of

Haiti threatened the Windward Passage; and Tobago and Trinidad in the Windward Isles channel, and Curaçao commanding the approach to that channel, also had great value.

Easily though the Caribbean lent itself to buccaneering, yet year after year the great *flota* made its way safely out into the Atlantic. But alongside buccaneering went a series of plans to settle in the West Indies in spite of Spain. When Thomas Warner, on a return voyage from North's dwindling colony on the Amazon, in 1622 touched at St Christopher in the Leeward Isles, he noted that it had a good soil for tobacco and, having secured financial support in London, returned in 1624 to make a plantation with about seventeen settlers. Warner's position was complicated by the need to fight the Caribs, by the arrival of the French privateer D'Esnambuc, and by an English company for the settlement of Barbados. That fertile and attractive island may well have been known to English sailors, but it was uninhabited when in 1624, or early 1625, a ship belonging to Sir William Courteen (a London merchant with Dutch connections) called there on a return voyage from Brazil. Courteen's captain forthwith annexed the island, and on his way back to England called at St Christopher. Warner, probably moved by the captain's report, in 1625 secured a royal grant making him governor of the four islands which he was alleged to have discovered—St Christopher, Nevis, Monserrat, and Barbados. But Warner had in fact no hold on Barbados while Courteen had formed a syndicate, sent out eighty men, and followed up with a hundred men and women, and with Indians, corn, tobacco and other plants, from the mainland.

With capital available from the capture of Spanish shipping, Courteen's plantation flourished so that by 1628 Barbados numbered 1,850 inhabitants. Warner, anxious to push his claim, made alliance with James Hay, earl of Carlisle, to whom Charles I granted both the Windward and the Leeward groups—all islands lying between 10° and 20° north of the equator—including Barbados. Courteen thereupon turned to the earl of Pembroke, who obtained a similar grant, conferring Trinidad and Tobago, an imaginary island called Fonseca, and again Barbados! Carlisle in turn secured a reaffirmation of his grant, clearly specifying Barbados. Thus strengthened, he sent out two parties of settlers in 1628 and virtually took over Barbados from Courteen's men, who were naturally confused by the irreconcilable grants but who recovered their position in 1629 when an expedition sent by Pembroke overthrew Carlisle's supporters, captured over £30,000 of tobacco, and brought the governor of the island in irons to London. The conflict of claims never came before a court of law, but after an investigation Lord Keeper Coventry issued a verdict against Pembroke and Courteen. The settlers seem to have been content, and Barbados moved into a period of prosperity, and of increase in population, based on tobacco.

Tobacco had also brought prosperity to St Christopher. Population had reached 3,000 by 1629, and some settlers were wealthy enough to charter their own shipping to take tobacco to the London market; but most were small men, dependent on the grantees or on their more wealthy neighbours. Great or small, they created such a demand for land that expansion to other islands soon followed, especially when, in 1626, D'Esnambuc induced Richelieu to set up a Compagnie de St Christophe, to develop unoccupied islands between 11° and 18°—which included all the Lesser Antilles so long as they were unoccupied. D'Esnambuc arranged an amicable partition of St Christopher with the English in 1627, the English taking the central area (to be known henceforth as St Kitts) and the French the two extremities. Though dispersed by a Spanish attack in 1629, the English returned and entered on a period of such continuous prosperity that population reached something like 20,000 in 1640. This included the neighbouring island of Nevis, to which they spread in 1628, and which had also recovered from the Spanish raid of 1629.

While the English took possession of the Leeward Islands, spreading from St Christopher to Nevis, to Antigua and Montserrat in 1632, and then attempting Tobago and St Lucia, the French concentrated on the Windward group. There also the Spaniards offered no opposition; but resistance from the Caribs was serious, and little was achieved until in 1635 Richelieu again stepped in, urged by a concept of a French Empire in which possessions in the West Indies would balance with tropical produce the northern colony of Canada. To the Compagnie des Isles d'Amèrique he granted St Christopher, and encouraged the company to begin settlement in other Leeward islands. On St Christopher the French continued their arrangement with the English, but they immediately and successfully colonized Martinique and Guadeloupe, overcoming Carib resistance there. When de Poincy was appointed governor-general in 1638 he rapidly organized the defence of his islands and established French control in St Croix, Martinique, Marie Galante, the Saints and Guadeloupe. Grenada, Dominica and St Lucia he left, but he asserted French authority over the buccaneers who were making Tortuga their headquarters and by 1642 he had established French settlements in fourteen islands. French population amounted to about 7,000, in addition there were numbers of slaves, and the wealth of the governor and the greater planters called for an enquiry on behalf of the company, which in 1646 ordered its governor to resign. This de Poincy refused to do, and he drove his successor-designate from St Christopher to Guadeloupe.

The struggle which ensued brought the company to the verge of ruin by 1647, when Mazarin decided to end the company and to distribute its possessions between the proprietors. Of these the greatest was the Order of the Knights of St John of Malta, for whom de Poincy acted. They now secured the French parts of St Christopher, and St Martin, Tortuga,

St Croix and St Bartholomew (a small island which, like Tortuga, was no more than a buccaneering stronghold). The French West Indies thus fell under the control of a group of wealthy proprietors, most of whom had no interest in their islands beyond their personal gain.

While the French West Indies had built up a greater European population than Canada, the English had over-ridden the confusion over proprietary patents, and had emigrated to the West Indies in considerable numbers. In some ways this movement resembled the Puritan emigration to North America, but it was controlled by proprietors rather than by companies, and it brought out many indentured labourers, men without sufficient capital for independent emigration, occasionally with an agricultural background, who engaged to serve for a period (usually from five to seven years) in return for their passage. Though then free to seek their fortunes, they often lacked capital and remained either as servants or share-croppers. Tobacco lent itself equally to growth on large or small plantations and was the basis of the small freeholds which grew up under this system as well as of the great estates. Maize was grown for food, salt fish was imported from New England and Newfoundland; and despite hardships and disappointments population soared. By 1643 the white population of Barbados was reckoned to be over 37,000 while that of St Kitts and Nevis together reached over 20,000.

These figures proved to be the highest ever reached for white settlement in the English islands. Not only had the emigrant tide turned strongly towards North America but by the middle years of the century sugar had replaced tobacco as the staple crop of the West Indies; and large plantations, worked by slave labour, proved the best units for the new crop. The sugar, the negro slave labour which went with it, and some of the capital for mills, as well as much of the shipping which transported the product, derived from the Dutch.

The Dutch West India Company's preoccupation with Brazil was part of a determined effort to take over the principal colony of settlement which existed in the first decade of the seventeenth century. The West India Company wished to establish a Dutch agricultural colony, to control the slave trade from the West African coast, and to undermine the Portuguese in the West as in the East. Brazil was therefore the company's first concern; but Brazil did not completely predominate. The West India Company organized raids on Spanish shipping so effectively that this was the chief source of its dividends and even offset the costs of the Brazilian war. Its efforts reached their climax when in 1628 Piet Heyn at last intercepted the great *flota* itself; in that year the West India Company paid a dividend of 50 per cent! Many of the buccaneers who 'swarmed on the rotting carcase of the Spanish empire' were Dutch; most of them had some sort of Protestantism at the back of their minds. But the Dutch formed the spearhead; they took the *flota*, and though 'more eager for conquest than for commerce' they carried much of the trade of the French and the English islands with the same disregard for prohibitions as they showed towards the Spaniards. There was indeed a Dutch settlement on the Essequibo, established in 1616, and on the Berbice, established in 1624; small colonies were set up in Tobago and Cayenne only to be destroyed by the Spaniards, and the Dutch settled on Curaçao in 1634 and on St Eustatius and St Martin in 1641. But though the Treaty of Münster in 1648 confirmed these colonies to the Dutch they were important as *entrepôts* rather than as colonies of settlement; for the Dutch were in the West Indies to trade rather than to farm.

The Dutch approach was all the more important because in the English islands, in a period when royal authority was under dispute, proprietors and planters sought their profit without regard to the regulations by which the home government tried to constrain them within a single economic system. Neither the English nor the French government could enforce its regulations, for both were embroiled in European wars and both had neglected their navies. Moreover the Dutch, valuable to both powers, would not accept any policy of exclusive trade and in 1625, in the Treaty of Southampton, they had won free access to all English possessions. In English and French colonies alike they assumed by treaty, or by right of commercial competence, that control of trade and shipping for which they had been prepared to fight the Portuguese and the Spaniards; and for which they would fight the English and the French also.

So, while the Dutch West India Company fought for Brazil and its sugar plantations it also captured the slave posts which were the complements of the Brazilian economy, taking in turn Arguin, Goree, São Thomè, Loanda and Elmina, and developing a slave-trade both to Brazil and to the English and French colonies. Little profit would be got from the West Indies unless the Dutch could be driven out and the products of the islands shipped under compulsion to the mother countries in their national-owned vessels. At Providence, for example, the Dutch were so strongly entrenched that in 1632 they offered to buy any crop produced, in 1638 the proprietors complained that only Dutch shipping served them, and in 1639 the Dutch even offered to buy the whole island. This was exceptional, but after the Spanish raid of 1629 St Kitts was to a large extent set going again by the Dutch, who brought a supply of slaves, and by 1659 the planters were complaining that the Dutch engrossed the whole trade of this important island. At Barbados too a new prosperity came with sugar and slavery. In 1640 'the Dutch came and taught the art of making sugar, and having free trade and plentiful supplies' firmly established the trade. The change was continuous; in 1636 Barbados had a white population of 6,000, in 1643 this had increased to 37,200 whites and there were 6,400 Negro slaves; and by 1660 the Negroes had risen to over 50,000. By 1654 the customs on the produce of Barbados came to £12,930 a year, there were usually sixty or seventy ships at anchor there, while the trade of the island was reported to occupy about 400 ships and about 10,000 seamen.

Before this increasingly important trade could profit either England or France the Dutch had to be driven out. Their great harbour at New Amsterdam made them able to control shipping from the mainland colonies while their possessions on the West African coast made them able to supply the West Indies. In the negotiations at The Hague which followed on the execution of Charles I they maintained their right to 'trade to all our Countries and plantations in America, and elsewhere, without any difference of people'. To this the English answer was equally direct: 'The Dutch cannot trade to the English islands and plantations out of Europe, nor can the English trade to theirs.' For the Dutch, it was said, 'prohibit the English to traffique in their Colonies in the East Indyes, or other parts, save in Europe. They exercise absolute dominion in India; where they are strongest at sea they search our ships . . . and confiscate not only contraband goods but all others'.

The period to the middle of the seventeenth century, therefore, had seen the establishment of permanent colonies of settlement in North America, the revelation of long-term rivalries there and of clearly defined national patterns of colonial government, with parallel but distinct and different settlement in the West Indies. It had also seen the Dutch mount to the position of 'most envied nation', succeeding Spain in that respect and working to a pattern of Atlantic and colonial trade which forced other colonial nations to adopt imperial policies, dominated by Navigation Acts, which set the mould in which the great period of European imperialism was shaped.

CHAPTER XXIII

LATIN AMERICA 1610–60

IN 1610 Philip III, *Rex Hispaniarum et Indiarum*, claimed sovereignty over two great empires in America, one governed from Madrid as part of his crown of Castile, the other governed from Lisbon as part of his crown of Portugal. Together the claimed dominions of the two empires covered all of America, stretching from the yet unknown lands that lay between the Gulf of Mexico and the mysterious Arctic, southward to the equally unknown lands of Tierra del Fuego on the far side of the Straits of Magellan. The territories of the crown of Castile were divided into two viceroyalties: that of New Spain, with its capital at Mexico City, comprised all of the Iberian possessions to the north of Panama, including the islands of the Caribbean and the territory of present-day Venezuela; that of Peru, with its capital at Lima, governed the Castilian possessions from Panama to Chile and Buenos Aires. The American Empire of the crown of Portugal was Brazil, then defined as all land east of the north–south line of demarcation set by the Treaty of Tordesillas, running from the eastern stretches of the Amazon delta to the Island of Santa Catarina on the coast of the present-day Brazilian state of Santa Catarina. This territory was governed by a captain-general at Bahia.

Effective occupation in the form of domination of the native population or direct settlement by Iberian subjects fell far short of Iberian claims, as other European governments did not fail to point out. Nevertheless, the area under effective occupation constituted immense territories. In North America, Spanish dominion touched the present areas of the United States and Canada at two points. In Florida, a small settlement at St Augustine, refounded permanently in 1597, attempted to keep foreign intruders away from the Bahama Channel and the return route of the Spanish fleets, and served as a base for missionary work among the Indians of Florida and Georgia. In the upper valley of the Rio Grande a new settlement, centred around the city of Santa Fé founded in 1609, constituted the most northward extension of Spanish settlement to be made during the next century and a half. The colonists and missions of New Mexico were separated from the settled area of Mexico by a long stretch of arid, relatively unpopulated country, and had to be supplied by great wagon trains. Of the islands of the Caribbean, the Greater Antilles were held by a thin population of Spaniards, Negroes, and various mixtures of races in settlements which exported sugar, hides, and cassia to Spain. The aboriginal population had been almost completely wiped out by the early decades of the sixteenth century. The fortified city of

Havana, with its excellent harbour, provided the gathering point for the fleets for the return voyage to Spain although the administrative seat for the Caribbean and Venezuela was Santo Domingo. The Lesser Antilles were largely unpopulated by the Spanish; they were left to such Indian remnants as survived a century of European proximity, and to the occasional fugitive use of non-Iberian Europeans. The major Spanish occupation—the core of the territories of Castile in the New World—covered the long western mountain backbone of North and South America from a line drawn between Sinaloa and southern Tamaulipas in Mexico to the Bío-Bío River in southern Chile. An eastward extension of Spanish occupation in northern South America followed the Andes into New Granada and Venezuela; and another thin eastward extension in southern South America crossed the continent through Tucuman, Paraguay, and the pampas to the sea at Buenos Aires. The mountains of middle America had been the seats of the most highly developed Indian civilizations at the time of the discovery of America, and their conquest placed at the disposal of the Spaniards organized societies that could be adapted to providing foodstuffs, labour, and services, the Europeans constituting a new upper stratum. The great cities, including the imperial city of Potosí at the foot of its mountain of silver, the mines that made Spanish America the source of Europe's specie, the bulk of Spanish agriculture, and the overwhelming majority of both Spanish and Indian population were in this zone. The dependence of Spanish settlement on the Indians was such that the former tended to be most dense where the native population was largest and sparse where it was small. In general, the coasts were held only by a thin settlement because of malaria and yellow fever, except for a relatively dense population raising cacao on the Sonsonate coast of Central America and the viceregal capital of Lima on the coast of Peru. The tropical rain forests also remained virtually untouched because of their impenetrability and lack of value relative to other regions. The largest area thus left vacant in 1610 lay in South America to the east of the great arc of the Pacific highlands, and included the immense valleys of the Amazon and upper Orinoco and the coast of the Guianas. It was a vast ill-known region, merging on the south into thorn thickets and highlands covered with scrub, with a thin population of nomadic and semi-nomadic tribes. It was assigned to the crown of Castile by the Treaty of Tordesillas.

On the Atlantic coast of South America, forming yet another arc of settlement on the eastward margin of the continent beyond the relatively vacant central area, lay the Portuguese territory of Brazil. In 1610 the area of effective occupation stretched approximately from Cape São Roque at the bulge of Brazil southward along the coast to the southern coast of São Paulo. Settlement was discontinuous, in small towns and plantations, farms, and ranches scattered along the coast on numerous small inland waterways that afforded easy transportation. Only on the uplands of São Paulo, in the valley of the São Francisco River, and at a few points in the north-eastern bulge had European occupation moved inland beyond the narrow coastal plain. The whole of Brazil was a small series of weak settlements compared to the wealth and power of New Spain and Peru, yet it already was the chief supplier of sugar to Europe. In 1610 there were almost no permanent settlements of other European powers in America although a number had been attempted.

The half-century between 1610 and 1660 witnessed relatively little change in the area of effective Spanish occupation and a very considerable extension of the Portuguese area as the Brazilians made ample use of the opportunity provided by the union of 1580–1640. Such change as there was in the Spanish territories took place at the northern and southern peripheries. From St Augustine, the Franciscans, continuing their missionary activity along the coast, by 1615 held more than twenty stations extending as far north as South Carolina. That was high water, soon to ebb as the English settlers farther north encouraged the tribes of the coast to resist. In northern Mexico, settlers and Jesuit missionaries continued a slow movement northward along the Pacific coast and inland into the ranges of the Sierra Madre Occidental, the rugged topography of which made the Indians difficult to reach so that there were relatively large pockets of independent aborigines in the Spanish rear as far south as Nayarit. In 1614 the Jesuits founded their first mission among the Tarahumara. Then in 1616 the great Tepehuán revolt forced retreat until resistance was crushed in 1622. In 1638 the Jesuits were able to move farther north among the Tarahumara and found their first mission in the mountains of Sonora. Their efforts were a precarious venture, backed by a few troops, with frequent setbacks. Yet farther north in the isolated settlements of New Mexico, Franciscan missionaries pressed work among the pueblo Indians of the United States south-west. By 1630 there were fifty friars at work. They had twenty-five missions, which included ninety pueblos and perhaps 50,000 converts. As was true of virtually all missions, each mission had a church, a school, workshops, dwellings, and fields. The neophytes were taught manual arts, and such accomplishments as were necessary for church services.

The most ambitious attempts to extend the area of Spanish occupation, as well as the most serious threats to Spanish dominion, took place in southern South America. In the vast plains extending from Mato Grosso to Patagonia and from Paraguay to the coast, the Jesuit missionaries found themselves at open warfare with the Brazilian subjects of the common king. In the southern part of the central valley of Chile, the long-existing Araucanian War continued its uncertain and bloody course.

In 1610 the Spanish in Chile were still attempting to cope with a reorganized Araucanian society·able to send forth large war parties equipped with horses, long lances, and even some firearms, and trained to deal with European soldiers. Of the eight cities founded in the sixteenth century between the Bío-Bío River and the Gulf of Reloncaví, the heavy Araucanian onslaughts of the years 1598–1605 had forced abandonment of seven. Araucanian successes also had forced abandonment of the militia system based on service by *encomenderos* and auxiliaries from the Indians around Santiago in favour of a professional army supplied and reinforced from Spain and Peru. The official strength of this army varied in this period from 1,500 to 2,500 men, but so many *plazas* were vacant or held by men old, sick or otherwise unfit for active service that the effective strength seldom exceeded 1,000. The most that the new army was able to do was to prevent the Araucanians from occupying land north of the Bío-Bío although their raiding parties crossed the river each year and sometimes penetrated as far as the Maule. The Spanish army, in turn, conducted annual raids that netted a valuable booty in slaves, who were sold in the Central Valley or shipped to Peru.

How to end the Araucanian raids and the heavy expenses of the War of Chile gave rise to prolonged debates in Santiago and Madrid. The Jesuits, who saw the Spanish part of the problem clearly, favoured establishment of a defensive line of posts along the Bío-Bío, an end to slaving raids, and pacification of the Araucanians through missionary activity. The colonial government, members of which derived substantial personal profits from slaving, favoured unrelenting prosecution of the war. A trial of the Jesuit plan, begun in 1611, failed when one group of Araucanians massacred the missionaries. Finally, in 1625 the crown ordered resumption of active prosecution of the war and formally renewed permission to enslave prisoners. In 1630 a new governor, Lazo de la Vega, having reinstituted military service for the male population of Santiago, was able to inflict a substantial series of defeats upon the Araucanians, who had been seriously weakened by murderous epidemics of smallpox and measles. But the incursions of the Spaniards aroused all of Araucania to resistance and led to a revival of Indian successes. In 1641, by the treaty of Quillén, the royal government recognized the independence of the Indians south of the Bío-Bío. The treaty could not put an end to raids on both sides, nor could new treaties, a second one of Quillén in 1647 and the Peace of Boroa in 1651. The profits of raids to Spanish soldiers and their commanders made the royal army a potent force against any policy aimed at peace. At the same time the peculiarly loose structure of Araucanian society, without any central authority, and the premium placed upon exhibitions of prowess in raids made it virtually impossible for the Indians to observe any agreements for a cessation of hostilities. In 1655 a concerted Araucanian effort, using the Andean passes to circle through Argentine territory and take the Spanish by surprise, threatened all Spanish settlements south of the Maule. The line of the Bío-Bío was not recovered by the Spanish until 1661 when a new governor, Porter Casanate, defeated the Indians in pitched battle at Curanilahué. Throughout this period the Spanish settlements in the Central Valley steadily increased in strength, while epidemics and losses through war and slaving slowly but steadily reduced the power of the Araucanians who, however, were able to redress the balance in part by recruiting among the Pehuelche tribes on the eastern slopes of the Andes. Meantime, the war required a heavy subsidy from the Peruvian treasury to meet the annual cost of over 200,000 ducats and helped to drain away treasure that the Spanish monarchy urgently needed in Europe.

On the Atlantic side of the Cordillera, in the broad band of territory stretching from Paraguay to the Atlantic, there took place the foundation of the so-called Jesuit state of Paraguay, which was to set the boundary in that area between Spanish and Portuguese America. There were already three small Spanish settlements in the upper valley of the Paraná, in the region of Guairá, and a few Franciscan missionaries in the upper valley of the Uruguay, but the major work was Jesuit. In 1604 the Jesuit general authorized the formation of a separate Jesuit province of Paraguay, and in 1607-8 missionary work was actually begun by sending pairs of missionaries to the Guaycurú Indians of the Chaco and to the semi-sedentary Indians of the upper and middle valleys of the Paraná. Under concessions embodied in the Ordinances of Governor Alfaro (1611), Indians in the missions, or reductions, were to be free from *encomienda*, from labour to private Spaniards, and for ten years even from payment of tribute to the crown. The missionaries sent to the Chaco were soon forced to leave, but those sent to the Guaraní were unusually successful. In 1610 the first permanent mission, San Ignacio Guazú, was founded in the middle Paraná Valley. Shortly thereafter two missions were founded on the Río Paranapanema in Guairá, north of two of the small Spanish settlements. The plan of the Spanish Jesuits and the civil government of Paraguay was to use the missions for ensuring Spanish control of all territory to the line of demarcation. Accordingly, in 1627 the mission of Yapeyú was founded on the Uruguay River as the first of a line that was to be extended to the ocean near Santa Catarina. By 1628 there were eleven Jesuit reductions in Guairá and ten in the area of the middle Paraná and Uruguay. But the very presence of these masses of manpower, temptingly presented in permanent reservations, brought attack from the *mestizo* slave hunters of the São Paulo. The first Paulista attack upon a Spanish Jesuit mission took place in 1611. In the 1620s, when the Portuguese slave trade with Angola was almost cut off by the Dutch, the raids became formidable military operations. Those of 1628-9 were carried out by four expeditions numbering perhaps 900 Paulistas and 2,000 Tupi Indian allies. In the years 1629-32 the Paulistas seized tens of thousands of Indians in Guairá from reductions and independent bands. The Jesuits could get little help from Spanish provincial authorities or the inhabitants of the small Spanish towns in the area. The latter were bitterly resentful of the exemption of the Indians from *encomienda* and service, while the provincial government resented the exemption of the Indians from tribute and the virtual autonomy of the missions. A new governor, Luis de Céspedes Jeria, who took office in 1628, actually attempted to make sure that the mission Indians remained unarmed. In 1630 the Jesuits decided upon the desperate measure of evacuating all mission Indians. Carried through despite opposition from the governor and civil population, the evacuation required nearly two years and entailed great loss of life; nearly half of the Indians died before they could be settled on the middle Paraná, south of the great Iguazú Falls, which interposed a long stretch of unnavigable river between the Paulistas and the missions. With the missions gone, the Spanish towns also had to be abandoned, so that in 1632 the uppermost Paraná Valley was left to unreduced Indians and the Paulista *bandeiras*.

After the great evacuation, the Jesuits continued successfully to expand their missions in the valleys of the middle Paraná and Uruguay rivers, and even began work in the region of Itatím, now in southernmost Mato Grosso. Since the Paulista raids did not stop, they used their salaries as curates and some of the proceeds of the sale of surplus crops for arms to train an Indian militia. In 1636 they were able to offer a Paulista raid heavy resistance even though the raiders made off with thousands of prisoners. The decisive success of the mission defence occurred in March 1641 when a large force of mission Indians, with perhaps 200 muskets, ambushed a *bandeira* on the Río Mbororé, a tributary of the Uruguay, and drove it back through the forests with very severe loss. Thereafter the raids became much less serious. The Jesuits received unexpected relief when the Brazilian war against the Dutch drew off many Paulistas to the north, including Antônio Raposo Tavares, the most active and formidable leader of *bandeiras*.

By the early 1640s, when the major expansive impulse was spent, the Jesuits had approximately twenty missions, or reductions, in the valleys of the middle Paraná and Uruguay rivers, most of them in the region of the present Argentine province of Misiones. The organization of the missions became the model for later ones elsewhere. Each mission had two Jesuits attached to it, one with the formal title of curate. The Indians were governed by a town government patterned after the Spanish: a town council, which chose a *corregidor* to preside over it and serve as military commander. The selection of *corregidor* had to be confirmed by the Spanish provincial governor. Real control, of course, rested with the missionaries. The towns were laid out in rectangular patterns, with church, official buildings, and storehouses in the centre and the fields and pastures on the outskirts. One crop, usually yerba maté or Paraguay tea, was raised for sale to buy items that could not be produced locally. The Indians, who had known a rudimentary, shifting agriculture, were taught the use of the plough and European techniques, crops, and stock-raising. The livestock multiplied especially rapidly. The very prosperity of the missions, their existence under Jesuit control, and an unwise resistance by the Jesuits to payment of tribute excited jealousy on the part of the Spanish population and the civil and ecclesiastical authorities, so that the Jesuits were under a steady stream of criticism only partly countered by their influence at court. In 1657 a judge of the Audiencia of Charcas carried out an official investigation. He upheld the Jesuits as able and loyal servants of the crown, and found with approval that the missions had 800 firearms for defence. He also determined that the population contained 7,500 males who should have been paying tribute and recommended that tribute be levied on them. A settlement of this troublesome dispute was not reached until 1667.

In contrast to Spanish America, the years 1610–60 were a period of active exploration and territorial expansion for the American dominions of the Portuguese crown. This process was aided by the Dutch, who drove part of the Portuguese population inland and forced development of inland routes of communication. The exploration and expansion were carried out especially by *bandeiras*, a term derived from the reformed Spanish army, where it was applied to subdivisions of the *tercios*, the major tactical groupings of various arms. In Brazil the term came to mean a semi-military expedition of Portuguese settlers, with Tupi auxiliaries, which set out on a long, wandering trek that might last for years and had as its purpose trade, hunting for deposits of precious metals (not found in this period), slaving, or colonization. The members of such a band were called *bandeirantes*. The most famous *bandeirante* centre was São Paulo, then a small *mestizo* settlement on the plateau, which found sugar unprofitable and turned to supplying the southern coastal plantations around Santos and Rio de Janeiro with Indian slaves. Indian slaves, although less efficient and shorter-lived than Negroes, sold for approximately a fifth as much and provided labour for the less flourishing sugar plantations of the south. São Paulo was on the edge of the Paraná drainage, with easy access to the excellent river communications of the Río de la Plata. Portages gave access also to the northward-flowing rivers of the Amazon system and enabled the *bandeirantes* to penetrate deep into the continent. In a famous three-year expedition Antônio Raposo Tavares led a *bandeira* from São Paulo to the territory of Itatím in southern Mato Grosso, up the Paraguay River, and by portage into the Guaporé in the Amazon system. The band drifted down the Guaporé to its confluence with the Mamoré, followed the Mamoré into the Madeira, and the latter to the Amazon. Coasting down the Amazon it finally arrived in 1651 at the outermost Portuguese post of Gurupá, at the confluence of the Xingú and the Amazon, completing a vast semi-circle through the heart of South America. Other notable *bandeirante* centres were Bahia and Pernambuco in the north, and the new settlements in Maranhão.

We have already mentioned the abandonment of Guairá and adjacent areas by Spanish settlers and missions under the pressure of Paulista *bandeiras*. The *bandeiras* also explored a broad band of territory inland from the Brazilian coast, carrying off or driving back the Indian population, the survivors of which fled hundreds of miles westward. Extensive, upland areas of the north-east bulge, beyond the São Francisco Valley, inland from Bahia and Pernambuco, and northward to Ceará, were thus opened for cattle-raising by a sparse settlement of ranchers, who supplied hides and meat to the plantations on the coast. Farther north, Portuguese penetration wrested the delta and lower valley of the Amazon from the crown of Castile. The French and English established small trading posts in the Amazon delta in the opening years of the seventeenth century; these were driven out in 1613–15 by expeditions sent from north-east Brazil with the consent of the crown of Castile. In 1616 a settlement was founded near the present site of Belém do Pará on the Spanish side of the line by the reckoning of the time. Thereafter a small number of Portuguese spread through the region as far as Gurupá, founded in 1623. Because the prevailing winds along the coast made communication with the rest of Brazil more difficult than direct communication with Portugal, the territory was organized in 1621 as a separate state of Maranhão, directly dependent upon Lisbon. In default of any other good economic possibility, the settlers turned to slaving and soon devastated the lower Amazon. One *bandeira*, sent out specially by the governor of Maranhão, explored the Amazon upstream to the Spanish outposts in the Andes of Quito and returned in 1639, claiming all of the intervening land for the crown of Portugal.

The *bandeirantes* were undoubtedly a tough, cruel, lawless lot. Although they could cloak their destruction of the Spanish missions as patriotic resistance to the hated Castilians, they showed an equal lack of mercy for missions founded by Portuguese Jesuits. Even the great Portuguese Jesuit, Father Antônio Vieira, who had approved the destruction of the Spanish missions, was arrested and sent back to Portugal with his companions, when in 1652–61 he attempted to set up a similar system of reservations in Maranhão and end slaving. But the operations of the *bandeirantes* did explore much of the continent and bent the line of demarcation far westward. The greatest losses of territory by the crown of Castile were to the Portuguese and, aside from Jamaica and Curaçao, were in this period the only permanent losses of territory under actual control.

The more important development of European settlement, even in Brazil, however, was not extension of the area of occupation but the steady increase of European and Europeanized populations—the non-

Indians—in the older areas. Immigration from the Iberian Peninsula continued in considerable volume, perhaps an average of two to three thousand a year, although that estimate is pure guess since the records of official licences have not been found, and if found, would be no real clue because many immigrants crossed without official leave. Migration from Spain was characterized by a growing proportion of men from the north, the so-called *vascongados*, actually from Galicia as well as the Basque Provinces. Rivalry between them and the *andaluces*, or immigrants from southern Spain, became an important element of politics in mining camps, and in Potosí gave rise to a prolonged riot in 1624. Migration from Portugal was characterized, as earlier, by a relatively large proportion of Christianized Jews, seeking in the New World respite from persecution by the Inquisition. Numbers of New Christians filtered across the Río de la Plata to the wealthy centres of Peru by the routes of illegal trade. Small numbers of Europeans from outside the Iberian Peninsula were also able, as before, to settle in the New World under the thin disguise of an Iberian surname. They were seldom disturbed unless heretics or New Christians, and were usually able to legitimize their stay by suitable monetary payment to the crown. Most of the European immigrants were men, who married local women and merged easily into the community. The major increase of white population, of course, was through the natural increase of whites and mixed bloods considered to be whites. Families were large and households abounded in servants so that, although the death rate was high, the number of native-born whites or Creoles rose very rapidly. By 1650 there were in Spanish and Portuguese America perhaps 600,000 people considered to be whites, both European-born and Creoles. Over a quarter were in Mexico, which steadily received the greater share of immigration from Europe; perhaps 100,000 were in Lower and Upper Peru (present-day Peru and Bolivia); and 70,000 in Brazil.

The emergence of the Creoles as the overwhelming element in the white population had a number of consequences that became manifest in the first half of the seventeenth century. One of the most important was the growth of a bitter rivalry for social and economic position between the Creoles and people of European birth, the latter dubbed disparagingly *gachupines* and *chapetones*, for the newcomers tended to enter at the top of the social pyramid and the crown continued to prefer European-born for higher official posts. In the Mexican and Peruvian church, where there was a substantial Creole clergy by the beginning of the seventeenth century, the rivalry between Creoles and Spanish-born led in most of the monastic orders to the adoption of the *alternativa*, a scheme by which the important posts were held alternately by members of one group and then the other. In some instances, the rotation was threefold: between Creoles, Spanish-born who had taken their vows in the colonies, and Spanish-born who had taken their vows in Europe. The development of a substantial secular clergy, heavily Creole in its lower ranks, led also to demands that the missionary orders turn over the older Indian parishes for administration by secular priests under normal diocesan jurisdiction. These demands flared into especially bitter strife in the disputes between Bishop Palafox of Puebla and the Jesuits in the 1640s. The increase in number of secular clergy also gave greater acrimony to the dispute between secular and regular clergy over payment of tithes by Indians and on properties of regular clergy since tithes were the mainstay of the seculars.

The increase of the whites was paralleled by an equally rapid increase among the Negroes and mixed bloods. Demand for labour on the plantations and ranches of the Caribbean and of the Brazilian coast led to continued heavy importation of Negro slaves, which was favoured on the whole rather than hindered when the Dutch used their seizure of Angola to enter the slave trade. Even though most of the involuntary immigrants were male and disease and hard labour in the tropics took heavy toll, the number of blacks steadily increased. By 1650 there were nearly as many of them in Spanish and Portuguese America as whites. Perhaps half of the total were on the Caribbean islands and coasts, and perhaps 100,000 in Brazil. Such estimates, of course, are mere guesses. *Mestizos*, mulattoes, and other mixed bloods became a major element of the population in America in the first half of the seventeenth century. In 1650 they were approximately equal in number in Spanish and Portuguese America to either the whites or the Negroes, the mulattoes tending to be concentrated on the islands and coasts where there were most Negroes, the *mestizos* tending to be concentrated on the uplands and in the temperate zone, where most of the Indians lived. Many of the mixed bloods were able farmers and artisans, who swelled the Europeanized segments of the population and gave able militia service in defence against foreign intruders. But many moved into the cities, where they formed the lowest element of the urban population, a new class of *léperos*, making a precarious living supplemented and enlivened by crime and brawling. They were disliked and feared by the magistrates, who never had sufficient force available to repress disorder and quell popular tumult.

In marked contrast to the increase among the non-Indian elements of Iberian America was the steady decrease in the number of Indians as wars, enslavement, the destruction of native systems and enforced change to new ones, and most deadly of all, diseases from Europe and Africa continued the attrition which began with the appearance of the white man in America. The destruction was not confined to the areas of white penetration but reached far beyond because of the flight of tribes, consequent wars for territory, and the spread of the new diseases. Unfortunately, the movement of Indian population in this period still remains to be studied in detail for most areas so that only very general statements can be made and statistics are very much subject to dispute. In the

Caribbean islands, where most of the Indians had vanished long before the seventeenth century, the destruction of the sparse native population of the Lesser Antilles was the work of the new English, Dutch, and French settlers. In Mexico and Central America, where the aboriginal population suffered very heavy loss in the sixteenth century, it may have reached demographic bottom early in the seventeenth century, have remained there for a number of decades, and by 1640 may have begun a very slow and halting recovery. In the Andean regions of the former Incan Empire, the native population slowly but steadily decreased throughout the seventeenth century. In Venezuela, Paraguay, Chile and north-western Argentina, decrease was more rapid. In 1633, for example, the bishop of Santiago, Chile, reported that his diocese, essentially the core of Spanish Chile, had more Negroes and mulattoes than Indians. By the middle of the century the majority of *encomiendas* in Venezuela and north-west Argentina, which began as relatively ample grants, had fewer than twenty adult Indian males and many had shrunk to five or six—far too few to support a Spanish family. The destruction of Indian population in Brazil has already been mentioned.

General decrease among the Indians, combined with increase in the strata of population dependent upon them for supplies and services, meant a steadily deepening shortage of labour in most of Spanish America. The Antilles, which had long since turned to Negro slaves, and Brazil, which either used Negro slaves or devastated large areas to secure Indian slaves, were exempt except for the difficulties of procurement and high costs of their form of labour. Elsewhere, the last decades of the sixteenth century and most of the seventeenth century, but especially the decades 1610–60, were notable for the failure of older forms of deriving labour from the Indians and the development of new forms. The oldest Spanish device, the *encomienda*, had lost importance by the middle of the sixteenth century in Mexico and by the end of the sixteenth century in Upper and Lower Peru; by the end of the sixteenth century most *encomiendas* in these areas had escheated to the crown. But the *encomienda* continued to be important in the marginal areas such as Venezuela, Chile, and the rest of southern South America, where Indian tributaries continued to pay all or part of their tribute in labour, the legal maximum varying from one to three months a year in the various regions. During the first half of the seventeenth century, as *encomienda* populations shrank, *encomienda* labour became unimportant even in these outlying areas. A second device for securing labour, the *mita, repartimiento, tanda* or *rueda* had become important in Spanish America during the second half of the sixteenth century. Under it the Indian towns were called upon to make available a fixed proportion of their adult males for wage labour in fields and mines. In Mexico, the quota was set in agriculture at 4 per cent in ordinary times and 10 per cent during the two peak agricultural seasons of weeding and harvest, in mining at three weeks' work a year for married men and four for unmarried adolescents. The quotas made available approximately 6 per cent of the Indian men as an annual average. In the viceroyalty of Peru the *mita* varied from region to region, but may be illustrated by the instance of the quota set for the sixteen provinces assigned to the service of the mines of Potosí, the famous *mita de Potosí*. The Indian towns had to provide workmen for periods of service of four months at a time. The quota is usually stated to have been a seventh but was actually a seventh for the three *turnos* of a year, so that the proportion was slightly under 5 per cent on annual average. The service was regarded as especially onerous because the workmen were kept from their families for such long periods and were forced to work under especially trying conditions at very high altitudes. It became even more hated in the first half of the seventeenth century as the miners began to require delivery of a fixed quota of ore for each day's work and the Indians had to work far beyond the legal day to meet the requirement. The *mita de Potosí* became steadily less effective as a means of supplying labour. In 1610 the number of workmen could still be set at 4,413 and in 1633 at 4,115, the latter quota presupposing a population of 86,415 tributaries in the sixteen provinces. But by the mid-century the *mita* yielded approximately half the quota, and by 1662 the sixteen provinces were estimated to have a population of only 16,000 tributaries. The Indian towns were required to make up the deficit by forcing their men to additional turns of service, sometimes as frequently as every two years instead of the legal seven, or had to provide money for hiring substitutes at the very much higher wage rate of free labour. The Potosí *mita* was so deeply hated that flight was more important than death in depleting the sixteen provinces. Elsewhere, in the viceroyalty of Peru, the *mita* had a less unfortunate history but also became less efficient as a form of deriving labour. A third device, which began early in the sixteenth century, was so-called free wage labour. Actually the workmen were bound to the employer by advances of money and goods and could not leave until they had cleared the debt. By renewing the advances, through force if necessary, the employer saw to it there was always a debt. The workmen were withdrawn from Indian towns and were settled either in Spanish towns or near the mines or on the farms and ranches where they worked. The device had the additional advantage that it could be used to secure labour from the *mestizos* and mixed-bloods. Free wage labour, with its concomitant device of debt peonage, was already prominent in Mexico by the end of the sixteenth century as large settlements of free labourers grew up around such mining camps as Zacatecas. During the first decades of the seventeenth century it was resorted to increasingly in Mexico and became the most important form of labour procurement. It was sufficiently successful for the viceroy of New Spain, in 1632, to order abandonment of the *repartimiento* in agriculture, although not in mining, which needed all labour that could be secured by whatever means. In the viceroyalty of Peru labour of the same kind became important in mining in the seventeenth century, and around such centres as Potosí there grew up substantial communities of Indians and mixed-bloods. The increase in the number of *yanaconas*, a term which earlier meant serfs, in the seventeenth century probably meant increase in debt peons bound to the estates and workshops. For the employer, wage labour, with or without debt peonage, had the great advantage that he secured all the working time of his employees and had a stable labour force. For the workmen, although they entered a form of bondage, there was at least the advantage that it was often relatively benign since the employer protected his workmen from the frequently much more merciless exploitation of the native nobility, the church, and civil officials. For the Indian towns, the device meant the steady loss of members to meet demands for labour and taxes and to maintain community services. The wage labourers seldom returned to their native towns and in new settlements took on European customs and mixed freely with other groups to swell the Hispanized *mestizo* element. As a labour device, wage labour and debt peonage were sufficiently successful for slavery to be able to compete only on the tropical coasts and on sugar plantations with their special needs. Nevertheless, the colonies passed through trying times, perhaps at their worst between 1620 and 1660.

It was shortage of labour, with its attendant factors of abandonment of agricultural land by the Indians and lessened production of food for the cities, that was perhaps most important in producing the economic stringency and depression that characterized the last quarter of the sixteenth century and much of the seventeenth century in the greater part of Iberian America. There were, of course, other factors increasingly operative in the seventeenth century that accentuated the depressive effects of labour shortage: the movement of the European economy, which entered a downward phase between 1630 and 1640 and the growing financial demands of the Spanish crown because of its participation in the Thirty Years' War. In addition, the entrance of non-Iberian nations into American trade on an increasing scale greatly affected established systems of trade. All factors combined to speed up a series of complex economic and social changes already under way. The net result, in the end, as in the solutions for labour, was greatly to strengthen the Europeanized segments of colonial society. Unfortunately, few studies have yet been made of most aspects of these changes for the various regions of Ibero-America so that our information is scanty and most statements, except those on the legal Atlantic trade, are largely conjecture. Our information is best for Mexico and Brazil.

In agriculture, the continued abandonment of land as the Indian population shrank led to continued and accelerating growth of large European landholdings. Such a growth would have taken place in any event because of the limited number of fields of economic activity open to an upper class in the seventeenth century and the economic security and social prestige attached to ownership of land, but it would have taken place much more slowly had the native population continued to occupy most of the land. In Mexico, where the phenomenon was well under way in the latter half of the sixteenth century, the bulk of land available for royal grant was given away or sold by the crown by the early decades of the seventeenth century. The largest number of grants was made between 1580 and 1610. Thereafter the formation of great estates took place by purchase and by the procedure of *composición*. The landholder who had occupied land secured a legal title through a compromise payment to the crown. In 1631 the crown, spurred on by its financial difficulties, ordered a general survey of land titles in the Spanish Indies in order to force such payments. As the surveys were carried out during the next twenty years, landholders were able to secure legal title to the large irregular tracts between former grants and to legitimize seizures from the Indians. Many of the new latifundia were owned by the clergy so that in 1631 the Mexico City council complained that a third of the land in Mexico was in mortmain. In Chile, where the development of large estates was equally rapid in this period, a survey carried out in 1604, ostensibly to protect the Indians in their lands, actually served to disclose the existence of large vacated tracts, all of which were occupied through grant or seizure by 1620. Throughout Iberian America, including Brazil, there was a similar development of large estates although at varying rate. The estates were kept intact by entail or by the custom of giving shares in common ownership to heirs rather than divide the inheritance. Much of the capital for the development of the estates in Spanish America came from the profits of office-holding and mining or from the very rapid development in this period of *censos*, funds put out on mortgage either for stipulated periods or permanently. Charitable and religious endowments consisted largely of funds invested in this way.

Many, perhaps most of the large estates, were devoted to stock-raising, which expanded very greatly in this period. It had the very important advantage of requiring little capital and labour and of being especially well suited for exploitation of large areas. We have already mentioned the great growth of stock-raising in Brazil and the Jesuit missions of the Río de la Plata. It was also true in Chile, which became a series of great cattle estates, in Cuba, northern Mexico, and in other areas. Stock-raising meant primarily cattle, although by no means exclusively so, and was characterized by a peculiar rhythm at its beginning. In the first years, the cattle increased very rapidly to such vast numbers that they passed the carrying capacity of the land. There was then a sharp contraction during which thousands and even millions of animals died, and the cattle came to balance at much lower numbers with the long-term carrying capacity of the land. In central Mexico the contraction was already evident by the end of the sixteenth century so that the great increase of the period 1610–60 took place on the new ranches of Sinaloa, Durango, Chihuahua and Coahuila. Throughout America, in general, there was little market for the meat; the major products were hides and tallow, which were exported or were used in large quantities by the mines. The ranches also supplied horses and mules for traction, and large quantities of wool for local production of coarser cloths.

The expansion of large European estates also made possible increased production of wheat, wine, and other foodstuffs for the cities and mines, taking advantage of the growing market left vacant by the decline in Indian production and enabling the Europeans to meet serious, and at times critical, problems of supply. Many of the large estates were devoted to sugar cane, the cultivation of which expanded greatly in the first half of the seventeenth century although profits fell off sharply after perhaps 1620. Brazil, already prominent in European supply of sugar at the opening of the century, increased deliveries rather steadily, the difficulties of the Portuguese after 1620 being more than made good through the expansion and reorganization of plantations by the Dutch. There was also a rapid expansion of sugar-cane-raising and extracting and processing mills in the Spanish Indies—in Santo Domingo, the Atlantic and Pacific coasts, and tropical mountain areas up to elevations of 1,500 metres. The very substantial production of Mexico and Peru was used locally; that of the Caribbean islands was exported to Spain. Sugar plantations were large industrial establishments requiring considerable amounts of capital if the owners controlled all processes. They needed large tracts of land for cane, pasture, and food; a heavy investment in expensive Negro slaves; complicated machinery for grinding the cane, concentrating the juice, and purifying it; and the hiring of skilled workmen to supervise the operations. In Brazil, much cane was raised by smaller planters, dependent on credit, who delivered their cane to the owner of the grinding mill for a percentage of the sugar. Other estates were self-contained enterprises. In general, the latter were the rule in the Spanish Indies. The Jesuits did much to develop sugar-raising in Mexico and Peru, and owned a number of unusually well-organized and eventually profitable plantations.

Another development in agriculture of the years 1610–60 was the extension of cacao-raising in the Spanish Indies. Aside from local production, the major source of supply during the sixteenth century was the Sonsonate area of Central America, which shipped to both Mexico and Peru. Shortly after the beginning of the seventeenth century, the viceroyalty of Peru developed its own supply on the coast around Guayaquil. At the same time, the low-lying areas of Venezuela finally found a profitable crop in cacao and opened an expanding export trade to Mexico. During this period the taste for drinking chocolate was still confined to America and to Spain so that there was relatively little shipment to Europe.

The course of mining is perhaps the most difficult to assess of all areas of economic activity. Mining in seventeenth-century America meant silver mining. It was regarded as the key industry since it furnished specie for exchange against imports and for remittances and the expenses of the Iberian crown in Europe. Receipts of treasure in Spain, for which excellent estimates are available to 1650, reached a peak in the decade 1591–1600, remained at a high level until 1630, and then fell off sharply. But, by the middle decades of the seventeenth century, shipments to Spain were no longer a clear indication of production. The increasing needs of the American colonies for circulating medium meant that much larger quantities of silver were retained there. Very large amounts of specie also reached Europe through illegal channels, either unregistered in Spanish shipping, or through trade with Portuguese and non-Iberian shipping. Buenos Aires and Brazil were especially important in siphoning off silver. Furthermore, the entire process of production and taxation was attended by a series of frauds that had become custom. In many districts of Peru, for example, it was customary to declare bars of newly processed silver at a fraction of their real value, as low as half, for purposes of assessment of the royal fifth. It is thus very difficult to determine the movement of silver production in this period. On the whole, it seems likely that production at least remained stationary and may well have declined in Mexico, especially in the 1640s and 1650s when many miners moved into stock-raising, and that production declined in Peru. It certainly did not expand greatly anywhere in America as it had done in the sixteenth century although there were still profitable new finds—in Mexico, the mines of the Parral district of Chihuahua 1631–4; in Peru, those of Pasco in 1630 and of Laicacota in 1657. The relatively static condition of the industry was brought about in part by the serious labour shortages already mentioned but also by the operation of an especially complex series of other factors: costs, taxes, credit, and technology inadequate for the problems encountered. The fundamental problem was that American mining was based upon quantity processing of ores of low grade. For a few years after each find, the miners worked in the weathered and relatively concentrated surface ores, which were easily dug and processed, with high yield. They soon reached water level, below which lay unweathered lodes with abundant supplies of ore of low concentration of metal. Excavating the ore involved extensive tunnelling and the difficult problem of drainage without pumps. Neither blasting by gunpowder nor drainage by horse-drawn whim was widely used until the beginning of the eighteenth century. The most effective solution known at this time was drainage by a tunnel driven below the level of the mine, an expensive and arduous undertaking but one carried out in Potosí in the great tunnel completed in 1636. The ore was usually carried on the backs of Indian workmen, who climbed series of ladders to reach the mouth of the shaft. Processing the ore was mostly by the patio process introduced and improved in the sixteenth century. The ore was ground, mixed with mercury, salt, and at times iron and copper pyrites, and at length the silver was extracted. Such treatment required a large investment in grinding and processing plants, and paid heavy tribute to the crown through the royal monopolies of mercury and salt. Few men were able to control the mining through the series of operations from extraction to processing. Usually, the miners who extracted ore sold it to middlemen, who in turn sold it to processing plants. At each link in the chain, the men were bound by advances of credit, without which they could not continue work, even to the owners of processing mills, who were usually heavily in debt to the crown for supplies of mercury and salt. The entire industry, furthermore, suffered from the rising prices of the sixteenth and early seventeenth centuries, which steadily drove up costs at the same time that output was sold for a fixed value of one *peso* (piece of eight reals or silver dollar) an ounce. When the financial needs of the crown led it to attempt to raise the price of mercury or to order early payment of the millions of *pesos* owing it, as happened in this period, the industry was threatened with ruin. In seventeenth-century Mexico, the term miner became synonymous with respectable poverty.

The greatest decay of production was at Potosí in Peru, whose mountain of silver earlier had provided the overwhelming proportion of Peruvian specie and rather more than half of American output. There the decline was bound up with the peculiar arrangement by which Indian towns made up shortages in their *mita* quotas through payment of the wages of a substitute at the rate of seven to seven and a half *pesos* a week. The arrangement was accepted by many towns as preferable to the hardships of work in the mines. The miners of Potosí accordingly were afforded the attractive prospect of having their labour supplied free or of simply pocketing the payments. A miner or processer with an allotment of forty *mitayos* (the average) could pay the royal taxes on a non-existent production and live on the remainder. The decay of the Potosí mines affected the extensive zones in Lower and Upper Peru and the Río de la Plata which supplied manufactures, foodstuffs, and animals, as indeed the decline of mining throughout America affected the workshops, farms, and ranches that had developed to supply the mines.

In trade, the period was marked by the increasingly static quality and eventual decline of the legal trade to Spanish America in the annual fleets. The system was cumbersome, monopolistic, and burdened with heavy taxes and the costs of defence. The merchant gild of Seville operated in collusion with the merchant gilds of Mexico City and Lima to keep prices high by storing merchandise and deliberately creating scarcity. As a defensive measure against foreign attack the fleets proved successful since, despite many attempts, only two were seized, one in 1628 by the Dutch and another in 1656-7 by the English; but as a commercial system they were increasingly unable to compete in greatly changed conditions. The largest fleet shipment of wares from Spain took place in 1608, with an estimated 45,000 maritime tons of approximately 54 cubic feet each. The average annual tonnage, calculated by five-year periods, continued to rise until 1616-20, largely through greater shipments to Mexico. From 1621 to 1650 there was a slow but rather steady decline in tonnage shipped, and after 1651 a precipitous drop. In the composition of the fleets themselves, there was a decrease in the number of ships, large numbers of which were lost in storms, but until the mid-century the decrease in number was made good in large part by the greater size of the new vessels built. In general, the fleets were able to sail each year until 1654 when the wars and lessened ability of defraying costs from the shipments led to suspension of the sailings in many years. The crown of Portugal did not have a fleet system for Brazil and permitted free sailings from all Portuguese ports. Only for a short period beginning in 1649 did it set up a semi-monopolistic company in order to ensure protection from Dutch attack.

The decline in the legal trade to Spanish America coincided in general with the downward movement of the European economy in the middle decades of the century. It was therefore due to many factors, of which two seem especially important: the growth of local manufactures and intercolonial trade and a vast increase in interloping or foreign contraband. There had been steady development of local agriculture and simpler manufactures during the sixteenth century in most of the colonies, many of which soon became self-sufficient or even developed surpluses for export to other colonies in wheat, olive oil, wine, and the coarser varieties of woollens. Chile and Mexico, for example, developed export trades in wheat and Peru one in wine, all to the detriment of fleet shipments from Spain. The Chinese trade via Manila also provided silks and finer wares for Mexico, and through transhipment at Acapulco for Peru and other colonies. As early as the 1590s the crown of Castile tried to protect the fleets, which were vital in imperial communication and finance, by limiting the Philippine trade, forbidding transhipment of Chinese wares, and ordering discouragement of competing colonial production of such items as silk, olive oil, and wine. When the early measures proved inadequate, the crown issued more stringent orders, such as forbidding Peruvian shipments of olive oil and wine to Panama and Guatemala (1614-15) and of wheat flour to Panama (1630). In 1634 it took the drastic step of prohibiting all trade between the viceroyalties of Mexico and Peru in an effort to cut off transhipment of Chinese wares. Evasion was widespread, however, and intercolonial trade prospered under a series of devices with the collusion of colonial administrators.

Foreign interloping or contraband also became very extensive in this period. The major centres were the Caribbean, which provided innumerable islands and inlets for illicit landings, and the Río de la Plata area with its excellent port at Buenos Aires and easy access by river and land to the great mining centres of Upper and Lower Peru. The principal interlopers at first were the Portuguese who, with the advantage of being common subjects during the crown union, made use of contracts for supplying Negro slaves for introduction of other wares and further built up a flourishing *entrepôt* trade through which wares of all European countries were shipped from Portugal to Brazil and then passed through the Río de la Plata. After the rupture of the crown union in 1640, the Portuguese were careful to avoid all hostilities with the Río de la Plata. The other major interlopers were the Dutch, who took the place of the Portuguese in the slave trade once they seized control of the African posts and early in the century engrossed a substantial part of Caribbean trade. Their seizure and settlement of islands in the Caribbean in the 1630s and occupation of part of Brazil 1624–54 gave them bases from which to carry on a trade in which the colonists enthusiastically participated. The French and English were of lesser importance in direct contraband trade in America although the French supplied an increasing proportion of the wares shipped in the legal trade from Seville.

The decline of the fleet shipments and the parallel decrease in receipts of American treasure in Spain indicated in general the growing failure of the crown of Castile to secure revenue from America in precisely the period when its needs became greater because of the Thirty Years War. This failure occurred despite strenuous efforts to increase fiscal yields, and was made worse by resort to whole or partial seizures of private shipments of treasure six times between 1621 and 1649. The reign of Philip IV was marked by repeated appeals to the generosity of his American subjects for voluntary contributions, there being ten such appeals in the years 1621–65; by the imposition of a series of new taxes; and by the sale of many of the higher offices in the colonies, such as accounting and treasury posts, which had hitherto been reserved from sale to ensure more honest administration and firmer royal control. The *composiciónes generales*, introduced in the 1630s, granted royal consent or pardon for seizures of land, maintenance of illegal liquor shops, and for a series of other infractions of laws. The net result of all these fiscal measures was increasing loss of royal control over colonial administrators, an even greater rapacity on the part of provincial and district governors, and the increasing absorption of the revenues of the empire through peculation, evasion, and smuggling. The profits of the Spanish Empire passed increasingly into the hands of colonial administrators in alliance with local magnates. In a somewhat parallel development in Brazil, where central control was weaker from the beginning, resistance to rule by the unpopular Habsburgs and the successful expulsion of the Dutch by the colonists, over initial opposition of João IV of the Braganza dynasty, created an especially vigorous, self-reliant, and defiant local spirit centred in the town councils. As in the expulsion of the Jesuits, they did not hesitate to over-ride royal command. In both Spanish and Portuguese America at the mid-century, impoverished and weakened central governments faced resistant, tenacious, and deep-rooted local interests.

INDEX

Aachen, 287
Abaza Hasan Pasha, revolt of (1658), 630, 642
Abaza Mehemmed, beglerbeg of Erzurum, revolt (1622-8), 629-30; battles of Kayseri (1624) and Erzurum (1627), 629; becomes beglerbeg of Bosnia, 630
Abbas I, shah of Persia, 645
  recovers territories ceded to the Ottoman Turks in the war of 1603-7, 630; and the Baghdad campaign (1624-6), 631
Abbot, George, archbishop of Canterbury, 546, 553
  suspension, 555; and Buckingham, 557; readmitted to the privy council (1628), 558; moderate church policy, 565
Abel, W., economic theories, 10, 15
Abyssinia, Jesuit mission to, 667
Académie Française, and Richelieu, 491
Académie royale des Sciences, France, founded (1666), 142
Acadia, Canada, 691
  Champlain and, 676
  French colonization, 697; granted to the earl of Stirling (1622), 697; colonization by the Kirks and the Nova Scotia Company, 698
Acapulco, Mexico, 79, 724
Acaya, marquess of, leads revolt in Naples, 55
Accademia degli Incogniti, Padua, 199
Accademia dei Lincei, Rome, 140
Accademia del Cimento, Florence, founded (1657), 140
Achin, Sumatra
  English accept rights to sovereignty of, 671, enemy of Portuguese in Malacca, 645, 655; political centre for Muslims, 655; conquests in Johore, Sumatra, Quedda and Perak (1620's), 655-6; attacks Jambi and the Dutch (1624-7), 656; attacks Indragiri (1632), 656; relations with Dutch, 646-7, 649, 655-7
  trade in cotton, 657, 661, and pepper, 653, 655-6
Acoustics, development, 158
Acta sanctorum, 378
Actors, *see* Drama
Aden, 646
Adharbayjan, 628, 633
Adirondacks, 676

Aegean Sea, Turco-Venetian wars in, 640-1, 643
Afrasiyab, House of, control Basra (c. 1600), 630
Africa
  botanical collections from, 164
  development of histories of, 1
  Dutch trade in Asian cotton, 661, 670; trade in slaves, 704-5, 725
  mines in, 78
  population, 70
  Portuguese in East Africa, risings against (c. 1600), 645; lose slave-trade centres, 725; position in West Africa, 664
Agra, cotton trade, 661
Agram, Jesuits in, 521
Agreement of the People (1647), 580
Agriculture
  dominant industry in the period, 91
  prices, 62-3, 89-91
  shift from grain to livestock, 93
  social effects of increased production, 15
  trends, 64-5, 89
  see also Grain, and *under* names of countries
Agung, sultan of Mataram, conquests in the East Indies (1619-25), 655; attacks Dutch in Batavia (1628-9), 655; Palembang submits to, 655; death (1646), 655
Ahmed I, sultan, 622
  accession (1603) and the law of fratricide, 621; army reform code, 629; and Iraq, 630; death (1617), 623, 636
Ahmed II, sultan, accession (1691), 622
Ahmed Köprülü, grand vizier, 643
  captures Candia (1669), 642; ends Turco-Venetian war, 642; reforms of, 61
Aiguillon, duchesse d', 493
Ai Island, *see* Pulo Ai Island
'Ajlun, 632
Akbar, Mughal emperor, supports Jesuit missions, 667
al-Ahsa; 630
Alais, Peace of (1629), 328
Álamos de Barrientos, Balthasar, political theorist, uses inductive methods, 130
Albania
  mercenaries of, 638; local resistance to the Ottoman Turks, 637
  pirates of, *see* Uskoks

INDEX

America (*cont.*)
population, 70
religion: Catholicism spreads to, 262; Puritan migration to, 704
trade, *see* Trade, trans-Atlantic
America, Central
numbers of Indians, 717
America, Iberian
increase in European population (1610–60), 714–15; type of emigrants from Spain and Portugal, 715; Creoles: increase of, 715; rivalry with European-born settlers, 715; increase in negro population, 716; *mestizos* and mulattoes 716; Indian decline, 716–17, 719–20
economic depression, 719; causes of the growth of European as opposed to native developments, 719–20; growth of European estates, 720; stock-raising, 720–1; wool production, 721; food-stuffs grown, 721; sugar-cane production, 721; cacao-raising, 721–2; silver mining, technical methods and exports, 722–3; poverty of miners, 723; exports, 721–2; contraband trade, 725
America, North, 682
Dutch claims, 675; French claims, 675; Dutch, French and English rivalry in, 690; relative positions by 1648, 701, 706; Spanish claims to, 6, 707; colonization methods, 677
America, South
and Portugal: 709–15; extent of territory, 707; exploration and acquisition by the Portuguese *bandeiras*, 713–14
America, Spanish
economic change in, 12
nobility in, 19
extent of Spanish occupation, 708–9
enquiry into Jesuit activities (1657), 713
encroachment by the Portuguese, 714
labour shortage and the *encomienda*, 717; and the *mita, repartimiento, tanda* or *rueda*, 717–18; free wage labour and debt peonage, 718–19; slave labour, 719
land surveys (1631–51), 720
decline of legal trade to, 723–4; and its causes, 724; imports and exports of the colonies, 708, 724; trade regulations, 724
fiscal measures by Castile increases power of colonies, 725–6
America, *see also* under countries and places
Amiens, taxation, 47; cloth industry, 64; municipal oligarchs, 65; economic position of peasants, 66; commerce, 477

Ammirato, Scipione, Italian historian, 261
theories of *raison d'état*, 116, and their influence, 117; his *Discorsi supra Cornelio Tacito* (1598), 117
Amoy, China, Dutch establish trade with Formosa, 659
Amsterdam, 78, 201, 365, 413
price trends, 62, 91; banking, 68, 84–5; immigration, 77–8, 366; bills of exchange, 83; marine insurance rates, 89; merchants' speculations, 100; Tulip Mania crash of 1636–7, 100; investment in armaments, 101; influx of *entrepreneurs*, 271, 292; economic growth of, 280, 366; German merchants in, 296; federal taxes, 362
plague in, 76
population, 71, 366
and the 1632 peace negotiations, 380; opposition to William II (1647), 383; the army crisis of 1649, 383
religion: Arminian school and seminary, Athenaeum Illustre, founded in, 180, 374; and the Gomarist-Arminian controversy, 372–4; toleration in, 201; English Separatists emigrate to (1608–9), 681
trade: centre for ammunitions, 367; facilities for grain trade in, 92; and the Dutch East India Company, 647; the London East India Company and the pepper trade, 653; and the Dutch West India Company, 691, 696
Amsterdam, Bank of (1609), 366
Amsterdam Exchange, building of (1611), 366
Amsterdam, Wisselbank, founded (1609), 68, 84
Amur river, 6, 616
Russian fur traders explore, 663
Amyraut, Moses (1596–1664), introduces Arminianism to the Huguenots, 181
Anabaptists, 176
Anatolia, revolts in, 1; population, 71; raids by the Cossacks, 596
Anatomy, teaching and development, 136–8, 164
Anchialos, Cossack raid (1621), 636
Ancre, Concino Concini, marquis of, 121
member of the secret council, 481; and the princes' revolt, 482–3; favourite of Henri IV, 481; assassination of (1617), 483
Andalusia, nobility, proportion of population, 18
revolt, 55
disease (1599–1600), 439; (1649), 471
famine (1647), 471

Argentina *(cont.)*
Indian population declines, 717; effect on the *encomiendas*, 717
crops grown in, 712–13
Argentina, *see also* Buenos Aires, Misiones, Rio de la Plata, Tucuman
Arguin Island, capture by Dutch West India Company, 705
Ariosto, *Orlando Furioso*, 28
Aristotle, 131, 147
status of occupations, 20
his system of physics, 139, 143–4, 154
distinction between artificial and natural bodies, 148
chemical theories, 159
his rules for drama, 257
Aristotelians, 156
Armenia, 628
Armies, *see* Warfare, armies
Arminianism, 195, 554
origins and beliefs, 177–8; views on toleration, 170, 181; political thought leads to conflict with the state, 179, 372; The Remonstrance, 179, 372; opposed by Maurice of Nassau, 123; the conflict in Holland, 372–4; defeated at the Synod of Dort (1618), 123, 180, 374; revived 180, 374; theories developed by Hugo Grotius, 180–1; summarized, 182
spreads abroad, 181–2, 558; foundation of church in Amsterdam (1630), 374; foundation of Athenaeum Illustre (1632), 374
Arminius, Jacobus, professor, divides Calvinism by his attack on predestination, 177; his beliefs, 177–8; accused of heresy, 188; and Gomarus, 371
Arnauld, mère Angélique, abbess of the Convent of Port-Royal, reforms convent, 188–9; and St Cyran, 188–9
Arnauld, Antoine, 188, 479
his *De la fréquente communion* (1643), 189–90, 501; religious and political beliefs, 191
Arndt, Johannes, his *True Christianity* (1605), 175
Arnim, Hans Georg von, besieges Stralsund (1628), 326; and the Edict of Restitution, 336; enters Saxon service, 336; invades Bohemia (1631), 336; negotiations with Wallenstein, 337–8, 343–4
Articuli Heinriciani, 585–6
Artois, occupied by French troops (1641), 350, 493; Treaty of the Pyrenees (1659), 428
Arumæus, Dominicus, professor at Jena University, his *Discursus Academici ad*

Auream Bullam (1617), 110; *Commentarius de Comitiis Romano-Germinanici imperii* (1630), 110
Arundel, Thomas Howard, second earl of Surrey and of, 345–6, and Buckingham, 553, 557
Aselli, Gasparo, anatomist, 136
Ash, John, clothier, 575, 582
Asia, 1, 2, 5
population, 70
spread of Catholicism to, 262, 667; Dutch provoke Islamic reaction, 670
extent and effect of European penetration into, 663–4, 670; influence of Asia on Europe, 670–1
relationships with Portugal (*c.* 1600), 644; port-to-port trading, 651; Dutch attempt to eliminate Asian traders, 651–3; pepper trade, 653; cotton trade, 657; Russian penetration, 663
see also under names of places
Asia Minor
and the Ottoman Turks, 639
recruitment of troops in, 625–6, 641; causes of unrest, 627–9; revolt (1607–10), 629; revolt against the janissaries (1622–8), 629–30; revolts of 1647, 1658 and 1687–8, 630, 642
Assada Association (Courteen Association), rivals East India Company, 562, 664
Aston, Sir Thomas, 574
and Presbyterianism, 572
Astrakhan, conquered by Ivan IV, 662
Astronomy, planetary theories, 2, 154–5; teaching, 134; chair founded at Oxford, 137; theories expounded at Oxford, 138; Accademia dei Lincei and research, 140; development of scientific instruments, 149–50
Atheism, 199–200
Atlantic coast, sugar production, 721
Augsburg
population losses due to war, 77
currency debasement, 82; index of silver values and the *Rechnungsgulden*, 86–7; changes in price trends, 88; linen trade, 293
Rathaus, 304
Augsburg, Confession of, 169
Augsburg, League of, formed by Maximilian I (1616), 291
Augsburg, Peace of (1555), 355
Augustine, Saint, 188, 190, 192, 197
Augustinianism, 201
as understood by the Jansenists, 191–2
Augustinians, missions to India, 669

INDEX

Barbary corsairs, 232, 303, 486, 638–9
Barbin, Claude, French controller of finances, made controller (1616), 482
Barcelona
and the Cardinal-Infant [Ferdinand] (1632), 466
resentment at the central government's taxation, 466
rising in (1640), 469
defeat of Marqués de los Vélez at (1641), 470
siege of (1651–2), 423, 425, 471–2
trade in silver, 81
Barnes, T. G., poor relief and the Book of Orders, 563
Baroja, J. Caro, 25, 29
Baronius, Caesar, cardinal, Vatican librarian, 7
Baroque art, as expression of economic stress, 9; in Italy, 2; in the Habsburg Empire, 528–9
Barrientos, Alamos de, 461
Bartholinus, Thomas, professor of anatomy at Copenhagen, 136
Bartolus, Italian jurist, theories about the nobility, 16, 22
Bärwalde, Treaty of (1631), 331–2, 395
renewed (1633), 342, 401
Basel University, 136
Basil Shuiskij, tsar, see Vasily Shuisky, tsar
Basque provinces
nobility, status of occupations, 21
taxation, 46
emigration to South America, 715
Basra, 645
House of Afrasiyab takes control (c. 1600), 630
Portuguese trade with, 662
Bassano, price trends in, 62
Bassompierre, François, baron de, marquis d'Harouel, marshal of France, imprisoned, 491
Bastille, the, 491
Bastwick, John, and the Star Chamber, 565
Batavia, formerly Jakarta, Java, United East India Company established in, 100; fortified, 649; resists English, and the regents of Bantam and Jakarta (1619), 649; renamed Batavia, 649; becomes centre for Dutch, 649, 658; Bandanese sent as slaves to (1621), 651; pepper trade, 653; Chinese sent by Dutch to (1620–1), 654; Bantam's hostility towards, 655; Sultan Agung of Mataram attacks on (1628–9), 655; Coen's plans for, 658; centre for trade in precious metals, 659–60

Bath, B. H. Slicher van, see Slicher, B. H. van Bath
Bathory, Sigismund, 296
Batjan, Molucca Islands, Dutch take Spanish fort of (c. 1609), 648
Batticaloa, Ceylon, Portuguese lose to Dutch (1639–40), 666
Bauhin, Caspar
establishes study of botany and anatomy, 136
his Prodromus theatri botanici (1620), 164
Bavaria
administration, 290
army development and changes: the Landrettung, 203
nobility, definition of, 23
population losses due to war, 77
prosperity in (1600–1621), 292
foreign affairs: annexes Donauwörth, (1607), 288–9; feared by Swabia, 289; joins the refounded Catholic League (1616), 291; invades Palatine (1621), 549–50; and Richelieu, 335; truce with Sweden (1632), 335; invasion by Sweden (1632), 337; Swedish devastation, 338; joins Wallenstein's invasion of Saxony, 340; defeat at Jankau (1645), 351; invasion by Turenne and Wrangel (1646), 351; devastation of, 351–2; defeat of Zusmarshausen (1648), 352; elector, Ferdinand Maria and the imperial succession (1657–8), 419; see also Maximilian I
peasant revolt (1633), 343
religion: Counter-Reformation in, 514
dukes of, see Maximilian I, duke, afterwards elector of Bavaria; William V
Baxter, Richard, and the Association movement, 582
Bayezid, son of Sultan Süleyman, 627
Bayning, Paul, London merchant, 533
Béarn
Luynes and, 483
Union with Navarre (1620), 483
Beauce, the, wool production, 477; disorder in (1652), 499
Beaufort, François de Vendôme, duke of
and the Cabale des Importants, 494
imprisonment (1643), 494
Beaumont, Francis, dramatist, wrote for the King's Men, 255
Beauvais
price trends, 62, 89; grain prices, 74; commerce of, 477; textile industry, 477–8
administration, 479
mortality in, 480
revolts, 480

734

Cape of Good Hope, 367
  ceded by Portugal, to the Dutch, 434;
    trade route, 640, 646, 660, 662; effects
    of Portuguese discovery, 670
Cape São Roque, Brazil, 708
Cape Verde, and the Barbary corsairs, 232
Capuchins, 521
  mission to Istanbul, 638
Caramanico, Bartolomeo Aquino, prince
    of, 48
Cárdenas, Iñigo de, Spanish ambassador,
    promotes Spanish party in France,
    268–9; in England (1652), 423
Carew, Thomas, poet and masque writer,
    his *Coelum Britannicum* (1634), 253
Caribbean, trade by Dutch and English,
    226, 446; Spanish fail to protect
    Caribbean from the Dutch, 229; centre
    for attacks on Spanish bullion fleet,
    701–2, and contraband trade, 725
Caribbean Islands, *see* West Indies
Caribs, fight English on St Christopher,
    702; resistance to colonization, 703;
    in the Lesser Antilles, 708, 717;
    decline of, 707–8, 716–17
Carinthia, constitution and administration,
    504–5; and archduke Ferdinand, 283
Carletti, Francisco, merchant, 5
Carlisle, James Hay, first earl of, granted the
    Windward and Leeward Islands, 702;
    aids Warner, 702; wins Barbados
    against rival claims (1629), 702
Carmelites, 521
  missions to India, 669
Carmelites, Discalced, 528
Carniola, ruled by archduke Ferdinand,
    283; constitution and administration,
    504–5
Carpenter, Nathanael, contributions to
    astronomy in his *Discorsi*, 154 and note
Carpio, duke of, *see* Haro, Don Luis de
Carr-Saunders, Sir Alexander, population
    estimates, 70
Cartagena, Colombia, 701
Cartesianism, 136, 142, 377–8
  its value, 148; weakness of its methodology,
    155–6
Casale, siege of (1629), 42–3, 328; in
    French control (1640s), 414; siege of
    (*c.* 1650), 423, 425
Casanate, Porter, governor of Chile,
    defeats Araucanians at Curanilahué
    (1661), 711
Casaubon, Isaac, scholar, refutation of
    Baronius, 7
Caspian Sea, 487, 662
Castelli, Benedetto, 136, 146
Castelnaudary, Battle of (1632), 489

Castile, 566
  sense of identity, 4; culture, 7; effects of
    war, 14, 532; the monarchy as protector,
    56; primacy in Spain, 438–9, 441, 443;
    bears major burden of the wars, 461–2;
    nationalism, 462
  agriculture, 438–9; sheep and wool
    production, 439
  class structure, 450–1
  Cortes and taxation, 439, 448, 456–7, 465
  disease, 439
  economic decline and its causes, 438,
    440–2, 448–9, 455, 457, 473; Olivares'
    economic reforms and, 461; economic
    crisis of 1626, 464; financial reforms,
    40; finances, 441–2, 458–9; monetary
    policy, 44–5, 444–5, 464; investments,
    449–50; industry, 439–40; prices, 444–
    5, 464, 470; taxation, 44–6, 439, 441–2,
    447–8, 461, 465–6; social results of
    taxation, 465–6; unemployment in,
    451; wages, 439
  immigrants, 450
  land held by peasants, nobles and the
    church, 449–51
  and the Moors, 37, 450, 452–6
  nobility: 20, 21, 451–2; proportion of
    population, 17, 18, 451; in urban
    areas, 17, 18; qualifications, 19;
    privileges, 19, 20, 60, 448; status of
    occupations, 21, 451; exploit war
    situation, 56; dominated by ad-
    ministrators, 60
  peasants, 448–9
  population, 439; rural depopulation,
    449
  rebellion, 56
  trade, 440; rivalry with Portugal, 462
  Crown's possessions in America: 707–8;
    losses in South America, 714; decline
    of revenue from, 725; loss of control
    over, 725–6; *see also* under names of
    places in America
  see also under names of places in Castile
Castillo, Alvaro, economic studies, 101–2
Castrillo, Conde de, and Olivares, 471
Castro, D. Martim Afonso de, Portuguese
    viceroy, breaks Dutch–Johore siege of
    Malacca (1606), 655
Casuistry, *see* Society of Jesus
Catalonia, 56, 438, 456
  administration: relations with the central
    government, 462, 466–7, 472; the Cortes
    and finance, 456, 466 and the Union of
    Arms, 464; the Senate, 52
  anarchy in (1600–15), 456; economic and
    political situation (1632), 466; (1640),
    469

INDEX

Chocim (Khotin), Battle of (1621), 41, 597, 609, 636
Christendom, 5
Christensen, Aksel, criticizes Baltic grain trade figures, 92
Christian I, see Anhalt-Bernburg, prince Christian I of
Christian IV, king of Denmark, duke of Holstein, 313, 355, 405
  character, and ability, 320-1
  court, 393
  and the control of the Baltic, 306, 322, 391
  and the Danish Sound, 387, 395
  and the German Protestants, 389; see also Christian IV and the Lower Saxon war
  and the Lower Saxon war: the Protestant bishoprics in Germany, 318, 321, 389; weakness of position, 322; alliance with England, 321, 322; joins the war, 321-2; League of The Hague (1625), 391; Treaty of The Hague (1625), 322; elected head of the Lower Saxon Circle (1626), 322, 391; withdraws to Verden, 323; defeat at Lutter (1626), 324, 391; position in 1627, 324-5, 391; defeat at Heiligenhafen (1627), 325; lands overrun, 325, 391; flees to Holstein and Fünen, 325; alliance with Gustavus Adolphus (1628), 326, 391; defeat in Pomerania, 326; Peace of Lübeck (1629), 326, 391; deserts German Protestants, 393
  and Sweden (and Gustavus Adolphus): merchants in Sweden, 387; declares war on Sweden (1611), 388; War of Kalmar (1611-13), 389; Peace of Knäred, 389-90; significance of the Swedish capture of Riga (1621), 390; crisis of 1624, 390; personal rivalry of the kings, 391; alliance (1628), 391; deserts Sweden (1629), 391; the Swedish invasion of Germany, 399; offers mediation in the German wars, [400], 402; plans anti-Swedish coalition (c. 1639), 402; gives refuge to Queen Christina, 402; provokes Sweden by tolls policy, 402; aids discontented Swedish colonels, 402; Peace of Brömsebro (1645), 403, 429-30
Christian of Brunswick see Brunswick-Wolfenbüttel, Christian, duke of
Christianity, movement against, in Japan, 659
Christina, queen of Sweden, 182, 433
  adopts theory of absolutism, 123; succeeds to throne (1632), 341; marriage proposals, 399
  and the peace negotiations at Osnabrück,

407; becomes a member of the Empire (1648), 408; the bishoprics of Bremen and Verden, 408; pro-Habsburg policy (1650s), 408-9
  abdication (1654), 429
Christina, widow of Gustavus II Adolphus, king of Sweden, flight to Denmark (1640), 402
Christina of France, duchess of Piedmont, afterwards duchess of Savoy, 427
Christopher, duke of Württemberg, see Württemberg, Christopher, duke of
Church of England, supports kingship, 125; liturgical revival, 192; Westminster assembly of Divines oppose 'Covenant' theology, 193; tolerance, 198
Churchyard, Thomas, writer, 211
Cicero, 479; De Officiis, 28
Cicognini, Giacinto Andrea, Italian playwright, 258
Cinq-Mars, Henry Coiffier de Ruzé, marquis of, revolts, 493; executed (1642), 493
Cîteaux, monastery of, 492
Clapmarius, his De arcanis rerum publicarum libra sex (1605), 116
Clarendon, Edward Hyde, first earl of, 559
  and the Civil War, 574-5
Claris, Pau, approaches to France (1640), 469
Clement VIII, Pope, Spanish domination and, 262; turns to France, 262-3
Clergy, status declines, 172; material position, 172-3, 535; education, 535; anti-clericalism, 536
Clermont, taxation in, 476
Clermont see Bar and Clermont, duchy of
Cleves, quartering of the army in, 209
Cleves, see Jülich-Cleves
Cloth industry, Royal Commission on the, 562
Clubmen, the, 577-8
Cluny, monastery of, 492
Coahuila, Mexico, stock-raising, 721
Coal industry, see Industry, metals and mining
Coblenz, and the Treaty of Trier (1632), 335
Coburg, population losses due to war, 77
Cocceius, Johannes, theologian, 193
Cochin, Malabar, Portuguese trade, 644, 646
Cockayne, William, alderman, his project for cloth finishing (1614), 94, 547-8
Cockpit theatre, 242
Cocq, Banningh, rise of, 366
Coddington, William, merchant, leaves Boston, 687; at Portsmouth (1639), 687; founds Newport (1639), 687
Coen, Jan Pietersz, director of Dutch East India Company

France (*cont.*)

481–2; meeting of the States General (1614), 481–2; Parlement of Paris attempts to revive the *Curia regis*, 482; Peace of London (1616) between government and princes, 482; murder of Concini, 483; government under Luynes (1617–21), 483; revolt of 1620, 483; Union of Béarn and Navarre, 483; revolt of Protestants (1620), 483; unrest in 1629–30, 488; revolts against taxation (1633–42), 492; internal government (1643–61), summarized, 415; the Fronde (1648–53): 57, 119, 121,418, 476; causes, 496–7, 416; edict of the Chambre Saint Louis, 496–7; popular support, 55; Paris rising [the Day of the Barricades] (1648), 416, 497–8; Peace of Rueil (1649), 497; arrest of Condé and the rise of the princes (1650), 498; Spain joins the Fronde, 425–7, 498; flight of Mazarin (1651), 498; dissension among Frondeurs (1651), 498–9; return of Mazarin with German troops (1651), 356, 498; renewal of civil war (1652), 498–9; breakdown of government, 499; end of war (1653), 499; economic effects, 499–500; significance for Louis XIV, 502; political history summarized from 1653–9, 221

political institutions: Assembly of Notables: financial policy, 40, 41; reforms of 1618, 483; reforms of 1626–7, 485; Cabale des Importants (1643), 494; Chambre Saint Louis, *see* France, Parlement de Paris; Council of the King, 485–6, 489; Council of State, 493–4, 497; Cour des Aide (Paris), 495; Parlement de Paris: and judicial absolutism, 121, and Gallicanism, 108–9, and the princes' rising (1615), 482; attempts to revive the *curia regis* (1615), 482, authorizes rebellion (1630), 489, and the financial deficit (1648), 496, Decree of Union and the Chambre Saint Louis, 496, and the Fronde, 496–9, and Jansenism, 501; States General: 481–2, 498, financial policy, 40, 46, the sovereignty of the king, 108

population, 71, 497

religion: dissidents allowed, 34; church relationships with state, 36; the Council of Trent, 106; atheism, 199, 484; Assembly of Clergy condemn Jansenism (1656, 1661), 501; Catholicism, 183–4, 484, 492; *see also* Jansenism

science, *see* Science in France

seapower: navy, 230–1

trade: import duty war with England, 235, 422–3; uses Dutch shipping for trade, 235; companies, 487; policy under Sully, 697; routes, 486–7

trade in cattle, 478; fur, 697; grain, 478; silver, 81, 89; textiles, 94, 422–3, 477; wine, 422, 478

see also Anne of Austria, queen consort; Francis I, king of France; Henri II, king of France; Henri IV, king of France; Louis XIII, king of France; Louis XIV, king of France; Marie de Medici, queen of France; political theory, absolutism in France; and under names of places

Francesco of Tuscany, *see* Tuscany, Francesco, grand duke of

Franche-Comté, used by Spanish troops as land route to the Netherlands, 261; occupied by Gallas (1636), 347; Treaty of the Pyrenees (1659), 428

Francis I, king of France, 24, 202, 213

Franciscan Recollect Order, represented on Condé's Canadian company (1615), 697; mission to Hurons, 697; support by duc de Montmorenci, 698

Franciscans

missions: to China from the Philippines, 668–9; from St Augustine to South Carolina, 709; in New Mexico to the Pueblo Indians, 709; in the Upper Uruguay, 711

condemn Jesuit missionary compromises, 668

Francis de Sales, Saint, bishop of Geneva, beliefs, 174, 183–4; influence on French society, 184, 188; *Traité de l'amour de Dieu*, 484

Francis Xavier, Saint, 171, 182

Franconia, population losses due to war, 77; and Gustavus Adolphus, 334; joins the League of Heilbronn, 341; Bernard of Saxe-Weimar becomes duke, 342

Frankenthal, 317

Frankfurt, Treaty of (1658), 421

Frankfurt-am-Main

devaluation, 82; index of silver values, 86–7; changes in price trends, 88; influx of *entrepreneurs*, 271, 292; fairs, 293, 295; economic prosperity (1570–1618), 304

and Gustavus Adolphus, 334

Franqueza, Don Pedro, 445

Franz, Günther, population estimates, 77, 357

Frederick III, king of Denmark, bishop of Verden

Le Bret, Cardin, counseller, 479
his *De la Souveraineté du Roi* (1632), 119;
theories on kingship, 120
Le Brun, Charles, painter, 500
Lech, Battle of (1632), 338
Lee, William, invents the knitting machine,
167
Leeds, attitude to the Civil War, 575; wool
industry, 582
Leeuwenhoek, Anton van, microscopist, 149
Leeward Islands, granted to the earl of
Carlisle (1628), 702; and the Com-
pagnie des Isles d'Amérique, 703
see also Antigua; Dominica; Guadeloupe;
Marie Galante; Montserrat; Nevis;
St Bartholomew; St Christopher; St
Eustatius; St Kitts; St Martin
Le Febure, councillor of state, 500
Leghorn, trade in silver, 81; corn imports,
301; the London East India Company
and the pepper trade, 653
Le Grangier, property dealer, 100–1
Le Havre, 493
Leibniz, Gottfred Wilhelm, mathematician,
uses calculating machines, 151
Leiden
cloth industry, 64, 95–6, 368; immigration of textile workers, 96
plague in, 76
immigration, 77–8
English Separatists emigrate to (1608–9),
681; but 35 leave for Massachusetts
(1620), 682
Leiden, University of, 371
centre for Protestant political thought,
104; and monarchism, 361; science in,
136; Arminianism starts at, 177; fame
of, 365
Leigh, Charles, settlement in Guiana
(1604–6), 701
Leighton, Alexander, 565
Leipzig, 513
devaluation, 82–3; changes in price
trends, 88; fairs, 293–5
economic prosperity (1600–18), 304; fur
trade, 663
Wallenstein at (1632), 341
Swedes at, 348
buys off Swedish attack (1642), 402
Leipzig, Convention of Protestant princes
at (1631), 331–2
Lei Timor, East Indies, attacked by Amboinese and Dutch, 646
Lemaire, Dutch explorer, voyage round the
world, 691
Le Mercier, Jacques, architect, builder of
Pavilion de l'Horloge, 491 and of
Chateau de Richelieu, 492

Lemnos, and the Turco-Venetian war
(1645–69), 641
Lemos, Don Pedro Fernandez de Castro,
marquis de Sarria, count de, financial
achievements, 37, 272
Lena river system, Russian fur traders
reach (1640), 663; conquered by
Russia, 616
Lennox, fourth duke of, *see* Richmond,
James Stuart, fourth duke of Lennox
and first duke of
Le Nôtre, André, 500
Lens, Battle of (1648), 352, 413, 497
Leo VI, pope, military writings, 216
Leo X, pope, drives French out of Italy
(1595), 261–2; election celebrated by
Henri IV, 263
Leopold I, 529
elected king of the Romans (1658), 419;
and the 'capitulation', of Münster,
420; relations with France, 420; aids
Spain in Italy, 420
Leopold William, archduke
occupies Jülich-Cleves (1609), 267
and the bishoprics, 318, 327
appointed governor of the Spanish
Netherlands (1647), 377, 413
defeated at Lens (1648), 352
the Peace of Westphalia (1648), 377
captures Dunkirk (1652), 423
Leopoldstat, 528
Lepanto, Battle of (1571), 273
Lerida, siege of (1645–6), 414
Lerma, François de Roxas de Sandoval,
marquis de Denia, duke of, 38
character, 443
administration, 456–7; dissolves Council
of India (1614), 664; patronage, 272;
and the nobility, 443–5
financial policy, 444–5, 448
as foreign minster, 263, 279, 446
dismissal of (1618), 278–9, 457
Le Roy Ladurie, E., economic theories, 11,
65
Leschassier, Jacques, French jurist, 105
Lesdiguières, François de Bonne, duc de,
Marshall of France, aids Savoy (1612),
274; and Luynes, 483; deserts Huguenots (1627), 487
Leslie, Sir Alexander, first earl of Leven,
leads Scottish regiment to relieve
Stralsund (1628), 326; and the Bohemian rebels (1634), 344
Leszczyński family, 589
Le Tellier, Michel, minister of war, military
reforms, 237
Le Tellier, Nicholas, receiver-general of the
gabelle, rising against (1639), 492

Mexico City, 720
 capital of New Spain, 707; merchant gild
  and the limitation of trans-Atlantic
  trade, 724
Mexico, Gulf of, 709
Meyzl, Jewish trader, 513
Michael Feodorovich Romanov, tsar, 614 ff.
 character, 603
 election (1613), 113, 388, 595, 602–3, 605
 internal policy, 603, 619
 foreign affairs: and the Peace of Stolbova
  (1617), 605; relationships with the
  Tatars, 611; isolationist foreign policy,
  613
 death (1645), 613
Michell, Sir Frances, condemnation by the
  House of Lords, 549
Michigan, Lake, 698–9
Middelburg, immigration, 77–8; bank
  founded 1616, 84, 366; cloth trade, 272;
  and the East India Company, 647
Middlesex, Lionel Cranfield, earl of,
  attitude to patronage, 38; and crown
  economies, 548; accusation of Chancellor Bacon, 549; becomes lord
  treasurer, 550; financial policy (after
  1621), 550–1; perquisites of office, 551;
  supervises Irish government reform,
  551; dissolution of the Virginia
  Company and, 551; impeachment
  (1624), 551; and Buckingham, 553
Middleton, Henry, reaches Banda (1605),
  650; reaches Tidore, 650
Middleton, Thomas, dramatist, 255
Mihriban, Battle of (1630), 631
Mikhail, Romanoff, czar
 see Michael Feodorovich Romanov
Milan, 107, 278
 economics: effects of war, 52; economic
  malaise, 53–4; price trends, 62;
  financial crisis in, 54; financial contributions to Spain, 462
 Spanish troops for, 228; depot for
  Spanish war supplies, 260
 foreign affairs: the Valtelline and, 278;
  threatened by France and Savoy (1610),
  268, 272; hostility to Venice, 273; the
  count of Fuentes and, 273–5; Franco-
  Italian Treaty to conquer (1636), 347;
  invasion of (1647), 414; see also
  Fuentes, Pedro Henriquez de Azevedo,
  count of
 nobility, status of occupations, 20, 52–3
 plague in, 76
 social changes, 52–3
 trade: linen imports, 293
Milford, Maine, colonization, 690; joins
  New England Confederation (1643), 690

Millenary Petition (1604), 536, 542
Milton, John, poet, 4
Minden, given to Brandenburg (1647), 354,
  412
Mines and mining see under Industry,
  metals and mining; names of countries;
  Trade in bullion; metals
Minuit, Peter, governor of New Netherland,
  appointment (1626), 692; withdraws
  garrisons against Mohawks, 692; re-
  called (1632), 693
Mirame, 249
Mirandola, annexed by Spain, 274
Mir Jumla, Coromandel official, and the
  cotton trade, 657
Missions, Argentina, Jesuit missions as
  models elsewhere, 712–13
Missions, Christian, 638, 659, 667–70,
  697–99, 707, 709–16
Mississippi river, 699
Mocenigo, Lazaro, 641
Modena, foreign policy, 269; annexed by
  Spain, 274; Mazarin and (1650), 426;
  threatens Spain (1658), 427
Modena, Francis d'Este, duke of, alliance
  with France (1647), 414; invasion of
  the duchy of Milan, 414
Mogila, Petr, bishop of Kiev, appointment
  confirmed by Władysław IV (1633),
  592; founds Kiev Academy, 593, 614
Mogilev, 597
Mogilev-Mstislavl', bishop of, recognized
  by the king, 592
Mohács, Battle of (1526), 506
Mohawks, Indian tribe, battle against the
  Hurons and French, 676; attack the
  Pequots at Pequot Hill, 689; attacked
  by Mohegans and Dutch (1626), 692;
  renew alliance with Dutch, 692; arms
  supply from colonists, 694; attack
  Algonquins (1643), 695
Mohegans, join Dutch in attacking Mohawks (1626), 692
Moldau (Vltava), river, 503
Moldavia, 586
 Polish and Turkish claims in, 596;
  Polish intervention in, 636; Peace of
  Buzsa (1617), to end Polish intervention, 636; Polish–Ottoman war in
  (1619–20), 597
Molinism, 185
Molière, pseud. Jean Baptiste Poquelin, 137,
  239, 244–5
 attempts to start a theatrical company
  (1640s), 243; his audience, 247; per-
  forms before the king (1658), 255;
  comedies not limited by dramatic rules,
  258

Molina, Luis, S.J., beliefs, 185
Molsheim, University of, 521
Molucca Islands, 650
 revolt affects spice trade, 644; Dutch
  encourage anti-Portuguese attacks, 648;
  revolt against Dutch (1646), 652;
  deportation of the population, 652
 trade: cotton imports from Coromandel,
  656; gold trade with Batavia, 659;
  Dutch monopoly of the Moluccan spice
  trade disrupts Indonesian trade, 670;
  English claims for a *Mare Librum*,
  671
 see also Amboina; Ceram; Ternate;
  Tidore
Mompesson, Sir Giles, condemnation by
 the House of Lords (1621), 549
Monaco, subjected to Spain, 274
Monaldeschi, equerry of Queen Christina of
 Sweden, executed, 123
Monarchomachs, 106
Monarchy, changes in the seventeenth
 century, 15, 39, 56
Moncada, Sancho de, economist, trans-
 Atlantic trade estimates (1619), 440;
 economic programme, 446
Monçon (Monzon), Treaty of (1626), 322,
 485
Money, shortage and the effects of, 11–12;
 bullion supplies, 78–81; currency de-
 basements, 81–3; gold appreciation,
 83–4; double monetary system evolves,
 84; and credit, 85; relative position of
 national economies shown by de-
 valuation, 85–6; contemporary theories
 about, 86
Monomotapa Empire, decline of and the
 Portuguese, 645
Monro, Robert, soldier, report on German
 prosperity (1631), 345
Montagnais Indians, tribe, trade with
 French, 675
Montagu, Henry *see* Manchester, Henry
 Montagu, first earl of
Montague, Richard, bishop of Chichester,
 and pamphleteer, Arminian writings,
 554; *Apello Caesarem*, 558
Montague, Walter, his *The Shepherd's
 Paradise* (1659), 250, 256
Montaigne, Michel de, comparison of
 European and Brazilian cultures, 5
Montauban, siege of (1620), 483
Montchrétien, Antoine de, mercantile ad-
 viser, 68; financial theories, 86
Montecuccoli, Raimondo, Austrian general,
 Battle of St Gotthard (1664), 62
Montenegro, local resistance to the Otto-
 man Turks, 637

Monteverdi, Claudio, writes operas at
 Mantua, 251; moves to Venice (1613),
 251; later works establish modern
 opera, 252
Montferrat, 262
 succession question (1612–18), 274–5;
 succession question in 1627, 42–3, 328;
 Treaty of Cherasco (1631), 329
Montmorenci (Montmorency), Henri II,
 duc de, obtains patent to maintain
 Franciscan Recollect mission in Canada
 and encourage emigration, 698
 revolts (1630), 489; defeat at Castle-
  naudary (1632), 489, execution (1632),
  489
Montpellier, 47
 taxation, 47
Montpellier, Peace of (1622), 484
Montpellier University, 136–7
Montpensier, Anne-Marie-Louise, 'La
 grande Demoiselle', proposed marriage
 with Ferdinand III (1649), 420
Montreal, Quebec, foundation (1642), 700;
 government, 700; and the Iroquois
 (1649), 700–1
Monts, Pierre du Gast, sieur de, patron of
 Samuel de Champlain, 676; builds fort
 at Quebec, 676
Montserrat, Leeward Islands, governorship
 of Thomas Warner (1625), 702;
 plantations on, 703
Monzon, Treaty of, *see* Monçon, Treaty of
 (1626)
Moors [Moriscos]
 in Spain; expulsion (*limpieza*), 4, 25, 37,
  271–2, 437, 452–6; Holy War against
  450; numbers of, 454–6; economic
  effects of expulsion, 453–6; encouraged
  by the French, 261 and Ottoman
  Turks, 261
Moravia, 503
 constitution and administration, 505–6
 used as an invasion route (1630–48), 522
 revolt (1619), 311; Cardinal Dietrichstein
  becomes governor (1620), 518; suppression of the Bohemian revolt
  (1618–20), 518
 land tenure, 525
 population, 71; war losses, 77, 523
 religion: Jesuit campaigns against the
  Protestants, 315, 514
Morbihan Trading Company, founded
 1626, 487
Morea, the, and the Ottoman Turks, 637,
 639, 641
Moreyra (y) Paz-Soldán, Manuel, his *En
 torno a dos valiosos documentos sobre
 Potosí*, 95

Naples *(cont.)*
nobility: 21, proportion of population, 17; status of occupations, 20, 21; codes of conduct, 26; numbers of, 48; revolts, 55; exploit war situation, 56
plague in, 76
trade: in silver, 81; the London East India Company and the pepper trade, 653
Banco dello Spirito Santo, 84–5
Napoleon Buonaparte, emperor of France, 396
Naragansett Bay, 687–8, 692
Naragansetts, Indian tribe, attack Massachusetts trade (1636), 689; defeat on Block Island by John Endecott, 689; join Pequots, 689; peace negotiated by Roger Williams, 689; join Massachusetts and Connecticut to exterminate Pequots (1638), 689
Narva, 390, 398
Naseby, Battle of (1645), 220
Nassau, army, development and changes, 203, 216
Nassau, House of, influence on stadholdership, 365
Nassau, John *de Middelste*, count of
military writings, 203, 204, 210; founds military college at Siegen (1616), 204; influences Swedish army when commander-in-chief, 217; organizer of the Nassau militia, and the Palatine *Landrettung*, 217
Nassau, John the elder, count of, 203
Nassau, Maurice, *see* Orange, Maurice of Nassau, prince of
National Covenant [of Scotland (1638)], 567
National Synod, Netherlands (1618), *see* Dort, Synod of
Nationalism, significance to modern non-European peoples, 3; used to interpret history, 3; development of, 3–5
Naumberg, Gustavus Adolphus at (1633), 340
Navarino, 639
Navarre, 438, 456
financial contributions to Spain, 462; union with Béarn (1620), 483
Navarrete, Fernández, economist, economic programme, 446
Navies, *see* Seapower
Navigation, development of techniques, 151, 166
Nayarit, Mexico, 709
Nef, John U., English coal production estimates, 97
Negapatam, Coromandel, Portuguese settlement in, 644, 656

Negombo, Ceylon, Portuguese lose to Dutch (1639–40), 666
Negroes, 19, 677, 680, 704–5, 707, 713
increase in America, 716–17
see also Trade in slaves
Neile, Richard, archbishop of York, 557 enforces Laudian innovations (1632), 565; attacks Puritans, 565; attack by Parliament, 565
Neisse, fortifications of, 222
Neo-Pythagoreans, philosophy, 131
Neo-stoicism, in the Spanish Netherlands, 124; philosophy, 198
Neo-Thomism, 105, 112, 118, 131
in the Spanish Netherlands, 124; deductive methods, 130–1
Neri, Philip, founds oratory in Rome (1564), 183
Neronov, I., leads 'zealots' *(revniteli)*, 615
Netherlands, the
situation in the early seventeenth century, 359; historical myths about, 360
agriculture: land reclamation, rise and decline, 64, 91–2; land rents, 65; agricultural prices, 91–2
army developments, 211–12
constitutional developments, 360–1
drama, *see* Drama in the Netherlands
economics: economic change, 12; impact of war, 14–15; situation in 1609, 36; price trends, 62, 64; economic tendencies, 360
emigrants to Sweden, 394
industry, textiles, 64, 94–6
nobility: wealth and poverty, 18; privileges, 20, 27; status of occupations, 20; codes of conduct, 26; definition, 30; revolts, 55
plague in, 76
and Poland, 'exploitation of', 11
political theories, 360–1; *see also* Political theory, absolutism in the Netherlands
population, 70, 71
religion, 359
technology, 167
trade: import of agricultural produce, 589; grain, 589; textiles, 94, 96, 293, 562; timber, 589
see also Science in the Netherlands
Netherlands, Dutch, 34, 82, 516
administrative and constitutional affairs: state identity achieved, 3; political power in towns, 15; economic involvement increases power of the state, 101–2; sovereignty in, 123–4; decentralization, 180; administration, 369; constitution, 361–3, 375; opposition to Holland, 382–3

Nicholas of Cusa, and the substance of matter, 162
Nice, 275
Nickolsburg, Peace of (1622), 520
Nicolet, Jean, explorations in Canada, 699
Nieuwpoort, Battle of (1600), 216, 224
Nipissing, Lake, Ontario, 697
Nobili, Roberto de, Jesuit missionary, at Madura, India, 668; compromise with Hinduism condemned (1610 and 1619), 668
Nobility
codes of conduct, 23–7
culture, 28–9, 476
effect of wars, 56, 58–60
equality and comparative wealth amongst, 18
European and the Chinese *shen-shih* compared, 30
political and seigneurial power, 17–18, 49–50, 52, 60, 285, 397, 443, 474–5, 490, 499, 525–6, 530, 585–8, 617–19
privileges: fiscal, 19, 45–6, 51, 52, 444–5, 448; legal, 19–20; inheritance, 19; exemption from certain punishments, 20; and recruitment to army, 20; position of bastards, 20; hunting rights, 26–7; economic, 513
proportion of the population, 17–18, 48, 451
qualifications, 16–18, 23, 29–31, 48, 53, 476, 510–11, 527, 547
rebellions, 49–50, 52, 55–6, 475–6, 481–3, 489, 494, 498–9
sale of titles, 48, 52–3, 56, 58–9, 476, 478, 547
status of occupations, 20–3, 52–3, 297, 451, 475–6, 486
see also nobility under names of countries
Nogat, 599
Nombre de Dios, Mexico, 701
Nördlingen, Battle of (1634), 34, 344, 489 significance of, 345, 400
Norfolk, gentry, 578; textile industry, 582
Normandy, and the Fronde, 498; risings against taxation (1639), 492; (1644), 494
Norris, Sir John, soldier, 219
North, Roger, and his Amazon company (1620), 701–2
Northampton, Henry Howard, first earl of, programme of reforms, 542
Northamptonshire, nobility, 578
Northern Company, Dutch, founded 1614, 99; attacked by English, 100
North-West Passage, 673, 675
'Norumbega', North America, 672

Norway
and Sweden: territory hems in port of Älvsborg, 387
trade, 99, 234, 299, 367
Norwich, weavers, 582
Nova, Matias de, 648
Nova Scotia, 699
charter granted to Sir William Stirling to colonize (1622), 697; renewed (1627), 698; Acadia colonized, 698
Nova Zembla, 675
Novgorod, 390
occupation by Swedes, 602, 604; and the Peace of Stolbova (1617), 605
Novgorod-Seversk, ceded to Poland (1619), 595
Novi, Heracles de, merchant, 513
Novigrad, 640
Noy, William, attorney-general, 559
Noyon, wool production and commerce of, 477
Nuremberg, 421, 513
economic prosperity (1600–18), 304
Gustavus Adolphus' meeting at (1632), 339, 421
industry: centre for metallurgy and mining, 294
population losses due to war, 77
trade: linen, 293–5; woollen, 296; Merchant Adventurers in, 294
Nuremberg, Battle of (1632), 339–40
Nuremberg Exchange Bank, founded 1621, 84, 295
Nüremburg, *see* Nuremberg
Nürnberg, *see* Nuremberg
Nutrition, in Europe, 74–5
Nyborg, Battle of (1659), 431

Ob river, 663
Occupations, status of, 21–2
Oceanography, development, 164
Ödenburg, Jesuits in, 521
Oder river, Peace of Westphalia and the, 354, 408
Oesel, ceded to Sweden (1645), 430
Offices, sale of, 23, 46: in Naples, 48; Castile, 444, 447; France, 476, 478, 488, 492; England, 547; Spanish America, 725
Okhotsk, Russians reach (1639), 616
Oldenbarnevelt, Johann von, advocate of Holland
asserts sovereignty of the provincial estates, 123
and the merchant companies, 367; founds Dutch East India Company (1602), 647
supports truce with Spain (1609), 267, 372
and the Arminian-Gomarist controversy, support of Arminians, 179, 373;

INDEX

Philip II, king of Spain, 34, 279, 371, 432, 435–6, 533
Belgian authors' views of, 360
economics: banking, 39, 58; taxation of Castile, 439; financial position, 441
internal affairs: the Jews, 58; the nobility, 443
foreign policy; 260; Bohemian policy, 277; proposes Anglo-Spanish marriage (1600), 262; proposes Franco-Spanish marriage (1600), 262; dominant in Italy, 261–2; league of Italian princes (1597), 273; Netherlands attack his Portuguese overseas possessions, 647 n.; and the papacy, 262
Philip III, king of Spain
character, 443
patronizes drama, 250
internal affairs: financial position, 37–8, 441–2; and the Council of State, 461; approves the political theories of Suarez, 106; relationship with the provinces, 456; persecution of the Jews and Moors, 37, 58, 60, 272; reign summarized, 435–6, 457
foreign policy: 260, 263; wishes to prolong Twelve Years Truce, 279; establishes Pax Hispanica (1610), 269–71
and Alsace, 277, 286, 309
and his American Empire, 707 ff.
and the Bohemian succession question, 277, 286, 308–9
and England: influence in (1600–10), 269; attempts to end war, 263; Anglo-Spanish marriage proposals, 264, 546
and Flanders: opposition from bourgeoisie (1615), 272; revolt in Brussels (1619), 272
and France: threatened by revived power of France, 263; alliance (1626), 325
and Hungary: succession question (1613–17), 286
and Italy: Italian hostility, 273; extends power in (1598–1610), 273
and the Netherlands, Dutch: the peace moves of Archduke Albert, 266; instructions to Spinola (1606), 266; opposes peace negotiations, 266
and the Lebanon: protects Fakhr al-Din II of the Lebanon, 632
and the Tyrol (1617), 277, 286
death (1621), 457
Philip IV, king of Spain, 36, 45, 457, 471, 473
as a hero, 34
financial position, 38, 46
marriage (1611), 268

patronage of the theatre, 247, 250
economic crises of, 725
foreign policy, 38, 42–3; and France (1628–35), 42–4, 414; and the Netherlands, 42–3, 376–8
Philippines
botanical collections from, 164
Spanish settlements, 6, 664
trade with Europe, 226; limitations by Spain, 724
Dutch attacks on shipping, 658; Dutch defeat, 666
missions to, 669
Dominican and Jesuit universities started (1611 and 1623), 669
see also Manila
Philippsburg, claims by France (1631–46), 335, 342, 353
Philosophy, European compared with Chinese, 33
Philosophy, 'the new', see Science, the 'new (scientific) philosophy'
Phoenix theatre (Cockpit), 242
Physics, teaching and development, 136, 143–4, 152–6
Physiocrats, agricultural theories, 93
Physiology, teaching and development, 136, 159–64
Piacenza, bills of exchange at fairs of, 83; the scudi d'oro, 84; Spanish garrisons in, 261
Piasecki, bishop, Chronica gestorum in Europa singularium, 593
Picardy, 497
resistance to tithes, 57; rent levels, 65; invasion of, 347
Piccolomini family, 527
Piccolomini, Ottavio d'Arragona, prince, duke of Amalfi, Austrian field-marshal, 351
and Wallenstein, 343–4; refuses battle in 1640, 349
Piedmont, nobility, proportion of population, 17
Pietism, 175, 183–4
Pilgrim Fathers, the, 686, 691
landing and settlement in Massachusetts, 682; secure grant of land from Council for New England (1621 and 1639), 683; Mayflower Compact replaced by the 'Fundamentals of Plymouth' (1629), 683; trade settlement at Windsor (1633), 688, 693
Pillau, Gustavus Adolphus lands at (1626), 599; ceded to Sweden (1629), 392
Pilsen, captured by Mansfeld (1619), 309–10
'Pilsen Revers' the, 344

Rhode Island (*cont.*)
and Plymouth, 687; known as Rogue's Island, 687; prosperity, 687–8
see also Newport; Providence; Warwick
Rhodes, 639
Ribeiro, comments on *Estado da India*, 665
Ricci, Matteo, Jesuit missionary, account of Chinese civilization, 5; mission to China, 668
Riccioli, Giovanni Battista, S.J., 136
studies the pendulum, 149
Rich, Sir Nathaniel, and Buckingham, 553; customs proposals, 557
Richelieu, Armand de Wignerod, Cardinal, 6, 35, 101–2, 123, 182, 415–17, 461, 471, 488
achievements, 493, 501
attitude to patronage, 38, 475
character, 484
friendship with Louis XIII, 484
patronizes drama, 248–9, 252, 258; art, 491–2; literature, 491; founds Académie Française, 491; contributes to the *Gazette*, 491
personal aggrandizement (1640–2), 493
political theories, 358; and Campanella, 105; orders textual comparison between Machiavelli and scripture, 185
secretary of state for foreign affairs (1616), 482; becomes chief minister (1624), 319, 484; favourite of Marie de Medici, 484; made cardinal (1622), 484
and the army, 348
the Catholics and, 189, 492
economics: financial policy, 40–1, 492; mercantile policy, 486–7; canal projects, 486–7
internal affairs: policy, 319; and the princes' revolt (1617), 482; opposition from the princes, 121, 476; proposals for reform of government (1625), 484–5, 488; plots against (1626), 485; and the Huguenot revolts (1626–9), 485; abandons plans for the nobility, 485; convenes assembly of notables (1627), 485; opposed by Marie de Medici over war (1630), 489; the Day of the Dupes, 489; centralizes government during war (1632 onwards), 489; uses political surveillance, 491; and revolts against taxation, 492–3
foreign policy: aims, 38–9, 42–3, 319, 328, 346, 392, 411, 485, 488; achievements, 350, 357
and America: forms Compagnie de la Nouvelle France (1627), with monopoly over trade and land in Canada, 698

policy towards Iroquois and Dutch (1641), 700
aims in the West Indies, 703; sets up Compagnie de St Christophe (1626), 703; and the Compagnie des Isles d'Amérique, 703
and the empire: Regensburg meeting (1630), 329; attempts negotiations with Bavaria and the Catholic League against Ferdinand II, 335; Treaty of Trier (1631), 335; aims after death of Gustavus Adolphus, 342; intrigues with Wallenstein, 343; effect of the Battle of Nördlingen, 346; relations with William of Hesse, 347; and Bernard of Saxe-Weimar, 347, 349, invasion of France (1636), 347; the Rhine campaign (1638–9), 348–9
and England: 320, 422; negotiations for marriage of Henrietta Maria Charles I, 319; the Palatine claims, 320
and Germany: liberties of, 418; prevents Protestants from helping French princes' revolt (1617), 482
and the Mantuan war: alliance with Venice to defend claims of Charles of Nevers (1627), 328; siege of Casale (1629), 328; leads troops and captures Pinerolo (1630), 328; defeated in, 328; Treaty of Cherasco (1631), 329; breaches the Treaty, 335
and the Netherlands, Dutch: aims, 422; alliance with (1630), 328; treaty to conquer the Spanish Netherlands (1635), 346, 380, 413
the papacy and, 108–9
and Parma: treaty (1635), 347
and Portugal: alliance with John IV, 414
and Savoy: treaty (1635), 347
and Spain: aims, 319, 328, 346; Mansfeld and the siege of Breda (1625), 320; alliance of 1626, 325; declares war (1635), 346; campaigns in Italy and the Netherlands, 347; secret peace negotiations, 349; occupies Artois and Roussillon (1641), 350
and Sweden: alliance negotiations, 331; Treaty of Bärwalde (1631), 331–2, 398; subsidizes Sweden, 396, 402; fears Swedish Rhineland successes, 335; relationships with Oxenstierna, 400; renews Treaty of Bärwalde, 342, 401; [Treaty of Compiègne] with Sweden, 346; Treaty of Hamburg (1638), 348; renews alliance (1641), 350
and the Valtelline: decides to intervene (1624), 319; expels Papal troops, 320;

Rupert of the Rhine, *see* Rupert, Palatine prince
Russell, Francis, *see* Bedford, Francis Russell, fourth earl of
Russia
boundaries defined, 6
outside European culture, 6
nationalism, 602
absolutism in, *see* Political theory, absolutism in Russia
Westernization of, 614
administration, 606–7; Code of Alexis (1649), 619
agriculture, 608, 617
army (*opolcheniye*), 602–3, 619; cavalry, 608; infantry, 608; mercenaries, 608–9
colonization in Asia, 616, 663
economic state of, 8, 615–16; Spanish bullion, 79; taxation, 604, 607–8, 617–18
famine, 73
internal affairs: revolts, 1; 'Time of Troubles', over the succession, 36, 386, 602; Vasily Shuisky as tsar and the Polish and Swedish candidates, 388, 594–5; effect of the 'Troubles', 385, 602, 604, 613–14, 617; Second National Rising, 388; election of Michael Romanov (1613), 388, 595, 602–3
foreign affairs: position abroad in 1560–80, 385; isolationist policy (1634–45), 613; situation in 1659, 433
and the Baltic, 605
and Brandenburg: negotiations over Prussia (1656), 430–1
and the Cossacks: the 'Time of Troubles', 602, 604; the Dnieper Cossacks seek protection, 609; relationships with the Don Cossacks, 612; the Azov war (1637, 1641), 612–13; Cossack fur traders cross Siberia to the Pacific, 663
and Denmark: negotiations against Sweden, 402; and the marriage of Irina and Valdemar, 613
and England, 609
and the Netherlands, 609
and the Ottoman Turks: Filaret plans joint attacks on Poland, 609–10; involvement over the Cossacks (1637–43), 612–13
and Poland: cedes Livonia (1581), 385; the succession 'Troubles', 388, 594–5; loss of Smolensk (1611), 595; Russo-Polish wars, 595, 599, 605; Peace of Stolbova (1617), 389, 605; Truce of Deulino (1619), 388–9, 595, 605; Filaret plans war, 609; attacks (1632), 389, 595, 610; Peace of Polyanovka (1634), 595, 611; results of the war,

611; Louis XIV offers mediation (1654), 433; threatens Warsaw (1659), 431
and Sweden: Sweden established at Reval, 385; threatens Swedish Finland, 386; the succession 'Troubles', 388; trade rivalry, 388; Treaty of Stolbova (1617) and its significance, 388–9, 599; grain trade (1630), 395 n., 609; Sweden establishes permanent diplomatic relations (1631), 609; plans for attack on Poland, 609; negotiations against (1638–9), 402
and the Tatars: relationships (1613–32), 611; attacked (1632), 610; and the Cossack capture of Azov (1641), 612–13
land tenure, 604, 608
law under Filaret, 606–7 n.
nobles (boyars): political power, 602–3, 617–19; provide cavalry, 608; status, 608; economic position, 617–19; revolts (1641, 1648–9), 619
peasants: revolts, 602, 615; 'black' and privately owned peasants, 607, 617–18; representation, 607; taxation, 607, 617–18; poverty, 615; status, 617–18; laws against fugitives, 618–19; the *slobody*, 618–19; the *zakladchiki*, 618–19
political institutions: Council of Nobles (*Duma*), 606; *Zemsky Sobor*, 113, 602–3, 606, 609, 613
population, 616–17
religion: Orthodox Church, chauvinistic attitude, 614; liturgical reforms, 614–15; the Great Schism (*Raskol*), 615; attitude to peasants, 618; Protestants in, 614
trade: 367, 616; and Asia, 662–3; England, 94, 367; Persia, 662–3; Sweden, 386; in furs, 6, 616, 662–3; spices, 295; textiles, 94, 295, 662–3; timber and wood products, 616
Russia Company, voyages to Persia, 650
Russian Grain Company (Dutch), founded (1608), 99
Ruvigny, leader of the French Protestants, in London (1660), 425
Ruyter, Michael de, Admiral, 232
capture of French ships, 425; Battle of Nyborg (1659), 431

Sa, archbishop de, condemns Nobili (1619), 668
Saavedra, Fajardo Diego, his *Political Idea of a Christian Prince Expressed in a Hundred and One Symbols* (Paris, 1660), 118
Sablat, Battle of (1619), 311

INDEX

Society of Jesus (*cont.*)
in Abyssinia, 667; Alsace, 521; America, central and south, 709–16; Austria, 514, 521; Bohemia, 308, 315, 516; Canada, 699–700; Ceylon, 669; China, 667–8; England, 264, 268; the (Habsburg) Empire, 514; France, 108, 268; Gujarat, 660; Hungary, 521; India, 667; Japan, 659, 667–8; the Netherlands, 271, 359, 370; Poland, 197, 590, Spain, 269–70; Sweden, 385; Transylvania, 197; Turkey, 637–8
Society of Notre Dame de Montreal, formation (1641) and aims, 700
Socinianism, *see* Unitarianism
Socinus, Faustus, establishes Unitarianism (Socinianism), 195–6
Soissonnais, disorder in (1652), 499
Soissons, wool production and commerce, 477
Soissons, Louis de Bourbon, count of, plots against the king (1626), 485; envoy to London (*c.* 1660), 425
Solis, Duarte Gomes, mercantile adviser, 68
Solomon of the North, *see* Mainz, John Philip von Schönborn, elector of
Solor Island, trade with and support from Macassar, 652
Somers, Sir George, expedition to Jamestown (1609–10), 674; claims Bermuda for England (1609), 674
Somerset
poor relief in, 563
local administration, 563
attitude to the Civil War, 575
Somerset, Edward, sixth earl, and second marquis of Worcester, publishes *A century of the names and scantlings of such inventions, as at present I can call to mind to have tried and perfected* (1663), 166
Sonora mountains, Mexico, 709
Sonsonate coast, Central America, Spanish settlement, 708
cacao raising in, 708, 721; export, 721
Sorbière, Samuel de, translates *Leviathan* by Hobbes, 130
Sorbonne, the, 137
Soubise, Benjamin de Rohan, Seigneur de, leads Huguenot rebellion (1626–7), 485
Sound, The, Danish control of tolls, 387, 395, 402–3, 405–6; Peace of Brömsebro (1645), 403, 429; Treaty of Roeskilde (1658), 430; shipping through, 63–4
South Molton, attitude to the Civil War, 574
Southampton, England, emigrants go to America, 682

Southampton, Henry Wriothesley, earl of, sponsors expedition to Virginia (1605), 673; the Virginia Company and (1618), 551, 677
Southampton, Long Island, colonization, 690, 693
Southampton, Treaty of (1625), 692, 705
South Carolina, Franciscan missions to, 709; *see also* Port Royal
Southwold, Long Island, colonization, 690
Spain, 107
nationalism, 4
as chosen instrument for Utopia, 5
its divine mission, 34
social results of the *Pax Hispanica*, 270–1
regional differences, 438
absolutism in, *see* Political theory, absolutism in Spain
decline (1598–1648), 6, 69, 435–6, 470; causes, 436–8; decadence by 1661, 432
administration: 32; disunity (1598–1621), 456; effect of *Pax Hispanica* on administration (1612–21), 271; administrative reforms of Olivares (1623), 460–4; rule by junta, 460–1; federal co-operation and the Union of Arms, 463; juntas abolished, 471; administration (1643–9), 471–3
agriculture: maize yields, 65
army: development and change, 204, 207, 210, 213, 218, 221–2; cost of, 445; the Union of Arms, 40, 463–4
class structure, 20–2; *see also* Spain, nobility
communications: sea and land routes to the Netherlands, 228, 260–1, 267, 273–4, 277–8, 280, 308, 314, 318–19, 349, 412
constitution: 443, 456, 464; power of the state increases, 102; constitutional effects of war, 39, 43
culture, 7
drama, *see* Drama in Spain
economics: banking, 39–40, 84–5, 445, 461; the economic decline and its causes (1596–1621), 8, 14, 87, 98–9, 440, 445–6; economic results of the *Pax Hispanica* (1609–21), 271; remedies of the *arbitristas*, 446–7, 461–2; economic reforms, 459–61; financiers mainly Genoese until 1627, 57; replaced by Portuguese Jews, 58; loans to monarchy increase (post 1610), 101; payment of *asientos*, 102, 459; financial weakness, 37, 39, 43, 54, 441–2, 458, 725; war finances, 39, 43–4, 459, 461–2, 464–7; fiscal grievances diverted to-

Spinola (*cont.*)
266; secret instructions from Philip III, peace negotiations at The Hague, 266; the Twelve Years' Truce (1609), 42, 359;
and the Netherlands, Spanish: peace policy, 376; resigns from army command (1627), 376
and the Palatine: re-establishes Spanish patronage (1614), 268; invasions (1620), 204, 278; (1621), 314; causes dissolution of Protestant Union, 316
Spinola family, Genoese bankers, 67, 81
Spitzbergen, English interests in whaling, 235
Sporck, Johann, count von, 59
Sprat, Thomas, 138
Springfield, Massachusetts, colony founded (1636–7), 688; sponsored by Roxbury, 688
Stade, 299, 324
Merchant Adventurers' 'factory', 294
Stadtlohn, Battle of (1623), 318
Staffordshire, attitude to the Civil War, 574
Stalin, Joseph, 4
Stamford, Maine, colonization, 690; joins New England Confederation (1643), 690
Star Chamber, 538, 565, 571
Stara Boleslav, the Virgin of, 527
Starodub, ceded to Poland (1619), 595
Staten Island
colonization of, 693; murder of Indians (1641), 694
Stelluti, Francesco, 140
publishes structure of the bee (1625), 149
Stettin, and Sweden (1647), 354, 407–8, 412; siege of (1659), 431
Stevin, Simon, 132
develops physics, 153; his *Haven-finding art*, 166; invents the Dutch sailing cart, 167; influences military thought, 216
Stirling, Sir William Alexander, earl of, 693
granted land in Acadia, 697; founds colony in Nova Scotia (1622), 697; charter renewed (1627), 698
Stolbova (Stolbovo), Treaty of (1617), 388–9, 390, 599, 605
Stone, L., 542 n., 543
Stone, William, emigration from Virginia, 680; governor of Maryland (1644), 680
Stow, John, *Survey* (1598), 72
Strafford, Sir Thomas Wentworth, first earl of, 102, 126, 550, 556, 563, 571
attitude to patronage, 38
opposition to Spanish war (1625), 554; exclusion from the Parliament of 1626,

554; imprisonment (1628), 555; made peer and president of the Council of the North (1628), 557; rule in Ireland, 565–6; raises army in Ireland (1640), 568; and the Short Parliament, 569; attacked by Irish Parliament (1640), 569; impeachment (1640), 570 and the political reasons for his execution (1641), 570
Stralsund, siege (1627–8), 325–6, 330, 391; alliance with Gustavus Adolphus (1628), 330–1, 393; ceded to Sweden, 412
merchant fleet, 234
Strasbourg
devaluation of currency, 83
the Reich court council and, 287
Richelieu's plans for, 328
and the negotiations at Münster, 353
Strasbourg, bishopric of, 411–12
Strasbourg, University of, centre for the teaching of the political theories of Lipsius, 104–5
Stroganov family, financiers, 67
Struve, J. A., his theories of law in *Syntagma Juris Civilis* (1658), 116
Stuart Bay, New England, 682
Stuarts, royal House of, causes of the fall of (1649), ch. xviii, 531–84
Stuhlweissenburg, 637
Stuhmsdorf, Treaty of (1635), 348, 401, 600
Stuttgart, population losses due to war, 77
Stuyvesant, Pieter, governor of Curaçao, 695; governor of New Netherland (1647), 695; aims, 695; and van Rensselaer, 695; and van der Dorick, 695–6
Styria, 503–4
constitution and administration, 504–5; Counter-Reformation in, 514; mining, 510
Styria, arch-dukes of, *see* Ferdinand II, emperor, arch-duke of
Suarez, Francisco, theologian and philosopher
political theories, 31, 106–7, 131; teaches neo-Thomism, 105; his *De Legibus* (1612), 106; his *Defensio Fidei* (1613), 106, condemned to be burnt by the hangman, 108; theory of the law of nations, 111; theory of the state, 112–13; theories have practical effects, 115–16; adopted in Spain, 117–18 and France, 119
uses deductive methods, 130
sees the state as an organism, 131
Suckling, Sir John, poet, 256
Suffolk, 578
attitude to the Civil War, 574

Sweden *(cont.)*
industry: 394; armaments, 101, 394; Kopparkompaniet founded (1619), 96; copper production, 97, 101, 394, 396, 410; iron production, 97, 101, 394
nobility: proportion of the population, 17; effect of wars, 56, 59; development of a service nobility, 60; struggle for power, 397
nutrition, 75
political institutions: *Standestaat* consolidated by Charter of 1612, 122
religion: strength given by Lutheranism, 397
seapower: naval strength in the Baltic, 231, 387, 389; naval finance, 396, 404–5; merchant fleets, 387, 404–6
trade: policy (post 1645), 404; exports: copper, 96, 297, 444, 670; iron, 97, 297; furs, 663; imports: grain, 395 n.
see also Charles IX; Charles X; Charles XI; Christina; Gustavus I; Gustavus II Adolphus; Oxenstierna, Axel; Sigismund III
Sweden, Bank of, issues first bank-notes in Europe, 82
Sweden, College of Commerce, established 1651, 404
Switzerland, 516
administration, 32
climatic change, 73
used by Spain as land route to the Netherlands, 261
independence recognized by the Peace of Westphalia, 358
nobility, proportion of population, 17; codes of conduct, 27; qualification, 30
political power in towns, 15
see also Grisons, the
Sylvius, *see* de la Boë, François
Syria, 640
recruitment of troops in, 625
Ottoman conquest (1516), 632
cause of revolts in, 670
Szön, the Peace of (1627 and 1642), 637

Tabriz, and the Persian-Ottoman campaigns (1635), 633
Tacitus, Cornelius, 360
Tacticus, Aelianus, military writings, 216–17
Tadoussac, Quebec province, fur trade centre, 675–6; French trade at, 676, 697
Tagus, Battle of the (1589), 300
Tamaulipas, Mexico, 708
Tangier, 434
dowry of Catherine of Braganza, 425
Tanjore, Coromandel, flouts Dutch *cartaz* system, 657

Taoism, 33
Tapp, John, 166
Tappans, Indian tribe, 694
Tarahumara, Indian tribe, Jesuit missions to, 709
Tartaglia, Niccolò, mathematician, theories of gunnery (1537), 166
Tasso, 7
Tassoni, Alessandro, poet, criticizes Spain, 273
Tatars
organization, 611 n., 612 n.
and Poland: raids, 596–7, 611, 636; invaded by Cossacks, 596–7, 611; Battle of Ţuţora (1620), 636; Battle of Chocim (1621), 41
and Russia: and the 'Time of Troubles', 602; relationships (1613–32), 611; receive annual payments, 611; attacks on Russia by Crimean and Nogai Tatars (1632–4), 610, 612; raids increase (1643), 613
Tavares, Antônio Raposo, Paulista *bandeira*, 712
explorations of, 713–14
Taxation
in Basque provinces, 46; Calabria, 50; Denmark, 44; England, 44, 583; France, 19, 44, 46–7, 56–7, 65, 476, 479, 481, 483, 485, 488, 490, 492, 494–6; Habsburg domains, 505; Naples, 48–9; Netherlands, Dutch, 44; Poland, 587; Russia, 604, 607–8, 617–18; Sicily, 50–2; Spain, 19, 40, 44–6, 439, 441–2, 447–9, 457, 461–2, 465–7; Sweden, 394; in the Turkish Empire, 626
Technology
development, 164–8
causes of the lack of progress, 165–7
application to dyeing, knitting, draining and steam power, 167–8
unites with philosophy to bring in unlimited improvements, 168
in England, 165–7; the Netherlands, 167; Scandinavia, 166
Tegengren, F. R., his *Sveriges ädlare malmer och bergwerk* (1924), 95
Tenedos, and the Turco-Venetian war (1645–69), 641
Tepehuá revolt (1616), 709
Terki, fortifications of, 222
Terlon, Chevalier de, French ambassador, negotiates at Copenhagen (1660), 431
Ternate, Molucca Islands
Portuguese encourage opposition to the Dutch (1601), 646; install garrison, 647; fleet fails to give support, 666